Atomic Masses of the Elements

Name	Symbol	Atomic Number	Atomic Mass[a]	Name	Symbol	Atomic Number	Atomic Mass[a]
Actinium	Ac	89	(227)[b]	Molybdenum	Mo		
Aluminum	Al	13	26.98	Neodymium	Nd		144.2
Americium	Am	95	(243)	Neon	Ne	10	20.18
Antimony	Sb	51	121.8	Neptunium	Np	93	(237)
Argon	Ar	18	39.95	Nickel	Ni	28	58.69
Arsenic	As	33	74.92	Niobium	Nb	41	92.91
Astatine	At	85	(210)	Nitrogen	N	7	14.01
Barium	Ba	56	137.3	Nobelium	No	102	(259)
Berkelium	Bk	97	(247)	Osmium	Os	76	190.2
Beryllium	Be	4	9.012	Oxygen	O	8	16.00
Bismuth	Bi	83	209.0	Palladium	Pd	46	106.4
Bohrium	Bh	107	(264)	Phosphorus	P	15	30.97
Boron	B	5	10.81	Platinum	Pt	78	195.1
Bromine	Br	35	79.90	Plutonium	Pu	94	(244)
Cadmium	Cd	48	112.4	Polonium	Po	84	(209)
Calcium	Ca	20	40.08	Potassium	K	19	39.10
Californium	Cf	98	(251)	Praseodymium	Pr	59	140.9
Carbon	C	6	12.01	Promethium	Pm	61	(145)
Cerium	Ce	58	140.1	Protactinium	Pa	91	231.0
Cesium	Cs	55	132.9	Radium	Ra	88	(226)
Chlorine	Cl	17	35.45	Radon	Rn	86	(222)
Chromium	Cr	24	52.00	Rhenium	Re	75	186.2
Cobalt	Co	27	58.93	Rhodium	Rh	45	102.9
Copernicium	Cn	112	(285)	Roentgenium	Rg	111	(272)
Copper	Cu	29	63.55	Rubidium	Rb	37	85.47
Curium	Cm	96	(247)	Ruthenium	Ru	44	101.1
Darmstadtium	Ds	110	(271)	Rutherfordium	Rf	104	(261)
Dubnium	Db	105	(262)	Samarium	Sm	62	150.4
Dysprosium	Dy	66	162.5	Scandium	Sc	21	44.96
Einsteinium	Es	99	(252)	Seaborgium	Sg	106	(266)
Erbium	Er	68	167.3	Selenium	Se	34	78.96
Europium	Eu	63	152.0	Silicon	Si	14	28.09
Fermium	Fm	100	(257)	Silver	Ag	47	107.9
Fluorine	F	9	19.00	Sodium	Na	11	22.99
Francium	Fr	87	(223)	Strontium	Sr	38	87.62
Gadolinium	Gd	64	157.3	Sulfur	S	16	32.07
Gallium	Ga	31	69.72	Tantalum	Ta	73	180.9
Germanium	Ge	32	72.64	Technetium	Tc	43	(99)
Gold	Au	79	197.0	Tellurium	Te	52	127.6
Hafnium	Hf	72	178.5	Terbium	Tb	65	158.9
Hassium	Hs	108	(265)	Thallium	Tl	81	204.4
Helium	He	2	4.003	Thorium	Th	90	232.0
Holmium	Ho	67	164.9	Thulium	Tm	69	168.9
Hydrogen	H	1	1.008	Tin	Sn	50	118.7
Indium	In	49	114.8	Titanium	Ti	22	47.87
Iodine	I	53	126.9	Tungsten	W	74	183.8
Iridium	Ir	77	192.2	Uranium	U	92	238.0
Iron	Fe	26	55.85	Vanadium	V	23	50.94
Krypton	Kr	36	83.80	Xenon	Xe	54	131.3
Lanthanum	La	57	138.9	Ytterbium	Yb	70	173.0
Lawrencium	Lr	103	(262)	Yttrium	Y	39	88.91
Lead	Pb	82	207.2	Zinc	Zn	30	65.41
Lithium	Li	3	6.941	Zirconium	Zr	40	91.22
Lutetium	Lu	71	175.0	—	—	113	(284)
Magnesium	Mg	12	24.31	—	—	114	(289)
Manganese	Mn	25	54.94	—	—	115	(288)
Meitnerium	Mt	109	(268)	—	—	116	(292)
Mendelevium	Md	101	(258)	—	—	117	(293)
Mercury	Hg	80	200.6	—	—	118	(294)

[a]Values for atomic masses are given to four significant figures.
[b]Values in parentheses are the mass number of an important radioactive isotope.

GENERAL, ORGANIC, AND BIOLOGICAL

CHEMISTRY

Structures of Life

GENERAL, ORGANIC, AND BIOLOGICAL

CHEMISTRY

Structures of Life

Fourth Edition

KAREN C. TIMBERLAKE

PEARSON

Boston   Columbus   Indianapolis   New York   San Francisco   Upper Saddle River
Amsterdam   Cape Town   Dubai   London   Madrid   Milan   Munich   Paris   Montréal   Toronto
Delhi   Mexico City   São Paulo   Sydney   Hong Kong   Seoul   Singapore   Taipei   Tokyo

Editor in Chief: Adam Jaworski
Executive Editor: Jeanne Zalesky
Marketing Manager: Jonathan Cottrell
Associate Editor: Jessica Neumann
Editorial Assistant: Lisa Tarabokjia
Marketing Assistant: Nicola Houston
Managing Editor, Chemistry and Geosciences: Gina M. Cheselka
Senior Production Project Manager: Beth Sweeten
Production Management: Andrea Stefanowicz, PreMediaGlobal
Compositor: PreMediaGlobal
Senior Technical Art Specialist: Connie Long
Illustrator: Imagineering
Image Lead: Maya Melenchuk
Photo Researcher: Eric Shrader
Text Research Manager: Beth Wollar
Text Researcher: Melissa Flamson
Design Manager: Derek Bacchus
Interior Designer: Gary Hespenheide
Cover Designer: Gary Hespenheide
Operations Specialist: Jeff Sargent
Cover Photo Credit: Fernando Alonso Herrero/iStockphoto

Credits and acknowledgments borrowed from other sources and reproduced, with permission, in this textbook appear on pp. C-1–C-4.

Library of Congress Cataloging-in-Publication Data
Timberlake, Karen C.
    General, organic, and biological chemistry : structures of life / Karen C. Timberlake. —4th ed.
        p. cm.
    Includes index.
    ISBN-13: 978-0-321-75089-1 (student ed.)
    ISBN-10: 0-321-75089-6 (student ed.)
    1. Chemistry—Textbooks. I. Title.
    QD33.2.T56 2013
    540—dc23   2011034499

ISBN-10: 0-321-75089-6; ISBN-13: 978-0-321-75089-1

Printed in the United States of America
1 2 3 4 5 6 7 8 9 10—CRK—17 16 15 14 13 12 11

Brief Contents

Contents

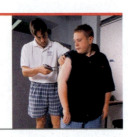
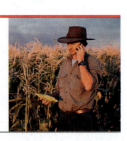

4

Nuclear Chemistry   127

5

Compounds and Their Bonds   158

6

Chemical Reactions and Quantities   204

7

Gases 259

8

Solutions 296

9

Reaction Rates and Chemical Equilibrium 340

10
Acids and Bases 368

11
Introduction to Organic Chemistry: Alkanes 411

12
Alkenes, Alkynes, and Aromatic Compounds 446

13

Alcohols, Phenols, Thiols, and Ethers 477

14

Aldehydes, Ketones, and Chiral Molecules 505

15

Carbohydrates 538

16
Carboxylic Acids and Esters 570

17
Lipids 598

18
Amines and Amides 639

19

Amino Acids and Proteins 674

20

Enzymes and Vitamins 708

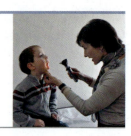

21

Nucleic Acids and Protein Synthesis 741

22
Metabolic Pathways for Carbohydrates   782

23
Metabolism and Energy Production   816

24
Metabolic Pathways for Lipids and Amino Acids   839

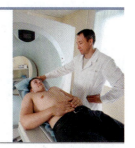

Applications and Activities

Explore Your World

Chemistry Link to Health

Chemistry Link to the Environment

Chemistry Link to Industry

Chemistry Link to History

Career Focus

Guide to Problem Solving

Preface

Welcome to the fourth edition of *General, Organic, and Biological Chemistry: Structures of Life*. This chemistry text was written and designed to help you prepare for a career in a health-related profession, such as nursing, dietetics, respiratory therapy, and environmental and agricultural science. This text assumes no prior knowledge of chemistry. My main objective in writing this text is to make the study of chemistry an engaging and positive experience for you by relating the structure and behavior of matter to its role in health and the environment. This new edition introduces more problem-solving strategies, including new Concept Checks, more problem-solving guides, new Analyze the Problem features, conceptual and challenge problems, and new sets of combined problems.

It is also my goal to encourage you become a critical thinker by understanding the scientific concepts with current issues concerning health and the environment. Thus, I have utilized materials that

- motivate you to learn and enjoy chemistry
- relate chemistry to careers that interest you
- develop problem-solving skills that lead to your success in chemistry
- promote your learning and success in your chosen career

I hope that this textbook helps you discover exciting new ideas and gives you a rewarding experience as you develop an understanding and appreciation of the role of chemistry in your life.

New for the Fourth Edition

New features have been added throughout this fourth edition, including the following:

- **All new chapter openers** provide engaging stories that illustrate how Chemistry is used daily in contemporary professions.
- **New Analyze the Problem** feature illustrates how to break down a word problem into the components required to solve a problem.
- A new **Chapter 1, Chemistry and Measurements**, offers a comprehensive overview of introductory Chemistry and a study plan for learning the fundamentals.
- **Learning Goals** are now included at the end of each chapter section with Questions and Problems to reinforce student retention of the main concepts.
- Problems with high difficulty in **MasteringChemistry** were moved to the Challenge Problems sections or revised, while problems that received low assign values from professors nationwide were rewritten and improved to better support student learning throughout the course. Additionally, over **30 new tutorials** specific to this text including activities incorporating **Concept Maps** will be available with MasteringChemistry for the Fourth Edition.
- Two new types of interest boxes, **Chemistry Link to Industry** and **Chemistry Link to History**, demonstrate connections between the chemical concepts and real events, then and now.
- **New Guides to Problem Solving** include Using Concentration to Calculate Mass or Volume, Using Density, Writing Formulas with Polyatomic Ions, Using Half-Lives, Drawing Electron-Dot Formulas, Determination of Polarity of a Molecule, and Calculating the Molar Mass of a Gas.
- **Chapter Reviews** now include bulleted lists and thumbnail art samples related to the content of each section.
- Statements in **Guides to Problem Solving** were rewritten and matched to steps of the corresponding *Sample Problems*.
- Problems were rewritten and added to give matched sets of problems for each odd number and its following even number.

Chapter-by-Chapter Changes to the Fourth Edition

Chapter 1, "Chemistry and Measurements," now introduces students to the concepts of chemicals and chemistry and asks students to develop a study plan for learning chemistry. Students learn measurement and the need to understand numerical structures of the metric system in the sciences.

- The *Chemistry Link to Health*, "Bone Density," has been updated to discuss changes in bone density with age and is now included in Chapter 1.
- New *Guide to Problem Solving*, "Using Density," uses color blocks as visual guides in the step-by-step solution pathway.
- Content in *Scientific Notation* was rewritten to clarify the coefficient and the power of 10.
- New photos added that include the standard kilogram, mass of a nickel, a virus, and ophthalmologist.
- New material identifies exact and measured numbers and their significant figures within equalities and conversion factors.
- New *Sample Problem* on percent body fat illustrates the use of a percent conversion factor as an equality and the formation of conversion factors.
- New numbers added to *Study Checks* to match the *Sample Problem* numbers.
- New problems added and problems paired to obtain similar content and questions.
- More emphasis on metric (SI) units and removed some problems that used U.S. system units.

Chapter 2, "Energy and Matter," now looks at energy, temperature, classification of matter, states of matter, physical and chemical changes, and nutritional energy values.

- The *Chemistry Link to the Environment* updates the content of "Carbon Dioxide and Global Warming."
- New *Guide to Problem Solving*, "Calculating Temperature," was added.
- New macro-to-micro art emphasizes the atomic level of compounds and changes of state.
- New problems relating the burning of fuel to product energy to light a light bulb were added while problems with heat of fusion, heat of vaporization, and multiple step calculations were deleted.

Chapter 3, "Atoms and Elements," looks at elements, atoms, subatomic particles, and atomic mass. The *Periodic Table* emphasizes the numbering of groups from 1–18.

- New element name and symbol Copernicium, Cn, was added to the periodic table.
- New atomic number 117 was added to the periodic table.
- New *Chemistry Link to Industry*, "Many Forms of Carbon," was added, which describes four forms of carbon: diamond, graphite, buckminsterfullerene, and nanotubes.

- New *Chemistry Link to Health*, "Elements Essential to Health," was added, which describes the essential elements in an adult and the position of each on the periodic table.
- New column added in Table 3.8, "Most Prevalent Isotope."
- New shapes of *d* orbitals added to *Shapes of Orbitals*.
- Material on mass number in Section 3.4 was rewritten.
- New *Metallic Character* text added to Section 3.8, *Trends in Periodic Properties*.
- New problems added that compare metallic character of elements.
- New summary of *Trends in Periodic Properties* added for valence electrons, atomic radius, ionization energy, and metallic character from top to bottom of a group and going left to right in a period.

Chapter 4, "Nuclear Chemistry," extends the concepts of subatomic particles, atomic number, and atomic mass to a discussion of the nucleus of radioisotopes including the positron. Nuclear equations are written and balanced for both naturally occurring and artificially produced radioisotopes. The topic of biological effects of radiation is part of the chapter content.

- New column "Type of Radiation" added to Tables 4.7 and 4.8.
- Increased the number of radioisotopes in Table 4.8.
- New problems added on measuring activity of a radioisotope, positron equation balancing, and positron decay.
- Updated to full symbols using mass number and atomic number in *Sample Problems* for balancing nuclear equations.
- Updated art including alpha and beta radiation.
- Placed bombarding particles at the beginning of nuclear equations involving bombardment.

Chapter 5, "Compounds and Their Bonds," describes how atoms form ionic and covalent bonds in compounds. Students learn to write chemical formulas and to name ionic compounds—including those with polyatomic ions—and covalent compounds. Students are introduced to the three-dimensional shape of molecules. The discussion of polyatomic ions, which includes more polyatomic ions, follows the formation of ionic compounds. The concept of resonance is discussed for the electron-dot formulas for compounds with multiple bonds. Electronegativity, bond polarity, and the shapes of molecules are discussed. *Attractive Forces in Compounds* compares the attractive forces between particles and their impact on physical properties and changes of state.

- Updated/added *Concept Checks* to clarify understanding of concepts for problem solving including "Drawing Electron-Dot Formulas" and "Using Electronegativity to Determine the Polarity of Bonds."
- Revised *Formation of Ions* to emphasize the stability of electron configurations.
- Updated/added art in ionic compounds with new colors for Na, Cl, Mg, and S, and to illustrate dispersion forces between two nonpolar molecules.

- Added more transition elements and their charges to Table 5.5.
- Reorganized polarity of molecules by presenting nonpolar molecules followed by polar molecules.
- New guides "Writing Formulas with Polyatomic Ions," "Determination of Polarity of a Molecule," and "Drawing Electron-Dot Formulas," were added.
- New table "Typical Bonding Patterns of Some Nonmetals in Covalent Compounds" was added.
- The discussion of exceptions to bonding patterns now includes models of BCl_3 and SF_6.
- Identification of molecular shape now emphasizes electron-group geometry.
- New wedge–dash notation was added to three-dimensional structures of methane and ammonia.

Chapter 6, "Chemical Reactions and Quantities," includes balancing chemical equations and classifying reaction types as combination, decomposition, single and double replacement, and combustion reactions. Calculations include the use of the mole, molar mass, and equation coefficients for problem solving involving mole and mass calculations for chemical reactions.

- Updated colors for atoms of H, C, O, and N in models of compounds undergoing reactions.
- New combustion reactions are now included in types of reactions. New problems were added for combustion to *Questions and Problems*.
- New number line added to illustrate direction of change in oxidation or reduction.
- Rewrote discussion of *Oxidation and Reduction in Biological Systems* to relate addition of O, loss of H, and loss of electrons to reduction with gain of H, loss of O, or gain of electrons.
- New *Concept Check*, "Calculating Percent Yield," was added.
- Rewrote limiting reactant problems to improve success in problem solving.
- Added list, "Three Conditions Required for a Reaction to Occur."
- Added tutorials include "Classifying Chemical Reactions by What Atoms Do," "Signs of a Chemical Reaction," "Limiting Reactant and Yield: Mole Calculations," "Limiting Reactant and Yield: Mass Calculations," and "The Mole as a Counting Unit."
- Added "draw the formulas of reactants and products" to problems with visual reactants and products.
- Added "predict products" of reactions to help students identify formation of products.

Chapter 7, "Gases," discusses the properties of a gas and asks the student to calculate changes in gases using the gas laws including the Ideal Gas Law.

- New/added *Concept Checks* for each of the gas laws and molar volume provide a conceptual transition between text information and problem solving.
- New guide "Calculating the Molar Mass of a Gas" was added.
- New gas properties that remain constant are now included in gas *Sample Problem* solutions.
- Gas problems were added that relate to real world gases or gas mixtures.

Chapter 8, "Solutions," describes solutions, solubility, saturation, concentrations, insoluble salts, and colligative properties. New problem-solving strategies clarify the use of concentration conversion factors to determine the volume of solution or mass of solute. The volumes and molarities of solutions are used to calculate product quantities in chemical reactions as well as in dilutions and titrations.

- Combined percent concentrations and molarity in Section 8.4 to give standard format for concentration calculations.
- New table "Summary of Types of Concentration Expressions and Their Units" clarifies the types of units in percent concentrations and molarity.
- New *Sample Problem* for volume/volume percent concentration was added.
- New guide "Using Concentration to Calculate Mass or Volume," was added.
- New *Explore Your World* activity, "Preparing Rock Candy," for students to experience an everyday saturated solution was added.
- Placed dilution in a separate Section 8.5 "Dilution of Solutions and Solution Reactions" that applies dilution to both percent and molarity solutions.
- New *Concept Check* about freezing point changes was added.
- New material and photo of the Alaskan Upis beetle that produces biological antifreeze to survive subfreezing environment.
- Updated/added tables on concentration factors that combine percent and molarity, organize solution problem data, and identify the type of solution as well as updated the table "Solubility Rules for Ionic Solids in Water."
- New material was added on the function of electrolytes in the cells and organs of the body, Pedialyte, and the impact of solute dissociation on freezing point lowering and boiling point elevation.

Chapter 9, "Chemical Equilibrium," looks at the rates of reactions and the equilibrium condition when forward and reverse rates for a reaction become equal. Equilibrium expressions for reactions are written and equilibrium constants are calculated. Le Châtelier's principle is used to evaluate the impact on concentrations when a stress is placed on the system.

- New photo added to content and *Sample Problems* that illustrate a biological example of enzymes (catalysts) in laundry detergents.
- Rewrote several problems to guide students through equilibrium concentration.
- Converted old Figures 9.9 and 9.10 to unnumbered art and updated to show correct proportions of reactants and products at equilibrium.
- Rewrote and updated *Concept Checks* and *Sample Problems* about concentration changes and equilibrium mixtures.
- Moved old Figure 9.8 of SO_2 and O_2 to Section 9.2 to illustrate reversible reactions and updated for more visuals on forward and reverse reactions reaching equilibrium.
- Revised Section 9.5 to be more qualitative and less quantitative and added content on the effect of volume changes on equilibrium systems.
- New art was added to illustrate Le Châtelier's Principle to show how adding water to one side of two connected water tanks reaches equilibrium, how addition of reactant places stress on an equilibrium system and how the system responds to reduce stress, and how a container shows shifts in equilibrium conditions when the piston increases or decreases volume.

Chapter 10, "Acids and Bases," discusses acids and bases, Brønsted–Lowry acids and bases, and conjugate acid–base pairs. The dissociation of strong and weak acids and bases is related to their strengths as acids or bases. The ionization of water leads to the ion-product constant of water, K_w, the pH scale, and the calculation of pH. Chemical equations for acids in reactions are balanced and titration of an acid is illustrated. Buffers are discussed along with their role in the blood.

- New *Concept Check* and photo illustrates the ionization of calcium hydroxide in the preparation of hominy and grits.
- New molecular models added to show atoms in carbonic acid, hydrogen carbonate, and carbonate ions, and atoms in formic acid and formate ion were added to illustrate their structures.
- New photos added to show use of calcium carbonate added to farm crops to reduce acidity of the soil, the chemical reaction of sodium bicarbonate with an acid and the products of carbon dioxide and a salt, calcium hydroxide as lime and dental filler, and how low dissociation of HF illustrates that hydrofluoric acid is a weak acid.
- New art illustrates the parietal cells in the lining of the stomach that secrete gastric acid HCl in *Chemistry Link to Health*.
- New guide "Calculating $[H_3O^+]$ from pH" was added.
- New list compares the effect of different ratios of $[H_2PO_4^-]/[HPO_4^{2-}]$ on pH.

Chapter 11, "Introduction to Organic Chemistry: Alkanes," discusses the structure, nomenclature, and reactions of alkanes. *Guides to Problem Solving (GPS)* clarify the rules for nomenclature. The chapter provides an overview of each family of organic compounds and their functional groups and forms a basis for understanding the biomolecules of living systems.

- Information on oil spills was updated to include recent British Petroleum oil spill.
- Updated colors for atoms of H, C, O, and N in models of compounds undergoing reactions.
- New representations of atoms with updated colors were added to Table 11.8.
- Updated and simplified the section and problems associated with *Naming of Alkanes with Substituents*.
- Converted *Sample Problem 11.3* to *Concept Check 11.4* to provide more detail on how to distinguish between structural formulas that are isomers or the same molecule.
- Updated the discussion of melting and boiling points of alkanes by adding analogies and photos of licorice sticks and tennis balls to illustrate impact of contact points on boiling points differences of straight-chain alkanes and branched alkanes.
- Changed *Sample Problem 11.8* to *Concept Check 11.7* in which students isolate functional groups in compounds and classify each class of compound.
- Rewrote and highlighted functional groups in various classes of organic compounds to help students identify a group of atoms that is a functional group on an alkane chain.

Chapter 12, "Alkenes, Alkynes, and Aromatic Compounds," discusses alkenes and alkynes, cis–trans isomers, addition reactions, polymers of alkenes found in everyday items, and aromatic compounds.

- Alkene examples were added to introductory paragraph.
- Bond angles were added in illustration of alkene and alkyne structures.
- Added skeletal formulas to the table of alkanes, alkenes, and alkynes, and added reactions for alkenes and alkynes.
- Changed instruction from *write* to *draw* a condensed structural formula.
- Color screens were added to *Sample Problem 12.1* to clarify "Naming Alkenes and Alkynes."
- Rewrote material in Section 12.2 to highlight cis and trans positions of groups attached to carbons and double bonds and discussion of benzene structure stability.
- New *Concept Check 12.3*, "Converting Formulas of Alkenes to Cis and Trans Isomers," illustrates how to draw groups in cis and trans isomers.
- Added photos and formulas of aromatic compounds.

Chapter 13, "Alcohols, Phenols, Ethers, and Thiols," discusses structures, names, properties, and reactions of alcohols, phenols, thiols, and ethers.

- New skeletal formulas for alcohols and ethers were added and the naming of alcohols was simplified.
- Changed instruction from *write* to *draw* a condensed structural formula.
- Moved classification of alcohols to Section 13.3.
- Updated the "Guide to Naming Alcohols."
- New color screens were added to *Sample Problems* that named alcohols and phenols and IUPAC naming of ethers.
- Rewrote *Sample Problem 13.4*, "Isomers of Alcohols and Ethers" including *Study Check*.
- Reorganized Table 13.1 to include solubility and boiling points of some typical alcohols and ethers and to include the number of carbon atoms and condensed structural formula with up to five carbon atoms.
- New *Chemistry Link to Health*, "Hand Sanitizers and Ethanol," has been added.
- Updated art in *Oxidation of Alcohols* to include level of oxidation of secondary alcohols.
- New colors for H and O atoms involved in oxidation and reduction were used.

Chapter 14, "Aldehydes, Ketones, and Chiral Molecules," discusses the nomenclature and structures of aldehydes and ketones. The discussion of Fischer projections, chiral molecules, and mirror images prepares students for the discussions on carbohydrates in Chapter 15.

- New skeletal formulas for aldehydes and ketones were added.
- Rewrote *Sample Problem 14.3*, "Boiling Point and Solubility."
- New problems on Tollens' and Benedict's reagents were added.
- New glucose example was added to *Chemistry Link to Health*, "Some Important Aldehydes and Ketones."
- IUPAC names used for alcohols, aldehydes, and ketones in addition reactions.
- Rewrote content on *Drawing Fischer Projections* and addition reactions that form hemiacetals and acetals.
- New photos and mirror images for ibuprofen and naproxen were added.

Chapter 15, "Carbohydrates," applies the organic chemistry of alcohols, aldehydes, and ketones to carbohydrates, which relates the study of chemistry to health and medicine.

- New art includes photo of iodine test for starch.
- Converted green spheres in types of carbohydrates to more representative hexagon shapes.
- Converted all CHO groups at top of Fischer projections to $C{=}O$ and $H{-}$.

- Rewrote the descriptions of the glycosidic bonds in monosaccharides, the definitions of anomers and anomeric carbons, and Fischer projections for clarity.
- Converted all open-chain structures to Fischer projections.
- New discussion of high-fructose corn syrup (HFCS) was included.
- Updated *Guide to Problem Solving* and discussion in *Sample Problem* for "Drawing Haworth Structures."
- New color coding of $-OH$ groups in open-chain and Haworth structures of D-glucose and of O in carbonyl groups and free hydroxyl group to highlight differences in alpha and beta anomers of monosaccharides.
- Described mutarotation for all the monosaccharides and disaccharides maltose and lactose.
- Highlighted hemiacetal and acetal linkage in monosaccharides and disaccharides along with $-OH$ groups in alpha and beta anomers.
- Ionized the structure of aspartame sweetener.
- Rewrote *Chemistry Link to Health*, "Blood Types and Carbohydrates," to clarify blood types and antigens.

Chapter 16, "Carboxylic Acids and Esters," discusses two more of the organic families that are important in biochemical systems. The chemical reactions discussed are most applicable to reactions in biochemical systems.

- Updated art with proper atom colors of H, O, and C.
- Rewrote "Guide to Naming Carboxylic Acids."
- New skeletal formulas and color-coded screens were added to *Sample Problem 16.1*, "Naming Carboxylic Acids."
- New photos of acetic acid crystals, facial with lactic acid, willow tree (aspirin), fingernail polish, aspirin, Dacron clothing, grapes, strawberries, and raspberries were added.
- Reworked naming for esters and turned all ester formulas to place acyl portion first.
- New color coding screens were added to *Sample Problem 16.6*, "Naming Esters."
- New problems for structural isomers of carboxylic acids and esters were added.

Chapter 17, "Lipids," contains the functional groups of alcohols, aldehydes, and ketones in larger molecules such as triacylglycerols, glycerophospholipids, and steroids.

- Updated melting points of fatty acids.
- New Table 17.3 now compares similarities of organic and lipid reactions of esterification, hydrogenation, hydrolysis, and saponification.
- Redesigned the art for the structure of a glycerophospholipid.
- New discussion of snake venom, which contains phospholipases, was added.
- Updated/added art on the olestra structure and adrenal glands and kidneys.
- Replaced Figure 17.10 with new art for lipoprotein transport of HDLs and LDLs.

- Added new material in *Chemistry Link to Health*, "Converting Unsaturated Fats to Saturated Fats: Hydrogenation and Interesterification" and added a new *Chemistry Link to Health*, "Infant Respiratory Distress Syndrome."

Chapter 18, "Amines and Amides,"

emphasizes the nitrogen atom in their functional groups and their names. Alkaloids are discussed as the naturally occurring amines in plants.

- Updated the "Guide to the IUPAC Naming of Amines."
- Rewrote *Naming Compounds with Two Functional Groups* to include names of amino substituents in alcohols, ketones, and carboxylic acid.
- New tables added on summarizing the priority of naming in molecules with two functional groups and comparing melting points of primary, secondary, and tertiary amines.
- New guide, "Naming Compounds with Two Functional Groups," was added.
- New *Sample Problem*, "IUPAC Names for Compounds with Two Functional Groups," was added.
- New photos include indigo related to aniline, Benadryl product for antihistamines, and Neo-Synephrine product.
- New models of amines showing number of hydrogen bonds between molecules of primary, secondary, and tertiary amines and showing the number of hydrogen bonds for solubility of primary, secondary, and tertiary amines in water.
- New section written on the role of amines in *Neurotransmitters*.
- New art on structures of neurotransmitters and over-the-counter products.
- New *Questions and Problems* and *Additional Problems* written on neurotransmitters.

Chapter 19, "Amino Acids and Proteins,"

discusses amino acids, formation of proteins, structural levels of proteins, hydrolysis, and denaturation of proteins.

- New one-letter abbreviations for amino acids were added to Table 19.2 and in problems.
- New list of amino acids, R groups, polarity, and behavior in water was added.
- Amino acids now drawn with bond line to H from α-C, and bond line from H to N.
- Reactions of zwitterions in acids and bases are now separated into two equations.
- Ammonium groups and carboxylate groups in amino acids are now color coded.
- New guide "Drawing a Peptide" has been added.
- New Table 19.7 "Protein Denaturation" has been added.
- Updated artwork of a prion to show both normal and abnormal protein structures.
- Updated myoglobin and hemoglobin structures to ribbon models.
- New art added including ribbon models of proteins, structures of pentapeptide met-enkephalin, and ball-and-stick models for some amino acids.

Chapter 20, "Enzymes and Vitamins,"

relates the importance of the three-dimensional shape of proteins to their function as enzymes. The shape of an enzyme and its substrate is a factor in enzyme regulation. End products of an enzyme-catalyzed sequence can increase or decrease the rate of an enzyme-catalyzed reaction. Proteins change shape and lose function when subjected to pH changes and high temperatures. The important role of water-soluble vitamins as coenzymes is related to enzyme function.

- Changed equation for carbonic anhydrase to
  $$CO_2 + H_2O \longrightarrow HCO_3^- + H^+.$$
- Combined art of enzyme with new pullout art to give more detail of active site.
- Added Enzyme–Product complex (EP complex) to enzyme-catalyzed reactions.
- New art added for enzyme-catalyzed reactions includes EP complex, enzymes using ribbon models to show active site with substrate, and proenzymes of proteases.
- New emphasis on the dynamic induced-fit model of substrate and active site.
- *Classification of Enzymes and Names* was moved from Section 20.1 to Section 20.2 and shortened.

Chapter 21, "Nucleic Acids and Protein Synthesis,"

describes the nucleic acids and their importance as biomolecules that store and direct information for cellular components, growth, and reproduction. The role of complementary base pairing is highlighted in both DNA replication and the formation of mRNA during protein synthesis. Discussions include the genetic code, its relationship to the order of amino acids in a protein, and how mutations can occur when the nucleotide sequence is altered. Recombinant DNA and viruses are also discussed.

- New Table 21.1 summarizes the components in DNA and RNA; Table 21.6 summarizes steps in protein synthesis, site and materials, and process; and Table 21.7 summarizes the nucleotide and amino acid sequences in protein synthesis.
- Section 21.3 now includes work of Rosalind Franklin on the DNA double helix.

Chapter 22, "Metabolic Pathways for Carbohydrates,"

describes the stages of metabolism and the digestion of carbohydrates, our most important fuel. The breakdown of glucose to pyruvate is described using the glycolytic pathway, which is followed under aerobic conditions by the decarboxylation of pyruvate to acetyl-CoA. The synthesis of glycogen and the synthesis of glucose from noncarbohydrate sources are discussed.

- Updated Figure 22.1 for stages of metabolism, Figure 22.3 for ATP structure, Figure 22.4 using color blocks to show ADP + P_i forms ATP, and Figure 22.10 to use color blocks for ATP in glycolysis.

- New tables added to summarize enzymes and coenzymes in metabolic reactions: "Characteristics of Oxidation and Reduction in Metabolic Pathways" (Table 22.2) and "Enzymes and Coenzymes in Metabolic Reactions" (Table 22.3).
- New color-coded art was added for structures of NAD and FAD in Figures 22.5 and 22.6.
- New art in Figure 22.12 adds glucose structures for reactions for glycogenesis.

Chapter 23, "Metabolic Pathways and Energy Production,"

looks at the entry of acetyl-CoA into the citric acid cycle and the production of reduced coenzymes for electron transport, oxidative phosphorylation, and the synthesis of ATP.

- Updated Figure 23.1 with new coding for components of citric acid cycle, Figure 23.3 to use same colors for components of the citric acid cycle, and Figures 23.5 and 23.7 to include complex notations and model of ATP synthase.
- New overall equation at Complex I written as $NADH + H^+ + CoQ \longrightarrow CoQH_2 + NAD^+$.
- Structure for oxidation/reduction of $CoQ/CoQH_2$ now included in Complex I discussion.
- New ribbon model for cytochrome c was added.
- Updated ATP formation at F_1 and F_o ATP synthase sites.
- Updated color screens for NADH, $FADH_2$, and ATP.

Chapter 24, "Metabolic Pathways for Lipids and Amino Acids,"

discusses the digestion of lipids and proteins and the metabolic pathways that convert fatty acids and amino acids into energy. Discussions include the conversion of excess carbohydrates to triacylglycerols in adipose tissue and how the intermediates of the citric acid cycle are converted to nonessential amino acids.

- Rewrote *Mobilization of Fat Stores* as *Utilization of Fat Stores*.
- Updated discussion for *Transport of Fatty Acids*.
- New chemical equations added for β-oxidation with the discussion of Reactions 1, 2, 3, and 4.
- Replaced vertical representation of β-oxidation.
- Changed fatty acids to give different fatty acids in text and in *Questions and Problems*.
- Updated Figure 24.4 with new color coding for components of β-oxidation of capric acid and Figure 24.10 for carbon atoms from degraded amino acids.
- Updated color screens for NADH, $FADH_2$, and ATP.
- New ribbon model of leptin added to *Chemistry Link to Health*, "Stored Fat and Obesity."
- Updated colors in Figures 24.8 and 24.12 to be consistent with earlier art of metabolic cycles.

Instructional Package

General, Organic, and Biological Chemistry: Structures of Life, fourth edition, provides an integrated teaching and learning package of support material for both students and professors.

For Students

Study Guide for *General, Organic, and Biological Chemistry: Structures of Life*, fourth edition, by Karen Timberlake. This manual is keyed to the learning goals in the text, and designed to promote active learning through a variety of exercises with answers as well as practice tests. (ISBN 0321767020)

Selected Solutions Manual for *General, Organic, and Biological Chemistry: Structures of Life*, fourth edition, by Mark Quirie. This manual contains the complete solutions to the odd-numbered problems. (ISBN 0321767039)

MasteringChemistry® (www.masteringchemistry.com) The most advanced, most widely used online chemistry tutorial and homework program is available for the fourth edition of *General, Organic, and Biological Chemistry: Structures of Life*. MasteringChemistry® utilizes the Socratic Method to coach students through problem-solving techniques, offering hints, and simpler questions on request to help students *learn*, not just practice. A powerful gradebook with diagnostics that gives instructors unprecedented insight into their students' learning is also available. For the Fourth Edition, 30 new tutorials have been created to guide students through the most challenging General, Organic, and Biological Chemistry topics and help them make connections between different concepts.

Pearson eText Pearson eText offers students the power to create notes, highlight text in different colors, create bookmarks, zoom, and view single or multiple pages. Access to the Pearson eText for *General, Organic, and Biological Chemistry: Structures of Life*, fourth edition, is available for purchase either as a stand-alone item (ISBN 0321768701) or within MasteringChemistry® (ISBN 0321638697).

Media Icons in the margins throughout the text direct you to tutorials within the Item Library and self-study activities and case studies in the Study Area located within MasteringChemistry® for *General, Organic, and Biological Chemistry: Structures of Life*, fourth edition.

Laboratory Manual for General, Organic, and Biological Chemistry 2e by Karen Timberlake. This best-selling lab manual coordinates 42 experiments with the topics in *General, Organic, and Biological Chemistry: Structures of Life*, fourth edition; uses new terms during the lab; and explores chemical concepts. Laboratory investigations develop skills of manipulating equipment, reporting data, solving problems, making calculations, and drawing conclusions. (ISBN 0321695291)

Essential Laboratory Manual for General, Organic, and Biological Chemistry 2e by Karen Timberlake. This manual contains 25 experiments for the standard course sequence of topics in *General, Organic, and Biological Chemistry: Structures of Life*, fourth edition. (ISBN 0136055478)

For Instructors

MasteringChemistry® (www.masteringchemistry.com) MasteringChemistry® is the first adaptive-learning online homework and tutorial system. Instructors can create online assignments for their students by choosing from a wide range of items, including end-of-chapter problems and research-enhanced tutorials. Assignments are automatically graded with up-to-date diagnostic information, helping instructors pinpoint where students struggle either individually or as a class as a whole. For the Fourth Edition, new tutorials have been created to guide students through the most challenging General, Organic, and Biological Chemistry topics and help them make connections between different concepts.

Instructor Resource DVD This DVD includes all the art and tables from the book in JPG format for use in classroom projection or creating study materials and tests. In addition, the instructor can access the PowerPoint™ lecture outlines, featuring over 2000 slides. Also available on the discs are downloadable files of the *Instructor Solutions Manual*, a set of "clicker questions" suitable for use with classroom-response systems, and the test bank. (ISBN 0321638700)

Instructor Solutions Manual Prepared by Mark Quirie, this manual highlights chapter topics and includes suggestions for the laboratory. Contains complete solution setups and answers to all problems in the text. (ISBN 0321767292)

Printed Test Bank Prepared by Bill Timberlake, this test bank contains over 2000 questions in multiple-choice, matching, true–false, and short-answer format. (ISBN 0321767306)

Online Instructor Manual to Laboratory Manual Contains answers to report pages for the *Laboratory Manual* and *Essential Laboratory Manual*. (ISBN 0321751035)

Also visit the Pearson Education catalog page for Timberlake's *General, Organic, and Biological Chemistry: Structures of Life*, fourth edition, at **www.pearsonhighered.com** to download available instructor supplements.

Acknowledgments

The preparation of a new edition is a continuous effort of many people. As in my work on other textbooks, I am thankful for the support, encouragement, and dedication of many people who put in hours of tireless effort to produce a high-quality book that provides an outstanding learning package. The editorial team at Pearson has done an exceptional job. I want to thank Adam Jaworski, editor in chief, and executive editor, Jeanne Zalesky, who supported my vision of this fourth edition and the addition of the new *Analyze the Problem* feature; more Guides to Problem Solving; new Chemistry Links to Health, History, Industry, and the Environment; new learning goals with section questions and problems; thumbnails in Chapter Review; matched problem sets; and an updated art program. I am in awe and much appreciate all the wonderful work of Jessica Neumann, associate editor, who was like an angel encouraging me at each step while skillfully coordinating reviews, art, website materials, and all the things it takes to make a book come together. I appreciate the work of Beth Sweeten, project manager, and Andrea Stefanowicz of PreMediaGlobal, who brilliantly coordinated all phases of the manuscript to the final pages of a beautiful book. Thanks to Mark Quirie and Vincent Dunlap, manuscript reviewers and accuracy checkers, and Denise Rubens, copy editor, who precisely reviewed and edited the manuscript to make sure the words and problems were correct to help students learn chemistry. Their keen eyes and thoughtful comments were extremely helpful in the development of this text.

I am especially proud of the art program in this text, which lends beauty and understanding to chemistry. I would like to thank Connie Long and Derek Bacchus, art director and book designer, whose creative ideas provided the outstanding design for the cover and pages of the book. Eric Schrader, photo researcher, was invaluable in researching and selecting vivid photos for the text so that students can see the beauty of chemistry. Thanks also to *Bio-Rad Laboratories* for their courtesy and use of *KnowItAll ChemWindows*, drawing software that helped me produce chemical structures for the manuscript. The macro-to-micro illustrations designed by Production Solutions and Precision Graphics give students visual impressions of the atomic and molecular organization of everyday things and are a fantastic learning tool. I want to thank Denne Wesolowski for the hours of proofreading all the pages. I also appreciate all the hard work in the field put in by the marketing team and Erin Gardner, marketing manager.

I am extremely grateful to an incredible group of peers for their careful assessment of all the new ideas for the text; for their suggested additions, corrections, changes, and deletions; and for providing an incredible amount of feedback about improvements for the book. In addition, I appreciate the time scientists took to let us take photos and discuss their work with them. I admire and appreciate every one of you.

If you would like to share your experience with chemistry or have questions and comments about this text, I would appreciate hearing from you.

Karen Timberlake

Email: khemist@aol.com

Reviewers

About the Author

KAREN TIMBERLAKE is Professor Emerita of Chemistry at Los Angeles Valley College, where she taught chemistry for allied health and preparatory chemistry for 36 years. She received her bachelor's degree in chemistry from the University of Washington and her master's degree in biochemistry from the University of California at Los Angeles.

Professor Timberlake has been writing chemistry textbooks for 35 years. During that time, her name has become associated with the strategic use of pedagogical tools that promote student success in chemistry and the application of chemistry to real-life situations. More than one million students have learned chemistry using texts, laboratory manuals, and study guides written by Karen Timberlake. In addition to *General, Organic, and Biological Chemistry: Structures of Life,* **Fourth Edition,** she is also the author of *Chemistry: An Introduction to General, Organic, and Biological Chemistry,* **Eleventh Edition,** and *Basic Chemistry,* **Third Edition.**

Professor Timberlake belongs to numerous scientific and educational organizations including the American Chemical Society (ACS) and the National Science Teachers Association (NSTA). She was the Western Regional Winner of Excellence in College Chemistry Teaching Award given by the Chemical Manufacturers Association. She received the McGuffey Award in Physical Sciences from the Textbook Authors Association for her textbook *Chemistry: An Introduction to General, Organic, and Biological Chemistry,* **Eighth Edition.** She received the "Texty" Textbook Excellence Award from the Textbook Authors Association for the first edition of *Basic Chemistry.* She has participated in education grants for science teaching including the Los Angeles Collaborative for Teaching Excellence (LACTE) and a Title III grant at her college. She speaks at conferences and educational meetings on the use of student-centered teaching methods in chemistry to promote the learning success of students.

Her husband, William Timberlake, who has contributed to writing this text, is Professor Emeritus of Chemistry at Los Angeles Harbor College, where he taught preparatory and organic chemistry for 36 years. He received his bachelor's degree in chemistry from Carnegie Mellon University and his master's degree in organic chemistry from the University of California at Los Angeles. When the Professors Timberlake are not writing textbooks, they relax by hiking, traveling, trying new restaurants, cooking, playing tennis, and taking care of their grandchildren, Daniel and Emily.

DEDICATION

I dedicate this book to

- My husband for his patience, loving support, and preparation of late meals

- My son, John, daughter-in-law, Cindy, grandson, Daniel, and granddaughter, Emily, for the precious things in life

- The wonderful students over many years whose hard work and commitment always motivated me and put purpose in my writing

Students learn chemistry using real-world examples

"Discovery consists of seeing what everybody has seen and thinking what nobody has thought."
—Albert Szent-Gyorgi

Feature	Description	Benefit	Page
NEW! Chapter Openers 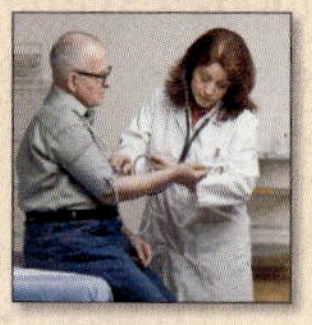	Chapters begin with **stories** involving careers such as nursing, physical therapy, dentistry, agriculture, and food science.	Show you how health professionals use chemistry every day	1
Explore Your World 	**Explore Your World** features are hands-on activities that use everyday materials to encourage you to explore selected chemistry topics.	Provide interactions with chemistry and support critical thinking	308
UPDATED! Chemistry Link to Health 	**Chemistry Links to Health** apply chemical concepts to relevant topics of health and medicine such as weight loss and weight gain, trans fats, anabolic steroids, alcohol abuse, genetic diseases, viruses, and cancer.	Provide you with connections that illustrate the importance of understanding chemistry in real life health and medical situations	28
UPDATED! Chemistry Link to the Environment 	**Chemistry Links to the Environment** relate chemistry to environmental topics such as global warming, radon in our homes, acid rain, and biodiesel.	Help you extend your understanding of the impact of chemistry on the environment	272
NEW! Chemistry Link to Industry 	**Chemistry Links to Industry** describe industrial and commercial applications in the oil industry and the commercial production of margarine and solid shortening.	Show you how chemistry is applied to industry and manufacturing	83
NEW! Chemistry Link to History 	**Chemistry Links to History** describe the historical development of chemical ideas.	Help you understand the role of chemistry in a historical setting	3
Career Focus	The **Career Focus** features within the chapters are additional examples of allied health professionals using chemistry.	Illustrate how chemistry is important in various fields within allied health	96

Engage students in the world of chemistry

"I never teach my pupils; I only attempt to provide the conditions in which they can learn."
—Albert Einstein

Feature	Description	Benefit	Page
Learning Goals LEARNING GOAL *Use the periodic table to identify the group and the period of an element; identify the element as a metal, nonmetal, or metalloid.*	**Learning Goals** at the beginning and end of each section identify the key concepts for that section and provide a roadmap for your study.	Help you focus your studying by emphasizing what is most important in each section	85
Writing Style The periodic table is an arrangement of the elements by increasing atomic number. A vertical column or group on the periodic table contains elements with similar properties. A horizontal row is called a period.	Timberlake's accessible **writing style** is based on careful development of chemical concepts suited to the skills and backgrounds of allied health students.	Helps you understand new terms and chemical concepts	120
UPDATED! Concept Maps	**Concept Maps** at the end of each chapter show how all the key concepts fit together.	Encourage learning by providing a **visual** guide to the interrelationship among all the concepts in each chapter	152
UPDATED! Macro-to-Micro Art	**Macro-to-Micro Art** utilizes photographs and drawings to illustrate recognizable objects and their atomic structure.	Helps you connect the world of atoms and molecules to the macroscopic world	210
UPDATED! Art Program	The **art program** is beautifully rendered, pedagogically effective, and includes questions with all the figures.	Helps you think critically using photos and illustrations	661
NEW! Chapter Review 3.5 Isotopes and Atomic Mass *LEARNING GOAL: Give the number of protons, neutrons, and electrons in one or more of the isotopes of an element; calculate the atomic mass of an element using the abundance and mass of its naturally occurring isotopes.* • Atoms that have the same number of protons but different numbers of neutrons are called isotopes. • The atomic mass of an element is the weighted average mass of all the atoms in a naturally occurring sample of that element.	The **Chapter Review** at the end of each chapter includes Learning Goals and new visual thumbnails to summarize the key points in each section.	Helps you determine your mastery of the chapter concepts and study for your tests	120

Many tools show students how to solve problems

"The whole art of teaching is only the art of awakening the natural curiosity of young minds."
—Anatole France

Feature	Description	Benefit	Page
UPDATED! Guide to Problem Solving (GPS) 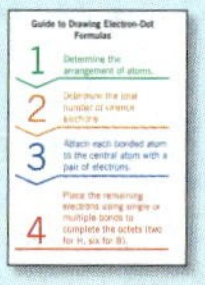	**Guides to Problem Solving (GPS)**	Visually guide you step-by-step through each problem solving strategy	177
End-of-Section Questions and Problems 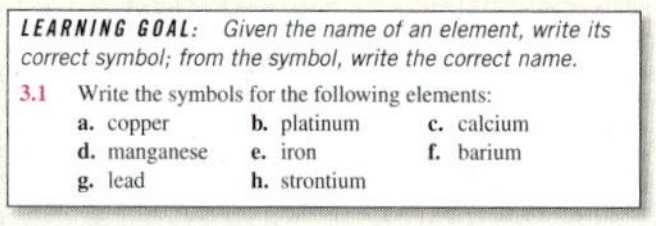	**Questions** and **Problems** are placed at the end of each section. Problems are paired and the Answers to the odd-numbered problems are given at the end of each chapter.	Encourage you to become involved immediately in the process of problem solving	85
Concept Checks 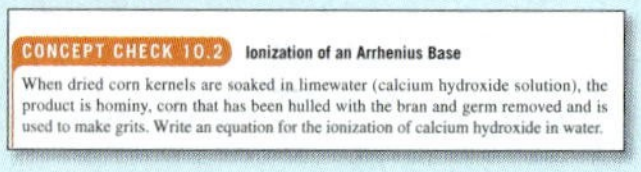	**Concept Checks** that transition from conceptual ideas to problem solving strategies are placed throughout each chapter.	Allow you to check your understanding of new chemical terms and ideas as they are introduced in the chapter	371
UPDATED! Sample Problems with Study Checks 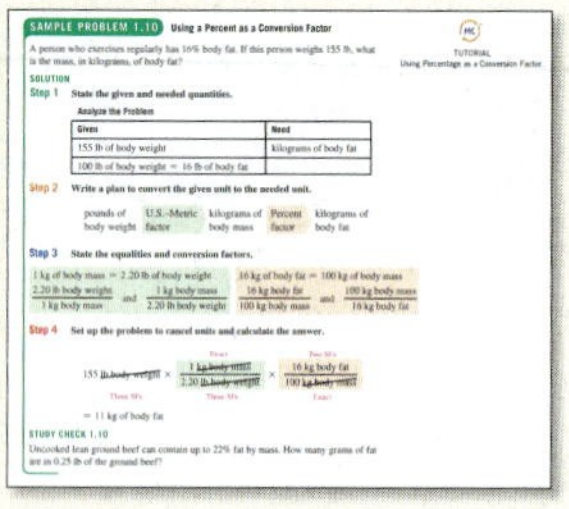	Numerous **Sample Problems** in each chapter demonstrate the application of each new concept to problem solving. The worked-out solutions give step-by-step explanations, provide a problem-solving model, and illustrate required calculations. **Study Checks** associated with each Sample Problem allow you to check your problem-solving strategies.	Provide the intermediate steps to guide you successfully through each type of problem	31
NEW! Analyze the Problem 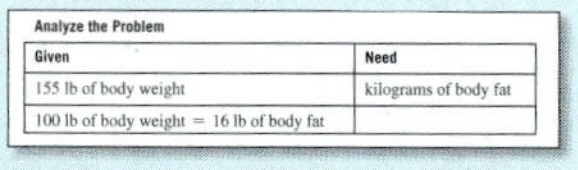	**Analyze the Problem** features now included in Sample Problem Solutions convert information in a word problem into components for problem solving.	Help you identify and utilize the components within a word problem to set up a solution strategy.	31
UPDATED! Understanding the Concepts 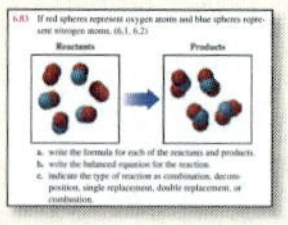	**Understanding the Concepts** are questions with visual representations placed at the end of each chapter.	Build an understanding of newly learned chemical concepts	249
UPDATED! Additional Questions 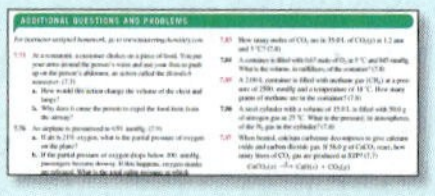	**Additional Questions** at the end of chapter provide further study and application of the topics from the entire chapter.	Promote critical thinking	293
Challenge Questions 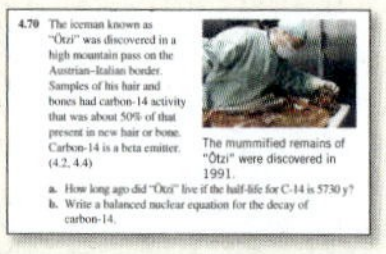	**Challenge Questions** at the end of each chapter provide complex questions.	Promote critical thinking, group work, and cooperative learning environments	156
UPDATED! Combining Ideas 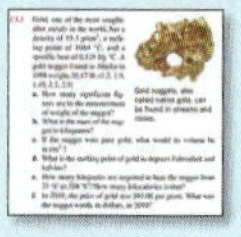	**Combining Ideas** are sets of integrated problems that are placed after every 2-4 chapters.	Test your understanding of the concepts from previous chapters by integrating topics	79

MasteringChemistry®

MasteringChemistry® is designed with a single purpose: to help students reach the moment of understanding. The Mastering online homework and tutoring system delivers self-paced tutorials that provide students with individualized coaching set to instructors' course objectives. MasteringChemistry helps students arrive better prepared for lecture and lab.

Engaging Experiences

MasteringChemistry® promotes interactivity and active learning in General, Organic, and Biological Chemistry. Research shows that Mastering's immediate feedback and tutorial assistance help students understand and master concepts and skills in Chemistry—allowing them to retain more knowledge and perform better in this course and beyond.

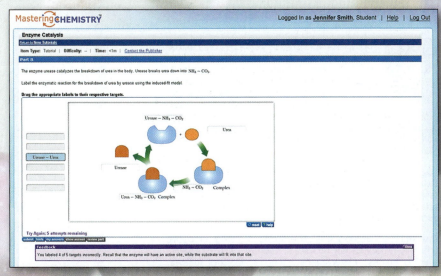

◀ NEW! Chemistry Tutorials

General, Organic, and Biological Chemistry Tutorials help students develop and refine their problem-solving skills in Chemistry by providing answer-specific feedback and coaching. For the **Fourth Edition,** new tutorials have been created to guide students through the most challenging General, Organic, and Biological Chemistry topics and help them make connections between different concepts.

NEW! Concept ▶ Map Quizzes

Concept Map Quizzes give students the opportunity to interactively make connections between important concepts.

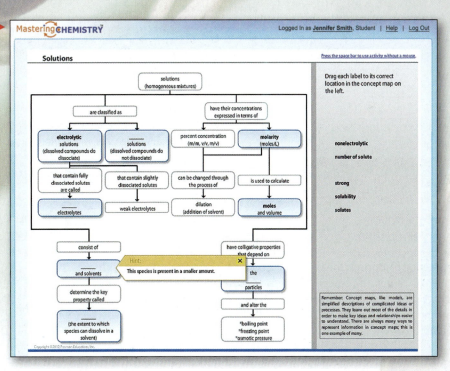

▼ Career Focus Links

Career Focus links, located in the Study Area of MasteringChemistry, expand on the book's Chapter Opening stories and provide insight into how science is used daily in modern careers.

Logged In as **Jennifer Smith**, Student | Help | Log Out

Chapter Guide
Learning Goals
Self Study Activities
PowerPoint Presentations
Review Questions
Quizzes
eText
Career Focus
Case Studies
Math Tools
Flashcards
Glossary
Periodic Table
Tutoring Services

OCCUPATIONAL THERAPIST

Career Focus: Occupational Therapist

Occupational therapist Leslie Wakasa builds self-confidence in patients by teaching them to live more independently. "Occupational therapists teach children and adults skills for the job of living. It's rewarding when you can show children how to feed themselves, which is a huge self-esteem issue for them. The possibility of helping people become more independent is very rewarding."

A child born with a birth defect, a person injured in an accident, or a person recovering from a stroke need the help of an occupational therapist to develop or regain basic mobility and reasoning skills. An occupational therapist also helps patients adjust to permanent disabilities.

You will see occupational therapists working in public schools, rehabilitation hospitals, mental health centers, nursing homes, government agencies, doctors' offices, and home health agencies. In these settings, occupational therapists use their background in biochemistry and anatomy to help people regain skills for living independently.

End of Chapter

The majority of end-of-chapter problems are now easily assignable within MasteringChemistry to help students prepare for the types of questions that may appear on a test.

Proven Results

The Mastering platform is the only online homework system with research showing that it improves student learning. A wide variety of published papers based on NSF-sponsored research and tests illustrate the benefits of the Mastering program. Results documented in scientifically valid efficacy papers are available at www.masteringchemistry.com/site/results

MasteringChemistry®

A Trusted Partner

The Mastering platform was developed by scientists for science students and instructors, and has a proven history with more than 10 years of student use. Mastering currently has more than 1.5 million active registrations with active users in 50 states and in 41 countries. The Mastering platform has 99.8% server reliability.

◄ NEW! Learning Outcomes

Let Mastering do the work in tracking student performance against your learning outcomes:

- Add your own or use the publisher-provided learning outcomes to track student performance and report it to your administration.
- View class performance against the specified learning outcomes.
- Export results to a spreadsheet that you can further customize and/or share with your chair, dean, administrator, or accreditation board.

Mastering offers a data supported measure to quantify students' learning gains and to share those results quickly and easily.

▼ Gradebook

The Gradebook records all scores for automatically graded assignments. At a glance, shades of red highlight struggling students and challenging assignments.

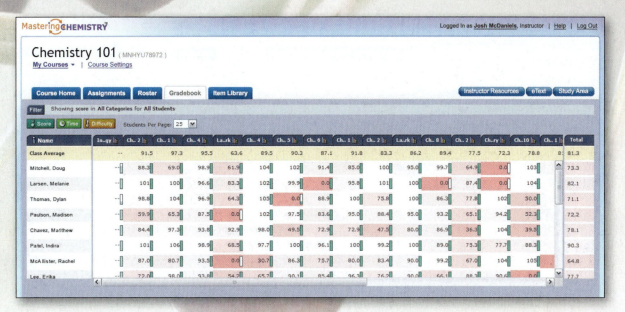

Gradebook Diagnostics

Gradebook diagnostics provide unique insight into class and student performance. With a single click, charts summarize the most difficult problems, vulnerable students, grade distribution, and even score improvement over the duration of the course.

Student Performance Data ▶

With a single click, Student Performance Data provides at-a-glance statistics on your class as well as national results. Wrong answer summaries give unique insight into your students' misconceptions and facilitate just-in-time teaching adjustments.

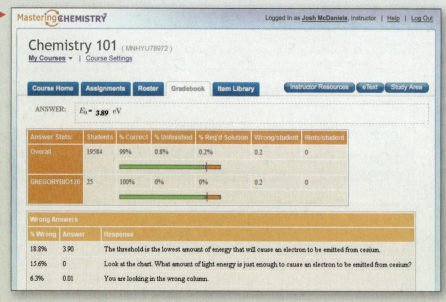

Chemistry and Measurements

1

Visit **www.masteringchemistry.com** for self-study materials and instructor-assigned homework.

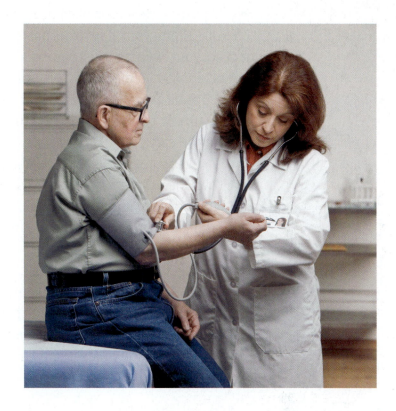

Within the past few months, Greg has been experiencing an increased number of headaches, and frequently feels dizzy and nauseous. He goes to his doctor's office where the registered nurse completes the initial part of the exam by recording several measurements: weight 88.5 kg, height 190.5 cm, temperature 37.2 °C, and blood pressure 155/95. A normal blood pressure is 120/80 or below.

When Greg sees his doctor, he is diagnosed as having high blood pressure (hypertension). The doctor prescribes 40 mg of Inderal (propranolol), which is used to treat hypertension and to be taken twice daily. The registered nurse fills the prescription at the pharmacy, which consists of 20-mg tablets. The nurse completes a calculation and determines that Greg needs to take 2 tablets each time.

Two weeks later, Greg visits his doctor again, who determines that his blood pressure is still elevated at 152/90. The doctor increases the dosage of Inderal to 60 mg, twice daily. The registered nurse informs Greg that he needs to increase his dosage to 3 tablets, twice daily.

Career: Registered Nurse

In addition to assisting physicians, registered nurses work to promote patient health, and prevent and treat disease. They provide patient care and help patients cope with illness. They take measurements such as a patient's weight, height, temperature, and blood pressure; make conversions; and calculate drug dosages. Registered nurses also maintain detailed medical records of patient symptoms, prescribed medications, and any reactions.

Chemistry and measurement are important parts of our everyday lives. Levels of toxic materials in the air, soil, and water are discussed in news reports. We read about radon in our homes, holes in the ozone layer, trans fats, and global climate change. We also read about nonpolluting fuels, solar energy, new techniques of DNA analysis, and new discoveries in medicine. Understanding chemistry and measurement helps us make informed choices about our world.

Think about your day; you probably made some measurements. Perhaps you checked your weight by stepping on a scale. If you did not feel well, you may have taken your temperature. If you made some rice for dinner, you added two cups of water to one cup of rice. If you stopped at the gas station, you watched the gas pump measure the number of gallons of gasoline you put in the car.

Measurement is an essential part of health careers such as nursing, dental hygiene, respiratory therapy, nutrition, and veterinary technology. The temperature, height, and weight of a patient are measured in degrees Celsius, meters, and kilograms, respectively. Samples of blood and urine are collected and sent to a laboratory where glucose, pH, urea, and protein levels are measured by the clinical technicians.

By learning about measurement, you will develop skills for solving problems and working with numbers in chemistry. If you intend to go into a health career, an understanding and assessment of measurements will be an important part of your evaluation of a patient's health.

Your weight on a bathroom scale is a measurement.

Define the term chemistry *and identify substances as chemicals.*

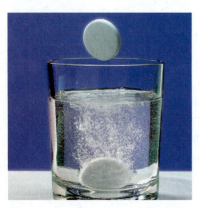

Antacid tablets undergo a chemical reaction when dropped into water.

1.1 Chemistry and Chemicals

Chemistry is the study of the composition, structure, properties, and reactions of matter. *Matter* is another word for all the substances that make up our world. Perhaps you imagine that chemistry is done only in a laboratory by a chemist wearing a lab coat and protective lab glasses. Actually, chemistry happens all around you every day and has an impact on everything you use and do. You are doing chemistry when you cook food, add chlorine to a swimming pool, or drop an antacid tablet into water. Plants grow because chemical reactions convert carbon dioxide, water, and energy to carbohydrates. Chemical reactions take place when you digest food and break it down into substances that you need for energy and health.

Branches of Chemistry

The field of chemistry is divided into several branches. Those of most interest to us are general, organic, and biological chemistry. General chemistry is the study of the composition, properties, and reactions of matter. Organic chemistry is the study of substances that contain the element carbon. Biological chemistry is the study of the chemical reactions that take place in biological systems.

Today, chemistry is often combined with other sciences such as geology and physics to form cross-disciplines such as geochemistry and physical chemistry. Geochemistry is the study of the chemical composition of ores, soils, and minerals of the surface of the Earth and other planets. Physical chemistry is the study of the physical nature of chemical systems, including energy changes.

A geochemist collects newly erupted lava samples from Kilauea Volcano, Hawaii.

Biochemists analyze laboratory samples.

Chemistry Link to History

EARLY CHEMISTS: THE ALCHEMISTS

For many centuries, chemists have studied changes in various substances. From the time of the ancient Greeks to about the sixteenth century, alchemists described a substance in terms of four components of nature: earth, air, fire, and water. By the eighth century, alchemists searched for an unknown substance called a philosopher's stone that they thought would turn metals into gold, as well as prolong youth and postpone death. Although these efforts failed, the alchemists did provide information on the processes and chemical reactions involved in the extraction of metals from ores. The alchemists also designed some of the first laboratory equipment and developed early laboratory procedures.

The alchemist Paracelsus (1493–1541) thought that alchemy should be about preparing new medicines, not about producing gold. Using observation and experimentation, he proposed that a healthy body was regulated by a series of chemical processes that could be unbalanced by certain chemical compounds and rebalanced by using minerals and medicines. For example, he determined that inhaled dust, not underground spirits, caused lung disease in miners. He also thought that goiter was a problem caused by contaminated water, and he treated syphilis with compounds of mercury. His opinion of medicines was that the right dose makes the difference between a poison and a cure. Today, this idea is part of the risk analysis of medicines.

Paracelsus changed alchemy in ways that helped to establish modern medicine and chemistry.

Alchemists in the Middle Ages developed laboratory procedures.

Swiss alchemist and physician Paracelsus (1493–1541) believed that chemicals and minerals could be used as medicines.

Chemicals

A **chemical** is a substance that always has the same composition and properties wherever it is found. All the things you see around you are composed of one or more chemicals. Chemical processes take place in chemistry laboratories, manufacturing plants, and pharmaceutical labs, as well as every day in nature and in our bodies. Often the terms *chemical* and *substance* are used interchangeably to describe a specific type of material.

Every day, you use products containing substances that were prepared by chemists. Soaps and shampoos contain chemicals that remove oils on your skin and scalp. When you brush your teeth, the substances in toothpaste clean your teeth, prevent plaque formation, and stop tooth decay. Some of the chemicals used to make toothpaste are listed in Table 1.1.

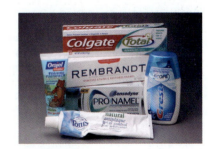

Toothpaste is a combination of many chemicals.

TABLE 1.1 Chemicals Commonly Used in Toothpaste

Chemical	Function
Calcium carbonate	Used as an abrasive to remove plaque
Sorbitol	Prevents loss of water and hardening of toothpaste
Sodium lauryl sulfate	Used to loosen plaque
Titanium dioxide	Makes toothpaste white and opaque
Triclosan	Inhibits bacteria that cause plaque and gum disease
Sodium fluorophosphate	Prevents formation of cavities by strengthening tooth enamel with fluoride
Methyl salicylate	Gives toothpaste a pleasant wintergreen flavor

In cosmetics and lotions, chemicals are used to moisturize, prevent deterioration of the product, fight bacteria, and thicken the product. Your clothes may be made of natural materials such as cotton, or synthetic substances such as nylon or polyester. Perhaps you wear a ring or watch made of gold, silver, or platinum. Your breakfast cereal is probably fortified with iron, calcium, and phosphorus, while the milk you drink is enriched with vitamins A and D. Antioxidants are chemicals added to your cereal to prevent it from spoiling. Chemicals you may encounter in the kitchen are shown in Figure 1.1.

Silicon dioxide (glass)
Chemically treated water
Metal alloy
Natural polymers
Natural gas
Fruits grown with fertilizers and pesticides

FIGURE 1.1 Many of the items found in a kitchen are chemicals or products of chemical reactions.
Q What are some other chemicals found in a kitchen?

CONCEPT CHECK 1.1 Chemicals

Why is the copper in copper wire an example of a chemical?

ANSWER

Copper has the same composition and properties wherever it is found. Thus, copper is a chemical.

QUESTIONS AND PROBLEMS

1.1 Chemistry and Chemicals

In every chapter, odd-numbered exercises in the *Questions and Problems* are paired with even-numbered exercises. The answers for the magenta, odd-numbered *Questions and Problems* are given at the end of this chapter. The complete solutions to the odd-numbered *Questions and Problems* are in the *Student Solutions Manual*.

LEARNING GOAL: *Define the term* chemistry *and identify substances as chemicals.*

1.1 Obtain a bottle of multivitamins, and read the list of ingredients. What are four chemicals from the list?

1.2 Obtain a box of breakfast cereal, and read the list of ingredients. What are four chemicals from the list?

1.3 A "chemical-free" shampoo includes the ingredients: water, cocomide, glycerin, and citric acid. Is the shampoo truly "chemical-free"?

1.4 A "chemical-free" sunscreen includes the ingredients: titanium dioxide, vitamin E, and vitamin C. Is the sunscreen truly "chemical-free"?

1.2 A Study Plan for Learning Chemistry

Here you are taking chemistry, perhaps for the first time. Whatever your reasons are for choosing to study chemistry, you can look forward to learning many new and exciting ideas.

Features in This Text Help You Study Chemistry

This text has been designed with study features to complement your individual learning style. On the inside of the front cover is a periodic table of the elements. On the inside of the back cover are tables that summarize useful information needed throughout your study of chemistry. Each chapter begins with *Looking Ahead*, which outlines the topics in the chapter. A *Learning Goal* at the beginning of each section previews the concepts you are to learn. At the end of the text, there is a comprehensive *Glossary and Index*, which lists and defines key terms used in the text.

Before you begin reading, obtain an overview of a chapter by reviewing the topics in *Looking Ahead*. As you prepare to read a section of the chapter, look at the section title and turn it into a question. For example, for Section 1.1 "Chemistry and Chemicals," you could ask "What is chemistry?" or "What are chemicals?" When you are ready to read through that section, review the *Learning Goal*, which tells you what to expect in that section. As you read, try to answer your question. Throughout the chapter, you will find *Concept Checks* that will help you understand key ideas. When you come to a *Sample Problem*, take the time to work it through and compare your solution to the one provided. Then try the associated *Study Check*. Many *Sample Problems* are accompanied by a *Guide to Problem Solving* (*GPS*), which gives the steps needed to work the problem. At the end of each section, you will find a set of *Questions and Problems* that allows you to apply problem solving immediately to the new concepts.

Throughout each chapter, boxes titled *Chemistry Link to Health*, *Chemistry Link to the Environment*, *Chemistry Link to Industry*, and *Chemistry Link to History* help you connect the chemical concepts you are learning to real-life situations. Many of the figures and diagrams use macro-to-micro illustrations to depict the atomic level of organization of ordinary objects. These visual models illustrate the concepts described in the text and allow you to "see" the world in a microscopic way.

At the end of each chapter, you will find several study aids that complete the chapter. *Concept Maps* show the connections between important concepts, and *Chapter Reviews* provide a summary. The *Key Terms*, which are in boldface type in the text, are listed with their definitions. *Understanding the Concepts*, a set of questions that use art and structures, helps you visualize concepts. *Additional Questions and Problems* and *Challenge Problems* provide additional problems to test your understanding of the topics in the chapter. The problems are paired, which means that each of the odd-numbered problems is similar to the following even-numbered problem. The answers to all the *Study Checks*, as well as the answers to the odd-numbered *Questions and Problems*, are provided at the end of each chapter. If the answers provided match your answers, you most likely understand the topic; if not, you need to study the section again.

After some chapters, problem sets called *Combining Ideas* test your ability to solve problems that combine material from more than one chapter.

Using Active Learning to Learn Chemistry

A student who is an active learner continually interacts with the chemical ideas while reading the text, working problems, and attending lecture. Let's see how this is done.

As you read and practice problem solving, you remain actively involved in studying, which enhances the learning process. In this way, you learn small bits of information at a time and establish the necessary foundation for understanding the next section. You should also note any questions you have about the reading to discuss

Students discuss a chemistry problem with their professor during office hours.

TABLE 1.2 Steps in Active Learning

1. Read each *Learning Goal* for an overview of the material.
2. Form a question from the title of the section you are going to read.
3. Read the section, looking for answers to your question.
4. Self-test by working *Concept Checks*, *Sample Problems*, and *Study Checks*.
5. Complete the *Questions and Problems* that follow that section, and check the answers for the magenta odd-numbered problems.
6. Work the exercises in the *Study Guide* and go to *www.masteringchemistry.com* for self-study materials and instructor-assigned homework (optional).
7. Proceed to the next section, and repeat the above steps.

with your professor and laboratory instructor. Table 1.2 summarizes these steps for active learning. The time you spend in lecture is also useful as a learning time. By keeping track of the class schedule and reading the assigned material before lecture, you become aware of the new terms and concepts you need to learn. Some questions that occur during your reading may be answered during the lecture. If not, you can ask for further clarification from your professor.

Many students find that studying with a group can be beneficial to learning. In a group, students motivate each other to study, fill in gaps, and correct misunderstandings by learning together. Studying alone does not allow the process of peer correction. In a group, you can cover the ideas more thoroughly as you discuss the reading and practice problem solving with other students. You may find it is easier to retain new material and new ideas if you study in short sessions throughout the week rather than all at once. Waiting to study until the night before an exam does not give you time to understand concepts and practice problem solving.

Studying in a group can be beneficial to learning.

Thinking About Your Study Plan

As you embark on your journey into the world of chemistry, think about your approach to studying and learning chemistry. You might consider some of the ideas in the following list. Check those ideas that will help you learn chemistry successfully. Commit to them now. *Your* success depends on *you*.

My study of chemistry will include the following:

_____ reading the chapter before a lecture

_____ going to lecture

_____ reviewing the *Learning Goals*

_____ keeping a problem notebook

_____ reading the text as an active learner

_____ self-testing by working *Questions and Problems* following each section and checking answers at the end of the chapter

_____ being an active learner during lecture

_____ organizing a study group

_____ seeing the professor during office hours

_____ completing exercises in the *Study Guide*

_____ working through the tutorials at *www.masteringchemistry.com*

_____ attending review sessions

_____ organizing my own review sessions

_____ studying as often as I can

CONCEPT CHECK 1.2 **A Study Plan for Learning Chemistry**

Which of the following activities would you include in your study plan for learning chemistry successfully?

a. skipping lecture
b. forming a study group
c. keeping a problem notebook
d. waiting to study the night before the exam
e. becoming an active learner

ANSWER

Your success in chemistry can be improved by:
b. forming a study group
c. keeping a problem notebook
e. becoming an active learner

QUESTIONS AND PROBLEMS

1.2 A Study Plan for Learning Chemistry

LEARNING GOAL: *Develop a study plan for learning chemistry.*

1.5 What are four things you can do to help yourself to succeed in chemistry?

1.6 What are four things that would make it difficult for you to succeed in chemistry?

1.7 A student in your class asks you for advice on learning chemistry. Which of the following might you suggest?
a. Form a study group.
b. Skip lecture.
c. Visit the professor during office hours.
d. Wait until the night before an exam to study.
e. Become an active learner.
f. Work the *Learning Exercises* in the *Study Guide.*

1.8 A student in your class asks you for advice on learning chemistry. Which of the following might you suggest?
a. Do the assigned problems.
b. Don't read the book; it's never on the test.
c. Attend review sessions.
d. Read the assignment before a lecture.
e. Keep a problem notebook.
f. Do the tutorials at *www.masteringchemistry.com.*

1.3 Units of Measurement

LEARNING GOAL

Write the names and abbreviations for metric or SI units used in measurements of length, volume, mass, temperature, and time.

Scientists and health professionals throughout the world use the **metric system** of measurement. The **International System of Units (SI)**, or Système International, is the official system of measurement throughout the world except for the United States. In chemistry, we use metric and SI units for length, volume, mass, temperature, and time (see Table 1.3).

TABLE 1.3 Units of Measurement

Measurement	Metric	SI
Length	meter (m)	meter (m)
Volume	liter (L)	cubic meter (m^3)
Mass	gram (g)	kilogram (kg)
Temperature	degree Celsius (°C)	kelvin (K)
Time	second (s)	second (s)

Suppose today, you walk 2.1 km to campus carrying a backpack that has a mass of 12 kg, when the temperature is 22 °C. Perhaps you have a mass of 58.2 kg and a height of 165 cm. You may be more familiar with these measurements stated in the U.S. system of measurement: Then you walk 1.3 mi carrying a backpack that weighs 26 lb. The temperature would be 72 °F. You have a weight of 128 lb and a height of 65 in.

There are many measurements in everyday life.

Length

The metric and SI unit of length is the **meter (m)**. A meter is 39.4 inches (in.), which makes it slightly longer than a yard (yd). The **centimeter (cm)**, a smaller unit of length, is commonly used in chemistry and is about as wide as your little finger. For comparison, there are 2.54 cm in 1 in. (see Figure 1.2). Some useful relationships between different units for length follow:

$$1 \text{ m} = 100 \text{ cm}$$
$$1 \text{ m} = 39.4 \text{ in.}$$
$$1 \text{ m} = 1.09 \text{ yd}$$
$$2.54 \text{ cm} = 1 \text{ in.}$$

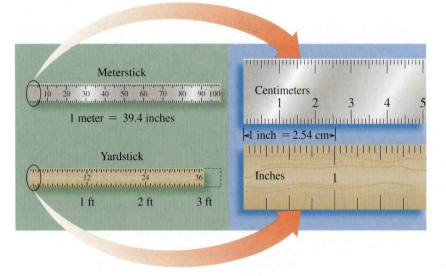

FIGURE 1.2 Length in the metric and SI systems is based on the meter, which is slightly longer than a yard.
Q How many centimeters are in a length of one inch?

Volume

Volume is the amount of space a substance occupies. A **liter (L)** is slightly larger than a quart (qt), (1 L = 1.06 qt). In a laboratory or a hospital, chemists work with metric units of volume that are smaller and more convenient, such as the **milliliter (mL)**. There are 1000 mL in 1 L (see Figure 1.3). The SI unit of volume is the cubic meter (m^3), a unit

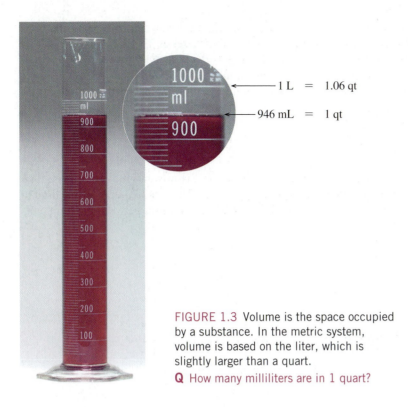

FIGURE 1.3 Volume is the space occupied by a substance. In the metric system, volume is based on the liter, which is slightly larger than a quart.
Q How many milliliters are in 1 quart?

1 L = 1.06 qt

946 mL = 1 qt

The standard kilogram for the United States is stored at the National Institute of Standards and Technology (NIST).

FIGURE 1.4 On an electronic balance, a nickel has a mass of 5.01 g in the digital readout.
Q What is the mass of 10 nickels?

FIGURE 1.5 A thermometer is used to determine temperature.
Q What kinds of temperature readings have you made today?

that is too large for practical use in the laboratory or hospital. Some useful relationships between different units for volume follow:

$$1 \text{ L} = 1000 \text{ mL}$$
$$1 \text{ L} = 1.06 \text{ qt}$$
$$946 \text{ mL} = 1 \text{ qt}$$
$$1000 \text{ L} = 1 \text{ m}^3$$

Mass

The **mass** of an object is a measure of the quantity of material it contains. The SI unit of mass, the **kilogram (kg)**, is used for large masses such as body weight. In the metric system, the unit for mass is the **gram (g)**, which is used for small masses. There are 1000 g in one kilogram. It takes 2.20 lb to make 1 kg, and 454 g are equal to one pound. Some useful relationships between different units for mass follow:

$$1 \text{ kg} = 1000 \text{ g}$$
$$1 \text{ kg} = 2.20 \text{ lb}$$
$$454 \text{ g} = 1 \text{ lb}$$

You may be more familiar with the term *weight* than with mass. Weight is a measure of the gravitational pull on an object. On Earth, an astronaut with a mass of 75.0 kg has a weight of 165 lb. On the Moon, where the gravitational pull is one-sixth that of Earth, the astronaut has a weight of 27.5 lb. However, the mass of the astronaut, 75.0 kg, is the same as on Earth. Scientists measure mass rather than weight because mass does not depend on gravity.

In a chemistry laboratory, an electronic balance is used to measure the mass of a substance in grams (see Figure 1.4).

Temperature

Temperature tells us how hot something is, how cold it is outside, or helps us determine if we have a fever (see Figure 1.5). In the metric system, temperature is measured using degrees Celsius. On the **Celsius (°C) temperature scale**, water freezes at 0 °C and boils at 100 °C, while on the Fahrenheit (°F) scale, water freezes at 32 °F and boils at 212 °F. In the SI system, temperature is measured using the **Kelvin (K) temperature scale**, on which the lowest temperature is 0 K. A unit on the Kelvin scale is called a kelvin and is not written with a degree sign. We will discuss the relationship between these three temperature scales in Chapter 2.

Time

The SI and metric basic unit of time is the **second (s)**. However, we also measure time in units of years (y), days, hours (h), or minutes (min). The standard device now used to determine a second is an atomic clock. Some useful relationships between different units for time follow:

$$1 \text{ day} = 24 \text{ h}$$
$$1 \text{ h} = 60 \text{ min}$$
$$1 \text{ min} = 60 \text{ s}$$

A stopwatch is used to measure the time of a race.

SAMPLE PROBLEM 1.1 Units of Measurement

State the type of measurement indicated by the unit in each of the following:

a. 25 g   **b.** 0.85 L   **c.** 36 m   **d.** 17 °C

SOLUTION

a. A gram (g) is a unit of mass.
b. A liter (L) is a unit of volume.
c. A meter (m) is a unit of length.
d. A degree Celsius (°C) is a unit of temperature.

STUDY CHECK 1.1

What type of measurement is indicated by the unit in 45 s?

QUESTIONS AND PROBLEMS

1.3 Units of Measurement

LEARNING GOAL: Write the names and abbreviations for metric or SI units used in measurements of length, volume, mass, temperature, and time.

1.9 State the type of measurement in each of the following statements:
  a. I filled my gas tank with 12 L of gasoline.
  b. My friend is 170 cm tall.
  c. We are 385 000 km away from the Moon.
  d. The horse won the race by 1.2 s.

1.10 State the type of measurement in each of the following statements:
  a. I rode my bicycle 15 km today.
  b. My dog weighs 12 kg.
  c. It is hot today. It is 30 °C.
  d. I used 2 L of water to fill my fish tank.

1.11 State the name of the unit and the type of measurement indicated for each of the following quantities:
  a. 4.8 m   **b.** 325 g   **c.** 1.5 L   **d.** 480 s   **e.** 28 °C

1.12 State the name of the unit and the type of measurement indicated for each of the following quantities:
  a. 0.8 mL   **b.** 3.6 cm   **c.** 14 kg   **d.** 35 h   **e.** 373 K

1.4 Scientific Notation

In chemistry, we use numbers that are very large or very small. We might measure something as tiny as the width of a human hair, which is about 0.000 008 m. Or perhaps we want to count the number of hairs in the average human scalp, which is about 100 000 hairs (see Figure 1.6). In this text, we add spaces between sets of three digits when it helps to make the places easier to count. However, we will see that it is more convenient to write small and large numbers in scientific notation.

Item	Value	Scientific Notation
Width of a human hair	0.000 008 m	8×10^{-6} m
Hairs on a human scalp	100 000 hairs	1×10^5 hairs

1×10^5 hairs

8×10^{-6} m

FIGURE 1.6 Humans have an average of 1×10^5 hairs on their scalps. Each hair is about 8×10^{-6} m wide.

Q Why are large and small numbers written in scientific notation?

TUTORIAL
Scientific Notation

Writing a Number in Scientific Notation

A number written in **scientific notation** has three parts: a coefficient, a power of 10, and a unit of measurement. For example, 2400 m is written in scientific notation as 2.4×10^3 m. The coefficient is 2.4, and 10^3 shows that the power of 10 is 3 and the unit of measurement is meter (m). The coefficient is obtained by moving the decimal point to the left to give a coefficient that is at least 1 but less than 10. Because we moved the decimal point three places, the power of 10 is 3, written as 10^3. When a number greater than 1 is converted to scientific notation, the power of 10 is positive. *A number greater than 1 written in scientific notation has a positive power of 10.*

$$2400. \text{ m} = 2.4 \times 1000 = 2.4 \times 10^3 \text{ m}$$

⟵—3 places   Coefficient   Power   Unit
of 10

When a number less than 1 is written in scientific notation, the power of 10 is a negative number. *A number less than 1 written in scientific notation has a negative power of 10.* For example, the number 0.000 86 is written in scientific notation by moving the decimal point four places to give a coefficient of 8.6. Because the decimal point was moved four places to the right, the power of 10 is a negative 4, written as 10^{-4}.

$$0.00086 \text{ g} = \frac{8.6}{10\,000} = \frac{8.6}{10 \times 10 \times 10 \times 10} = 8.6 \times 10^{-4} \text{ g}$$

4 places →   Coefficient   Power   Unit
of 10

Table 1.4 gives some examples of numbers written as positive and negative powers of 10. The powers of 10 are a way to keep track of the decimal point in the decimal number. Table 1.5 gives several examples of writing measurements in scientific notation.

TABLE 1.4 Some Powers of 10

Number	Multiples of 10	Scientific Notation	Powers of Ten
10 000	$10 \times 10 \times 10 \times 10$	1×10^4	
1 000	$10 \times 10 \times 10$	1×10^3	
100	10×10	1×10^2	Some positive powers of 10
10	10	1×10^1	
1	0	1×10^0	
0.1	$\dfrac{1}{10}$	1×10^{-1}	
0.01	$\dfrac{1}{10} \times \dfrac{1}{10} = \dfrac{1}{100}$	1×10^{-2}	Some negative powers of 10
0.001	$\dfrac{1}{10} \times \dfrac{1}{10} \times \dfrac{1}{10} = \dfrac{1}{1000}$	1×10^{-3}	
0.0001	$\dfrac{1}{10} \times \dfrac{1}{10} \times \dfrac{1}{10} \times \dfrac{1}{10} = \dfrac{1}{10\,000}$	1×10^{-4}	

A chickenpox virus has a diameter of 3×10^{-7} m.

TABLE 1.5 Some Measurements Written in Scientific Notation

Measured Quantity	Measurement	Scientific Notation
Volume of gasoline used in the United States each year	550 000 000 000 L	5.5×10^{11} L
Diameter of Earth	12 800 000 m	1.28×10^7 m
Time for light to travel from the Sun to Earth	500 s	5×10^2 s
Mass of a typical human	68 kg	6.8×10^1 kg
Mass of a hummingbird	0.002 kg	2×10^{-3} kg
Diameter of a chickenpox (*varicella zoster*) virus	0.000 000 3 m	3×10^{-7} m
Mass of a bacterium (mycoplasma)	0.000 000 000 000 000 000 1 kg	1×10^{-19} kg

TUTORIAL
Using Scientific Notation

Scientific Notation and Calculators

You can enter a number in scientific notation on many calculators using the EE or EXP key. After you enter the coefficient, press the EXP (or EE) key and enter only the power of 10, because the EXP function key already includes the $\times$ 10 value. To enter a negative power of 10, press the plus/minus $(+/-)$ key or the minus $(-)$ key, depending on your calculator. As you work through these problems, read the instruction manual for your particular calculator to determine the proper sequence for using the keys.

Number to Enter	Method	Display Reads	
4×10^6	4 EXP (EE) 6	4 06 or 4⁰⁶ or 4 E06	
2.5×10^{-4}	2.5 EXP (EE) +/− 4	2.5−04 or 2.5⁻⁰⁴ or 2.5 E−04	

When a calculator display appears in scientific notation, it is shown as a number between 1 and 10, followed by a space and the power of 10. To express this display in scientific notation, write the coefficient value, write $\times$ 10, and use the power of 10 as an exponent.

Calculator Display	Expressed in Scientific Notation
7.52 04 or 7.52⁰⁴ or 7.52 E04	7.52×10^4
5.8−02 or 5.8⁻⁰² or 5.8 E−02	5.8×10^{-2}

On many scientific calculators, a number is converted into scientific notation using the appropriate keys. For example, the number 0.000 52 can be entered, followed by pressing the 2nd or 3rd function key and the SCI key. The scientific notation appears in the calculator display as a coefficient and the power of 10.

0.000 52 [2nd or 3rd function key] [SCI] = $5.2-04$ or 5.2^{-04} or $5.2\ E-04$ = 5.2×10^{-4}

Key   Key

Converting Scientific Notation to a Standard Number

When a number in scientific notation has a positive power of 10, the standard number is written by moving the decimal point to the right for the same number of places as the power of 10. Placeholder zeros are used to give additional decimal places.

$$8.2 \times 10^2 = 8.2 \times 100 = 820$$

When a number written in scientific notation has a negative power of 10, the standard number is written by moving the decimal point to the left for the same number of places. Placeholder zeros are added in front of the coefficient as needed.

$$4.3 \times 10^{-3} = 4.3 \times \frac{1}{1000} = 0.0043$$

SAMPLE PROBLEM 1.2 **Scientific Notation**

Write each of the following in scientific notation:

a. 45 000 m   **b.** 0.0092 g   **c.** 143 mL

SOLUTION

a. To write a coefficient greater than 1 but less than 10, move the decimal point four places to the left to give 4.5×10^4 m.

b. To write a coefficient greater than 1 but less than 10, move the decimal point three places to the right to give 9.2×10^{-3} g.

c. To write a coefficient greater than 1 but less than 10, move the decimal point two places to the left to give 1.43×10^2 mL.

STUDY CHECK 1.2

Write the following measurements in scientific notation:

a. 425 000 m   **b.** 0.000 000 8 g

QUESTIONS AND PROBLEMS

1.4 Scientific Notation

LEARNING GOAL: *Write a number in scientific notation.*

1.13 Write each of the following measurements in scientific notation:
  a. 55 000 m   **b.** 480 g   **c.** 0.000 005 cm
  d. 0.000 14 s   **e.** 0.007 85 L   **f.** 670 000 kg

1.14 Write each of the following measurements in scientific notation:
  a. 180 000 000 g   **b.** 0.000 06 m
  c. 750 °C   **d.** 0.15 mL
  e. 0.024 s   **f.** 1500 cm

1.15 Which number in each of the following pairs is larger?
  a. 7.2×10^3 cm or 8.2×10^2 cm
  b. 4.5×10^{-4} kg or 3.2×10^{-2} kg
  c. 1×10^4 L or 1×10^{-4} L
  d. 0.000 52 m or 6.8×10^{-2} m

1.16 Which number in each of the following pairs is smaller?
  a. 4.9×10^{-3} s or 5.5×10^{-9} s
  b. 1250 kg or 3.4×10^2 kg
  c. 0.000 000 4 m or 5×10^{-8} m
  d. 2.50×10^2 g or 4×10^{-2} g

1.17 Write each of the following as standard numbers:
  a. 1.2×10^4 s
  b. 8.25×10^{-2} kg
  c. 4×10^6 g
  d. 5×10^{-3} m

1.18 Write each of the following as standard numbers:
  a. 3.6×10^{-5} L
  b. 8.75×10^4 cm
  c. 3×10^{-2} mL
  d. 2.12×10^5 kg

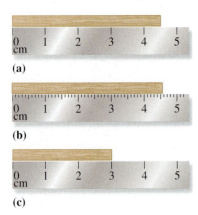

FIGURE 1.7 The lengths of the rectangular objects are measured as **(a)** 4.5 cm and **(b)** 4.55 cm.

Q What is the length of the object in (c)?

SELF-STUDY ACTIVITY
Significant Figures

TUTORIAL
Counting Significant Figures

1.5 Measured Numbers and Significant Figures

When you make a measurement, you use some type of measuring device. For example, you may use a meterstick to measure your height, a scale to check your weight, or a thermometer to take your temperature.

Measured Numbers

Measured numbers are the numbers you obtain when you measure a quantity using a measuring tool. Suppose you are going to measure the lengths of the objects in Figure 1.7. You would select a metric ruler that may have lines marked in 1 cm divisions, or perhaps in divisions of 0.1 cm. To report the length of each object, you observe the numerical values of the marked lines at the end of the object. Then, you *estimate* the final number by visually dividing the space between the marked lines. This estimated number is the final digit that is reported for any measured number.

For example, in Figure 1.7a, the end of the object is between the marks of 4 cm and 5 cm. Thus, you know that its length is more than 4 cm but less than 5 cm. Now you could estimate that the end is halfway between 4 cm and 5 cm and report its length as 4.5 cm. However, another student might report the length of this object as 4.4 cm because people do not estimate the same way. Therefore, there is always some uncertainty about the estimated number in every measurement.

The metric ruler shown in Figure 1.7b is marked at every 0.1 cm. With this ruler, you can now estimate the value of the hundredths place (0.01 cm). Now you could know that the end of the object is between 4.5 and 4.6 cm. Perhaps you report the length of the object as 4.55 cm, while another student may report its length as 4.56 cm. Both results are acceptable.

In Figure 1.7c, the end of the object appears to line up with the 3-cm mark. Because the divisions are marked in units of 1 cm, the estimated digit in the tenths place (0.1 cm) is 0. The reported measurement for length is reported as 3.0 cm, not 3. This means that the uncertainty of the measurement (the last digit) is in the tenths place (0.1 cm).

Significant Figures

In a measured number, the **significant figures (SFs)** *are all the digits including the estimated digit.* Nonzero numbers are always counted as significant figures. However, a zero may or may not be significant, depending on its position in a number. Table 1.6 gives the rules and examples of counting significant figures.

TABLE 1.6 Significant Figures in Measured Numbers

Rule	Measured Number	Number of Significant Figures
1. A number is a *significant figure* if it is		
a. not a zero	4.5 g	2
	122.35 m	5
b. one or more zeros between nonzero digits	205 m	3
	5.008 kg	4
c. one or more zeros at the end of a decimal number	50. L	2
	25.0 °C	3
	16.00 g	4
d. in the coefficient of a number written in scientific notation	4.8×10^5 m	2
	5.70×10^{-3} g	3
2. A zero is *not significant* if it is		
a. at the beginning of a decimal number	0.0004 s	1
	0.075 m	2
b. used as a placeholder in a large number without a decimal point	850 000 m	2
	1 250 000 g	3

Scientific Notation and Significant Zeros

When one or more zeros in a large number are significant, they are shown more clearly by writing the number in scientific notation. For example, if the first zero in the measurement 500 m is significant, it is written as 5.0×10^2 m. In this text, we will place a decimal point after a significant zero at the end of a number. For example, a measurement written as 500. g indicates that *both zeros* are significant figures. To show this clearly, we can write it as 5.00×10^2 g. We will assume that zeros at the end of large numbers without a decimal point are not significant. Therefore, we write 400 000 g as 4×10^5 g, which has only one significant figure.

> **CONCEPT CHECK 1.3** **Significant Zeros**
>
> Identify the significant and nonsignificant zeros in each of the following measured numbers:
>
> **a.** 0.000 250 m **b.** 70.040 g **c.** 1 020 000 L
>
> **ANSWER**
>
> **a.** The zeros preceding the first nonzero digit of 2 are not significant. The zero in the last decimal place following the 5 is significant.
> **b.** The zeros between nonzero digits or at the end of decimal numbers are significant. All zeros in 70.040 g are significant.
> **c.** The zeros between nonzero digits are significant. The zero between 1 and 2 is significant, but the four zeros following the 2 are not significant.

Exact Numbers

Exact numbers *are those numbers obtained by counting items or using a definition that compares two units in the same measuring system.* Suppose a friend asks you to tell her the number of coats in your closet or the number of classes you are taking in school. Your answer would be given by counting the items. It was not necessary for you to use any type of measuring tool. Suppose someone asks you to state the number of seconds in one minute. Without using any measuring device, you would give the definition: 60 seconds in one minute. *Exact numbers are not measured, do not have a limited number of significant figures, and do not affect the number of significant figures in a calculated answer.* For more examples of exact numbers, see Table 1.7.

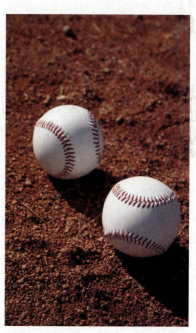

The number of baseballs is counted, which means 2 is an exact number.

TABLE 1.7 Examples of Some Exact Numbers

Items	Defined Equalities	
Counted Numbers	U.S. System	Metric System
8 doughnuts	1 ft = 12 in.	1 L = 1000 mL
2 baseballs	1 qt = 4 cups	1 m = 100 cm
5 capsules	1 lb = 16 oz	1 kg = 1000 g

> **CONCEPT CHECK 1.4** **Measured Numbers and Significant Figures**
>
> Identify each of the following numbers as measured or exact, and give the number of significant figures in each measured number:
>
> **a.** 42.2 g **b.** 3 eggs **c.** 5.0×10^{-3} cm **d.** 450 000 km **e.** 1 ft = 12 in.
>
> **ANSWER**
>
> **a.** The mass of 42.2 g is a measured number because it is obtained with a measuring tool. There are three SFs in 42.2 g because non-zero digits are always significant.
> **b.** The value of 3 eggs is an exact number because it is obtained by counting rather than using a measuring tool.

c. The length of 5.0×10^{-3} cm is a measured number because it is obtained with a measuring tool. There are two SFs in 5.0×10^{-3} cm because all the numbers in the coefficient of a number written in scientific notation are significant.

d. The distance of 450 000 km is a measured number because it is obtained with a measuring tool. There are only two SFs in 450 000 km because the zeros at the end of a large number without a decimal point are not significant.

e. The lengths of 1 ft and 12 in. contain exact numbers because the relationship 1 ft = 12 in. is a definition in the U.S. system of measurement. The relationship of number of inches in one foot was obtained by definition; no measuring tool was used.

QUESTIONS AND PROBLEMS

1.5 Measured Numbers and Significant Figures

LEARNING GOAL: Identify a number as measured or exact; determine the number of significant figures in a measured number.

1.19 Identify the number in each of the following as measured or exact and give the reason for your choice:
a. A person weighs 67.5 kg.
b. A patient is given 2 tablets of medication.
c. In the metric system, 1 m is equal to 1000 mm.
d. The distance from Denver, Colorado, to Houston, Texas, is 1720 km.

1.20 Identify the number in each of the following as measured or exact and give the reason for your choice:
a. There are 31 students in the laboratory.
b. The oldest known flower lived 1.2×10^8 y ago.
c. The largest gem ever found, an aquamarine, has a mass of 104 kg.
d. A laboratory test shows a blood cholesterol level of 184 mg/100 mL.

1.21 Identify the measured number(s), if any, in each of the following pairs of numbers:
a. 3 hamburgers and 6 oz of meat
b. 1 table and 4 chairs
c. 0.75 lb of grapes and 350 g of butter
d. 60 s = 1 min

1.22 Identify the measured number(s), if any, in each of the following pairs of numbers:
a. 5 pizzas and 50.0 g of cheese
b. 6 nickels and 16 g of nickel
c. 3 onions and 3 lb of onions
d. 5 miles and 5 cars

1.23 Indicate the significant zeros, if any, in each of the following measurements:
a. 0.00380 m
b. 5.04 cm
c. 800. L
d. 3.0×10^{-3} kg
e. 85 000 g

1.24 Indicate the significant zeros, if any, in each of the following measurements:
a. 20.5 °C
b. 5.00 m
c. 0.000 070 L
d. 120 000 y
e. 6.003×10^2 g

1.25 How many significant figures are in each of the following measurements?
a. 11.005 g
b. 0.000 32 m
c. 36 000 000 m
d. 1.80×10^4 g
e. 0.8250 L
f. 30.0 °C

1.26 How many significant figures are in each of the following measurements?
a. 20.60 L
b. 1036.48 g
c. 4.00 m
d. 18.4 °C
e. 60 800 000 g
f. 5.0×10^{-3} L

1.27 Identify the number in each of the following pairs that contains more significant figures:
a. 11.0 m and 11.00 m
b. 405 K and 405.0 K
c. 0.0120 s and 12 000 s
d. 250.0 L and 2.5×10^{-2} L

1.28 Identify the number in each of the following pairs that contains fewer significant figures:
a. 28.33 g and 2.8×10^{-3} g
b. 0.0250 m and 0.2005 m
c. 150 000 s and 1.50×10^4 s
d. 3.8×10^{-2} L and 3.80×10^5 L

1.6 Significant Figures in Calculations

In the sciences, we measure many things: the length of a bacterium, the volume of a gas sample, the temperature of a reaction mixture, or the mass of iron in a sample. The numbers obtained from these types of measurements are often used in calculations. The number of significant figures in the measured numbers limits the number of significant figures that can be given in the calculated answer.

Using a calculator will usually help you do calculations faster. However, calculators cannot think for you. It is up to you to enter the numbers properly, press the correct function keys, and give an answer with the correct number of significant figures.

Rounding Off

Suppose you decide to buy carpeting for a room that measures 5.52 m by 3.58 m. Each measurement of length has three significant figures because the measuring tape limits your estimated place to 0.01 m. To determine how much carpeting you need, you would calculate the area of the room by multiplying 5.52 times 3.58. If you used a calculator, the display shows the numbers 19.7616. However, the display has too many numbers, which is the result of the multiplication process. Because each of the original measurements has three significant figures, the display numbers of 19.7616 must be *rounded off* to three significant figures, 19.8. Therefore, you can order carpeting that will cover an area of 19.8 m^2 (square meters).

    Each time you use a calculator, it is important to look at the original measurements and determine the number of significant figures that can be used for the answer. You can use the following rules to round off the numbers in a calculator display:

A technician uses a calculator in the laboratory.

Rules for Rounding Off

1. If the first digit to be dropped is *4 or less*, then it and all following digits are simply dropped from the number.
2. If the first digit to be dropped is *5 or greater*, then the last retained digit of the number is increased by 1.

Number to Round Off	Three Significant Figures	Two Significant Figures
8.4234	8.42 (drop 34)	8.4 (drop 234)
14.780	14.8 (drop 80, increase the last retained digit by 1)	15 (drop 780, increase the last retained digit by 1)
3262	3260* (drop 2, add 0) 3.26 × 10^3	3300* (drop 62, increase the last retained digit by 1, add 00) 3.3 × 10^3

*The value of a large number is retained by using placeholder zeros to replace dropped digits.

CONCEPT CHECK 1.5   Rounding Off

Identify the digits to drop, whether the last retained digit increases by 1 or not, and give the correctly rounded-off value of 2.8456 m to each of the following:

a. three significant figures
b. two significant figures

ANSWER

a. To round off 2.8456 m to three significant figures, drop the last two digits, 56. Because the first digit dropped is 5, the last retained digit is increased by 1 to give 2.85 m.
b. To round off 2.8456 m to two significant figures, drop the final three digits, 456. Because the first digit dropped is 4, the last retained digit does not change to give 2.8 m.

SAMPLE PROBLEM 1.3   Rounding Off

Round off each of the following calculator displays to three significant figures:

a. 35.7823 m   b. 0.002 625 L
c. 3.8268 × 10^3 g   d. 1.2836 kg

SOLUTION

a. 35.8 m   b. 0.002 63 L
c. 3.83 × 10^3 g   d. 1.28 kg

STUDY CHECK 1.3

Round off each of the numbers in Sample Problem 1.3 to two significant figures.

A calculator is helpful in working problems and doing calculations faster.

Multiplication and Division

In multiplication or division, the final answer is written so it has the same number of significant figures as the measurement with the fewest significant figures (SFs). Some examples of rounding off numbers from multiplication and division follow:

Example 1

Multiply the following measured numbers: 24.65×0.67

$$24.65 \quad \boxed{\times} \quad 0.67 \quad \boxed{=} \qquad \textit{16.5155} \quad \longrightarrow \quad 17$$

Four SFs · · · · · · · Two SFs · · · · · · · · · Calculator · · · · · Final answer,
· display · · · · · · · rounded off to two SFs

The answer in the calculator display has more digits than the measured numbers allow. The measurement 0.67 has the fewer number of significant figures, two. Therefore, the numbers in the calculator display are rounded off to give two significant figures in the answer.

Example 2

Solve the following using measured numbers:

$$\frac{2.85 \times 67.4}{4.39}$$

A problem with multiple steps is worked on a calculator by multiplying the numbers in the numerator, and then dividing by the numbers in the denominator. We might press the keys in the following order, but be sure to use the correct operation process for your calculation:

$$2.85 \quad \boxed{\times} \quad 67.4 \quad \boxed{\div} \quad 4.39 \quad \boxed{=} \qquad \textit{43.75626424} \quad \longrightarrow \quad 43.8$$

Three SFs · · · Three SFs · · · Three SFs · · · Calculator · · Final answer, rounded
· display · · · · · · off to three SFs

All of the original measurements in this problem have three significant figures. Therefore, the calculator result is rounded off to give an answer with three significant figures, 43.8.

Adding Significant Zeros

Sometimes, a calculator display consists of a small whole number. Then we add one or more significant zeros to the calculator display to obtain the correct number of significant figures. For example, suppose the calculator display is 4, but you used measurements that have three significant numbers. Then two significant zeros are added to give 4.00 as the correct answer.

Three SFs
$$\frac{8.00}{2.00} \quad \boxed{=} \qquad \textit{4} \quad \longrightarrow \quad 4.00$$
Three SFs · · · · · · · Calculator · · · · · Final answer, two zeros
· · · · · · · · · · · · · · display · · · · · · added to give three SFs

---

CONCEPT CHECK 1.6 **Significant Figures in Multiplication and Division**

Perform the following calculations of measured numbers. Give each answer with the correct number of significant figures.

a. $\dfrac{2.075}{(8.42)(0.0045)}$ 　　　　**b.** $\dfrac{2.0 \times 6.00}{4.00}$

ANSWER

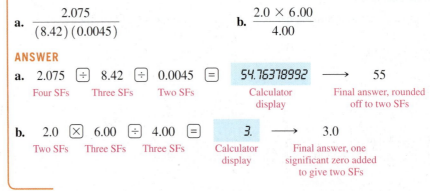

a. $2.075 \quad \boxed{\div} \quad 8.42 \quad \boxed{\div} \quad 0.0045 \quad \boxed{=} \qquad \textit{54.76378992} \quad \longrightarrow \quad 55$

Four SFs · · · Three SFs · · Two SFs · · · · · · · Calculator · · · · Final answer, rounded
· display · · · · · · off to two SFs

b. $2.0 \quad \boxed{\times} \quad 6.00 \quad \boxed{\div} \quad 4.00 \quad \boxed{=} \qquad \textit{3.} \quad \longrightarrow \quad 3.0$

Two SFs · · · Three SFs · · Three SFs · · · · · Calculator · · · Final answer, one
· display · · · · · significant zero added
· to give two SFs

Addition and Subtraction

In addition or subtraction, the final answer is written so that it has the same number of decimal places as the measurement having the fewest decimal places. Some examples of addition and subtraction follow:

Example 3

Add:

	2.045	Three decimal places
+	34.1	One decimal place
	36.145	Calculator display
	36.1	Answer, rounded off to one decimal place

When numbers are added or subtracted to give answers ending in zero, the zero does not appear after the decimal point in the calculator display. For example, if you do the subtraction 14.5 g − 2.5 g on your calculator, the display shows 12. The correct answer, 12.0 g, is obtained by placing a significant zero after the decimal point.

Example 4

Subtract:

	14.5 g	One decimal place
−	2.5 g	One decimal place
	12.	Calculator display
	12.0 g	Answer, one zero added to give one decimal place

SAMPLE PROBLEM 1.4 Addition and Subtraction

Perform each of the following calculations and give the answers with the correct number of decimal places:

a. 27.8 cm + 0.235 cm **b.** 153.247 g − 14.82 g

SOLUTION

a. 28.0 cm **b.** 138.43 g

STUDY CHECK 1.4

Perform each of the following calculations and give the answers with the correct number of decimal places:

a. 82.45 mg + 1.245 mg + 0.000 56 mg **b.** 4.259 L − 3.8 L

QUESTIONS AND PROBLEMS

1.6 Significant Figures in Calculations

LEARNING GOAL: *Give the correct number of significant figures in a final answer by adding or removing digits in a calculator result.*

1.29 Round off each of the following measurements to three significant figures:
  a. 1.854 kg **b.** 184.2038 L **c.** 0.004 738 265 cm
  d. 8807 m **e.** 1.832×10^5 s

1.30 Round off each of the measurements in Problem 1.29 to two significant figures.

1.31 Perform each of the following calculations and give answers with the correct number of significant figures:
  a. 45.7×0.034 **b.** $0.002\ 78 \times 5$
  c. $\dfrac{34.56}{1.25}$ **d.** $\dfrac{(0.2465)(25)}{1.78}$

1.32 Perform each of the following calculations and give answers with the correct number of significant figures:
  a. 400×185 **b.** $\dfrac{2.40}{(4)(125)}$
  c. $0.825 \times 3.6 \times 5.1$ **d.** $\dfrac{3.5 \times 0.261}{8.24 \times 20.0}$

1.33 Perform each of the following calculations, and give answers with the correct number of decimal places:
  a. 45.48 cm + 8.057 cm
  b. 23.45 g + 104.1 g + 0.025 g
  c. 145.675 mL − 24.2 mL **d.** 1.08 L − 0.585 L

1.34 Perform each of the following calculations, and give answers with the correct number of decimal places:
  a. 5.08 g + 25.1 g
  b. 85.66 cm + 104.10 cm + 0.025 cm
  c. 24.568 mL − 14.25 mL **d.** 0.2654 L − 0.2585 L

SELF-STUDY ACTIVITY
Metric System

TUTORIAL
SI Prefixes and Units

1.7 Prefixes and Equalities

In the metric and SI systems of units, a **prefix** attached to any unit increases or decreases its size by some factor of 10. For example, the prefixes *milli* and *micro* are used to make the smaller units milligram (mg) and microgram (μg). Table 1.8 lists some of the metric prefixes, their symbols, and their decimal values.

TABLE 1.8 Metric and SI Prefixes

Prefix	Symbol	Numerical Value	Scientific Notation	Equality
Prefixes That Increase the Size of the Unit				
peta	P	1 000 000 000 000 000	10^{15}	$1 \text{ Pg} = 10^{15} \text{ g}$ $1 \text{ g} = 10^{-15} \text{ Pg}$
tera	T	1 000 000 000 000	10^{12}	$1 \text{ Tg} = 10^{12} \text{ g}$ $1 \text{ g} = 10^{-12} \text{ Tg}$
giga	G	1 000 000 000	10^{9}	$1 \text{ Gm} = 10^{9} \text{ m}$ $1 \text{ m} = 10^{-9} \text{ Gm}$
mega	M	1 000 000	10^{6}	$1 \text{ Mg} = 10^{6} \text{ g}$ $1 \text{ g} = 10^{-6} \text{ Mg}$
kilo	k	1 000	10^{3}	$1 \text{ km} = 10^{3} \text{ m}$ $1 \text{ m} = 10^{-3} \text{ km}$
Prefixes That Decrease the Size of the Unit				
deci	d	0.1	10^{-1}	$1 \text{ dL} = 10^{-1} \text{ L}$ $1 \text{ L} = 10 \text{ dL}$
centi	c	0.01	10^{-2}	$1 \text{ cm} = 10^{-2} \text{ m}$ $1 \text{ m} = 100 \text{ cm}$
milli	m	0.001	10^{-3}	$1 \text{ ms} = 10^{-3} \text{ s}$ $1 \text{ s} = 10^{3} \text{ ms}$
micro	μ	0.000 001	10^{-6}	$1 \text{ }\mu\text{g} = 10^{-6} \text{ g}$ $1 \text{ g} = 10^{6} \text{ }\mu\text{g}$
nano	n	0.000 000 001	10^{-9}	$1 \text{ nm} = 10^{-9} \text{ m}$ $1 \text{ m} = 10^{9} \text{ nm}$
pico	p	0.000 000 000 001	10^{-12}	$1 \text{ ps} = 10^{-12} \text{ s}$ $1 \text{ s} = 10^{12} \text{ ps}$
femto	f	0.000 000 000 000 001	10^{-15}	$1 \text{ fs} = 10^{-15} \text{ s}$ $1 \text{ s} = 10^{15} \text{ fs}$

TABLE 1.9 Daily Values for Selected Nutrients

Nutrient	Amount Recommended
Vitamin B$_{12}$	6 μg
Vitamin C	60 mg
Calcium	1000 mg
Copper	2 mg
Iodine	150 μg
Iron	18 mg
Magnesium	400 mg
Niacin	20 mg
Potassium	3500 mg
Sodium	2400 mg
Zinc	15 mg

The prefix *centi* is like cents in a dollar. One cent would be a "centidollar" or 0.01 of a dollar. That also means that one dollar is the same as 100 cents. The prefix *deci* is like the value of a dime in a dollar. One dime would be a "decidollar" or 0.1 of a dollar. That also means that one dollar is the same as 10 dimes.

The relationship of a prefix to a unit can be expressed by replacing the prefix with its numerical value. For example, when the prefix *kilo* in kilometer is replaced with its value of 1000, we find that a kilometer is equal to 1000 meters. Some relationships using the prefix *kilo* follow:

1 **kilo**meter (1 km) = **1000** meters (1000 m $= 10^{3}$ m)

1 **kilo**liter (1 kL)   = **1000** liters (1000 L $= 10^{3}$ L)

1 **kilo**gram (1 kg) = **1000** grams (1000 g $= 10^{3}$ g)

The U.S. Food and Drug Administration (FDA) has determined the daily values (DVs) of nutrients for adults and children age 4 or older. Some examples of the daily values that have prefixes are listed in Table 1.9.

CONCEPT CHECK 1.7 **Prefixes**

Fill in each of the blanks with the correct prefix:

a. 1000 g = 1 _____ g   **b.** 0.01 m = 1 _____ m   **c.** 1×10^6 L = 1 _____ L

ANSWER

a. The prefix for 1000 is *kilo*; 1000 g = 1 kg
b. The prefix for 0.01 is *centi*; 0.01 m = 1 cm
c. The prefix for 1×10^6 is *mega*; 1×10^6 L = 1 ML

SAMPLE PROBLEM 1.5 **Prefixes**

The storage capacity for a hard disk drive (HDD) is specified using prefixes: megabyte (MB), gigabyte (GB), or terabyte (TB). Indicate the storage capacity in bytes of each of the following hard disk drives. Suggest a reason for describing a HDD storage capacity in gigabytes or terabytes.

a. 5 MB   **b.** 2 GB

SOLUTION

a. The prefix *mega* (M) in MB is equal to 1 000 000 or 1×10^6. Thus, 5 MB is equal to 5 000 000 (5×10^6) bytes.
b. The prefix *giga* (G) in GB is equal to 1 000 000 000 or 1×10^9. Thus, 2 GB is equal to 2 000 000 000 (2×10^9) bytes.

Expressing HDD capacity in gigabytes or terabytes gives a more reasonable number to work with than a number with many zeros or a large power of 10.

STUDY CHECK 1.5

A hard drive has a storage capacity of 1.5 TB. How many bytes are stored?

A 1 terabyte hard disk drive stores 10^{12} bytes of information.

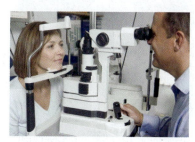

Using a retinal camera, an ophthalmologist photographs the retina of an eye.

Measuring Length

An ophthalmologist may measure the diameter of the retina of an eye in centimeters (cm), whereas a surgeon may need to know the length of a nerve in millimeters (mm). When the prefix *centi* is used with the unit meter, it becomes *centimeter*, a length that is one-hundredth of a meter (0.01 m). When the prefix *milli* is used with the unit meter, it becomes *millimeter*, a length that is one-thousandth of a meter (0.001 m). There are 100 cm and 1000 mm in a meter (see Figure 1.8).

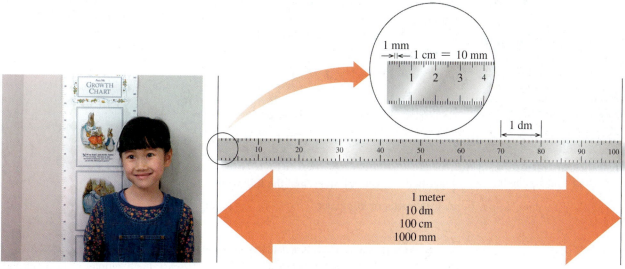

FIGURE 1.8 The metric length of 1 meter is the same length as 10 dm, 100 cm, and 1000 mm.
Q How many millimeters (mm) are in 1 centimeter (cm)?

First Quantity		Second Quantity	
1	m =	100	cm

Number + unit   Number + unit

This example of an equality shows the relationship between meters and centimeters.

TABLE 1.10 Some Typical Laboratory Test Values

Substance in Blood	Typical Range
Albumin	3.5–5.0 g/dL
Ammonia	20–150 μg/dL
Calcium	8.5–10.5 mg/dL
Cholesterol	105–250 mg/dL
Iron (male)	80–160 μg/dL
Protein (total)	6.0–8.0 g/dL

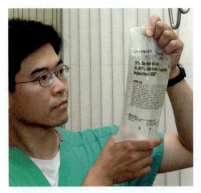

FIGURE 1.9 A plastic intravenous fluid bag contains 1000 mL.

Q How many liters of solution are in the intravenous fluid bag?

A laboratory technician transfers a small volume using a micropipette.

An **equality** shows the relationship between two units that measure the same quantity. For example, we know that 1 m is the same length as 100 cm. Then the equality for this relationship is written as 1 m = 100 cm. Each quantity in this equality describes the same length but in a different unit. Every time we write an equality, we show each quantity as both a number and a unit.

Other examples of equalities between different metric units of length follow:

$$1 \text{ m} = 100 \text{ cm} = 1 \times 10^2 \text{ cm}$$
$$1 \text{ m} = 1000 \text{ mm} = 1 \times 10^3 \text{ mm}$$
$$1 \text{ cm} = 10 \text{ mm} = 1 \times 10^1 \text{ mm}$$

Measuring Volume

Volumes of 1 L or smaller are common in the health sciences. When a liter is divided into 10 equal portions, each portion is a deciliter (dL). There are 10 dL in 1 L. Laboratory results for blood work are often reported in mass per deciliter. Table 1.10 lists typical laboratory test values for some substances in the blood.

When a liter is divided into a thousand equal parts, each smaller part is a milliliter (mL). In a 1-L container of physiological saline, there are 1000 mL of solution (see Figure 1.9). Other examples of equalities between different metric units of volume follow:

$$1\text{L} = 10 \text{ dL} = 1 \times 10^1 \text{ dL}$$
$$1 \text{ L} = 1000 \text{ mL} = 1 \times 10^3 \text{ mL}$$
$$1 \text{ dL} = 100 \text{ mL} = 1 \times 10^2 \text{ mL}$$

The **cubic centimeter** (abbreviated as cm^3 or **cc**) is the volume of a cube with dimensions of 1 cm on each side. A cubic centimeter has the same volume as a milliliter, and the units are often used interchangeably.

$$1 \text{ cm}^3 = 1 \text{ cc} = 1 \text{ mL}$$

When you see *1 cm*, you are reading about length; when you see *1 cc* or *1 cm³* or *1 mL*, you are reading about volume. A comparison of units of volume is illustrated in Figure 1.10.

Measuring Mass

When you go to a doctor for a physical examination, your mass is recorded in kilograms, whereas the results of your laboratory tests are reported in grams, milligrams (mg), or micrograms (μg). A kilogram is equal to 1000 g. As an equality, this is written as 1 kg = 1000 g. One gram represents the same mass as 1000 mg. Some examples of equalities between different metric units of mass follow:

$$1 \text{ kg} = 1000 \text{ g} = 1 \times 10^3 \text{ g}$$
$$1 \text{ g} = 1000 \text{ mg} = 1 \times 10^3 \text{ mg}$$
$$1 \text{ mg} = 1000 \mu\text{g} = 1 \times 10^3 \mu\text{g}$$

CONCEPT CHECK 1.8   **Metric Prefixes**

Identify the larger unit in each of the following:

a. centimeter or kilometer   **b.** mg or μg

ANSWER

a. A kilometer (1000 m) is larger than a centimeter (0.01 m).
b. A mg (0.001 g) is larger than a μg (0.000 001 g)

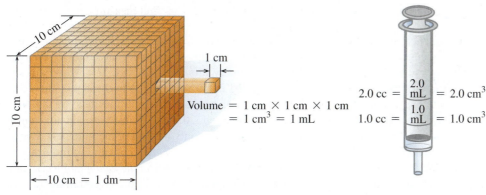

Volume = 1 cm × 1 cm × 1 cm
= 1 cm^3 = 1 mL

2.0 cc = 2.0 mL = 2.0 cm^3
1.0 cc = 1.0 mL = 1.0 cm^3

←10 cm = 1 dm→

Volume = 10 cm × 10 cm × 10 cm
= 1000 cm^3
= 1000 mL
= 1 L

FIGURE 1.10 A cube measuring 10 cm on each side has a volume of 1000 cm^3, or 1 L; a cube measuring 1 cm on each side has a volume of 1 cm^3 (cc), or 1 mL.

Q What is the relationship between a milliliter (mL) and a cubic centimeter (cm^3)?

SAMPLE PROBLEM 1.6 **Writing Metric Relationships**

Complete the following list of metric equalities:

a. 1 L = _____ dL   **b.** 1 km = _____ m   **c.** 1 cm^3 = _____ mL

SOLUTION

a. 10 dL   **b.** 1000 m   **c.** 1 mL

STUDY CHECK 1.6

Complete the following metric equalities:

a. 1 kg = _____ g   **b.** 1 mL = _____ L

QUESTIONS AND PROBLEMS

1.7 Prefixes and Equalities

LEARNING GOAL: Use the numerical values of prefixes to write a metric equality.

1.35 The speedometer is marked in both km/h and mi/h. What is the meaning of each abbreviation?

1.36 In a French car, the odometer reads 2250. What units would this be? What units would it be if this were an odometer in a car made for the United States?

1.37 Write the abbreviation for each of the following units:
  a. milligram   **b.** deciliter   **c.** kilometer
  d. picogram   **e.** microliter   **f.** nanosecond

1.38 Write the complete name for each of the following units:
  a. cm   **b.** ks   **c.** dL   **d.** Gm   **e.** μg   **f.** ps

1.39 Write the numerical values for each of the following prefixes:
  a. centi   **b.** kilo   **c.** milli **d.** tera   **e.** mega   **f.** pico

1.40 Write the complete name (prefix + unit) for each of the following numerical values:
  a. 0.1 g   **b.** 1 × 10^{-6} g   **c.** 1000 g   **d.** 0.01 g
  e. 0.001 g   **f.** 1 × 10^{12} g

1.41 Complete the following metric relationships:
  a. 1 m = _____ cm   **b.** 1 m = _____ nm
  c. 1 mm = _____ m   **d.** 1 L = _____ mL

1.42 Complete the following metric relationships:
  a. 1 Mg = _____ g   **b.** 1 mL = _____ μL
  c. 1 g = _____ kg   **d.** 1 g = _____ mg

1.43 For each of the following pairs, which is the larger unit?
  a. milligram or kilogram   **b.** milliliter or microliter
  c. m or km   **d.** kL or dL   **e.** nanometer or picometer

1.44 For each of the following pairs, which is the smaller unit?
  a. mg or g   **b.** centimeter or millimeter
  c. mm or μm   **d.** mL or dL   **e.** mg or Mg

1.8 Writing Conversion Factors

Many problems in chemistry and the health sciences require a change of units. You make changes in units every day. For example, suppose you spent 2.0 hours (h) on your homework, and someone asked you how many minutes that was. You would answer 120 minutes (min). You must have multiplied 2.0 h × 60 min/h, because you knew that one hour is equal to 60 minutes. The relationship between two units that measure the same quantity is called an **equality**. When you expressed 2.0 h as 120 min, you did not change the amount of time you spent studying. You changed only the unit of measurement used to express the time. *Any equality can be written as fractions called* **conversion factors** *with one of the quantities in the numerator, and the other quantity in the denominator.* Be sure to include the units when you write the conversion factors. Two conversion factors are always possible from any equality.

Two Conversion Factors for the Equality 60 min = 1 h

$$\frac{\text{Numerator} \longrightarrow}{\text{Denominator} \longrightarrow} \qquad \frac{60 \text{ min}}{1 \text{ h}} \quad \text{and} \quad \frac{1 \text{ h}}{60 \text{ min}}$$

These conversion factors are read as "60 minutes per 1 hour," and "1 hour per 60 minutes." The term *per* means "divide." This relationship may also be written as 60 min/h. Some common relationships are given in Table 1.11. It is important that the equality you select to form a conversion factor is an actual relationship between the two units.

TABLE 1.11 Some Common Equalities

Quantity	Metric (SI)	U.S.	Metric–U.S.
Length	1 km = 1000 m 1 m = 1000 mm 1 cm = 10 mm	1 ft = 12 in. 1 yd = 3 ft 1 mi = 5280 ft	2.54 cm = 1 in. (exact) 1 m = 39.4 in. 1 km = 0.621 mi
Volume	1 L = 1000 mL 1 dL = 100 mL 1 mL = 1 cm^3	1 qt = 4 cups 1 qt = 2 pt 1 gal = 4 qt	946 mL = 1 qt 1 L = 1.06 qt
Mass	1 kg = 1000 g 1 g = 1000 mg	1 lb = 16 oz	1 kg = 2.20 lb 454 g = 1 lb
Time	1 h = 60 min 1 min = 60 s	1 h = 60 min 1 min = 60 s	

Exact and Measured Numbers in Equalities

The numbers in any equality between metric units or between U.S. system units are obtained by definition. Because numbers in a definition are exact, they are not used to determine significant figures. For example, the equality of 1 g = 1000 mg is defined, which means that both of the numbers 1 and 1000 are exact. *However, equalities between metric and U.S. units are obtained by measurement.* For example, the equality of 1 lb = 454 g is obtained by measuring the grams in exactly 1 lb. In this equality, the measured quantity 454 has three significant figures, whereas the 1 is exact. An exception is the relationship of 1 in. = 2.54 cm where 2.54 has been defined as exact.

Metric Conversion Factors

We can write conversion factors for the metric relationships we have studied. For example, from the equality for meters and centimeters, we can write the following factors:

Metric Equality	Conversion Factors		
1 m = 100 cm	$\dfrac{100 \text{ cm}}{1 \text{ m}}$	and	$\dfrac{1 \text{ m}}{100 \text{ cm}}$

Both of these conversion factors represent the same equality; one is just the inverse of the other. *The usefulness of conversion factors is enhanced by the fact that we can turn a conversion factor over and use its inverse.* The numbers 100 and 1 in this equality between metric units and its conversion factors are *exact* numbers.

CONCEPT CHECK 1.9   **Conversion Factors**

Identify the correct conversion factors for the equality for gigagrams and grams.

a. $\dfrac{1\ \text{Gg}}{1 \times 10^9\ \text{g}}$ **b.** $\dfrac{1 \times 10^{-9}\ \text{g}}{1\ \text{Gg}}$ **c.** $\dfrac{1 \times 10^9\ \text{Gg}}{1\ \text{g}}$ **d.** $\dfrac{1 \times 10^9\ \text{g}}{1\ \text{Gg}}$

ANSWER

Using the prefix table, we can write the equality for gigagrams and grams as $1\ \text{Gg} = 1 \times 10^9$ g. Answers **a** and **d** are correctly written conversion factors that represent this equality.

Metric–U.S. System Conversion Factors

Suppose you need to convert from pounds, a unit in the U.S. system, to kilograms in the metric (or SI) system. A relationship you could use is:

$$1\ \text{kg} = 2.20\ \text{lb}$$

The corresponding conversion factors would be:

$$\frac{2.20\ \text{lb}}{1\ \text{kg}} \quad \text{and} \quad \frac{1\ \text{kg}}{2.20\ \text{lb}}$$

In this metric–U.S. equality, the number in 2.20 lb is obtained from the measurement of exactly 1 kg.

In the United States, the contents of many packaged foods are listed in both U.S. and metric units.

CONCEPT CHECK 1.10   **Writing Conversion Factors from Equalities**

Write an equality and its conversion factors, and state whether the numbers are exact or measured for each of the following:

a. millimeters and meters
b. quarts and milliliters

ANSWER

Equality	Conversion Factors	Exact or Measured Quantities
a. 1 m = 1000 mm	$\dfrac{1000\ \text{mm}}{1\ \text{m}}$ and $\dfrac{1\ \text{m}}{1000\ \text{mm}}$	In the definition of a metric equality, both 1 and 1000 are exact quantities.
b. 1 qt = 946 mL	$\dfrac{946\ \text{mL}}{1\ \text{qt}}$ and $\dfrac{1\ \text{qt}}{946\ \text{mL}}$	In a U.S–metric equality, the 1 is exact and the 946 is measured (three significant figures).

Equalities and Conversion Factors Stated Within a Problem

An equality may also be stated within a problem that applies only to that problem. For example, the cost of 1 kilogram of oranges or the speed of a car in kilometers per hour would be specific relationships for that problem only. However, it is still possible to identify these relationships within a problem and to write corresponding conversion factors.

Explore Your World

SI AND METRIC EQUALITIES ON PRODUCT LABELS

Read the labels on some food products. List the amount of product given in different units. Write a relationship for two of the amounts for the same product and container. Look for measurements of grams and pounds or quarts and milliliters.

QUESTIONS

1. Use the stated measurement to derive a metric–U.S. conversion factor.
2. How do your results compare to the conversion factors we have described in this text?

From each of the following statements, we can write an equality, and its conversion factors, and identify each number as exact or give its significant figures:

1. The motorcycle was traveling at a speed of 85 km/h.

Equality	Conversion Factors	Significant Figures or Exact
85 km = 1 h	$\dfrac{85\ km}{1\ h}$ and $\dfrac{1\ h}{85\ km}$	The 85 in 85 km is measured: It has two significant figures. The 1 in 1 h is exact.

2. One tablet contains 500 mg of vitamin C.

Equality	Conversion Factors	Significant Figures or Exact
1 tablet = 500 mg of vitamin C	$\dfrac{500\ mg\ vitamin\ C}{1\ tablet}$ and $\dfrac{1\ tablet}{500\ mg\ vitamin\ C}$	The 500 in 500 mg is measured: It has one significant figure. The 1 in 1 tablet is exact.

Vitamin C, an antioxidant needed by the body, is found in fruits such as lemons.

TUTORIAL
Using Percentage as a Conversion Factor

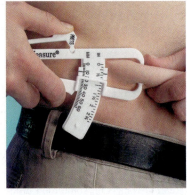

The thickness of the skin fold at the waist is used to determine the percent body fat.

Conversion Factors from Percent, ppm, and ppb

When a *percent* (%) is given in a problem, it gives the parts of a specific substance in 100 parts of the total. *To write a percentage as a conversion factor, we choose a unit and express the numerical relationship of the parts of this unit to 100 parts of the whole.* For example, a person might have 18% body fat by mass. The percent quantity can be written as 18 mass units of body fat in every 100 mass units of body mass. Different mass units such as grams, kilograms (kg), or pounds (lb) can be used, but both units in the factor must be the same.

CONCEPT CHECK 1.11   **Equalities and Conversion Factors Stated in a Problem**

A person has 18% body fat by mass. What equality and conversion factors can be written for this statement using the unit of kilogram? State the equality, write the conversion factors, and identify each number as exact or give its significant figures.

ANSWER

Equality	Conversion Factors	Significant Figures or Exact
18 kg of body fat = 100 kg of body mass	$\dfrac{100\ kg\ body\ mass}{18\ kg\ body\ fat}$ and $\dfrac{18\ kg\ body\ fat}{100\ kg\ body\ mass}$	The 18 in 18 kg is measured: It has two significant figures. The 100 in 100 kg is exact.

When scientists want to indicate very small ratios, they use numerical relationships called *parts per million* (ppm) or *parts per billion* (ppb). The ratio of parts per million is the same as the milligrams of a substance per kilogram (mg/kg). The ratio of parts per billion equals the micrograms of a substance per kilogram (μg/kg).

Ratio	Units
parts per million (ppm)	milligrams per kilogram (mg/kg)
parts per billion (ppb)	micrograms per kilogram (μg/kg)

For example, the maximum amount of lead that is allowed by the Food and Drug Administration (FDA) in glazed pottery bowls is 2 ppm.

Equality	Conversion Factors	Significant Figures or Exact
2 mg of lead = 1 kg of glaze	$\dfrac{2\text{ mg lead}}{1\text{ kg glaze}}$ and $\dfrac{1\text{ kg glaze}}{2\text{ mg lead}}$	The 2 in 2 mg is measured: It has one significant figure. The 1 in 1 kg is exact.

SAMPLE PROBLEM 1.7   Conversion Factors Stated in a Problem

Write the equality and its corresponding conversion factors, and identify each number as exact or give its significant figures for each of the following statements:

a. There are 325 mg of aspirin in 1 tablet.
b. One kilogram of bananas costs $1.25 at the grocery store.
c. The EPA has set the maximum level for mercury in tuna at 0.5 ppm.

SOLUTION

a. There are 325 mg of aspirin in 1 tablet.

Equality	Conversion Factors	Significant Figures or Exact
325 mg of aspirin = 1 tablet	$\dfrac{325\text{ mg aspirin}}{1\text{ tablet}}$ and $\dfrac{1\text{ tablet}}{325\text{ mg aspirin}}$	The 325 in 325 mg is measured: It has three significant figures. The 1 in 1 tablet is exact.

b. One kilogram of bananas costs $1.25 at the grocery store.

Equality	Conversion Factors	Significant Figures or Exact
1 kg of bananas = $1.25	$\dfrac{\$1.25}{1\text{ kg bananas}}$ and $\dfrac{1\text{ kg bananas}}{\$1.25}$	The 1.25 in $1.25 is measured: It has three significant figures. The 1 in 1 kg is exact.

The maximum amount of mercury allowed by the EPA in tuna is 0.5 ppm.

c. The EPA has set the maximum level for mercury in tuna at 0.5 ppm.

Equality	Conversion Factors	Significant Figures or Exact
0.5 mg of mercury = 1 kg of tuna	$\dfrac{0.5\text{ mg mercury}}{1\text{ kg tuna}}$ and $\dfrac{1\text{ kg tuna}}{0.5\text{ mg mercury}}$	The 0.5 in 0.5 mg is measured: It has one significant figure. The 1 in 1 kg is exact.

STUDY CHECK 1.7

Write the equality and its corresponding conversion factors, and identify each number as exact or give its significant figures for each of the following statements:

a. A cyclist in the Tour de France bicycle race reaches a top speed of 62.2 km/h.
b. The permissible level of arsenic in water is 10 ppb.

Chemistry Link to Health

TOXICOLOGY AND RISK-BENEFIT ASSESSMENT

Each day we make choices about what we do or what we eat, often without thinking about the risks associated with these choices. We are aware of the risks of cancer from smoking, and we know there is a greater risk of having an accident if we cross a street where there is no light or crosswalk.

A basic concept of toxicology is the statement of Paracelsus that the right dose is the difference between a poison and a cure. To evaluate the level of danger from various substances, natural or synthetic, a risk assessment is made by exposing laboratory animals to the substances and monitoring the health effects. Often, doses much greater than humans might encounter are given to the test animals.

Many hazardous chemicals or substances have been identified by these tests. One measure of toxicity is the LD_{50} or lethal dose, which is the concentration of the substance that causes death in 50% of the test animals. A dose is typically measured in ppm (mg/kg) of body mass or ppb (μg/kg).

Other evaluations also need to be made, but it is easy to compare LD_{50} values. Parathion, a pesticide, with an LD_{50} of 3 ppm would be highly toxic. That means that half the test animals given 3 mg of parathion per kg of body mass would be expected to die. Salt (sodium chloride) with an LD_{50} of 3750 ppm has a much lower toxicity. You would need to ingest a huge amount of salt before any toxic effect would be observed. Although the risk to animals based on dose can be evaluated in the laboratory, it is more difficult to determine the impact in the environment because there is also a difference between continued exposure and a single, large dose of the substance.

Table 1.12 lists some LD_{50} values and compares pesticides and common substances in our everyday lives, in order of increasing toxicity.

The LD_{50} of caffeine is 192 ppm.

TABLE 1.12 Some LD_{50} Values for Pesticides and Common Materials Tested in Rats

Substance	LD_{50} (ppm)
Table sugar	29 700
Boric acid	5140
Baking soda	4220
Table salt	3750
Ethanol	2080
Aspirin	1100
Caffeine	192
DDT	113
Dichlorvos (pesticide strips)	56
Sodium cyanide	6
Parathion	3

QUESTIONS AND PROBLEMS

1.8 Writing Conversion Factors

LEARNING GOAL: *Write a conversion factor for two units that describe the same quantity.*

1.45 Write the equality and conversion factors for each of the following pairs of units:
   a. centimeters and meters **b.** milligrams and grams
   c. liters and milliliters **d.** deciliters and milliliters

1.46 Write the equality and conversion factors for each of the following pairs of units:
   a. centimeters and inches **b.** pounds and kilograms
   c. pounds and grams **d.** quarts and liters

1.47 Write the equality and conversion factors, and identify the numbers as exact or give the number of significant figures for each of the following statements:
   a. One yard is 3 ft. **b.** One kilogram is 2.20 lb.
   c. One minute is 60 s. **d.** A car goes 27 miles on
   e. Sterling silver is 93% 1 gal of gas.
      by mass silver.

1.48 Write the equality and conversion factors, and identify the numbers as exact or give the number of significant figures for each of the following statements:
   a. One liter is 1.06 qt.

b. At the store, oranges are $1.29 per lb.
   c. There are 7 days in 1 week.
   d. One deciliter contains 100 mL.
   e. An 18-carat gold ring contains 75% gold by mass.

1.49 Write the equality and conversion factors, and identify the numbers as exact or give the number of significant figures for each of the following statements:
   a. A bee flies at an average speed of 3.5 m per second.
   b. The daily requirement for potassium is 3500 mg.
   c. An automobile traveled 46.0 km on 1 gal of gasoline.
   d. The label on a bottle reads 50. mg of Atenolol per tablet.
   e. The pesticide level in plums was 29 ppb.
   f. A low-dose aspirin tablet contains 81 mg of aspirin.

1.50 Write the equality and conversion factors, and identify the numbers as exact or give the number of significant figures for each of the following statements:
   a. The label on a bottle reads 10 mg of furosemide per mL.
   b. The daily requirement for iodine is 150 μg.
   c. The nitrate level in well water was 32 ppm.
   d. Gold jewelry contains 58% by mass gold.
   e. The price of a gallon of gasoline is $3.19.
   f. One capsule of fish oil contains 360 mg of omega-3 fatty acids.

1.9 Problem Solving

The process of problem solving in chemistry often requires the conversion of an initial quantity given in one unit to the same quantity but in different units. By multiplying the given unit by one or more conversion factors, it can be converted to the needed unit as shown in Sample Problem 1.8.

TUTORIAL
Unit Conversions

TUTORIAL
Metric Conversions

TUTORIAL
Introduction to Unit Analysis Method

SAMPLE PROBLEM 1.8 **Problem Solving Using Conversion Factors**

In radiological imaging such as PET or CT scans, dosages of pharmaceuticals are based on body mass. If a person weighs 164 lb, what is that body mass in kilograms?

SOLUTION

Step 1 **State the given and needed quantities.**

Analyze the Problem

Given	Need
164 lb	kilograms

Step 2 **Write a plan to convert the given unit to the needed unit.** In our problem analysis, we see that the given unit is in the U.S. system of measurement and the needed unit is in the metric system. Therefore, we use the conversion factor that relates the U.S. unit lb to the metric unit kg.

$$\text{pounds} \quad \boxed{\text{U.S.–Metric factor}} \quad \text{kilograms}$$

Step 3 **State the equalities and conversion factors.**

$$1 \text{ kg} = 2.20 \text{ lb}$$
$$\frac{2.20 \text{ lb}}{1 \text{ kg}} \quad \text{and} \quad \frac{1 \text{ kg}}{2.20 \text{ lb}}$$

Step 4 **Set up the problem to cancel units and calculate the answer.** Write the given, 164 lb, and the conversion factor with the unit lb in the denominator (bottom number), which cancels the unit lb of the given unit.

Unit for answer goes here

$$164 \ \cancel{\text{lb}} \quad \times \quad \frac{1 \text{ kg}}{2.20 \ \cancel{\text{lb}}} \quad = \quad 74.5 \text{ kg}$$

Given   Conversion factor   Answer

Look at how the units cancel. The unit lb cancels out and the needed unit kg is the one that remains. This is a helpful way to check that a problem is set up properly.

$$\cancel{\text{lb}} \times \frac{\text{kg}}{\cancel{\text{lb}}} = \text{kg} \quad \text{Unit needed for answer}$$

The calculator display gives a numerical answer, which is rounded off to give a final answer with the proper number of significant figures (SFs).

$$164 \ \boxed{\times} \ \frac{1}{2.20} \ \boxed{=} \ 164 \ \boxed{\div} \ 2.20 \ \boxed{=} \ \boxed{74.54545455} \longrightarrow 74.5$$

Three SFs   Three SFs   Calculator display   Three SFs (rounded off)

When the value of 74.5 is combined with the unit, kg, the final answer of 74.5 kg is obtained. With few exceptions, answers to numerical problems contain a number and a unit.

STUDY CHECK 1.8

If 1890 mL of orange juice is prepared from orange juice concentrate, how many liters of orange juice is that?

Guide to Problem Solving Using Conversion Factors

1 State the given and needed quantities.

2 Write a plan to convert the given unit to the needed unit.

3 State the equalities and conversion factors.

4 Set up the problem to cancel units and calculate the answer.

Using Two or More Conversion Factors

In problem solving, two or more conversion factors are often needed to complete the change of units. In setting up these problems, one factor follows the other. Each factor is arranged to cancel the preceding unit until the needed unit is obtained. Once the problem is set up to cancel units properly, the calculations can be done without writing intermediate results. The process is worth practicing until you understand unit cancellation, the steps on the calculator, and rounding off to give a final answer. In this text, the final answer will be based on obtaining a final calculator display and rounding off (or adding zeros) to give the correct number of significant figures.

CONCEPT CHECK 1.12   Cancellation of Units

Cancel the units in the following set up and give the unit needed in the answer.

$$3.5 \text{ L} \times \frac{1000 \text{ mL}}{1 \text{ L}} \times \frac{0.48 \text{ g}}{1 \text{ mL}} \times \frac{1000 \text{ mg}}{1 \text{ g}} =$$

ANSWER

All units in both the numerator and denominator cancel except for mg in the numerator, which is the unit needed for the answer.

$$3.5 \text{ L} \times \frac{1000 \text{ mL}}{1 \text{ L}} \times \frac{0.48 \text{ g}}{1 \text{ mL}} \times \frac{1000 \text{ mg}}{1 \text{ g}} = \text{ needed unit is mg}$$

MC

TUTORIAL
Determining the Correct Dosage

Clinical Calculations Using Conversion Factors

Conversion factors are also useful for calculating medications. For example, if an antibiotic is available in 5-mg tablets, the dosage can be written as a conversion factor: 5 mg/1 tablet. When you do a clinical problem, you often start with a doctor's order that contains the quantity you need to give to the patient, and use the dosage as a conversion factor as shown in Sample Problem 1.9.

SAMPLE PROBLEM 1.9   Problem Solving Using Two Conversion Factors

Synthroid is a synthetic thyroid hormone that is used as a replacement or supplemental therapy for diminished thyroid function. A dosage of 0.200 mg is prescribed. One tablet contains 50 μg of Synthroid. How many tablets are required to provide the prescribed dosage?

SOLUTION

Step 1   State the given and needed quantities.

Analyze the Problem

Given	Need
0.200 mg of Synthroid	tablets for dosage
1 tablet = 50 μg of Synthroid	

Step 2   Write a plan to convert the given unit to the needed unit.

milligrams ⟶ Metric factor ⟶ micrograms ⟶ Clinical factor ⟶ number of tablets

Step 3   State the equalities and conversion factors.

1 mg = 1000 μg	1 tablet = 50 μg of Synthroid
$\dfrac{1 \text{ mg}}{1000 \mu\text{g}}$ and $\dfrac{1000 \mu\text{g}}{1 \text{ mg}}$	$\dfrac{1 \text{ tablet}}{50 \mu\text{g Synthroid}}$ and $\dfrac{50 \mu\text{g Synthroid}}{1 \text{ tablet}}$

Step 4 **Set up the problem to cancel units and calculate the answer.**

$$0.200 \text{ mg} \times \frac{1000 \text{ } \mu g \text{ Synthroid}}{1 \text{ mg}} \times \frac{1 \text{ tablet}}{50 \text{ } \mu g \text{ Synthroid}} = 4 \text{ tablets}$$

Three SFs · Exact · Exact · Exact · One SF · Exact (counting number)

Using a sequence of two or more conversion factors is an efficient way to set up and solve problems, especially if you are using a calculator. Once you have the problem set up, the calculations can be done without writing out the intermediate values. This process is worth practicing until you understand unit cancellation and the mathematical calculations.

STUDY CHECK 1.9

One medium bran muffin contains 4.2 g of fiber. How many ounces (oz) of fiber are obtained by eating three medium bran muffins?

SAMPLE PROBLEM 1.10 **Using a Percent as a Conversion Factor**

TUTORIAL
Using Percentage as a Conversion Factor

A person who exercises regularly has 16% body fat. If this person weighs 155 lb, what is the mass, in kilograms, of body fat?

SOLUTION

Step 1 **State the given and needed quantities.**

Analyze the Problem

Given	Need
155 lb of body weight	kilograms of body fat
100 lb of body weight = 16 lb of body fat	

Step 2 **Write a plan to convert the given unit to the needed unit.**

pounds of body weight → U.S.–Metric factor → kilograms of body mass → Percent factor → kilograms of body fat

Step 3 **State the equalities and conversion factors.**

1 kg of body mass = 2.20 lb of body weight	16 kg of body fat = 100 kg of body mass
$\dfrac{2.20 \text{ lb body weight}}{1 \text{ kg body mass}}$ and $\dfrac{1 \text{ kg body mass}}{2.20 \text{ lb body weight}}$	$\dfrac{16 \text{ kg body fat}}{100 \text{ kg body mass}}$ and $\dfrac{100 \text{ kg body mass}}{16 \text{ kg body fat}}$

Step 4 **Set up the problem to cancel units and calculate the answer.**

$$155 \text{ lb body weight} \times \frac{1 \text{ kg body mass}}{2.20 \text{ lb body weight}} \times \frac{16 \text{ kg body fat}}{100 \text{ kg body mass}}$$

Three SFs · Exact · Three SFs · Two SFs · Exact

$$= 11 \text{ kg of body fat}$$

STUDY CHECK 1.10

Uncooked lean ground beef can contain up to 22% fat by mass. How many grams of fat are in 0.25 lb of the ground beef?

QUESTIONS AND PROBLEMS

1.9 Problem Solving

LEARNING GOAL: *Use conversion factors to change from one unit to another.*

1.51 Use metric conversion factors to solve the following problems:
   a. The height of a student is 175 cm. How tall is the student in meters?
   b. A cooler has a volume of 5500 mL. What is the capacity of the cooler in liters?
   c. A hummingbird has a mass of 0.0055 kg. What is the mass of the hummingbird in grams?

1.52 Use metric conversion factors to solve the following problems:
   a. The daily requirement of phosphorus is 800 mg. How many grams of phosphorus are needed?
   b. A glass of orange juice contains 0.85 dL of juice. How many milliliters of orange juice are in the glass?
   c. A package of chocolate instant pudding contains 2840 mg of sodium. How many grams of sodium are in the pudding?

1.53 Solve each of the following problems using one or more conversion factors:
   a. A container holds 0.750 qt of liquid. How many milliliters of lemonade will it hold?
   b. In England, a person is weighed in stones. If one stone has a weight of 14.0 lb, what is the mass, in kilograms, of a person who weighs 11.8 stones?
   c. The femur, or thighbone, is the longest bone in the body. In a 6-ft-tall person, the femur is 19.5 in. long. What is the length of that femur in millimeters?
   d. How many inches thick is an arterial wall that measures 0.50 μm?

1.54 Solve each of the following problems using one or more conversion factors:
   a. You need 4.0 oz of a steroid ointment. If there are 16 oz in 1 lb, how many grams of ointment does the pharmacist need to prepare?
   b. During surgery, a person receives 5.0 pt of plasma. How many milliliters of plasma were given?
   c. Solar flares containing hot gases can rise to 120 000 miles above the surface of the Sun. What is that distance in kilometers?
   d. A filled gas tank contains 18.5 gallons of unleaded fuel. If a car uses 46.0 L, how many gallons of fuel remain in the tank?

1.55 The singles portion of a tennis court is 27.0 ft wide and 78.0 ft long.

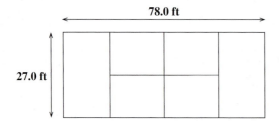

a. What is the length of the court in meters?
b. What is the area of the court in square meters (m^2)?
c. If a serve is measured at 185 km/h, how many seconds does it take for the tennis ball to travel the length of the court?

1.56 A football field is 300. feet long between goal lines.

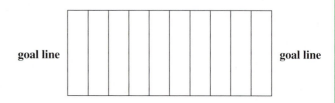

a. What distance, in meters, does a player run if he catches the ball on his own goal line and scores a touchdown?
b. If a player catches the football and runs 45 yards, how many meters did he gain?
c. If a player runs at a speed of 36 km/h, how many seconds does it take to run from the 50-yard line to the 20-yard line?

1.57 Use conversion factors to solve the following clinical problems:
   a. You need 250 L of distilled water for a dialysis patient. How many gallons of water is that?
   b. A patient needs 0.024 g of a sulfa drug. There are 8-mg tablets in stock. How many tablets should be given?
   c. The daily dose of ampicillin for the treatment of an ear infection is 115 mg/kg of body weight. What is the daily dose, in mg, for a 34-lb child?

1.58 Use conversion factors to solve the following clinical problems:
   a. A physician has ordered 1.0 g of tetracycline to be given every 6 h to a patient. If your stock on hand is 500-mg tablets, how many will you need for 1 day's treatment?
   b. An intramuscular medication is given at 5.00 mg/kg of body weight. If you give 425 mg of medication to a patient, what is the patient's weight in pounds?
   c. A physician orders 325 mg of atropine, intramuscularly. If atropine were available as 0.50 g/mL of solution, how many milliliters would you need to give?

1.59 **a.** Oxygen makes up 46.7% by mass of Earth's crust. How many grams of oxygen are present if a sample of Earth's crust has a mass of 325 g?
   b. Magnesium makes up 2.1% by mass of Earth's crust. How many grams of magnesium are present if a sample of Earth's crust has a mass of 1.25 g?
   c. A plant fertilizer contains 15% by mass nitrogen (N). In a container of soluble plant food, there are 10.0 oz of fertilizer. How many grams of nitrogen are in the container?
   d. In a candy factory, nutty chocolate bars contain 22.0% by mass pecans. If 5.0 kg of pecans were used for candy last Tuesday, how many pounds of nutty chocolate bars were made?

Agricultural fertilizers applied to a field provide nitrogen for plant growth.

1.60 a. Water is 11.2% by mass hydrogen. How many kilograms of water would contain 5.0 g of hydrogen?
b. Water is 88.8% by mass oxygen. How many grams of water would contain 2.25 kg of oxygen?
c. Blueberry high-fiber muffins contain 51% dietary fiber. If a package with a net weight of 12 oz contains 6 muffins, how many grams of fiber are in each muffin?
d. A jar of crunchy peanut butter contains 1.43 kg of peanut butter. If you use 8.0% of the peanut butter for a sandwich, how many ounces of peanut butter did you take out of the container?

1.10 Density

The mass and volume of any object can be measured. If we compare the mass of the object to its volume, we obtain a relationship called **density**.

$$\text{Density} = \frac{\text{mass of substance}}{\text{volume of substance}}$$

Every substance has a unique density, which distinguishes it from other substances. For example, lead has a density of 11.3 g/mL, whereas cork has a density of 0.26 g/mL. From these densities, we can predict if these substances will sink or float in water. If a substance, such as cork, is less dense than water, it will float. However, a lead object sinks in water because its density is greater than that of water (see Figure 1.11). A lead object would float on liquid mercury, because lead is less dense than the liquid.

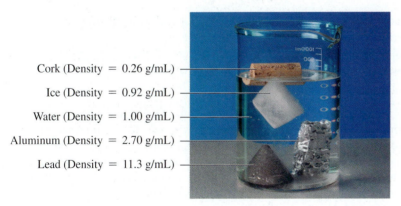

Cork (Density = 0.26 g/mL)
Ice (Density = 0.92 g/mL)
Water (Density = 1.00 g/mL)
Aluminum (Density = 2.70 g/mL)
Lead (Density = 11.3 g/mL)

FIGURE 1.11 Objects that sink in water are more dense than water; objects that float are less dense.
Q Why does an ice cube float and a piece of aluminum sink?

Density is used in chemistry and medicine in many ways. For example, density can be used to identify an unknown substance. If we calculate a density of a pure metal as 10.5 g/mL, then we might identify it as silver, but not lead or aluminum.

Metals such as gold and lead tend to have higher densities, whereas gases have very low densities. In the metric system, the densities of solids and liquids are usually expressed as grams per cubic centimeter (g/cm^3) or grams per milliliter (g/mL). The densities of gases are usually stated as grams per liter (g/L). Table 1.13 gives the densities of some common substances.

TABLE 1.13 Densities of Some Common Substances

Solids (at 25 °C)	Density (g/mL)	Liquids (at 25 °C)	Density (g/mL)	Gases (at 0 °C, 1 atm)	Density (g/L)
Cork	0.26	Gasoline	0.74	Hydrogen	0.090
Wood (maple)	0.75	Ethanol	0.79	Helium	0.179
Ice (at 0 °C)	0.92	Olive oil	0.92	Methane	0.714
Sugar	1.59	Water (at 4 °C)	1.00	Neon	0.902
Bone	1.80	Urine	1.003–1.030	Nitrogen	1.25
Salt (NaCl)	2.16	Plasma (blood)	1.03	Air (dry)	1.29
Aluminum	2.70	Milk	1.04	Oxygen	1.43
Cement	3.00	Mercury	13.6	Carbon dioxide	1.96
Diamond	3.52				
Iron	7.86				
Silver	10.5				
Lead	11.3				
Gold	19.3				

CONCEPT CHECK 1.13 Density

A   B

a. In diagram **A**, the gray cube has a density of 4.5 g/cm^3. Is the density of the green cube the same, lower than, or higher than the gray cube?

b. In diagram **B**, the gray cube has a density of 4.5 g/cm^3. Is the density of the green cube the same, lower than, or higher than the gray cube?

ANSWER

a. The green cube has the same volume as the gray cube. However, the green cube has a larger mass on the scale, which means that its mass/volume ratio is larger. Thus, the density of the green cube is higher than the density of the gray cube.

b. The green cube has the same mass as the gray cube. However, the green cube has a greater volume, which means that its mass/volume ratio is smaller. Thus, the density of the green cube is lower than the density of the gray cube.

Guide to Calculating Density

1 State the given and needed quantities.

2 Write the density expression.

3 Express mass in grams and volume in milliliters (mL) or cm^3.

4 Substitute mass and volume into the density expression and calculate the density.

SAMPLE PROBLEM 1.11 Calculating Density

High-density lipoprotein (HDL) contains large amounts of proteins and small amounts of cholesterol. If a 0.258-g sample of HDL has a volume of 0.215 cm^3, what is the density, in g/cm^3, of the HDL sample?

SOLUTION

Step 1 **State the given and needed quantities.**

Analyze the Problem

Given	Need
0.258 g of HDL	density (g/cm^3) of HDL
0.215 cm^3 of HDL	

Step 2   Write the density expression.

$$\text{Density} = \frac{\text{mass of substance}}{\text{volume of substance}}$$

Step 3   Express mass in grams and volume in cm³.

Mass of HDL sample $= 0.258$ g

Volume of HDL sample $= 0.215$ cm³

Step 4   Substitute mass and volume into the density expression and calculate the density.

Three SFs

$$\text{Density} = \frac{0.258 \text{ g}}{0.215 \text{ cm}^3} = \frac{1.20 \text{ g}}{1 \text{ cm}^3} = 1.20 \text{ g/cm}^3$$

Three SFs   Three SFs

STUDY CHECK 1.11

Low-density lipoprotein (LDL) contains small amounts of proteins and large amounts of cholesterol. If a 0.380-g sample of LDL has a volume of 0.362 cm³, what is the density of the LDL sample, in g/cm³?

Density of Solids

The density of a solid is calculated from its mass and volume. When a solid is completely submerged, it displaces a volume of water that is equal to the volume of the solid. In Figure 1.12, the water level rises from 35.5 mL to 45.0 mL. This means that 9.5 mL of water is displaced and that the volume of the object is 9.5 mL. The density of the zinc is calculated as follows:

Four SFs

$$\text{Density} = \frac{68.60 \text{ g zinc}}{9.5 \text{ mL}} = 7.2 \text{ g/mL}$$

Two SFs   Two SFs

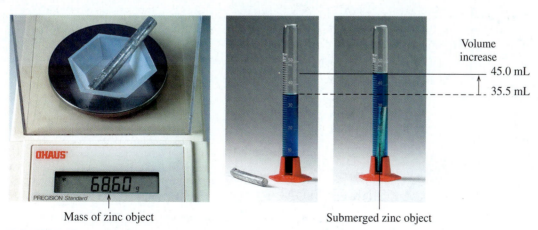

Mass of zinc object   Submerged zinc object

FIGURE 1.12 The density of a solid can be determined by volume displacement because a submerged object displaces a volume of water equal to its own volume.

Q How is the volume of the zinc object determined?

Lead weights in a belt counteract the buoyancy of a scuba diver.

SAMPLE PROBLEM 1.12 Using Volume Displacement to Calculate Density

A lead weight used in the belt of a scuba diver has a mass of 226 g. When the lead weight is placed in a graduated cylinder containing 200.0 mL of water, the water level rises to 220.0 mL. What is the density of the lead weight (g/mL)?

SOLUTION

Step 1 State the given and needed quantities.

Analyze the Problem

Given	Need
226 g of lead	density (g/mL) of lead
water level + lead = 220.0 mL	
water level (initial) = 200.0 mL	

Step 2 Write the density expression.

$$\text{Density} = \frac{\text{mass of substance}}{\text{volume of substance}}$$

Step 3 Express mass in grams and volume in milliliters (mL).

Mass of lead weight = 226 g

The volume of the lead weight is equal to the volume of water displaced, which is calculated as follows:

Water level after object submerged	=	220.0 mL
Water level before object submerged	=	−200.0 mL
Water displaced (volume of lead weight)	=	20.0 mL

Step 4 Substitute mass and volume into the density expression and calculate the density. The density is calculated by dividing the mass (g) by the volume (mL). Be sure to use the volume of water displaced and *not* the original volume of water.

$$\text{Density} = \frac{\overset{\text{Three SFs}}{226 \text{ g}}}{\underset{\text{Three SFs}}{20.0 \text{ mL}}} = \frac{11.3 \text{ g}}{1 \text{ mL}} = \underset{\text{Three SFs}}{11.3 \text{ g/mL}}$$

STUDY CHECK 1.12

A total of 0.500 lb of glass marbles is added to 425 mL of water. The water level rises to a volume of 528 mL. What is the density (g/mL) of the glass marbles?

Explore Your World

SINK OR FLOAT

1. Fill a large container or bucket with water. Place a can of diet and a can of nondiet soft drink in the water. What happens? Using information on the label, how might you account for your observations?

2. Design an experiment to determine the substance that is the most dense in each of the following:
   a. water and vegetable oil
   b. water and ice
   c. rubbing alcohol and ice
   d. vegetable oil, water, and ice

Chemistry Link to Health

BONE DENSITY

The density of our bones determines their health and strength. Our bones are constantly gaining and losing minerals such as calcium, magnesium, and phosphate. In childhood, bones form at a faster rate than they break down. As we age, the breakdown of bone occurs more rapidly than new bone forms. As the loss of bone minerals increases, bones begin to thin, causing a decrease in mass and density. Thinner bones lack strength, which increases the risk of fracture. Hormonal changes, disease, and certain medications can also contribute to the thinning of bone. Eventually, a condition of severe thinning of bone known as *osteoporosis* may occur. *Scanning electron micrographs* (SEMs) show (a) normal bone and (b) bone in osteoporosis caused by the loss of bone minerals.

Bone density is often determined by passing low-dose X-rays through the narrow part at the top of the femur (hip) and the spine (c). These locations are where fractures are more likely to occur, especially as we age. Bones with high density will block more of the X-rays compared to bones that are less dense. The results of a bone density test are compared to a healthy young adult, as well as to other people of the same age.

Recommendations to improve bone strength include supplements of calcium and vitamin D. Weight-bearing exercise such as walking and lifting weights can also improve muscle strength, which in turn, increases bone strength.

(a) Normal bone

(b) Bone with osteoporosis

(c) Viewing a low-dose X-ray of the spine

Problem Solving Using Density

Density can be used as a conversion factor. For example, if the volume and the density of a sample are known, the mass in grams of the sample can be calculated as shown in Sample Problem 1.13.

SAMPLE PROBLEM 1.13   Problem Solving Using Density

If the density of milk is 1.04 g/mL, how many grams of milk are in 0.50 qt of milk?

SOLUTION

Step 1   **State the given and needed quantities.**

Analyze the Problem

Given	Need
0.50 qt of milk	grams of milk
density of milk = 1.04 g/mL	
(1 mL of milk = 1.04 g)	

Step 2   **Write a plan to calculate the needed quantity.**

quarts → U.S.–Metric factor → liters → Metric factor → milliliters → Density factor → grams

Step 3   **Write equalities and their conversion factors, including density.**

1 L = 1.06 qt	1 L = 1000 mL	1 mL = 1.04 g
$\dfrac{1\ L}{1.06\ qt}$ and $\dfrac{1.06\ qt}{1\ L}$	$\dfrac{1\ L}{1000\ mL}$ and $\dfrac{1000\ mL}{1\ L}$	$\dfrac{1\ mL}{1.04\ g}$ and $\dfrac{1.04\ g}{1\ mL}$

Guide to Using Density

1 State the given and needed quantities.

2 Write a plan to calculate the needed quantity.

3 Write equalities and their conversion factors, including density.

4 Set up the problem to calculate the needed quantity.

Step 4   **Set up the problem to calculate the needed quantity.**

Exact   Exact   Three SFs

$$0.50 \ \cancel{qt} \times \frac{1 \ \cancel{L}}{1.06 \ \cancel{qt}} \times \frac{1000 \ \cancel{mL}}{1 \ \cancel{L}} \times \frac{1.04 \ g}{1 \ \cancel{mL}} = 490 \ g \ (4.9 \times 10^2 \ g)$$

Two SFs   Three SFs   Exact   Exact   Two SFs

STUDY CHECK 1.13

The density of maple syrup is 1.33 g/mL. A bottle of maple syrup contains 740 mL of syrup. What is the mass of the syrup?

Specific Gravity

Specific gravity (sp gr) *is a relationship between the density of a substance and the density of water.* Specific gravity is calculated by dividing the density of a sample by the density of water, which is 1.00 g/mL at 4 °C. A substance with a specific gravity of 1.00 has the same density as water. A substance with a specific gravity of 3.00 is three times as dense as water, whereas a substance with a specific gravity of 0.50 is just one-half as dense as water.

$$\text{Specific gravity} = \frac{\text{density of sample}}{\text{density of water}}$$

Specific gravity is one of the few unitless values you will use in chemistry. An instrument called a *hydrometer* is often used to measure the specific gravity of fluids such as battery fluid or a sample of urine. In Figure 1.13, a hydrometer is used to measure the specific gravity of a fluid. In the calculations for specific gravity, the units of density must match. Then all units cancel to leave only a number as the answer.

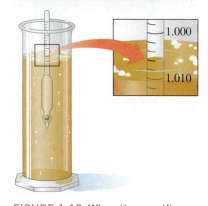

FIGURE 1.13 When the specific gravity of beer measures 1.010 or less with a hydrometer, the fermentation process is complete.

Q If the hydrometer reading is 1.006, what is the density, in g/mL, of the liquid?

| **SAMPLE PROBLEM 1.14** | **Problem Solving with Specific Gravity** |

John took 2.0 teaspoons (tsp) of cough syrup. If the syrup has a specific gravity (sp gr) of 1.20, and there are 5.0 mL in 1 tsp, what was the mass, in grams, of the cough syrup?

SOLUTION

Step 1   **State the given and needed quantities.**

Analyze the Problem

Given	Need
2.0 tsp of cough syrup	grams of cough syrup
sp gr 1.20	
1 tsp = 5.0 mL	

Step 2   **Write a plan to calculate the needed quantity.**

teaspoons → U.S.–Metric factor → milliliters → Density factor → grams

Step 3   **Write equalities and their conversion factors, including density.** For problem solving, it is convenient to convert the specific gravity value (1.20) to density.

$$\text{Density} = (\text{sp gr}) \times 1.00 \ g/mL = 1.20 \ g/mL$$

1 tsp = 5.0 mL	1 mL = 1.20 g
$\dfrac{1 \ tsp}{5.0 \ mL}$ and $\dfrac{5.0 \ mL}{1 \ tsp}$	$\dfrac{1 \ mL}{1.20 \ g}$ and $\dfrac{1.20 \ g}{1 \ mL}$

Step 4 **Set up the problem to calculate the needed quantity.**

Two SFs   Three SFs

$$2.0 \ \text{tsp} \ \times \ \frac{5.0 \ \text{mL}}{1 \ \text{tsp}} \ \times \ \frac{1.20 \ \text{g}}{1 \ \text{mL}} = 12 \ \text{g of cough syrup}$$

Two SFs   Exact   Exact   Two SFs

STUDY CHECK 1.14

An ebony carving has a mass of 275 g. If ebony has a specific gravity of 1.12, what is the volume, in milliliters, of the carving?

QUESTIONS AND PROBLEMS

1.10 Density

LEARNING GOAL: *Calculate the density or specific gravity of a substance; use the density or specific gravity to calculate the mass or volume of a substance.*

1.61 In an old trunk, you find a piece of metal that you think may be aluminum, silver, or lead. After laboratory testing, you find it has a mass of 217 g and a volume of 19.2 cm^3. Using Table 1.13, what is the metal you found?

1.62 Suppose you have two 100-mL graduated cylinders. In each cylinder, there is 40.0 mL of water. You also have two cubes: One is lead, and the other is aluminum. Each cube measures 2.0 cm on each side. After you carefully lower each cube into the water of its own cylinder, what will the new water level be in each of the cylinders?

1.63 What is the density (g/mL) for each of the following samples?
  a. A 20.0-mL sample of a salt solution that has a mass of 24.0 g.
  b. A cube of butter weighs 0.250 lb and has a volume of 130. mL.
  c. A gem has a mass of 45.0 g. When the gem is placed in a graduated cylinder containing 20.0 mL of water, the water level rises to 34.5 mL.

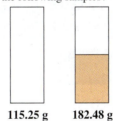

115.25 g   **182.48 g**

  d. A liquid is added to an empty container with a mass of 115.25 g. When 0.100 pt of liquid is added, the total mass of the container and liquid is 182.48 g.

1.64 What is the density (g/mL) for each of the following samples?
  a. The fluid in a car battery, if it has a volume of 125 mL and a mass of 155 g.
  b. A plastic material weighs 2.68 lb and has a volume of 3.5 L.

Titanium is used to make heads of drivers.

  c. A 5.00-mL urine sample from a patient suffering from symptoms resembling those of diabetes mellitus. The mass of the urine sample is 5.025 g.
  d. A lightweight head on the driver of a golf club is made of titanium. If the volume of a sample of titanium is 114 cm^3 and the mass is 514.1 g, what is the density of titanium?

1.65 Use the density values in Table 1.13 to solve each of the following problems:
  a. How many liters of ethanol contain 1.5 kg of ethanol?
  b. How many grams of mercury are present in a barometer that holds 6.5 mL of mercury?
  c. A sculptor has prepared a mold for casting a bronze figure. The figure has a volume of 225 mL. If bronze has a density of 7.8 g/mL, how many ounces of bronze are needed in the preparation of the bronze figure?
  d. How many kilograms of gasoline fill a 12.0-gallon gas tank? (1 gallon = 4 qt)

1.66 Use the density values in Table 1.13 to solve each of the following problems:
  a. A graduated cylinder contains 18.0 mL of water. What is the new water level, in milliliters, after 35.6 g of silver metal is submerged in the water?
  b. A fish tank holds 35 gallons of water. How many pounds of water are in the fish tank?
  c. The mass of an empty container is 88.25 g. The mass of the container and a liquid with a density of 0.758 g/mL is 150.50 g. What is the volume, in milliliters, of the liquid in the container?
  d. A cannon ball made of iron has a volume of 115 cm^3. What is the mass, in kilograms, of the cannon ball?

1.67 Solve each of the following specific gravity problems:
  a. A urine sample has a density of 1.030 g/mL. What is the specific gravity of the sample?
  b. A liquid has a volume of 40.0 mL and a mass of 45.0 g. What is the specific gravity of the liquid?
  c. The specific gravity of a vegetable oil is 0.85. What is its density?

1.68 Solve each of the following specific gravity problems:
  a. A glucose solution has a density of 1.02 g/mL. What is its specific gravity?
  b. A bottle containing 325 g of cleaning solution is used for carpets. If the cleaning solution has a specific gravity of 0.850, what volume, in milliliters, of solution was used?
  c. Butter has a specific gravity of 0.86. What is the mass, in grams, of 2.15 L of butter?

CONCEPT MAP

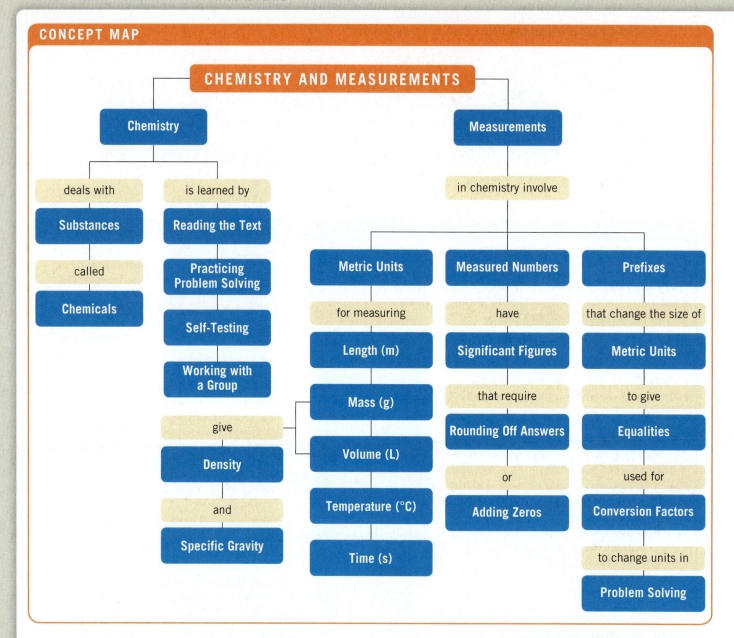

CHEMISTRY AND MEASUREMENTS

Chemistry

deals with

Substances

called

Chemicals

is learned by

Reading the Text

Practicing Problem Solving

Self-Testing

Working with a Group

give

Density

and

Specific Gravity

Measurements

in chemistry involve

Metric Units

for measuring

Length (m)

Mass (g)

Volume (L)

Temperature (°C)

Time (s)

Measured Numbers

have

Significant Figures

that require

Rounding Off Answers

or

Adding Zeros

Prefixes

that change the size of

Metric Units

to give

Equalities

used for

Conversion Factors

to change units in

Problem Solving

CHAPTER REVIEW

1.1 Chemistry and Chemicals

LEARNING GOAL: Define the term chemistry *and identify substances as chemicals.*

- Chemistry is the study of the composition, structure, properties, and reactions of matter.
- A chemical is any substance that always has the same composition and properties wherever it is found.

1.2 A Study Plan for Learning Chemistry

LEARNING GOAL: Develop a study plan for learning chemistry.

- A study plan for learning chemistry utilizes the features in this text and develops an active learning approach to the study of chemistry.
- By using the *Learning Goals* in the chapter and working the *Concept Checks, Sample Problems, Study Checks,* and the *Questions and Problems* that follow each section, you can successfully learn chemistry.

1.3 Units of Measurement

LEARNING GOAL: Write the names and abbreviations for metric or SI units used in measurements of length, volume, mass, temperature, and time.

- In science, physical quantities are described in units of the metric system or International System (SI).
- Some important units are meter (m) for length, liter (L) for volume, gram (g) and kilogram (kg) for mass, and degree Celsius (°C) and Kelvin (K) for temperature.

1.4 Scientific Notation

LEARNING GOAL: Write a number in scientific notation.

- Large and small numbers can be written using scientific notation in which the decimal point is moved to give a coefficient of at least 1 but less than 10, and the number of spaces moved is shown as a power of 10.
- A large number will have a positive power of 10, while a small number will have a negative power of 10.

1.5 Measured Numbers and Significant Figures

LEARNING GOAL: Identify a number as measured or exact; determine the number of significant figures in a measured number.

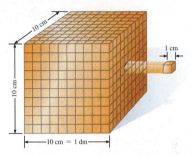

- A measured number is any number obtained by using a measuring device.
- An exact number is obtained by counting items or from a definition; no measuring device is needed.
- Significant figures are the numbers reported in a measurement including the estimated digit. Zeros in front of a decimal number or at the end of a nondecimal number are not significant.

1.6 Significant Figures in Calculations

LEARNING GOAL: Give the correct number of significant figures in a final answer by adding or removing digits in a calculator result.

- In multiplication or division, the final answer is written so that it has the same number of significant figures as the measurement with the fewest significant figures.

- In addition and subtraction, the final answer is written so that it has the same number of decimal places as the measurement with the fewest decimal places.

1.7 Prefixes and Equalities

LEARNING GOAL: Use the numerical values of prefixes to write a metric equality.

- A prefix placed in front of a metric or SI unit changes the size of the unit by factors of 10.
- Prefixes such as *centi*, *milli*, and *micro* provide smaller units; prefixes such as *kilo*, *mega*, and *tera* provide larger units.
- An equality shows the relationship between two units that measure the same quantity of length, volume, mass, or time.
- Examples of equalities are 1 m = 100 cm, 1 qt = 946 mL, 1 kg = 1000 g, and 1 min = 60 s.

1.8 Writing Conversion Factors

LEARNING GOAL: Write a conversion factor for two units that describe the same quantity.

- Conversion factors are used to express an equality in the form of a fraction.
- Two conversion factors can be written for any relationship in the metric or U.S. system.
- A percentage is written as a conversion factor by expressing matching units in the relationship as the parts to 100 parts of the whole.
- Extremely small percentage values are written as parts per million (ppm) or parts per billion (ppb).

1.9 Problem Solving

LEARNING GOAL: Use conversion factors to change from one unit to another.

- Conversion factors are useful when changing a quantity expressed in one unit to a quantity expressed in another unit.
- In the process, a given unit is multiplied by one or more conversion factors that cancel units until the needed unit for the answer is obtained.

$$164 \text{ lb} \quad \times \quad \frac{1 \text{ kg}}{2.20 \text{ lb}} \quad = \quad 74.5 \text{ kg}$$

Unit for answer goes here

Given   Conversion factor   Answer

1.10 Density

LEARNING GOAL: *Calculate the density or specific gravity of a substance; use the density or specific gravity to calculate the mass or volume of a substance.*

- The density of a substance is a ratio of its mass to its volume, usually g/mL or g/cm^3.
- The units of density can be used to write conversion factors that convert between the mass and volume of a substance.
- Specific gravity (sp gr) compares the density of a substance to the density of water, 1.00 g/mL.

KEY TERMS

Celsius (°C) temperature scale A temperature scale on which water has a freezing point of 0 °C and a boiling point of 100 °C.

centimeter (cm) A unit of length in the metric system; there are 2.54 cm in 1 in.

chemical A substance that has the same composition and properties wherever it is found.

chemistry The science that studies the composition, structure, properties, and reactions of matter.

conversion factor A ratio in which the numerator and denominator are quantities from an equality or given relationship. For example, the conversion factors for the relationship 1 kg = 2.20 lb are written:

$$\frac{2.20 \text{ lb}}{1 \text{ kg}} \quad \text{and} \quad \frac{1 \text{ kg}}{2.20 \text{ lb}}$$

cubic centimeter (cm^3 or cc) The volume of a cube that has 1-cm sides; 1 cm^3 is equal to 1 mL.

density The relationship of the mass of an object to its volume expressed as grams per cubic centimeter (g/cm^3), grams per milliliter (g/mL), or grams per liter (g/L).

equality A relationship between two units that measure the same quantity.

exact number A number obtained by counting or by definition.

gram (g) The metric unit used in measurements of mass.

International System of Units (SI) A system of units that modifies the metric system.

Kelvin (K) temperature scale A temperature scale on which the lowest possible temperature is 0 K.

kilogram (kg) A metric mass of 1000 g and equal to 2.20 lb. The kilogram is the SI standard unit of mass.

liter (L) The metric unit for volume that is slightly larger than a quart.

mass A measure of the quantity of material in an object.

measured number A number obtained when a quantity is determined by using a measuring device.

meter (m) The metric unit for length that is slightly longer than a yard. The meter is the SI standard unit of length.

metric system A system of measurement used by scientists and in most countries of the world.

milliliter (mL) A metric unit of volume equal to one-thousandth of a liter (0.001 L).

prefix The part of the name of a metric unit that precedes the base unit and specifies the size of the measurement. All prefixes are related on a decimal scale.

scientific notation A form of writing large and small numbers using a coefficient that is at least 1 but less than 10, followed by a power of 10.

second (s) The standard unit of time in the SI and metric system.

significant figures (SFs) The numbers recorded in a measurement.

specific gravity (sp gr) A relationship between the density of a substance and the density of water:

$$\text{sp gr} = \frac{\text{density of sample}}{\text{density of water}}$$

temperature An indicator of the hotness or coldness of an object.

volume The amount of space occupied by a substance.

UNDERSTANDING THE CONCEPTS

The chapter sections to review are shown in parentheses at the end of each question.

1.69 Which of the following will help you develop a successful study plan? (1.2)
- **a.** Skip lecture and just read the text.
- **b.** Work the *Sample Problems* as you go through a chapter.
- **c.** Go to your professor's office hours.
- **d.** Read through the chapter, but work the problems later.

1.70 Which of the following will help you develop a successful study plan? (1.2)
- **a.** Study all night before the exam.
- **b.** Form a study group and discuss the problems together.
- **c.** Work problems in a notebook for easy reference.
- **d.** Copy the answers to homework from a friend.

1.71 A balance measures mass to 0.001 g. If you determine the mass of an object that weighs about 30 g, would you record the mass as 30 g, 32 g, 32.1 g, or 32.075 g? Explain your choice by writing two to three complete sentences that describe your thinking. (1.5)

1.72 When three students use the same meterstick to measure the length of a paper clip, they obtain results of 5.8 cm, 5.75 cm, and 5.76 cm. If the meterstick has millimeter markings, what are some reasons for the different values? (1.5)

1.73 In the following pairs, which measurement has more significant figures? (1.4, 1.5)

    a. 2.0500 m and 0.0205 m

    b. 600.0 K and 60 K

    c. 0.000 705 s and 75 000 s

    d. 2550 L and 2.550×10^{-2} L

1.74 In the following pairs, which measurement has fewer significant figures? (1.4, 1.5)

    a. 2.80×10^{-3} g and 0.0028 g

    b. 8.005 m and 0.00805 m

    c. 163 000 s and 1.630×10^2 s

    d. 0.03080 cm and 308 cm

1.75 Indicate if each of the following is an exact number or a measured number: (1.5)

    a. number of legs

    b. height of the table

    c. number of chairs at the table

    d. area of tabletop

1.76 Measure the length of each of the objects in diagrams (**a**), (**b**), and (**c**) using the metric rule in the figure. Indicate the number of significant figures for each and the estimated digit for each. (1.5)

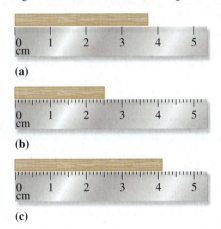

    (a)

    (b)

    (c)

1.77 Measure the length and width of the rectangle, including the estimated digit, using a metric rule. (1.5)

    a. What is the length and width of this rectangle measured in centimeters?

    b. What is the length and width of this rectangle measured in millimeters?

    c. How many significant figures are in the length measurement?

    d. How many significant figures are in the width measurement?

    e. What is the area of the rectangle in cm^2?

    f. How many significant figures are in the calculated answer for area?

1.78 Each of the following represents a container of water and a cube. Some cubes float while others sink. Match diagrams **1**, **2**, **3**, or **4** with one of the following descriptions and explain your choices: (1.10)

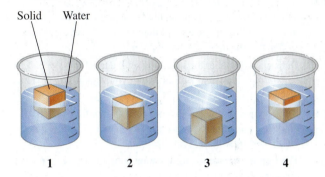

    a. The cube has a greater density than water.

    b. The cube has a density that is 0.60–0.80 g/mL.

    c. The cube has a density that is 1/2 the density of water.

    d. The cube has the same density as water.

1.79 What is the density of the solid object that is weighed and submerged in water? (1.10)

1.80 Consider the following solids. The solids **A**, **B**, and **C** represent aluminum, gold, and silver. If each has a mass of 10.0 g, what is the identity of each solid? (1.10)

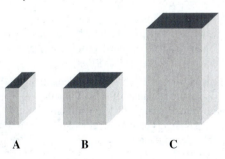

    Density of aluminum = 2.70 g/mL

    Density of gold = 19.3 g/mL

    Density of silver = 10.5 g/mL

ADDITIONAL QUESTIONS AND PROBLEMS

For instructor-assigned homework, go to www.masteringchemistry.com.

1.81 Round off or add zeros to the following calculated answers to give a final answer with three significant figures: (1.4, 1.5)
   a. 0.000 012 58 L   **b.** 3.528×10^2 kg
   c. 125 111 m   **d.** 58.703 g

1.82 Round off or add zeros to the following calculated answers to give a final answer with two significant figures: (1.4, 1.5)
   a. 0.004 mL   **b.** 34 677 g
   c. 4.393 cm   **d.** 1.74×10^3 ms

1.83 What is the total mass, in grams, of a dessert containing 137.25 g of vanilla ice cream, 84 g of fudge sauce, and 43.7 g of nuts? (1.6)

1.84 A fish company delivers 22 kg of salmon, 5.5 kg of crab, and 3.48 kg of oysters to your seafood restaurant. (1.3, 1.6)
   a. What is the total mass, in kilograms, of the seafood?
   b. What is the total number of pounds?

1.85 During a workout at the gym, you set the treadmill at a pace of 55.0 m/min. How many minutes will you walk if you cover a distance of 7500 ft? (1.3, 1.9)

1.86 Bill's recipe for onion soup calls for 4.0 lb of thinly sliced onions. If an onion has an average mass of 115 g, how many onions does Bill need? (1.3, 1.9)

1.87 The following nutrition information is listed on a box of crackers: (1.9)

Serving size 0.50 oz (6 crackers)

Fat 4 g per serving

Sodium 140 mg per serving
   a. If the box has a net weight (contents only) of 8.0 oz, about how many crackers are in the box?
   b. If you ate 10 crackers, how many ounces of fat did you consume?
   c. How many grams of sodium are used to prepare 50 boxes of crackers in part **a**?

1.88 The price of 1 lb of potatoes is $1.75. If all the potatoes sold today at the store bring in $1420, how many kilograms of potatoes did grocery shoppers buy? (1.9)

1.89 In Mexico, avocados are 48 pesos per kilogram. What is the cost, in cents, of an avocado that weighs 0.45 lb if the exchange rate is 13.0 pesos to the dollar? (1.9)

1.90 An aquarium store unit requires 75 000 mL of water. How many gallons (1 gal = 4 qt) of water are needed? (1.9)

1.91 **a.** Some athletes have as little as 3.0% body fat. If such a person has a body mass of 65 kg, how many pounds of body fat does that person have? (1.9)
   b. In a process called *liposuction*, a doctor removes fat deposits from a person's body. If body fat has a density of 0.94 g/mL and 3.0 liters of fat are removed, how many pounds of fat were removed from the patient? (1.9)

1.92 Celeste's diet restricts her intake of protein to 24 g per day. If she eats an 8.0-oz burger that is 15.0% protein, has she exceeded her protein limit for the day? How many ounces of a burger would be allowed for Celeste? (1.3, 1.7, 1.9)

1.93 The water level in a graduated cylinder initially at 215 mL rises to 285 mL after a piece of lead is submerged. What is the mass, in grams, of the lead (see Table 1.13)? (1.9, 1.10)

1.94 A graduated cylinder contains 155 mL of water. A 15.0-g piece of iron and a 20.0-g piece of lead are added. What is the new water level, in milliliters, in the cylinder (see Table 1.13)? (1.9, 1.10)

1.95 Sterling silver is 92.5% silver by mass, with a density of 10.3 g/cm^3. If a cube of sterling silver has a volume of 27.0 cm^3, how many ounces of pure silver are present? (1.9, 1.10)

1.96 A typical adult body contains 55% water. If a person has a mass of 65 kg, how many pounds of water does she have in her body? (1.9)

CHALLENGE QUESTIONS

The following groups of questions and problems are related to the topics in this chapter. However, they do not all follow the chapter order, and they require you to combine concepts and skills from several sections. These problems will help you increase your critical thinking skills and prepare for your next exam.

1.97 A sunscreen preparation contains 2.50% by mass benzyl salicylate. If a tube contains 4.0 oz of sunscreen, how many kilograms of benzyl salicylate are needed to manufacture 325 tubes of sunscreen? (1.9)

1.98 A mouthwash is 21.6% by mass alcohol. If one bottle contains 0.358 pt of mouthwash with a density of 0.876 g/mL, how many kilograms of alcohol are in 180 bottles of the mouthwash? (1.9, 1.10)

A mouthwash may contain ethyl alcohol.

1.99 A car travels at 55 mi/h and travels 11 kilometers on one liter of gasoline. How many gallons of gasoline are needed for a 3.0-h trip? (1.9, 1.10)

1.100 If a recycling center collects 1254 aluminum cans and there are 22 aluminum cans in 1 lb, what volume, in liters, of aluminum was collected (see Table 1.13)? (1.9, 1.10)

1.101 For a 180-lb person, calculate the quantities of each of the following that must be ingested to provide the LD$_{50}$ for caffeine given in Table 1.12: (1.8, 1.9)
   a. cups of coffee if one cup is 12 fl oz and there are 100. mg of caffeine per 6.0 fl oz of drip-brewed coffee
   b. cans of cola if one can contains 50. mg of caffeine
   c. tablets of No-Doz if one tablet contains 100. mg of caffeine

1.102 The label on a 1-pt bottle of mineral water lists the following components. If the density is the same as pure water and you drink three bottles of water in one day, how many milligrams of each component will you obtain? (1.8, 1.9, 1.10)
   a. calcium 28 ppm   **b.** fluoride 0.08 ppm
   c. magnesium 12 ppm   **d.** potassium 3.2 ppm
   e. sodium 15 ppm

1.103 In the manufacturing of computer chips, cylinders of silicon are cut into thin wafers that are 3.00 inches in diameter and have a mass of 1.50 g of silicon. How thick (mm) is each wafer if silicon has a density of 2.33 g/cm³? (1.8, 1.9, 1.10) (The volume of a cylinder is $V = \pi r^2 h$.)

1.104 A circular pool with a diameter of 27 ft is filled to a depth of 50. in. Assume the pool is a cylinder ($V = \pi r^2 h$). (1.8, 1.9, 1.10)
- **a.** What is the volume of water in the pool in cubic meters?
- **b.** The density of water is 1.00 g/cm³. What is the mass, in kilograms, of the water in the pool?

1.105 A package of aluminum foil is 66.7 yd long, 12 in. wide, and 0.000 30 in. thick. If aluminum has a density of 2.70 g/cm³, what is the mass, in grams, of the foil? (1.8, 1.9, 1.10)

1.106 An 18-karat gold necklace is 75% gold by mass, 16% silver, and 9.0% copper. (1.8, 1.9, 1.10)
- **a.** What is the mass, in grams, of the necklace if it contains 0.24 oz of silver?
- **b.** How many grams of copper are in the necklace?
- **c.** If 18-karat gold has a density of 15.5 g/cm³, what is the volume in cubic centimeters?

1.107 What is a cholesterol level of 1.85 g/L in units of mg/dL? (1.7, 1.8, 1.9, 1.10)

1.108 An object has a mass of 3.15 oz. When it is submerged in a graduated cylinder initially containing 325.2 mL of water, the water level rises to 442.5 mL. What is the density (g/mL) of the object? (1.8, 1.9, 1.10)

ANSWERS

Answers to Study Checks

1.1 time

1.2 a. 4.25×10^5 m **b.** 8×10^{-7} g

1.3 a. 36 m **b.** 0.0026 L
c. 3.8×10^3 g **d.** 1.3 kg

1.4 a. 83.70 mg **b.** 0.5 L

1.5 1.5×10^{12} bytes

1.6 a. 1000 g (1×10^3 g) **b.** 0.001 L (1×10^{-3} L)

1.7 a. 62.2 km = 1 h; $\dfrac{62.2 \text{ km}}{1 \text{ h}}$ and $\dfrac{1 \text{ h}}{62.2 \text{ km}}$
The 1 h is exact; the 62.2 has three SFs.
b. 1 μg of arsenic = 1 kg of water;
$\dfrac{1 \,\mu\text{g arsenic}}{1 \text{ kg water}}$ and $\dfrac{1 \text{ kg water}}{1 \,\mu\text{g arsenic}}$
The 1 in 1 kg of water is exact; the 1 in 1 μg has one SF.

1.8 1.89 L

1.9 0.44 oz

1.10 25 g of fat

1.11 1.05 g/cm³

1.12 2.20 g/mL

1.13 980 g of syrup

1.14 246 mL

Answers to Selected Questions and Problems

1.1 Many chemicals are listed on a vitamin bottle such as vitamin A, vitamin B₃, vitamin B₁₂, folic acid, etc.

1.3 No. All of the ingredients listed are chemicals.

1.5 Among the things you can do to help yourself succeed in chemistry are: form a study group, review the *Learning Goals*, attend class regularly, go to office hours, work the problems in the text, and become an active learner.

1.7 a, c, e, f

1.9 a. volume **b.** length **c.** length **d.** time

1.11 a. meter; length **b.** gram; mass
c. liter; volume **d.** second; time
e. degree Celsius; temperature

1.13 a. 5.5×10^4 m **b.** 4.8×10^2 g
c. 5×10^{-6} cm **d.** 1.4×10^{-4} s
e. 7.85×10^{-3} L **f.** 6.7×10^5 kg

1.15 a. 7.2×10^3 cm **b.** 3.2×10^{-2} kg
c. 1×10^4 L **d.** 6.8×10^{-2} m

1.17 a. 12 000 s **b.** 0.0825 kg
c. 4 000 000 g **d.** 0.005 m

1.19 a. Measured; measurement of mass requires a measuring device.
b. Exact; tablets are counted.
c. Exact; both numbers in a metric definition are exact.
d. Measured; distance is measured with a measuring device.

1.21 a. 6 oz of meat **b.** none
c. 0.75 lb; 350 g **d.** none (definitions are exact)

1.23 a. The zero following the 8 is significant.
b. The zero between nonzero digits is significant.
c. Both zeros in a number with a decimal point are significant.
d. The zero in the coefficient is significant.
e. None; zeros in a large number with no decimal point are not significant.

1.25 a. five SFs **b.** two SFs **c.** two SFs
d. three SFs **e.** four SFs **f.** three SFs

1.27 a. 11.00 m **b.** 405.0 K **c.** 0.0120 s **d.** 250.0 L

1.29 a. 1.85 kg **b.** 184 L **c.** 0.004 74 cm
d. 8810 m **e.** 1.83×10^5 s

1.31 a. 1.6 **b.** 0.01 **c.** 27.6 **d.** 3.5

1.33 a. 53.54 cm **b.** 127.6 g **c.** 121.5 mL **d.** 0.50 L

1.35 km/h is kilometers per hour; mi/h is miles per hour.

1.37 a. mg **b.** dL **c.** km
d. pg **e.** μL **f.** ns

1.39 a. 0.01 **b.** 1000
c. 0.001 (1×10^{-3}) **d.** 1×10^{12}
e. 1 000 000 (1×10^6) **f.** 1×10^{-12}

1.41 a. 100 cm **b.** 1×10^9 nm
c. 0.001 m **d.** 1000 mL

1.43 a. kilogram   **b.** milliliter   **c.** km
      d. kL   **e.** nanometer

1.45 a. $1 \text{ m} = 100 \text{ cm}$; $\dfrac{100 \text{ cm}}{1 \text{ m}}$ and $\dfrac{1 \text{ m}}{100 \text{ cm}}$

     b. $1 \text{ g} = 1000 \text{ mg}$; $\dfrac{1000 \text{ mg}}{1 \text{ g}}$ and $\dfrac{1 \text{ g}}{1000 \text{ mg}}$

     c. $1 \text{ L} = 1000 \text{ mL}$; $\dfrac{1000 \text{ mL}}{1 \text{ L}}$ and $\dfrac{1 \text{ L}}{1000 \text{ mL}}$

     d. $1 \text{ dL} = 100 \text{ mL}$; $\dfrac{100 \text{ mL}}{1 \text{ dL}}$ and $\dfrac{1 \text{ dL}}{100 \text{ mL}}$

1.47 a. $1 \text{ yd} = 3 \text{ ft}$; $\dfrac{3 \text{ ft}}{1 \text{ yd}}$ and $\dfrac{1 \text{ yd}}{3 \text{ ft}}$
     The numbers 1 and 3 are both exact.

     b. $1 \text{ kg} = 2.20 \text{ lb}$; $\dfrac{2.20 \text{ lb}}{1 \text{ kg}}$ and $\dfrac{1 \text{ kg}}{2.20 \text{ lb}}$
     The number 1 is exact; the number 2.20 has three SFs.

     c. $1 \text{ min} = 60 \text{ sec}$; $\dfrac{60 \text{ sec}}{1 \text{ min}}$ and $\dfrac{1 \text{ min}}{60 \text{ sec}}$
     The numbers 1 and 60 are both exact.

     d. $1 \text{ gal} = 27 \text{ mi}$; $\dfrac{1 \text{ gal}}{27 \text{ mi}}$ and $\dfrac{27 \text{ mi}}{1 \text{ gal}}$
     The number 1 is exact; the number 27 has two SFs.

     e. 93 g of silver = 100 g of sterling;
     $\dfrac{93 \text{ g silver}}{100 \text{ g sterling}}$ and $\dfrac{100 \text{ g sterling}}{93 \text{ g silver}}$
     The number 100 is exact; the number 93 has two SFs.

1.49 a. $3.5 \text{ m} = 1 \text{ s}$; $\dfrac{3.5 \text{ m}}{1 \text{ s}}$ and $\dfrac{1 \text{ s}}{3.5 \text{ m}}$
     The number 1 is exact; the number 3.5 has two SFs.

     b. 3500 mg of potassium = 1 day;
     $\dfrac{3500 \text{ mg potassium}}{1 \text{ day}}$ and $\dfrac{1 \text{ day}}{3500 \text{ mg potassium}}$
     The number 1 is exact; the number 3500 has two SFs.

     c. $46.0 \text{ km} = 1 \text{ gal}$; $\dfrac{46.0 \text{ km}}{1 \text{ gal}}$ and $\dfrac{1 \text{ gal}}{46.0 \text{ km}}$
     The number 1 is exact; the number 46.0 has three SFs.

     d. 50. mg of Atenolol = 1 tablet;
     $\dfrac{50. \text{ mg Atenolol}}{1 \text{ tablet}}$ and $\dfrac{1 \text{ tablet}}{50. \text{ mg Atenolol}}$
     The number 1 is exact; the number 50. has two SFs.

     e. 29 μg of pesticide = 1 kg of plums;
     $\dfrac{29 \ \mu\text{g pesticide}}{1 \text{ kg plums}}$ and $\dfrac{1 \text{ kg plums}}{29 \ \mu\text{g pesticide}}$
     The number 1 is exact; the number 29 has two SFs.

     f. 81 mg of aspirin = 1 tablet;
     $\dfrac{81 \text{ mg aspirin}}{1 \text{ tablet}}$ and $\dfrac{1 \text{ tablet}}{81 \text{ mg aspirin}}$
     The number 1 is exact; the number 81 has two SFs.

1.51 a. 1.75 m   **b.** 5.5 L   **c.** 5.5 g

1.53 a. 710. mL   **b.** 75.1 kg   **c.** 495 mm
     d. 2.0×10^{-5} in.

1.55 a. 23.8 m   **b.** 196 m^2 **c.** 0.463 s

1.57 a. 66 gal   **b.** 3 tablets
     c. 1800 mg (1.8×10^3 mg)

1.59 a. 152 g of oxygen   **b.** 0.026 g of magnesium
     c. 43 g of N   **d.** 50. lb of chocolate bars

1.61 lead; 11.3 g/mL

1.63 a. 1.20 g/mL   **b.** 0.877 g/mL
     c. 3.10 g/mL   **d.** 1.42 g/mL

1.65 a. 1.9 L   **b.** 88 g
     c. 62 oz   **d.** 34 kg

1.67 a. 1.03   **b.** 1.13
     c. 0.85 g/mL

1.69 b and c

1.71 You should record the mass as 32.075 g. Because your balance will weigh to the nearest 0.001 g, the mass values should be reported to 0.001 g.

1.73 a. 2.0500 m   **b.** 600.0 K
     c. 0.000 705 s   **d.** 2.550×10^{-2} L

1.75 a. exact   **b.** measured
     c. exact   **d.** measured

1.77 a. length = 6.96 cm; width = 4.75 cm
     b. length = 69.6 mm; width = 47.5 mm
     c. three SFs
     d. three SFs
     e. 33.1 cm^2
     f. three SFs

1.79 1.8 g/mL

1.81 a. 0.000 0126 L   **b.** 3.53×10^2 kg
     c. 125 000 m   **d.** 58.7 g

1.83 265 g

1.85 42 min

1.87 a. 96 crackers
     b. 0.2 oz of fat
     c. 110 g of sodium

1.89 76 cents

1.91 a. 4.3 lb of body fat   **b.** 6.2 lb

1.93 790 g

1.95 9.07 oz of pure silver

1.97 0.92 kg

1.99 6.4 gal

1.101 a. 79 cups   **b.** 310 cans
     c. 160 tablets

1.103 0.141 mm

1.105 3.8×10^2 g of aluminum foil

1.107 185 mg/dL

Energy and Matter

Visit **www.masteringchemistry.com**
for self-study materials and instructor-
assigned homework.

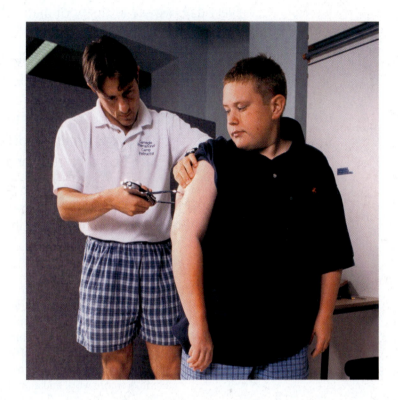

Charles is 13 years old and overweight

for his age. His doctor is worried that Charles is at risk for type 2 diabetes and advises his mother to make an appointment with a dietician. Daniel, a dietician, explains to them that choosing the appropriate foods is important to living a healthy lifestyle, losing weight, and preventing or managing diabetes.

Daniel also explains that food contains potential or stored energy, and different foods contain different amounts of potential energy. For instance, carbohydrates contain 4 kcal/g while fats contain 9 kcal/g. He then explains that diets high in fat require more exercise to burn the fats, as they contain more potential energy. Daniel encourages Charles and his mother to include whole grains, fruits, and vegetables in their diet instead of foods high in fat or sugar. They also discuss food labels and that smaller serving sizes of healthy foods are necessary in order to lose weight. Before leaving, Charles and his mother are given a menu for the following two weeks, and a diary to keep track of what, and how much, they actually consume.

Career: Dietician

Dieticians specialize in helping individuals learn about good nutrition and the need for a balanced diet. This requires them to understand biochemical processes, the importance of vitamins, and food labels, as well as the differences between carbohydrates, fats, and proteins in terms of their energy content and how they are metabolized. Dieticians work in a variety of environments including hospitals, nursing homes, school cafeterias, and public health clinics. In these environments, they create personalized diets for individuals diagnosed with a specific disease, or create meal plans for those in a nursing home.

Almost everything we do involves energy. We use energy when we walk, play tennis, study, and breathe. We use energy when we warm water, cook food, turn on lights, use a washing machine, and drive our cars. Of course, that energy has to come from something. In our bodies, the food we eat provides us with energy. Energy from fossil fuels or the Sun is used to heat a home or water for a pool.

Every day, we see a variety of materials with many different shapes and forms. To a scientist, all of this material is *matter*. Matter is everywhere around us: the orange juice we had for breakfast, the water we put in the coffee maker, the plastic bag we put our sandwich in, our toothbrush and toothpaste, the oxygen we inhale, and the carbon dioxide we exhale are all forms of matter.

When we look around us, we see that matter takes the physical state of a solid, a liquid, or a gas. Water is a familiar substance that we observe in all three states. In the solid state, water can be an ice cube or a snowflake. It is a liquid when it comes out of a faucet or fills a pool. We will also see that a substance can change state. For example, water changes state when ice melts, liquid evaporates from a pond, or water boils to form a gas. When water vapor in the atmosphere condenses, clouds are formed.

LEARNING GOAL

Identify energy as potential or kinetic; convert between units of energy.

2.1 Energy

When you are running, walking, dancing, or thinking, you are using energy to do **work**, which is any activity that requires energy. In fact, **energy** is defined as the ability to do work. Suppose you are climbing a steep hill and you become too tired to go on. At that moment, you do not have sufficient energy to do any more work. Perhaps you sit down and have lunch. In a while, you will have obtained energy from the food, and you will be able to do more work and complete the climb (see Figure 2.1).

Potential and Kinetic Energy

All energy can be classified as potential energy or kinetic energy. **Kinetic energy** is the energy of motion. Any object that is moving has kinetic energy. **Potential energy** is determined by the position of an object or by the chemical composition of a substance. A boulder resting on top of a mountain has potential energy because of its location. If the boulder rolls down the mountain, the potential energy becomes kinetic energy. Water stored in a reservoir has potential energy. When the water goes over the dam and falls to the stream below, its potential energy becomes kinetic energy. Foods and fossil fuels have potential energy stored in the bonds of their molecules. When you digest food or burn gasoline in your car, potential energy is converted to kinetic energy to do work.

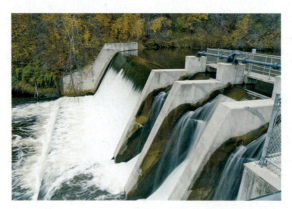

FIGURE 2.1 Water at the top of dam stores potential energy.

Q What happens to the potential energy of the water at the top of the dam when the water goes over the dam and falls to the stream below?

Heat and Energy

Heat, also known as *thermal energy*, is associated with the motion of particles. A frozen pizza feels cold because heat flows from your hand to the pizza. The faster the particles move, the greater the heat or thermal energy of the substance. In the frozen pizza, the particles are moving very slowly. As heat is added and the pizza becomes warmer, the motions of the particles in the pizza increase. Eventually, the particles have enough energy to make the pizza hot and ready to eat.

TUTORIAL
Heat

TUTORIAL
Energy Conversions

Units of Energy

The SI unit of energy and work is the **joule (J)** (pronounced like "jewel"). The joule is a small amount of energy, so scientists often use the kilojoule (kJ), 1000 joules. To heat water for one cup of tea, you need about 75 000 J or 75 kJ of heat. Table 2.1 shows a comparison of energy in joules for several energy sources.

You may be more familiar with the unit **calorie (cal)**, from the Latin *calor*, meaning "heat." The calorie was originally defined as the amount of energy (heat) needed to raise the temperature of 1 g of water by 1 °C. Now one calorie is defined as *exactly* 4.184 J. This equality can also be written as two conversion factors:

$$1 \text{ cal} = 4.184 \text{ J (exact)}$$

$$\frac{4.184 \text{ J}}{1 \text{ cal}} \quad \text{and} \quad \frac{1 \text{ cal}}{4.184 \text{ J}}$$

One *kilocalorie* (kcal) is equal to 1000 calories, and one *kilojoule* (kJ) is equal to 1000 joules.

$$1 \text{ kcal} = 1000 \text{ cal}$$
$$1 \text{ kJ} = 1000 \text{ J}$$

TABLE 2.1 **A Comparison of Energy for Various Resources**

Energy in Joules

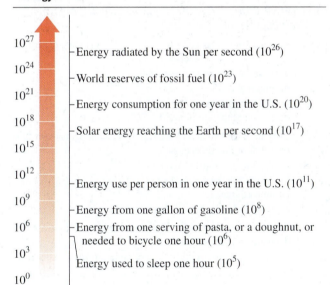

- Energy radiated by the Sun per second (10^{26})
- World reserves of fossil fuel (10^{23})
- Energy consumption for one year in the U.S. (10^{20})
- Solar energy reaching the Earth per second (10^{17})
- Energy use per person in one year in the U.S. (10^{11})
- Energy from one gallon of gasoline (10^{8})
- Energy from one serving of pasta, or a doughnut, or needed to bicycle one hour (10^{6})
- Energy used to sleep one hour (10^{5})

SAMPLE PROBLEM 2.1   **Energy Units**

When 1.0 g of diesel fuel burns in a diesel car engine, 48 000 J are released. What is this energy in calories?

SOLUTION

Step 1   **State the given and needed quantities.**

Analyze the Problem

Given	Need
48 000 J	calories

Diesel fuel reacts in a car engine to produce energy.

Step 2 Write a plan to convert the given unit to the needed unit.

$$\text{joules} \xrightarrow[\text{factor}]{\text{Energy}} \text{calories}$$

Step 3 State the equalities and conversion factors.

$$1 \text{ cal} = 4.184 \text{ J}$$

$$\frac{4.184 \text{ J}}{1 \text{ cal}} \quad \text{and} \quad \frac{1 \text{ cal}}{4.184 \text{ J}}$$

Step 4 Set up the problem to calculate the needed quantity.

$$48\,000 \text{ J} \quad \times \quad \underset{\text{Exact}}{\frac{1 \text{ cal}}{4.184 \text{ J}}} \quad = \quad 11\,000 \text{ cal } (1.1 \times 10^4 \text{ cal})$$

Two SFs   Exact   Two SFs

STUDY CHECK 2.1

The burning of 1.0 g of coal produces 8.4 kcal. How many kilojoules are produced?

QUESTIONS AND PROBLEMS

2.1 Energy

LEARNING GOAL: *Identify energy as potential or kinetic; convert between units of energy.*

2.1 Indicate whether each of the following statements describes potential or kinetic energy:
 a. water at the top of a waterfall
 b. kicking a ball
 c. the energy in a lump of coal
 d. a skier at the top of a hill

2.2 Indicate whether each of the following statements describes potential or kinetic energy:
 a. the energy in your food
 b. a tightly wound spring
 c. an earthquake
 d. a car speeding down the freeway

2.3 State whether each of the following involves an increase or decrease in potential energy:
 a. A roller coaster climbs up a ramp in a roller-coaster ride.

 b. A skier at the top of the jump begins to ski down the course.
 c. Water at the top of a waterfall drops to the pool below.

2.4 State whether each of the following involves an increase or decrease in potential energy:
 a. A gondola goes to the top of a mountain.
 b. Water is pumped up to a high water tower.
 c. Gasoline is added to a gas tank.

2.5 The energy needed to keep a 75-watt lightbulb burning for 1.0 h is 270 kJ. Calculate the energy required to keep the lightbulb burning for 3.0 h in each of the following energy units:
 a. joules   **b.** kilocalories

2.6 A person uses 750 kcal on a long hike. Calculate the energy used for the hike in each of the following energy units:
 a. joules   **b.** kilojoules

Given a temperature, calculate a corresponding value on another temperature scale.

TUTORIAL
Temperature Conversions

2.2 Temperature

Temperatures in science are measured and reported in *Celsius* (°C) units. On the Celsius scale, the reference points are the freezing point of water, defined as 0 °C, and the boiling point of water, 100 °C. In the United States, everyday temperatures are commonly reported in *Fahrenheit* (°F) units. On the Fahrenheit scale, pure water freezes at exactly 32 °F and boils at exactly 212 °F. A typical room temperature of 22 °C would be the same as 72 °F. Normal human body temperature is 37.0 °C, which is the same temperature as 98.6 °F.

On the Celsius and Fahrenheit temperature scales, the temperature difference between freezing and boiling is divided into smaller units called *degrees*. On the Celsius scale, there are 100 degrees Celsius between the freezing and boiling points of water. On the Fahrenheit scale, there are 180 degrees Fahrenheit between the freezing and boiling points of water. That makes a degree Celsius almost twice the size of a degree Fahrenheit: 1 °C = 1.8 °F (see Figure 2.2).

180 degrees Fahrenheit = 100 degrees Celsius

$$\frac{180 \text{ degrees Fahrenheit}}{100 \text{ degrees Celsius}} = \frac{1.8 \text{ °F}}{1 \text{ °C}}$$

We can write a temperature equation that relates a Fahrenheit temperature and its corresponding Celsius temperature.

$$T_F = 1.8(T_C) + 32$$

Changes   Adjusts
°C to °F   freezing point

In this equation, the Celsius temperature is multiplied by 1.8 to change °C to °F; then 32 is added to adjust the freezing point from 0 °C to 32 °F. Both values, 1.8 and 32, are exact numbers.

To convert from Fahrenheit to Celsius, the temperature equation is rearranged to obtain T_C.

$$T_C = \frac{T_F - 32}{1.8}$$

Scientists have learned that the coldest temperature possible is −273 °C (more precisely, −273.15 °C). On the *Kelvin* scale, this temperature, called *absolute zero*, has the value of 0 K. Temperature units on the Kelvin scale are called kelvins (K); no degree

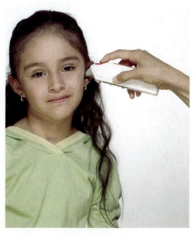

A digital ear thermometer is used to measure body temperature.

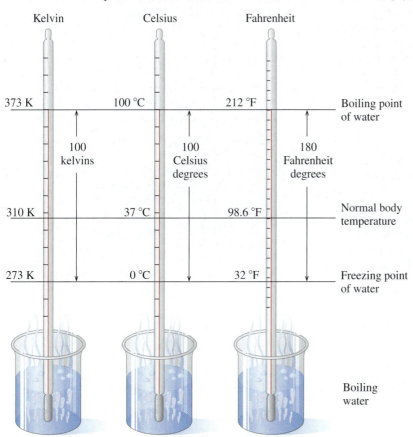

FIGURE 2.2 A comparison of the Fahrenheit, Celsius, and Kelvin temperature scales between the freezing and boiling points of water.

Q What are the values for the freezing point of water on the Fahrenheit, Celsius, and Kelvin temperature scales?

symbol is used. Because there are no lower temperatures, the Kelvin scale has no negative temperature values. Between the freezing point of water, 273 K, and the boiling point, 373 K, there are 100 kelvins, which makes a kelvin equal in size to a Celsius unit.

1 K = 1 °C

We can write an equation that relates a Celsius temperature to its corresponding Kelvin temperature by adding 273. Table 2.2 gives a comparison of some temperatures on the three scales.

$$T_K = T_C + 273$$

TABLE 2.2 A Comparison of Temperatures

Example	Fahrenheit (°F)	Celsius (°C)	Kelvin (K)
Sun	9937	5503	5776
A hot oven	450	232	505
A desert	120	49	322
A high fever	104	40	313
Room temperature	70	21	294
Water freezes	32	0	273
An Alaskan winter	−66	−54	219
Helium boils	−452	−269	4
Absolute zero	−459	−273	0

Chemistry Link to Health

VARIATION IN BODY TEMPERATURE

Normal human body temperature is considered to be 37.0 °C, although it varies throughout the day and from person to person. Oral temperatures of 36.1 °C are common in the morning and climb to a high of 37.2 °C between 6 P.M. and 10 P.M. Temperatures above 37.2 °C for a person at rest are usually an indication of disease. Individuals who are involved in prolonged exercise may also experience elevated temperatures. Body temperatures of marathon runners can range from 39 °C to 41 °C because heat production during exercise exceeds the body's ability to release heat.

Changes of more than 3.5 °C from the normal body temperature begin to interfere with bodily functions. Body temperatures above 41 °C, *hyperthermia*, can lead to convulsions, particularly in children, which may cause permanent brain damage. Heatstroke occurs above 41.1 °C. Sweat production stops, and the skin becomes hot and dry. The pulse rate is elevated, and respiration becomes weak and rapid. The person can become lethargic and lapse into a coma. Damage to internal organs is a major concern, and treatment, which must be immediate, may include immersing the person in an ice-water bath.

At the low temperature extreme of *hypothermia*, body temperature can drop as low as 28.5 °C. The person may appear cold and pale and have an irregular heartbeat. Unconsciousness can occur if the body temperature drops below 26.7 °C. Respiration becomes slow and shallow, and oxygenation of the tissues decreases. Treatment involves providing oxygen and increasing blood volume with glucose and saline fluids. Injecting warm fluids (37.0 °C) into the peritoneal cavity may restore the internal temperature.

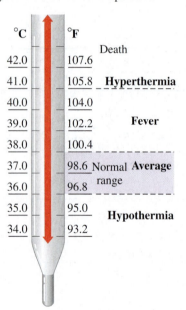

SAMPLE PROBLEM 2.2 Converting from Celsius to Fahrenheit Temperature

During the winter, the thermostat in a room is set at 21 °C. To what temperature, in Fahrenheit degrees, should you set the thermostat?

SOLUTION

Step 1 State the given and needed quantities.

Analyze the Problem

Given	Need
21 °C	*T* in degrees Fahrenheit

Step 2 **Write a temperature equation.**

$$T_F = 1.8(T_C) + 32$$

Step 3 **Substitute in the known values and calculate the new temperature.** In the equation, *the values of 1.8 and 32 are exact numbers*, which do not affect the number of SFs.

$$T_F = 1.8(21) + 32 \quad \text{1.8 is exact; 32 is exact}$$

$$= 70. \,°F \quad \text{Answer to the ones place}$$

STUDY CHECK 2.2

In the process of making ice cream, rock salt is added to crushed ice to chill the ice cream mixture. If the temperature drops to $-11 \,°C$, what is the temperature in degrees Fahrenheit?

Guide to Calculating Temperature

1 State the given and needed quantities.

2 Write a temperature equation.

3 Substitute in the known values and calculate the new temperature.

SAMPLE PROBLEM 2.3 **Converting from Fahrenheit to Celsius Temperature**

In a type of cancer treatment called *thermotherapy*, temperatures as high as 113 °F are used to destroy cancer cells. What is that temperature in degrees Celsius?

SOLUTION

Step 1 **State the given and needed quantities.**

Analyze the Problem

Given	Need
113 °F	T in degrees Celsius

Step 2 **Write a temperature equation.**

$$T_C = \frac{T_F - 32}{1.8}$$

Step 3 **Substitute in the known values and calculate the new temperature.**

$$T_C = \frac{(113 - 32)}{1.8} \quad \text{32 is exact; 1.8 is exact}$$

$$= \frac{81}{1.8} = 45 \,°C \quad \text{Answer to the ones place}$$

STUDY CHECK 2.3

A child has a temperature of 103.6 °F. What is this temperature on a Celsius thermometer?

SAMPLE PROBLEM 2.4 **Converting from Celsius to Kelvin Temperature**

A dermatologist may use cryogenic liquid nitrogen at $-196 \,°C$ to remove skin lesions and some skin cancers. What is the temperature, in kelvins, of the liquid nitrogen?

SOLUTION

Step 1 **State the given and needed quantities.**

Analyze the Problem

Given	Need
$-196 \,°C$	T in kelvins

Step 2 **Write a temperature equation.** To calculate the Kelvin temperature, we use the equation that relates Celsius and Kelvin temperatures.

$$T_K = T_C + 273$$

Step 3 **Substitute in the known values and calculate the new temperature.**

$$T_K = -196 + 273$$
$$= 77 \text{ K}$$

STUDY CHECK 2.4

On the planet Mercury, the average night temperature is 13 K, and the average day temperature is 683 K. What are these temperatures in degrees Celsius?

Chemistry Link to the Environment

CARBON DIOXIDE AND GLOBAL WARMING

Earth's climate is a product of interactions between sunlight, the atmosphere, and the oceans. The Sun provides us with energy in the form of solar radiation. Some of this radiation is reflected back into space. The rest is absorbed by the clouds, atmospheric gases including carbon dioxide, and Earth's surface. For millions of years, concentrations of carbon dioxide have fluctuated. However, in the past 100 years, the amount of carbon dioxide (CO_2) gas in our atmosphere has increased significantly. From the years 1000 to 1800, the atmospheric carbon dioxide averaged 280 ppm. But since the beginning of the Industrial Revolution in 1800, the level of atmospheric carbon dioxide has risen from about 280 ppm to about 390 ppm, a 40% increase.

As the atmospheric CO_2 level increases, more solar radiation is trapped by atmospheric gases, which raises the temperature at Earth's surface. Some scientists have estimated that if the carbon dioxide level doubles from its level before the Industrial Revolution, the average global temperature could increase by 2.0 °C to 4.4 °C. Although this seems to be a small temperature change, it could have dramatic impact worldwide. Even now, glaciers and snow cover in much of the world have diminished. Ice sheets in Antarctica and Greenland are melting rapidly and breaking apart. Although no one

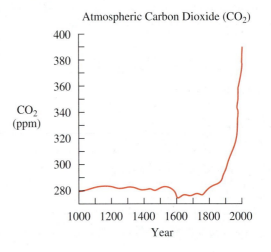

knows for sure how rapidly the ice in the polar regions is melting, this accelerating change will contribute to a rise in sea level. In the twentieth century, the sea level rose 15 to 23 cm, and some scientists predict the sea level will rise 1 m in this century. Such an increase will have a major impact on coastal areas.

Until recently, the carbon dioxide level was maintained as algae in the oceans and trees in the forests utilized the carbon dioxide. However, the ability of these and other forms of plant life to absorb carbon dioxide is not keeping up with the increase in carbon dioxide levels. Most scientists agree that the primary source of the increase of carbon dioxide is the burning of fossil fuels such as gasoline, coal, and natural gas. The cutting and burning of trees in the rain forests (deforestation) also reduces the amount of carbon dioxide removed from the atmosphere.

Worldwide efforts are being made to reduce the carbon dioxide produced by burning fossil fuels that heat our homes, run our cars, and provide energy for industries. Scientists are exploring ways to provide alternative energy sources and to reduce the effects of deforestation. Meanwhile, we can reduce energy use in our homes by using appliances that are more energy efficient, such as replacing incandescent light bulbs with fluorescent lights. Such an effort worldwide will reduce the possible impact of global warming, and at the same time, save our fuel resources.

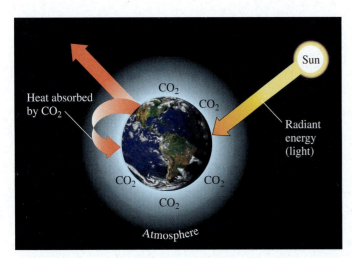

Heat from the Sun is trapped by the CO_2 layer in the atmosphere.

QUESTIONS AND PROBLEMS

2.2 Temperature

LEARNING GOAL: *Given a temperature, calculate a corresponding value on another temperature scale.*

2.7 Your friend who is visiting from Canada just took her temperature. When it reads 99.8, she becomes concerned that she is quite ill. How would you explain this temperature to your friend?

2.8 You have a friend who is using a recipe for flan from a Mexican cookbook. You notice that he set your oven temperature at 175 °F. What would you advise him to do?

2.9 Solve the following temperature conversions:
a. 37.0 °C = _____ °F **b.** 65.3 °F = _____ °C
c. −27 °C = _____ K **d.** 224 K = _____ °C
e. 114 °F = _____ °C

2.10 Solve the following temperature conversions:
a. 25 °C = _____ °F **b.** 155 °C = _____ °F
c. −25 °F = _____ °C **d.** 62 °C = _____ K
e. 545 K = _____ °C

2.11 **a.** A patient with hyperthermia has a temperature of 106 °F. What does this read on a Celsius thermometer?
b. Because high fevers can cause convulsions in children, a doctor wants to be called if a child's temperature goes over 40.0 °C. Should the doctor be called if a child has a temperature of 103 °F?

2.12 **a.** Hot compresses are prepared with water heated to 145 °F. What is the temperature of the hot water in degrees Celsius?
b. During extreme hypothermia, a boy's temperature dropped to 20.6 °C. What was his temperature on the Fahrenheit scale?

2.3 Classification of Matter

LEARNING GOAL

Classify examples of matter as pure substances or mixtures.

Matter is anything that has mass and occupies space. Matter makes up all the things we use, such as water, wood, plates, plastic bags, clothes, and shoes. The different types of matter are classified by their composition.

Pure Substances

There are two kinds of pure substances: elements and compounds. A **pure substance** is matter that has a fixed or constant composition. An **element**, the simplest type of a pure substance, is composed of only one kind of material such as silver, iron, or aluminum. Every element is composed of *atoms*, which are extremely tiny particles that make up each type of matter. Silver is composed of silver atoms, iron of iron atoms, and aluminum of aluminum atoms. A full list of the elements is found on the inside front cover of this text.

TUTORIAL
Classification of Matter

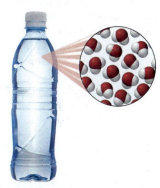

A molecule of water consists of two atoms of hydrogen (white) for one atom of oxygen (red) and has a formula of H_2O.

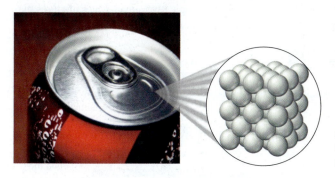

An aluminum can consists of many atoms of aluminum.

A **compound** is also a pure substance, but it consists of two or more elements chemically combined in the same proportion. In many compounds, the atoms of the elements are held together by attractions called *bonds*, which form small groups of atoms called molecules. For example, a molecule of the compound water, H_2O, has two hydrogen atoms for every one oxygen atom, and is represented by the formula H_2O. This means that water found anywhere always has the same composition of H_2O. Another compound that consists of a combination of hydrogen and oxygen is called hydrogen peroxide. However, it has two hydrogen atoms for every two oxygen atoms, and is represented by the formula H_2O_2. Thus, water (H_2O) and hydrogen peroxide (H_2O_2) are different compounds, which means they have different properties.

Pure substances that are compounds can be broken down by chemical processes into their elements. They cannot be broken down through physical methods such as boiling or sifting. For example, the compound in ordinary table salt, NaCl, is chemically broken down into the elements sodium and chlorine as seen in Figure 2.3. Elements cannot be broken down further.

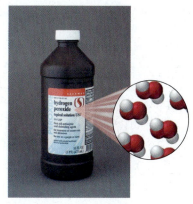

A molecule of hydrogen peroxide consists of two atoms of hydrogen (white) for two atoms of oxygen (red) and has a formula of H_2O_2.

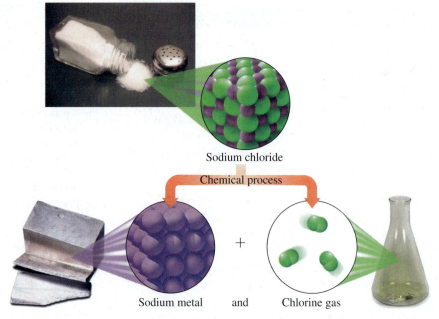

FIGURE 2.3 A chemical process called decomposition breaks down NaCl to produce the elements sodium and chlorine.

Q How do elements and compounds differ?

TUTORIAL
Classifying Matter

Mixtures

In a **mixture**, two or more substances are physically mixed, but not chemically combined. Much of the matter in our everyday lives consists of mixtures (see Figure 2.4). The air we breathe is a mixture of mostly oxygen and nitrogen gases. The steel in buildings and railroad tracks is a mixture of iron, nickel, carbon, and chromium. The brass in doorknobs and fixtures is a mixture of zinc and copper. There are different types of brass, which contain between 20% zinc to 50% zinc. Different types of brass have different properties, depending on the ratio of copper to zinc. Tea, coffee, and ocean water are mixtures, too. Unlike compounds, the composition of a mixture is not consistent, but can vary. For example, two sugar–water mixtures may look the same, but the one with the higher ratio of sugar to water would taste sweeter.

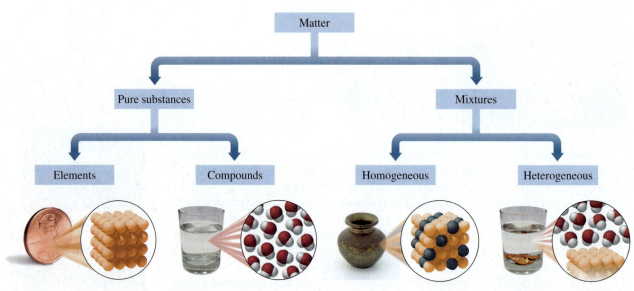

FIGURE 2.4 Matter is organized by its components: elements, compounds, and mixtures. **(a)** The element copper consists of copper atoms. **(b)** The compound water consists of H_2O molecules. **(c)** Brass is a homogeneous mixture of copper and zinc atoms. **(d)** Copper metal in water is a heterogeneous mixture of copper atoms and H_2O molecules.

Q Why are copper and water pure substances, but brass is a mixture?

Physical processes can be used to separate mixtures because there are no chemical interactions between the components. For example, different coins such as nickels, dimes, and quarters can be separated by size; iron particles mixed with sand can be picked up with a magnet; and water is separated from cooked spaghetti by using a strainer (see Figure 2.5).

CONCEPT CHECK 2.2 Pure Substances and Mixtures

Classify each of the following as a pure substance or a mixture:

a. sugar in a sugar bowl
b. a collection of nickels and dimes
c. coffee with milk and sugar

ANSWER

a. Sugar is a compound, which is a pure substance.
b. The nickels and dimes are physically mixed, but not chemically combined, which makes the collection a mixture.
c. The coffee, milk, and sugar are physically mixed, but not chemically combined, which makes it a mixture.

Physical method of separation

Types of Mixtures

Mixtures are classified as homogeneous or heterogeneous. In a *homogeneous mixture*, also called a *solution*, the composition is uniform throughout the sample. Familiar examples of homogeneous mixtures are air, which contains oxygen and nitrogen gases; and salt water, a solution of salt and water.

In a *heterogeneous mixture*, the components do not have a uniform composition. For example, a mixture of oil and water is heterogeneous because the oil floats on the surface of the water. Other examples of heterogeneous mixtures include the raisins in a cookie and the pulp in orange juice.

In the chemistry laboratory, mixtures are separated by various methods. Solids are separated from liquids by *filtration*, which involves pouring a mixture through a filter paper set in a funnel. In *chromatography*, different components of a liquid mixture separate as they move at different rates up the surface of a piece of chromatography paper.

FIGURE 2.5 A mixture of spaghetti and water is separated using a strainer, a physical method of separation.

Q Why can physical methods be used to separate mixtures but not compounds?

SAMPLE PROBLEM 2.5 Classifying Mixtures

Classify each of the following as a pure substance (element or compound) or as a mixture (homogeneous or heterogeneous):

a. copper wire
b. a chocolate chip cookie
c. Nitrox, a breathing mixture of oxygen and nitrogen for scuba

SOLUTION

a. Copper is an element, which is a pure substance.
b. A chocolate chip cookie does not have a uniform composition, which makes it a heterogeneous mixture.
c. The gases oxygen and nitrogen have a uniform composition in Nitrox, which makes it a homogeneous mixture.

STUDY CHECK 2.5

A salad dressing is prepared with oil, vinegar, and chunks of blue cheese. Is this a homogeneous or heterogeneous mixture?

Oil and water form a heterogeneous mixture.

A mixture of a liquid and a solid is separated by filtration.

Different substances are separated as they travel at different rates up the surface of chromatography paper.

Chemistry Link to Health

BREATHING MIXTURES FOR SCUBA

The air we breathe is composed mostly of the gases oxygen (21%) and nitrogen (79%). The homogeneous breathing mixtures used by scuba divers differ from the air we breathe, depending on the depth of the dive. For example, a breathing mixture known as Nitrox contains more oxygen gas (up to 32%) and less nitrogen gas (68%) than air. A breathing mixture with less nitrogen gas decreases the risk of *nitrogen narcosis*, which causes mental confusion and is associated with breathing regular air while diving. With deep dives, there is more chance of nitrogen narcosis. Another breathing mixture, Heliox, contains oxygen and helium, which is typically used for diving to more than 200 feet. By replacing nitrogen with helium, nitrogen narcosis does not occur. However, at dive depths over 300 ft, helium is associated with severe shaking and body temperature drop.

A breathing mixture used for dives over 400 ft is Trimix, which contains oxygen, helium, and some nitrogen. The addition of nitrogen lessens the problem of shaking that comes with breathing high levels of helium. Both Heliox and Trimix are used by only professional, military, or other highly trained divers.

A Nitrox mixture is used to fill scuba tanks.

QUESTIONS AND PROBLEMS

2.3 Classification of Matter

LEARNING GOAL: *Classify examples of matter as pure substances or mixtures.*

2.13 Classify each of the following as an element, compound, or mixture:
a. baking soda ($NaHCO_3$)   **b.** a blueberry muffin
c. ice (H_2O)   **d.** zinc (Zn)
e. Trimix (oxygen, nitrogen, and helium) in a scuba tank

2.14 Classify each of the following as an element, compound, or mixture:
a. a soft drink   **b.** propane (C_3H_8)
c. a cheese sandwich   **d.** an iron (Fe) nail
e. salt substitute (KCl)

2.15 Classify each of the following mixtures as homogeneous or heterogeneous:
a. vegetable soup
b. seawater
c. tea
d. tea with ice and lemon slices
e. fruit salad

2.16 Classify each of the following mixtures as homogeneous or heterogeneous:
a. nonfat milk
b. chocolate-chip ice cream
c. gasoline
d. peanut butter sandwich
e. cranberry juice

LEARNING GOAL

Identify the states and the physical and chemical properties of matter.

(MC)

TUTORIAL
Properties and Changes of Matter

2.4 States and Properties of Matter

On Earth, matter exists in one of three physical states called the *states of matter*: solids, liquids, and gases. A **solid**, such as a pebble or a baseball, has a definite shape and volume. You can probably recognize several solids within your reach right now such as books, pencils, or a computer mouse. In a solid, strong attractive forces hold the particles, such as atoms or molecules, close together. The particles in a solid are arranged in such a rigid pattern, their only movement is to vibrate slowly in their fixed positions. For many solids, their rigid structures produce crystals.

A **liquid** has a definite volume, but not a definite shape. In a liquid, the particles move slowly in random directions but are sufficiently attracted to each other to maintain a definite volume, although not a rigid structure. Thus, when oil, water, or vinegar is poured from one container to another, the liquid maintains its own volume but takes the shape of the new container.

A **gas** does not have a definite shape or volume. In a gas, the particles are far apart, have little attraction to each other, and move at extremely high speeds, taking the shape and volume of their container. The helium gas in a balloon fills the entire volume of the balloon. Table 2.3 compares the three states of matter.

Amethyst, a solid, is a purple form of quartz (SiO_2).

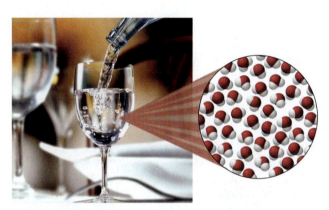

Water as a liquid takes the shape of its container.

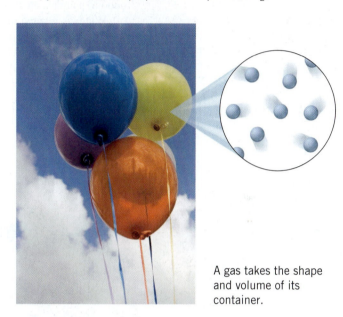

A gas takes the shape and volume of its container.

TABLE 2.3 A Comparison of Solids, Liquids, and Gases

Characteristic	Solid	Liquid	Gas
Shape	Has a definite shape	Takes the shape of the container	Takes the shape of the container
Volume	Has a definite volume	Has a definite volume	Fills the volume of the container
Arrangement of Particles	Fixed, very close	Random, close	Random, far apart
Interaction Between Particles	Very strong	Strong	Essentially none
Movement of Particles	Very slow	Moderate	Very fast
Examples	Ice, salt, iron	Water, oil, vinegar	Water vapor, helium, air

CONCEPT CHECK 2.3   **States of Matter**

Identify the state(s) of matter described by the substance in each of the following:

a. no change in volume when placed in a different container
b. has an especially low density
c. shape depends on the container
d. has a definite shape and volume

ANSWER

a. Both a solid and a liquid have their own volume that does not depend on the volume of their container.
b. In a gas, the particles are far apart, which gives a small mass per volume, or a low density.
c. Both a liquid and a gas take the shape of their containers.
d. A solid has a rigid arrangement of particles that gives it a definite shape and volume.

Copper, used in cookware, is a good conductor of heat.

TABLE 2.4 **Some Physical Properties of Copper**

Characteristic	Physical Property
Color	Orange-red
Odor	Odorless
Melting point	1083 °C
Boiling point	2567 °C
State at 25 °C	Solid
Luster	Shiny
Conduction of electricity	Excellent
Conduction of heat	Excellent

Physical Properties and Physical Changes

One way to describe matter is to observe its physical properties. If you were asked to describe yourself, you might list your characteristics such as the color of your eyes and skin, or the length, color, and texture of your hair.

Physical properties are those characteristics that can be observed or measured without affecting the identity of a substance. Typical physical properties include the shape, state, color, melting point, and boiling point of a substance. For example, you might observe that a penny has the physical properties of a round shape, an orange-red color, a solid state, and a shiny luster. Table 2.4 gives examples of physical properties of copper found in pennies, electrical wiring, and copper pans.

Water is a substance that is commonly found in all three states: solid, liquid, and gas. When matter undergoes a **physical change**, its state or its appearance changes, but its composition remains the same. The solid form of water—snow or ice—has a different appearance than its liquid or gaseous form, but all three states are water (see Figure 2.6).

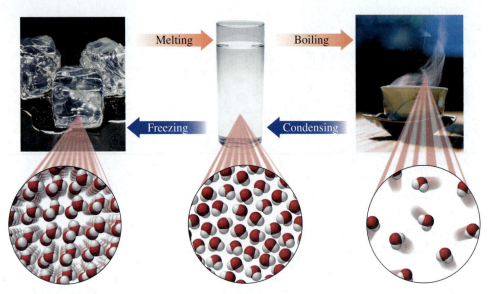

FIGURE 2.6 Water changes state from a solid to a liquid and from a liquid to a gas as heat is added.
Q Is heat added or released when liquid water freezes?

Melting and Freezing

Matter undergoes a **change of state** when it is converted from one state to another state (see Figure 2.6). As heat is added to a solid, the particles in the rigid structure move faster. At a temperature called the **melting point (mp)**, the solid is converted to a liquid. During **melting**, energy is absorbed to overcome the attractive forces that hold the particles together in the solid; the rigid solid structure changes to a random association of particles in the liquid. During a change of state, the temperature of a substance remains constant. We will look at the specific types of attractive forces between particles in Chapter 5.

If the temperature of a liquid is lowered, the reverse process takes place. Heat is removed from the liquid, which causes its particles to move slower. Eventually, the attractive forces are sufficient to form a solid. The substance is in the process of **freezing**, changing from a liquid to a solid. The temperature at which a liquid changes to a solid is its **freezing point (fp)**, which is the same temperature as the melting point.

Every substance has its own freezing (melting) point: Solid water (ice) melts at 0 °C when heat is added, and freezes at 0 °C when heat is removed. Gold melts at 1064 °C and freezes at 1064 °C. Nitrogen melts at −210 °C and freezes at −210 °C.

Melting and freezing are reversible processes.

Evaporation, Boiling, and Condensation

Water in a mud puddle disappears, unwrapped food dries out, and clothes hung on a clothesline dry. **Evaporation** occurs when water molecules at the surface acquire sufficient kinetic energy to escape from the liquid and form a gas. As the warmer water molecules leave the liquid, heat is removed, which cools the remaining liquid water. At higher temperatures, more water molecules evaporate. At the **boiling point (bp)**, all the molecules within a liquid gain enough energy to overcome the attractive forces between them and become a gas. We can observe the **boiling** of a liquid such as water as gas bubbles form throughout the liquid, rise to the surface, and escape.

When heat is removed from a gas, a reverse process takes place. In **condensation**, water vapor is converted back to liquid as the water molecules lose energy and slow down. Condensation occurs at the same temperature as boiling but differs because heat is removed. You may have noticed that condensation occurs when you take a hot shower and the water vapor forms droplets on your mirror.

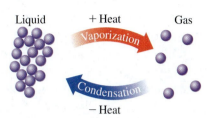

Vaporization and condensation are reversible processes.

Temperature Curves

A *heating curve* can be drawn to illustrate the changes of temperature and changes of state as heat is added to a substance. A diagonal line indicates a warming of a solid as heat is added. When the temperature of the solid reaches the melting point, it begins to change to liquid. This melting process, which occurs at constant temperature, is drawn as a horizontal line.

As heat is added to the liquid, its temperature begins to rise, which is shown as a diagonal line. At the boiling point, the liquid obtains enough energy to change to a gas, which is drawn as a horizontal line. At the boiling point, the temperature is constant. Once all the liquid becomes a gas, another diagonal line shows the temperature increase as heat is added to the gas.

In a *cooling curve*, the temperature of a substance decreases as heat is removed. If we begin with a gas sample of water vapor (steam) at 140 °C, a diagonal line shows the decrease in temperature to the boiling (condensation) point. Then a change from gas to liquid takes place, which is shown as a horizontal line. The temperature at condensation remains constant until all of the water vapor has changed into liquid water. Another diagonal line then shows the decrease in temperature as liquid water cools until it reaches the freezing point. At the freezing point of water (0 °C), a horizontal line indicates that water is freezing. Once all of the water is frozen, a diagonal line is drawn below the freezing point as more heat is removed from the solid water (ice).

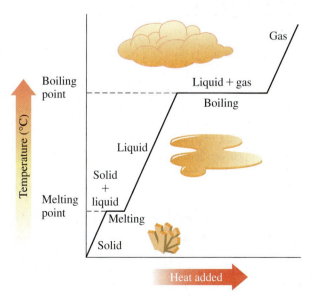

A heating curve illustrates the change in temperature and changes in state as heat is added.

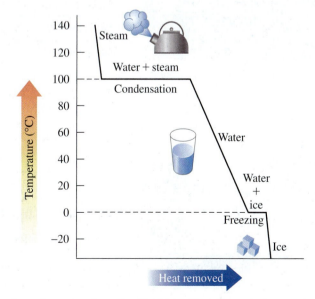

A cooling curve for water illustrates the change in temperature and changes in state as heat is removed.

Sublimation and Deposition

In a process called **sublimation**, the particles on the surface of a solid change directly to a gas with no temperature change and without going through the liquid state. In the reverse process called **deposition**, gas particles change directly to a solid.

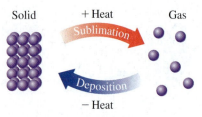

Dry ice sublimes at −78 °C.

Water vapor will change to a solid on contact with a cold surface, such as these frozen peas.

Sublimation and deposition are reversible processes.

For example, dry ice, which is solid carbon dioxide (CO_2), undergoes sublimation at −78 °C. It is called "dry" because it does not form a liquid as it warms. In extremely cold areas, snow does not melt, but sublimes directly to water vapor. In a frost-free refrigerator, the water in the ice on the walls of the freezer and in frozen foods sublimes when warm air is circulated through the compartment during the defrost cycle. When frozen foods are left in the freezer for a long time, so much water sublimes that foods, especially meat, become dry and shrunken, a condition called *freezer burn*. Deposition occurs in a freezer when water vapor forms ice crystals on the surface of freezer bags and frozen food.

Freeze-dried foods have a long shelf life because they contain no water.

Freeze-dried foods prepared by sublimation are convenient for long-term storage and for camping and hiking. A food that has been frozen is placed in a vacuum chamber where it dries as the ice sublimes. The dried food retains all of its nutritional value and needs only water to be edible. A food that is freeze-dried does not need refrigeration because bacteria cannot grow without moisture.

The physical appearance of a substance can change in other ways, too. Suppose that you dissolve some salt in water. The appearance of the salt changes, but you could re-form the salt crystals by heating the mixture and evaporating the water. Thus, in a physical change, there are no new substances produced. Table 2.5 gives more examples of physical changes.

Salt crystals form as water evaporates from seawater.

TABLE 2.5 **Examples of Some Physical Changes**	
Type of Physical Change	**Example**
Change of State	Boiling water
	Freezing of liquid water to solid water (ice)
Change of Appearance	Dissolving sugar in water
Change of Shape	Hammering a gold ingot into shiny gold leaf
	Drawing copper into thin copper wire
Change of Size	Cutting paper into tiny pieces for confetti
	Grinding pepper into smaller particles

Chemical Properties and Chemical Changes

Chemical properties are those that describe the ability of a substance to change into a new substance. When a **chemical change** takes place, the original substance is converted into a new substance, which has different physical and chemical properties. For example, the rusting or corrosion of a metal such as iron is a chemical property. In the rain, an iron (Fe) nail reacts with oxygen (O_2) to form rust (Fe_2O_3). A chemical change has taken place: Rust is a new substance with new physical and chemical properties. Table 2.6 gives examples of chemical changes.

In a physical change, a gold ingot is hammered to form gold leaf.

TABLE 2.6 Examples of Some Chemical Changes

Type of Chemical Change	Changes in Properties
Tarnishing of Silver	Shiny, silver metal reacts in air to give a black, grainy coating.
Burning Wood	A piece of pine burns with a bright flame, producing heat, ashes, carbon dioxide, and water vapor.
Caramelizing Sugar	At high temperatures, white, granular sugar changes to a smooth, caramel-colored substance.
Formation of Rust	Iron, which is gray and shiny, combines with oxygen to form orange-red rust.

In a chemical change, the iron on the surface of nails reacts with oxygen to form rust.

Table 2.7 summarizes physical and chemical properties, and physical and chemical changes.

TABLE 2.7 Summary of Physical and Chemical Properties and Changes

	Physical	Chemical
Property	A characteristic of a substance such as color, shape, odor, luster, size, melting point, and density.	A characteristic that indicates the ability of a substance to form another substance: Paper can burn, iron can rust, and silver can tarnish.
Change	A change in a physical property that retains the identity of the substance: A change of state, a change in size, or a change in shape and appearance.	A change in which the original substance is converted to one or more new substances: Paper burns, iron rusts, and silver tarnishes.

Flan has a topping of caramelized sugar.

CONCEPT CHECK 2.4   Physical and Chemical Properties

Classify each of the following as a physical or chemical property:

a. Gasoline is a liquid at room temperature.
b. Gasoline burns in air.
c. Gasoline has a pungent odor.

ANSWER

a. A liquid is a state of matter, which makes it a physical property.
b. When gasoline burns, it changes to different substances with new properties, which is a chemical property.
c. The odor of gasoline is a physical property.

SAMPLE PROBLEM 2.6   Physical and Chemical Changes

Classify each of the following as a physical or chemical change:

a. An ice cube melts to form liquid water.
b. An enzyme breaks down the lactose in milk.
c. Peppercorns are ground into flakes.

SOLUTION

a. A physical change occurs when the ice cube changes state from solid to liquid.
b. A chemical change occurs when an enzyme breaks down lactose into simpler substances.
c. A physical change occurs when the size of an object changes.

STUDY CHECK 2.6

Which of the following are chemical changes?

a. Gas bubbles form when baking powder is mixed with vinegar.
b. A log is chopped for firewood.
c. A log is burned in a fireplace.

QUESTIONS AND PROBLEMS

2.4 States and Properties of Matter

LEARNING GOAL: Identify the states and the physical and chemical properties of matter.

2.17 Indicate whether each of the following describes a gas, a liquid, or a solid:
  a. This substance has no definite volume or shape.
  b. The particles in a substance do not interact with each other.
  c. The particles in a substance are held in a rigid structure.

2.18 Indicate whether each of the following describes a gas, a liquid, or a solid:
  a. The substance has a definite volume but takes the shape of the container.
  b. The particles in this substance are very far apart.
  c. This substance occupies the entire volume of the container.

2.19 Describe each of the following as a physical or chemical property:
  a. Chromium is a steel-gray solid.
  b. Hydrogen reacts readily with oxygen.
  c. Nitrogen freezes at −210 °C.
  d. Milk will sour when left in a warm room.

2.20 Describe each of the following as a physical or chemical property:
  a. Neon is a colorless gas at room temperature.
  b. Apple slices turn brown when exposed to air.
  c. Phosphorus will ignite when exposed to air.
  d. At room temperature, mercury is a liquid.

2.21 What type of change, physical or chemical, takes place in each of the following?
  a. Water vapor condenses to form rain.
  b. Cesium metal reacts explosively with water.
  c. Gold melts at 1064 °C.
  d. A puzzle is cut into 1000 pieces.
  e. Cheese is grated on top of pasta.

2.22 What type of change, physical or chemical, takes place in each of the following?
  a. Gold is hammered into thin sheets.
  b. A silver pin tarnishes in the air.
  c. A tree is cut into boards at a sawmill.
  d. Food is digested.
  e. A chocolate bar melts.

2.23 Describe each property of the element fluorine as physical or chemical.
  a. is highly reactive
  b. is a gas at room temperature
  c. has a pale, yellow color
  d. will explode in the presence of hydrogen
  e. has a melting point of −220 °C

2.24 Describe each property of the element zirconium as physical or chemical.
  a. melts at 1852 °C
  b. is resistant to corrosion
  c. has a grayish-white color
  d. ignites spontaneously in air when finely divided
  e. is a shiny metal

2.25 Identify each of the following changes of state as melting, freezing, sublimation, or deposition:
  a. The solid structure of a substance breaks down as liquid forms.
  b. Coffee is freeze-dried.
  c. Water on the street turns to ice during a cold wintry night.
  d. Ice crystals form on a package of frozen corn.

2.26 Identify each of the following changes of state as melting, freezing, sublimation, or deposition:
  a. Dry ice in an ice-cream cart disappears.
  b. Snow on the ground turns to liquid water.
  c. Heat is removed from 125 g of liquid water at 0 °C.
  d. Frost forms on a cold morning.

2.27 Identify each of the following changes of state as evaporation, boiling, or condensation:
  a. The water vapor in the clouds changes to rain.
  b. Wet clothes dry on a clothesline.
  c. Lava flows into the ocean and steam forms.
  d. After a hot shower, your bathroom mirror is covered with water.

2.28 Identify each of the following changes of state as evaporation, boiling, or condensation:
  a. At 100 °C, the water in a pan changes to steam.
  b. On a cool morning, the windows in your car fog up.
  c. A shallow pond dries up in the summer.
  d. A teakettle whistles when the water is ready for tea.

2.29 Draw a heating curve for a sample of ice that is heated from −20 °C to 140 °C. Indicate the segment of the graph that corresponds to each of the following:
  a. solid   **b.** melting   **c.** liquid
  d. boiling   **e.** gas

2.30 Draw a cooling curve for a sample of steam that cools from 110 °C to −10 °C. Indicate the segment of the graph that corresponds to each of the following:
  a. solid   **b.** freezing   **c.** liquid
  d. condensing   **e.** gas

LEARNING GOAL

Use specific heat to calculate the quantity of heat lost or gained during a temperature change.

TUTORIAL
Specific Heat Calculations

2.5 Specific Heat

Every substance can absorb or lose heat. When you bake a potato, you place it in a hot oven. If you are cooking pasta, you add the pasta to boiling water. You already know that adding heat to water increases its temperature until it boils. Every substance has its own characteristic ability to absorb heat. Certain substances absorb more heat than others to reach a certain temperature.

The energy requirements for different substances are described in terms of a physical property called *specific heat*. The **specific heat (SH)** for a substance is defined as the number of joules (or calories) needed to change the temperature of exactly 1 g of a substance by exactly 1 °C. To calculate the specific heat of a substance, we measure the heat in joules (or calories), the mass in grams, and the ΔT, which is the change in temperature, in degrees Celsius. The symbol delta in ΔT means "change in."

$$\text{Specific heat } (SH) = \frac{\text{heat}}{\text{mass} \times \Delta T} = \frac{\text{J (or cal)}}{1\text{ g} \times 1\text{ °C}}$$

Now we can write the specific heat for water using our definition in Section 2.1 for the joule and calorie, which is 1.00 cal = 4.184 J.

$$\text{Specific heat } (SH) \text{ of } H_2O(l) = \frac{4.184\text{ J}}{\text{g °C}} = \frac{1.00\text{ cal}}{\text{g °C}}$$

If we look at Table 2.8, we see that 1 g of water requires 4.184 J (or 1.00 cal) to increase its temperature by 1 °C. Water has a large specific heat that is about five times the specific heat of aluminum. Aluminum has a specific heat that is about twice that of copper. Therefore, the absorption of 4.184 J (or 1.00 cal) by 1 g of water will raise its temperature by 1 °C. However, adding the same amount of heat (4.184 J or 1.00 cal) will also raise the temperature of 1 g of aluminum by about 5 °C and 1 g of copper by about 10 °C. The low specific heats of aluminum and copper mean they transfer heat efficiently, which makes them useful in cookware.

The high specific heat of water has a major impact on the temperatures in a coastal city compared to an inland city. A large mass of water near a coastal city can absorb or release five times the energy absorbed or released by the same mass of rock near an inland city. This means that in the summer, a body of water absorbs large quantities of heat, which cools a coastal city, and then in the winter that same body of water releases large quantities of heat, which provides warmer temperatures. A similar effect happens with our bodies, which contain 70% by mass water. Water in the body absorbs or releases large quantities of heat in order to maintain an almost constant body temperature.

TABLE 2.8 Specific Heats of Some Substances

Substance	(J/g °C)	(cal/g °C)
Elements		
Aluminum, Al(s)	0.897	0.214
Copper, Cu(s)	0.385	0.0920
Gold, Au(s)	0.129	0.0308
Iron, Fe(s)	0.452	0.108
Silver, Ag(s)	0.235	0.0562
Titanium, Ti(s)	0.523	0.125
Compounds		
Ammonia, NH₃(g)	2.04	0.488
Ethanol, C₂H₅OH(l)	2.46	0.588
Sodium chloride, NaCl(s)	0.864	0.207
Water, H₂O(l)	4.184	1.00

CONCEPT CHECK 2.5   Comparing Specific Heats

Water has a specific heat that is about six times larger than that of sandstone. How would the temperature change during the day and night if you live in a house next to a large lake compared to a house built in the desert on sandstone?

ANSWER

In the day, the water in the lake will absorb six times the quantity of energy that sandstone will, which will keep the temperature in a house on a large lake more comfortable and cooler than a house in the desert. In the night, the water in the lake will release energy that warms the surrounding air so that the temperature will not drop as much as in the desert.

SAMPLE PROBLEM 2.7   Calculating Specific Heat

What is the specific heat, in cal/g °C, of lead if 13.6 cal will raise the temperature of 35.6 g of lead by 12.5 °C?

SOLUTION

Step 1   State the given and needed quantities.

Analyze the Problem

Given	Need
13.6 cal absorbed	specific heat of lead (cal/g °C)
35.6 g of lead	
$\Delta T = 12.5$ °C	

Guide to Calculating Specific Heat

1 State the given and needed quantities.

2 Write the relationship for specific heat.

3 Set up the problem to calculate the specific heat.

Step 2   **Write the relationship for specific heat.** In the relationship for specific heat (*SH*), the quantity of heat is divided by the mass and by the temperature change (ΔT).

$$\text{Specific heat } (SH) = \frac{\text{heat}}{\text{mass} \quad \Delta T}$$

Step 3   **Set up the problem to calculate the specific heat.** Substitute the quantity of heat, in calories, the mass, in grams, and the temperature change (ΔT), in degrees Celsius, into the relationship for specific heat.

$$\text{Specific heat } (SH) = \frac{13.6 \text{ cal}}{35.6 \text{ g} \quad 12.5 \text{ °C}} = 0.0306 \frac{\text{cal}}{\text{g °C}}$$

STUDY CHECK 2.7

What is the specific heat of sodium metal (J/g °C) if 123 J are needed to raise the temperature of 4.00 g of sodium by 25.0 °C?

Calculations Using Specific Heat

TUTORIAL
Specific Heat Calculations

When we know the specific heat relationship for a substance, we can rearrange it to obtain a useful expression called the *heat equation*.

$$\text{Specific heat } (SH) = \frac{\text{heat}}{\text{mass} \times \Delta T}$$

$$\text{Heat} = \text{mass} \times \Delta T \times \text{specific heat } (SH) \qquad \text{Heat equation}$$

Using the heat equation, we can calculate the quantity of heat lost or gained by a substance by substituting in the known quantities for the mass, the change in temperature, and its specific heat.

$$\text{Heat} \quad = \quad \text{mass} \quad \times \text{ temperature change} \times \text{ specific heat}$$

Heat	=	mass	×	ΔT	×	SH
cal	=	g	×	°C	×	$\frac{\text{cal}}{\text{g °C}}$
J	=	g	×	°C	×	$\frac{\text{J}}{\text{g °C}}$

Guide to Calculations Using Specific Heat

1 State the given and needed quantities.

2 Calculate the temperature change (ΔT).

3 Write the heat equation.

4 Substitute in the given values and solve, making sure units cancel.

SAMPLE PROBLEM 2.8   **Calculating Heat with an Increase in Temperature**

How many joules are absorbed by 45.2 g of aluminum (Al) if its temperature rises from 12.5 °C to 76.8 °C (see Table 2.8)?

SOLUTION

Step 1   **State the given and needed quantities.**

Analyze the Problem

Given	Need
45.2 g of aluminum	joules absorbed by aluminum
SH for aluminum = 0.897 J/g °C	
T_{initial} = 12.5 °C	
T_{final} = 76.8 °C	

Step 2 **Calculate the temperature change (ΔT).** The temperature change ΔT is the difference between the final and initial temperatures.

$$\Delta T = T_{\text{final}} - T_{\text{initial}} = 76.8\,°C - 12.5\,°C = 64.3\,°C$$

Step 3 **Write the heat equation.**

$$\text{Heat} = \text{mass} \times \Delta T \times SH$$

Step 4 **Substitute in the given values and solve, making sure units cancel.**

$$\text{Heat} = 45.2\,\cancel{g} \times 64.3\,\cancel{°C} \times \frac{0.897\text{ J}}{\cancel{g}\,\cancel{°C}} = 2610\text{ J }(2.61 \times 10^3\text{ J})$$

The copper on a pan conducts heat rapidly to the food in the pan.

STUDY CHECK 2.8

Some cooking pans have a layer of copper on the bottom. How many kilojoules are needed to raise the temperature of 125 g of copper from 22 °C to 325 °C (see Table 2.8)?

Chemistry Link to Health

STEAM BURNS

Hot water at 100 °C will cause burns and damage to the skin. If 25 g of hot water at 100 °C falls on a person's skin, the temperature of the water will drop to body temperature, 37 °C. The heat released can cause severe burns. This amount of heat can be calculated from the temperature change, 100 °C − 37 °C = 63 °C.

$$25\,\cancel{g} \times 63\,\cancel{°C} \times \frac{4.184\text{ J}}{\cancel{g}\,\cancel{°C}} = 6600\text{ J}$$

However, getting steam on the skin is even more dangerous. The condensation of the same quantity of steam to liquid at 100 °C releases much more heat—almost ten times as much. This amount of heat can be calculated using the heat of vaporization, which is 2260 J/g for water.

$$25\,\cancel{g} \times \frac{2260\text{ J}}{1\,\cancel{g}} = 57\,000\text{ J}$$

When we combine the quantity of heat released from the condensation and cooling of the water from 100 °C to 37 °C, we see that most of the heat is from the condensation of steam. This large amount of heat released on the skin is what causes damage from steam burns.

Condensation (100 °C)	= 57 000 J
Cooling (100 °C to 37 °C)	= 6 600 J
Heat released	= 64 000 J (rounded off)

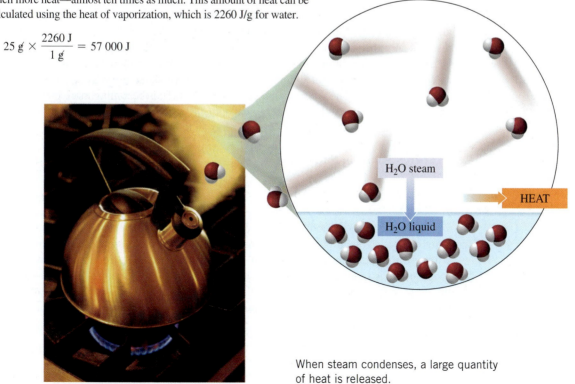

When steam condenses, a large quantity of heat is released.

QUESTIONS AND PROBLEMS

2.5 Specific Heat

LEARNING GOAL: *Use specific heat to calculate the quantity of heat lost or gained during a temperature change.*

2.31 If the same amount of heat is supplied to samples of 10.0 g each of aluminum, iron, and copper, all at 15 °C, which sample would reach the highest temperature (see Table 2.8)?

2.32 Substances A and B are the same mass and at the same initial temperature. When the same amount of heat is added to each, the final temperature of A is 55 °C higher than the temperature of B. What does this tell you about the specific heats of A and B?

2.33 Calculate the specific heat (J/g °C) for each of the following:
  a. a 13.5-g sample of zinc heated from 24.2 °C to 83.6 °C that absorbs 312 J of heat
  b. a 48.2-g sample of a metal that absorbs 345 J when its temperature increases from 35.0 °C to 57.9 °C

2.34 Calculate the specific heat (J/g °C) for each of the following:
  a. an 18.5-g sample of tin that absorbs 183 J when its temperature increases from 35.0 °C to 78.6 °C
  b. a 22.5-g sample of a metal that absorbs 645 J when its temperature increases from 36.2 °C to 92.0 °C

2.35 What is the amount of energy involved in each of the following?
  a. calories to heat 25 g of water from 15 °C to 25 °C
  b. joules to heat 15 g of water from 22 °C to 75 °C
  c. kilocalories to heat 150 g of water in a kettle from 15 °C to 77 °C

2.36 What is the amount of energy involved in each of the following?
  a. calories given off when 85 g of water cools from 45 °C to 25 °C
  b. joules given off when 25 g of water cools from 86 °C to 61 °C
  c. kilocalories absorbed when 5.0 kg of water warms from 22 °C to 28 °C

2.37 Calculate the energy, in joules and calories, for each of the following (see Table 2.8):
  a. required to heat 25.0 g of water from 12.5 °C to 25.7 °C
  b. required to heat 38.0 g of copper from 122 °C to 246 °C
  c. lost when 15.0 g of ethanol cools from 60.5 °C to −42.0 °C
  d. lost when 112 g of iron cools from 118 °C to 55 °C

2.38 Calculate the energy in joules and calories, for each of the following (see Table 2.8):
  a. required to heat 5.25 g of water from 5.5 °C to 64.8 °C
  b. lost when 75.0 g of water cools from 86.4 °C to 2.1 °C
  c. required to heat 10.0 g of silver from 112 °C to 275 °C
  d. lost when 18.0 g of gold cools from 224 °C to 118 °C

LEARNING GOAL

Use the energy values to calculate the kilojoules (kJ) or kilocalories (kcal) in a food.

MC

TUTORIAL
Nutritional Energy

CASE STUDY
Calories from Hidden Sugar

2.6 Energy and Nutrition

The food we eat provides energy to do work in the body, which includes the growth and repair of cells. Carbohydrates are the primary fuel for the body, but if carbohydrate reserves are exhausted, fats and then proteins can be used for energy.

For many years in the field of nutrition, the energy from food was measured in Calories or kilocalories. The nutritional unit **Calorie, Cal** (with an uppercase C), is the same as 1000 cal, or 1 kcal. The international unit, kilojoule (kJ), is becoming more prevalent. For example, a baked potato has an energy value of 110 Calories, which is 110 kcal or 460 kJ. A typical diet of 2100 Cal (kcal) is the same as an 8800 kJ diet.

Energy Values in Nutrition

1 Cal = 1 kcal = 1000 cal
1 Cal = 4.184 kJ = 4184 J

In the laboratory, foods are burned in a calorimeter to determine their energy value (kJ/g or kcal/g) (see Figure 2.7). A sample of food is placed in a steel container filled with oxygen with a measured amount of water that fills the surrounding chamber. The food sample is ignited, releasing heat that increases the temperature of the water. From the mass of the food and water as well as the temperature increase, the energy value of the food is calculated. We will assume that the energy absorbed by the calorimeter is negligible.

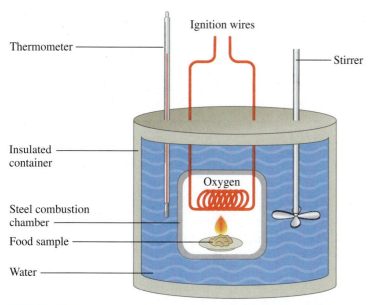

FIGURE 2.7 Heat released from burning a food sample in a calorimeter is used to determine the energy value of the food.

Q What happens to the temperature of water in a calorimeter during the combustion of a food sample?

CONCEPT CHECK 2.6   Energy Values of Food

When 55 g of pasta is burned in a calorimeter, 220 Cal of heat is released. What is the energy value of pasta in kcal/g?

ANSWER

Using the equality of 1 Cal = 1 kcal, we can calculate the energy value of the pasta.

$$\frac{220 \text{ Cal}}{55 \text{ g}} \times \frac{1 \text{ kcal}}{1 \text{ Cal}} = 4.0 \text{ kcal/g}$$

Energy Values for Foods

The **energy (caloric) values** of food are the kilojoules or kilocalories obtained from burning 1 g of a carbohydrate, fat, or protein (see Table 2.9).

Using the energy values in Table 2.9, we can calculate the total energy of a food if the mass of each food type is known.

$$\text{kilojoules} = \text{g} \times \frac{\text{kJ}}{\text{g}} \qquad \text{kilocalories} = \text{g} \times \frac{\text{kcal}}{\text{g}}$$

On packaged food, the energy content is listed in the Nutrition Facts label on the package, usually in terms of the number of Calories for one serving. The general composition and caloric content of some foods are given in Table 2.10.

TABLE 2.9 **Typical Energy (Caloric) Values for the Three Food Types**

Food Type	kJ/g	kcal/g
Carbohydrate	17	4
Fat	38	9
Protein	17	4

The nutrition facts include the total Calories, Calories from fat, and total grams of carbohydrate.

TABLE 2.10	General Composition and Energy Content of Some Foods			
Food	Carbohydrate (g)	Fat (g)	Protein (g)	Energy*
Banana, 1 medium	26	0	1	460 kJ (110 kcal)
Beef, ground, 3 oz	0	14	22	910 kJ (220 kcal)
Carrots, raw, 1 cup	11	0	1	200 kJ (50 kcal)
Chicken, no skin, 3 oz	0	3	20	460 kJ (110 kcal)
Egg, 1 large	0	6	6	330 kJ (80 kcal)
Milk, 4% fat, 1 cup	12	9	9	700 kJ (170 kcal)
Milk, nonfat, 1 cup	12	0	9	360 kJ (90 kcal)
Potato, baked	23	0	3	440 kJ (100 kcal)
Salmon, 3 oz	0	5	16	460 kJ (110 kcal)
Steak, 3 oz	0	27	19	1350 kJ (320 kcal)

*Energy values are rounded off to the tens place.

Guide to Calculating the Energy Content for a Food

1 State the given and needed quantities.

2 Use the energy value of each food type and calculate the kJ or kcal rounded off to the tens place.

3 Add the energy for each food type to give the total energy for the food.

Explore Your World

COUNTING CALORIES

Obtain a food item that has a nutrition label. From the information on the label, determine the number of grams of carbohydrate, fat, and protein in one serving. Using energy values, calculate the total Calories for one serving. (For most products, the kilocalories for each food type are rounded off to the tens place.)

QUESTION

How does your total for the Calories in one serving compare to the Calories stated on the label for a single serving?

SAMPLE PROBLEM 2.9 Energy Content for a Food

At a fast-food restaurant, a hamburger contains 37 g of carbohydrate, 19 g of fat, and 24 g of protein. What is the energy content for each food type and the total energy content, in kcal? Round off the kilocalories for each food type to the tens place.

SOLUTION

Step 1 **State the given and needed quantities.**

Analyze the Problem

Given	Need
Carbohydrate, 37 g	kilocalories for each food and the total number of kilocalories
Fat, 19 g	
Protein, 24 g	

Using the energy values for carbohydrate, fat, and protein (see Table 2.9), we can calculate the energy for each type of food.

Step 2 **Use the energy value of each food type and calculate the kJ or kcal rounded off to the tens place.**

Food Type	Mass	Energy Value	Energy
Carbohydrate	37 g	$\times \dfrac{4 \text{ kcal}}{1 \text{ g}} =$	150 kcal
Fat	19 g	$\times \dfrac{9 \text{ kcal}}{1 \text{ g}} =$	170 kcal
Protein	24 g	$\times \dfrac{4 \text{ kcal}}{1 \text{ g}} =$	100 kcal

Step 3 **Add the energy for each food type to give the total energy for the food.**

Total energy content = 150 kcal + 170 kcal + 100 kcal

= 420 kcal

STUDY CHECK 2.9

If you buy the same hamburger as described in Sample Problem 2.9 at a fast-food restaurant in Canada, what is the energy content for each food type and the total energy content, in kJ? Round off the kilojoules for each food type to the tens place.

Chemistry Link to Health

LOSING AND GAINING WEIGHT

The number of kilocalories or kilojoules needed in the daily diet of an adult depends on gender, age, and level of physical activity. Some general levels of energy needs are given in Table 2.11.

The amount of food a person eats is regulated by the hunger center in the hypothalamus, located in the brain. Food intake is normally proportional to the nutrient stores in the body. If these nutrient stores are low, you feel hungry; if they are high, you do not feel like eating. The hunger signal is governed by blood sugar (and insulin).

A person gains weight when food intake exceeds energy output, and loses weight when food intake is less than energy output. Many diet products contain cellulose, which has no nutritive value but provides bulk and makes you feel full. Some diet drugs depress the hunger center and must be used with caution, because they excite the nervous system and can elevate blood pressure. Because muscular

One hour of swimming uses 2100 kJ of energy.

exercise is an important way to expend energy, an increase in daily exercise aids weight loss. Table 2.12 lists some activities and the amount of energy they require.

TABLE 2.11 Typical Energy Requirements for Adults

Gender	Age	Moderately Active kJ (kcal)	Highly Active kJ (kcal)
Female	19–30	8800 (2100)	10 000 (2400)
	31–50	8400 (2000)	9200 (2200)
Male	19–30	11 300 (2700)	12 600 (3000)
	31–50	10 500 (2500)	12 100 (2900)

TABLE 2.12 Energy Expended by a 70.0-kg (154-lb) Adult

Activity	Energy (kJ/h)	Energy (kcal/h)
Sleeping	250	60
Sitting	420	100
Walking	840	200
Swimming	2100	500
Running	3100	750

QUESTIONS AND PROBLEMS

2.6 Energy and Nutrition

LEARNING GOAL: *Use the energy values to calculate the kilojoules (kJ) or kilocalories (kcal) in a food.*

2.39 Using the following data, determine the kilojoules and kilocalories for each food burned in a calorimeter:
   a. one stalk of celery that produces energy to heat 505 g of water from 25.2 °C to 35.7 °C
   b. a waffle that produces energy to heat 4980 g of water from 20.6 °C to 62.4 °C

2.40 Using the following data, calculate the kilojoules and kilocalories for each food burned in a calorimeter:
   a. 1 cup of popcorn that produces energy to change the temperature of 1250 g of water from 25.5 °C to 50.8 °C
   b. a sample of butter that produces energy to increase the temperature of 357 g of water from 22.7 °C to 38.8 °C

2.41 Using the energy values for foods (see Table 2.9), determine each of the following (round off the answers for kilojoules and kilocalories to the tens place):
   a. the kilojoules for 1 cup of orange juice that contains 26 g of carbohydrate, no fat, and 2 g of protein
   b. the grams of carbohydrate in one apple if the apple has no fat and no protein and provides 72 kcal of energy

   c. the kilocalories in 1 tablespoon of vegetable oil, which contains 14 g of fat and no carbohydrate or protein
   d. the kilocalories for a diet that consists of 68 g of carbohydrate, 9.0 g of fat, and 150 g of protein

2.42 Using the energy values for foods (see Table 2.9), determine each of the following (round off the answers for kilojoules and kilocalories to the tens place):
   a. the kilojoules in 2 tablespoons of crunchy peanut butter that contains 6 g of carbohydrate, 16 g of fat, and 7 g of protein
   b. the grams of protein in a cup of soup that has 110 kcal with 9 g of carbohydrate and 7 g of fat
   c. the grams of sugar (carbohydrate) in a can of cola if it has 140 Cal and no fat and no protein
   d. the grams of fat in one avocado if it has 405 kcal, 13 g of carbohydrate, and 5 g of protein

2.43 One cup of clam chowder contains 16 g of carbohydrate, 12 g of fat, and 9 g of protein. How much energy, in kilojoules and kilocalories, is in the clam chowder? (Round off the kilojoules and kilocalories to the tens place.)

2.44 A high-protein diet contains 70. g of carbohydrate, 5.0 g of fat, and 150 g of protein. How much energy, in kilojoules and kilocalories, does this diet provide? (Round off the kilojoules or kilocalories to the tens place.)

CONCEPT MAP

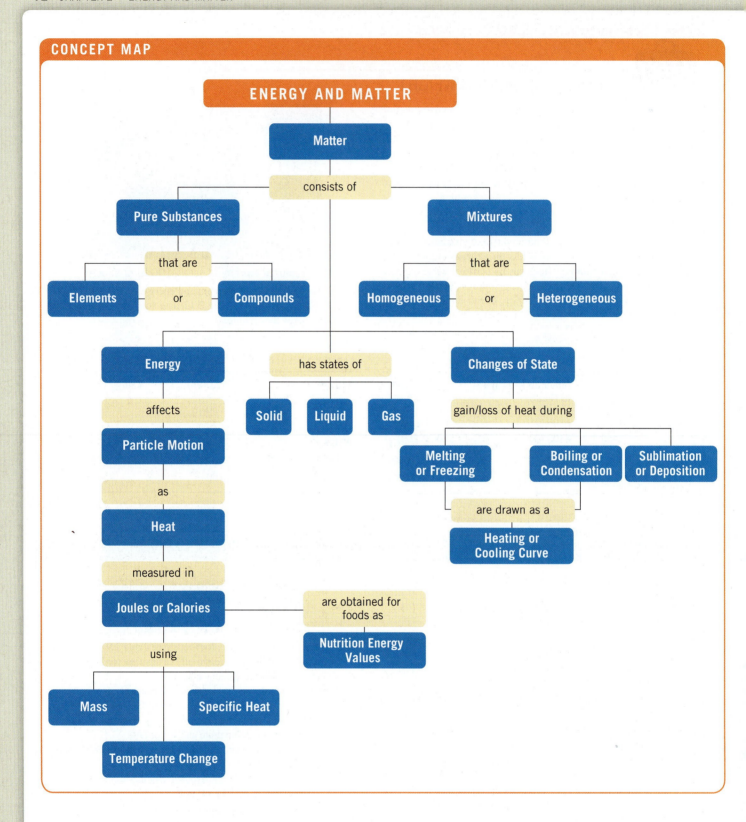

CHAPTER REVIEW

2.1 Energy

LEARNING GOAL: Identify energy as potential or kinetic; convert between units of energy.

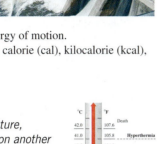

- Energy is the ability to do work.
- Potential energy is stored energy; kinetic energy is the energy of motion.
- Common units of energy are the calorie (cal), kilocalorie (kcal), joule (J), and kilojoule (kJ).
- One cal is equal to 4.184 J.

2.2 Temperature

LEARNING GOAL: Given a temperature, calculate a corresponding value on another temperature scale.

- In science, temperature is measured in degrees Celsius (°C) or kelvins (K).
- On the Celsius scale, there are 100 units between the freezing point (0 °C) and the boiling point (100 °C) of water.
- On the Fahrenheit scale used in the United States, there are 180 units between the freezing point (32 °F) and the boiling point (212 °F) of water.
- A Fahrenheit temperature is related to its Celsius temperature by the equation $T_F = 1.8\,T_C + 32$.
- The SI unit, kelvin, is related to the Celsius temperature by the equation $T_K = T_C + 273$.

2.3 Classification of Matter

LEARNING GOAL: Classify examples of matter as pure substances or mixtures.

- Matter is anything that has mass and occupies space.
- Matter is classified as pure substances or mixtures.
- Pure substances, which are elements or compounds, have fixed compositions, and mixtures have variable compositions.
- The substances in mixtures can be separated using physical methods.

2.4 States and Properties of Matter

LEARNING GOAL: Identify the states and the physical and chemical properties of matter.

- The three states of matter are solid, liquid, and gas.
- A physical property is a characteristic of a substance in which the identity of the substance does not change.
- A physical change occurs when physical properties change, but not the identity of the substance.
- A chemical property indicates the ability of a substance to change into another substance.
- A chemical change occurs when one or more substances react to form a substance with new physical and chemical properties.

2.5 Specific Heat

LEARNING GOAL: Use specific heat to calculate the quantity of heat lost or gained during a temperature change.

- Specific heat is the amount of energy required to raise the temperature of exactly 1 g of a substance by exactly 1 °C.
- The heat gained or lost by a substance is calculated by multiplying its mass, its temperature change, and its specific heat (cal/g °C or J/g °C).

2.6 Energy and Nutrition

LEARNING GOAL: Use the energy values to calculate the kilojoules (kJ) or kilocalories (kcal) in a food.

- The nutritional Calorie is the same amount of energy as 1 kcal or 1000 cal.
- The energy content of a food is the sum of kilojoules or kilocalories from carbohydrate, fat, and protein.

TABLE 2.9 Typical Energy (Caloric) Values for the Three Food Types

Food Type	kJ/g	kcal/g
Carbohydrate	17	4
Fat	38	9
Protein	17	4

KEY TERMS

boiling The formation of bubbles of gas throughout a liquid.

boiling point (bp) The temperature at which a liquid changes to gas (boils) and gas changes to liquid (condenses).

calorie (cal) The amount of heat energy that raises the temperature of exactly 1 g of water exactly 1 °C; 1 cal = 4.184 J.

Calorie (Cal) A nutritional unit of energy equal to 1000 cal, or 1 kcal.

change of state The transformation of one state of matter to another; for example, from solid to liquid, liquid to solid, and liquid to gas.

chemical change A change during which the original substance is converted into a new substance with a different composition and new physical and chemical properties.

chemical properties The properties that indicate the ability of a substance to change to a new substance.

compound A pure substance consisting of two or more elements, with a definite composition, that can be broken down into a simpler substance only by chemical methods.

condensation The change of state of a gas to a liquid.

deposition The reverse process of sublimation, with gas particles changing directly into a solid.

element A pure substance containing only one type of matter, which cannot be broken down by chemical methods.

energy The ability to do work.

energy (caloric) value The kilojoules or kilocalories obtained per gram of the three food types: carbohydrate, fat, and protein.

evaporation The formation of a gas (vapor) by the escape of high-energy molecules from the surface of a liquid.

freezing A change of state from liquid to solid.

freezing point (fp) The temperature at which a liquid changes to a solid (freezes) and a solid changes to a liquid (melts).

gas A state of matter characterized by no definite shape or volume. Particles in a gas move rapidly.

heat The energy associated with the motion of particles in a substance.

joule (J) The SI unit of heat energy; 4.184 J = 1 cal.

kinetic energy The energy of motion.

liquid A state of matter that takes the shape of its container but has a definite volume.

matter Anything that has mass and occupies space.

melting A change of state that involves the conversion of a solid to a liquid.

melting point (mp) The temperature at which a solid becomes a liquid (melts). It is the same temperature as the freezing point.

mixture The physical combination of two or more substances that does not change the identities of the substances.

physical change The change in which the physical appearance of a substance changes, but the chemical composition stays the same.

physical properties The properties that can be observed or measured without affecting the identity of a substance.

potential energy An inactive type of energy that is stored for future use.

pure substance Matter composed of elements or compounds that has a definite composition.

solid A state of matter that has its own shape and volume.

specific heat (SH) A quantity of heat that changes the temperature of exactly 1 g of a substance by exactly 1 °C.

sublimation The change of state in which a solid is transformed directly to a gas without forming a liquid first.

work An activity that requires energy.

UNDERSTANDING THE CONCEPTS

The chapter sections to review are shown in parentheses at the end of each question.

2.45 Select the warmer temperature in each of the following pairs: (2.2)
   a. 10 °C or 10 °F   **b.** 30 °C or 15 °F
   c. −10 °C or 32 °F   **d.** 200 °C or 200 K

2.46 State the temperature, including the estimated digit, on each of the following Celsius thermometers: (2.2)

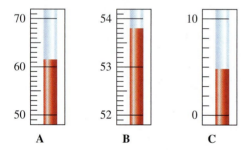

A   B   C

2.47 Compost can be made at home from grass clippings, some kitchen scraps, and dry leaves. As microbes break down organic matter, heat is generated and the compost can reach a temperature of 155 °F, which kills most pathogens. What is this temperature in degrees Celsius and kelvins? (2.2)

2.48 After a week, biochemical reactions in compost slow, and the temperature drops to 45 °C. The dark brown organic-rich mixture is ready for use in the garden. What is this temperature in Fahrenheit degrees and kelvins? (2.2)

Compost produced from decayed plant material is used to enrich the soil.

2.49 Identify each of the following as an element, compound, or mixture: (2.3)

a.
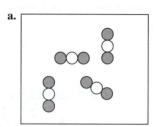
b.
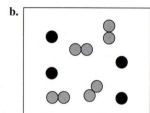

c.
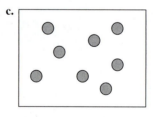

2.50 Which diagram illustrates a heterogeneous mixture? Explain your choice. Which diagrams illustrate a homogeneous mixture? Explain your choice. (2.3)

    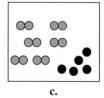

a.   b.   c.

2.51 Classify each of the following as a homogeneous or heterogeneous mixture: (2.3)
   a. lemon-flavored water   **b.** stuffed mushrooms
   c. eye drops

2.52 Classify each of the following as a homogeneous or heterogeneous mixture: (2.3)

    a. ketchup   **b.** tortilla soup   **c.** hard-boiled egg

2.53 Indicate if heat is added or removed in each of the following: (2.4)

    a. water freezing   **b.** copper melting

    c. dry ice subliming

2.54 Indicate if heat is added or removed in each of the following: (2.4)

    a. water boiling   **b.** water condensing

    c. alcohol evaporating

2.55 Use your knowledge of changes of state to explain the following: (2.4)

    a. How does perspiration during heavy exercise cool the body?

    b. Why do towels dry more quickly on a hot summer day than on a cold winter day?

Perspiration forms on the skin during heavy exercise.

2.56 Use your knowledge of changes of state to explain the following: (2.4)

    a. When a sports injury occurs during a game, a spray such as ethyl chloride (chloroethane) may be used to numb an area of the skin. Explain how a substance such as ethyl chloride that evaporates quickly can numb the skin.

    b. Why does water in a wide, flat, shallow dish evaporate more quickly than the same amount of water in a tall, narrow glass?

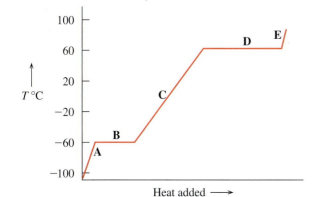

A spray is used to numb a sports injury.

2.57 The following is a heating curve for chloroform, a solvent for fats, oils, and waxes. (2.4)

a. What is the melting point of chloroform?

b. What is the boiling point of chloroform?

c. On the heating curve, identify the segments **A**, **B**, **C**, **D**, and **E** as solid, liquid, gas, melting, or boiling.

d. At the following temperatures, is chloroform a solid, liquid, or gas? $-80\ °C$; $-40\ °C$; $25\ °C$; $80\ °C$

2.58 Match the contents of the beakers (**1–5**) with segments (**A–E**) on the heating curve for water. (2.4)

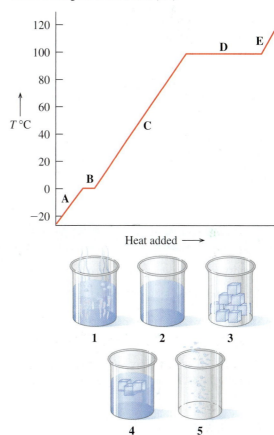

2.59 On a hot day, the beach sand gets hot, but the water stays cool. Would you predict the specific heat of sand is higher or lower than that of water? Explain. (2.5)

The water, sand, and air gain energy from the Sun.

2.60 Determine the energy to heat three cubes (gold, aluminum, and silver), each with a volume of 10.0 cm³, from 15 °C to 25 °C. Refer to Tables 1.13 and 2.8. What do you notice about the energy needed for each? (2.5)

2.61 A 70.0-kg person has just eaten a quarter-pound cheeseburger, french fries, and a chocolate shake. (2.6)

　　a. Using Table 2.9, calculate the total kilocalories for each food type in this meal (round off the kilocalories to the tens place).

Item	Carbohydrate (g)	Fat (g)	Protein (g)
Cheeseburger	34	29	31
French fries	26	11	3
Chocolate shake	60	9	11

b. Using Table 2.12, determine the number of hours of sleeping needed to burn off the kilocalories in this meal.

c. Using Table 2.12, determine the number of hours of running needed to burn off the kilocalories in this meal.

2.62 For lunch, your friend, who has a mass of 70.0 kg, has a slice of pizza, a cola soft drink, and ice cream. (2.6)

　　a. Using Table 2.9, calculate the total kilocalories for each food type in this meal (round off the kilocalories to the tens place).

Item	Carbohydrate (g)	Fat (g)	Protein (g)
Pizza	29	10	13
Cola	51	0	0
Ice cream	44	28	8

b. Using Table 2.12, determine the number of hours of sitting needed to burn off the kilocalories in this meal.

c. Using Table 2.12, determine the number of hours of swimming needed to burn off the kilocalories in this meal.

ADDITIONAL QUESTIONS AND PROBLEMS

For instructor-assigned homework, go to www.masteringchemistry.com.

2.63 Calculate each of the following temperatures in degrees Celsius: (2.2)

　　a. The highest recorded temperature in the continental United States was 134 °F in Death Valley, California, on July 10, 1913.

　　b. The lowest recorded temperature in the continental United States was −69.7 °F in Rodgers Pass, Montana, January 20, 1954.

2.64 Calculate each of the following temperatures in degrees Fahrenheit: (2.2)

　　a. The highest recorded temperature in the world was 58.0 °C in El Azizia, Libya, on September 13, 1922.

　　b. The lowest recorded temperature in the world was −89.2 °C in Vostok, Antarctica, on July 21, 1983.

2.65 What is −15 °F in degrees Celsius and in kelvins? (2.2)

2.66 The highest recorded body temperature that a person has survived is 46.5 °C. Calculate that temperature in degrees Fahrenheit and in kelvins. (2.2)

2.67 Classify each of the following as an element, a compound, or a mixture: (2.3)

　　a. carbon in pencils

　　b. carbon dioxide (CO_2) we exhale

　　c. orange juice

　　d. neon gas in lights

　　e. salad dressing of oil and vinegar

2.68 Classify each of the following as a homogeneous or heterogeneous mixture: (2.3)

　　a. hot fudge sundae　　**b.** herbal tea

　　c. vegetable oil　　　　**d.** water and sand

　　e. mustard

2.69 Identify each of the following as a solid, a liquid, or a gas: (2.4)

　　a. vitamin tablets in a bottle　**b.** helium in a balloon

　　c. milk in a glass　　　　　　**d.** the air you breathe

　　e. charcoal briquettes on a barbecue

2.70 Identify each of the following as a solid, a liquid, or a gas: (2.4)

　　a. popcorn in a bag　　　**b.** water in a garden hose

　　c. a computer mouse　　**d.** air in a tire

　　e. hot tea

2.71 Identify each of the following as a physical or chemical property: (2.4)

　　a. Gold is shiny.

　　b. Gold melts at 1064 °C.

　　c. Gold is a good conductor of electricity.

　　d. When gold reacts with yellow sulfur, a black compound forms.

2.72 Identify each of the following as a physical or chemical property of a candle: (2.4)

　　a. The candle is 20 cm high with a diameter of 3 cm.

　　b. The candle burns.

　　c. The wax of the candle softens on a hot day.

　　d. The candle is blue.

2.73 Identify each of the following as a physical or chemical change: (2.4)

　　a. A plant grows a new leaf.

　　b. Chocolate is melted for a dessert.

　　c. Wood is chopped for the fireplace.

　　d. Wood burns in a fireplace.

2.74 Identify each of the following as a physical or chemical change: (2.4)

　　a. A medication tablet is broken in two.

　　b. Carrots are grated for use in a salad.

　　c. Malt undergoes fermentation to make beer.

　　d. A copper pipe reacts with air and turns green.

2.75 A hot-water bottle contains 725 g of water at 65 °C. If the water cools to body temperature (37 °C), how many kilocalories of heat could be transferred to sore muscles? (2.5)

2.76 A pitcher containing 0.75 L of water at 4 °C is removed from the refrigerator. How many kilojoules are needed to warm the water to a room temperature of 22 °C? (2.5)

2.77 Calculate the Cal (kcal) in 1 cup of whole milk: 12 g of carbohydrate, 8 g of fat, and 8 g of protein. (Round off the answers to the tens place). (2.6)

2.78 Calculate the Cal (kcal) in 1/2 cup of soft ice cream that contains 18 g of carbohydrate, 11 g of fat, and 4 g of protein. (Round off the answers to the tens place). (2.6)

CHALLENGE QUESTIONS

2.79 The combustion of 1.0 g of gasoline releases 11 kcal of heat (density of gasoline = 0.74 g/mL). (2.5)
   a. How many megajoules are released when 1.0 gal of gasoline burns?
   b. When a color television is on for 2.0 h, 300 kJ are used. How long can a color television run on the energy from 1.0 gal of gasoline?

2.80 In a large building, oil is used in a steam boiler heating system. The combustion of 1.0 lb of oil provides 2.4×10^7 J. How many kilograms of oil are needed to heat 150 kg of water from 22 °C to 100 °C? (2.5)

2.81 The melting point of carbon tetrachloride is −23 °C and its boiling point is 77 °C. Sketch a heating curve for carbon tetrachloride from −100 °C to 100 °C. (2.4)
   a. What is the state of carbon tetrachloride at −50 °C?
   b. What happens on the curve at −23 °C?
   c. What is the state of carbon tetrachloride at 20 °C?
   d. What is the state of carbon tetrachloride at 90 °C?
   e. At what temperature will both solid and liquid be present?

2.82 The melting point of benzene is 5.5 °C and its boiling point is 80.1 °C. Sketch a heating curve for benzene from 0 °C to 100 °C. (2.4)
   a. What is the state of benzene at 15 °C?
   b. What happens on the curve at 5.5 °C?
   c. What is the state of benzene at 63 °C?
   d. What is the state of benzene at 98 °C?
   e. At what temperature will both liquid and gas be present?

2.83 A 70.0-g piece of copper metal at 86.0 °C is placed in 50.0 g of water at 16.0 °C. The metal and water come to the same temperature of 24.0 °C. What is the specific heat, in J/g °C, of copper? (2.5)

2.84 A 125-g piece of metal is heated to 288 °C and dropped into 85.0 g of water at 26 °C. If the final temperature of the water and metal is 58.0 °C, what is the specific heat (J/g °C) of the metal? (2.5)

2.85 A metal is thought to be titanium or aluminum. When 4.7 g of the metal absorbs 11 J, its temperature rises by 4.5 °C. (2.5)
   a. What is the specific heat, in J/g °C, of the metal?
   b. Would you identify the metal as titanium or aluminum (see Table 2.8)?

2.86 A metal is thought to be copper or gold. When 18 g of the metal absorbs 58 cal, its temperature rises by 35 °C. (2.5)
   a. What is the specific heat, in cal/g °C, of the metal?
   b. Would you identify the metal as copper or gold (see Table 2.8)?

2.87 When a 0.660-g sample of olive oil is burned in a calorimeter, the heat released increases the temperature of 370. g of water in the calorimeter from 22.7 °C to 38.8 °C. What is the energy value, in kJ/g and kcal/g, of the olive oil? (2.6)

2.88 When a 1.30-g sample of ethanol (alcohol) is burned in a calorimeter, the heat released increases the temperature of 870. g of water in the calorimeter from 18.5 °C to 28.9 °C. What is the energy value, in kJ/g and kcal/g, of ethanol? (2.6)

2.89 If you want to lose 1 pound of "fat," which is 15% water, how many kilocalories do you need to expend? (2.6)

2.90 A patient receives 2500 mL of an IV solution containing 5 g of glucose per 100 mL. How much energy, in kilojoules and kilocalories, does the patient obtain from glucose, a carbohydrate? (2.6)

ANSWERS

Answers to Study Checks

2.1 35 kJ

2.2 12 °F

2.3 39.8 °C

2.4 night −260. °C; day 410. °C

2.5 This salad dressing is a heterogeneous mixture with a nonuniform composition.

2.6 a and c are chemical changes.

2.7 SH = 1.23 J/g °C

2.8 14.6 kJ

2.9 carbohydrate 630 kJ, fat 720 kJ, protein 410 kJ; total = 1760 kJ

Answers to Selected Questions and Problems

2.1 a. potential   **b.** kinetic
   c. potential   **d.** potential

2.3 a. increase   **b.** decrease   **c.** decrease

2.5 a. 8.1×10^5 J   **b.** 190 kcal

2.7 In the United States, the Fahrenheit scale is in common use. On a Fahrenheit thermometer, normal body temperature is 98.6 °F. A temperature of 99.8 °F would indicate a mild fever. On the Celsius scale, her temperature is 37.7 °C.

2.9 a. 98.6 °F   **b.** 18.5 °C   **c.** 246 K
   d. −49 °C   **e.** 46 °C

2.11 a. 41 °C
   b. No. The temperature is equivalent to 39 °C.

2.13 a. compound; contains four elements in a definite composition
   b. mixture
   c. compound; consists of two elements in a definite composition
   d. element; consists of one type of pure substance
   e. mixture

2.15 a. heterogeneous   **b.** homogeneous
   c. homogeneous   **d.** heterogeneous
   e. heterogeneous

2.17 a. gas   **b.** gas   **c.** solid

2.19 a. physical   **b.** chemical
   c. physical   **d.** chemical

2.21 a. physical   **b.** chemical   **c.** physical
   d. physical   **e.** physical

2.23 a. chemical   **b.** physical   **c.** physical
   d. chemical   **e.** physical

2.25 a. melting   **b.** sublimation
   c. freezing   **d.** deposition

2.27 a. condensation   **b.** evaporation
   c. boiling   **d.** condensation

2.29

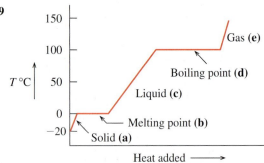

2.31 Copper has the lowest specific heat of the samples and will reach the highest temperature.

2.33 a. 0.389 J/g °C   **b.** 0.313 J/g °C

2.35 a. 250 cal   **b.** 3300 J   **c.** 9.3 kcal

2.37 a. 1380 J; 330. cal   **b.** 1810 J; 434 cal
   c. 3780 J; 904 cal   **d.** 3200 J; 760 cal

2.39 a. 5.30 kcal; 22.2 kJ   **b.** 208 kcal; 871 kJ

2.41 a. 470 kJ   **b.** 18 g
   c. 130 kcal   **d.** 950 kcal

2.43 880 kJ; 210 kcal

2.45 a. 10 °C   **b.** 30 °C
   c. 32 °F   **d.** 200 °C

2.47 68.3 °C; 341 K

2.49 a. compound   **b.** mixture   **c.** element

2.51 a. homogeneous   **b.** heterogeneous
   c. homogeneous

2.53 a. removed   **b.** added   **c.** added

2.55 a. The heat from the skin is used to evaporate the water (perspiration). Therefore, the skin is cooled.
   b. On a hot day, there are more molecules with sufficient energy to become water vapor.

2.57 a. about −60 °C
   b. about 60 °C
   c. **A** is solid. **B** is melting. **C** is liquid. **D** is boiling. **E** is gas.
   d. At −80 °C, it is solid; at −40 °C, it is liquid; at 25 °C, it is liquid; at 80 °C, it is gas.

2.59 Sand must have a lower specific heat than water. When both substances absorb the same amount of heat, the final temperature of the sand will be higher than that of water.

2.61 a. 1100 kcal
   b. 18 h of sleeping
   c. 1.5 h of running

2.63 a. 56.7 °C   **b.** −56.5 °C

2.65 a. −26 °C, 247 K

2.67 a. element   **b.** compound   **c.** mixture
   d. element   **e.** mixture

2.69 a. solid   **b.** gas   **c.** liquid
   d. gas   **e.** solid

2.71 a. physical property   **b.** physical property
   c. physical property   **d.** chemical property

2.73 a. chemical change   **b.** physical change
   c. physical change   **d.** chemical change

2.75 20. kcal

2.77 150 Cal

2.79 a. 130 MJ   **b.** 860 h

2.81 a. solid   **b.** solid carbon tetrachloride melts
   c. liquid   **d.** gas   **e.** −23 °C

2.83 Specific heat = 0.39 J/g °C

2.85 a. 0.52 J/g °C
   b. titanium

2.87 37.8 kJ/g; 9.03 kcal/g

2.89 3500 kcal

Combining Ideas from Chapters 1 and 2

The chapter sections to review are shown in parentheses at the end of each question.

CI.1 Gold, one of the most sought-after metals in the world, has a density of 19.3 g/cm³, a melting point of 1064 °C, and a specific heat of 0.129 J/g °C. A gold nugget found in Alaska in 1998 weighs 20.17 lb. (1.5, 1.9, 1.10, 2.2, 2.5)

Gold nuggets, also called native gold, can be found in streams and mines.

   a. How many significant figures are in the measurement of weight of the nugget?

   b. What is the mass of the nugget in kilograms?

   c. If the nugget were pure gold, what would its volume be in cm³ ?

   d. What is the melting point of gold in degrees Fahrenheit and kelvins?

   e. How many kilojoules are required to heat the nugget from 27 °C to 358 °C? How many kilocalories is that?

   f. In 2010, the price of gold was $61.08 per gram. What was the nugget worth, in dollars, in 2010?

CI.2 The mileage for a motorcycle with a fuel-tank capacity of 22 L is 35 mi/gal. The density of gasoline is 0.74 g/mL. (1.9, 1.10, 2.5)

   a. How long a trip, in kilometers, can be made on one full tank of gasoline?

   b. If the price of gasoline is $3.59 per gallon, what would be the cost of fuel for the trip?

   c. If the average speed during the trip is 44 mi/h, how many hours will it take to reach the destination?

   d. What is the mass, in grams, of the fuel in the tank?

   e. When 1.0 g of gasoline burns, 47 kJ of energy is released. How many kilojoules are produced when the fuel in one full tank is completely burned?

When 1.0 g of gasoline burns in a motorcycle, 47 kJ of energy is released.

CI.3

Answer the following for diagrams **A** and **B**: (2.4)

   a. In which sample (**A** or **B**) does the water have its own shape?

   b. Which diagram (**1**, **2**, or **3**) represents the arrangement of particles in water sample **A**?

   c. Which diagram (**1**, **2**, or **3**) represents the arrangement of particles in water sample **B**?

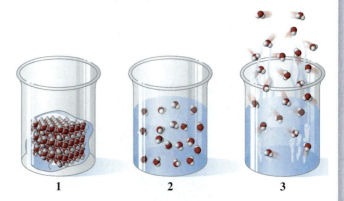

Answer the following for diagrams **1**, **2**, and **3**: (2.4, 2.5)

   d. The state of matter indicated in diagram **1** is a _____; in diagram **2**, it is a _____; and in diagram **3**, it is a _____.

   e. The motion of the particles is slowest in diagram _____.

   f. The arrangement of particles is farthest apart in diagram _____.

   g. The particles fill the volume of the container in diagram _____.

   h. If the water in diagram **2** has a mass of 19 g and a temperature of 45 °C, how much heat, in kilojoules, is removed to cool the liquid to 0 °C?

CI.4 The label of a black cherry almond energy bar with a mass of 68 g lists the "nutrition facts" as 39 g of carbohydrate, 5 g of fat, and 10 g of protein. (2.1, 2.6)

   a. Using the energy values of carbohydrates, fats, and proteins (see Table 2.9), what are the kilocalories (Calories) listed for the black cherry almond bar? (Round off answers for each food type to the tens place.)

   b. What are the kilojoules for the black cherry almond bar? (Round off answers for each food type to the tens place.)

   c. If you obtain 160 kJ, how many grams of the black cherry almond bar did you eat?

   d. If you are walking and using energy at a rate of 840 kJ/h, how many minutes will you need to walk to expend the energy from two bars?

An energy bar contains carbohydrate, fat, and protein.

CI.5 In a box of nails, there are 75 iron nails weighing 0.250 lb. The density of iron is 7.86 g/cm³. The specific heat of iron is 0.452 J/g °C. (1.10, 2.5)
  a. What is the volume, in cm³, of the iron nails in the box?
  b. If 30 nails are added to a graduated cylinder containing 17.6 mL of water, what is the new level of water in the cylinder?
  c. How many joules must be added to the nails in the box to raise their temperature from 16 °C to 125 °C?

Nails made of iron have a density of 7.86 g/cm³.

CI.6 A hot tub is filled with 450 gal of water. (1.9, 1.10, 2.5)
  a. What is the volume, in liters, of water in the tub?
  b. What is the mass, in kilograms, of water in the tub?
  c. How many kilocalories are needed to heat the water from 62 °F to 105 °F?
  d. If the hot tub heater provides 1400 kcal/min, how long, in minutes, will it take to heat the water in the hot tub from 62 °F to 105 °F?

A hot tub filled with water is heated to 105 °F.

ANSWERS

CI.1 **a.** Four significant figures are in the measurement.
  b. 9.17 kg
  c. 475 cm³
  d. 1947 °F; 1337 K
  e. 392 kJ; 93.6 kcal
  f. $560 000 or 5.60×10^5

CI.3 **a.** B
  b. A is represented by diagram 2.
  c. B is represented by diagram 1.

  d. solid, liquid, gas
  e. diagram 1
  f. diagram 3
  g. diagram 3
  h. 3.6 kJ

CI.5 **a.** 14.4 cm³
  b. 23.4 mL
  c. 5590 J or 5.59 $\times 10^3$ J

Atoms and Elements

Mastering**CHEMISTRY**™

Visit **www.masteringchemistry.com** for self-study materials and instructor-assigned homework.

John is preparing for the next growing season as he decides how much of each crop should be planted and their location on his farm. Part of this decision is determined by the quality of the soil including the pH, the amount of moisture, and the nutrient content in the soil. He begins by sampling the soil and performing a few chemical tests on the samples. John determines that several of his fields need additional fertilizer before the crops can be planted.

John considers several different types of fertilizers, as each kind supplies nutrients to the soil to help increase crop production. Plants need three basic elements for plant growth. These elements are potassium, nitrogen, and phosphorus. Potassium (K on the periodic table) is a metal, while nitrogen (N) and phosphorus (P) are nonmetals. Fertilizers may also contain several other elements including calcium (Ca), magnesium (Mg), and sulfur (S). John applies a fertilizer containing a mixture of all of these elements to his soil, and plans to retest the soil nutrient content in a few days.

Career: Farmer
Farming involves much more than growing crops and raising animals. Farmers must understand how to perform chemical tests, apply fertilizer to soil, and pesticides or herbicides to crops. Pesticides are chemicals used to kill insects that could destroy the crop, while herbicides are chemicals used to kill weeds that would compete for the crop's water and nutrient supply. This requires a knowledge of how these chemicals work, their safety, effectiveness, and their storage. In using this information, farmers are able to grow crops that produce a higher yield, greater nutritional value, and better taste.

All matter is composed of *elements*, of which there are 118 different kinds. Of these, 88 elements occur naturally and make up all the substances in our world. Many elements are already familiar to you. Perhaps you use aluminum in the form of foil or drink soft drinks from aluminum cans. You may have a ring or necklace made of gold, silver, or perhaps platinum. If you play tennis or golf, your racket or clubs may be made from the elements titanium or carbon. In our bodies, compounds of calcium and phosphorus form the structure of bones and teeth, iron and copper are needed for the formation of red blood cells, and iodine is required for the proper functioning of the thyroid.

The amounts of certain elements are crucial for the proper growth and function of the body. Low levels of iron can lead to anemia, while lack of iodine can cause hypothyroidism and goiter. Some elements known as microminerals, such as chromium, cobalt, and selenium, are needed in our bodies in very small amounts. Laboratory tests are used to confirm that these elements are within normal ranges in our bodies.

LEARNING GOAL

Given the name of an element, write its correct symbol; from the symbol, write the correct name.

TUTORIAL
Elements and Symbols in the Periodic Table

3.1 Elements and Symbols

Elements are pure substances from which all other things are built. As we discussed in Section 2.3, elements cannot be broken down into simpler substances. Over the centuries, elements have been named for planets, mythological figures, colors, minerals, geographic locations, and famous people. Some sources of names of elements are listed in Table 3.1. A complete list of all the elements and their symbols appears on the inside front cover of this text.

TABLE 3.1 Some Elements, Symbols, Sources of Names, and Atomic Numbers

Element	Symbol	Source of Name	Atomic Number
Uranium	U	The planet Uranus	92
Titanium	Ti	Titans (mythology)	22
Chlorine	Cl	*Chloros*: "greenish yellow" (Greek)	17
Iodine	I	*Ioeides*: "violet" (Greek)	53
Magnesium	Mg	Magnesia, a mineral	12
Californium	Cf	California	98
Curium	Cm	Marie and Pierre Curie	96
Copernicium	Cn	Nicolaus Copernicus	112

One-Letter Symbols		Two-Letter Symbols	
C	carbon	Co	cobalt
S	sulfur	Si	silicon
N	nitrogen	Ne	neon
I	iodine	Ni	nickel

Chemical symbols are one- and two-letter abbreviations for the names of the elements. Only the first letter of an element's symbol is capitalized. If the symbol has a second letter, it is lowercase so that we know when a different element is indicated. If two letters are capitalized, they represent the symbols of two different elements. For example, the element cobalt has the symbol Co. However, the two capital letters CO specify two elements, carbon (C) and oxygen (O).

Chemistry Link to Industry

MANY FORMS OF CARBON

Carbon has the symbol C and atomic number 6. However, carbon atoms can be arranged in different ways to give several different kinds of carbon substances. Two forms—diamond and graphite—have been known since prehistoric times. A diamond is transparent and harder than any other substance, whereas graphite is black and soft. In diamond, carbon atoms are arranged in a rigid structure, while in graphite, carbon atoms are arranged in sheets that slide easily over each other. Graphite is used as pencil lead, as a lubricant, and in the manufacture of carbon fibers used for lightweight golf clubs and tennis rackets.

Two other forms of carbon have been discovered more recently. In the form called *buckminsterfullerene* or *buckyball* (named after R. Buckminster "Bucky" Fuller, who popularized the geodesic dome), 60 carbon atoms are arranged as rings of 5 and 6 atoms to give a spherical, cage-like structure. When the buckyball structure is stretched out, it produces a cylinder called a *nanotube*, which has a diameter of a few nanometers. Practical uses for buckyballs and nanotubes have not yet been developed, but they are expected to find use in lightweight structural materials, heat conductors, computer parts, and medicine.

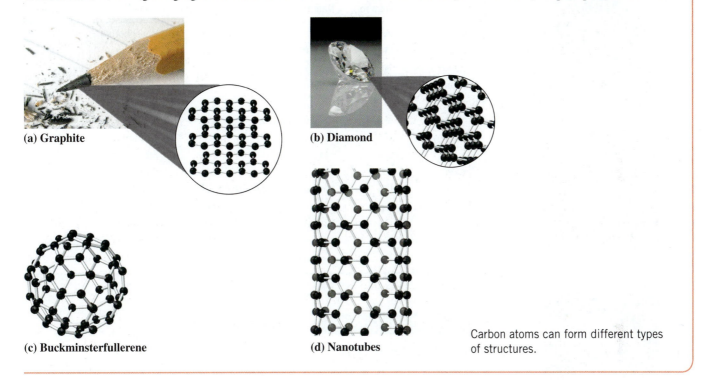

(a) Graphite

(b) Diamond

(c) Buckminsterfullerene

(d) Nanotubes

Carbon atoms can form different types of structures.

Although most of the symbols use letters from their English names, some are derived from their ancient names. For example, Na, the symbol for sodium, comes from the Latin word *natrium*. The symbol for iron, Fe, is derived from the Latin name *ferrum*. Table 3.2 lists the names and symbols of some common elements. Learning their names and symbols will greatly help your learning of chemistry.

Chemistry Link to Health

LATIN NAMES FOR ELEMENTS IN CLINICAL USAGE

In medicine, the Latin name *natrium* is often used for sodium, an important electrolyte in body fluids and cells. An increase in serum sodium, a condition called *hypernatremia*, may occur when water is lost because of profuse sweating, severe diarrhea, or vomiting, or when there is inadequate water intake. A decrease in sodium, a condition called *hyponatremia*, may occur when a person takes in a large amount of water or fluid-replacement solutions. Conditions that occur in cardiac failure, liver failure, and malnutrition can also cause hyponatremia.

The Latin name *kalium* is often used for potassium, the most common electrolyte inside the cells. Potassium regulates osmotic pressure, acid–base balance, nerve and muscle excitability, and the function of cellular enzymes. Serum potassium measures potassium outside the cells, which amounts to only 2% of total body potassium. An increase in serum potassium (*hyperkalemia* or *hyperpotassemia*) may occur when cells are severely injured, in renal failure when potassium is not properly excreted, and in Addison's disease. A severe loss of potassium (*hypokalemia* or *hypopotassemia*) may occur during excessive vomiting, diarrhea, renal tubular defects, and glucose or insulin therapy.

Aluminum

Carbon

Gold

Silver

Sulfur

CONCEPT CHECK 3.1 Symbols of the Elements

The symbol for carbon is C, and the symbol for sulfur is S. However, the symbol for cesium is Cs, not CS. Why?

ANSWER

When the symbol for an element has two letters, the first letter is capitalized, but the second letter is lowercase. If both letters are capitalized such as in CS, then two elements—carbon and sulfur—are indicated.

TABLE 3.2 Names and Symbols of Some Common Elements

Name*	Symbol	Name*	Symbol	Name*	Symbol
Aluminum	Al	Gold (*aurum*)	Au	Phosphorus	P
Argon	Ar	Helium	He	Platinum	Pt
Arsenic	As	Hydrogen	H	Potassium (*kalium*)	K
Barium	Ba	Iodine	I	Radium	Ra
Boron	B	Iron (*ferrum*)	Fe	Silicon	Si
Bromine	Br	Lead (*plumbum*)	Pb	Silver (*argentum*)	Ag
Cadmium	Cd	Lithium	Li	Sodium (*natrium*)	Na
Calcium	Ca	Magnesium	Mg	Strontium	Sr
Carbon	C	Manganese	Mn	Sulfur	S
Chlorine	Cl	Mercury (*hydrargyrum*)	Hg	Tin (*stannum*)	Sn
Chromium	Cr	Neon	Ne	Titanium	Ti
Cobalt	Co	Nickel	Ni	Uranium	U
Copper (*cuprum*)	Cu	Nitrogen	N	Zinc	Zn
Fluorine	F	Oxygen	O		

*Names given in parentheses are ancient Latin or Greek words from which the symbols are derived.

SAMPLE PROBLEM 3.1 Writing Chemical Symbols

What are the chemical symbols for each of the following elements?

a. nickel **b.** nitrogen **c.** neon

SOLUTION

a. Ni **b.** N **c.** Ne

STUDY CHECK 3.1

What are the chemical symbols for silicon, sulfur, and silver?

SAMPLE PROBLEM 3.2 Names and Symbols of Chemical Elements

Give the name of the element that corresponds to each of the following chemical symbols:

a. Zn **b.** K **c.** H **d.** Fe

SOLUTION

a. zinc **b.** potassium **c.** hydrogen **d.** iron

STUDY CHECK 3.2

What are the names of the elements with the chemical symbols Mg, Al, and F?

Chemistry Link to the Environment

TOXICITY OF MERCURY

Mercury is a silvery, shiny element that is a liquid at room temperature. Mercury can enter the body through inhalation as a vapor, contact with the skin, or foods or water that have been contaminated with mercury. In the body, mercury destroys proteins and disrupts cell function. Long-term exposure to mercury can damage the brain and kidneys, cause mental retardation, and decrease physical development. Blood, urine, and hair samples are used to test for mercury.

In both freshwater and seawater, bacteria convert mercury into toxic methylmercury, which attacks the central nervous system (CNS). Because fish absorb methylmercury, we are exposed to mercury when we eat mercury-contaminated fish. The Food and Drug Administration (FDA) has set a maximum level of one part mercury per million parts seafood (1 ppm), which is the same as 1 mg of mercury in every kilogram of seafood. Fish higher in the food chain such as swordfish, tuna, and shark can have such high levels of mercury that the Environmental Protection Agency (EPA) recommends they be consumed no more than once a week.

One of the worst incidents of mercury poisoning occurred in Minamata and Niigata, Japan, in 1950. At that time, the ocean was polluted with high levels of mercury from industrial wastes. Because fish were a major food in the Japanese diet, more than 2000 people were affected with mercury poisoning and many died or developed neural damage. In the United States, between 1988 and 1997, the use of mercury decreased by 75% when mercury was banned in paints and pesticides, and regulated in batteries and other products. Certain batteries and CFL bulbs contain mercury and instructions for their safe disposal should be followed.

This mercury fountain, housed in glass, was designed by Alexander Calder for the 1937 World's Fair in Paris.

QUESTIONS AND PROBLEMS

3.1 Elements and Symbols

LEARNING GOAL: *Given the name of an element, write its correct symbol; from the symbol, write the correct name.*

3.1 Write the symbols for the following elements:
   a. copper   **b.** platinum   **c.** calcium
   d. manganese   **e.** iron   **f.** barium
   g. lead   **h.** strontium

3.2 Write the symbols for the following elements:
   a. oxygen   **b.** lithium   **c.** uranium
   d. titanium   **e.** hydrogen   **f.** chromium
   g. tin   **h.** gold

3.3 Write the name of the element for each of the following symbols:
   a. C   **b.** Cl   **c.** I   **d.** Hg
   e. Ag   **f.** Ar   **g.** B   **h.** Ni

3.4 Write the name of the element for each of the following symbols:
   a. He   **b.** P   **c.** Na   **d.** As
   e. Ca   **f.** Br   **g.** Cd   **h.** Si

3.5 What elements are represented by the symbols in each of the following substances?
   a. table salt, $NaCl$
   b. plaster cast, $CaSO_4$
   c. Demerol, $C_{15}H_{22}ClNO_2$
   d. antacid, $CaCO_3$

3.6 What elements are represented by the symbols in each of the following substances?
   a. water, H_2O
   b. baking soda, $NaHCO_3$
   c. lye, $NaOH$
   d. sugar, $C_{12}H_{22}O_{11}$

3.2 The Periodic Table

As more elements were discovered, it became necessary to organize them into some type of classification system. By the late 1800s, scientists recognized that certain elements looked alike and behaved in much the same way. In 1872, a Russian chemist, Dmitri Mendeleev, arranged the 60 elements known at that time into groups with similar properties and placed them in order of increasing mass. Today, this arrangement of 118 elements is known as the **periodic table** (see Figure 3.1).

LEARNING GOAL

Use the periodic table to identify the group and the period of an element; identify the element as a metal, nonmetal, or metalloid.

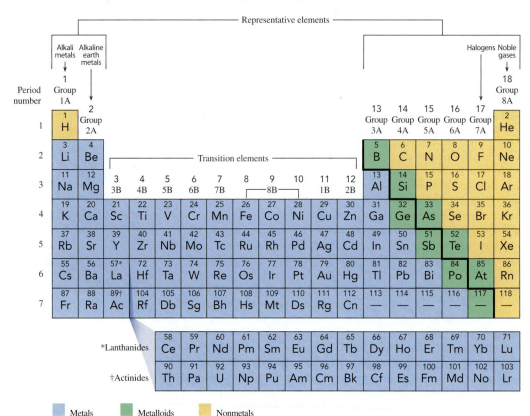

FIGURE 3.1 On the periodic table, groups are elements arranged as vertical columns, and periods are the elements in each horizontal row.

Q What is the symbol and name of the alkali metal in Period 3?

Periods and Groups

Each horizontal row in the periodic table is a **period** (see Figure 3.2). The periods are counted from the top of the table as Period 1 to Period 7. The first period contains two elements: hydrogen (H) and helium (He). The second period contains eight elements: lithium (Li), beryllium (Be), boron (B), carbon (C), nitrogen (N), oxygen (O), fluorine (F), and neon (Ne). The third period also contains eight elements, beginning with sodium (Na) and ending with argon (Ar). The fourth period, which begins with potassium (K), and the fifth period, which begins with rubidium (Rb), have 18 elements each. The sixth period, which begins with cesium (Cs), has 32 elements. The seventh period contains 32 elements, for a total of 118 elements.

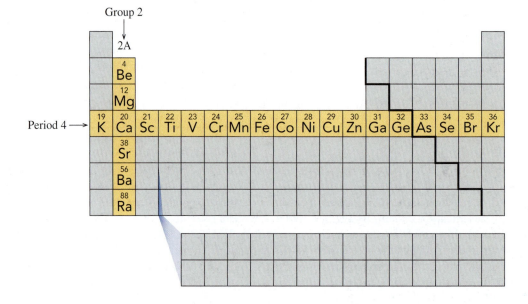

FIGURE 3.2 On the periodic table, each vertical column represents a group of elements, and each horizontal row of elements represents a period.

Q Are the elements Si, P, and S part of a group or a period?

Each vertical column on the periodic table contains a **group** (or family) of elements that have similar properties. At the top of each column is a number that is assigned to each group. The elements in the first two columns on the left of the periodic table and the last six columns on the right are called the **representative elements**. For many years, they have been given **group numbers** 1A–8A. In the center of the periodic table is a block of elements known as the **transition elements**, which are designated with the letter "B." A newer system assigns numbers 1 to 18 to the groups going left to right across the periodic table. Because both systems of group numbers are currently in use, they are both shown on the periodic table in this text and are included in our discussions of elements and group numbers. Below the periodic table, there are two rows of 14 elements, which are part of Periods 6 and 7. These elements, called the lanthanides and actinides (or the inner transition elements), are placed below the periodic table to allow it to fit on a page.

Names of Groups

Several groups in the periodic table have special names (see Figure 3.3). Group 1A (1) elements—lithium (Li), sodium (Na), potassium (K), rubidium (Rb), cesium (Cs), and francium (Fr)—are a family of elements known as the **alkali metals** (see Figure 3.4). The elements within this group are soft, shiny metals that are good conductors of heat and electricity, and have relatively low melting points. Alkali metals react vigorously with water and form white products when they combine with oxygen.

Although hydrogen (H) is at the top of Group 1A (1), it is not an alkali metal and has very different properties than the rest of the elements in this group. Thus, hydrogen is not included in the classification of alkali metals.

The **alkaline earth metals** are found in Group 2A (2). They include the elements beryllium (Be), magnesium (Mg), calcium (Ca), strontium (Sr), barium (Ba), and radium (Ra). The alkaline earth metals are shiny metals like those in Group 1A (1), but they are not as reactive.

The **halogens** are found on the right side of the periodic table in Group 7A (17). They include the elements fluorine (F), chlorine (Cl), bromine (Br), iodine (I), and astatine (At) (see Figure 3.5). The halogens, especially fluorine and chlorine, are highly reactive and form compounds with most of the elements.

The **noble gases** are found in Group 8A (18). They include helium (He), neon (Ne), argon (Ar), krypton (Kr), xenon (Xe), and radon (Rn). The noble gases are quite unreactive and are seldom found in combination with other elements.

Group 1A (1)

3 Li
11 Na
19 K
37 Rb
55 Cs

Lithium (Li)

Sodium (Na)

Potassium (K)

FIGURE 3.4 Lithium (Li), sodium (Na), and potassium (K) are some alkali metals from Group 1A (1).

Q What physical properties do these alkali metals have in common?

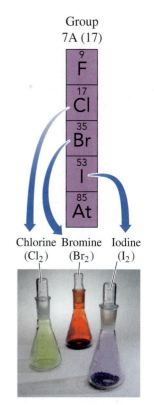

Group 7A (17)

9 F
17 Cl
35 Br
53 I
85 At

Chlorine (Cl_2) Bromine (Br_2) Iodine (I_2)

FIGURE 3.5 Chlorine (Cl_2), bromine (Br_2), and iodine (I_2) are examples of halogens from Group 7A (17).

Q What elements are in the halogen group?

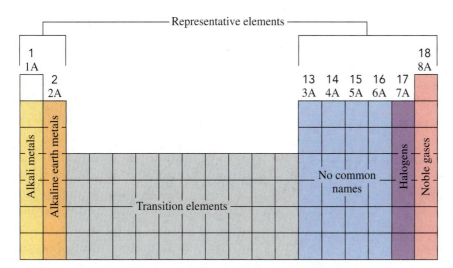

FIGURE 3.3 Certain groups on the periodic table have common names.

Q What is the common name for the group of elements that includes helium and argon?

SAMPLE PROBLEM 3.3   Period and Group Numbers of Some Elements

Give the period and group number for each of the following elements, and identify each as a representative or transition element:

a. iodine   **b.** manganese   **c.** barium   **d.** gold

SOLUTION

a. Iodine (I), Period 5, Group 7A (17), is a representative element.
b. Manganese (Mn), Period 4, Group 7B (7), is a transition element.
c. Barium (Ba), Period 6, Group 2A (2), is a representative element.
d. Gold (Au), Period 6, Group 1B (11), is a transition element.

STUDY CHECK 3.3

Strontium is an element that gives a brilliant red color to fireworks.

a. In what group is strontium found?
b. In what chemical family is strontium found?
c. In what period is strontium found?
d. What is the name and symbol of the element in Period 3 that is in the same group as strontium?
e. What alkali metal, halogen, and noble gas are in the same period as strontium?

Strontium provides the red color in fireworks.

Metals, Nonmetals, and Metalloids

The heavy zigzag line on the periodic table separates the *metals* from the *nonmetals. Except for hydrogen*, the metals are to the left of the line with the nonmetals to the right (see Figure 3.6). In general, most **metals** are shiny solids, such as copper (Cu), gold (Au), and silver (Ag). Metals can be shaped into wires (ductile) or hammered into flat sheets (malleable). Metals are good conductors of heat and electricity. They usually melt at higher temperatures than nonmetals. All of the metals are solids at room temperature, except for mercury (Hg), which is a liquid.

Nonmetals are not especially shiny, ductile, or malleable, and they are often poor conductors of heat and electricity. They typically have low melting points and low densities. Some examples of nonmetals are hydrogen (H), carbon (C), nitrogen (N), oxygen (O), chlorine (Cl), and sulfur (S).

Except for aluminum, the elements located along the heavy zigzag line are **metalloids**: B, Si, Ge, As, Sb, Te, Po, and At. Metalloids exhibit some properties that are typical

TUTORIAL
Metals, Nonmetals, and Metalloids

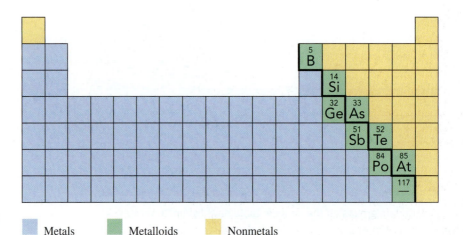

FIGURE 3.6 The metalloids that border the heavy zigzag line on the periodic table exhibit characteristics of both metals and nonmetals.

Q On which side of the heavy zigzag line are the nonmetals located?

of the metals, and other properties that are characteristic of the nonmetals. For example, metalloids are better conductors of heat and electricity than the nonmetals, but not as good as the metals. The metalloids are semiconductors because they can be modified to function as conductors or insulators. Table 3.3 compares some characteristics of silver, a metal, with those of antimony, a metalloid, and sulfur, a nonmetal.

TABLE 3.3 Some Characteristics of a Metal, a Metalloid, and a Nonmetal

Silver (Ag)	Antimony (Sb)	Sulfur (S)
Metal	Metalloid	Nonmetal
Shiny	Blue-gray, shiny	Dull, yellow
Extremely ductile	Brittle	Brittle
Can be hammered into sheets (malleable)	Shatters when hammered	Shatters when hammered
Good conductor of heat and electricity	Poor conductor of heat and electricity	Poor conductor, good insulator
Used in coins, jewelry, tableware	Used to harden lead, color glass and plastics	Used in gunpowder, rubber, fungicides
Density 10.5 g/mL	Density 6.7 g/mL	Density 2.1 g/mL
Melting point 962 °C	Melting point 630 °C	Melting point 113 °C

A silver cup is shiny, antimony is a blue-gray solid, and sulfur is a dull, yellow color.

SAMPLE PROBLEM 3.4 **Names and Classification of Elements**

Use the periodic table to classify each of the following elements by its group, group name (if any), and as a metal, nonmetal, or metalloid:

a. Na   **b.** I   **c.** B

SOLUTION

a. Na (sodium), Group 1A (1), an alkali metal, is a metal.
b. I (iodine), Group 7A (17), a halogen, is a nonmetal.
c. B (boron), Group 3A (13), is a metalloid.

STUDY CHECK 3.4

Identify each of the following as a metal, nonmetal, or metalloid:

a. germanium   **b.** radon   **c.** chromium

Chemistry Link to Health

ELEMENTS ESSENTIAL TO HEALTH

Of all the elements, only about 20 are essential for the well-being and survival of the human body. Of those, four elements—oxygen, carbon, hydrogen, and nitrogen—which are representative elements in Period 1 and Period 2 on the periodic table, make up 96% of our body mass. Most of the food in our daily diet consists of these elements, which are found in carbohydrates, fats, and proteins. Much of the hydrogen and oxygen is found in water, which makes up 55–60% of our body mass.

The *macrominerals*—Ca, P, K, Cl, S, Na, and Mg—are representative elements located in Period 3 and Period 4 of the periodic table. They are involved in the formation of bones and teeth, maintenance of heart and blood vessels, muscle contraction, nerve impulses, acid–base balance of body fluids, and regulation of cellular metabolism.

The macrominerals are present in lower amounts than the major elements, so that smaller amounts are required in our daily diets.

The other essential elements, called *microminerals* or *trace elements*, are mostly transition elements in Period 4 along with Mo and I in Period 5. They are present in the human body in small amounts, some less than 100 mg. In recent years, the detection of such small amounts has improved so that researchers can more easily identify the roles of trace elements. Some trace elements such as arsenic, chromium, and selenium are toxic at higher levels in the body, but are still required by the body. Other elements such as tin and nickel are thought to be essential, but their metabolic role has not yet been determined. Some examples and the amounts present in a 60-kg person are listed in Table 3.4.

TABLE 3.4 Typical Amounts of Essential Elements in a 60-kg Adult

Element	Quantity	Function
Major Elements		
Oxygen (O)	39 kg	Building block of biomolecules and water (H_2O)
Carbon (C)	11 kg	Building block of organic molecules and biomolecules
Hydrogen (H)	6 kg	Component of biomolecules, water (H_2O), and pH of body fluids, stomach acid (HCl)
Nitrogen (N)	1.5 kg	Component of proteins and nucleic acids
Macrominerals		
Calcium (Ca)	1000 g	Needed for bone and teeth, muscle contraction, nerve impulses
Phosphorus (P)	600 g	Needed for bone and teeth, nucleic acids, ATP
Potassium (K)	120 g	Most abundant positive ion (K^+) in cells, muscle contraction, nerve impulses
Chlorine (Cl)	100 g	Most abundant negative ion (Cl^-) in fluids outside cells, stomach acid (HCl)
Sulfur (S)	86 g	Component of proteins, liver, vitamin B_1, insulin
Sodium (Na)	60 g	Most abundant positive ion (Na^+) in fluids outside cells, water balance, functions in muscle contraction, nerve impulses
Magnesium (Mg)	36 g	Component of bone, required for metabolic reactions
Microminerals (trace elements)		
Iron (Fe)	3600 mg	Component of oxygen carrier hemoglobin
Silicon (Si)	3000 mg	Needed for growth and maintenance of bone and teeth, tendons and ligaments, hair and skin
Zinc (Zn)	2000 mg	Used in metabolic reactions in cells, DNA synthesis, growth of bone, teeth, connective tissue, immune system
Copper (Cu)	240 mg	Needed for blood vessels, blood pressure, immune system
Manganese (Mn)	60 mg	Needed for bone growth, blood clotting, necessary for metabolic reactions
Iodine (I)	20 mg	Needed for proper thyroid function
Molybdenum (Mo)	12 mg	Needed to process Fe and N from diets
Arsenic (As)	3 mg	Needed for growth and reproduction
Chromium (Cr)	3 mg	Needed for maintenance of blood sugar levels, synthesis of biomolecules
Cobalt (Co)	3 mg	Component of vitamin B_{12}, red blood cells
Selenium (Se)	2 mg	Used in the immune system, health of heart and pancreas
Vanadium (V)	2 mg	Needed in the formation of bone and teeth, energy from food

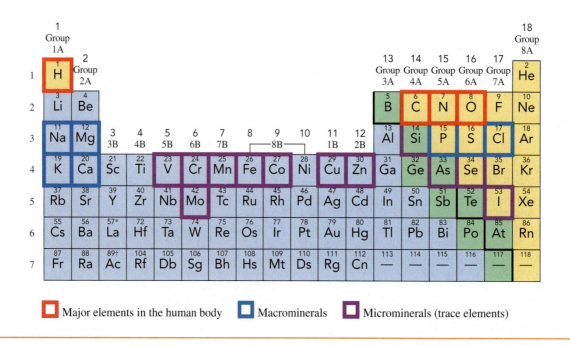

QUESTIONS AND PROBLEMS

3.2 The Periodic Table

LEARNING GOAL: *Use the periodic table to identify the group and the period of an element; identify the element as a metal, nonmetal, or metalloid.*

3.7 Identify the period or group number described by each of the following:
   a. contains the elements C, N, and O
   b. begins with helium
   c. contains the alkali metals
   d. ends with neon

3.8 Identify the period or group number described by each of the following:
   a. contains Na, K, and Rb
   b. the row that begins with Li
   c. the noble gases
   d. contains F, Cl, Br, and I

3.9 Classify each of the following as an alkali metal, alkaline earth metal, transition element, halogen, or noble gas:
   a. Ca   **b.** Fe   **c.** Xe
   d. K   **e.** Cl

3.10 Classify each of the following as an alkali metal, alkaline earth metal, transition element, halogen, or noble gas:
   a. Ne   **b.** Mg   **c.** Cu
   d. Br   **e.** Cs

3.11 Give the symbol of the element described by each of the following:
   a. Group 4A (14), Period 2
   b. a noble gas in Period 1
   c. an alkali metal in Period 3
   d. Group 2A (2), Period 4
   e. Group 3A (13), Period 3

3.12 Give the symbol of the element described by each of the following:
   a. an alkaline earth metal in Period 2
   b. Group 5A (15), Period 3
   c. a noble gas in Period 4
   d. a halogen in Period 5
   e. Group 4A (14), Period 4

3.13 Is each of the following elements a metal, nonmetal, or metalloid?
   a. calcium
   b. sulfur
   c. a shiny element
   d. an element that is a gas at room temperature
   e. located in Group 8A (18)
   f. bromine
   g. tellurium
   h. silver

3.14 Is each of the following elements a metal, nonmetal, or metalloid?
   a. located in Group 2A (2)
   b. a good conductor of electricity
   c. chlorine
   d. silicon
   e. an element that is not shiny
   f. oxygen
   g. nitrogen
   h. tin

3.3 The Atom

All the elements listed in the periodic table are made up of atoms. In Section 2.3, we described an **atom** as the smallest particle of an element. Imagine that you are dividing a piece of aluminum foil into smaller and smaller pieces. Now imagine that you have a piece so small that you cannot divide it further. Then you would have a single atom of aluminum.

LEARNING GOAL

Describe the electrical charge and location in an atom for a proton, a neutron, and an electron.

SELF-STUDY ACTIVITY
Atoms and Isotopes

TUTORIAL
The Anatomy of Atoms

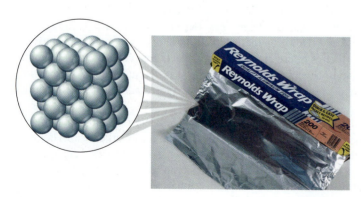

Aluminum foil consists of atoms of aluminum.

The concept of the atom is relatively recent. Although the Greek philosophers in 500 B.C.E. reasoned that everything must contain minute particles they called *atomos*, the idea of atoms did not become a scientific theory until 1808. Then John Dalton

(1766–1844) developed an atomic theory that proposed that atoms were responsible for the combinations of elements found in compounds.

Dalton's Atomic Theory

1. All matter is made up of tiny particles called atoms.
2. All atoms of a given element are similar to one another and different from atoms of other elements.
3. Atoms of two or more different elements combine to form compounds. A particular compound is always made up of the same kinds of atoms and always has the same number of each kind of atom.
4. A chemical reaction involves the rearrangement, separation, or combination of atoms. Atoms are never created or destroyed during a chemical reaction.

Dalton's atomic theory formed the basis of current atomic theory, although we have modified some of Dalton's statements. We now know that atoms of the same element are not completely identical to each other and consist of even smaller particles. However, an atom is still the smallest particle of any element.

Although atoms are the building blocks of everything we see around us, we cannot see an atom or even a billion atoms with the naked eye. However, when billions and billions of atoms are packed together, the characteristics of each atom are added to those of the next until we can see the characteristics we associate with the element. For example, a small piece of the shiny element nickel consists of many, many nickel atoms. A special kind of microscope called a *scanning tunneling microscope* (STM) produces images of individual atoms (see Figure 3.7).

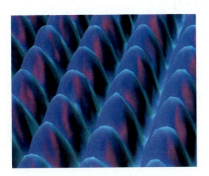

FIGURE 3.7 Images of nickel atoms are produced when nickel is magnified millions of times by a scanning tunneling microscope (STM). This instrument generates an image of the atomic structure.

Q Why is a microscope with extremely high magnification needed to see these atoms?

Electrical Charges in an Atom

By the end of the 1800s, experiments with electricity showed that atoms were not solid spheres, but were composed of even smaller bits of matter called **subatomic particles**, three of which are the proton, electron, and neutron. Some of these subatomic particles were discovered because they have electrical charges.

An electrical charge can be positive or negative. Experiments show that like charges repel, or push away from each other. When you brush your hair on a dry day, electrical charges that are alike build up on the brush and in your hair. As a result, your hair flies away from the brush. Opposite or unlike charges attract. The crackle of clothes taken from the clothes dryer indicates the presence of electrical charges. The clinginess of the clothing results from the attraction of opposite, unlike charges, as shown in Figure 3.8.

Positive charges repel

Negative charges repel

Unlike charges attract

FIGURE 3.8 Like charges repel, and unlike charges attract.

Q Why are electrons attracted to the protons in the nucleus of an atom?

Structure of the Atom

In 1897, J. J. Thomson, an English physicist, applied electricity to a glass tube and produced streams of small particles called *cathode rays*. Because these rays were attracted to a positively charged electrode, Thomson realized that these particles must be negatively charged. In further experiments, these particles called **electrons** were found to be much smaller than the atom and to have an extremely small mass. Because atoms are neutral, scientists soon discovered that atoms contain positively charged particles called **protons** that are much heavier than the electrons.

Thomson proposed a model for the atom in which the electrons and protons were randomly distributed through the atom. In 1911, Ernest Rutherford worked with Thomson to test this model. In Rutherford's experiment, positively charged particles were aimed at a thin sheet of gold foil (see Figure 3.9). If the Thomson model was correct, the particles would travel in straight paths through the gold foil. Rutherford was greatly surprised to find that some of the particles were deflected slightly as they passed through the gold foil, and a few particles were deflected so much that they went back in the opposite direction. According to Rutherford, it was as though he had shot a cannonball at a piece of tissue paper, and it bounced back at him.

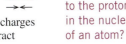

Positive electrode

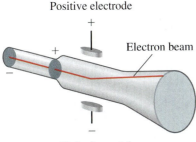

Electron beam

Cathode ray tube

Negatively charged cathode rays (electrons) are attracted to the positive electrode.

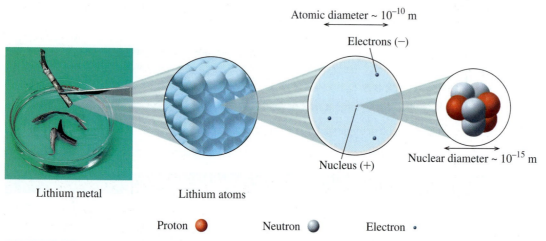

(a)   **(b)**

FIGURE 3.9 **(a)** Positive particles are aimed at a piece of gold foil. **(b)** Particles that come close to the atomic nuclei of gold are deflected from their straight path.

Q Why are some particles deflected while most pass through the gold foil undeflected?

From his gold-foil experiments, Rutherford realized that the protons must be contained in a small, positively charged region at the center of the atom, which he called the **nucleus**. He proposed that the electrons in the atom occupy the space surrounding the nucleus through which most of the particles traveled undisturbed. Only the particles that came near this dense, positive center within the gold atoms were deflected. If an atom were the size of a football stadium, the nucleus would be about the size of a golf ball placed in the center of the field.

Scientists knew that the nucleus was heavier than the mass of the protons and looked for another subatomic particle. Eventually, James Chadwick, in 1932, discovered that the nucleus also contained a particle called a **neutron**, which is neutral. Thus, the masses of the protons and neutrons in the nucleus determine its mass (see Figure 3.10).

FIGURE 3.10 In an atom, the protons and neutrons that make up almost all the mass of the atom are packed into the tiny volume of the nucleus. The rapidly moving electrons surround the nucleus and account for the large volume of the atom.

Q Why can we say that an atom is mostly empty space?

Mass of the Atom

All the subatomic particles are extremely small compared with the things you see around you. One proton has a mass of 1.7×10^{-24} g, and the neutron is about the same. The mass of the electron is 9.1×10^{-28} g, which is about 1/2000th of the mass of either a proton or a neutron. Because the masses of subatomic particles are so small, chemists use a unit called an **atomic mass unit (amu)**. An amu is defined as one-twelfth of the mass of the carbon atom with six protons and six neutrons, a standard with which the mass of every other atom is compared. In biology, the atomic mass unit is called a *Dalton* (Da) in honor of

TUTORIAL
Atomic Structure and Properties
of Subatomic Particles

John Dalton. On the amu scale, the proton and neutron each have a mass of about 1 amu. Because the electron mass is so small, it is usually ignored in atomic mass calculations. Table 3.5 summarizes some information about the subatomic particles in an atom.

TABLE 3.5 Particles in the Atom

Subatomic Particle	Symbol	Electrical Charge	Mass (amu)	Location in Atom
Proton	p or p^+	1+	1.007	Nucleus
Neutron	n or n^0	0	1.008	Nucleus
Electron	e^-	1−	0.000 55	Outside nucleus

CONCEPT CHECK 3.2 Subatomic Particles

Is each of the following statements *true* or *false*? If false, explain your reason.

a. Protons are heavier than electrons.
b. Protons are attracted to neutrons.
c. Electrons are so small that they have no electrical charge.
d. The nucleus contains all the protons and neutrons of an atom.

ANSWER

a. True
b. False; protons are attracted to electrons.
c. False; electrons have a 1− charge.
d. True

SAMPLE PROBLEM 3.5 Identifying Subatomic Particles

Identify the subatomic particle that has the following characteristics:

a. no charge
b. a mass of 0.000 55 amu
c. a mass about the same as a neutron

SOLUTION

a. neutron   b. electron   c. proton

STUDY CHECK 3.5

Is the following statement *true* or *false*?

The nucleus occupies a large volume in an atom.

QUESTIONS AND PROBLEMS

3.3 The Atom

LEARNING GOAL: *Describe the electrical charge and location in an atom for a proton, a neutron, and an electron.*

3.15 Identify each of the following as describing a proton, a neutron, or an electron:
  a. has the smallest mass
  b. has a 1+ charge
  c. is found outside the nucleus
  d. is electrically neutral

3.16 Identify each of the following as describing a proton, a neutron, or an electron:
  a. has a mass about the same as a proton
  b. is found in the nucleus
  c. is attracted to the protons
  d. has a 1− charge

3.17 Is each of the following statements *true* or *false*?
  a. A proton and an electron have opposite charges.
  b. The nucleus contains most of the mass of an atom.
  c. Electrons repel each other.
  d. A proton is attracted to a neutron.

3.18 Is each of the following statements *true* or *false*?
  a. A proton is attracted to an electron.
  b. A neutron has twice the mass of a proton.
  c. Neutrons repel each other.
  d. Electrons and neutrons have opposite charges.

3.19 How did Thomson determine that the electrons have a negative charge?

3.20 What did Rutherford determine about the structure of the atom from his gold-foil experiment?

3.4 Atomic Number and Mass Number

All of the atoms of the same element always have the same number of protons. This feature distinguishes atoms of one element from atoms of all the other elements.

Atomic Number

The **atomic number** of an element is equal to the number of protons in every atom of that element. The atomic number is the whole number that appears above the symbol of each element on the periodic table.

    Atomic number = number of protons in an atom

The periodic table on the inside front cover of this text shows the elements in order of atomic number from 1 to 118. We can use an atomic number to identify the number of protons in an atom of any element. For example, a lithium atom, with atomic number 3, has 3 protons. Every lithium atom has 3 and only 3 protons. Any atom with 3 protons is always a lithium atom. In the same way, we determine that a carbon atom, with atomic number 6, has 6 protons. Every carbon atom has 6 protons and any atom with 6 protons is carbon.

An atom is electrically neutral. That means that the number of protons in an atom is equal to the number of electrons, which gives every atom an overall electrical charge of zero. Thus, for any atom, the atomic number also gives the number of electrons.

LEARNING GOAL

Given the atomic number and the mass number of an atom, state the number of protons, neutrons, and electrons.

TUTORIAL
Atomic Number and Mass Number

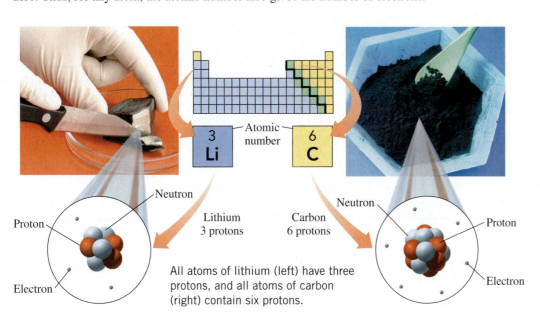

All atoms of lithium (left) have three protons, and all atoms of carbon (right) contain six protons.

SAMPLE PROBLEM 3.6   **Atomic Number, Protons, and Electrons**

Using the periodic table, state the atomic number, number of protons, and number of electrons for an atom of each of the following elements:

a. nitrogen   **b.** magnesium   **c.** bromine

SOLUTION

a. atomic number 7; 7 protons and 7 electrons
b. atomic number 12; 12 protons and 12 electrons
c. atomic number 35; 35 protons and 35 electrons

STUDY CHECK 3.6

Consider an atom that has 79 electrons.

a. How many protons are in its nucleus?
b. What is its atomic number?
c. What is its name, and what is its symbol?

Career Focus

OPTICIAN

Opticians fit and adjust eyewear for patients who have had their eyesight tested by an ophthalmologist or optometrist. Optics and mathematics are used to select materials for frames and lenses that are compatible with patients' facial measurements and lifestyles.

Mass Number

We now know that protons and neutrons determine the mass of any nucleus. Thus, a **mass number** is written for any single atom, which is the total number of protons and neutrons in its nucleus. However, the mass number of a single atom does not appear on the periodic table.

$$\text{Mass number} = \text{number of protons} + \text{number of neutrons in a nucleus}$$

For example, the nucleus of a single oxygen atom that contains 8 protons and 8 neutrons has a mass number of 16. If the nucleus of a single iron atom contains 26 protons and 32 neutrons, it would have a mass number of 58.

If we are given the mass number of an atom and its atomic number, we can calculate the number of neutrons in its nucleus.

$$\text{Number of neutrons in a nucleus} = \text{mass number} - \text{number of protons}$$

For example, if we are given a mass number of 37 for an atom of chlorine (atomic number 17), we can calculate the number of neutrons in its nucleus.

$$\text{Number of neutrons} = 37 \text{ (mass number)} - 17 \text{ (protons)} = 20 \text{ neutrons}$$

Table 3.6 illustrates these relationships between atomic number, mass number, and the number of protons, neutrons, and electrons in examples of single atoms for different elements.

TABLE 3.6 Composition of Some Atoms of Different Elements

Element	Symbol	Atomic Number	Mass Number	Number of Protons	Number of Neutrons	Number of Electrons
Hydrogen	H	1	1	1	0	1
Nitrogen	N	7	14	7	7	7
Oxygen	O	8	16	8	8	8
Chlorine	Cl	17	37	17	20	17
Iron	Fe	26	58	26	32	26
Gold	Au	79	197	79	118	79

CONCEPT CHECK 3.3 Subatomic Particles in Atoms

An atom of silver has a mass number of 109.

a. How many protons are in the nucleus?
b. How many neutrons are in the nucleus?
c. How many electrons are in the atom?

ANSWER

a. Silver (Ag), with atomic number 47, has 47 protons.
b. The number of neutrons is calculated by subtracting the number of protons from the mass number.

$$109 - 47 = 62 \text{ neutrons for an atom of Ag with a mass number of 109.}$$

c. In a neutral atom, the number of electrons is equal to the number of protons. An atom of silver with 47 protons has 47 electrons.

SAMPLE PROBLEM 3.7 Calculating Numbers of Protons, Neutrons, and Electrons

For an atom of zinc that has a mass number of 68, determine the following:

a. the number of protons
b. the number of neutrons
c. the number of electrons

SOLUTION

Analyze the Problem

Element	Atomic Number	Number of Protons	Mass Number	Number of Neutrons	Number of Electrons
Zinc (Zn)	30	Equal to atomic number	68	Mass number – number of protons	Equal to number of protons

a. Zinc (Zn), with an atomic number of 30, has 30 protons.

b. The number of neutrons in this zinc atom is found by subtracting the number of protons (atomic number) from the mass number.

Mass number − atomic number = number of neutrons

68 − 30 = 38

c. Because the zinc atom is neutral, the number of electrons is equal to the number of protons. A zinc atom has 30 electrons.

STUDY CHECK 3.7

How many neutrons are in the nucleus of a bromine atom that has a mass number of 80?

QUESTIONS AND PROBLEMS

3.4 Atomic Number and Mass Number

LEARNING GOAL: Given the atomic number and the mass number of an atom, state the number of protons, neutrons, and electrons.

3.21 Would you use atomic number, mass number, or both to obtain the following?
a. number of protons in an atom
b. number of neutrons in an atom
c. number of particles in the nucleus
d. number of electrons in a neutral atom

3.22 What do you know about the subatomic particles from the following?
a. atomic number **b.** mass number
c. mass number − atomic number
d. mass number + atomic number

3.23 Write the names and symbols of the elements with the following atomic numbers:
a. 3 **b.** 9 **c.** 20 **d.** 30
e. 10 **f.** 14 **g.** 53 **h.** 8

3.24 Write the names and symbols of the elements with the following atomic numbers:
a. 1 **b.** 11 **c.** 19 **d.** 82
e. 35 **f.** 47 **g.** 15 **h.** 2

3.25 How many protons and electrons are there in a neutral atom of the following?
a. argon **b.** zinc
c. iodine **d.** cadmium

3.26 How many protons and electrons are there in a neutral atom of the following?
a. carbon **b.** fluorine
c. tin **d.** nickel

3.27 Complete the following table for each neutral atom:

Name of the Element	Symbol	Atomic Number	Mass Number	Number of Protons	Number of Neutrons	Number of Electrons
	Al		27			
		12			12	
Potassium					20	
				16	15	
			56			26

3.28 Complete the following table for each neutral atom:

Name of the Element	Symbol	Atomic Number	Mass Number	Number of Protons	Number of Neutrons	Number of Electrons
	N		15			
Calcium			42			
				38	50	
		14			16	
		56	138			

3.5 Isotopes and Atomic Mass

We have seen that all atoms of the same element have the same number of protons and electrons. Although Dalton could not know it at the time, scientists eventually discovered in 1913 that atoms of any one element are not entirely identical because the atoms of most elements have different numbers of neutrons. When a sample of an element consists of

LEARNING GOAL

Give the number of protons, neutrons, and electrons in one or more of the isotopes of an element; calculate the atomic mass of an element using the abundance and mass of its naturally occurring isotopes.

SELF-STUDY ACTIVITY
Atoms and Isotopes

TUTORIAL
Isotopes

two or more atoms with differing numbers of neutrons, those atoms are called *isotopes*. In Section 4.1, we will see that some isotopes of an element are stable, whereas others are radioactive, breaking down and emitting radiation particles.

Isotopes

Isotopes are atoms of the same element that have the same atomic number but different numbers of neutrons. For example, all atoms of the element magnesium (Mg) have an atomic number of 12. Thus every magnesium atom always has 12 protons. However, some of the magnesium atoms have 12 neutrons, others have 13 neutrons, and still others have 14 neutrons. These different numbers of neutrons give the magnesium atoms different mass numbers but do not change their chemical behavior.

To distinguish between the different isotopes of an element, we write an **atomic symbol** for a particular isotope with its mass number in the upper left corner and its atomic number in the lower left corner.

Mass number — Symbol of element

$^{24}_{12}\text{Mg}$

Atomic number

Atomic symbol for an isotope of magnesium, Mg-24.

An isotope may be referred to by its name or symbol, followed by the mass number, such as magnesium-24 or Mg-24. Magnesium has three naturally occurring isotopes, as shown in Table 3.7.

TABLE 3.7 Isotopes of Magnesium

Atomic Symbol	$^{24}_{12}\text{Mg}$	$^{25}_{12}\text{Mg}$	$^{26}_{12}\text{Mg}$
Name	Mg-24	Mg-25	Mg-26
Number of Protons	12	12	12
Number of Electrons	12	12	12
Mass Number	**24**	**25**	**26**
Number of Neutrons	**12**	**13**	**14**
Mass of Isotope (amu)	23.99	24.99	25.98
% Abundance	78.70	10.13	11.17

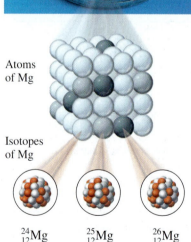

Atoms of Mg

Isotopes of Mg

$^{24}_{12}\text{Mg}$ $^{25}_{12}\text{Mg}$ $^{26}_{12}\text{Mg}$

The nuclei of the three naturally occurring magnesium isotopes have the same number of protons, but different numbers of neutrons.

SAMPLE PROBLEM 3.8 Identifying Protons and Neutrons in Isotopes

The element neon has three naturally occurring stable isotopes: Ne-20, Ne-21, and Ne-22. State the number of protons and neutrons in the stable isotopes of neon (Ne):

a. $^{20}_{10}\text{Ne}$ **b.** $^{21}_{10}\text{Ne}$ **c.** $^{22}_{10}\text{Ne}$

SOLUTION

The atomic number of Ne is 10, which means that each isotope has 10 protons. The number of neutrons in each isotope is found by subtracting the number of protons (10) from each of their mass numbers.

a. 10 protons; 10 neutrons $(20 - 10)$
b. 10 protons; 11 neutrons $(21 - 10)$
c. 10 protons; 12 neutrons $(22 - 10)$

STUDY CHECK 3.8

Write an atomic symbol for each of the following isotopes:

a. a nitrogen atom with 8 neutrons
b. an atom with 35 protons and 46 neutrons
c. an atom with mass number 27 and 13 neutrons

Atomic Mass

In laboratory work, a chemist generally uses samples with many atoms that contain all the different isotopes of an element. Because each kind of isotope has a different mass, chemists have calculated an **atomic mass** for an "average atom," which is a *weighted average* of the masses of all the naturally occurring isotopes of that element. On the periodic table, the atomic mass is the number including decimal places that is shown below the symbol of each element. Most of the elements consist of two or more isotopes, which is one reason why atomic masses on the periodic table are seldom whole numbers.

Calculating Atomic Mass Using Isotopes

To calculate the atomic mass of an element, we need to know the percent abundance of each isotope and its mass, which are determined experimentally. For example, a large sample of naturally occurring chlorine consists of 75.76% of $^{35}_{17}Cl$ atoms and 24.24% of $^{37}_{17}Cl$ atoms. The atomic mass is a *weighted average* because it is calculated from the percent abundance of each isotope and its mass: the isotope $^{35}_{17}Cl$ has a mass of 34.97 amu, and the isotope $^{37}_{17}Cl$ has a mass of 36.97 amu.

$$\text{Atomic mass of Cl} = \text{mass of } ^{35}_{17}Cl \times \underbrace{\frac{^{35}_{17}Cl\%}{100\%}}_{\text{mass from } ^{35}_{17}Cl} + \text{mass of } ^{37}_{17}Cl \times \underbrace{\frac{^{37}_{17}Cl\%}{100\%}}_{\text{mass from } ^{37}_{17}Cl}$$

Isotope	Mass (amu)		Abundance (%)		Contribution to Average Cl Atom
$^{35}_{17}Cl$	34.97	×	$\dfrac{75.76}{100}$	=	26.49 amu
$^{37}_{17}Cl$	36.97	×	$\dfrac{24.24}{100}$	=	8.962 amu
			Atomic mass of Cl	=	35.45 amu (weighted average mass)

The atomic mass of 35.45 amu is the weighted average mass of a sample of Cl atoms, although no individual Cl atom actually has this mass. An atomic mass of 35.45, which is closer to the mass number of Cl-35, indicates there is a higher percentage of $^{35}_{17}Cl$ atoms in the chlorine sample. In fact, there are about three atoms of $^{35}_{17}Cl$ for every one atom of $^{37}_{17}Cl$ in a sample of chlorine atoms.

Table 3.8 lists the naturally occurring isotopes of selected elements, their atomic mass, and their most prevalent isotope.

TABLE 3.8	The Atomic Mass of Some Elements		
Element	**Stable Isotopes**	**Atomic Mass (weighted average)**	**Most Prevalent Isotope**
Lithium	$^{6}_{3}Li$, $^{7}_{3}Li$	6.941 amu	$^{7}_{3}Li$
Carbon	$^{12}_{6}C$, $^{13}_{6}C$, $^{14}_{6}C$	12.01 amu	$^{12}_{6}C$
Oxygen	$^{16}_{8}O$, $^{17}_{8}O$, $^{18}_{8}O$	16.00 amu	$^{16}_{8}O$
Fluorine	$^{19}_{9}F$	19.00 amu	$^{19}_{9}F$
Sulfur	$^{32}_{16}S$, $^{33}_{16}S$, $^{34}_{16}S$, $^{36}_{16}S$	32.07 amu	$^{32}_{16}S$
Copper	$^{63}_{29}Cu$, $^{65}_{29}Cu$	63.55 amu	$^{63}_{29}Cu$

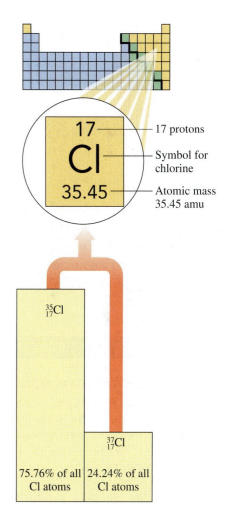

17 — 17 protons

Cl — Symbol for chlorine

35.45 — Atomic mass 35.45 amu

$^{35}_{17}Cl$

$^{37}_{17}Cl$

75.76% of all Cl atoms | 24.24% of all Cl atoms

Chlorine, with two naturally occurring isotopes, has an atomic mass of 35.45 amu.

TUTORIAL
Atomic Mass Calculations

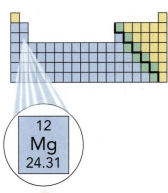

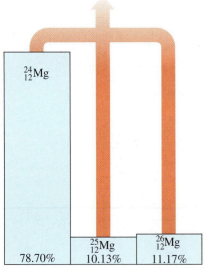

$^{24}_{12}\text{Mg}$ 78.70% $^{25}_{12}\text{Mg}$ 10.13% $^{26}_{12}\text{Mg}$ 11.17%

Magnesium, with three naturally occuring isotopes, has an atomic mass of 24.31 amu.

CONCEPT CHECK 3.4 **Average Atomic Mass**

Neon consists of three naturally occurring isotopes: $^{20}_{10}\text{Ne}$, $^{21}_{10}\text{Ne}$, and $^{22}_{10}\text{Ne}$. Using the atomic mass on the periodic table, which isotope of neon is likely to be the most prevalent?

ANSWER

Using the periodic table, we find that the atomic mass for all the naturally occurring isotopes of neon is 20.18 amu. Since this number is very close to the mass number of 20, the isotope Ne-20 is the most prevalent isotope in a naturally occurring sample of neon atoms.

SAMPLE PROBLEM 3.9 **Calculating Atomic Mass**

Using Table 3.7, calculate the atomic mass for magnesium.

SOLUTION

Isotope	Mass (amu)	Abundance (%)		Contribution to the Atomic Mass
$^{24}_{12}\text{Mg}$	23.99	$\times$ $\dfrac{78.70}{100}$	=	18.88 amu
$^{25}_{12}\text{Mg}$	24.99	$\times$ $\dfrac{10.13}{100}$	=	2.531 amu
$^{26}_{12}\text{Mg}$	25.98	$\times$ $\dfrac{11.17}{100}$	=	2.902 amu
		Atomic mass of Mg	=	24.31 amu (weighted average mass)

STUDY CHECK 3.9

There are two naturally occurring isotopes of boron. The isotope $^{10}_{5}\text{B}$ has a mass of 10.01 amu with an abundance of 19.80%, and the isotope $^{11}_{5}\text{B}$ has a mass of 11.01 amu with an abundance of 80.20%. What is the atomic mass of boron?

QUESTIONS AND PROBLEMS

3.5 Isotopes and Atomic Mass

LEARNING GOAL: *Give the number of protons, neutrons, and electrons in one or more of the isotopes of an element; calculate the atomic mass of an element using the abundance and mass of its naturally occurring isotopes.*

3.29 What are the number of protons, neutrons, and electrons in the following isotopes?
a. $^{89}_{38}\text{Sr}$ **b.** $^{52}_{24}\text{Cr}$ **c.** $^{34}_{16}\text{S}$ **d.** $^{81}_{35}\text{Br}$

3.30 What are the number of protons, neutrons, and electrons in the following isotopes?
a. $^{2}_{1}\text{H}$ **b.** $^{14}_{7}\text{N}$ **c.** $^{26}_{14}\text{Si}$ **d.** $^{70}_{30}\text{Zn}$

3.31 Write the atomic symbols for isotopes with the following:
a. 15 protons and 16 neutrons
b. 35 protons and 45 neutrons
c. 50 electrons and 72 neutrons
d. a chlorine atom with 18 neutrons
e. a mercury atom with 122 neutrons

3.32 Write the atomic symbols for isotopes with the following:
a. an oxygen atom with 10 neutrons
b. 4 protons and 5 neutrons

c. 25 electrons and 28 neutrons
d. a mass number of 24 and 13 neutrons
e. a nickel atom with 32 neutrons

3.33 Argon has three naturally occurring isotopes, with mass numbers 36, 38, and 40.
a. Write the atomic symbol for each of these atoms.
b. How are these isotopes alike?
c. How are they different?
d. Why is the atomic mass of argon on the periodic table not a whole number?
e. Which isotope is most prevalent in a sample of argon?

3.34 Strontium has four naturally occurring isotopes, with mass numbers 84, 86, 87, and 88.
a. Write the atomic symbol for each of these atoms.
b. How are these isotopes alike?
c. How are they different?
d. Why is the atomic mass of strontium on the periodic table not a whole number?
e. Which isotope is the most prevalent in a sample of strontium?

3.35 Two isotopes of gallium are naturally occurring. The isotope $^{69}_{31}$Ga has a percent abundance of 60.11% and a mass of 68.93 amu, and the isotope $^{71}_{31}$Ga has a percent abundance of 39.89% and a mass of 70.92 amu. Calculate the atomic mass of gallium.

3.36 Two isotopes of copper are naturally occurring. The isotope $^{63}_{29}$Cu has a percent abundance of 69.09% and a mass of 62.93 amu, and the isotope $^{65}_{29}$Cu has a percent abundance of 30.91% and a mass of 64.93 amu. Calculate the atomic mass of copper.

3.6 Electron Arrangement in Atoms

We have seen that the protons and neutrons are contained in the small, dense nucleus of an atom. However, it is the electrons within the atoms that determine the physical and chemical properties of the elements. Therefore, we need to understand how electrons are arranged within the large volume of space surrounding the nucleus.

LEARNING GOAL

Describe the energy levels, sublevels, and orbitals for the electrons in an atom.

Electron Energy Levels

Scientists have now determined that every electron occupies an **energy level**, which has a specific energy. Each energy level has a *principal quantum number* (n), starting with the lowest energy level $n = 1$ up to the highest energy level $n = 7$.

Electrons in the lower energy levels are usually closer to the nucleus, while electrons in the higher energy levels are farther away. As an analogy, we can think of the energy levels of an atom as similar to the shelves in a bookcase (see Figure 3.11). The first shelf is the lowest energy level; the second shelf would be the second energy level. If we are arranging books on the shelves, it would take less energy to fill the bottom shelf first, and then the second shelf, and so on. However, we could never put a book in the space between any of the shelves. Similarly, an electron must be at one of the specific energy levels, and not between them.

Unlike bookcases, there is a large difference between the energy of the first and second energy levels, but then the higher levels are closer together. Another difference is that the higher electron energy levels hold more electrons than the lower energy levels.

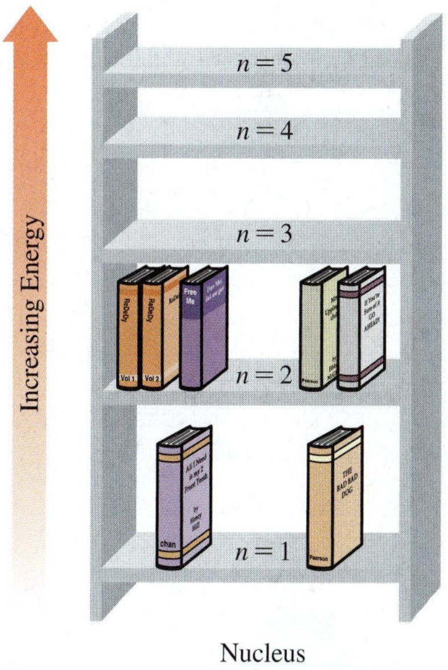

FIGURE 3.11 An electron can have the energy of only one of the energy levels in an atom.

Q Does an electron in $n = 3$ have less or greater energy than an electron in $n = 1$?

Electron Sublevels

Each of the energy levels consists of one or more **sublevels**, in which electrons with identical energy are found. The sublevels are identified by the letters s, p, d, and f. The number of sublevels within each energy level is equal to its principal quantum number, n (see Figure 3.12). For example, the first energy level ($n = 1$) has one sublevel, $1s$. The second energy level ($n = 2$) has two sublevels, $2s$ and $2p$. The third energy level ($n = 3$) has three sublevels, $3s$, $3p$, and $3d$. The fourth energy level ($n = 4$) has four sublevels: $4s$, $4p$, $4d$, and $4f$. Energy levels $n = 5$, $n = 6$, and $n = 7$ also have as many sublevels as the value of n, but only s, p, d, and f sublevels are utilized to hold the electrons of atoms of the 118 elements known today. Within each energy level, the s sublevel has the lowest energy, the p sublevel has the next lowest energy, then the d sublevel, and finally the f sublevel.

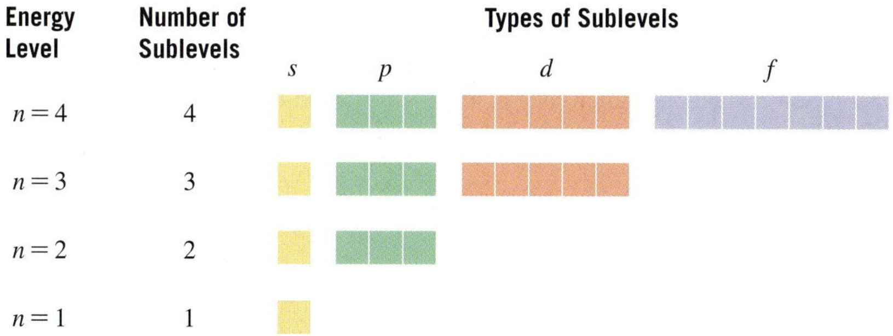

Energy Level	Number of Sublevels	Types of Sublevels
$n = 4$	4	s p d f
$n = 3$	3	s p d
$n = 2$	2	s p
$n = 1$	1	s

FIGURE 3.12 The number of sublevels in an energy level is the same as the principal quantum number n.

Q How many sublevels are in energy level $n = 5$?

Chemistry Link to the Environment

ENERGY-SAVING FLUORESCENT BULBS

The compact fluorescent light (CFL) is replacing the standard light-bulb we use in our homes and workplaces. Compared to a standard lightbulb, the CFL has a longer life and uses less electricity. Within about 20 days of use, the fluorescent bulb saves enough money in electricity costs to pay for its higher initial cost.

A standard incandescent lightbulb has a thin tungsten filament inside a sealed glass bulb. When the light is switched on, electricity flows through this filament, and electrical energy is converted to heat energy. When the filament reaches a temperature around 2300 °C, we see white light.

A fluorescent bulb produces light in a different way. When the switch is turned on, electrons move between two electrodes and collide with mercury atoms in a mixture of mercury and argon gas inside the bulb. When the electrons in the mercury atoms absorb energy from the collisions, electrons are raised to higher energy levels. As electrons fall to lower levels, energy is emitted that leads to the emission of visible light (fluorescence) by the phosphor coating inside the tube.

The production of light in a fluorescent bulb is more efficient than in an incandescent lightbulb. A 75-watt incandescent bulb can be replaced by a 20-watt CFL that gives the same amount of light, providing a 70% reduction in electricity costs. A typical incandescent lightbulb lasts for one to two months, whereas a CFL lasts from one to two years. One drawback of the CFL is that each contains about 4 mg of mercury. As long as the bulb stays intact, no mercury is released. However, used CFL bulbs should not be disposed of in household trash, but should be taken to a recycling center.

A compact fluorescent light (CFL) uses up to 70% less energy.

Orbitals

Imagine that you could draw a circle with a 100-m radius around your chemistry classroom. There is a high probability of finding you within that circle when your chemistry class is in session. But once in a while, you may be found outside that circle because you were sick or your car did not start. In a similar way, we do not know the exact location of an electron in an atom at any given time. However, we can describe a three-dimensional space called an **orbital** in which there is a high probability of finding an electron.

Each type of orbital has a unique three-dimensional shape. Electrons in s orbitals are most likely found in a region with a spherical shape. Imagine that you take a picture of the electron in an s orbital every second for an hour. When all these photos are overlaid, the result would look like the electron cloud shown in Figure 3.13a. For convenience, we draw this type of electron cloud as a sphere called an s orbital. There is one s orbital for every energy level starting with $n = 1$. For example, in the first, second, and third energy levels, there are s orbitals designated as $1s$, $2s$, and $3s$. As the principal quantum number increases, there is an increase in the size of the s orbitals (see Figure 3.13b). For all energy levels, a single orbital can hold up to two electrons, which allows an s orbital in any energy level to hold two electrons.

The orbitals occupied by p, d, and f electrons have different three-dimensional shapes than that of the s electrons. There are three p orbitals in each sublevel, starting with $n = 2$. Each p orbital has two lobes like a balloon tied in the middle. The three p orbitals in each p sublevel are arranged along the x, y, and z axes around the nucleus (see Figure 3.14). As with the s orbital, each p orbital can hold two electrons, which means that three p orbitals can hold up to six electrons. At higher energy levels, the shape of p orbitals is the same, but their volume increases.

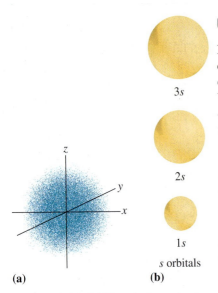

(a)   **(b)**

FIGURE 3.13 **(a)** The electron cloud of an s orbital represents the highest probability of finding an s electron. **(b)** The s orbitals are shown as spheres. The sizes of the s orbitals increase because they contain electrons at higher energy levels.

Q Is the probability high or low of finding an s electron outside an s orbital?

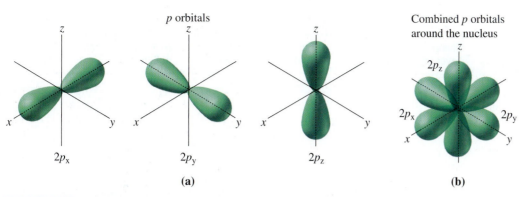

(a)   **(b)**

FIGURE 3.14 A *p* orbital has two regions of high probability, which gives a "dumb-bell" shape. **(a)** Each of the *p* orbitals is aligned along a different axis from other *p* orbitals. **(b)** All three *p* orbitals are shown around the nucleus.

Q What is the maximum number of electrons possible in a *p* sublevel?

In summary, energy level $n = 2$, which has 2*s* and 2*p* sublevels, contains one *s* orbital and three *p* orbitals. Thus, the $n = 2$ energy level can hold a maximum of eight electrons.

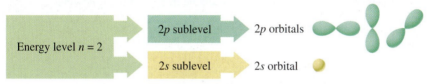

Energy level $n = 2$ is made up of one 2*s* orbital and three 2*p* orbitals.

Energy level $n = 3$ consists of three sublevels *s*, *p*, and *d*. A *d* sublevel consists of five *d* orbitals. Because each *d* orbital can hold two electrons, a *d* sublevel can have a maximum of ten electrons (see Figure 3.15).

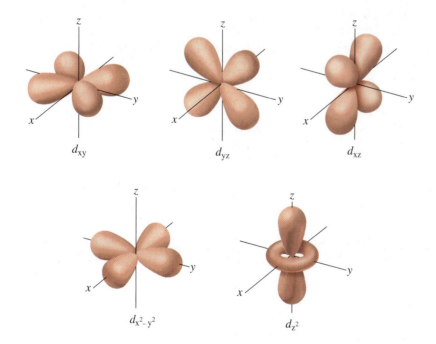

FIGURE 3.15 Four of the five *d* orbitals consist of four lobes that are aligned along or between different axes. One *d* orbital consists of two lobes and a doughnut-shaped ring around its center.

Q What is the maximum number of electrons possible in the 5*d* sublevel?

Energy level $n = 4$ consists of four sublevels *s*, *p*, *d*, and *f*. In the *f* sublevel, there are seven *f* orbitals. Because each *f* orbital can hold two electrons, the *f* sublevel can have a maximum of 14 electrons (see Table 3.9). The shapes of *f* orbitals are more complex, and we have not included them in this text.

TABLE 3.9 Electron Capacity in Sublevels for Energy Levels 1–4

Energy Level (n)	Number of Sublevels	Type of Sublevel	Number of Orbitals	Maximum Number of Electrons	Total Electrons
4	4	$4f$	7	14	32
		$4d$	5	10	
		$4p$	3	6	
		$4s$	1	2	
3	3	$3d$	5	10	18
		$3p$	3	6	
		$3s$	1	2	
2	2	$2p$	3	6	8
		$2s$	1	2	
1	1	$1s$	1	2	2

CONCEPT CHECK 3.5 **Energy Levels, Sublevels, and Orbitals**

Indicate the type and number of orbitals available in each of the following:

a. $3p$ sublevel **b.** $n = 2$
c. $1s$ sublevel **d.** $4d$ sublevel

ANSWER

a. The $3p$ sublevel contains three $3p$ orbitals.
b. The $n = 2$ energy level consists of one $2s$ orbital and three $2p$ orbitals.
c. The $1s$ sublevel consists of one s orbital.
d. The $4d$ sublevel contains five $4d$ orbitals.

SAMPLE PROBLEM 3.10 **Electrons**

Indicate the maximum number of electrons in each of the following:

a. $2p$ orbital **b.** $n = 2$ **c.** $3d$ sublevel

SOLUTION

a. A $2p$ orbital can hold two electrons.
b. The $n = 2$ energy level with one $2s$ orbital (two electrons) and three $2p$ orbitals (six electrons) can hold a maximum of 8 electrons.
c. The $3d$ sublevel with five d orbitals can hold 10 electrons.

STUDY CHECK 3.10

What is the maximum number of electrons in the $4s$ sublevel?

QUESTIONS AND PROBLEMS

3.6 Electron Arrangement in Atoms

LEARNING GOAL: *Describe the energy levels, sublevels, and orbitals for the electrons in an atom.*

3.37 Describe the shape of each of the following orbitals:
   a. $1s$ **b.** $2p$ **c.** $5s$

3.38 Describe the shape of each of the following orbitals:
   a. $3p$ **b.** $6s$ **c.** $4p$

3.39 Identify what is the same for **a–d**:
   1. They have the same shape.
   2. The maximum number of electrons is the same.
   3. They are in the same energy level.

   a. $1s$ and $2s$ orbitals
   b. $3s$ and $3p$ sublevels
   c. $3p$ and $4p$ sublevels
   d. three $3p$ orbitals

3.40 Identify what is the same for **a–d**:
   1. They have the same shape.
   2. The maximum number of electrons is the same.
   3. They are in the same energy level.

   a. $5s$ and $6s$ orbitals
   b. $3p$ and $4p$ orbitals
   c. $3s$ and $4s$ sublevels
   d. $2s$ and $2p$ orbitals

3.41 Indicate the number of each in the following:
a. orbitals in the 3*d* sublevel
b. sublevels in the *n* = 1 energy level
c. orbitals in the 6*s* sublevel
d. orbitals in the *n* = 3 energy level

3.42 Indicate the number of each in the following:
a. orbitals in the *n* = 2 energy level
b. sublevels in the *n* = 4 energy level
c. orbitals in the 5*f* sublevel
d. orbitals in the 6*p* sublevel

3.43 Indicate the maximum number of electrons in the following:
a. 3*p* orbital
b. 3*p* sublevel
c. *n* = 4 energy level
d. 5*d* sublevel

3.44 Indicate the maximum number of electrons in the following:
a. 3*s* sublevel
b. 4*p* orbital
c. *n* = 3 energy level
d. 4*f* sublevel

3.7 Orbital Diagrams and Electron Configurations

We can now look at how electrons are arranged in the orbitals within an atom. An **electron configuration** shows the placement of the electrons in the orbitals in order of increasing energy (see Figure 3.16). In this energy diagram, we see that the electrons in the 1*s* orbital have the lowest energy level. The energy level is higher for the 2*s* orbital and is even higher for the 2*p* orbitals.

We can begin our discussion of electron configuration by using **orbital diagrams** in which boxes represent the orbitals. Any orbital can have a maximum of two electrons.

To draw an orbital diagram, the lowest energy orbitals are filled in first. For example, in the diagram for a carbon atom with six electrons, the first two electrons fill the 1*s* orbital; the next two electrons go into the 2*s* orbital. When an orbital contains two electrons, the arrows representing the electrons are drawn in opposite directions, one up and one down.

LEARNING GOAL

Draw the orbital diagram and write the electron configuration for an element.

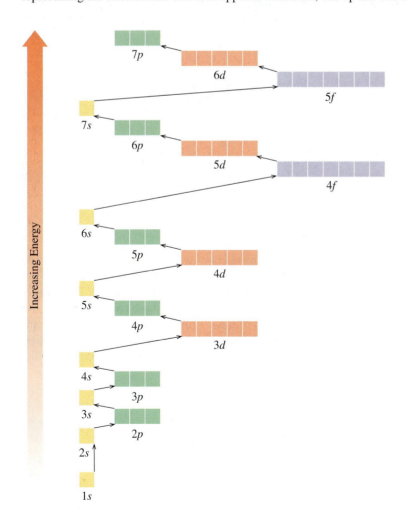

FIGURE 3.16 The orbitals in an atom fill in order of increasing energy, beginning with 1*s*.

Q Why does the 3*d* sublevel fill after the 4*s* sublevel?

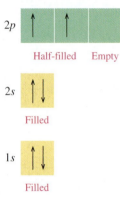

Orbital diagram for carbon

TUTORIAL
Electron Configurations

The last two electrons in carbon begin to fill the $2p$ orbitals, which have the next lowest energy. However, there are three $2p$ orbitals of equal energy. Because the negatively charged electrons repel each other, they go into separate $2p$ orbitals.

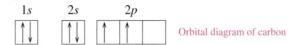

Orbital diagram of carbon

Electron Configurations

Chemists use a notation called the **electron configuration** to indicate the placement of the electrons of an atom in order of increasing energy. For example, the electron configuration for carbon is obtained by writing the lowest energy orbital first, followed by the orbitals of the next lower energy sublevel. The total number of electrons in each orbital is shown as a superscript.

Electron Configuration for Carbon

Type of orbital   Number of electrons

$1s^2 2s^2 2p^2$ Read as "one s two, two s two, two p two"

Period 1 Hydrogen and Helium

We can now draw the orbital diagrams and write the electron configurations for the elements H and He in Period 1. The $1s$ orbital (which is also the $1s$ sublevel) is written first because it has the lowest energy. Hydrogen has one electron in the $1s$ sublevel; helium has two. In the orbital diagram, the electrons for helium are drawn as arrows in opposite directions.

Atomic Number	Element	Orbital Diagram	Electron Configuration
		$1s$	
1	H	↑	$1s^1$
2	He	↑↓	$1s^2$

Period 2 Lithium to Neon

Period 2 begins with lithium, which has three electrons. The first two electrons fill the $1s$ orbital, while the third electron goes into the $2s$ orbital, the sublevel with the next lowest energy. In beryllium, another electron is added to complete the $2s$ orbital. The next six electrons are used to fill the $2p$ orbitals. The electrons are added one at a time from boron to nitrogen, which gives three half-filled $2p$ orbitals. From oxygen to neon, the remaining three electrons pair up to complete the $2p$ sublevel. In writing the complete electron configurations for the elements in Period 2, begin with the $1s$ followed by the $2s$ and the $2p$ orbitals.

An electron configuration can also be written in an *abbreviated configuration*. The electron configuration of the preceding noble gas is replaced by writing its symbol inside square brackets. For example, the electron configuration for lithium, $1s^2 2s^1$, can be abbreviated as $[\text{He}]2s^1$, where $[\text{He}]$ replaces $1s^2$.

Atomic Number	Element	Orbital Diagram	Electron Configuration	Abbreviated Electron Configuration
3	Li	$1s$ $2s$	$1s^2 2s^1$	$[He]2s^1$
4	Be	$1s$ $2s$	$1s^2 2s^2$	$[He]2s^2$
5	B	$1s$ $2s$ $2p$	$1s^2 2s^2 2p^1$	$[He]2s^2 2p^1$
6	C	$1s$ $2s$ $2p$	$1s^2 2s^2 2p^2$	$[He]2s^2 2p^2$
7	N	$1s$ $2s$ $2p$	$1s^2 2s^2 2p^3$	$[He]2s^2 2p^3$
8	O	$1s$ $2s$ $2p$	$1s^2 2s^2 2p^4$	$[He]2s^2 2p^4$
9	F	$1s$ $2s$ $2p$	$1s^2 2s^2 2p^5$	$[He]2s^2 2p^5$
10	Ne	$1s$ $2s$ $2p$	$1s^2 2s^2 2p^6$	$[He]2s^2 2p^6$

Unpaired electrons

CONCEPT CHECK 3.6   **Orbital Diagrams and Electron Configurations**

Draw or write each of the following for a nitrogen atom:

a. orbital diagram **b.** electron configuration
c. abbreviated electron configuration

ANSWER

On the periodic table, nitrogen has atomic number 7, which means it has seven electrons.

a. For the orbital diagram, we draw boxes to represent the $1s$, $2s$, and $2p$ orbitals.

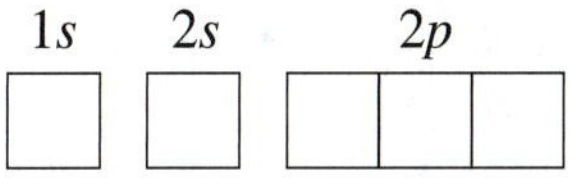

$1s$ $2s$ $2p$

First, we place a pair of electrons in both the $1s$ and $2s$ orbitals. Then, we place the three remaining electrons in three separate $2p$ orbitals with arrows drawn in the same direction.

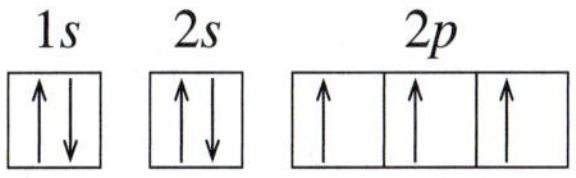

$1s$ $2s$ $2p$ Orbital diagram for nitrogen (N)

b. The electron configuration for nitrogen is written to show the orbitals and electrons in order of increasing energy.

$1s^2 2s^2 2p^3$ Electron configuration for nitrogen (N)

c. The abbreviated electron configuration for nitrogen is written by substituting the symbol of $[He]$, the noble gas that precedes Period 2, for the $1s^2$ notation in the electron configuration.

$[He]2s^2 2p^3$ Abbreviated electron configuration for nitrogen (N)

Period 3 Sodium to Argon

In Period 3, electrons enter the orbitals of the $3s$ and $3p$ sublevels, but not the $3d$ sublevel. We notice that the elements sodium to argon, which are directly below the elements lithium to neon in Period 2, have a similar pattern of filling their s and p orbitals. In sodium and magnesium, one and two electrons go into the $3s$ orbital. The electrons for aluminum, silicon, and phosphorus go into separate $3p$ orbitals. We can draw the orbital diagram for phosphorus with three half-filled $3p$ orbitals as follows:

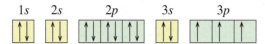

For elements in Period 3 through Period 7, we abbreviate the orbital diagram by using the symbol from the preceding noble gas followed by the boxes for the remaining electrons in the last filled period. In Period 3, the symbol $[\text{Ne}]$ replaces the electron configuration of neon, $1s^2 2s^2 2p^6$. The abbreviated orbital diagram for phosphorus is as follows:

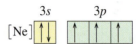

Atomic Number	Element	Orbital Diagram (3s and 3p orbitals only)	Electron Configuration	Abbreviated Electron Configuration
11	Na	$[\text{Ne}]$	$1s^2 2s^2 2p^6 3s^1$	$[\text{Ne}]3s^1$
12	Mg	$[\text{Ne}]$	$1s^2 2s^2 2p^6 3s^2$	$[\text{Ne}]3s^2$
13	Al	$[\text{Ne}]$	$1s^2 2s^2 2p^6 3s^2 3p^1$	$[\text{Ne}]3s^2 3p^1$
14	Si	$[\text{Ne}]$	$1s^2 2s^2 2p^6 3s^2 3p^2$	$[\text{Ne}]3s^2 3p^2$
15	P	$[\text{Ne}]$	$1s^2 2s^2 2p^6 3s^2 3p^3$	$[\text{Ne}]3s^2 3p^3$
16	S	$[\text{Ne}]$	$1s^2 2s^2 2p^6 3s^2 3p^4$	$[\text{Ne}]3s^2 3p^4$
17	Cl	$[\text{Ne}]$	$1s^2 2s^2 2p^6 3s^2 3p^5$	$[\text{Ne}]3s^2 3p^5$
18	Ar	$[\text{Ne}]$	$1s^2 2s^2 2p^6 3s^2 3p^6$	$[\text{Ne}]3s^2 3p^6$

SAMPLE PROBLEM 3.11 Drawing Orbital Diagrams and Writing Electron Configurations

For the element silicon, draw or write each of the following:

a. orbital diagram **b.** electron configuration
c. abbreviated electron configuration

SOLUTION

Analyze the Problem

Given	Atomic Number	Orbital Diagram	Electron Configuration	Abbreviated Electron Configuration
Silicon (Si)	14	Use the order of filling, placing two electrons in separate boxes, and single electrons in highest level.	List the sublevels in order of filling.	Substitute the symbol of the noble gas followed by the remaining order of filling.

a. Starting with the $1s$ orbital, add paired electrons through the $3s$ orbital. Then, place the last two electrons in separate $3p$ orbitals.

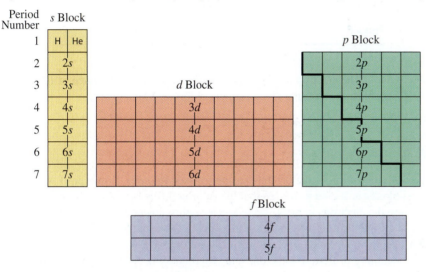

Complete orbital diagram for Si

b. The electron configuration shows the electrons that fill the orbitals, which are listed in order of increasing energy.

$1s^2 2s^2 2p^6 3s^2 3p^2$ Electron configuration for Si

c. For silicon, the preceding noble gas is neon. For the abbreviated electron configuration of silicon, we replace $1s^2 2s^2 2p^6$ with $[\text{Ne}]$.

$[\text{Ne}] 3s^2 3p^2$ Abbreviated electron configuration for Si

STUDY CHECK 3.11

Write the complete and abbreviated electron configurations for sulfur.

Electron Configurations and the Periodic Table

The position of the elements on the periodic table is also related to their electron configurations. Different sections or blocks within the table correspond to the s, p, d, and f sublevels and the filling of their orbitals (see Figure 3.17). Thus, we can also write the electron configuration of an element by reading the periodic table from left to right across each period.

SELF-STUDY ACTIVITY
Bohr's Shell Model

Period Number	s Block		d Block			p Block	
1	H	He					
2	2s					2p	
3	3s					3p	
4	4s		3d			4p	
5	5s		4d			5p	
6	6s		5d			6p	
7	7s		6d			7p	

f Block

4f

5f

FIGURE 3.17 Electron configuration follows the order of sublevels on the periodic table.

Q How many electrons are in the $1s$, $2s$, and $2p$ sublevels of neon?

Blocks on the Periodic Table

1. The **s block** includes hydrogen and helium as well as the elements in Group 1A (1) and Group 2A (2). This means that the final one or two electrons in the elements of the s block are located in an s orbital. The period number indicates the particular s orbital that is filling: $1s$, $2s$, and so on.

2. The **p block** consists of the elements in Group 3A (13) to Group 8A (18). There are six p block elements in each period because three p orbitals can hold up to six electrons. The period number indicates the particular p sublevel that is filling: $2p$, $3p$, and so on.

3. The **d block**, which contains the transition elements, first appears after calcium (atomic number 20). There are 10 elements in each period of the d block because five d orbitals can hold up to 10 electrons. The particular d sublevel is one less $(n - 1)$ than the period number. For example, in Period 4, the first d block is the $3d$ sublevel. In Period 5, the second d block is the $4d$ sublevel.

4. The **f block** includes the inner transition elements in the two rows at the bottom of the periodic table. There are 14 elements in each f block because seven f orbitals can hold up to 14 electrons. Elements that have atomic numbers higher than 57 (La) have electrons in the $4f$ block. The particular f sublevel is two less $(n - 2)$ than the period number. For example, in Period 6, the first f block is the $4f$ sublevel. In Period 7, the second f block is the $5f$ sublevel.

Writing Electron Configurations Using Sublevel Blocks

Now we can write electron configurations using the sublevel blocks on the periodic table as a guide. As before, each configuration begins at H. But now we move across the table, writing down each sublevel block we come to until we reach the element for which we are writing an electron configuration. For example, we will write the electron configuration for chlorine (atomic number 17) from the sublevel blocks on the periodic table.

Step 1 **Locate the element on the periodic table.**
Chlorine (atomic number 17) is in Group 7A (17) and Period 3.

Step 2 **Write the filled sublevels in order, going across each period.** Beginning with $1s$, and reading from left to right across the periodic table, write the electron configuration for each filled sublevel block as follows:

Period		Sublevel Blocks Filled
1	$1s$ sublevel $(\text{H} \rightarrow \text{He})$	$1s^2$
2	$2s$ sublevel $(\text{Li} \rightarrow \text{Be})$	$2s^2$
	$2p$ sublevel $(\text{B} \rightarrow \text{Ne})$	$2p^6$
3	$3s$ sublevel $(\text{Na} \rightarrow \text{Mg})$	$3s^2$

Step 3 **Complete the configuration by counting the electrons in the unfilled block.** Because chlorine is the fifth element in the $3p$ block, there are five electrons in the $3p$ sublevel.

Period		Last Sublevel Block
3	$3p$ sublevel $(\text{Al} \rightarrow \text{Cl})$	$3p^5$

The electron configuration is written with the sequence of filled sublevel blocks for the given element chlorine, which gives:

$$1s^2 2s^2 2p^6 3s^2 3p^5$$

Period 4

Up to Period 4, the filling of the orbitals has progressed in order. However, if we look at the sublevel blocks in Period 4, we see that the $4s$ orbital fills before the $3d$ orbitals. This occurs because the electrons in the $4s$ orbital have slightly lower energy than the electrons in the $3d$ orbitals. This order occurs again in Period 5 when the $5s$ orbital fills before the $4d$ orbitals, and again in Period 6 when the $6s$ fills before the $5d$.

At the beginning of Period 4, the one and two remaining electrons in potassium (19) and calcium (20) go into the $4s$ orbital. In scandium, the electron following the filled $4s$ orbital goes into the $3d$ block. The $3d$ block continues to fill until it is complete with 10 electrons at zinc (30). Once the $3d$ block is complete, the next six electrons, gallium to krypton, go into the orbitals in the $4p$ block.

CONCEPT CHECK 3.7 **Electron Configurations**

Give the symbol and name of the element with each of the following electron configurations:

a. $1s^2 2s^2 2p^5$ **b.** $1s^2 2s^2 2p^6 3s^2 3p^6 4s^2 3d^{10} 4p^2$ **c.** $[\text{Ar}] 4s^2 3d^6$

ANSWER

a. In the p block, Period 2, the fifth element across is F, fluorine.
b. In the p block, Period 4, the second element across is Ge, germanium.
c. In the d block, Period 4, the sixth element across is Fe, iron.

Atomic Number	Element	Electron Configuration	Abbreviated Electron Configuration
4s Block			
19	K	$1s^2 2s^2 2p^6 3s^2 3p^6 4s^1$	$[\text{Ar}]4s^1$
20	Ca	$1s^2 2s^2 2p^6 3s^2 3p^6 4s^2$	$[\text{Ar}]4s^2$
3d Block			
21	Sc	$1s^2 2s^2 2p^6 3s^2 3p^6 4s^2 3d^1$	$[\text{Ar}]4s^2 3d^1$
22	Ti	$1s^2 2s^2 2p^6 3s^2 3p^6 4s^2 3d^2$	$[\text{Ar}]4s^2 3d^2$
23	V	$1s^2 2s^2 2p^6 3s^2 3p^6 4s^2 3d^3$	$[\text{Ar}]4s^2 3d^3$
24	Cr*	$1s^2 2s^2 2p^6 3s^2 3p^6 4s^1 3d^5$	$[\text{Ar}]4s^1 3d^5$ (half-filled d sublevel is stable)
25	Mn	$1s^2 2s^2 2p^6 3s^2 3p^6 4s^2 3d^5$	$[\text{Ar}]4s^2 3d^5$
26	Fe	$1s^2 2s^2 2p^6 3s^2 3p^6 4s^2 3d^6$	$[\text{Ar}]4s^2 3d^6$
27	Co	$1s^2 2s^2 2p^6 3s^2 3p^6 4s^2 3d^7$	$[\text{Ar}]4s^2 3d^7$
28	Ni	$1s^2 2s^2 2p^6 3s^2 3p^6 4s^2 3d^8$	$[\text{Ar}]4s^2 3d^8$
29	Cu*	$1s^2 2s^2 2p^6 3s^2 3p^6 4s^1 3d^{10}$	$[\text{Ar}]4s^1 3d^{10}$ (filled d sublevel is stable)
30	Zn	$1s^2 2s^2 2p^6 3s^2 3p^6 4s^2 3d^{10}$	$[\text{Ar}]4s^2 3d^{10}$
4p Block			
31	Ga	$1s^2 2s^2 2p^6 3s^2 3p^6 4s^2 3d^{10} 4p^1$	$[\text{Ar}]4s^2 3d^{10} 4p^1$
32	Ge	$1s^2 2s^2 2p^6 3s^2 3p^6 4s^2 3d^{10} 4p^2$	$[\text{Ar}]4s^2 3d^{10} 4p^2$
33	As	$1s^2 2s^2 2p^6 3s^2 3p^6 4s^2 3d^{10} 4p^3$	$[\text{Ar}]4s^2 3d^{10} 4p^3$
34	Se	$1s^2 2s^2 2p^6 3s^2 3p^6 4s^2 3d^{10} 4p^4$	$[\text{Ar}]4s^2 3d^{10} 4p^4$
35	Br	$1s^2 2s^2 2p^6 3s^2 3p^6 4s^2 3d^{10} 4p^5$	$[\text{Ar}]4s^2 3d^{10} 4p^5$
36	Kr	$1s^2 2s^2 2p^6 3s^2 3p^6 4s^2 3d^{10} 4p^6$	$[\text{Ar}]4s^2 3d^{10} 4p^6$

*Exceptions to the order of filling.

SAMPLE PROBLEM 3.12   Using Sublevel Blocks to Write Electron Configurations

Use the sublevel blocks on the periodic table to write the complete electron configuration for selenium.

SOLUTION

Step 1   **Locate the element on the periodic table.** Selenium is in Period 4 and Group 6A (16), which is in the fourth column of the p block.

Step 2   **Write the filled sublevels in order, going across each period.** Beginning with $1s$, and reading from left to right across the periodic table, write the electron configuration for each filled sublevel block as follows:

Period 1 $1s^2$
Period 2 $2s^2 \rightarrow 2p^6$
Period 3 $3s^2 \rightarrow 3p^6$
Period 4 $4s^2 \rightarrow 3d^{10}$

Step 3   **Complete the configuration by counting the electrons in the unfilled block.** There are four electrons in the $4p$ sublevel for Se $(4p^4)$, which completes the electron configuration for Se: $1s^2 2s^2 2p^6 3s^2 3p^6 4s^2 3d^{10} 4p^4$.

STUDY CHECK 3.12

Write the complete electron configuration for tin.

Guide to Writing Electron Configurations using Sublevel Blocks

1 Locate the element on the periodic table.

2 Write the filled sublevels in order, going across each period.

3 Complete the configuration by counting the electrons in the unfilled block.

Exceptions in Sublevel Block Order

Within the filling of the $3d$ sublevel, exceptions occur for chromium and copper. In Cr and Cu, the $3d$ sublevel is close to being a half-filled or filled sublevel, which is particularly stable. Thus, the electron configuration of chromium has only one electron in the $4s$ and five electrons in the $3d$ sublevel, which gives the added stability of a half-filled d sublevel. This is shown in the abbreviated orbital diagram for chromium that follows:

Orbital diagram for chromium

A similar exception occurs for copper, which achieves a stable, filled $3d$ sublevel with ten electrons and only one electron in the $4s$ orbital. This is shown in the abbreviated orbital diagram for copper that follows:

Orbital diagram for copper

After the $4s$ and $3d$ sublevels are completed, the $4p$ sublevel fills as expected from gallium to krypton, the noble gas that completes Period 4.

QUESTIONS AND PROBLEMS

3.7 Orbital Diagrams and Electron Configurations

LEARNING GOAL: *Draw the orbital diagram and write the electron configuration for an element.*

3.45 Draw an orbital diagram for an atom of each of the following:
    a. boron   **b.** aluminum
    c. phosphorus   **d.** argon

3.46 Draw an orbital diagram for an atom of each of the following:
    a. fluorine   **b.** sodium
    c. magnesium   **d.** sulfur

3.47 Write a complete electron configuration for an atom of each of the following:
    a. iron   **b.** sodium
    c. rubidium   **d.** arsenic

3.48 Write a complete electron configuration for an atom of each of the following:
    a. gallium   **b.** fluorine
    c. phosphorus   **d.** cobalt

3.49 Write an abbreviated electron configuration for an atom of each of the following:
    a. magnesium   **b.** barium
    c. aluminum   **d.** titanium

3.50 Write an abbreviated electron configuration for an atom of each of the following:
    a. sodium
    b. oxygen
    c. nickel
    d. silver

3.51 Give the symbol of the element with each of the following electron configurations:
    a. $1s^22s^22p^63s^23p^4$ **b.** $1s^22s^22p^63s^23p^64s^23d^7$
    c. $[\text{Ne}]3s^23p^2$ **d.** $[\text{Ar}]4s^23d^{10}4p^5$

3.52 Give the symbol of the element with each of the following electron configurations:
    a. $1s^22s^22p^4$ **b.** $1s^22s^22p^63s^23p^6$
    c. $[\text{Ne}]3s^23p^1$ **d.** $[\text{Ar}]4s^23d^4$

3.53 Give the symbol of the element that meets the following conditions:
    a. has three electrons in the $n = 3$ energy level
    b. has two $2p$ electrons
    c. completes the $3p$ sublevel
    d. has two electrons in the $4d$ sublevel

3.54 Give the symbol of the element that meets the following conditions:
    a. has five electrons in the $3p$ sublevel
    b. has three $2p$ electrons
    c. completes the $3s$ sublevel
    d. has four $5p$ electrons

3.55 Give the number of electrons in the indicated orbitals for the following:
    a. $3d$ in zinc   **b.** $2p$ in sodium
    c. $4p$ in arsenic   **d.** $5s$ in rubidium

3.56 Give the number of electrons in the indicated orbitals for the following:
    a. $3d$ in manganese   **b.** $5p$ in antimony
    c. $6p$ in lead   **d.** $3s$ in magnesium

LEARNING GOAL

Use the electron configurations of elements to explain the trends in periodic properties.

3.8 Trends in Periodic Properties

The electron configurations of atoms are an important factor in the physical and chemical properties of the elements. Now we will look at the *valence electrons* in atoms, *atomic size, ionization energy,* and *metallic character*. Known as *periodic properties*, each increases or decreases across a period, and then the trend is repeated again in each successive period. We can use the seasonal changes in temperatures as an analogy for periodic properties. In the winter, temperatures are cold and become warmer in the spring. By summer, the outdoor temperatures are high, but begin to cool in the fall. By winter, we expect low temperatures again as the pattern of decreasing and increasing temperatures repeats for another year.

Group Number and Valence Electrons

The chemical properties of representative elements are mostly due to the **valence electrons**, which are the electrons in the outermost energy level. The *group number* gives the number of valence electrons for each group (vertical column) of representative elements. These valence electrons occupy the s and p orbitals with the highest principal quantum number n. For example, all the elements in Group 1A (1) have one valence electron in an s orbital. All the elements in Group 2A (2) have two (2) valence electrons in an s orbital. The halogens in Group 7A (17) all have seven valence electrons in s and p orbitals.

We can see the repetition of the outermost s and p electrons for the representative elements in Periods 1 to 4 in Table 3.10. Helium is included in Group 8A (18) because it is a noble gas, but it has only two electrons in its complete energy level.

TABLE 3.10 Valence Electrons for Representative Elements in Periods 1–4

1A (1)	2A (2)	3A (13)	4A (14)	5A (15)	6A (16)	7A (17)	8A (18)
1 H $1s^1$							2 He $1s^2$
3 Li $2s^1$	4 Be $2s^2$	5 B $2s^22p^1$	6 C $2s^22p^2$	7 N $2s^22p^3$	8 O $2s^22p^4$	9 F $2s^22p^5$	10 Ne $2s^22p^6$
11 Na $3s^1$	12 Mg $3s^2$	13 Al $3s^23p^1$	14 Si $3s^23p^2$	15 P $3s^23p^3$	16 S $3s^23p^4$	17 Cl $3s^23p^5$	18 Ar $3s^23p^6$
19 K $4s^1$	20 Ca $4s^2$	31 Ga $4s^24p^1$	32 Ge $4s^24p^2$	33 As $4s^24p^3$	34 Se $4s^24p^4$	35 Br $4s^24p^5$	36 Kr $4s^24p^6$

CONCEPT CHECK 3.8 **Using Group Numbers**

Using the periodic table, write the group number and the number of valence electrons for each of the following:

a. cesium   **b.** iodine   **c.** magnesium

ANSWER

a. Cesium (Cs) is in Group 1A (1). Because the group number is the same as the number of valence electrons, cesium has one valence electron.
b. Iodine (I) is in Group 7A (17). Because the group number is the same as the number of valence electrons, iodine has seven valence electrons.
c. Magnesium (Mg) is in Group 2A (2). Because the group number is the same as the number of valence electrons, magnesium has two valence electrons.

Electron-Dot Symbols

An **electron-dot symbol** is a convenient way to represent the valence electrons, which are shown as dots placed on the sides, top, or bottom of the symbol for the element. One to four valence electrons are arranged as single dots. When there are five to eight electrons,

(MC)™

TUTORIAL
Periodic Trends

TUTORIAL
Electron Configurations and the
Periodic Table

(MC)™

TUTORIAL
Electron-Dot Symbols for Elements

Atoms of
magnesium

Mg·
Electron-dot symbol

$1s^22s^22p^6\boxed{3s^2}$

Electron configuration of magnesium

one or more electrons are paired. Any of the following would be an acceptable electron-dot symbol for magnesium, which has two valence electrons:

Possible Electron-Dot Symbols for the Two Valence Electrons in Magnesium

$\overset{\cdot}{Mg}\cdot \quad \overset{\cdot}{Mg} \quad \cdot\overset{\cdot}{Mg} \quad \cdot Mg\cdot \quad Mg\overset{\cdot}{\cdot} \quad \cdot\underset{\cdot}{Mg}$

Electron-dot symbols for selected elements are given in Table 3.11.

Increasing Number of Valence Electrons →

TABLE 3.11 Electron-Dot Symbols for Selected Elements in Periods 1–4

	Group Number							
	1A (1)	2A (2)	3A (13)	4A (14)	5A (15)	6A (16)	7A (17)	8A (18)
Number of Valence Electrons	1	2	3	4	5	6	7	8*
Electron-Dot Symbol	H·							He:
	Li·	Be·	·B·	·C·	·N·	·O·	·F:	:Ne:
	Na·	Mg·	·Al·	·Si·	·P·	·S:	·Cl:	:Ar:
	K·	Ca·	·Ga·	·Ge·	·As·	·Se:	·Br:	:Kr:

* Helium (He) is stable with 2 valence electrons.

SAMPLE PROBLEM 3.13 **Writing Electron-Dot Symbols**

Write the electron-dot symbol for each of the following elements:

a. bromine **b.** aluminum

SOLUTION

a. Because the group number for bromine is 7A (17), bromine has seven valence electrons, which are drawn as seven dots, three pairs and one single dot, around the symbol Br.

·Br:

b. Aluminum, in Group 3A (13), has three valence electrons, which are drawn as three single dots around the symbol Al.

·Al·

STUDY CHECK 3.13

What is the electron-dot symbol for phosphorus?

Atomic Size

The size of an atom is determined by its *atomic radius*, which is the distance of the valence electrons from the nucleus. For each group of representative elements, the atomic size *increases* going from the top to the bottom because the outermost electrons in each energy level are farther from the nucleus. For example, in Group 1A (1), Li has a valence electron in energy level 2; Na has a valence electron in energy level 3; and K has a valence electron in energy level 4. This means that a K atom is larger than a Na atom, and a Na atom is larger than a Li atom (see Figure 3.18).

The atomic radius of representative elements is affected by the attractive forces of the protons in the nucleus on the valence electrons. For the elements going across a period, the increase in the number of protons in the nucleus increases the positive charge of the nucleus.

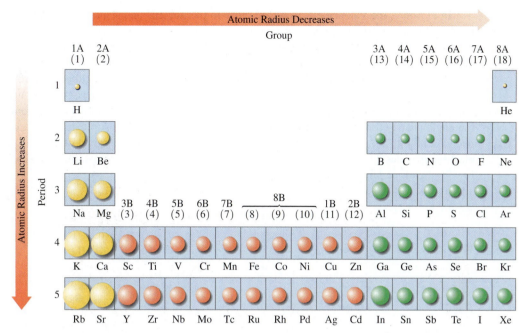

FIGURE 3.18 The atomic radius increases going down a group but decreases going from left to right across a period.

Q Why does the atomic radius increase going down a group?

As a result, the electrons are pulled closer to the nucleus, which means that the atomic sizes of representative elements decrease going from left to right across a period.

The atomic radii of the transition elements within a period change only slightly because electrons add to *d* orbitals rather than to the outermost energy level. Because the increase in nuclear charge is canceled by an increase in *d* electrons, the attraction of the nucleus for the outermost electrons remains about the same. Thus, the atomic radii of the transition elements are fairly constant.

CONCEPT CHECK 3.9   Atomic Radius

Why is the radius of a phosphorus atom larger than the radius of a nitrogen atom but smaller than the radius of a silicon atom?

ANSWER

The radius of a phosphorus atom is larger than the radius of a nitrogen atom because phosphorus has valence electrons in a higher energy level, which is farther from the nucleus. A phosphorus atom has one more proton than a silicon atom, which makes its nucleus more positive. This gives the nucleus in phosphorus a stronger attraction for the valence electrons, which decreases its radius compared to a silicon atom.

Ionization Energy

In an atom, negatively charged electrons are attracted to the positive charge of the protons in the nucleus. Therefore, energy is required to remove an electron from an atom. The **ionization energy** is the energy needed to remove the least tightly bound electron from an atom in the gaseous (*g*) state. When an electron is removed from a neutral atom, a particle called a *cation*, with a 1+ charge, is formed.

$$Na(g) + \text{energy (ionization)} \rightarrow Na^+(g) + e^-$$

The ionization energy decreases going down a group. Less energy is needed to remove an electron because nuclear attraction decreases when electrons are farther from the nucleus. Going across a period from left to right, the ionization energy increases. As the positive charge of the nucleus increases, more energy is needed to remove an electron (see Figure 3.19).

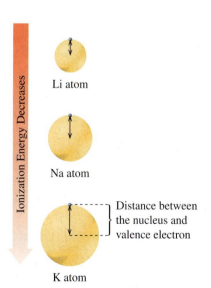

FIGURE 3.19 As the distance from the nucleus to a valence electron increases in Group 1A (1), the ionization energy decreases.

Q Is it easier to remove an electron from a K atom or from a Li atom?

MC ™

TUTORIAL
Ionization Energy

In Period 1, the valence electrons are close to the nucleus and strongly held. H and He have high ionization energies because a large amount of energy is required to remove an electron. The ionization energy for He is the highest of any element because He has a full, stable, energy level that requires a very large amount of energy in order to remove an electron. The high ionization energies of the noble gases indicate that their electron arrangements are especially stable. The slight decrease in ionization energy for Group 3A (13) compared to Group 2A (2), occurs because the single p electron is farther from the nucleus and more easily removed than the electrons in the full s sublevel. The next decrease in ionization energy occurs for Group 6A (16) because the removal of a single p electron provides a half-filled, more stable p sublevel. In general, the ionization energy is low for metals and high for nonmetals (see Figure 3.20).

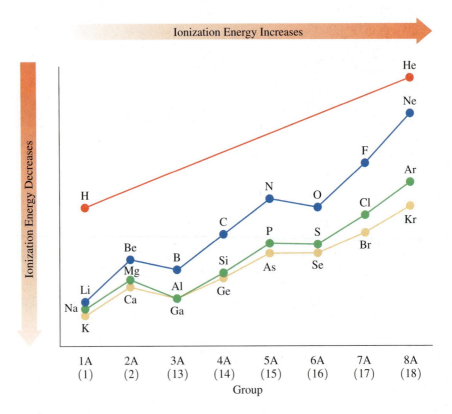

FIGURE 3.20 Ionization energies for the representative elements tend to decrease going down a group and increase going left to right across a period.

Q Why is the ionization energy for Li less than that for O?

SAMPLE PROBLEM 3.14 Ionization Energy

Indicate the element in each set that has the higher ionization energy and explain your choice.

a. K or Na **b.** Mg or Cl **c.** F, N, or C

SOLUTION

a. Na. In Na, the valence electron is closer to the nucleus.
b. Cl. Attraction for the valence electrons increases across a period, going left to right.
c. F. Because fluorine has more protons than nitrogen or carbon, more energy is needed to remove a valence electron from the fluorine atom.

STUDY CHECK 3.14

Arrange Sn, Sr, and I in order of increasing ionization energy.

Metallic Character

In Section 3.2, we identified elements as metals, nonmetals, and metalloids. An element that has **metallic character** is an element that loses valence electrons easily. Metallic character is more prevalent in the elements (metals) on the left side of the periodic table, and decreases going from the left side to the right side of the periodic table. The elements (nonmetals) on the right side of the periodic table do not easily lose electrons, which means they are the least metallic. Most of the metalloids between the metals and nonmetals tend to lose electrons, but not as easily as the metals. Thus, in Period 3, sodium, which loses electrons most easily, would be the most metallic. Going across from left to right in Period 3, metallic character decreases to argon, which has the least metallic character.

For elements in the same group of representative elements, metallic character increases going from top to bottom. Atoms at the bottom of any group have more electron levels, which makes it easier to lose electrons. Thus, the elements at the bottom of a group on the periodic table have lower ionization energy and are more metallic compared to the elements at the top (see Figure 3.21).

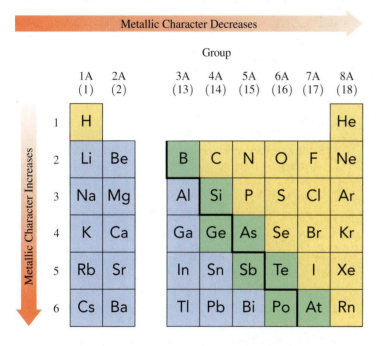

FIGURE 3.21 Metallic character of the representative elements increases going down a group and decreases going from left to right across a period.

Q Why is the metallic character greater for Rb than for Li?

A summary of the trends in periodic properties we have discussed is given in Table 3.12.

TABLE 3.12 Summary of Trends in Periodic Properties of Representative Elements

Periodic Property	Top to Bottom of a Group	Left to Right Across a Period
Valence Electrons	Remains the same	Increases
Atomic Radius	Increases due to the increase in the number of energy levels	Decreases as the increase of protons strengthens the attraction of the nucleus for the valence electrons, and pulls them closer to the nucleus
Ionization Energy	Decreases because the valence electrons are easier to remove when they are farther from the nucleus	Increases as the increase of protons strengthens the attraction between the nucleus for the valence electrons, and more energy is needed to remove an electron
Metallic Character	Increases because the valence electrons are easier to remove when they are farther from the nucleus	Decreases as the attraction of the protons makes it more difficult to remove a valence electron

CONCEPT CHECK 3.10 Metallic Character

Identify the element that has more metallic character in each of the following:

a. Mg or Al   **b.** Na or K

ANSWER

a. Mg is more metallic than Al because metallic character decreases going from left to right across a period.

b. K is more metallic than Na because metallic character increases going down a group.

QUESTIONS AND PROBLEMS

3.8 Trends in Periodic Properties

LEARNING GOAL: *Use the electron configurations of elements to explain the trends in periodic properties.*

3.57 Indicate the number of valence electrons in each of the following:
  a. aluminum
  b. Group 5A
  c. F, Cl, Br, and I

3.58 Indicate the number of valence electrons in each of the following:
  a. Li, Na, K, Rb, and Cs
  b. C, Si, Ge, Sn, and Pb
  c. Group 8A

3.59 Write the group number and electron-dot symbol for each element:
  a. sulfur   **b.** nitrogen
  c. calcium   **d.** sodium
  e. gallium

3.60 Write the group number and electron-dot symbol for each element:
  a. carbon   **b.** oxygen
  c. argon   **d.** lithium
  e. chlorine

3.61 Select the larger atom in each pair.
  a. Na or Cl   **b.** Na or Rb
  c. Na or Mg   **d.** Rb or I

3.62 Select the larger atom in each pair.
  a. S or Ar   **b.** S or O
  c. S or K   **d.** S or Mg

3.63 Place the elements in each set in order of decreasing atomic radius.
  a. Al, Si, Mg   **b.** Cl, Br, I
  c. Sr, Sb, I   **d.** P, Si, Na

3.64 Place the elements in each set in order of decreasing atomic radius.
  a. Cl, S, P   **b.** Ge, Si, C
  c. Ba, Ca, Sr   **d.** S, O, Se

3.65 Select the element in each pair with the higher ionization energy.
  a. Br or I
  b. Mg or Sr
  c. Si or P
  d. I or Xe

3.66 Select the element in each pair with the higher ionization energy.
  a. O or Ne   **b.** K or Br
  c. Ca or Ba   **d.** N or Ne

3.67 Arrange each set of elements in order of increasing ionization energy.
  a. F, Cl, Br   **b.** Na, Cl, Al
  c. Na, K, Cs   **d.** As, Ca, Br

3.68 Arrange each set of elements in order of increasing ionization energy.
  a. O, N, C   **b.** S, P, Cl
  c. As, P, N   **d.** Al, Si, P

3.69 Fill in each of the following blanks using *larger* or *smaller*, *more* or *less*: Na has a _____ atomic size and is _____ metallic than P.

3.70 Fill in each of the following blanks using *larger* or *smaller*, *lower* or *higher:* Mg has a _____ atomic size and a _____ ionization energy than Ba.

3.71 Place the following in order of decreasing metallic character: Br, Ge, Ca, Ga

3.72 Place the following in order of increasing metallic character: Na, P, Al, Ar

3.73 Fill in each of the following blanks using *higher* or *lower*, *more* or *less*: Sr has a _____ ionization energy and is _____ metallic than Sb.

3.74 Fill in each of the following blanks using *higher* or *lower*, *more* or *less*: N has a _____ ionization energy and is _____ metallic than As.

3.75 Complete each of the statements **a–d** using **1, 2,** or **3:**
  1. decreases   **2.** increases   **3.** remains the same

  Going down Group 6A (16),
  a. the ionization energy _____
  b. the atomic size _____
  c. the metallic character _____
  d. the number of valence electrons _____

3.76 Complete each of the statements **a–d** using **1, 2,** or **3:**
  1. decreases   **2.** increases   **3.** remains the same

  Going from left to right across Period 4,
  a. the ionization energy _____
  b. the atomic size _____
  c. the metallic character _____
  d. the number of valence electrons _____

3.77 Which statements completed with **a–e** will be *true* and which will be *false*?

In Period 2, an atom of N compared to an atom of Li has a larger (greater)
a. atomic size
b. ionization energy
c. number of protons
d. metallic character
e. number of valence electrons

3.78 Which statements completed with **a–e** will be *true* and which will be *false*?

In Group 4A (14), an atom of C compared to an atom of Sn has a larger (greater)
a. atomic size
b. ionization energy
c. number of protons
d. metallic character
e. number of valence electrons

CONCEPT MAP

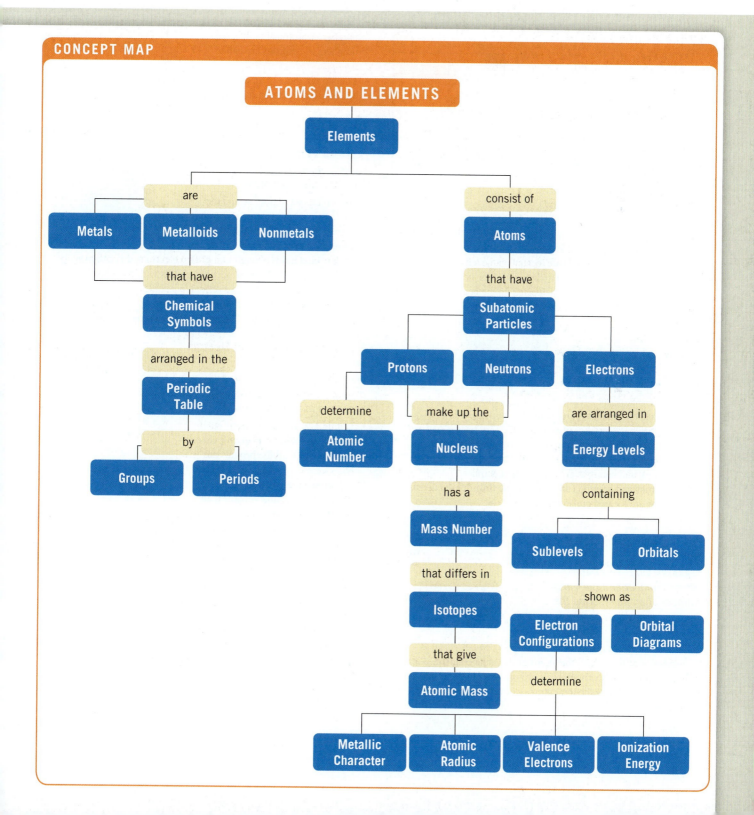

CHAPTER REVIEW

3.1 Elements and Symbols

LEARNING GOAL: Given the name of an element, write its correct symbol; from the symbol, write the correct name.

- Elements are the primary substances of matter.
- Chemical symbols are one- or two-letter abbreviations of the names of the elements.

3.2 The Periodic Table

LEARNING GOAL: Use the periodic table to identify the group and the period of an element; identify the element as a metal, nonmetal, or metalloid.

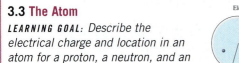

- The periodic table is an arrangement of the elements by increasing atomic number.
- A vertical column on the periodic table containing elements with similar properties is called a *group*. A horizontal row is called a *period*.
- Elements in Group 1A (1) are called the *alkali metals*; Group 2A (2), the *alkaline earth metals*; Group 7A (17), the *halogens*; and Group 8A (18), the *noble gases*.
- On the periodic table, metals are located on the left of the heavy zigzag line, and nonmetals are to the right of the heavy zigzag line.
- Except for aluminum, elements located on the heavy zigzag line are called *metalloids*.

3.3 The Atom

LEARNING GOAL: Describe the electrical charge and location in an atom for a proton, a neutron, and an electron.

- An atom is the smallest particle that retains the characteristics of an element.
- Atoms are composed of three types of subatomic particles.
- Protons have a positive charge (+), electrons carry a negative charge (−), and neutrons are electrically neutral.
- The protons and neutrons are found in the tiny, dense nucleus. Electrons are located outside the nucleus.

3.4 Atomic Number and Mass Number

LEARNING GOAL: Given the atomic number and the mass number of an atom, state the number of protons, neutrons, and electrons.

- The atomic number gives the number of protons in all the atoms of the same element.
- In a neutral atom, the number of protons and electrons is equal.
- The mass number is the total number of protons and neutrons in an atom.

3.5 Isotopes and Atomic Mass

LEARNING GOAL: Give the number of protons, neutrons, and electrons in one or more of the isotopes of an element; calculate the atomic mass of an element using the abundance and mass of its naturally occurring isotopes.

- Atoms that have the same number of protons but different numbers of neutrons are called *isotopes*.
- The atomic mass of an element is the weighted average mass of all the atoms in a naturally occurring sample of that element.

3.6 Electron Arrangement in Atoms

LEARNING GOAL: Describe the energy levels, sublevels, and orbitals for the electrons in an atom.

- An orbital is a region around the nucleus in which an electron with a specific energy is most likely to be found.
- Each orbital holds a maximum of two electrons. In each principal energy level (n), electrons occupy orbitals within sublevels.
- An s sublevel contains one s orbital, a p sublevel contains three p orbitals, a d sublevel contains five d orbitals, and an f sublevel contains seven f orbitals. Each type of orbital has a unique shape.

3.7 Orbital Diagrams and Electron Configurations

LEARNING GOAL: Draw the orbital diagram and write the electron configuration for an element.

- Within a sublevel, electrons enter orbitals in the same energy level one at a time until all the orbitals are half-filled.
- Additional electrons enter until the orbitals in that sublevel are filled with two electrons each.
- The electron arrangement in an atom can be drawn as an orbital diagram, which shows the orbitals that are occupied by paired and unpaired electrons.
- The electron configuration shows the number of electrons in each sublevel. In an abbreviated electron configuration, the symbol of a noble gas in brackets represents the filled sublevels.
- The periodic table consists of s, p, d, and f sublevel blocks. Beginning with $1s$, an electron configuration is obtained by writing the sublevel blocks in order going across the periodic table until the element is reached.

3.8 Trends in Periodic Properties

LEARNING GOAL: Use the electron configurations of elements to explain the trends in periodic properties.

Li atom

Na atom

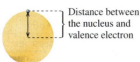
Distance between the nucleus and valence electron

K atom

- The properties of elements are related to the valence electrons of the atoms.
- With only a few minor exceptions, each group of elements has the same number of valence electrons, differing only in the energy level.

- Valence electrons are represented as dots around the symbol of the element.
- The radius of an atom increases going down a group and decreases going left to right across a period.
- The energy required to remove a valence electron is the ionization energy, which generally decreases going down a group and generally increases going left to right across a period.
- The metallic character increases going down a group and decreases going left to right across a period.

KEY TERMS

alkali metal An element in Group 1A (1), except hydrogen, that is a soft, shiny metal with one electron in its outermost energy level.

alkaline earth metal An element in Group 2A (2) that has two electrons in its outermost energy level.

atom The smallest particle of an element that retains the characteristics of the element.

atomic mass The weighted average mass of all the naturally occurring isotopes of an element.

atomic mass unit (amu) A small mass unit used to describe the mass of extremely small particles such as atoms and subatomic particles; 1 amu is equal to one-twelfth the mass of a $^{12}_{6}C$ atom.

atomic number A number that is equal to the number of protons in an atom.

atomic symbol An abbreviation used to indicate the mass number and atomic number of an isotope.

chemical symbol An abbreviation that represents the name of an element.

d **block** The block of ten elements from Groups 3B (3) to 2B (12) in which electrons fill the five *d* orbitals in the *d* sublevels.

electron A negatively charged subatomic particle having a minute mass that is usually ignored in mass calculations; its symbol is e^-.

electron configuration A list of the number of electrons in each sublevel within an atom, arranged by increasing energy.

electron-dot symbol The representation of an atom that shows valence electrons as dots around the symbol of the element.

energy level A group of electrons with similar energy.

f **block** The block of 14 elements in the rows at the bottom of the periodic table in which electrons fill the seven *f* orbitals in the 4*f* and 5*f* sublevels.

group A vertical column in the periodic table that contains elements having similar physical and chemical properties.

group number A number that appears at the top of each vertical column (group) in the periodic table and indicates the number of electrons in the outermost energy level.

halogen An element in Group 7A (17)—fluorine, chlorine, bromine, iodine, and astatine—that has seven electrons in its outermost energy level.

ionization energy The energy needed to remove the least tightly bound electron from the outermost energy level of an atom.

isotope An atom that differs only in mass number from another atom of the same element. Isotopes have the same atomic number (number of protons) but different numbers of neutrons.

mass number The total number of protons and neutrons in the nucleus of an atom.

metal An element that is shiny, malleable, ductile, and a good conductor of heat and electricity. The metals are located to the left of the heavy zigzag line on the periodic table.

metallic character A measure of how easily an element loses a valence electron.

metalloid Elements with properties of both metals and nonmetals located along the heavy zigzag line on the periodic table.

neutron A neutral subatomic particle having a mass of about 1 amu and found in the nucleus of an atom; its symbol is n or n^0.

noble gas An element in Group 8A (18) of the periodic table, generally unreactive and seldom found in combination with other elements, that has eight electrons (helium has two electrons) in its outermost energy level.

nonmetal An element with little or no luster that is a poor conductor of heat and electricity. The nonmetals are located to the right of the heavy zigzag line on the periodic table.

nucleus The compact, extremely dense center of an atom, containing the protons and neutrons of the atom.

orbital The region around the nucleus where electrons of a certain energy are more likely to be found. The *s* orbitals are spherical; the *p* orbitals have two lobes.

orbital diagram A diagram that shows the distribution of electrons in the orbitals of the energy levels.

p **block** The elements in Groups 3A (13) to 8A (18) in which electrons fill the *p* orbitals in the *p* sublevels.

period A horizontal row of elements in the periodic table.

periodic table An arrangement of elements by increasing atomic number such that elements having similar chemical behavior are grouped in vertical columns.

proton A positively charged subatomic particle having a mass of about 1 amu and found in the nucleus of an atom; its symbol is p or p^+.

representative element An element in the first two columns on the left of the periodic table and the last six columns on the right that has a group number of 1A through 8A or 1, 2, and 13 through 18.

s **block** The elements in Groups 1A (1) and 2A (2) in which electrons fill the *s* orbitals.

subatomic particle A particle within an atom; protons, neutrons, and electrons are subatomic particles.

sublevel A group of orbitals of equal energy within principal energy levels. The number of sublevels in each energy level is the same as the principal quantum number (n).

transition element An element in the center of the periodic table that is designated with the letter "B" or the group number of 3 through 12.

valence electrons Electrons in the highest energy level of an atom.

UNDERSTANDING THE CONCEPTS

The chapter sections to review are shown in parentheses at the end of each question.

3.79 According to Dalton's atomic theory, which of the following are *true*? (3.3)

  a. Atoms of an element are identical to atoms of other elements.

  b. Every element is made of atoms.

  c. Atoms of two different elements combine to form compounds.

  d. In a chemical reaction, some atoms disappear and new atoms appear.

3.80 Use Rutherford's gold-foil experiment to answer each of the following: (3.3)

  a. What did Rutherford expect to happen when he aimed particles at the gold foil?

  b. How did the results differ from what he expected?

  c. How did he use the results to propose a model of the atom?

3.81 Match the subatomic particles (**1–3**) to each of the descriptions below: (3.3)

  1. protons   **2.** neutrons   **3.** electrons

  a. atomic mass   **b.** atomic number

  c. positive charge   **d.** negative charge

  e. mass number – atomic number

3.82 Match the subatomic particles (**1–3**) to each of the descriptions below: (3.3)

  1. protons   **2.** neutrons   **3.** electrons

  a. mass number   **b.** surround the nucleus

  c. nucleus   **d.** charge of 0

  e. equal to number of electrons

3.83 Consider the following atoms in which X represents the chemical symbol of the element: $^{16}_{8}X$ $^{16}_{9}X$ $^{18}_{10}X$ $^{17}_{8}X$ $^{18}_{8}X$ (3.4, 3.5)

  a. What atoms have the same number of protons?

  b. Which atoms are isotopes? Of what element?

  c. Which atoms have the same mass number?

  d. What atoms have the same number of neutrons?

3.84 For each of the following, write the symbol and name for X and the number of protons and neutrons. Which are isotopes of each other? (3.4, 3.5)

  a. $^{80}_{35}X$ **b.** $^{56}_{26}X$ **c.** $^{116}_{50}X$

  d. $^{124}_{50}X$ **e.** $^{116}_{48}X$

3.85 Indicate if the atoms in each pair have the same number of protons, neutrons, and electrons. (3.4)

  a. $^{37}_{17}Cl$, $^{38}_{18}Ar$ **b.** $^{36}_{14}Si$, $^{35}_{14}Si$

  c. $^{40}_{18}Ar$, $^{39}_{17}Cl$

3.86 Complete the following table for the three naturally occurring isotopes of silicon, the major component in computer chips: (3.5)

Computer chips consist primarily of the element silicon.

	Isotope		
	$^{28}_{14}Si$	$^{29}_{14}Si$	$^{30}_{14}Si$
Number of protons			
Number of neutrons			
Number of electrons			
Atomic number			
Mass number			

3.87 For each representation of a nucleus **A–E**, write the atomic symbol, and identify which are isotopes. (3.4, 3.5)

Proton

Neutron

  A   **B**   **C**   **D**   **E**

3.88 Identify the element represented by each nucleus **A–E** in Problem 3.87 as a metal, nonmetal, or metalloid. (3.2)

3.89 Match the spheres **A–D** with atoms of Li, Na, K, and Rb. (3.8)

  A   **B**   **C**   **D**

3.90 Match the spheres **A–D** with atoms of K, Ge, Ca, and Kr. (3.8)

  A   **B**   **C**   **D**

3.91 Of the elements Na, Mg, Si, S, Cl, and Ar, identify one that fits each of the following: (3.2, 3.7, 3.8)

  a. largest atomic size

  b. a halogen

  c. electron configuration $1s^2 2s^2 2p^6 3s^2 3p^4$

  d. highest ionization energy

  e. is a metalloid

  f. most metallic character

  g. two valence electrons

3.92 Of the elements Sn, Xe, Te, Sr, I, and Rb, identify one that fits each of the following: (3.2, 3.8)

  a. smallest atomic size

  b. in Group 2A (2)

  c. a metalloid

  d. lowest ionization energy

  e. in Group 4A (14)

  f. least metallic character

  g. seven valence electrons

ADDITIONAL QUESTIONS AND PROBLEMS

For instructor-assigned homework, go to www.masteringchemistry.com.

3.93 Give the period and group number for each of the following elements: (3.2)
   a. bromine
   b. argon
   c. potassium
   d. radium

3.94 Give the period and group number for each of the following elements: (3.2)
   a. radon
   b. lead
   c. carbon
   d. neon

3.95 The following trace elements have been found to be crucial to the functions of the body. Indicate each as a metal, nonmetal, or metalloid. (3.2)
   a. zinc
   b. cobalt
   c. manganese
   d. iodine

3.96 The following trace elements have been found to be crucial to the functions of the body. Indicate each as a metal, nonmetal, or metalloid. (3.2)
   a. copper
   b. selenium
   c. arsenic
   d. chromium

3.97 Indicate if each of the following statements is *true* or *false*: (3.3)
   a. The proton is a negatively charged particle.
   b. The neutron is 2000 times as heavy as a proton.
   c. The atomic mass unit is based on a carbon atom with 6 protons and 6 neutrons.
   d. The nucleus is the largest part of the atom.
   e. The electrons are located outside the nucleus.

3.98 Indicate if each of the following statements is *true* or *false*: (3.3)
   a. The neutron is electrically neutral.
   b. Most of the mass of an atom is due to the protons and neutrons.
   c. The charge of an electron is equal, but opposite, to the charge of a neutron.
   d. The proton and the electron have about the same mass.
   e. The mass number is the number of protons.

3.99 For the following atoms, give the number of protons, neutrons, and electrons: (3.3)
   a. $^{114}_{48}Cd$
   b. $^{98}_{43}Tc$
   c. $^{199}_{79}Au$
   d. $^{222}_{86}Rn$
   e. $^{136}_{54}Xe$

3.100 For the following atoms, give the number of protons, neutrons, and electrons: (3.3)
   a. $^{202}_{80}Hg$
   b. $^{127}_{53}I$
   c. $^{75}_{35}Br$
   d. $^{133}_{55}Cs$
   e. $^{195}_{78}Pt$

3.101 Complete the following table: (3.3)

Name of the Element	Atomic Symbol	Number of Protons	Number of Neutrons	Number of Electrons
	$^{34}_{16}S$			
		28	34	
Magnesium			14	
	$^{228}_{88}Ra$			

3.102 Complete the following table: (3.3)

Name of the Element	Atomic Symbol	Number of Protons	Number of Neutrons	Number of Electrons
Potassium			22	
	$^{51}_{23}V$			
		48	64	
Barium			82	

3.103 **a.** What electron sublevel starts to fill after completion of the 3*s* sublevel? (3.7)
   b. What electron sublevel starts to fill after completion of the 4*p* sublevel?
   c. What electron sublevel starts to fill after completion of the 3*d* sublevel?
   d. What electron sublevel starts to fill after completion of the 3*p* sublevel?

3.104 **a.** What electron sublevel starts to fill after completion of the 5*s* sublevel? (3.7)
   b. What electron sublevel starts to fill after completion of the 4*d* sublevel?
   c. What electron sublevel starts to fill after completion of the 4*f* sublevel?
   d. What electron sublevel starts to fill after completion of the 5*p* sublevel?

3.105 **a.** How many 3*d* electrons are in Fe? (3.7)
   b. How many 5*p* electrons are in Ba?
   c. How many 4*d* electrons are in I?
   d. How many 7*s* electrons are in Ra?

3.106 **a.** How many 4*d* electrons are in Cd? (3.7)
   b. How many 4*p* electrons are in Br?
   c. How many 6*p* electrons are in Bi?
   d. How many 5*s* electrons are in Zn?

3.107 Name the element that corresponds to each of the following: (3.7, 3.8)
   a. $1s^2 2s^2 2p^6 3s^2 3p^3$
   b. alkali metal with the smallest atomic radius
   c. $[Kr]5s^2 4d^{10}$
   d. Group 5A (15) element with the highest ionization energy
   e. Period 3 element with the largest atomic radius

3.108 Name the element that corresponds to each of the following: (3.7, 3.8)
   a. $1s^2 2s^2 2p^6 3s^2 3p^6 4s^1 3d^5$
   b. $[Xe]6s^2 4f^{14} 5d^{10} 6p^5$
   c. halogen with the highest ionization energy
   d. Group 2A (2) element with the smallest ionization energy
   e. Period 4 element with the smallest atomic radius

3.109 Of the elements Na, P, Cl, and F, which (3.2, 3.8)
   a. is a metal?
   b. is in Group 5A (15)?
   c. has the highest ionization energy?
   d. loses an electron most easily?
   e. is found in Group 7A (17), Period 3?

3.110 Of the elements K, Ca, Br, and Kr, which (3.2, 3.8)
    a. is a noble gas?
    b. has the smallest atomic radius?

    c. has the lowest ionization energy?
    d. requires the most energy to remove an electron?
    e. is found in Group 2A (2), Period 4?

CHALLENGE QUESTIONS

3.111 The most abundant isotope of lead is $^{208}_{82}Pb$. (3.4)
    a. How many protons, neutrons, and electrons are in $^{208}_{82}Pb$?
    b. What is the atomic symbol of another isotope of lead with 132 neutrons?
    c. What is the name and symbol of an atom with the same mass number as in part **b** and 131 neutrons?

3.112 The most abundant isotope of silver is $^{107}_{47}Ag$. (3.4)
    a. How many protons, neutrons, and electrons are in $^{107}_{47}Ag$?
    b. What is the symbol of another isotope of silver with 62 neutrons?
    c. What is the name and symbol of an atom with the same mass number as in part **b** and 61 neutrons?

3.113 Give the symbol of the element that has the (3.8)
    a. smallest atomic size in Group 6A (16)
    b. smallest atomic size in Period 3
    c. highest ionization energy in Group 4A (14)
    d. lowest ionization energy in Period 3
    e. most metallic character in Group 2A (2)

3.114 Give the symbol of the element that has the (3.8)
    a. largest atomic size in Group 1A (1)
    b. largest atomic size in Period 4
    c. highest ionization energy in Group 2A (2)
    d. lowest ionization energy in Group 7A (17)
    e. least metallic character in Group 4A (14)

3.115 Silicon has three naturally occurring isotopes: Si-28 that has a percent abundance of 92.23% and a mass of 27.977 amu, Si-29 that has a 4.68% abundance and a mass of 28.976 amu, and Si-30 that has a percent abundance of 3.09% and a mass of 29.974 amu. What is the atomic mass of silicon? (3.5)

3.116 Antimony (Sb), has two naturally occurring isotopes: Sb-121 that has a percent abundance of 57.30% and a mass of 120.9 amu, and Sb-123 that has a percent abundance of 42.70% and a mass of 122.9 amu. What is the atomic mass of antimony? (3.5)

3.117 Consider three elements with the following abbreviated electron configurations: (3.2, 3.8)

$$X = [Ar]4s^2 \qquad Y = [Ne]3s^23p^4$$
$$Z = [Ar]4s^23d^{10}4p^4$$

    a. Identify each element as a metal, nonmetal, or metalloid.
    b. Which element has the largest atomic radius?
    c. Which elements have similar properties?
    d. Which element has the highest ionization energy?
    e. Which element has the smallest atomic radius?

3.118 Consider three elements with the following abbreviated electron configurations: (3.2, 3.8)

$$X = [Ar]4s^23d^5 \qquad Y = [Ar]4s^23d^{10}4p^1$$
$$Z = [Ar]4s^23d^{10}4p^6$$

    a. Identify each element as a metal, nonmetal, or metalloid.
    b. Which element has the smallest atomic radius?
    c. Which elements have similar properties?
    d. Which element has the highest ionization energy?
    e. Which element has a half-filled sublevel?

ANSWERS

Answers to Study Checks

3.1 Si, S, Ag

3.2 magnesium, aluminum, fluorine

3.3 a. Group 2A (2)   **b.** alkaline earth metals
    c. Period 5   **d.** magnesium, Mg
    e. alkali metal, Rb; halogen, I; noble gas, Xe

3.4 a. metalloid   **b.** nonmetal   **c.** metal

3.5 False; most of the volume in an atom is outside the nucleus.

3.6 a. 79   **b.** 79   **c.** gold, Au

3.7 45 neutrons

3.8 a. $^{15}_{7}N$ **b.** $^{81}_{35}Br$ **c.** $^{27}_{14}Si$

3.9 10.81 amu

3.10 The 4s sublevel can hold a maximum of 2 electrons.

3.11 $1s^22s^22p^63s^23p^4$ Complete electron configuration for sulfur (S)
    $[Ne]3s^23p^4$ Abbreviated electron configuration for sulfur (S)

3.12 Tin has the electron configuration:
$1s^22s^22p^63s^23p^64s^23d^{10}4p^65s^24d^{10}5p^2$

3.13 $\cdot \ddot{P} \cdot$

3.14 Ionization energy increases going across a period from left to right: Sr is lowest, Sn is higher, and I is the highest of this set.

Answers to Selected Questions and Problems

3.1 a. Cu   **b.** Pt   **c.** Ca   **d.** Mn
    e. Fe   **f.** Ba   **g.** Pb   **h.** Sr

3.3 a. carbon   **b.** chlorine   **c.** iodine   **d.** mercury
    e. silver   **f.** argon   **g.** boron   **h.** nickel

3.5 a. sodium, chlorine
    b. calcium, sulfur, oxygen
    c. carbon, hydrogen, chlorine, nitrogen, oxygen
    d. calcium, carbon, oxygen

3.7 a. Period 2   **b.** Group 8A (18)
    c. Group 1A (1)   **d.** Period 2

3.9 a. alkaline earth metal   **b.** transition element
c. noble gas   **d.** alkali metal
e. halogen

3.11 a. C   **b.** He   **c.** Na
d. Ca   **e.** Al

3.13 a. metal   **b.** nonmetal   **c.** metal
d. nonmetal   **e.** nonmetal   **f.** nonmetal
g. metalloid   **h.** metal

3.15 a. electron
b. proton
c. electron
d. neutron

3.17 a, **b**, and **c** are *true*, but **d** is *false*. A proton is attracted to an electron, not a neutron.

3.19 Thomson determined that electrons had a negative charge when he observed they were attracted to a positive electrode in a cathode ray tube.

3.21 a. atomic number
b. both
c. mass number
d. atomic number

3.23 a. lithium, Li   **b.** fluorine, F
c. calcium, Ca   **d.** zinc, Zn
e. neon, Ne   **f.** silicon, Si
g. iodine, I   **h.** oxygen, O

3.25 a. 18 protons and 18 electrons
b. 30 protons and 30 electrons
c. 53 protons and 53 electrons
d. 48 protons and 48 electrons

3.27 See the table at the bottom of the page.

3.29 a. 38 protons, 51 neutrons, 38 electrons
b. 24 protons, 28 neutrons, 24 electrons
c. 16 protons, 18 neutrons, 16 electrons
d. 35 protons, 46 neutrons, 35 electrons

3.31 a. $^{31}_{15}P$ **b.** $^{80}_{35}Br$ **c.** $^{122}_{50}Sn$
d. $^{35}_{17}Cl$ **e.** $^{202}_{80}Hg$

3.33 a. $^{36}_{18}Ar$ $^{38}_{18}Ar$ $^{40}_{18}Ar$
b. They all have the same number of protons and electrons.
c. They have different numbers of neutrons, which gives them different mass numbers.
d. The atomic mass of Ar listed on the periodic table is the average atomic mass of all the isotopes.
e. Because argon has an atomic mass of 39.95, the isotope $^{40}_{18}Ar$ would be the most prevalent.

3.35 69.72 amu

3.37 a. spherical   **b.** two lobes
c. spherical

3.39 a. 1 and 2   **b.** 3
c. 1 and 2   **d.** 1, 2, and 3

3.41 a. There are five orbitals in the $3d$ sublevel.
b. There is one sublevel in the $n = 1$ energy level.
c. There is one orbital in the $6s$ sublevel.
d. There are nine orbitals in the $n = 3$ energy level.

3.43 a. There is a maximum of two electrons in a $3p$ orbital.
b. There is a maximum of six electrons in the $3p$ sublevel.
c. There is a maximum of 32 electrons in the $n = 4$ energy level.
d. There is a maximum of 10 electrons in the $5d$ sublevel.

3.45

3.47 a. $1s^2 2s^2 2p^6 3s^2 3p^6 4s^2 3d^6$
b. $1s^2 2s^2 2p^6 3s^1$
c. $1s^2 2s^2 2p^6 3s^2 3p^6 4s^2 3d^{10} 4p^6 5s^1$
d. $1s^2 2s^2 2p^6 3s^2 3p^6 4s^2 3d^{10} 4p^3$

3.49 a. $[Ne]3s^2$ **b.** $[Xe]6s^2$
c. $[Ne]3s^2 3p^1$ **d.** $[Ar]4s^2 3d^2$

3.51 a. S   **b.** Co   **c.** Si   **d.** Br

3.53 a. Al   **b.** C   **c.** Ar   **d.** Zr

3.55 a. 10   **b.** 6   **c.** 3   **d.** 1

3.57 a. 3   **b.** 5   **c.** 7

3.59 a. Group 6A (16) $\cdot \overset{\cdot\cdot}{\underset{\cdot\cdot}{S}} :$ **b.** Group 5A (15) $\cdot \overset{\cdot\cdot}{N} \cdot$
c. Group 2A (2) $Ca \cdot$ **d.** Group 1A (1) $Na \cdot$
e. Group 3A (13) $\cdot Ga \cdot$

3.61 a. Na   **b.** Rb   **c.** Na   **d.** Rb

3.63 a. Mg, Al, Si   **b.** I, Br, Cl
c. Sr, Sb, I   **d.** Na, Si, P

3.65 a. Br   **b.** Mg
c. P   **d.** Xe

3.67 a. Br, Cl, F   **b.** Na, Al, Cl
c. Cs, K, Na   **d.** Ca, As, Br

3.69 larger, more

3.71 Ca, Ga, Ge, Br

Answer to 3.27

Name of the Element	Symbol	Atomic Number	Mass Number	Number of Protons	Number of Neutrons	Number of Electrons
Aluminum	Al	13	27	13	14	13
Magnesium	Mg	12	24	12	12	12
Potassium	K	19	39	19	20	19
Sulfur	S	16	31	16	15	16
Iron	Fe	26	56	26	30	26

3.73 lower, more

3.75 a. 1 **b.** 2 **c.** 2 **d.** 3

3.77 a. false **b.** true **c.** true
d. false **e.** true

3.79 Statements **b** and **c** are true.

3.81 a. 1 and 2 **b.** 1 **c.** 1
d. 3 **e.** 2

3.83 a. $^{16}_8X$, $^{17}_8X$, and $^{18}_8X$ have eight protons.
b. $^{16}_8X$, $^{17}_8X$, and $^{18}_8X$ are isotopes of oxygen.
c. $^{16}_8X$ and $^{16}_9X$ have mass number 16, whereas $^{18}_8X$ and $^{18}_{10}X$ have mass number 18.
d. $^{16}_8X$ and $^{18}_{10}X$ both have eight neutrons.

3.85 a. Both atoms have 20 neutrons.
b. Both atoms have 14 protons and 14 electrons.
c. Both atoms have 22 neutrons.

3.87 a. ^9_4Be **b.** $^{11}_5B$ **c.** $^{13}_6C$
d. $^{10}_5B$ **e.** $^{12}_6C$
Representations **B** and **D** are isotopes of boron; **C** and **E** are isotopes of carbon.

3.89 **A** is Na, **B** is Rb, **C** is K, and **D** is Li.

3.91 a. Na **b.** Cl **c.** S **d.** Ar
e. Si **f.** Na **g.** Mg

3.93 a. Period 4, Group 7A (17)
b. Period 3, Group 8A (18)
c. Period 4, Group 1A (1)
d. Period 7, Group 2A (2)

3.95 a. metal **b.** metal **c.** metal **d.** nonmetal

3.97 a. false **b.** false **c.** true
d. false **e.** true

3.99 a. 48 protons, 66 neutrons, 48 electrons
b. 43 protons, 55 neutrons, 43 electrons
c. 79 protons, 120 neutrons, 79 electrons
d. 86 protons, 136 neutrons, 86 electrons
e. 54 protons, 82 neutrons, 54 electrons

3.101 See the table at the bottom of the page.

3.103 a. $3p$ **b.** $5s$ **c.** $4p$ **d.** $4s$

3.105 a. 6 **b.** 6 **c.** 10 **d.** 2

3.107 a. phosphorus **b.** lithium (H is a nonmetal)
c. cadmium **d.** nitrogen
e. sodium

3.109 a. Na **b.** Na **c.** F
d. Na **e.** Cl

3.111 a. 82 protons, 126 neutrons, 82 electrons
b. $^{214}_{82}Pb$ **c.** $^{214}_{83}Bi$

3.113 a. O **b.** Ar **c.** C
d. Na **e.** Ra

3.115 28.09 amu

3.117 a. X is a metal; Y and Z are nonmetals.
b. X has the largest atomic radius.
c. Y and Z have six valence electrons and are in Group 6A (16).
d. Y has the highest ionization energy.
e. Y has the smallest atomic radius.

Answer to 3.101

Name of the Element	Atomic Symbol	Number of Protons	Number of Neutrons	Number of Electrons
Sulfur	$^{34}_{16}S$	16	18	16
Nickel	$^{62}_{28}Ni$	28	34	28
Magnesium	$^{26}_{12}Mg$	12	14	12
Radon	$^{228}_{88}Ra$	88	140	88

Nuclear Chemistry

Visit **www.masteringchemistry.com** for self-study materials and instructor-assigned homework.

Simone's doctor is concerned about her

elevated cholesterol, which could lead to coronary heart disease and a heart attack. He sends her to a nuclear medicine center to undergo a cardiac stress test.

Paul, the nuclear medicine technician, explains to Simone that he will inject Technetium-99m (Tc-99m) into her bloodstream. He explains that Tc-99m is a radioactive isotope that has a half-life of 6 h and is a gamma emitter. Simone is curious about the term "half-life". Paul explains that a half-life is the amount of time it takes for one-half of a radioactive sample to break down. He assures her that after four half-lives (one day), the radiation emitted will be almost zero.

Paul tells Simone that when the Tc-99m reaches her heart that any area with restricted blood supply will pick up only small amounts of the radioisotope, which can indicate coronary heart disease. Later, Simone will

undergo an active stress test to compare her cardiac blood flow during rest and under stress.

Career: Nuclear Medicine Technician

Nuclear medicine is frequently used to diagnose and treat a variety of medical conditions. A variety of techniques are employed for imaging, including Computed Tomography (CT), Magnetic Resonance Imaging (MRI), and Positron Emission Tomography (PET). Nuclear medicine technicians operate the instrumentation and computers associated with the various techniques in nuclear medicine. Nuclear medicine technicians safely handle radioisotopes, employ the necessary type of shielding, and administer radioactive isotopes to patients. In addition, they must physically and mentally prepare patients for imaging by explaining the procedure to them.

A female patient, age 50, complains of nervousness, irritability, increased perspiration, brittle hair, and muscle weakness. Her hands are shaky at times, and her heart often beats rapidly. She has been experiencing weight loss. The doctor decides to test her thyroid. To get a detailed look, a thyroid scan is ordered. The patient is given a small amount of an iodine radioisotope, which will be taken up by the thyroid. The scan shows a higher than normal rate of uptake of the radioactive iodine, which indicates an overactive thyroid gland, a condition called *hyperthyroidism*. Treatment for hyperthyroidism includes the use of drugs to lower the level of thyroid hormone, the use of radioactive iodine to destroy thyroid cells, or surgical removal of part or the entire thyroid. In our case, the nuclear physician decides to use radioactive iodine. To begin treatment, the patient drinks a solution containing radioactive iodine. In the following few weeks, the cells that take up the radioactive iodine are destroyed by the radiation. After treatment, further tests show that the patient's thyroid is smaller and the blood level of thyroid hormone is normal.

With the production of artificial radioactive substances in 1934, the field of nuclear medicine was established. In 1937, the first radioactive isotope was used to treat a patient with leukemia at the University of California at Berkeley. Major strides in the use of radioactivity in medicine occurred in 1946, when a radioactive iodine isotope was successfully used to diagnose thyroid function and to treat hyperthyroidism and thyroid cancer. During the 1970s and 1980s, a variety of radioactive substances were used to produce images of organs such as the liver, spleen, thyroid, kidney, and brain, and to detect heart disease. Today, procedures in nuclear medicine provide information about the function and structure of every organ in the body, allowing physicians to diagnose and treat diseases early.

4.1 Natural Radioactivity

Most naturally occurring isotopes of elements up to atomic number 19 have stable nuclei. An atom has a stable nucleus when the forces of attraction and repulsion are balanced. Elements with atomic numbers 20 and higher usually have one or more isotopes that have unstable nuclei. An unstable nucleus has too many or too few protons compared to the number of neutrons, which means the forces between protons and neutrons are unbalanced. An unstable nucleus is *radioactive*, which means that it spontaneously emits small particles of energy called **radiation**, to become more stable.

Radiation may take the form of alpha (α) and beta (β) particles, positrons (β^+), or pure energy such as gamma (γ) rays. An isotope that emits radiation is called a *radioisotope*. For most types of radiation, there is a change in the number of protons in the nucleus. This change, called *transmutation*, occurs when an atom of one element is converted into an atom of a different element. This kind of nuclear change was not evident to Dalton when he made his predictions about atoms. Elements with atomic numbers of 93 and higher are produced artificially in nuclear laboratories and consist only of radioactive isotopes.

In Section 3.5, we wrote symbols for the different isotopes of an element. These symbols had their mass numbers written in the upper left corner and their atomic number in the lower left corner. Recall that the mass number is equal to the number of protons and neutrons in the nucleus, and that the atomic number is equal to the number of protons. For example, a radioactive isotope of iodine used in the diagnosis and treatment of thyroid conditions has a symbol with a mass number of 131 and an atomic number of 53.

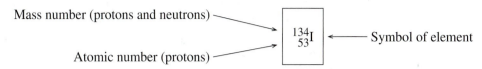

Mass number (protons and neutrons) $\longrightarrow$ $^{134}_{53}\text{I}$ $\longleftarrow$ Symbol of element

Atomic number (protons) $\longrightarrow$

Radioactive isotopes are identified by writing the mass number after the element's name or symbol. Thus, in this example, the isotope is called iodine-131 or I-131. Table 4.1 compares some stable, nonradioactive isotopes with some radioactive isotopes.

TABLE 4.1 Stable and Radioactive Isotopes of Some Elements

Magnesium	Iodine	Uranium
Stable Isotopes		
$^{24}_{12}\text{Mg}$	$^{127}_{53}\text{I}$	None
Magnesium-24	Iodine-127	
Radioactive Isotopes		
$^{23}_{12}\text{Mg}$	$^{125}_{53}\text{I}$	$^{235}_{92}\text{U}$
Magnesium-23	Iodine-125	Uranium-235
$^{27}_{12}\text{Mg}$	$^{131}_{53}\text{I}$	$^{238}_{92}\text{U}$
Magnesium-27	Iodine-131	Uranium-238

Types of Radiation

By emitting radiation, an unstable nucleus forms a more stable, lower energy nucleus. One type of radiation consists of *alpha particles*. An **alpha particle** is identical to a helium (He) nucleus, which has two protons and two neutrons. An alpha particle has a mass number of 4, an atomic number of 2, and a charge of 2+. It is represented as the Greek letter alpha (α) or the atomic symbol of a helium nucleus.

Another type of radiation occurs when a radioisotope emits a *beta particle*. A **beta particle** is a high-energy electron with a charge of 1−, and because its mass is so much less than the mass of a proton, it has a mass number of 0. It is represented by the Greek letter beta (β) or by the symbol for the electron including the mass number and the charge, $^{0}_{-1}e$. A beta particle forms when a neutron in an unstable nucleus changes to a proton and an electron.

A **positron**, similar to a beta particle, has a positive (1+) charge with a mass number of 0. It is represented by the Greek letter beta with a 1+ charge, β^{+}, or by the symbol for the electron, which includes the mass number and the charge, $^{0}_{+1}e$. A positron is produced by an unstable nucleus when a proton is transformed into a neutron and a positron.

A positron is an example of *antimatter*, a term physicists use to describe a particle that is the exact opposite of another particle, in this case, an electron. When an electron and a positron collide, their minute masses are completely converted to energy in the form of gamma rays.

$$^{0}_{-1}e + {}^{0}_{+1}e \longrightarrow 2{}^{0}_{0}\gamma$$

Gamma rays are high-energy radiation, released when an unstable nucleus undergoes a rearrangement of its particles to give a more stable, lower-energy nucleus. Gamma rays are often emitted along with other types of radiation. A gamma ray is represented by the Greek letter gamma (γ). Because gamma rays are energy only, zeros are used to show that a gamma ray has no mass or charge.

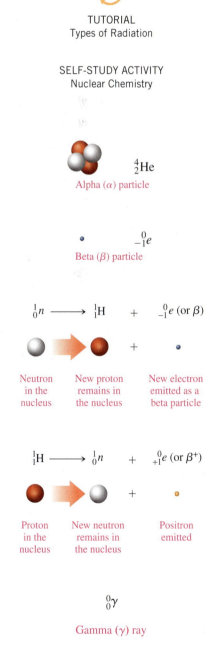

MC

TUTORIAL
Types of Radiation

SELF-STUDY ACTIVITY
Nuclear Chemistry

$^{4}_{2}\text{He}$

Alpha (α) particle

$^{0}_{-1}e$

Beta (β) particle

$^{1}_{0}n \longrightarrow {}^{1}_{1}\text{H} + {}^{0}_{-1}e \text{ (or } \beta)$

| Neutron in the nucleus | New proton remains in the nucleus | New electron emitted as a beta particle |

$^{1}_{1}\text{H} \longrightarrow {}^{1}_{0}n + {}^{0}_{+1}e \text{ (or } \beta^{+})$

| Proton in the nucleus | New neutron remains in the nucleus | Positron emitted |

$^{0}_{0}\gamma$

Gamma (γ) ray

Table 4.2 summarizes the types of radiation we will use in nuclear equations.

TABLE 4.2 Some Forms of Radiation

Type of Radiation	Symbol		Change in Nucleus	Mass Number	Charge
Alpha particle	α	^4_2He	Two protons and two neutrons are emitted as an alpha particle.	4	2+
Beta particle	β	$^0_{-1}e$	A neutron changes to a proton and an electron is emitted.	0	1−
Positron	β^+	$^0_{+1}e$	A proton changes to a neutron and a positron is emitted.	0	1+
Gamma ray	γ	$^0_0\gamma$	Energy is lost to stabilize the nucleus.	0	0
Proton	p	^1_1H	A proton is emitted.	1	1+
Neutron	n	^1_0n	A neutron is emitted.	1	0

CONCEPT CHECK 4.1 **Radiation Particles**

Give the name and write the symbol for each of the following types of radiation:

a. contains two protons and two neutrons
b. has a mass number of 0 and a 1− charge

ANSWER

a. An alpha (α) particle, ^4_2He, has two protons and two neutrons.
b. A beta (β) particle, $^0_{-1}e$, is like an electron with a mass number of 0 and a 1− charge.

SELF-STUDY ACTIVITY
Radiation and Its Biological Effects

Biological Effects of Radiation

When radiation strikes molecules in its path, electrons may be knocked away, forming unstable ions. If this *ionizing radiation* passes through the human body, it may interact with water molecules, removing electrons, and producing H_2O^+, which can cause undesirable chemical reactions.

The cells most sensitive to ionizing radiation are the ones undergoing rapid division—those of the bone marrow, skin, reproductive organs, and intestinal lining, as well as all cells of growing children. Damaged cells may lose their ability to produce necessary materials. For example, if radiation damages cells of the bone marrow, red blood cells may no longer be produced. If sperm cells, ova, or the cells of a fetus are damaged, birth defects may result. In contrast, cells of the nerves, muscles, liver, and adult bones are much less sensitive to radiation because they undergo little or no cellular division.

Cancer cells are another example of rapidly dividing cells. Because cancer cells are highly sensitive to radiation, large doses of radiation are used to destroy them. The normal tissue that surrounds cancer cells divides at a slower rate and suffers less damage from radiation. However, radiation, due to its high penetrating energy, may itself cause malignant tumors, leukemia, anemia, and genetic mutations.

Radiation Protection

Radiologists, chemists, doctors, and nurses who work with radioactive isotopes must use proper radiation protection. Proper **shielding** is necessary to prevent exposure. Alpha particles, which have the largest mass and charge of the radiation particles, travel only a few centimeters in the air before they collide with air molecules, acquire electrons, and become helium atoms. A piece of paper, clothing, and our skin are protection against alpha particles. Lab coats and gloves will also provide sufficient shielding. However, if alpha emitters are ingested or inhaled, the alpha particles they give off can cause serious internal damage.

Beta particles have a very small mass and move much faster and farther than alpha particles, traveling as far as several meters through air. They can pass through paper and penetrate as far as 4–5 mm into body tissue. External exposure to beta particles can burn the surface of the skin, but they do not travel far enough to reach the internal organs. Heavy clothing such as lab coats and gloves are needed to protect the skin from beta particles.

Gamma rays travel great distances through the air and pass through many materials, including body tissues. Because gamma rays penetrate so deeply, exposure to these rays is extremely hazardous. Only very dense shielding from substances such as lead and concrete will stop them. Syringes used for injections of radioactive materials use shielding made of lead or heavy-weight materials such as tungsten and plastic composites.

When working with radioactive materials, medical personnel wear protective clothing and gloves and stand behind a shield (see Figure 4.1). Long tongs may be used to pick up vials of radioactive material, keeping them away from the hands and body.

Table 4.3 summarizes the shielding materials required for the various types of radiation.

If you work in an environment where radioactive materials are present, such as a nuclear medicine facility, try to keep the time you must spend in a radioactive area to a minimum. Remaining in a radioactive area twice as long exposes you to twice as much radiation.

Keep your distance! The greater the distance from the radioactive source, the lower the intensity of radiation you receive. Just by doubling your distance from the radiation source, the intensity of the radiation drops to $\left(\frac{1}{2}\right)^2$ or one-fourth of its previous value.

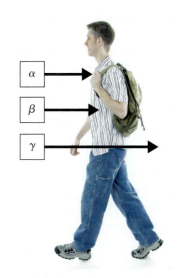

FIGURE 4.1 A person working with radioisotopes wears protective clothing and gloves and stands behind a shield.

Q What types of radiation does a lead shield block?

TABLE 4.3 Properties of Ionizing Radiation and Shielding Required

Property	Alpha (α) Particle	Beta (β) Particle	Gamma (γ) Ray
Travel Distance in Air	2–4 cm	200–300 cm	500 m
Tissue Depth	0.05 mm	4–5 mm	50 cm or more
Shielding	Paper, clothing	Heavy clothing, lab coats, gloves	Lead, thick concrete
Typical Source	Radium-226	Carbon-14	Technetium-99m

SAMPLE PROBLEM 4.1   Radiation Protection

How does the type of shielding for alpha radiation differ from that used for gamma radiation?

SOLUTION

Alpha radiation is stopped by paper and clothing. However, lead or concrete is needed for protection from gamma radiation.

STUDY CHECK 4.1

Besides shielding, what other methods help reduce exposure to radiation?

QUESTIONS AND PROBLEMS

4.1 Natural Radioactivity

LEARNING GOAL: *Describe alpha, beta, positron, and gamma radiation.*

4.1 Identify the type of particle or radiation for each of the following:
  a. $_2^4\text{He}$ **b.** $_{+1}^{0}e$ **c.** $_0^0\gamma$

4.2 Identify the type of particle or radiation for each of the following:
  a. $_{-1}^{0}e$ **b.** $_1^1\text{H}$ **c.** $_0^1n$

4.3 Naturally occurring potassium consists of three isotopes: potassium-39, potassium-40, and potassium-41.
  a. Write the atomic symbol for each isotope.
  b. In what ways are the isotopes similar and in what ways do they differ?

4.4 Naturally occurring iodine is iodine-127. Medically, radioactive isotopes of iodine-125 and iodine-130 are used.
   a. Write the atomic symbol for each isotope.
   b. In what ways are the isotopes similar and in what ways do they differ?

4.5 Supply the missing information in the following table:

Medical Use	Atomic Symbol	Mass Number	Number of Protons	Number of Neutrons
Heart imaging	$^{201}_{81}\text{Tl}$			
Radiation therapy		60	27	
Abdominal scan			31	36
Hyperthyroidism	$^{131}_{53}\text{I}$			
Leukemia treatment			32	17

4.6 Supply the missing information in the following table:

Medical Use	Atomic Symbol	Mass Number	Number of Protons	Number of Neutrons
Cancer treatment	$^{131}_{55}\text{Cs}$			
Brain scan		99	43	
Blood flow		141	58	
Bone scan		85		47
Lung function	$^{133}_{54}\text{Xe}$			

4.7 Write the symbol for each of the following isotopes used in nuclear medicine:
   a. copper-64   **b.** selenium-75
   c. sodium-24   **d.** nitrogen-15

4.8 Write the symbol for each of the following isotopes used in nuclear medicine:
   a. indium-111   **b.** palladium-103
   c. barium-131   **d.** rubidium-82

4.9 Identify each of the following:
   a. $^{0}_{-1}\text{X}$ **b.** $^{4}_{2}\text{X}$ **c.** $^{1}_{0}\text{X}$
   d. $^{38}_{18}\text{X}$ **e.** $^{14}_{6}\text{X}$

4.10 Identify each of the following:
   a. $^{1}_{1}\text{X}$ **b.** $^{81}_{35}\text{X}$ **c.** $^{0}_{0}\text{X}$
   d. $^{59}_{26}\text{X}$ **e.** $^{0}_{+1}\text{X}$

4.11 Match the type of radiation with each of the following statements:
   1. alpha particle
   2. beta particle
   3. gamma radiation

   a. does not penetrate skin
   b. shielding protection includes lead or thick concrete
   c. can be very harmful if ingested

4.12 Match the type of radiation with each of the following statements:
   1. alpha particle
   2. beta particle
   3. gamma radiation

   a. penetrates farthest into skin and body tissues
   b. shielding protection includes lab coats and gloves
   c. travels only a short distance in air

4.2 Nuclear Reactions

In a process called **radioactive decay**, a nucleus spontaneously breaks down by emitting radiation. This process can be written as a nuclear equation with the atomic symbols of the original radioactive nucleus on the left, an arrow, and the new nucleus and radiation emitted on the right.

$$\text{Radioactive nucleus} \longrightarrow \text{new nucleus} + \text{radiation}(\alpha, \beta, \beta^+, \gamma)$$

In a nuclear equation, the total of the mass numbers and the total of the atomic numbers on one side of the arrow must equal the total of the mass numbers and the total of the atomic numbers on the other side.

Alpha Decay

In alpha decay, an unstable nucleus emits an alpha particle, which consists of 2 protons and 2 neutrons. Thus, the mass number of the radioactive nucleus decreases by 4, and its atomic number decreases by 2. For example, when uranium-238 emits an alpha particle, the new nucleus that forms has a mass number of 234. Compared to uranium with 92 protons, the new nucleus has 90 protons, which is thorium.

Radioactive uranium nucleus

Alpha particle

Radiation

$^{4}_{2}\text{He}$

Thorium-234 nucleus

New nucleus

$^{238}_{92}\text{U}$

○ Neutron

● Proton

$^{234}_{90}\text{Th}$

| 146 neutrons | 144 neutrons | 2 neutrons |
| 92 protons | 90 protons | 2 protons |

$$^{238}_{92}\text{U} \longrightarrow \quad ^{234}_{90}\text{Th} + ^{4}_{2}\text{He}$$

Radioactive nucleus — New nucleus — Alpha particle

In alpha decay, the mass number of the new nucleus decreases by 4 and its atomic number decreases by 2.

CONCEPT CHECK 4.2   **Alpha Decay**

When francium-221 undergoes alpha decay, an alpha particle is emitted.

a. Does the new nucleus have a larger or smaller mass number? By how much?
b. Does the new nucleus have a larger or smaller atomic number? By how much?

ANSWER

a. The loss of an alpha particle will give the new nucleus a smaller mass number. Because an alpha particle is a helium nucleus, $^4_2$He, the mass number of the new nucleus will decrease by four from 221 to 217.
b. The loss of an alpha particle will give the new nucleus a smaller atomic number. Because an alpha particle is a helium nucleus, $^4_2$He, the atomic number of the new nucleus will decrease by two from 87 to 85.

We can look at writing a balanced nuclear equation for americium-241, which undergoes alpha decay as shown in Sample Problem 4.2.

SAMPLE PROBLEM 4.2   **Writing an Equation for Alpha Decay**

Smoke detectors that are used in homes and apartments contain americium-241, which undergoes alpha decay. When alpha particles collide with air molecules, charged particles are produced that generate an electrical current. If smoke particles enter the detector, they interfere with the formation of charged particles in the air, and the electrical current is interrupted. This causes the alarm to sound and warns the occupants of the danger of fire. Complete the following nuclear equation for the decay of americium-241:

$$^{241}_{95}\text{Am} \longrightarrow ? + {}^4_2\text{He}$$

SOLUTION

Step 1   **Write the incomplete nuclear equation.**

$$^{241}_{95}\text{Am} \longrightarrow ? + {}^4_2\text{He}$$

Step 2   **Determine the missing mass number.** In the equation, the mass number of the americium, 241, is equal to the sum of the mass numbers of the new nucleus and the alpha particle.

$$241 \quad = ? + 4$$
$$241 - 4 = ?$$
$$241 - 4 = 237 \text{ (mass number of new nucleus)}$$

Step 3   **Determine the missing atomic number.** The atomic number of americium, 95, must equal the sum of the atomic numbers of the new nucleus and the alpha particle.

$$95 \quad = ? + 2$$
$$95 - 2 = ?$$
$$95 - 2 = 93 \text{ (atomic number of new nucleus)}$$

Step 4   **Determine the symbol of the new nucleus.** On the periodic table, the element that has atomic number 93 is neptunium, Np. The nucleus of this isotope of Np is written as $^{237}_{93}$Np.

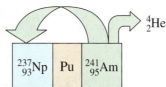

Step 5   **Complete the nuclear equation.**

$$^{241}_{95}\text{Am} \longrightarrow {}^{237}_{93}\text{Np} + {}^4_2\text{He}$$

STUDY CHECK 4.2

Write a balanced nuclear equation for the alpha decay of Po-214.

A smoke detector sounds an alarm when smoke enters its ionization chamber.

Guide to Completing a Nuclear Equation

1 Write the incomplete nuclear equation.

2 Determine the missing mass number.

3 Determine the missing atomic number.

4 Determine the symbol of the new nucleus.

5 Complete the nuclear equation.

Beta Decay

As we learned in Section 4.1, the formation of a beta particle is the result of the breakdown of a neutron into a proton and an electron (beta particle). Because the proton remains in the nucleus, the number of protons increases by one, while the number of neutrons decreases by one. Thus, in a nuclear equation for beta decay, the mass number of the radioactive nucleus and the mass number of the new nucleus are the same. However, the atomic number of the new nucleus increases by one, which makes it a nucleus of a different element (*transmutation*). For example, the beta decay of a carbon-14 nucleus produces a nitrogen-14 nucleus.

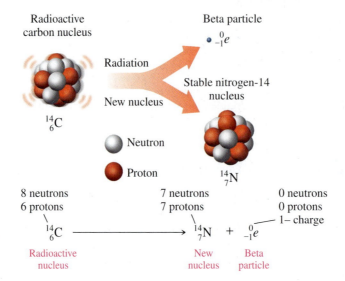

In beta decay, the mass number of the new nucleus remains the same and its atomic number increases by 1.

$$_{6}^{14}\text{C} \longrightarrow {}_{7}^{14}\text{N} + {}_{-1}^{0}e$$

Radioactive nucleus   New nucleus   Beta particle

Chemistry Link to the Environment

RADON IN OUR HOMES

The presence of radon has become a much publicized environmental and health issue because of the radiation danger it poses. Radioactive isotopes such as radium-226 are naturally present in many types of rocks and soils. Radium-226 emits an alpha particle and is converted into radon gas, which diffuses out of the rocks and soil.

$$_{88}^{226}\text{Ra} \longrightarrow {}_{86}^{222}\text{Rn} + {}_{2}^{4}\text{He}$$

Outdoors, radon gas poses little danger because it disperses in the air. However, if the radioactive source is under a house or building, the radon gas can enter the house through cracks in the foundation or other openings. Those who live or work there may inhale the radon. Inside the lungs, radon-222 emits alpha particles to form polonium-218, which is known to cause lung cancer.

$$_{86}^{222}\text{Rn} \longrightarrow {}_{84}^{218}\text{Po} + {}_{2}^{4}\text{He}$$

The Environmental Protection Agency (EPA) estimates that in 2003, exposure to radon caused 21 000 lung cancer deaths in the United States. The EPA recommends that the maximum level of radon not exceed 4 picocuries (pCi) per liter of air in a home. One picocurie (pCi) is equal to 1×10^{-12} curies (Ci); curies are described in Section 4.3. In California, 1 percent of all the houses surveyed exceeded the EPA's recommended maximum radon level.

A radon gas detector is used to determine radon levels in buildings.

TUTORIAL
Writing Nuclear Equations

SAMPLE PROBLEM 4.3   Writing an Equation for Beta Decay

Write the balanced nuclear equation for the beta decay of cobalt-60.

SOLUTION

Step 1   **Write the incomplete nuclear equation.**

$$_{27}^{60}\text{Co} \longrightarrow ? + {}_{-1}^{0}e$$

Step 2   **Determine the missing mass number.** In the equation, the mass number of the cobalt, 60, is equal to the sum of the mass numbers of the new nucleus and the beta particle.

$$60 \quad = ? + 0$$
$$60 - 0 = ?$$
$$60 - 0 = 60 \text{ (mass number of new nucleus)}$$

Step 3   **Determine the missing atomic number.** The atomic number of cobalt, 27, must equal the sum of the atomic numbers of the new nucleus and the beta particle.

$$27 \quad = ? - 1$$
$$27 + 1 = ?$$
$$27 + 1 = 28 \text{ (atomic number of new nucleus)}$$

Step 4   **Determine the symbol of the new nucleus.** On the periodic table, the element that has atomic number 28 is nickel (Ni). The nucleus of this isotope of Ni is written as $^{60}_{28}\text{Ni}$.

Step 5   **Complete the nuclear equation.**

$$^{60}_{27}\text{Co} \longrightarrow {}^{60}_{28}\text{Ni} + {}^{0}_{-1}e$$

STUDY CHECK 4.3

Write the balanced nuclear equation for the beta decay of chromium-51.

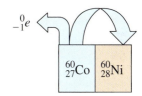

Positron Emission

As we learned in Section 4.1, positron emission occurs when a proton in an unstable nucleus is converted to a neutron and a positron. The neutron remains in the nucleus, but the positron is emitted. In a nuclear equation for positron emission, the mass number of the radioactive nucleus and the mass number of the new nucleus are the same. However, the atomic number of the new nucleus decreases by one, indicating a change of one element into another (*transmutation*). For example, an aluminum-24 nucleus undergoes positron emission to produce a magnesium-24 nucleus. The atomic number of magnesium, 12, and the charge of the positron (1+) give the atomic number of aluminum, 13.

$$^{24}_{13}\text{Al} \longrightarrow {}^{24}_{12}\text{Mg} + {}^{0}_{+1}e$$

SAMPLE PROBLEM 4.4   **Writing an Equation for Positron Emission**

Write the balanced nuclear equation for manganese-49, which decays by emitting a positron.

SOLUTION

Step 1   **Write the incomplete nuclear equation.**

$$^{49}_{25}\text{Mn} \longrightarrow ? + {}^{0}_{+1}e$$

Step 2   **Determine the missing mass number.** In the equation, the mass number of the manganese, 49, is equal to the sum of the mass numbers of the new nucleus and the positron.

$$49 \quad = ? + 0$$
$$49 - 0 = ?$$
$$49 - 0 = 49 \text{ (mass number of new nucleus)}$$

Step 3   **Determine the missing atomic number.** The atomic number of manganese, 25, must equal the sum of the atomic numbers of the new nucleus and the positron.

$$25 \quad = ? + 1$$
$$25 - 1 = ?$$
$$25 - 1 = 24 \text{ (atomic number of new nucleus)}$$

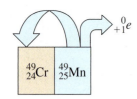

Step 4 **Determine the symbol of the new nucleus.** On the periodic table, the element that has atomic number 24 is chromium, Cr. The nucleus of this isotope of Cr is written as $^{49}_{24}\text{Cr}$.

Step 5 **Complete the nuclear equation.**

$$^{49}_{25}\text{Mn} \longrightarrow {}^{49}_{24}\text{Cr} + {}^{0}_{+1}e$$

STUDY CHECK 4.4

Write the balanced nuclear equation for xenon-118, which undergoes positron emission.

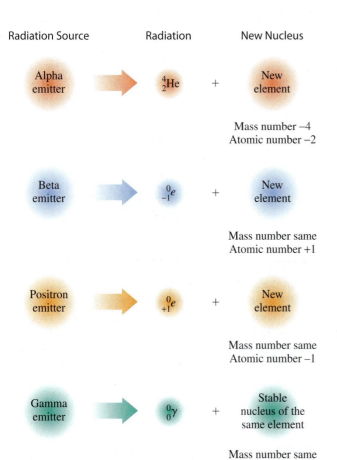

Radiation Source	Radiation	New Nucleus
Alpha emitter	$^{4}_{2}\text{He}$ +	New element
		Mass number −4 Atomic number −2
Beta emitter	$^{0}_{-1}e$ +	New element
		Mass number same Atomic number +1
Positron emitter	$^{0}_{+1}e$ +	New element
		Mass number same Atomic number −1
Gamma emitter	$^{0}_{0}\gamma$ +	Stable nucleus of the same element
		Mass number same Atomic number same

FIGURE 4.2 When the nuclei of alpha, beta, positron, and gamma emitters emit radiation, new and more stable nuclei are produced.

Q What changes occur in the number of protons and neutrons of an unstable nucleus that undergoes alpha decay?

Gamma Emission

Pure gamma emitters are rare, although some gamma radiation accompanies most alpha and beta radiation. In radiology, one of the most commonly used gamma emitters is technetium (Tc). The unstable isotope of technetium is written as the *metastable* (symbol m) isotope technetium-99m, Tc-99m, or $^{99m}_{43}\text{Tc}$. By emitting energy in the form of gamma rays, the unstable nucleus becomes more stable.

$$^{99m}_{43}\text{Tc} \longrightarrow {}^{99}_{43}\text{Tc} + {}^{0}_{0}\gamma$$

Figure 4.2 summarizes the changes in the nucleus for alpha, beta, positron, and gamma radiation.

Producing Radioactive Isotopes

Today, many radioisotopes are produced in small amounts by converting stable, nonradioactive isotopes into radioactive ones. In the process called *transmutation*, a stable nucleus is bombarded by high-speed particles such as alpha particles, protons, neutrons, and small nuclei. When one of these particles is absorbed, the stable nucleus is converted to a radioactive isotope and usually some type of radiation particle.

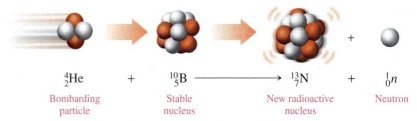

$$^{4}_{2}\text{He} + {}^{10}_{5}\text{B} \longrightarrow {}^{13}_{7}\text{N} + {}^{1}_{0}n$$

Bombarding particle   Stable nucleus   New radioactive nucleus   Neutron

When nonradioactive B-10 is bombarded by an alpha particle, the products are radioactive N-13 and a neutron.

All elements that have an atomic number greater than 92 have been produced artificially by bombardment. Most have been produced in small amounts and exist for only a short time, making it difficult to study their properties. For example, when californium-249 is bombarded with nitrogen-15, the radioactive element 105, dubnium (Db), and some neutrons are produced.

$$^{15}_{7}\text{N} + {}^{249}_{98}\text{Cf} \longrightarrow {}^{260}_{105}\text{Db} + 4{}^{1}_{0}n$$

Technetium-99m is a radioisotope used in nuclear medicine for several diagnostic procedures, including the detection of brain tumors and examinations of the liver and spleen. The source of technetium-99m is molybdenum-99, which is produced in a nuclear reactor by neutron bombardment of molybdenum-98.

$$_{0}^{1}n + _{42}^{98}\text{Mo} \longrightarrow _{42}^{99}\text{Mo}$$

Many radiology laboratories have small generators containing molybdenum-99, which decays to technetium-99m.

$$_{42}^{99}\text{Mo} \longrightarrow _{43}^{99m}\text{Tc} + _{-1}^{0}e$$

The technetium-99m radioisotope decays by emitting gamma rays. Gamma emission is desirable for diagnostic work because the gamma rays pass through the body to the detection equipment.

$$_{43}^{99m}\text{Tc} \longrightarrow _{43}^{99}\text{Tc} + _{0}^{0}\gamma$$

A generator is used to prepare technetium-99m.

TUTORIAL
Alpha, Beta, and Gamma Emitters

CONCEPT CHECK 4.3   Writing an Isotope Produced by Bombardment

Sulfur-32 is bombarded with a neutron to produce a new radioactive isotope and an alpha particle. What is the symbol for the new isotope?

$$_{0}^{1}n + _{16}^{32}\text{S} \longrightarrow \; ? + _{2}^{4}\text{He}$$

ANSWER

To determine the new isotope, we need to calculate its mass number and atomic number. On the left side of the equation, the sum of the mass numbers of one neutron, 1, and the sulfur isotope, 32, gives a total of 33. On the right side, the sum of the mass number of the new isotope and that of the alpha particle, 4, must equal 33. Thus, the new isotope has a mass number of 29.

$$_{0}^{1}n + _{16}^{32}\text{S} \longrightarrow \; _{?}^{29}? + _{2}^{4}\text{He}$$

On the left side of the equation, the sum of the atomic numbers of a neutron, 0, and the sulfur, 16, gives a total of 16. On the right side, the sum of the atomic number of the new isotope and the atomic number of the alpha particle, 2, must equal 16. Thus, the new isotope has an atomic number of 14. On the periodic table, the element that has atomic number 14 is silicon. Thus, the symbol for the new isotope is $_{14}^{29}\text{Si}$.

$$_{0}^{1}n + _{16}^{32}\text{S} \longrightarrow \; _{14}^{29}\text{Si} + _{2}^{4}\text{He}$$

SAMPLE PROBLEM 4.5   Writing Equations for Isotope Production

Write the balanced nuclear equation for the bombardment of nickel-58 by a proton ($_{1}^{1}\text{H}$), which produces a radioactive isotope and an alpha particle.

SOLUTION

Step 1   Write the incomplete nuclear equation.

$$_{1}^{1}\text{H} + _{28}^{58}\text{Ni} \longrightarrow \; ? + _{2}^{4}\text{He}$$

Step 2   Determine the missing mass number. In the equation, the sum of the mass numbers of the proton, 1, and the nickel, 58, gives a total of 59, which must equal the sum of the mass numbers of the new nucleus and the alpha particle, 4.

$$1 + 58 = \; ? + 4$$
$$59 - 4 = \; ?$$
$$59 - 4 = 55 \text{ (mass number of new nucleus)}$$

Step 3   **Determine the missing atomic number.** The sum of the atomic numbers of the proton, 1, and nickel, 28, gives a total of 29, which must equal the sum of the atomic numbers of the new nucleus and the alpha particle, 2.

$$1 + 28 = ? + 2$$
$$29 - 2 = ?$$
$$29 - 2 = 27 \text{ (atomic number of new nucleus)}$$

Step 4   **Determine the symbol of the new nucleus.** On the periodic table, the element that has atomic number 27 is cobalt, Co. The nucleus of this isotope is written as $^{55}_{27}\text{Co}$.

Step 5   **Complete the nuclear equation.**

$$^{1}_{1}\text{H} + {}^{58}_{28}\text{Ni} \longrightarrow {}^{55}_{27}\text{Co} + {}^{4}_{2}\text{He}$$

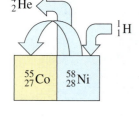

STUDY CHECK 4.5

The first radioactive isotope was produced in 1934 by the bombardment of aluminum-27 by an alpha particle to produce a radioactive isotope and one neutron. What is the balanced nuclear equation for this transmutation?

QUESTIONS AND PROBLEMS

4.2 Nuclear Reactions

LEARNING GOAL: Write a balanced nuclear equation showing mass numbers and atomic numbers for radioactive decay.

4.13 Write a balanced nuclear equation for the alpha decay of each of the following radioactive isotopes:
   a. $^{208}_{84}\text{Po}$ **b.** $^{232}_{90}\text{Th}$
   c. $^{251}_{102}\text{No}$ **d.** radon-220

4.14 Write a balanced nuclear equation for the alpha decay of each of the following radioactive isotopes:
   a. curium-243   **b.** $^{252}_{99}\text{Es}$
   c. $^{251}_{98}\text{Cf}$ **d.** $^{261}_{107}\text{Bh}$

4.15 Write a balanced nuclear equation for the beta decay of each of the following radioactive isotopes:
   a. $^{25}_{11}\text{Na}$ **b.** $^{20}_{8}\text{O}$
   c. strontium-92   **d.** iron-60

4.16 Write a balanced nuclear equation for the beta decay of each of the following radioactive isotopes:
   a. $^{44}_{19}\text{K}$ **b.** iron-59
   c. potassium-42   **d.** $^{141}_{56}\text{Ba}$

4.17 Write a balanced nuclear equation for the positron emission of each of the following radioactive isotopes:
   a. silicon-26   **b.** cobalt-54
   c. $^{77}_{37}\text{Rb}$ **d.** $^{93}_{45}\text{Rh}$

4.18 Write a balanced nuclear equation for the positron emission of each of the following radioactive isotopes:
   a. boron-8   **b.** $^{15}_{8}\text{O}$
   c. $^{40}_{19}\text{K}$ **d.** nitrogen-13

4.19 Complete each of the following nuclear equations and describe the type of radiation:
   a. $^{28}_{13}\text{Al} \longrightarrow ? + {}^{0}_{-1}e$ **b.** $^{180m}_{73}\text{Ta} \longrightarrow {}^{180}_{73}\text{Ta} + ?$
   c. $^{66}_{29}\text{Cu} \longrightarrow {}^{66}_{30}\text{Zn} + ?$ **d.** $? \longrightarrow {}^{234}_{90}\text{Th} + {}^{4}_{2}\text{He}$
   e. $^{188}_{80}\text{Hg} \longrightarrow ? + {}^{0}_{+1}e$

4.20 Complete each of the following nuclear equations and describe the type of radiation:
   a. $^{11}_{6}\text{C} \longrightarrow {}^{11}_{5}\text{B} + ?$ **b.** $^{35}_{16}\text{S} \longrightarrow ? + {}^{0}_{-1}e$
   c. $? \longrightarrow {}^{90}_{39}\text{Y} + {}^{0}_{-1}e$ **d.** $^{210}_{83}\text{Bi} \longrightarrow ? + {}^{4}_{2}\text{He}$
   e. $? \longrightarrow {}^{89}_{39}\text{Y} + {}^{0}_{+1}e$

4.21 Complete each of the following bombardment reactions:
   a. $^{1}_{0}n + {}^{9}_{4}\text{Be} \longrightarrow ?$
   b. $^{1}_{0}n + {}^{131}_{52}\text{Te} \longrightarrow ? + {}^{0}_{-1}e$
   c. $^{1}_{0}n + ? \longrightarrow {}^{24}_{11}\text{Na} + {}^{4}_{2}\text{He}$
   d. $^{4}_{2}\text{He} + {}^{27}_{13}\text{Al} \longrightarrow ? + {}^{1}_{0}n$

4.22 Complete each of the following bombardment reactions:
   a. $? + {}^{40}_{18}\text{Ar} \longrightarrow {}^{43}_{19}\text{K} + {}^{1}_{1}\text{H}$
   b. $^{1}_{0}n + {}^{238}_{92}\text{U} \longrightarrow ?$
   c. $^{1}_{0}n + ? \longrightarrow {}^{14}_{6}\text{C} + {}^{1}_{1}\text{H}$
   d. $? + {}^{64}_{28}\text{Ni} \longrightarrow {}^{272}_{111}\text{Rg} + {}^{1}_{0}n$

4.3 Radiation Measurement

LEARNING GOAL

Describe the detection and measurement of radiation.

One of the most common instruments for detecting beta and gamma radiation is the Geiger counter. It consists of a metal tube filled with a gas such as argon. When radiation enters a window on the end of the tube, it produces charged particles in the gas, which produce an electrical current. Each burst of current is amplified to give a click and a reading on a meter.

$$\text{Ar} + \text{radiation} \longrightarrow \text{Ar}^+ + e^-$$

A radiation technician uses a Geiger counter to check radiation levels.

Measuring Radiation

Radiation is measured in several different ways. When a radiology laboratory obtains a radioisotope, the *activity* of the sample is measured in terms of the number of nuclear disintegrations per second. The **curie (Ci)**, the original unit of activity, was defined as the number of disintegrations that occur in 1 second for 1 gram of radium, which is equal to 3.7×10^{10} disintegrations/s. The unit was named for the Polish scientist Marie Curie, who along with her husband, Pierre, discovered the radioactive elements radium and polonium. The SI unit of radiation activity is the **becquerel (Bq)**, which is 1 disintegration/s.

The **rad (radiation absorbed dose)** is a unit that measures the amount of radiation absorbed by a gram of material such as body tissue. The SI unit for absorbed dose is the **gray (Gy)**, which is defined as the joules of energy absorbed by 1 kilogram of body tissue. The gray is equal to 100 rad.

The **rem (radiation equivalent in humans)** is a unit that measures the biological effects of different kinds of radiation. Although alpha particles do not penetrate the skin, if they should enter the body by some other route, they can cause extensive damage within a short distance in tissue. High-energy radiation, such as beta particles, high-energy protons, and neutrons that penetrate the skin and travel into tissue cause more damage. Gamma rays are damaging because they travel a long way through body tissue.

To determine the **equivalent dose** or rem dose, the absorbed dose (rads) is multiplied by a factor that adjusts for biological damage caused by a particular form of radiation. For beta and gamma radiation, the factor is 1, so the biological damage in rems is the same as the absorbed radiation (rads). For high-energy protons and neutrons, the factor is about 10, and for alpha particles it is 20.

Biological damage (rems) = absorbed dose (rads) × factor

Often the measurement for an equivalent dose will be in units of millirems (mrems). One rem is equal to 1000 mrem. The SI unit is the **sievert (Sv)**. One sievert is equal to 100 rem. Table 4.4 summarizes the units used to measure radiation.

TUTORIAL
Measuring Radiation

SELF-STUDY ACTIVITY
Nuclear Chemistry

TABLE 4.4 **Some Units of Radiation Measurement**			
Measurement	**Common Unit**	**SI Unit**	**Relationship**
Activity	curie (Ci)	becquerel (Bq)	$1 \text{ Ci} = 3.7 \times 10^{10} \text{ Bq}$
Absorbed Dose	rad	gray (Gy)	$1 \text{ Gy} = 100 \text{ rad}$
Biological Damage	rem	sievert (Sv)	$1 \text{ Sv} = 100 \text{ rem}$

A film badge measures radiation exposure.

People who work in radiology laboratories wear film badges to monitor their exposure to radiation. A film badge consists of radiation-sensitive film in a holder that is attached to clothing. If gamma rays, X-rays, or beta particles strike the film, it appears darker upon development. Periodically, the film is collected to determine if any exposure to radiation has occurred.

Chemistry Link to Health

RADIATION AND FOOD

Food-borne illnesses caused by pathogenic bacteria such as *Salmonella*, *Listeria*, and *Escherichia coli* have become a major health concern in the United States. The Centers for Disease Control and Prevention (CDC) estimates that each year, *E. coli* in contaminated foods infects 20 000 people in the United States, and that 500 people die. *E. coli* has been responsible for outbreaks of illness from contaminated ground beef, eggs, fruit juices, lettuce, spinach, and alfalfa sprouts.

The Food and Drug Administration (FDA) has approved the use of 0.3 kGy to 1 kGy of radiation produced by cobalt-60 or cesium-137 for the treatment of foods. The irradiation technology is much like that used to sterilize medical supplies. Cobalt pellets are placed in stainless steel tubes, which are arranged in racks. When food moves through the series of racks, the gamma rays pass through the food and kill the bacteria.

It is important for consumers to understand that when food is irradiated, it never comes into contact with the radioactive source. The gamma rays pass through the food to kill bacteria, but that does not make the food radioactive. The radiation kills bacteria because it stops their ability to divide and grow. We cook or heat food thoroughly for the same purpose. Radiation has little effect on the food itself because its cells are no longer dividing or growing. Thus, irradiated food is not harmed although small amounts of vitamins B_1 and C may be lost.

Currently, tomatoes, blueberries, strawberries, and mushrooms are being irradiated to allow them to be harvested when completely ripe and extend their shelf life (see Figure 4.3). The FDA has also approved the irradiation of pork, poultry, and beef to decrease potential infections and to extend shelf life. Currently, irradiated vegetable and meat products are available in more than 40 countries. In the United States, irradiated foods such as tropical fruits, spinach,

and ground meats are found in some stores. *Apollo 17* astronauts ate irradiated foods on the Moon, and some U.S. hospitals and nursing homes now use irradiated poultry to reduce the possibility of salmonella infections among patients. The extended shelf life of irradiated food also makes it useful for campers and military personnel. Soon, consumers concerned about food safety will have a choice of irradiated meats, fruits, and vegetables at the market.

(a)

(b)

FIGURE 4.3 **(a)** The FDA requires this symbol to appear on irradiated retail foods. **(b)** After two weeks, the irradiated strawberries on the right show no spoilage. Mold is growing on the nonirradiated ones on the left.

Q Why are irradiated foods used on spaceships and in nursing homes?

SAMPLE PROBLEM 4.6   Radiation Measurement

One treatment for bone pain involves intravenous administration of the radioisotope phosphorus-32, which is primarily incorporated into bone. A typical dose of 7 mCi can produce up to 450 rad in the bone. What is the difference between the units of mCi and rad?

SOLUTION

The millicuries (mCi) indicate the activity of the P-32 in terms of nuclei that break down in 1 second. The radiation absorbed dose (rads) is a measure of the amount of radiation absorbed by the bone.

STUDY CHECK 4.6

If P-32 is a beta emitter, how do the number of rems compare to the rads?

Exposure to Radiation

Every day, we are exposed to low levels of radiation from naturally occurring radioactive isotopes in the buildings where we live and work, in our food and water, and in the air we breathe. For example, potassium-40 is a naturally occurring isotope that is present in any potassium-containing food. Other naturally occurring radioisotopes in air and food are carbon-14, radon-222, strontium-90, and iodine-131. The average person in the United States is exposed to about 360 mrem of radiation annually. Medical sources of radiation, including dental, hip, spine, and chest X-rays and mammograms, add to our radiation exposure. Table 4.5 lists some common sources of radiation.

Another source of background radiation is cosmic radiation produced in space by the Sun. People who live at high altitudes or travel by airplane receive a greater amount of cosmic radiation because there are fewer molecules in the atmosphere to absorb the radiation. For example, a person living in Denver receives about twice the cosmic radiation as a person living in Los Angeles. A person living close to a nuclear power plant normally does not receive much additional radiation, perhaps 0.1 mrem in one year. (One rem equals 1000 mrem.) However, in the accident at the Chernobyl nuclear power plant in 1986 in Ukraine, it is estimated that people in a nearby town received as much as 1 rem/h.

Radiation Sickness

The larger the amount of radiation received at one time, the greater the effect on the body. Exposure to radiation of less than 25 rem is usually not detected. Whole-body exposure of 100 rem produces a temporary decrease in the number of white blood cells. If the exposure to radiation is greater than 100 rem, a person may experience symptoms of radiation sickness: nausea, vomiting, fatigue, and a reduction in white-cell count. A whole-body dosage greater than 300 rem can decrease the white-cell count to zero. The victim may have diarrhea, hair loss, and infection. Exposure to radiation of 500 rem is expected to cause death in 50% of the people receiving that dose. This amount of radiation to the whole body is called the *lethal dose for one-half the population*, or the LD_{50}. The LD_{50} varies for different life forms, as Table 4.6 shows. Whole body radiation of 600 rem or greater would be fatal to all humans within a few weeks.

TABLE 4.5 Average Annual Radiation Received by a Person in the United States

Source	Dose (mrem)
Natural	
Ground	20
Air, water, food	30
Cosmic rays	40
Wood, concrete, brick	50
Medical	
Chest X-ray	20
Dental X-ray	20
Mammogram	40
Hip X-ray	60
Lumbar spine X-ray	70
Upper gastrointestinal tract X-ray	200
Other	
Nuclear power plants	0.1
Air travel	10
Television	20
Radon	200*

*Varies widely.

TABLE 4.6 Lethal Doses of Whole-Body Radiation for Some Life Forms

Life Form	LD_{50} (rem)
Insect	100 000
Bacterium	50 000
Rat	800
Human	500
Dog	300

QUESTIONS AND PROBLEMS

4.3 Radiation Measurement

LEARNING GOAL: *Describe the detection and measurement of radiation.*

4.23 Match each property (**1–3**) with its unit of measurement.
1. activity
2. absorbed dose
3. biological damage

   a. rad   **b.** mrem
   c. μCi   **d.** Gy

4.24 Match each property (**1–3**) with its unit of measurement.
1. activity
2. absorbed dose
3. biological damage

   a. mrad   **b.** gray
   c. becquerel   **d.** Sv

4.25 Two technicians in a nuclear laboratory were accidentally exposed to radiation. If one was exposed to 8 mGy and the other to 5 rad, which technician received more radiation?

4.26 Two samples of a radioisotope were spilled in a nuclear laboratory. The activity of one sample was 8 kBq and the other 15 μCi. Which sample produced the higher amount of radiation?

4.27 a. The recommended dosage of iodine-131 is 4.20 μCi/kg of body mass. How many microcuries of iodine-131 are needed for a 70.0-kg patient with hyperthyroidism?

   b. A person receives 50 rad of gamma radiation. What is that amount in grays?

4.28 a. The dosage of technetium-99m for a lung scan is 20. μCi/kg of body mass. How many millicuries of technetium-99m are needed for a 50.0-kg patient?

   b. Suppose a person absorbed 50 mrad of alpha radiation. What would be the equivalent dose in millirems?

SELF-STUDY ACTIVITY
Nuclear Chemistry

4.4 Half-Life of a Radioisotope

The **half-life** of a radioisotope is the amount of time it takes for one-half of a sample to decay. For example, $^{131}_{53}I$ has a half-life of 8.0 days. As $^{131}_{53}I$ decays, it produces the non-radioactive isotope $^{131}_{54}Xe$ and a beta particle.

$$^{131}_{53}I \longrightarrow ^{131}_{54}Xe + ^{0}_{-1}e$$

Suppose we have a sample that initially contains 20. mg of $^{131}_{53}I$. In 8.0 days, one-half (10. mg) of the I-131 nuclei in the sample will decay, which leaves 10. mg of I-131. After 16 days (two half-lives), 5.0 mg of the remaining I-131 decays, which leaves 5.0 mg of I-131. After 24 days (three half-lives), 2.5 mg of the remaining I-131 decays, which leaves 2.5 mg of I-131 still capable of producing radiation.

As the I-131 undergoes beta decay, there is a buildup of the decay product Xe-131. That means that after the first half-life, the decay process produces 10. mg of Xe-131, and after a second half-life, there is a total of 15. mg of the product Xe-131. After the third half-life, there is a total of 17.5 mg of Xe-131.

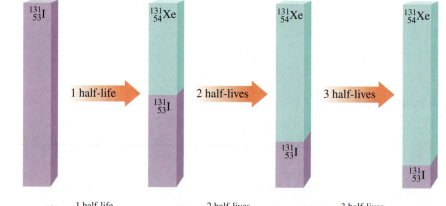

$$20.\text{ mg of } ^{131}_{53}I \xrightarrow{\text{1 half-life}} 10.\text{ mg of } ^{131}_{53}I \xrightarrow{\text{2 half-lives}} 5.0\text{ mg of } ^{131}_{53}I \xrightarrow{\text{3 half-lives}} 2.5\text{ mg of } ^{131}_{53}I$$

A **decay curve** is a diagram of the decay of a radioactive isotope. Figure 4.4 shows such a curve for the $^{131}_{53}I$ we have discussed.

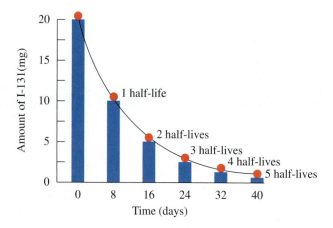

FIGURE 4.4 The decay curve for iodine-131 shows that one-half of the radioactive sample decays and one-half remains radioactive, after each half-life of 8.0 days.

Q How many milligrams of the 20.-mg sample remain radioactive after 2 half-lives?

TUTORIAL
Radioactive Half-Lives

CONCEPT CHECK 4.4 **Half-Lives**

Iridium-192, used to treat breast and prostate cancer, has a half-life of 74 days. What is the activity of the Ir-192 after 74 days if the activity of the initial sample of Ir-192 is 8×10^4 Bq?

ANSWER

In 74 days, which is one half-life of iridium-192, one-half of the iridium-192 atoms will decay. Thus, after 74 days, the activity is half of the initial activity of 8×10^4 Bq, which is 4×10^4 Bq.

SAMPLE PROBLEM 4.7   Using Half-Lives of a Radioisotope

Phosphorus-32, a radioisotope used in the treatment of leukemia, has a half-life of 14.3 days. If a sample contains 8.0 mg of phosphorus-32, how many milligrams of phosphorus-32 remain after 42.9 days?

SOLUTION

Step 1   State the given and needed quantities.

Analyze the Problem

Given	Equality	Need
8.0 mg of P-32 42.9 days elapsed	1 half-life = 14.3 days	milligrams of P-32 remaining

Step 2   Write a plan to calculate the unknown quantity.

days ⟶ Half-life ⟶ number of half-lives

milligrams of $^{32}_{15}P$ ⟶ Number of half-lives ⟶ milligrams of $^{32}_{15}P$ remaining

Step 3   Write the half-life equality and conversion factors.

1 half-life = 14.3 days

$$\frac{14.3 \text{ days}}{1 \text{ half-life}} \quad \text{and} \quad \frac{1 \text{ half-life}}{14.3 \text{ days}}$$

Step 4   **Set up the problem to calculate the needed quantity.** First, we determine the number of half-lives in the amount of time that has elapsed.

$$\text{Number of half-lives} = 42.9 \text{ days} \times \frac{1 \text{ half-life}}{14.3 \text{ days}} = 3 \text{ half-lives}$$

Now we can calculate how much of the sample decays in 3 half-lives, and how many milligrams of the phosphorus remain.

8.0 mg of $^{32}_{15}P$ $\xrightarrow{\text{1 half-life}}$ 4.0 mg of $^{32}_{15}P$ $\xrightarrow{\text{2 half-lives}}$ 2.0 mg of $^{32}_{15}P$ $\xrightarrow{\text{3 half-lives}}$ 1.0 mg of $^{32}_{15}P$

STUDY CHECK 4.7

Fe-59 has a half-life of 44 days. If a laboratory received 8.0 μg of Fe-59, how many micrograms of Fe-59 are still active after 176 days?

Naturally occurring isotopes of the elements usually have long half-lives, as shown in Table 4.7. They disintegrate slowly and produce radiation over a long period of time, even hundreds or millions of years. In contrast, the radioisotopes used in nuclear medicine have much shorter half-lives. They disintegrate rapidly and produce almost all their radiation in a short period of time. For example, technetium-99m emits half of its radiation in the first six hours. This means that a small amount of the radioisotope given to a patient is essentially gone within two days. The decay products of technetium-99m are totally eliminated by the body.

Guide to Using Half-Lives

1 State the given and needed quantities.

2 Write a plan to calculate the unknown quantity.

3 Write the half-life equality and conversion factors.

4 Set up the problem to calculate the needed quantity.

Explore Your World

MODELING HALF-LIVES

Obtain a piece of paper and a licorice stick or celery stalk. Draw a vertical and a horizontal axis on the paper. Label the vertical axis as radioactive atoms and the horizontal axis as minutes. Place the licorice stick or celery against the vertical axis and mark its height at zero minutes. In the next minute, cut the licorice stick or celery in two. (You can eat the half if you are hungry.) Place the shortened licorice stick or celery at 1 minute on the horizontal axis and mark its height. Every minute, cut the licorice stick or celery in half again and mark the height at the corresponding time. Keep reducing the length by half until you cannot divide the licorice or celery in half any more. Connect the points you made for each minute. What does the curve look like? How does this curve represent the concept of a half-life for a radioisotope?

TABLE 4.7 Half-Lives of Some Radioisotopes

Element	Radioisotope	Half-Life	Type of Radiation
Naturally Occurring Radioisotopes			
Carbon-14	$^{14}_{6}C$	5730 y	Beta
Potassium-40	$^{40}_{19}K$	1.3×10^9 y	Beta, gamma
Radium-226	$^{226}_{88}Ra$	1600 y	Alpha
Strontium-90	$^{90}_{38}Sr$	38.1 y	Alpha
Uranium-238	$^{238}_{92}U$	4.5×10^9 y	Alpha
Some Medical Radioisotopes			
Chromium-51	$^{51}_{24}Cr$	28 d	Gamma
Iodine-131	$^{131}_{53}I$	8.0 d	Beta, gamma
Iridium-192	$^{192}_{77}Ir$	74 d	Beta, gamma
Iron-59	$^{59}_{26}Fe$	44 d	Beta, gamma
Radon-222	$^{222}_{86}Rn$	3.8 d	Alpha
Technetium-99m	$^{99m}_{43}Tc$	6.0 h	Gamma

TUTORIAL
Radiocarbon Dating

Chemistry Link to the Environment

DATING ANCIENT OBJECTS

Radiological dating is a technique used by geologists, archaeologists, and historians to determine the age of ancient objects. The age of an object derived from plants or animals (such as wood, fiber, natural pigments, bone, and cotton and woolen clothing) is determined by measuring the amount of carbon-14, a naturally occurring radioactive form of carbon. In 1960, Willard Libby received the Nobel Prize for his work developing carbon-14 dating techniques during the 1940s. Carbon-14 is produced in the upper atmosphere by the bombardment of $^{14}_{7}N$ by high-energy neutrons from cosmic rays.

$$^{1}_{0}n + ^{14}_{7}N \longrightarrow ^{14}_{6}C + ^{1}_{1}H$$

Neutron from cosmic rays | Nitrogen in atmosphere | Radioactive carbon-14 | Proton

The carbon-14 reacts with oxygen to form radioactive carbon dioxide, $^{14}_{6}CO_2$. Living plants continuously absorb carbon dioxide, which incorporates carbon-14 into the plant material. The uptake of carbon-14 stops when the plant dies.

$$^{14}_{6}C \longrightarrow ^{14}_{7}N + ^{0}_{-1}e$$

As the carbon-14 decays, the amount of radioactive carbon-14 in the plant material steadily decreases. In a process called **carbon dating**, scientists use the half-life of carbon-14 (5730 years) to calculate the length of time since the plant died. For example, a wooden beam found in an ancient dwelling might have one-half of the carbon-14 found in a living tree. Because one half-life of carbon-14 is 5730 years, this tells us that the tree was cut down about 5730 years ago. Carbon-14 dating was used to determine that the Dead Sea Scrolls are about 2000 years old.

A radiological dating method used for determining the age of much older items is based on the radioisotope uranium-238,

The age of the Dead Sea Scrolls was determined using carbon-14 dating.

which decays through a series of reactions to lead-206. The uranium-238 isotope has an incredibly long half-life, about 4×10^9 (4 billion) years. Measurements of the amounts of uranium-238 and lead-206 enable geologists to determine the age of rock samples. The older rocks will have a higher percentage of lead-206 because more of the uranium-238 has decayed. The age of rocks brought back from the moon by the *Apollo* missions, for example, was determined using uranium-238. They were found to be about 4×10^9 years old, approximately the same age calculated for Earth.

SAMPLE PROBLEM 4.8   Carbon Dating Using Half-Lives

Carbon material in the bones of humans and animals assimilates carbon until death. Using radiocarbon dating, the number of half-lives of carbon-14 from a bone sample determine the age of the bone. Suppose a sample is obtained from a prehistoric animal and used for radiocarbon dating. We can calculate the age of the bone or the years elapsed since the animal died by using the half-life of carbon-14, which is 5730 years. If the sample shows that four half-lives have passed, how much time has elapsed since the animal died?

The age of a bone sample from a skeleton can be determined by carbon dating.

SOLUTION

Step 1   **State the given and needed quantities.**

Analyze the Problem

Given	Equality	Need
4 half-lives elapsed	1 half-life = 5730 y	years elapsed

Step 2   **Write a plan to calculate the unknown quantity.**

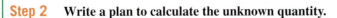

4 half-lives   Half-life   years elapsed

Step 3   **Write the half-life equality and conversion factors.**

$$1 \text{ half-life} = 5730 \text{ y}$$

$$\frac{5730 \text{ y}}{1 \text{ half-life}} \quad \text{and} \quad \frac{1 \text{ half-life}}{5730 \text{ y}}$$

Step 4   **Set up the problem to calculate the needed quantity.**

$$\text{Years elapsed} = 4.0 \text{ half-lives} \times \frac{5730 \text{ y}}{1 \text{ half-life}} = 23\,000 \text{ y}$$

We would estimate that the animal lived 23 000 years ago.

STUDY CHECK 4.8

Suppose that a piece of wood found in a tomb had $\frac{1}{8}$ of its original carbon-14 activity. About how many years ago was the wood part of a living tree?

QUESTIONS AND PROBLEMS

4.4 Half-Life of a Radioisotope

LEARNING GOAL: *Given the half-life of a radioisotope, calculate the amount of radioisotope remaining after one or more half-lives.*

4.29 For each of the following, indicate if the number of half-lives elapsed is:

1. one half-life   **2.** two half-lives   **3.** three half-lives

a. a sample of Pd-103 with a half-life of 17 days after 34 days

b. a sample of C-11 with a half-life of 20 min after 20 min

c. a sample of At-211 with a half-life of 7 h after 21 h

4.30 For each of the following, indicate if the number of half-lives elapsed is:

1. one half-life   **2.** two half-lives   **3.** three half-lives

a. a sample of Ce-141 with a half-life of 32.5 days after 32.5 days

b. a sample of F-18 with a half-life of 110 min after 330 min

c. a sample of Au-198 with a half-life of 2.7 days after 5.4 days

4.31 Technetium-99m is an ideal radioisotope for scanning organs because it has a half-life of 6.0 h and is a pure gamma emitter. Suppose that 80.0 mg were prepared in the technetium generator this morning. How many milligrams of technetium-99m would remain active after the following intervals?

a. one half-life   **b.** two half-lives

c. 18 h   **d.** 24 h

4.32 A sample of sodium-24 with an activity of 12 mCi is used to study the rate of blood flow in the circulatory system. If sodium-24 has a half-life of 15 h, what is the activity of the sodium after 2.5 days?

4.33 Strontium-85, used for bone scans, has a half-life of 65 days. How long will it take for the radiation level of strontium-85 to drop to one-fourth of its original level? To one-eighth?

4.34 Fluorine-18, which has a half-life of 110 min, is used in PET scans (see Section 4.5). If 100. mg of fluorine-18 is shipped at 8 A.M., how many milligrams of the radioisotope are still active if the sample arrives at the radiology laboratory at 1:30 P.M.?

4.5 Medical Applications Using Radioactivity

To determine the condition of an organ in the body, a radiologist may use a radioisotope that concentrates in that organ. The cells in the body cannot differentiate between a nonradioactive atom and a radioactive one, so these radioisotopes are easily incorporated. Then the radioactive atoms can be detected because they emit radiation. Some radioisotopes used in nuclear medicine are listed in Table 4.8.

TABLE 4.8 Medical Applications of Some Common Radioisotopes

Isotope	Half-Life	Radiation	Medical Application
Au-198	2.7 d	Beta	Liver imaging; treatment of abdominal carcinoma
Ce-141	32.5 d	Gamma	Gastrointestinal tract diagnosis; measuring blood flow to the heart
Cs-131	9.7 d	Gamma	Prostate brachytherapy
F-18	110 min	Positron	Positron emission tomography (PET)
Ga-67	78 h	Gamma	Abdominal imaging; tumor detection
Ga-68	68 min	Gamma	Detection of pancreatic cancer
I-123	13.2 h	Gamma	Treatment of thyroid, brain, and prostate cancer
I-131	8.0 d	Beta	Treatment of Graves' disease, goiter, hyperthyroidism, thyroid and prostate cancer
Ir-192	74 d	Gamma	Treatment of breast and prostate cancer
P-32	14.3 d	Beta	Treatment of leukemia, excess red blood cells, pancreatic cancer
Pd-103	17 d	Gamma	Prostate brachytherapy
Sr-85	65 d	Gamma	Detection of bone lesions; brain scans
Tc-99m	6 h	Gamma	Imaging of skeleton and heart muscle, brain, liver, heart, lungs, bone, spleen, kidney, and thyroid; most widely used radioisotope in nuclear medicine
Y-90	2.7 d	Beta	Treatment of liver cancer

Chemistry Link to Health

RADIATION DOSES IN DIAGNOSTIC AND THERAPEUTIC PROCEDURES

We can compare the levels of radiation exposure commonly used during diagnostic and therapeutic procedures in nuclear medicine. In diagnostic procedures, the radiologist uses the minimum amount of radioactive isotope needed to evaluate the condition of an organ or tissue. The doses used in radiation therapy are much greater than those used for diagnostic procedures. For example, a therapeutic dose would be used to destroy the cells in a malignant tumor. Although there will be some damage to surrounding tissue, the healthy cells are more resistant to radiation and can repair themselves (see Table 4.9).

TABLE 4.9 Radiation Doses Used for Diagnostic and Therapeutic Procedures

Organ/Condition	Dose (rem)
Diagnostic	
Liver	0.3
Lung	2.0
Thyroid	50.0
Therapeutic	
Lymphoma	4500
Skin cancer	5000–6000
Lung cancer	6000
Brain tumor	6000–7000

Scans with Radioisotopes

After a person receives a radioisotope, the radiologist determines the level and location of radioactivity emitted by the radioisotope. An apparatus called a *scanner* is used to produce an image of the organ. The scanner moves slowly across the patient's body above the region where the organ containing the radioisotope is located. The gamma rays emitted from the radioisotope in the organ can be used to expose a photographic plate, producing a **scan** of the organ. On a scan, an area of decreased or increased radiation can indicate conditions such as a disease of the organ, a tumor, a blood clot, or edema.

A common method of determining thyroid function is the use of *radioactive iodine uptake (RAIU)*. Taken orally, the radioisotope iodine-131 mixes with the iodine already present in the thyroid. Twenty-four hours later, the amount of iodine taken up by the thyroid is determined. A detection tube held up to the area of the thyroid gland detects the radiation coming from the iodine-131 that has located there (see Figure 4.5).

A person with a hyperactive thyroid will have a higher than normal level of radioactive iodine, whereas a person with a hypoactive thyroid will have low values. If the person has hyperthyroidism, treatment is begun to lower the activity of the thyroid. One treatment involves giving a therapeutic dosage of radioactive iodine, which has a higher radiation level than the diagnostic dose. The radioactive iodine accumulates in the thyroid, where its radiation permanently destroys some of the thyroid cells. The thyroid produces less thyroid hormone, bringing the hyperthyroid condition under control.

Positron Emission Tomography (PET)

Positron emitters with short half-lives such as carbon-11, nitrogen-13, oxygen-15, and fluorine-18 are used in an imaging method called *positron emission tomography* (*PET*). A positron-emitting isotope such as fluorine-18 is used to study brain function, metabolism, and blood flow.

$$^{18}_{9}F \longrightarrow {}^{18}_{8}O + {}^{0}_{+1}e$$

As positrons are emitted, they combine with electrons to produce gamma rays that are detected by computerized equipment to create a three-dimensional image of the organ (see Figure 4.6).

(a)

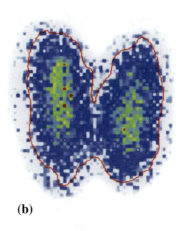
(b)

FIGURE 4.5 **(a)** A scanner is used to detect radiation from a radioisotope that has accumulated in an organ. **(b)** A scan of the thyroid shows the accumulation of radioactive iodine-131 in the thyroid.

Q What type of radiation would move through body tissues, exposing a photographic plate and creating a scan?

SAMPLE PROBLEM 4.9 Medical Applications of Radioisotopes

In the treatment of abdominal carcinoma, a person is treated with gold-198, a beta emitter. Write the balanced nuclear equation for the beta decay of gold-198.

SOLUTION

We can write the incomplete nuclear equation starting with gold-198.

$$^{198}_{79}Au \longrightarrow ? + {}^{0}_{-1}e$$

In beta decay, the mass number, 198, does not change, but the atomic number of the new nucleus increases by one. The new atomic number is 80, which is mercury, Hg.

$$^{198}_{79}Au \longrightarrow {}^{198}_{80}Hg + {}^{0}_{-1}e$$

STUDY CHECK 4.9

An experimental treatment uses boron-10, which is taken up by malignant tumors. When bombarded with neutrons, boron-10 decays by emitting alpha particles that destroy the surrounding tumor cells. Write the balanced equation for the nuclear reaction for this experimental procedure.

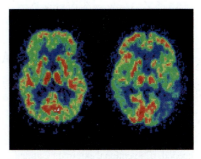

FIGURE 4.6 These PET scans of the brain show a normal brain on the left and a brain affected by Alzheimer's disease on the right.

Q When positrons collide with electrons, what type of radiation is produced that gives an image of an organ?

Chemistry Link to Health

OTHER IMAGING METHODS

Computed Tomography (CT)

Another medical imaging method used to scan organs such as the brain, lungs, and heart is *computed tomography* (*CT*). A computer monitors the degree of absorption of 30 000 X-ray beams directed at successive layers of the target organ. Based on the densities of the tissues and fluids in the organ, the differences in absorption of the X-rays provide a series of images of the organ. This technique is successful in the identification of brain hemorrhages, tumors, and atrophy (see Figure 4.7).

Magnetic Resonance Imaging (MRI)

Magnetic resonance imaging (*MRI*) is a powerful imaging technique that does not involve X-ray radiation. It is the least invasive imaging

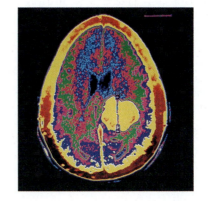

FIGURE 4.7 A CT scan shows a tumor (yellow) in the brain.

Q What is the type of radiation used to give a CT scan?

method available. MRI is based on the absorption of energy when the protons in hydrogen atoms are placed in a strong magnetic field. Hydrogen atoms make up 63% of all the atoms in the body. In the hydrogen nuclei, the protons act like tiny bar magnets. With no external magnetic field, the protons have random orientations. However, when placed within a strong magnetic field, the protons align with the field. A proton aligned with the field has a lower energy than one that is aligned against the field. As the MRI scan proceeds, pulses of radio waves that are specific only to hydrogen are applied, and the hydrogen nuclei resonate at a certain frequency. Then the radio waves are quickly turned off and the hydrogen protons slowly return to their natural alignment within the magnetic field, and resonate at a different frequency. They release the energy absorbed from the radio wave pulses. The difference in energy between the two states is released as photons, which produce the electromagnetic signal that the scanner detects. These signals are sent to a computer system, where a color image of the body is generated. Because hydrogen atoms in the body are in different chemical environments, different energies are absorbed. MRI is particularly useful in obtaining images of soft tissues, which contain large amounts of hydrogen atoms in the form of water (see Figure 4.8).

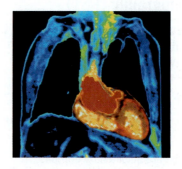

FIGURE 4.8 An MRI scan of the heart and lungs, with the left ventricle shown in red.

Q What is the source of energy in an MRI?

Chemistry Link to Health

BRACHYTHERAPY

The process called *brachytherapy*, or seed implantation, uses an internal form of radiation therapy. The prefix *brachy* is from the Greek word for short distance. With internal radiation, a high dose of radiation is delivered to a cancerous area, while normal tissue sustains minimal damage. Because higher doses are used, fewer treatments of shorter duration are needed. Conventional external treatment delivers a lower dose per treatment but requires six to eight weeks of treatments.

Permanent Brachytherapy

One of the most common forms of cancer in males is prostate cancer. In addition to surgery and chemotherapy, one treatment option is to place 40 or more titanium capsules, or "seeds," in the malignant area. Each seed, which is the size of a small grain of rice, contains radioactive iodine-125, palladium-103, or cesium-131. The radiation from the seeds interferes with the reproduction of cancer cells with minimal damage to adjacent normal tissues. Ninety percent (90%) of the radioisotopes decay within a few months because they have short half-lives.

Isotope	I-125	Pd-103	Cs-131
Radiation	Gamma	Gamma	Gamma
Half-Life	60 days	17 days	10 days
Time to Deliver 90% of Radiation	7 months	2 months	1 month

Almost no radiation passes out of the patient's body. The amount of radiation received by a family member is no greater than that received on a long plane flight. Because the radioisotopes decay to products that are not radioactive, the inert titanium capsules can be left in the body.

Temporary Brachytherapy

In another type of treatment for prostate cancer, long needles containing iridium-192 are placed in the tumor. However, the needles are removed after 5 to 10 minutes, depending on the activity of the iridium isotope. Compared to permanent brachytherapy, temporary brachytherapy can deliver a higher dose of radiation over a shorter time. The procedure may be repeated in a few days.

Brachytherapy is also used following breast cancer lumpectomy. An iridium-192 isotope is inserted into a catheter that is implanted in the space left by the removal of the tumor. The isotope is removed after 5 to 10 minutes, depending on the activity of the iridium source. Radiation is delivered primarily to the tissue surrounding the cavity that contained the tumor and where the cancer is most likely to reoccur. The procedure is repeated twice a day for five days to give an absorbed dose of 34 Gy (3400 rad). The catheter is then removed, and no radioactive material remains in the body.

In conventional external beam therapy for breast cancer, a patient is given 2 Gy once a day for six to seven weeks, which gives a total absorbed dose of about 80 Gy or 8000 rad. The external beam therapy irradiates the entire breast, including the tumor cavity.

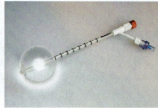

A catheter placed temporarily in the breast supplies radiation from Ir-192.

QUESTIONS AND PROBLEMS

4.5 Medical Applications Using Radioactivity

LEARNING GOAL: *Describe the use of radioisotopes in medicine.*

4.35 Bone and bony structures contain calcium and phosphorus.
  a. Why would the radioisotopes calcium-47 and phosphorus-32 be used in the diagnosis and treatment of bone diseases?
  b. The radioisotope strontium-89, a beta emitter, is used to treat bone cancer. Write the balanced nuclear equation and explain why a strontium radioisotope would be used to treat bone cancer.

4.36 **a.** Technetium-99m emits only gamma radiation. Why would this type of radiation be used in diagnostic imaging rather than an isotope that also emits beta or alpha radiation?

b. A patient with polycythemia vera (excess production of red blood cells) receives radioactive phosphorus-32. Why would this treatment reduce the production of red blood cells in the bone marrow of the patient?

4.37 In a diagnostic test for leukemia, a patient receives 4.0 mL of a solution containing selenium-75. If the activity of the selenium-75 is 45 μCi/mL, what is the dose received by the patient?

4.38 A vial contains radioactive iodine-131 with an activity of 2.0 mCi/mL. If a thyroid test requires 3.0 mCi in an "atomic cocktail," how many milliliters are used to prepare the iodine-131 solution?

4.6 Nuclear Fission and Fusion

During the 1930s, scientists bombarding uranium-235 with neutrons discovered that the U-235 nucleus splits into two medium-weight nuclei and produces a great amount of energy. This was the discovery of nuclear **fission**. The energy generated by splitting the atom was called *atomic* energy. A typical equation for nuclear fission is:

LEARNING GOAL

Describe the processes of nuclear fission and fusion.

TUTORIAL
Fission and Fusion

TUTORIAL
Nuclear Fission and Fusion Reactions

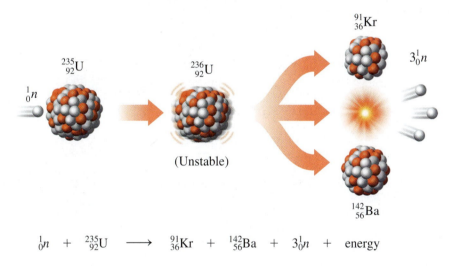

$$\,^{1}_{0}n \;+\; \,^{235}_{92}U \;\longrightarrow\; \,^{91}_{36}Kr \;+\; \,^{142}_{56}Ba \;+\; 3\,^{1}_{0}n \;+\; \text{energy}$$

If we could determine the mass of the products, krypton, barium, and 3 neutrons, with great accuracy, we would find that their total mass is slightly less than the mass of the starting materials. The missing mass has been converted into an enormous amount of energy, consistent with the famous equation derived by Albert Einstein:

$$E = mc^2$$

where E is the energy released, m is the mass lost, and c is the speed of light, 3×10^8 m/s. Even though the mass loss is very small, when it is multiplied by the speed of light squared, the result is a large value for the energy released. The fission of 1 g of uranium-235 produces about as much energy as the burning of 3 tons of coal.

Chain Reaction

Fission begins when a neutron collides with the nucleus of a uranium atom. The resulting nucleus is unstable and splits into smaller nuclei. This fission process also releases neutrons and large amounts of gamma radiation and energy. The neutrons emitted have high energies

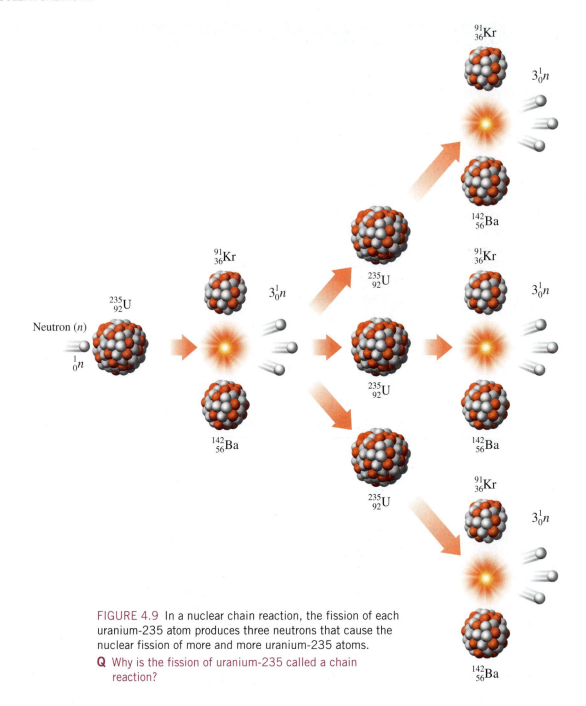

FIGURE 4.9 In a nuclear chain reaction, the fission of each uranium-235 atom produces three neutrons that cause the nuclear fission of more and more uranium-235 atoms.

Q Why is the fission of uranium-235 called a chain reaction?

and bombard other uranium-235 nuclei. In a **chain reaction**, there is a rapid increase in the number of high-energy neutrons available to react with more uranium. To sustain a nuclear chain reaction, sufficient quantities of uranium-235 must be brought together to provide a *critical mass* in which almost all the neutrons collide with more uranium-235 nuclei. So much heat and energy are released that an atomic explosion can occur (see Figure 4.9).

Nuclear Fusion

In **fusion**, two small nuclei such as those in hydrogen combine to form a larger nucleus. Mass is lost, and a tremendous amount of energy is released, even more than the energy released from nuclear fission. However, a fusion reaction requires a temperature of 100 000 000 °C to overcome the repulsion of the hydrogen nuclei and cause them to undergo fusion. Fusion reactions occur continuously in the Sun and other stars, providing us with heat and light. The huge amounts of energy produced by our Sun come from the fusion of 6×10^{11} kg of hydrogen every second. The following fusion reaction involves the combination of two isotopes of hydrogen:

$$_1^3\text{H} \quad + \quad _1^2\text{H} \quad \longrightarrow \quad _2^4\text{He} \quad + \quad _0^1n \quad + \quad \text{energy}$$

Scientists expect less radioactive waste with shorter half-lives from fusion reactors. However, fusion is still in the experimental stage because the extremely high temperatures needed have been difficult to reach and even more difficult to maintain. Research groups around the world are attempting to develop the technology needed to make the harnessing of the fusion reaction for energy a reality in our lifetime.

CONCEPT CHECK 4.5   Identifying Fission and Fusion

Classify the following as pertaining to nuclear fission, nuclear fusion, or both:

a. Small nuclei combine to form larger nuclei.
b. Large amounts of energy are released.
c. Extremely high temperatures are needed for reaction.

ANSWER

a. When small nuclei are combined, the process is fusion.
b. Large amounts of energy are generated in both the fission and fusion processes.
c. An extremely high temperature is required for fusion.

Chemistry Link to the Environment

NUCLEAR POWER PLANTS

In a nuclear power plant, the quantity of uranium-235 is held below a critical mass so that it cannot sustain a chain reaction. The fission reactions are slowed by placing control rods among the uranium samples to absorb some of the fast-moving neutrons. In this way, there is a slower, controlled production of energy. The heat from the controlled fission is used to produce steam. The steam drives a generator, which produces electricity. Approximately 10% of the electrical energy produced in the United States is generated by nuclear power plants.

Although nuclear power plants help meet our energy needs, there are some problems. One of the most serious is the production of radioactive by-products that have long half-lives, such as plutonium-239 with a half-life of 24 000 y. It is essential that these waste products be stored safely in a place where they do not contaminate the environment. Several countries are now in the process of selecting areas where nuclear waste can be placed in caverns 1000 m below the surface of the Earth. In the United States, a current proposed repository site for nuclear waste is Yucca Mountain, Nevada.

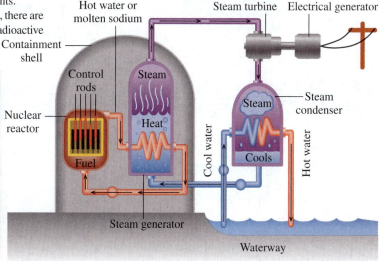

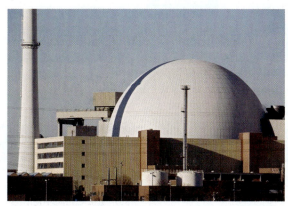

Nuclear power plants supply about 10% of the electricity in the United States.

Heat from nuclear fission is used to generate electricity.

QUESTIONS AND PROBLEMS

4.6 Nuclear Fission and Fusion

LEARNING GOAL: *Describe the processes of nuclear fission and fusion.*

4.39 What is nuclear fission?

4.40 How does a chain reaction occur in nuclear fission?

4.41 Complete the following fission reaction:

$$\,_0^1 n + \,_{92}^{235}U \longrightarrow \,_{50}^{131}Sn + ? + 2\,_0^1 n + \text{energy}$$

4.42 In another fission reaction, uranium-235 bombarded with a neutron produces strontium-94, another nucleus, and 3 neutrons. Write the balanced equation for the fission reaction.

4.43 Indicate whether each of the following is characteristic of the fission process, the fusion process, or both:
   a. Neutrons bombard a nucleus.
   b. The nuclear process occurring in the Sun.
   c. A large nucleus splits into smaller nuclei.
   d. Small nuclei combine to form larger nuclei.

4.44 Indicate whether each of the following is characteristic of the fission process, the fusion process, or both:
   a. Extremely high temperatures are required to initiate the reaction.
   b. Less radioactive waste is produced.
   c. Hydrogen nuclei are the reactants.
   d. Large amounts of energy are released when the nuclear reaction occurs.

CONCEPT MAP

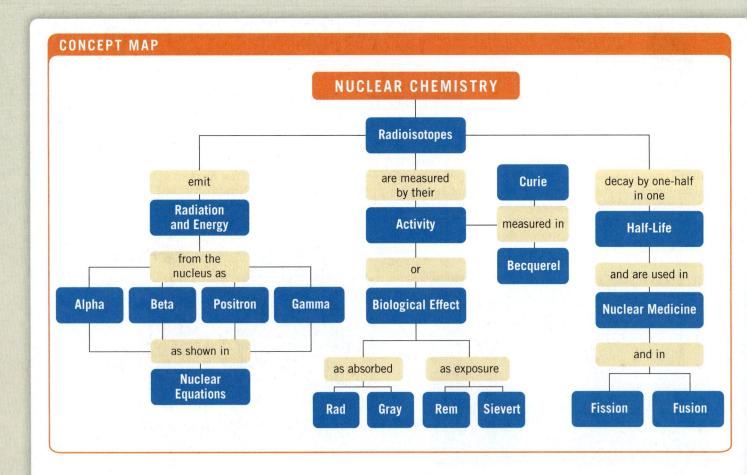

CHAPTER REVIEW

4.1 Natural Radioactivity

LEARNING GOAL: Describe alpha, beta, positron, and gamma radiation.

^4_2He

Alpha (α) particle

- Radioactive isotopes have unstable nuclei that break down (decay), spontaneously emitting alpha (α), beta (β), positron (β^+), and gamma (γ) radiation.
- Because radiation can damage the cells in the body, proper protection must be used: shielding, limiting the time of exposure, and distance.

4.2 Nuclear Reactions

LEARNING GOAL: Write a balanced nuclear equation showing mass numbers and atomic numbers for radioactive decay.

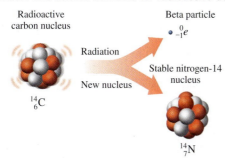

Radioactive carbon nucleus

Radiation

New nucleus

$^{14}_6\text{C}$

Beta particle

$^0_{-1}e$

Stable nitrogen-14 nucleus

$^{14}_7\text{N}$

- A balanced equation is used to represent the changes that take place in the nuclei of the reactants and products.
- The new isotopes and the type of radiation emitted can be determined from the symbols that show the mass numbers and atomic numbers of the isotopes in the nuclear reaction.
- A radioisotope is produced artificially when a nonradioactive isotope is bombarded by a small particle.

4.3 Radiation Measurement

LEARNING GOAL: Describe the detection and measurement of radiation.

- In a Geiger counter, radiation produces charged particles in the gas contained in the tube, which generates an electrical current.
- The curie (Ci) measures the number of nuclear transformations of a radioactive sample. Activity is also measured in becquerel (Bq) units.
- The amount of radiation absorbed by a substance is measured in rads or the gray (Gy).
- The rem and the sievert (Sv) are units used to determine the biological damage from the different types of radiation.

4.4 Half-Life of a Radioisotope

LEARNING GOAL: Given the half-life of a radioisotope, calculate the amount of radioisotope remaining after one or more half-lives.

- Every radioisotope has its own rate of emitting radiation.
- The time it takes for one-half of a radioactive sample to decay is called its half-life.

- For many medical radioisotopes, such as Tc-99m and I-131, half-lives are short.
- For other isotopes, usually naturally occurring ones such as C-14, Ra-226, and U-238, half-lives are extremely long.

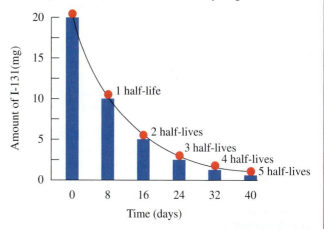

- 1 half-life
- 2 half-lives
- 3 half-lives
- 4 half-lives
- 5 half-lives

Amount of I-131 (mg) vs Time (days)

4.5 Medical Applications Using Radioactivity

LEARNING GOAL: Describe the use of radioisotopes in medicine.

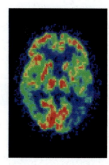

- In nuclear medicine, radioisotopes that go to specific sites in the body are given to the patient.
- By detecting the radiation they emit, an evaluation can be made about the location and extent of an injury, disease, tumor, or the level of function of a particular organ.
- Higher levels of radiation are used to treat or destroy tumors.

4.6 Nuclear Fission and Fusion

LEARNING GOAL: Describe the processes of nuclear fission and fusion.

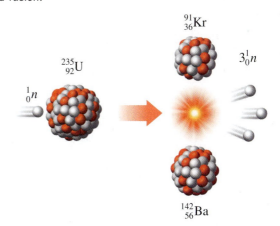

$^{235}_{92}\text{U}$

^1_0n

$^{91}_{36}\text{Kr}$

3^1_0n

$^{142}_{56}\text{Ba}$

- In fission, a large nucleus breaks apart into smaller pieces, releasing one or more types of radiation and a great amount of energy.
- In fusion, small nuclei combine to form a larger nucleus while great amounts of energy are released.

KEY TERMS

alpha particle A nuclear particle identical to a helium nucleus, symbol α or ^4_2He.

becquerel (Bq) A unit of activity of a radioactive sample equal to one disintegration per second.

beta particle A particle identical to an electron, symbol β or $^{0}_{-1}e$, that forms in the nucleus when a neutron changes to a proton and an electron.

carbon dating A technique used to date ancient specimens that contain carbon. The age is determined by the amount of active carbon-14 that remains in the samples.

chain reaction A fission reaction that will continue once it has been initiated by a high-energy neutron bombarding a heavy nucleus such as uranium-235.

curie (Ci) A unit of radiation equal to 3.7×10^{10} disintegrations/s.

decay curve A diagram of the decay of a radioactive element.

equivalent dose The measure of biological damage from an absorbed dose that has been adjusted for the type of radiation.

fission A process in which large nuclei are split into smaller pieces, releasing large amounts of energy.

fusion A reaction in which large amounts of energy are released when small nuclei combine to form larger nuclei.

gamma ray High-energy radiation, symbol $^0_0\gamma$, that is emitted by an unstable nucleus.

gray (Gy) A unit of absorbed dose equal to 100 rad.

half-life The length of time it takes for one-half of a radioactive sample to decay.

positron A particle with no mass and a positive charge, symbol β^+ or $^{0}_{+1}e$, produced when a proton is transformed into a neutron and a positron.

rad (radiation absorbed dose) A measure of an amount of radiation absorbed by the body.

radiation Energy or particles released by radioactive atoms.

radioactive decay The process by which an unstable nucleus breaks down and releases high-energy radiation.

rem (radiation equivalent in humans) A measure of the biological damage caused by the various kinds of radiation (rad $\times$ radiation biological factor).

scan The image of a site in the body created by the detection of radiation from radioactive isotopes that have accumulated in that site.

shielding Materials used to provide protection from radioactive sources.

sievert (Sv) A unit of biological damage (equivalent dose) equal to 100 rem.

UNDERSTANDING THE CONCEPTS

The chapter sections to review are shown in parentheses at the end of each question.

In Problems 4.45 to 4.48, a nucleus is shown with protons and neutrons.

● proton
○ neutron

4.45 Draw the new nucleus when this isotope emits a positron to complete the following figure: (4.2)

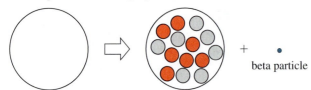
+ positron

4.46 Draw the nucleus of an isotope that emits a beta particle to complete the following figure: (4.2)

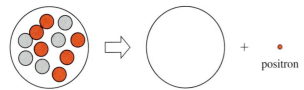
+ beta particle

4.47 Draw the nucleus of the isotope that is bombarded in the following figure: (4.2)

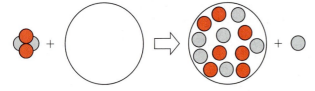

4.48 Complete the following bombardment reaction by drawing the nucleus of the new isotope that is produced in the following figure: (4.2)

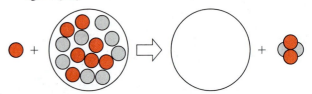

4.49 Carbon dating of small bits of charcoal used in cave paintings has determined that some of the paintings are from 10 000 to 30 000 y old. Carbon-14 has a half-life of 5730 y. In a 1 μg-sample of carbon from a live tree, the activity of $^{14}_6C$ is 6.4 μCi. If researchers determine that 1 μg of charcoal from a prehistoric cave painting in France has an activity of 0.80 μCi, what is the age of the painting? (4.4)

The technique of carbon dating is used to determine the age of ancient cave paintings.

4.50 Use the following decay curve for iodine-131 to answer Questions **a**–**c**: (4.4)

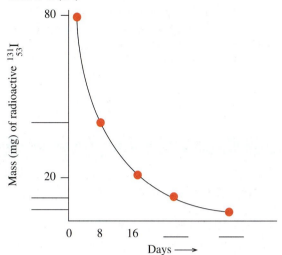

a. Complete the values for the mass of radioactive $^{131}_{53}I$ on the vertical axis.

b. Complete the number of days on the horizontal axis.

c. Use the graph to determine the half-life, in days, of iodine-131.

ADDITIONAL QUESTIONS AND PROBLEMS

For instructor-assigned homework, go to www.masteringchemistry.com.

4.51 State the number of protons and number of neutrons in the nucleus of each of the following: (4.1)
  a. sodium-25   **b.** nickel-61
  c. rubidium-84   **d.** silver-110

4.52 State the number of protons and number of neutrons in the nucleus of each of the following: (4.1)
  a. boron-10   **b.** zinc-72
  c. iron-59   **d.** gold-198

4.53 Identify each of the following as alpha decay, beta decay, positron emission, or gamma emission: (4.1)
  a. $^{27m}_{13}Al \longrightarrow ^{27}_{13}Al + ^{0}_{0}\gamma$
  b. $^{8}_{5}B \longrightarrow ^{8}_{4}Be + ^{0}_{+1}e$
  c. $^{220}_{86}Rn \longrightarrow ^{216}_{84}Po + ^{4}_{2}He$

4.54 Identify each of the following as alpha decay, beta decay, positron emission, or gamma emission: (4.1)
  a. $^{127}_{55}Cs \longrightarrow ^{127}_{54}Xe + ^{0}_{+1}e$
  b. $^{90}_{38}Sr \longrightarrow ^{90}_{39}Y + ^{0}_{-1}e$
  c. $^{218}_{85}At \longrightarrow ^{214}_{83}Bi + ^{4}_{2}He$

4.55 Write a balanced nuclear equation for each of the following: (4.2)
  a. Th-225 (α decay)   **b.** Bi-210 (α decay)
  c. cesium-137 (β decay)   **d.** tin-126 (β decay)
  e. F-18 (β^+ emission)

4.56 Write a balanced nuclear equation for each of the following: (4.2)
  a. potassium-40 (β decay)
  b. sulfur-35 (β decay)
  c. platinum-190 (α decay)
  d. Ra-210 (α decay)
  e. In-113m (γ emission)

4.57 Complete each of the following nuclear equations: (4.2)
  a. $^{4}_{2}He + ^{14}_{7}N \longrightarrow ? + ^{1}_{1}H$
  b. $^{4}_{2}He + ^{27}_{13}Al \longrightarrow ^{30}_{14}Si + ?$
  c. $^{1}_{0}n + ^{235}_{92}U \longrightarrow ^{90}_{38}Sr + 3^{1}_{0}n + ?$
  d. $^{23m}_{12}Mg \longrightarrow ? + ^{0}_{0}\gamma$

4.58 Complete each of the following nuclear equations: (4.2)
  a. $? + ^{59}_{27}Co \longrightarrow ^{56}_{25}Mn + ^{4}_{2}He$
  b. $? \longrightarrow ^{14}_{7}N + ^{0}_{-1}e$
  c. $^{0}_{-1}e + ^{76}_{36}Kr \longrightarrow ?$
  d. $^{4}_{2}He + ^{241}_{95}Am \longrightarrow ? + 2^{1}_{0}n$

4.59 Write the balanced nuclear equation for each of the following: (4.2)
  a. When two oxygen-16 atoms collide, one of the products is an alpha particle.
  b. When californium-249 is bombarded by oxygen-18, a new isotope and four neutrons are produced.
  c. Radon-222 undergoes alpha decay.

4.60 Write the balanced nuclear equation for each of the following: (4.2)
  a. Polonium-210 decays to give lead-206.
  b. Bismuth-211 emits an alpha particle.
  c. A radioisotope emits a positron to form titanium-48.

4.61 If the amount of radioactive phosphorus-32 in a sample decreases from 1.2 mg to 0.30 mg in 28.6 days, what is the half-life, in days, of phosphorus-32? (4.4)

4.62 If the amount of radioactive iodine-123 in a sample decreases from 0.4 g to 0.1 g in 26.4 h, what is the half-life, in hours, of iodine-123? (4.4)

4.63 Calcium-47, a beta emitter, has a half-life of 4.5 days. (4.2, 4.4)
  a. Write the balanced nuclear equation for the beta decay of calcium-47.
  b. How much, in milligrams, of a 16-mg sample of calcium-47 remains after 18 days?
  c. How many days have passed if 4.8 mg of calcium-47 decayed to 1.2 mg of calcium-47?

4.64 Cesium-137, a beta emitter, has a half-life of 30 y. (4.2, 4.4)
  a. Write the balanced nuclear equation for the beta decay of cesium-137.
  b. How many grams of a 16-mg sample of cesium-137 would remain after 90 y?
  c. How many years are required for 28 mg of cesium-137 to decay to 3.5 mg of cesium-137?

4.65 A thyroid scan used 320 mCi of I-123, which has a half-life of 13.2 h. How long, in hours, would it take for the activity to be reduced to 40. mCi? (4.4)

4.66 A wooden object from the site of an ancient temple has a carbon-14 activity of 10 counts/min, compared with a reference piece of wood cut today that has an activity of 40 counts/min. If the half-life for carbon-14 is 5730 y, what is the age of the object? (4.4)

4.67 A 120-mg sample of technetium-99m is used for a diagnostic test. If technetium-99m has a half-life of 6.0 h, how much of the technetium-99m sample remains 24 h after the test? (4.4)

4.68 The half-life of oxygen-15 is 124 s. If a sample of oxygen-15 has an activity of 4000 Bq, how many minutes will elapse before it reaches an activity of 500 Bq? (4.4)

CHALLENGE QUESTIONS

4.69 Uranium-238 decays in a series of nuclear changes until stable $^{206}_{82}\text{Pb}$ is produced. Complete the following nuclear equations that are part of the $^{238}_{92}\text{U}$ decay series: (4.2)

    a. $^{238}_{92}\text{U} \longrightarrow {}^{234}_{90}\text{Th} + ?$ **b.** $^{234}_{90}\text{Th} \longrightarrow ? + {}^{0}_{-1}e$

    c. $? \longrightarrow {}^{222}_{86}\text{Rn} + {}^{4}_{2}\text{He}$

4.70 The iceman known as "Ötzi" was discovered in a high mountain pass on the Austrian–Italian border. Samples of his hair and bones had carbon-14 activity that was about 50% of that present in new hair or bone. Carbon-14 is a beta emitter. (4.2, 4.4)

The mummified remains of "Ötzi" were discovered in 1991.

    a. How long ago did "Ötzi" live if the half-life for C-14 is 5730 y?

    b. Write a balanced nuclear equation for the decay of carbon-14.

4.71 The half-life for the radioactive decay of Ce-141 is 32.5 days. If a sample has an activity of 4.0 μCi after 130 days have elapsed, what was the initial activity, in microcuries, of the sample? (4.4)

4.72 A technician was accidentally exposed to potassium-42 while doing some brain scans for possible tumors. The error was not discovered until 36 h later when the activity of the potassium-42 sample was 2.0 μCi. If potassium-42 has a half-life of 12 h, what was the activity of the sample at the time the technician was exposed? (4.4)

4.73 A 64-μCi sample of Tl-201 decays to 4.0 μCi in 12 days. What is the half-life, in days, of Tl-201? (4.4)

4.74 A 16-μg sample of sodium-24 decays to 2.0 μg in 45 h. What is the half-life, in hours, of sodium-24? (4.4)

4.75 The activity of K-40 in a 70.-kg human body is estimated to be 120 nCi. What is this activity in becquerels? (4.3)

4.76 The activity of C-14 in a 70.-kg human body is estimated to be 3.7 kBq. What is this activity in microcuries? (4.3)

4.77 Write a balanced equation for each of the following radioactive emissions: (4.2)

    a. an alpha particle from Hg-180

    b. a beta particle from Au-198

    c. a positron from Rb-82

4.78 Write a balanced equation for each of the following radioactive emissions: (4.2)

    a. an alpha particle from Gd-148

    b. a beta particle from Ni-64

    c. a positron from Al-25

4.79 All the elements beyond uranium, the transuranium elements, have been prepared by bombardment and are not naturally occurring elements. The first transuranium element, neptunium, Np, was prepared by bombarding U-238 with neutrons to form a neptunium atom and a beta particle. Complete the following equation: (4.2)

$$^{1}_{0}n + {}^{238}_{92}\text{U} \longrightarrow ? + ?$$

4.80 One of the most recent transuranium elements, ununoctium-294 (Uuo-294), atomic number 118, was prepared by bombarding californium-249 with another isotope. Complete the following equation for the preparation of this new element: (4.2)

$$? + {}^{249}_{98}\text{Cf} \longrightarrow {}^{294}_{118}\text{Uuo} + 3{}^{1}_{0}n$$

ANSWERS

Answers to Study Checks

4.1 distance from the radioactive source and minimizing the time of exposure

4.2 $^{214}_{84}\text{Po} \longrightarrow {}^{210}_{82}\text{Pb} + {}^{4}_{2}\text{He}$

4.3 $^{51}_{24}\text{Cr} \longrightarrow {}^{51}_{25}\text{Mn} + {}^{0}_{-1}e$

4.4 $^{118}_{54}\text{Xe} \longrightarrow {}^{118}_{53}\text{I} + {}^{0}_{+1}e$

4.5 $^{4}_{2}\text{He} + {}^{27}_{13}\text{Al} \longrightarrow {}^{30}_{15}\text{P} + {}^{1}_{0}n$

4.6 For β, the factor is 1; rads and rems are equal.

4.7 0.50 μg

4.8 17 200 y

4.9 $^{1}_{0}n + {}^{10}_{5}\text{B} \longrightarrow {}^{7}_{3}\text{Li} + {}^{4}_{2}\text{He}$

Answers to Selected Questions and Problems

4.1 **a.** alpha particle

    b. positron

    c. gamma radiation

4.3 **a.** $^{39}_{19}\text{K}, {}^{40}_{19}\text{K}, {}^{41}_{19}\text{K}$

    b. They all have 19 protons and 19 electrons, but they differ in the number of neutrons.

4.5

Medical Use	Atomic Symbol	Mass Number	Number of Protons	Number of Neutrons
Heart imaging	$^{201}_{81}$Tl	201	81	120
Radiation therapy	$^{60}_{27}$Co	60	27	33
Abdominal scan	$^{67}_{31}$Ga	67	31	36
Hyperthyroidism	$^{131}_{53}$I	131	53	78
Leukemia treatment	$^{32}_{15}$P	32	15	17

4.7 a. $^{64}_{29}$Cu   **b.** $^{75}_{34}$Se   **c.** $^{24}_{11}$Na   **d.** $^{15}_{7}$N

4.9 a. β or $^{0}_{-1}e$ **b.** α or $^{4}_{2}$He   **c.** n or $^{1}_{0}n$
d. $^{38}_{18}$Ar   **e.** $^{14}_{6}$C

4.11 a. 1. alpha particle
   b. 3. gamma radiation
   c. 1. alpha particle

4.13 a. $^{208}_{84}$Po $\longrightarrow$ $^{204}_{82}$Pb + $^{4}_{2}$He
   b. $^{232}_{90}$Th $\longrightarrow$ $^{228}_{88}$Ra + $^{4}_{2}$He
   c. $^{251}_{102}$No $\longrightarrow$ $^{247}_{100}$Fm + $^{4}_{2}$He
   d. $^{220}_{86}$Rn $\longrightarrow$ $^{216}_{84}$Po + $^{4}_{2}$He

4.15 a. $^{25}_{11}$Na $\longrightarrow$ $^{25}_{12}$Mg + $^{0}_{-1}e$
   b. $^{20}_{8}$O $\longrightarrow$ $^{20}_{9}$F + $^{0}_{-1}e$
   c. $^{92}_{38}$Sr $\longrightarrow$ $^{92}_{39}$Y + $^{0}_{-1}e$
   d. $^{60}_{26}$Fe $\longrightarrow$ $^{60}_{27}$Co + $^{0}_{-1}e$

4.17 a. $^{26}_{14}$Si $\longrightarrow$ $^{26}_{13}$Al + $^{0}_{+1}e$
   b. $^{54}_{27}$Co $\longrightarrow$ $^{54}_{26}$Fe + $^{0}_{+1}e$
   c. $^{77}_{37}$Rb $\longrightarrow$ $^{77}_{36}$Kr + $^{0}_{+1}e$
   d. $^{93}_{45}$Rh $\longrightarrow$ $^{93}_{44}$Ru + $^{0}_{+1}e$

4.19 a. $^{28}_{14}$Si, beta decay
   b. $^{0}_{0}\gamma$, gamma emission
   c. $^{0}_{-1}e$, beta decay
   d. $^{238}_{92}$U, alpha decay
   e. $^{188}_{79}$Au, positron emission

4.21 a. $^{10}_{4}$Be   **b.** $^{132}_{53}$I   **c.** $^{27}_{13}$Al   **d.** $^{30}_{15}$P

4.23 a. 2   **b.** 3   **c.** 1   **d.** 2

4.25 The technician exposed to 5 rad received the higher amount of radiation.

4.27 a. 294 μCi   **b.** 0.5 Gy

4.29 a. two half-lives   **b.** one half-life
   c. three half-lives

4.31 a. 40.0 mg   **b.** 20.0 mg
   c. 10.0 mg   **d.** 5.00 mg

4.33 130 days, 195 days

4.35 a. Because the elements Ca and P are part of bone, their radio-active isotopes will also become part of the bony structures of the body, where their radiation can be used to diagnose or treat bone diseases.
   b. $^{89}_{38}$Sr $\longrightarrow$ $^{89}_{39}$Y + $^{0}_{-1}e$
   Strontium (Sr) acts much like calcium (Ca) because both are Group 2A (2) elements. The body will accumulate radioactive strontium in bones in the same way that it incorporates calcium. Once the strontium isotope is absorbed by the bone, the beta radiation will destroy cancer cells.

4.37 180 μCi

4.39 Nuclear fission is the splitting of a large atom into smaller fragments with the release of large amounts of energy.

4.41 $^{103}_{42}$Mo

4.43 a. fission   **b.** fusion
   c. fission   **d.** fusion

4.45

 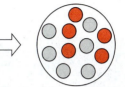

positron

4.47

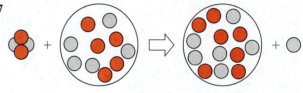

4.49 17 200 y old

4.51 a. 11 protons and 14 neutrons
   b. 28 protons and 33 neutrons
   c. 37 protons and 47 neutrons
   d. 47 protons and 63 neutrons

4.53 a. gamma emission
   b. positron emission
   c. alpha decay

4.55 a. $^{225}_{90}$Th $\longrightarrow$ $^{221}_{88}$Ra + $^{4}_{2}$He
   b. $^{210}_{83}$Bi $\longrightarrow$ $^{206}_{81}$Tl + $^{4}_{2}$He
   c. $^{137}_{55}$Cs $\longrightarrow$ $^{137}_{56}$Ba + $^{0}_{-1}e$
   d. $^{126}_{50}$Sn $\longrightarrow$ $^{126}_{51}$Sb + $^{0}_{-1}e$
   e. $^{18}_{9}$F $\longrightarrow$ $^{18}_{8}$O + $^{0}_{+1}e$

4.57 a. $^{17}_{8}$O   **b.** $^{1}_{1}$H   **c.** $^{143}_{54}$Xe   **d.** $^{23}_{12}$Mg

4.59 a. $^{16}_{8}$O + $^{16}_{8}$O $\longrightarrow$ $^{28}_{14}$Si + $^{4}_{2}$He
   b. $^{18}_{8}$O + $^{249}_{98}$Cf $\longrightarrow$ $^{263}_{106}$Sg + 4$^{1}_{0}n$
   c. $^{222}_{86}$Rn $\longrightarrow$ $^{218}_{84}$Po + $^{4}_{2}$He

4.61 14.3 days

4.63 a. $^{47}_{20}$Ca $\longrightarrow$ $^{47}_{21}$Sc + $^{0}_{-1}e$
   b. 1.0 mg of Ca-47   **c.** 9.0 days

4.65 39.6 h

4.67 7.5 mg

4.69 a. $^{238}_{92}$U $\longrightarrow$ $^{234}_{90}$Th + $^{4}_{2}$He
   b. $^{234}_{90}$Th $\longrightarrow$ $^{234}_{91}$Pa + $^{0}_{-1}e$
   c. $^{226}_{88}$Ra $\longrightarrow$ $^{222}_{86}$Rn + $^{4}_{2}$He

4.71 64 μCi

4.73 3.0 days

4.75 4.4 $\times$ 10^3 Bq

4.77 a. $^{180}_{80}$Hg $\longrightarrow$ $^{176}_{78}$Pt + $^{4}_{2}$He
   b. $^{198}_{79}$Au $\longrightarrow$ $^{198}_{80}$Hg + $^{0}_{-1}e$
   c. $^{82}_{37}$Rb $\longrightarrow$ $^{82}_{36}$Kr + $^{0}_{+1}e$

4.79 $^{1}_{0}n$ + $^{238}_{92}$U $\longrightarrow$ $^{239}_{93}$Np + $^{0}_{-1}e$

5

Compounds and Their Bonds

Sarah, a pharmacy technician, is working at a local drug store. A customer asks Sarah about the effects of aspirin, as his doctor has recommended that he take a low-dose aspirin (81 mg) every day to prevent a heart attack or stroke.

Sarah informs her customer that aspirin is acetylsalicylic acid, and has the chemical formula, $C_9H_8O_4$. Aspirin is a covalent compound, often referred to as an organic molecule because it contains the nonmetals carbon (C), hydrogen (H), and oxygen (O). Sarah shows the customer the chemical structure of aspirin, and explains that aspirin is used to relieve minor pains, to reduce inflammation and fever, and to slow blood clotting. Some potential side effects of aspirin may include heartburn, upset stomach, nausea, and an increased risk of a stomach ulcer. Sarah then refers the customer to the licensed pharmacist on duty for additional information.

Mastering CHEMISTRY™

Visit **www.masteringchemistry.com** for self-study materials and instructor-assigned homework.

Career: Pharmacy Technician

Pharmacy technicians work under the supervision of a pharmacist, and their main responsibility is to fill prescriptions by preparing pharmaceutical medications. They obtain the proper medication, calculate, measure, and label the patient's medication, which is then approved by the pharmacist. After the prescription is filled, the technicians price and file the prescription. Pharmacy technicians also provide customer service by receiving prescription requests, interacting with customers, and answering any questions they may have about the drugs and their health condition. Pharmacy technicians may also prepare insurance claims, and create and maintain patient profiles.

Aspirin

In nature, atoms of almost all the elements on the periodic table are found in combination with other atoms. Only the atoms of the noble gases—He, Ne, Ar, Kr, Xe, and Rn—do not combine in nature with other atoms. As discussed in Section 2.3, a compound is a pure substance, composed of two or more elements, with a definite composition. Compounds are either ionic or covalent. In an ionic compound, one or more electrons are transferred from the atoms of metals to atoms of nonmetals. The attractions that result are called *ionic bonds*.

We use many ionic compounds every day, such as salt (NaCl) and baking soda ($NaHCO_3$). Milk of magnesia ($Mg(OH)_2$) or calcium carbonate ($CaCO_3$) may be taken to settle an upset stomach. In a mineral supplement, iron may be present as iron(II) sulfate ($FeSO_4$), iodine as potassium iodide (KI), and manganese as manganese(II) sulfate ($MnSO_4$). Some sunscreens contain zinc oxide (ZnO), and the tin(II) fluoride (SnF_2) in toothpaste provides fluoride to help prevent tooth decay.

Small amounts of metals cause the different colors of gemstones.

Precious and semiprecious gemstones are examples of ionic compounds called minerals that are cut and polished to make jewelry. Sapphires and rubies are made of a crystalline form of aluminum oxide (Al_2O_3). Impurities of chromium make rubies red, and iron and titanium make sapphires blue.

In compounds of nonmetals, *covalent bonds* occur when atoms share one or more valence electrons. There are many more covalent compounds than there are ionic ones, and many simple covalent compounds are present in our everyday lives. For example, water (H_2O), oxygen (O_2), and carbon dioxide (CO_2) are covalent compounds.

Covalent compounds consist of molecules, which are discrete groups of atoms. A molecule of water (H_2O) consists of two atoms of hydrogen and one atom of oxygen. When you have iced tea, perhaps you add molecules of sugar ($C_{12}H_{22}O_{11}$). Other covalent compounds include propane (C_3H_8), alcohol (C_2H_6O), and the antibiotic amoxicillin ($C_{16}H_{19}N_3O_5S$).

5.1 Ions: Transfer of Electrons

Most of the elements, except the noble gases, are found in nature combined as compounds. The noble gases are so stable that they form compounds only under extreme conditions. One explanation for their stability is that they have a filled valence energy level. Helium is stable with two valence electrons that fill its outermost electron level. All the other noble gases are stable because they have eight valence electrons, called an *octet*.

Compounds are the result of a transfer or sharing of electrons to give the atoms in the compound stable electron configurations. A few atoms, such as hydrogen, are stable with two electrons, but most are stable when they have eight electrons. *Ionic bonds* occur when the electrons of atoms of a metal are transferred to atoms of nonmetals. *Covalent bonds* form when atoms of nonmetals share valence electrons. This tendency for the atoms to obtain a stable electron configuration is called the

LEARNING GOAL

Using the octet rule, write the symbols for the simple ions of the representative elements.

TUTORIAL
Octet Rule and Ions

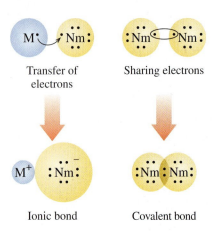

Transfer of electrons

Sharing electrons

Ionic bond

Covalent bond

M is a metal
Nm is a nonmetal

octet rule and provides a key to our understanding of the ways in which atoms of representative elements bond and form compounds. The octet rule does not apply to transition elements.

Positive Ions: Loss of Electrons

In ionic bonding, **ions**, which have electrical charges, form when atoms lose or gain electrons to obtain a stable electron configuration. As we have seen in Section 3.8, the ionization energies of metals of Groups 1A (1), 2A (2), and 3A (13) are low. Thus, metal atoms readily lose their valence electrons. In doing so, they form ions with positive charges. For example, when a sodium atom loses its one valence electron, the remaining electrons have a stable electron configuration. By losing an electron, sodium has 10 electrons instead of 11. Because there are still 11 protons in its nucleus, the atom is no longer neutral. It is now a sodium ion with an electrical charge, called an **ionic charge**, of 1+. In the symbol for the sodium ion, the ionic charge of 1+ is written in the upper right-hand corner, Na^+, where the 1 is understood. The sodium ion is smaller than the sodium atom because the ion has lost its outermost electron from the third energy level. The positively charged ions of metals are called **cations** (pronounced *cat-eye-uns*) and use the name of the element.

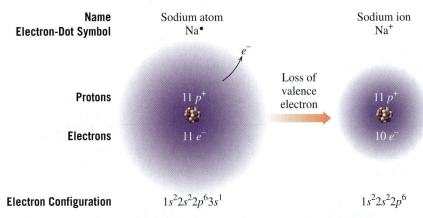

Name	Sodium atom Na•		Sodium ion Na^+
Electron-Dot Symbol			
Protons	$11\,p^+$	Loss of valence electron	$11\,p^+$
Electrons	$11\,e^-$		$10\,e^-$
Electron Configuration	$1s^22s^22p^63s^1$		$1s^22s^22p^6$

Magnesium, a metal in Group 2A (2), obtains a stable electron configuration by losing two valence electrons to form a magnesium ion with a 2+ ionic charge, Mg^{2+}. The magnesium ion is smaller than the magnesium atom because the outermost electrons

 ## Chemistry Link to Health

SOME USES FOR NOBLE GASES

Noble gases may be used when it is necessary to have a substance that is unreactive. Scuba divers normally use a pressurized mixture of nitrogen and oxygen gases for breathing under water. However, when the air mixture is used at depths where pressure is high, the nitrogen gas is absorbed into the blood, where it can cause mental disorientation. To avoid nitrogen narcosis, a breathing mixture of oxygen and helium may be substituted (see *Breathing Mixtures for Scuba* in Section 2.3). The diver still obtains the necessary oxygen, but the unreactive helium that dissolves in the blood does not cause mental disorientation. However, its lower density does change the vibrations of the vocal cords, and the diver will sound like Donald Duck.

Helium is also used to fill blimps and balloons. When dirigibles were first designed, they were filled with hydrogen, a very light gas. However, when they came in contact with any type of spark or heating source, they exploded violently because of the extreme reactivity of hydrogen gas with oxygen present in the air. Today,

blimps are filled with unreactive helium gas, which presents no danger of explosion.

Lighting tubes are generally filled with a noble gas such as neon or argon. While the electrically heated filaments that produce the light get very hot, the surrounding noble gases do not react with the hot filament. If heated in air, the elements that constitute the filament will quickly burn out when oxygen is present.

The helium in a blimp is much less dense than air, which allows the blimp to fly above the ground.

in the third energy level were removed. The octet in the magnesium ion is made up of electrons that fill its second energy level.

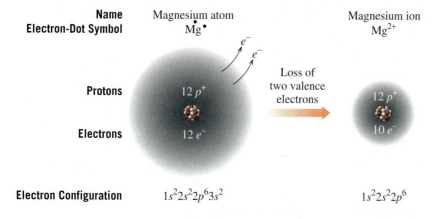

| Name Electron-Dot Symbol | Magnesium atom $\overset{\bullet}{Mg}{}^{\bullet}$ | | Magnesium ion Mg^{2+} |

Loss of two valence electrons

| | Protons | 12 p^+ | | 12 p^+ |
| | Electrons | 12 e^- | | 10 e^- |

| Electron Configuration | $1s^2 2s^2 2p^6 3s^2$ | | $1s^2 2s^2 2p^6$ |

Negative Ions: Gain of Electrons

In Section 3.8, we learned that the ionization energy of a nonmetal atom in Group 5A (15), 6A (16), or 7A (17) is high. Rather than lose electrons to form ions, a nonmetal atom gains one or more valence electrons to obtain a stable electron configuration. For example, an atom of chlorine with seven valence electrons gains one more electron to form an octet. Because there are now 18 electrons and 17 protons, the chlorine atom is no longer neutral. It becomes a chloride ion with an ionic charge of 1−, which is written as Cl^-. A negatively charged ion, called an **anion** (pronounced *an-eye-un*), is named by using the first syllable of its element name followed by *ide*. The chloride ion is larger than a chlorine atom because the ion has an additional electron, which completes its outermost energy level.

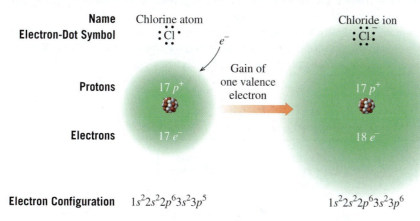

| Name Electron-Dot Symbol | Chlorine atom $:\overset{\bullet\bullet}{\underset{\bullet\bullet}{Cl}}\,\bullet$ | | Chloride ion $:\overset{\bullet\bullet}{\underset{\bullet\bullet}{Cl}}:$ |

Gain of one valence electron

| | Protons | 17 p^+ | | 17 p^+ |
| | Electrons | 17 e^- | | 18 e^- |

| Electron Configuration | $1s^2 2s^2 2p^6 3s^2 3p^5$ | | $1s^2 2s^2 2p^6 3s^2 3p^6$ |

Table 5.1 lists the names of some important metal and nonmetal ions.

TABLE 5.1	**Symbols and Names of Some Common Ions**				
Group Number	Cation	Name of Cation	Group Number	Anion	Name of Anion
	Metals			**Nonmetals**	
1A (1)	Li^+	Lithium	5A (15)	N^{3-}	Nitride
	Na^+	Sodium		P^{3-}	Phosphide
	K^+	Potassium	6A (16)	O^{2-}	Oxide
2A (2)	Mg^{2+}	Magnesium		S^{2-}	Sulfide
	Ca^{2+}	Calcium	7A (17)	F^-	Fluoride
	Ba^{2+}	Barium		Cl^-	Chloride
3A (13)	Al^{3+}	Aluminum		Br^-	Bromide
				I^-	Iodide

TUTORIAL
Ions

a. Write the symbol and name for the ion that has 7 protons and 10 electrons.
b. Write the symbol and name for the ion that has 20 protons and 18 electrons.

ANSWER

a. The element with 7 protons is nitrogen. In an ion of nitrogen with 10 electrons, the ionic charge is 3−, $(7+) + (10−) = 3−$. The ion, written as N^{3-}, is the *nitride* ion.
b. The element with 20 protons is calcium. In an ion of calcium with 18 electrons, the ionic charge is 2+, $(20+) + (18−) = 2+$. The ion, written as Ca^{2+}, is the *calcium* ion.

Ionic Charges from Group Numbers

As we learned in Section 3.8, we can obtain the number of valence electrons of the representative elements from their group numbers on the periodic table. Now we can use group numbers to determine the charges for their ions, which acquire eight valence electrons like the nearest noble gas, or two for helium. The elements in Group 1A (1) lose one electron to form ions with a 1+ charge. The atoms of the elements in Group 2A (2) lose two electrons to form ions with a 2+ charge. The atoms of the elements in Group 3A (13) lose three electrons to form ions with a 3+ charge. In this text, we do not use the group numbers of the transition elements to determine their ionic charges.

In ionic compounds, the atoms of the nonmetals in Group 7A (17) gain one electron to form ions with a 1− charge. The atoms of the elements in Group 6A (16) gain two electrons to form ions with a 2− charge. The atoms of the elements in Group 5A (15) typically gain three electrons to form ions with a 3− charge.

The nonmetals of Group 4A (14) do not typically form ions. However, the metals Sn and Pb in Group 4A (14) lose electrons to form positive ions. Table 5.2 lists the ionic charges for some common monatomic ions of representative elements.

TABLE 5.2 Examples of Monatomic Ions and Their Nearest Noble Gases

Noble Gases		Metals Lose Valence Electrons			Nonmetals Gain Valence Electrons				Noble Gases
		1A (1)	2A (2)	3A (13)	5A (15)	6A (16)	7A (17)		
He	⇐	Li^+							
Ne	⇐	Na^+	Mg^{2+}	Al^{3+}	N^{3-}	O^{2-}	F^-	⇒	Ne
Ar	⇐	K^+	Ca^{2+}		P^{3-}	S^{2-}	Cl^-	⇒	Ar
Kr	⇐	Rb^+	Sr^{2+}				Br^-	⇒	Kr
Xe	⇐	Cs^+	Ba^{2+}				I^-	⇒	Xe

Chemistry Link to Health

SOME IMPORTANT IONS IN THE BODY

Several ions in body fluids have important physiological and metabolic functions. Some of them are listed in Table 5.3.

Foods such as bananas, milk, cheese, and potatoes provide the body with ions that are important in regulating body functions.

TABLE 5.3 Ions in the Body

Ion	Occurrence	Function	Source	Result of Too Little	Result of Too Much
Na^+	Principal cation outside the cell	Regulates and controls body fluids	Salt, cheese, pickles, potato chips, pretzels	Hyponatremia, anxiety, diarrhea, circulatory failure, decrease in body fluid	Hypernatremia, little urine, thirst, edema
K^+	Principal cation inside the cell	Regulates body fluids and cellular functions	Bananas, orange juice, milk, prunes, potatoes	Hypokalemia (hypopotassemia), lethargy, muscle weakness, failure of neurological impulses	Hyperkalemia (hyperpotassemia), irritability, nausea, little urine, cardiac arrest
Ca^{2+}	Cation outside the cell; 90% of calcium in the body in bone occurs as $Ca_3(PO_4)_2$ or $CaCO_3$	Major cation of bone; needed for muscle contraction	Milk, yogurt, cheese, greens, spinach	Hypocalcemia, tingling fingertips, muscle cramps, osteoporosis	Hypercalcemia, relaxed muscles, kidney stones, deep bone pain
Mg^{2+}	Cation outside the cell; 70% of magnesium in the body is in the bones	Essential for certain enzymes, muscles, nerve control	Widely distributed (part of chlorophyll of all green plants), nuts, whole grains	Disorientation, hypertension, tremors, slow pulse	Drowsiness
Cl^-	Principal anion outside the cell	Major anion of gastric juice, regulates body fluids	Salt	Same as for Na^+	Same as for Na^+

QUESTIONS AND PROBLEMS

5.1 Ions: Transfer of Electrons

LEARNING GOAL: *Using the octet rule, write the symbols for the simple ions of the representative elements.*

5.1 State the number of electrons that must be lost by atoms of each of the following to obtain a stable electron configuration:
    a. Li   **b.** Ca   **c.** Ga
    d. Cs   **e.** Ba

5.2 State the number of electrons that must be gained by atoms of each of the following to obtain a stable electron configuration:
    a. Cl   **b.** Se   **c.** N
    d. I   **e.** S

5.3 Write the symbols for the ions with the following number of protons and electrons:
    a. 3 protons, 2 electrons
    b. 9 protons, 10 electrons
    c. 12 protons, 10 electrons
    d. 26 protons, 23 electrons

5.4 Write the symbols for the ions with the following number of protons and electrons:
    a. 30 protons, 28 electrons
    b. 53 protons, 54 electrons
    c. 82 protons, 78 electrons
    d. 15 protons, 18 electrons

5.5 How many protons and electrons are in each of the following ions?
a. O^{2-} b. K^+ c. Br^- d. S^{2-}

5.6 How many protons and electrons are in each of the following ions?
a. Sr^{2+} b. F^- c. Au^{3+} d. Cs^+

5.7 Write the symbol for the ion of each of the following:
a. chlorine   b. potassium   c. oxygen
d. aluminum   e. selenium

5.8 Write the symbol for the ion of each of the following:
a. fluorine   b. calcium   c. sodium
d. iodine   e. barium

5.2 Ionic Compounds

LEARNING GOAL

Using charge balance, write the correct formula for an ionic compound.

TUTORIAL
Ionic Compounds

Ionic compounds consist of positive and negative ions. The ions are held together by strong attractions between the oppositely charged ions, called **ionic bonds**.

Properties of Ionic Compounds

The physical and chemical properties of an ionic compound such as NaCl are very different from those of the original elements. For example, the original elements of NaCl were sodium, which is a soft, shiny metal, and chlorine, which is a yellow-green poisonous gas. However, when they react and form positive and negative ions, they produce ordinary table salt, NaCl, a hard, white, crystalline substance that is important in our diet.

In a crystal of NaCl, every Na^+ ion (shown in purple) is surrounded by six Cl^- ions (shown in green), and every Cl^- ion is surrounded by six Na^+ ions (see Figure 5.1). Thus,

Sodium metal   and   Chlorine gas

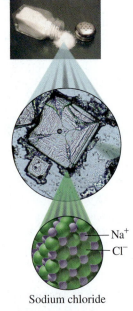

Na^+
Cl^-

Sodium chloride

FIGURE 5.1 The elements sodium and chlorine react to form the ionic compound sodium chloride, which makes up table salt. The magnification of NaCl crystals shows the arrangements of Na^+ and Cl^- ions in a NaCl crystal.

Q What is the type of bonding between Na^+ and Cl^- ions in NaCl?

there are many strong attractions between the positive and negative ions, which account for the high melting points of ionic compounds. For example, the melting point of NaCl is 801 °C. At room temperature, ionic compounds are solids.

Formulas of Ionic Compounds

The **chemical formula** of a compound represents the symbols and subscripts in the lowest whole-number ratio of the atoms or ions. In the formula of an ionic compound, the sum of the ionic charges is always zero, which means that the total amount of positive charge is equal to the total amount of negative charge. For example, the formula NaCl indicates that this compound consists of one sodium ion, Na^+, for every chloride ion, Cl^-. Although the ions have positive or negative charges, their ionic charges are not shown in the formula of the compound.

Loses 1 e^- Gains 1 e^-

One sodium ion   One chloride ion
Na^+ Cl^-
$1(1+) + 1(1-) = 0$
NaCl, sodium chloride

Subscripts in Formulas

Consider a compound of magnesium and chlorine. To achieve an octet, a Mg atom loses its two valence electrons to form Mg^{2+}. Two Cl atoms each gain one electron to form two Cl^- ions. The two Cl^- ions are needed to balance the positive charge of Mg^{2+}. This gives the formula $MgCl_2$, magnesium chloride, in which the subscript 2 shows that two Cl^- ions are needed for charge balance.

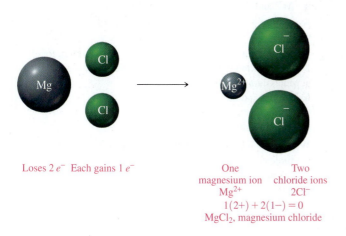

Loses 2 e^- Each gains 1 e^-

One magnesium ion   Two chloride ions
Mg^{2+} $2Cl^-$
$1(2+) + 2(1-) = 0$
$MgCl_2$, magnesium chloride

Writing Ionic Formulas from Ionic Charges

The subscripts in the formula of an ionic compound represent the number of positive and negative ions that give an overall charge of zero. Thus, we can now write a formula directly from the ionic charges of the positive and negative ions. In the formula of an ionic compound, the cation is written first and is followed by the anion. Suppose we wish to write the formula for the ionic compound containing Na^+ and S^{2-} ions. To balance the ionic charge of the S^{2-} ion, we show two Na^+ ions by using a subscript 2 in the formula. This gives the formula Na_2S, which has an overall charge of zero. When there is no subscript for a symbol such as the S in Na_2S, it assumed to be 1.

The group of ions that has the lowest ratio of the ions in an ionic compound is called a *formula unit*.

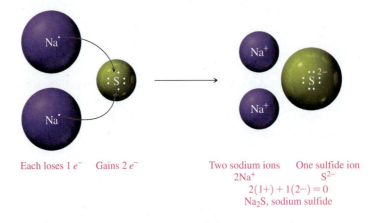

Each loses 1 e^- Gains 2 e^-

Two sodium ions   One sulfide ion
2Na$^+$ S^{2-}
2(1+) + 1(2−) = 0
Na$_2$S, sodium sulfide

CONCEPT CHECK 5.2   **Writing Formulas from Ionic Charges**

Determine the ionic charges, and write the formula for the ionic compound formed when lithium and nitrogen react.

ANSWER

Lithium in Group 1A (1) forms Li$^+$; nitrogen in Group 5A (15) forms N^{3-}. The charge of 3− for N^{3-} is balanced by three Li$^+$ ions. Writing the positive ion first gives the formula Li$_3$N.

QUESTIONS AND PROBLEMS

5.2 Ionic Compounds

LEARNING GOAL: *Using charge balance, write the correct formula for an ionic compound.*

5.9 Which of the following pairs of elements are likely to form ionic compounds?
   a. lithium and chlorine   **b.** oxygen and bromine
   c. potassium and oxygen   **d.** sodium and neon
   e. cesium and magnesium   **f.** nitrogen and fluorine

5.10 Which of the following pairs of elements are likely to form ionic compounds?
   a. helium and oxygen   **b.** magnesium and chlorine
   c. chlorine and bromine   **d.** potassium and sulfur
   e. sodium and potassium   **f.** nitrogen and iodine

5.11 Write the correct ionic formula for the compound formed between the following:
   a. Na$^+$ and O^{2-} **b.** Al^{3+} and Br$^-$
   c. Ba^{2+} and N^{3-} **d.** Mg^{2+} and F$^-$
   e. Al^{3+} and S^{2-}

5.12 Write the correct ionic formula for the compound formed between the following:
   a. Al^{3+} and Cl$^-$ **b.** Ca^{2+} and S^{2-}
   c. Li$^+$ and S^{2-} **d.** Rb$^+$ and P^{3-}
   e. Cs$^+$ and I$^-$

5.13 Write the symbols for the ions and the correct formula for the ionic compound formed by each of the following:
   a. potassium and sulfur
   b. sodium and nitrogen
   c. aluminum and iodine
   d. gallium and oxygen

5.14 Write the symbols for the ions and the correct formula for the ionic compound formed by each of the following:
   a. calcium and chlorine
   b. rubidium and sulfur
   c. sodium and phosphorus
   d. magnesium and oxygen

LEARNING GOAL

Given the formula of an ionic compound, write the correct name; given the name of an ionic compound, write the correct formula.

5.3 Naming and Writing Ionic Formulas

In the name of an ionic compound made up of two elements, the name of the metal ion, which is written first, is the same as its element name. The name of the nonmetal ion is obtained by using the first syllable of its element name followed by *ide*. In the name of any ionic compound, a space separates the name of the cation from the name of the anion.

Subscripts are not used; they are understood because of the charge balance of the ions in the compound (see Table 5.4).

TABLE 5.4 Names of Some Ionic Compounds

Compound	Metal Ion	Nonmetal Ion	Name of Ionic Compound
KI	K^+ Potassium	I^- Iodide	Potassium iodide
$MgBr_2$	Mg^{2+} Magnesium	Br^- Bromide	Magnesium bromide
Al_2O_3	Al^{3+} Aluminum	O^{2-} Oxide	Aluminum oxide

Iodized salt contains KI to prevent iodine deficiency.

SAMPLE PROBLEM 5.1   **Naming Ionic Compounds**

Write the name for the ionic compound Mg_3N_2.

SOLUTION

Step 1   **Identify the cation and anion.** The cation from Group 2A (2) is Mg^{2+}, and the anion from Group 5A (15) is N^{3-}.

Step 2   **Name the cation by its element name.** The cation Mg^{2+} is magnesium.

Step 3   **Name the anion by using the first syllable of its element name followed by *ide*.** The anion N^{3-} is nitride.

Step 4   **Write the name for the cation first and the name for the anion second.** Mg_3N_2 is magnesium nitride.

STUDY CHECK 5.1

Name the compound Ga_2S_3.

Metals with Variable Charge

We have seen that the charge of an ion of a representative element can be obtained from its group number. However, it is not as easy to determine the charge of a transition element because they typically form two or more positive ions. The transition elements can lose *s* electrons from the highest energy level as well as *d* electrons from a lower energy level. This is also true for metals of representative elements in Groups 4A (14) and 5A (15), such as Pb, Sn, and Bi.

In some ionic compounds, iron is in the Fe^{2+} form; but in other compounds, it has the Fe^{3+} form. Copper also forms two different ions: Cu^+ and Cu^{2+}. When a metal can form two or more ions, it has a *variable charge*. Thus, for these metals, we cannot predict the ionic charge from the group number.

When different ions are possible, a naming system is used to identify the particular cation. To do this, a Roman numeral that is equal to the ionic charge is placed in parentheses immediately after its element name. For example, Fe^{2+} is named iron(II), and Fe^{3+} is named iron(III). Table 5.5 lists the ions of some transition elements that have two or more ions.

Figure 5.2 shows some ions and their location on the periodic table. The transition elements form more than one positive ion except for zinc (Zn^{2+}), cadmium (Cd^{2+}), and silver (Ag^+), which form only one ion. Thus, the names of zinc, cadmium, and silver are sufficient when naming their cations in ionic compounds. Metals in Group 4A (14) also form more than one positive ion. For example, lead and tin in Group 4A (14) form cations with charges of 2+ and 4+.

Guide to Naming Ionic Compounds with Metals That Form a Single Ion

1   Identify the cation and anion.

2   Name the cation by its element name.

3   Name the anion by using the first syllable of its element name followed by *ide*.

4   Write the name for the cation first and the name for the anion second.

TUTORIAL
Writing Ionic Formulas

TABLE 5.5 Some Metals That Form More Than One Positive Ion

Element	Ions	Name of Ion	Element	Ions	Name of Ion
Chromium	Cr^{2+}	Chromium(II)	Lead	Pb^{2+}	Lead(II)
	Cr^{3+}	Chromium(III)		Pb^{4+}	Lead(IV)
Cobalt	Co^{2+}	Cobalt(II)	Manganese	Mn^{2+}	Manganese(II)
	Co^{3+}	Cobalt(III)		Mn^{3+}	Manganese(III)
Copper	Cu^{+}	Copper(I)	Mercury	Hg_2^{2+}	Mercury(I)*
	Cu^{2+}	Copper(II)		Hg^{2+}	Mercury(II)
Gold	Au^{+}	Gold(I)	Nickel	Ni^{2+}	Nickel(II)
	Au^{3+}	Gold(III)		Ni^{3+}	Nickel(III)
Iron	Fe^{2+}	Iron(II)	Tin	Sn^{2+}	Tin(II)
	Fe^{3+}	Iron(III)		Sn^{4+}	Tin(IV)

*Mercury(I) ions form an ion pair with a 2+ charge.

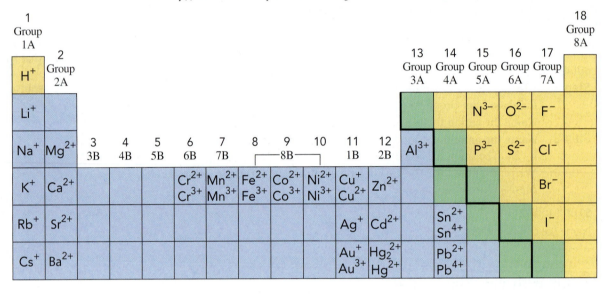

Metals   Metalloids   Nonmetals

FIGURE 5.2 On the periodic table, positive ions are produced from metals and negative ions are produced from nonmetals.

Q What are the ions produced by calcium, copper, and oxygen?

Determination of Variable Charge

When you name an ionic compound, you need to determine if the metal is a representative element or a transition element. If it is a transition element, except for zinc, cadmium, or silver, you will need to write its ionic charge as a Roman numeral for part of its name. The calculation of ionic charge depends on the negative charge of the anions in the formula. For example, we use charge balance to calculate the charge of the copper cation in the formula $CuCl_2$. Because there are two chloride ions, each with a 1− charge, the total negative charge is 2−. To balance the 2− charge, the copper ion must have a charge of 2+, which is a Cu^{2+} ion:

$CuCl_2$

Cu charge + 2Cl⁻ charge = 0

? + 2(1−) = 0

2+ + 2− = 0

To indicate the 2+ charge for the copper ion Cu^{2+}, we place the Roman numeral (II) immediately after copper when naming the compound: copper(II) chloride.

Table 5.6 lists the names of some ionic compounds in which the transition elements and metals from Group 4A (14) have more than one positive ion.

TABLE 5.6 Some Ionic Compounds of Metals That Form Two Kinds of Positive Ions

Compound	Systematic Name
$FeCl_2$	Iron(II) chloride
Fe_2O_3	Iron(III) oxide
Cu_3P	Copper(I) phosphide
$CuBr_2$	Copper(II) bromide
$SnCl_2$	Tin(II) chloride
PbS_2	Lead(IV) sulfide

SAMPLE PROBLEM 5.2 Naming Ionic Compounds with Variable Charge Metal Ions

Antifouling paint contains Cu_2O, which prevents the growth of barnacles and algae on the bottoms of boats. What is the name of Cu_2O?

SOLUTION

Step 1 **Determine the charge of the cation from the anion.** The nonmetal O in Group 6A (16) forms the O^{2-} ion. Because there are two Cu ions to balance the O^{2-}, the charge of each Cu ion must be 1+.

Analyze the Problem

	Metal	Nonmetal
Element	Copper	Oxygen
Location on the Periodic Table	Transition element	Group 6A (16)
Ion	Cu?	O^{2-}
Charge balance	2 (1+) +	(2−) = 0
Ion	Cu^+	O^{2-}

Step 2 **Name the cation by its element name, and use a Roman numeral in parentheses for the charge.** copper(I)

Step 3 **Name the anion by using the first syllable of its element name followed by** *ide.* oxide

Step 4 **Write the name for the cation first and the name for the anion second.** copper(I) oxide

STUDY CHECK 5.2

Write the name for the compound with the formula Mn_2S_3.

Guide to Naming Ionic Compounds with Variable Charge Metals

1 Determine the charge of the cation from the anion.

2 Name the cation by its element name, and use a Roman numeral in parentheses for the charge.

3 Name the anion by using the first syllable of its element name followed by *ide*.

4 Write the name for the cation first and the name for the anion second.

SAMPLE PROBLEM 5.3 Writing Formulas for Ionic Compounds

Write the formula for iron(III) chloride.

SOLUTION

Step 1 **Identify the cation and anion.** The Roman numeral (III) indicates that the charge of the iron ion is 3+, Fe^{3+}.

Analyze the Problem

	Metal	Nonmetal
Ion	Iron(III)	Chloride
Group	Transition	7A (17)
Symbol	Fe^{3+}	Cl^-

Step 2 **Balance the charges.**

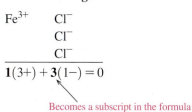

$$Fe^{3+} \quad Cl^-$$
$$Cl^-$$
$$Cl^-$$
$$\overline{1(3+) + 3(1-) = 0}$$

Becomes a subscript in the formula

Guide to Writing Formulas from the Name of an Ionic Compound

1 Identify the cation and anion.

2 Balance the charges.

3 Write the formula, cation first, using subscripts from the charge balance.

The pigment chrome oxide green contains chromium(III) oxide.

Step 3 **Write the formula, cation first, using subscripts from the charge balance.**

$FeCl_3$

STUDY CHECK 5.3

Write the correct formula for chromium(III) oxide.

QUESTIONS AND PROBLEMS

5.3 Naming and Writing Ionic Formulas

LEARNING GOAL: *Given the formula of an ionic compound, write the correct name; given the name of an ionic compound, write the correct formula.*

5.15 Write the name for each of the following:
  a. Al_2O_3 **b.** $CaCl_2$ **c.** Na_2O
  d. Mg_3P_2 **e.** KI **f.** BaF_2

5.16 Write the name for each of the following:
  a. $MgCl_2$ **b.** K_3P **c.** Li_2S
  d. CsF **e.** MgO **f.** $SrBr_2$

5.17 Why is a Roman numeral placed after the name of the ions of most transition elements?

5.18 The compound $CaCl_2$ is named calcium chloride; the compound $CuCl_2$ is named copper(II) chloride. Explain why a Roman numeral is used in one name but not in the other.

5.19 Write the name for each of the following (include the Roman numeral when necessary):
  a. Fe^{2+} **b.** Cu^{2+} **c.** Zn^{2+}
  d. Pb^{4+} **e.** Cr^{3+} **f.** Mn^{2+}

5.20 Write the name for each of the following (include the Roman numeral when necessary):
  a. Ag^+ **b.** Cu^+ **c.** Fe^{3+}
  d. Sn^{2+} **e.** Au^{3+} **f.** Ni^{2+}

5.21 Write the name for each of the following:
  a. $SnCl_2$ **b.** FeO **c.** Cu_2S
  d. CuS **e.** $CrBr_3$ **f.** $ZnCl_2$

5.22 Write the name for each of the following:
  a. Ag_3P **b.** PbS
  c. SnO_2 **d.** $MnCl_3$
  e. FeS **f.** $CoCl_2$

5.23 Write the symbol for the cation in each of the following:
  a. $AuCl_3$ **b.** Fe_2O_3
  c. PbI_4 **d.** $SnCl_2$

5.24 Write the symbol for the cation in each of the following:
  a. $FeCl_2$ **b.** CrO
  c. Ni_2S_3 **d.** AlP

5.25 Write formulas for the following ionic compounds:
  a. magnesium chloride
  b. sodium sulfide
  c. copper(I) oxide
  d. zinc phosphide
  e. gold(III) nitride
  f. chromium(II) chloride

5.26 Write formulas for the following ionic compounds:
  a. nickel(III) oxide
  b. barium fluoride
  c. tin(IV) chloride
  d. silver sulfide
  e. copper(II) chloride
  f. lithium nitride

LEARNING GOAL

Write the name and formula for a compound containing a polyatomic ion.

TUTORIAL
Polyatomic Ions

5.4 Polyatomic Ions

A **polyatomic ion** is a group of covalently bonded atoms that has an overall ionic charge. Most polyatomic ions consist of a nonmetal such as phosphorus, sulfur, carbon, or nitrogen bonded to oxygen atoms.

Almost all of the polyatomic ions are anions with charges of 1−, 2−, or 3−, which indicate that the group of atoms has gained 1, 2, or 3 electrons to complete a stable electron configuration, usually an octet. Only one common polyatomic ion, NH_4^+, has a positive charge. Some models of common polyatomic ions are shown in Figure 5.3.

Names of Polyatomic Ions

The names of the most common negatively charged polyatomic ions end in *ate* such as nitrate and sulfate. When a related ion has one less oxygen atom, the *ite* ending is used for its name such as nitrite and sulfite. Recognizing these endings will help you identify polyatomic ions in the names of compounds. The hydroxide ion (OH^-) and cyanide ion (CN^-) are exceptions to this naming pattern.

Plaster molding
$CaSO_4$

Fertilizer
NH_4NO_3

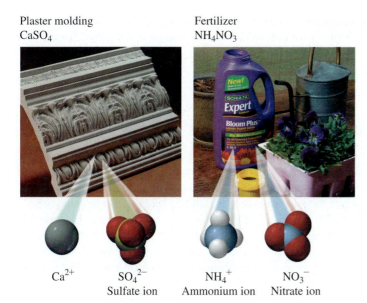

Ca^{2+} SO_4^{2-} NH_4^+ NO_3^-
            Sulfate ion   Ammonium ion   Nitrate ion

FIGURE 5.3 Many products contain polyatomic ions, which are groups of bonded atoms that carry an ionic charge.

Q Why does the sulfate ion have a 2– charge?

By learning the formulas, charges, and the names of the polyatomic ions shown in bold type in Table 5.7, you can derive the related ions. Note that the *ate* and *ite* ions of a particular nonmetal have the same ionic charge. For example, the sulfate ion is SO_4^{2-}, and the sulfite ion, which has one less oxygen atom, is SO_3^{2-}. Phosphate and phosphite ions each have a 3– charge; nitrate and nitrite each have a 1– charge. The elements in Group 7A (17) form four different polyatomic ions with oxygen. Prefixes are added to the names, and the ending is changed to distinguish among these ions. The prefix *per* is used for the polyatomic ion that has one more oxygen than the *ate* form. The prefix *hypo* is used for the polyatomic ion that has one oxygen less than the *ite* form. For example, the polyatomic ions of chlorine—perchlorate, chlorate, chlorite, and hypochlorite—each have a 1– charge.

TABLE 5.7   Names and Formulas of Some Common Polyatomic Ions

Nonmetal	Formula of Ion*	Name of Ion
Hydrogen	OH^-	Hydroxide
Nitrogen	NH_4^+	Ammonium
	NO_3^-	**Nitrate**
	NO_2^-	Nitrite
Chlorine	ClO_4^-	Perchlorate
	ClO_3^-	**Chlorate**
	ClO_2^-	Chlorite
	ClO^-	Hypochlorite
Carbon	**CO_3^{2-}**	**Carbonate**
	HCO_3^-	Hydrogen carbonate (or bicarbonate)
	CN^-	Cyanide
	$H_2C_3O_2^-$	Acetate
Sulfur	**SO_4^{2-}**	**Sulfate**
	HSO_4^-	Hydrogen sulfate (or bisulfate)
	SO_3^{2-}	Sulfite
	HSO_3^-	Hydrogen sulfite (or bisulfite)
Phosphorus	**PO_4^{3-}**	**Phosphate**
	HPO_4^{2-}	Hydrogen phosphate
	$H_2PO_4^-$	Dihydrogen phosphate
	PO_3^{3-}	Phosphite

*Formulas and names in bold show the most common polyatomic ion for that element.

Sodium chlorite is used in the processing and bleaching of pulp from wood fibers and recycled cardboard.

The formula of hydrogen carbonate, or *bicarbonate*, is written with a hydrogen in front of the polyatomic formula for carbonate, and the charge is decreased from 2− to 1− to give HCO_3^-.

$$CO_3^{2-} + H^+ = HCO_3^-$$

Compounds Containing Polyatomic Ions

No polyatomic ion exists by itself. Like any other ion, a polyatomic ion must be associated with ions of opposite charge. The bonding between polyatomic ions and other ions is one of electrical attraction. For example, the compound sodium chlorite, used in bleaching wood pulp, consists of sodium ions (Na^+) and chlorite ions (ClO_2^-) held together by ionic bonds.

To write correct formulas for compounds containing a polyatomic ion, we follow the same rules of charge balance that we used when writing the formulas for ionic compounds. The total negative and positive charges must equal zero. For example, consider the formula for a compound containing sodium ions and chlorite ions. The ions are written:

$$Na^+ \qquad ClO_2^-$$

Sodium ion   Chlorite ion

Ionic charge $(1+) + (1-) = 0$

Because it takes one ion of each to balance the charge, the formula is written:

$NaClO_2$
Sodium chlorite

When more than one polyatomic ion is needed for charge balance, parentheses are used to enclose the formula of the ion. A subscript is written outside the closing parenthesis of the polyatomic ion to indicate the number needed for charge balance. The formula for magnesium nitrate contains the magnesium ion and the polyatomic nitrate ion.

$$Mg^{2+} \qquad NO_3^-$$

Magnesium ion   Nitrate ion

To balance the positive charge of 2+ on the magnesium ion, two nitrate ions are needed. In the formula of the compound, parentheses are placed around the nitrate ion, and the subscript 2 is written outside the closing parenthesis.

$$NO_3^-$$
$$Mg^{2+}$$
$$NO_3^-$$
$(2+) + 2(1-) = 0$

Magnesium nitrate

$Mg(NO_3)_2$

Parentheses enclose the formula of the nitrate ion

Subscript outside the parenthesis indicates the use of two nitrate ions

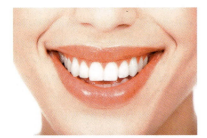

The mineral substance in teeth contains phosphate and hydroxide ions.

CONCEPT CHECK 5.3 Polyatomic Ions in Bones and Teeth

Bones and teeth contain a solid mineral substance called hydroxyapatite, $Ca_{10}(PO_4)_6(OH)_2$. What are the names and formulas of the polyatomic ions contained in the mineral substance of bones and teeth?

ANSWER

The polyatomic ions are phosphate, PO_4^{3-}, and hydroxide, OH^-.

Naming Compounds Containing Polyatomic Ions

When naming ionic compounds containing polyatomic ions, we first write the positive ion, usually a metal, and then we write the name for the polyatomic ion. It is important that you learn to recognize the polyatomic ion in the formula and name it correctly. As with other ionic compounds, no prefixes are used.

$$Na_2SO_4 \qquad FePO_4 \qquad Al_2(CO_3)_3$$

$$Na_2\boxed{SO_4} \qquad Fe\boxed{PO_4} \qquad Al_2(\boxed{CO_3})_3$$

Sodium sulfate   Iron(III) phosphate   Aluminum carbonate

Table 5.8 lists the formulas and names of some ionic compounds that include polyatomic ions and also gives their uses in medicine and industry.

TABLE 5.8 Some Compounds That Contain Polyatomic Ions

Formula	Name	Use
$BaSO_4$	Barium sulfate	Contrast medium for X-rays
$CaCO_3$	Calcium carbonate	Antacid, calcium supplement
$Ca_3(PO_4)_2$	Calcium phosphate	Calcium dietary supplement
$CaSO_3$	Calcium sulfite	Preservative in cider and fruit juices
$CaSO_4$	Calcium sulfate	Plaster casts
$AgNO_3$	Silver nitrate	Topical anti-infective
$NaHCO_3$	Sodium bicarbonate *or* Sodium hydrogen carbonate	Antacid
$Zn_3(PO_4)_2$	Zinc phosphate	Dental cement
$FePO_4$	Iron(III) phosphate	Food additive
K_2CO_3	Potassium carbonate	Alkalizer, diuretic
$Al_2(SO_4)_3$	Aluminum sulfate	Antiperspirant, anti-infective
$AlPO_4$	Aluminum phosphate	Antacid
$MgSO_4$	Magnesium sulfate	Cathartic, Epsom salts

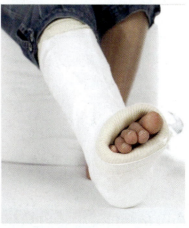

A plaster cast made of $CaSO_4$ immobilizes a broken leg.

SAMPLE PROBLEM 5.4 Naming Compounds Containing Polyatomic Ions

Name the following ionic compounds:

a. $KClO_3$
b. $Cu(NO_2)_2$

SOLUTION

	Step 1		Step 2	Step 3 Name of	Step 4
Formula	Cation	Anion	Name of Cation	Polyatomic Ion	Name of Compound
a. $KClO_3$	K^+	ClO_3^-	Potassium ion	Chlorate ion	Potassium chlorate
b. $Cu(NO_2)_2$	Cu^{2+}	NO_2^-	Copper(II) ion	Nitrite ion	Copper(II) nitrite

STUDY CHECK 5.4

What is the name of $Co_3(PO_4)_2$?

Guide to Naming Ionic Compounds with Polyatomic Ions

1 Identify the cation and polyatomic ion (anion).

2 Name the cation using a Roman numeral, if needed.

3 Name the polyatomic ion.

4 Write the name for the compound, cation first and the polyatomic ion second.

SAMPLE PROBLEM 5.5   Writing Formulas for Ionic Compounds Containing Polyatomic Ions

Write the formula for aluminum bicarbonate.

SOLUTION

Step 1   Identify the cation and polyatomic ion (anion).

Cation	Polyatomic Ion (Anion)
Al^{3+}	HCO_3^-

Step 2   Balance the charges.

$$Al^{3+} \qquad \begin{matrix} HCO_3^- \\ HCO_3^- \\ HCO_3^- \end{matrix}$$

$$\overline{\mathbf{1}(3+) \quad + \quad \mathbf{3}(1-) = 0}$$

Becomes a subscript in the formula

Step 3   Write the formula, cation first, using the subscripts from charge balance.
The formula for the compound is written by enclosing the formula of the bicarbonate ion, HCO_3^-, in parentheses, and writing the subscript 3 outside the closing parenthesis.

$$Al(HCO_3)_3$$

STUDY CHECK 5.5

Write the formula for a compound containing ammonium ion(s) and phosphate ion(s).

Guide to Writing Formulas with Polyatomic Ions

1   Identify the cation and polyatomic ion (anion).

2   Balance the charges.

3   Write the formula, cation first, using the subscripts from charge balance.

QUESTIONS AND PROBLEMS

5.4 Polyatomic Ions

LEARNING GOAL: Write the name and formula for a compound containing a polyatomic ion.

5.27 Write the formula, including the charge, for each of the following polyatomic ions:
  a. hydrogen carbonate (bicarbonate)
  b. ammonium
  c. phosphate
  d. hydrogen sulfate
  e. perchlorate

5.28 Write the formula, including the charge, for each of the following polyatomic ions:
  a. nitrite   **b.** sulfite
  c. hydroxide   **d.** hypophosphite
  e. bromate

5.29 Name each of the following polyatomic ions:
  a. SO_4^{2-} **b.** ClO^- **c.** PO_4^{3-} **d.** NO_3^-

5.30 Name each of the following polyatomic ions:
  a. OH^- **b.** HSO_3^- **c.** CN^- **d.** NO_2^-

5.31 Complete the following table with the formula of the compound that forms between each pair of ions:

	NO_2^-	CO_3^{2-}	HSO_4^-	PO_4^{3-}
Li^+				
Cu^{2+}				
Ba^{2+}				

5.32 Complete the following table with the formula of the compound that forms between each pair of ions:

	NO_3^-	HCO_3^-	SO_3^{2-}	HPO_4^{2-}
NH_4^+				
Al^{3+}				
Pb^{4+}				

5.33 Write the formula for the polyatomic ion in each of the following and name each compound:
  a. Na_2CO_3 **b.** NH_4Cl **c.** K_3PO_4
  d. $Cr(NO_2)_2$ **e.** $FeSO_3$

5.34 Write the formula for the polyatomic ion in each of the following and name each compound:
  a. KOH **b.** $NaNO_3$ **c.** Au_2CO_3
  d. $NaHCO_3$ **e.** $BaSO_4$

5.35 Write the correct formula for each of the following compounds:
  a. barium hydroxide   **b.** sodium sulfate
  c. iron(II) nitrate   **d.** zinc phosphate
  e. iron(III) carbonate

5.36 Write the correct formula for each of the following compounds:
  a. aluminum chlorate   **b.** ammonium oxide
  c. magnesium bicarbonate   **d.** sodium nitrite
  e. copper(I) sulfate

5.5 Covalent Compounds: Sharing Electrons

A **covalent compound** forms when atoms of two nonmetals share electrons. Because of the high ionization energies of the nonmetals, electrons are not transferred between atoms of nonmetals, but are shared to achieve stability. When nonmetal atoms share electrons, the bond is a **covalent bond**. When two or more atoms share electrons, they form a **molecule**.

LEARNING GOAL

Draw the electron-dot formulas for covalent compounds, including multiple bonds and resonance structures.

SELF-STUDY ACTIVITY
Covalent Bonds

Formation of a Hydrogen Molecule

The simplest covalent molecule is hydrogen, H_2. When two H atoms are far apart, there are no attractions between them. As the H atoms move closer, the positive charge of each nucleus attracts the electron of the other atom. This attraction, which is greater than the repulsion between the valence electrons, pulls the atoms closer until they share a pair of valence electrons. The result is called a *covalent bond*, in which each H atom has a stable electron configuration. The atoms bonded in H_2 are more stable than two individual H atoms.

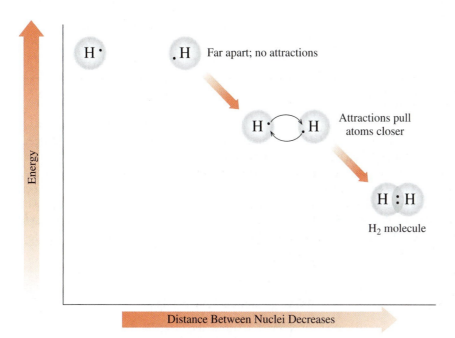

Electron-Dot Formulas of Covalent Molecules

The valence electrons in covalent molecules are shown using an electron-dot formula, also called a Lewis structure. The shared electrons, or *bonding pairs*, are shown as two dots or a single line between atoms. The nonbonding pairs of electrons, or *lone pairs*, are placed on the outside. For example, a fluorine molecule, F_2, consists of two fluorine atoms, Group 7A (17), each with seven valence electrons. In the F_2 molecule, each F atom achieves an octet by sharing its unpaired valence electron.

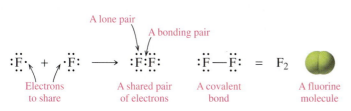

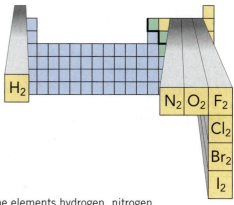

The elements hydrogen, nitrogen, oxygen, fluorine, chlorine, bromine, and iodine exist as diatomic molecules.

Hydrogen (H_2) and fluorine (F_2) are examples of nonmetal elements whose natural state is diatomic; that is, they contain two like atoms. The elements that exist as diatomic molecules are listed in Table 5.9.

Sharing Electrons between Atoms of Different Elements

The number of covalent bonds that a nonmetal forms is usually equal to the number of electrons it needs to acquire a stable electron configuration. Table 5.10 gives the most typical bonding patterns for several of the nonmetals.

TABLE 5.10 **Typical Bonding Patterns of Some Nonmetals in Covalent Compounds**					
1A (1)	**3A (13)**	**4A (14)**	**5A (15)**	**6A (16)**	**7A (17)**
*H 1 bond					
	*B 3 bonds	C 4 bonds	N 3 bonds	O 2 bonds	F 1 bond
		Si 4 bonds	P 3 bonds	S 2 bonds	Cl, Br, I 1 bond

*H and B do not form eight-electron octets. H atoms share one electron pair; B atoms share three electron pairs for a set of 6 electrons.

Methane, CH_4, a component of natural gas, is a compound of carbon and hydrogen. By sharing electrons, each carbon atom forms four bonds, and each hydrogen atom forms one bond. The carbon atom obtains an octet and each hydrogen atom is complete with two shared electrons. As seen in Table 5.11, the electron-dot formula for methane is drawn with the carbon atom as the center atom with the hydrogen atoms on all four sides. The bonding pairs of electrons, which are single covalent bonds, may also be shown as single lines between the carbon atom and each of the hydrogen atoms. Table 5.11 gives the formulas of some covalent molecules for Period 2 elements.

CONCEPT CHECK 5.4 **Drawing Electron-Dot Formulas**

Use the electron-dot symbols of S and F to draw the electron-dot formula for SF_2, sulfur difluoride, in which sulfur is the central atom.

ANSWER

To draw the electron-dot formula for SF_2, we need the electron-dot symbols of sulfur with six valence electrons, and fluorine with seven valence electrons.

$$:\overset{..}{\underset{.}{S}}\cdot \qquad \cdot \overset{..}{\underset{..}{F}}:$$

A sulfur atom will form two bonds by sharing each of its two unpaired electrons with the unpaired electron in each of two fluorine atoms. In this way, both the S atom and the two F atoms obtain stable electron configurations. The electron-dot formula for SF_2 shows the central S atom attached to two fluorine atoms using electron pairs or single bonds.

$$\begin{matrix} :\overset{..}{\underset{..}{S}}:\overset{..}{\underset{..}{F}}: \\ :\underset{..}{F}: \end{matrix} \quad \text{or} \quad \begin{matrix} :\overset{..}{\underset{..}{S}}—\overset{..}{\underset{..}{F}}: \\ | \\ :\underset{..}{F}: \end{matrix}$$

TUTORIAL
Covalent Molecules and the Octet Rule

TUTORIAL
Writing Electron-Dot Formulas

TUTORIAL
Covalent Lewis-Dot Formulas

TABLE 5.11 **Electron-Dot Formulas for Some Covalent Compounds**

CH_4	NH_3	H_2O

Formulas Using Electron Dots

$$\begin{matrix} & H & & & & \\ H&:\!\overset{..}{C}\!:&H \quad H\!:\!\overset{..}{N}\!:\!H \quad :\!\overset{..}{O}\!:\!H \\ & H & & H & & H \end{matrix}$$

Formulas Using Bonds and Electron Dots

$$\begin{matrix} & H & & & & \\ & | & & & & \\ H&—C—&H \quad H—\overset{..}{N}—H \quad :\overset{..}{O}—H \\ & | & & | & & \\ & H & & H & & H \end{matrix}$$

Molecular Models

Methane molecule   Ammonia molecule   Water molecule

SAMPLE PROBLEM 5.6 **Drawing Electron-Dot Formulas for Covalent Compounds**

Draw the electron-dot formula for PCl_3, phosphorus trichloride.

SOLUTION

Step 1 **Determine the arrangement of atoms.** In PCl_3, the central atom is P because it needs the most electrons.

Cl P Cl
   Cl

Step 2 **Determine the total number of valence electrons.** We use the group numbers to determine the valence electrons for each of the atoms in the molecule.

Element	Group	Atoms	Valence Electrons	=	Total
P	5A (15)	1 P	$\times\, 5\, e^-$	=	$5\, e^-$
Cl	7A (17)	3 Cl	$\times\, 7\, e^-$	=	$21\, e^-$
		Total valence electrons for PCl_3		=	$26\, e^-$

Step 3 **Attach each bonded atom to the central atom with a pair of electrons.**

Cl:P:Cl   or   Cl—P—Cl
  Cl   Cl

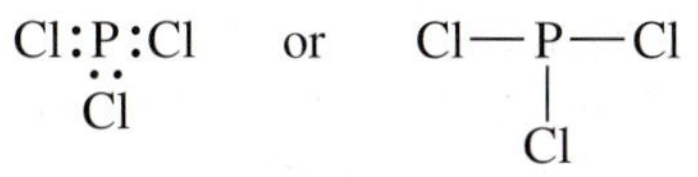

Step 4 **Place the remaining electrons using single or multiple bonds to complete the octets.** A total of six electrons ($3 \times 2\, e^-$) are needed to bond the central P atom to three Cl atoms. Twenty valence electrons are left:

26 valence e^- − 6 bonding e^- = 20 e^- remaining

The remaining electrons are placed as lone pairs of electrons around the outer Cl atoms first, which uses 18 more electrons.

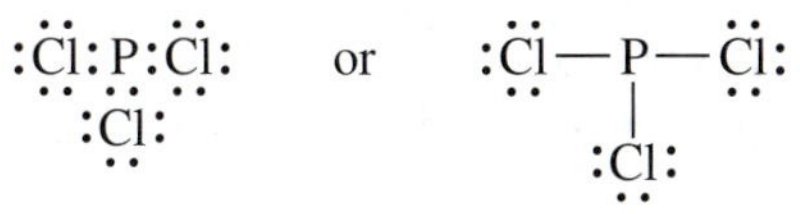

:Cl:P:Cl: or   :Cl—P—Cl:
  :Cl: :Cl:

Use the remaining two electrons to complete the octet for the P atom.

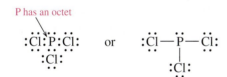

P has an octet

:Cl:P:Cl: or   :Cl—P—Cl:
  :Cl: :Cl:

STUDY CHECK 5.6

Draw the electron-dot formula for Cl_2O (O is the central atom).

Guide to Drawing Electron-Dot Formulas

1 Determine the arrangement of atoms.

2 Determine the total number of valence electrons.

3 Attach each bonded atom to the central atom with a pair of electrons.

4 Place the remaining electrons using single or multiple bonds to complete the octets (two for H, six for B).

The ball-and-stick model of PCl_3 consists of P (blue) and Cl atoms (green).

Exceptions to the Octet Rule

While the octet rule is useful, there are exceptions. We have already seen that a hydrogen (H_2) molecule requires just two electrons or a single bond to achieve stability. In $BeCl_2$, Be forms only two covalent bonds. In BCl_3, the B atom has only three valence electrons to share. Boron compounds typically have three electron groups around the central B atom and form three covalent bonds. Although the nonmetals typically form octets, atoms such as P, S, Cl, Br, and I can form compounds with 10, 12, or even 14 valence electrons. For example, in PCl_3, the P atom has an octet, but in PCl_5, the P atom has 10 valence electrons or five covalent bonds. In H_2S, the S atom has an octet, but in SF_6, there are 12 valence electrons or six bonds to the sulfur atom. In this text, we will encounter formulas with expanded octets, but we do not represent them with electron-dot formulas.

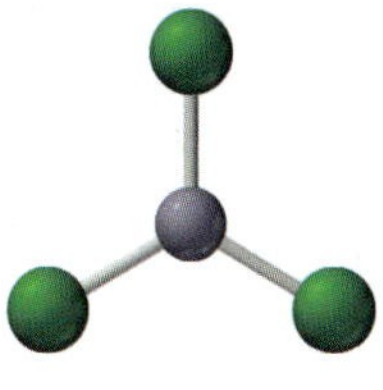

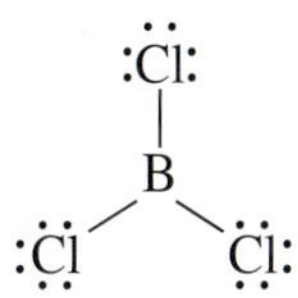

In BCl_3, the central B atom (purple) is bonded to three Cl atoms (green).

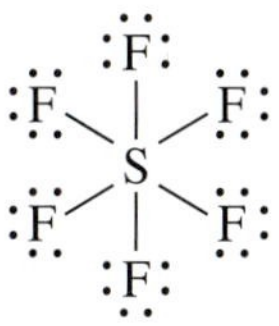

In SF_6, the central S atom (yellow) is bonded to six F atoms (yellow-green).

Double and Triple Covalent Bonds

Up to now, we have looked at covalent bonding in molecules having only single bonds. In many covalent compounds, atoms share two or three pairs of electrons to complete their octets. A **double bond** occurs when two pairs of electrons are shared; in a **triple bond**, three pairs of electrons are shared. Atoms of carbon, oxygen, nitrogen, and sulfur are most likely to form multiple bonds. Atoms of hydrogen and the halogens do not form double or triple bonds.

Double or triple bonds form when there are not enough valence electrons to complete the octets of some of the atoms in the molecule. Then one or more lone pairs of electrons from the atoms attached to the central atom are shared with the central atom.

For example, there are double bonds in CO_2 because two pairs of electrons are shared between the carbon atom and each oxygen atom to give octets. The process of drawing an electron-dot formula for CO_2 is shown in Sample Problem 5.7.

SAMPLE PROBLEM 5.7 **Drawing Electron-Dot Formulas with Multiple Bonds**

Draw the electron-dot formula for carbon dioxide, CO_2, in which the central atom is C.

SOLUTION

Step 1 **Determine the arrangement of atoms.** O C O

Step 2 **Determine the total number of valence electrons.** Using the group numbers to determine valence electrons, each oxygen atom has six valence electrons, and one carbon atom has four valence electrons, which gives a total of 16 valence electrons for the molecule.

Element	Group	Atoms	Valence Electrons	=	Total
O	6A (16)	2 O	$\times 6\ e^-$	=	$12\ e^-$
C	4A (14)	1 C	$\times 4\ e^-$	=	$4\ e^-$
		Total valence electrons for CO_2		=	$16\ e^-$

Step 3 **Attach each bonded atom to the central atom by a pair of electrons.** A pair of bonding electrons (single bond) is placed between each O atom and the central C atom.

$$\text{O:C:O} \quad \text{or} \quad \text{O—C—O}$$

Step 4 **Place the remaining electrons using single or multiple bonds to complete the octets.** Because we used four valence electrons to attach the C atom to two O atoms, there are 12 valence electrons remaining.

$$16 \text{ valence } e^- - 4 \text{ bonding } e^- = 12\ e^- \text{ remaining}$$

The remaining 12 electrons are placed as six lone pairs of electrons on the O atoms. However, this does not complete the octet for the C atom.

$$\text{:Ö:C:Ö:} \quad \text{or} \quad \text{:Ö—C—Ö:}$$

To complete the octet for the C atom, it shares a lone pair of electrons from each of the O atoms. When two bonding pairs occur between atoms, it is a double bond.

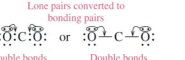

Lone pairs converted to bonding pairs

Double bonds   Double bonds

Molecule of carbon dioxide

$$\text{:O::C::O:} \quad \text{or} \quad \text{:O=C=O:}$$

STUDY CHECK 5.7

Draw the electron-dot formula for HCN (atoms arranged as H C N).

To draw the electron-dot formula for the covalent compound N_2, an octet is achieved when each nitrogen atom shares three pairs of electrons. Three covalent bonds between atoms is a triple bond as shown in Concept Check 5.5.

CONCEPT CHECK 5.5   **Drawing Triple Bonds in Covalent Molecules**

The covalent molecule N_2 contains a triple bond. Show how the atoms of N achieve octets to form a triple bond.

ANSWER

Step 1   **Determine the arrangement of atoms.** N N

Step 2   **Determine the total number of valence electrons.** Because nitrogen is in Group 5A (15), each N atom has five valence electrons.

Element	Group	Atoms	Valence Electrons	=	Total
N	5A (15)	2 N	$\times 5\ e^-$	=	$10\ e^-$

Step 3   **Attach each bonded atom to the central atom by a pair of electrons.** A pair of bonding electrons (single bond) is placed between the N atoms. However, this does not provide an octet for each N atom.

$$\cdot \ddot{N} : \ddot{N} \cdot \quad \text{or} \quad \cdot \ddot{N} - \ddot{N} \cdot$$

Step 4   **Place the remaining electrons using single or multiple bonds to complete the octets.** Each N atom achieves an octet by sharing three bonding pairs of electrons to form a triple bond.

Octets

$$\cdot \ddot{N} : \ddot{N} \cdot \quad \longrightarrow \quad : N \vdots N : \quad : N \equiv N : \quad N_2$$

Three shared   Triple bond   Nitrogen
pairs   molecule

Resonance Structures

When a molecule contains multiple bonds, it may be possible to draw more than one electron-dot formula. We can see how this happens when we try to draw the electron-dot formula for ozone, O_3, a component in the stratosphere that protects us from the ultraviolet rays of the Sun.

To draw the electron-dot formula, we need to determine the number of valence electrons for an O atom, and then the total number of valence electrons for O_3. Because O is in Group 6A (16), it has six valence electrons. Therefore, the compound O_3 would have a total of 18 valence electrons. To draw the electron-dot formula for O_3, we place three O atoms in a row and identify the O atom in the middle as the central atom.

Using four of the available valence electrons, we draw a bonding pair between the O atoms on the end and the central O atom.

$$O - O - O$$

These bonding pairs use four valence electrons and 14 valence electrons remain. We now place three lone pairs of electrons around the O atoms on both ends of the electron-dot formula, which uses 12 more valence electrons. The two remaining valence electrons are placed as a lone pair of electrons on the central O atom.

$$: \ddot{O} - \ddot{O} - \ddot{O} :$$

However, this use of all the remaining valence electrons does not complete an octet for the central O atom. To achieve an octet for the central O atom, one lone pair

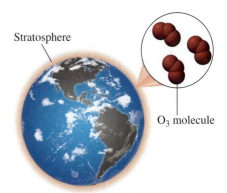

Stratosphere

O_3 molecule

Ozone, O_3, is a component in the stratosphere that protects us from the ultraviolet rays of the Sun.

of electrons from an end O atom is shared. But which one should be used? One possibility is to form a double bond on the left and the other possibility is to form a double bond on the right.

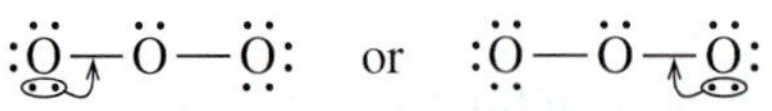

$$:\ddot{\text{O}}{\rightharpoonup}\ddot{\text{O}}—\ddot{\text{O}}: \quad \text{or} \quad :\ddot{\text{O}}—\ddot{\text{O}}{\rightharpoonup}\ddot{\text{O}}:$$

Now we see that we can draw more than one electron-dot formula for O_3. When this happens, all the possible electron-dot formulas are called **resonance structures**, which are shown with a double-headed arrow. Because the electrons in resonance structures are delocalized, they are not associated with a single atom. Thus, the bonding of these electrons is drawn with more than one electron-dot formula.

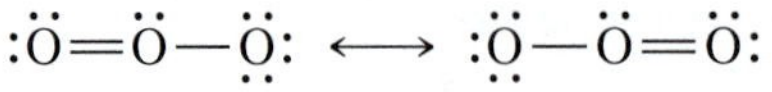

$$:\ddot{\text{O}}=\ddot{\text{O}}—\ddot{\text{O}}: \longleftrightarrow :\ddot{\text{O}}—\ddot{\text{O}}=\ddot{\text{O}}:$$

Resonance structures

Experiments show that the actual bond lengths are equivalent to a molecule with a "one and a half" bond between the central O atom and each outside O atom. In the actual ozone molecules, the electrons are shown spread equally over all the O atoms. When we draw resonance structures, the true structure is really an average of those structures.

CONCEPT CHECK 5.6   Resonance Structures

Explain why SCl_2 does not have resonance structures, but SO_2 does.

ANSWER

In the electron-dot formula of SCl_2, the unpaired valence electrons of each chlorine atom complete the octet of the sulfur atom. However, in SO_2, the central sulfur atom must form a double bond with one of the oxygen atoms. Thus, two electron-dot formulas, or resonance structures, are possible.

SAMPLE PROBLEM 5.8   Drawing Resonance Structures

Sulfur dioxide is produced naturally from volcanic activity and the burning of sulfur-containing coal. Once in the atmosphere, the SO_2 is converted to SO_3, which combines with water to form sulfuric acid, H_2SO_4, a component of acid rain. Draw two resonance structures for sulfur dioxide, SO_2.

SOLUTION

Step 1   **Determine the arrangement of atoms.** In SO_2, the S atom is the central atom.

O S O

Step 2   **Determine the total number of valence electrons.**

Element	Group	Atoms	Valence Electrons	=	Total
S	6A (16)	1 S	$\times 6\,e^-$	=	$6\,e^-$
O	6A (16)	2 O	$\times 6\,e^-$	=	$12\,e^-$
			Total valence electrons for SO_2	=	$18\,e^-$

Step 3   **Attach each bonded atom to the central atom with a pair of electrons.**

O—S—O

Step 4   **Place the remaining electrons using single or multiple bonds to complete the octets.** After four electrons are used to form single bonds between the

S atom and the O atoms, the remaining 14 electrons are drawn as lone pairs of electrons to complete the octets of the O atoms but not the S atom.

$$:\ddot{O}-\ddot{S}-\ddot{O}:$$

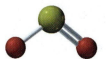

To complete the octet for S, one lone pair of electrons from one of the O atoms is shared to form a double bond. Because the lone pair of electrons that is shared can come from either O atom, two resonance structures can be drawn.

The ball-and-stick model of SO_2, which consists of S (yellow) and O atoms (red).

$$:\underset{..}{O}=\ddot{S}-\ddot{O}: \quad \longleftrightarrow \quad :\ddot{O}-\ddot{S}=\underset{..}{O}:$$

STUDY CHECK 5.8

Draw three resonance structures for SO_3.

QUESTIONS AND PROBLEMS

5.5 Covalent Compounds: Sharing Electrons

LEARNING GOAL: *Draw the electron-dot formulas for covalent compounds, including multiple bonds and resonance structures.*

5.37 Which of the following pairs of elements are most likely to form covalent compounds?
   a. oxygen and chlorine
   b. calcium and bromine
   c. nitrogen and oxygen
   d. iodine and iodine
   e. sodium and iodine
   f. carbon and sulfur

5.38 Which of the following pairs of elements are most likely to form covalent compounds?
   a. chlorine and bromine
   b. phosphorus and oxygen
   c. cesium and fluorine
   d. barium and iodine
   e. nitrogen and bromine
   f. potassium and sulfur

5.39 State the number of valence electrons, bonding pairs, and lone pairs in each of the following electron-dot formulas:
   a. H:H   **b.** $H:\ddot{Br}:$ **c.** $:\ddot{Br}:\ddot{Br}:$

5.40 State the number of valence electrons, bonding pairs, and lone pairs in each of the following electron-dot formulas:
   a. $H:\overset{H}{\underset{..}{\ddot{O}}:}$ **b.** $H:\overset{..}{\underset{H}{N}}:H$ **c.** $:\ddot{Br}:\overset{:\ddot{Br}:}{\underset{..}{\ddot{O}}}:$

5.41 Draw the electron-dot formula for each of the following molecules:
   a. HF
   b. NBr_3
   c. CH_3OH (methyl alcohol) $H\ \underset{H}{\overset{H}{C}}\ O\ H$
   d. N_2H_4 (hydrazine) $H\ \underset{H}{\overset{H\ H}{N}}\ N\ H$

5.42 Draw the electron-dot formula for each of the following molecules:
   a. H_2O
   b. SiF_4
   c. CF_2Cl_2
   d. C_2H_6 (ethane) $H\ \underset{H\ H}{\overset{H\ H}{C}}\ C\ H$

5.43 Draw the electron-dot formula, including multiple bonds, for each of the following molecules:
   a. CO (carbon monoxide)
   b. H_2CCH_2 (ethylene)
   c. H_2CO (C is the central atom)

5.44 Draw the electron-dot formula, including multiple bonds, for each of the following molecules:
   a. HCCH (acetylene)
   b. CS_2 (C is the central atom)
   c. $COCl_2$ (C is the central atom)

5.45 Draw resonance structures for $ClNO_2$ (N is the central atom).

5.46 Draw resonance structures for N_2O (N N O).

5.6 Naming and Writing Covalent Formulas

LEARNING GOAL

Given the formula of a covalent compound, write its correct name; given the name of a covalent compound, write its formula.

When naming a covalent compound, the first nonmetal in the formula is named by its element name; the second nonmetal is named using the first syllable of its element name, followed by *ide*. When a subscript indicates two or more atoms of an element, a prefix is shown in front of its name. Table 5.12 lists prefixes used in naming covalent compounds. The names of covalent compounds need prefixes because it is possible for atoms of two nonmetals to form two or more different compounds. For example, atoms of carbon and

TUTORIAL
Naming Covalent Compounds

TUTORIAL
Naming Molecular Compounds

oxygen form carbon monoxide (CO) and carbon dioxide (CO_2), in which the number of atoms of oxygen in each compound is indicated by the prefixes *mono* or *di* in their names.

When the vowels *o* and *o* or *a* and *o* appear together, the first vowel is omitted as in carbon monoxide. In the name of a covalent compound, the prefix *mono* is usually omitted, as in NO, nitrogen oxide. Traditionally, however, CO is named carbon monoxide. Table 5.13 lists the formulas, names, and commercial uses of some covalent compounds.

TABLE 5.12 Prefixes Used in Naming Covalent Compounds

1	mono	6	hexa
2	di	7	hepta
3	tri	8	octa
4	tetra	9	nona
5	penta	10	deca

TABLE 5.13 Some Common Covalent Compounds

Formula	Name	Commercial Uses
CS_2	Carbon disulfide	Manufacture of rayon
CO_2	Carbon dioxide	Carbonation of beverages; fire extinguishers; propellant in aerosols; dry ice
NO	Nitrogen oxide	Stabilizer
N_2O	Dinitrogen oxide	Inhalation anesthetic: "laughing gas"
SiO_2	Silicon dioxide	Manufacture of glass
SO_2	Sulfur dioxide	Preserving fruits, vegetables; disinfectant in breweries; bleaching textiles
SF_6	Sulfur hexafluoride	Electrical circuits

CONCEPT CHECK 5.7 **Naming Covalent Compounds**

Why is it that the name of the covalent compound BrCl, bromine chloride, does not include a prefix, but the name of OCl_2, oxygen dichloride, does?

ANSWER

When a formula has one atom of each element, the prefix (*mono*) is not used in the name. Thus, the name of BrCl is bromine chloride. However, two or more atoms of an element are indicated by using a prefix. Thus, the name of OCl_2 contains the prefix *di*, oxygen dichloride.

SAMPLE PROBLEM 5.9 **Naming Covalent Compounds**

Name the covalent compound NCl_3.

SOLUTION

Analyze the Problem

Symbol of Element	N	Cl
Name	Nitrogen	Chloride
Subscript	1	3
Prefix	none (understood)	tri

Guide to Naming Covalent Compounds

1 Name the first nonmetal by its element name.

2 Name the second nonmetal by using the first syllable of its name followed by *ide*.

3 Add prefixes to indicate the number of atoms (subscripts).

Step 1 **Name the first nonmetal by its element name.** In NCl_3, the first nonmetal (N) is nitrogen.

Step 2 **Name the second nonmetal by using the first syllable of its name followed by *ide*.** The second nonmetal (Cl) is named chloride.

Step 3 **Add prefixes to indicate the number of atoms (subscripts).** Because there is one nitrogen atom, no prefix is needed. The subscript 3 for the Cl atoms is written as the prefix *tri*. The name of NCl_3 is nitrogen trichloride.

STUDY CHECK 5.9

Write the name for each of the following compounds:

a. $SiBr_4$ **b.** Br_2O

Writing Formulas from the Names of Covalent Compounds

In the name of a covalent compound, the names of two nonmetals are given along with prefixes for the number of atoms of each. To write its formula, we use the element symbol for each element and a subscript when a prefix indicates two or more atoms, as shown in Sample Problem 5.10.

SAMPLE PROBLEM 5.10 Writing Formulas for Covalent Compounds

Write the formula for diboron trioxide.

SOLUTION

Analyze the Problem

Name	Diboron	Trioxide
Symbol of Element	B	O
Subscript	2 (from *di*)	3 (from *tri*)

Step 1 **Write the symbols in order of the elements in the name.** In this covalent compound of two nonmetals, the first nonmetal is boron (B) and the second nonmetal is oxygen (O).

B O

Step 2 **Write any prefixes as subscripts.** The prefix *di* in *diboron* indicates that there are two atoms of boron, shown as a subscript 2 in the formula. The prefix *tri* in *trioxide* indicates that there are three atoms of oxygen, shown as a subscript 3 in the formula.

B_2O_3

STUDY CHECK 5.10

What is the formula of iodine heptafluoride?

Guide to Writing Formulas for Covalent Compounds

1 Write the symbols in the order of the elements in the name.

2 Write any prefixes as subscripts.

Summary of Naming Ionic and Covalent Compounds

We have now examined strategies for naming ionic and covalent compounds. In general, compounds having two elements are named by stating the first element name, followed by the name of the second element with an *ide* ending. If the first element is a metal, the compound is usually ionic; if the first element is a nonmetal, the compound is usually covalent. For ionic compounds, it is necessary to determine whether the metal can form more than one type of positive ion; if so, a Roman numeral following the name of the metal indicates the particular ionic charge. One exception is the ammonium ion, NH_4^+, which is also written first as a positively charged polyatomic ion. Ionic compounds having three or more elements include some type of polyatomic ion. They are named by ionic rules but have an *ate* or *ite* ending when the polyatomic ion has a negative charge.

In naming covalent compounds having two elements, prefixes are necessary to indicate two or more atoms of each nonmetal as shown in that particular formula (see Figure 5.4). Organic compounds of C and H, such as CH_4 and C_2H_6, use a different system of naming that we will discuss in a later chapter.

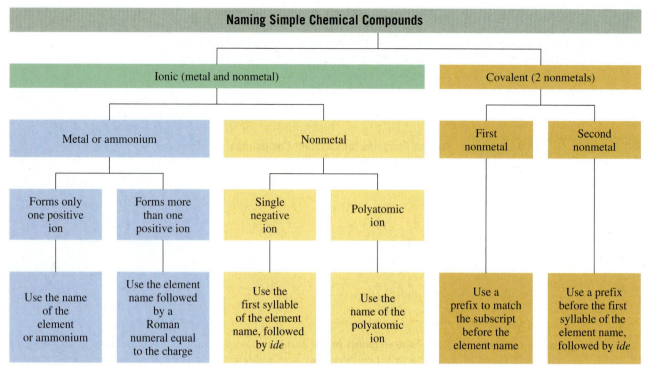

FIGURE 5.4 A flowchart shows a strategy for naming ionic and covalent compounds.

Q Why does the name sulfur dichloride have a prefix but the name magnesium chloride does not?

CONCEPT CHECK 5.8 **Naming Ionic and Covalent Compounds**

Identify each of the following compounds as ionic or covalent and give its name:

a. Na_3P **b.** $NiSO_4$ **c.** SO_3

ANSWER

a. Na_3P, consisting of a metal and nonmetal, is an ionic compound. As a representative element in Group 1A (1), Na forms the sodium ion, Na^+. Phosphorus, as a representative element in Group 5A (15), forms a phosphide ion, P^{3-}. Writing the name for the cation followed by the name for the anion gives the name sodium phosphide.

b. $NiSO_4$, consisting of a cation of a transition element and an anion, SO_4^{2-}, of a polyatomic ion is an ionic compound. As a transition element, Ni forms more than one type of ion. In this formula, the 2− charge of SO_4^{2-} is balanced by one nickel ion, Ni^{2+}. In the name, a Roman numeral written after the metal name, nickel(II), specifies the 2+ charge. The anion SO_4^{2-} is a polyatomic ion named sulfate. The compound is named nickel(II) sulfate.

c. SO_3 consists of two nonmetals, which indicates that it is a covalent compound. The first element, S, is *sulfur* (no prefix is needed). The second element O, *oxide*, has a subscript 3, which requires a prefix of *tri* in the name. The compound is named sulfur trioxide.

QUESTIONS AND PROBLEMS

5.6 Naming and Writing Covalent Formulas

LEARNING GOAL: *Given the formula of a covalent compound, write its correct name; given the name of a covalent compound, write its formula.*

5.47 Name each of the following:
    a. PBr_3 **b.** CBr_4 **c.** SiO_2 **d.** N_2O_3 **e.** PCl_5

5.48 Name each of the following:
    a. CS_2 **b.** P_2O_5 **c.** Cl_2O **d.** PCl_3 **e.** IBr_3

5.49 Write the formula for each of the following:
    a. carbon tetrachloride
    b. carbon monoxide
    c. phosphorus trichloride
    d. dinitrogen tetroxide
    e. boron trifluoride
    f. sulfur hexafluoride

5.50 Write the formula for each of the following:
  a. sulfur dioxide
  b. silicon tetrachloride
  c. iodine pentafluoride
  d. dinitrogen oxide
  e. tetraphosphorus hexoxide
  f. dinitrogen pentoxide

5.51 Name each of the following ionic or covalent compounds:
  a. $Al_2(SO_4)_3$ antiperspirant
  b. $CaCO_3$ antacid
  c. N_2O "laughing gas" (inhaled anesthetic)

  d. Na_3PO_4 cathartic
  e. $(NH_4)_2SO_4$ fertilizer
  f. Fe_2O_3 pigment

5.52 Name each of the following ionic or covalent compounds:
  a. N_2 Earth's atmosphere
  b. $Mg_3(PO_4)_2$ antacid
  c. $FeSO_4$ iron supplement in vitamins
  d. N_2O_4 rocket fuel
  e. Cu_2O fungicide
  f. NI_3 contact explosive

5.7 Electronegativity and Bond Polarity

We can learn more about the chemistry of compounds by looking at how electrons are shared between atoms. Although we have discussed covalent bonds as one or more bonding pairs of electrons, we do not know if those electrons are shared equally or unequally.

To do this, we use **electronegativity**, which is the ability of an atom to attract the shared electrons in a chemical bond (see Figure 5.5). Nonmetals have higher electronegativities than do metals, because nonmetals have a great attraction for electrons. The nonmetal fluorine, which has the highest electronegativity (4.0), is located in the upper right corner of the periodic table. The metal cesium, which has the lowest electronegativity (0.7), is located in the lower left corner of the periodic table. Note that there are no electronegativity values for the noble gases because they do not typically form bonds. The electronegativity values for transition elements are also low, but we have not included them in our discussion.

LEARNING GOAL

Use electronegativity to determine the polarity of a bond.

TUTORIAL
Electronegativity

SELF-STUDY ACTIVITY
Bonds and Bond Polarities

Electronegativity Increases →

1 Group 1A	2 Group 2A				13 Group 3A	14 Group 4A	15 Group 5A	16 Group 6A	17 Group 7A
							H 2.1		
Li 1.0	Be 1.5				B 2.0	C 2.5	N 3.0	O 3.5	F 4.0
Na 0.9	Mg 1.2				Al 1.5	Si 1.8	P 2.1	S 2.5	Cl 3.0
K 0.8	Ca 1.0				Ga 1.6	Ge 1.8	As 2.0	Se 2.4	Br 2.8
Rb 0.8	Sr 1.0				In 1.7	Sn 1.8	Sb 1.9	Te 2.1	I 2.5
Cs 0.7	Ba 0.9				Tl 1.8	Pb 1.9	Bi 1.9	Po 2.0	At 2.1

↓ Electronegativity Decreases

18 Group 8A

FIGURE 5.5 The electronegativities of the representative elements in Group 1A (1) to Group 7A (17), which indicate the ability of atoms to attract shared electrons, increase across a period and decrease going down a group.

Q What element on the periodic table has the strongest attraction for shared electrons?

Types of Bonding

The difference in the electronegativity of two atoms can be used to predict the type of bond, ionic or covalent, that forms. For the H—H bond, the electronegativity difference is zero $(2.1 - 2.1 = 0.0)$, which means that the bonding electrons are shared equally. Thus, we see a symmetrical electron cloud around the H atoms. A covalent bond between atoms with identical or very similar electronegativity values is a **nonpolar covalent bond**. However, when bonds are between atoms with different electronegativity values, the electrons are shared unequally; the bond is a **polar covalent bond**. The electron cloud for a polar covalent bond is unsymmetrical. For the H—Cl bond, there is an electronegativity difference of 0.9 (3.0 − 2.1 = 0.9), which means that the H—Cl bond is polar covalent (see Figure 5.6).

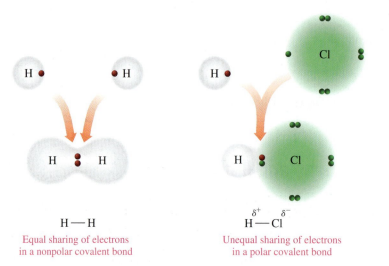

FIGURE 5.6 In the nonpolar covalent bond of H_2, electrons are shared equally. In the polar covalent bond of HCl, electrons are shared unequally.

Q H_2 has a nonpolar covalent bond, but HCl has a polar covalent bond. Explain.

H—H

Equal sharing of electrons
in a nonpolar covalent bond

$\overset{\delta^+}{H}—\overset{\delta^-}{Cl}$

Unequal sharing of electrons
in a polar covalent bond

Dipoles and Bond Polarity

The *polarity* of a bond depends on its electronegativity difference. In a polar covalent bond, the shared electrons are attracted to the more electronegative atom, which makes it partially negative, due to the negatively charged electrons around that atom. At the other end of the bond, the atom with the lower electronegativity becomes partially positive due to a lack of electrons around that atom. A bond becomes more *polar* as the electronegativity difference increases. A polar covalent bond that has a separation of charges is called a **dipole**. The positive and negative ends of the dipole are indicated by the lowercase Greek letter delta with a positive or negative sign, δ^+ and δ^-. Sometimes we use an arrow that points from the positive charge to the negative charge (⟼) to indicate the dipole.

Examples of Dipoles in Polar Covalent Bonds

$\overset{\delta^+}{C}—\overset{\delta^-}{O}$ $\overset{\delta^+}{N}—\overset{\delta^-}{O}$ $\overset{\delta^+}{Cl}—\overset{\delta^-}{F}$

Variations in Bonding

The variations in bonding are continuous; there is no definite point at which one type of bond stops and the next starts. When the electronegativity difference is from 0.0 to 0.4, the electrons are considered to be shared equally in a *nonpolar covalent bond*. For example, the H—H bond with an electronegativity difference of 0.0 (2.1 − 2.1 = 0.0) and the C—H bond with an electronegativity difference of 0.4 (2.5 − 2.1 = 0.4) are classified as nonpolar covalent bonds. As the electronegativity difference increases, the shared electrons are attracted more closely to the more electronegative atom, which increases the polarity of the bond. When the electronegativity difference is from 0.5 to 1.8, the bond is classified as a *polar covalent bond* (see Table 5.14).

TABLE 5.14 Electronegativity Difference and Types of Bonds

Electronegativity Difference	0	0.4	1.8	3.3
Bond Type	Covalent nonpolar		Covalent polar	Ionic
Electron Bonding	Electrons shared equally		Electrons shared unequally δ^+ δ^-	Electron transfer + −

When the electronegativity difference is greater than 1.8, electrons are transferred from one atom to another, which results in an ionic bond. For example, the electronegativity difference for the ionic compound NaCl is $2.1\,(3.0 - 0.9 = 2.1)$. Thus, for large differences in electronegativity, we would predict an ionic bond (see Table 5.15).

TABLE 5.15 Predicting Bond Type from Electronegativity Differences

Molecule	Bond	Type of Electron Sharing	Electronegativity Difference*	Type of Bond	Reason
H_2	H—H	Shared equally	$2.1 - 2.1 = 0.0$	Nonpolar covalent	Less than 0.4
Cl_2	Cl—Cl	Shared equally	$3.0 - 3.0 = 0.0$	Nonpolar covalent	Less than 0.4
HBr	$\overset{\delta^+}{H}$—$\overset{\delta^-}{Br}$	Shared unequally	$2.8 - 2.1 = 0.7$	Polar covalent	Greater than 0.4, but less than 1.8
HCl	$\overset{\delta^+}{H}$—$\overset{\delta^-}{Cl}$	Shared unequally	$3.0 - 2.1 = 0.9$	Polar covalent	Greater than 0.4, but less than 1.8
NaCl	$Na^+\ Cl^-$	Electron transfer	$3.0 - 0.9 = 2.1$	Ionic	Greater than 1.8
MgO	$Mg^{2+}\ O^{2-}$	Electron transfer	$3.5 - 1.2 = 2.3$	Ionic	Greater than 1.8

*Values are taken from Figure 5.5.

CONCEPT CHECK 5.9 **Using Electronegativity to Determine the Polarity of Bonds**

Complete the following table for each of the bonds indicated:

Bond	Electronegativity Difference	Type of Bond	Reason
Si—P			
Si—S			
Cs—Cl			

ANSWER

Bond	Electronegativity Difference	Type of Bond	Reason
Si—P	$2.1 - 1.8 = 0.3$	Nonpolar covalent	Less than 0.4
Si—S	$2.5 - 1.8 = 0.7$	Polar covalent	Greater than 0.4, but less than 1.8
Cs—Cl	$3.0 - 0.7 = 2.3$	Ionic	Greater than 1.8

SAMPLE PROBLEM 5.11 **Bond Polarity**

Using electronegativity values, classify each bond as nonpolar covalent, polar covalent, or ionic:

N—N, O—H, Cl—As, O—K

SOLUTION

For each bond, we obtain the electronegativity values and calculate the difference.

Bond	Electronegativity Difference	Type of Bond
N—N	$3.0 - 3.0 = 0.0$	Nonpolar covalent
O—H	$3.5 - 2.1 = 1.4$	Polar covalent
Cl—As	$3.0 - 2.0 = 1.0$	Polar covalent
O—K	$3.5 - 0.8 = 2.7$	Ionic

STUDY CHECK 5.11

Using electronegativity values, classify each bond as nonpolar covalent, polar covalent, or ionic:

a. P—Cl   **b.** Br—Br   **c.** Na—O

QUESTIONS AND PROBLEMS

5.7 Electronegativity and Bond Polarity

LEARNING GOAL: *Use electronegativity to determine the polarity of a bond.*

5.53   Using the periodic table, describe the trend in electronegativity as *increases* or *decreases* for each of the following:
   a. from B to F   **b.** from Mg to Ba
   c. from F to I

5.54   Using the periodic table, describe the trend in electronegativity as *increases* or *decreases* for each of the following:
   a. from Al to Cl   **b.** from N to Bi
   c. from Li to Cs

5.55   State the electronegativity difference for each of the following pairs of elements:
   a. Rb and Cl   **b.** Cl and Cl
   c. N and O   **d.** C and H

5.56   State the electronegativity difference for each of the following pairs of elements:
   a. Sr and S   **b.** N and S
   c. Cl and Br   **d.** K and F

5.57   Using the periodic table, arrange the atoms in each set in order of increasing electronegativity:
   a. Li, Na, K   **b.** Na, Cl, P   **c.** Se, Ca, O

5.58   Using the periodic table, arrange the atoms in each set in order of increasing electronegativity:
   a. Cl, F, Br   **b.** B, O, N   **c.** Mg, F, S

5.59   Predict whether each of the following bonds is nonpolar covalent, polar covalent, or ionic:
   a. Si—Br   **b.** Li—F   **c.** Br—F
   d. I—I   **e.** N—P   **f.** C—O

5.60   Predict whether each of the following bonds is nonpolar covalent, polar covalent, or ionic:
   a. Si—O   **b.** K—Cl   **c.** S—F
   d. P—Br   **e.** Li—S   **f.** N—S

5.61   For each of the following bonds, indicate the positive end with δ^+ and the negative end with δ^-. Draw an arrow to show the dipole for each.
   a. N—F   **b.** Si—Br   **c.** C—O
   d. P—Br   **e.** N—P

5.62   For each of the following bonds, indicate the positive end with δ^+ and the negative end with δ^-. Draw an arrow to show the dipole for each.
   a. P—Cl   **b.** Se—F   **c.** Br—F
   d. N—H   **e.** B—Cl

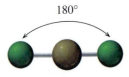

180°

Linear shape

:C̈l—Be—C̈l:

Linear electron-group geometry

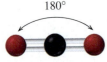

180°

Linear shape

:Ö=C=Ö:

Linear electron-group geometry

5.8 Shapes and Polarity of Molecules

Using the information in Section 5.7, we can now predict the three-dimensional shapes of many molecules. The shape is important to our understanding of how molecules interact with enzymes and certain antibiotics, or produce our sense of taste and smell.

The three-dimensional shape of a molecule is determined by drawing an electron-dot formula and identifying the number of electron groups and their geometry around a central atom. In the **valence-shell electron-pair repulsion (VSEPR) theory**, the electron groups are arranged as far apart as possible to minimize the repulsion between them. The specific shape of the molecule is determined from the number of atoms attached to the central atom.

Central Atoms with Two Electron Groups

In $BeCl_2$, two chlorine atoms are bonded to a central Be atom. Because an atom of Be has a strong attraction for valence electrons, it forms a covalent rather than ionic compound. With only two electron groups (two electron pairs) around the central atom, the electron-dot formula of $BeCl_2$ is an exception to the octet rule. The best geometry for two electron groups for minimal repulsion is to place them on opposite sides of the central Be atom. This gives the $BeCl_2$ molecule a linear electron-group geometry and a **linear** shape with a bond angle of 180°.

Another example of a linear molecule is CO_2. To predict geometry, we count a double or triple bond as *one electron group*. In the electron-dot formula of CO_2, the two electron groups (two double bonds) are on opposite sides of the central C atom, which is a linear electron-group geometry. With two atoms attached to the central C, the shape of the CO_2 molecule is *linear* with a bond angle of 180°.

Central Atoms with Three Electron Groups

In the electron-dot formula for BF_3, the central B atom has three electron groups attached to three fluorine atoms, which is another exception to the octet rule. In the electron-group geometry, the three electron groups are placed as far apart as possible around the central B atom at 120° bond angles. This type of electron-group geometry is *trigonal planar*. In BF_3, the three electron groups around the central B atom are each bonded to a fluorine atom, which gives a shape called **trigonal planar** with bond angles of 120°.

MC™

TUTORIAL
Molecular Shape

TUTORIAL
Shapes of Molecules

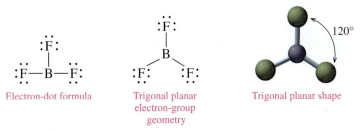

Electron-dot formula   Trigonal planar   Trigonal planar shape
                            electron-group
                            geometry

In the electron-dot formula for SO_2, there are also three electron groups around the central S atom: a single bond, a double bond, and a lone pair of electrons. As in BF_3, three electron groups have minimal repulsion by forming a trigonal planar electron-group geometry. However, in SO_2 one of the electron groups is a lone pair of electrons. Therefore, the shape of SO_2 is determined by the two oxygen atoms bonded to the central S atom, which gives the SO_2 molecule a **bent** shape with a bond angle of 120°. When there are one or more lone pairs on the central atom, the shape of the molecule is different than that of the electron-group geometry.

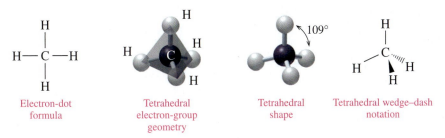

Electron-dot formula   Trigonal planar   Bent shape
                            electron-group
                            geometry

Central Atoms with Four Electron Groups

In a molecule of CH_4, the central C atom is bonded to four H atoms. From the electron-dot formula, you may think that CH_4 is planar with 90° bond angles. However, the best geometry for minimal repulsion is *tetrahedral*, which places the bonded atoms at the corners of a tetrahedron, giving bond angles of 109°. When there are four atoms attached to four electron groups, the shape of the molecule is **tetrahedral**.

A way to represent the three-dimensional structure of methane is to use the wedge–dash notation. In this notation, the two bonds connecting carbon to hydrogen by solid lines are in the plane of the paper. The wedge represents a carbon-to-hydrogen bond coming out of the page towards us, whereas the dash represents a carbon-to-hydrogen bond going into the page away from us.

Electron-dot   Tetrahedral   Tetrahedral   Tetrahedral wedge–dash
formula   electron-group   shape   notation
                      geometry

Now we can look at molecules that also have four electron groups of which one or more are lone pairs. Then the central atom is attached to only two or three atoms. For example, in the electron-dot formula of ammonia, NH_3, four electron groups have a tetrahedral electron-group geometry. However, in NH_3 one of the electron groups is a lone pair of electrons. Therefore, the shape of NH_3 is determined by the three hydrogen atoms bonded to the central N atom, which gives the NH_3 molecule a **trigonal pyramidal** shape with a bond angle of 109°. The wedge–dash notation can also represent this three-dimensional structure of ammonia with one N—H bond in the plane, one N—H bond coming towards us, and one N—H bond going away from us.

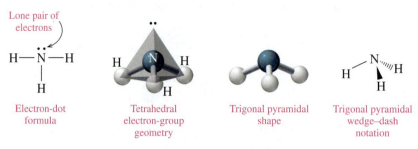

Lone pair of electrons

| Electron-dot formula | Tetrahedral electron-group geometry | Trigonal pyramidal shape | Trigonal pyramidal wedge–dash notation |

In the electron-dot formula of water, H_2O, there are also four electron groups, which have minimal repulsion when the electron-group geometry is tetrahedral. However, in H_2O, two of the electron groups are lone pairs of electrons. Because the shape of H_2O is determined by the two hydrogen atoms bonded to the central O atom, the H_2O molecule has a **bent** shape with a bond angle of 109°. Table 5.16 gives the molecular shapes for molecules with two, three, and four electron groups.

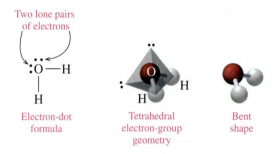

Two lone pairs of electrons

| Electron-dot formula | Tetrahedral electron-group geometry | Bent shape |

CONCEPT CHECK 5.10 Shapes of Molecules

If the four electron groups in a PH_3 molecule form a tetrahedron, why does a PH_3 molecule have a trigonal pyramidal shape?

ANSWER

Four electron groups achieve minimal repulsion when the electron-group geometry is a tetrahedron. However, one of the electron groups is a lone pair of electrons. Because the shape of the PH_3 molecule is determined by the three H atoms bonded to the central P atom, the shape of PH_3 is trigonal pyramidal.

SAMPLE PROBLEM 5.12 Predicting Shapes

Predict the shape of a molecule of H_2Se.

SOLUTION

Guide to Predicting Molecular Shape (VSEPR Theory)

1 Draw the electron-dot formula.

2 Arrange the electron groups around the central atom to minimize repulsion.

3 Use the atoms bonded to the central atom to determine the molecular shape.

Step 1   **Draw the electron-dot formula.** In the electron-dot formula for H_2Se, there are four electron groups, including two lone pairs of electrons.

$$:\!\overset{..}{Se}\!-\!H$$
$$|$$
$$H$$

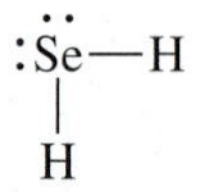

Step 2   **Arrange the electron groups around the central atom to minimize repulsion.** The four electron groups around Se would have a tetrahedral arrangement.

Step 3   **Use the atoms bonded to the central atom to determine the molecular shape.** Two bonded atoms give H_2Se a bent shape with a bond angle of 109°.

STUDY CHECK 5.12

Predict the shape of CBr_4.

TABLE 5.16 Molecular Shapes for a Central Atom with Two, Three, and Four Bonded Atoms

Electron Groups	Electron-Group Arrangement	Bonded Atoms	Lone Pairs	Bond Angle	Molecular Shape	Example	Three-Dimensional Model
2	Linear	2	0	180°	Linear	$BeCl_2$	
3	Trigonal planar	3	0	120°	Trigonal planar	BF_3	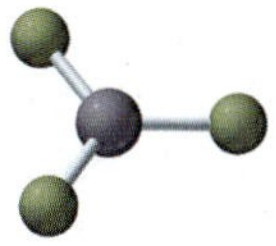
		2	1	120°	Bent	SO_2	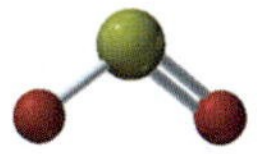
4	Tetrahedral	4	0	109°	Tetrahedral	CH_4	
		3	1	109°	Trigonal pyramidal	NH_3	
		2	2	109°	Bent	H_2O	

Polarity of Molecules

We have seen that covalent bonds can be polar or nonpolar. The bond polarities and shape of a molecule determines whether that molecule is polar or nonpolar.

TUTORIAL
Distinguishing Polar and Nonpolar Molecules

Nonpolar Molecules

In a **nonpolar molecule**, all the bonds are nonpolar or the polar bonds cancel each other out. Molecules such as H_2, Cl_2, and CH_4 are nonpolar because they contain only nonpolar covalent bonds.

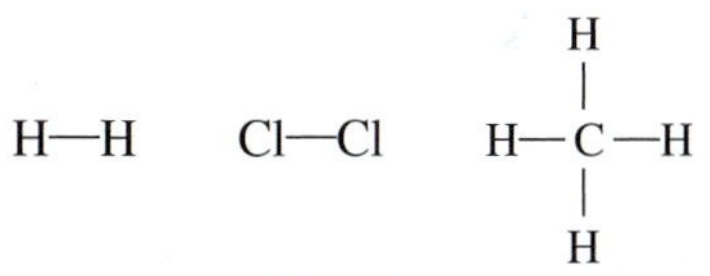

$$H—H \quad Cl—Cl \quad H—\overset{\displaystyle H}{\underset{\displaystyle H}{C}}—H$$

Nonpolar

A *nonpolar molecule* also occurs when polar bonds or dipoles in a molecule cancel each other because they are in a symmetrical arrangement. For example, CO_2, a linear molecule, contains two polar covalent bonds whose dipoles point in opposite directions. As a result, the dipoles cancel out, which makes a CO_2 molecule nonpolar.

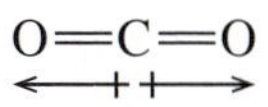

$$O═C═O$$

Dipoles cancel

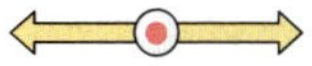

CO_2 is a nonpolar molecule.

Other examples of nonpolar molecules with symmetrical arrangements of polar bonds include BF_3 and CCl_4. In BF_3, the dipoles of three polar bonds in a trigonal planar shape cancel out to give a nonpolar molecule. The CCl_4 molecule is also nonpolar because its four polar bonds are symmetrically arranged around the central C atom with the dipoles pointing away from each other and canceling out.

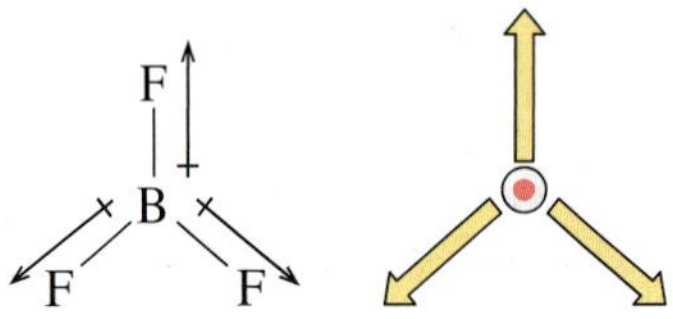

BF₃ is a nonpolar molecule.

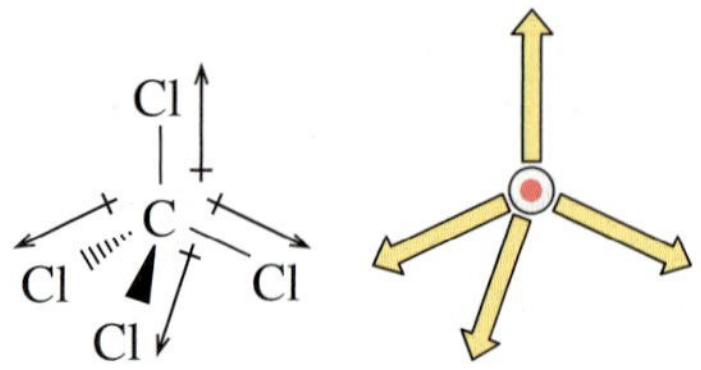

CCl₄ is a nonpolar molecule.

Polar Molecules

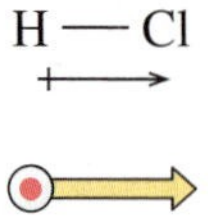

H — Cl

A single dipole does not cancel.

In a **polar molecule**, one end of the molecule is more negatively charged than another end. Polarity in a molecule occurs when the polar bonds or dipoles do not cancel out. For example, the HCl molecule is polar because electrons are shared unequally in the polar H—Cl bond.

In polar molecules with three or more atoms, the shape of the molecule determines whether the dipoles cancel or not. Often, there are lone pairs of electrons around the central atom. In H_2O, the dipoles point in the same direction, which means they do not cancel, but add together. The result is a molecule positive at one end and negative at the other end. Thus, water is a polar molecule.

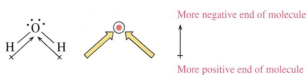

More negative end of molecule

More positive end of molecule

H_2O is a polar molecule because its dipoles do not cancel.

In the molecule NH_3, there are three dipoles, but they do not cancel.

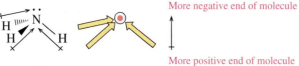

More negative end of molecule

More positive end of molecule

NH_3 is a polar molecule because its dipoles do not cancel.

In the molecule CH_3F, the C—F bond is polar but the three C—H bonds are nonpolar, which makes CH_3F a polar molecule.

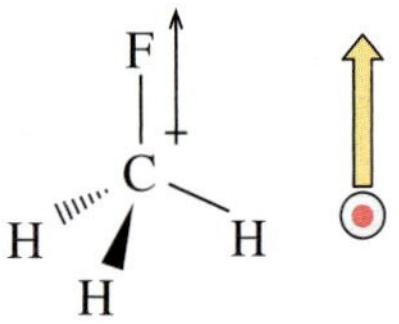

CH₃F is a polar molecule.

Guide to Determination of Polarity of a Molecule

1 Determine if the bonds are polar covalent or nonpolar covalent.

2 If the bonds are polar covalent, draw the electron-dot formula and determine if the dipoles cancel or not.

SAMPLE PROBLEM 5.13   Polarity of Molecules

Determine whether each of the following molecules is polar or nonpolar:

a. $SiCl_4$ **b.** OF_2

SOLUTION

a. Step 1 **Determine if the bonds are polar covalent or nonpolar covalent.** From the electronegativity table, Cl 3.0 and Si 1.8 gives a difference of 1.2, which makes the Si—Cl bonds polar covalent.

Step 2 **If the bonds are polar covalent, draw the electron-dot formula and determine if the dipoles cancel or not.** The electron-dot formula for $SiCl_4$ has four electron groups and four bonded atoms. The molecule has a tetrahedral shape. The dipoles of the Si—Cl bonds point away from each other and cancel out, which makes $SiCl_4$ a nonpolar molecule.

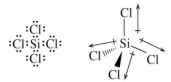

$SiCl_4$ is a nonpolar molecule.

b. Step 1 **Determine if the bonds are polar covalent or nonpolar covalent.** From the electronegativity table, F 4.0 and O 3.5 gives a difference of 0.5, which makes the O—F bonds polar covalent.

Step 2 **If the bonds are polar covalent, draw the electron-dot formula and determine if the dipoles cancel or not.** The electron-dot formula for OF_2 has four electron groups and two bonded atoms. The molecule has a bent shape in which the dipoles of the O—F bonds point in the same direction. This makes one end of the molecule positive and the other end negative. The OF_2 molecule would be a polar molecule.

OF_2 is a polar molecule.

STUDY CHECK 5.13

Would PCl_3 be a polar or nonpolar molecule?

QUESTIONS AND PROBLEMS

5.8 Shapes and Polarity of Molecules

LEARNING GOAL: Predict the three-dimensional structure of a molecule and classify it as polar or nonpolar.

5.63 Choose the shape (**1–6**) that matches with each of the following three descriptions:
1. linear   **2.** bent (109°)   **3.** trigonal planar
4. bent (120°)   **5.** trigonal pyramidal   **6.** tetrahedral

a. a molecule with a central atom that has four electron groups and four bonded atoms
b. a molecule with a central atom that has four electron groups and three bonded atoms
c. a molecule with a central atom that has three electron groups and three bonded atoms

5.64 Choose the shape (**1–6**) that matches with each of the following three descriptions:
1. linear   **2.** bent (109°)   **3.** trigonal planar
4. bent (120°)   **5.** trigonal pyramidal   **6.** tetrahedral

a. a molecule with a central atom that has four electron groups and two bonded atoms
b. a molecule with a central atom that has two electron groups and two bonded atoms
c. a molecule with a central atom that has three electron groups and two bonded atoms

5.65 Complete each of the following statements for a molecule of SeO_3:
a. There are _____ electron groups around the central atom.
b. The electron-group geometry is _____.

c. The shape of the molecule is _____.
d. The molecule is (polar/nonpolar) _____.

5.66 Complete each of the following statements for a molecule of $SeCl_2$:
a. There are _____ electron groups around the central atom.
b. The electron-group geometry is _____.
c. The shape of the molecule is _____.
d. The molecule is (polar/nonpolar) _____.

5.67 Which of the following molecules has the same shape as PH_3?
a. NCl_3 b. PCl_3 c. BF_3

5.68 Which of the following molecules has the same shape as CO_2?
a. BeF_2 b. H_2O c. OF_2

5.69 Use the VSEPR theory to predict the shape of each molecule:
a. OF_2 b. CCl_4
c. $GaCl_3$ d. SeO_2

5.70 Use the VSEPR theory to predict the shape of each molecule:
a. NCl_3 b. SCl_2
c. SiF_2Cl_2 d. $BeBr_2$

5.71 The molecule Cl_2 is nonpolar, but HCl is polar. Explain.

5.72 The molecules CH_4 and CH_3Cl both contain four bonds. Why is CH_4 nonpolar whereas CH_3Cl is polar?

5.73 Identify each of the following molecules as polar or nonpolar:
a. HBr   b. NF_3
c. CHF_3 d. SO_3

5.74 Identify each of the following molecules as polar or nonpolar:
a. SeF_2 b. PBr_3
c. SiF_4 d. SeO_2

TUTORIAL
Intermolecular Forces

TUTORIAL
Forces between Molecules

5.9 Attractive Forces in Compounds

Now we will look at the attractive forces that hold molecules and ions close together in liquids and solids. A solid melts and a liquid boils when the quantity of heat added exceeds the strength of the attractive forces between the particles. When attractive forces are weak, the substance undergoes a change of state at relatively low melting and boiling points. If the attractive forces are strong, the substance changes state at higher temperatures.

In gases, the attractions between particles are minimal, which allows gas molecules to move far apart from each other. In solids and liquids, there are sufficient attractions between the particles to hold them close together, although some solids have low melting points whereas others have extremely high melting points. Such differences in properties are explained by looking at the various kinds of attractive forces between particles.

Ionic compounds typically have high melting points. Large amounts of energy are needed to overcome the strong attractive forces between positive and negative ions and to melt the ionic solid. For example, solid NaCl melts at 801 °C. In solids containing molecules with covalent bonds, there are also attractive forces, but they are weaker than those of ionic compounds. The attractive forces we will discuss are *dipole–dipole attractions*, *hydrogen bonds*, and *dispersion forces*.

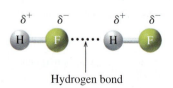

Dipole–dipole
attraction

Dipole–Dipole Attractions and Hydrogen Bonds

Attractive forces called **dipole–dipole attractions** occur between polar molecules in which a partially positive charge of one molecule is attracted to the partially negative charge in another molecule. For example, in the polar molecule HCl, the partially positive H atom of one HCl molecule attracts the partially negative Cl atom in another molecule.

When a hydrogen atom is attached to a highly electronegative atom of fluorine, oxygen, or nitrogen, there are strong dipole–dipole attractions between the polar molecules. This type of attraction, called a **hydrogen bond**, occurs between the partially positive hydrogen atom of one molecule and a lone pair of electrons on a nitrogen, oxygen, or fluorine atom in another molecule. Hydrogen bonds are not true chemical bonds, but represent the strongest type of dipole–dipole attraction. They are a major factor in the formation and structure of biological molecules such as proteins and DNA.

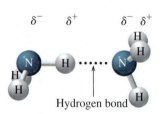

Hydrogen bond

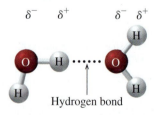

Hydrogen bond

Dispersion Forces

Nonpolar compounds can form solids or liquids, but only at low temperatures. Very weak attractions called **dispersion forces** occur between nonpolar molecules. Usually, the electrons in a nonpolar molecule are distributed symmetrically. However, electrons may accumulate more in one part of the molecule than another, which forms a temporary dipole. Although dispersion forces are especially weak, they make it possible for nonpolar molecules to form liquids and solids.

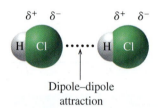

Hydrogen bond

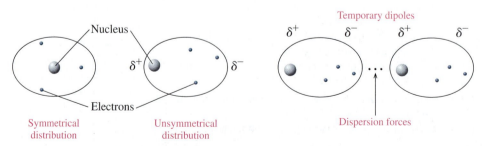

Nonpolar molecules form attractions when they form temporary dipoles.

The various types of attractions within ionic and covalent compounds, and between the particles in solids and liquids are summarized in Table 5.17.

TABLE 5.17 Comparison of Bonding and Attractive Forces

Type of Force	Particle Arrangement	Example	Strength
Between Atoms or Ions Ionic bond		Na^+Cl^-	Strong
Covalent bond (X = nonmetal)	X : X	Cl—Cl	
Between Molecules Hydrogen bond (X = F, O, or N)	$\delta^+ \delta^-$ $\delta^+ \delta^-$ H X ⋯ H X	δ^+ δ^- δ^+ δ^- H—F⋯H—F	
Dipole–dipole attractions (X and Y = nonmetals)	$\delta^+ \delta^-$ $\delta^+ \delta^-$ Y X ⋯ Y X	δ^+ δ^- δ^+ δ^- Br—Cl⋯Br—Cl	
Dispersion forces (temporary shift of electrons in nonpolar bonds)	$\delta^+ \delta^-$ $\delta^+ \delta^-$ (temporary dipoles) X : X ⋯ X : X	δ^+ δ^- δ^+ δ^- F—F⋯F—F	Weak

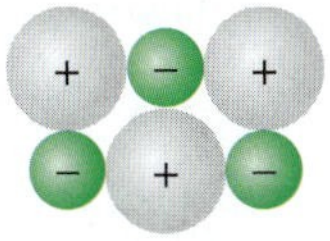

<table>
<tr><td>

CONCEPT CHECK 5.11   Attractive Forces between Particles

Indicate the major type of molecular interaction expected of each of the following:

1. dipole–dipole attractions   **2.** hydrogen bonding   **3.** dispersion forces

a. HF   **b.** Br_2 **c.** PCl_3

ANSWER
a. **2**; HF is a polar molecule that interacts with other HF molecules by hydrogen bonding.
b. **3**; Br_2 is nonpolar; the only molecular interactions would be from dispersion forces.
c. **1**; The polarity of the PCl_3 molecules provides dipole–dipole attractions.

</td></tr>
</table>

Attractive Forces and Melting Point

The melting point of a substance is related to the strength of the attractive forces between its particles. A compound with weak attractive forces such as dispersion forces has a low melting point because only a small amount of energy is needed to separate its molecules and form a liquid. A compound with dipole–dipole attractions requires more energy to break the attractive forces that hold its particles together. A compound that forms hydrogen bonds requires even more energy to overcome the attractive forces that exist between its molecules. The highest melting points are seen with ionic compounds that have very strong attractions between positive and negative ions. Table 5.18 compares the melting points of some substances with different kinds of attractive forces.

TABLE 5.18 Melting Points of Selected Substances

Substance	Melting Point (°C)
Ionic Bonds	
MgF_2	1248
NaCl	801
Hydrogen Bonds	
H_2O	0
NH_3	−78
Dipole–Dipole Attractions	
HI	−51
HBr	−89
HCl	−115
Dispersion Forces	
Br_2	−7
Cl_2	−101
F_2	−220
CH_4	−182

QUESTIONS AND PROBLEMS

5.9 Attractive Forces in Compounds

LEARNING GOAL: *Describe the attractive forces between ions, polar molecules, and nonpolar molecules.*

5.75 Identify the major type of interactive force between particles in each of the following:
  a. BrF   **b.** KCl   **c.** CCl_4 **d.** Cl_2

5.76 Identify the major type of interactive force between particles in each of the following:
  a. HCl   **b.** MgF_2 **c.** PBr_3 **d.** NH_3

5.77 Identify the strongest attractive forces between molecules of each of the following:
  a. CH_3OH **b.** N_2 **c.** HBr
  d. CH_4 **e.** CH_3CH_3

5.78 Identify the strongest attractive forces between molecules of each of the following:
  a. O_2 **b.** CBr_4
  c. CH_3Cl **d.** H_2O
  e. NF_3

5.79 Identify the substance in each of the following pairs that would have the higher boiling point and explain your choice:
  a. HF or HBr   **b.** HF or NaF
  c. $MgBr_2$ or PBr_3 **d.** CH_4 or CH_3OH

5.80 Identify the substance in each of the following pairs that would have the higher boiling point and explain your choice:
  a. NaCl or HCl   **b.** H_2O or H_2Se
  c. NH_3 or PH_3 **d.** F_2 or HF

CONCEPT MAP

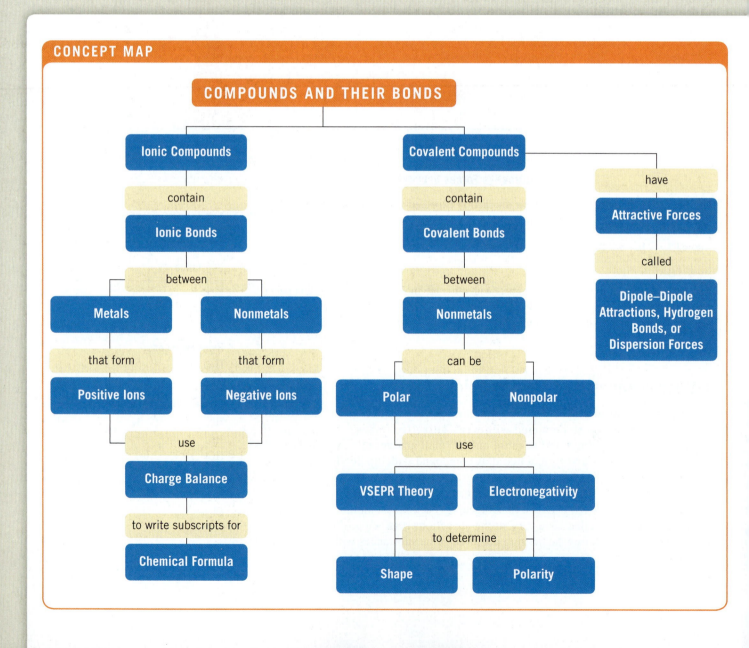

CHAPTER REVIEW

5.1 Ions: Transfer of Electrons

LEARNING GOAL: Using the octet rule, write the symbols for the simple ions of the representative elements.

Transfer of electrons

Ionic bond

- The stability of the noble gases is associated with a complete electron configuration in the outermost energy level.
- With the exception of helium, which needs two electrons for stability, noble gases have eight valence electrons, which is an octet.
- Atoms of elements in Groups 1A–7A (1, 2, 13–17) achieve stability by losing, gaining, or sharing their valence electrons in the formation of compounds.
- Metals of the representative elements lose valence electrons to form positively charged ions (cations): Group 1A (1), 1+; Group 2A (2), 2+; and Group 3A (13), 3+.
- When reacting with metals, nonmetals gain electrons to form octets and form negatively charged ions (anions): Group 5A (15), 3−; Group 6A (16), 2−; and Group 7A (17), 1−.

5.2 Ionic Compounds

LEARNING GOAL: Using charge balance, write the correct formula for an ionic compound.

- The total positive and negative ionic charge is balanced in the formula for an ionic compound.
- Charge balance in a formula is achieved by using subscripts after each symbol so that the overall charge is zero.

Sodium chloride

5.3 Naming and Writing Ionic Formulas

LEARNING GOAL: Given the formula of an ionic compound, write the correct name; given the name of an ionic compound, write the correct formula.

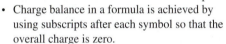
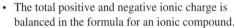

- In naming ionic compounds, the name of the positive ion is given first, followed by the name of the negative ion.
- Ionic compounds containing two elements end with *ide*.
- Except for Ag, Cd, and Zn, transition elements form cations with two or more ionic charges.
- The charge of a cation of a transition element is determined from the total negative charge in the formula and included as a Roman numeral following the name.

5.4 Polyatomic Ions

LEARNING GOAL: Write the name and formula for a compound containing a polyatomic ion.

Fertilizer NH_4NO_3

- A polyatomic ion is a group of nonmetal atoms that carries an electrical charge; for example, the carbonate ion has the formula CO_3^{2-}.
- Most polyatomic ions have names that end with *ate* or *ite*.

NH_4^+ NO_3^-

5.5 Covalent Compounds: Sharing Electrons

LEARNING GOAL: Draw the electron-dot formulas for covalent compounds, including multiple bonds and resonance structures.

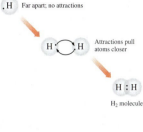

H   Far apart; no attractions

H   H   Attractions pull atoms closer

H : H
H_2 molecule

- In a covalent bond, electrons are shared by atoms of two nonmetals such that each atom has a stable electron configuration.
- In some covalent compounds, double or triple bonds provide an octet (or a pair of electrons for H.)
- Resonance structures are possible when more than one electron-dot formula can be drawn for a molecule with a multiple bond.

5.6 Naming and Writing Covalent Formulas

LEARNING GOAL: Given the formula of a covalent compound, write its correct name; given the name of a covalent compound, write its formula.

1	mono	6	hexa
2	di	7	hepta
3	tri	8	octa
4	tetra	9	nona
5	penta	10	deca

- The first nonmetal in a covalent compound uses its element name; the second nonmetal uses the first syllable of its element name followed by *ide*.
- The name of a covalent compound with two different atoms uses prefixes to indicate the number of atoms of each nonmetal in the formula.

5.7 Electronegativity and Bond Polarity

LEARNING GOAL: Use electronegativity to determine the polarity of a bond.

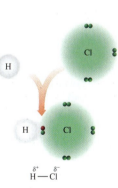

Cl

H

H   Cl

δ^+ δ^-
H — Cl

- Electronegativity is the ability of an atom to attract shared pairs of electrons.
- The electronegativity values of the metals are low, whereas nonmetals have high electronegativities.
- Atoms that form ionic bonds have large differences in electronegativity.
- If atoms share the bonding pair of electrons equally, it is called a nonpolar covalent bond.
- If the bonding electrons in a covalent bond are unequally shared, it is called a polar covalent bond.
- In polar covalent bonds, the atom with the lower electronegativity is partially positive and the atom with the higher electronegativity is partially negative.

5.8 Shapes and Polarity of Molecules

LEARNING GOAL: Predict the three-dimensional structure of a molecule and classify it as polar or nonpolar.

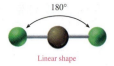

$:\ddot{C}l—Be—\ddot{C}l:$

180°

Linear shape

- The VSEPR theory indicates that the arrangement of electron groups around a central atom is minimized when the electron groups are as far apart as possible.
- The shape of a molecule with two electron groups and two bonded atoms is linear.
- The shape of a molecule with three electron groups and three bonded atoms is trigonal planar.
- The shape of a molecule with three electron groups and two bonded atoms is bent, 120°.
- The shape of a molecule with four electron groups and four bonded atoms is tetrahedral.
- The shape of a molecule with four electron groups and three bonded atoms is trigonal pyramidal.
- The shape of a molecule with four electron groups and two bonded atoms is bent, 109°.
- Molecules are nonpolar if they contain nonpolar covalent bonds or have an arrangement of polar covalent bonds with dipoles that cancel out.
- In polar molecules, the dipoles do not cancel.

5.9 Attractive Forces in Compounds

LEARNING GOAL: Describe the attractive forces between ions, polar molecules, and nonpolar molecules.

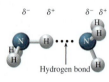

Hydrogen bond

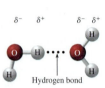

Hydrogen bond

- Ionic bonds consist of very strong attractive forces between oppositely charged ions.
- Attractive forces in polar covalent compounds are weaker than ionic bonds and include dipole–dipole attractions and hydrogen bonds.
- Nonpolar covalent compounds form solids using temporary dipoles called dispersion forces.

KEY TERMS

anion A negatively charged ion such as Cl^-, O^{2-}, or $SO_4{}^{2-}$.

bent The shape of a molecule with four electron groups, but only two bonded atoms; or three electron groups but only two bonded atoms.

cation A positively charged ion such as Na^+, Mg^{2+}, Al^{3+}, or $NH_4{}^+$.

chemical formula The symbols and subscripts that represent the lowest whole-number ratio of the atoms or ions in a compound.

covalent bond A bond created by the sharing of valence electrons by two nonmetal atoms.

covalent compound A combination of nonmetals that share electrons to obtain a stable electron configuration.

dipole The separation of positive and negative charge in a polar bond indicated by an arrow that is drawn from the more positive atom to the more negative atom.

dipole–dipole attractions Attractive forces between oppositely charged ends of polar molecules.

dispersion forces Weak dipole attractions that result from a momentary polarization of nonpolar molecules.

double bond A sharing of two pairs of electrons by two atoms.

electronegativity The relative ability of an element to attract electrons in a bond.

hydrogen bond The attraction between a partially positive H in one molecule and a strongly electronegative atom of F, O, or N in a nearby molecule.

ion An atom or group of atoms having an electrical charge because of a loss or gain of electrons.

ionic bond The attraction between positively charged metal ions and negatively charged nonmetal ions.

ionic charge The difference between the number of protons (positive) and the number of electrons (negative) written in the upper right corner of the symbol for the element or polyatomic ion.

ionic compound A compound of positive and negative ions held together by ionic bonds.

linear The shape of a molecule that has two electron groups and two bonded atoms.

molecule The smallest unit of two or more nonmetal atoms held together by covalent bonds.

nonpolar covalent bond A covalent bond in which the electrons are shared equally between atoms.

nonpolar molecule A molecule that has only nonpolar bonds or in which the bond dipoles cancel.

octet rule The tendency for elements in Groups 1A–7A (1, 2, 13–17) to react with other elements to produce a stable electron configuration, usually eight electrons in the outer shell.

polar covalent bond A covalent bond in which the electrons are shared unequally between two nonmetal atoms.

polar molecule A molecule containing polar bonds with dipoles that do not cancel.

polyatomic ion A group of covalently bonded nonmetal atoms that has an overall electrical charge.

resonance structures Two or more electron-dot formulas that can be drawn for a molecule by placing a multiple bond between different atoms.

tetrahedral The shape of a molecule with four electron groups and four bonded atoms.

trigonal planar The shape of a molecule with three electron groups and three bonded atoms.

trigonal pyramidal The shape of a molecule that has four electron groups, but only three bonded atoms.

triple bond A sharing of three pairs of electrons by two nonmetal atoms.

valence-shell electron-pair repulsion (VSEPR) theory A theory that predicts the shape of a molecule by placing the electron pairs on a central atom as far apart as possible to minimize the mutual repulsion of the electrons.

UNDERSTANDING THE CONCEPTS

The chapter sections to review are shown in parentheses at the end of each question.

5.81 Identify each of the following atoms or ions: (5.1)

18 e^-	8 e^-	28 e^-	23 e^-
15 p^+	8 p^+	30 p^+	26 p^+
16 n	8 n	35 n	28 n
a.	**b.**	**c.**	**d.**

5.82 Identify each of the following atoms or ions: (5.1)

2 e^-	0 e^-	3 e^-	10 e^-
3 p^+	1 p^+	3 p^+	7 p^+
4 n		4 n	8 n
a.	**b.**	**c.**	**d.**

5.83 Identify each of the following atoms or ions: (5.1)
  a. 35 protons, 45 neutrons, and 36 electrons
  b. 47 protons, 60 neutrons, and 46 electrons
  c. 50 protons, 68 neutrons, and 46 electrons

5.84 Identify each of the following atoms or ions: (5.1)
  a. 28 protons, 31 neutrons, and 26 electrons
  b. 82 protons, 126 neutrons, and 82 electrons
  c. 34 protons, 46 neutrons, and 36 electrons

5.85 Consider an ion with the symbol X^{2+} formed from a representative element. (5.2, 5.3)
  a. What is the group number of the element?
  b. What is the electron-dot symbol of the element?
  c. If X is in Period 3, what is the element?
  d. What is the formula of the compound formed from X and the nitride ion?

5.86 Consider an ion with the symbol Y^{3-} formed from a representative element. (5.2, 5.3)
  a. What is the group number of the element?
  b. What is the electron-dot symbol of the element?
  c. If Y is in Period 3, what is the element?

  d. What is the formula of the compound formed from the barium ion and Y?

5.87 Match each of the electron-dot formulas (**a–c**) with the correct diagram (**1–3**) of its shape, and name the shape; indicate if each molecule is polar or nonpolar. Assume X and Y are non-metals and all bonds are polar covalent. (5.7, 5.8)

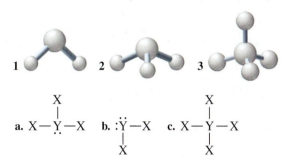

a. X—Y—X **b.** :Ÿ—X **c.** X—Y—X

5.88 Match each of the formulas (**a–c**) with the correct diagram (**1–3**) of its shape, and name the shape; indicate if each molecule is polar or nonpolar. (5.7, 5.8)

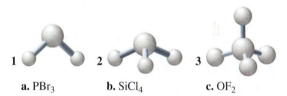

  a. PBr$_3$ **b.** SiCl$_4$ **c.** OF$_2$

5.89 Consider the following bonds: Ca—O, C—O, K—O, O—O, and N—O. (5.7)
  a. Which bonds are polar covalent?
  b. Which bonds are nonpolar covalent?
  c. Which bonds are ionic?
  d. Arrange the covalent bonds in order of decreasing polarity.

5.90 Consider the following bonds: F—Cl, Cl—Cl, Cs—Cl, O—Cl, and Ca—Cl. (5.7)
  a. Which bonds are polar covalent?
  b. Which bonds are nonpolar covalent?
  c. Which bonds are ionic?
  d. Arrange the covalent bonds in order of decreasing polarity.

ADDITIONAL QUESTIONS AND PROBLEMS

For instructor-assigned homework, go to www.masteringchemistry.com.

5.91 Write the electron configuration for each of the following: (5.1)
  a. N^{3-} **b.** Mg^{2+} **c.** P^{3-}
  d. Al^{3+} **e.** Li$^+$

5.92 Write the electron configuration for each of the following: (5.1)
  a. K$^+$ **b.** Na$^+$ **c.** S^{2-}
  d. Cl$^-$ **e.** Ca^{2+}

5.93 One of the ions of tin is tin(IV). (5.1, 5.2, 5.3, 5.4)
  a. What is the symbol for this ion?
  b. How many protons and electrons are in the ion?
  c. What is the formula of tin(IV) oxide?
  d. What is the formula of tin(IV) phosphate?

5.94 One of the ions of gold is gold(III). (5.1, 5.2, 5.3, 5.4)
  a. What is the symbol for this ion?
  b. How many protons and electrons are in the ion?
  c. What is the formula of gold(III) sulfate?
  d. What is the formula of gold(III) nitrate?

5.95 Write the symbol for the ion of each of the following: (5.1)
  a. chloride   **b.** potassium
  c. oxide   **d.** aluminum

5.96 Write the symbol for the ion of each of the following: (5.1)
  a. fluoride   **b.** calcium
  c. sodium   **d.** phosphide

5.97 What is the name of each of the following ions? (5.1)
  a. K$^+$ **b.** S^{2-} **c.** Ca^{2+} **d.** N^{3-}

5.98 What is the name of each of the following ions? (5.1)
  a. Mg^{2+} **b.** Ba^{2+} **c.** I^- **d.** Cl^-

5.99 Write the formula for each of the following ionic compounds: (5.3)
  a. tin(II) sulfide **b.** lead(IV) oxide
  c. silver chloride **d.** calcium nitride
  e. copper(I) phosphide **f.** chromium(II) bromide

5.100 Write the formula for each of the following ionic compounds: (5.3)
  a. nickel(III) oxide **b.** iron(III) sulfide
  c. lead(II) sulfide **d.** chromium(III) iodide
  e. lithium nitride **f.** gold(I) oxide

5.101 Draw the electron-dot formula for each of the following: (5.5)
  a. Cl_2O **b.** CF_4
  c. H_2NOH (N is the central atom)
  d. H_2CCCl_2

5.102 Draw the electron-dot formula for each of the following: (5.5)
  a. H_3COCH_3; the atoms are in the order C O C
  b. CS_2; the atoms are in the order S C S
  c. NH_3
  d. H_2CCHCN; the atoms are in the order C C C N

5.103 Name each of the following covalent compounds: (5.6)
  a. NCl_3 **b.** N_2S_3 **c.** N_2O
  d. F_2 **e.** SO_2 **f.** P_2O_5

5.104 Name each of the following covalent compounds: (5.6)
  a. CBr_4 **b.** SF_6 **c.** Br_2
  d. N_2O_4 **e.** PCl_5 **f.** CS_2

5.105 Write the formula for each of the following: (5.6)
  a. carbon monoxide **b.** diphosphorus pentoxide
  c. dihydrogen sulfide **d.** sulfur dichloride

5.106 Write the formula for each of the following: (5.6)
  a. silicon dioxide
  b. carbon tetrabromide
  c. diphosphorus tetraiodide
  d. dinitrogen oxide

5.107 Classify each of the following compounds as ionic or covalent, and give its name: (5.2, 5.3, 5.4, 5.6)
  a. $FeCl_3$ **b.** Na_2SO_4 **c.** NO_2
  d. N_2 **e.** PF_5 **f.** CF_4

5.108 Classify each of the following compounds as ionic or covalent, and give its name: (5.2, 5.3, 5.4, 5.6)
  a. $Al_2(CO_3)_3$ **b.** ClF_5 **c.** H_2
  d. Mg_3N_2 **e.** ClO_2 **f.** $CrPO_4$

5.109 Write the formulas for the following: (5.2, 5.3, 5.4, 5.6)
  a. tin(II) carbonate **b.** lithium phosphide
  c. silicon tetrachloride **d.** manganese(III) oxide
  e. iodine **f.** calcium bromide

5.110 Write the formulas for the following: (5.2, 5.3, 5.4, 5.6)
  a. sodium carbonate **b.** nitrogen dioxide
  c. aluminum nitrate **d.** copper(I) nitride
  e. potassium phosphate **f.** cobalt(III) sulfate

5.111 Select the more polar bond in each of the following pairs: (5.7)
  a. C—N or C—O
  b. N—F or N—Br
  c. Br—Cl or S—Cl
  d. Br—Cl or Br—I
  e. N—F or N—O

5.112 Select the more polar bond in each of the following pairs: (5.7)
  a. C—C or C—O
  b. P—Cl or P—Br
  c. Si—S or Si—Cl
  d. F—Cl or F—Br
  e. P—O or P—S

5.113 Show the dipole arrow for each of the following bonds: (5.7)
  a. Si—Cl **b.** C—N **c.** F—Cl
  d. C—F **e.** N—O

5.114 Show the dipole arrow for each of the following bonds: (5.7)
  a. C—O **b.** N—F **c.** O—Cl
  d. S—Cl **e.** P—F

5.115 Classify each of the following bonds as nonpolar covalent, polar covalent, or ionic: (5.7)
  a. Si—Cl **b.** C—C **c.** Na—Cl
  d. C—H **e.** F—F

5.116 Classify each of the following bonds as nonpolar covalent, polar covalent, or ionic: (5.7)
  a. C—N **b.** Cl—Cl **c.** K—Br
  d. H—H **e.** N—F

5.117 For each of the following, draw the electron-dot formula and determine the shape of the molecule: (5.8)
  a. NF_3 **b.** $SiBr_4$ **c.** $BeCl_2$ **d.** SO_2

5.118 For each of the following, draw the electron-dot formula and determine the shape of the molecule: (5.8)
  a. SiH_4 **b.** HCCH
  c. $COCl_2$ (C is the central atom) **d.** BCl_3

CHALLENGE QUESTIONS

5.119 Write the formula and name for the compound that forms for each pair of elements (X = metal, Y = nonmetal) indicated by the period and electron-dot symbols in the following table: (5.2, 5.3, 5.5, 5.6)

Period	Electron-Dot Symbols	Formula of Compound	Name of Compound
3	·X· and ·Ÿ·		
3	·Ẋ· and ·Ÿ:		
3	·Ÿ: and ·Ÿ:		
3	·Ÿ· and ·Ÿ:		

5.120 Write the formula and name for the compound that forms for each pair of elements (X = metal, Y = nonmetal) indicated by the period and electron-dot symbols in the following table: (5.2, 5.3, 5.5, 5.6)

Period	Electron-Dot Symbols	Formula of Compound	Name of Compound
2	X· and ·Ÿ·		
2	·Ẏ· and ·Ÿ:		
4	·X· and ·Ÿ:		
4	·Ẋ· and ·Ÿ:		

5.121 Write the symbols of ions, formulas, and names for their ionic compounds using their electron configurations. (5.2, 5.3)

Electron Configurations		Symbols of Ions			
Metal	Nonmetal	Cation	Anion	Formula of Compound	Name of Compound
$1s^22s^1$	$1s^22s^22p^63s^23p^4$				
$1s^22s^22p^63s^23p^64s^2$	$1s^22s^22p^63s^23p^3$				
$1s^22s^22p^63s^1$	$1s^22s^22p^63s^23p^5$				

5.122 Write the symbols of ions, formulas, and names for their ionic compounds using the electron configurations. (5.2, 5.3)

Electron Configurations		Symbols of Ions			
Metal	Nonmetal	Cation	Anion	Formula of Compound	Name of Compound
$1s^22s^22p^63s^2$	$1s^22s^22p^3$				
$1s^22s^22p^63s^23p^64s^1$	$1s^22s^22p^4$				
$1s^22s^22p^63s^23p^1$	$1s^22s^22p^5$				

5.123 Consider the following electron-dot formulas for elements X and Y: (5.2, 5.3, 5.5, 5.6)

$$X\cdot \quad \cdot \ddot{Y}:$$

a. What are the group numbers of X and Y?
b. Will a compound of X and Y be ionic or covalent?
c. What ions would be formed by X and Y?
d. What would be the formula of a compound of X and Y?
e. What would be the formula of a compound of X and chlorine?
f. What would be the formula of a compound of Y and sodium?
g. Is the compound in part **f** ionic or covalent?

5.124 Consider the following electron-dot formulas for elements X and Y: (5.2, 5.3, 5.5, 5.6)

$$\cdot X\cdot \text{ and } \cdot \ddot{Y}\cdot$$

a. What are the group numbers of X and Y?
b. Will a compound of X and Y be ionic or covalent?
c. What ions would be formed by X and Y?
d. What would be the formula of a compound of X and Y?
e. What would be the formula of a compound of X and chlorine?
f. What would be the formula of a compound of Y and sulfur?
g. Is the compound in part **f** ionic or covalent?

5.125 Classify the following compounds as ionic or covalent and name each: (5.2, 5.3, 5.5, 5.6)
a. Li_2O **b.** N_2O
c. CF_4 **d.** Cl_2O

5.126 Classify the following compounds as ionic or covalent and name each: (5.2, 5.3, 5.5, 5.6)
a. MgF_2 **b.** CO **c.** $CaCl_2$ **d.** K_3PO_4

5.127 Name the following compounds: (5.3, 5.4, 5.6)
a. $FeCl_2$ **b.** Cl_2O_7 **c.** N_2
d. $Ca_3(PO_4)_2$ **e.** PCl_3 **f.** $Ca(ClO)_2$

5.128 Name the following compounds: (5.3, 5.4, 5.6)
a. $PbCl_4$ **b.** $MgCO_3$ **c.** NO_2
d. $SnSO_4$ **e.** $Ba(NO_3)_2$ **f.** CuS

5.129 Predict the shape and polarity of each of the following molecules: (5.8)
a. H_2S **b.** NF_3 **c.** NH_3
d. CH_3Cl **e.** SiF_4

5.130 Predict the shape and polarity of each of the following molecules: (5.8)
a. H_2O **b.** CF_4 **c.** GeH_4
d. PCl_3 **e.** SCl_2

5.131 Indicate the major type of attractive forces—(1) ionic bonds, (2) dipole–dipole attractions, (3) hydrogen bonds, (4) dispersion forces—that occurs between particles of the following: (5.9)
a. NH_3 **b.** ClF **c.** Br_2
d. Cs_2O **e.** C_3H_8 **f.** CH_3OH

5.132 Indicate the major type of attractive force—(1) ionic bonds, (2) dipole–dipole attraction, (3) hydrogen bonds, (4) dispersion forces—that occurs between particles of the following: (5.9)
a. $CHCl_3$ **b.** H_2O **c.** LiCl
d. Cl_2 **e.** HBr **f.** IBr

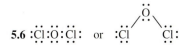

ANSWERS

Answers to Study Checks

5.1 gallium sulfide

5.2 manganese(III) sulfide

5.3 Cr_2O_3

5.4 cobalt(II) phosphate

5.5 $(NH_4)_3PO_4$

5.6 $:\ddot{C}l:\ddot{O}:\ddot{C}l:$ or

$$\ddot{O} \quad \text{with } :\ddot{C}l \quad \ddot{C}l:$$

5.7 $H:C::N:$ or $H—C\equiv N:$
In HCN, there is a triple bond between C and N atoms.

5.8 $:\ddot{O}=S—\ddot{O}: \longleftrightarrow :\ddot{O}—S—\ddot{O}: \longleftrightarrow :\ddot{O}—S=\ddot{O}:$
with $:\ddot{O}:$ below each sulfur

5.9 a. silicon tetrabromide **b.** dibromine oxide

5.10 IF_7

5.11 a. polar covalent **b.** nonpolar covalent **c.** ionic

5.12 tetrahedral

5.13 polar

Answers to Selected Questions and Problems

5.1 a. 1   **b.** 2   **c.** 3   **d.** 1   **e.** 2

5.3 a. Li^+ **b.** F^- **c.** Mg^{2+} **d.** Fe^{3+}

5.5 a. 8 protons, 10 electrons   **b.** 19 protons, 18 electrons
    c. 35 protons, 36 electrons   **d.** 16 protons, 18 electrons

5.7 a. Cl^- **b.** K^+ **c.** O^{2-} **d.** Al^{3+} **e.** Se^{2-}

5.9 a and c

5.11 a. Na_2O **b.** $AlBr_3$ **c.** Ba_3N_2 **d.** MgF_2 **e.** Al_2S_3

5.13 a. K^+, S^{2-} K_2S **b.** Na^+, N^{3-} Na_3N
    c. Al^{3+}, I^- AlI_3 **d.** Ga^{3+}, O^{2-} Ga_2O_3

5.15 a. aluminum oxide   **b.** calcium chloride
    c. sodium oxide   **d.** magnesium phosphide
    e. potassium iodide   **f.** barium fluoride

5.17 Most of the transition elements form more than one positive ion. The specific ion is indicated in the name by writing
a Roman numeral that is the same as the ionic charge. For
example, iron forms Fe^{2+} and Fe^{3+} ions, which are named
iron(II) and iron(III).

5.19 a. iron(II)   **b.** copper(II)   **c.** zinc
    d. lead(IV)   **e.** chromium(III)   **f.** manganese(II)

5.21 a. tin(II) chloride   **b.** iron(II) oxide
    c. copper(I) sulfide   **d.** copper(II) sulfide
    e. chromium(III) bromide   **f.** zinc chloride

5.23 a. Au^{3+} **b.** Fe^{3+} **c.** Pb^{4+} **d.** Sn^{2+}

5.25 a. $MgCl_2$ **b.** Na_2S **c.** Cu_2O
    d. Zn_3P_2 **e.** AuN **f.** $CrCl_2$

5.27 a. HCO_3^- **b.** NH_4^+ **c.** PO_4^{3-}
    d. HSO_4^- **e.** ClO_4^-

5.29 a. sulfate   **b.** hypochlorite
    c. phosphate   **d.** nitrate

5.31

	NO_2^-	CO_3^{2-}	HSO_4^-	PO_4^{3-}
Li^+	$LiNO_2$	Li_2CO_3	$LiHSO_4$	Li_3PO_4
Cu^{2+}	$Cu(NO_2)_2$	$CuCO_3$	$Cu(HSO_4)_2$	$Cu_3(PO_4)_2$
Ba^{2+}	$Ba(NO_2)_2$	$BaCO_3$	$Ba(HSO_4)_2$	$Ba_3(PO_4)_2$

5.33 a. CO_3^{2-}, sodium carbonate
    b. NH_4^+, ammonium chloride
    c. PO_4^{3-}, potassium phosphate
    d. NO_2^-, chromium(II) nitrite
    e. SO_3^{2-}, iron(II) sulfite

5.35 a. $Ba(OH)_2$ **b.** Na_2SO_4 **c.** $Fe(NO_3)_2$
    d. $Zn_3(PO_4)_2$ **e.** $Fe_2(CO_3)_3$

5.37 a, c, d, and f

5.39 a. 2 valence electrons: 1 bonding pair and 0 lone pairs
    b. 8 valence electrons: 1 bonding pair and 3 lone pairs
    c. 14 valence electrons: 1 bonding pair and 6 lone pairs

5.41 a. HF $(8\ e^-)$ H:F̈:   or   H—F̈:

    b. NBr_3 $(26\ e^-)$:B̈r:N̈:B̈r: or   :B̈r—N̈—B̈r:

5.43 a. CO $(10\ e^-)$:C::O: or   :C≡O:

    b. H_2CCH_2 $(12\ e^-)$ H:C::C:H   or   H—C=C—H

    c. H_2CO $(12\ e^-)$ H:C:H   or   H—C—H

5.45 $ClNO_2$ $(24\ e^-)$:C̈l—N—Ö: ⟷ :C̈l—N=Ö:

5.47 a. phosphorus tribromide   **b.** carbon tetrabromide
    c. silicon dioxide   **d.** dinitrogen trioxide
    e. phosphorus pentachloride

5.49 a. CCl_4 **b.** CO   **c.** PCl_3
    d. N_2O_4 **e.** BF_3 **f.** SF_6

5.51 a. aluminum sulfate   **b.** calcium carbonate
    c. dinitrogen oxide   **d.** sodium phosphate
    e. ammonium sulfate   **f.** iron(III) oxide

5.53 a. increases   **b.** decreases   **c.** decreases

5.55 a. 2.2   **b.** 0.0   **c.** 0.5   **d.** 0.4

5.57 a. K, Na, Li   **b.** Na, P, Cl   **c.** Ca, Se, O

5.59 a. polar covalent   **b.** ionic
    c. polar covalent   **d.** nonpolar covalent
    e. polar covalent   **f.** polar covalent

5.61 a. $\overset{\delta^+}{N}—\overset{\delta^-}{F}$ **b.** $\overset{\delta^+}{Si}—\overset{\delta^-}{Br}$ **c.** $\overset{\delta^+}{C}—\overset{\delta^-}{O}$

    d. $\overset{\delta^+}{P}—\overset{\delta^-}{Br}$ **e.** $\overset{\delta^-}{N}—\overset{\delta^+}{P}$

5.63 a. 6   **b.** 5   **c.** 3

5.65 a. 3   **b.** trigonal planar
    c. trigonal planar   **d.** nonpolar

5.67 a and b

5.69 a. bent (109°)   **b.** tetrahedral
    c. trigonal planar   **d.** bent (120°)

5.71 Cl_2 is a nonpolar molecule because there is a nonpolar covalent
bond between Cl atoms, which have identical electronegativity
values. In HCl, the bond is a polar bond because there is a large
electronegativity difference, which makes HCl a polar molecule.

5.73 a. polar   **b.** polar   **c.** polar   **d.** nonpolar

5.75 a. dipole–dipole attractions   **b.** ionic bonds
    c. dispersion forces   **d.** dispersion forces

5.77 a. hydrogen bonding   **b.** dispersion forces
    c. dipole–dipole attractions   **d.** dispersion forces
    e. dispersion forces

5.79 a. HF; hydrogen bonds are stronger than the dipole–dipole
attractions in HBr.
    b. NaF; ionic bonds are stronger than the hydrogen bonds in HF.

c. CH_3OH $(14\ e^-)$ H:C:O:H   or   H—C—O—H
(with H above and below C)

d. N_2H_4 $(14\ e^-)$ H:N:N:H   or   H—N—N—H
(with H above each N)

c. $MgBr_2$; ionic bonds are stronger than the dipole–dipole attractions in PBr_3.

d. CH_3OH; hydrogen bonds are stronger than the dispersion forces in CH_4.

5.81 a. P^{3-} **b.** O atom   **c.** Zn^{2+} **d.** Fe^{3+}

5.83 a. Br^- **b.** Ag^+ **c.** Sn^{4+}

5.85 a. 2A (2)   **b.** $\dot{X}\cdot$ **c.** Mg   **d.** X_3N_2

5.87 a. 2, trigonal pyramidal, polar
b. 1, bent (109°), polar
c. 3, tetrahedral, nonpolar

5.89 a. C—O and N—O   **b.** O—O
c. Ca—O and K—O   **d.** C—O, N—O, O—O

5.91 a. $1s^2 2s^2 2p^6$ **b.** $1s^2 2s^2 2p^6$ **c.** $1s^2 2s^2 2p^6 3s^2 3p^6$
d. $1s^2 2s^2 2p^6$ **e.** $1s^2$

5.93 a. Sn^{4+} **b.** 50 protons, 46 electrons
c. SnO_2 **d.** $Sn_3(PO_4)_4$

5.95 a. Cl^- **b.** K^+ **c.** O^{2-} **d.** Al^{3+}

5.97 a. potassium   **b.** sulfide   **c.** calcium   **d.** nitride

5.99 a. SnS   **b.** PbO_2 **c.** AgCl
d. Ca_3N_2 **e.** Cu_3P **f.** $CrBr_2$

5.101 a. Cl_2O $(20\ e^-)$:Cl:O:Cl: or   Cl—O—Cl structures

b. CF_4 $(32\ e^-)$:F:C:F: or   F—C—F structures

c. H_2NOH $(14\ e^-)$ H:N:O:H   or   H—N—O—H structures

d. H_2CCCl_2 $(24\ e^-)$ H:C::C:Cl: or   H—C=C—Cl structures

5.103 a. nitrogen trichloride   **b.** dinitrogen trisulfide
c. dinitrogen oxide   **d.** fluorine
e. sulfur dioxide   **f.** diphosphorus pentoxide

5.105 a. CO   **b.** P_2O_5 **c.** H_2S **d.** SCl_2

5.107 a. ionic, iron(III) chloride
b. ionic, sodium sulfate
c. covalent, nitrogen dioxide
d. covalent, nitrogen
e. covalent, phosphorus pentafluoride
f. covalent, carbon tetrafluoride

5.109 a. $SnCO_3$ **b.** Li_3P **c.** $SiCl_4$
d. Mn_2O_3 **e.** I_2 **f.** $CaBr_2$

5.111 a. C—O   **b.** N—F   **c.** S—Cl
d. Br—I   **e.** N—F

5.113 a. Si—Cl   **b.** C—N   **c.** F—Cl
d. C—F   **e.** N—O

5.115 a. polar covalent   **b.** nonpolar covalent
c. ionic   **d.** nonpolar covalent
e. nonpolar covalent

5.117 a. NF_3 $(26\ e^-)$:F—N—F: with :F: below   trigonal pyramidal

b. $SiBr_4$ $(32\ e^-)$:Br—Si—Br: with :Br: above and below   tetrahedral

c. $BeCl_2$ $(16\ e^-)$:Cl—Be—Cl: linear

d. SO_2 $(18\ e^-)$ $[:\ddot{O}=\ddot{S}-\ddot{O}:] \longleftrightarrow [:\ddot{O}-\ddot{S}=\ddot{O}:]$ bent (120°)

5.119

Period	Electron-Dot Symbols	Formula of Compound	Name of Compound
3	$\cdot X\cdot$ and $\cdot \ddot{Y}\cdot$	Mg_3P_2	Magnesium phosphide
3	$\cdot X\cdot$ and $\cdot \ddot{Y}:$	Al_2S_3	Aluminum sulfide
3	$\cdot \ddot{Y}:$ and $\cdot \ddot{Y}:$	Cl_2	Chlorine
3	$\cdot \ddot{Y}\cdot$ and $\cdot \ddot{Y}:$	PCl_3	Phosphorus trichloride

5.121 See the table at the bottom of the page.

5.123 a. X is in Group 1A (1); Y is in Group 6A (16)
b. ionic   **c.** X^+, Y^{2-} **d.** X_2Y
e. XCl   **f.** Na_2Y **g.** ionic

5.125 a. ionic, lithium oxide
b. covalent, dinitrogen oxide
c. covalent, carbon tetrafluoride
d. covalent, dichlorine oxide

5.127 a. iron(II) chloride   **b.** dichlorine heptoxide
c. nitrogen   **d.** calcium phosphate
e. phosphorus trichloride   **f.** calcium hypochlorite

5.129 a. bent (109°), nonpolar   **b.** trigonal pyramidal, polar
c. trigonal pyramidal, polar   **d.** tetrahedral, polar
e. tetrahedral, nonpolar

5.131 a. (3) hydrogen bonds   **b.** (2) dipole–dipole attractions
c. (4) dispersion forces   **d.** (1) ionic bonds
e. (4) dispersion forces   **f.** (3) hydrogen bonds

Answer to 5.121

Electron Configurations		Symbols of Ions			
Metal	Nonmetal	Cation	Anion	Formula of Compound	Name of Compound
$1s^2 2s^1$	$1s^2 2s^2 2p^6 3s^2 3p^4$	Li^+	S^{2-}	Li_2S	Lithium sulfide
$1s^2 2s^2 2p^6 3s^2 3p^6 4s^2$	$1s^2 2s^2 2p^6 3s^2 3p^3$	Ca^{2+}	P^{3-}	Ca_3P_2	Calcium phosphide
$1s^2 2s^2 2p^6 3s^1$	$1s^2 2s^2 2p^6 3s^2 3p^5$	Na^+	Cl^-	NaCl	Sodium chloride

6 Chemical Reactions and Quantities

Visit **www.masteringchemistry.com** for self-study materials and instructor-assigned homework.

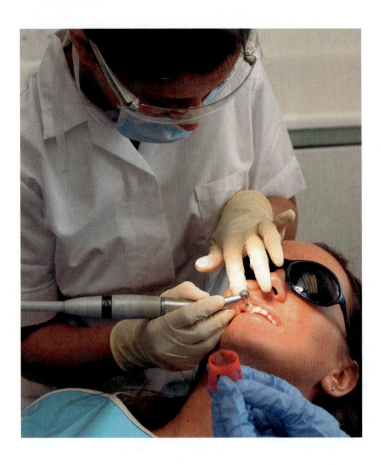

Kimberly's teeth have become badly stained

due to drinking excessive amounts of coffee. She makes an appointment to have her teeth whitened with her dental hygienist. First, Kimberly's teeth are cleaned by the dental hygienist, and the dentist then checks her teeth for any cavities.

After that, the hygienist begins the process of whitening Kimberly's teeth. She explains to Kimberly that she uses a gel of 15–35% hydrogen peroxide which penetrates into the enamel of the tooth, where it causes a chemical reaction that whitens the teeth. The chemical reaction is referred to as a redox reaction where one chemical (hydrogen peroxide) is reduced and the other chemical (the coffee stain) is oxidized. During the oxidation, the coffee stains on the teeth become lighter or colorless, and therefore, the teeth are whiter.

Career: Dental Hygienist

A visit to the dentist frequently begins with a dental hygienist who cleans and polishes the patient's teeth by removing tartar, stains and plaque. This requires the hygienist to use a variety of tools, including hand and rotary instruments, as well as ultrasonic equipment. The hygienist also discusses the proper technique for brushing and flossing with each patient. The dental hygienist may also take X-rays of a patient's teeth in order to detect any abnormalities. A dental hygienist must be knowledgeable about the proper safety procedures for taking X-rays and how to protect themselves from disease transmission by wearing the proper safety attire like safety glasses, surgical masks and gloves.

The fuel in our cars burns with oxygen to provide energy to make the car move or run the air conditioner. When we cook our food or bleach our hair, chemical reactions take place. In our bodies, chemical reactions convert food substances into molecules to build muscles and move them. In the leaves of trees and plants, carbon dioxide and water are converted into carbohydrates.

Some chemical reactions are simple, whereas others are quite complex. However, they can all be written with equations used to describe chemical reactions. In every chemical reaction, the atoms in the reacting substances, called *reactants*, are rearranged to give new substances called *products*.

In this chapter, we will see how equations are written and how we can determine the amount of reactant or product involved. When we cook, we follow a recipe that gives the correct amounts of ingredients (reactants) to mix together and how much bread or cookies (products) we will obtain. At the automotive repair shop, a mechanic does essentially the same thing when adjusting the fuel system of an engine to allow for the correct amounts of fuel and oxygen. In the hospital, a respiratory therapist evaluates the levels of CO_2 and O_2 in the blood. A certain amount of O_2 must reach the tissues for efficient metabolic reactions. If the oxygenation of the blood is low, then the therapist will oxygenate the patient and recheck the blood oxygen levels.

6.1 Equations for Chemical Reactions

As we discussed in Section 2.4, a *chemical change* occurs when a substance is converted into one or more new substances. There may be a change in color or the formation of bubbles or a solid. For example, when silver tarnishes, the shiny silver metal (Ag) reacts with sulfur (S) to form the dull, black substance we call tarnish (Ag_2S) (see Figure 6.1).

SELF-STUDY ACTIVITY
Chemical Reactions and Equations

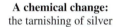

A chemical change:
the tarnishing of silver

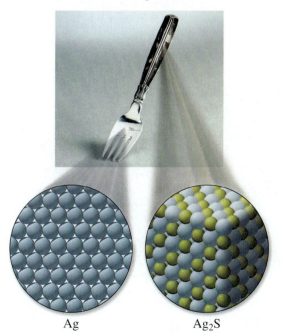

Ag Ag_2S

FIGURE 6.1 A chemical change produces new substances.

Q Why is the formation of tarnish a chemical change?

FIGURE 6.2 A chemical reaction forms new products with different properties. An antacid ($NaHCO_3$) tablet in water forms bubbles of carbon dioxide (CO_2).

Q What is the evidence for chemical change in this chemical reaction?

TABLE 6.1 Types of Visible Evidence of a Chemical Reaction

1. Change in the color
2. Formation of a gas (bubbles)
3. Formation of a solid (precipitate)
4. Heat (or a flame) produced or heat absorbed

SELF-STUDY ACTIVITY
What is Chemistry?

TUTORIAL
Chemical Reactions and Equations

A Chemical Equation Describes a Chemical Reaction

A **chemical reaction** always involves chemical change because atoms of the reacting substances form new combinations with new properties. For example, a chemical reaction takes place when an antacid tablet is dropped into a glass of water. The tablet fizzes and bubbles as $NaHCO_3$ and citric acid ($C_6H_8O_7$) in the tablet react to form carbon dioxide (CO_2) gas (see Figure 6.2). During a chemical change, new properties become visible, which are an indication that a chemical reaction has taken place (see Table 6.1).

CONCEPT CHECK 6.1 **Evidence of a Chemical Reaction**

Indicate why each of the following is a chemical reaction:

a. burning propane fuel in a barbecue
b. using peroxide to change the color of hair

ANSWER

a. The production of heat during the burning of propane fuel is evidence of a chemical reaction.
b. The change in hair color is evidence of a chemical reaction.

When you install a new computer program, cook using a recipe, or prepare a medication, you follow a set of directions. These directions tell you what materials to use and the products you will obtain. In chemistry, a *chemical equation* tells us the materials we need and the products that will form in a chemical reaction.

Writing a Chemical Equation

Suppose you work in a bicycle shop, assembling wheels and frames into bicycles. You could represent this process by an equation:

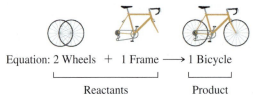

Equation: 2 Wheels + 1 Frame ⟶ 1 Bicycle

Reactants   Product

When you burn charcoal in a grill, the carbon in the charcoal combines with oxygen to form carbon dioxide. We can represent this reaction by a chemical equation that is much like the one for the bicycle:

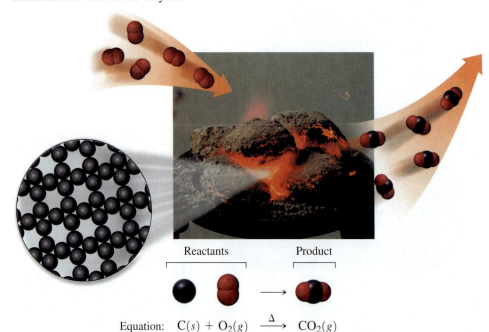

Reactants   Product

Equation: $C(s) + O_2(g) \xrightarrow{\Delta} CO_2(g)$

In a **chemical equation**, the formulas of the **reactants** are written on the left of the arrow and the formulas of the **products** on the right. When there are two or more formulas on the same side, they are separated by plus ($+$) signs. The delta sign (Δ) over the reaction arrow indicates that heat was used to start the reaction.

Generally, each formula in an equation is followed by an abbreviation, in parentheses, that gives the physical state of the substance: solid (s), liquid (l), or gas or vapor (g). If a substance is dissolved in water, it is an aqueous (aq) solution. Table 6.2 summarizes some of the symbols used in equations.

Identifying a Balanced Chemical Equation

When a chemical reaction takes place, the bonds between the atoms of the reactants are broken, and new bonds are formed to give the products. All atoms are conserved, which means that atoms cannot be gained, lost, or changed into other types of atoms during the reaction. Every chemical reaction must be written as a **balanced equation**, which shows the same number of atoms for each element in the reactants as well as in the products.

Now consider the reaction in which hydrogen reacts with oxygen to form water. The formulas of the reactants and products are written as follows:

$$H_2(g) + O_2(g) \longrightarrow H_2O(g)$$

When we add up the atoms of each element on each side, we find that the equation is *not balanced*. There are two oxygen atoms to the left side of the arrow, but only one to the right. To balance this equation, we place whole numbers called **coefficients** in front of the formulas. If we write a coefficient of 2 in front of the H_2O formula, it represents two molecules of water. Because the coefficient multiplies all the atoms in H_2O, there are now four hydrogen atoms and two oxygen atoms in the products. To obtain four hydrogen atoms in the reactants, we must write a coefficient of 2 in front of H_2. However, we *do not change any subscripts*, which would alter the chemical identity of a reactant or product. Now the number of hydrogen atoms and the number of oxygen atoms are the same in the reactants as in the products. The equation is *balanced*.

TABLE 6.2 **Some Symbols Used in Writing Equations**	
Symbol	**Meaning**
$+$	Separates two or more formulas
$\longrightarrow$	Reacts to form products
$\xrightarrow{\Delta}$	Reactants are heated
(s)	Solid
(l)	Liquid
(g)	Gas or vapor
(aq)	Aqueous

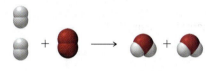

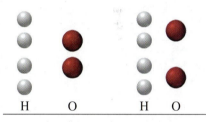

$$2H_2(g) + O_2(g) \longrightarrow 2H_2O(g)$$

Reactant atoms $=$ Product atoms

CONCEPT CHECK 6.2 **Balancing Chemical Equations**

Indicate the number of each atom in the reactants and in the products for the following equation:

$$Fe_2S_3(s) + 6HCl(aq) \longrightarrow 2FeCl_3(aq) + 3H_2S(g)$$

	Reactants	Products
Atoms of Fe		
Atoms of S		
Atoms of H		
Atoms of Cl		

ANSWER

The total number of atoms in each formula is obtained by multiplying through by its coefficient.

	Reactants	Products
Atoms of Fe	2	2
Atoms of S	3	3
Atoms of H	6	6
Atoms of Cl	6	6

TUTORIAL
Balancing Chemical Equations

TUTORIAL
Signs of a Chemical Reaction

Balancing a Chemical Equation

The chemical reaction that occurs in the flame of a gas burner you use in the laboratory or a gas cooktop is the reaction of methane gas, CH_4, and oxygen to produce carbon dioxide and water. We show the process of balancing a chemical equation in Sample Problem 6.1.

SAMPLE PROBLEM 6.1   **Balancing a Chemical Equation**

The chemical reaction of methane, CH_4, and oxygen gas, O_2, produces carbon dioxide, CO_2, and water, H_2O. Write a balanced chemical equation for this reaction.

SOLUTION

Guide to Balancing a Chemical Equation

1 Write an equation using the correct formulas of the reactants and products.

2 Count the atoms of each element in the reactants and products.

3 Use coefficients to balance each element.

4 Check the final equation to confirm it is balanced.

Step 1   **Write an equation using the correct formulas of the reactants and products.**

$$CH_4(g) + O_2(g) \xrightarrow{\Delta} CO_2(g) + H_2O(g)$$

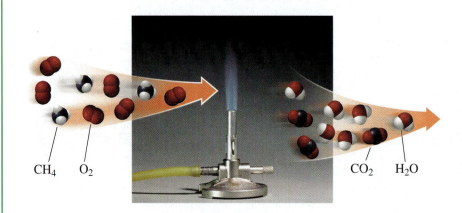

CH_4 O_2 CO_2 H_2O

Step 2   **Count the atoms of each element in the reactants and products.** In the initial unbalanced equation, a coefficient of 1 is understood and not usually written. When we compare the atoms on the reactant side with the atoms on the product side, we see that there are more H atoms in the reactants and more O atoms in the products.

$$CH_4(g) + O_2(g) \xrightarrow{\Delta} CO_2(g) + H_2O(g)$$

Reactants	Products	
1 C atom	1 C atom	Balanced
4 H atoms	2 H atoms	Not balanced
2 O atoms	3 O atoms	Not balanced

Step 3   **Use coefficients to balance each element.** We will start by balancing the H atoms in CH_4 because it has the most atoms. By placing a coefficient of 2 in front of the formula for water, a total of 4 H atoms in the products is obtained.

$$CH_4(g) + O_2(g) \xrightarrow{\Delta} CO_2(g) + 2H_2O(g)$$

Reactants	Products	
1 C atom	1 C atom	Balanced
4 H atoms	4 H atoms	Balanced
2 O atoms	4 O atoms	Not balanced

We can balance the O atoms on the reactant side by placing a coefficient of 2 in front of the formula O_2. There are now 4 O atoms and 4 H atoms in both the reactants and products.

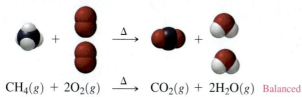

$$CH_4(g) + 2O_2(g) \xrightarrow{\Delta} CO_2(g) + 2H_2O(g) \quad \text{Balanced}$$

Step 4   **Check the final equation to confirm it is balanced.** In the final equation, the numbers of C, H, and O atoms are the same in both the reactants and products. The equation is balanced.

$$CH_4(g) + 2O_2(g) \xrightarrow{\Delta} CO_2(g) + 2H_2O(g)$$

Reactants	Products	
1 C atom	1 C atom	Balanced
4 H atoms	4 H atoms	Balanced
4 O atoms	4 O atoms	Balanced

In a balanced equation, the coefficients must be the lowest whole numbers possible. Suppose you had obtained the following:

$$2CH_4(g) + 4O_2(g) \xrightarrow{\Delta} 2CO_2(g) + 4H_2O(g) \quad \text{Incorrect}$$

Although there are equal numbers of atoms in the reactants and in the products, this is not balanced correctly. The correctly balanced equation is obtained by dividing all the coefficients by 2.

STUDY CHECK 6.1

Balance the following equation:

$$Al(s) + Cl_2(g) \longrightarrow AlCl_3(s)$$

SAMPLE PROBLEM 6.2   Balancing Chemical Equations with Polyatomic Ions

Balance the following equation:

$$Na_3PO_4(aq) + MgCl_2(aq) \longrightarrow Mg_3(PO_4)_2(s) + NaCl(aq)$$

SOLUTION

Step 1   **Write an equation using the correct formulas of the reactants and products.**

$$Na_3PO_4(aq) + MgCl_2(aq) \longrightarrow Mg_3(PO_4)_2(s) + NaCl(aq)$$

Step 2   **Count the atoms of each element in the reactants and products.** When we compare the number of ions on the reactant and product sides, we find they are not balanced. In this equation, we can balance the phosphate ion as a group because it appears on both sides of the equation.

$$Na_3PO_4(aq) + MgCl_2(aq) \longrightarrow Mg_3(PO_4)_2(s) + NaCl(aq)$$

Reactants	Products	
3 Na^+	1 Na^+	Not balanced
1 PO_4^{3-}	2 PO_4^{3-}	Not balanced
1 Mg^{2+}	3 Mg^{2+}	Not balanced
2 Cl^-	1 Cl^-	Not balanced

Step 3 **Use coefficients to balance each element.** We begin with the formula that has the highest subscript values, which in this equation is $Mg_3(PO_4)_2$. The subscript 3 in $Mg_3(PO_4)_2$ is used as a coefficient for $MgCl_2$ to balance magnesium. The subscript 2 in $Mg_3(PO_4)_2$ is used as a coefficient for Na_3PO_4 to balance the phosphate ion.

$$2Na_3PO_4(aq) + 3MgCl_2(aq) \longrightarrow Mg_3(PO_4)_2(s) + NaCl(aq)$$

Reactants	Products	
$6\ Na^+$	$1\ Na^+$	Not balanced
$2\ PO_4^{3-}$	$2\ PO_4^{3-}$	Balanced
$3\ Mg^{2+}$	$3\ Mg^{2+}$	Balanced
$6\ Cl^-$	$1\ Cl^-$	Not balanced

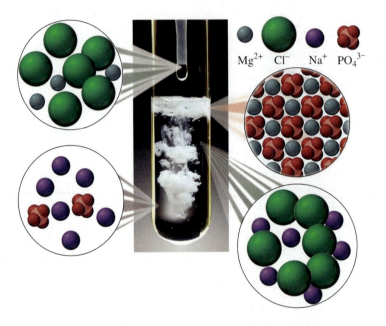

Mg^{2+} Cl^- Na^+ PO_4^{3-}

Looking again at each of the ions in the reactants and products, we see that the sodium and chloride ions are not yet equal. A coefficient of 6 for the NaCl balances the equation.

$$2Na_3PO_4(aq) + 3MgCl_2(aq) \longrightarrow Mg_3(PO_4)_2(s) + 6NaCl(aq)$$

Step 4 **Check the final equation to confirm it is balanced.** A check of the total number of atoms indicates that the equation is balanced. A coefficient of 1 is understood and not usually written.

$$2Na_3PO_4(aq) + 3MgCl_2(aq) \longrightarrow Mg_3(PO_4)_2(s) + 6NaCl(aq) \quad \text{Balanced}$$

Reactants	Products	
$6\ Na^+$	$6\ Na^+$	Balanced
$2\ PO_4^{3-}$	$2\ PO_4^{3-}$	Balanced
$3\ Mg^{2+}$	$3\ Mg^{2+}$	Balanced
$6\ Cl^-$	$6\ Cl^-$	Balanced

STUDY CHECK 6.2

Balance the following equation:

$$Sb_2S_3(s) + HCl(aq) \longrightarrow SbCl_3(s) + H_2S(g)$$

QUESTIONS AND PROBLEMS

6.1 Equations for Chemical Reactions

LEARNING GOAL: *Write a balanced chemical equation from the formulas of the reactants and products for a chemical reaction.*

6.1 Determine whether each of the following equations is balanced or not balanced:
a. $S(s) + O_2(g) \longrightarrow SO_3(g)$
b. $2Al(s) + 3Cl_2(g) \longrightarrow 2AlCl_3(s)$
c. $2NaOH(s) + H_2SO_4(aq) \longrightarrow Na_2SO_4(aq) + H_2O(l)$
d. $C_3H_8(g) + 5O_2(g) \xrightarrow{\Delta} 3CO_2(g) + 4H_2O(g)$

6.2 Determine whether each of the following equations is balanced or not balanced:
a. $PCl_3(s) + Cl_2(g) \longrightarrow PCl_5(s)$
b. $CO(g) + 2H_2(g) \longrightarrow CH_3OH(g)$
c. $2KClO_3(s) \xrightarrow{\Delta} 2KCl(s) + O_2(g)$
d. $Mg(s) + N_2(g) \longrightarrow Mg_3N_2(s)$

6.3 Balance each of the following equations:
a. $N_2(g) + O_2(g) \longrightarrow NO(g)$
b. $HgO(s) \longrightarrow Hg(l) + O_2(g)$
c. $Fe(s) + O_2(g) \longrightarrow Fe_2O_3(s)$
d. $Na(s) + Cl_2(g) \longrightarrow NaCl(s)$
e. $Cu_2O(s) + O_2(g) \longrightarrow CuO(s)$

6.4 Balance each of the following equations:
a. $Ca(s) + Br_2(l) \longrightarrow CaBr_2(s)$
b. $P_4(s) + O_2(g) \longrightarrow P_4O_{10}(s)$
c. $C_4H_8(g) + O_2(g) \xrightarrow{\Delta} CO_2(g) + H_2O(g)$
d. $Sb_2S_3(s) + HCl(aq) \longrightarrow SbCl_3(s) + H_2S(g)$
e. $Fe_2O_3(s) + C(s) \longrightarrow Fe(s) + CO(g)$

6.5 Balance each of the following equations:
a. $Mg(s) + AgNO_3(aq) \longrightarrow Mg(NO_3)_2(aq) + Ag(s)$
b. $CuCO_3(s) \longrightarrow CuO(s) + CO_2(g)$
c. $C_5H_{12}(g) + O_2(g) \xrightarrow{\Delta} CO_2(g) + H_2O(g)$
d. $Pb(NO_3)_2(aq) + NaCl(aq) \longrightarrow$
$$PbCl_2(s) + NaNO_3(aq)$$
e. $Al(s) + HCl(aq) \longrightarrow AlCl_3(aq) + H_2(g)$

6.6 Balance each of the following equations:
a. $Zn(s) + H_2SO_4(aq) \longrightarrow ZnSO_4(aq) + H_2(g)$
b. $N_2(g) + I_2(g) \longrightarrow NI_3(g)$
c. $K_2SO_4(aq) + BaCl_2(aq) \longrightarrow BaSO_4(s) + KCl(aq)$
d. $CaCO_3(s) \xrightarrow{\Delta} CaO(s) + CO_2(g)$
e. $Al_2(SO_4)_3(aq) + KOH(aq) \longrightarrow$
$$Al(OH)_3(s) + K_2SO_4(aq)$$

6.2 Types of Reactions

A great number of reactions occur in nature, in biological systems, and in the laboratory. However, some general patterns among all reactions help us to classify them. Most fit into five general reaction types.

Combination Reactions

In a **combination reaction**, two or more elements or compounds bond to form one product. For example, sulfur and oxygen combine to form the product sulfur dioxide.

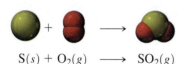

$$S(s) + O_2(g) \longrightarrow SO_2(g)$$

In Figure 6.3, the elements magnesium and oxygen combine to form a single product, magnesium oxide.

$$2Mg(s) + O_2(g) \xrightarrow{\Delta} 2MgO(s)$$

In other examples of combination reactions, elements or compounds combine to form a single product.

$$N_2(g) + 3H_2(g) \longrightarrow 2NH_3(g)$$
Ammonia

$$Cu(s) + S(s) \longrightarrow CuS(s)$$
$$MgO(s) + CO_2(g) \longrightarrow MgCO_3(s)$$

MC

TUTORIAL
Classifying Chemical Reactions
by What Atoms Do

Combination

Two or more   combine   a single
reactants   to yield   product

 +

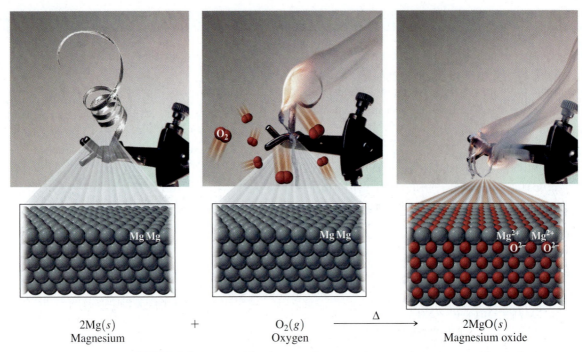

$$2Mg(s) \quad + \quad O_2(g) \quad \xrightarrow{\Delta} \quad 2MgO(s)$$

Magnesium   Oxygen   Magnesium oxide

FIGURE 6.3 In a combination reaction, two or more substances combine to form one substance as product.

Q What happens to the atoms of the reactants in a combination reaction?

Decomposition

A   splits   two or more
reactant   into   products

A B $\longrightarrow$ A   +   B

FIGURE 6.4 In a decomposition reaction, one reactant breaks down into two or more products.

Q How do the differences in the reactant and products classify this as a decomposition reaction?

Decomposition Reactions

In a **decomposition reaction**, a reactant splits into two or more simpler products. For example, when mercury(II) oxide is heated, the compound breaks apart into mercury atoms and oxygen (see Figure 6.4).

$$2HgO(s) \xrightarrow{\Delta} 2Hg(l) + O_2(g)$$

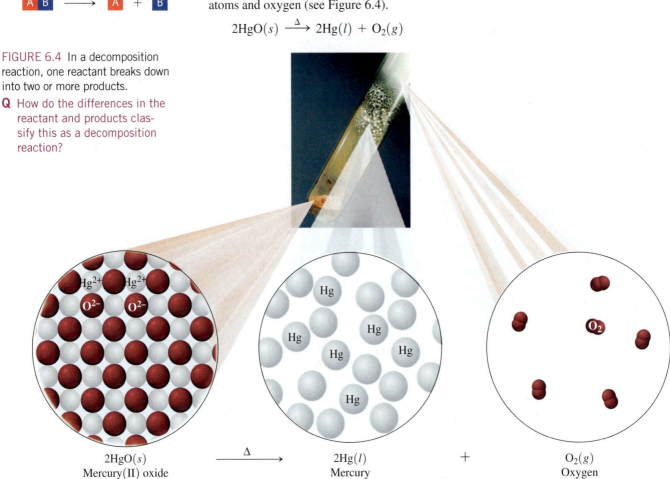

$$2HgO(s) \quad \xrightarrow{\Delta} \quad 2Hg(l) \quad + \quad O_2(g)$$

Mercury(II) oxide   Mercury   Oxygen

In another example of a decomposition reaction, calcium carbonate breaks apart into simpler compounds of calcium oxide and carbon dioxide.

$$CaCO_3(s) \xrightarrow{\Delta} CaO(s) + CO_2(g)$$

Single Replacement Reactions

In a replacement reaction, elements in a compound are replaced by other elements. In a **single replacement reaction**, a reacting element switches place with an element in the other reacting compound. In the single replacement reaction shown in Figure 6.5, zinc replaces hydrogen in hydrochloric acid, $HCl(aq)$.

Single replacement

One element   replaces   another element

A + B C ⟶ A C + B

$$Zn(s) + 2HCl(aq) \longrightarrow ZnCl_2(aq) + H_2(g)$$

In another single replacement reaction, chlorine replaces bromine in the compound potassium bromide.

$$Cl_2(g) + 2KBr(aq) \longrightarrow 2KCl(s) + Br_2(l)$$

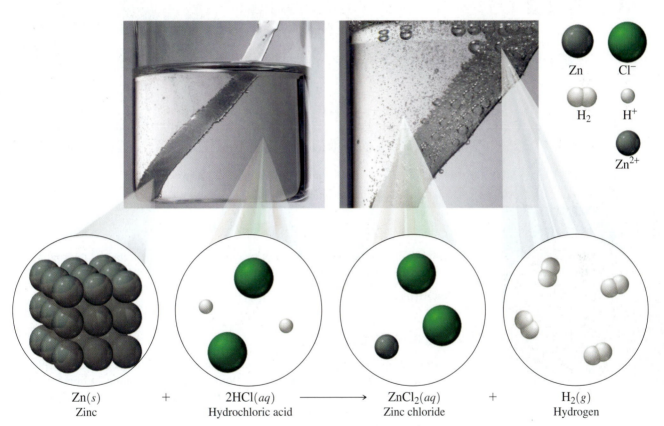

| $Zn(s)$ | + | $2HCl(aq)$ | ⟶ | $ZnCl_2(aq)$ | + | $H_2(g)$ |
| Zinc | | Hydrochloric acid | | Zinc chloride | | Hydrogen |

FIGURE 6.5 In a single replacement reaction, an atom or ion replaces an atom or ion in a compound.

Q What changes in the formulas of the reactants identify this equation as a single replacement?

Double Replacement Reactions

In a **double replacement reaction**, the positive ions in the reacting compounds switch places.

In the reaction shown in Figure 6.6, barium ions change places with sodium ions in the reactants to form sodium chloride and a white solid precipitate of barium sulfate. The formulas of the products depend on the charges of the ions.

$$BaCl_2(aq) + Na_2SO_4(aq) \longrightarrow BaSO_4(s) + 2NaCl(aq)$$

Double replacement

Two elements   replace   each other

A B + C D ⟶ A D + C B

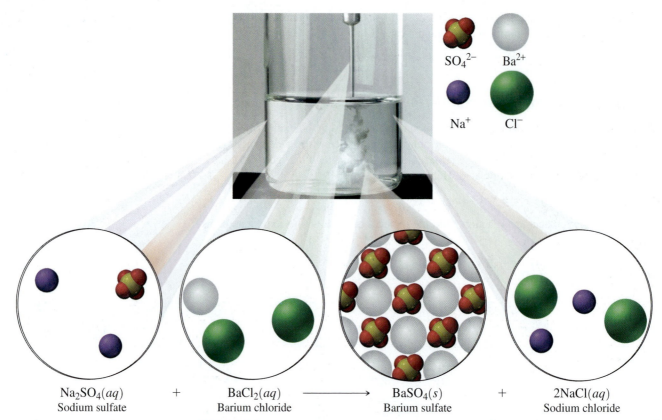

$$\underset{\text{Sodium sulfate}}{Na_2SO_4(aq)} \quad + \quad \underset{\text{Barium chloride}}{BaCl_2(aq)} \quad \longrightarrow \quad \underset{\text{Barium sulfate}}{BaSO_4(s)} \quad + \quad \underset{\text{Sodium chloride}}{2NaCl(aq)}$$

FIGURE 6.6 In a double replacement reaction, the positive ions in the reactants replace each other.

Q How do the changes in the formulas of the reactants identify this equation as a double replacement reaction?

When sodium hydroxide and hydrochloric acid (HCl) react, sodium and hydrogen ions switch places, forming sodium chloride and water.

$$NaOH(aq) + HCl(aq) \longrightarrow NaCl(aq) + HOH(l)$$

Combustion Reactions

The burning of a candle and the burning of fuel in the engine of a car are examples of combustion reactions. In a **combustion reaction**, a carbon-containing compound that is the fuel burns in oxygen from the air to produce carbon dioxide (CO_2), water (H_2O), and energy in the form of heat or a flame. For example, methane gas (CH_4) undergoes combustion when used to cook our food on a gas cooktop and to heat our homes. In the equation for the combustion of methane, each element in the fuel (CH_4) forms a compound with oxygen.

$$\underset{\text{Methane}}{CH_4(g)} + 2O_2(g) \xrightarrow{\Delta} CO_2(g) + 2H_2O(g) + \text{energy}$$

The balanced equation for the combustion of propane (C_3H_8) is:

$$C_3H_8(g) + 5O_2(g) \xrightarrow{\Delta} 3CO_2(g) + 4H_2O(g) + \text{energy}$$

Propane is the fuel used in portable heaters and gas barbecues. Gasoline, a mixture of liquid hydrocarbons, is the fuel that powers our cars, lawn mowers, and snow blowers.

Table 6.3 summarizes the reaction types and gives examples.

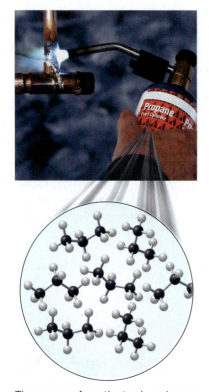

The propane from the torch undergoes combustion, which provides energy to solder metals.

CONCEPT CHECK 6.3 **Identifying the Type of Reaction**

Classify the following reactions as combination, decomposition, single replacement, double replacement, or combustion:

a. $2Fe_2O_3(s) + 3C(s) \longrightarrow 3CO_2(g) + 4Fe(s)$

b. $2KClO_3(s) \xrightarrow{\Delta} 2KCl(s) + 3O_2(g)$

c. $C_2H_4(g) + 3O_2(g) \xrightarrow{\Delta} 2CO_2(g) + 2H_2O(g) + energy$

ANSWER

a. In this single replacement reaction, a C atom replaces Fe in Fe_2O_3 to form the compound CO_2 and Fe atoms.

b. When one reactant breaks down to produce two products, the reaction is decomposition.

c. The reaction of a carbon compound with oxygen to produce carbon dioxide, water, and energy makes this a combustion reaction.

In a combustion reaction, a candle burns using the oxygen in the air.

TABLE 6.3 Summary of Reaction Types

Reaction Type	Example
Combination	
$A + B \longrightarrow AB$	$Ca(s) + Cl_2(g) \longrightarrow CaCl_2(s)$
Decomposition	
$AB \longrightarrow A + B$	$Fe_2S_3(s) \longrightarrow 2Fe(s) + 3S(s)$
Single Replacement	
$A + BC \longrightarrow AC + B$	$Cu(s) + 2AgNO_3(aq) \longrightarrow Cu(NO_3)_2(aq) + 2Ag(s)$
Double Replacement	
$AB + CD \longrightarrow AD + CB$	$BaCl_2(aq) + K_2SO_4(aq) \longrightarrow BaSO_4(s) + 2KCl(aq)$
Combustion	
$C_XH_Y + ZO_2(g) \xrightarrow{\Delta} XCO_2(g) + Y/2\ H_2O(g) + energy$	$CH_4(g) + 2O_2(g) \xrightarrow{\Delta} CO_2(g) + 2H_2O(g) + energy$

Chemistry Link to Health

SMOG AND HEALTH CONCERNS

There are two types of smog. One, photochemical smog, requires sunlight to initiate reactions that produce pollutants such as nitrogen oxides and ozone. The other type of smog, industrial or London smog, occurs in areas where coal that contains sulfur is burned and the unwanted product, sulfur dioxide, is emitted.

Photochemical smog is most prevalent in cities where people are dependent on cars for transportation. On a typical day in Los Angeles, for example, nitrogen oxide (NO) emissions from car exhausts increase as traffic increases on the roads. When N_2 and O_2 react at high temperatures in car and truck engines, the product is nitrogen oxide.

$$N_2(g) + O_2(g) \xrightarrow{\Delta} 2NO(g)$$

Then NO reacts with oxygen in the air to produce NO_2, a reddish-brown gas that is irritating to the eyes and damaging to the respiratory tract.

$$2NO(g) + O_2(g) \xrightarrow{\Delta} 2NO_2(g)$$

The reddish-brown color of smog is due to nitrogen dioxide.

When NO_2 molecules are exposed to sunlight, they are converted into NO and an oxygen atom (O).

$$NO_2(g) \xrightarrow{Sunlight} NO(g) + O(g)$$

Oxygen atom

Oxygen atoms are so reactive that they combine with oxygen molecules in the atmosphere, forming ozone.

$$O(g) + O_2(g) \longrightarrow O_3(g)$$
Ozone

In the upper atmosphere (the stratosphere), ozone is beneficial because it protects us from harmful ultraviolet radiation that comes from the Sun. However, in the lower atmosphere, ozone irritates the eyes and respiratory tract, where it causes coughing, decreased lung function, and fatigue. It also causes deterioration of fabrics, cracks rubber, and damages trees and crops.

Industrial smog is prevalent in areas where sulfur is converted to sulfur dioxide during the burning of coal or other sulfur-containing fuels.

$$S(s) + O_2(g) \longrightarrow SO_2(g)$$

The SO_2 is damaging to plants and is corrosive to metals such as steel. SO_2 is also damaging to humans and can cause lung impairment and respiratory difficulties. In the air, the SO_2 reacts with more oxygen to form SO_3, which can combine with water to form sulfuric acid. When rain falls, it absorbs the sulfuric acid, which makes acid rain.

$$2SO_2(g) + O_2(g) \longrightarrow 2SO_3(g)$$
$$SO_3(g) + H_2O(l) \longrightarrow H_2SO_4(aq)$$
Sulfuric acid

The presence of sulfuric acid in rivers and lakes causes an increase in the acidity of the water, reducing the ability of animals and plants to survive.

QUESTIONS AND PROBLEMS

6.2 Types of Reactions

LEARNING GOAL: *Identify a chemical reaction as a combination, decomposition, single replacement, double replacement, or combustion reaction.*

6.7 Classify each of the following as a combination, decomposition, single replacement, double replacement, or combustion reaction:
   a. $2Al_2O_3(s) \xrightarrow{\Delta} 4Al(s) + 3O_2(g)$
   b. $Br_2(g) + BaI_2(s) \longrightarrow BaBr_2(s) + I_2(g)$
   c. $2C_2H_2(g) + 5O_2(g) \xrightarrow{\Delta} 4CO_2(g) + 2H_2O(g)$
   d. $BaCl_2(aq) + K_2CO_3(aq) \longrightarrow BaCO_3(s) + 2KCl(aq)$

6.8 Classify each of the following as a combination, decomposition, single replacement, double replacement, or combustion reaction:
   a. $H_2(g) + Br_2(g) \longrightarrow 2HBr(g)$
   b. $AgNO_3(aq) + NaCl(aq) \longrightarrow AgCl(s) + NaNO_3(aq)$
   c. $2H_2O_2(aq) \longrightarrow 2H_2O(g) + O_2(g)$
   d. $Zn(s) + CuCl_2(aq) \longrightarrow Cu(s) + ZnCl_2(aq)$

6.9 Classify each of the following as a combination, decomposition, single replacement, double replacement, or combustion reaction:
   a. $Mg(s) + 2AgNO_3(aq) \longrightarrow Mg(NO_3)_2(aq) + 2Ag(s)$
   b. $4Fe(s) + 3O_2(g) \longrightarrow 2Fe_2O_3(s)$
   c. $CuCO_3(s) \xrightarrow{\Delta} CuO(s) + CO_2(g)$
   d. $2C_6H_6(l) + 15O_2(g) \xrightarrow{\Delta} 12CO_2(g) + 6H_2O(g)$
   e. $Al_2(SO_4)_3(aq) + 6KOH(aq) \longrightarrow$
      $\qquad\qquad\qquad 2Al(OH)_3(s) + 3K_2SO_4(aq)$
   f. $KOH(aq) + HBr(aq) \longrightarrow KBr(aq) + H_2O(l)$

6.10 Classify each of the following as a combination, decomposition, single replacement, double replacement or combustion reaction:
   a. $CuO(s) + 2HCl(aq) \longrightarrow CuCl_2(aq) + H_2O(l)$
   b. $2Al(s) + 3Br_2(g) \longrightarrow 2AlBr_3(s)$
   c. $Pb(NO_3)_2(aq) + 2NaCl(aq) \longrightarrow$
      $\qquad\qquad\qquad PbCl_2(s) + 2NaNO_3(aq)$
   d. $C_6H_{12}O_6(aq) \longrightarrow 2C_2H_6O(aq) + 2CO_2(g)$
   e. $NaOH(aq) + HCl(aq) \longrightarrow NaCl(aq) + H_2O(l)$
   f. $C_6H_{12}(l) + 9O_2(g) \xrightarrow{\Delta} 6CO_2(g) + 6H_2O(g)$

6.11 Complete the equation for each of the following types of reactions, and then balance:
   a. combination: $Mg(s) + Cl_2(g) \longrightarrow$ _____
   b. decomposition: $HBr(g) \longrightarrow$ _____ $+ Br_2(g)$
   c. single replacement: $Mg(s) + Zn(NO_3)_2(aq) \longrightarrow$
      _____ $+$ _____
   d. double replacement: $K_2S(aq) + Pb(NO_3)_2(aq) \longrightarrow$
      _____ $+$ _____
   e. combustion: $C_5H_{10}(l) + O_2(g) \xrightarrow{\Delta}$
      $\qquad\qquad\qquad CO_2(g) +$ _____

6.12 Complete the equation for each of the following types of reactions, and then balance:
   a. combination: $Ca(s) + O_2(g) \longrightarrow$ _____
   b. combustion: $C_3H_4(g) + O_2(g) \xrightarrow{\Delta}$
      _____ $+ H_2O(g)$
   c. decomposition: $PbO_2(s) \longrightarrow$ _____ $+$ _____
   d. single replacement: $KI(s) + Cl_2(g) \longrightarrow$
      _____ $+$ _____
   e. double replacement: $CuCl_2(aq) + Na_2S(aq) \longrightarrow$
      _____ $+ NaCl(aq)$

6.3 Oxidation–Reduction Reactions

Perhaps you have never heard of an oxidation and reduction reaction. However, this type of reaction has many important applications in your everyday life. When you see a rusty nail, tarnish on a silver spoon, or corrosion on iron metal, you are observing oxidation.

$$4Fe(s) + 3O_2(g) \longrightarrow 2Fe_2O_3(s)$$
Rust

When we turn the lights on in our automobiles, an oxidation–reduction reaction within the car battery provides the electricity. On a cold, wintry day, we might build a fire. As the wood burns, oxygen combines with carbon and hydrogen to produce carbon dioxide, water, and heat. In the last section, we called this a combustion reaction, but it is also an oxidation–reduction reaction. When we eat foods with starches in them, the starches break down to give glucose, which is oxidized in our cells to give us energy along with carbon dioxide and water. Every breath we take provides oxygen to carry out oxidation in our cells.

$$C_6H_{12}O_6(aq) + 6O_2(g) \longrightarrow 6CO_2(g) + 6H_2O(l) + energy$$

Oxidation–Reduction Reactions

In an **oxidation–reduction reaction** (*redox*), electrons are transferred from one substance to another. If one substance loses electrons, another substance must gain electrons. **Oxidation** is defined as the *loss* of electrons; **reduction** is defined as the *gain* of electrons.

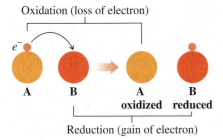

One way to remember these definitions is to use the following:

OIL RIG

Oxidation **I**s **L**oss of electrons.

Reduction **I**s **G**ain of electrons.

In the formation of ionic compounds, we have seen that metals lose electrons to become positive ions and nonmetals gain electrons to become negative ions. We can identify oxidation and reduction by looking at their charges in the reactants and the products. We can write a number line that goes from 0 up to 4+ and down from 0 to 4−. Using the value of 0 for any element by itself, we can determine whether each change is an oxidation or reduction reaction.

Let's look at the formation of the ionic compound CaS from its elements Ca and S.

$$Ca(s) + S(s) \longrightarrow CaS(s)$$

The element Ca in the reactants has a charge of 0, but in the CaS product, it is present as a Ca^{2+} ion. Because the charge is more positive, we know that the calcium atom lost two electrons, which means that an oxidation reaction took place.

$$Ca^0(s) \longrightarrow Ca^{2+}(s) + 2\,e^- \quad \text{Oxidation; loss of electrons}$$

At the same time, the element S in the reactants has a charge of 0, but in the CaS product, it is present as a S^{2-} ion. Because the charge is more negative, we know that the sulfur atom gained two electrons, which means that a reduction reaction took place.

$$S^0(s) + 2\,e^- \longrightarrow S^{2-}(s) \quad \text{Reduction; gain of electrons}$$

Thus, the overall equation for the formation of CaS involves an oxidation and a reduction reaction that occur simultaneously. In every oxidation and reduction, the number of electrons lost must be equal to the number of electrons gained. Because each shows a loss or gain of two electrons, we can add them and write the overall equation for the formation of CaS.

$$Ca^0(s) \longrightarrow Ca^{2+}(s) + 2\,e^-$$
$$S^0(s) + 2\,e^- \longrightarrow S^{2-}(s)$$
$$\overline{Ca^0(s) + S^0(s) \longrightarrow Ca^{2+}S^{2-}(s)}$$

Rust forms when the oxygen in the air reacts with iron.

TUTORIAL
Identifying Oxidation–Reduction Reactions

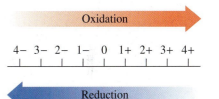

An oxidation reaction occurs when the charge becomes more positive. A reduction reaction occurs when the charge becomes more negative.

The overall equation without the charges is written as:

$$Ca(s) + S(s) \longrightarrow CaS(s)$$

As we can see in the next reaction between zinc and copper(II) sulfate, there is always an oxidation with every reduction (see Figure 6.7).

$$Zn(s) + CuSO_4(aq) \longrightarrow ZnSO_4(aq) + Cu(s)$$

We can rewrite the equation to show the atoms and ions that react as:

$$Zn^0(s) + Cu^{2+}(aq) + SO_4{}^{2-}(aq) \longrightarrow Zn^{2+}(aq) + SO_4{}^{2-}(aq) + Cu^0(s)$$

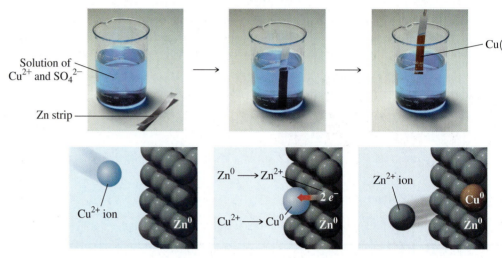

Solution of Cu^{2+} and $SO_4{}^{2-}$

Zn strip

Cu(

FIGURE 6.7 In this single replacement reaction, $Zn^0(s)$ is oxidized to Zn^{2+} when it provides two electrons to reduce Cu^{2+} to $Cu^0(s)$:

$$Zn^0(s) + Cu^{2+}(aq) \longrightarrow Cu^0(s) + Zn^{2+}(aq)$$

Q In the oxidation, does $Zn(s)$ lose or gain electrons?

In this reaction, Zn atoms lose two electrons to form Zn^{2+}. The increase in positive charge indicates that $Zn(s)$ is oxidized. At the same time, Cu^{2+} gains two electrons to form $Cu(s)$. The decrease in charge indicates that Cu^{2+} is reduced. The $SO_4{}^{2-}$ ions are *spectator ions*, which means they are present in both the reactants and products and do not change.

$$Zn^0(s) \longrightarrow Zn^{2+}(aq) + 2\,e^- \qquad \text{Oxidation of Zn}$$
$$Cu^{2+}(aq) + 2\,e^- \longrightarrow Cu^0(s) \qquad \text{Reduction of } Cu^{2+}$$

CONCEPT CHECK 6.4 **Oxidation and Reduction**

The following unbalanced reaction takes place in a NiCad battery used in cameras and toys:

$$Cd^0(s) \longrightarrow Cd^{2+}(aq)$$

a. Complete the equation by showing the electron loss or gain.
b. Is this reaction an oxidation or a reduction? Why?

ANSWER

a. $Cd(s)$ loses electrons to form $Cd^{2+}(aq)$.

$$Cd^0(s) \longrightarrow Cd^{2+}(aq) + 2\,e^-$$

b. There is an increase in the positive charge, which means that the reaction of Cd is an oxidation.

Batteries come in many shapes and sizes.

CONCEPT CHECK 6.5   **Identifying Oxidation–Reduction Reactions**

In photographic film, the following decomposition reaction occurs in the presence of light. What is oxidized, and what is reduced?

$$2AgBr(s) \xrightarrow{\text{Light}} 2Ag(s) + Br_2(g)$$

ANSWER

To determine the substances oxidized and reduced, we need to look at the ions and charges in the reactants and products. In AgBr, there is a silver ion (Ag^+) with a 1+ charge and a bromide ion (Br^-) with a charge of $1-$. By writing AgBr as ions, we obtain the following reaction:

$$2Ag^+(s) + 2Br^-(s) \longrightarrow 2Ag^0(s) + Br_2^{\,0}(g)$$

Now we can compare Ag^+ with the product Ag atom. We see that each Ag^+ gained an electron; Ag^+ is reduced.

$$2Ag^+(s) + 2\,e^- \longrightarrow 2Ag^0(s) \quad \text{Reduction}$$

When we compare Br^- in the reactant with the Br atom in the product Br_2, we see that each Br^- lost an electron; Br_2 is oxidized.

$$2Br^-(s) \longrightarrow Br_2^{\,0}(g) + 2\,e^- \quad \text{Oxidation}$$

A vintage photograph has a sepia tone that is caused by the reaction of light with silver in the film.

Explore Your World

OXIDATION OF FRUITS AND VEGETABLES

Freshly cut surfaces of fruits and vegetables discolor when exposed to oxygen in the air. Cut three slices of a fruit or vegetable such as apple, potato, avocado, or banana. Leave one piece on the kitchen counter (uncovered). Wrap one piece in plastic wrap and leave on the kitchen counter. Dip one piece in lemon juice and leave uncovered.

QUESTIONS

1. What changes take place in each sample after 1–2 h?
2. Why would wrapping fruits and vegetables slow the rate of discoloration?

3. If lemon juice contains vitamin C (an antioxidant), why would dipping a fruit or vegetable in lemon juice affect the oxidation reaction on its surface?
4. Other kinds of antioxidants are vitamin E, citric acid, and BHT. Look for these antioxidants on the labels of cereals, potato chips, and other foods in your kitchen. Why are antioxidants added to food products that will be stored on our kitchen shelves?

Oxidation and Reduction in Biological Systems

Oxidation may also involve the addition of oxygen or the loss of hydrogen, whereas reduction may involve the loss of oxygen or the gain of hydrogen. In the cells of the body, oxidation of organic (carbon) compounds involves the transfer of hydrogen atoms (H), which are composed of electrons and protons. For example, the oxidation of a typical biological molecule can involve the transfer of two hydrogen atoms (or $2H^+$ and $2\,e^-$) to a proton acceptor such as the coenzyme FAD (flavin adenine dinucleotide). The coenzyme is reduced to $FADH_2$.

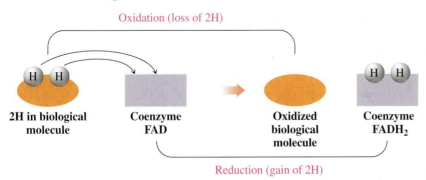

In biological systems, oxidation is identified as a gain of O atoms or a loss of H atoms; reduction is identified as a loss of O atoms or a gain of H atoms.

In many biochemical oxidation–reduction reactions, the transfer of hydrogen atoms is necessary for the production of energy in the cells. For example, when methanol (CH_3OH), a poisonous substance, is metabolized in the body, it loses two H atoms to form the oxidized product methanal. The H atoms reduce the coenzyme NAD^+ to NADH and H^+.

$$CH_3OH \longrightarrow H_2CO + 2H \qquad\qquad NAD^+ + 2H \longrightarrow NADH + H^+$$
Methanol   Methanal

The methanal is oxidized further to methanoic acid by gaining oxygen, which is itself reduced.

$$2H_2CO + O_2 \longrightarrow 2H_2CO_2$$
Methanal   Methanoic acid

Finally, methanoic acid is oxidized to carbon dioxide and water as O_2 is reduced.

$$2H_2CO_2 + O_2 \longrightarrow 2CO_2 + 2H_2O$$
Methanoic acid

The intermediate products of the oxidation of methanol are quite toxic, causing blindness and possibly death as they interfere with key reactions in the cells of the body.

In summary, we find that the particular definition of oxidation and reduction we use depends on the process that occurs in the reaction. All of these definitions are summarized in Table 6.4. Oxidation always involves a loss of electrons, but it may also be seen as an addition of oxygen, or the loss of hydrogen atoms. A reduction always involves a gain of electrons and may also be seen as the loss of oxygen, or the gain of hydrogen.

TABLE 6.4 Characteristics of Oxidation and Reduction

Oxidation	
Always Involves	**May Involve**
Loss of electrons	Addition of oxygen
	Loss of hydrogen

Reduction	
Always Involves	**May Involve**
Gain of electrons	Loss of oxygen
	Gain of hydrogen

QUESTIONS AND PROBLEMS

6.3 Oxidation–Reduction Reactions

LEARNING GOAL: *Define the terms oxidation and reduction; identify the reactant that is oxidized and the reactant that is reduced.*

6.13 Indicate whether each of the following is an oxidation or a reduction reaction:
    a. $Na^+(aq) + e^- \longrightarrow Na(s)$
    b. $Ni(s) \longrightarrow Ni^{2+}(aq) + 2\,e^-$
    c. $Cr^{3+}(aq) + 3\,e^- \longrightarrow Cr(s)$
    d. $2H^+(aq) + 2\,e^- \longrightarrow H_2(g)$

6.14 Indicate whether each of the following is an oxidation or a reduction reaction:
    a. $O_2(g) + 4\,e^- \longrightarrow 2O^{2-}(aq)$
    b. $Al(s) \longrightarrow Al^{3+}(aq) + 3\,e^-$
    c. $Fe^{3+}(aq) + e^- \longrightarrow Fe^{2+}(aq)$
    d. $2Br^-(aq) \longrightarrow Br_2(l) + 2\,e^-$

6.15 In the following reactions, identify which reactant is oxidized and which is reduced:
    a. $Zn(s) + Cl_2(g) \longrightarrow ZnCl_2(s)$
    b. $Cl_2(g) + 2NaBr(aq) \longrightarrow 2NaCl(aq) + Br_2(l)$
    c. $2PbO(s) \longrightarrow 2Pb(s) + O_2(g)$
    d. $2Fe^{3+}(aq) + Sn^{2+}(aq) \longrightarrow 2Fe^{2+}(aq) + Sn^{4+}(aq)$

6.16 In the following reactions, identify which reactant is oxidized and which is reduced:
    a. $2Li(s) + F_2(g) \longrightarrow 2LiF(s)$
    b. $Cl_2(g) + 2KI(aq) \longrightarrow 2KCl(aq) + I_2(s)$
    c. $Mg(s) + Cu^{2+}(aq) \longrightarrow Mg^{2+}(aq) + Cu(s)$
    d. $Fe(s) + CuSO_4(aq) \longrightarrow FeSO_4(aq) + Cu(s)$

6.17 In the mitochondria of human cells, energy for the production of ATP is provided by the oxidation and reduction reactions of the iron ions in the cytochromes that function in electron transport. Identify each of the following reactions as an oxidation or reduction:
    a. $Fe^{3+} + e^- \longrightarrow Fe^{2+}$
    b. $Fe^{2+} \longrightarrow Fe^{3+} + e^-$

6.18 Chlorine (Cl_2) is a strong germicide used to disinfect drinking water and to kill microbes in swimming pools. If the product is Cl^-, was the Cl_2 oxidized or reduced?

6.19 When linoleic acid, an unsaturated fatty acid, reacts with hydrogen, it forms a saturated fatty acid. Is linoleic acid oxidized or reduced in the hydrogenation reaction?

$$C_{18}H_{32}O_2 + 2H_2 \longrightarrow C_{18}H_{36}O_2$$
Linoleic acid

6.20 In one of the reactions in the citric acid cycle, which provides energy for ATP synthesis, succinic acid is converted to fumaric acid.

$$C_4H_6O_4 \longrightarrow C_4H_4O_4 + 2H$$
Succinic acid   Fumaric acid

The reaction is accompanied by a coenzyme, flavin adenine dinucleotide (FAD):

$$FAD + 2H \longrightarrow FADH_2$$

    a. Is succinic acid oxidized or reduced?
    b. Is FAD oxidized or reduced?
    c. Why would the two reactions occur together?

Chemistry Link to the Environment

FUEL CELLS: CLEAN ENERGY FOR THE FUTURE

Fuel cells are of interest to scientists because they provide an alternative source of electrical energy that is more efficient, does not use up oil reserves, and generates products that do not pollute the atmosphere. Fuel cells are considered a clean way to produce energy.

In a fuel cell, the reactants continuously enter the cell, which generates an electrical current. One type of hydrogen–oxygen fuel cell has been used in automobile prototypes. In this cell, hydrogen gas enters the fuel cell and comes in contact with platinum embedded in a plastic membrane. The platinum assists in the oxidation of hydrogen atoms to hydrogen ions and electrons.

The electrons produce an electric current as they travel through the wire. The hydrogen ions move through the plastic membrane to react with oxygen molecules. The oxygen molecules are reduced to oxide ions that combine with the hydrogen ions to form water.

The overall hydrogen–oxygen fuel cell reaction can be written as:

$$2H_2(g) + O_2(g) \longrightarrow 2H_2O(l)$$

Fuel cells have already been used to power the space shuttle. A major drawback to the practical use of fuel cells is the economic impact of converting cars to fuel cell operation. The storage and cost of producing hydrogen are also problems. Some manufacturers are experimenting with systems that convert gasoline or methanol to hydrogen for use in fuel cells. Energy must be expended to produce the hydrogen fuel for these cells. However, this can be accomplished using solar or wind power, which means there is a minimum of pollution and fossil fuels are not needed. In addition, the output from the fuel cell is water, a nonpollutant.

In homes, fuel cells may one day replace the batteries currently used to provide electrical power for cell phones, CD and DVD players, and laptop computers. Fuel cell design is still in the prototype phase, although there is much interest in development of these cells. We already know they can work, but modifications must still be made before they become reasonably priced and part of our everyday lives.

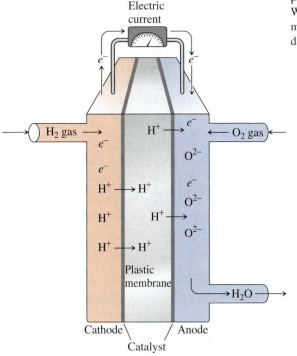

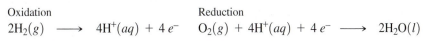

Oxidation
$$2H_2(g) \longrightarrow 4H^+(aq) + 4\,e^-$$

Reduction
$$O_2(g) + 4H^+(aq) + 4\,e^- \longrightarrow 2H_2O(l)$$

A fuel cell uses a continuous supply of hydrogen and oxygen to generate electricity.

Fuel cells are used to supply power on the space shuttle orbiter.

6.4 The Mole

At the grocery store, you buy eggs by the dozen or soda by the case. In an office-supply store, pencils are ordered by the gross and paper by the ream. The terms such as dozen, gross, ream, and case are used to count the number of items present. For example, when you buy a dozen eggs, you know you will get 12 eggs in the carton.

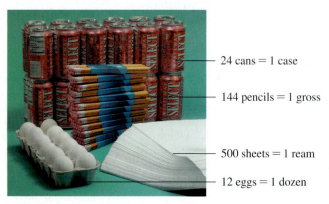

24 cans = 1 case

144 pencils = 1 gross

500 sheets = 1 ream

12 eggs = 1 dozen

Collections of items include dozen, gross, and mole.

Avogadro's Number

In chemistry, particles such as atoms, molecules, and ions are counted by the **mole**, a unit that contains 6.02×10^{23} of those particles. Avogadro's number is a very big number because atoms are so small that it takes an extremely large number of atoms to provide a sufficient amount to weigh and use in chemical reactions. **Avogadro's number** is named for Amedeo Avogadro, an Italian physicist.

Avogadro's number

$602\,000\,000\,000\,000\,000\,000\,000 = 6.02 \times 10^{23}$

One mole of any element always contains Avogadro's number of atoms. In one mole of carbon, there are 6.02×10^{23} carbon atoms; in one mole of aluminum, there are 6.02×10^{23} aluminum atoms; and in one mole of sulfur, there are 6.02×10^{23} sulfur atoms.

1 mole of an element = 6.02×10^{23} atoms of that element

Avogadro's number tells us that one mole of a compound contains 6.02×10^{23} of the particular type of particles that make up that compound. One mole of a covalent compound contains Avogadro's number of molecules. For example, one mole of CO_2 contains 6.02×10^{23} molecules of CO_2. One mole of an ionic compound contains Avogadro's number of **formula units**, which are the groups of ions represented by the formula of an ionic compound. One mole of NaCl contains 6.02×10^{23} formula units of NaCl (Na^+, Cl^-). Table 6.5 gives examples of the number of particles in some one-mole quantities.

TUTORIAL
Using Avogadro's Number

TUTORIAL
The Mole as a Counting Unit

One mole of sulfur contains 6.02×10^{23} sulfur atoms.

TABLE 6.5 Number of Particles in One-Mole Samples

Substance	Number and Type of Particles
1 mole of Al	6.02×10^{23} atoms of Al
1 mole of S	6.02×10^{23} atoms of S
1 mole of water (H_2O)	6.02×10^{23} molecules of H_2O
1 mole of vitamin C ($C_6H_8O_6$)	6.02×10^{23} molecules of vitamin C
1 mole of NaCl	6.02×10^{23} formula units of NaCl

We can use Avogadro's number as a conversion factor to convert between the moles of a substance and the number of particles it contains.

$$\frac{6.02 \times 10^{23} \text{ particles}}{1 \text{ mole}} \quad \text{and} \quad \frac{1 \text{ mole}}{6.02 \times 10^{23} \text{ particles}}$$

For example, we use Avogadro's number to convert 4.00 moles of iron to atoms of iron.

$$4.00 \text{ moles Fe atoms} \times \frac{6.02 \times 10^{23} \text{ Fe atoms}}{1 \text{ mole Fe atoms}} = 2.41 \times 10^{24} \text{ Fe atoms}$$

Avogadro's number as a conversion factor

We can also use Avogadro's number to convert 3.01×10^{24} molecules of CO_2 to moles of CO_2.

$$3.01 \times 10^{24} \text{ CO}_2 \text{ molecules} \times \frac{1 \text{ mole CO}_2 \text{ molecules}}{6.02 \times 10^{23} \text{ CO}_2 \text{ molecules}} = 5.00 \text{ moles of CO}_2 \text{ molecules}$$

Avogadro's number as a conversion factor

Generally, in calculations that convert between moles and particles, the number of moles will be a small number compared to the number of atoms or molecules, which will be a large number.

CONCEPT CHECK 6.6   Moles and Particles

Explain why 0.20 mole of aluminum is a small number, but the number of atoms in 0.20 mole is a large number: 1.2×10^{23} atoms of aluminum.

ANSWER

The term *mole* is used as a collection term that represents 6.02×10^{23} particles. Because atoms are submicroscopic particles, a large number of atoms are in one mole of aluminum.

SAMPLE PROBLEM 6.3   Calculating the Number of Molecules

How many molecules are present in 1.75 moles of carbon dioxide, CO_2?

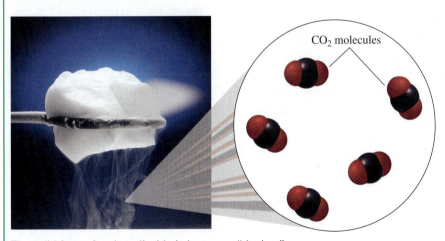

CO$_2$ molecules

The solid form of carbon dioxide is known as "dry ice."

SOLUTION

Step 1   **State the given and needed quantities.**

Analyze the Problem

Given	Need
1.75 moles of CO_2	molecules of CO_2

Guide to Calculating the Atoms or Molecules of a Substance

1 State the given and needed quantities.

2 Write a plan to convert moles to atoms or molecules.

3 Use Avogadro's number to write conversion factors.

4 Set up the problem to calculate the number of particles.

Step 2 Write a plan to convert moles to atoms or molecules.

$$\text{moles of } CO_2 \quad \boxed{\text{Avogadro's number}} \quad \text{molecules of } CO_2$$

Step 3 Use Avogadro's number to write conversion factors.

$$1 \text{ mole of } CO_2 = 6.02 \times 10^{23} \text{ molecules of } CO_2$$

$$\frac{6.02 \times 10^{23} \text{ molecules } CO_2}{1 \text{ mole } CO_2} \quad \text{and} \quad \frac{1 \text{ mole } CO_2}{6.02 \times 10^{23} \text{ molecules } CO_2}$$

Step 4 Set up the problem to calculate the number of particles.

$$1.75 \cancel{\text{ moles } CO_2} \times \frac{6.02 \times 10^{23} \text{ molecules } CO_2}{1 \cancel{\text{ mole } CO_2}} = 1.05 \times 10^{24} \text{ molecules of } CO_2$$

STUDY CHECK 6.3

How many moles of water, H_2O, contain 2.60×10^{23} molecules of water?

TUTORIAL
Moles and the Chemical Formula

Moles of Elements in a Formula

We have seen that the subscripts in a chemical formula of a compound indicate the number of atoms of each type of element. For example, in a molecule of aspirin, chemical formula $C_9H_8O_4$, there are 9 carbon atoms, 8 hydrogen atoms, and 4 oxygen atoms. The subscripts also state the number of moles of each element in one mole of aspirin: 9 moles of C atoms, 8 moles of H atoms, and 4 moles of O atoms.

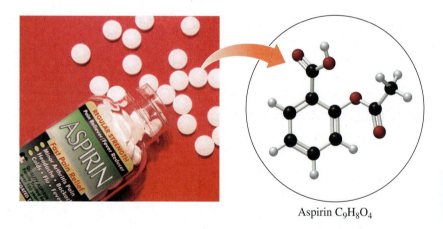

Number of atoms in one molecule

Carbon (C)   Hydrogen (H)   Oxygen (O)

Aspirin $C_9H_8O_4$

Using the subscripts in the formula of aspirin, $C_9H_8O_4$, we can write the number of atoms of C, H, and O in one molecule of aspirin, or the moles of C, H, and O in one mole of aspirin.

$$C_9H_8O_4$$

Carbon	**Hydrogen**	**Oxygen**
9 atoms of C	8 atoms of H	4 atoms of O
9 moles of C	8 moles of H	4 moles of O

Using the subscripts from the formula, $C_9H_8O_4$, we can write the conversion factors for each of the elements in one mole of aspirin:

$$\frac{9 \text{ moles C}}{1 \text{ mole } C_9H_8O_4} \quad \frac{8 \text{ moles H}}{1 \text{ mole } C_9H_8O_4} \quad \frac{4 \text{ moles O}}{1 \text{ mole } C_9H_8O_4}$$

$$\frac{1 \text{ mole } C_9H_8O_4}{9 \text{ moles C}} \quad \frac{1 \text{ mole } C_9H_8O_4}{8 \text{ moles H}} \quad \frac{1 \text{ mole } C_9H_8O_4}{4 \text{ moles O}}$$

CONCEPT CHECK 6.7 Using Subscripts of a Formula

Indicate the moles of each type of atom in one mole of each of the following:

a. $C_5H_{10}O_2$, propyl acetate, odor and taste of pears
b. $Zn(C_2H_3O_2)_2$, zinc dietary supplement

ANSWER

a. The subscripts in the formula indicate that there are 5 moles of C atoms, 10 moles of H atoms, and 2 moles of O atoms in 1 mole of propyl acetate.
b. The subscript 2 outside the parentheses indicates there are 2 moles of the ion $C_2H_3O_2^-$ in the formula. Thus, there is 1 mole of Zn^{2+} ions, 4 (2×2) moles of C atoms, 6 (2×3) moles of H atoms, and 4 (2×2) moles of O atoms in 1 mole of $Zn(C_2H_3O_2)_2$.

The compound propyl acetate provides the odor and taste of pears.

SAMPLE PROBLEM 6.4 Calculating the Moles of an Element

How many moles of carbon are present in 1.50 moles of aspirin, $C_9H_8O_4$?

SOLUTION

Step 1 State the given and needed quantities.

Analyze the Problem

Given	Need
1.50 moles of aspirin	moles of C
molecular formula $C_9H_8O_4$	

Step 2 Write a plan to convert moles of compound to moles of an element.

moles of $C_9H_8O_4$ | Subscript | moles of C atoms

Step 3 Write equalities and conversion factors using subscripts.

1 mole of $C_9H_8O_4$ = 9 moles of C atoms

$$\frac{9 \text{ moles C}}{1 \text{ mole } C_9H_8O_4} \quad \text{and} \quad \frac{1 \text{ mole } C_9H_8O_4}{9 \text{ moles C}}$$

Step 4 Set up the problem to calculate the moles of an element.

$$1.50 \text{ moles } C_9H_8O_4 \times \frac{9 \text{ moles C}}{1 \text{ mole } C_9H_8O_4} = 13.5 \text{ moles of C}$$

STUDY CHECK 6.4

How many moles of aspirin, $C_9H_8O_4$, contain 0.480 mole of O?

Guide to Calculating Moles

1 State the given and needed quantities.

2 Write a plan to convert moles of compound to moles of an element.

3 Write equalities and conversion factors using subscripts.

4 Set up the problem to calculate the moles of an element.

QUESTIONS AND PROBLEMS

6.4 The Mole

LEARNING GOAL: Use Avogadro's number to determine the number of particles in a given amount of moles.

6.21 Calculate each of the following:
  a. number of Ag atoms in 0.200 mole of Ag
  b. number of C_3H_8O molecules in 0.750 mole of C_3H_8O
  c. number of Cr atoms in 1.25 moles of Cr

6.22 Calculate each of the following:
  a. number of Ni atoms in 3.4 moles of Ni
  b. number of $Mg(OH)_2$ formula units in 1.20 moles of $Mg(OH)_2$
  c. number of Li atoms in 4.5 moles of Li

6.23 Calculate each of the following:
  a. moles of Al in 3.26×10^{24} atoms of Al
  b. moles of C_2H_5OH in 8.50×10^{24} molecules of C_2H_5OH
  c. moles of Au in 2.88×10^{23} atoms of Au

6.24 Calculate each of the following:
  a. moles of Cu in 7.8×10^{21} atoms of Cu
  b. moles of C_2H_6 in 3.75×10^{23} molecules of C_2H_6
  c. moles of Zn in 5.6×10^{24} atoms of Zn

6.25 Quinine, $C_{20}H_{24}N_2O_2$, is a component of tonic water and bitter lemon.
  a. How many moles of hydrogen are in 1.0 mole of quinine?
  b. How many moles of carbon are in 5.0 moles of quinine?
  c. How many moles of nitrogen are in 0.020 mole of quinine?

6.26   Aluminum sulfate, $Al_2(SO_4)_3$, is used in some antiperspirants.
  a. How many moles of sulfur are present in 3.0 moles of $Al_2(SO_4)_3$?
  b. How many moles of aluminum ions are present in 0.40 mole of $Al_2(SO_4)_3$?
  c. How many moles of sulfate ions $(SO_4{}^{2-})$ are present in 1.5 moles of $Al_2(SO_4)_3$?

6.27   Calculate each of the following:
  a. number of C atoms in 0.500 mole of C
  b. number of SO_2 molecules in 1.28 moles of SO_2
  c. moles of Fe in 5.22×10^{22} atoms of Fe

6.28   Calculate each of the following:
  a. number of Co atoms in 2.2 moles of Co
  b. number of CO_2 molecules in 0.0180 mole of CO_2
  c. moles of Cr in 4.58×10^{23} atoms of Cr

6.29   Calculate each of the following quantities in 2.00 moles of H_3PO_4:
  a. moles of H   **b.** moles of O
  c. atoms of P   **d.** atoms of O

6.30   Calculate each of the following quantities in 0.185 mole of $(C_3H_7)_2O$:
  a. moles of C   **b.** moles of O
  c. atoms of H   **d.** atoms of C

LEARNING GOAL

Determine the molar mass of a substance and use the molar mass to convert between grams and moles.

6.5 Molar Mass

A single atom or molecule is much too small to weigh, even on the most sensitive laboratory balance. In fact, it takes a huge number of atoms or molecules to make enough of a substance for you to see. An amount of water that contains Avogadro's number of water molecules is only a few sips. In the laboratory, we can use a balance to weigh out Avogadro's number of particles or one mole of a substance.

For any element, the quantity called **molar mass** is the number of grams that equals the atomic mass of that element. We are counting 6.02×10^{23} atoms of an element when we weigh out the number of grams equal to its molar mass. For example, carbon has an atomic mass of 12.01 on the periodic table. Then to obtain one mole of carbon atoms, we would weigh out 12.01 g of carbon. Thus, the molar mass of carbon is found by looking at its atomic mass on the periodic table.

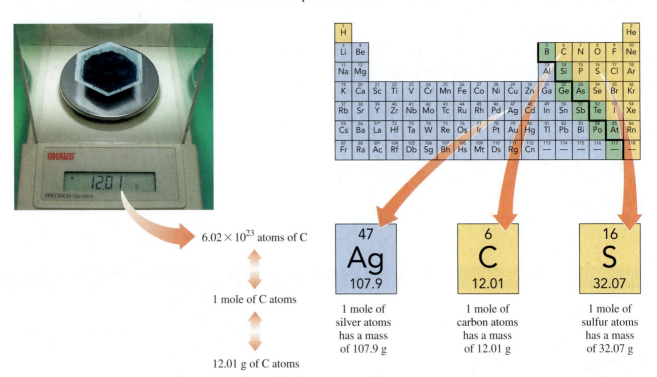

6.02×10^{23} atoms of C

1 mole of C atoms

12.01 g of C atoms

47	6	16
Ag	**C**	**S**
107.9	12.01	32.07

1 mole of silver atoms has a mass of 107.9 g

1 mole of carbon atoms has a mass of 12.01 g

1 mole of sulfur atoms has a mass of 32.07 g

Molar Mass of a Compound

To determine the molar mass of a compound, multiply the molar mass of each element by its subscript in the formula, and add the results as shown in Sample Problem 6.5. *In this text, we round the molar mass of an element to the tenths (0.1 g) place or use at least three significant figures for calculations.*

SAMPLE PROBLEM 6.5 Calculating the Molar Mass of a Compound

Find the molar mass of Li_2CO_3 used to produce the red color in fireworks.

SOLUTION

Analyze the Problem

Given	Need
molecular formula Li_2CO_3	molar mass of Li_2CO_3

Step 1 **Obtain the molar mass of each element.**

$$\frac{6.94 \text{ g Li}}{1 \text{ mole Li}} \quad \frac{12.0 \text{ g C}}{1 \text{ mole C}} \quad \frac{16.0 \text{ g O}}{1 \text{ mole O}}$$

Step 2 **Multiply each molar mass by the number of moles (subscript) in the formula.**

Grams from 2 moles of Li

$$2 \text{ moles Li} \times \frac{6.94 \text{ g Li}}{1 \text{ mole Li}} = 13.9 \text{ g of Li}$$

Grams from 1 mole of C

$$1 \text{ mole C} \times \frac{12.0 \text{ g C}}{1 \text{ mole C}} = 12.0 \text{ g of C}$$

Grams from 3 moles of O

$$3 \text{ moles O} \times \frac{16.0 \text{ g O}}{1 \text{ mole O}} = 48.0 \text{ g of O}$$

Step 3 **Calculate the molar mass by adding the masses of the elements.**

$$\begin{align}
2 \text{ moles of Li} &= \quad 13.9 \text{ g of Li} \\
1 \text{ mole of C} &= \quad 12.0 \text{ g of C} \\
3 \text{ moles of O} &= +48.0 \text{ g of O} \\
\hline
\text{Molar mass of } Li_2CO_3 &= \quad 73.9 \text{ g}
\end{align}$$

STUDY CHECK 6.5

Calculate the molar mass of salicylic acid, $C_7H_6O_3$.

Guide to Calculating Molar Mass

1 Obtain the molar mass of each element.

2 Multiply each molar mass by the number of moles (subscript) in the formula.

3 Calculate the molar mass by adding the masses of the elements.

Lithium carbonate produces a red color in fireworks.

Calculations Using Molar Mass

The molar mass of an element or a compound is a useful conversion factor because it converts moles of a substance to grams, or grams to moles. For example, 1 mole of magnesium has a mass of 24.3 g. To express its molar mass as an equality, we can write:

1 mole of Mg = 24.3 g of Mg

From this equality, two conversion factors can be written.

$$\frac{24.3 \text{ g Mg}}{1 \text{ mole Mg}} \quad \text{and} \quad \frac{1 \text{ mole Mg}}{24.3 \text{ g Mg}}$$

Figure 6.8 shows some one-mole quantities of substances. Table 6.6 lists the molar mass for several one-mole samples.

TABLE 6.6 The Molar Mass of Selected Elements and Compounds

Substance	Molar Mass
1 mole of C	12.0 g
1 mole of Na	23.0 g
1 mole of Fe	55.9 g
1 mole of NaF	42.0 g
1 mole of $CaCO_3$	100.1 g
1 mole of $C_6H_{12}O_6$ (glucose)	180.1 g
1 mole of $C_8H_{10}N_4O_2$ (caffeine)	194.1 g

S   Fe   NaCl $K_2Cr_2O_7$ $C_{12}H_{22}O_{11}$

FIGURE 6.8 One-mole samples: sulfur, S (32.1 g); iron, Fe (55.9 g); salt, NaCl (58.5 g); potassium dichromate, $K_2Cr_2O_7$ (294 g); and sugar, sucrose, $C_{12}H_{22}O_{11}$ (342 g).
Q How is the molar mass for $K_2Cr_2O_7$ obtained?

TUTORIAL
Converting Between Grams and Moles

Conversion factors are written for compounds in the same way. For example, the equality for the molar mass of the compound H_2O is written:

1 mole of H_2O = 18.0 g of H_2O

From this equality, the conversion factors from the molar mass of H_2O are written as:

$$\frac{18.0 \text{ g } H_2O}{1 \text{ mole } H_2O} \quad \text{and} \quad \frac{1 \text{ mole } H_2O}{18.0 \text{ g } H_2O}$$

We can now change from moles to grams, or grams to moles, using the conversion factors derived from the molar mass as shown in Sample Problem 6.6. (Remember, you must determine the molar mass of the substance first.)

SAMPLE PROBLEM 6.6 **Converting Mass of a Compound to Moles**

A box of salt contains 737 g of NaCl. How many moles of NaCl are present in the box?

SOLUTION

Step 1 **State the given and needed quantities.**

Analyze the Problem

Given	Need
737 g of NaCl	moles of NaCl

Step 2 **Write a plan to convert grams to moles.**

grams of NaCl   Molar mass   moles of NaCl

Step 3 **Determine the molar mass and write conversion factors.**

1 mole of NaCl = 58.5 g of NaCl
$$\frac{58.5 \text{ g NaCl}}{1 \text{ mole NaCl}} \quad \text{and} \quad \frac{1 \text{ mole NaCl}}{58.5 \text{ g NaCl}}$$

Step 4 **Set up the problem to convert grams to moles.**

$$737 \text{ g NaCl} \times \frac{1 \text{ mole NaCl}}{58.5 \text{ g NaCl}} = 12.6 \text{ moles of NaCl}$$

Guide to Calculating the Moles (or Grams) of a Substance from Grams (or Moles)

1 State the given and needed quantities.

2 Write a plan to convert moles to grams (or grams to moles).

3 Determine the molar mass and write conversion factors.

4 Set up the problem to convert moles to grams (or grams to moles).

Table salt is sodium chloride, NaCl.

STUDY CHECK 6.6

Silver metal is used in the manufacture of tableware, mirrors, jewelry, and dental alloys. If the design for a piece of jewelry requires 0.750 mole of silver, how many grams of silver are needed?

Silver metal is used to make jewelry.

Explore Your World

CALCULATING MOLES IN THE KITCHEN

The labels on food products list the components in grams and milligrams. Read the labels of some products in the kitchen and convert the amounts given in grams or milligrams to moles using molar mass.

QUESTIONS

1. How many moles of NaCl are in a 4-oz salt shaker?
2. How many moles of sugar are contained in a 5-lb bag of sugar if sugar has the formula $C_{12}H_{22}O_{11}$?
3. A serving of cereal contains 90 mg of potassium. If there are 11 servings of cereal in the box, how many moles of K^+ are present in the cereal in the box?

Figure 6.9 shows the connections between the moles of a compound, its mass in grams, the number of molecules (or formula units if ionic), and the moles and atoms of each element in that compound.

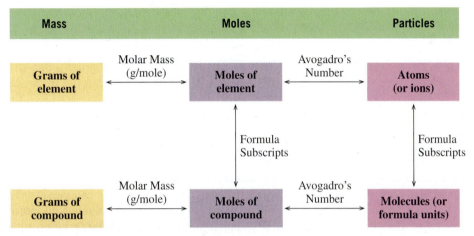

FIGURE 6.9 The moles of a compound are related to its mass in grams by molar mass, to the number of molecules (or formula units) by Avogadro's number, and to the moles of each element by the subscripts in the formula.

Q What steps are needed to calculate the number of H atoms in 5.00 g of CH_4?

QUESTIONS AND PROBLEMS

6.5 Molar Mass

LEARNING GOAL: Determine the molar mass of a substance and use the molar mass to convert between grams and moles.

6.31 Calculate the molar mass for each of the following:
a. $KC_4H_5O_6$ (cream of tartar)
b. Fe_2O_3 (rust)
c. $C_{19}H_{20}FNO_3$ (Paxil, an antidepressant)
d. $Al_2(SO_4)_3$ (antiperspirant)
e. $Mg(OH)_2$ (antacid)
f. $C_{16}H_{19}N_3O_5S$ (amoxicillin, an antibiotic)

6.32 Calculate the molar mass for each of the following:
a. $FeSO_4$ (iron supplement)
b. Al_2O_3 (absorbent and abrasive)
c. $C_7H_5NO_3S$ (saccharin)
d. C_3H_8O (rubbing alcohol)
e. $(NH_4)_2CO_3$ (baking powder)
f. $Zn(C_2H_3O_2)_2$ (dietary supplement)

6.33 Calculate the mass, in grams, for each of the following:
a. 2.00 moles of Na
b. 2.80 moles of Ca
c. 0.125 mole of Sn
d. 1.76 moles of Cu

6.34 Calculate the mass, in grams, for each of the following:
a. 1.50 moles of K
b. 2.5 moles of C
c. 0.25 mole of P
d. 12.5 moles of He

6.35 Calculate the mass, in grams, for each of the following:
a. 0.500 mole of NaCl
b. 1.75 moles of Na_2O
c. 0.225 mole of H_2O
d. 4.42 moles of CO_2

6.36 Calculate the mass, in grams, for each of the following:
a. 2.0 moles of $MgCl_2$
b. 3.5 moles of C_3H_8
c. 5.00 moles of C_2H_6O
d. 0.488 mole of $C_3H_6O_3$

6.37 a. The compound $MgSO_4$ is called Epsom salts. How many grams will you need to prepare a bath containing 5.00 moles of Epsom salts?
b. In a bottle of soda, there is 0.25 mole of CO_2. How many grams of CO_2 are in the bottle?

6.38 a. Cyclopropane, C_3H_6, is an anesthetic given by inhalation. How many grams are in 0.25 mole of cyclopropane?
b. The sedative Demerol hydrochloride has the formula $C_{15}H_{22}ClNO_2$. How many grams are in 0.025 mole of Demerol hydrochloride?

6.39 How many moles are contained in each of the following?
a. 50.0 g of Ag
b. 0.200 g of C
c. 15.0 g of NH_3
d. 75.0 g of SO_2

6.40 How many moles are contained in each of the following?
a. 25.0 g of Ca
b. 5.00 g of S
c. 40.0 g of H_2O
d. 12.2 g of O_2

6.41 How many moles of S are in each of the following quantities?
  a. 25 g of S   **b.** 125 g of SO₂   **c.** 30.1 g of Al₂S₃

6.42 How many moles of C are in each of the following quantities?
  a. 75 g of C   **b.** 32.6 g of C₂H₆   **c.** 88 g of CO₂

6.43 Caffeine, $C_8H_{10}N_4O_2$, is obtained from tea, coffee, and energy drinks.

Coffee beans
are a source
of caffeine.

  a. How many grams of caffeine are in 0.850 mole?
  b. How many moles of caffeine are in 28.0 g of caffeine?
  c. How many moles of carbon are in 28.0 g of caffeine?
  d. How many grams of nitrogen are in 28.0 g of caffeine?

6.44 Fructose, $C_6H_{12}O_6$, a monosaccharide, is found in honey and fruits.
  a. How many grams of fructose are in 1.20 moles of fructose?
  b. How many moles of fructose are in 15.0 g of fructose?
  c. How many moles of carbon are in 15.0 g of fructose?
  d. How many grams of oxygen are in 15.0 g of fructose?

TUTORIAL
Moles of Reactants and Products

TUTORIAL
Law of Conservation of Mass

SELF-STUDY ACTIVITY
Stoichiometry

6.6 Mole Relationships in Chemical Equations

In Section 6.1, we saw that equations are balanced in terms of the numbers of each type of atom in the reactants and products. However, when experiments are done in the laboratory or medications are prepared in the pharmacy, the samples we use contain billions of atoms and molecules, making it impossible to count them. What we can measure is their mass using a balance. Because mass is related to the number of particles through the molar mass, measuring the mass is equivalent to counting the number of particles or moles.

Conservation of Mass

In any chemical reaction, the total amount of matter in the reactants is equal to the total amount of matter in the products. Thus, the total mass of all the reactants must be equal to the total mass of all the products. This is known as the *law of conservation of mass*, which says that there is no change in the total mass of the substances reacting in a balanced chemical reaction. Thus, no material is lost or gained as original substances are changed to new substances.

For example, tarnish forms when silver reacts with sulfur to form silver sulfide.

$$2Ag(s) + S(s) \longrightarrow Ag_2S(s)$$

2Ag(s)   +   S(s)   ⟶   Ag₂S(s)

Mass of reactants   =   Mass of product

The law of conservation of mass states that there is no matter lost or gained in a chemical reaction.

In this reaction, the number of silver atoms that reacts is two times the number of sulfur atoms. When 200 silver atoms react, 100 sulfur atoms are required. However, in the actual chemical reaction, many more atoms of both silver and sulfur would react. If we are dealing with molar amounts, then the coefficients in the equation can be interpreted in terms of moles. Thus, 2 moles of Ag react with 1 mole of S to produce 1 mole of Ag_2S. Because the molar mass of each can be determined, the moles of Ag, S, and Ag_2S can also be stated in terms of mass in grams of each. Thus, 215.8 g of Ag and 32.1 g of S react to form 247.9 g of Ag_2S. The total mass of the reactants (247.9 g) is equal to the mass of the product, 247.9 g. The various ways in which a chemical equation can be interpreted are seen in Table 6.7.

TABLE 6.7 Information Available from a Balanced Equation

	Reactants		Product
Equation	$2Ag(s)$	$+ S(s)$	$\longrightarrow Ag_2S(s)$
Atoms	2 Ag atoms	+ 1 S atom	$\longrightarrow$ Ag_2S formula unit
	200 Ag atoms	+ 100 S atoms	$\longrightarrow$ 100 Ag_2S formula units
Avogadro's Number of Atoms	$2(6.02 \times 10^{23})$ Ag atoms	$+ 1(6.02 \times 10^{23})$ S atoms	$\longrightarrow$ $1(6.02 \times 10^{23})$ Ag_2S formula units
Moles	2 moles of Ag	+ 1 mole of S	$\longrightarrow$ 1 mole of Ag_2S
Mass (g)	$2(107.9$ g$)$ of Ag	$+ 1(32.1$ g$)$ of S	$\longrightarrow$ $1(247.9$ g$)$ of Ag_2S
Total Mass (g)	247.9 g		$\longrightarrow$ 247.9 g

Mole–Mole Factors from an Equation

When iron reacts with sulfur, the product is iron(III) sulfide.

$$2Fe(s) + 3S(s) \longrightarrow Fe_2S_3(s)$$

Iron (Fe)		Sulfur (S)		Iron(III) sulfide (Fe_2S_3)
$2Fe(s)$	+	$3S(s)$	$\longrightarrow$	$Fe_2S_3(s)$

In the chemical reaction of Fe and S, the mass of the reactants is the same as the mass of the product, Fe_2S_3.

Because the equation is balanced, we know the proportions of iron and sulfur in the reaction. For this reaction, we see that 2 moles of iron react with 3 moles of sulfur to form 1 mole of iron(III) sulfide. Actually, any amount of iron or sulfur may be used but the *ratio* of iron reacting with sulfur will be the same. From the coefficients, we can write **mole–mole factors** between reactants and between reactants and products.

The coefficients used in the mole–mole factors are exact numbers; they do not limit the number of significant figures.

Fe and S: $\dfrac{2 \text{ moles Fe}}{3 \text{ moles S}}$ and $\dfrac{3 \text{ moles S}}{2 \text{ moles Fe}}$

Fe and Fe_2S_3: $\dfrac{2 \text{ moles Fe}}{1 \text{ mole } Fe_2S_3}$ and $\dfrac{1 \text{ mole } Fe_2S_3}{2 \text{ moles Fe}}$

S and Fe_2S_3: $\dfrac{3 \text{ moles S}}{1 \text{ mole } Fe_2S_3}$ and $\dfrac{1 \text{ mole } Fe_2S_3}{3 \text{ moles S}}$

CONCEPT CHECK 6.8 **Writing Mole–Mole Factors**

Consider the following balanced equation:

$$4Na(s) + O_2(g) \longrightarrow 2Na_2O(s)$$

Write the mole–mole factors for each of the following relationships:

a. Na and O_2 **b.** Na and Na_2O

ANSWER

a. The mole–mole factors for Na and O_2 use the coefficient of Na to write 4 moles of Na, and the coefficient of 1 (understood) to write 1 mole of O_2.

$$4 \text{ moles of Na} \quad = \quad 1 \text{ mole of } O_2$$

$$\dfrac{4 \text{ moles Na}}{1 \text{ mole } O_2} \quad \text{and} \quad \dfrac{1 \text{ mole } O_2}{4 \text{ moles Na}}$$

b. The mole–mole factors for Na and Na_2O use the coefficient of Na to write 4 moles of Na, and the coefficient of Na_2O to write 2 moles of Na_2O.

$$4 \text{ moles of Na} \quad = \quad 2 \text{ moles of } Na_2O$$

$$\dfrac{4 \text{ moles Na}}{2 \text{ moles } Na_2O} \quad \text{and} \quad \dfrac{2 \text{ moles } Na_2O}{4 \text{ moles Na}}$$

Using Mole–Mole Factors in Calculations

Whenever you prepare a recipe, adjust an engine for the proper mixture of fuel and air, or prepare medicines in a pharmaceutical laboratory, you need to know the proper amounts of reactants to use and how much of the product will form. Earlier, we wrote all the possible conversion factors that can be obtained from this balanced equation: $2Fe(s) + 3S(s) \longrightarrow Fe_2S_3(s)$. Now we will use mole–mole factors in chemical calculations in Sample Problem 6.7.

Propane fuel reacts with O_2 in the air to produce CO_2, H_2O, and energy.

SAMPLE PROBLEM 6.7 **Using Mole–Mole Factors**

Propane gas (C_3H_8), a fuel used in camp stoves, soldering torches, and specially equipped automobiles, reacts with oxygen to produce carbon dioxide, water, and energy. How many moles of CO_2 can be produced when 2.25 moles of C_3H_8 react?

$$C_3H_8(g) + 5O_2(g) \xrightarrow{\Delta} 3CO_2(g) + 4H_2O(g) + \text{energy}$$
Propane

SOLUTION

Step 1 State the given and needed quantities.

Analyze the Problem

Given	Need
2.25 moles of C_3H_8	moles of CO_2

Equation
$C_3H_8(g) + 5O_2(g) \xrightarrow{\Delta} 3CO_2(g) + 4H_2O(g) + $ energy Propane

Step 2 Write a plan to convert the given to the needed quantity (moles or grams).

moles of C_3H_8 → Mole–mole factor → moles of CO_2

Step 3 Use coefficients to write mole–mole factors; write molar mass factors if needed.

$$1 \text{ mole of } C_3H_8 = 3 \text{ moles of } CO_2$$
$$\frac{1 \text{ mole } C_3H_8}{3 \text{ moles } CO_2} \quad \text{and} \quad \frac{3 \text{ moles } CO_2}{1 \text{ mole } C_3H_8}$$

Step 4 Set up the problem to give the needed quantity (moles or grams).

$$2.25 \text{ moles } C_3H_8 \times \frac{3 \text{ moles } CO_2}{1 \text{ mole } C_3H_8} = 6.75 \text{ moles of } CO_2$$

The answer is given with three SFs because the given quantity, 2.25 moles of C_3H_8, has three SFs. The values in the mole–mole factor are exact.

STUDY CHECK 6.7

Using the equation in Sample Problem 6.7, calculate the number of moles of oxygen that must react to produce 0.756 mole of water.

Guide to Calculating the Quantities of Reactants and Products in a Chemical Reaction

1 State the given and needed quantities.

2 Write a plan to convert the given to the needed quantity (moles or grams).

3 Use coefficients to write mole–mole factors; write molar mass factors if needed.

4 Set up the problem to give the needed quantity (moles or grams).

QUESTIONS AND PROBLEMS

6.6 Mole Relationships in Chemical Equations

LEARNING GOAL: Given a quantity in moles of reactant or product, use a mole–mole factor from the balanced equation to calculate the moles of another substance in the reaction.

6.45 Write all of the mole–mole factors for each of the following equations:
 a. $2SO_2(g) + O_2(g) \longrightarrow 2SO_3(g)$
 b. $4P(s) + 5O_2(s) \longrightarrow 2P_2O_5(s)$

6.46 Write all of the mole–mole factors for each of the following equations:
 a. $2Al(s) + 3Cl_2(g) \longrightarrow 2AlCl_3(s)$
 b. $4HCl(g) + O_2(g) \longrightarrow 2Cl_2(g) + 2H_2O(g)$

6.47 The reaction of hydrogen with oxygen produces water.

$$2H_2(g) + O_2(g) \longrightarrow 2H_2O(g)$$

 a. How many moles of O_2 are required to react with 2.0 moles of H_2?

 b. If you have 5.0 moles of O_2, how many moles of H_2 are needed for the reaction?
 c. How many moles of H_2O form when 2.5 moles of O_2 react?

6.48 Ammonia is produced by the reaction of hydrogen and nitrogen.

$$N_2(g) + 3H_2(g) \longrightarrow 2NH_3(g)$$
Ammonia

 a. How many moles of H_2 are needed to react with 1.0 mole of N_2?
 b. How many moles of N_2 reacted if 0.60 mole of NH_3 is produced?
 c. How many moles of NH_3 are produced when 1.4 moles of H_2 react?

6.49 Carbon disulfide and carbon monoxide are produced when carbon is heated with sulfur dioxide.

$$5C(s) + 2SO_2(g) \longrightarrow CS_2(l) + 4CO(g)$$

a. How many moles of C are needed to react with 0.500 mole of SO_2?

b. How many moles of CO are produced when 1.2 moles of C react?

c. How many moles of SO_2 are required to produce 0.50 mole of CS_2?

d. How many moles of CS_2 are produced when 2.5 moles of C react?

6.50 In the acetylene torch, acetylene gas (C_2H_2) burns in oxygen to produce carbon dioxide and water.

$$2C_2H_2(g) + 5O_2(g) \xrightarrow{\Delta} 4CO_2(g) + 2H_2O(g)$$

a. How many moles of O_2 are needed to react with 2.00 moles of C_2H_2?

b. How many moles of CO_2 are produced when 3.5 moles of C_2H_2 react?

c. How many moles of C_2H_2 are required to produce 0.50 mole of H_2O?

d. How many moles of CO_2 are produced from 0.100 mole of O_2?

TUTORIAL
Masses of Reactants and Products

A mixture of acetylene and oxygen undergoes combustion during the welding of metals.

6.7 Mass Calculations for Reactions

When you perform a chemistry experiment in the laboratory, you measure a specific mass of reactant. From the mass in grams, you can calculate the number of moles of reactant. By using mole–mole factors, you can predict the moles of product that can be produced. Then the molar mass of the product is used to convert moles to grams as seen in Sample Problem 6.8.

SAMPLE PROBLEM 6.8 **Mass of Product from Mass of Reactant**

When acetylene, C_2H_2, burns in oxygen, high temperatures are produced that are used for welding metals.

$$2C_2H_2(g) + 5O_2(g) \xrightarrow{\Delta} 4CO_2(g) + 2H_2O(g)$$

How many grams of CO_2 are produced when 54.6 g of C_2H_2 is burned?

SOLUTION

Step 1 **State the given and needed quantities.**

Analyze the Problem

Given	Need
54.6 g of C_2H_2	grams of CO_2
Equation	
$2C_2H_2(g) + 5O_2(g) \xrightarrow{\Delta} 4CO_2(g) + 2H_2O(g) +$ energy	

Step 2 **Write a plan to convert the given to the needed quantity (mole or grams).**

grams of C_2H_2 → [Molar mass] → moles of C_2H_2 → [Mole–mole factor] → moles of CO_2 → [Molar mass] → grams of CO_2

Step 3 **Use coefficients to write mole–mole factors; write molar mass factors if needed.**

1 mole of $C_2H_2 = 26.0$ g of C_2H_2

$$\frac{26.0 \text{ g } C_2H_2}{1 \text{ mole } C_2H_2} \quad \text{and} \quad \frac{1 \text{ mole } C_2H_2}{26.0 \text{ g } C_2H_2}$$

2 moles of $C_2H_2 = 4$ moles of CO_2

$$\frac{2 \text{ moles } C_2H_2}{4 \text{ moles } CO_2} \quad \text{and} \quad \frac{4 \text{ moles } CO_2}{2 \text{ moles } C_2H_2}$$

1 mole of $CO_2 = 44.0$ g of CO_2

$$\frac{44.0 \text{ g } CO_2}{1 \text{ mole } CO_2} \quad \text{and} \quad \frac{1 \text{ mole } CO_2}{44.0 \text{ g } CO_2}$$

Step 4   **Set up the problem to give the needed quantity (moles or grams).**

$$54.6 \text{ g } C_2H_2 \times \frac{1 \text{ mole } C_2H_2}{26.0 \text{ g } C_2H_2} \times \frac{4 \text{ moles } CO_2}{2 \text{ moles } C_2H_2} \times \frac{44.0 \text{ g } CO_2}{1 \text{ mole } CO_2} = 185 \text{ g of } CO_2$$

STUDY CHECK 6.8

Using the equation in Sample Problem 6.8, calculate the grams of CO_2 that can be produced when 25.0 g of O_2 reacts.

QUESTIONS AND PROBLEMS

6.7 Mass Calculations for Reactions

LEARNING GOAL: *Given the mass in grams of a substance in a reaction, calculate the mass in grams of another substance in the reaction.*

6.51 Sodium reacts with oxygen to produce sodium oxide.

$$4Na(s) + O_2(g) \longrightarrow 2Na_2O(s)$$

    a. How many grams of Na_2O are produced when 57.5 g of Na reacts?
    b. If you have 18.0 g of Na, how many grams of O_2 are required for reaction?
    c. How many grams of O_2 are needed in a reaction that produces 75.0 g of Na_2O?

6.52 Nitrogen gas reacts with hydrogen gas to produce ammonia by the following equation:

$$N_2(g) + 3H_2(g) \longrightarrow 2NH_3(g)$$

    a. If you have 3.64 g of H_2, how many grams of NH_3 can be produced?
    b. How many grams of H_2 are needed to react with 2.80 g of N_2?
    c. How many grams of NH_3 can be produced from 12.0 g of H_2?

6.53 Ammonia and oxygen react to form nitrogen and water.

$$4NH_3(g) + 3O_2(g) \longrightarrow 2N_2(g) + 6H_2O(g)$$

    a. How many grams of O_2 are needed to react with 13.6 g of NH_3?
    b. How many grams of N_2 can be produced when 6.50 g of O_2 reacts?
    c. How many grams of water are formed from the reaction of 34.0 g of NH_3?

6.54 Iron(III) oxide reacts with carbon to give iron and carbon monoxide.

$$Fe_2O_3(s) + 3C(s) \longrightarrow 2Fe(s) + 3CO(g)$$

    a. How many grams of C are required to react with 16.5 g of Fe_2O_3?
    b. How many grams of CO are produced when 36.0 g of C reacts?
    c. How many grams of Fe can be produced when 6.00 g of Fe_2O_3 reacts?

6.55 Nitrogen dioxide and water react to produce nitric acid, HNO_3, and nitrogen oxide.

$$3NO_2(g) + H_2O(l) \longrightarrow 2HNO_3(aq) + NO(g)$$

    a. How many grams of H_2O are required to react with 28.0 g of NO_2?
    b. How many grams of NO are obtained from 15.8 g of NO_2?
    c. How many grams of HNO_3 are produced from 8.25 g of NO_2?

6.56 Calcium cyanamide reacts with water to form calcium carbonate and ammonia.

$$CaCN_2(s) + 3H_2O(l) \longrightarrow CaCO_3(s) + 2NH_3(g)$$

    a. How many grams of water are needed to react with 75.0 g of $CaCN_2$?
    b. How many grams of NH_3 are produced from 5.24 g of $CaCN_2$?
    c. How many grams of $CaCO_3$ form if 155 g of water reacts?

6.57 When the ore lead(II) sulfide burns in oxygen, the products are solid lead(II) oxide and sulfur dioxide gas.

    a. Write the balanced equation for the reaction.
    b. How many grams of oxygen are required to react with 29.9 g of lead(II) sulfide?
    c. How many grams of sulfur dioxide can be produced when 65.0 g of lead(II) sulfide reacts?
    d. How many grams of lead(II) sulfide are used to produce 128 g of lead(II) oxide?

6.58 When the gases dihydrogen sulfide and oxygen react, they form the gases sulfur dioxide and water.

    a. Write the balanced equation for the reaction.
    b. How many grams of oxygen are required to react with 2.50 g of dihydrogen sulfide?
    c. How many grams of sulfur dioxide can be produced when 38.5 g of oxygen reacts?
    d. How many grams of oxygen are required to produce 55.8 g of water vapor?

6.8 Percent Yield and Limiting Reactants

In our problems up to now, we assumed that all of the reactants were changed completely to product. Thus, we have calculated the amount of product as the maximum quantity possible, or 100%. While this would be an ideal situation, it does not usually happen. As we run a reaction and transfer products from one container to another, some product is usually lost. In the lab as well as commercially, the starting materials may not be completely pure, and side reactions may use some of the reactants to give unwanted products. Thus, 100% of the desired product is not actually obtained.

When we run a chemical reaction in the laboratory, we measure out specific quantities of the reactants and place them in a reaction flask. We calculate the **theoretical yield** for the reaction, which is the amount of product (100%) we would expect if all the reactants are converted to the desired product. When the reaction ends, we collect and measure the mass of the product, which is the **actual yield** for the product. Because some product is usually lost, the actual yield is less than the theoretical yield. Using the actual yield and the theoretical yield, we can calculate the **percent yield**.

$$\text{Percent yield } (\%) = \frac{\text{Actual yield}}{\text{Theoretical yield}} \times 100\%$$

CONCEPT CHECK 6.9 **Calculating Percent Yield**

For your chemistry class party, you have prepared cookie dough from a recipe that makes 5 dozen cookies. You place dough for 12 cookies on a baking sheet, and place it in the oven. But then the phone rings, and you answer. While you are talking, the cookies on the baking sheet burn and you have to throw them out. You proceed to prepare four more baking sheets with 12 cookies each. If the rest of the cookies are edible, what is the percent yield of cookies you provide for the chemistry party?

ANSWER

The theoretical yield of cookies is 5 dozen or 60 cookies, which is the maximum or 100% of the possible number of cookies. The actual yield is 48 edible cookies, which is 60 cookies minus the 12 cookies that burned. The percent yield is the ratio of 48 edible cookies divided by the theoretical yield of 60 cookies that were possible, multiplied by 100%.

Theoretical yield:	60 cookies possible
Actual yield:	48 cookies to eat
Percent yield:	$\dfrac{48 \text{ cookies (actual)}}{60 \text{ cookies (theoretical)}} \times 100\% = 80\%$

Guide to Calculations for Percent Yield

1 State the given and needed quantities.

2 Write a plan to calculate the theoretical yield and the percent yield.

3 Write the molar mass for the reactant and the mole–mole factor from the balanced equation.

4 Solve for the percent yield ratio by dividing the actual yield (given) by the theoretical yield and multiplying the result by 100%.

SAMPLE PROBLEM 6.9 **Calculating Percent Yield**

On a space shuttle, LiOH is used to absorb exhaled CO_2 from breathing air to form $LiHCO_3$.

$$LiOH(s) + CO_2(g) \longrightarrow LiHCO_3(s)$$

What is the percent yield of the reaction if 50.0 g of LiOH gives 72.8 g of $LiHCO_3$?

On a space shuttle, the LiOH in the canisters removes CO_2 from the air.

SOLUTION

Step 1 **State the given and needed quantities.**

Analyze the Problem

Given	Need
50.0 g of LiOH (reactant)	theoretical yield of $LiHCO_3$
72.8 g of $LiHCO_3$ (actual product)	percent yield of $LiHCO_3$
Equation	
$LiOH(s) + CO_2(g) \longrightarrow LiHCO_3(s)$	

Step 2 **Write a plan to calculate the theoretical yield and the percent yield.**

Calculation of theoretical yield:

grams of LiOH | Molar mass | moles of LiOH | Mole–mole factor | moles of $LiHCO_3$ | Molar mass | grams of $LiHCO_3$ (theoretical yield)

Calculation of percent yield:

$$\text{Percent yield } (\%) = \frac{\text{Actual yield}}{\text{Theoretical yield}} \times 100\%$$

Step 3 **Write the molar mass for the reactant and the mole–mole factor from the balanced equation.**

1 mole of LiOH = 24.0 g of LiOH
$$\frac{1 \text{ mole LiOH}}{24.0 \text{ g LiOH}} \quad \text{and} \quad \frac{24.0 \text{ g LiOH}}{1 \text{ mole LiOH}}$$

1 mole of $LiHCO_3$ = 1 mole of LiOH
$$\frac{1 \text{ mole } LiHCO_3}{1 \text{ mole LiOH}} \quad \text{and} \quad \frac{1 \text{ mole LiOH}}{1 \text{ mole } LiHCO_3}$$

1 mole of $LiHCO_3$ = 68.0 g of $LiHCO_3$
$$\frac{68.0 \text{ g } LiHCO_3}{1 \text{ mole } LiHCO_3} \quad \text{and} \quad \frac{1 \text{ mole } LiHCO_3}{68.0 \text{ g } LiHCO_3}$$

Step 4 **Solve for the percent yield ratio by dividing the actual yield (given) by the theoretical yield and multiplying the result by 100%.**

Calculation of theoretical yield:

$$50.0 \text{ g LiOH} \times \frac{1 \text{ mole LiOH}}{24.0 \text{ g LiOH}} \times \frac{1 \text{ mole } LiHCO_3}{1 \text{ mole LiOH}} \times \frac{68.0 \text{ g } LiHCO_3}{1 \text{ mole } LiHCO_3} = 142 \text{ g of } LiHCO_3 \text{ (theoretical yield)}$$

Calculation of percent yield:

$$\frac{\text{Actual yield (given)}}{\text{Theoretical yield (calculated)}} \times 100\% = \frac{72.8 \text{ g } LiHCO_3}{142 \text{ g } LiHCO_3} \times 100\% = 51.3\%$$

A percent yield of 51.3% means that 72.8 g of the theoretical amount of 142 g of $LiHCO_3$ was actually produced by the reaction.

STUDY CHECK 6.9

For the reaction in Sample Problem 6.9, what is the percent yield if 8.00 g of CO_2 produces 10.5 g of $LiHCO_3$?

Limiting Reactants

When you make peanut butter sandwiches for lunch, you need 2 slices of bread and 1 tablespoon of peanut butter for each sandwich. As an equation, we could write:

2 slices of bread + 1 tablespoon of peanut butter $\longrightarrow$ 1 peanut butter sandwich

If you have 8 slices of bread and a full jar of peanut butter, you will run out of bread after you make 4 peanut butter sandwiches. You cannot make any more sandwiches once the bread is used up, even though there is a lot of peanut butter left in the jar. The number of slices of bread has limited the number of sandwiches you can make.

On a different day, you might have 8 slices of bread but only a tablespoon of peanut butter left in the peanut butter jar. You will run out of peanut butter after you make just 1 peanut butter sandwich with 6 slices of bread left over. The small amount of peanut butter available has limited the number of sandwiches you can make.

8 slices of bread	+	1 jar of peanut butter	make	4 peanut butter sandwiches	+	peanut butter left over
8 slices of bread	+	1 tablespoon of peanut butter	make	1 peanut butter sandwich	+	6 slices of bread left over

The reactant that is used up first is the **limiting reactant**. The other reactant, called the **excess reactant**, is left over.

Bread	Peanut Butter	Sandwiches	Limiting Reactant	Excess Reactant
8 slices	1 full jar	4	bread	peanut butter
8 slices	1 tablespoon	1	peanut butter	bread

CONCEPT CHECK 6.10 **Limiting Reactants**

For a picnic that you are planning, you have 10 spoons, 8 forks, and 6 knives. If each person including yourself requires 1 spoon, 1 fork, and 1 knife, how many people can be served at your picnic?

ANSWER

The relationship of utensils required by each person can be written:

1 person = 1 spoon, 1 fork, and 1 knife

The maximum number of people for each utensil can be calculated as follows:

$$10 \text{ spoons} \times \frac{1 \text{ person}}{1 \text{ spoon}} = 10 \text{ people}$$

$$8 \text{ forks} \times \frac{1 \text{ person}}{1 \text{ fork}} = 8 \text{ people}$$

$$6 \text{ knives} \times \frac{1 \text{ person}}{1 \text{ knife}} = 6 \text{ people} \quad \text{(smallest number of people)}$$

The limiting utensil is 6 knives, which means that 6 people, including yourself, can be at your picnic.

Calculating Moles of Product from a Limiting Reactant

In a similar way, the availability of reactants in a chemical reaction can limit the amount of product that forms. In many reactions, the reactants are not combined in quantities that allow each to be used up at exactly the same time. Consider the reaction in which hydrogen and chlorine form hydrogen chloride:

$$H_2(g) + Cl_2(g) \longrightarrow 2HCl(g)$$

Suppose the reaction mixture contains 2 moles of H_2 and 5 moles of Cl_2. From the equation, we see that 1 mole of hydrogen reacts with 1 mole of chlorine to produce 2 moles of hydrogen chloride. Now we need to calculate the amount of product that is possible from each of the reactants. We are looking for the limiting reactant, which is the one that runs out first, producing the smaller amount of product.

The mole–mole factors from the equation are written as follows:

$$2 \text{ moles of HCl} = 1 \text{ mole of } H_2 \qquad\qquad 2 \text{ moles of HCl} = 1 \text{ mole of } Cl_2$$

$$\frac{2 \text{ moles HCl}}{1 \text{ mole } H_2} \quad \text{and} \quad \frac{1 \text{ mole } H_2}{2 \text{ moles HCl}} \qquad \frac{2 \text{ moles HCl}}{1 \text{ mole } Cl_2} \quad \text{and} \quad \frac{1 \text{ mole } Cl_2}{2 \text{ moles HCl}}$$

Moles of HCl from H_2:

$$2 \text{ moles } H_2 \times \frac{2 \text{ moles HCl}}{1 \text{ mole } H_2} = 4 \text{ moles of HCl } \text{(smaller amount of product)}$$

Moles of HCl from Cl_2:

$$5 \text{ moles } Cl_2 \times \frac{2 \text{ moles HCl}}{1 \text{ mole } Cl_2} = 10 \text{ moles of HCl } \text{(not possible)}$$

In this reaction mixture, H_2 is the limiting reactant. When 2 moles of H_2 are used up, the reaction stops. The excess reactant, 3 moles of Cl_2, is left over and cannot react. We can show the changes in each reactant and the product as follows:

	Reactants			Product
Equation	**H_2**	+	**Cl_2** $\longrightarrow$	**2HCl**
Initial Moles	2 moles		5 moles	0 mole
Moles Used/Formed	−2 moles		−2 moles	+4 moles
Moles Left	0 mole (2 − 2)		3 moles (5 − 2)	4 moles (0 + 4)
Identify As	Limiting reactant		Excess reactant	Product possible

CONCEPT CHECK 6.11   **Moles of Product from Limiting Reactant**

Consider the reaction for the synthesis of methanol (CH_3OH):

$$CO(g) + 2H_2(g) \longrightarrow CH_3OH(g)$$

In the laboratory, 3.00 moles of reactant CO and 5.00 moles of reactant H_2 are combined. Calculate the number of moles of CH_3OH that can form and identify the limiting reactant.

a. What mole–mole equalities will be needed in the calculation?
b. What are the mole–mole factors from the equalities you wrote in **a**?
c. What is the number of moles of CH_3OH from each reactant?
d. What is the liming reactant for the reaction?

TUTORIAL
What Will Run Out First?

TUTORIAL
Limiting Reactant and Yield:
Mole Calculations

ANSWER

a. Two equalities are needed: one for the mole–mole relationship between CO and CH₃OH and another for the mole–mole relationship between H₂ and CH₃OH using the coefficients from the balanced equation.

$$1 \text{ mole of CO} = 1 \text{ mole of CH}_3\text{OH} \qquad 2 \text{ moles of H}_2 = 1 \text{ mole of CH}_3\text{OH}$$

b. From each equality, two mole–mole factors can be written:

$$\frac{1 \text{ mole CH}_3\text{OH}}{1 \text{ mole CO}} \quad \text{and} \quad \frac{1 \text{ mole CO}}{1 \text{ mole CH}_3\text{OH}} \qquad \frac{1 \text{ mole CH}_3\text{OH}}{2 \text{ moles H}_2} \quad \text{and} \quad \frac{2 \text{ moles H}_2}{1 \text{ mole CH}_3\text{OH}}$$

c. Using separate calculations, calculate the moles of CH₃OH that are possible from each of the reactants.

$$3.00 \text{ moles CO} \times \frac{1 \text{ mole CH}_3\text{OH}}{1 \text{ mole CO}} = 3.00 \text{ moles of CH}_3\text{OH}$$

$$5.00 \text{ moles H}_2 \times \frac{1 \text{ mole CH}_3\text{OH}}{2 \text{ moles H}_2} = 2.50 \text{ moles of CH}_3\text{OH}$$

d. The smaller amount, which is 2.50 moles of CH₃OH, is the maximum number of moles of methanol that can be produced. Because this smaller quantity is produced from H₂, the limiting reactant is H₂. Thus, H₂ is the limiting reactant and CO is in excess.

	Reactants			Product
Equation	**CO**	**+**	**2H₂** ⟶	**CH₃OH**
Initial Moles	3.0 moles		5.0 moles	0 mole
Moles Used/Formed	−2.5 moles		−5.0 moles	+2.5 moles
Moles Left	0.5 mole		0 mole	2.5 moles
Identify As	Excess reactant		Limiting reactant	Product possible

TUTORIAL
Limiting Reactant and Yield:
Mass Calculations

A ceramic brake disc in a sports car withstands temperatures of 1400 °C.

Calculating Mass of Product from a Limiting Reactant

The quantities of the reactants can also be given in grams. The calculations to identify the limiting reactant are the same as before, but the grams of each reactant must first be converted to moles. Once the limiting reactant is determined, the smaller number of moles of product is converted to grams using molar mass. This calculation is shown in Sample Problem 6.10.

SAMPLE PROBLEM 6.10   Mass of Product from a Limiting Reactant

When silicon dioxide (sand) and carbon are heated, the products are silicon carbide, SiC, and carbon monoxide. Silicon carbide is a ceramic material, which tolerates extreme temperatures, and is used as an abrasive and in the brake discs of sports cars. How many grams of CO are produced from a mixture of 70.0 g of SiO₂ and 50.0 g of C?

$$\text{SiO}_2(s) + 3\text{C}(s) \xrightarrow{\text{Heat}} \text{SiC}(s) + 2\text{CO}(g)$$

SOLUTION

Step 1   State the given and needed quantities.

Analyze the Problem

Given	Need
70.0 g of SiO₂	grams of CO from limiting reactant
50.0 g of C	
Equation	
$\text{SiO}_2(s) + 3\text{C}(s) \xrightarrow{\text{Heat}} \text{SiC}(s) + 2\text{CO}(g)$	

Step 2 **Use coefficients to write mole–mole factors; write molar mass factors, if needed.**

Guide to Calculating Product from a Limiting Reactant

1 mole of SiO_2 = 60.1 g of SiO_2

$$\dfrac{1 \text{ mole } SiO_2}{60.1 \text{ g } SiO_2} \quad \text{and} \quad \dfrac{60.1 \text{ g } SiO_2}{1 \text{ mole } SiO_2}$$

1 mole of C = 12.0 g of C

$$\dfrac{1 \text{ mole } C}{12.0 \text{ g } C} \quad \text{and} \quad \dfrac{12.0 \text{ g } C}{1 \text{ mole } C}$$

1 State the given and needed quantities.

2 moles of CO = 1 mole of SiO_2

$$\dfrac{2 \text{ moles } CO}{1 \text{ mole } SiO_2} \quad \text{and} \quad \dfrac{1 \text{ mole } SiO_2}{2 \text{ moles } CO}$$

3 moles of C = 2 moles of CO

$$\dfrac{2 \text{ moles } CO}{3 \text{ moles } C} \quad \text{and} \quad \dfrac{3 \text{ moles } C}{2 \text{ moles } CO}$$

2 Use coefficients to write mole–mole factors; write molar mass factors, if needed.

Step 3 **Calculate the number of moles of product from each reactant and determine the limiting reactant.**

$$70.0 \text{ g } SiO_2 \times \dfrac{1 \text{ mole } SiO_2}{60.1 \text{ g } SiO_2} \times \dfrac{2 \text{ moles } CO}{1 \text{ mole } SiO_2} = 2.32 \text{ moles of CO} \quad \text{(smaller amount)}$$

3 Calculate the number of moles of product from each reactant and determine the limiting reactant.

$$50.0 \text{ g } C \times \dfrac{1 \text{ mole } C}{12.0 \text{ g } C} \times \dfrac{2 \text{ moles } CO}{3 \text{ moles } C} = 2.77 \text{ moles of CO}$$

4 Use the molar mass to convert the smaller number of moles of product to grams.

Step 4 **Use the molar mass to convert the smaller number of moles of product to grams.**

1 mole of CO = 28.0 g of CO

$$\dfrac{1 \text{ mole } CO}{28.0 \text{ g } CO} \quad \text{and} \quad \dfrac{28.0 \text{ g } CO}{1 \text{ mole } CO}$$

$$2.32 \text{ moles } CO \times \dfrac{28.0 \text{ g } CO}{1 \text{ mole } CO} = 65.0 \text{ g of CO}$$

STUDY CHECK 6.10

Hydrogen sulfide burns with oxygen to give sulfur dioxide and water. How many grams of sulfur dioxide can be produced from the reaction of 8.52 g of H_2S and 10.6 g of O_2?

QUESTIONS AND PROBLEMS

6.8 Percent Yield and Limiting Reactants

LEARNING GOAL: *Given the actual quantity of product, determine the percent yield for a reaction. Identify a limiting reactant when given the quantities of two or more reactants; calculate the amount of product formed from the limiting reactant.*

6.59 Carbon disulfide is produced by the reaction of carbon and sulfur dioxide.

$$5C(s) + 2SO_2(g) \longrightarrow CS_2(g) + 4CO(g)$$

a. What is the percent yield for carbon disulfide if the reaction of 40.0 g of carbon produces 36.0 g of carbon disulfide?
b. What is the percent yield for carbon disulfide if the reaction of 32.0 g of sulfur dioxide produces 12.0 g of carbon disulfide?

6.60 Iron(III) oxide reacts with carbon monoxide to produce iron and carbon dioxide.

$$Fe_2O_3(s) + 3CO(g) \longrightarrow 2Fe(s) + 3CO_2(g)$$

a. What is the percent yield for iron if the reaction of 65.0 g of iron(III) oxide produces 38.0 g of iron?
b. What is the percent yield for carbon dioxide if a reaction of 75.0 g of carbon monoxide produces 85.0 g of carbon dioxide?

6.61 Aluminum reacts with oxygen to produce aluminum oxide.

$$4Al(s) + 3O_2(g) \longrightarrow 2Al_2O_3(s)$$

Calculate the mass of Al_2O_3 that can be produced if the reaction of 50.0 g of aluminum and excess oxygen has a 75.0% yield.

6.62 Propane (C_3H_8) burns in oxygen to produce carbon dioxide and water.

$$C_3H_8(g) + 5O_2(g) \xrightarrow{\Delta} 3CO_2(g) + 4H_2O(g)$$

Calculate the mass of CO_2 that can be produced if the reaction of 45.0 g of propane and excess oxygen has a 60.0% yield.

6.63 When 30.0 g of carbon is heated with silicon dioxide, 28.2 g of carbon monoxide is produced. What is the percent yield of carbon monoxide for this reaction?

$$3C(s) + SiO_2(s) \xrightarrow{\Delta} SiC(s) + 2CO(g)$$

6.64 When 56.6 g of calcium is reacted with nitrogen gas, 32.4 g of calcium nitride is produced. What is the percent yield of calcium nitride for this reaction?

$$3Ca(s) + N_2(g) \longrightarrow Ca_3N_2(s)$$

6.65 A taxi company has 10 taxis.
a. On a certain day, only eight taxi drivers show up for work. How many taxis can be used to pick up passengers?
b. On another day, 10 taxi drivers show up for work but three taxis are in the repair shop. How many taxis can be driven?

6.66 A clock maker has 15 clock faces. Each clock requires one clock face and two hands.
a. If the clock maker has 42 hands, how many clocks can be produced?
b. If the clock maker has only eight hands, how many clocks can be produced?

6.67 Nitrogen and hydrogen react to form ammonia.

$$N_2(g) + 3H_2(g) \longrightarrow 2NH_3(g)$$

Determine the limiting reactant in each of the following mixtures of reactants:
a. 3.0 moles of N_2 and 5.0 moles of H_2
b. 8.0 moles of N_2 and 4.0 moles of H_2
c. 3.0 moles of N_2 and 12.0 moles of H_2

6.68 Iron and oxygen react to form iron(III) oxide.

$$4Fe(s) + 3O_2(g) \longrightarrow 2Fe_2O_3(s)$$

Determine the limiting reactant in each of the following mixtures of reactants:
a. 2.0 moles of Fe and 6.0 moles of O_2
b. 5.0 moles of Fe and 4.0 moles of O_2
c. 16.0 moles of Fe and 20.0 moles of O_2

6.69 For each of the following reactions, 2.00 moles of each reactant is present initially. Determine the limiting reactant, and calculate the moles of product in parentheses that would form.
a. $2SO_2(g) + O_2(g) \longrightarrow 2SO_3(g)$ (SO_3)
b. $3Fe(s) + 4H_2O(l) \longrightarrow Fe_3O_4(s) + 4H_2(g)$ (Fe_3O_4)
c. $C_7H_{16}(g) + 11O_2(g) \xrightarrow{\Delta}$
$$7CO_2(g) + 8H_2O(g)$$ (CO_2)

6.70 For each of the following reactions, 3.00 moles of each reactant is present initially. Determine the limiting reactant, and calculate the moles of product in parentheses that would form.
a. $4Li(s) + O_2(g) \longrightarrow 2Li_2O(s)$ (Li_2O)
b. $Fe_2O_3(s) + 3H_2(g) \longrightarrow 2Fe(s) + 3H_2O(l)$ (Fe)
c. $Al_2S_3(s) + 6H_2O(l) \longrightarrow$
$$2Al(OH)_3(aq) + 3H_2S(g)$$ (H_2S)

6.71 For each of the following reactions, 20.0 g of each reactant is present initially. Determine the limiting reactant, and calculate the grams of product in parentheses that would be produced.
a. $2Al(s) + 3Cl_2(g) \longrightarrow 2AlCl_3(s)$ ($AlCl_3$)
b. $4NH_3(g) + 5O_2(g) \longrightarrow 4NO(g) + 6H_2O(g)$ (H_2O)
c. $CS_2(g) + 3O_2(g) \longrightarrow CO_2(g) + 2SO_2(g)$ (SO_2)

6.72 For each of the following reactions, 20.0 g of each reactant is present initially. Determine the limiting reactant, and calculate the grams of product in parentheses that would be produced.
a. $4Al(s) + 3O_2(g) \longrightarrow 2Al_2O_3(s)$ (Al_2O_3)
b. $3NO_2(g) + H_2O(l) \longrightarrow$
$$2HNO_3(aq) + NO(g)$$ (HNO_3)
c. $C_2H_5OH(l) + 3O_2(g) \longrightarrow$
$$2CO_2(g) + 3H_2O(g)$$ (H_2O)

6.9 Energy Changes in Chemical Reactions

For a chemical reaction to take place, the molecules of the reactants must collide with each other and have the proper orientation and energy. Even when a collision has the proper orientation, there still must be sufficient energy to break the bonds of the reactants. The **activation energy** is the amount of energy required to break the bonds between atoms of the reactants. If the energy of a collision is less than the activation energy, the molecules bounce apart without reacting. Many collisions occur, but only a few actually lead to the formation of product.

The concept of activation energy is analogous to climbing over a hill. To reach a destination on the other side, we must expend energy to climb to the top of the hill. Once we are at the top, we can easily run down the other side. The energy needed to get us from our starting point to the top of the hill would be the activation energy.

Three Conditions Required for a Reaction to Occur

1. Collision The reactants must collide.
2. Orientation The reactants must align properly to break and form bonds.
3. Energy The collision must provide the energy of activation.

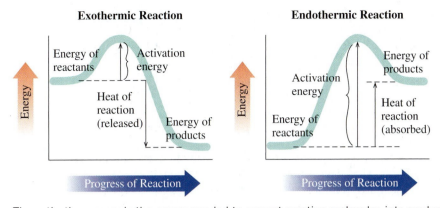

Exothermic Reaction

Energy of reactants

Activation energy

Heat of reaction (released)

Energy of products

Energy

Progress of Reaction

Endothermic Reaction

Activation energy

Energy of reactants

Energy of products

Heat of reaction (absorbed)

Energy

Progress of Reaction

The activation energy is the energy needed to convert reacting molecules into products.

Heat of Reaction

In every chemical reaction, heat is absorbed or released as bonds in the reactants are broken, and new bonds are formed in the products. The **heat of reaction**, symbol ΔH, is the difference between the energy of breaking bonds in the reactants and forming bonds in the products. The direction of heat flow depends on whether the products in the reaction have more or less energy than the reactants.

$$\Delta H = H_{products} - H_{reactants}$$

Exothermic Reactions

In an **exothermic reaction** (*exo* means out), the energy of the reactants is greater than that of the products. Thus, heat is released along with the formation of the products. In an exothermic reaction, the heat of reaction (ΔH) value is written with a negative sign ($-$), indicating that heat is emitted or lost. For example, in the thermite reaction, the reaction of aluminum and iron(III) oxide produces so much heat that temperatures of 2500 °C are reached. The thermite reaction has been used to cut or weld railroad tracks.

Exothermic, Heat Released (Given Off)   **Heat Is a Product**

$$2Al(s) + Fe_2O_3(s) \longrightarrow 2Fe(s) + Al_2O_3(s) + 850 \text{ kJ}$$

$$2Al(s) + Fe_2O_3(s) \longrightarrow 2Fe(s) + Al_2O_3(s) \qquad \Delta H = -850 \text{ kJ}$$

Negative sign

Endothermic Reactions

In an **endothermic reaction** (*endo* means within), the energy of the reactants is lower than that of the products. Thus, heat is absorbed and used to convert the reactants to products. For an endothermic reaction, the heat of reaction can be written on the same side as the reactants. In an endothermic reaction, the heat of reaction (ΔH) value is written with a positive sign ($+$) indicating that heat is absorbed. For example, in the breakdown of water to hydrogen and oxygen, the ΔH is +137 kcal, which is the energy required to break down 2 moles of water into 2 moles of hydrogen and 1 mole of oxygen.

Endothermic, Heat Required   **Heat Is a Reactant**

$$2H_2O(l) + 137 \text{ kcal} \longrightarrow 2H_2(g) + O_2(g)$$

$$2H_2O(l) \longrightarrow 2H_2(g) + O_2(g) \qquad \Delta H = +137 \text{ kcal}$$

Positive sign

Reaction	Energy Change	Heat in the Equation	Sign of ΔH
Exothermic	Heat released	Product side	Negative sign ($-$)
Endothermic	Heat absorbed	Reactant side	Positive sign ($+$)

TUTORIAL
Heat of Reaction

The high temperature of the thermite reaction has been used to cut or weld railroad tracks.

CONCEPT CHECK 6.12   **Exothermic and Endothermic Reactions**

In the reaction of one mole of carbon with oxygen gas, the energy of the carbon dioxide product is 393 kJ lower than the energy of the reactants.

a. Is the reaction exothermic or endothermic?
b. Write the equation for the reaction, including the heat of the reaction.
c. What is the value, in kilojoules, of the ΔH for this reaction?

ANSWER

a. When the energy of the products is lower than that of the reactants, the reaction gives off heat, which means it is an exothermic reaction.
b. In an exothermic reaction, heat is written as a product.

$$C(s) + O_2(g) \longrightarrow CO_2(g) + 393 \text{ kJ}$$

c. The heat of reaction for an exothermic reaction has a negative sign: $\Delta H = -393 \text{ kJ}$

Calculations of Heat in Reactions

The value of ΔH refers to the heat change for the number of moles of each substance in the balanced equation for the reaction. Consider the following decomposition reaction:

$$2H_2O(l) \longrightarrow 2H_2(g) + O_2(g) \qquad \Delta H = +572 \text{ kJ}$$

$$2H_2O(l) + 572 \text{ kJ} \longrightarrow 2H_2(g) + O_2(g)$$

For this reaction, 572 kJ are absorbed by 2 moles of H_2O to produce 2 moles of H_2 and 1 mole of O_2. We can write heat conversion factors for each substance in this reaction:

$$\frac{+572 \text{ kJ}}{2 \text{ moles } H_2O} \qquad \frac{+572 \text{ kJ}}{2 \text{ moles } H_2} \qquad \frac{+572 \text{ kJ}}{1 \text{ mole } O_2}$$

Suppose in this reaction that 9.00 g of H_2O undergoes reaction. We can calculate the heat absorbed as:

$$9.00 \text{ g } H_2O \times \frac{1 \text{ mole } H_2O}{18.0 \text{ g } H_2O} \times \frac{+572 \text{ kJ}}{2 \text{ moles } H_2O} = +143 \text{ kJ}$$

SAMPLE PROBLEM 6.11   **Calculating the Heat in a Reaction**

In the formation of two moles of ammonia, NH_3, from hydrogen and nitrogen, 92.2 kJ of heat is released.

$$N_2(g) + 3H_2(g) \longrightarrow 2NH_3(g) \quad \Delta H = -92.2 \text{ kJ}$$

How much heat, in kilojoules, is released when 50.0 g of ammonia is produced?

Guide to Calculations Using Heat of Reaction (ΔH)

1 State the given and needed quantities.

2 Write a plan using heat of reaction and any molar mass needed.

3 Write the conversion factors including heat of reaction.

4 Set up the problem to calculate the heat.

SOLUTION

Step 1   **State the given and needed quantities.**

Analyze the Problem

Given	Need
50.0 g of ammonia, NH_3	kilojoules produced
$\Delta H = -92.2$ kJ	
Equation	
$N_2(g) + 3H_2(g) \longrightarrow 2NH_3(g)$	

Step 2   **Write a plan using heat of reaction and any molar mass needed.**

grams of NH_3 [Molar mass] moles of NH_3 [Heat of reaction] kilojoules

Step 3 **Write the conversion factors including heat of reaction.**

1 mole of NH_3 = 17.0 g of NH_3		2 moles of NH_3 = −92.2 kJ	
$\dfrac{1 \text{ mole } NH_3}{17.0 \text{ g } NH_3}$ and $\dfrac{17.0 \text{ g } NH_3}{1 \text{ mole } NH_3}$		$\dfrac{-92.2 \text{ kJ}}{2 \text{ moles } NH_3}$ and $\dfrac{2 \text{ moles } NH_3}{-92.2 \text{ kJ}}$	

Step 4 **Set up the problem to calculate the heat.**

$$50.0 \text{ g } NH_3 \times \frac{1 \text{ mole } NH_3}{17.0 \text{ g } NH_3} \times \frac{-92.2 \text{ kJ}}{2 \text{ moles } NH_3} = -136 \text{ kJ}$$

STUDY CHECK 6.11

Mercury(II) oxide decomposes to mercury and oxygen.

$$2HgO(s) \xrightarrow{\Delta} 2Hg(l) + O_2(g) \quad \Delta H = +182 \text{ kJ}$$

a. Is the reaction exothermic or endothermic?
b. How many kilojoules are needed to react 25.0 g of mercury(II) oxide?

Chemistry Link to Health

COLD PACKS AND HOT PACKS

In a hospital, at a first-aid station, or at an athletic event, an instant *cold pack* may be used to reduce swelling from an injury, remove heat from inflammation, or decrease capillary size to lessen the effect of hemorrhaging. Inside the plastic container of a cold pack, there is a compartment containing solid ammonium nitrate (NH_4NO_3) that is separated from a compartment containing water. The pack is activated when it is hit or squeezed hard enough to break the walls between the compartments and cause the ammonium nitrate to mix with the water (shown as H_2O over the reaction arrow). In an endothermic process, one mole of NH_4NO_3 that dissolves absorbs 26 kJ. The temperature drops to about 4–5 °C to give a cold pack that is ready to use.

Endothermic Reaction in a Cold Pack

$$NH_4NO_3(s) + 26 \text{ kJ} \xrightarrow{H_2O} NH_4NO_3(aq)$$

Exothermic Reaction in a Hot Pack

$$CaCl_2(s) \xrightarrow{H_2O} CaCl_2(aq) + 82 \text{ kJ}$$

Hot packs are used to relax muscles, lessen aches and cramps, and increase circulation by expanding capillary size. Constructed in the same way as cold packs, a hot pack contains a salt such as $CaCl_2$. When one mole of $CaCl_2$ dissolves in water, 82 kJ are released. The temperature changes as much as 66 °C to give a hot pack that is ready to use.

Cold packs use an endothermic reaction.

QUESTIONS AND PROBLEMS

6.9 Energy Changes in Chemical Reactions

LEARNING GOAL: *Describe the energy changes in exothermic and endothermic reactions.*

6.73 **a.** Why do chemical reactions require activation energy?
  b. In an exothermic reaction, is the energy of the products higher or lower than that of the reactants?
  c. Draw an energy diagram for an exothermic reaction.

6.74 **a.** What is measured by the heat of reaction?
  b. In an endothermic reaction, is the energy of the products higher or lower than that of the reactants?
  c. Draw an energy diagram for an endothermic reaction.

6.75 Classify the following as exothermic or endothermic reactions:
  a. A reaction releases 550 kJ.
  b. The energy level of the products is higher than that of the reactants.
  c. The metabolism of glucose in the body provides energy.

6.76 Classify the following as exothermic or endothermic reactions:
  a. The energy level of the products is lower than that of the reactants.
  b. In the body, the synthesis of proteins requires energy.
  c. A reaction absorbs 125 kJ.

6.77 Classify the following as exothermic or endothermic reactions and give ΔH for each:
   a. $CH_4(g) + 2O_2(g) \xrightarrow{\Delta} CO_2(g) + 2H_2O(g) + 890 \text{ kJ}$
   b. $Ca(OH)_2(s) + 65.3 \text{ kJ} \longrightarrow CaO(s) + H_2O(l)$
   c. $2Al(s) + Fe_2O_3(s) \longrightarrow$
                       $Al_2O_3(s) + 2Fe(s) + 205 \text{ kcal}$

6.78 Classify the following as exothermic or endothermic reactions and give ΔH for each:
   a. $C_3H_8(g) + 5O_2(g) \xrightarrow{\Delta}$
                       $3CO_2(g) + 4H_2O(g) + 530 \text{ kcal}$
   b. $2Na(s) + Cl_2(g) \longrightarrow 2NaCl(s) + 819 \text{ kJ}$
   c. $PCl_5(g) + 67 \text{ kJ} \longrightarrow PCl_3(g) + Cl_2(g)$

6.79 The equation for the formation of silicon tetrachloride from silicon and chlorine is:

$$Si(s) + 2Cl_2(g) \longrightarrow SiCl_4(g) \quad \Delta H = -657 \text{ kJ}$$

How many kilojoules are released when 125 g of Cl_2 reacts with silicon?

6.80 Methanol (CH_3OH), which is used as a cooking fuel, undergoes combustion to produce carbon dioxide and water.

$$2CH_3OH(l) + 3O_2(g) \xrightarrow{\Delta} 2CO_2(g) + 4H_2O(g)$$
$$\Delta H = -726 \text{ kJ}$$

How many kilojoules are released when 75.0 g of methanol is burned?

CONCEPT MAP

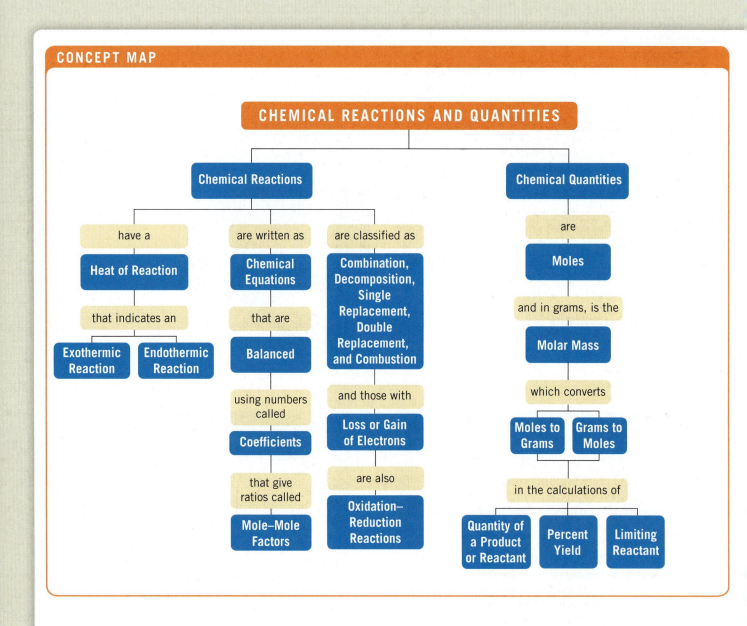

CHAPTER REVIEW

6.1 Equations for Chemical Reactions

LEARNING GOAL: *Write a balanced chemical equation from the formulas of the reactants and products for a chemical reaction.*

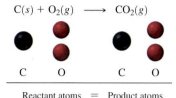

$$C(s) + O_2(g) \longrightarrow CO_2(g)$$

Reactant atoms = Product atoms

- A chemical change occurs when the atoms of the initial substances rearrange to form new substances.
- A chemical equation shows the formulas of the substances that react on the left side of a reaction arrow and the products that form on the right side of the reaction arrow.
- A chemical equation is balanced by writing coefficients, small whole numbers, in front of formulas to equalize the atoms of each of the elements in the reactants and the products.

6.2 Types of Reactions

LEARNING GOAL: *Identify a chemical reaction as a combination, decomposition, single replacement, double replacement, or combustion reaction.*

Single replacement

One element replaces another element

- Many chemical reactions can be organized by reaction type: combination, decomposition, single replacement, double replacement, or combustion.

6.3 Oxidation–Reduction Reactions

LEARNING GOAL: *Define the terms oxidation and reduction; identify the reactant that is oxidized and the reactant that is reduced.*

Oxidation (loss of electron)

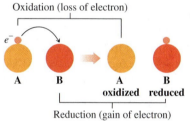

Reduction (gain of electron)

- When electrons are transferred in a reaction, it is an oxidation–reduction reaction.
- The reactant that is oxidized loses electrons, and may also gain oxygen atoms or lose hydrogen atoms.
- The reactant that is reduced gains electrons, and may also lose oxygen atoms or gain hydrogen atoms.
- Overall, the number of electrons lost and gained is equal in any oxidation–reduction reaction.

6.4 The Mole

LEARNING GOAL: *Use Avogadro's number to determine the number of particles in a given amount of moles.*

TABLE 6.5 Number of Particles in One-Mole Samples

Substance	Number and Type of Particles
1 mole of Al	6.02×10^{23} atoms of Al
1 mole of S	6.02×10^{23} atoms of S
1 mole of water (H_2O)	6.02×10^{23} molecules of H_2O
1 mole of vitamin C ($C_6H_8O_6$)	6.02×10^{23} molecules of vitamin C
1 mole of NaCl	6.02×10^{23} formula units of NaCl

- One mole of an element contains 6.02×10^{23} atoms.
- One mole of a compound contains 6.02×10^{23} molecules or formula units.

6.5 Molar Mass

LEARNING GOAL: *Determine the molar mass of a substance and use the molar mass to convert between grams and moles.*

TABLE 6.6 The Molar Mass of Selected Elements and Compounds

Substance	Molar Mass
1 mole of C	12.0 g
1 mole of Na	23.0 g
1 mole of Fe	55.9 g
1 mole of NaF	42.0 g
1 mole of $CaCO_3$	100.1 g
1 mole of $C_6H_{12}O_6$ (glucose)	180.1 g
1 mole of $C_8H_{10}N_4O_2$ (caffeine)	194.1 g

- The molar mass (g/mole) of any substance is the mass in grams equal numerically to its atomic mass, or the sum of the atomic masses, which have been multiplied by their subscripts in a formula.
- The molar mass is used as a conversion factor to change a quantity in grams to moles or to change a given number of moles to grams.

6.6 Mole Relationships in Chemical Equations

LEARNING GOAL: *Given a quantity in moles of reactant or product, use a mole–mole factor from the balanced equation to calculate the moles of another substance in the reaction.*

$$1 \text{ mole of } C_3H_8 = 3 \text{ moles of } CO_2$$

$$\frac{1 \text{ mole } C_3H_8}{3 \text{ moles } CO_2} \quad \text{and} \quad \frac{3 \text{ moles } CO_2}{1 \text{ mole } C_3H_8}$$

- In a balanced equation, the total mass of the reactants is equal to the total mass of the products.
- The coefficients in an equation describing the relationship between the moles of any two components are used to write mole–mole factors.
- When the number of moles for one substance is known, a mole–mole factor is used to find the moles of a different substance in the reaction.

6.7 Mass Calculations for Reactions

LEARNING GOAL: *Given the mass in grams of a substance in a reaction, calculate the mass in grams of another substance in the reaction.*

$$1 \text{ mole of } CO_2 = 44.0 \text{ g of } CO_2$$

$$\frac{44.0 \text{ g } CO_2}{1 \text{ mole } CO_2} \quad \text{and} \quad \frac{1 \text{ mole } CO_2}{44.0 \text{ g } CO_2}$$

- In calculations using equations, molar masses and mole–mole factors are used to change the number of grams of one substance to the corresponding grams of a different substance.

6.8 Percent Yield and Limiting Reactants

LEARNING GOAL: *Given the actual quantity of product, determine the percent yield for a reaction. Identify a limiting reactant when given the quantities of two or more reactants; calculate the amount of product formed from the limiting reactant.*

$$\text{Percent yield (\%)} = \frac{\text{Actual yield}}{\text{Theoretical yield}} \times 100\%$$

- The percent yield of a reaction indicates the percent of product that is actually produced by a reaction.
- The percent yield is calculated by dividing the actual yield in grams of a product by the theoretical yield in grams, which is expressed as a percent.
- A limiting reactant is the reactant in the reaction that produces the smaller amount of product.
- When the mass of two or more reactants is given, the actual mass of a product is calculated from the limiting reactant.

6.9 Energy Changes in Chemical Reactions

LEARNING GOAL: Describe the energy changes in exothermic and endothermic reactions.

- In a reaction, the reacting particles must collide with energy equal to or greater than the energy of activation.
- The heat of reaction is the energy difference between the initial energy of the reactants and the final energy of the products.

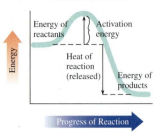

- In an exothermic reaction, the energy of the reactants is greater than that of the products; heat is released and ΔH is negative.
- In an endothermic reaction, the energy of the reactants is lower than that of the products; heat is absorbed and ΔH is positive.

KEY TERMS

activation energy The energy needed upon collision to break the bonds of the reacting molecules.

actual yield The actual amount of product produced by a reaction.

Avogadro's number The number of items in a mole, equal to 6.02×10^{23}.

balanced equation The final form of a chemical equation that shows the same number of atoms of each element in the reactants and products.

chemical equation A shorthand way to represent a chemical reaction using chemical formulas to indicate the reactants and products, and coefficients to show reacting ratios.

chemical reaction The process by which a chemical change takes place.

coefficients Whole numbers placed in front of the formulas to balance the number of atoms or moles of atoms of each element on both sides of an equation.

combination reaction A chemical reaction in which reactants combine to form a single product.

combustion reaction A chemical reaction in which a carbon-containing compound burns in oxygen from the air to produce carbon dioxide, water, and energy.

decomposition reaction A chemical reaction in which a single reactant splits into two or more simpler substances.

double replacement reaction A chemical reaction in which parts of two different reactants exchange places.

endothermic reaction A reaction in which the energy of the reactants is less than that of the products.

excess reactant The reactant that remains when the limiting reactant is used up in a reaction.

exothermic reaction A reaction in which the energy of the reactants is greater than that of the products.

formula unit The group of ions represented by the formula of an ionic compound.

heat of reaction The heat (symbol ΔH) absorbed or released when a reaction takes place.

limiting reactant The reactant used up during a chemical reaction; it limits the amount of product that can form.

molar mass The mass in grams of 1 mole of an element equal numerically to its atomic mass. The molar mass of a compound is equal to the sum of the masses of the elements multiplied by their subscripts in the formula.

mole A group of atoms, molecules, or formula units that contains 6.02×10^{23} of these items.

mole–mole factor A conversion factor that relates the number of moles of two compounds derived from the coefficients in a balanced equation.

oxidation The loss of electrons by a substance. Biological oxidation is indicated by the addition of oxygen or the loss of hydrogen.

oxidation–reduction reaction A reaction in which the oxidation of one reactant is always accompanied by the reduction of another reactant.

percent yield The ratio of the actual yield of a reaction to the theoretical yield possible for the reaction that is multiplied by 100%.

products The substances formed as a result of a chemical reaction.

reactants The initial substances that undergo change in a chemical reaction.

reduction The gain of electrons by a substance. Biological reduction is indicated by the loss of oxygen or the gain of hydrogen.

single replacement reaction A reaction in which an element replaces a different element in a compound.

theoretical yield The maximum amount of product that a reaction can produce from a given amount of reactant.

UNDERSTANDING THE CONCEPTS

The chapter sections to review are shown in parentheses at the end of each question.

6.81 Balance each of the following by adding coefficients; identify the type of reaction for each: (6.1, 6.2)

a.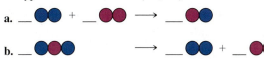

b.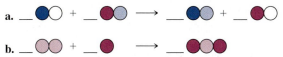

6.82 Balance each of the following by adding coefficients; identify the type of reaction for each: (6.1, 6.2)

a.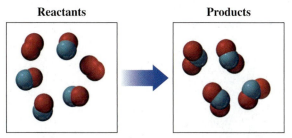

b.

6.83 If red spheres represent oxygen atoms and blue spheres represent nitrogen atoms, (6.1, 6.2)

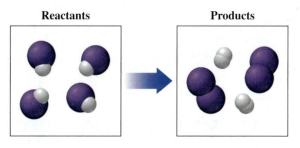

    Reactants   **Products**

a. write the formula for each of the reactants and products.
b. write the balanced equation for the reaction.
c. indicate the type of reaction as combination, decomposition, single replacement, double replacement, or combustion.

6.84 If purple spheres represent iodine atoms and white spheres represent hydrogen atoms, (6.1, 6.2)

    Reactants   **Products**

a. write the formula for each of the reactants and products.
b. write the balanced equation for the reaction.
c. indicate the type of reaction as combination, decomposition, single replacement, double replacement, or combustion.

6.85 If blue spheres represent nitrogen atoms and purple spheres represent iodine atoms, (6.1, 6.2)

    Reactants   **Products**

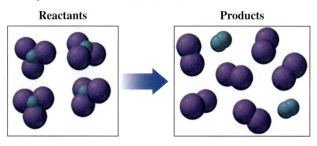

a. write the formula for each of the reactants (solid) and products.
b. write the balanced equation for the reaction.
c. indicate the type of reaction as combination, decomposition, single replacement, double replacement, or combustion.

6.86 If green spheres represent chlorine atoms, yellow-green spheres represent fluorine atoms, and white spheres represent hydrogen atoms, (6.1, 6.2)

    Reactants   **Products**

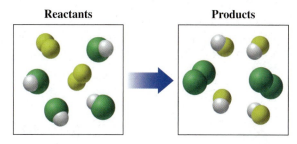

a. write the formula for each of the reactants and products.
b. write the balanced equation for the reaction.
c. indicate the type of reaction as combination, decomposition, single replacement, double replacement, or combustion.

6.87 If green spheres represent chlorine atoms and red spheres represent oxygen atoms, (6.1, 6.2)

    Reactants   **Products**

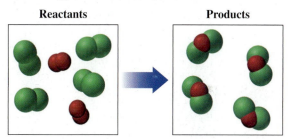

a. write the formula for each of the reactants and products.
b. write the balanced equation for the reaction.
c. indicate the type of reaction as combination, decomposition, single replacement, double replacement, or combustion.

6.88 If blue spheres represent nitrogen atoms and purple spheres represent iodine atoms, (6.1, 6.2)

    Reactants   **Products**

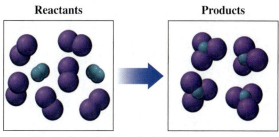

a. write the formula for each of the reactants and products.
b. write the balanced equation for the reaction.
c. indicate the type of reaction as combination, decomposition, single replacement, double replacement, or combustion.

6.89 Using the models of the molecules, (black = C, white = H, yellow = S, green = Cl), determine each of the following: (6.4, 6.5)

1.

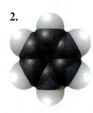

2.

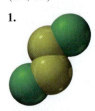

a. molecular formula
b. molar mass
c. number of moles in 10.0 g

6.90 Using the models of the molecules, (black = C, white = H, yellow = S, red = O), determine each of the following: (6.4, 6.5)

1.

2.

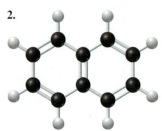

a. molecular formula
b. molar mass
c. number of moles in 10.0 g

6.91 A dandruff shampoo contains dipyrithione, $C_{10}H_8N_2O_2S_2$, an antibacterial and antifungal agent. (6.5)

This dandruff shampoo contains dipyrithione.

a. What is the molar mass of dipyrithione?
b. How many moles of dipyrithione are in 25.0 g?
c. How many moles of carbon are in 25.0 g of dipyrithione?

6.92 Ammonium sulfate, $(NH_4)_2SO_4$, is used in fertilizers to provide nitrogen for the soil. (6.4, 6.5)
a. How many formula units are in 0.200 mole of ammonium sulfate?
b. How many H atoms are in 0.100 mole of ammonium sulfate?
c. How many moles of ammonium sulfate contain 7.4×10^{25} atoms of N?
d. What is the molar mass of ammonium sulfate?

6.93 Propane gas, C_3H_8, a hydrocarbon, is used as a fuel for many barbecues. (6.4, 6.5)
a. How many grams of the compound are in 1.50 moles of propane?
b. How many moles of the compound are in 34.0 g of propane?
c. How many grams of carbon are in 34.0 g of propane?
d. How many atoms of H are in 0.254 g of propane?

6.94 Allyl sulfide, $(C_3H_5)_2S$, is the substance that gives garlic its characteristic odor. (6.4, 6.5)

The characteristic odor of garlic is due to a sulfur-containing compound.

a. How many moles of sulfur are in 23.2 g of $(C_3H_5)_2S$?
b. How many atoms of H are in 0.75 mole of $(C_3H_5)_2S$?
c. How many grams of carbon are in 4.20×10^{23} molecules of $(C_3H_5)_2S$?
d. How many atoms of C are in 15.0 g of $(C_3H_5)_2S$?

ADDITIONAL QUESTIONS AND PROBLEMS

For instructor-assigned homework, go to www.masteringchemistry.com.

6.95 Balance each of the following equations and identify the type of reaction: (6.1, 6.2)
a. $NH_3(g) + HCl(g) \longrightarrow NH_4Cl(s)$
b. $Fe_3O_4(s) + H_2(g) \longrightarrow Fe(s) + H_2O(g)$
c. $Sb(s) + Cl_2(g) \longrightarrow SbCl_3(s)$
d. $C_5H_{12}(g) + O_2(g) \xrightarrow{\Delta} CO_2(g) + H_2O(g)$
e. $KBr(aq) + Cl_2(aq) \longrightarrow KCl(aq) + Br_2(l)$
f. $Al_2(SO_4)_3(aq) + NaOH(aq) \longrightarrow$
$Na_2SO_4(aq) + Al(OH)_3(s)$

6.96 Balance each of the following equations and identify the type of reaction: (6.1, 6.2)
a. $Li_3N(s) \longrightarrow Li(s) + N_2(g)$
b. $Mg(s) + N_2(g) \longrightarrow Mg_3N_2(s)$
c. $Mg(s) + H_3PO_4(aq) \longrightarrow Mg_3(PO_4)_2(s) + H_2(g)$
d. $C_4H_6(g) + O_2(g) \xrightarrow{\Delta} CO_2(g) + H_2O(g)$
e. $Al(s) + Cl_2(g) \longrightarrow AlCl_3(s)$
f. $MgCl_2(aq) + AgNO_3(aq) \longrightarrow$
$Mg(NO_3)_2(aq) + AgCl(s)$

6.97 Predict the products and write a balanced equation for each of the following: (6.1, 6.2)

  a. single replacement:
   $Zn(s) + HCl(aq) \longrightarrow$ _____ + _____

  b. decomposition:
   $BaCO_3(s) \xrightarrow{\Delta}$ _____ + _____

  c. double replacement:
   $NaOH(aq) + HCl(aq) \longrightarrow$ _____ + _____

  d. combination:
   $Al(s) + F_2(g) \longrightarrow$ _____

6.98 Predict the products and write a balanced equation for each of the following: (6.1, 6.2)

  a. decomposition:
   $NaCl(s) \xrightarrow{Electricity}$ _____ + _____

  b. combination:
   $Ca(s) + Br_2(g) \longrightarrow$ _____

  c. combustion:
   $C_2H_4(g) + O_2(g) \xrightarrow{\Delta}$ _____ + _____

  d. double replacement:
   $NiCl_2(aq) + NaOH(aq) \longrightarrow Ni(OH)_2(s) +$ _____

6.99 For each of the following reactions, predict which reactant is oxidized and which reactant is reduced: (6.3)

  a. $Cu(s) + 2H^+(aq) \longrightarrow Cu^{2+}(aq) + H_2(g)$
  b. $Ni^{2+}(aq) + Fe(s) \longrightarrow Fe^{2+}(aq) + Ni(s)$
  c. $2Ag(s) + Cu^{2+}(aq) \longrightarrow 2Ag^+(aq) + Cu(s)$
  d. $3Ni^{2+}(aq) + 2Cr(s) \longrightarrow 3Ni(s) + 2Cr^{3+}(aq)$
  e. $Zn(s) + Cu^{2+}(aq) \longrightarrow Zn^{2+}(aq) + Cu(s)$
  f. $Pb^{2+}(aq) + Zn(s) \longrightarrow Pb(s) + Zn^{2+}(aq)$

6.100 For each of the following reactions, predict which reactant is oxidized and which reactant is reduced: (6.3)

  a. $2Ag(s) + 2H^+(aq) \longrightarrow 2Ag^+(aq) + H_2(g)$
  b. $Mg(s) + Cu^{2+}(aq) \longrightarrow Mg^{2+}(aq) + Cu(s)$
  c. $2Al(s) + 3Cu^{2+}(aq) \longrightarrow 2Al^{3+}(aq) + 3Cu(s)$
  d. $Mg^{2+}(aq) + Zn(s) \longrightarrow Mg(s) + Zn^{2+}(aq)$
  e. $Al^{3+}(aq) + 3Na(s) \longrightarrow Al(s) + 3Na^+(aq)$
  f. $Ni^{2+}(aq) + Mg(s) \longrightarrow Mg^{2+}(aq) + Ni(s)$

6.101 During heavy exercise and workouts, lactic acid, $C_3H_6O_3$, accumulates in the muscles, where it can cause pain and soreness. (6.4, 6.5)

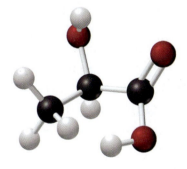

In the ball-and-stick model of lactic acid, black spheres = C, white spheres = H, and red spheres = O.

  a. What is the molar mass of lactic acid?
  b. How many molecules are in 0.500 mole of lactic acid?
  c. How many atoms of C are in 1.50 moles of lactic acid?
  d. How many grams of lactic acid contain 4.5×10^{24} atoms of O?

6.102 Ibuprofen, the anti-inflammatory ingredient in Advil, has the formula $C_{13}H_{18}O_2$. (6.4, 6.5)

Ibuprofen is an anti-inflammatory drug.

  a. What is the molar mass of ibuprofen?
  b. How many molecules are in 0.200 mole of ibuprofen?
  c. How many atoms of H are in 0.100 mole of ibuprofen?
  d. How many grams of ibuprofen contain 7.4×10^{25} atoms of C?

6.103 Calculate the molar mass of each of the following: (6.5)

  a. $ZnSO_4$, zinc sulfate, zinc supplement
  b. $Ca(IO_3)_2$, calcium iodate, iodine source in table salt
  c. $C_5H_8NNaO_4$, monosodium glutamate, flavor enhancer

6.104 Calculate the molar mass of each of the following: (6.5)

  a. $Mg(HCO_3)_2$, magnesium hydrogen carbonate
  b. $Au(OH)_3$, gold(III) hydroxide, used in gold plating
  c. $C_{18}H_{34}O_2$, oleic acid from olive oil

6.105 How many grams are in 0.150 mole of each of the following? (6.5)

  a. K   **b.** Cl_2 **c.** Na_2CO_3

6.106 How many grams are in 2.25 moles of each of the following? (6.5)

  a. N_2 **b.** NaBr   **c.** C_6H_{14}

6.107 How many moles are in 25.0 g of each of the following compounds? (6.5)

  a. CO_2 **b.** $Al(OH)_3$ **c.** $MgCl_2$

6.108 How many moles are in 4.00 g of each of the following compounds? (6.5)

  a. NH_3 **b.** $Ca(NO_3)_2$ **c.** SO_3

6.109 At a winery, glucose ($C_6H_{12}O_6$) in grapes undergoes fermentation to produce ethanol (C_2H_6O) and carbon dioxide. (6.6, 6.7)

$$C_6H_{12}O_6(aq) \longrightarrow 2C_2H_6O(l) + 2CO_2(g)$$
   Glucose   Ethanol

Glucose in grapes ferments to produce ethanol.

  a. How many grams of glucose are required to form 124 g of ethanol?
  b. How many grams of ethanol would be formed from the reaction of 0.240 kg of glucose?

6.110 Gasohol is a fuel that contains ethanol (C_2H_6O), which burns in oxygen (O_2) to give carbon dioxide and water. (6.6, 6.7)
  a. Write the balanced equation for the combustion of ethanol.
  b. How many moles of O_2 are needed to completely react with 4.0 moles of C_2H_6O?
  c. If a car produces 88 g of CO_2, how many grams of O_2 are used up in the reaction?
  d. If you add 125 g of C_2H_6O to your fuel, how many grams of CO_2 and H_2O can be produced from the ethanol?

6.111 When ammonia (NH_3) reacts with fluorine, the products are dinitrogen tetrafluoride and hydrogen fluoride. (6.1, 6.6, 6.7)
  a. Write the balanced equation for the reaction.
  b. How many moles of each reactant are needed to produce 4.00 moles of HF?
  c. How many grams of F_2 are required to react with 25.5 g of NH_3?
  d. How many grams of N_2F_4 can be produced when 3.40 g of NH_3 reacts?

6.112 When peroxide (H_2O_2) is used in rocket fuels, it produces water and oxygen (O_2). (6.1, 6.6, 6.7)
  a. Write the balanced equation for the reaction.
  b. How many moles of peroxide are needed to produce 3.00 moles of water?
  c. How many grams of peroxide are required to produce 36.5 g of O_2?
  d. How many grams of water can be produced when 12.2 g of peroxide reacts?

6.113 Ethane gas, C_2H_6, reacts with chlorine gas, Cl_2, to form hexachloroethane gas, C_2Cl_6, and hydrogen chloride gas. (6.1, 6.6, 6.7)
  a. Write the balanced equation for the reaction.
  b. How many moles of chlorine gas must react to produce 1.60 moles of hexachloroethane?
  c. How many grams of hydrogen chloride are produced when 50.0 g of ethane reacts?
  d. How many grams of hexachloroethane are produced when 50.0 g of ethane reacts?

6.114 Propane gas, C_3H_8, a fuel for many barbecues, reacts with oxygen to produce water and carbon dioxide. Propane has a density of 2.02 g/L at room temperature. (6.1, 6.4, 6.6, 6.7)

Propane is converted to carbon dioxide and water when used as a fuel in a barbecue.

  a. Write the balanced equation for the reaction.
  b. How many grams of water form when 5.00 L of propane gas completely react?
  c. How many grams of CO_2 are produced from 18.5 g of oxygen gas and excess propane?
  d. How many grams of H_2O can be produced from the reaction of 8.50×10^{22} molecules of propane gas?

6.115 Acetylene gas, C_2H_2, burns in oxygen to produce carbon dioxide and water. If 62.0 g of CO_2 is produced when 22.5 g of C_2H_2 reacts with sufficient oxygen, what is the percent yield of CO_2 for the reaction? (6.1, 6.6, 6.7, 6.8)

6.116 When 50.0 g of iron(III) oxide reacts with carbon monoxide, 32.8 g of iron is produced. What is the percent yield of Fe for the reaction? (6.6, 6.7, 6.8)

$$Fe_2O_3(s) + 3CO(g) \longrightarrow 2Fe(s) + 3CO_2(g)$$

CHALLENGE QUESTIONS

6.117 Pentane gas, C_5H_{12}, reacts with oxygen to produce carbon dioxide and water. (6.6, 6.7, 6.8)

$$C_5H_{12}(g) + 8O_2(g) \xrightarrow{\Delta} 5CO_2(g) + 6H_2O(g)$$
Pentane

  a. How many grams of pentane must react to produce 4.0 moles of water?
  b. How many grams of CO_2 are produced from 32.0 g of oxygen and excess pentane?
  c. How many grams of CO_2 are formed if 44.5 g of C_5H_{12} is reacted with 108 g of O_2?

6.118 When nitrogen dioxide (NO_2) from car exhaust combines with water in the air, it forms nitric acid (HNO_3), which causes acid rain, and nitrogen oxide. (6.6, 6.7, 6.8)

$$3NO_2(g) + H_2O(l) \longrightarrow 2HNO_3(aq) + NO(g)$$

  a. How many molecules of NO_2 are needed to react with 0.250 mole of H_2O?
  b. How many grams of HNO_3 are produced when 60.0 g of NO_2 completely reacts?
  c. How many grams of HNO_3 can be produced if 225 g of NO_2 is reacted with 55.2 g of H_2O?

6.119 When a mixture of 12.8 g of Na and 10.2 g of Cl_2 reacts, what is the mass of NaCl that is produced? (6.6, 6.7, 6.8)

$$2Na(s) + Cl_2(g) \longrightarrow 2NaCl(s)$$

6.120 If a mixture of 35.8 g of CH_4 and 75.5 g of S reacts, how many grams of H_2S are produced? (6.6, 6.7, 6.8)

$$CH_4(g) + 4S(g) \longrightarrow CS_2(g) + 2H_2S(g)$$

6.121 The formation of nitrogen oxide, NO, from $N_2(g)$ and $O_2(g)$, requires 21.6 kcal of heat. (6.9)

$$N_2(g) + O_2(g) \longrightarrow 2NO(g) \quad \Delta H = +21.6 \text{ kcal}$$

  a. How many kilocalories are required to form 3.00 g of NO?
  b. What is the complete equation (including heat) for the decomposition of NO?
  c. How many kilocalories are released when 5.00 g of NO decomposes to N_2 and O_2?

6.122 The formation of rust (Fe_2O_3) from solid iron and oxygen gas releases 1.7×10^3 kJ. (6.9)

$$4Fe(s) + 3O_2(g) \longrightarrow 2Fe_2O_3(s) \quad \Delta H = -1.7 \times 10^3 \text{ kJ}$$

a. How many kilojoules are released when 2.00 g of Fe reacts?

b. How many grams of rust form when 150 kcal are released?

c. What is the complete equation (including heat) for the formation of rust?

6.123 Write a balanced equation for each of the following reaction descriptions and identify each type of reaction: (6.1, 6.2)

a. An aqueous solution of lead(II) nitrate is mixed with aqueous sodium phosphate to produce solid lead(II) phosphate and aqueous sodium nitrate.

b. Gallium metal heated in oxygen gas forms solid gallium(III) oxide.

c. When solid sodium nitrate is heated, solid sodium nitrite and oxygen gas are produced.

d. Solid bismuth(III) oxide and solid carbon react to form bismuth metal and carbon monoxide gas.

6.124 A toothpaste contains 0.24% by mass sodium fluoride (NaF) used to prevent dental caries and 0.30% by mass triclosan, $C_{12}H_7Cl_3O_2$, a preservative and antigingivitis agent. One tube contains 119 g of toothpaste. (6.4, 6.5)

 Components in toothpaste include triclosan and NaF.

a. How many moles of NaF are in the tube of toothpaste?

b. How many fluoride ions (F^-) are in the tube of toothpaste?

c. How many grams of sodium ion (Na^+) are in 1.50 g of toothpaste?

d. How many molecules of triclosan are in the tube of toothpaste?

6.125 A gold bar is 2.31 cm long, 1.48 cm wide, and 0.0758 cm thick. (6.4, 6.5)

a. If gold has a density of 19.3 g/mL, what is the mass, in grams, of the gold bar?

b. How many atoms of gold are in the bar?

c. When the same mass of gold combines with oxygen, the oxide product has a mass of 5.61 g. How many moles of O are combined with the gold?

6.126 The gaseous hydrocarbon acetylene, C_2H_2, used in welders' torches, releases a large amount of heat when it burns according to the following equation: (6.6, 6.7, 6.8)

$$2C_2H_2(g) + 5O_2(g) \xrightarrow{\Delta} 4CO_2(g) + 2H_2O(g)$$

a. How many moles of water are produced from the complete reaction of 2.50 moles of oxygen?

b. How many grams of oxygen are needed to react completely with 2.25 g of acetylene?

c. How many grams of carbon dioxide are produced from the complete reaction of 78.0 g of acetylene?

d. If the reaction in part **c** produces 186 g of CO_2, what is the percent yield of CO_2 for the reaction?

6.127 Consider the following equation: (6.1, 6.2, 6.6, 6.7, 6.8)

$$Al(s) + O_2(g) \longrightarrow Al_2O_3(s)$$

a. Balance the equation.

b. Identify the type of reaction.

c. How many moles of oxygen are needed to react with 4.50 moles of Al?

d. How many grams of aluminum oxide are produced when 50.2 g of aluminum reacts?

e. When 13.5 g of aluminum is reacted with 8.00 g of oxygen, how many grams of aluminum oxide can form?

f. If 45.0 g of aluminum and 62.0 g of oxygen undergo a reaction that has a 70.0% yield, what mass of aluminum oxide forms?

6.128 Consider the equation for the reaction of sodium and nitrogen to form sodium nitride. (6.1, 6.2, 6.6, 6.7, 6.8)

$$Na(s) + N_2(g) \longrightarrow Na_3N(s)$$

a. Balance the equation.

b. If 80.0 g of sodium is reacted with 20.0 g of nitrogen gas, what mass of sodium nitride forms?

c. If the reaction in part **b** has a percent yield of 75.0%, how many grams of sodium nitride are actually produced?

ANSWERS

Answers to Study Checks

6.1 $2Al(s) + 3Cl_2(g) \longrightarrow 2AlCl_3(s)$

6.2 $Sb_2S_3(s) + 6HCl(aq) \longrightarrow 2SbCl_3(s) + 3H_2S(g)$

6.3 0.432 mole of H_2O

6.4 0.120 mole of aspirin

6.5 138.1 g/mole

6.6 80.9 g of Ag

6.7 0.945 mole of O_2

6.8 27.5 g of CO_2

6.9 84.7% yield

6.10 14.2 g of SO_2

6.11 a. endothermic   **b.** 10.5 kJ

Answers to Selected Questions and Problems

6.1 a. not balanced   **b.** balanced
     c. not balanced   **d.** balanced

6.3 a. $N_2(g) + O_2(g) \longrightarrow 2NO(g)$
     b. $2HgO(s) \longrightarrow 2Hg(l) + O_2(g)$
     c. $4Fe(s) + 3O_2(g) \longrightarrow 2Fe_2O_3(s)$
     d. $2Na(s) + Cl_2(g) \longrightarrow 2NaCl(s)$
     e. $2Cu_2O(s) + O_2(g) \longrightarrow 4CuO(s)$

6.5 a. $Mg(s) + 2AgNO_3(aq) \longrightarrow Mg(NO_3)_2(aq) + 2Ag(s)$
     b. $CuCO_3(s) \longrightarrow CuO(s) + CO_2(g)$
     c. $C_5H_{12}(g) + 8O_2(g) \xrightarrow{\Delta} 5CO_2(g) + 6H_2O(g)$
     d. $Pb(NO_3)_2(aq) + 2NaCl(aq) \longrightarrow$
$$PbCl_2(s) + 2NaNO_3(aq)$$
     e. $2Al(s) + 6HCl(aq) \longrightarrow 2AlCl_3(aq) + 3H_2(g)$

6.7 a. decomposition reaction
b. single replacement reaction
c. combustion reaction
d. double replacement reaction

6.9 a. single replacement reaction
b. combination reaction
c. decomposition reaction
d. combustion reaction
e. double replacement reaction
f. double replacement reaction

6.11 a. $Mg(s) + Cl_2(g) \longrightarrow MgCl_2(s)$
b. $2HBr(g) \longrightarrow H_2(g) + Br_2(g)$
c. $Mg(s) + Zn(NO_3)_2(aq) \longrightarrow$
$$Zn(s) + Mg(NO_3)_2(aq)$$
d. $K_2S(aq) + Pb(NO_3)_2(aq) \longrightarrow$
$$2KNO_3(aq) + PbS(s)$$
e. $2C_5H_{10}(l) + 15O_2(g) \xrightarrow{\Delta} 10CO_2(g) + 10H_2O(g)$

6.13 a. reduction   **b.** oxidation
c. reduction   **d.** reduction

6.15 a. Zn is oxidized; Cl_2 is reduced.
b. Br^- in NaBr is oxidized; Cl_2 is reduced.
c. The O^{2-} in PbO is oxidized; the Pb^{2+} is reduced.
d. Sn^{2+} is oxidized; Fe^{3+} is reduced.

6.17 a. reduction   **b.** oxidation

6.19 Linoleic acid gains hydrogen atoms and is reduced.

6.21 a. 1.20×10^{23} atoms of Ag
b. 4.52×10^{23} molecules of C_3H_8O
c. 7.53×10^{23} atoms of Cr

6.23 a. 5.42 moles of Al   **b.** 14.1 moles of C_2H_5OH
c. 0.478 mole of Au

6.25 a. 24 moles of H   **b.** 1.0×10^2 moles of C
c. 0.040 mole of N

6.27 a. 3.01×10^{23} atoms of C
b. 7.71×10^{23} molecules of SO_2
c. 0.0867 mole of Fe

6.29 a. 6.00 moles of H   **b.** 8.00 moles of O
c. 1.20×10^{24} atoms of P   **d.** 4.82×10^{24} atoms of O

6.31 a. 188.2 g/mole   **b.** 159.8 g/mole
c. 329.2 g/mole   **d.** 342.3 g/mole
e. 58.3 g/mole   **f.** 365.3 g/mole

6.33 a. 46.0 g   **b.** 112 g
c. 14.8 g   **d.** 112 g

6.35 a. 29.3 g   **b.** 109 g
c. 4.05 g   **d.** 194 g

6.37 a. 602 g   **b.** 11 g

6.39 a. 0.463 mole of Ag   **b.** 0.0167 mole of C
c. 0.882 mole of NH_3 **d.** 1.17 moles of SO_2

6.41 a. 0.78 mole of S   **b.** 1.95 moles of S
c. 0.601 mole of S

6.43 a. 165 g of caffeine   **b.** 0.144 mole of caffeine
c. 1.15 moles of C   **d.** 8.08 g of N

6.45 a. $\dfrac{2 \text{ moles } SO_2}{1 \text{ mole } O_2}$ and $\dfrac{1 \text{ mole } O_2}{2 \text{ moles } SO_2}$

$\dfrac{2 \text{ moles } SO_2}{2 \text{ moles } SO_3}$ and $\dfrac{2 \text{ moles } SO_3}{2 \text{ moles } SO_2}$

$\dfrac{2 \text{ moles } SO_3}{1 \text{ mole } O_2}$ and $\dfrac{1 \text{ mole } O_2}{2 \text{ moles } SO_3}$

b. $\dfrac{4 \text{ moles } P}{5 \text{ moles } O_2}$ and $\dfrac{5 \text{ moles } O_2}{4 \text{ moles } P}$

$\dfrac{4 \text{ moles } P}{2 \text{ moles } P_2O_5}$ and $\dfrac{2 \text{ moles } P_2O_5}{4 \text{ moles } P}$

$\dfrac{5 \text{ moles } O_2}{2 \text{ moles } P_2O_5}$ and $\dfrac{2 \text{ moles } P_2O_5}{5 \text{ moles } O_2}$

6.47 a. 1.0 mole of O_2 **b.** 10. moles of H_2 **c.** 5.0 moles of H_2O

6.49 a. 1.25 moles of C   **b.** 0.96 mole of CO
c. 1.0 mole of SO_2 **d.** 0.50 mole of CS_2

6.51 a. 77.5 g of Na_2O **b.** 6.26 g of O_2 **c.** 19.4 g of O_2

6.53 a. 19.2 g of O_2 **b.** 3.79 g of N_2 **c.** 54.0 g of H_2O

6.55 a. 3.65 g of H_2O **b.** 3.43 g of NO   **c.** 7.53 g of HNO_3

6.57 a. $2PbS(s) + 3O_2(g) \longrightarrow 2PbO(s) + 2SO_2(g)$
b. 6.00 g of O_2
c. 17.4 g of SO_2
d. 137 g of PbS

6.59 a. 70.9%   **b.** 63.2%

6.61 70.8 g of Al_2O_3

6.63 60.4%

6.65 a. Eight taxis can be used to pick up passengers.
b. Seven taxis can be driven.

6.67 a. 5.0 moles of H_2 **b.** 4.0 moles of H_2 **c.** 3.0 moles of N_2

6.69 a. limiting reactant SO_2; 2.00 moles of SO_3
b. limiting reactant H_2O; 0.500 mole of Fe_3O_4
c. limiting reactant O_2; 1.27 moles of CO_2

6.71 a. limiting reactant Cl_2; 25.1 g of $AlCl_3$
b. limiting reactant O_2; 13.5 g of H_2O
c. limiting reactant O_2; 26.7 g of SO_2

6.73 a. The activation energy is the energy required to break the bonds of the reacting molecules.
b. In exothermic reactions, the energy of the products is lower than that of the reactants.
c.

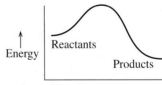

6.75 a. exothermic   **b.** endothermic   **c.** exothermic

6.77 a. exothermic; $\Delta H = -890$ kJ
b. endothermic; $\Delta H = +65.3$ kJ
c. exothermic; $\Delta H = -205$ kcal

6.79 578 kJ are released

6.81 a. 1, 1, 2 combination reaction
  b. 2, 2, 1 decomposition reaction

6.83 a. reactants NO, O_2; product NO_2
  b. $2NO(g) + O_2(g) \longrightarrow 2NO_2(g)$
  c. combination reaction

6.85 a. reactant NI_3; products N_2, I_2
  b. $2NI_3(s) \longrightarrow N_2(g) + 3I_2(g)$
  c. decomposition reaction

6.87 a. reactants Cl_2, O_2; product OCl_2
  b. $2Cl_2(g) + O_2(g) \longrightarrow 2OCl_2(g)$
  c. combination reaction

6.89 1. a. S_2Cl_2 **b.** 135.2 g/mole **c.** 0.0740 mole
   2. a. C_6H_6 **b.** 78.1 g/mole **c.** 0.128 mole

6.91 a. 252 g/mole **b.** 0.0991 mole **c.** 0.991 mole of C

6.93 a. 66.2 g of propane
  b. 0.771 mole of propane
  c. 27.8 g of C
  d. 2.77×10^{22} atoms of H

6.95 a. $NH_3(g) + HCl(g) \longrightarrow NH_4Cl(s)$ Combination
  b. $Fe_3O_4(s) + 4H_2(g) \longrightarrow 3Fe(s) + 4H_2O(g)$
    Single replacement
  c. $2Sb(s) + 3Cl_2(g) \longrightarrow 2SbCl_3(s)$ Combination
  d. $C_5H_{12}(g) + 8O_2(g) \xrightarrow{\Delta} 5CO_2(g) + 6H_2O(g)$
    Combustion
  e. $2KBr(aq) + Cl_2(aq) \longrightarrow 2KCl(aq) + Br_2(l)$
    Single replacement
  f. $Al_2(SO_4)_3(aq) + 6NaOH(aq) \longrightarrow$
    $3Na_2SO_4(aq) + 2Al(OH)_3(s)$ Double replacement

6.97 a. $Zn(s) + 2HCl(aq) \longrightarrow ZnCl_2(aq) + H_2(g)$
  b. $BaCO_3(s) \xrightarrow{\Delta} BaO(s) + CO_2(g)$
  c. $NaOH(aq) + HCl(aq) \longrightarrow NaCl(aq) + H_2O(l)$
  d. $2Al(s) + 3F_2(g) \longrightarrow 2AlF_3(s)$

6.99 a. $Cu^0(s)$ is oxidized and $H^+(aq)$ is reduced.
  b. $Fe^0(s)$ is oxidized and $Ni^{2+}(aq)$ is reduced.
  c. $Ag^0(s)$ is oxidized and $Cu^{2+}(aq)$ is reduced.
  d. $Cr^0(s)$ is oxidized and $Ni^{2+}(aq)$ is reduced.
  e. $Zn^0(s)$ is oxidized and $Cu^{2+}(aq)$ is reduced.
  f. $Zn^0(s)$ is oxidized and $Pb^{2+}(aq)$ is reduced.

6.101 a. 90.1 g/mole
  b. 3.01×10^{23} molecules
  c. 2.71×10^{24} atoms of C
  d. 220 g of lactic acid

6.103 a. 161.5 g/mole **b.** 389.9 g/mole **c.** 169.1 g/mole

6.105 a. 5.87 g **b.** 10.7 g **c.** 15.9 g

6.107 a. 0.568 mole **b.** 0.321 mole **c.** 0.262 mole

6.109 a. 242 g of glucose
  b. 123 g of ethanol

6.111 a. $2NH_3(g) + 5F_2(g) \longrightarrow N_2F_4(g) + 6HF(g)$
  b. 1.33 moles of NH_3 and 3.33 moles of F_2
  c. 143 g of F_2
  d. 10.4 g of N_2F_4

6.113 a. $C_2H_6(g) + 6Cl_2(g) \longrightarrow C_2Cl_6(g) + 6HCl(g)$
  b. 9.60 moles of chlorine
  c. 364 g of HCl
  d. 394 g of hexachloroethane

6.115 81.4%

6.117 a. 48 g of C_5H_{12} **b.** 27.5 g of CO_2 **c.** 92.8 g of CO_2

6.119 16.8 g of NaCl

6.121 a. 1.08 kcal are released
  b. $2NO(g) \longrightarrow N_2(g) + O_2(g) + 21.6$ kcal
  c. 1.80 kcal are required

6.123 a. $3Pb(NO_3)_2(aq) + 2Na_3PO_4(aq) \longrightarrow$
    $Pb_3(PO_4)_2(s) + 6NaNO_3(aq)$ Double replacement
  b. $4Ga(s) + 3O_2(g) \xrightarrow{\Delta} 2Ga_2O_3(s)$ Combination
  c. $2NaNO_3(s) \xrightarrow{\Delta} 2NaNO_2(s) + O_2(g)$ Decomposition
  d. $Bi_2O_3(s) + 3C(s) \longrightarrow 2Bi(s) + 3CO(g)$
    Single replacement

6.125 a. 5.00 g of gold
  b. 1.53×10^{22} atoms of Au
  c. 0.038 mole of oxygen

6.127 a. $4Al(s) + 3O_2(g) \longrightarrow 2Al_2O_3(s)$
  b. combination reaction
  c. 3.38 moles of oxygen
  d. 94.8 g of aluminum oxide
  e. 17.0 g of aluminum oxide
  f. 59.5 g of aluminum oxide

Combining Ideas from Chapters 3 to 6

CI.7 Some of the isotopes of silicon are listed in the following table: (3.4, 3.5, 3.7, 4.2, 4.4, 5.8)

Isotope	% Natural Abundance	Atomic Mass (amu)	Half-Life	Radiation Emitted
$^{27}_{14}Si$		26.99	4.2 s	Positron
$^{28}_{14}Si$	92.23	27.98	Stable	None
$^{29}_{14}Si$	4.67	28.98	Stable	None
$^{30}_{14}Si$	3.10	29.97	Stable	None
$^{31}_{14}Si$		30.98	2.6 h	Beta

a. In the following table, indicate the number of protons, neutrons, and electrons for each isotope listed:

Isotope	Number of Protons	Number of Neutrons	Number of Electrons
$^{27}_{14}Si$			
$^{28}_{14}Si$			
$^{29}_{14}Si$			
$^{30}_{14}Si$			
$^{31}_{14}Si$			

b. What is the electron configuration of silicon?
c. Calculate the atomic mass for silicon, using the isotopes that have a natural abundance.
d. Write the balanced nuclear equations for the decay of $^{27}_{14}Si$ and $^{31}_{14}Si$.
e. Draw the electron-dot formula and predict the shape of $SiCl_4$.
f. How many hours are needed for a sample of $^{31}_{14}Si$ with an activity of 16 μCi to decay to 2.0 μCi?

CI.8 K^+, an electrolyte required by the human body, is found in many foods, and in salt substitutes. One isotope of potassium is $^{40}_{19}K$, which has a natural abundance of 0.012% and a half-life of 1.30×10^9 y, and an activity of 7.0 μCi per gram. The isotope $^{40}_{19}K$ decays to $^{40}_{20}Ca$ or to $^{40}_{18}Ar$. (4.2, 4.3, 4.4, 6.4)

Potassium chloride is used as a salt substitute.

a. Write a balanced nuclear equation for each type of decay.
b. Identify the particle emitted for each type of decay.
c. How many K^+ ions are in 3.5 oz of KCl?
d. What is the activity of 25 g of KCl, in becquerels?

CI.9 Of much concern to environmentalists is the radioactive noble gas radon-222, which can seep from the ground into basements of homes and buildings. Radon-222 is a product of the decay of radium-226 that occurs naturally in rocks and soil in much of the United States. Radon-222, which has a half-life of 3.8 days, decays by emitting an alpha particle. Radon-222, which is a gas, can be inhaled into the lungs where it is strongly associated with lung cancer. Environmental agencies have set the maximum level of radon-222 in a home at 4 pico-curies per liter (pCi/L) of air. (4.2, 4.3, 4.4)

A home detection kit is used to measure the level of radon-222.

a. Write the balanced nuclear equation for the decay of Ra-226.
b. Write the balanced nuclear equation for the decay of Rn-222.
c. If a room contains 24 000 atoms of radon-222, how many atoms of radon-222 remain after 15.2 days?
d. Suppose a room in a home has a volume of 72 000 L (7.2×10^4 L). If the radon level is 2.5 pCi/L, how many alpha particles are emitted in one day?

CI.10 A sterling silver bracelet, which is 92.5% silver by mass, has a volume of 25.6 cm^3 and a density of 10.2 g/cm^3. (1.8, 1.9, 1.10, 3.5, 6.4)

Sterling silver is 92.5% silver by mass.

a. What is the mass, in kilograms, of the bracelet?
b. How many atoms of silver are in the bracelet?
c. Determine the number of protons and neutrons in each of the two stable isotopes of silver: $^{107}_{47}Ag$ and $^{109}_{47}Ag$

CI.11 Consider the loss of electrons by atoms of element X in Group 2A (2), Period 3, and a gain of electrons by atoms of element Y in Group 7A (17), Period 3. (3.6, 3.7, 5.1, 5.2, 5.3, 5.7)

X   Y   Y

a. Which reactant has the higher electronegativity?

b. What are the ionic charges of X and Y in the product?

c. Write the electron configurations of the atoms X and Y.

d. Write the electron configurations of the ions of X and Y.

e. Write the formula and name for the ionic compound formed by the ions of X and Y.

CI.12 The active ingredient in Tums is calcium carbonate. One Tums tablet contains 500. mg of calcium carbonate. (1.8, 1.9, 5.2, 5.3, 5.4, 6.4, 6.5, 6.6)

The active ingredient in Tums neutralizes excess stomach acid.

a. What is the formula for calcium carbonate?

b. What is the molar mass of calcium carbonate?

c. How many moles of calcium carbonate are in one roll of Tums that contains 12 tablets?

d. If a person takes two Tums tablets, how many grams of calcium are obtained?

e. If the daily recommended quantity of Ca^{2+} to maintain bone strength in older women is 1500 mg, how many tablets will supply the needed calcium?

CI.13 Acetone (propanone), a clear liquid solvent with an acrid odor, is used to remove nail polish, paints, and resins. It has a low boiling point and is highly flammable. The combustion of acetone has a ΔH of -28.5 kJ/g. Acetone has a density of 0.786 g/mL. (1.10, 5.5, 5.7, 6.1, 6.2, 6.4, 6.5, 6.7, 6.9)

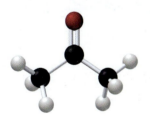

Acetone consists of carbon atoms (black), hydrogen atoms (white), and an oxygen atom (red).

a. What is the molecular formula of acetone?

b. What is the molar mass of acetone?

c. Identify the bonds $C-C$, $C-H$, and $C-O$ in a molecule of acetone as polar covalent or nonpolar covalent.

d. Write the balanced equation for the combustion of acetone.

e. How many grams of oxygen gas are needed to react with 15.0 mL of acetone?

f. How much heat, in kilojoules, is given off for the reaction in part **e**?

CI.14 The compound butyric acid gives rancid butter its characteristic odor. (1.10, 5.5, 5.7, 6.1, 6.2, 6.4, 6.5, 6.7, 6.8)

Butyric acid

Butyric acid produces the characteristic odor of rancid butter.

a. If black spheres are carbon atoms, white spheres are hydrogen atoms, and red spheres are oxygen atoms, what is the formula of butyric acid?

b. What is the molar mass of butyric acid?

c. How many grams of butyric acid contain 3.28×10^{23} atoms of O?

d. How many grams of carbon are in 5.28 g of butyric acid?

e. Butyric acid has a density of 0.959 g/mL at 20 °C. How many moles of butyric acid are contained in 1.56 mL of butyric acid?

f. Write a balanced equation for the combustion of butyric acid with oxygen gas to form carbon dioxide and water.

g. How many grams of oxygen are needed to completely react 1.58 g of butyric acid?

h. What mass of carbon dioxide is formed when 100. g of butyric acid and 100. g of oxygen react?

CI.15 Tamiflu®(Oseltamivir), $C_{16}H_{28}N_2O_4$, is an antiviral drug used to treat influenza. The preparation of Tamiflu begins with the extraction of shikimic acid from the seedpods of the Chinese spice, star anise (*Illicium verum*). From 2.6 g of star anise, 0.13 g of shikimic acid can be obtained and used to produce one capsule containing 75 mg of Tamiflu. The usual adult dosage for treatment of influenza is two capsules of Tamiflu daily for 5 days. (5.5, 5.7, 6.1, 6.2, 6.4, 6.5)

Shikimic acid

Shikimic acid is the basis for the antiviral drug in Tamiflu.

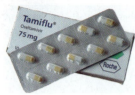

The spice called star anise is a plant source of shikimic acid.

a. What is the formula of shikimic acid?
   (Black spheres = C, white spheres = H, and red spheres = O)
b. What is the molar mass of shikimic acid?
c. How many moles of shikimic acid are contained in 130 g of shikimic acid?
d. How many capsules containing 75 mg of Tamiflu could be produced from 155 g of star anise?
e. What is the molar mass of Tamiflu?
f. How many kilograms of Tamiflu would be needed to treat all the people in a city with a population of 500 000 if each person takes two Tamiflu capsules a day for 5 days?

CI.16 When clothes have stains, bleach is often added to the wash to react with the soil and make the stains colorless.

One brand of bleach contains 5.25% sodium hypochlorite by mass (active ingredient) with a density of 1.08 g/mL. The liquid bleach solution is prepared by bubbling chlorine gas into a solution of sodium hydroxide to produce sodium hypochlorite, sodium chloride, and water. (1.10, 5.2, 5.4, 6.1, 6.4, 6.5, 6.8)

The active component of bleach is sodium hypochlorite.

a. What is the chemical formula and molar mass of sodium hypochlorite?
b. How many hypochlorite ions are present in 1.00 gallon of bleach solution?
c. Write the balanced equation for the preparation of bleach.
d. How many grams of NaOH are required to produce the mass of sodium hypochlorite in 1.00 gallon of bleach?
e. If 165 g of Cl_2 is passed through a solution containing 275 g of NaOH and 162 g of sodium hypochlorite is produced, what is the percent yield of sodium hypochlorite for the reaction?

ANSWERS

CI.7 a.

Isotope	Number of Protons	Number of Neutrons	Number of Electrons
$^{27}_{14}Si$	14	13	14
$^{28}_{14}Si$	14	14	14
$^{29}_{14}Si$	14	15	14
$^{30}_{14}Si$	14	16	14
$^{31}_{14}Si$	14	17	14

b. $1s^22s^22p^63s^23p^2$
c. Atomic mass calculated from the three stable isotopes is 28.09 amu.
d. $^{27}_{14}Si \longrightarrow {}^{27}_{13}Al + {}^{0}_{+1}e$ and $^{31}_{14}Si \longrightarrow {}^{31}_{15}P + {}^{0}_{-1}e$
e.

$$:\ddot{C}l:$$
$$:\ddot{C}l\!-\!Si\!-\!\ddot{C}l: \quad \text{Tetrahedral}$$
$$:\ddot{C}l:$$

f. 7.8 h

CI.9 a. $^{226}_{88}Ra \longrightarrow {}^{222}_{86}Rn + {}^{4}_{2}He$
b. $^{222}_{86}Rn \longrightarrow {}^{218}_{84}Po + {}^{4}_{2}He$
c. 1500 atoms of radon-222 remain.
d. 5.8×10^8 alpha particles

CI.11 a. Y has the higher electronegativity.
b. X^{2+}, Y^-
c. $X = 1s^22s^22p^63s^2$ $Y = 1s^22s^22p^63s^23p^5$
d. $X^{2+} = 1s^22s^22p^6$ $Y^- = 1s^22s^22p^63s^23p^6$
e. $MgCl_2$, magnesium chloride

CI.13 a. C_3H_6O
b. 58.1 g/mole
c. nonpolar covalent bonds: C—C, C—H;
   polar covalent bond: C—O
d. $C_3H_6O(l) + 4O_2(g) \xrightarrow{\Delta} 3CO_2(g) + 3H_2O(g) + energy$
e. 26.0 g of O_2
f. 336 kJ

CI.15 a. $C_7H_{10}O_5$
b. 174.1 g/mole
c. 0.75 mole
d. 59 capsules
e. 312 g/mole
f. 400 kg

Gases

7

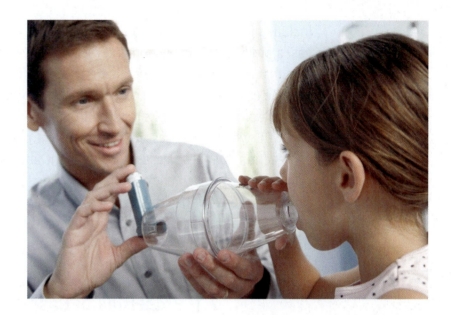

Visit **www.masteringchemistry.com** for self-study materials and instructor-assigned homework.

After soccer practice, Whitney complained that she was having difficulty breathing. Her father quickly took her to the emergency room where she was seen by a respiratory therapist. The respiratory therapist listened to Whitney's chest and then tested her breathing capacity using a spirometer. Based on her limited breathing capacity and the wheezing noise in her chest, Whitney was diagnosed as having asthma.

The therapist gave Whitney a nebulizer containing a bronchodilator that opens the airways and allows more air to go into the lungs. During the breathing treatment, the respiratory therapist measured the amount of oxygen (O_2) in her blood and explained to Whitney and her father that air is a mixture of gases containing 78% nitrogen (N_2) gas and 21% O_2 gas. Because Whitney had difficulty obtaining sufficient oxygen breathing air, the respiratory therapist gave her supplemental oxygen through an oxygen mask. Within a short period of time, Whitney's breathing returned to normal. The therapist then explained that the lungs work according to Boyle's Law: the volume of the lungs increases upon inhalation and the pressure decreases to make air flow in. However, during an asthma attack, the airways become restricted, and it becomes more difficult to expand the volume of the lungs.

Career: Respiratory Therapist

Respiratory therapists assess and treat a range of patients, including premature infants whose lungs have not developed and asthmatics or patients with emphysema or cystic fibrosis. In assessing patients, they perform a variety of diagnostic tests including breathing capacity, concentrations of oxygen and carbon dioxide in a patient's blood, as well as blood pH. In order to treat patients, therapists provide oxygen or aerosol medications to the patient, and chest physiotherapy to remove mucus from their lungs. Respiratory therapists also educate patients on how to correctly use their inhalers.

W e all live at the bottom of a sea of gases called the atmosphere. The most important of these gases is oxygen, which constitutes about 21% of the atmosphere. Without oxygen, life on this planet would be impossible because oxygen is vital to all life processes of plants and animals. Ozone (O_3), formed in the upper atmosphere by the interaction of oxygen with ultraviolet light, absorbs some of the harmful radiation from space before it can strike Earth's surface. The other gases in the atmosphere include nitrogen (78%), argon, carbon dioxide (CO_2), and water vapor. Carbon dioxide gas, a product of combustion and metabolism, is used by plants in photosynthesis, a process that produces the oxygen that is essential for humans and animals.

The atmosphere has become a dumping ground for other gases, such as methane, chlorofluorocarbons (CFCs), and nitrogen oxides, as well as volatile organic compounds (VOCs), which are gases from paints, paint thinners, and cleaning supplies. The chemical reactions of these gases with sunlight and oxygen in the air are contributing to air pollution, ozone depletion, global warming, and acid rain. Such chemical changes can seriously affect our health and our lifestyle. An understanding of gases and the laws that govern gas behavior can help us understand the nature of matter and allow us to make decisions concerning important environmental and health issues.

7.1 Properties of Gases

We are surrounded by gases, but not often aware of their presence. Of the elements on the periodic table, only a few exist as gases at room temperature: H_2, N_2, O_2, F_2, Cl_2, and the noble gases. Another group of gases includes the oxides of the nonmetals on the upper right corner of the periodic table, such as CO, CO_2, NO, NO_2, SO_2, and SO_3. Generally, molecules that are gases at room temperature have fewer than five atoms, which are from elements found in the first or second period.

The behavior of gases is quite different from that of liquids and solids. As we learned in Section 2.4, gas particles are far apart, whereas particles of both liquids and solids are held close together. A gas has no definite shape or volume, and will completely fill any container. As we discussed in Section 5.9, the attractive forces between gas particles are minimal. Thus, there are great distances between gas particles, which make a gas less dense than a solid or liquid, and easy to compress. A model for the behavior of a gas, called the **kinetic molecular theory of gases**, helps us understand gas behavior.

Kinetic Molecular Theory of Gases

1. **A gas consists of small particles (atoms or molecules) that move randomly with high velocities.** Gas molecules moving in random directions at high speeds cause a gas to fill the entire volume of a container.
2. **The attractive forces between the particles of a gas are usually very small.** Gas particles are far apart and fill a container of any size and shape.
3. **The actual volume of the gas molecules is extremely small compared to the volume that the gas occupies.** The volume of the gas is considered equal to the volume of the container. Most of the volume of a gas is empty space, which allows gases to be easily compressed.
4. **Gas particles are in constant motion, moving rapidly in straight paths.** When gas particles collide, they rebound and travel in new directions. Every time they hit the walls of a container, they exert pressure. An increase in the number or force of collisions against the walls of a container causes an increase in the pressure of the gas.

5. **The average kinetic energy of gas molecules is proportional to the Kelvin temperature.** Gas particles move faster as the temperature increases. At higher temperatures, gas particles hit the walls of the container with more force, producing higher pressures.

The kinetic molecular theory of gases helps explain some of the characteristics of gases. For example, we can quickly smell perfume when a bottle is opened on the opposite side of a room because its particles move rapidly in all directions. At room temperatures, the molecules of air are moving at about 450 m/s, which is 1000 mi/h. They move faster at higher temperatures and more slowly at lower temperatures. Sometimes tires and gas-filled containers explode when temperatures are too high. From the kinetic molecular theory of gases, we know that gas particles move faster when heated, hit the walls of a container with more force, and cause a buildup of pressure inside a container.

CONCEPT CHECK 7.1 **Properties of Gases**

Use the kinetic molecular theory of gases to explain each of the following:

a. You can smell the odor of cooking onions from far away.
b. The volume of a balloon filled with helium gas increases when left in the sun.

ANSWER

a. Molecules of gas, which carry the aroma of cooking food, move at high speeds in random directions and great distances to reach you in a different location.
b. Raising the temperature of a gas causes the gas particles to move faster, hitting the walls of the balloon more often and with more force, which increases its volume.

When we talk about a gas, we describe it in terms of four properties: pressure, volume, temperature, and the amount of gas.

Pressure (*P*)

Gas particles are extremely small and move rapidly. When they hit the walls of a container, they exert a **pressure** (see Figure 7.1). If we heat the container, the molecules move faster and smash into the walls more often and with increased force, thus increasing the pressure. The gas particles in the air, mostly oxygen and nitrogen, exert a pressure on us called **atmospheric pressure** (see Figure 7.2). As you go to higher altitudes, the atmospheric pressure decreases because the atmosphere thins out and there are fewer particles in the air. The most common units used for gas pressure measurement are *atmosphere* (atm) and *millimeters of mercury* (mmHg). On the TV weather report, you may hear or see the atmospheric pressure given in inches of mercury, or in countries other than the United States, kilopascals. In a hospital, the unit *torr* may be used.

Volume (*V*)

The volume of gas equals the size of the container in which the gas is placed. When you inflate a tire or a basketball, you are adding more gas particles. The increase in the number of particles hitting the walls of the tire or basketball increases the volume. Sometimes, on a cool morning, a tire looks flat. The volume of the tire has decreased because a lower temperature decreases the speed of the molecules, which in turn reduces the force of their impacts on the walls of the tire. The most common units for volume measurement are liters (L) and milliliters (mL).

Temperature (*T*)

The temperature of a gas is related to the kinetic energy of its particles. For example, if we have a gas at 200 K in a rigid container and heat it to a temperature of 400 K, the gas particles will have twice the kinetic energy that they did at 200 K. This also means that the gas at 400 K exerts twice the pressure of the gas at 200 K. Although you measure gas

FIGURE 7.1 Gas particles move in straight lines within a container. The gas particles exert pressure when they collide with the walls of the container.

Q Why does heating the container increase the pressure of the gas within it?

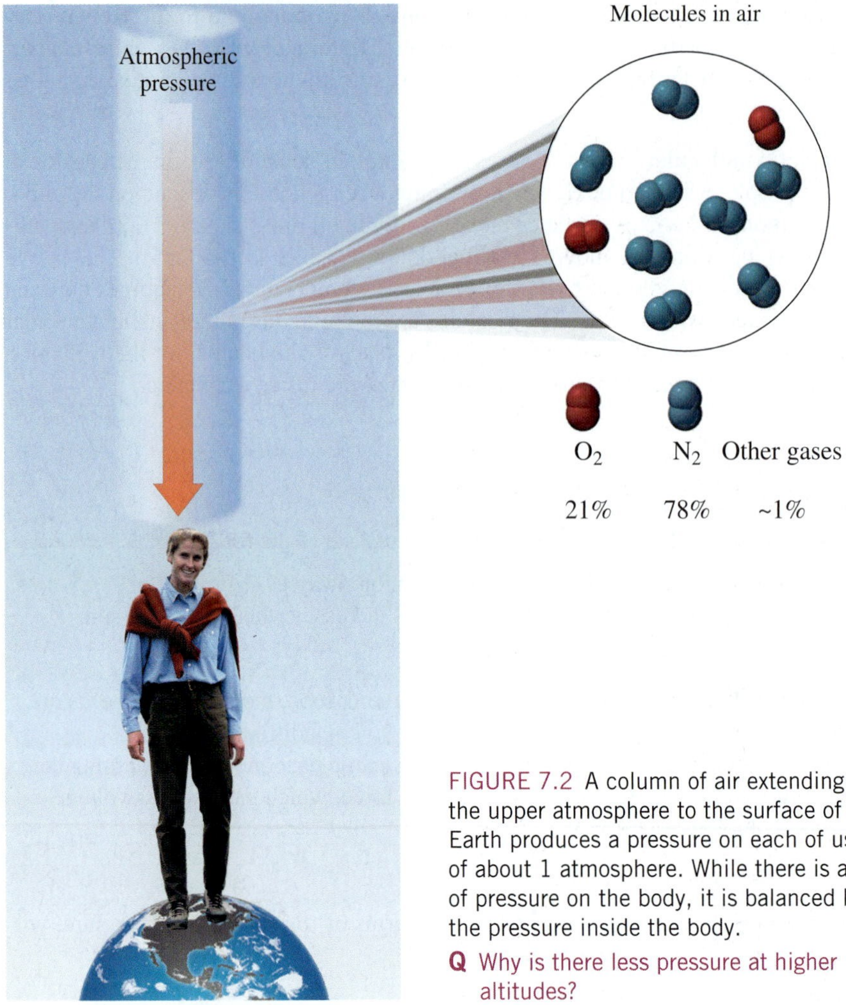

Atmospheric pressure

Molecules in air

O_2 N_2 Other gases

21%   78%   ~1%

FIGURE 7.2 A column of air extending from the upper atmosphere to the surface of the Earth produces a pressure on each of us of about 1 atmosphere. While there is a lot of pressure on the body, it is balanced by the pressure inside the body.

Q Why is there less pressure at higher altitudes?

Explore Your World

FORMING A GAS

Obtain baking soda and a jar or a plastic bottle. You will also need an elastic glove that will fit over the mouth of the jar or a balloon that will fit snugly over the top of the plastic bottle. Place a cup of vinegar in the jar or bottle. Sprinkle some baking soda into the fingertips of the glove or into the balloon. Carefully fit the glove or balloon over the top of the jar or bottle. Slowly lift the fingers of the glove or the balloon so that the baking soda falls into the vinegar. Watch what happens. Squeeze the glove or balloon.

QUESTIONS

1. Describe the properties of gas that you observe as the reaction takes place between vinegar and baking soda.
2. How do you know that a gas was formed?

temperature using a Celsius thermometer, all comparisons of gas behavior and all calculations related to temperature must use the Kelvin temperature scale. No one has yet achieved the conditions for absolute zero (0 K), but we predict that the particles will have zero kinetic energy and exert zero pressure at absolute zero.

Amount of Gas (n)

When you add air to a bicycle tire, you increase the amount of gas, which results in a higher pressure in the tire. Usually, we measure the amount of gas by its mass (grams). In gas law calculations, we need to change the grams of gas to moles.

A summary of the four properties of a gas is given in Table 7.1.

TABLE 7.1 Properties That Describe a Gas

Property	Description	Unit(s) of Measurement
Pressure (P)	The force exerted by gas against the walls of its container	atmosphere (atm); millimeters of mercury (mmHg); torr; pascal (Pa)
Volume (V)	The space occupied by a gas	liter (L); milliliter (mL); cubic meter (m^3)
Temperature (T)	The factor that determines the kinetic energy and rate of motion of gas particles	degree Celsius (°C); kelvin (K) *is required in calculations*
Amount (n)	The quantity of gas present in a container	grams (g); moles (n) *is required in calculations*

SAMPLE PROBLEM 7.1 Properties of Gases

Identify the property of a gas that is described by each of the following:

a. increases the kinetic energy of gas particles
b. the force of the gas particles hitting the walls of the container
c. the space that is occupied by a gas

SOLUTION

a. temperature   **b.** pressure   **c.** volume

STUDY CHECK 7.1

As more helium gas is added to a balloon, the number of grams of helium increases. What property of a gas is described?

QUESTIONS AND PROBLEMS

7.1 Properties of Gases

LEARNING GOAL: Describe the kinetic molecular theory of gases and the properties of gases.

7.1   Use the kinetic molecular theory of gases to explain each of the following:
  a. Gas particles move faster at higher temperatures.
  b. Gases can be compressed much more than liquids or solids.

7.2   Use the kinetic molecular theory of gases to explain each of the following:
  a. A container of nonstick cooking spray explodes when thrown into a fire.
  b. The air in a hot-air balloon is heated to make the balloon rise.

7.3   Identify the property of a gas that is measured in each of the following:
  a. 350 K
  b. 125 mL
  c. 2.00 g of O_2
  d. 755 mmHg

7.4   Identify the property of a gas that is measured in each of the following:
  a. 425 K
  b. 1.0 atm
  c. 10.0 L
  d. 0.50 mole of He

7.2 Gas Pressure

When billions and billions of gas particles hit against the walls of a container, they exert **pressure**, which is defined as a force acting on a certain area.

$$\text{Pressure } (P) = \frac{\text{force}}{\text{area}}$$

The atmospheric pressure can be measured using a barometer (see Figure 7.3). At a pressure of exactly 1 atmosphere (atm), a mercury column in an inverted glass tube would be *exactly* 760 mm high. One **atmosphere (atm)** is defined as *exactly* 760 mmHg (millimeters of mercury). One atmosphere is also 760 torr, a pressure unit named to honor Evangelista Torricelli, the inventor of the barometer. Because the units of torr and mmHg are equal, they are used interchangeably.

1 atm = 760 mmHg = 760 torr (exact)

1 mmHg = 1 torr (exact)

In SI units, pressure is measured in pascals (Pa); 1 atm is equal to 101 325 Pa. Because a pascal is a very small unit, pressures can be reported in kilopascals.

1 atm = 101 325 Pa = 101.325 kPa

LEARNING GOAL

Describe the units of measurement used for pressure, and change from one unit to another.

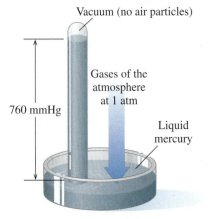

Vacuum (no air particles)

Gases of the atmosphere at 1 atm

760 mmHg

Liquid mercury

FIGURE 7.3 **A barometer:** The pressure exerted by the gases in the atmosphere is equal to the downward pressure of a mercury column in a closed glass tube. The height of the mercury column measured in mmHg is called atmospheric pressure.

Q Why does the height of the mercury column change from day to day?

MC

TUTORIAL
Converting Between Units of Pressure

CASE STUDY
Scuba Diving and Blood Gases

The U.S. equivalent of 1 atm is 14.7 pounds per square inch (psi). When you use a pressure gauge to check the air pressure in the tires of a car, it may read 30–35 psi. This measurement is actually 30–35 psi above the pressure that the atmosphere exerts on the outside of the tire. Table 7.2 summarizes the various units used in the measurement of pressure.

TABLE 7.2 Units for Measuring Pressure

Unit	Abbreviation	Unit Equivalent to 1 atm
Atmosphere	atm	1 atm (exact)
Millimeters of Hg	mmHg	760 mmHg (exact)
Torr	torr	760 torr (exact)
Inches of Hg	in. Hg	29.9 in. Hg
Pounds per square inch	lb/in.^{2} (psi)	14.7 lb/in.^{2}
Pascal	Pa	101 325 Pa
Kilopascal	kPa	101.325 kPa

If you have a barometer in your home, it probably measures pressure in inches of mercury. Atmospheric pressure changes with variations in weather and altitude. On a hot, sunny day, a column of air has more particles, which increases the pressure on the surface of the mercury. The mercury column rises, indicating a higher atmospheric pressure. On a rainy day, the atmosphere exerts less pressure, which causes the mercury column to fall. In the weather report, this type of weather is called a *low-pressure system*. Above sea level, the density of the gases in the air decreases, which causes lower atmospheric pressures; the atmospheric pressure is greater than 760 mmHg at the Dead Sea because it is below sea level and the column of air above it is taller (see Table 7.3).

TABLE 7.3 Altitude and Atmospheric Pressure

Location	Altitude (km)	Atmospheric Pressure (mmHg)
Dead Sea	−0.40	800
Sea level	0.00	760
Los Angeles	0.09	750
Las Vegas	0.70	700
Denver	1.60	630
Mount Whitney	4.50	440
Mount Everest	8.90	250

Divers must be concerned about increasing pressures on their ears and lungs when they dive below the surface of the ocean. Because water is more dense than air, the pressure on a diver increases rapidly as the diver descends. At a depth of 33 ft below the surface of the ocean, an additional 1 atm of pressure is exerted by the water on a diver, for a total of 2 atm. At 100 ft down, there is a total pressure of about 4 atm on a diver. The regulator that a diver carries continuously adjusts the pressure of the breathing mixture to match the increase in pressure.

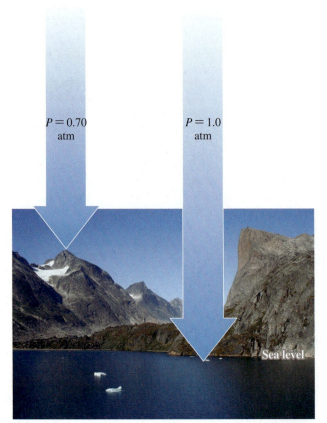

$P = 0.70$ atm

$P = 1.0$ atm

Sea level

The atmospheric pressure decreases as the altitude increases.

CONCEPT CHECK 7.2   **Units of Pressure**

A sample of neon gas has a pressure of 0.50 atm. Calculate the pressure, in mmHg, of the neon.

ANSWER

The equality 1 atm = 760 mmHg can be written as two conversion factors:

$$\frac{760 \text{ mmHg}}{1 \text{ atm}} \quad \text{and} \quad \frac{1 \text{ atm}}{760 \text{ mmHg}}$$

Using the conversion factor that cancels atm and gives mmHg, we can set up the problem as:

$$0.50 \text{ atm} \times \frac{760 \text{ mmHg}}{1 \text{ atm}} = 380 \text{ mmHg}$$

Chemistry Link to Health

MEASURING BLOOD PRESSURE

Your blood pressure is one of the vital signs a doctor or nurse checks during a physical examination. It actually consists of two separate measurements. Acting as a pump, the heart contracts to create the pressure that pushes blood through the circulatory system. During contraction, the blood pressure is at its highest; this is your *systolic* pressure. When the heart muscles relax, the blood pressure falls; this is your *diastolic* pressure. The normal range for systolic pressure is 100–120 mmHg. For diastolic pressure, it is 60–80 mmHg. These two measurements are usually expressed as a ratio such as 100/80. These values are somewhat higher in older people. When blood pressures are elevated, say, 140/90, there is a greater risk of stroke, heart attack, or kidney damage. Low blood pressure prevents the brain from receiving adequate oxygen, causing dizziness and fainting.

The blood pressures are measured by a sphygmomanometer, an instrument consisting of a stethoscope and an inflatable cuff connected to a tube of mercury called a manometer. After the cuff is wrapped around the upper arm, it is pumped up with air until it cuts off the flow of blood through the arm. With the stethoscope over the artery, the air is slowly released from the cuff, decreasing the pressure on the artery. When blood flow first starts again in the artery, a noise can be heard through the stethoscope, signifying the systolic blood pressure as the pressure shown on the manometer. As air continues to be released, the cuff deflates until no sound is heard in the artery. A second pressure reading is taken at the moment of silence and denotes the diastolic pressure, the pressure when the heart is not contracting.

The use of digital blood pressure monitors is becoming more common. However, they have not been validated for use in all situations and can sometimes give inaccurate readings.

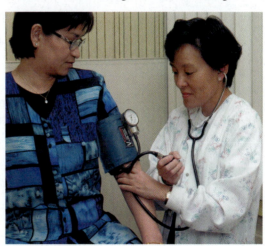

The measurement of blood pressure is part of a routine physical examination.

QUESTIONS AND PROBLEMS

7.2 Gas Pressure

LEARNING GOAL: *Describe the units of measurement used for pressure, and change from one unit to another.*

7.5 What units are used to measure the pressure of a gas?

7.6 Which of the following statement(s) describes the pressure of a gas?
  a. the force of the gas particles on the walls of the container
  b. the number of gas particles in a container
  c. the volume of the container
  d. 3.00 atm   **e.** 750 torr

7.7 An oxygen tank contains oxygen (O_2) at a pressure of 2.00 atm. What is the pressure in the tank in terms of the following units?
  a. torr   **b.** mmHg

7.8 On a climb up Mt. Whitney, the atmospheric pressure is 467 mmHg. What is the pressure in terms of the following units?
  a. atm   **b.** torr

TUTORIAL
Pressure and Volume

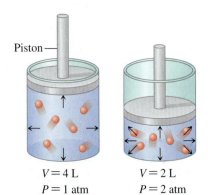

Piston

$V = 4$ L
$P = 1$ atm

$V = 2$ L
$P = 2$ atm

FIGURE 7.4 Boyle's law: As volume decreases, gas molecules become more crowded, which causes the pressure to increase. Pressure (*P*) and volume (*V*) are inversely related.

Q If the volume of a gas increases, what will happen to its pressure?

7.3 Pressure and Volume (Boyle's Law)

Imagine that you can see air particles hitting the walls inside a bicycle tire pump. What happens to the pressure inside the pump as you push down on the handle? As the volume decreases, there is a decrease in the surface area of the container. The air particles are crowded together, more collisions occur, and the pressure increases within the container.

When a change in one property (in this case, volume) causes a change in another property (in this case, pressure), the two properties are related. If the changes occur in opposite directions, the properties have an **inverse relationship**. The inverse relationship between the pressure and volume of a gas is known as **Boyle's law**. The law states that the volume (*V*) of a sample of gas changes inversely with the pressure (*P*) of the gas as long as there has been no change in the temperature (*T*) or amount of gas (*n*), as illustrated in Figure 7.4.

If the volume or pressure of a gas sample changes without any change in the temperature or in the amount of the gas, then the new pressure and volume will give the same *PV* product as the initial pressure and volume. Therefore, we can set the initial and final *PV* products equal to each other.

Boyle's Law

$$P_1 V_1 = P_2 V_2 \quad \text{No change in number of moles and temperature}$$

CONCEPT CHECK 7.3 Boyle's Law

State and explain the reason for the change (*increases*, *decreases*) in the pressure of a gas that occurs in each of the following when *n* and *T* do not change:

	Pressure (*P*)	Volume (*V*)	Amount (*n*)	Temperature (*T*)
a.		decreases	constant	constant
b.		increases	constant	constant

ANSWER

a. When the volume of a gas decreases at constant *n* and *T*, the gas particles are closer together, which increases the number of collisions with the container walls. Therefore, pressure increases when volume decreases with no change in *n* and *T*.

b. When the volume of a gas increases at constant *n* and *T*, the gas particles move farther apart, which decreases the number of collisions with the container walls. Therefore, pressure decreases when the volume increases with no change in *n* and *T*.

	Pressure (*P*)	Volume (*V*)	Amount (*n*)	Temperature (*T*)
a.	increases	decreases	constant	constant
b.	decreases	increases	constant	constant

SAMPLE PROBLEM 7.2 Calculating Pressure When Volume Changes

A sample of hydrogen gas (H_2) has a volume of 5.0 L and a pressure of 1.0 atm. What is the new pressure, in atmospheres, if the volume is decreased to 2.0 L with no change in temperature and the amount of gas?

SOLUTION

Step 1 **Organize the data in a table of initial and final conditions.** In this problem, we want to know the final pressure (P_2) for the change in volume. We place the properties that change, which are the volume and pressure, in a table. The properties that do not change, which are temperature and amount of gas, are shown below the table. Because we are given the initial and final volume of the gas, we know that the volume decreases. We can predict that the pressure will increase. The properties that remain constant, in this case, are temperature (T) and the amount of gas (n).

Analyze the Problem

Conditions 1	Conditions 2	Know	Predict
$V_1 = 5.0$ L	$V_2 = 2.0$ L	V decreases	
$P_1 = 1.0$ atm	$P_2 = ?$ atm		P increases

Factors that remain constant: T and n

Guide to Using the Gas Laws

1 Organize the data in a table of initial and final conditions.

2 Rearrange the gas law equation to solve for the unknown quantity.

3 Substitute values into the gas law equation and calculate.

Step 2   **Rearrange the gas law equation to solve for the unknown quantity.** For a PV relationship, we use Boyle's law and solve for P_2 by dividing both sides by V_2.

$$P_1V_1 = P_2V_2$$

$$\frac{P_1V_1}{V_2} = \frac{P_2V_2}{V_2}$$

$$P_2 = P_1 \times \frac{V_1}{V_2}$$

Step 3   **Substitute values into the gas law equation and calculate.** When we substitute in the values, we see that the ratio of the volumes (volume factor) is greater than 1, which increases the pressure as we predicted in Step 1. Note that the units of volume (L) cancel to give the final pressure in atmospheres.

$$P_2 = 1.0 \text{ atm} \times \frac{5.0 \text{ L}}{2.0 \text{ L}} = 2.5 \text{ atm}$$

Volume factor
increases pressure

STUDY CHECK 7.2

A sample of helium gas has a volume of 150 mL at 750 torr. If the volume expands to 450 mL at constant temperature, what is the new pressure in torr?

SAMPLE PROBLEM 7.3   **Calculating Volume When Pressure Changes**

The gauge on a 12-L tank of compressed oxygen reads 3800 mmHg. How many liters would this same gas occupy at a pressure of 0.75 atm at constant temperature and amount of gas?

SOLUTION

Step 1   **Organize the data in a table of initial and final conditions.** To match the units for initial and final pressures, we can either convert atm to mmHg, or mmHg to atm.

$$0.75 \text{ atm} \times \frac{760 \text{ mmHg}}{1 \text{ atm}} = 570 \text{ mmHg}$$

$$3800 \text{ mmHg} \times \frac{1 \text{ atm}}{760 \text{ mmHg}} = 5.0 \text{ atm}$$

We place the gas data using units of mmHg for pressure and liters for volume in a table. (We could have both pressures in units of atm as well.) We know that pressure decreases. We can predict that the volume increases.

A gauge indicates the pressure in a tank.

Analyze the Problem

Conditions 1	Conditions 2	Know	Predict
$P_1 = 3800$ mmHg (5.0 atm)	$P_2 = 570$ mmHg (0.75 atm)	P decreases	
$V_1 = 12$ L	$V_2 = ?$ L		V increases

Factors that remain constant: T and n

Step 2 **Rearrange the gas law equation to solve for the unknown quantity.** For a *PV* relationship, we use Boyle's law and solve for V_2 by dividing both sides by P_2. According to Boyle's law, a decrease in the pressure will cause an increase in the volume when T and n remain constant.

$$P_1 V_1 = P_2 V_2$$

$$\frac{P_1 V_1}{P_2} = \frac{P_2 V_2}{P_2}$$

$$V_2 = V_1 \times \frac{P_1}{P_2}$$

Step 3 **Substitute values into the gas law equation and calculate.** When we substitute in the values with pressures in units of mmHg or atm, the ratio of pressures (pressure factor) is greater than 1, which increases the volume as predicted in Step 1.

$$V_2 = 12 \text{ L} \times \frac{3800 \text{ mmHg}}{570 \text{ mmHg}} = 80. \text{ L}$$

Pressure factor increases volume

or

$$V_2 = 12 \text{ L} \times \frac{5.0 \text{ atm}}{0.75 \text{ atm}} = 80. \text{ L}$$

Pressure factor increases volume

STUDY CHECK 7.3

In an underground gas reserve, a bubble of methane gas (CH_4) has a volume of 45.0 mL at 1.60 atm. What volume, in milliliters, will it occupy when it reaches the surface where the atmospheric pressure is 745 mmHg, if there is no change in the temperature and amount of gas?

Chemistry Link to Health

PRESSURE–VOLUME RELATIONSHIP IN BREATHING

The importance of Boyle's law becomes more apparent when you consider the mechanics of breathing. Our lungs are elastic, balloon-like structures contained within an airtight chamber called the thoracic cavity. The diaphragm, a muscle, forms the flexible floor of the cavity.

Inspiration

The process of taking a breath of air begins when the diaphragm contracts and the rib cage expands, causing an increase in the volume of the thoracic cavity. The elasticity of the lungs allows them to expand when the thoracic cavity expands. According to Boyle's law, the pressure inside the lungs decreases when their volume increases, causing the pressure inside the lungs to fall below the pressure of the atmosphere. This difference in pressures produces a *pressure gradient* between the lungs and the atmosphere. In a pressure gradient, molecules

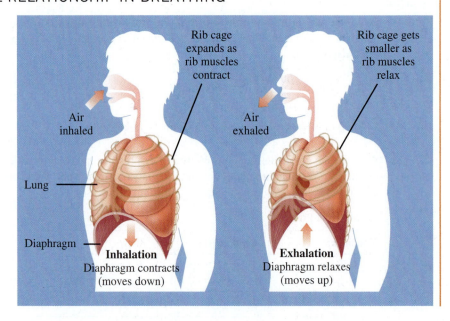

Rib cage expands as rib muscles contract

Rib cage gets smaller as rib muscles relax

Air inhaled

Air exhaled

Lung

Diaphragm

Inhalation
Diaphragm contracts
(moves down)

Exhalation
Diaphragm relaxes
(moves up)

flow from an area of greater pressure to an area of lower pressure. Thus, we inhale as air flows into the lungs (*inspiration*), until the pressure within the lungs becomes equal to the pressure of the atmosphere.

Expiration
Expiration, or the exhalation phase of breathing, occurs when the diaphragm relaxes and moves back up into the thoracic cavity to its

resting position. The volume of the thoracic cavity decreases, which squeezes the lungs and decreases their volume. Now the pressure in the lungs is greater than the pressure of the atmosphere, so air flows out of the lungs. Thus, breathing is a process in which pressure gradients are continuously created between the lungs and the environment because of the changes in the volume.

QUESTIONS AND PROBLEMS

7.3 Pressure and Volume (Boyle's Law)

LEARNING GOAL: Use the pressure–volume relationship (Boyle's law) to determine the new pressure or volume when the temperature and amount of gas are constant.

7.9 Why do scuba divers need to exhale air (and not hold their breath) when they ascend to the surface of the water?

7.10 Why does a sealed bag of chips expand when you take it to a higher altitude?

7.11 The air in a cylinder with a piston has a volume of 220 mL and a pressure of 650 mmHg.
a. To obtain a higher pressure inside the cylinder at constant temperature and amount of gas, should the cylinder change as shown in **A** or **B**? Explain your choice.

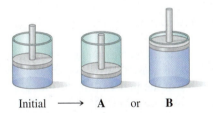

Initial ⟶ **A** or **B**

b. If the pressure inside the cylinder increases to 1.2 atm, what is the final volume, in milliliters, of the cylinder? Complete the following data table:

Property	Conditions 1	Conditions 2	Know	Predict
Pressure (P)				
Volume (V)				

7.12 A balloon is filled with helium gas. When the following changes are made at constant temperature, which of the diagrams (**A**, **B**, or **C**) shows the new volume of the balloon?

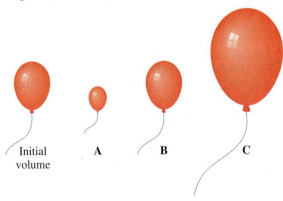

Initial volume   **A**   **B**   **C**

a. The balloon floats to a higher altitude where the outside pressure is lower.

b. The balloon is taken inside the house, but the atmospheric pressure remains the same.
c. The balloon is put in a hyperbaric chamber in which the pressure is increased.

7.13 A gas with a volume of 4.0 L is in a closed container. Indicate what changes (*increases, decreases, does not change*) in pressure must have occurred if the volume undergoes the following changes at constant temperature and amount of gas:
a. The volume is compressed to 2.0 L.
b. The volume expands to 12 L.
c. The volume is compressed to 0.40 mL.

7.14 A gas at a pressure of 2.0 atm is in a closed container. Indicate the changes (*increases, decreases, does not change*) in its volume when the pressure undergoes the following changes at constant temperature and amount of gas:
a. The pressure increases to 6.0 atm.
b. The pressure remains at 2.0 atm.
c. The pressure drops to 0.40 atm.

7.15 A 10.0-L balloon contains helium gas at a pressure of 655 mmHg. What is the new pressure, in mmHg, of the helium gas at each of the following volumes, if there is no change in temperature and amount of gas?
a. 20.0 L   b. 2.50 L   c. 1500. mL

7.16 The air in a 5.00-L tank has a pressure of 1.20 atm. What is the new pressure, in atm, of the air when the air is placed in tanks that have the following volumes, if there is no change in temperature and amount of gas?
a. 1.00 L   b. 2500. mL   c. 750. mL

7.17 A sample of nitrogen (N_2) has a volume of 50.0 L at a pressure of 760. mmHg. What is the volume, in liters, of the gas at each of the following pressures, if there is no change in temperature and amount of gas?
a. 1500 mmHg   b. 4.00 atm   c. 0.500 atm

7.18 A sample of methane (CH_4) has a volume of 25 mL at a pressure of 0.80 atm. What is the volume of the gas at each of the following pressures, if there is no change in temperature and amount of gas?
a. 0.40 atm   b. 2.00 atm   c. 2500 mmHg

7.19 Cyclopropane, C_3H_6, is a general anesthetic. A 5.0-L sample has a pressure of 5.0 atm. What is the volume of the anesthetic given to a patient at a pressure of 1.0 atm with no change in temperature and amount of gas?

7.20 The volume of air in a person's lungs is 615 mL at a pressure of 760. mmHg. Inhalation occurs as the pressure in the lungs drops to 752 mmHg with no change in temperature and amount of gas. To what volume, in milliliters, did the lungs expand?

7.21 Use the words *inspiration* or *expiration* to describe the part of the breathing cycle that occurs because of each of the following:
   a. The diaphragm contracts (flattens out).
   b. The volume of the lungs decreases.
   c. The pressure within the lungs is less than that of the atmosphere.

7.22 Use the words *inspiration* or *expiration* to describe the part of the breathing cycle that occurs because of each of the following:
   a. The diaphragm relaxes, moving up into the thoracic cavity.
   b. The volume of the lungs expands.
   c. The pressure within the lungs is greater than that of the atmosphere.

As a gas in a hot-air balloon is heated, it expands.

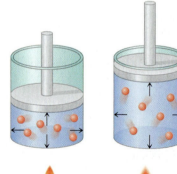

$T = 200$ K $T = 400$ K
$V = 1$ L $V = 2$ L

FIGURE 7.5 **Charles's law:** The Kelvin temperature of a gas is directly related to the volume of the gas when there is no change in the pressure and amount of gas. When the temperature increases, making the molecules move faster, the volume must increase to maintain constant pressure.

Q If the temperature of a gas decreases at constant pressure and amount of gas, how will the volume change?

7.4 Temperature and Volume (Charles's Law)

Suppose that you are going to take a ride in a hot-air balloon. The captain turns on a propane burner to heat the air inside the balloon. As the temperature rises, the air particles move faster and spread out, causing the volume of the balloon to increase. The hot air becomes less dense than the air outside, causing the balloon and its passengers to lift off. In 1787, Jacques Charles, a balloonist as well as a physicist, proposed that the volume of a gas is related to the temperature. This proposal became **Charles's law**, which states that the volume (V) of a gas is directly related to the temperature (T) when there is no change in the pressure (P) or amount (n) of gas (see Figure 7.5). A **direct relationship** is one in which the related properties increase or decrease together. For two conditions, we can write Charles's law as follows:

Charles's Law

$$\frac{V_1}{T_1} = \frac{V_2}{T_2} \qquad \text{No change in number of moles and pressure}$$

All temperatures used in gas law calculations must be converted to their corresponding Kelvin (K) temperatures.

To determine the effect of changing temperature on the volume of a gas, the pressure and the amount of gas are kept constant. If we increase the temperature of a gas sample, we know from the kinetic molecular theory that the motion (kinetic energy) of the gas particles will also increase. To keep the pressure constant, the volume of the container must increase. If the temperature of the gas decreases, the volume of the container must decrease to maintain the same pressure when the amount of gas is constant.

CONCEPT CHECK 7.4   **Charles's Law**

State and explain the reason for the change (*increases*, *decreases*) in the volume of a gas that occurs for the following when P and n do not change:

Temperature (T)	Volume (V)	Pressure (P)	Amount (n)
a. increases		constant	constant
b. decreases		constant	constant

ANSWER

a. When the temperature of a gas increases at constant P and n, the gas particles move faster. To keep the pressure constant, the volume of the container must increase when temperature increases with no change in P and n.

b. When the temperature of a gas decreases at constant P and n, the gas particles move more slowly. To keep the pressure constant, the volume of the container must decrease when the temperature decreases with no change in P and n.

Temperature (T)	Volume (V)	Pressure (P)	Amount (n)
a. increases	increases	constant	constant
b. decreases	decreases	constant	constant

SAMPLE PROBLEM 7.4 **Calculating Volume When Temperature Changes**

A sample of argon gas has a volume of 5.40 L and a temperature of 15 °C. Find the new volume, in liters, of the gas after the temperature increases to 42 °C at constant pressure and amount of gas.

SOLUTION

Step 1 **Organize the data in a table of initial and final conditions.** The properties that change, which are the temperature and volume, are listed in the table. The properties that do not change, which are pressure and amount of gas, are shown below the table. When the temperature is given in degrees Celsius, it must be changed to kelvins. Because we know the initial and final temperatures of the gas, we know that the temperature increases. Thus, we can predict that the volume increases.

$$T_1 = 15 \,°C + 273 = 288 \text{ K}$$
$$T_2 = 42 \,°C + 273 = 315 \text{ K}$$

Analyze the Problem

Conditions 1	Conditions 2	Know	Predict
$T_1 = 288$ K	$T_2 = 315$ K	T increases	
$V_1 = 5.40$ L	$V_2 = ?$ L		V increases

Factors that remain constant: P and n

Step 2 **Rearrange the gas law equation to solve for the unknown quantity.** In this problem, we want to know the final volume (V_2) when the temperature increases. Using Charles's law, we solve for V_2 by multiplying both sides by T_2.

$$\frac{V_1}{T_1} = \frac{V_2}{T_2}$$

$$\frac{V_1}{T_1} \times T_2 = \frac{V_2}{\cancel{T_2}} \times \cancel{T_2}$$

$$V_2 = V_1 \times \frac{T_2}{T_1}$$

Step 3 **Substitute values into the gas law equation and calculate.** We see that the temperature has increased. Because temperature is directly related to volume, the volume must increase. When we substitute in the values, we see that the ratio of the temperatures (temperature factor) is greater than 1, which increases the volume, as predicted in Step 1.

$$V_2 = 5.40 \text{ L} \times \frac{315 \text{ K}}{288 \text{ K}} = 5.91 \text{ L}$$

Temperature factor
increases volume

STUDY CHECK 7.4

A mountain climber with a body temperature of 37 °C inhales 486 mL of air at a temperature of −8 °C. What volume, in milliliters, will the air occupy in the lungs, if the pressure and amount of gas do not change?

Chemistry Link to the Environment

GREENHOUSE GASES

The term *greenhouse gases* was first used during the early 1800s for the gases in the atmosphere that trap heat. Among the greenhouse gases are carbon dioxide (CO_2), methane (CH_4), dinitrogen oxide (N_2O), and chlorofluorocarbons (CFCs). The molecules of greenhouse gases consist of more than two atoms that vibrate when heat is absorbed. By contrast, oxygen and nitrogen do not trap heat and are not greenhouse gases. Because the two atoms in their molecules are so tightly bonded, they do not absorb heat.

Greenhouse gases are beneficial in keeping the average surface temperature of the Earth at 15 °C. Without greenhouse gases, it is estimated that the average surface temperature of Earth would be −18 °C. Most scientists say that the concentration of greenhouse gases in the atmosphere and the surface temperature of Earth are increasing because of human activities. As we discussed in Section 2.2, the increase in atmospheric carbon dioxide is mostly a result of the burning of fossil fuels and wood.

Methane (CH_4) is a colorless, odorless gas that is released by livestock, rice farming, the decomposition of organic plant material in landfills, and the mining, drilling, and transport of coal and oil. The contribution from livestock comes from the breakdown of organic material in the digestive tracts of cows, sheep, and camels. The level of methane in the atmosphere has increased about 150% since industrialization. In one year, as much as 5×10^{11} kg of methane are added to the atmosphere. Livestock produce about 20% of the greenhouse gases. In one day, one cow emits about 200 g of methane. For a global population of 1.5 billion livestock, a total of 3×10^8 kg of methane is produced every day. In the past few years, methane levels have stabilized due to improvements in the recovery of methane. Methane remains in the atmosphere for about ten years, but its molecular structure causes it to trap 20 times more heat than does carbon dioxide.

Dinitrogen oxide (N_2O), commonly called nitrous oxide, is a colorless greenhouse gas that has a sweet odor. Most people recognize it as an anesthetic used in dentistry called "laughing gas." Although some dinitrogen oxide is released naturally from soil bacteria, its major sources are from agricultural and industrial processes. Atmospheric dinitrogen oxide has increased by about 15% since industrialization, caused by the extensive use of fertilizers, sewage treatment plants, and car exhaust. Each year, 1×10^{10} kg of dinitrogen oxide is added to the atmosphere. Dinitrogen oxide released today will remain in the atmosphere for about 150–180 years, where it has a greenhouse effect that is 300 times greater than that of carbon dioxide.

Chlorofluorinated gases (CFCs) are synthetic compounds containing chlorine, fluorine, and carbon. Chlorofluorocarbons were used as propellants in aerosol cans and as refrigerants in refrigerators and air conditioners. During the 1970s, scientists determined that CFCs in the atmosphere were destroying the protective ozone layer. Since then, many countries have banned the production and use of CFCs, and their levels in the atmosphere have declined slightly. Hydrofluorocarbons (HFCs), in which hydrogen atoms replace chlorine atoms, are now used as refrigerants. Although HFCs do not destroy the ozone layer, they are greenhouse gases because they trap heat in the atmosphere.

Based on current trends and climate models, scientists estimate that levels of atmospheric carbon dioxide will increase by about 2% each year up through 2025. As long as the greenhouse gases trap more heat than is reflected back into space, average surface temperatures on Earth will continue to rise. Efforts are taking place around the world to slow or decrease the emissions of greenhouse gases into the atmosphere. It is anticipated that temperatures will stabilize only when the amount of energy that reaches the surface of Earth is equal to the heat that is reflected back into space.

In 2007, former U.S. Vice President Al Gore and the United Nations Panel on Climate Change were awarded the Nobel Peace Prize for increasing global awareness of the relationship between human activities and global warming.

Percentages of Greenhouse Gases in the Atmosphere

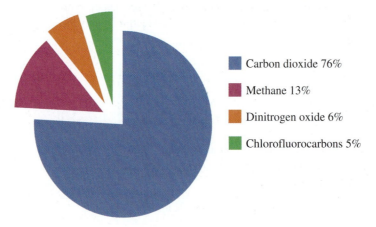

- Carbon dioxide 76%
- Methane 13%
- Dinitrogen oxide 6%
- Chlorofluorocarbons 5%

QUESTIONS AND PROBLEMS

7.4 Temperature and Volume (Charles's Law)

LEARNING GOAL: *Use the temperature–volume relationship (Charles's law) to determine the new temperature or volume when the pressure and amount of gas are constant.*

7.23 Select the diagram that shows the new volume of a balloon when the following changes are made at constant pressure:

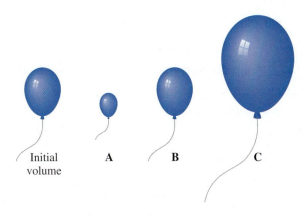

Initial volume   **A**   **B**   **C**

a. The temperature is changed from 100 K to 300 K.
b. The balloon is placed in a freezer.
c. The balloon is first warmed, and then returned to its starting temperature.

7.24 Indicate whether the final volume in each of the following is *the same*, *larger*, or *smaller* than the initial volume, if pressure and amount of gas do not change:
a. A volume of 505 mL of air on a cold winter day at $-15\ °C$ is breathed into the lungs, when body temperature is 37 °C.
b. The heater used to heat the air in a hot-air balloon is turned off.
c. A balloon filled with helium at the amusement park is left in a car on a hot day.

7.25 A sample of neon initially has a volume of 2.50 L at 15 °C. What final temperature, in degrees Celsius, is needed to change the volume of the gas to each of the following, if P and n do not change?
a. 5.00 L   b. 1250 mL   c. 7.50 L   d. 3550 mL

7.26 A gas has a volume of 4.00 L at 0 °C. What final temperature, in degrees Celsius, is needed to change the volume of the gas to each of the following, if P and n do not change?
a. 1.50 L   b. 1200 mL   c. 250 L   d. 50.0 mL

7.27 A balloon contains 2500 mL of helium gas at 75 °C. What is the final volume, in milliliters, of the gas when the temperature changes to each of the following, if P and n do not change?
a. 55 °C   b. 680. K   c. $-25\ °C$ d. 240. K

7.28 An air bubble has a volume of 0.500 L at 18 °C. What is the final volume, in liters, of the gas when the temperature changes to each of the following, if P and n do not change?
a. 0 °C   b. 425 K   c. $-12\ °C$ d. 575 K

7.5 Temperature and Pressure (Gay-Lussac's Law)

If we could observe the molecules of a gas as the temperature rises, we would notice that they move faster and hit the sides of the container more often and with greater force. If we maintain a constant volume and amount of gas, the pressure will increase. In the temperature–pressure relationship known as **Gay-Lussac's law**, the pressure of a gas is directly related to its Kelvin temperature. This means that an increase in temperature increases the pressure of a gas, and a decrease in temperature decreases the pressure of the gas as long as the volume and amount of gas do not change (see Figure 7.6).

Gay-Lussac's Law

$$\frac{P_1}{T_1} = \frac{P_2}{T_2}$$ No change in number of moles and volume

All temperatures used in gas law calculations must be converted to their corresponding Kelvin (K) temperatures.

CONCEPT CHECK 7.5   **Gay-Lussac's Law**

State and explain the reason for the change (*increases*, *decreases*) in the pressure of a gas that occurs for the following when V and n do not change:

Temperature (T)	Pressure (P)	Volume (V)	Amount (n)
a. increases		constant	constant
b. decreases		constant	constant

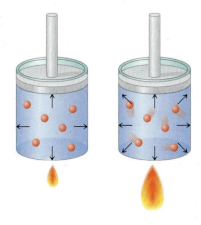

$T = 200\ K$ $T = 400\ K$
$P = 1\ atm$ $P = 2\ atm$

FIGURE 7.6 **Gay-Lussac's law:** When the Kelvin temperature of a gas doubles at constant volume and amount of gas, the pressure also doubles.

Q How does a decrease in the temperature of a gas affect its pressure at constant volume and amount of gas?

(MC)

TUTORIAL
Temperature and Pressure

ANSWER

a. When the temperature of a gas increases with no change in V and n, the particles of gas move faster. When the volume does not change, the gas particles collide more often with the container walls and with more force, increasing the pressure.

b. When the temperature of a gas decreases at constant V and n, the particles of gas move slower. When the volume does not change, the gas particles do not collide as often with the container walls and with less force, decreasing the pressure.

	Temperature (T)	Pressure (P)	Volume (V)	Amount (n)
a.	increases	increases	constant	constant
b.	decreases	decreases	constant	constant

SAMPLE PROBLEM 7.5 Calculating Pressure When Temperature Changes

Aerosol containers can be dangerous if they are heated, because they can explode. Suppose a container of hair spray with a pressure of 4.0 atm at a room temperature of 25 °C is thrown into a fire. If the temperature of the gas inside the aerosol can reaches 402 °C, what will be its pressure in atmospheres? The aerosol container may explode if the pressure inside exceeds 8.0 atm. Would you expect it to explode?

SOLUTION

Step 1 **Organize the data in a table of initial and final conditions.** We list the properties that change, which are the pressure and temperature, in a table. The properties that do not change, which are volume and amount of gas, are shown below the table. The temperatures given in degrees Celsius must be changed to kelvins. Because we know the initial and final temperatures of the gas, we know that the temperature increases. Thus, we can predict that the pressure increases.

$$T_1 = 25\,°C + 273 = 298\ K$$
$$T_2 = 402\,°C + 273 = 675\ K$$

Analyze the Problem

Conditions 1	Conditions 2	Know	Predict
$P_1 = 4.0$ atm	$P_2 = ?$ atm		P increases
$T_1 = 298$ K	$T_2 = 675$ K	T increases	

Factors that remain constant: V and n

Step 2 **Rearrange the gas law equation to solve for the unknown quantity.** Using Gay-Lussac's law, we can solve for P_2 by multiplying both sides by T_2.

$$\frac{P_1}{T_1} = \frac{P_2}{T_2}$$

$$\frac{P_1}{T_1} \times T_2 = \frac{P_2}{\cancel{T_2}} \times \cancel{T_2}$$

$$P_2 = P_1 \times \frac{T_2}{T_1}$$

Step 3 **Substitute values into the gas law equation and calculate.** When we substitute in the values, we see that the ratio of the temperatures (temperature factor) is greater than 1, which increases pressure as predicted in Step 1.

$$P_2 = 4.0 \text{ atm} \times \frac{675\ \cancel{K}}{298\ \cancel{K}} = 9.1 \text{ atm}$$

Temperature factor
increases pressure

Because the calculated pressure of 9.1 atm exceeds the limit of 8.0 atm for the can, we would expect the can to explode.

STUDY CHECK 7.5

In a storage area where the temperature has reached 55 °C, the pressure of oxygen gas in a 15.0-L steel cylinder is 965 torr. To what temperature, in degrees Celsius, would the gas have to be cooled to reduce the pressure to 850. torr?

Vapor Pressure and Boiling Point

In Section 2.4, we learned that liquid molecules with sufficient kinetic energy can break away from the surface of the liquid to become gas particles or vapor. In an open container, all the liquid will eventually evaporate. In a closed container, the vapor accumulates and creates pressure called **vapor pressure**. Each liquid exerts its own vapor pressure at a given temperature. As temperature increases, more vapor forms, and vapor pressure increases. Table 7.4 lists the vapor pressure of water at various temperatures.

A liquid reaches its boiling point when its vapor pressure becomes equal to the external pressure. As boiling occurs, bubbles of the gas form within the liquid and quickly rise to the surface. For example, at an atmospheric pressure of 760 mmHg, water will boil at 100 °C, the temperature at which its vapor pressure reaches 760 mmHg (see Table 7.5).

TABLE 7.4 **Vapor Pressure of Water**	
Temperature (°C)	**Vapor Pressure (mmHg)**
0	5
10	9
20	18
30	32
37*	47
40	55
50	93
60	149
70	234
80	355
90	528
95	634
100	760

*At body temperature.

TABLE 7.5 **Pressure and the Boiling Point of Water**	
Pressure (mmHg)	**Boiling Point (°C)**
270	70
467	87
630	95
752	99
760	100
800	100.4
1075	110
1520 (2 atm)	120
3800 (5 atm)	160
7600 (10 atm)	180

TUTORIAL
Vapor Pressure and Boiling Point

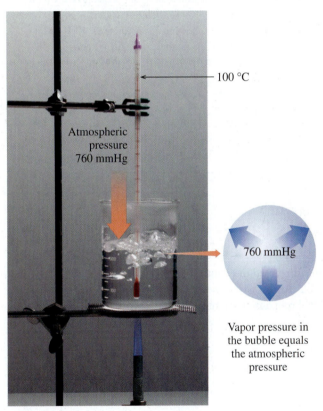

Water boils when its vapor pressure is equal to the pressure of the atmosphere.

At high altitudes, where atmospheric pressures are lower than 760 mmHg, the boiling point of water is lower than 100 °C. Earlier, we saw that the typical atmospheric pressure in Denver is 630 mmHg. This means that water in Denver needs a vapor pressure of 630 mmHg to boil. Because water has a vapor pressure of 630 mmHg at 95 °C, water boils at 95 °C in Denver.

In a closed container such as a pressure cooker, a pressure greater than 1 atm can be obtained, which means that water boils at a temperature higher than 100 °C. Laboratories and hospitals use closed containers called *autoclaves* to sterilize laboratory and surgical equipment.

An autoclave used to sterilize equipment attains a temperature higher than 100 °C.

QUESTIONS AND PROBLEMS

7.5 Temperature and Pressure (Gay-Lussac's Law)

LEARNING GOAL: *Use the temperature–pressure relationship (Gay-Lussac's law) to determine the new temperature or pressure when the volume and amount of gas are constant.*

7.29 Why do aerosol cans explode if heated?

7.30 Why is there an increased danger of the tires on a car having a blowout when the car is driven on hot pavement in the desert?

7.31 For the following, calculate the final temperature of the gas, in degrees Celsius, when initial pressure is changed, with V and n constant:
   a. A sample of xenon at 25 °C and 745 mmHg is cooled to give a pressure of 625 mmHg.
   b. A tank of argon gas with a pressure of 0.950 atm at −18 °C is heated to give a pressure of 1250 torr.

7.32 For the following, calculate the final temperature of the gas, in degrees Celsius, when initial pressure is changed, with V and n constant:
   a. A tank of helium gas with a pressure of 250 torr at 0 °C is heated to give a pressure of 1500 torr.
   b. A sample of air at 40. °C and 745 mmHg is cooled to give a pressure of 685 mmHg.

7.33 Solve for the final pressure when each of the following temperature changes occurs, with V and n constant:
   a. A gas with an initial pressure of 1200 torr at 155 °C is cooled to 0 °C.

b. A gas in an aerosol container at an initial pressure of 1.40 atm at 12 °C is heated to 35 °C.

7.34 Solve for the final pressure when each of the following temperature changes occurs, with V and n constant:
   a. A gas with an initial pressure of 1.20 atm at 75 °C is cooled to −22 °C.
   b. A sample of N_2 with an initial pressure of 780. mmHg at −75 °C is heated to 28 °C.

7.35 Match the terms *vapor pressure*, *atmospheric pressure*, and *boiling point* to the following descriptions:
   a. the temperature at which bubbles of vapor appear within the liquid
   b. the pressure exerted by a gas above the surface of its liquid

7.36 Match the terms *vapor pressure*, *atmospheric pressure*, and *boiling point* to the following descriptions:
   a. the pressure exerted on Earth by the particles in the air
   b. the temperature at which the vapor pressure of a liquid becomes equal to the external pressure

7.37 Explain each of the following observations:
   a. Water boils at 87 °C on the top of Mt. Whitney.
   b. Food cooks more quickly in a pressure cooker than in an open pan.

7.38 Explain each of the following observations:
   a. Boiling water at sea level is hotter than boiling water in the mountains.
   b. Water used to sterilize surgical equipment is heated to 120 °C at 2.0 atm in an autoclave.

LEARNING GOAL

Use the combined gas law to find the new pressure, volume, or temperature of a gas when changes in two of these properties are given and the amount of gas is constant.

7.6 The Combined Gas Law

All the pressure–volume–temperature relationships for gases that we have studied may be combined into a single relationship called the **combined gas law**. This expression is useful for studying the effect of changes in two of these variables on the third as long as the amount of gas (number of moles) remains constant.

Combined Gas Law

$$\frac{P_1 V_1}{T_1} = \frac{P_2 V_2}{T_2} \qquad \text{No change in moles of gas}$$

By using the combined gas law, we can derive any of the gas laws by omitting those properties that do not change, as seen in Table 7.6.

TUTORIAL
The Combined Gas Law

TABLE 7.6 Summary of Gas Laws

Combined Gas Law	Properties Held Constant	Relationship	Name of Gas Law
$\dfrac{P_1 V_1}{\cancel{T_1}} = \dfrac{P_2 V_2}{\cancel{T_2}}$	T, n	$P_1 V_1 = P_2 V_2$	Boyle's
$\dfrac{\cancel{P_1} V_1}{T_1} = \dfrac{\cancel{P_2} V_2}{T_2}$	P, n	$\dfrac{V_1}{T_1} = \dfrac{V_2}{T_2}$	Charles's
$\dfrac{P_1 \cancel{V_1}}{T_1} = \dfrac{P_2 \cancel{V_2}}{T_2}$	V, n	$\dfrac{P_1}{T_1} = \dfrac{P_2}{T_2}$	Gay-Lussac's

CONCEPT CHECK 7.6   **Combined Gas Law**

State and explain the reason for the change (*increases, decreases, no change*) in a gas that occurs for the following when n does not change:

	Pressure (P)	Volume (V)	Temperature (K)	Amount (n)
a.		twice as large	half the Kelvin temperature	constant
b.	twice as large		twice as large	constant

ANSWER

a. Pressure decreases by one-half when the volume (at constant n) doubles. If the temperature in Kelvin is halved, the pressure is also halved. The changes in both V and T decrease the pressure to one-fourth its initial value.

b. No change. When the Kelvin temperature of a gas (at constant n) is doubled, the volume is doubled. But when the pressure is twice as much, the volume must decrease to one-half. The changes offset each other, and no change occurs in the volume.

	Pressure (P)	Volume (V)	Temperature (K)	Amount (n)
a.	one-fourth as large	twice as large	half the Kelvin temperature	constant
b.	twice as large	no change	twice as large	constant

SAMPLE PROBLEM 7.6   **Using the Combined Gas Law**

A 25.0-mL bubble is released from a diver's air tank at a pressure of 4.00 atm and a temperature of 11 °C. What is the volume, in milliliters, of the bubble when it reaches the ocean surface where the pressure is 1.00 atm and the temperature is 18 °C (assume the amount of gas in the bubble remains the same)?

SOLUTION

Step 1   **Organize the data in a table of initial and final conditions.** We list the properties that change, which are the pressure, volume, and temperature, in a table. The property that remains constant, which is the amount of gas, is shown below the table. The temperatures in degrees Celsius must be changed to kelvins.

$$T_1 = 11\,°C + 273 = 284\ K$$
$$T_2 = 18\,°C + 273 = 291\ K$$

Analyze the Problem

Conditions 1	Conditions 2
$P_1 = 4.00$ atm	$P_2 = 1.00$ atm
$V_1 = 25.0$ mL	$V_2 = ?$ mL
$T_1 = 284$ K	$T_2 = 291$ K

Factor that remains constant: n

Step 2   **Rearrange the gas law equation to solve for the unknown quantity.** For changes in two conditions, we rearrange the combined gas law to solve for V_2.

$$\frac{P_1V_1}{T_1} = \frac{P_2V_2}{T_2}$$

$$\frac{P_1V_1}{T_1} \times \frac{T_2}{P_2} = \frac{\cancel{P_2}V_2 \times \cancel{T_2}}{\cancel{T_2} \times \cancel{P_2}}$$

$$V_2 = V_1 \times \frac{P_1}{P_2} \times \frac{T_2}{T_1}$$

Under water, the pressure on a diver is greater than the atmospheric pressure.

Step 3 **Substitute values into the gas law equation and calculate.** From the data table, we determine that both the pressure decrease and the temperature increase will increase the volume.

$$V_2 = 25.0 \text{ mL} \times \frac{4.00 \text{ atm}}{1.00 \text{ atm}} \times \frac{291 \text{ K}}{284 \text{ K}} = 102 \text{ mL}$$

Pressure
factor
increases
volume

Temperature
factor
increases
volume

However, when the unknown value is decreased by one change but increased by the second change, it is not possible to predict the overall change.

STUDY CHECK 7.6

A weather balloon is filled with 15.0 L of helium at a temperature of 25 °C and a pressure of 685 mmHg. What is the pressure (mmHg) of the helium in the balloon in the upper atmosphere when the temperature is −35 °C and the volume becomes 34.0 L, if the amount of He does not change?

QUESTIONS AND PROBLEMS

7.6 The Combined Gas Law

LEARNING GOAL: *Use the combined gas law to find the new pressure, volume, or temperature of a gas when changes in two of these properties are given and the amount of gas is constant.*

7.39 A sample of helium gas has a volume of 6.50 L at a pressure of 845 mmHg and a temperature of 25 °C. What is the final pressure of the gas, in atmospheres, when the volume and temperature of the gas sample are changed to the following, if the amount of gas does not change?
  a. 1850 mL and 325 K
  b. 2.25 L and 12 °C
  c. 12.8 L and 47 °C

7.40 A sample of argon gas has a volume of 735 mL at a pressure of 1.20 atm and a temperature of 112 °C. What is the final volume of the gas, in milliliters, when the pressure and

temperature of the gas sample are changed to the following, if the amount of gas does not change?
  a. 658 mmHg and 281 K
  b. 0.55 atm and 75 °C
  c. 15.4 atm and −15 °C

7.41 A 124-mL bubble of hot gas at 212 °C and 1.80 atm is emitted from an active volcano. What is the final temperature, in °C, of the gas in the bubble outside the volcano if the final volume of the bubble is 138 mL and the final pressure is 0.800 atm, if the amount of gas remains constant?

7.42 A scuba diver 60 ft below the ocean surface inhales 50.0 mL of compressed air from a scuba tank at an initial pressure of 3.00 atm and temperature of 8 °C. What is the final pressure of air, in atmospheres, in the lungs when the gas expands to 150.0 mL at a body temperature of 37 °C, and the amount of gas remains constant?

7.7 Volume and Moles (Avogadro's Law)

LEARNING GOAL

Use Avogadro's law to determine the amount or volume of a gas when the pressure and temperature are constant.

TUTORIAL
Volume and Moles

In our study of the gas laws, we have looked at changes in properties for a specified amount (*n*) of gas. Now we will consider how the properties of a gas change when there is a change in the number of moles or grams of the gas.

When you blow up a balloon, its volume increases because you are adding more air molecules. If the balloon has a hole in it, air leaks out, causing its volume to decrease. In 1811, Amedeo Avogadro formulated **Avogadro's law**, which states that the volume of a gas is directly related to the number of moles of a gas when pressure and temperature are not changed. For example, if the number of moles of a gas is doubled, then the volume will double as long as we do not change the pressure or the temperature (see Figure 7.7). At constant pressure and temperature, we can write Avogadro's law as follows:

Avogadro's Law

$$\frac{V_1}{n_1} = \frac{V_2}{n_2} \qquad \text{No change in pressure and temperature}$$

SAMPLE PROBLEM 7.7   Calculating Volume When There Is a Change in Moles

A weather balloon with a volume of 44 L is filled with 2.0 moles of helium. To what volume, in liters, will the balloon expand if 3.0 moles of helium are added, to give a total of 5.0 moles of helium, if the pressure and temperature do not change?

SOLUTION

Step 1   **Organize the data in a table of initial and final conditions.** We list those properties that change, which are volume and amount (moles) of gas, in a table. The properties that do not change, which are pressure and temperature, are shown below the table. Because there is an increase in the number of moles of gas, we can predict that the volume increases.

Analyze the Problem

Conditions 1	Conditions 2	Know	Predict
$V_1 = 44$ L	$V_2 = ?$ L		V increases
$n_1 = 2.0$ moles	$n_2 = 5.0$ moles	n increases	

Factors that remain constant: P and T

Step 2   **Rearrange the gas law equation to solve for the unknown quantity.** Using Avogadro's law, we can solve for V_2.

$$\frac{V_1}{n_1} = \frac{V_2}{n_2}$$

$$n_2 \times \frac{V_1}{n_1} = \frac{V_2}{n_2} \times n_2$$

$$V_2 = V_1 \times \frac{n_2}{n_1}$$

Step 3   **Substitute values into the gas law equation and calculate.** When we substitute in the values, we see that the mole factor is greater than 1, which increases volume as predicted in Step 1.

$$V_2 = 44 \text{ L} \times \frac{5.0 \text{ moles}}{2.0 \text{ moles}} = 110 \text{ L}$$

Mole factor
increases volume

STUDY CHECK 7.7

A sample containing 8.00 g of oxygen gas has a volume of 5.00 L. What is the volume, in liters, after 4.00 g of oxygen gas is added to the 8.00 g in the balloon, if temperature and pressure do not change?

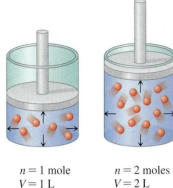

$n = 1$ mole $n = 2$ moles
$V = 1$ L $V = 2$ L

FIGURE 7.7 **Avogadro's law:** The volume of a gas is directly related to the number of moles of the gas. If the number of moles is doubled, the volume must double at constant pressure and temperature.

Q If a balloon has a leak, what happens to its volume?

The molar volume of a gas at STP is about the same as the volume of three basketballs.

STP and Molar Volume

Using Avogadro's law, we can say that any two gases will have equal volumes if they contain the same number of moles of gas at the same temperature and pressure. To help us make comparisons between different gases, arbitrary conditions called *standard temperature* (273 K) and *standard pressure* (1 atm), together abbreviated **STP**, were selected by scientists.

STP Conditions

Standard temperature is *exactly* 0 °C (273 K).

Standard pressure is *exactly* 1 atm (760 mmHg).

At STP, one mole of any gas occupies a volume of 22.4 L, which is about the same as the volume of three basketballs. This volume of 22.4 L of any gas at STP is called the **molar volume** (see Figure 7.8).

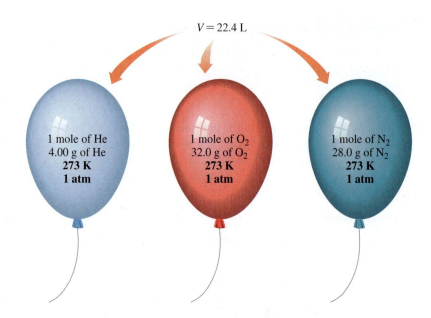

$V = 22.4$ L

1 mole of He
4.00 g of He
273 K
1 atm

1 mole of O_2
32.0 g of O_2
273 K
1 atm

1 mole of N_2
28.0 g of N_2
273 K
1 atm

FIGURE 7.8 Avogadro's law indicates that 1 mole of any gas at STP has a volume of 22.4 L.

Q What volume of gas, in liters, is occupied by 16.0 g of methane gas, CH_4, at STP?

When a gas is at STP conditions (0 °C and 1 atm), its molar volume can be written as a conversion factor and used to convert between the number of moles of gas and its volume, in liters.

1 mole of gas at STP = 22.4 L

Molar Volume Conversion Factors

$$\frac{1 \text{ mole gas}}{22.4 \text{ L (STP)}} \quad \text{and} \quad \frac{22.4 \text{ L (STP)}}{1 \text{ mole gas}}$$

CONCEPT CHECK 7.7 **Molar Volume**

Write the equality and conversion factors for the molar volume of helium at STP.

ANSWER

The equality for the molar volume of helium at STP is:

1 mole of He = 22.4 L of He

Because an equality has two conversion factors, we write the factors for the molar volume for helium as:

$$\frac{22.4 \text{ L He (STP)}}{1 \text{ mole He}} \quad \text{and} \quad \frac{1 \text{ mole He}}{22.4 \text{ L He (STP)}}$$

Guide to Using Molar Volume

1 State the given and needed quantities.

2 Write a plan to calculate the needed quantity.

3 Write the equalities and conversion factors including 22.4 L/mole at STP.

4 Set up the problem with factors to cancel units.

SAMPLE PROBLEM 7.8 **Using Molar Volume to Find Volume at STP**

What is the volume, in liters, of 64.0 g of O_2 gas at STP?

SOLUTION

Step 1 **State the given and needed quantities.**

Analyze the Problem

Given	Need
64.0 g of O_2 gas at STP	liters of O_2 gas at STP

Step 2 **Write a plan to calculate the needed quantity.**

grams of O_2 Molar mass moles of O_2 Molar volume liters of O_2

Step 3 **Write the equalities and conversion factors including 22.4 L/mole at STP.**

1 mole of O_2 = 32.0 g of O_2	1 mole of O_2 = 22.4 L of O_2 (STP)
$\dfrac{32.0 \text{ g } O_2}{1 \text{ mole } O_2}$ and $\dfrac{1 \text{ mole } O_2}{32.0 \text{ g } O_2}$	$\dfrac{22.4 \text{ L } O_2 \text{ (STP)}}{1 \text{ mole } O_2}$ and $\dfrac{1 \text{ mole } O_2}{22.4 \text{ L } O_2 \text{ (STP)}}$

Step 4 **Set up the problem with factors to cancel units.**

$$64.0 \text{ g } O_2 \times \frac{1 \text{ mole } O_2}{32.0 \text{ g } O_2} \times \frac{22.4 \text{ L } O_2 \text{ (STP)}}{1 \text{ mole } O_2} = 44.8 \text{ L of } O_2 \text{ at STP}$$

STUDY CHECK 7.8

How many grams of $N_2(g)$ are in 5.6 L of $N_2(g)$ at STP?

Gases in Reactions at STP

We can use the molar volume at STP to determine the moles of a gas in a reaction. Once we know the moles of gas in a reaction, we can use a mole–mole factor to determine the moles of any other substance as we have done before.

SAMPLE PROBLEM 7.9 **Gases in Chemical Reactions at STP**

When potassium metal reacts with chlorine gas, the product is solid potassium chloride.

$$2K(s) + Cl_2(g) \longrightarrow 2KCl(s)$$

How many grams of potassium chloride are produced when 7.25 L of chlorine gas at STP reacts with potassium?

SOLUTION

Step 1 **State the given and needed quantities.**

Analyze the Problem

Given	Need
7.25 L of Cl_2 at STP	grams of KCl
Equation	
$2K(s) + Cl_2(g) \longrightarrow 2KCl(s)$	

Guide to Reactions Involving Gases

1 State the given and needed quantities.

2 Write a plan to calculate the needed quantity.

3 Write the equalities and conversion factors including the molar volume.

4 Set up the problem and calculate.

Step 2 **Write a plan to calculate the needed quantity.**

liters of Cl_2 Molar volume moles of Cl_2 Mole–mole factor moles of KCl Molar mass grams of KCl

Step 3 **Write the equalities and conversion factors including the molar volume.**

1 mole of Cl_2 = 22.4 L of Cl_2 (STP)
$\dfrac{22.4 \text{ L } Cl_2 \text{ (STP)}}{1 \text{ mole } Cl_2}$ and $\dfrac{1 \text{ mole } Cl_2}{22.4 \text{ L } Cl_2 \text{ (STP)}}$

1 mole of Cl_2 = 2 moles of KCl
$\dfrac{2 \text{ moles KCl}}{1 \text{ mole } Cl_2}$ and $\dfrac{1 \text{ mole } Cl_2}{2 \text{ moles KCl}}$

1 mole of KCl = 74.6 g of KCl
$\dfrac{1 \text{ mole KCl}}{74.6 \text{ g KCl}}$ and $\dfrac{74.6 \text{ g KCl}}{1 \text{ mole KCl}}$

Step 4   Set up the problem and calculate.

$$7.25 \ \text{L} \ \text{Cl}_2 \ \text{(STP)} \times \frac{1 \ \text{mole} \ \text{Cl}_2}{22.4 \ \text{L} \ \text{Cl}_2 \ \text{(STP)}} \times \frac{2 \ \text{moles} \ \text{KCl}}{1 \ \text{mole} \ \text{Cl}_2} \times \frac{74.6 \ \text{g} \ \text{KCl}}{1 \ \text{mole} \ \text{KCl}} = 48.3 \ \text{g of KCl}$$

STUDY CHECK 7.9

H_2 gas forms when zinc metal reacts with aqueous HCl according to the following equation:

$$Zn(s) + 2HCl(aq) \longrightarrow ZnCl_2(aq) + H_2(g)$$

How many liters of H_2 gas at STP are produced when 15.8 g of zinc reacts?

QUESTIONS AND PROBLEMS

7.7 Volume and Moles (Avogadro's Law)

LEARNING GOAL: Use Avogadro's law to determine the amount or volume of a gas when the pressure and temperature are constant.

7.43 What happens to the volume of a bicycle tire or a basketball when you use an air pump to add air?

7.44 Sometimes when you blow up a balloon and release it, it flies around the room. What is happening to the air that was in the balloon and its volume?

7.45 A sample containing 1.50 moles of neon gas has an initial volume of 8.00 L. What is the final volume of gas, in liters, when the following changes occur in the quantity of the gas at constant pressure and temperature?
a. A leak allows one-half of the neon atoms to escape.
b. A sample of 25.0 g of neon is added to the 1.50 moles of neon gas in the container.
c. A sample of 3.50 moles of O_2 is added to the 1.50 moles of neon gas in the container.

7.46 A sample containing 4.80 g of O_2 gas has an initial volume of 15.0 L. Pressure and temperature remain constant.
a. What is the final volume if 0.500 mole of O_2 gas is added?

b. Oxygen is released until the volume is 10.0 L. How many moles of O_2 remain?
c. What is the final volume after 4.00 g of He is added to the 4.80 g of O_2 gas in the container?

7.47 Use the molar volume of a gas to solve the following at STP:
a. the number of moles of O_2 in 44.8 L of O_2 gas
b. the number of moles of CO_2 in 4.00 L of CO_2 gas
c. the volume (L) of 6.40 g of O_2
d. the volume (mL) occupied by 50.0 g of neon

7.48 Use the molar volume of a gas to solve the following at STP:
a. the volume (L) occupied by 2.50 moles of N_2
b. the volume (mL) occupied by 0.420 mole of He
c. the number of grams of neon contained in 11.2 L of Ne gas
d. the number of grams of H_2 in 1620 mL of H_2 gas

7.49 Mg metal reacts with HCl to produce hydrogen gas.

$$Mg(s) + 2HCl(aq) \longrightarrow MgCl_2(aq) + H_2(g)$$

What volume, in liters, of H_2 at STP is released when 8.25 g of Mg reacts?

7.50 Aluminum oxide can be formed from its elements.

$$4Al(s) + 3O_2(g) \xrightarrow{\Delta} 2Al_2O_3(s)$$

How many grams of Al will react with 12.0 L of O_2 at STP?

LEARNING GOAL

Use the ideal gas law equation to solve for P, V, T, or n of a gas when given three of the four values in the ideal gas law.

TUTORIAL
Introduction to the Ideal Gas Law

7.8 The Ideal Gas Law

The **ideal gas law** is the combination of the four properties used in the measurement of a gas—pressure (P), volume (V), temperature (T), and amount (n)—to give a single expression, which is written as follows:

Ideal Gas Law

$$PV = nRT$$

Rearranging the ideal gas law equation shows that the four gas properties equal a constant, R.

$$\frac{PV}{nT} = R$$

To calculate the value of R, we substitute the STP conditions for molar volume into the expression: 1 mole of any gas occupies 22.4 L at STP (273 K and 1 atm).

$$R = \frac{(1.00 \ \text{atm})(22.4 \ \text{L})}{(1.00 \ \text{mole})(273 \ \text{K})} = \frac{0.0821 \ \text{L} \cdot \text{atm}}{\text{mole} \cdot \text{K}}$$

The value for R, the **ideal gas constant**, is 0.0821 L · atm per mole · K. If we use 760. mmHg for the pressure, we obtain another useful value for R: 62.4 L · mmHg per mole · K.

$$R = \frac{(760.\, \text{mmHg})(22.4\, \text{L})}{(1.00\, \text{mole})(273\, \text{K})} = \frac{62.4\, \text{L} \cdot \text{mmHg}}{\text{mole} \cdot \text{K}}$$

The ideal gas law is a useful expression when you are given the values for any three of the four properties of a gas. In working problems using the ideal gas law, the units of each variable must match the units in the R you select.

SELF-STUDY ACTIVITY
The Ideal Gas Law

Ideal Gas Constant (R)	$\dfrac{0.0821\, \text{L} \cdot \text{atm}}{\text{mole} \cdot \text{K}}$	$\dfrac{62.4\, \text{L} \cdot \text{mmHg}}{\text{mole} \cdot \text{K}}$
Pressure (P)	atm	mmHg
Volume (V)	L	L
Amount (n)	moles	moles
Temperature (T)	K	K

SAMPLE PROBLEM 7.10   Using the Ideal Gas Law

Dinitrogen oxide, N_2O, which is used in dentistry, is an anesthetic also called "laughing gas." What is the pressure, in atmospheres, of 0.350 mole of N_2O at 22 °C in a 5.00 L container?

SOLUTION

Step 1   **State the given and needed quantities.** When three of the four quantities (P, V, n, and T) are known, we use the ideal gas law equation to solve for the unknown quantity. It is helpful to organize the data in a table. The temperature is converted from degrees Celsius to kelvins so that the units of V, n, and T match the units of the gas constant R.

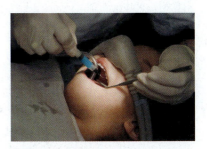

Dinitrogen oxide is used as an anesthetic in dentistry.

Analyze the Problem

Property	P	V	n	R	T
Given		5.00 L	0.350 mole	$\dfrac{0.0821\, \text{L} \cdot \text{atm}}{\text{mole} \cdot \text{K}}$	22 °C 22 °C + 273 = 295 K
Need	? atm				

Step 2   **Rearrange the ideal gas law equation to solve for the needed quantity.** By dividing both sides of the ideal gas law equation by V, we solve for pressure, P.

$$PV = nRT \quad \text{Ideal gas law equation}$$

$$P\frac{\cancel{V}}{\cancel{V}} = \frac{nRT}{V}$$

$$P = \frac{nRT}{V}$$

Step 3   **Substitute the gas data into the equation and calculate the needed quantity.**

$$P = \frac{0.350\, \cancel{\text{mole}} \times \dfrac{0.0821\, \cancel{\text{L}} \cdot \text{atm}}{\cancel{\text{mole}} \cdot \cancel{\text{K}}} \times 295\, \cancel{\text{K}}}{5.00\, \cancel{\text{L}}} = 1.70\, \text{atm}$$

Guide to Using the Ideal Gas Law

1 State the given and needed quantities.

2 Rearrange the ideal gas law equation to solve for the needed quantity.

3 Substitute the gas data into the equation and calculate the needed quantity.

STUDY CHECK 7.10

Chlorine gas, Cl_2, is used to purify water. How many moles of chlorine gas are in a 7.00 L tank if the gas has a pressure of 865 mmHg and a temperature of 24 °C?

SAMPLE PROBLEM 7.11   Calculating Mass Using the Ideal Gas Law Equation

Butane, C_4H_{10}, is used as a fuel for barbecues and as an aerosol propellant. If you have 108 mL of butane at 715 mmHg and 25 °C, what is the mass, in grams, of the butane?

SOLUTION

Step 1   **State the given and needed quantities.** When three of the four quantities (P, V, n, and T) are known, we use the ideal gas law equation to solve for the unknown quantity. It is helpful to organize the data in a table. Because the pressure is given in mmHg, we will use R in mmHg. The volume given in milliliters (mL) is converted to a volume in liters (L). The temperature is converted from degrees Celsius to kelvins.

Analyze the Problem

Property	P	V	n	R	T
Given	715 mmHg	108 mL (0.108 L)		$\dfrac{62.4 \text{ L} \cdot \text{mmHg}}{\text{mole} \cdot \text{K}}$	25 °C 25 °C + 273 = 298 K
Need			? mole (? g)		

Step 2   **Rearrange the ideal gas law equation to solve for the needed quantity.** By dividing both sides of the ideal gas law equation by RT, we solve for moles, n.

$$PV = \boxed{n}\, RT \quad \text{Ideal gas law equation}$$

$$\frac{PV}{RT} = n\frac{RT}{RT}$$

$$\boxed{n} = \frac{PV}{RT}$$

Step 3   **Substitute the gas data into the equation and calculate the needed quantity.**

$$n = \frac{715 \text{ mmHg} \times 0.108 \text{ L}}{\dfrac{62.4 \text{ L} \cdot \text{mmHg}}{\text{mole} \cdot \text{K}} \times 298 \text{ K}} = 0.00415 \text{ mole } (4.15 \times 10^{-3} \text{ mole})$$

Now we convert the moles of butane to grams using its molar mass of 58.1 g/mole.

$$0.00415 \text{ mole } C_4H_{10} \times \frac{58.1 \text{ g } C_4H_{10}}{1 \text{ mole } C_4H_{10}} = 0.241 \text{ g of } C_4H_{10}$$

STUDY CHECK 7.11

What is the volume of 1.20 g of carbon monoxide at 8 °C if it has a pressure of 724 mmHg?

SAMPLE PROBLEM 7.12   Molar Mass of a Gas Using the Ideal Gas Law

What is the molar mass of a gas if a 3.16-g sample at 0.750 atm and 45 °C occupies a volume of 2.05 L?

SOLUTION

Step 1   **State the given and needed quantities.** It is helpful to organize the data in a table.

Analyze the Problem

Property	P	V	n	R	T	Mass
Given	0.750 atm	2.05 L		$\dfrac{0.0821 \text{ L} \cdot \text{atm}}{\text{mole} \cdot \text{K}}$	45 °C 45 °C + 273 = 318 K	3.16 g
Need			? mole (? molar mass)			

Step 2 **Rearrange the ideal gas law equation to solve for the number of moles.**

$$PV = nRT \quad \text{Ideal gas law equation}$$

To solve the ideal gas law equation for n, we divide both sides by RT.

$$\frac{PV}{RT} = \frac{nRT}{RT}$$

$$n = \frac{PV}{RT}$$

$$n = \frac{0.750 \text{ atm} \times 2.05 \text{ L}}{\dfrac{0.0821 \text{ L} \cdot \text{atm}}{\text{mole} \cdot \text{K}} \times 318 \text{ K}} = 0.0589 \text{ mole}$$

Guide to Calculating the Molar Mass of a Gas

1 State the given and needed quantities.

2 Rearrange the ideal gas law equation to solve for the number of moles.

3 Obtain the molar mass by dividing the given number of grams by the number of moles.

Step 3 **Obtain the molar mass by dividing the given number of grams by the number of moles.**

$$\text{Molar mass} = \frac{\text{mass}}{\text{moles}} = \frac{3.16 \text{ g}}{0.0589 \text{ mole}} = 53.7 \text{ g/mole}$$

STUDY CHECK 7.12

What is the molar mass of an unknown gas in a 1.50-L container if 0.488 g of the gas has a pressure of 0.0750 atm at 19 °C?

Chemical Reactions and the Ideal Gas Law

If a gas is not at STP, we use its pressure (P), volume (V), and temperature (T) to determine the moles of that gas involved in a reaction. Then we can determine the moles of any other substance by using the mole–mole factors as we did in Section 6.6.

SAMPLE PROBLEM 7.13   **Chemical Equations Using the Ideal Gas Law**

Limestone ($CaCO_3$) reacts with HCl to produce aqueous calcium chloride and carbon dioxide gas.

$$CaCO_3(s) + 2HCl(aq) \longrightarrow CaCl_2(aq) + CO_2(g) + H_2O(l)$$

How many liters of CO_2 are produced at 752 mmHg and 24 °C from a 25.0-g sample of limestone?

SOLUTION

Step 1 **State the given and needed quantities.**

Analyze the Problem

Given		Need
Reactant:	25.0 g of $CaCO_3$	liters of $CO_2(g)$
Product:	$CO_2(g)$ at 752 mmHg, 24 °C (24 °C + 273 = 297 K)	
Equation		
$CaCO_3(s) + 2HCl(aq) \longrightarrow CaCl_2(aq) + CO_2(g) + H_2O(l)$		

Step 2 **Write a plan to convert the given quantity to the needed moles.**

grams of $CaCO_3$ ⟩Molar mass⟩ moles of $CaCO_3$ ⟩Mole–mole factor⟩ moles of CO_2

Guide to Reactions Involving the Ideal Gas Law

1 State the given and needed quantities.

2 Write a plan to convert the given quantity to the needed moles.

3 Write the equalities for molar mass and mole–mole factors.

4 Set up the problem to calculate moles of needed quantity.

5 Convert the moles of needed to mass or volume using the molar mass or the ideal gas law equation.

Step 3 **Write the equalities for molar mass and mole–mole factors.**

1 mole of $CaCO_3$ = 100.1 g of $CaCO_3$

$$\frac{100.1 \text{ g } CaCO_3}{1 \text{ mole } CaCO_3} \quad \text{and} \quad \frac{1 \text{ mole } CaCO_3}{100.1 \text{ g } CaCO_3}$$

1 mole of $CaCO_3$ = 1 mole of CO_2

$$\frac{1 \text{ mole } CaCO_3}{1 \text{ mole } CO_2} \quad \text{and} \quad \frac{1 \text{ mole } CO_2}{1 \text{ mole } CaCO_3}$$

Step 4 **Set up the problem to calculate moles of needed quantity.**

$$25.0 \text{ g } CaCO_3 \times \frac{1 \text{ mole } CaCO_3}{100.1 \text{ g } CaCO_3} \times \frac{1 \text{ mole } CO_2}{1 \text{ mole } CaCO_3} = 0.250 \text{ mole of } CO_2$$

Step 5 **Convert the moles of needed to volume using the ideal gas law equation.** Now the ideal gas law equation is rearranged to solve for volume (L) of gas. Then substitute in the given quantities and calculate V.

$$V = \frac{nRT}{P}$$

$$V = \frac{0.250 \text{ mole} \times \dfrac{62.4 \text{ L} \cdot \text{mmHg}}{\text{mole} \cdot \text{K}} \times 297 \text{ K}}{752 \text{ mmHg}} = 6.16 \text{ L of } CO_2$$

STUDY CHECK 7.13

If 12.8 g of aluminum reacts with HCl, how many liters of H_2 would be formed at 715 mmHg and 19 °C?

$$2Al(s) + 6HCl(aq) \longrightarrow 2AlCl_3(aq) + 3H_2(g)$$

QUESTIONS AND PROBLEMS

7.8 The Ideal Gas Law

LEARNING GOAL: Use the ideal gas law equation to solve for P, V, T, or n of a gas when given three of the four values in the ideal gas law.

7.51 Calculate the pressure, in atmospheres, of 2.00 moles of helium gas in a 10.0-L container at 27 °C.

7.52 What is the volume, in liters, of 4.0 moles of methane gas, CH_4, at 18 °C and 1.40 atm?

7.53 An oxygen gas container has a volume of 20.0 L. How many grams of oxygen are in the container if the gas has a pressure of 845 mmHg at 22 °C?

7.54 A 10.0-g sample of krypton gas has a temperature of 25 °C at 575 mmHg. What is the volume, in milliliters, of the krypton gas?

7.55 A 25.0-g sample of nitrogen, N_2, has a volume of 50.0 L and a pressure of 630. mmHg. What is the temperature, in kelvins and degrees Celsius, of the gas?

7.56 A 0.226-g sample of carbon dioxide, CO_2, has a volume of 525 mL and a pressure of 455 mmHg. What is the temperature, in kelvins and degrees Celsius, of the gas?

7.57 Using molar volume (STP) or the ideal gas law equation, determine the molar mass, g/mole, of each of the following:
   a. 0.84 g of a gas that has a volume of 450 mL at STP
   b. 1.48 g of a gas that has a volume of 1.00 L at 685 mmHg and 22 °C
   c. 2.96 g of a gas that has a volume of 2.30 L at 0.95 atm and 24 °C

7.58 Using molar volume (STP) or the ideal gas law equation, determine the molar mass, g/mole, of each of the following:
   a. 11.6 g of a gas that has a volume of 2.00 L at STP
   b. 0.726 g of a gas that has a volume of 855 mL at 1.20 atm and 18 °C
   c. 2.32 g of a gas that has a volume of 1.23 L at 685 mmHg and 25 °C

7.59 Butane undergoes combustion when it reacts with oxygen to produce carbon dioxide and water. Using the ideal gas law equation, calculate the volume, in liters, of oxygen needed to burn all the butane at 0.850 atm and 25 °C if a tank contains 55.2 g of butane.
$$2C_4H_{10}(g) + 13O_2(g) \xrightarrow{\Delta} 8CO_2(g) + 10H_2O(g)$$

7.60 When heated to 350. °C at 0.950 atm, ammonium nitrate decomposes to produce nitrogen, water, and oxygen gases. Using the ideal gas law equation, calculate the volume, in liters, of water vapor produced when 25.8 g of NH_4NO_3 decomposes.
$$2NH_4NO_3(s) \xrightarrow{\Delta} 2N_2(g) + 4H_2O(g) + O_2(g)$$

7.61 Potassium nitrate decomposes to potassium nitrite and oxygen. Using the ideal gas law equation, calculate the volume, in liters, of the O_2 produced if the decomposition of 50.0 g of KNO_3 takes place at 35 °C and 1.19 atm.
$$2KNO_3(s) \xrightarrow{\Delta} 2KNO_2(s) + O_2(g)$$

7.62 Nitrogen dioxide reacts with water to produce oxygen and ammonia. Using the ideal gas law equation, calculate the grams of NH_3 that can be produced when 4.00 L of NO_2 react at a temperature of 415 °C and a pressure of 725 mmHg.
$$4NO_2(g) + 6H_2O(g) \xrightarrow{\Delta} 7O_2(g) + 4NH_3(g)$$

7.9 Partial Pressures (Dalton's Law)

LEARNING GOAL

Use Dalton's law of partial pressures to calculate the total pressure of a mixture of gases.

Many gas samples are a mixture of gases. For example, the air you breathe is a mixture of mostly oxygen and nitrogen gases. Scientists have observed that all gas particles in ideal gas mixtures behave in the same way. Therefore, the total pressure of the gases in a mixture is a result of the collisions of the gas particles, regardless of what type of gas they are.

In a gas mixture, each gas exerts its **partial pressure**, which is the pressure it would exert if it were the only gas in the container. **Dalton's law** states that the total pressure of a gas mixture is the sum of the partial pressures of the gases in the mixture.

TUTORIAL
Mixture of Gases

Dalton's Law

$$P_{total} = P_1 + P_2 + P_3 + \cdots$$
Total pressure of = Sum of the partial pressures
a gas mixture   of the gases in the mixture

Suppose we have two separate tanks, one filled with helium at 2.0 atm and the other filled with argon at 4.0 atm. When the gases are combined in a single tank with the same volume and temperature, the number of gas molecules, not the type of gas, determines the pressure in a container. The pressure of the gases in the gas mixture would be 6.0 atm, which is the sum of their individual or partial pressures.

$$P_{total} = P_{He} + P_{Ar}$$
$$= 2.0 \text{ atm} + 4.0 \text{ atm}$$
$$= 6.0 \text{ atm}$$

$P_{He} = 2.0$ atm $P_{Ar} = 4.0$ atm

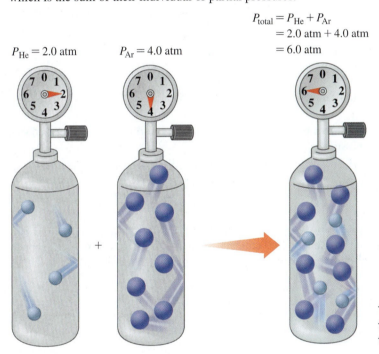

The total pressure of two gases is the sum of their partial pressures.

CONCEPT CHECK 7.8   **Pressure of a Gas Mixture**

A scuba tank is filled with Trimix, a breathing gas mixture for deep scuba diving. The tank contains oxygen with a partial pressure of 20. atm, nitrogen with a partial pressure of 40. atm, and helium with a partial pressure of 140. atm. What is the total pressure of the breathing mixture, in atmospheres?

ANSWER

Using Dalton's law of partial pressures, we add together the partial pressures of oxygen, nitrogen, and helium present in the mixture.

$$P_{total} = P_{oxygen} + P_{nitrogen} + P_{helium}$$
$$P_{total} = 20. \text{ atm} + 40. \text{ atm} + 140. \text{ atm}$$
$$= 200. \text{ atm}$$

Therefore, when oxygen, nitrogen, and helium are placed in the same container, the sum of their partial pressures is the total pressure of the mixture, which is 200. atm.

TABLE 7.7 Typical Composition of Air

Gas	Partial Pressure (mmHg)	Percentage (%)
Nitrogen, N_2	594	78.2
Oxygen, O_2	160.	21.0
Carbon dioxide, CO_2		
Argon, Ar	6	0.8
Water vapor, H_2O		
Total air	760.	100

Guide to Solving for Partial Pressure

1 Write the equation for the sum of the partial pressures.

2 Rearrange the equation to solve for the unknown pressure.

3 Substitute known pressures into the equation and calculate the unknown partial pressure.

Air Is a Gas Mixture

The air you breathe is a mixture of gases. What we call the *atmospheric pressure* is actually the sum of the partial pressures of all the gases in the air. Table 7.7 lists partial pressures for the gases in air on a typical day.

SAMPLE PROBLEM 7.14 **Partial Pressure of a Gas in a Mixture**

A Heliox breathing mixture of oxygen and helium is prepared for a scuba diver who is going to descend 200 ft below the ocean surface. At that depth, the diver breathes a gas mixture that has a total pressure of 7.00 atm. If the partial pressure of the oxygen in the tank at that depth is 1140 mmHg, what is the partial pressure of the helium in the breathing mixture?

SOLUTION

Step 1 **Write the equation for the sum of the partial pressures.** From Dalton's law of partial pressures, we know that the total pressure is equal to the sum of the partial pressures.

$$P_{total} = P_{O_2} + P_{He}$$

Step 2 **Rearrange the equation to solve for the unknown pressure.** To solve for the partial pressure of helium (P_{He}), we rearrange the expression to give the following:

$$P_{He} = P_{total} - P_{O_2}$$

Convert units to match.

$$P_{O_2} = 1140 \text{ mmHg} \times \frac{1 \text{ atm}}{760 \text{ mmHg}} = 1.50 \text{ atm}$$

Step 3 **Substitute known pressures into the equation and calculate the unknown partial pressure.**

$$P_{He} = P_{total} - P_{O_2}$$
$$P_{He} = 7.00 \text{ atm} - 1.50 \text{ atm} = 5.50 \text{ atm}$$

STUDY CHECK 7.14

An anesthetic consists of a mixture of cyclopropane gas, C_3H_6, and oxygen gas, O_2. If the mixture has a total pressure of 1.09 atm, and the partial pressure of the cyclopropane is 73 torr, what is the partial pressure (torr) of the oxygen in the anesthetic?

Chemistry Link to Health

BLOOD GASES

Our cells continuously use oxygen and produce carbon dioxide. Both gases move in and out of the lungs through the membranes of the alveoli, the tiny air sacs at the ends of the airways in the lungs. An exchange of gases occurs in which oxygen from the air diffuses into the lungs and into the blood, while carbon dioxide produced in the cells is carried to the lungs to be exhaled. In Table 7.8, partial pressures are given for the gases in the air that we inhale (inspired air), the air in the alveoli, and the air that we exhale (expired air).

At sea level, oxygen normally has a partial pressure of 100 mmHg in the alveoli of the lungs. Because the partial pressure of oxygen in venous blood is 40 mmHg, oxygen diffuses from the alveoli into the bloodstream. The oxygen combines with hemoglobin, which carries it to the tissues of the body, where the partial pressure of oxygen can be very low, less than 30 mmHg. Oxygen

diffuses from the blood where the partial pressure of O_2 is high into the tissues, where O_2 pressure is low.

TABLE 7.8 Partial Pressures of Gases During Breathing

Gas	Partial Pressure (mmHg)		
	Inspired Air	Alveolar Air	Expired Air
Nitrogen, N_2	594	573	569
Oxygen, O_2	160	100	116
Carbon dioxide, CO_2	0.3	40	28
Water vapor, H_2O	5.7	47	47
Total	760.	760.	760.

As oxygen is used in the cells of the body during metabolic processes, carbon dioxide is produced, so the partial pressure of CO_2 may be as high as 50 mmHg or more. Carbon dioxide diffuses from the tissues into the bloodstream and is carried to the lungs. There it diffuses out of the blood, where CO_2 has a partial pressure of 46 mmHg, into the alveoli, where the CO_2 is at 40 mmHg, and is exhaled. Table 7.9 gives the partial pressures of blood gases in the tissues, and in oxygenated and deoxygenated blood.

TABLE 7.9 Partial Pressures of Oxygen and Carbon Dioxide in Blood and Tissues

Gas	Partial Pressure (mmHg)		
	Oxygenated Blood	Deoxygenated Blood	Tissues
O_2	100	40	30 or less
CO_2	40	46	50 or greater

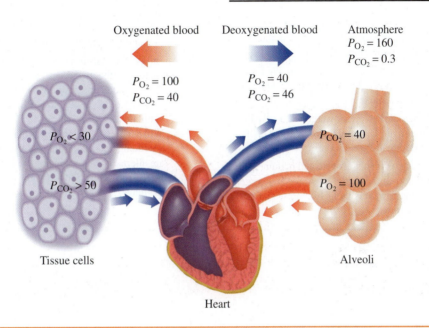

Oxygenated blood

$P_{O_2} = 100$
$P_{CO_2} = 40$

$P_{O_2} < 30$

$P_{CO_2} > 50$

Tissue cells

Deoxygenated blood

$P_{O_2} = 40$
$P_{CO_2} = 46$

Atmosphere
$P_{O_2} = 160$
$P_{CO_2} = 0.3$

$P_{CO_2} = 40$

$P_{O_2} = 100$

Alveoli

Heart

Chemistry Link to Health

HYPERBARIC CHAMBERS

A burn patient may undergo treatment for burns and infections in a hyperbaric chamber, a device in which pressures can be obtained that are two to three times greater than atmospheric pressure. A greater oxygen pressure increases the level of dissolved oxygen in the blood and tissues. Because high levels of oxygen are toxic to many strains of bacteria, this helps fight bacterial infections. The hyperbaric chamber may also be used to counteract carbon monoxide (CO) poisoning and to treat some cancers. In carbon monoxide poisoning, CO has a much stronger affinity for hemoglobin than oxygen does.

The blood is normally capable of dissolving up to 95% of the oxygen available to it. Thus, if the partial pressure of the oxygen in the hyperbaric chamber is 2280 mmHg (3 atm), about 2170 mmHg of oxygen can dissolve in the blood, saturating the tissues. In the treatment for carbon monoxide poisoning, oxygen at high pressure is used to displace the CO from the hemoglobin faster than breathing pure oxygen at 1 atm.

A patient undergoing treatment in a hyperbaric chamber must also undergo decompression (reduction of pressure) at a rate that slowly reduces the concentration of dissolved oxygen in the blood. If decompression is too rapid, the oxygen dissolved in the blood may form gas bubbles in the circulatory system.

Similarly, if a scuba diver does not decompress slowly, a condition called the "bends" may occur. While below the surface of the ocean, a diver uses a breathing mixture with higher pressures. If there is nitrogen in the mixture, higher quantities of nitrogen gas will dissolve in the blood. If the diver ascends to the surface too quickly, the dissolved nitrogen forms gas bubbles that can block a blood vessel and cut off the flow of blood in the joints and tissues of the body and be quite painful. A diver suffering from the bends is placed immediately into a hyperbaric chamber, where pressure is first increased and then slowly decreased. The dissolved nitrogen can then diffuse through the lungs as the pressure is decreasing until atmospheric pressure is reached. See also Section 2.3, Chemistry Link to Health "Breathing Mixtures for Scuba."

A hyperbaric chamber is used in the treatment of certain diseases.

QUESTIONS AND PROBLEMS

7.9 Partial Pressures (Dalton's Law)

LEARNING GOAL: *Use Dalton's law of partial pressures to calculate the total pressure of a mixture of gases.*

7.63 A typical air sample in the lungs contains oxygen at 98 mmHg, nitrogen at 573 mmHg, carbon dioxide at 40. mmHg, and water vapor at 47 mmHg. What is the total pressure, in mmHg, of the gas sample?

7.64 A Nitrox II gas mixture for scuba diving contains oxygen gas at 53 atm and nitrogen gas at 94 atm. What is the total pressure, in atm, of the scuba gas mixture?

7.65 In a gas mixture, the partial pressures are nitrogen 425 torr, oxygen 115 torr, and helium 225 torr. What is the total pressure (torr) exerted by the gas mixture?

7.66 In a gas mixture, the partial pressures are argon 415 mmHg, neon 75 mmHg, and nitrogen 125 mmHg. What is the total pressure (mmHg) exerted by the gas mixture?

7.67 A gas mixture containing oxygen, nitrogen, and helium exerts a total pressure of 925 torr. If the partial pressures are oxygen 425 torr and helium 75 torr, what is the partial pressure (atm) of the nitrogen in the mixture?

7.68 A gas mixture containing oxygen, nitrogen, and neon exerts a total pressure of 1.20 atm. If helium added to the mixture increases the pressure to 1.50 atm, what is the partial pressure (mmHg) of the helium?

7.69 In certain lung ailments such as emphysema, there is a decrease in the ability of oxygen to diffuse into the blood.
a. How would the partial pressure of oxygen in the blood change?
b. Why does a person with severe emphysema sometimes use a portable oxygen tank?

7.70 An injury to the head can affect the ability of a person to ventilate (breathe in and out), and so can certain drugs.
a. What would happen to the partial pressures of oxygen and carbon dioxide in the blood if a person cannot properly ventilate?
b. When a person with hypoventilation is placed on a ventilator, an air mixture is delivered at pressures that are alternately above and below the air pressure in the person's lung. How will this move oxygen gas into the lungs, and carbon dioxide out?

CONCEPT MAP

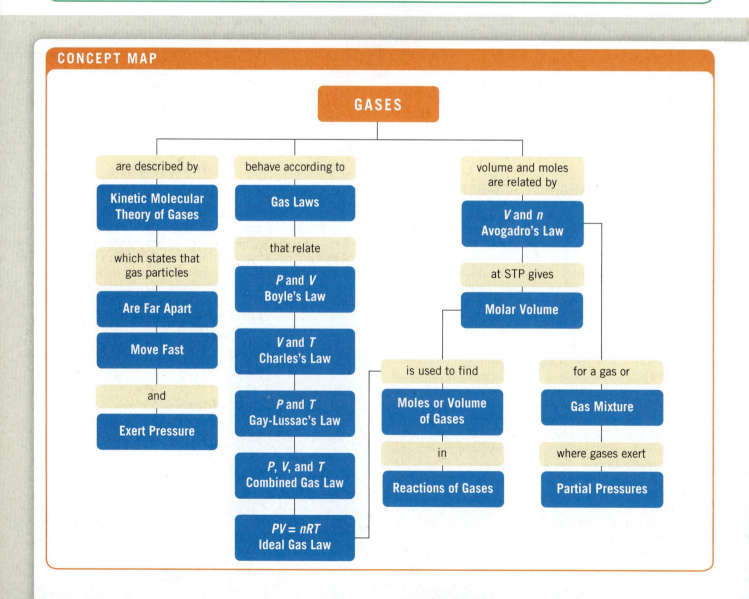

CHAPTER REVIEW

7.1 Properties of Gases

LEARNING GOAL: Describe the kinetic molecular theory of gases and the properties of gases.

- In a gas, particles are so far apart and moving so fast that their attractions are negligible.
- A gas is described by the physical properties of pressure (P), volume (V), temperature (T), and amount in moles (n).

7.2 Gas Pressure

LEARNING GOAL: Describe the units of measurement used for pressure, and change from one unit to another.

Vacuum (no air particles)

760 mmHg

Gases of the atmosphere at 1 atm

Liquid mercury

- A gas exerts pressure, the force of the gas particles striking the walls of a container.
- Gas pressure is measured in units such as torr, mmHg, atm, and Pa.

7.3 Pressure and Volume (Boyle's Law)

LEARNING GOAL: Use the pressure–volume relationship (Boyle's law) to determine the new pressure or volume when the temperature and amount of gas are constant.

Piston

$V = 4$ L
$P = 1$ atm

$V = 2$ L
$P = 2$ atm

- The volume (V) of a gas changes inversely with the pressure (P) of the gas if there is no change in the temperature and the amount of gas.

$$P_1V_1 = P_2V_2$$

- This means that the pressure increases if volume decreases; pressure decreases if volume increases.

7.4 Temperature and Volume (Charles's Law)

LEARNING GOAL: Use the temperature–volume relationship (Charles's law) to determine the new temperature or volume when the pressure and amount of gas are constant.

$T = 200$ K
$V = 1$ L

$T = 400$ K
$V = 2$ L

- The volume (V) of a gas is directly related to its Kelvin temperature (T) when there is no change in the pressure and amount of the gas.

$$\frac{V_1}{T_1} = \frac{V_2}{T_2}$$

- Therefore, if temperature increases, the volume of the gas increases; if temperature decreases, volume decreases.

7.5 Temperature and Pressure (Gay-Lussac's Law)

LEARNING GOAL: Use the temperature–pressure relationship (Gay-Lussac's law) to determine the new temperature or pressure when the volume and amount of gas are constant.

$T = 200$ K
$P = 1$ atm

$T = 400$ K
$P = 2$ atm

- The pressure (P) of a gas is directly related to its Kelvin temperature (T).

$$\frac{P_1}{T_1} = \frac{P_2}{T_2}$$

- This relationship means that an increase in temperature increases the pressure of a gas, and a decrease in temperature decreases the pressure, as long as the volume and amount of gas remain constant.

- Vapor pressure is the pressure of the gas that forms when a liquid evaporates.
- At the boiling point of a liquid, the vapor pressure equals the external pressure.

7.6 The Combined Gas Law

LEARNING GOAL: Use the combined gas law to find the new pressure, volume, or temperature of a gas when changes in two of these properties are given and the amount of gas is constant.

- The combined gas law is the relationship of pressure (P), volume (V), and temperature (T) for a constant amount of gas.
- This expression is used to determine the effect of changes in two of the variables on the third.

$$\frac{P_1V_1}{T_1} = \frac{P_2V_2}{T_2}$$

7.7 Volume and Moles (Avogadro's Law)

LEARNING GOAL: Use Avogadro's law to determine the amount or volume of a gas when the pressure and temperature are constant.

$V = 22.4$ L

1 mole of O_2
32.0 g of O_2
273 K
1 atm

- The volume (V) of a gas is directly related to the number of moles (n) of the gas when the pressure and temperature of the gas do not change.

$$\frac{V_1}{n_1} = \frac{V_2}{n_2}$$

- If the moles of gas increase, the volume must increase; if the moles of gas decrease, the volume must decrease.
- At standard temperature (273 K) and standard pressure (1 atm), abbreviated STP, one mole of any gas has a volume of 22.4 L.

7.8 The Ideal Gas Law

LEARNING GOAL: Use the ideal gas law equation to solve for P, V, T, or n of a gas when given three of the four values in the ideal gas law.

- The ideal gas law equation gives the relationship of all the quantities P, V, n, and T that describe and measure a gas:

$$PV = nRT.$$

- Any of the four variables can be calculated if the other three are known.

7.9 Partial Pressures (Dalton's Law)

LEARNING GOAL: Use Dalton's law of partial pressures to calculate the total pressure of a mixture of gases.

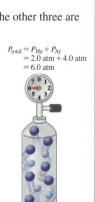

$P_{total} = P_{He} + P_{Ar}$
$= 2.0$ atm $+ 4.0$ atm
$= 6.0$ atm

- In a mixture of two or more gases, the total pressure is the sum of the partial pressures of the individual gases.

$$P_{total} = P_1 + P_2 + P_3 + \cdots$$

- The partial pressure of a gas in a mixture is the pressure it would exert if it were the only gas in the container.

KEY TERMS

atmosphere (atm) The pressure exerted by a column of mercury 760 mm high.

atmospheric pressure The pressure exerted by the atmosphere.

Avogadro's law A gas law stating that the volume of a gas is directly related to the number of moles of the gas when pressure and temperature do not change.

Boyle's law A gas law stating that the pressure of a gas is inversely related to the volume when temperature (K) and amount (moles) of the gas do not change.

Charles's law A gas law stating that the volume of a gas changes directly with a change in Kelvin temperature when pressure and amount (moles) of the gas do not change.

combined gas law A relationship that combines several gas laws relating pressure, volume, and temperature, when the amount of gas does not change.

$$\frac{P_1 V_1}{T_1} = \frac{P_2 V_2}{T_2}$$

Dalton's law A gas law stating that the total pressure exerted by a mixture of gases in a container is the sum of the partial pressures that each gas would exert alone.

direct relationship A relationship in which two properties increase or decrease together.

Gay-Lussac's law A gas law stating that the pressure of a gas changes directly with a change in Kelvin temperature when the number of moles of the gas and its volume do not change.

ideal gas constant, R A numerical value that relates the quantities P, V, n, and T in the ideal gas law equation, $PV = nRT$.

ideal gas law A law that combines the four measured properties of a gas in the equation $PV = nRT$.

inverse relationship A relationship in which two properties change in opposite directions.

kinetic molecular theory of gases A model used to explain the behavior of gases.

molar volume A volume of 22.4 L occupied by 1 mole of a gas at STP conditions of 0 °C (273 K) and 1 atm.

partial pressure The pressure exerted by a single gas in a gas mixture.

pressure The force exerted by gas particles that hit the walls of a container.

STP Standard conditions of exactly 0 °C (273 K) temperature and 1 atm pressure used for the comparison of gases.

vapor pressure The pressure exerted by the particles of vapor above a liquid.

UNDERSTANDING THE CONCEPTS

The chapter sections to review are shown in parentheses at the end of each question.

7.71 At 100 °C, which of the following diagrams (**1**, **2**, or **3**) represents a gas sample that exerts the: (7.7)
   a. lowest pressure?   **b.** highest pressure?

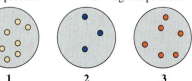

7.72 Indicate which diagram (**1**, **2**, or **3**) represents the volume of a gas sample in a flexible container when each of the following changes (**a–e**) takes place: (7.3, 7.4)

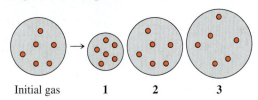

   a. Temperature increases at constant pressure.
   b. Temperature decreases at constant pressure.
   c. Atmospheric pressure increases at constant temperature.
   d. Atmospheric pressure decreases at constant temperature.
   e. Doubling the atmospheric pressure and doubling the Kelvin temperature.

7.73 A balloon is filled with helium gas with a partial pressure of 1.00 atm, and neon gas with a partial pressure of 0.50 atm. For each of the following changes of the initial balloon, select the diagram (**A**, **B**, or **C**) that shows the final volume of the balloon: (7.3, 7.4, 7.7)
   a. The balloon is put in a cold storage unit (*P* and *n* constant).
   b. The balloon floats to a higher altitude where the pressure is less (*n* and *T* are constant).

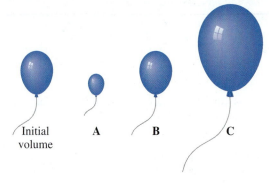

   c. All of the neon gas is removed (*T* and *P* constant).
   d. The Kelvin temperature doubles and one-half of the gas atoms leak out (*P* is constant).
   e. 2.0 moles of O_2 gas is added at constant *T* and *P*.

7.74 Indicate if pressure *increases*, *decreases*, or *does not change* in each of the following: (7.3, 7.5, 7.7)

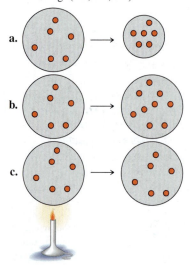

ADDITIONAL QUESTIONS AND PROBLEMS

For instructor-assigned homework, go to www.masteringchemistry.com.

7.75 At a restaurant, a customer chokes on a piece of food. You put your arms around the person's waist and use your fists to push up on the person's abdomen, an action called the *Heimlich maneuver*. (7.3)
   a. How would this action change the volume of the chest and lungs?
   b. Why does it cause the person to expel the food item from the airway?

7.76 An airplane is pressurized to 650. mmHg. (7.9)
   a. If air is 21% oxygen, what is the partial pressure of oxygen on the plane?
   b. If the partial pressure of oxygen drops below 100. mmHg, passengers become drowsy. If this happens, oxygen masks are released. What is the total cabin pressure at which oxygen masks are dropped?

7.77 In 1783, Jacques Charles launched his first balloon filled with hydrogen gas, which he chose because it was lighter than air. The balloon had a volume of 31 000 L when it reached an altitude of 1000 m, where the pressure was 658 mmHg and the temperature was $-8\,°C$. How many kilograms of hydrogen were used to fill the balloon at STP? (7.7)

Jacques Charles used hydrogen to launch his balloon in 1783.

7.78 Your spaceship has docked at a space station above Mars. The temperature inside the space station is a carefully controlled $24\,°C$ at a pressure of 745 mmHg. A balloon with a volume of 425 mL drifts into the airlock where the temperature is $-95\,°C$ and the pressure is 0.115 atm. What is the new volume, in milliliters, of the balloon if n remains constant and the balloon is very elastic? (7.6)

7.79 A fire extinguisher has a pressure of 10. atm at $25\,°C$. What is the pressure, in atmospheres, if the fire extinguisher is used at a temperature of $75\,°C$ and V and n remain constant? (7.5)

7.80 A weather balloon has a volume of 750 L when filled with helium at $8\,°C$ at a pressure of 380 torr. What is the new volume of the balloon when the pressure is 0.20 atm, the temperature is $-45\,°C$, and n remains constant? (7.6)

7.81 A sample of hydrogen (H_2) gas at $127\,°C$ has a pressure of 2.00 atm. At what temperature ($°C$) will the pressure of the H_2 decrease to 0.25 atm, if V and n remain constant? (7.5)

7.82 A sample of nitrogen (N_2) gas has a pressure of 745 mmHg at $30.\,°C$. What is the pressure when the temperature rises to $125\,°C$? (7.5)

7.83 How many moles of CO_2 are in 35.0 L of $CO_2(g)$ at 1.2 atm and $5\,°C$? (7.8)

7.84 A container is filled with 0.67 mole of O_2 at $5\,°C$ and 845 mmHg. What is the volume, in milliliters, of the container? (7.8)

7.85 A 2.00-L container is filled with methane gas (CH_4) at a pressure of 2500. mmHg and a temperature of $18\,°C$. How many grams of methane are in the container? (7.8)

7.86 A steel cylinder with a volume of 15.0 L is filled with 50.0 g of nitrogen gas at $25\,°C$. What is the pressure, in atmospheres, of the N_2 gas in the cylinder? (7.8)

7.87 When heated, calcium carbonate decomposes to give calcium oxide and carbon dioxide gas. If 56.0 g of $CaCO_3$ react, how many liters of CO_2 gas are produced at STP? (7.7)

$$CaCO_3(s) \xrightarrow{\Delta} CaO(s) + CO_2(g)$$

7.88 Magnesium reacts with oxygen to form magnesium oxide. How many liters of oxygen gas at STP are needed to react completely with 8.0 g of magnesium? (7.7)

$$2Mg(s) + O_2(g) \xrightarrow{\Delta} 2MgO(s)$$

7.89 In the Haber process, H_2 and N_2 react to produce ammonia (NH_3). How many grams of N_2 are needed to produce 150 L of ammonia at STP? (7.6)

$$3H_2(g) + N_2(g) \longrightarrow 2NH_3(g)$$

7.90 How many liters of H_2 gas at STP can be produced from the reaction of 2.45 g of Al with excess HCl? (7.6)

$$2Al(s) + 6HCl(aq) \longrightarrow 2AlCl_3(aq) + 3H_2(g)$$

7.91 Aluminum oxide can be formed from its elements. What volume, in liters, of oxygen at STP is needed to completely react 5.4 g of Al? (7.6)

$$4Al(s) + 3O_2(g) \xrightarrow{\Delta} 2Al_2O_3(s)$$

7.92 Glucose, $C_6H_{12}O_6$, is metabolized in living systems to CO_2 and H_2O. How many grams of water can be produced from 12.5 L of O_2 at STP? (7.6)

$$C_6H_{12}O_6(s) + 6O_2(g) \longrightarrow 6CO_2(g) + 6H_2O(l)$$

7.93 A sample of gas with a mass of 1.62 g has a volume of 941 mL at a pressure of 748 torr and a temperature of $20\,°C$. What is the molar mass, g/mole, of the gas? (7.8)

7.94 What is the molar mass, g/mole, of a gas if 1.15 g of the gas has a volume of 225 mL at STP? (7.7, 7.8)

7.95 Nitrogen dioxide reacts with water to produce oxygen and ammonia. How many liters of O_2 are produced when 0.42 mole of NO_2 reacts at STP? (7.7, 7.8)

$$4NO_2(g) + 6H_2O(g) \xrightarrow{\Delta} 7O_2(g) + 4NH_3(g)$$

7.96 What is the volume, in liters, of H_2 gas produced at STP from the reaction of 25.0 g of Al? (7.7)

$$2Al(s) + 3H_2SO_4(aq) \longrightarrow Al_2(SO_4)_3(aq) + 3H_2(g)$$

7.97 A weather balloon is partially filled with helium to allow for expansion at high altitudes. At STP, a weather balloon is filled with enough helium to give a volume of 25.0 L. How many grams of helium were added to the balloon? (7.6, 7.7)

7.98 At an altitude of 30.0 km, where the temperature is $-35\,°C$, a weather balloon containing 1.75 moles of helium has a volume of 2460 L. What is the pressure, in mmHg, of the helium inside the balloon? (7.8)

7.99 A gas mixture contains oxygen and argon at partial pressures of 0.60 atm and 425 mmHg. If nitrogen gas added to the sample increases the total pressure to 1250 torr, what is the partial pressure, in torr, of the nitrogen added? (7.9)

7.100 A gas mixture contains helium and oxygen at partial pressures of 255 torr and 0.450 atm. What is the total pressure, in mmHg, of the mixture after it is placed in a container one-half the volume of the original container? (7.9)

CHALLENGE QUESTIONS

7.101 A gas sample has a volume of 4250 mL at 15 °C and 745 mmHg. What is the new temperature (°C) after the sample is transferred to a new container with a volume of 2.50 L and a pressure of 1.20 atm? (7.6)

7.102 In the fermentation of glucose (wine making), a volume of 780 mL of CO_2 gas was produced at 37 °C and 1.00 atm. What is the volume (L) of the gas when measured at 22 °C and 675 mmHg? (7.6)

7.103 When a car is involved in a collision, sodium azide, NaN_3, in the airbags reacts to produce nitrogen gas, which fills the airbags within 0.03 s. How many liters of N_2 are produced at STP if one airbag contains 132 g of NaN_3? (7.7)

$$2NaN_3(s) \longrightarrow 2Na(s) + 3N_2(g)$$

7.104 Ammonia reacts with oxygen to produce nitrogen oxide and water. How many liters of nitrogen oxide at STP are produced from the reaction of 50. g of NH_3? (7.7, 7.8)

$$4NH_3(g) + 5O_2(g) \longrightarrow 4NO(g) + 6H_2O(g)$$

7.105 A 1.00-g sample of dry ice (CO_2) is placed in a container that has a volume of 4.60 L and a temperature of 24 °C. What is the pressure of CO_2, in mmHg, inside the container after all the dry ice changes to a gas? (7.8)

$$CO_2(s) \longrightarrow CO_2(g)$$

7.106 A 250-mL sample of nitrogen (N_2) has a pressure of 745 mmHg at 30. °C. What is the mass, in grams, of the nitrogen gas? (7.8)

7.107 Hydrogen gas can be produced in the laboratory through the reaction of magnesium metal with hydrochloric acid. What is the volume, in liters, of H_2 gas produced at 24 °C and 835 mmHg, from the reaction of 12.0 g of Mg? (7.8)

$$Mg(s) + 2HCl(aq) \longrightarrow MgCl_2(aq) + H_2(g)$$

7.108 In the formation of smog, nitrogen and oxygen gas react to form nitrogen dioxide. How many grams of nitrogen dioxide will be produced when 2.0 L of nitrogen at 840 mmHg and 24 °C are completely reacted? (7.8)

$$N_2(g) + 2O_2(g) \longrightarrow 2NO_2(g)$$

7.109 Solid aluminum reacts with H_2SO_4 to form H_2 gas and aluminum sulfate. How many grams of Al can react when 415 mL of H_2 gas is produced at 23 °C at a pressure of 734 mmHg? (7.8)

$$2Al(s) + 3H_2SO_4(aq) \longrightarrow 3H_2(g) + Al_2(SO_4)_3(aq)$$

7.110 When heated, solid $KClO_3$ forms solid KCl and O_2 gas. When a sample of $KClO_3$ is heated, 226 mL of O_2 gas is produced with a pressure of 719 mmHg and a temperature of 26 °C. How many grams of $KClO_3$ reacted? (7.8)

$$2KClO_3(s) \xrightarrow{\Delta} 2KCl(s) + 3O_2(g)$$

ANSWERS

Answers to Study Checks

7.1 The mass, in grams, gives the amount of gas.

7.2 250 torr

7.3 73.5 mL

7.4 569 mL

7.5 16 °C

7.6 241 mmHg

7.7 7.50 L

7.8 7.0 g of N_2

7.9 5.41 L of H_2

7.10 0.327 mole of Cl_2

7.11 1.04 L

7.12 104 g/mole

7.13 18.1 L of H_2

7.14 755 torr

Answers to Selected Questions and Problems

7.1 a. At a higher temperature, gas particles have greater kinetic energy, which makes them move faster.
  b. Because there are great distances between the particles of a gas, they can be pushed closer together and still remain a gas.

7.3 a. temperature
  b. volume
  c. amount
  d. pressure

7.5 atmospheres (atm), mmHg, torr, lb/in.^{2}, kPa

7.7 a. 1520 torr
  b. 1520 mmHg

7.9 As the scuba diver ascends to the surface, external pressure decreases. If the air in the lungs, which is at a higher pressure, were not exhaled, its volume would expand and severely damage the lungs. The pressure of the gas in the lungs must adjust to changes in the external pressure.

7.11 a. The pressure is greater in cylinder **A**. According to Boyle's law, a decrease in volume pushes the gas particles closer together, which will cause an increase in the pressure.

b.

Property	Conditions 1	Conditions 2	Know	Predict
Pressure (P)	650 mmHg	1.2 atm (910 mmHg)	P increases	
Volume (V)	220 mL	160 mL		V decreases

7.13 a. increases   **b.** decreases   **c.** increases

7.15 a. 328 mmHg   **b.** 2620 mmHg   **c.** 4370 mmHg

7.17 a. 25 L   **b.** 12.5 L   **c.** 100. L

7.19 25 L

7.21 a. inspiration   **b.** expiration   **c.** inspiration

7.23 a. C   **b.** A   **c.** B

7.25 a. 303 °C   **b.** −129 °C
     c. 591 °C   **d.** 136 °C

7.27 a. 2400 mL   **b.** 4900 mL
     c. 1800 mL   **d.** 1700 mL

7.29 An increase in temperature increases the pressure inside the can. When the pressure exceeds the pressure limit of the can, it explodes.

7.31 a. −23 °C   **b.** 168 °C

7.33 a. 770 torr   **b.** 1.51 atm

7.35 a. boiling point   **b.** vapor pressure

7.37 a. On top of a mountain, water boils below 100 °C because the atmospheric (external) pressure is less than 1 atm.
     b. Because the pressure inside a pressure cooker is greater than 1 atm, water boils above 100 °C. At a higher temperature, food cooks faster.

7.39 a. 4.26 atm   **b.** 3.07 atm   **c.** 0.606 atm

7.41 −33 °C

7.43 The volume increases because the number of gas particles is increased.

7.45 a. 4.00 L   **b.** 14.6 L   **c.** 26.7 L

7.47 a. 2.00 moles of O_2
     b. 0.179 mole of CO_2
     c. 4.48 L
     d. 55 400 mL

7.49 7.60 L of H_2

7.51 4.93 atm

7.53 29.4 g of O_2

7.55 565 K (292 °C)

7.57 a. 42 g/mole   **b.** 39.8 g/mole   **c.** 33 g/mole

7.59 178 L of O_2

7.61 5.25 L of O_2

7.63 758 mmHg

7.65 765 torr

7.67 0.559 atm

7.69 a. The partial pressure of oxygen will be lower than normal.
     b. Breathing a higher concentration of oxygen will help to increase the supply of oxygen in the lungs and blood and raise the partial pressure of oxygen in the blood.

7.71 a. 2   **b.** 1

7.73 a. A   **b.** C
     c. A   **d.** B
     e. C

7.75 a. The volume of the chest and lungs is decreased.
     b. The decrease in volume increases the pressure, which can dislodge the food in the trachea.

7.77 2.5 kg of H_2

7.79 12 atm

7.81 −223 °C

7.83 1.8 moles of CO_2

7.85 4.40 g

7.87 12.5 L of CO_2

7.89 94 g of N_2

7.91 3.4 L of O_2

7.93 42.1 g/mole

7.95 16 L of O_2

7.97 4.46 g of helium

7.99 370 torr

7.101 −66 °C

7.103 68.2 L of N_2

7.105 91.5 mmHg

7.107 11.0 L of H_2

7.109 0.297 g of Al

8 Solutions

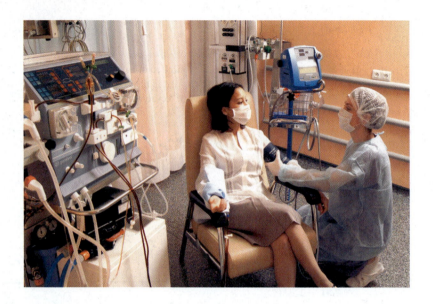

Visit **www.masteringchemistry.com** for self-study materials and instructor-assigned homework.

When Michelle's kidneys stopped

functioning, she was placed on dialysis three times a week. As she enters the dialysis unit, her dialysis nurse, Amanda, asks Michelle how she is feeling. Michelle indicates that she feels tired today and has considerable swelling around her ankles.

The dialysis nurse informs Michelle that her side effects are due to her body's inability to regulate the amount of water in her cells. She explains that the amount of water is regulated by the concentration of electrolytes in her body fluids and the rate at which waste products are removed from her body. Amanda explains that although water is essential for the many chemical reactions that occur in the body, the amount of water can become too high or too low, due to various diseases and conditions.

Because Michelle's kidneys no longer perform dialysis, she cannot regulate the amount of electrolytes or waste products in her body fluids. As a result, she has an electrolyte imbalance and a build-up of waste products, so her body is retaining water. Amanda then explains that the dialysis machine does the work of her kidneys to reduce the high levels of electrolytes and waste products.

Career: Dialysis Nurse

A dialysis nurse specializes in assisting patients with kidney disease undergoing dialysis. This requires monitoring the patient before, during, and after dialysis for any complications such as a drop in blood pressure or cramping. The dialysis nurse connects the patient to the dialysis unit via a dialysis catheter that is inserted into the neck or chest, which must be kept clean to prevent infection. A dialysis nurse must have considerable knowledge about how the dialysis machine functions to ensure that it is operating correctly at all times.

Solutions are everywhere around us. Most consist of one substance dissolved in another. The air we breathe is a solution of primarily oxygen and nitrogen gases. Carbon dioxide gas dissolved in water makes carbonated drinks. When we make solutions of coffee or tea, we use hot water to dissolve substances from coffee beans or tea leaves. The ocean is also a solution, consisting of many salts, such as sodium chloride, dissolved in water. In a hospital, antiseptic tincture of iodine is a solution of iodine dissolved in ethanol.

Our body fluids contain water and dissolved substances, such as glucose and urea, and ions called electrolytes, such as K^+, Na^+, Cl^-, Mg^{2+}, HCO_3^-, and HPO_4^{2-}. Proper amounts of each of these dissolved substances and water must be maintained in the body fluids. Small changes in electrolyte levels can seriously disrupt cellular processes, endangering our health. Therefore, the measurement of their concentrations is a valuable diagnostic tool.

Through the processes of osmosis and dialysis, water, essential nutrients, and waste products enter and leave the cells of the body. In osmosis, water flows in and out of the cells of the body. In dialysis, small particles in solution as well as water diffuse through semipermeable membranes. The kidneys utilize osmosis and dialysis to regulate the amount of water and electrolytes that are excreted.

8.1 Solutions

A **solution** is a homogeneous mixture in which one substance called the **solute** is uniformly dispersed in another substance called the **solvent** (see Figure 8.1). When a small amount of salt is dissolved in water, the salt-water solution tastes slightly salty. When more salt is dissolved, the salt-water solution tastes very salty. Usually, the solute (in this case, salt) is the substance present in the smaller amount, whereas the solvent (in this case, water) is present in the larger amount. For example, when a solution is composed of 5.0 g of salt and 50. g of water, salt is the solute, and water is the solvent.

LEARNING GOAL

Identify the solute and solvent in a solution; describe the formation of a solution.

Solute: The substance present in lesser amount

Salt

Water

Solvent: The substance present in greater amount

A solution consists of at least one solute dispersed in a solvent.

CONCEPT CHECK 8.1   Identifying a Solute and a Solvent

Identify the solute and the solvent in each of the following solutions:

a. 15 g of sugar dissolved in 500 g of water
b. 75 mL of water mixed with 25 mL of isopropyl alcohol
c. a tincture of iodine prepared with 0.10 g of I_2 and 10.0 g of ethanol

ANSWER

a. Sugar, the smaller quantity, is the solute; water is the solvent.
b. Isopropyl alcohol, which has the smaller volume, is the solute; water is the solvent.
c. Iodine, the smaller quantity, is the solute; ethanol is the solvent.

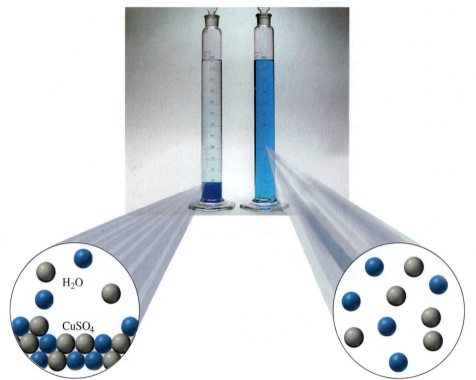

FIGURE 8.1 A solution of copper(II) sulfate ($CuSO_4$) forms as particles of solute dissolve, move away from the crystals, and become evenly dispersed among the solvent (water) molecules.

Q What does the uniform blue color in the graduated cylinder on the right indicate about the $CuSO_4$ solution?

Types of Solutes and Solvents

Solutes and solvents may be solids, liquids, or gases. The solution that forms has the same physical state as the solvent. When sugar crystals are dissolved in water, the resulting sugar solution is liquid. Sugar is the solute, and water is the solvent. Soda water and soft drinks are prepared by dissolving carbon dioxide gas in water. The carbon dioxide gas is the solute, and water is the solvent. Table 8.1 lists some solutes and solvents and their solutions.

TABLE 8.1 Some Examples of Solutions

Type	Example	Primary Solute	Solvent
Gas Solutions			
Gas in a gas	Air	Oxygen (gas)	Nitrogen (gas)
Liquid Solutions			
Gas in a liquid	Soda water	Carbon dioxide (gas)	Water (liquid)
	Household ammonia	Ammonia (gas)	Water (liquid)
Liquid in a liquid	Vinegar	Acetic acid (liquid)	Water (liquid)
Solid in a liquid	Seawater	Sodium chloride (solid)	Water (liquid)
	Tincture of iodine	Iodine (solid)	Ethanol (liquid)
Solid Solutions			
Solid in a solid	Brass	Zinc (solid)	Copper (solid)
	Steel	Carbon (solid)	Iron (solid)

SELF-STUDY ACTIVITY
Hydrogen Bonding

Water as a Solvent

Water is one of the most common solvents in nature. In the H_2O molecule, an oxygen atom shares electrons with two hydrogen atoms. Because oxygen is much more electronegative than hydrogen, the O—H bonds are polar. In each polar bond, the oxygen atom has a partial negative (δ^-) charge, and the hydrogen atom has a partial positive (δ^+) charge. Because the water molecule has a bent shape, water is a *polar solvent*.

In Section 5.9, we learned that *hydrogen bonds* are interactions between molecules where partially positive hydrogen atoms are attracted to the partially negative atoms of O, N, or F. In the diagram to the right, hydrogen bonds are shown as dotted lines. Although hydrogen bonds are much weaker than covalent or ionic bonds, there are many of them linking water molecules together. Hydrogen bonds also are important in the properties of biological compounds such as proteins, carbohydrates, and DNA.

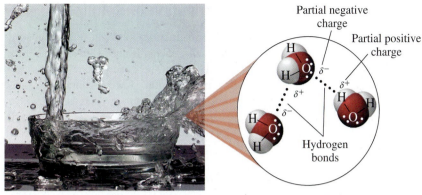

In water, hydrogen bonds form between a partially positive hydrogen atom in one water molecule and a partially negative oxygen atom in another.

Chemistry Link to Health

WATER IN THE BODY

The average adult body contains about 60% water by mass, and the average infant about 75%. About 60% of the body's water is contained within the cells as intracellular fluids; the other 40% makes up extracellular fluids, which include the interstitial fluid in tissue and the plasma in the blood. These external fluids carry nutrients and waste materials between the cells and the circulatory system.

Every day you lose between 1500 and 3000 mL of water from the kidneys as urine, from the skin as perspiration, from the lungs as you exhale, and from the gastrointestinal tract. Serious dehydration can occur in an adult if there is a 10% loss in total body fluid. A 20% loss of fluid can be fatal. An infant suffers severe dehydration with a 5–10% loss in body fluid.

24 Hours

Water gain		Water loss	
Liquid	1000 mL	Urine	1500 mL
Food	1200 mL	Perspiration	300 mL
Metabolism	300 mL	Breath	600 mL
		Feces	100 mL
Total	2500 mL	Total	2500 mL

Water loss is continually replaced by the liquids and foods in the diet, and from metabolic processes that produce water in the cells of the body. Table 8.2 lists the percentage by mass of water contained in some foods.

The water lost from the body is replaced by the intake of fluids.

TABLE 8.2 Percentage of Water in Some Foods

Food	Water (% by mass)	Food	Water (% by mass)
Vegetables		**Meats/Fish**	
Carrot	88	Chicken, cooked	71
Celery	94	Hamburger, broiled	60
Cucumber	96	Salmon	71
Tomato	94		
Fruits		**Milk Products**	
Apple	85	Cottage cheese	78
Cantaloupe	91	Milk, whole	87
Orange	86	Yogurt	88
Strawberry	90		
Watermelon	93		

Formation of Solutions

The interactions between solute and solvent will determine whether a solution will form. Initially, energy is needed to separate the particles in the solute and to move the solvent particles apart. Then, energy is released as solute particles move between the solvent particles to form a solution. However, attractive forces between the solute and the solvent particles must be strong enough to provide the energy for the initial separation. These attractive forces only occur when the solute and the solvent have similar polarities. If there is no attraction between a solute and a solvent, there is not sufficient energy to form a solution (see Table 8.3).

TABLE 8.3 Possible Combinations of Solutes and Solvents

Solutions Will Form		Solutions Will Not Form	
Solute	Solvent	Solute	Solvent
Polar	Polar	Polar	Nonpolar
Nonpolar	Nonpolar	Nonpolar	Polar

Solutions with Ionic and Polar Solutes

In ionic solutes such as sodium chloride, NaCl, there are strong solute–solute attractions between positively charged Na^+ ions and negatively charged Cl^- ions. When NaCl crystals are placed in water, the process of dissolution begins as the partially negatively charged oxygen atoms in water molecules attract positive Na^+ ions, and the partially positive hydrogen atoms in other water molecules attract negative Cl^- ions (see Figure 8.2). This process called **hydration** diminishes the attractions between the Na^+ and Cl^- ions and keeps them in solution. The strong solute–solvent attractions between the Na^+ and Cl^- ions and the polar water molecules provide the energy to form the solution.

In the equation for the formation of the NaCl solution, the solid and aqueous NaCl are shown with the formula H_2O over the arrow, which indicates that water is needed for the dissociation process but is not a reactant.

$$NaCl(s) \xrightarrow{H_2O} Na^+(aq) + Cl^-(aq)$$

In another example, we find that a polar covalent compound such as methanol, CH_3-OH, is soluble in water because methanol has a polar $-OH$ group that forms hydrogen bonds with water.

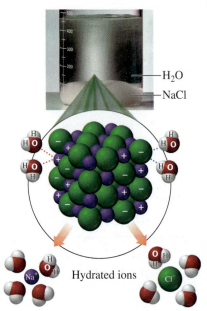

FIGURE 8.2 Ions on the surface of a crystal of NaCl dissolve in water as they are attracted to the polar water molecules that pull the ions into solution and surround them.

Q What helps keep the Na^+ and Cl^- ions in solution?

Molecules of polar covalent compound methanol, CH_3-OH, form hydrogen bonds with polar water molecules to form a methanol–water solution.

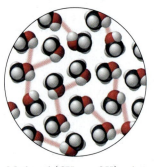
Methanol (CH_3-OH) solute

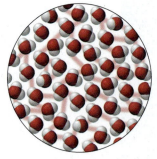
Water solvent

Methanol–water solution with hydrogen bonding

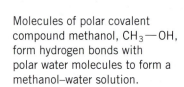
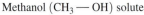

Solutions with Nonpolar Solutes

Compounds containing nonpolar molecules such as iodine (I_2), oil, or grease do not dissolve in water, because there is little or no interaction between the particles of a nonpolar solute and a polar solvent. Nonpolar solutes require nonpolar solvents for a solution to form. The expression "*like dissolves like*" is a way of saying that the polarities of a solute and a solvent must be similar to form a solution. Figure 8.3 illustrates the formation of some polar and nonpolar solutions.

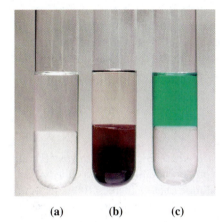

(a)   **(b)**   **(c)**

FIGURE 8.3 Like dissolves like. In each test tube, the lower layer is CH_2Cl_2 (more dense), and the upper layer is water (less dense). **(a)** CH_2Cl_2 is nonpolar and water is polar; the two layers do not mix. **(b)** The nonpolar solute I_2 (purple) is soluble in the nonpolar CH_2Cl_2 layer. **(c)** The ionic solute $Ni(NO_3)_2$ (green) is soluble in the polar water layer.

Q In which layer would polar molecules of sugar be soluble?

CONCEPT CHECK 8.2   **Polar and Nonpolar Solutes**

Indicate whether each of the following substances will form solutions with water. Explain.

a. KCl   **b.** octane, C_8H_{18}, a compound in gasoline
c. ethanol, C_2H_5OH, in mouthwash

ANSWER

a. Yes. KCl is an ionic compound. The solute–solvent attractions between the ions K^+ and Cl^- and polar water molecules provide the energy to break solute–solute and solvent–solvent bonds. Thus, a KCl solution will form.

b. No. Octane, C_8H_{18}, is a nonpolar compound of carbon and hydrogen, which means it does not form a solution with the polar water molecules. There are no attractions between a nonpolar solute and a polar solvent. Thus, no solution forms.

c. C_2H_5OH is a polar solute. Because attractions between a polar solute and the polar solvent water release energy to break solute–solute and solvent–solvent bonds, a C_2H_5OH solution will form.

Explore
Your World

LIKE DISSOLVES LIKE

Mix together small amounts of the following substances:

a. oil and water
b. water and vinegar
c. salt and water
d. sugar and water
e. salt and oil

QUESTIONS

1. Which of the mixtures formed a solution? Which did not?
2. Why do some mixtures form solutions, but others do not?

QUESTIONS AND PROBLEMS

8.1 Solutions

LEARNING GOAL: *Identify the solute and solvent in a solution; describe the formation of a solution.*

8.1 Identify the solute and the solvent in each solution composed of the following:
  a. 10.0 g of NaCl and 100.0 g of H_2O
  b. 50.0 mL of ethanol, C_2H_5OH, and 10.0 mL of H_2O
  c. 0.20 L of O_2 and 0.80 L of N_2 at STP

8.2 Identify the solute and the solvent in each solution composed of the following:
  a. 10 mL of acetic acid and 200 mL of water
  b. 100.0 g of water and 5.0 g of sugar
  c. 1.0 mL of Br_2 and 50.0 mL of methylene chloride

8.3 Describe the formation of an aqueous KI solution when KI dissolves in water.

8.4 Describe the formation of an aqueous LiBr solution when LiBr dissolves in water.

8.5 Water is a polar solvent and carbon tetrachloride, CCl_4, is a nonpolar solvent. In which solvent is each of the following more likely to be soluble?
  a. $NaNO_3$, ionic   **b.** I_2, nonpolar
  c. sucrose (table sugar), polar   **d.** gasoline, nonpolar

8.6 Water is a polar solvent; hexane is a nonpolar solvent. In which solvent is each of the following more likely to be soluble?
  a. vegetable oil, nonpolar   **b.** benzene, nonpolar
  c. LiCl, ionic   **d.** Na_2SO_4, ionic

8.2 Electrolytes and Nonelectrolytes

Solutes can be classified by their ability to conduct an electrical current. When **electrolytes** dissolve in water, they separate into ions that conduct electricity. When **nonelectrolytes** dissolve in water, they dissolve as molecules, not as ions. The solutions of nonelectrolytes do not conduct electricity.

To test solutions for the presence of ions, we can use an apparatus that consists of a battery and a pair of electrodes connected by wires to a light bulb. The light bulb glows when electricity flows, which can only happen when the electrolytes provide ions that move between the electrodes to complete the circuit.

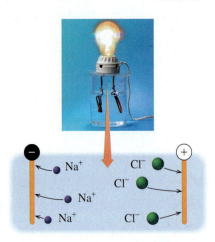

Strong electrolyte

A strong electrolyte completely dissociates into ions in an aqueous solution.

Electrolytes

Electrolytes can be further classified as *strong electrolytes* and *weak electrolytes*. For all electrolytes, some or all of the solute that dissolves produces ions, a process called *dissociation*. For a **strong electrolyte**, such as sodium chloride (NaCl), there is 100% dissociation of the solute into ions. When the electrodes from the light bulb apparatus are placed in a NaCl solution, the light bulb is very bright.

In an equation for dissociation, the charges must balance. For example, magnesium nitrate dissociates to give one magnesium ion for every two nitrate ions. Only the ionic bonds between Mg^{2+} and NO_3^- are broken; the covalent bonds within the polyatomic ion are retained. The dissociation for $Mg(NO_3)_2$ is written as follows:

$$Mg(NO_3)_2(s) \xrightarrow{H_2O} Mg^{2+}(aq) + 2NO_3^-(aq)$$

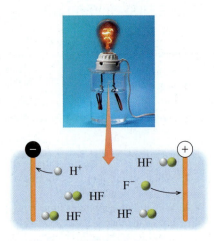

Weak electrolyte

A weak electrolyte forms mostly molecules and a few ions in an aqueous solution.

Weak Electrolytes

A **weak electrolyte** is a compound that dissolves in water mostly as molecules. Only a few of the dissolved solute molecules separate, producing a small number of ions in solution. Thus, solutions of weak electrolytes do not conduct electrical current as well as solutions of strong electrolytes. For example, an aqueous solution of the weak electrolyte HF contains mostly HF molecules and only a few H^+ and F^- ions. When the electrodes of the light bulb apparatus are placed in a solution of a weak electrolyte, the glow of the light bulb is very dim. As more H^+ and F^- ions form, some recombine to give HF molecules. These forward and reverse reactions of molecules to ions and back again are indicated by two arrows between reactant and products that point in opposite directions.

$$HF(aq) \underset{\text{Recombination}}{\overset{\text{Dissociation}}{\rightleftharpoons}} H^+(aq) + F^-(aq)$$

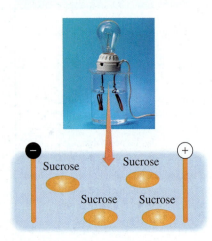

Nonelectrolyte

A nonelectrolyte dissolves as molecules in an aqueous solution.

Nonelectrolytes

A nonelectrolyte such as sucrose (sugar) dissolves in water as molecules, which do not dissociate into ions. When electrodes of the light bulb apparatus are placed in a solution of a nonelectrolyte, the light bulb does not glow, because the solution does not contain ions and cannot conduct electricity.

$$C_{12}H_{22}O_{11}(s) \xrightarrow{H_2O} C_{12}H_{22}O_{11}(aq)$$
Sucrose   Solution of sucrose molecules

Table 8.4 summarizes the classification of solutes in aqueous solutions.

TABLE 8.4 Classification of Solutes in Aqueous Solutions

Type of Solute	Dissociates	Types of Particles in Solution	Conducts Electricity?	Examples
Strong electrolyte	Completely	Ions only	Yes	Ionic compounds such as NaCl, KBr, MgCl$_2$, NaNO$_3$, NaOH, KOH, HCl, HBr, HI, HNO$_3$, HClO$_4$, H$_2$SO$_4$
Weak electrolyte	Partially	Mostly molecules and a few ions	Weakly	HF, H$_2$O, NH$_3$, HC$_2$H$_3$O$_2$ (acetic acid)
Nonelectrolyte	None	Molecules only	No	Carbon compounds such as CH$_3$OH (methanol), C$_2$H$_5$OH (ethanol), C$_{12}$H$_{22}$O$_{11}$ (sucrose), CH$_4$N$_2$O (urea)

CONCEPT CHECK 8.3   Solutions of Electrolytes and Nonelectrolytes

Indicate whether solutions of each of the following contain only ions, only molecules, or mostly molecules and a few ions:

a. Na$_2$SO$_4$, a strong electrolyte   **b.** CH$_3$OH, a nonelectrolyte
c. hypochlorous acid, HClO, a weak electrolyte

ANSWER

a. An aqueous solution of Na$_2$SO$_4$ contains only the ions Na$^+$ and SO$_4{}^{2-}$.
b. A nonelectrolyte such as CH$_3$OH produces only molecules when it dissolves in water.
c. A solution of HClO contains mostly HClO molecules and a few ions of H$^+$ and ClO$^-$.

TUTORIAL
Electrolytes and Ionization

Equivalents

Body fluids contain a mixture of several electrolytes, such as Na$^+$, Cl$^-$, K$^+$, and Ca^{2+}. We measure each individual ion in terms of an **equivalent (Eq)**, which is the amount of that ion equal to 1 mole of positive or negative electrical charge. For example, 1 mole of Na$^+$ ions and 1 mole of Cl$^-$ ions are each 1 equivalent or 1000 milliequivalents (mEq) because they each contain 1 mole of charge. For an ion with a charge of 2+ or 2−, there are 2 equivalents for each mole. Some examples of ions and equivalents are shown in Table 8.5.

TABLE 8.5 Equivalents of Electrolytes

Ion	Electrical Charge	Number of Equivalents in 1 Mole
Na$^+$	1+	1 Eq
Ca^{2+}	2+	2 Eq
Fe^{3+}	3+	3 Eq
Cl$^-$	1−	1 Eq
SO$_4{}^{2-}$	2−	2 Eq

In any solution, the charge of the positive ions is always balanced by the charge of the negative ions. For example, a solution containing 25 mEq/L of Na$^+$ and 4 mEq/L of K$^+$ has a total positive charge of 29 mEq/L. If Cl$^-$ is the only anion in the solution, its concentration must be 29 mEq/L.

SAMPLE PROBLEM 8.1 | Electrolyte Concentration

The laboratory tests for a patient indicate a blood calcium (Ca^{2+}) level of 8.8 mEq/L.

a. How many moles of calcium ion are in 0.50 L of blood?
b. If chloride ion is the only other ion present, what is its concentration in mEq/L?

SOLUTION

a. Using the volume and the electrolyte concentration (in mEq/L), we can find the number of equivalents in 0.50 L of blood.

$$0.50\ \cancel{L} \times \frac{8.8\ \cancel{mEq\ Ca^{2+}}}{1\ \cancel{L}} \times \frac{1\ Eq\ Ca^{2+}}{1000\ \cancel{mEq\ Ca^{2+}}} = 0.0044\ Eq\ of\ Ca^{2+}$$

We can then convert equivalents to moles (for Ca^{2+}, there are 2 Eq/mole).

$$0.0044\ \cancel{Eq\ Ca^{2+}} \times \frac{1\ mole\ Ca^{2+}}{2\ \cancel{Eq\ Ca^{2+}}} = 0.0022\ mole\ of\ Ca^{2+}$$

b. If the concentration of Ca^{2+} is 8.8 mEq/L, then the concentration of Cl^- must be 8.8 mEq/L to balance the charge.

STUDY CHECK 8.1

A Ringer's solution for intravenous fluid replacement contains 155 mEq of Cl^- per liter of solution. If a patient receives 1250 mL of Ringer's solution, how many moles of chloride ion were given?

QUESTIONS AND PROBLEMS

8.2 Electrolytes and Nonelectrolytes

LEARNING GOAL: Identify solutes as electrolytes or nonelectrolytes.

8.7 KF is a strong electrolyte, and HF is a weak electrolyte. How is the solution of KF different from that of HF?

8.8 NaOH is a strong electrolyte, and CH_3OH is a nonelectrolyte. How is the solution of NaOH different from that of CH_3OH?

8.9 Write a balanced equation for the dissociation of each of the following strong electrolytes in water:
  a. KCl   **b.** $CaCl_2$
  c. K_3PO_4 **d.** $Fe(NO_3)_3$

8.10 Write a balanced equation for the dissociation of each of the following strong electrolytes in water:
  a. LiBr   **b.** $NaNO_3$
  c. $CuCl_2$ **d.** K_2CO_3

8.11 Indicate whether aqueous solutions of each of the following contain only ions, only molecules, or mostly molecules and a few ions:
  a. acetic acid ($HC_2H_3O_2$), a weak electrolyte
  b. NaBr, a strong electrolyte
  c. fructose ($C_6H_{12}O_6$), a nonelectrolyte

8.12 Indicate whether aqueous solutions of each of the following contain only ions, only molecules, or mostly molecules and a few ions:
  a. NH_4Cl, a strong electrolyte
  b. ethanol (C_2H_5OH), a nonelectrolyte
  c. hydrocyanic acid (HCN), a weak electrolyte

8.13 Classify each solute represented in the following equations as a strong, weak, or nonelectrolyte:

  a. $K_2SO_4(s) \xrightarrow{H_2O} 2K^+(aq) + SO_4^{2-}(aq)$

  b. $NH_4OH(aq) \underset{\longleftarrow}{\overset{H_2O}{\rightleftharpoons}} NH_4^+(aq) + OH^-(aq)$

  c. $C_6H_{12}O_6(s) \xrightarrow{H_2O} C_6H_{12}O_6(aq)$

8.14 Classify each solute represented in the following equations as a strong, weak, or nonelectrolyte:

  a. $CH_3OH(l) \xrightarrow{H_2O} CH_3OH(aq)$

  b. $MgCl_2(s) \xrightarrow{H_2O} Mg^{2+}(aq) + 2Cl^-(aq)$

  c. $HClO(aq) \underset{\longleftarrow}{\overset{H_2O}{\rightleftharpoons}} H^+(aq) + ClO^-(aq)$

8.15 Indicate the number of equivalents in each of the following:
  a. 1 mole of K^+ **b.** 2 moles of OH^-
  c. 1 mole of Ca^{2+} **d.** 3 moles of CO_3^{2-}

8.16 Indicate the number of equivalents in each of the following:
  a. 1 mole of Mg^{2+} **b.** 0.5 mole of H^+
  c. 4 moles of Cl^- **d.** 2 moles of Fe^{3+}

8.17 A physiological saline solution contains 154 mEq/L, each of Na^+ and Cl^-. How many moles each of Na^+ and Cl^- are in 1.00 L of the saline solution?

8.18 A solution to replace potassium loss contains 40. mEq/L, each of K^+ and Cl^-. How many moles each of K^+ and Cl^- are in 1.5 L of the solution?

8.19 A solution contains 40. mEq/L of Cl^- and 15 mEq/L of HPO_4^{2-}. If Na^+ is the only cation in the solution, what is the Na^+ concentration, in milliequivalents per liter?

8.20 A sample of Ringer's solution contains the following concentrations (mEq/L) of cations: Na^+ 147, K^+ 4, and Ca^{2+} 4. If Cl^- is the only anion in the solution, what is the Cl^- concentration, in milliequivalents per liter?

Chemistry Link to Health

ELECTROLYTES IN BODY FLUIDS

Electrolytes in the body play an important role in maintaining the proper function of the cells and organs in the body. Typically, the electrolytes sodium, potassium, chloride, and bicarbonate are measured in a blood test. Sodium ions regulate the water content in the body and are important in carrying electrical impulses through the nervous system. Potassium ions are also involved in the transmission of electrical impulses and play a role in the maintenance of a regular heartbeat. Chloride ions balance the charges of the positive ions and also control the balance of fluids in the body. Bicarbonate

is important in maintaining the proper pH of the blood. Sometimes when vomiting, diarrhea, or sweating is excessive, the concentrations of certain electrolytes may decrease. Then fluids such as Pedialyte may be given to return electrolyte levels to normal.

The concentrations of electrolytes present in body fluids and in intravenous fluids given to a patient are often expressed in milliequivalents per liter (mEq/L) of solution: 1 Eq = 1000 mEq. For example, one liter of Pedialyte contains the following electrolytes: Na^+ 45 mEq, K^+ 20 mEq, Cl^- 35 mEq, and $citrate^{3-}$ 30 mEq.

Table 8.6 gives the concentrations of some typical electrolytes in blood plasma. There is a charge balance because the total number of positive charges is equal to the total number of negative charges. The use of a specific intravenous solution depends on the nutritional, electrolyte, and fluid needs of the individual patient. Examples of various types of solutions are given in Table 8.7.

TABLE 8.6 Some Typical Concentrations of Electrolytes in Blood Plasma

Electrolyte	Concentration (mEq/L)
Cations	
Na^+	138
K^+	5
Mg^{2+}	3
Ca^{2+}	4
Total	150
Anions	
Cl^-	110
HCO_3^-	30
HPO_4^{2-}	4
Proteins	6
Total	150

An intravenous solution is used to replace electrolytes in the body.

TABLE 8.7 Electrolyte Concentrations in Intravenous Replacement Solutions

Solution	Electrolytes (mEq/L)	Use
Sodium chloride (0.9%)	Na^+ 154, Cl^- 154	Replacement of fluid loss
Potassium chloride with 5% dextrose	K^+ 40, Cl^- 40	Treatment of malnutrition (low potassium levels)
Ringer's solution	Na^+ 147, K^+ 4, Ca^{2+} 4, Cl^- 155	Replacement of fluids and electrolytes lost through dehydration
Maintenance solution with 5% dextrose	Na^+ 40, K^+ 35, Cl^- 40, $lactate^-$ 20, HPO_4^{2-} 15	Maintenance of fluid and electrolyte levels
Replacement solution (extracellular)	Na^+ 140, K^+ 10, Ca^{2+} 5, Mg^{2+} 3, Cl^- 103, $acetate^-$ 47, $citrate^{3-}$ 8	Replacement of electrolytes in extracellular fluids

8.3 Solubility

The term *solubility* is used to describe the amount of a solute that can dissolve in a given amount of solvent. Many factors, such as the type of solute, the type of solvent, and the temperature, affect the solubility of a solute. **Solubility**, usually expressed in grams of solute in 100 grams of solvent, is the maximum amount of solute that can be dissolved at a certain temperature. If a solute readily dissolves when added to the solvent, the solution does not contain the maximum amount of solute. We call this solution an **unsaturated solution**.

LEARNING GOAL

Define solubility. Distinguish between an unsaturated and a saturated solution; identify a salt as soluble or insoluble.

SELF-STUDY ACTIVITY
Solubility

TUTORIAL
Introduction to Solubility and Solution
Formation

A solution that contains all the solute that can dissolve is a **saturated solution**. When a solution is saturated, the rate at which solute dissolves becomes equal to the rate at which solid forms, a process known as recrystallization. Then there is no further change in the amount of dissolved solute in solution.

Solute dissolves

Solute + solvent ⇌ Saturated solution

Solute recrystallizes

We can prepare a saturated solution by adding an amount of solute greater than that needed to reach maximum solubility (saturation). Stirring the solution will dissolve the maximum amount of solute and leave the excess on the bottom of the container. Once we have a saturated solution, the addition of more solute will increase only the amount of undissolved solute.

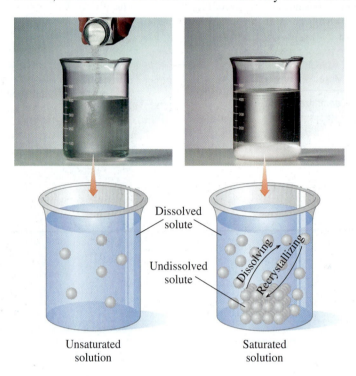

Dissolved solute

Undissolved solute

Unsaturated solution

Saturated solution

More solute can dissolve in an unsaturated solution, but not in a saturated solution.

SAMPLE PROBLEM 8.2 Saturated Solutions

At 20 °C, the solubility of KCl is 34 g/100 g of water. In the laboratory, a student mixes 75 g of KCl with 200. g of water at a temperature of 20 °C.

a. How much of the KCl can dissolve?
b. Is the solution saturated or unsaturated?
c. What is the mass, in grams, of any solid KCl on the bottom of the container?

SOLUTION

a. KCl has a solubility of 34 g of KCl in 100 g of water. Using its solubility as a conversion factor, we can calculate the maximum amount of KCl that can dissolve in 200. g of water as follows:

$$200. \text{ g } H_2O \times \frac{34 \text{ g KCl}}{100 \text{ g } H_2O} = 68 \text{ g of KCl}$$

b. Because 75 g of KCl exceeds the maximum amount (68 g) that can dissolve in 200. g of water, the KCl solution is saturated.

c. If we add 75 g of KCl to 200. g of water and only 68 g of KCl can dissolve, there is 7 g (75 g − 68 g) of solid (undissolved) KCl on the bottom of the container.

STUDY CHECK 8.2

At 40 °C, the solubility of KNO_3 is 65 g/100 g of water. How many grams of KNO_3 will dissolve in 120 g of water at 40 °C?

Chemistry Link to Health

GOUT AND KIDNEY STONES: A PROBLEM OF SATURATION IN BODY FLUIDS

The conditions of gout and kidney stones involve compounds in the body that exceed their solubility levels and form solid products. Gout affects adults, primarily men, over the age of 40. Attacks of gout may occur when the concentration of uric acid in blood plasma exceeds its solubility, which is 7 mg/100 mL of plasma at 37 °C. Insoluble deposits of needle-like crystals of uric acid can form in the cartilage, tendons, and soft tissues, where they cause painful gout attacks. They may also form in the tissues of the kidneys, where they can cause renal damage. High levels of uric acid in the body can be caused by an increase in uric acid production, failure of the kidneys to remove uric acid, or by a diet with an overabundance of foods containing purines, which are metabolized to uric acid in the body. Foods in the diet that contribute to high levels of uric acid include certain meats, sardines, mushrooms,

asparagus, and beans. Drinking alcoholic beverages such as beer may significantly increase uric acid levels and bring about gout attacks.

Treatment for gout involves dietary changes and drugs. Depending on the levels of uric acid, a medication such as probenecid can be used to help the kidneys eliminate uric acid, or allopurinol can be administered to block the production of uric acid by the body.

Kidney stones are solid materials that form in the urinary tract. Most kidney stones are composed of calcium phosphate and calcium oxalate, although they can be solid uric acid. The excessive ingestion of minerals and insufficient water intake can cause the concentration of mineral salts to exceed their solubility and lead to the formation of kidney stones. When a kidney stone passes through the urinary tract, it causes considerable pain and discomfort, necessitating the use of painkillers and possibly surgery. Sometimes ultrasound is used to break up kidney stones. Persons prone to kidney stones are advised to drink six to eight glasses of water every day to prevent saturation levels of minerals in the urine.

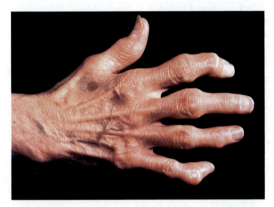

Gout occurs when uric acid exceeds its solubility.

Kidney stones form when calcium phosphate exceeds its solubility.

Effect of Temperature on Solubility

MC TUTORIAL Solubility

The solubility of most solids becomes greater as temperature increases, which means that solutions usually can contain more dissolved solute at higher temperatures. A few substances show little change in solubility at higher temperatures, and a few are less soluble (see Figure 8.4). For example, when you add sugar to iced tea, some undissolved sugar may quickly collect on the bottom of the glass. But if you add sugar to hot tea, many teaspoons of sugar are needed before solid sugar appears. Hot tea dissolves more sugar than does cold tea because the solubility of sugar is much greater at a higher temperature.

When a saturated solution is carefully cooled, it becomes a *supersaturated solution* because it contains more solute than the solubility allows, although it is still completely liquid. Such a solution is unstable, and if the solution is agitated or if a solute crystal is added, the excess solute will recrystallize to give a saturated solution again.

Conversely, the solubility of a gas in water decreases as the temperature increases. At higher temperatures, more gas molecules have the energy to escape from the solution. Perhaps you have observed the bubbles

FIGURE 8.4 In water, most common solids are more soluble as the temperature increases.

Q Compare the solubility of $NaNO_3$ at 20 °C and 60 °C.

TUTORIAL
Solubility of Gases and Solids in Water

escaping from a cold carbonated soft drink as it warms. At high temperatures, bottles containing carbonated solutions may burst as more gas molecules leave the solution and increase the gas pressure inside the bottle. Biologists have found that increased temperatures in rivers and lakes cause the amount of dissolved oxygen to decrease until the warm water can no longer support a biological community. In the early morning, the surface of a lake or pond contains cooler water, which has more dissolved oxygen and therefore more fish. Electricity-generating plants are required to have their own ponds to use with their cooling towers to lessen the threat of thermal pollution to surrounding waterways.

Explore Your World

PREPARING ROCK CANDY

Need: 1 cup of water, 3 cups of granulated sugar, clean narrow glass or jar, wooden stick (skewer) or thick string that is the height of the glass, pencil, and food coloring (optional)

Rock candy can be made from a saturated solution of sugar (sucrose).

Process:

1. Place the water and two cups of sugar in a pan and begin heating and stirring. The sugar should all dissolve. Continue heating, but not boiling, adding small amounts of the remaining sugar and stirring thoroughly each time, until some of the sugar no longer dissolves. There may be some sugar crystals on the bottom of the pan. Carefully pour the sugar solution into the glass or jar. Add 2–3 drops of food coloring, if desired.

2. Wet the wooden stick and roll it in granulated sugar to provide crystals for the sugar solution to attach to. Place the stick in the sugar solution. If using string, tape it to a pencil so it will hang slightly above the bottom of the glass. Wet the lower half of the string, roll it in the granulated sugar, and place the pencil across the top of the glass with the string in the sugar solution. Place the glass and wooden stick or string in a place where it will not be disturbed. You should see sugar crystals grow over the next several days.

QUESTIONS

1. Why did more sugar dissolve as the solution was heated?
2. How did you know when you obtained a saturated solution?
3. Why did you see crystals forming on the stick or string over time?

Henry's Law

Henry's law states that the solubility of gas in a liquid is directly related to the pressure of that gas above the liquid. At higher pressures, there are more gas molecules available to enter and dissolve in the liquid. A can of soda is carbonated by using CO_2 gas at high pressure to increase the solubility of the CO_2 in the beverage. When you open the soda can at atmospheric pressure, the pressure on the CO_2 drops, which decreases the solubility of CO_2. As a result, bubbles of CO_2 rapidly escape from the solution. The burst of bubbles is even more noticeable when you open a warm can of soda.

CONCEPT CHECK 8.4   **Factors Affecting Solubility**

Indicate whether there is an increase or decrease in each of the following:

a. the solubility of sugar in water at 45 °C compared to its solubility in water at 25 °C

b. the solubility of O_2 in a lake as the water warms

ANSWER

a. A decrease in the temperature of the water from 45 °C to 25 °C decreases the solubility of the sugar.

b. An increase in the temperature of the water decreases the solubility of O_2 gas.

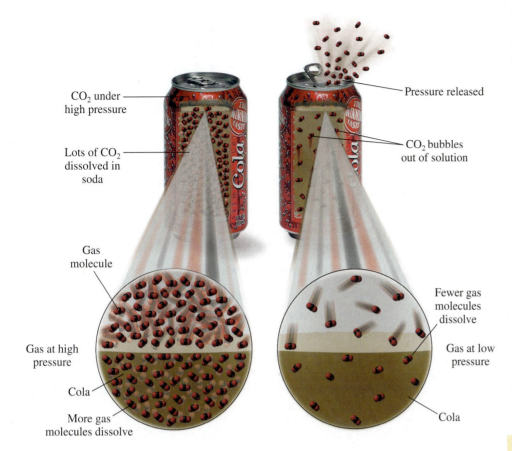

When the pressure of a gas above a solution decreases, the solubility of that gas in the solution also decreases.

CO₂ under high pressure

Lots of CO₂ dissolved in soda

Pressure released

CO₂ bubbles out of solution

Gas molecule

Fewer gas molecules dissolve

Gas at high pressure

Gas at low pressure

Cola

Cola

More gas molecules dissolve

Soluble and Insoluble Salts

Up to now, we have considered ionic compounds that dissolve in water: They are **soluble salts**. However, some ionic compounds do not separate into ions in water. They are **insoluble salts** that remain as solids even in contact with water.

Salts that are soluble in water typically contain at least one of the following ions: Li^+, Na^+, K^+, NH_4^+, NO_3^-, or $C_2H_3O_2^-$. *Only a salt containing a soluble cation or anion will dissolve in water.* Salts containing Cl^-, Br^-, or I^- are soluble unless combined with Ag^+, Pb^{2+}, or Hg_2^{2+}; then they are insoluble. Similarly, most salts containing SO_4^{2-} are soluble, but a few are insoluble as shown in Table 8.8. Most other salts including those containing the anions CO_3^{2-}, S^{2-}, PO_4^{3-}, or OH^- are insoluble (see Figure 8.5). In an insoluble salt, attractions between its positive and negative ions are too strong for the polar water molecules to break. We can use the solubility rules to predict whether a salt (a solid ionic compound) would be expected to dissolve in water. Table 8.9 illustrates the use of these rules.

TABLE 8.8 Solubility Rules for Ionic Solids in Water

An ionic solid is:	
Soluble if it contains:	**Insoluble if it contains:**
Li^+, Na^+, K^+	None
NH_4^+	None
NO_3^-, $C_2H_3O_2^-$	None
Cl^-, Br^-, I^-	Ag^+, Pb^{2+}, or Hg_2^{2+}
SO_4^{2-}	Ba^{2+}, Pb^{2+}, Ca^{2+}, Sr^{2+}, CO_3^{2-}, S^{2-}, PO_4^{3-}, OH^-

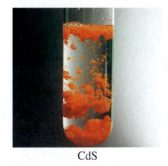

CdS

FeS

PbI_2

$Ni(OH)_2$

FIGURE 8.5 If a salt contains a cation and anion that are not soluble, that salt is insoluble. For example, combinations of cadmium and sulfide, iron and sulfide, lead and iodide, and nickel and hydroxide do not contain any soluble ions. Thus, they form insoluble salts.

Q What makes each of these salts insoluble in water?

TABLE 8.9 Using Solubility Rules

Ionic Compound	Solubility in Water	Reasoning
K_2S	Soluble	Contains K^+
$Ca(NO_3)_2$	Soluble	Contains NO_3^-
$PbCl_2$	Insoluble	Forms an insoluble chloride with Pb^{2+}
NaOH	Soluble	Contains Na^+
$AlPO_4$	Insoluble	Contains no soluble ions

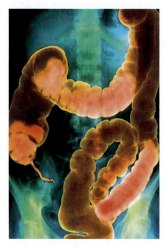

FIGURE 8.6 A barium sulfate-enhanced X-ray of the abdomen shows the large intestine.

Q Is $BaSO_4$ a soluble or an insoluble substance?

In medicine, the insoluble salt $BaSO_4$ is used as an opaque substance to enhance X-rays of the gastrointestinal tract. $BaSO_4$ is so insoluble that it does not dissolve in gastric fluids (see Figure 8.6). Other barium salts cannot be used; they would dissolve in water, releasing Ba^{2+}, which is poisonous.

CONCEPT CHECK 8.5 **Soluble and Insoluble Salts**

Predict whether each of the following salts is soluble in water and explain why:

a. Na_3PO_4 **b.** $CaCO_3$

ANSWER

a. The salt Na_3PO_4 is soluble in water because any compound that contains Na^+ is soluble.

b. The salt $CaCO_3$ is insoluble in water because it does not contain a soluble positive ion or a soluble negative ion.

TUTORIAL
Writing Net Ionic Equations

Formation of a Solid

We can use solubility rules to predict whether a solid, called a *precipitate*, forms when two solutions of ionic compounds are mixed as shown in Sample Problem 8.3.

SAMPLE PROBLEM 8.3 **Writing Equations for the Formation of an Insoluble Salt**

When solutions of NaCl and $AgNO_3$ are mixed, a white solid forms. Write the ionic and net ionic equations for the reaction.

SOLUTION

Guide to Writing the Formation of Equations for an Insoluble Salt

1 Write the ions of the reactants.

2 Write the combinations of ions and determine if any are insoluble.

3 Write the ionic equation including any solid.

4 Write the net ionic equation.

Step 1 Write the ions of the reactants.

Reactants
(initial combinations)

$$Ag^+(aq) + NO_3^-(aq)$$

$$Na^+(aq) + Cl^-(aq)$$

Step 2 Write the combinations of ions and determine if any are insoluble. When we look at the ions of each solution, we see that the combination of Ag^+ and Cl^- forms an insoluble salt.

Mixture (new combinations)	Product	Soluble
$Ag^+(aq) + Cl^-(aq)$	$AgCl(s)$	No
$Na^+(aq) + NO_3^-(aq)$	$NaNO_3$	Yes

Step 3 **Write the ionic equation including any solid.** In the **ionic equation**, we show all the ions of the reactants. The products include the solid AgCl that forms along with the remaining ions Na^+ and NO_3^-.

$$Ag^+(aq) + NO_3^-(aq) + Na^+(aq) + Cl^-(aq) \longrightarrow AgCl(s) + Na^+(aq) + NO_3^-(aq)$$

Step 4 **Write the net ionic equation.** To write a **net ionic equation**, we remove the Na^+ and NO_3^- ions, known as *spectator ions*, which are unchanged. This leaves only the ions and solid of the chemical reaction.

$$Ag^+(aq) + \underbrace{NO_3^-(aq) + Na^+(aq)}_{\text{Spectator ions}} + Cl^-(aq) \longrightarrow AgCl(s) + \underbrace{Na^+(aq) + NO_3^-(aq)}_{\text{Spectator ions}}$$

$$Ag^+(aq) + Cl^-(aq) \longrightarrow AgCl(s) \quad \text{Net ionic equation}$$

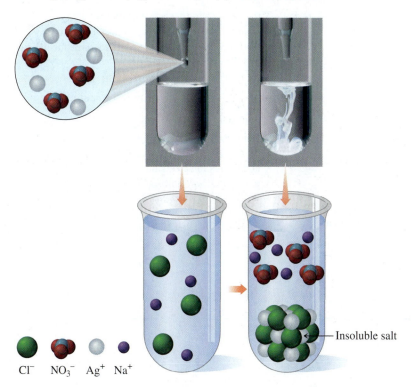

Insoluble salt

Cl^- NO_3^- Ag^+ Na^+

Type of Equation			
Chemical	$AgNO_3(aq)$	$+ NaCl(aq)$ ⟶	$AgCl(s) + NaNO_3(aq)$
Ionic	$Ag^+(aq) + NO_3^-(aq)$	$+ Na^+(aq) + Cl^-(aq) \rightarrow$	$AgCl(s) + Na^+(aq) + NO_3^-(aq)$
Net ionic	$Ag^+(aq)$	$+ Cl^-(aq)$ ⟶	$AgCl(s)$

STUDY CHECK 8.3

Predict whether a solid might form in each of the following mixtures of solutions. If so, write the net ionic equation for the reaction.

a. $NH_4Cl(aq) + Ca(NO_3)_2(aq)$ **b.** $Pb(NO_3)_2(aq) + KCl(aq)$

QUESTIONS AND PROBLEMS

8.3 Solubility

LEARNING GOAL: *Define solubility. Distinguish between an unsaturated and a saturated solution; identify a salt as soluble or insoluble.*

8.21 State whether each of the following refers to a saturated or unsaturated solution:
   a. A crystal added to a solution does not change in size.

   b. A sugar cube completely dissolves when added to a cup of coffee.

8.22 State whether each of the following refers to a saturated or unsaturated solution:
   a. A spoonful of salt added to boiling water dissolves.
   b. A layer of sugar forms on the bottom of a glass of tea as ice is added.

Use the following table for Problems 8.23–8.26.

	Solubility (g/100 g H₂O)	
Substance	**20 °C**	**50 °C**
KCl	34	43
NaNO₃	88	110
C₁₂H₂₂O₁₁ (sugar)	204	260

8.23 Use the previous table to determine whether each of the following solutions will be saturated or unsaturated at 20 °C:
   a. adding 25 g of KCl to 100. g of H₂O
   b. adding 11 g of NaNO₃ to 25 g of H₂O
   c. adding 400. g of sugar to 125 g of H₂O

8.24 Use the previous table to determine whether each of the following solutions will be saturated or unsaturated at 50 °C:
   a. adding 25 g of KCl to 50. g of H₂O
   b. adding 150. g of NaNO₃ to 75 g of H₂O
   c. adding 80. g of sugar to 25 g of H₂O

8.25 A solution containing 80. g of KCl in 200. g of H₂O at 50 °C is cooled to 20 °C.
   a. How many grams of KCl remain in solution at 20 °C?
   b. How many grams of solid KCl crystallized after cooling?

8.26 A solution containing 80. g of NaNO₃ in 75 g of H₂O at 50 °C is cooled to 20 °C.
   a. How many grams of NaNO₃ remain in solution at 20 °C?
   b. How many grams of solid NaNO₃ crystallized after cooling?

8.27 Explain the following observations:
   a. More sugar dissolves in hot tea than in iced tea.
   b. Champagne in a warm room goes flat.
   c. A warm can of soda has more spray when opened than a cold one.

8.28 Explain the following observations:
   a. An open can of soda loses its "fizz" quicker at room temperature than in the refrigerator.
   b. Chlorine gas in tap water escapes as the water warms to room temperature.
   c. Less sugar dissolves in iced coffee than in hot coffee.

8.29 Predict whether each of the following ionic compounds is soluble in water:
   a. LiCl   **b.** AgCl   **c.** BaCO₃
   d. K₂O   **e.** Fe(NO₃)₃

8.30 Predict whether each of the following ionic compounds is soluble in water:
   a. PbS   **b.** KI   **c.** Na₂S
   d. Ag₂O   **e.** CaSO₄

8.31 Determine whether a solid forms when solutions containing the following salts are mixed. If so, write the ionic equation and the net ionic equation.
   a. KCl(*aq*) and Na₂S(*aq*)
   b. AgNO₃(*aq*) and K₂S(*aq*)
   c. CaCl₂(*aq*) and Na₂SO₄(*aq*)
   d. CuCl₂(*aq*) and Li₃PO₄(*aq*)

8.32 Determine whether a solid forms when solutions containing the following salts are mixed. If so, write the ionic equation and the net ionic equation.
   a. Na₃PO₄(*aq*) and AgNO₃(*aq*)
   b. K₂SO₄(*aq*) and Na₂CO₃(*aq*)
   c. Pb(NO₃)₂(*aq*) and Na₂CO₃(*aq*)
   d. BaCl₂(*aq*) and KOH(*aq*)

8.4 Solution Concentration

The amount of solute dissolved in a certain amount of solution is called the **concentration** of the solution. We will look at the concentrations that are a ratio of a certain amount of solute in a given amount of solution:

$$\text{Concentration of a solution} = \frac{\text{amount of solute}}{\text{amount of solution}}$$

Mass Percent (m/m) Concentration

Mass percent (m/m) describes the mass of the solute in grams for exactly 100 g of solution. In the calculation of mass percent (m/m), the units of mass of the solute and solution must be the same. If the mass of the solute is given as grams, then the mass of the solution must also be grams. The mass of the solution is the sum of the mass of the solute and the mass of the solvent.

$$\text{Mass percent (m/m)} = \frac{\text{mass of solute (g)}}{\text{mass of solute (g)} + \text{mass of solvent (g)}} \times 100\%$$

$$= \frac{\text{mass of solute (g)}}{\text{mass of solution (g)}} \times 100\%$$

Suppose we prepared a solution by mixing 8.00 g of KCl (solute) with 42.00 g of water (solvent). Together, the mass of the solute and mass of solvent give the mass of the solution (8.00 g + 42.00 g = 50.00 g). Mass percent is calculated by substituting the mass of the solute and the mass of the solution into the mass percent expression.

$$\frac{8.00 \text{ g KCl}}{50.00 \text{ g solution}} \times 100\% = 16.0\% \text{ (m/m) KCl solution}$$

$$\underbrace{8.00 \text{ g KCl} + 42.00 \text{ g H}_2\text{O}}$$
$$\text{(Solute} \quad + \quad \text{Solvent)}$$

Add 8.00 g of KCl

CONCEPT CHECK 8.6 Mass Percent Concentration

A NaBr solution is prepared by adding 4.0 g of NaBr to 50.0 g of H_2O.

a. What is the mass of the solution?
b. Is the final concentration of the NaBr solution equal to 7.4% (m/m), 8.0% (m/m), or 80.% (m/m)?

ANSWER

a. The mass of the NaBr solution is the sum of 4.0 g of NaBr solute and 50.0 g of H_2O solvent, which is 54.0 g (4.0 g NaBr + 50.0 g H_2O).
b. The mass percent of the NaBr solution is equal to 7.4% (m/m).

$$\frac{4.0 \text{ g NaBr}}{54.0 \text{ g solution}} \times 100\% = 7.4\% \text{ (m/m) NaBr solution}$$

Add water until the solution weighs 50.00 g

When water is added to 8.00 g of KCl to form 50.00 g of KCl solution, the mass percent concentration is 16.0% (m/m).

SAMPLE PROBLEM 8.4 Calculating Mass Percent (m/m) Concentration

What is the mass percent (m/m) of NaOH in a solution prepared by dissolving 30.0 g of NaOH in 120.0 g of H_2O?

SOLUTION

Step 1 **State the given and needed quantities.** Using the following table, we can organize the information in the problem:

Analyze the Problem

Given	Need
30.0 g of NaOH solute	Mass percent (m/m)
30.0 g NaOH + 120.0 g H_2O = 150.0 g of NaOH solution	

Step 2 **Write the concentration expression.**

$$\text{Mass percent (m/m)} = \frac{\text{grams of solute}}{\text{grams of solution}} \times 100\%$$

Step 3 **Substitute solute and solution quantities into the expression and calculate.**

$$\text{Mass percent (m/m)} = \frac{\overset{\text{mass of solute}}{30.0 \text{ g NaOH}}}{\underset{\text{mass of solution}}{150.0 \text{ g NaOH solution}}} \times 100\%$$

$$= 20.0\% \text{ (m/m) NaOH solution}$$

Guide to Calculating Solution Concentration

1 State the given and needed quantities.

2 Write the concentration expression.

3 Substitute solute and solution quantities into the expression and calculate.

STUDY CHECK 8.4

What is the mass percent (m/m) of NaCl in a solution made by dissolving 2.0 g of NaCl in 56.0 g of H_2O?

The label indicates that vanilla extract contains 35% (v/v) alcohol.

Volume Percent (v/v) Concentration

Because the volumes of liquids or gases are easily measured, the concentrations of their solutions are often expressed as **volume percent (v/v)**. The units of volume used in the ratio must be the same; for example, both in milliliters or both in liters.

$$\text{Volume percent (v/v)} = \frac{\text{volume of solute}}{\text{volume of solution}} \times 100\%$$

We interpret a volume percent (v/v) as the volume of solute in exactly 100 mL of solution. On a bottle of extract of vanilla, a label that reads alcohol 35% (v/v) means 35 mL of ethanol solute in exactly 100 mL of vanilla solution.

SAMPLE PROBLEM 8.5   Calculating Volume Percent (v/v) Concentration

A bottle contains 59 mL of lemon extract. If the extract solution contains 49 mL of alcohol, what is the volume percent (v/v) of the alcohol in the extract solution?

SOLUTION

Step 1   **State the given and needed quantities.**

Analyze the Problem

Given	Need
49 mL of alcohol solute	Volume percent (v/v)
59 mL of lemon extract solution	

Step 2   **Write the concentration expression.**

$$\text{Volume percent (v/v)} = \frac{\text{volume of solute}}{\text{volume of solution}} \times 100\%$$

Step 3   **Substitute solute and solution quantities into the expression and calculate.**

$$\text{Volume percent (v/v)} = \frac{\overset{\text{volume of solute}}{49 \text{ mL alcohol}}}{\underset{\text{volume of solution}}{59 \text{ mL solution}}} \times 100\%$$

$$= 83\% \text{ (v/v) alcohol solution}$$

STUDY CHECK 8.5

What is the volume percent (v/v) of bromine in a solution prepared by dissolving 12 mL of bromine in the solvent carbon tetrachloride to make 250 mL of solution?

Lemon extract is a mixture of lemon flavor and alcohol.

TUTORIAL
Calculating Percent Concentration

Mass/Volume Percent (m/v) Concentration

Mass/volume percent (m/v) describes the mass of the solute in grams for exactly 100 mL of solution. In the calculation of mass/volume percent, the unit of mass of the solute is grams and the unit of volume is milliliters.

$$\text{Mass/volume percent (m/v)} = \frac{\text{grams of solute}}{\text{milliliters of solution}} \times 100\%$$

The mass/volume percent is widely used in hospitals and pharmacies for the preparation of intravenous solutions and medicines. For example, a 5% (m/v) glucose solution contains 5 g of glucose in exactly 100 mL of solution. The volume of solution represents the combined volumes of the glucose and H_2O.

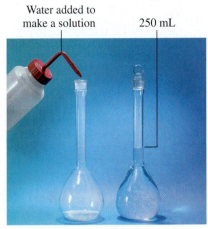

Water is added to 5.0 g of KI to make 250 mL of KI solution.

SAMPLE PROBLEM 8.6 Calculating Mass/Volume Percent (m/v) Concentration

A student prepared a solution by dissolving 5.0 g of KI in enough water to give a final volume of 250 mL. What is the mass/volume percent (m/v) of the KI in the solution?

SOLUTION

Step 1 State the given and needed quantities.

Analyze the Problem

Given	Need
5.0 g of KI solute	Mass/volume percent (m/v)
250 mL of KI solution	

Step 2 Write the concentration expression.

$$\text{Mass/volume percent (m/v)} = \frac{\text{grams of solute}}{\text{milliliters of solution}} \times 100\%$$

Step 3 Substitute solute and solution quantities into the expression and calculate.

$$\text{Mass/volume percent (m/v)} = \frac{\overset{\text{Mass of solute}}{5.0 \text{ g KI}}}{\underset{\text{Volume of solution}}{250 \text{ mL solution}}} \times 100\%$$

$$= 2.0\% \text{ (m/v) KI solution}$$

STUDY CHECK 8.6

What is the mass/volume percent (m/v) of NaOH in a solution prepared by dissolving 12 g of NaOH in enough water to make 220 mL of solution?

Molarity (M) Concentration

When chemists work with solutions, they often use **molarity (M)**, a concentration that states the number of moles of solute in exactly 1 liter of solution.

$$\text{Molarity (M)} = \frac{\text{moles of solute}}{\text{liters of solution}}$$

For example, if 2.0 moles of NaCl is dissolved in enough water to prepare 1.0 L of solution, the resulting NaCl solution has a molarity of 2.0 M. The abbreviation M indicates the units of moles per liter (moles/L).

$$M = \frac{\text{moles of solute}}{\text{liters of solution}} = \frac{2.0 \text{ moles NaCl}}{1.0 \text{ L solution}} = 2.0 \text{ M NaCl solution}$$

The molarity of a solution can be calculated knowing the moles of solute and the volume of solution in liters as shown in Sample Problem 8.7.

SAMPLE PROBLEM 8.7 Calculating Molarity

What is the molarity (M) of 60.0 g of NaOH in 0.250 L of solution?

SOLUTION

Step 1 State the given and needed quantities. For molarity, we need the quantity, in moles, and the volume of the solution in liters.

Analyze the Problem

Given	Need
60.0 g of NaOH solute	Molarity
0.250 L of NaOH solution	

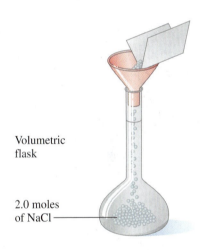

Volumetric flask

2.0 moles of NaCl

Add water until the 1.0-L mark is reached

Mix

A 2.0 M NaCl solution

A solution of 2.0 moles of NaCl and water added to the 1-L mark is a 2.0 M NaCl solution.

To calculate the moles of NaOH, we need to write the equality and conversion factors for the molar mass of NaOH. Then the moles in 60.0 g of NaOH can be determined.

$$1 \text{ mole of NaOH} = 40.0 \text{ g of NaOH}$$

$$\frac{1 \text{ mole NaOH}}{40.0 \text{ g NaOH}} \quad \text{and} \quad \frac{40.0 \text{ g NaOH}}{1 \text{ mole NaOH}}$$

$$\text{moles of NaOH} = 60.0 \text{ g NaOH} \times \frac{1 \text{ mole NaOH}}{40.0 \text{ g NaOH}}$$

$$= 1.50 \text{ moles of NaOH}$$

Step 2 **Write the concentration expression.**

$$\text{Molarity (M)} = \frac{\text{moles of solute}}{\text{liters of solution}}$$

Step 3 **Substitute solute and solution quantities into the expression and calculate.**

$$M = \frac{1.50 \text{ moles NaOH}}{0.250 \text{ L solution}} = \frac{6.00 \text{ moles NaOH}}{1 \text{ L solution}} = 6.00 \text{ M NaOH solution}$$

STUDY CHECK 8.7

What is the molarity of a solution that contains 75.0 g of KNO_3 dissolved in 0.350 L of solution?

Table 8.10 summarizes the types of units used in the various types of concentration expressions for solutions.

TABLE 8.10 Summary of Types of Concentration Expressions and Their Units

Concentration Units	Mass Percent (m/m)	Volume Percent (v/v)	Mass/Volume Percent (m/v)	Molarity (M)
Solute	g	mL	g	mole
Solution	g	mL	mL	L

Using Concentrations as Conversion Factors

In the preparation of solutions, we often need to calculate the amount of solute or volume of solution. Then the concentration of that solution is useful as a conversion factor. The value of 100 in the denominator of a percent expression is an *exact* number. Some examples of percent concentrations and molarity, their meanings, and possible conversion factors are given in Table 8.11. Some examples of using percent concentration or molarity as conversion factors are given in Sample Problems 8.8 and 8.9.

TABLE 8.11 Conversion Factors from Percent Concentrations

Percent Concentration	Meaning	Conversion Factors	
15% (m/m) KCl solution	15 g of KCl in 100 g of KCl solution	$\dfrac{15 \text{ g KCl}}{100 \text{ g solution}}$ and	$\dfrac{100 \text{ g solution}}{15 \text{ g KCl}}$
12% (v/v) ethanol solution	12 mL of ethanol in 100 mL of ethanol solution	$\dfrac{12 \text{ mL ethanol}}{100 \text{ mL solution}}$ and	$\dfrac{100 \text{ mL solution}}{12 \text{ mL ethanol}}$
5% (m/v) glucose solution	5 g of glucose in 100 mL of glucose solution	$\dfrac{5 \text{ g glucose}}{100 \text{ mL solution}}$ and	$\dfrac{100 \text{ mL solution}}{5 \text{ g glucose}}$
Molarity			
6.0 M HCl solution	6.0 moles of HCl in 1 liter of HCl solution	$\dfrac{6.0 \text{ moles HCl}}{1 \text{ L solution}}$ and	$\dfrac{1 \text{ L solution}}{6.0 \text{ moles HCl}}$

SAMPLE PROBLEM 8.8   **Using Mass/Volume Percent to Find Mass of Solute**

A topical antibiotic is 1.0% (m/v) clindamycin. How many grams of clindamycin are in 60. mL of the 1.0% (m/v) solution?

SOLUTION

Step 1   **State the given and needed quantities.**

Analyze the Problem

Given	Need
60. mL of 1.0% (m/v) clindamycin solution	grams of clindamycin

Step 2   **Write a plan to calculate the mass or volume.**

milliliters of solution → % (m/v) factor → grams of clindamycin

Step 3   **Write equalities and conversion factors.** The mass/volume percent (m/v) indicates the grams of a solute in every 100 mL of a solution. The 1.0% (m/v) can be written as two conversion factors.

$$1.0 \text{ g of clindamycin} = 100 \text{ mL of solution}$$

$$\frac{1.0 \text{ g clindamycin}}{100 \text{ mL solution}} \quad \text{and} \quad \frac{100 \text{ mL solution}}{1.0 \text{ g clindamycin}}$$

Step 4   **Set up the problem to calculate the mass or volume.** The volume of the solution is converted to mass of solute using the conversion factor that cancels mL.

$$60. \text{ mL solution} \times \frac{1.0 \text{ g clindamycin}}{100 \text{ mL solution}} = 0.60 \text{ g of clindamycin}$$

STUDY CHECK 8.8

Calculate the grams of KCl in 225 g of an 8.00% (m/m) KCl solution.

Guide to Using Concentration to Calculate Mass or Volume

1 State the given and needed quantities.

2 Write a plan to calculate the mass or volume.

3 Write equalities and conversion factors.

4 Set up the problem to calculate the mass or volume.

SAMPLE PROBLEM 8.9   **Using Molarity to Find Volume**

How many liters of a 2.00 M NaCl solution are needed to provide 67.3 g of NaCl?

SOLUTION

Step 1   **State the given and needed quantities.**

Analyze the Problem

Given	Need
67.3 g of NaCl	liters of NaCl solution
2.00 M NaCl solution	

Step 2   **Write a plan to calculate the mass or volume.**

grams of NaCl → Molar mass → moles of NaCl → Molarity → liters of NaCl solution

Step 3   **Write equalities and conversion factors.**

$$1 \text{ mole of NaCl} = 58.5 \text{ g of NaCl}$$

$$\frac{1 \text{ mole NaCl}}{58.5 \text{ g NaCl}} \quad \text{and} \quad \frac{58.5 \text{ g NaCl}}{1 \text{ mole NaCl}}$$

The molarity of any solution can be written as two conversion factors.

$$1 \text{ L of NaCl solution} = 2.00 \text{ moles of NaCl}$$

$$\frac{1 \text{ L NaCl solution}}{2.00 \text{ moles NaCl}} \quad \text{and} \quad \frac{2.00 \text{ moles NaCl}}{1 \text{ L NaCl solution}}$$

Step 4   **Set up the problem to calculate the mass or volume.**

$$\text{liters of NaCl solution} = 67.3 \text{ g NaCl} \times \frac{1 \text{ mole NaCl}}{58.5 \text{ g NaCl}} \times \frac{1 \text{ L NaCl solution}}{2.00 \text{ moles NaCl}}$$

$$= 0.575 \text{ L of NaCl solution}$$

STUDY CHECK 8.9

How many milliliters of a 6.00 M HCl solution will provide 10.4 g of HCl?

QUESTIONS AND PROBLEMS

8.4 Solution Concentration

LEARNING GOAL: *Calculate the concentration of a solute in a solution; use concentration to calculate the amount of solute or solution.*

8.33 Calculate the mass percent (m/m) for the solute in each of the following solutions:
   a. 25 g of KCl and 125 g of H_2O
   b. 12 g of sugar in 225 g of tea solution with sugar
   c. 8.0 g of $CaCl_2$ in 80.0 g of $CaCl_2$ solution

8.34 Calculate the mass percent (m/m) for the solute in each of the following solutions:
   a. 75 g of NaOH in 325 g of NaOH solution
   b. 2.0 g of KOH and 20.0 g of H_2O
   c. 48.5 g of Na_2CO_3 in 250.0 g of Na_2CO_3 solution

8.35 Calculate the mass/volume percent (m/v) for the solute in each of the following solutions:
   a. 75 g of Na_2SO_4 in 250 mL of Na_2SO_4 solution
   b. 39 g of sucrose in 355 mL of a carbonated drink

8.36 Calculate the mass/volume percent (m/v) for the solute in each of the following solutions:
   a. 2.50 g of LiCl in 50.0 mL of LiCl solution
   b. 7.5 g of casein in 120 mL of low-fat milk

8.37 Calculate the molarity (M) of the following solutions:
   a. 2.00 moles of glucose in 4.00 L of glucose solution
   b. 4.00 g of KOH in 2.00 L of KOH solution
   c. 5.85 g of NaCl in 400. mL of NaCl solution

8.38 Calculate the molarity (M) of the following solutions:
   a. 0.500 mole of glucose in 0.200 L of glucose solution
   b. 36.5 g of HCl in 1.00 L of HCl solution
   c. 30.0 g of NaOH in 350. mL of NaOH solution

8.39 Calculate the amount of solute, in grams or milliliters, needed to prepare the following solutions:
   a. 50.0 mL of a 5.0% (m/v) KCl solution
   b. 1250 mL of a 4.0% (m/v) NH_4Cl solution
   c. 250. mL of a 10.0% (v/v) acetic acid solution

8.40 Calculate the amount of solute, in grams or milliliters, needed to prepare the following solutions:
   a. 150 mL of a 40.0% (m/v) $LiNO_3$ solution
   b. 450 mL of a 2.0% (m/v) KOH solution
   c. 225 mL of a 15% (v/v) isopropyl alcohol solution

8.41 A mouthwash contains 22.5% (v/v) alcohol. If the bottle of mouthwash contains 355 mL, what is the volume, in milliliters, of the alcohol?

8.42 Champagne is an 11% (v/v) alcohol solution. If there are 750 mL of champagne in a bottle, how many milliliters of alcohol are present?

8.43 A patient receives 100. mL of a 20.% (m/v) mannitol solution every hour.
   a. How many grams of mannitol are given in 1 h?
   b. How many grams of mannitol does the patient receive in 12 h?

8.44 A patient receives 250 mL of a 4.0% (m/v) amino acid solution twice a day.
   a. How many grams of amino acids are in 250 mL of solution?
   b. How many grams of amino acids does the patient receive in 1 day?

8.45 A patient needs 100. g of glucose in the next 12 h. How many liters of a 5% (m/v) glucose solution must be given?

8.46 A patient received 2.0 g of NaCl in 8 h. How many milliliters of a 0.9% (m/v) NaCl (saline) solution were delivered?

8.47 Calculate the amount of solution (g or mL) that contains each of the following amounts of solute:
   a. 5.0 g of $LiNO_3$ from a 25% (m/m) $LiNO_3$ solution
   b. 40.0 g of KOH from a 10.0% (m/v) KOH solution
   c. 2.0 mL of formic acid from a 10.0% (v/v) formic acid solution

8.48 Calculate the amount of solution (g or mL) that contains each of the following amounts of solute:
   a. 7.50 g of NaCl from a 2.0% (m/m) NaCl solution
   b. 4.0 g of NaF from a 25% (m/v) NaF solution
   c. 20.0 g of KBr from an 8.0% (m/m) KBr solution

8.49 Calculate the moles of solute needed to prepare each of the following:
   a. 1.00 L of a 3.00 M NaCl solution
   b. 0.400 L of a 1.00 M KBr solution
   c. 125 mL of a 2.00 M MgCl$_2$ solution

8.50 Calculate the moles of solute needed to prepare each of the following:
   a. 5.00 L of a 2.00 M CaCl$_2$ solution
   b. 4.00 L of a 0.100 M NaOH solution
   c. 215 mL of a 4.00 M HNO$_3$ solution

8.51 Calculate the grams of solute needed to prepare each of the following:
   a. 2.00 L of a 1.50 M NaOH solution
   b. 4.00 L of a 0.200 M KCl solution
   c. 25.0 mL of a 6.00 M HCl solution

8.52 Calculate the grams of solute needed to prepare each of the following:
   a. 2.00 L of a 6.00 M NaOH solution
   b. 5.00 L of a 0.100 M CaCl$_2$ solution
   c. 175 mL of a 3.00 M NaNO$_3$ solution

8.53 Calculate the volume indicated for each of the following:
   a. liters of a 2.00 M KBr solution to obtain 3.00 moles of KBr
   b. milliliters of a 1.50 M NaCl solution to obtain 4.78 g of NaCl
   c. milliliters of a 0.800 M Ca(NO$_3$)$_2$ solution to obtain 0.0500 mole of Ca(NO$_3$)$_2$

8.54 Calculate the volume indicated for each of the following:
   a. liters of a 4.00 M KCl solution to obtain 0.100 mole of KCl
   b. milliliters of a 6.00 M HCl solution to obtain 18.3 g of HCl
   c. milliliters of a 2.50 M K$_2$SO$_4$ solution to obtain 1.20 moles of K$_2$SO$_4$

8.5 Dilution of Solutions and Solution Reactions

LEARNING GOAL

Calculate the new concentration or volume of a diluted solution. Given the volume and concentration of a solution, calculate the amount of another reactant or product in a reaction.

In chemistry and biology, we often prepare diluted solutions from more concentrated (stock) solutions. In a process called **dilution**, a solvent, usually water, is added to a solution, which increases the volume. As a result, the concentration of the solution decreases. In an everyday example, you are making a dilution when you add three cans of water to a can of concentrated orange juice.

1 can of orange juice concentrate   +   3 cans of water   =   4 cans of orange juice

One can of orange juice concentrate will make four cans of orange juice.

Although the addition of solvent increases the volume, the amount of solute doesn't change; it is the same in the concentrated solution and the diluted solution (see Figure 8.7).

Grams or moles of solute = grams or moles of solute
   Concentrated solution   Diluted solution

We can write this equality in terms of the concentration, C, and the volume, V. The concentration, C, may be percent concentration or molarity.

$$C_1 V_1 = C_2 V_2$$
   Concentrated   Diluted
   solution   solution

TUTORIAL
Dilution

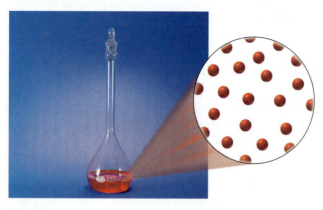 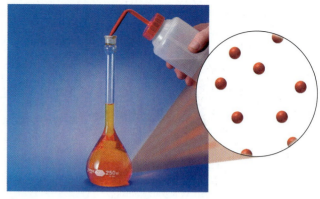

FIGURE 8.7 When water is added to a concentrated solution, there is no change in the number of particles, but the solute particles spread out as the volume of the diluted solution increases.

Q What is the concentration of the diluted solution after an equal volume of water is added to a sample of a 6 M HCl solution?

If we are given any three of the four variables, we can rearrange the dilution expression to solve for the unknown quantity as seen in Concept Check 8.7 and Sample Problem 8.10.

CONCEPT CHECK 8.7 **Volume of a Diluted Solution**

A 50.0-mL sample of a 20.0% (m/v) $SrCl_2$ solution is diluted with water to give a 5.00% (m/v) $SrCl_2$ solution. Use this data to complete the following table with the given concentrations and volumes of the solutions. Indicate what we know as *increases* or *decreases*, and predict the change in the unknown as *increases* or *decreases*.

Analyze the Problem

Concentrated Solution	Diluted Solution	Know	Predict
$C_1 =$	$C_2 =$		
$V_1 =$	$V_2 =$		

ANSWER

Analyze the Problem

Concentrated Solution	Diluted Solution	Know	Predict
$C_1 = 20.0\%$ (m/v)	$C_2 = 5.00\%$ (m/v)	C decreases	
$V_1 = 50.0$ mL	$V_2 = ?$ mL		*V* increases

SAMPLE PROBLEM 8.10 **Volume of a Diluted Solution**

What volume, in milliliters, of a 2.5% (m/v) KOH solution can be prepared by diluting 50.0 mL of a 12% (m/v) KOH solution?

Guide to Calculating Dilution Quantities

1 Prepare a table of the concentrations and volumes of the solutions.

2 Rearrange the dilution expression to solve for the unknown quantity.

3 Substitute the known quantities into the dilution expression and calculate.

SOLUTION

Step 1 **Prepare a table of the concentrations and volumes of the solutions.** For our problem analysis, we organize the solution data in a table, making sure that the units of concentration and volume are the same.

Analyze the Problem

Concentrated Solution	Diluted Solution	Know	Predict
$C_1 = 12\%$ (m/v)	$C_2 = 2.5\%$ (m/v)	C decreases	
$V_1 = 50.0$ mL	$V_2 = ?$ mL		*V* increases

Step 2 **Rearrange the dilution expression to solve for the unknown quantity.**

$$C_1V_1 = C_2V_2$$

Divide both sides by C_2.
$$\frac{C_1V_1}{C_2} = \frac{C_2V_2}{C_2}$$

$$V_2 = V_1 \times \frac{C_1}{C_2}$$

Step 3 **Substitute the known quantities into the dilution expression and calculate.**

$$V_2 = 50.0 \text{ mL} \times \frac{12\%}{2.5\%} = 240 \text{ mL of diluted KOH solution}$$

Concentration factor increases volume

When the initial volume (V_1) is multiplied by a ratio of the percent concentrations (concentration factor) that is greater than 1, the volume of the solution increases as predicted in Step 1.

STUDY CHECK 8.10

What is the final volume, in milliliters, when 25.0 mL of a 15% (m/v) KCl solution is diluted to a 3.0% (m/v) KCl solution?

SAMPLE PROBLEM 8.11 Molarity of a Diluted Solution

What is the molarity of a solution that is prepared by diluting 75.0 mL of a 4.00 M KCl solution to a volume of 500. mL?

SOLUTION

Step 1 **Prepare a table of the concentrations and volumes of the solutions.** We organize the solution data in a table, making sure that the units of concentration and volume are the same.

Analyze the Problem

Concentrated Solution	Diluted Solution	Know	Predict
$C_1 = 4.00$ M	$C_2 = ?$ M		C (molarity) decreases
$V_1 = 75.0$ mL	$V_2 = 500.$ mL	V increases	

Step 2 **Rearrange the dilution expression to solve for the unknown quantity.**

$$C_1V_1 = C_2 V_2$$

Divide both sides by V_2.
$$\frac{C_1V_1}{V_2} = C_2 \frac{V_2}{V_2}$$

$$C_2 = C_1 \times \frac{V_1}{V_2}$$

Step 3 **Substitute the known quantities into the dilution expression and calculate.**

$$C_2 = 4.00 \text{ M} \times \frac{75 \text{ mL}}{500. \text{ mL}} = 0.600 \text{ M (diluted KCl solution)}$$

Volume factor decreases concentration

When the initial molarity is multiplied by a ratio of the volumes (volume factor) that is less than 1, the molarity of the solution decreases as predicted in Step 1.

STUDY CHECK 8.11

What is the molarity of a solution prepared when 75.0 mL of a 10.0 M NaNO$_3$ solution is diluted to a volume of 600. mL?

TUTORIAL
Solution Stoichiometry

Solutions and Chemical Reactions

When chemical reactions involve aqueous solutions, we use molarity and volume to determine the moles or grams of the substances required or produced. Using the balanced chemical equation, we can determine the volume of a solution from the molarity and moles or grams of a solute as seen in Sample Problem 8.12. This is the same type of calculation that we did in Sections 6.6 and 6.7, when we calculated moles or grams of product from the given amount of reactant.

SAMPLE PROBLEM 8.12 Volume of a Solution in a Reaction

Zinc reacts with HCl to produce $ZnCl_2$ and hydrogen gas H_2.

$$Zn(s) + 2HCl(aq) \longrightarrow ZnCl_2(aq) + H_2(g)$$

How many liters of a 1.50 M HCl solution completely react with 5.32 g of zinc?

SOLUTION

Step 1 State the given and needed quantities.

Analyze the Proble

Given	Need
5.32 g of Zn	
1.50 M HCl solution	liters of HCl solution
Equation	
$Zn(s) + 2HCl(aq) \longrightarrow ZnCl_2(aq) + H_2(g)$	

Photo caption: Zn(s) in HCl produces bubbles of hydrogen gas and $ZnCl_2$.

Step 2 Write a plan to calculate the needed quantity or concentration.

grams of Zn → [Molar mass] → moles of Zn → [Mole–mole factor] → moles of HCl → [Molarity] → liters of HCl solution

Guide to Calculations Involving Solutions in Chemical Reactions

1 State the given and needed quantities.

2 Write a plan to calculate the needed quantity or concentration.

3 Write equalities and conversion factors including mole–mole and concentration factors.

4 Set up the problem to calculate the needed quantity or concentration.

Step 3 Write equalities and conversion factors including mole–mole and concentration factors.

1 mole of Zn = 65.4 g of Zn

$$\frac{1 \text{ mole Zn}}{65.4 \text{ g Zn}} \quad \text{and} \quad \frac{65.4 \text{ g Zn}}{1 \text{ mole Zn}}$$

1 mole of Zn = 2 moles of HCl

$$\frac{1 \text{ mole Zn}}{2 \text{ moles HCl}} \quad \text{and} \quad \frac{2 \text{ moles HCl}}{1 \text{ mole Zn}}$$

1 L of HCl solution = 1.50 moles of HCl

$$\frac{1 \text{ L HCl solution}}{1.50 \text{ moles HCl}} \quad \text{and} \quad \frac{1.50 \text{ moles HCl}}{1 \text{ L HCl solution}}$$

Step 4 Set up the problem to calculate the needed quantity or concentration. We can write the problem setup as seen in our plan:

$$5.32 \text{ g Zn} \times \frac{1 \text{ mole Zn}}{65.4 \text{ g Zn}} \times \frac{2 \text{ moles HCl}}{1 \text{ mole Zn}} \times \frac{1 \text{ L HCl solution}}{1.50 \text{ moles HCl}} = 0.108 \text{ L of HCl solution}$$

STUDY CHECK 8.12

Using the reaction in Sample Problem 8.12, how many grams of zinc can react with 225 mL of a 0.200 M HCl solution?

SAMPLE PROBLEM 8.13 Volume of a Reactant in a Solution

How many liters of a 0.250 M $BaCl_2$ solution are needed to react with 0.0325 L of a 0.160 M Na_2SO_4 solution?

$$Na_2SO_4(aq) + BaCl_2(aq) \longrightarrow BaSO_4(s) + 2NaCl(aq)$$

SOLUTION

Step 1   State the given and needed quantities.

Analyze the Problem

Given	Need
0.0325 L of 0.160 M Na$_2$SO$_4$ solution	
0.250 M BaCl$_2$ solution	liters of BaCl$_2$ solution
Equation	
Na$_2$SO$_4$(aq) + BaCl$_2$(aq) $\longrightarrow$ BaSO$_4$(s) + 2NaCl(aq)	

Step 2   Write a plan to calculate the needed quantity or concentration.

liters of Na$_2$SO$_4$ solution   **Molarity**   moles of Na$_2$SO$_4$ **Mole–mole factor**   moles of BaCl$_2$ **Molarity**   liters of BaCl$_2$ solution

Step 3   Write equalities and conversion factors including mole–mole and concentration factors.

1 L of Na$_2$SO$_4$ solution = 0.160 mole of Na$_2$SO$_4$

$$\frac{1 \text{ L Na}_2\text{SO}_4 \text{ solution}}{0.160 \text{ mole Na}_2\text{SO}_4} \quad \text{and} \quad \frac{0.160 \text{ mole Na}_2\text{SO}_4}{1 \text{ L Na}_2\text{SO}_4 \text{ solution}}$$

1 mole of Na$_2$SO$_4$ = 1 mole of BaCl$_2$

$$\frac{1 \text{ mole Na}_2\text{SO}_4}{1 \text{ mole BaCl}_2} \quad \text{and} \quad \frac{1 \text{ mole BaCl}_2}{1 \text{ mole Na}_2\text{SO}_4}$$

1 L BaCl$_2$ solution = 0.250 mole of BaCl$_2$

$$\frac{1 \text{ L BaCl}_2 \text{ solution}}{0.250 \text{ mole BaCl}_2} \quad \text{and} \quad \frac{0.250 \text{ mole BaCl}_2}{1 \text{ L BaCl}_2 \text{ solution}}$$

Step 4   Set up the problem to calculate the needed quantity or concentration.

$$0.0325 \text{ L Na}_2\text{SO}_4 \text{ solution} \times \frac{0.160 \text{ mole Na}_2\text{SO}_4}{1 \text{ L Na}_2\text{SO}_4 \text{ solution}} \times \frac{1 \text{ mole BaCl}_2}{1 \text{ mole Na}_2\text{SO}_4} \times \frac{1 \text{ L BaCl}_2 \text{ solution}}{0.250 \text{ mole BaCl}_2} = 0.0208 \text{ L of BaCl}_2 \text{ solution}$$

STUDY CHECK 8.13

For the reaction in Sample Problem 8.13, how many liters of a 0.330 M Na$_2$SO$_4$ solution are needed to react with 0.0268 L of a 0.216 M BaCl$_2$ solution?

Figure 8.8 gives a summary of the pathways and conversion factors needed for substances, including solutions, involved in chemical reactions.

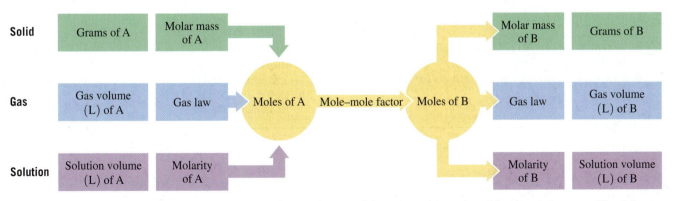

FIGURE 8.8 In calculations involving chemical reactions, substance A is converted to moles of A using molar mass (if solid), gas laws (if gas), or molarity (if solution). Then moles of A are converted to moles of substance B, which are converted to grams of solid, liters of gas, or liters of solution, as needed.

Q What sequence of conversion factors would you use to calculate the number of grams of CaCO$_3$ needed to react with 1.50 L of a 2.00 M HCl solution in the reaction: 2HCl(aq) + CaCO$_3$(s) $\longrightarrow$ CaCl$_2$(aq) + CO$_2$(g) + H$_2$O(l)?

QUESTIONS AND PROBLEMS

8.5 Dilution of Solutions and Solution Reactions

LEARNING GOAL: *Calculate the new concentration or volume of a diluted solution. Given the volume and concentration of a solution, calculate the amount of another reactant or product in a reaction.*

8.55 Calculate the final concentration of each of the following diluted solutions:
   a. 2.0 L of a 6.0 M HCl solution is added to water so that the final volume is 6.0 L.
   b. Water is added to 0.50 L of a 12 M NaOH solution to make 3.0 L of a diluted NaOH solution.
   c. A 10.0-mL sample of a 25% (m/v) KOH solution is diluted with water so that the final volume is 100.0 mL.
   d. A 50.0-mL sample of a 15% (m/v) H_2SO_4 solution is added to water to give a final volume of 250 mL.

8.56 Calculate the final concentration of each of the following diluted solutions:
   a. 1.0 L of a 4.0 M HNO_3 solution is added to water so that the final volume is 8.0 L.
   b. Water is added to 0.25 L of a 6.0 M NaF solution to make 2.0 L of a diluted NaF solution.
   c. A 50.0-mL sample of an 8.0% (m/v) KBr solution is diluted with water so that the final volume is 200.0 mL.
   d. A 5.0-mL sample of a 50.0% (m/v) acetic acid ($HC_2H_3O_2$) solution is added to water to give a final volume of 25 mL.

8.57 What is the volume, in milliliters, of each of the following diluted solutions?
   a. a 1.50 M HCl solution prepared from 20.0 mL of a 6.00 M HCl solution
   b. a 2.0% (m/v) LiCl solution prepared from 50.0 mL of a 10.0% (m/v) LiCl solution
   c. a 0.500 M H_3PO_4 solution prepared from 50.0 mL of a 6.00 M H_3PO_4 solution
   d. a 5.0% (m/v) glucose solution prepared from 75 mL of a 12% (m/v) glucose solution

8.58 What is the volume, in milliliters, of each of the following diluted solutions?
   a. a 1.00% (m/v) H_2SO_4 solution prepared from 10.0 mL of a 20.0% H_2SO_4 solution
   b. a 0.10 M HCl solution prepared from 25 mL of a 6.0 M HCl solution
   c. a 1.0 M NaOH solution prepared from 50.0 mL of a 12 M NaOH solution
   d. a 1.0% (m/v) $CaCl_2$ solution prepared from 18 mL of a 4.0% (m/v) $CaCl_2$ solution

8.59 Determine the volume, in milliliters, required to prepare each of the following diluted solutions:
   a. 255 mL of a 0.200 M HNO_3 solution using a 4.00 M HNO_3 solution
   b. 715 mL of a 0.100 M $MgCl_2$ solution using a 6.00 M $MgCl_2$ solution
   c. 0.100 L of a 0.150 M KCl solution using an 8.00 M KCl solution

8.60 Determine the volume, in milliliters, required to prepare each of the following diluted solutions:
   a. 20.0 mL of a 0.250 M KNO_3 solution using a 6.00 M KNO_3 solution
   b. 25.0 mL of a 2.50 M H_2SO_4 solution using a 12.0 M H_2SO_4 solution
   c. 0.500 L of a 1.50 M NH_4Cl solution using a 10.0 M NH_4Cl solution

8.61 Answer the following for the reaction:

$$Pb(NO_3)_2(aq) + 2KCl(aq) \longrightarrow PbCl_2(s) + 2KNO_3(aq)$$

   a. How many grams of $PbCl_2$ will be formed from 50.0 mL of a 1.50 M KCl solution?
   b. How many milliliters of a 2.00 M $Pb(NO_3)_2$ solution will react with 50.0 mL of a 1.50 M KCl solution?

8.62 Answer the following for the reaction:

$$NiCl_2(aq) + 2NaOH(aq) \longrightarrow Ni(OH)_2(s) + 2NaCl(aq)$$

   a. How many milliliters of a 0.200 M NaOH solution are needed to react with 18.0 mL of a 0.500 M $NiCl_2$ solution?
   b. How many grams of $Ni(OH)_2$ are produced from the reaction of 35.0 mL of a 0.200 M NaOH solution?

8.63 Answer the following for the reaction:

$$Mg(s) + 2HCl(aq) \longrightarrow MgCl_2(aq) + H_2(g)$$

   a. How many milliliters of a 6.00 M HCl solution are required to react with 15.0 g of magnesium?
   b. How many moles of hydrogen gas form when 0.500 L of a 2.00 M HCl solution reacts?

8.64 The calcium carbonate in limestone reacts with HCl to produce a calcium chloride solution, liquid water, and carbon dioxide gas.

$$CaCO_3(s) + 2HCl(aq) \longrightarrow CaCl_2(aq) + H_2O(l) + CO_2(g)$$

   a. How many milliliters of a 0.200 M HCl solution can react with 8.25 g of $CaCO_3$?
   b. How many moles of CO_2 form when 15.5 mL of a 3.00 M HCl solution react?

LEARNING GOAL

Identify a mixture as a solution, a colloid, or a suspension. Describe how the number of particles in a solution affects the freezing point, boiling point, and osmotic pressure of a solution.

8.6 Properties of Solutions

The solute particles in a solution play an important role in determining the properties of that solution. In most of the solutions discussed so far, the solute is dissolved as small particles that are uniformly dispersed throughout the solvent to give a homogeneous solution. When you observe a solution, such as salt water, you cannot visually distinguish the solute from the solvent. The solution appears transparent, although it may have a color. The particles are so small that they go through filters and through semipermeable membranes. A **semipermeable membrane** allows solvent molecules such as water and very small solute particles to pass through, but does not allow the passage of large solute molecules.

Colloids

The particles in a colloidal dispersion, or **colloid**, are much larger than solute particles in a solution. Colloidal particles are large molecules, such as proteins, or groups of molecules or ions. Colloids are homogeneous mixtures that do not separate or settle out. Colloidal particles are small enough to pass through filters but too large to pass through semipermeable membranes. Table 8.12 lists several examples of colloids.

TABLE 8.12 Examples of Colloids		
	Substance Dispersed	**Dispersing Medium**
Fog, clouds, sprays	Liquid	Gas
Dust, smoke	Solid	Gas
Shaving cream, whipped cream, soapsuds	Gas	Liquid
Styrofoam, marshmallows	Gas	Solid
Mayonnaise, homogenized milk, hand lotions	Liquid	Liquid
Cheese, butter	Liquid	Solid
Blood plasma, paints (latex), gelatin	Solid	Liquid

 Chemistry Link to Health

COLLOIDS AND SOLUTIONS IN THE BODY

In the body, colloids are retained by semipermeable membranes. For example, the intestinal lining allows solution particles to pass into the blood and lymph circulatory systems. However, the colloids from foods are too large to pass through the membrane, and they remain in the intestinal tract. Digestion breaks down large colloidal particles, such as starch and protein, into smaller particles, such as glucose and amino acids, that can pass through the intestinal membrane and enter the circulatory system. However, human digestive processes cannot break down certain foods, such as bran, a form of fiber, and they move through the intestine intact.

Because large proteins, such as enzymes, are colloids, they remain inside cells. However, many of the substances that must be obtained by cells, such as oxygen, amino acids, electrolytes, glucose, and minerals, can pass through cellular membranes. Waste products, such as urea and carbon dioxide, pass out of the cell to be excreted.

Suspensions

Suspensions are heterogeneous, nonuniform mixtures that are very different from solutions or colloids. The particles of a suspension are so large that they can often be seen with the naked eye. These particles are trapped by filters and semipermeable membranes.

The weight of the suspended solute particles causes them to settle out soon after mixing. If you stir muddy water, it mixes but then quickly separates as the suspended particles settle to the bottom and leave clear liquid at the top. You can find suspensions among the medications in a hospital or in your medicine cabinet. These include Kaopectate, calamine lotion, antacid mixtures, and liquid penicillin. It is important to "shake well before using" to suspend all the particles before giving a medication that is a suspension.

Water-treatment plants make use of the properties of suspensions to purify water. When flocculants such as aluminum sulfate or iron(III) sulfate are added to untreated water, they react with small particles of impurities to form large suspended particles called *floc.* In the water-treatment plant, a system of filters traps the suspended particles but allows clean water to pass through.

Table 8.13 compares the different types of mixtures, and Figure 8.9 illustrates some properties of solutions, colloids, and suspensions.

TABLE 8.13 Comparison of Solutions, Colloids, and Suspensions

Type of Mixture	Type of Particle	Settling	Separation
Solution	Small particles such as atoms, ions, or small molecules	Particles do not settle	Particles cannot be separated by filters or semipermeable membranes
Colloid	Larger molecules or groups of molecules or ions	Particles do not settle	Particles can be separated by semipermeable membranes but not by filters
Suspension	Very large particles that may be visible	Particles settle rapidly	Particles can be separated by filters

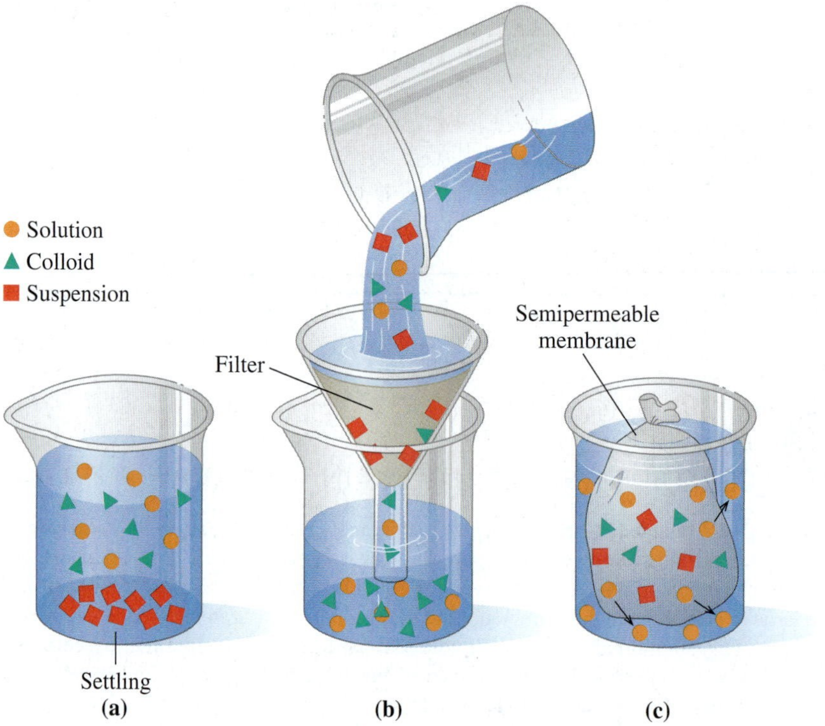

FIGURE 8.9 Properties of different types of mixtures: **(a)** Suspensions settle out; **(b)** suspensions are separated by a filter; **(c)** solution particles go through a semipermeable membrane, but colloids and suspensions do not.

Q A filter can be used to separate suspension particles from a solution, but a semipermeable membrane is needed to separate colloids from a solution. Explain.

CONCEPT CHECK 8.8   **Classifying Types of Mixtures**

Classify each of the following as a solution, a colloid, or a suspension:

a. a mixture that has particles that settle upon standing
b. a mixture whose solute particles pass through both filters and membranes
c. an enzyme, which is a large protein molecule, that cannot pass through cellular membranes, but does pass through a filter

ANSWER

a. A suspension has very large particles that settle upon standing.
b. A solution contains particles small enough to pass through both filters and membranes.
c. A colloid contains particles that are small enough to pass through a filter, but too large to pass through a membrane.

Freezing Point Lowering and Boiling Point Elevation

When a solute is added to water, the physical properties such as freezing point and boiling point change. The freezing point is lowered and boiling point is raised. These types of changes, known as *colligative properties*, depend only upon the number of molecules or solute particles in a given volume of solvent and not on the kind of particles.

Probably one familiar example of lowering the freezing point is the process of spreading salt on icy sidewalks and roads when temperatures drop below freezing. The particles from the salt combine with water to lower the freezing point, which causes the ice to melt. Another example is the addition of antifreeze, such as ethylene glycol, $C_2H_6O_2$, to the water in a car radiator. If the ethylene glycol and water mixture is about 50% water by mass, it does not freeze until the temperature drops to about $-37\,°C$ ($-34\,°F$) and does not boil unless the temperature goes above $124\,°C$ ($255\,°F$). The solution in the radiator prevents the water from forming ice in cold weather and boiling over on a hot desert highway.

Insects and fish in climates with subfreezing temperatures control ice formation by producing biological antifreezes made of glycerol, proteins, and sugars such as glucose, within their bodies. Some insects can survive temperatures below $-60\,°C$. These forms of biological antifreezes may one day be applied to the long-term preservation of human organs.

The lowering of the freezing point is due to solute particles, which disrupt the formation of the solid ice structure. When a solute is added to a solvent, the solvent molecules are prevented from forming a solid. In order to freeze the solution, the temperature must be lower than the freezing point of the solvent. The greater the solute concentration, the lower the freezing point will be. A similar effect happens to the boiling point of a solvent. When a solute is added to a solvent, the vapor pressure of the solvent is decreased. In order to boil the solution, the temperature must be higher than that of the solvent to attain the vapor pressure necessary to boil.

One mole of particles in 1000 g of water lowers the freezing point from $0\,°C$ to $-1.86\,°C$. If there are 2 moles of particles in 1000 g of water, the freezing point drops to $-3.72\,°C$. A similar change occurs with the boiling point of water. One mole of particles in 1000 g of water raises the boiling point by $0.52\,°C$, from $100.\,°C$ to $100.52\,°C$.

As we discussed in Section 8.2, a solute that is a nonelectrolyte dissolves as molecules, whereas a solute that is a strong electrolyte dissolves entirely as ions. The solute in antifreeze, which is ethylene glycol, $C_2H_6O_2$, dissolves as molecules. The salt $CaCl_2$ used to melt ice on roads and sidewalks produces 3 moles of particles, 1 mole of Ca^{2+} and 2 moles of Cl^-, from 1 mole of $CaCl_2$, which will lower the freezing point of water three times more than one mole of ethylene glycol. The effect of solute particles on the freezing point and the boiling point is summarized in Table 8.14.

A truck spreads calcium chloride on the road to melt ice and snow.

The Alaskan Upis beetle produces biological antifreeze to survive subfreezing temperatures.

Nonelectrolyte:

   1 mole of $C_2H_6O_2(l)$ = 1 mole of $C_2H_6O_2(aq)$

Strong electrolytes:

   1 mole of NaCl(s) = $\underbrace{\text{1 mole of } Na^+(aq) + \text{1 mole of } Cl^-(aq)}_{\text{2 moles of particles }(aq)}$

   1 mole of $CaCl_2$(s) = $\underbrace{\text{1 mole of } Ca^{2+}(aq) + \text{2 moles of } Cl^-(aq)}_{\text{3 moles of particles }(aq)}$

TABLE 8.14 **Effect of Solute Concentration on Freezing and Boiling Points of 1000 g of Water**

Substance	Type of Solute	Moles of Solute Particles	Freezing Point	Boiling Point
Pure water	None	0	$0\,°C$	$100\,°C$
1 mole of ethylene glycol	Nonelectrolyte	1 mole	$-1.86\,°C$	$100.52\,°C$
1 mole of NaCl	Strong electrolyte	2 moles	$-3.72\,°C$	$101.04\,°C$
1 mole of $CaCl_2$	Strong electrolyte	3 moles	$-5.58\,°C$	$101.56\,°C$

Ethylene glycol is added to a car radiator to form a solution that has a lower freezing point and a higher boiling point than water.

SELF-STUDY ACTIVITY
Diffusion

TUTORIAL
Osmosis

CONCEPT CHECK 8.9 Freezing Point Changes

In each pair, identify the solution that will have a lower freezing point. Explain.

a. 1.0 mole of NaOH (strong electrolyte) and 1.0 mole of ethylene glycol (nonelectrolyte) each in 1.0 L of water.

b. 0.20 mole of KNO_3 (strong electrolyte) and 0.20 mole of $Ca(NO_3)_2$ (strong electrolyte) each in 1.0 L of water.

ANSWER

a. When 1.0 mole of NaOH dissolves in water, it will produce 2.0 moles of particles because each NaOH dissociates to give two particles, Na^+ and OH^-. However, 1.0 mole of ethylene glycol dissolves as molecules to produce only 1.0 mole of particles. Thus, 1.0 mole of NaOH in 1.0 L of water will have the lower freezing point.

b. When 0.20 mole of KNO_3 dissolves in water, it will produce 0.40 mole of particles because each KNO_3 dissociates to give two particles, K^+ and NO_3^-. When 0.20 mole of $Ca(NO_3)_2$ dissolves in water, it will produce 0.60 mole of particles because each $Ca(NO_3)_2$ dissociates to give three particles, Ca^{2+} and $2NO_3^-$. Thus, 0.20 mole of $Ca(NO_3)_2$ in 1.0 L of water will have the lower freezing point.

Osmotic Pressure

In **osmosis**, a semipermeable membrane allows molecules of the solvent, water, to move through but retains the solute molecules. In this process of diffusion, water moves from the compartment where its concentration is higher to the side where it has a lower concentration. In terms of solute concentration, water flows through the membrane in the direction that will equalize or attempt to equalize the concentrations of solute on both sides. Although water can flow in both directions through the semipermeable membrane, the net flow of water is from the side with the lower solute concentration into the side with the higher solute concentration.

If an osmosis apparatus contains water on one side and a sucrose solution on the other side, the net flow of water will be from the pure water into the sucrose solution, which increases its volume and lowers its sucrose concentration. In the case where two sucrose solutions with different concentrations are placed on each side of the semipermeable membrane, water will flow from the side containing the lower sucrose concentration into the side containing the higher sucrose concentration.

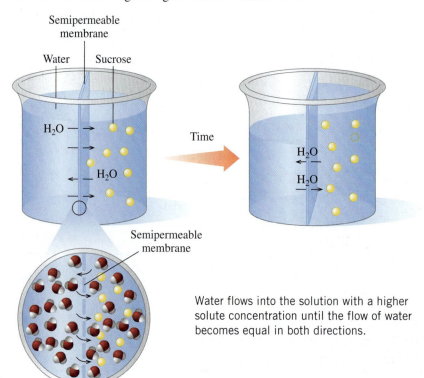

Water flows into the solution with a higher solute concentration until the flow of water becomes equal in both directions.

Eventually, the height of the sucrose solution creates sufficient pressure to equalize the flow of water between the two compartments. This pressure, called **osmotic pressure**, prevents the flow of additional water into the more concentrated solution. Then there is no further change in the volumes of the two solutions. The osmotic pressure depends on the concentration of solute particles in the solution. The greater the number of particles dissolved, the higher its osmotic pressure. In this example, the sucrose solution has a higher osmotic pressure than pure water, which has an osmotic pressure of zero.

In a process called *reverse osmosis*, a pressure greater than the osmotic pressure is applied to a solution so that it is forced through a purification membrane. The flow of water is reversed because water flows from an area of lower water concentration to an area of higher water concentration. The molecules and ions in solution stay behind, trapped by the membrane, while water passes through the membrane. This process of reverse osmosis is used in a few desalination plants to obtain pure water from sea (salt) water. However, the pressure that must be applied requires so much energy that reverse osmosis is not yet an economical method for obtaining pure water in most parts of the world.

CONCEPT CHECK 8.10 Osmotic Pressure

A 2% (m/v) sucrose solution and an 8% (m/v) sucrose solution are separated by a semi-permeable membrane.

a. Which sucrose solution exerts the greater osmotic pressure?
b. In what direction does water flow initially?
c. Which solution will have the higher level of liquid at equilibrium?

ANSWER

a. The 8% (m/v) sucrose solution has the higher solute concentration, more solute particles, and the greater osmotic pressure.
b. Initially, water will flow out of the 2% (m/v) solution into the more concentrated 8% (m/v) solution.
c. The level of the 8% (m/v) solution will be higher.

Isotonic Solutions

Because the cell membranes in biological systems are semipermeable, osmosis is an ongoing process. The solutes in body solutions such as blood, tissue fluids, lymph, and plasma all exert osmotic pressure. Most intravenous solutions are **isotonic solutions**, which exert the same osmotic pressure as body fluids, such as blood. *Iso* means "equal to," and *tonic* refers to the osmotic pressure of the solution in the cell. Isotonic solutions include 0.9% (m/v) NaCl solution and 5% (m/v) glucose solution. Although they do not contain the same particles, a 0.9% (m/v) NaCl solution as well as a 5% (m/v) glucose solution are both 0.3 M (Na^+ and Cl^- ions or glucose molecules). A red blood cell placed in an isotonic solution retains its volume because there is an equal flow of water into and out of the cell (see Figure 8.10a).

A 0.9% NaCl solution is isotonic with the solute concentration of the blood cells of the body.

Hypotonic and Hypertonic Solutions

If a red blood cell is placed in a solution that is not isotonic, the differences in osmotic pressure inside and outside the cell can drastically alter the volume of the cell. When a red blood cell is placed in a **hypotonic solution**, which has a lower solute concentration (*hypo* means "lower than"), water flows into the cell by osmosis in order to dilute the solutes within the cell (see Figure 8.10b). The increase in fluid causes the cell to swell, and possibly burst—a process called **hemolysis**. A similar process occurs when you place dehydrated food, such as raisins or dried fruit, in water. The water enters the cells, and the food becomes plump and smooth.

Isotonic solution   Hypotonic solution   Hypertonic solution

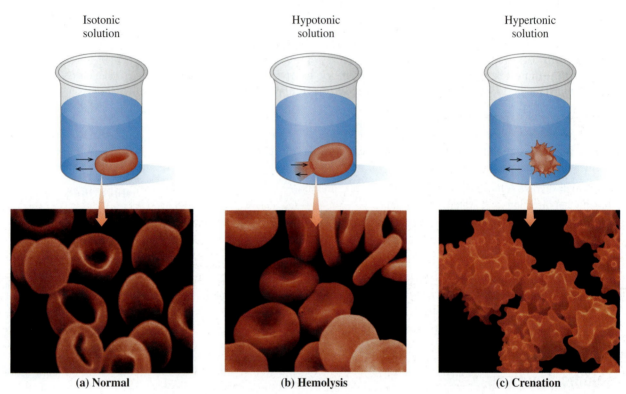

(a) Normal   **(b) Hemolysis**   **(c) Crenation**

FIGURE 8.10 **(a)** In an isotonic solution, a red blood cell retains its normal volume. **(b)** Hemolysis: In a hypotonic solution, water flows into a red blood cell, causing it to swell and burst. **(c)** Crenation: In a hypertonic solution, water leaves the red blood cell, causing it to shrink.
Q What happens to a red blood cell placed in a 4% (m/v) NaCl solution?

If a red blood cell is placed in a **hypertonic solution**, which has a higher solute concentration than that inside the red blood cell (*hyper* means "greater than"), water molecules flow out of the cell by osmosis to dilute the solutes outside the cell. Suppose a red blood cell is placed in a 10% (m/v) NaCl solution. Because the osmotic pressure in the red blood cell is equal to that of a 0.9% (m/v) NaCl solution, the 10% (m/v) NaCl solution has a much greater osmotic pressure. As water is lost, the cell shrinks—a process called **crenation** (see Figure 8.10c). A similar process occurs when making pickles, which uses a hypertonic salt solution that causes the cucumbers to shrivel as they lose water.

SAMPLE PROBLEM 8.14   Isotonic, Hypotonic, and Hypertonic Solutions

Describe each of the following solutions as isotonic, hypotonic, or hypertonic. Indicate whether a red blood cell placed in each solution will undergo hemolysis, crenation, or no change.

a. a 5% (m/v) glucose solution   **b.** a 0.2% (m/v) NaCl solution

SOLUTION

a. A 5% (m/v) glucose solution is isotonic. A red blood cell will not undergo any change.
b. A 0.2% (m/v) NaCl solution is hypotonic. A red blood cell will undergo hemolysis.

STUDY CHECK 8.14

What will happen to a red blood cell placed in a 10% (m/v) glucose solution?

Dialysis

Dialysis is a process that is similar to osmosis. In dialysis, a semipermeable membrane, called a *dialyzing membrane*, has small holes that permit small solute molecules and ions as well as solvent water molecules to pass through, but still retain large particles, such as colloids. Dialysis is a way to separate solution particles from colloids.

Suppose we fill a cellophane bag with a solution containing NaCl, glucose, starch, and protein and place it in pure water. Cellophane is a dialyzing membrane, and the sodium ions, chloride ions, and glucose molecules will pass through it into the surrounding water. However, starch and protein remain inside because they are colloids. Water molecules will flow by osmosis into the cellophane bag. Eventually the concentrations of sodium ions, chloride ions, and glucose molecules inside and outside the dialysis bag become equal. To remove more NaCl or glucose, the cellophane bag must be placed in a fresh sample of pure water.

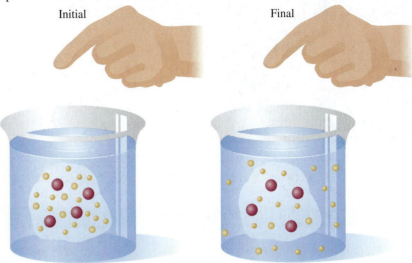

Initial   Final

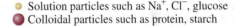

- ○ Solution particles such as Na^+, Cl^-, glucose
- ● Colloidal particles such as protein, starch

Chemistry Link to Health

DIALYSIS BY THE KIDNEYS AND THE ARTIFICIAL KIDNEY

The fluids of the body undergo dialysis by the membranes of the kidneys, which remove waste materials, excess salts, and water. In an adult, each kidney contains about 2 million nephrons, the functional unit of the kidney. At the top of each nephron, there is a network of arterial capillaries called the *glomerulus*.

As blood flows into the nephron, small particles, such as amino acids, glucose, urea, water, and certain ions, will move through the capillary membranes of the glomerulus. As this solution moves through the membrane of the glomerulus, substances still of value to the body (such as amino acids, glucose, certain ions, and 99% of the water) are reabsorbed. The major waste product, urea, is excreted in the urine.

Hemodialysis

If the kidneys fail to dialyze waste products, increased levels of urea can become life-threatening in a relatively short time. A person with kidney failure must use an artificial kidney, which cleanses the blood by **hemodialysis**.

A typical artificial kidney machine contains a large tank filled with water containing selected electrolytes. In the center of this dialyzing bath (dialysate), there is a dialyzing coil or membrane made of cellulose tubing. As the patient's blood flows through the dialyzing coil, the highly concentrated waste products dialyze out of the blood. No blood is lost, because the membrane is not permeable to large particles such as red blood cells.

Dialysis patients do not produce much urine. As a result, they retain large amounts of water between dialysis treatments, which produces a strain on the heart. The intake of fluids for a dialysis patient may be restricted to as little as a few teaspoons of water a day. In the dialysis procedure, the pressure of the blood is increased as it circulates through the dialyzing coil so water can be squeezed out of the blood. For some dialysis patients, 2–10 L of water may be removed during one treatment. Dialysis patients typically have from two to three treatments a week, each treatment requiring about 5–7 h. Some of the newer treatments require less time. For many patients, dialysis is done at home with a home dialysis unit.

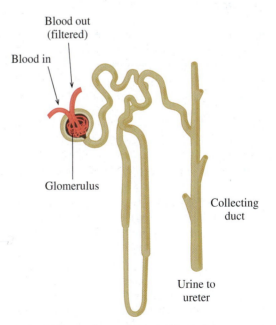

In the kidneys, the nephrons each contain a glomerulus where urea and waste products are removed from the blood to form urine.

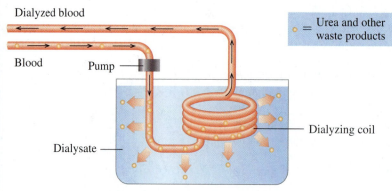

Dialyzed blood

Blood

Pump

Dialysate

Dialyzing coil

= Urea and other waste products

During dialysis, waste products and excess water are removed from the blood.

QUESTIONS AND PROBLEMS

8.6 Properties of Solutions

LEARNING GOAL: *Identify a mixture as a solution, a colloid, or a suspension. Describe how the number of particles in a solution affects the freezing point, boiling point, and osmotic pressure of a solution.*

8.65 Identify the following as characteristic of a solution, a colloid, or a suspension:
   a. a mixture that cannot be separated by a semipermeable membrane
   b. a mixture that settles out upon standing

8.66 Identify the following as characteristic of a solution, a colloid, or a suspension:
   a. Particles of this mixture remain inside a semipermeable membrane but pass through filters.
   b. The particles of solute in this mixture are very large and visible.

8.67 In each pair, identify the solution that will have a lower freezing point. Explain.
   a. 1.0 mole of glycerol (nonelectrolyte) and 2.0 moles of ethylene glycol (nonelectrolyte) each in 1.0 L of water
   b. 0.50 mole of KCl (strong electrolyte) and 0.50 mole of $MgCl_2$ (strong electrolyte) each in 2.0 L of water

8.68 In each pair, identify the solution that will have a higher boiling point. Explain.
   a. 1.50 moles of LiOH (strong electrolyte) and 3.00 moles of KOH (strong electrolyte) each in 0.50 L of water
   b. 0.40 mole of $Al(NO_3)_3$ (strong electrolyte) and 0.40 mole of CsCl (strong electrolyte) each in 0.50 L of water

8.69 A 10% (m/v) starch solution is separated from a 1% (m/v) starch solution by a semipermeable membrane. (Starch is a colloid.)
   a. Which compartment has the higher osmotic pressure?
   b. In which direction will water flow initially?
   c. In which compartment will the volume level rise?

8.70 Two solutions, a 0.1% (m/v) albumin solution and a 2% (m/v) albumin solution, are separated by a semipermeable membrane. (Albumin is a colloid.)
   a. Which compartment has the higher osmotic pressure?
   b. In which direction will water flow initially?
   c. In which compartment will the volume level rise?

8.71 Indicate the compartment (A or B) that will increase in volume for each of the following pairs of solutions separated by semipermeable membranes:

Solution in A	Solution in B
a. 5% (m/v) starch	10% (m/v) starch
b. 8% (m/v) albumin	4% (m/v) albumin
c. 0.1% (m/v) sucrose	10% (m/v) sucrose

8.72 Indicate the compartment (A or B) that will increase in volume for each of the following pairs of solutions separated by semipermeable membranes:

Solution in A	Solution in B
a. 20% (m/v) starch	10% (m/v) starch
b. 10% (m/v) albumin	2% (m/v) albumin
c. 0.5% (m/v) sucrose	5% (m/v) sucrose

8.73 Are the following solutions isotonic, hypotonic, or hypertonic compared with a red blood cell?
   a. distilled H_2O **b.** 1% (m/v) glucose
   c. 0.9% (m/v) NaCl   **d.** 15% (m/v) glucose

8.74 Will a red blood cell undergo crenation, hemolysis, or no change in each of the following solutions?
   a. 1% (m/v) glucose   **b.** 2% (m/v) NaCl
   c. 5% (m/v) glucose   **d.** 0.1% (m/v) NaCl

8.75 Each of the following mixtures is placed in a dialyzing bag and immersed in distilled water. Which substances will be found outside the bag in the distilled water?
   a. NaCl solution
   b. starch solution (colloid) and alanine, an amino acid, solution
   c. NaCl solution and starch solution (colloid)
   d. urea solution

8.76 Each of the following mixtures is placed in a dialyzing bag and immersed in distilled water. Which substances will be found outside the bag in the distilled water?
   a. KCl solution and glucose solution
   b. an albumin solution (colloid)
   c. an albumin solution (colloid), KCl solution, and glucose solution
   d. urea solution and NaCl solution

CONCEPT MAP

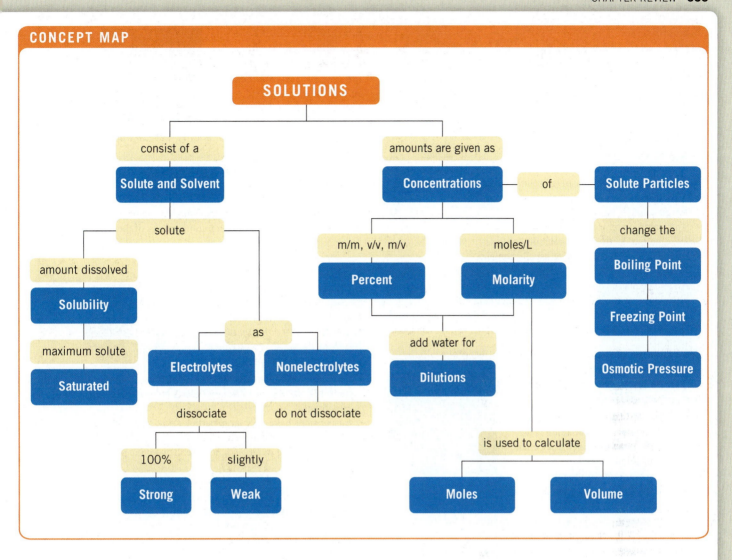

CHAPTER REVIEW

8.1 Solutions

LEARNING GOAL: Identify the solute and solvent in a solution; describe the formation of a solution.

- A solution forms when a solute, usually the smaller quantity, dissolves in a solvent.
- In a solution, the particles of solute are evenly dispersed in the solvent.
- The solute and solvent may be solid, liquid, or gas.
- The polar O—H groups form hydrogen bonds between water molecules.
- An ionic solute dissolves in water—a polar solvent—because the polar water molecules attract and pull the ions into solution, where they become hydrated.
- The expression "like dissolves like" means that a polar or ionic solute dissolves in a polar solvent while a nonpolar solute requires a nonpolar solvent.

Solute: The substance present in lesser amount

Salt

Water

Solvent: The substance present in greater amount

8.2 Electrolytes and Nonelectrolytes

LEARNING GOAL: Identify solutes as electrolytes or nonelectrolytes.

- Substances that release ions in water are called electrolytes because the solution will conduct an electrical current.
- Strong electrolytes are completely ionized, whereas weak electrolytes are only partially ionized.
- Nonelectrolytes are substances that dissolve in water to produce molecules and cannot conduct electrical currents.
- An equivalent (Eq) is the amount of an electrolyte that carries 1 mole of positive or negative charge.
- In fluid replacement solutions, the concentrations of electrolytes are expressed as mEq/L of solution.

Strong electrolyte

8.3 Solubility

LEARNING GOAL: Define solubility. Distinguish between an unsaturated and a saturated solution; identify a salt as soluble or insoluble.

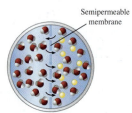

Dissolved solute

Undissolved solute

Dissolving

Recrystallizing

Saturated solution

- The solubility of a solute is the maximum amount of a solute that can dissolve in 100 g of solvent.
- A solution that contains the maximum amount of dissolved solute is a saturated solution.
- A solution containing less than the maximum amount of dissolved solute is unsaturated.
- An increase in temperature increases the solubility of most solids in water, but decreases the solubility of gases in water.
- Salts that are soluble in water usually contain Li^+, Na^+, K^+, NH_4^+, NO_3^-, or acetate $C_2H_3O_2^-$.
- An ionic equation consists of writing the reactants as ions and the products as an insoluble salt and the remaining ions.
- A net ionic equation is written by removing all the ions that do not change during the reaction (spectator ions) from the ionic equation.

8.4 Solution Concentration

LEARNING GOAL: Calculate the concentration of a solute in a solution; use concentration to calculate the amount of solute or solution.

Water added to make a solution

250 mL

5.0 g of KI

- The concentration of a solution is the amount of solute dissolved in a certain amount of solution.
- Mass percent (m/m) is the ratio of the mass of the solute to the mass of the solution multiplied by 100%.
- Volume percent (v/v) is the ratio of the volume of the solute to the volume of the solution multiplied by 100%.
- Mass/volume percent (m/v) is the ratio of the mass of the solute to the volume of the solution multiplied by 100%.
- Molarity (M) is the ratio of the moles of the solute to the volume in liters of the solution.
- In calculations of grams or milliliters of solute or solution, the percent concentration is used as a conversion factor.
- In calculations with moles of solute and liters of solution, the molarity is used as a conversion factor.

8.5 Dilution of Solutions and Solution Reactions

LEARNING GOAL: Calculate the new concentration or volume of a diluted solution. Given the volume and concentration of a solution, calculate the amount of another reactant or product in a reaction.

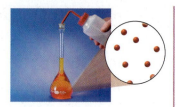

- In a dilution, a solvent such as water is added to a solution, which increases its volume and decreases its concentration.
- If the mass or solution volume and molarity of substances in a reaction are given, the balanced equation can be used to determine the quantities or concentrations of any of the other substances in the reaction.

8.6 Properties of Solutions

LEARNING GOAL: Identify a mixture as a solution, a colloid, or a suspension. Describe how the number of particles in a solution affects the freezing point, boiling point, and osmotic pressure of a solution.

Semipermeable membrane

- Colloids contain particles that do not settle out; they pass through filters but not semipermeable membranes.
- Suspensions have very large particles that settle out of solution.
- The particles of solute in a solution lower the freezing point, raise the boiling point, and increase the osmotic pressure of the solution.
- In osmosis, solvent (water) passes through a semipermeable membrane from a solution with a lower osmotic pressure (lower solute concentration) to a solution with a higher osmotic pressure (higher solute concentration).
- Isotonic solutions have osmotic pressures equal to that of body fluids.
- A red blood cell maintains its volume in an isotonic solution, but swells and may burst (hemolyze) in a hypotonic solution and shrinks (crenates) in a hypertonic solution.
- In dialysis, water and small solute particles pass through a dialyzing membrane, while larger solute particles are retained.

KEY TERMS

colloids Mixtures having particles that are moderately large. Colloids pass through filters but cannot pass through semipermeable membranes.

concentration A measure of the amount of solute that is dissolved in a specified amount of solution.

crenation The shriveling of a cell due to water leaving the cell when the cell is placed in a hypertonic solution.

dialysis A process in which water and small solute particles pass through a semipermeable membrane.

dilution A process by which water (solvent) is added to a solution to increase the volume and decrease (dilute) the concentration of the solute.

electrolyte A substance that produces ions when dissolved in water; its solution conducts electricity.

equivalent (Eq) The amount of a positive or negative ion that supplies 1 mole of electrical charge.

hemodialysis A cleansing of the blood by an artificial kidney using the principle of dialysis.

hemolysis A swelling and bursting of red blood cells in a hypotonic solution due to an increase in fluid volume.

Henry's law The solubility of a gas in a liquid is directly related to the pressure of that gas above the liquid.

hydration The process of surrounding dissolved ions by water molecules.

hypertonic solution A solution that has a higher osmotic pressure than the red blood cells of the body.

hypotonic solution A solution that has a lower osmotic pressure than the red blood cells of the body.

insoluble salt An ionic compound that does not dissolve in water.

ionic equation An equation for a reaction in solution that gives all the individual ions, both reacting ions and spectator ions.

isotonic solution A solution that has the same osmotic pressure as that of the red blood cells of the body.

mass percent (m/m) The grams of solute in exactly 100 g of solution.

mass/volume percent (m/v) The grams of solute in exactly 100 mL of solution.

molarity (M) The number of moles of solute in exactly 1 L of solution.

net ionic equation An equation for a reaction in solution that gives only the reactants and products involved in a chemical change.

nonelectrolyte A substance that dissolves in water as molecules; its solution does not conduct an electrical current.

osmosis The flow of a solvent, usually water, through a semipermeable membrane into a solution of higher solute concentration.

osmotic pressure The pressure that prevents the flow of water into the more concentrated solution.

saturated solution A solution containing the maximum amount of solute that can dissolve at a given temperature. Any additional solute will remain undissolved in the container.

semipermeable membrane A membrane that permits the passage of certain substances while blocking or retaining others.

solubility The maximum amount of solute that can dissolve in exactly 100 g of solvent, usually water, at a given temperature.

soluble salt An ionic compound that dissolves in water.

solute The component in a solution that is present in the smaller quantity.

solution A homogeneous mixture in which the solute is made up of small particles (ions or molecules) that can pass through filters and semipermeable membranes.

solvent The substance in which the solute dissolves; usually the component present in the greatest amount.

strong electrolyte A polar or ionic compound that ionizes completely when it dissolves in water. Its solution is a good conductor of electricity.

suspension A mixture in which the solute particles are large enough and heavy enough to settle out and be retained by both filters and semipermeable membranes.

unsaturated solution A solution that contains less solute than can be dissolved.

volume percent (v/v) A percent concentration that relates the volume of the solute to the volume of the solution.

weak electrolyte A substance that produces only a few ions along with many molecules when it dissolves in water. Its solution is a weak conductor of electricity.

UNDERSTANDING THE CONCEPTS

The chapter sections to review are shown in parentheses at the end of each question.

8.77 Select the diagram that represents the solution formed by a solute ◯◯ that is a: (8.2)
  a. nonelectrolyte   **b.** weak electrolyte
  c. strong electrolyte

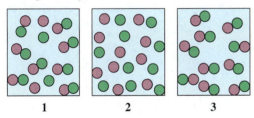

8.78 Match the diagrams with each of the following: (8.1)
  a. a polar solute and a polar solvent
  b. a nonpolar solute and a polar solvent
  c. a nonpolar solute and a nonpolar solvent

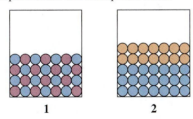

8.79 Select the container that represents the dilution of a 4% (m/v) NaCl solution to each of the following: (8.5)
  a. a 2% (m/v) NaCl solution
  b. a 1% (m/v) NaCl solution

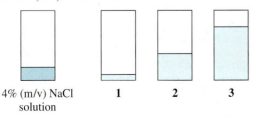

8.80 If all the solute is dissolved in Figure 1, how would heating or cooling the solution cause each of the following changes? (8.3)
  a. 2 to 3
  b. 2 to 1

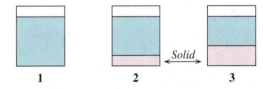

8.81 A pickle is made by soaking a cucumber in brine, a salt-water solution. What makes the smooth cucumber become wrinkled like a prune? (8.6)

8.82 Why do the lettuce leaves in a salad wilt after a vinaigrette dressing containing salt is added? (8.6)

Use the following beakers and solutions for Questions 8.83 and 8.84:

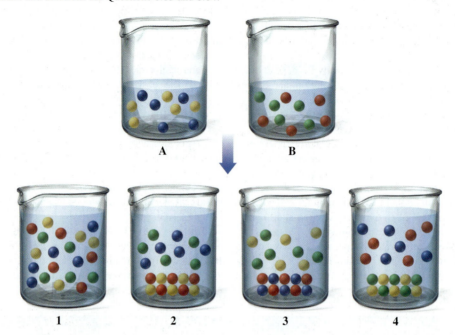

8.83 Use the following types of ions: (8.3)

Na^+ ⚪ Cl^- 🔵 Ag^+ 🔴 NO_3^- 🟢

a. Select the beaker (1, 2, 3, or 4) that contains the products after the solutions in beakers A and B are mixed.
b. If an insoluble salt forms, write the ionic equation.
c. If a reaction occurs, write the net ionic equation.

8.84 Use the following types of ions: (8.3)

K^+ ⚪ NO_3^- 🔵 NH_4^+ 🔴 Br^- 🟢

a. Select the beaker (1, 2, 3, or 4) that contains the products after the solutions in beakers A and B are mixed.
b. If an insoluble salt forms, write the ionic equation.
c. If a reaction occurs, write the net ionic equation.

8.85 A semipermeable membrane separates two compartments, A and B. If the levels of solutions in A and B are equal initially, select the diagram that illustrates the final levels for each of the following: (8.6)

A B	A B	A B
1	2	3

	Solution in A	Solution in B
a.	2% (m/v) starch	8% (m/v) starch
b.	1% (m/v) starch	1% (m/v) starch
c.	5% (m/v) sucrose	1% (m/v) sucrose
d.	0.1% (m/v) sucrose	1% (m/v) sucrose

8.86 Select the diagram that represents the shape of a red blood cell when placed in each of the following solutions: (8.6)

1   2   3

Normal red blood cell

a. 0.9% (m/v) NaCl solution
b. 10% (m/v) glucose solution
c. 0.01% (m/v) NaCl solution
d. 5% (m/v) glucose solution
e. 1% (m/v) glucose solution

ADDITIONAL QUESTIONS AND PROBLEMS

For instructor-assigned homework, go to www.masteringchemistry.com.

8.87 If sodium chloride has a solubility of 36.0 g of NaCl in 100 g of H_2O at 20 °C, how many grams of water are needed to prepare a saturated solution containing 80.0 g of NaCl? (8.3)

8.88 If the solid NaCl in a saturated solution of NaCl continues to dissolve, why is there no change in the concentration of the NaCl solution? (8.3)

8.89 Potassium nitrate has a solubility of 32 g of KNO_3 in 100 g of H_2O at 20 °C. State if each of the following forms an unsaturated or saturated solution at 20 °C: (8.3)
  a. 32 g of KNO_3 and 200. g of H_2O
  b. 19 g of KNO_3 and 50. g of H_2O
  c. 68 g of KNO_3 and 150. g of H_2O

8.90 Potassium fluoride has a solubility of 92 g of KF in 100 g of H_2O at 18 °C. State if each of the following forms an unsaturated or saturated solution at 18 °C: (8.3)
  a. 46 g of KF and 100. g of H_2O
  b. 46 g of KF and 50. g of H_2O
  c. 184 g of KF and 150. g of H_2O

8.91 Indicate whether each of the following ionic compounds is soluble or insoluble in water: (8.3)
  a. $CuCO_3$ **b.** $NaHCO_3$
  c. $Mg_3(PO_4)_2$ **d.** $(NH_4)_2SO_4$
  e. FeO   **f.** $Ca(OH)_2$

8.92 Indicate whether each of the following ionic compounds is soluble or insoluble in water: (8.3)
  a. Na_3PO_4 **b.** $PbBr_2$
  c. KCl   **d.** $(NH_4)_2S$
  e. $MgCO_3$ **f.** $FePO_4$

8.93 Write the net ionic equation to show the formation of a solid (insoluble salt) when the following solutions are mixed. Write *none* if there is no precipitate. (8.3)
  a. $AgNO_3(aq)$ and $LiCl(aq)$
  b. $NaCl(aq)$ and $KNO_3(aq)$
  c. $Na_2SO_4(aq)$ and $BaCl_2(aq)$

8.94 Write the net ionic equation to show the formation of a solid (insoluble salt) when the following solutions are mixed. Write *none* if there is no precipitate. (8.3)
  a. $Ca(NO_3)_2(aq)$ and $Na_2S(aq)$
  b. $Na_3PO_4(aq)$ and $Pb(NO_3)_2(aq)$
  c. $FeCl_3(aq)$ and $NH_4NO_3(aq)$

8.95 Calculate the mass percent (m/m) of a solution containing 15.5 g of Na_2SO_4 and 75.5 g of H_2O. (8.4)

8.96 Calculate the mass percent (m/m) of a solution containing 26 g of K_2CO_3 and 724 g of H_2O. (8.4)

8.97 What is the molarity of a solution containing 8.0 g of NaOH in 400. mL of NaOH solution? (8.5)

8.98 What is the molarity of a solution containing 15.6 g of KCl in 274 mL of KCl solution? (8.5)

8.99 How many grams of solute are in each of the following solutions? (8.5)
  a. 2.20 L of a 3.00 M $Al(NO_3)_3$ solution
  b. 75.0 mL of a 0.500 M $C_6H_{12}O_6$ solution
  c. 0.150 L of a 0.320 M NH_4Cl solution

8.100 How many grams of solute are in each of the following solutions? (8.5)
  a. 428 mL of a 0.450 M Na_2SO_4 solution
  b. 10.5 mL of a 2.50 M $AgNO_3$ solution
  c. 28.4 mL of a 6.00 M H_3PO_4 solution

8.101 A patient receives all her nutrition from fluids given through the vena cava. Every 12 h, 750 mL of a solution that is 4% (m/v) amino acids (protein) and 25% (m/v) glucose (carbohydrate) is given along with 500 mL of a 10% (m/v) lipid (fat) solution. (8.4)
  a. In 1 day, how many grams of amino acids, glucose, and lipid are given to the patient?
  b. How many kilocalories does she obtain in 1 day?

8.102 A patient receives an intravenous solution of a 5.0% (m/v) glucose solution. How many liters of the glucose solution would the patient be given to obtain 75 g of glucose? (8.4)

8.103 How many milliliters of a 12% (v/v) propyl alcohol solution would you need to obtain 4.5 mL of propyl alcohol? (8.4)

8.104 An 80-proof brandy is 40.0% (v/v) ethyl alcohol. The "proof" is twice the percent concentration of alcohol in the beverage. How many milliliters of alcohol are present in 750 mL of brandy? (8.4)

8.105 Calculate the concentration, percent or molarity, of the solution when water is added to prepare each of the following solutions: (8.5)
  a. 25.0 mL of a 0.200 M NaBr solution diluted to 50.0 mL
  b. 15.0 mL of a 12.0% (m/v) K_2SO_4 solution diluted to 40.0 mL
  c. 75.0 mL of a 6.00 M NaOH solution diluted to 255 mL

8.106 Calculate the concentration, percent or molarity, of the solution when water is added to prepare each of the following solutions: (8.5)
  a. 25.0 mL of an 18.0 M HCl solution diluted to 500. mL
  b. 50.0 mL of a 15.0% (m/v) NH_4Cl solution diluted to 125 mL
  c. 4.50 mL of an 8.50 M KOH solution diluted to 75.0 mL

8.107 What is the final volume, in milliliters, when 25.0 mL of each of the following solutions is diluted to provide the given concentration? (8.5)
  a. 10.0% (m/v) HCl solution to give a 2.50% (m/v) HCl solution
  b. 5.00 M HCl solution to give a 1.00 M HCl solution
  c. 6.00 M HCl solution to give a 0.500 M HCl solution

8.108 What is the final volume, in milliliters, when 5.00 mL of each of the following solutions is diluted to provide the given concentration? (8.5)
  a. 20.0% (m/v) NaOH solution to give a 4.00% (m/v) NaOH solution
  b. 0.600 M NaOH solution to give a 0.100 M NaOH solution
  c. 16.0% (m/v) NaOH solution to give a 2.00% (m/v) NaOH solution

CHALLENGE QUESTIONS

8.109 A solution is prepared with 70.0 g of HNO_3 and 130.0 g of H_2O. The HNO_3 solution has a density of 1.21 g/mL. (8.4, 8.5)
  a. What is the mass percent (m/m) of the HNO_3 solution?
  b. What is the total volume of the solution?
  c. What is the mass/volume percent (m/v)?
  d. What is its molarity (M)?

8.110 A solution is prepared by dissolving 22.0 g of NaOH in 118.0 g of water. The NaOH solution has a density of 1.15 g/mL. (8.4, 8.5)
  a. What is the mass percent (m/m) of the NaOH solution?
  b. What is the total volume of the solution?
  c. What is the mass/volume percent (m/v)?
  d. What is its molarity (M)?

8.111 The antacid Amphogel contains aluminum hydroxide $Al(OH)_3$. How many milliliters of a 6.00 M HCl solution are required to react with 60.0 mL of a 1.00 M $Al(OH)_3$ solution? (8.5)

$$Al(OH)_3(s) + 3HCl(aq) \longrightarrow AlCl_3(aq) + 3H_2O(l)$$

8.112 Calcium carbonate, $CaCO_3$, reacts with stomach acid (HCl, hydrochloric acid) according to the following equation: (8.5)

$$CaCO_3(s) + 2HCl(aq) \longrightarrow$$
$$CaCl_2(aq) + H_2O(l) + CO_2(g)$$

Tums, an antacid, contains $CaCO_3$. If Tums is added to 20.0 mL of a 0.400 M HCl solution, how many grams of CO_2 gas are produced?

8.113 How many grams of NO gas can be produced from 80.0 mL of a 4.00 M HNO_3 solution and excess Cu? (8.5)

$$3Cu(s) + 8HNO_3(aq) \longrightarrow$$
$$3Cu(NO_3)_2(aq) + 4H_2O(l) + 2NO(g)$$

8.114 A 355-mL sample of a HCl solution reacts with excess Mg to produce 4.20 L of H_2 gas measured at 745 mmHg and 35 °C. What is the molarity of the HCl solution? (8.5)

$$Mg(s) + 2HCl(aq) \longrightarrow MgCl_2(aq) + H_2(g)$$

8.115 Write the net ionic equation to show the formation of a solid (insoluble salt) when the following solutions are mixed. Write *none* if there is no precipitate. (8.3)

a. $AgNO_3(aq) + Na_2SO_4(aq)$
b. $KCl(aq) + Pb(NO_3)_2(aq)$
c. $CaCl_2(aq) + (NH_4)_3PO_4(aq)$
d. $K_2SO_4(aq) + BaCl_2(aq)$

8.116 Write the net ionic equation to show the formation of a solid (insoluble salt) when the following solutions are mixed. Write *none* if there is no precipitate. (8.3)

a. $Pb(NO_3)_2(aq) + NaBr(aq)$
b. $AgNO_3(aq) + (NH_4)_2CO_3(aq)$
c. $Na_3PO_4(aq) + Al(NO_3)_3(aq)$
d. $NaOH(aq) + CuCl_2(aq)$

8.117 In a laboratory experiment, a 10.0-mL sample of NaCl solution is poured into an evaporating dish with a mass of 24.10 g. The combined mass of the evaporating dish and NaCl solution is 36.15 g. After heating, the evaporating dish and dry NaCl have a combined mass of 25.50 g. (8.4, 8.5)

a. What is the mass percent (m/m) of the NaCl solution?
b. What is the molarity (M) of the NaCl solution?
c. If water is added to 10.0 mL of the initial NaCl solution to give a final volume of 60.0 mL, what is the molarity (M) of the diluted NaCl solution?

8.118 In a laboratory experiment, a 15.0-mL sample of KCl solution is poured into an evaporating dish with a mass of 24.10 g. The combined mass of the evaporating dish and KCl solution is 41.50 g. After heating, the evaporating dish and dry KCl have a combined mass of 28.28 g. (8.4, 8.5)

a. What is the mass percent (m/m) of the KCl solution?
b. What is the molarity (M) of the KCl solution?
c. If water is added to 10.0 mL of the initial KCl solution to give a final volume of 60.0 mL, what is the molarity of the diluted KCl solution?

ANSWERS

Answers to Study Checks

8.1 0.194 mole of Cl^-

8.2 78 g of KNO_3

8.3 a. No solid forms.
b. $Pb^{2+}(aq) + 2Cl^-(aq) \longrightarrow PbCl_2(s)$

8.4 3.4% (m/m) NaCl solution

8.5 4.8% (m/v) Br_2 in CCl_4

8.6 5.5% (m/v) NaOH solution

8.7 2.12 M KNO_3 solution

8.8 18.0 g of KCl

8.9 47.5 mL of HCl solution

8.10 125 mL of KCl solution

8.11 1.25 M $NaNO_3$ solution

8.12 1.47 g of Zn

8.13 0.0175 L of Na_2SO_4 solution

8.14 The red blood cell will shrink (crenate).

Answers to Selected Questions and Problems

8.1 a. NaCl, solute; water, solvent
b. water, solute; ethanol, solvent
c. oxygen, solute; nitrogen, solvent

8.3 The polar water molecules pull the K^+ and I^- ions away from the solid and into solution, where they are hydrated.

8.5 a. water   **b.** CCl_4 **c.** water   **d.** CCl_4

8.7 In a solution of KF, only the ions of K^+ and F^- are present in the solvent. In an HF solution, there are a few ions of H^+ and F^- present, but mostly dissolved HF molecules.

8.9 a. $KCl(s) \xrightarrow{H_2O} K^+(aq) + Cl^-(aq)$

b. $CaCl_2(s) \xrightarrow{H_2O} Ca^{2+}(aq) + 2Cl^-(aq)$

c. $K_3PO_4(s) \xrightarrow{H_2O} 3K^+(aq) + PO_4^{3-}(aq)$

d. $Fe(NO_3)_3(s) \xrightarrow{H_2O} Fe^{3+}(aq) + 3NO_3^-(aq)$

8.11 a. mostly molecules and a few ions
b. ions only   **c.** molecules only

8.13 a. strong electrolyte
b. weak electrolyte   **c.** nonelectrolyte

8.15 a. 1 Eq   **b.** 2 Eq   **c.** 2 Eq   **d.** 6 Eq

8.17 0.154 mole of Na^+, 0.154 mole of Cl^-

8.19 55 mEq/L

8.21 a. saturated   **b.** unsaturated

8.23 a. unsaturated   **b.** unsaturated
c. saturated

8.25 a. 68 g of KCl   **b.** 12 g of KCl

8.27 a. The solubility of solid solutes typically increases as temperature increases.
   b. The solubility of a gas is less at a higher temperature.
   c. Gas solubility is less at a higher temperature and the CO_2 pressure in the can is increased.

8.29 a. soluble   **b.** insoluble   **c.** insoluble
   d. soluble   **e.** soluble

8.31 a. No solid forms.
   b. $2Ag^+(aq) + 2NO_3^-(aq) + 2K^+(aq) + S^{2-}(aq) \longrightarrow$
   $$Ag_2S(s) + 2K^+(aq) + 2NO_3^-(aq)$$
   $2Ag^+(aq) + S^{2-}(aq) \longrightarrow Ag_2S(s)$
   c. $Ca^{2+}(aq) + 2Cl^-(aq) + 2Na^+(aq) + SO_4^{2-}(aq) \longrightarrow$
   $$CaSO_4(s) + 2Na^+(aq) + 2Cl^-(aq)$$
   $Ca^{2+}(aq) + SO_4^{2-}(aq) \longrightarrow CaSO_4(s)$
   d. $3Cu^{2+}(aq) + 6Cl^-(aq) + 6Li^+(aq) + 2PO_4^{3-}(aq) \longrightarrow$
   $$Cu_3(PO_4)_2(s) + 6Li^+(aq) + 6Cl^-(aq)$$
   $3Cu^{2+}(aq) + 2PO_4^{3-}(aq) \longrightarrow Cu_3(PO_4)_2(s)$

8.33 a. 17% (m/m) KCl solution   **b.** 5.3% (m/m) sugar solution
   c. 10.% (m/m) $CaCl_2$ solution

8.35 a. 30.% (m/v) Na_2SO_4 solution
   b. 11% (m/v) sucrose solution

8.37 a. 0.500 M glucose solution   **b.** 0.0357 M KOH solution
   c. 0.250 M NaCl solution

8.39 a. 2.5 g of KCl   **b.** 50. g of NH_4Cl
   c. 25.0 mL of acetic acid

8.41 79.9 mL of alcohol

8.43 a. 20. g of mannitol   **b.** 240 g of mannitol

8.45 2 L of glucose solution

8.47 a. 20. g of $LiNO_3$ solution   **b.** 400. mL of KOH solution
   c. 20. mL of formic acid solution

8.49 a. 3.00 moles of NaCl   **b.** 0.400 mole of KBr
   c. 0.250 mole of $MgCl_2$

8.51 a. 120. g of NaOH   **b.** 59.7 g of KCl
   c. 5.48 g of HCl

8.53 a. 1.50 L   **b.** 54.5 mL   **c.** 62.5 mL

8.55 a. 2.0 M HCl solution   **b.** 2.0 M NaOH solution
   c. 2.5% (m/v) KOH solution
   d. 3.0% (m/v) H_2SO_4 solution

8.57 a. 80.0 mL of HCl solution   **b.** 250 mL of LiCl solution
   c. 600. mL of H_3PO_4 solution
   d. 180 mL of glucose solution

8.59 a. 12.8 mL of HNO_3 solution   **b.** 11.9 mL of $MgCl_2$ solution
   c. 1.88 mL of KCl solution

8.61 a. 10.4 g of $PbCl_2$
   b. 18.8 mL of $Pb(NO_3)_2$ solution

8.63 a. 206 mL of HCl solution   **b.** 0.500 mole of H_2 gas

8.65 a. solution   **b.** suspension

8.67 a. 2.0 moles of ethylene glycol in 1.0 L of water will have a lower freezing point because it has more particles in solution.
   b. 0.50 mole of $MgCl_2$ in 2.0 L of water has a lower freezing point because each formula unit of $MgCl_2$ dissociates in water to give three particles, whereas each formula unit of KCl dissociates to give only two particles.

8.69 a. 10% (m/v) starch solution
   b. from the 1% (m/v) starch solution into the 10% (m/v) starch solution
   c. 10% (m/v) starch solution

8.71 a. **B** 10% (m/v) starch solution
   b. **A** 8% (m/v) albumin solution
   c. **B** 10% (m/v) sucrose solution

8.73 a. hypotonic   **b.** hypotonic
   c. isotonic   **d.** hypertonic

8.75 a. NaCl   **b.** alanine
   c. NaCl   **d.** urea

8.77 a. 3   **b.** 1   **c.** 2

8.79 a. 2   **b.** 3

8.81 The skin of the cucumber acts like a semipermeable membrane through which the pickle loses water to the hypertonic brine solution.

8.83 a. beaker 3
   b. $Na^+(aq) + Cl^-(aq) + Ag^+(aq) + NO_3^-(aq) \longrightarrow$
   $$AgCl(s) + Na^+(aq) + NO_3^-(aq)$$
   c. $Ag^+(aq) + Cl^-(aq) \longrightarrow AgCl(s)$

8.85 a. 2   **b.** 1   **c.** 3   **d.** 2

8.87 222 g of water

8.89 a. unsaturated   **b.** saturated   **c.** saturated

8.91 a. insoluble   **b.** soluble   **c.** insoluble
   d. soluble   **e.** insoluble   **f.** insoluble

8.93 a. $Ag^+(aq) + Cl^-(aq) \longrightarrow AgCl(s)$ **b.** none
   c. $Ba^{2+}(aq) + SO_4^{2-}(aq) \longrightarrow BaSO_4(s)$

8.95 17.0% (m/m) Na_2SO_4 solution

8.97 0.50 M NaOH solution

8.99 a. 1410 g of $Al(NO_3)_3$ **b.** 6.75 g of $C_6H_{12}O_6$
   c. 2.57 g of NH_4Cl

8.101 a. 60 g of amino acids, 380 g of glucose, and 100 g of lipids
   b. 2700 kcal

8.103 38 mL of propyl alcohol solution

8.105 a. 0.100 M NaBr solution   **b.** 4.50% (m/v) K_2SO_4 solution
   c. 1.76 M NaOH solution

8.107 a. 100. mL   **b.** 125 mL   **c.** 300. mL

8.109 a. 35.0% (m/m) HNO_3 solution
   b. 165 mL
   c. 42.4% (m/v) HNO_3 solution
   d. 6.73 M HNO_3 solution

8.111 30.0 mL of HCl solution

8.113 2.40 g of NO

8.115 a. $2Ag^+(aq) + SO_4^{2-}(aq) \longrightarrow Ag_2SO_4(s)$
   b. $Pb^{2+}(aq) + 2Cl^-(aq) \longrightarrow PbCl_2(s)$
   c. $3Ca^{2+}(aq) + 2PO_4^{3-}(aq) \longrightarrow Ca_3(PO_4)_2(s)$
   d. $Ba^{2+}(aq) + SO_4^{2-}(aq) \longrightarrow BaSO_4(s)$

8.117 a. 11.6% (m/m) NaCl solution
   b. 2.39 M NaCl solution
   c. 0.398 M NaCl solution

9 Reaction Rates and Chemical Equilibrium

Visit **www.masteringchemistry.com** for self-study materials and instructor-assigned homework.

Peter, a chemical oceanographer, is collecting data concerning the amount of dissolved gases, specifically carbon dioxide (CO_2), in the Atlantic Ocean. Studies indicate that CO_2 in the atmosphere has increased as much as 25% since the 18th century, which has resulted in a scientific debate regarding its effects. The exact role of the oceans in this debate is currently unknown. Peter's research involves measuring the amount of dissolved CO_2 in the oceans and determining its impact on global conditions such as temperature.

The oceans are a complex mixture of many different chemicals including gases, elements and minerals, organic and particulate matter. Due to this, the oceans have been called a "chemical soup" which can complicate a study like Peter's. Peter understands that CO_2 is absorbed in the ocean via a series of equilibrium reactions. An equilibrium reaction is a reversible reaction in which both the products and the reactants are present. If the equilibrium reactions shift according to Le Châtelier's principle, an increase in the CO_2 concentration could eventually increase the amount of dissolved calcium carbonate, $CaCO_3$, which makes up coral reefs and shells. However, Peter must first determine the rate at which CO_2 is absorbed into the seawater and how it affects the amount of $CaCO_3$ in the water to determine if this is occurring.

Career: Chemical Oceanographer

A chemical oceanographer, also called a marine chemist, studies the chemistry of the ocean. One area of study includes how chemicals or pollutants enter into and affect the ocean. This can range from sewage and oil or fuels, to chemical fertilizers and storm drain overflows. Oceanographers analyze how these chemicals interact with seawater, marine life and sediments, as they can behave differently due to the ocean's varied environmental conditions. Chemical oceanographers also study how the various elements are cycled within the ocean. For instance, oceanographers quantify the amount and rate at which carbon dioxide is absorbed from the ocean's surface and eventually transferred to deep waters. Chemical oceanographers also aid ocean engineers in the development of instruments and vessels that enable researchers to collect data and discover previously unknown marine life.

E arlier, we looked at chemical reactions and determined the amounts of substances that react and the products that form. Now we are interested in how fast a reaction goes. If we know how fast a medication acts on the body, we can adjust the time over which the medication is taken. In construction, substances are added to cement to make it dry faster so work can continue. Some reactions, such as explosions or the formation of precipitates in a solution, are very fast. We know that when we roast a turkey or bake a cake, the reaction is slower. Some reactions, such as the tarnishing of silver or the aging of the body, are even slower (see Figure 9.1). We will see that some reactions need energy to keep running, whereas other reactions produce energy. We burn gasoline in our automobile engines to produce energy to make our cars move. In a similar way, we metabolize components from the foods in our diet to obtain the energy we need to make our bodies move. We will also look at the effect of changing the concentrations of reactants or products on the rate of reaction.

Up to now, we have considered a reaction as proceeding in a forward direction from reactants to products. However, in many reactions a reverse reaction also takes place as products collide to reform reactants. When the forward and reverse reactions take place at the same rates, the amounts of reactants and products stay the same. When this balance in the forward and reverse rate is reached, we say that the reaction has reached *equilibrium*. At equilibrium, both reactants and products are present, though some reaction mixtures contain mostly reactants and form only a few products, while others contain mostly products and few reactants.

5 days

5 months

50 years

Reaction Rate Increases

FIGURE 9.1 Reaction rates vary greatly for everyday processes. A banana ripens in a few days, silver tarnishes in a few months, while the aging process of humans takes many years.

Q How would you compare the rates of the reaction that forms sugars in plants by photosynthesis with the reactions that digest sugars in the body?

9.1 **Rates of Reactions**

For a chemical reaction to take place, the molecules of the reactants must come in contact with each other. The **collision theory** indicates that a reaction takes place only when molecules collide with the proper orientation and with sufficient energy. Many collisions can occur, but only a few actually lead to the formation of product. For example, consider the reaction of

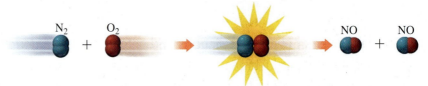

Collision that forms products

Collisions that do not form products

Insufficient energy

Wrong orientation

FIGURE 9.2 Reacting molecules must collide, have a minimum amount of energy, and have the proper orientation to form products.

FIGURE 9.2 Reacting molecules must collide, have a minimum amount of energy, and have the proper orientation to form products.

Q What happens when reacting molecules collide with the minimum energy but do not have the proper orientation?

nitrogen (N_2) and oxygen (O_2) molecules (see Figure 9.2). To form the nitrogen oxide (NO) product, the collisions between the N_2 and the O_2 molecules must place the atoms in the proper orientation. If the molecules are not aligned properly, no reaction takes place.

Activation Energy

Even when a collision has the proper orientation, there still must be sufficient energy to break the bonds between the atoms of the reactants. The **activation energy** is the minimum amount of energy required to break the bonds between atoms of reactants. In Figure 9.3, activation energy appears as an energy hill. The concept of activation energy is analogous to climbing a hill. To reach a destination on the other side, we must have the energy needed to climb to the top of the hill. Once we are at the top, we can run down the other side. The energy needed to get us from our starting point to the top of the hill would be our activation energy.

In the same way, a collision must provide enough energy to push the reactants to the top of the energy hill. Then the reactants may be converted to products. If the

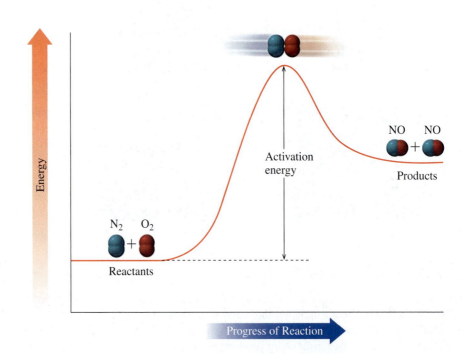

FIGURE 9.3 The activation energy is the minimum energy needed to convert the colliding molecules into product.

Q What happens in a collision of reacting molecules that have the proper orientation but not the energy of activation?

energy provided by the collision is less than the activation energy, the molecules simply bounce apart, and no reaction occurs. The features that lead to a successful reaction are summarized as follows:

Three Conditions Required for a Reaction to Occur

1. Collision   The reactants must collide.
2. Orientation   The reactants must align properly to break and form bonds.
3. Energy   The collision must provide the energy of activation.

Reaction Rates

The **rate** (or speed) **of reaction** is determined by measuring the amount of a reactant used up, or the amount of a product formed, in a certain period of time.

$$\text{Rate of reaction} = \frac{\text{change in concentration of reactant or product}}{\text{change in time}}$$

Perhaps we can describe the rate of reaction by the analogy of eating a pizza. When we start to eat, we have a whole pizza. As time goes by, there are fewer slices of pizza left. If we know how long it took to eat the pizza, we could determine the rate at which the pizza was consumed. Let's assume 4 slices are eaten every 8 minutes. That gives a rate of $\frac{1}{2}$ slice per minute. After 16 minutes, all 8 slices are gone.

Rate at Which Pizza Slices Are Eaten

Slices Eaten	0	4 slices	6 slices	8 slices
Time (min)	0	8 min	12 min	16 min

$$\text{Rate} = \frac{4\ \text{slices}}{8\ \text{min}} = \frac{1\ \text{slice}}{2\ \text{min}} = \frac{\frac{1}{2}\ \text{slice}}{1\ \text{min}}$$

Factors That Affect the Rate of a Reaction

Some reactions go very fast, while others are very slow. For any reaction, the rate is affected by changes in temperature, changes in the concentrations of the reactants, and the addition of catalysts.

Temperature At higher temperatures, the increase in kinetic energy makes the reacting molecules move faster. As a result, more collisions occur, and more colliding molecules have sufficient energy to react and form products. If we want food to cook faster, we use more heat to raise the temperature. When body temperature rises, there is an increase in the pulse rate, rate of breathing, and metabolic rate. On the other hand, we slow down reactions by lowering the temperature. We refrigerate perishable foods to retard spoilage and make them last longer. For some injuries, we apply ice to lessen the bruising process.

Concentrations of Reactants For virtually all reactions, the rate of a reaction increases when the concentrations of the reactants increase. When there are more reacting molecules, more collisions that form products can occur, and the reaction goes faster (see Figure 9.4). For example, a person having difficulty breathing may be given oxygen. The increase in the number of oxygen molecules in the lungs increases the rate at which oxygen combines with hemoglobin and helps the patient breathe more easily.

Catalysts Another way to speed up a reaction is to lower the activation energy. We saw that the activation energy is the minimum energy needed to break apart the bonds of the reacting molecules. If a collision provides less energy than the activation energy, the

TUTORIAL
Factors That Affect Rate

Reaction:

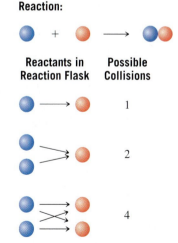

FIGURE 9.4 Increasing the concentration of the reactants increases the number of collisions that are possible.

Q Why does doubling the number of reactants increase the rate of reaction?

TUTORIAL
Activation Energy and Catalysis

TUTORIAL
Factors That Affect the Rate of a
Chemical Reaction

bonds do not break apart and the molecules bounce apart. A **catalyst** speeds up a reaction by lowering the activation energy, which allows more collisions of the reactants to have sufficient energy to form products. During any catalyzed reaction, the catalyst is not changed or consumed.

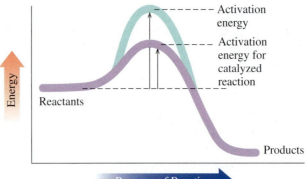

Catalysts have many uses in industry. In the manufacturing of margarine, hydrogen (H_2) is added to vegetable oils. Normally, the reaction is very slow because it has a high activation energy. However, when platinum (Pt) is used as a catalyst, the reaction occurs rapidly. In the body, biocatalysts called enzymes make most metabolic reactions proceed at rates necessary for proper cellular activity. Enzymes are added to laundry detergents to break down proteins (proteases), starches (amylases), or greases (lipases) that have stained clothes. Such enzymes function at the low temperatures that are used in home washing machines, and are reusable and biodegradable as well.

A summary of the factors affecting reaction rates is given in Table 9.1.

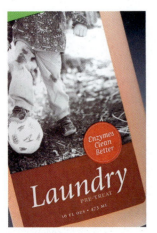

Enzymes in laundry detergent catalyze the removal of stains at low temperatures.

TABLE 9.1 Factors That Increase Reaction Rate

Factor	Reason
Higher temperature	More collisions, more collisions with energy of activation
More reactants	More collisions
Adding a catalyst	Lowers energy of activation

CONCEPT CHECK 9.1   **Rate of Reactions**

Describe how decreasing the concentration of a reactant would change the rate of a reaction.

ANSWER

If the concentration of a reactant is decreased, there will be fewer collisions of the reactant molecules, which would slow the rate of reaction.

SAMPLE PROBLEM 9.1   **Factors That Affect the Rate of Reaction**

Indicate whether the following changes will increase, decrease, or have no effect upon the rate of reaction:

a. increase in temperature
b. increase in the number of reactant molecules
c. adding a catalyst

SOLUTION

a. increase   **b.** increase   **c.** increase

STUDY CHECK 9.1

How does the lowering of temperature affect the rate of reaction?

Chemistry Link to the Environment

CATALYTIC CONVERTERS

For over 30 years, manufacturers have been required to include catalytic converters on the exhaust systems of gasoline automobile engines. When gasoline burns, the products found in the exhaust of a car contain high levels of pollutants. These include carbon monoxide (CO) from incomplete combustion, hydrocarbons such as C_8H_{18} (octane) from unburned fuel, and nitrogen oxide (NO) from the reaction of N_2 and O_2 at the high temperatures reached within the engine. Carbon monoxide is toxic, and unburned hydrocarbons and nitrogen oxide are involved in the formation of smog and acid rain.

The purpose of a catalytic converter is to lower the activation energy for reactions that convert each of these pollutants into substances such as CO_2, N_2, O_2, and H_2O, which are already present in the atmosphere.

$$2CO(g) + O_2(g) \longrightarrow 2CO_2(g)$$

$$2C_8H_{18}(g) + 25O_2(g) \longrightarrow 16CO_2(g) + 18H_2O(g)$$

$$2NO(g) \longrightarrow N_2(g) + O_2(g)$$

A catalytic converter consists of solid-particle catalysts, such as platinum (Pt) and palladium (Pd), on a ceramic honeycomb that provides a large surface area and facilitates contact with pollutants.

As the pollutants pass through the converter, they react with the catalysts. Today, we all use unleaded gasoline because lead interferes with the ability of the Pt and Pd catalysts in the converter to react with the pollutants.

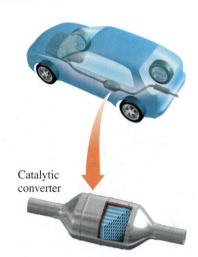

Catalytic converter

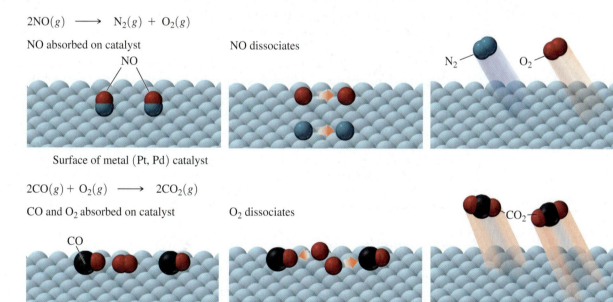

$$2NO(g) \longrightarrow N_2(g) + O_2(g)$$

NO absorbed on catalyst
NO
Surface of metal (Pt, Pd) catalyst

NO dissociates

N_2 O_2

$$2CO(g) + O_2(g) \longrightarrow 2CO_2(g)$$

CO and O_2 absorbed on catalyst
CO
Surface of metal (Pt, Pd) catalyst

O_2 dissociates

CO_2

QUESTIONS AND PROBLEMS

9.1 Rates of Reactions

LEARNING GOAL: Describe how temperature, concentration, and catalysts affect the rate of a reaction.

9.1 Why does bread grow mold more quickly at room temperature than in the refrigerator?

9.2 Why is pure oxygen used in cases of respiratory distress?

9.3 In the following reaction, what happens to the number of collisions between the reactants when more Br_2 molecules are added?

$$H_2(g) + Br_2(g) \longrightarrow 2HBr(g)$$

9.4 In the following reaction, what happens to the number of collisions between the reactants when the volume of the reaction container is increased?

$$H_2(g) + Br_2(g) \longrightarrow 2HBr(g)$$

9.5 In the following reaction, what happens to the number of collisions between the reactants when the temperature of the reaction is increased?

$$N_2(g) + O_2(g) \longrightarrow 2NO(g)$$

9.6 In the following reaction, what happens to the number of collisions between the reactants when the volume of the reaction container is decreased?

$$N_2(g) + O_2(g) \longrightarrow 2NO(g)$$

9.7 A catalytic converter accelerates the reaction of carbon monoxide with oxygen to produce carbon dioxide. How would each of the following changes affect the rate of the reaction shown here?

$$2CO(g) + O_2(g) \longrightarrow 2CO_2(g)$$

a. adding more $CO(g)$
b. raising the temperature
c. removing the catalyst
d. removing some $O_2(g)$

9.8 How would each of the following changes affect the rate of the reaction shown here?

$$2NO(g) + 2H_2(g) \longrightarrow N_2(g) + 2H_2O(g)$$

a. adding more $NO(g)$
b. lowering the temperature
c. removing some $H_2(g)$
d. adding a catalyst

LEARNING GOAL

Use the concept of reversible reactions to explain chemical equilibrium.

9.2 Chemical Equilibrium

In earlier chapters, we considered only the *forward reaction* in an equation and assumed that all of the reactants were converted to products. However, most of the time, reactants are not completely converted to products because a *reverse reaction* takes place in which products come together and form the reactants. When a reaction proceeds in both a forward and reverse direction, it is said to be reversible. We have looked at other reversible processes. For example, the melting of solids to form liquids and the freezing of liquids into solids is a reversible physical change. Even in our daily life, we have reversible events. We go from home to school, and we return from school to home. We go up an escalator and come back down. We put money in our bank account and take money out.

An analogy for a forward and reverse reaction can be found in the phrase "We are going to the grocery store." Although we mention our trip in one direction, we know that we will also return home from the grocery store. Because our trip has both a forward and reverse direction, we can say the trip is reversible. It is not very likely that we would stay at the grocery store forever.

A trip to the grocery store can be used to illustrate another aspect of reversible reactions. Perhaps the grocery store is nearby and we usually walk. However, we can change our rate. Suppose that one day we drive to the store, which increases our rate and gets us to the store faster. Correspondingly, a car also increases the rate at which we return home.

Reversible Reactions

A **reversible reaction** proceeds in both the forward and reverse directions. That means there are two reaction rates: the rate of the forward reaction and the rate of the reverse reaction. When molecules begin to react, the rate of the forward reaction is faster than the rate of the reverse reaction. As reactants are consumed and products accumulate, the rate of the forward reaction decreases, whereas the rate of the reverse reaction increases.

SAMPLE PROBLEM 9.2 Reversible Reactions

Write the forward and reverse reactions for each of the following:

a. $N_2(g) + 3H_2(g) \rightleftharpoons 2NH_3(g)$
b. $2CO(g) + O_2 \rightleftharpoons 2CO_2(g)$

SOLUTION

The equations are separated into forward and reverse reactions.

a. Forward reaction: $N_2(g) + 3H_2(g) \longrightarrow 2NH_3(g)$
Reverse reaction: $N_2(g) + 3H_2(g) \longleftarrow 2NH_3(g)$

b. Forward reaction: $2CO(g) + O_2(g) \longrightarrow 2CO_2(g)$
Reverse reaction: $2CO(g) + O_2(g) \longleftarrow 2CO_2(g)$

STUDY CHECK 9.2

Write the equation for the equilibrium reaction that contains the following reverse reaction:

$$H_2(g) + Br_2(g) \longleftarrow 2HBr(g)$$

SELF-STUDY ACTIVITY
Equilibrium

TUTORIAL
Chemical Equilibrium

Chemical Equilibrium

Eventually, the rates of the forward and reverse reactions are equal; the reactants form products as often as products form reactants. A reaction reaches **chemical equilibrium** when there is no further change in the concentrations of the reactants or products even though the two reactions continue at equal but opposite rates.

At equilibrium:

The rate of the forward reaction is equal to the rate of the reverse reaction.

No further changes occur in the concentrations of the reactants or products; the forward and reverse reactions continue at equal rates.

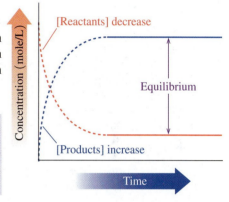

Let us look at the process as the reaction of H_2 and I_2 proceeds to equilibrium. Initially, only the reactants H_2 and I_2 are present. Soon, a few molecules of HI are produced by the forward reaction. With more time, additional HI molecules are produced. As the concentration of HI increases, more HI molecules collide and react in the reverse direction.

Forward reaction: $H_2(g) + I_2(g) \longrightarrow 2HI(g)$

Reverse reaction: $H_2(g) + I_2(g) \longleftarrow 2HI(g)$

As HI product builds up, the rate of the reverse reaction increases, while the rate of the forward reaction decreases. Eventually the rates become equal, which means the reaction has reached equilibrium. Even though the concentrations remain constant at equilibrium, the forward and reverse reactions continue to occur. The forward and reverse reactions are usually shown together in a single equation by using a double arrow. A reversible reaction is two opposing reactions that occur at the same time (see Figure 9.5).

$$H_2(g) + I_2(g) \quad \underset{\text{Reverse reaction}}{\overset{\text{Forward reaction}}{\rightleftarrows}} \quad 2HI(g)$$

We might also set up a reaction starting with only reactants or starting with only products. Let's look at the initial reactions in each, the forward and reverse reactions, and the equilibrium mixture from each for the following reaction:

$$2SO_2(g) + O_2(g) \rightleftarrows 2SO_3(g)$$

In the container with only the reactants SO_2 and O_2, the forward reaction takes place initially. As product SO_3 is formed, the rate of the reverse reaction increases. In the container with only the product SO_3, the reverse reaction takes place initially. As reactants are formed, the rate of the forward reaction increases. Eventually, the rates of both the forward and reverse reactions become equal. Then the equilibrium mixtures contain the same amounts of SO_2, O_2, and SO_3 in each.

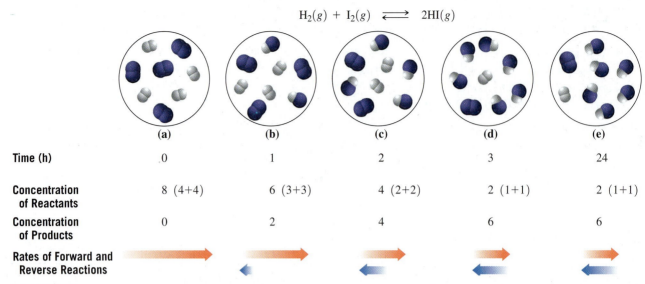

$$H_2(g) + I_2(g) \rightleftharpoons 2HI(g)$$

	(a)	(b)	(c)	(d)	(e)
Time (h)	0	1	2	3	24
Concentration of Reactants	8 (4+4)	6 (3+3)	4 (2+2)	2 (1+1)	2 (1+1)
Concentration of Products	0	2	4	6	6
Rates of Forward and Reverse Reactions					

FIGURE 9.5 (a) Initially, the reaction flask contains only the reactants H_2 and I_2. **(b)** The forward reaction between H_2 and I_2 begins to produce HI. **(c)** As the reaction proceeds, there are fewer molecules of H_2 and I_2 and more molecules of HI, which increases the rate of the reverse reaction. **(d)** At equilibrium, the concentrations of reactants H_2 and I_2 and product HI are constant. **(e)** The reaction continues, with the rate of the forward reaction equal to the rate of the reverse reaction.

Q How do the rates of the forward and reverse reactions compare once a chemical reaction reaches equilibrium?

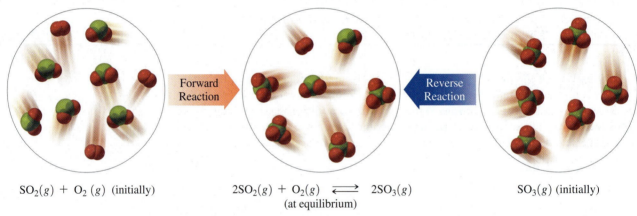

$SO_2(g) + O_2(g)$ (initially)	$2SO_2(g) + O_2(g) \rightleftharpoons 2SO_3(g)$ (at equilibrium)	$SO_3(g)$ (initially)

One sample initially contains SO_2 and O_2. Another sample contains only SO_3. At equilibrium, both mixtures contain small amounts of reactants SO_2 and O_2 and a large amount of product SO_3.

CONCEPT CHECK 9.2   **Reaction Rates and Equilibrium**

Complete each of the following with *equal* or *not equal*, *faster* or *slower*, *change* or *do not change*:

a. Before equilibrium is reached, the concentrations of the reactants and products _____.

b. Initially, reactants placed in a container have a _____ rate of reaction than the rate of reaction of the products.

c. At equilibrium, the rate of the forward reaction is _____ to the rate of the reverse reaction.

d. At equilibrium, the concentrations of the reactants and products _____.

ANSWER

a. Before equilibrium is reached, the concentrations of the reactants and products *change*.

b. Initially, reactants placed in a container have a *faster* rate of reaction than the rate of reaction of the products.

c. At equilibrium, the rate of the forward reaction is *equal* to the rate of the reverse reaction.

d. At equilibrium, the concentrations of the reactants and products *do not change*.

QUESTIONS AND PROBLEMS

9.2 Chemical Equilibrium

LEARNING GOAL: *Use the concept of reversible reactions to explain chemical equilibrium.*

9.9 What is meant by the term "reversible reaction"?

9.10 When does a reversible reaction reach equilibrium?

9.11 Which of the following processes are reversible?
    a. breaking a glass   **b.** melting snow
    c. heating a pan

9.12 Which of the following processes are not reversible?
    a. boiling water   **b.** eating a pizza
    c. walking up a hill

9.13 Which of the following are at equilibrium?
    a. The rate of the forward reaction is twice as fast as the rate of the reverse reaction.
    b. The concentrations of the reactants and the products do not change.
    c. The rate of the reverse reaction does not change.

9.14 Which of the following are not at equilibrium?
    a. The rates of the forward and reverse reactions are equal.
    b. The rate of the forward reaction does not change.
    c. The concentrations of reactants and the products are not constant.

9.3 Equilibrium Constants

At equilibrium, reactions occur in opposite directions at the same rate, which means the concentrations of the reactants and products remain constant. We can use a ski lift as an analogy. Early in the morning, skiers at the bottom of the mountain begin to ride the ski lift up to the slopes. As skiers reach the top of the mountain, they ski down. Eventually, the number of people riding up the ski lift becomes equal to the number of people skiing down the mountain. When there is no further change in the number of skiers on the slopes; the system is at equilibrium.

Equilibrium Constant Expression

Because the concentrations in a reaction at equilibrium no longer change, they can be used to set up a relationship between the products and the reactants. Suppose we write a general equation for reactants A and B that form products C and D. The small italic letters are the coefficients in the balanced equation.

$$a\text{A} + b\text{B} \rightleftharpoons c\text{C} + d\text{D}$$

An **equilibrium constant expression** can be written that multiplies the concentrations of the products and divides by the concentrations of the reactants. Each concentration is raised to a power that is its coefficient in the balanced chemical equation. The square bracket around each substance indicates that the concentration is expressed in moles per liter (M). The **equilibrium constant**, K_c, is the numerical value obtained by substituting molar concentrations at equilibrium into the expression. For our general reaction, the equilibrium constant expression is:

$$K_c = \frac{[\text{Products}]}{[\text{Reactants}]} = \frac{[\text{C}]^c [\text{D}]^d}{[\text{A}]^a [\text{B}]^b} \overset{\text{Coefficients}}{\nwarrow}$$

Equilibrium constant   Equilibrium constant expression

We can now describe how to write the equilibrium constant expression for the reaction of H_2 and I_2 that forms HI. First, we need to write the balanced chemical equation with a double arrow between the reactants and the products.

$$H_2(g) + I_2(g) \rightleftharpoons 2HI(g)$$

Second, we show the concentration of the products using brackets in the numerator and the concentrations of the reactants in brackets in the denominator.

$$\frac{[\text{Products}]}{[\text{Reactants}]} \longrightarrow \frac{[\text{HI}]}{[\text{H}_2][\text{I}_2]}$$

At equilibrium, the number of people riding the lift and the number of people skiing on the slope are constant.

TUTORIAL
Equilibrium Constant

Finally, we write any coefficient in the balanced chemical equation as an exponent of its concentration (the coefficient 1 is understood) and set it equal to K_c.

$$K_c = \frac{[\text{Products}]}{[\text{Reactants}]} = \frac{[\text{HI}]^2}{[\text{H}_2][\text{I}_2]}$$

CONCEPT CHECK 9.3 **Equilibrium Constant Expression**

Select the correctly written equilibrium constant expression for the following reaction, and explain your choice:

$$CH_4(g) + H_2O(g) \rightleftharpoons CO(g) + 3H_2(g)$$

a. $K_c = \dfrac{[\text{CO}][3\text{H}_2]}{[\text{CH}_4][\text{H}_2\text{O}]}$ **b.** $K_c = \dfrac{[\text{CO}][\text{H}_2]^3}{[\text{CH}_4][\text{H}_2\text{O}]}$

c. $K_c = \dfrac{[\text{CH}_4][\text{H}_2\text{O}]}{[\text{CO}][\text{H}_2]^3}$ **d.** $K_c = \dfrac{[\text{CO}][\text{H}_2]}{[\text{CH}_4][\text{H}_2\text{O}]}$

ANSWER

The correct equilibrium constant expression is **b**. The products are written in the numerator and the reactants are in the denominator. Because H_2 has a coefficient of 3 in the balanced equation, an exponent of 3 is used with the concentration of H_2.

SAMPLE PROBLEM 9.3 **Writing an Equilibrium Constant Expression**

Write the equilibrium constant expression for the following:

$$2SO_2(g) + O_2(g) \rightleftharpoons 2SO_3(g)$$

SOLUTION

Guide to Writing the K_c Expression

1 Write the balanced chemical equation.

2 Write the concentrations of the products as the numerator and the reactants as the denominator.

3 Write any coefficient in the equation as an exponent.

Step 1 **Write the balanced chemical equation.**

$$2SO_2(g) + O_2(g) \rightleftharpoons 2SO_3(g)$$

Step 2 **Write the concentrations of the products as the numerator and the reactants as the denominator.** Write the concentration of the product SO_3 in the numerator and the concentrations of the reactants SO_2 and O_2 each in the denominator.

$$\frac{[\text{Products}]}{[\text{Reactants}]} \longrightarrow \frac{[\text{SO}_3]}{[\text{SO}_2][\text{O}_2]}$$

Step 3 **Write any coefficient in the equation as an exponent.** Write the coefficient 2 as an exponent of the concentration of SO_2 and the coefficient 2 as an exponent of the concentration of SO_3.

$$K_c = \frac{[\text{SO}_3]^2}{[\text{SO}_2]^2[\text{O}_2]}$$

STUDY CHECK 9.3

Write the balanced chemical equation that would give the following equilibrium constant expression:

$$K_c = \frac{[\text{NO}_2]^2}{[\text{NO}]^2[\text{O}_2]}$$

Heterogeneous Equilibrium

Up to now, our examples have been reactions that involve only gases. A reaction in which all the reactants and products are gases is a **homogeneous equilibrium**. When the reactants and products are in two or more physical states, the equilibrium is termed a **heterogeneous equilibrium**. In the following example, solid calcium carbonate reaches equilibrium with solid calcium oxide and carbon dioxide gas; this is a heterogeneous equilibrium (see Figure 9.6).

$$CaCO_3(s) \rightleftharpoons CaO(s) + CO_2(g)$$

In contrast to gases, the concentrations of pure solids and pure liquids in a heterogeneous equilibrium are constant; they do not change. Therefore, pure solids and liquids are not included in the equilibrium constant expression. For this heterogeneous equilibrium, the K_c expression does not include the concentration of $CaCO_3(s)$ or $CaO(s)$. It is written as $K_c = [CO_2]$.

$$CaCO_3(s) \rightleftharpoons CaO(s) + CO_2(g)$$

$T = 800\ °C$

SAMPLE PROBLEM 9.4   Heterogeneous Equilibrium Constant Expression

Write the equilibrium constant expression for the following reaction at equilibrium:

$$4HCl(g) + O_2(g) \rightleftharpoons 2H_2O(l) + 2Cl_2(g)$$

SOLUTION

Step 1 **Write the balanced chemical equation.**

$$4HCl(g) + O_2(g) \rightleftharpoons 2H_2O(l) + 2Cl_2(g)$$

Step 2 **Write the concentrations of the products as the numerator and the reactants as the denominator.** In this heterogeneous reaction, the concentration of the liquid H_2O is not included in the equilibrium constant expression.

$$\frac{[Products]}{[Reactants]} \longrightarrow \frac{[Cl_2]}{[HCl][O_2]}$$

Step 3 **Write any coefficient in the equation as an exponent.**

$$K_c = \frac{[Cl_2]^2}{[HCl]^4[O_2]}$$

STUDY CHECK 9.4

Solid iron(II) oxide and carbon monoxide gas react to produce solid iron and carbon dioxide gas. Write the balanced chemical equation and the equilibrium constant expression for this reaction at equilibrium.

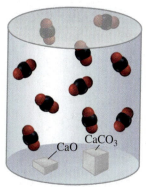

$T = 800\ °C$

FIGURE 9.6 At equilibrium at constant temperature, the concentration of CO_2 is the same regardless of the amounts of $CaCO_3(s)$ and $CaO(s)$ in the container.

Q Why are the concentrations of $CaO(s)$ and $CaCO_3(s)$ not included in K_c for the decomposition of $CaCO_3$?

Calculating Equilibrium Constants

The numerical value of the equilibrium constant is calculated from the equilibrium constant expression by substituting experimentally measured concentrations of the reactants and products at equilibrium into the expression. For example, the equilibrium constant expression for the reaction of H_2 and I_2 is written:

$$H_2(g) + I_2(g) \rightleftharpoons 2HI(g) \qquad K_c = \frac{[HI]^2}{[H_2][I_2]}$$

In the first experiment, the molar concentrations for the reactants and products at equilibrium are found to be $[H_2] = 0.10$ M, $[I_2] = 0.20$ M, and $[HI] = 1.04$ M. When we substitute these values into the equilibrium constant expression, we obtain its numerical value.

In additional experiments 2 and 3, the mixtures have different equilibrium concentrations. However, when these concentrations are used to calculate the equilibrium constant, we obtain the same value of K_c for each (see Table 9.2). *Thus, a reaction at a specific temperature has only one value for the equilibrium constant.*

The units of K_c depend on the specific equation. In this example, the units of $[M]^2/[M]^2$ cancel out to give a value of 54. In other equations, the concentration units do not cancel. However, in this text, the numerical value will be given without any units as shown in Sample Problem 9.5.

TABLE 9.2 Equilibrium Constant for $H_2(g) + I_2(g) \rightleftharpoons 2HI(g)$ at 427 °C

Experiment	Concentrations at Equilibrium			Equilibrium Constant
	$[H_2]$	$[I_2]$	$[HI]$	$K_c = \dfrac{[HI]^2}{[H_2][I_2]}$
1	0.10 M	0.20 M	1.04 M	$K_c = \dfrac{[1.04]^2}{[0.10][0.20]} = 54$
2	0.20 M	0.20 M	1.47 M	$K_c = \dfrac{[1.47]^2}{[0.20][0.20]} = 54$
3	0.30 M	0.17 M	1.66 M	$K_c = \dfrac{[1.66]^2}{[0.30][0.17]} = 54$

SAMPLE PROBLEM 9.5   Calculating an Equilibrium Constant

The decomposition of dinitrogen tetroxide forms nitrogen dioxide.

$$N_2O_4(g) \rightleftharpoons 2NO_2(g)$$

What is the value of K_c at 100 °C if a reaction mixture at equilibrium contains $[N_2O_4] = 0.45$ M and $[NO_2] = 0.31$ M?

SOLUTION

Analyze the Problem

	Reactant	Product	Equilibrium Constant
Chemical Reaction	$N_2O_4(g) \rightleftharpoons 2NO_2(g)$		
Equilibrium	0.45 M N_2O_4	0.31 M NO_2	K_c

Guide to Calculating the K_c Value

1 Write the K_c expression for the equilibrium.

2 Substitute equilibrium (molar) concentrations and calculate K_c.

Step 1   Write the K_c expression for the equilibrium.

$$K_c = \frac{[\text{Products}]}{[\text{Reactants}]} = \frac{[NO_2]^2}{[N_2O_4]}$$

Step 2   Substitute equilibrium (molar) concentrations and calculate K_c. Note that the numerical value of K_c is given without any units.

$$K_c = \frac{[0.31]^2}{[0.45]} = 0.21$$

STUDY CHECK 9.5

Ammonia decomposes when heated to give nitrogen and hydrogen.

$$2NH_3(g) \rightleftharpoons 3H_2(g) + N_2(g)$$

Calculate the equilibrium constant if an equilibrium mixture contains $[NH_3] = 0.040$ M, $[H_2] = 0.60$ M, and $[N_2] = 0.20$ M.

QUESTIONS AND PROBLEMS

9.3 Equilibrium Constants

LEARNING GOAL: *Calculate the equilibrium constant for a reversible reaction given the concentrations of reactants and products at equilibrium.*

9.15   Write the equilibrium constant expression for each of the following reactions:

    a. $CH_4(g) + 2H_2S(g) \rightleftharpoons CS_2(g) + 4H_2(g)$

    b. $2NO(g) \rightleftharpoons N_2(g) + O_2(g)$

    c. $2SO_3(g) + CO_2(g) \rightleftharpoons CS_2(g) + 4O_2(g)$

9.16   Write the equilibrium constant expression for each of the following reactions:

    a. $2HBr(g) \rightleftharpoons H_2(g) + Br_2(g)$

    b. $CO(g) + 2H_2(g) \rightleftharpoons CH_3OH(g)$

    c. $CH_4(g) + Cl_2(g) \rightleftharpoons CH_3Cl(g) + HCl(g)$

9.17 Identify each of the following as a homogeneous or heterogeneous equilibrium:

a. $2O_3(g) \rightleftharpoons 3O_2(g)$

b. $2NaHCO_3(s) \rightleftharpoons Na_2CO_3(s) + CO_2(g) + H_2O(g)$

c. $CH_4(g) + H_2O(g) \rightleftharpoons 3H_2(g) + CO(g)$

d. $4HCl(g) + Si(s) \rightleftharpoons SiCl_4(g) + 2H_2(g)$

9.18 Identify each of the following as a homogeneous or heterogeneous equilibrium:

a. $CO(g) + H_2(g) \rightleftharpoons C(s) + H_2O(g)$

b. $CO(g) + 2H_2(g) \rightleftharpoons CH_3OH(l)$

c. $CS_2(g) + 4H_2(g) \rightleftharpoons CH_4(g) + 2H_2S(g)$

d. $Br_2(g) + Cl_2(g) \rightleftharpoons 2BrCl(g)$

9.19 Write the equilibrium constant expression for each of the reactions in Problem 9.17.

9.20 Write the equilibrium constant expression for each of the reactions in Problem 9.18.

9.21 What is the K_c for the following reaction at equilibrium if $[N_2O_4] = 0.030$ M and $[NO_2] = 0.21$ M?

$$N_2O_4(g) \rightleftharpoons 2NO_2(g)$$

9.22 What is the K_c for the following reaction at equilibrium if $[CO_2] = 0.30$ M, $[H_2] = 0.033$ M, $[CO] = 0.20$ M, and $[H_2O] = 0.30$ M?

$$CO_2(g) + H_2(g) \rightleftharpoons CO(g) + H_2O(g)$$

9.23 What is the K_c for the following reaction at equilibrium at 1000 °C if $[CO] = 0.50$ M, $[H_2] = 0.30$ M, $[CH_4] = 1.8$ M, and $[H_2O] = 2.0$ M?

$$CO(g) + 3H_2(g) \rightleftharpoons CH_4(g) + H_2O(g)$$

9.24 What is the K_c for the following reaction at equilibrium at 500 °C if $[N_2] = 0.44$ M, $[H_2] = 0.40$ M, and $[NH_3] = 2.2$ M?

$$N_2(g) + 3H_2(g) \rightleftharpoons 2NH_3(g)$$

9.25 What is the K_c for the following reaction at equilibrium at 750 °C if $[CO] = 0.20$ M and $[CO_2] = 0.052$ M?

$$FeO(s) + CO(g) \rightleftharpoons Fe(s) + CO_2(g)$$

9.26 What is the K_c for the following reaction at equilibrium at 800 °C if $[CO_2] = 0.030$ M?

$$CaCO_3(s) \rightleftharpoons CaO(s) + CO_2(g)$$

9.4 Using Equilibrium Constants

LEARNING GOAL

Use an equilibrium constant to predict the extent of reaction and to calculate equilibrium concentrations.

The values of equilibrium constants can be large or small. The size of the constant depends on whether equilibrium is reached with more products than reactants, or more reactants than products. *However, the size of an equilibrium constant does not effect how fast equilibrium is reached.*

Equilibrium with a Large K_c

When a reaction has a large equilibrium constant, it means that the forward reaction produced a large amount of products when equilibrium was reached. Then the equilibrium mixture contains mostly products, which makes the concentrations of the products in the numerator larger than the concentrations of the reactants in the denominator. Thus at equilibrium, this reaction has a large K_c.

$$2SO_2(g) + O_2(g) \rightleftharpoons 2SO_3(g)$$

$$K_c = \frac{[SO_3]^2}{[SO_2]^2[O_2]} \quad \frac{\text{Mostly products}}{\text{Few reactants}} = 3.4 \times 10^2$$

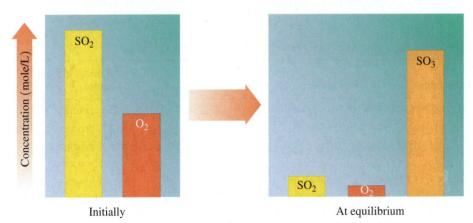

The equilibrium mixture contains a large amount of the product SO_3 and only a small amount of the reactants SO_2 and O_2, which results in a large K_c.

Equilibrium with a Small K_c

When a reaction has a small equilibrium constant, it means that the reverse reaction converted most of the products back to reactants when equilibrium was reached. Thus, the equilibrium mixture contains mostly reactants, which makes the concentrations of the products in the numerator much smaller than the concentrations of the reactants in the denominator. For example, the reaction of N_2 and O_2 to form NO has a small K_c. When equilibrium is reached for this reaction, the equilibrium mixture contains mostly reactants, N_2 and O_2, and only a few molecules of the product NO. Reactions with very small K_c produce essentially no products.

$$N_2(g) + O_2(g) \rightleftharpoons 2NO(g)$$

$$K_c = \frac{[NO]^2}{[N_2][O_2]} \quad \frac{\text{Few products}}{\text{Mostly reactants}} = 2 \times 10^{-9}$$

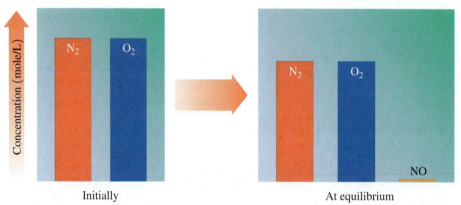

The equilibrium mixture contains a very small amount of the product NO and a large amount of the reactants N_2 and O_2, which results in a small K_c.

Only a few reactions have equilibrium constants close to 1, which means they have about equal concentrations of reactants and products. Moderate amounts of reactants have been converted to products when equilibrium was reached (see Figure 9.7). Table 9.3 lists some equilibrium constants and the extent of their reaction.

FIGURE 9.7 At equilibrium, a reaction with a large K_c contains mostly products, whereas a reaction with a small K_c contains mostly reactants.

Q Does a reaction with a $K_c = 1.2 \times 10^{15}$ contain mostly reactants or products at equilibrium?

Small K_c	$K_c \approx 1$	Large K_c
Favors Reactants		Favors Products
Reactants >> Products Little reaction takes place	Reactants ≈ Products Moderate reaction	Reactants << Products Reaction almost complete

TABLE 9.3 Examples of Reactions with Large and Small K_c Values

Reactants	Products	K_c	Equilibrium Mixture Contains
$2CO(g) + O_2(g) \rightleftharpoons$	$2CO_2(g)$	2×10^{11}	Mostly products
$2H_2(g) + S_2(g) \rightleftharpoons$	$2H_2S(g)$	1.1×10^7	Mostly products
$N_2(g) + 3H_2(g) \rightleftharpoons$	$2NH_3(g)$	1.6×10^2	Mostly products
$PCl_5(g) \rightleftharpoons$	$PCl_3(g) + Cl_2(g)$	1.2×10^{-2}	Mostly reactants
$N_2(g) + O_2(g) \rightleftharpoons$	$2NO(g)$	2×10^{-9}	Mostly reactants

Calculating Concentrations at Equilibrium

We have seen that reactions can reach equilibrium without using up all the reactants. Then we need to use the equilibrium constant to calculate the amount of a reactant or product that would be found in the equilibrium mixture. In this type of problem, we are given the value of the equilibrium constant for a specific reaction and all the concentrations except one, as shown in Sample Problem 9.6.

TUTORIAL
Calculations Using the Equilibrium
Constant

SAMPLE PROBLEM 9.6 Calculating Concentration Using an Equilibrium Constant

Phosgene ($COCl_2$) is a toxic substance that is produced by the reaction of carbon monoxide and chlorine; the K_c for the reaction is 5.0.

$$CO(g) + Cl_2(g) \rightleftharpoons COCl_2(g)$$

If the concentrations for the reaction at equilibrium are $[CO] = 0.64$ M and $[Cl_2] = 0.25$ M, what is the concentration of $COCl_2(g)$?

SOLUTION

Analyze the Problem

	Reactants		Product	Equilibrium Constant
Reaction	$CO(g) + Cl_2(g) \rightleftharpoons COCl_2(g)$			
Equilibrium	0.64 M	0.25 M	M $COCl_2$	$K_c = 5.0$

Step 1   **Write the K_c expression for the equilibrium equation.** Using the balanced chemical equation, the equilibrium constant expression is written as:

$$K_c = \frac{[\text{Products}]}{[\text{Reactants}]} = \frac{[COCl_2]}{[CO][Cl_2]}$$

Step 2   **Solve the K_c expression for the unknown concentration.** To rearrange the expression for $[COCl_2]$, we multiply both sides by $[CO][Cl_2]$, which cancels $[CO][Cl_2]$ on the right side.

$$K_c[CO][Cl_2] = \frac{[COCl_2]\cancel{[CO]}\cancel{[Cl_2]}}{\cancel{[CO]}\cancel{[Cl_2]}} = [COCl_2]$$

Step 3   **Substitute the known values into the rearranged K_c expression and calculate.** Substituting the molar concentrations for the equilibrium mixture and the K_c value into the equilibrium constant expression gives the $COCl_2$ concentration.

$$[COCl_2] = K_c[CO][Cl_2] = 5.0[0.64][0.25] = 0.80 \text{ M}$$

Guide to Using the K_c Value

1 Write the K_c expression for the equilibrium equation.

2 Solve the K_c expression for the unknown concentration.

3 Substitute the known values into the rearranged K_c expression and calculate.

STUDY CHECK 9.6

Ethanol can be produced by reacting ethylene (C_2H_4) with water vapor. At 327 °C, the reaction has a K_c of 9.0×10^3.

$$C_2H_4(g) + H_2O(g) \rightleftharpoons C_2H_5OH(g)$$

If the concentrations at equilibrium are $[C_2H_4] = 0.020$ M and $[H_2O] = 0.015$ M, what is the concentration of C_2H_5OH?

QUESTIONS AND PROBLEMS

9.4 Using Equilibrium Constants

LEARNING GOAL: *Use an equilibrium constant to predict the extent of reaction and to calculate equilibrium concentrations.*

9.27 Indicate whether each of the following reactions contains mostly products, mostly reactants, or both reactants and products at equilibrium:
   a. $Cl_2(g) + 2NO(g) \rightleftharpoons 2NOCl(g)$ $K_c = 3.7 \times 10^8$
   b. $H_2O(g) + CH_4(g) \rightleftharpoons CO(g) + 3H_2(g)$ $K_c = 4.7$
   c. $3O_2(g) \rightleftharpoons 2O_3(g)$ $K_c = 1.7 \times 10^{-56}$

9.28 Indicate whether each of the following reactions contains mostly products, mostly reactants, or both reactants and products at equilibrium:
   a. $CO(g) + Cl_2(g) \rightleftharpoons COCl_2(g)$ $K_c = 5.0$
   b. $2HF(g) \rightleftharpoons H_2(g) + F_2(g)$ $K_c = 1.0 \times 10^{-95}$
   c. $2NO(g) + O_2(g) \rightleftharpoons 2NO_2(g)$ $K_c = 6.0 \times 10^{13}$

9.29 The equilibrium constant, K_c, for the reaction of H_2 and I_2 is 54 at 425 °C. If the equilibrium mixture contains 0.015 M I_2 and 0.030 M HI, what is the concentration of H_2?
$$H_2(g) + I_2(g) \rightleftharpoons 2HI(g)$$

9.30 The equilibrium constant, K_c, for the decomposition of N_2O_4 is 4.6×10^{-3}. If the equilibrium mixture contains 0.050 M NO_2, what is the concentration of N_2O_4?
$$N_2O_4(g) \rightleftharpoons 2NO_2(g)$$

9.31 The equilibrium constant, K_c, for the decomposition of NOBr is 2.0 at 100 °C. If the system at equilibrium contains 2.0 M NO and 1.0 M Br_2, what is the concentration of NOBr?
$$2NOBr(g) \rightleftharpoons 2NO(g) + Br_2(g)$$

9.32 The equilibrium constant, K_c, for the reaction of H_2 and N_2 is 1.7×10^2 at 225 °C. If the system at equilibrium contains 0.18 M H_2 and 0.020 M N_2, what is the concentration of NH_3?
$$3H_2(g) + N_2(g) \rightleftharpoons 2NH_3(g)$$

LEARNING GOAL

Use Le Châtelier's principle to describe the changes made in equilibrium concentrations when reaction conditions change.

TUTORIAL
Le Châtelier's Principle

9.5 Changing Equilibrium Conditions: Le Châtelier's Principle

We have seen that when a reaction reaches equilibrium, the rates of the forward and reverse reactions are equal, and the concentrations remain constant. Now we will look at how a system at equilibrium responds to changes in concentration, pressure, and temperature. There are several ways to disturb the equilibrium, including removing or adding one of the reactants or products, or decreasing or increasing the volume or temperature.

Le Châtelier's Principle

When we alter any of the conditions of a system at equilibrium, the rates of the forward and reverse reactions will no longer be equal. We say that a *stress* is placed on the equilibrium. Then the system responds by changing the rate of the forward or reverse reaction in the direction that relieves that stress to reestablish equilibrium. We can use **Le Châtelier's principle**, which states that when a system at equilibrium is disturbed, the system will shift in the direction that will reduce that stress.

Water at equilibrium

Stress as water is added to first tank
Increasing rate of forward direction

New equilibrium established

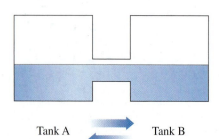

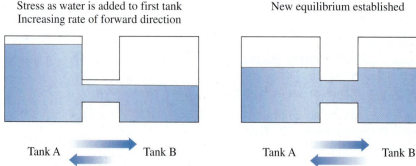

When water is added to one tank, the levels readjust to equalize.

Suppose we have two water tanks connected by a pipe. When the water levels are equal, water moves equally in the forward direction (Tank A to Tank B) and in the reverse direction (Tank B to Tank A). Suppose we add more water to Tank A. With a higher level of water in Tank A, more water moves in the forward direction from Tank A to Tank B than in the reverse direction from Tank B to Tank A, which is shown with a longer arrow. Eventually, equilibrium is reached as the levels in both tanks again become equal, but higher than before.

Effect of Concentration Changes on Equilibrium

We will now use the reaction of H_2 and I_2 to illustrate how a change in concentration disturbs the equilibrium, and how the system responds to that stress.

$$H_2(g) + I_2(g) \rightleftharpoons 2HI(g)$$

Suppose that more of the reactant H_2 is added to the equilibrium mixture, which increases the concentration of H_2. Because a K_c cannot change for a reaction at a given temperature, adding more H_2 places a stress on the system (see Figure 9.8). Then the system relieves this stress by increasing the rate of the forward reaction. Thus, more products are formed until the system is again at equilibrium. According to Le Châtelier's principle, adding more reactant causes the system to *shift* in the direction of the products until equilibrium is reestablished.

Add H_2

$$H_2(g) + I_2(g) \rightleftharpoons 2HI(g)$$

Suppose now that some H_2 is removed from the reaction mixture at equilibrium, which lowers the concentration of H_2. To relieve this stress, the rate of the forward reaction is slowed. From using Le Châtelier's principle, we know that when some of the reactants are removed, the system will *shift* in the direction of the reactants until equilibrium is reestablished.

Remove H_2

$$H_2(g) + I_2(g) \rightleftharpoons 2HI(g)$$

There can also be an increase or decrease in the concentrations of the products of an equilibrium mixture. For example, if more HI is added, there is an increase in the rate of the reaction in the reverse direction, which converts some of the products to reactants. The concentration of the products decreases and the concentration of the reactants increases until equilibrium is reestablished. Using Le Châtelier's principle, we see that the addition of a product causes the system to *shift* in the direction of the reactants.

Add HI

$$H_2(g) + I_2(g) \rightleftharpoons 2HI(g)$$

In another example, some HI is removed from an equilibrium mixture, which decreases the concentration of the products. Then there is a *shift* in the direction of the products to reestablish equilibrium.

Remove HI

$$H_2(g) + I_2(g) \rightleftharpoons 2HI(g)$$

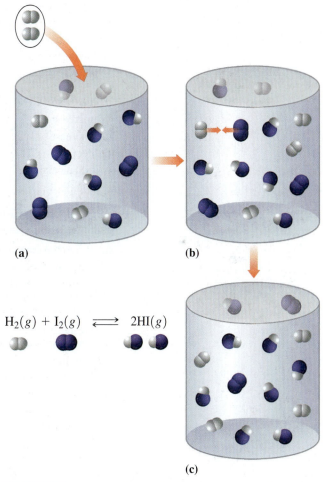

$$H_2(g) + I_2(g) \rightleftharpoons 2HI(g)$$

FIGURE 9.8 **(a)** The addition of H_2 places stress on the equilibrium system of $H_2(g) + I_2(g) \rightleftharpoons 2HI(g)$. **(b)** To relieve the stress, the forward reaction converts some reactants H_2 and I_2 to product HI. **(c)** A new equilibrium is established when the rates of the forward reaction and the reverse reaction become equal.

Q If more product HI is added, will the equilibrium shift in the direction of the products or reactants? Why?

TUTORIAL
Predicting Equilibrium Shifts

TABLE 9.4 Effect of Concentration Change on Equilibrium
$H_2(g) + I_2(g) \rightleftharpoons 2HI(g)$

Stress	Shift in the Direction of
Increase $[H_2]$	Products
Decrease $[H_2]$	Reactants
Increase $[I_2]$	Products
Decrease $[I_2]$	Reactants
Increase $[HI]$	Reactants
Decrease $[HI]$	Products

In summary, Le Châtelier's principle indicates that a stress caused by adding a substance at equilibrium is relieved when the equilibrium system shifts the reaction away from that substance. Adding more reactant causes an increase in the forward reaction to products. Adding more product causes an increase in the reverse reaction to reactants. When some of a substance is removed, the equilibrium system shifts in the direction of that substance. These features of Le Châtelier's principle are summarized in Table 9.4.

Effect of a Catalyst on Equilibrium

Sometimes a catalyst is added to a reaction. Earlier, in Section 9.1, we showed that a catalyst speeds up a reaction by lowering the activation energy. As a result, the rates of the forward and reverse reactions both increase. The time required to reach equilibrium is shorter, but the same ratios of products and reactants are attained. Therefore, a catalyst speeds up the forward and reverse reactions, but it has no effect on the concentrations of the reactants and products in the equilibrium mixture.

CONCEPT CHECK 9.4 Effect of Changes in Concentrations on Equilibrium

Describe the effect of each of the following changes on the equilibrium mixture of the following reaction:

$$CO(g) + H_2O(g) \rightleftharpoons CO_2(g) + H_2(g)$$

a. increase $[CO]$
b. increase $[H_2]$
c. decrease $[H_2O]$
d. decrease $[CO_2]$
e. add a catalyst

ANSWER

According to Le Châtelier's principle, when stress is applied to a reaction at equilibrium, the equilibrium will shift to relieve the stress.

a. When the concentration of the reactant CO increases, the rate of the forward reaction increases to shift the equilibrium in the direction of the products until equilibrium is reestablished.
b. When the concentration of the product H_2 increases, the rate of the reverse reaction increases to shift the equilibrium in the direction of the reactants until equilibrium is reestablished.
c. When the concentration of the reactant H_2O decreases, the rate of the reverse reaction increases to shift the equilibrium in the direction of the reactants until equilibrium is reestablished.
d. When the concentration of the product CO_2 decreases, the rate of the forward reaction increases to shift the equilibrium in the direction of the products until equilibrium is reestablished.
e. When a catalyst is added, it changes the rates of the forward and reverse reactions equally, which does not cause any shift in the equilibrium system.

Effect of Volume Change on Equilibrium

If there is a change in the volume of a gas mixture at equilibrium, there will also be a change in the concentrations of those gases. Decreasing the volume will increase the concentration of gases, whereas increasing the volume will decrease their concentration. Then the system responds to reestablish equilibrium.

Let's look at the effect of decreasing the volume of the equilibrium mixture of the following reaction:

$$2CO(g) + O_2(g) \rightleftharpoons 2CO_2(g)$$

If we decrease the volume, there is an increase in all the concentrations. According to Le Châtelier's principle, the increase in concentration is relieved when the system shifts in the direction of the fewer number of moles.

Decrease V

$$2CO(g) + O_2(g) \rightleftharpoons 2CO_2(g)$$

3 moles   2 moles

On the other hand, when the volume of the equilibrium gas mixture increases, the concentrations of all the gases decrease. Then the system shifts in the direction of the greater number of moles to reestablish equilibrium (see Figure 9.9).

Increase V

$$2CO(g) + O_2(g) \rightleftharpoons 2CO_2(g)$$

3 moles   2 moles

When a reaction has the same number of moles of reactants as products, a volume change does not affect the equilibrium mixture because the concentrations of the reactants and products change in the same way.

$$H_2(g) + I_2(g) \rightleftharpoons 2HI(g)$$

2 moles   2 moles

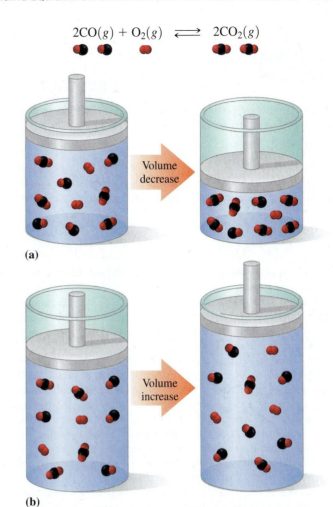

$$2CO(g) + O_2(g) \rightleftharpoons 2CO_2(g)$$

(a)

(b)

FIGURE 9.9 **(a)** A decrease in the volume of the container causes the system to shift in the direction of fewer moles of gas. **(b)** An increase in the volume of the container causes the system to shift in the direction of more moles of gas.

Q If you want to increase the products, would you increase or decrease the volume of the reaction container?

SAMPLE PROBLEM 9.7   **Effect of Changes in Volume on Equilibrium**

Indicate the effect of decreasing the volume of the container for each of the following at equilibrium:

a. $C_2H_2(g) + 2H_2(g) \rightleftharpoons C_2H_6(g)$
b. $2NO_2(g) \rightleftharpoons 2NO(g) + O_2(g)$
c. $CO(g) + H_2O(g) \rightleftharpoons CO_2(g) + H_2(g)$

SOLUTION

a. The system shifts in the direction of the product, which has fewer moles of gas.

$$C_2H_2(g) + 2H_2(g) \longrightarrow C_2H_6(g)$$

3 moles   1 mole

b. The system shifts in the direction of the reactant, which has fewer moles of gas.

$$2NO_2(g) \longleftarrow 2NO(g) + O_2(g)$$

2 moles   3 moles

c. There is no shift in the system because the moles of reactant are equal to the moles of product.

$$CO(g) + H_2O(g) \rightleftharpoons CO_2(g) + H_2(g)$$

2 moles   2 moles

STUDY CHECK 9.7

Suppose you want to increase the yield of product in the following reaction. Would you increase or decrease the volume of the reaction container?

$$CO(g) + 2H_2(g) \rightleftharpoons CH_3OH(g)$$

Chemistry Link to Health

OXYGEN–HEMOGLOBIN EQUILIBRIUM AND HYPOXIA

The transport of oxygen involves an equilibrium between hemoglobin (Hb), oxygen, and oxyhemoglobin (HbO_2).

$$Hb + O_2 \rightleftharpoons HbO_2$$

When the O_2 level is high in the alveoli of the lung, the reaction favors the product HbO_2. In the tissues where O_2 concentration is low, the reverse reaction releases the oxygen from the hemoglobin. The equilibrium constant expression is written:

$$K_c = \frac{[HbO_2]}{[Hb][O_2]}$$

At normal atmospheric pressure, oxygen diffuses into the blood because the partial pressure of oxygen in the alveoli is higher than that in the blood. At an altitude above 8000 ft, a decrease in the atmospheric pressure results in a significant reduction in the partial pressure of oxygen, which means that there is less oxygen available for the blood and body tissues. The fall in atmospheric pressure at higher altitudes decreases the partial pressure of inhaled oxygen, and there is less driving pressure for gas exchange in the lungs. At an altitude of 18 000 feet, a person will obtain 29% less oxygen. When oxygen levels are lowered, a person may experience *hypoxia*, which has symptoms that include increased respiratory rate, headache, decreased mental acuteness, fatigue, decreased physical coordination, nausea, vomiting, and cyanosis. A similar problem occurs in persons with a history of lung disease that impairs gas diffusion in the alveoli or in persons who have a reduced number of red blood cells, such as smokers.

According to Le Châtelier's principle, we see that a decrease in oxygen will shift the equilibrium in the direction of the reactants. Such a shift depletes the concentration of HbO_2 and causes the hypoxia condition.

$$Hb + O_2 \longleftarrow HbO_2$$

Immediate treatment of altitude sickness includes hydration, rest, and if necessary, descending to a lower altitude. The adaptation to lowered oxygen levels requires about 10 days. During this time, the bone marrow increases red blood cell production, providing more hemoglobin. A person living at a high altitude can have 50% more red blood cells than someone at sea level. This increase in hemoglobin causes a shift in the equilibrium in the direction of the HbO_2 product. Eventually, the higher concentration of HbO_2 will provide more oxygen to the tissues and the symptoms of hypoxia will lessen.

$$Hb + O_2 \longrightarrow HbO_2$$

For some who climb high mountains, it is important to stop and acclimatize for several days at increasing altitudes. At very high altitudes, it may be necessary to use an oxygen tank.

Hypoxia may occur at high altitudes where the oxygen concentration is lower.

Effect of Temperature Change on Equilibrium

We can think of heat as a reactant or a product in a reaction. For example, in the equation for an endothermic reaction, heat is written on the reactant side. When the temperature of an endothermic reaction increases, the system responds by shifting in the direction of the products to remove heat.

Increase T

$$N_2(g) + O_2(g) + heat \rightleftharpoons 2NO(g)$$

If the temperature is lowered for an endothermic reaction, there is a decrease in heat. Then the system shifts in the direction of the reactants to add heat.

Decrease T

$$N_2(g) + O_2(g) + heat \rightleftharpoons 2NO(g)$$

In the equation for an exothermic reaction, heat is written on the product side. When the temperature of an exothermic reaction increases, the system responds by shifting in the direction of the reactants to remove heat.

Increase T

$$2SO_2(g) + O_2(g) \rightleftarrows 2SO_3(g) + \text{heat}$$

If the temperature is lowered for an exothermic reaction, there is a decrease in heat. Then the system shifts in the direction of the products to add heat.

Decrease T

$$2SO_2(g) + O_2(g) \rightleftarrows 2SO_3(g) + \text{heat}$$

SAMPLE PROBLEM 9.8 Effect of Temperature Change on Equilibrium

Indicate the change that takes place when the temperature is increased for each of the following systems at equilibrium:

a. $N_2(g) + 3H_2(g) \rightleftarrows 2NH_3(g) + 92 \text{ kJ}$
b. $N_2(g) + O_2(g) + 180 \text{ kJ} \rightleftarrows 2NO(g)$

SOLUTION

a. When the temperature is increased for an exothermic reaction, the system shifts in the direction of the reactants to remove heat.
b. When the temperature is increased for an endothermic reaction, the system shifts in the direction of the products to remove heat.

STUDY CHECK 9.8

Indicate the change that takes place when the temperature is decreased for each of the reactions at equilibrium in Sample Problem 9.8.

Table 9.5 summarizes the ways we can use Le Châtelier's principle to determine the shift in equilibrium that relieves stress caused by the change in a condition.

TABLE 9.5 Effects of Condition Changes on Equilibrium

Condition	Change (stress)	Remove Stress in the Direction of
Concentration	Add a reactant	Products (forward reaction)
	Remove a reactant	Reactants (reverse reaction)
	Add a product	Reactants (reverse reaction)
	Remove a product	Products (forward reaction)
Volume (container)	Decrease volume	Fewer number of moles
	Increase volume	Greater number of moles
Temperature	**Endothermic reaction**	
	Raise T	Products (forward reaction to remove heat)
	Lower T	Reactants (reverse reaction to add heat)
	Exothermic reaction	
	Raise T	Reactants (reverse reaction to remove heat)
	Lower T	Products (forward reaction to add heat)
Catalyst	Increase rates equally	No effect

Chemistry Link to Health

HOMEOSTASIS: REGULATION OF BODY TEMPERATURE

In a physiological system of equilibrium called *homeostasis*, changes in our environment are balanced by changes in our bodies. It is crucial to our survival that we balance heat gain with heat loss. If we do not lose enough heat, our body temperature rises. At high temperatures, the body can no longer regulate our metabolic reactions. If we lose too much heat, body temperature drops. At low temperatures, essential functions proceed too slowly.

The skin plays an important role in the maintenance of body temperature. When the outside temperature rises, receptors in the skin send signals to the brain. The temperature-regulating part of the brain stimulates the sweat glands to produce perspiration. As perspiration evaporates from the skin, heat is removed, and the body temperature is lowered.

In cold temperatures, epinephrine is released, causing an increase in metabolic rate, which increases the production of heat. Receptors on the skin signal the brain to constrict the blood vessels. Less blood flows through the skin, and heat is conserved. The production of perspiration stops to lessen the heat lost by evaporation.

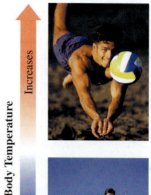

Blood vessels dilate
• sweat production increases
• sweat evaporates
• skin cools

Blood vessels constrict and epinephrine is released
• metabolic activity increases
• muscular activity increases
• shivering occurs
• sweat production stops

QUESTIONS AND PROBLEMS

9.5 Changing Equilibrium Conditions: Le Châtelier's Principle

LEARNING GOAL: *Use Le Châtelier's principle to describe the changes made in equilibrium concentrations when reaction conditions change.*

9.33 In the lower atmosphere, oxygen is converted to ozone (O_3) by the energy provided from lightning.

$$3O_2(g) + \text{heat} \rightleftharpoons 2O_3(g)$$

For each of the following changes at equilibrium, indicate whether the system shifts in the direction of the products, reactants, or does not change:
a. add more $O_2(g)$
b. add more $O_3(g)$
c. increase the temperature
d. increase the volume of the container
e. add a catalyst

9.34 Ammonia is produced by reacting nitrogen gas and hydrogen gas.

$$N_2(g) + 3H_2(g) \rightleftharpoons 2NH_3(g) + 92 \text{ kJ}$$

For each of the following changes at equilibrium, indicate whether the system shifts in the direction of the products, reactants, or does not change:
a. remove some $N_2(g)$
b. lower the temperature
c. add more $NH_3(g)$

d. add more $H_2(g)$
e. increase the volume of the container

9.35 Hydrogen chloride can be made by reacting hydrogen gas and chlorine gas.

$$H_2(g) + Cl_2(g) + \text{heat} \rightleftharpoons 2HCl(g)$$

For each of the following changes at equilibrium, indicate whether the system shifts in the direction of the products, reactants, or does not change:
a. add more $H_2(g)$
b. increase the temperature
c. remove some $HCl(g)$
d. add a catalyst
e. remove some $Cl_2(g)$

9.36 When heated, carbon reacts with water to produce carbon monoxide and hydrogen.

$$C(s) + H_2O(g) + \text{heat} \rightleftharpoons CO(g) + H_2(g)$$

For each of the following changes at equilibrium, indicate whether the system shifts in the direction of the products, reactants, or does not change:
a. decrease the temperature
b. add more $C(s)$
c. remove $CO(g)$ as it forms
d. add more $H_2O(g)$
e. decrease the volume of the container

CONCEPT MAP

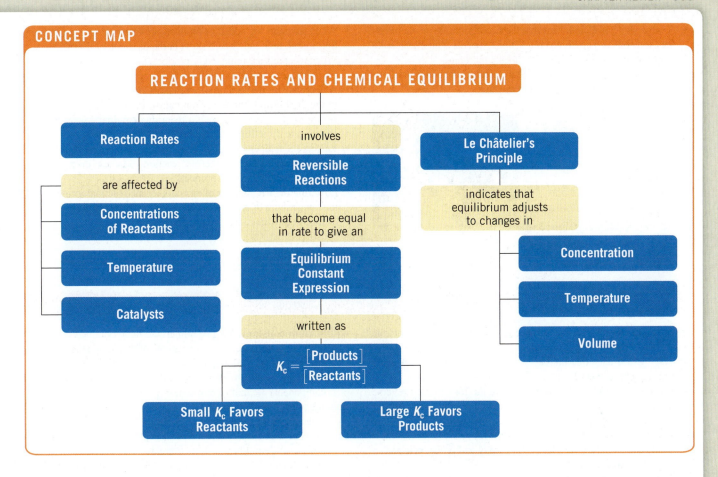

REACTION RATES AND CHEMICAL EQUILIBRIUM

Reaction Rates

are affected by

Concentrations of Reactants

Temperature

Catalysts

involves

Reversible Reactions

that become equal in rate to give an

Equilibrium Constant Expression

written as

$$K_c = \frac{[\text{Products}]}{[\text{Reactants}]}$$

Small K_c Favors Reactants

Large K_c Favors Products

Le Châtelier's Principle

indicates that equilibrium adjusts to changes in

Concentration

Temperature

Volume

CHAPTER REVIEW

9.1 Rates of Reactions

LEARNING GOAL: Describe how temperature, concentration, and catalysts affect the rate of a reaction.

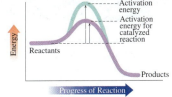

- The rate of a reaction is the speed at which the reactants are converted to products.
- Increasing the concentrations of reactants, raising the temperature, or adding a catalyst can increase the rate of a reaction.

9.2 Chemical Equilibrium

LEARNING GOAL: Use the concept of reversible reactions to explain chemical equilibrium.

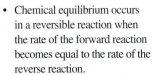

- Chemical equilibrium occurs in a reversible reaction when the rate of the forward reaction becomes equal to the rate of the reverse reaction.
- At equilibrium, no further change occurs in the concentrations of the reactants and products as the forward and reverse reactions continue.

9.3 Equilibrium Constants

LEARNING GOAL: Calculate the equilibrium constant for a reversible reaction given the concentrations of reactants and products at equilibrium.

- An equilibrium constant, K_c, is the ratio of the concentrations of the products to the concentrations of the reactants, with each concentration raised to a power equal to its coefficient in the chemical equation.
- For heterogeneous reactions, only gases are placed in the equilibrium expression.

9.4 Using Equilibrium Constants

LEARNING GOAL: Use an equilibrium constant to predict the extent of reaction and to calculate equilibrium concentrations.

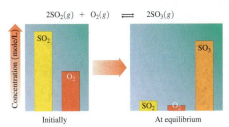

- A large value of K_c indicates that the equilibrium favors the products and could go nearly to completion, whereas a small value of K_c shows that the equilibrium favors the reactants.
- Equilibrium constants can be used to calculate the concentration of a component in the equilibrium mixture.

- When reactants are added or products are removed from an equilibrium mixture, the system shifts in the direction of the products.
- When reactants are removed or products are added to an equilibrium mixture, the system shifts in the direction of the reactants.
- A decrease in the volume of a reaction container causes a shift in the direction of the fewer number of moles.
- An increase in the volume of a reaction container causes a shift in the direction of the greater number of moles.
- Raising the temperature of an endothermic reaction or lowering the temperature of an exothermic reaction will cause the system to shift in the direction of products.
- Lowering the temperature of an endothermic reaction or raising the temperature of an exothermic reaction will cause the system to shift in the direction of reactants.

9.5 Changing Equilibrium Conditions: Le Châtelier's Principle

LEARNING GOAL: Use Le Châtelier's principle to describe the changes made in equilibrium concentrations when reaction conditions change.

KEY TERMS

activation energy The minimum energy required to break apart the bonds of the reacting molecules.

catalyst A substance that increases the rate of reaction by lowering the activation energy.

chemical equilibrium The point at which the forward and reverse reactions take place at the same rate so that there is no further change in concentrations of reactants and products.

collision theory A model for a chemical reaction that states that molecules must collide with sufficient energy and proper orientation in order to form products.

equilibrium constant expression The ratio of the concentrations of products to the concentrations of reactants with each component raised to an exponent equal to the coefficient of that compound in the balanced chemical equation.

equilibrium constant, K_c The numerical value obtained by substituting the equilibrium concentrations of the components into the equilibrium constant expression.

heterogeneous equilibrium An equilibrium system in which the components are in different states.

homogeneous equilibrium An equilibrium system in which all components are in the same state.

Le Châtelier's principle When a stress is placed on a system at equilibrium, the equilibrium shifts to relieve that stress.

rate of reaction The speed at which reactants are used to form product(s).

reversible reaction A reaction in which a forward reaction occurs from reactants to products, and a reverse reaction occurs from products back to reactants.

UNDERSTANDING THE CONCEPTS

The chapter sections to review are shown in parentheses at the end of each question.

9.37 Would the equilibrium constant, K_c, for the reaction in the diagrams have a large or small value? (9.4)

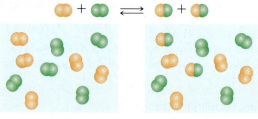

Initially   At Equilibrium

9.38 Would the equilibrium constant, K_c, for the reaction in the diagrams have a large or small value? (9.4)

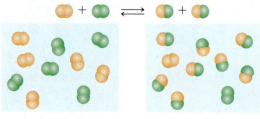

Initially   At Equilibrium

9.39 Would T_2 be higher or lower than T_1 for the reaction shown in the diagrams? (9.5)

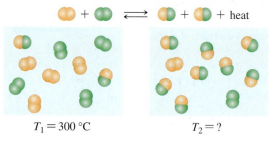

$T_1 = 300\ °C$ $T_2 = ?$

9.40 Would the reaction shown in the diagrams be exothermic or endothermic? (9.5)

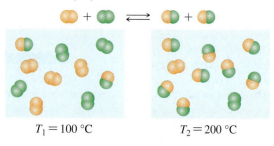

$T_1 = 100\ °C$ $T_2 = 200\ °C$

9.41 Indicate any changes that **a–d** will cause for the following reaction initially at equilibrium: (9.5)

$$C_2H_4(g) + Cl_2(g) \rightleftharpoons C_2H_4Cl_2(g) + \text{heat}$$

a. raise the temperature of the reaction
b. decrease the volume of the reaction container
c. add a catalyst
d. add more $Cl_2(g)$

9.42 Indicate any changes that **a–d** will cause for the following reaction initially at equilibrium: (9.5)

$$N_2(g) + O_2(g) + \text{heat} \rightleftharpoons 2NO(g)$$

a. raise the temperature of the reaction
b. decrease the volume of the reaction container
c. add a catalyst
d. remove some $N_2(g)$

ADDITIONAL QUESTIONS AND PROBLEMS

For instructor-assigned homework, go to www.masteringchemistry.com.

9.43 Write the equilibrium constant expression for each of the following reactions: (9.3)
a. $CH_4(g) + 2O_2(g) \rightleftharpoons CO_2(g) + 2H_2O(g)$
b. $4NH_3(g) + 3O_2(g) \rightleftharpoons 2N_2(g) + 6H_2O(g)$
c. $C(s) + 2H_2(g) \rightleftharpoons CH_4(g)$

9.44 Write the equilibrium constant expression for each of the following reactions: (9.3)
a. $2C_2H_6(g) + 7O_2(g) \rightleftharpoons 4CO_2(g) + 6H_2O(g)$
b. $2NaHCO_3(s) \rightleftharpoons Na_2CO_3(s) + CO_2(g) + H_2O(g)$
c. $4NH_3(g) + 5O_2(g) \rightleftharpoons 4NO(g) + 6H_2O(g)$

9.45 For each of the following reactions, indicate if the equilibrium mixture contains mostly products, mostly reactants, or both reactants and products: (9.4)
a. $H_2(g) + Cl_2(g) \rightleftharpoons 2HCl(g)$ $\quad K_c = 1.3 \times 10^{34}$
b. $2NOBr(g) \rightleftharpoons 2NO(g) + Br_2(g)$ $\quad K_c = 2.0$
c. $2NOCl(g) \rightleftharpoons Cl_2(g) + 2NO(g)$ $\quad K_c = 2.7 \times 10^{-9}$
d. $C(s) + H_2O(g) \rightleftharpoons CO(g) + H_2(g)$ $\quad K_c = 6.3 \times 10^{-1}$

9.46 For each of the following reactions, indicate if the equilibrium mixture contains mostly products, mostly reactants, or both reactants and products: (9.4)
a. $2H_2O(g) \rightleftharpoons 2H_2(g) + O_2(g)$ $\quad K_c = 4 \times 10^{-48}$
b. $N_2(g) + 3H_2(g) \rightleftharpoons 2NH_3(g)$ $\quad K_c = 0.30$
c. $2SO_2(g) + O_2(g) \rightleftharpoons 2SO_3(g)$ $\quad K_c = 1.2 \times 10^9$
d. $H_2(g) + S(s) \rightleftharpoons H_2S(g)$ $\quad K_c = 7.8 \times 10^5$

9.47 Write the equilibrium constant expression for the reactions **a–d** in Problem 9.45. (9.3)

9.48 Write the equilibrium constant expression for the reactions **a–d** in Problem 9.46. (9.3)

9.49 Write the balanced chemical equations that would give each of the following equilibrium constant expressions: (9.3)

a. $K_c = \dfrac{[SO_2][Cl_2]}{[SO_2Cl_2]}$ $\qquad$ **b.** $K_c = \dfrac{[BrCl]^2}{[Br_2][Cl_2]}$

c. $K_c = \dfrac{[CH_4][H_2O]}{[CO][H_2]^3}$ $\qquad$ **d.** $K_c = \dfrac{[N_2O][H_2O]^3}{[O_2]^2[NH_3]^2}$

9.50 Write the balanced chemical equations that would give each of the following equilibrium constant expressions: (9.3)

a. $K_c = \dfrac{[CO_2][H_2]}{[CO][H_2O]}$ $\qquad$ **b.** $K_c = \dfrac{[H_2][F_2]}{[HF]^2}$

c. $K_c = \dfrac{[O_2][HCl]^4}{[Cl_2]^2[H_2O]^2}$ $\qquad$ **d.** $K_c = \dfrac{[CS_2][H_2]^4}{[CH_4][H_2S]^2}$

9.51 Consider the reaction: (9.3)

$$2NH_3(g) \rightleftharpoons N_2(g) + 3H_2(g)$$

a. Write the equilibrium constant expression.

b. What is the K_c for the reaction if the concentrations at equilibrium are 0.20 M NH_3, 3.0 M N_2, and 0.50 M H_2?

9.52 Consider the reaction: (9.3)

$$2SO_2(g) + O_2(g) \rightleftharpoons 2SO_3(g)$$

a. Write the equilibrium constant expression.
b. What is the K_c for the reaction if the concentrations at equilibrium are 0.10 M SO_2, 0.12 M O_2, and 0.60 M SO_3?

9.53 The equilibrium constant for the combination reaction of NO_2 is 5.0 at 100 °C. If an equilibrium mixture contains 0.50 M NO_2, what is the concentration of N_2O_4? (9.3, 9.4)

$$2NO_2(g) \rightleftharpoons N_2O_4(g)$$

9.54 The equilibrium constant for the reaction of carbon and water to form carbon monoxide and hydrogen is 0.20 at 1000 °C. If an equilibrium mixture contains solid carbon, 0.40 M H_2O, and 0.40 M CO, what is the concentration of H_2? (9.3, 9.4)

$$C(s) + H_2O(g) \rightleftharpoons CO(g) + H_2(g)$$

9.55 According to Le Châtelier's principle, what is the effect when more O_2 is added to an equilibrium mixture of each of the following? (9.5)
a. $3O_2(g) \rightleftharpoons 2O_3(g)$
b. $2CO_2(g) \rightleftharpoons 2CO(g) + O_2(g)$
c. $P_4(g) + 5O_2(g) \rightleftharpoons P_4O_{10}(s)$
d. $2SO_2(g) + 2H_2O(g) \rightleftharpoons 2H_2S(g) + 3O_2(g)$

9.56 According to Le Châtelier's principle, what is the effect when more N_2 is added to an equilibrium mixture of each of the following? (9.5)
a. $2NH_3(g) \rightleftharpoons 3H_2(g) + N_2(g)$
b. $N_2(g) + O_2(g) \rightleftharpoons 2NO(g)$
c. $2NO_2(g) \rightleftharpoons N_2(g) + 2O_2(g)$
d. $4NH_3(g) + 3O_2(g) \rightleftharpoons 2N_2(g) + 6H_2O(g)$

9.57 Would decreasing the volume of the container for each of the following reactions at equilibrium cause the system to shift in the direction of the products or the reactants? (9.5)
a. $3O_2(g) \rightleftharpoons 2O_3(g)$
b. $2CO_2(g) \rightleftharpoons 2CO(g) + O_2(g)$
c. $P_4(g) + 5O_2(g) \rightleftharpoons P_4O_{10}(s)$
d. $2SO_2(g) + 2H_2O(g) \rightleftharpoons 2H_2S(g) + 3O_2(g)$

9.58 Would increasing the volume of the container for each of the following reactions at equilibrium cause the system to shift in the direction of the products or the reactants? (9.5)
a. $2NH_3(g) \rightleftharpoons 3H_2(g) + N_2(g)$
b. $N_2(g) + O_2(g) \rightleftharpoons 2NO(g)$
c. $N_2(g) + 2O_2(g) \rightleftharpoons 2NO_2(g)$
d. $4NH_3(g) + 3O_2(g) \rightleftharpoons 2N_2(g) + 6H_2O(g)$

9.59 For each of the following K_c values, indicate whether the equilibrium mixture contains mostly reactants, mostly products, or similar amounts of reactants and products: (9.4)
 a. $N_2(g) + O_2(g) \rightleftharpoons 2NO(g)$ $K_c = 1 \times 10^{-30}$
 b. $H_2(g) + Br_2(g) \rightleftharpoons 2HBr(g)$ $K_c = 2.0 \times 10^{19}$

9.60 For each of the following K_c values, indicate whether the equilibrium mixture contains mostly reactants, mostly products, or similar amounts of reactants and products: (9.4)
 a. $Cl_2(g) + 2NO(g) \rightleftharpoons 2NOCl(g)$ $K_c = 3.7 \times 10^8$
 b. $N_2(g) + 2H_2(g) \rightleftharpoons N_2H_4(g)$ $K_c = 7.4 \times 10^{-26}$

9.61 Indicate if you would increase or decrease the volume of the container to *increase* the yield of the products in each of the following: (9.5)
 a. $2C(s) + O_2(g) \rightleftharpoons 2CO(g)$
 b. $2CH_4(g) \rightleftharpoons C_2H_2(g) + 3H_2(g)$
 c. $2H_2(g) + O_2(g) \rightleftharpoons 2H_2O(g)$

9.62 Indicate if you would increase or decrease the volume of the container to *increase* the yield of the products in each of the following: (9.5)
 a. $Cl_2(g) + 2NO(g) \rightleftharpoons 2NOCl(g)$
 b. $N_2(g) + 2H_2(g) \rightleftharpoons N_2H_4(g)$
 c. $N_2O_4(g) \rightleftharpoons 2NO_2(g)$

CHALLENGE QUESTIONS

9.63 You mix 0.10 mole of PCl_5 with 0.050 mole of PCl_3 and 0.050 mole of Cl_2 in a 1.0 L container. (9.3, 9.4)

$$PCl_5(g) \rightleftharpoons PCl_3(g) + Cl_2(g) \qquad K_c = 4.2 \times 10^{-2}$$

 a. Is the reaction at equilibrium?
 b. If not, will the reaction proceed in the forward or reverse direction?

9.64 You mix 0.10 mole of NOBr, 0.10 mole of NO, and 0.10 mole of Br_2 in a 1.0 L container. (9.3, 9.4)

$$2NOBr(g) \rightleftharpoons 2NO(g) + Br_2(g) \qquad K_c = 2.0 \text{ at } 100\,°C$$

 a. Is the reaction at equilibrium?
 b. If not, will the reaction proceed in the forward or reverse direction?

9.65 Consider the following reaction: (9.3, 9.4, 9.5)

$$PCl_5(g) \rightleftharpoons PCl_3(g) + Cl_2(g)$$

 a. Write the equilibrium constant expression for the reaction.
 b. Initially, 0.60 mole of PCl_5 is placed in a 1.00 L flask. At equilibrium, there is 0.16 mole of PCl_3 in the flask. What are the equilibrium concentrations of the PCl_5 and Cl_2?
 c. What is the value of the equilibrium constant, K_c, for the reaction?
 d. If 0.20 mole of Cl_2 is added to the equilibrium mixture, will the concentration of PCl_5 increase or decrease?

9.66 The K_c for the decomposition of NOBr is 2.0 at 100 °C. (9.1, 9.2, 9.3, 9.4)

$$2NOBr(g) \rightleftharpoons 2NO(g) + Br_2(g)$$

 In an experiment, 1.0 mole of NOBr, 1.0 mole of NO, and 1.0 mole of Br_2 was placed in a 1.0 L container.
 a. Write the equilibrium constant expression for the reaction.
 b. Is the system at equilibrium?
 c. If not, will the rate of the forward or reverse reaction initially speed up?
 d. At equilibrium, which concentration(s) will be greater than 1.0 mole/L, and which will be less than 1.0 mole/L?

9.67 The combination reaction of solid carbon and carbon dioxide produces carbon monoxide. An equilibrium mixture contains solid carbon, 0.060 M CO_2, and 0.030 M CO. (9.3, 9.5)

$$C(s) + CO_2(g) \rightleftharpoons 2CO(g)$$

 a. What is the value of the equilibrium constant, K_c, for the reaction?
 b. What is the effect of adding more CO_2 to the equilibrium mixture?
 c. What is the effect of decreasing the volume of the container?

9.68 The solid NH_4HS is in equilibrium with the gases NH_3 and H_2S. An equilibrium mixture contains solid NH_4HS, 0.12 M NH_3, and 0.021 M H_2S. (9.3, 9.5)

$$NH_4HS(s) \rightleftharpoons NH_3(g) + H_2S(g)$$

 a. What is the value of the equilibrium constant, K_c, for the reaction?
 b. What is the effect of adding more solid NH_4HS to the equilibrium mixture?
 c. What is the effect of increasing the volume of the container?

9.69 Indicate how each of the following will affect the equilibrium concentration of CO in the following reaction: (9.3, 9.5)

$$C(s) + H_2O(g) + 31 \text{ kcal} \rightleftharpoons CO(g) + H_2(g)$$

 a. add more $H_2(g)$
 b. increase the temperature of the reaction
 c. increase the volume of the container
 d. decrease the volume of the container
 e. add a catalyst
 f. decrease the temperature of the reaction
 g. remove some $H_2O(g)$

9.70 Indicate how each of the following will affect the equilibrium concentration of NH_3 in the following reaction: (9.3, 9.5)

$$NH_3(g) + 5O_2(g) \rightleftharpoons 4NO(g) + 6H_2O(g) + 906 \text{ kJ}$$

 a. add more $O_2(g)$
 b. increase the temperature of the reaction
 c. increase the volume of the container
 d. add more NO(g)
 e. decrease the volume of the container
 f. decrease the temperature of the reaction
 g. remove some $H_2O(g)$

ANSWERS

Answers to Study Checks

9.1 Lowering the temperature will decrease the rate of reaction.

9.2 $H_2(g) + Br_2(g) \rightleftharpoons 2HBr(g)$

9.3 $2NO(g) + O_2(g) \rightleftharpoons 2NO_2(g)$

9.4 $FeO(s) + CO(g) \rightleftharpoons Fe(s) + CO_2(g)$ $K_c = \dfrac{[CO_2]}{[CO]}$

9.5 $K_c = 27$

9.6 $[C_2H_5OH] = 2.7$ M

9.7 Decreasing the volume will increase the yield of product.

9.8 a. When the temperature is decreased for an exothermic reaction, the system shifts in the direction of products to add heat.
  b. When the temperature is decreased for an endothermic reaction, the system shifts in the direction of reactants to add heat.

Answers to Selected Questions and Problems

9.1 Reactions go faster at higher temperatures.

9.3 The number of collisions between reactants will increase when the number of Br_2 molecules is increased.

9.5 The number of collisions between reactants will increase when the temperature is increased.

9.7 a. increase **b.** increase **c.** decrease **d.** decrease

9.9 A reversible reaction is one in which a forward reaction converts reactants to products, while a reverse reaction converts products to reactants.

9.11 a. not reversible **b.** reversible **c.** reversible

9.13 a. not at equilibrium **b.** at equilibrium **c.** at equilibrium

9.15 a. $K_c = \dfrac{[CS_2][H_2]^4}{[CH_4][H_2S]^2}$ **b.** $K_c = \dfrac{[N_2][O_2]}{[NO]^2}$

  c. $K_c = \dfrac{[CS_2][O_2]^4}{[SO_3]^2[CO_2]}$

9.17 a. homogeneous equilibrium **b.** heterogeneous equilibrium
  c. homogeneous equilibrium **d.** heterogeneous equilibrium

9.19 a. $K_c = \dfrac{[O_2]^3}{[O_3]^2}$ **b.** $K_c = [CO_2][H_2O]$

  c. $K_c = \dfrac{[H_2]^3[CO]}{[CH_4][H_2O]}$ **d.** $K_c = \dfrac{[SiCl_4][H_2]^2}{[HCl]^4}$

9.21 $K_c = 1.5$

9.23 $K_c = 270$

9.25 $K_c = 0.26$

9.27 a. mostly products **b.** both reactants and products
  c. mostly reactants

9.29 $[H_2] = 1.1 \times 10^{-3}$ M

9.31 $[NOBr] = 1.4$ M

9.33 a. The system shifts in the direction of the products.
  b. The system shifts in the direction of the reactants.
  c. The system shifts in the direction of the products.
  d. The system shifts in the direction of the reactants.
  e. No shift in system occurs.

9.35 a. The system shifts in the direction of the products.
  b. The system shifts in the direction of the products.
  c. The system shifts in the direction of the products.
  d. No shift in system occurs.
  e. The system shifts in the direction of the reactants.

9.37 The equilibrium constant would have a small value.

9.39 T_2 is lower than T_1.

9.41 a. shift in the direction of reactants
  b. shift in the direction of products
  c. no change
  d. shift in the direction of products

9.43 a. $K_c = \dfrac{[CO_2][H_2O]^2}{[CH_4][O_2]^2}$ **b.** $K_c = \dfrac{[N_2]^2[H_2O]^6}{[NH_3]^4[O_2]^3}$

  c. $K_c = \dfrac{[CH_4]}{[H_2]^2}$

9.45 a. mostly products **b.** both reactants and products
  c. mostly reactants **d.** both reactants and products

9.47 a. $K_c = \dfrac{[HCl]^2}{[H_2][Cl_2]}$ **b.** $K_c = \dfrac{[NO]^2[Br_2]}{[NOBr]^2}$

  c. $K_c = \dfrac{[Cl_2][NO]^2}{[NOCl]^2}$ **d.** $K_c = \dfrac{[CO][H_2]}{[H_2O]}$

9.49 a. $SO_2Cl_2(g) \rightleftharpoons SO_2(g) + Cl_2(g)$
  b. $Br_2(g) + Cl_2(g) \rightleftharpoons 2BrCl(g)$
  c. $CO(g) + 3H_2(g) \rightleftharpoons CH_4(g) + H_2O(g)$
  d. $2O_2(g) + 2NH_3(g) \rightleftharpoons N_2O(g) + 3H_2O(g)$

9.51 a. $K_c = \dfrac{[N_2][H_2]^3}{[NH_3]^2}$ **b.** $K_c = 9.4$

9.53 $[N_2O_4] = 1.3$ M

9.55 a. The system shifts in the direction of the products.
  b. The system shifts in the direction of the reactants.
  c. The system shifts in the direction of the products.
  d. The system shifts in the direction of the reactants.

9.57 a. The system shifts in the direction of the products.
  b. The system shifts in the direction of the reactants.
  c. The system shifts in the direction of the products.
  d. The system shifts in the direction of the reactants.

9.59 a. A small K_c indicates that the equilibrium mixture contains mostly reactants.
  b. A large K_c indicates that the equilibrium mixture contains mostly products.

9.61 a. increase **b.** increase **c.** decrease

9.63 a. The reaction is not at equilibrium.
  b. The reaction will proceed in the forward direction.

9.65 a. $K_c = \dfrac{[PCl_3][Cl_2]}{[PCl_5]}$
  b. At equilibrium, the concentrations are $[PCl_3] = 0.16$ M, $[Cl_2] = 0.16$ M, and $[PCl_5] = 0.44$ M.
  c. $K_c = 0.058$
  d. $[PCl_5]$ will increase.

9.67 a. $K_c = 0.015$
  b. If more CO_2 is added, the equilibrium will shift in the direction of the products.
  c. If the container volume is decreased, the equilibrium will shift in the direction of the reactants.

9.69 a. decrease **b.** increase **c.** increase
  d. decrease **e.** no change **f.** decrease
  g. decrease

10 Acids and Bases

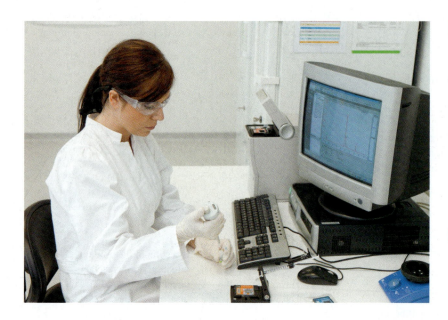

Mastering**CHEMISTRY**™

Visit **www.masteringchemistry.com** for self-study materials and instructor-assigned homework.

A 30-year-old man has been brought to the emergency room after a severe car crash. The emergency room nurses are tending to the patient, who is unresponsive. A blood sample is taken, which is sent to Brianna, a clinical laboratory technician, who begins the process of analyzing the blood's pH, the partial pressure of O_2 and CO_2 gas, and the concentrations of glucose and electrolytes.

Within minutes, Brianna determines that the patient's blood pH is 7.30 and the partial pressure of CO_2 gas is above the desired level. Blood pH is typically in the range of 7.35–7.45, and a value less than 7.35 indicates a state of acidosis. Respiratory acidosis occurs due to an increase in the partial pressure of CO_2 gas in the bloodstream which prevents the biochemical buffers in blood from making a change in the pH. Brianna recognizes these signs and immediately contacts the emergency room to inform them that the patient's airway must be blocked. In the emergency room, they provide the patient with an IV containing bicarbonate to increase the blood pH and begin the process of unblocking the patient's airway. Shortly afterward, the patient's airway is cleared, and his blood pH and partial pressure of CO_2 gas return to normal.

Career: Clinical Laboratory Technician

Clinical laboratory technicians, also known as medical laboratory technicians, perform a wide variety of tests on body fluids and cells that help in the diagnosis and treatment of patients. These tests range from determining blood concentrations, such as glucose and cholesterol, to determining drug levels in the blood for transplant patients or a patient undergoing treatment. Clinical laboratory technicians also prepare specimens in the detection of cancerous tumors, and type blood samples for transfusions using microscopes, cell counters, and computerized instruments. Clinical laboratory technicians must also interpret and analyze the results, which are then passed on to the physician.

Lemons, grapefruit, and vinegar taste sour because they contain acids. We have acid in our stomach that helps us digest food. We produce lactic acid in our muscles when we exercise. Acid from bacteria turns milk sour to make cottage cheese or yogurt. Bases are solutions that neutralize acids. Sometimes we take antacids such as milk of magnesia to offset the effects of too much stomach acid.

The pH of a solution describes its acidity. The lungs and the kidneys are the primary organs that regulate the pH of body fluids, including blood and urine. Major changes in the pH of the body fluids can severely affect biological activities within the cells. Buffers are present to prevent large fluctuations in pH.

In the environment, the pH of rain, water, and soil can have significant effects. When rain becomes too acidic, it can dissolve marble statues and accelerate the corrosion of metals. In lakes and ponds, the acidity of water can affect the ability of fish to survive. The acidity of the soil around plants affects their growth. If the soil pH is too acidic or too basic, the roots of the plant cannot take up some nutrients. Most plants thrive in soil with a nearly neutral pH, although certain plants such as orchids, camellias, and blueberries require a more acidic soil.

Citrus fruits are sour because of the presence of acids.

10.1 Acids and Bases

The term *acid* comes from the Latin word *acidus*, which means "sour." We are familiar with the sour tastes of vinegar, lemons, and other common acidic foods.

In 1887, the Swedish chemist Svante Arrhenius was the first to describe **acids** as substances that produce hydrogen ions (H^+) when they dissolve in water. For example, hydrogen chloride ionizes in water to give hydrogen ions, H^+, and chloride ions, Cl^-. The hydrogen ions give acids a sour taste, change blue litmus indicator to red, and corrode some metals.

LEARNING GOAL

Describe and name Arrhenius and Brønsted–Lowry acids and bases; identify conjugate acid–base pairs.

$$HCl(g) \xrightarrow{\text{H}_2\text{O}} H^+(aq) + Cl^-(aq)$$

Polar covalent   Ionization   Hydrogen
compound   ion

Naming Acids

Acids dissolve in water to produce hydrogen ions, along with a negative ion that may be a simple nonmetal anion or a polyatomic ion.

When an acid dissolves in water to produce a hydrogen ion and a simple nonmetal anion, the prefix *hydro* is used before the name of the nonmetal, and its *ide* ending is changed to *ic acid*. For example, hydrogen chloride (HCl) dissolves in water to form HCl(*aq*), which is named hydrochloric acid. When an acid contains an oxygen-containing polyatomic ion, the name of the acid comes from the name of the polyatomic ion. The *ate* in the name is replaced with *ic acid*. If the acid contains a polyatomic ion with an *ite* ending, its name ends with *ous acid*. The names of some common acids and their anions are listed in Table 10.1.

TABLE 10.1 Naming Common Acids

Acid	Name of Acid	Anion	Name of Anion
HCl	Hydrochloric acid	Cl^-	Chloride
HBr	Hydrobromic acid	Br^-	Bromide
HNO_3	Nitric acid	NO_3^-	Nitrate
HNO_2	Nitrous acid	NO_2^-	Nitrite
H_2SO_4	Sulfuric acid	SO_4^{2-}	Sulfate
H_2SO_3	Sulfurous acid	SO_3^{2-}	Sulfite
H_2CO_3	Carbonic acid	CO_3^{2-}	Carbonate
H_3PO_4	Phosphoric acid	PO_4^{3-}	Phosphate
$HClO_4$	Perchloric acid	ClO_4^-	Perchlorate
$HClO_3$	Chloric acid	ClO_3^-	Chlorate
$HClO_2$	Chlorous acid	ClO_2^-	Chlorite
HClO	Hypochlorous acid	ClO^-	Hypochlorite
$HC_2H_3O_2$	Acetic acid	$C_2H_3O_2^-$	Acetate

Sulfuric acid contains two H atoms that can dissociate in aqueous solution.

CONCEPT CHECK 10.1   Naming Acids

a. If H_2SO_4 is named sulfuric acid, what is the name of H_2SO_3? Why?
b. In part **a**, why is the prefix *hydro* not used at the beginning of either name?

ANSWER

a. H_2SO_3 is named sulfurous acid. The acid of the polyatomic anion that ends in *ite* replaces the *ite* ending with *ous acid*.
b. The prefix *hydro* is used only when the anion is a simple nonmetal anion, and not with an acid that includes a polyatomic anion.

Bases

You may be familiar with some household bases such as antacids, window cleaner, drain openers, and oven cleaners. According to the Arrhenius theory, **bases** are ionic compounds that dissociate into cations and hydroxide ions (OH^-) when they dissolve in water. They are another example of strong electrolytes, which we discussed in Section 8.2. For example, sodium hydroxide is an Arrhenius base that ionizes in water to give sodium ions, Na^+, and hydroxide ions, OH^-.

Most Arrhenius bases are formed from Groups 1A (1) and 2A (2) metals, such as NaOH, KOH, LiOH, and $Ca(OH)_2$. The hydroxide ions (OH^-) give Arrhenius bases common characteristics such as a bitter taste and a slippery feel. A base turns litmus indicator blue and phenolphthalein indicator pink.

NaOH(*s*)

— OH^-
 Na^+

— Water

$$NaOH(s) \xrightarrow{H_2O} Na^+(aq) + OH^-(aq)$$

Ionic   Ionization   Hydroxide
compound   ion

An Arrhenius base produces a cation and an OH^- anion in an aqueous solution.

MC

TUTORIAL
Acid and Base Formulas

TUTORIAL
Naming Acids and Bases

Naming Bases

Typical Arrhenius bases are named as *hydroxides*.

Base	Name
NaOH	Sodium **hydroxide**
KOH	Potassium **hydroxide**
$Ca(OH)_2$	Calcium **hydroxide**
$Al(OH)_3$	Aluminum **hydroxide**

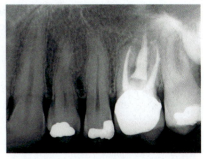

Calcium hydroxide, $Ca(OH)_2$, also called slaked lime, is used in the food industry to produce beverages, in tanning to neutralize acids, and in dentistry as a filler for root canals.

CONCEPT CHECK 10.2   Ionization of an Arrhenius Base

When dried corn kernels are soaked in limewater (calcium hydroxide solution), the product is hominy, corn that has been hulled with the bran and germ removed and is used to make grits. Write an equation for the ionization of calcium hydroxide in water.

ANSWER

When calcium hydroxide, $Ca(OH)_2$, dissolves in water, the solution contains calcium ions (Ca^{2+}) and twice as many hydroxide ions (OH^-). The equation is written as:

$$Ca(OH)_2(s) \xrightarrow{H_2O} Ca^{2+}(aq) + 2OH^-(aq)$$

Hominy for grits is prepared by soaking corn kernels in a calcium hydroxide solution.

SAMPLE PROBLEM 10.1   Names and Formulas of Acids and Bases

a. Identify each of the following as an acid or a base and give its name:
  1. H_3PO_4, ingredient in soft drinks
  2. NaOH, ingredient in oven cleaner
b. Write the formula for each of the following:
  1. magnesium hydroxide, ingredient in antacids
  2. hydrobromic acid, used industrially to prepare bromide compounds

SOLUTION

a. 1. acid; phosphoric acid   **2.** base; sodium hydroxide
b. 1. $Mg(OH)_2$ **2.** HBr

STUDY CHECK 10.1

a. Identify as an acid or base and give the name for $HClO_3$.
b. Write the formula for iron(III) hydroxide.

A soft drink contains H_3PO_4 and H_2CO_3.

Brønsted–Lowry Acids and Bases

In 1923, J. N. Brønsted in Denmark and T. M. Lowry in Great Britain expanded the definition of acids and bases to include bases that do not contain OH^- ions. A **Brønsted–Lowry acid** can donate a hydrogen ion, H^+, to another substance, and a **Brønsted–Lowry base** can accept a hydrogen ion.

> A Brønsted–Lowry acid is a substance that donates H^+.
>
> A Brønsted–Lowry base is a substance that accepts H^+.

MC

TUTORIAL
Definitions of Acids and Bases

A free hydrogen ion, H^+, does not actually exist in water. Its attraction to polar water molecules is so strong that the H^+ bonds to the water molecule and forms a **hydronium ion, H_3O^+.**

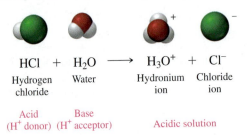

Water   Hydrogen ion   Hydronium ion

We can write the formation of a hydrochloric acid solution as a transfer of H^+ from hydrogen chloride to water. By accepting an H^+ in the reaction, water is acting as a base according to the Brønsted–Lowry concept.

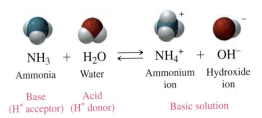

$$HCl \ + \ H_2O \ \longrightarrow \ H_3O^+ \ + \ Cl^-$$

Hydrogen chloride   Water   Hydronium ion   Chloride ion

Acid (H^+ donor)   Base (H^+ acceptor)   Acidic solution

In another reaction, ammonia (NH_3) reacts with water. Because the nitrogen atom of NH_3 has a stronger attraction for H^+, water acts as an acid by donating H^+.

$$NH_3 \ + \ H_2O \ \rightleftharpoons \ NH_4^+ \ + \ OH^-$$

Ammonia   Water   Ammonium ion   Hydroxide ion

Base (H^+ acceptor)   Acid (H^+ donor)   Basic solution

TUTORIAL
Properties of Acids and Bases

Table 10.2 compares some characteristics of acids and bases.

TABLE 10.2 Some Characteristics of Acids and Bases

Characteristic	Acids	Bases
Arrhenius	Produce H^+	Produce OH^-
Brønsted–Lowry	Donate H^+	Accept H^+
Electrolytes	Yes	Yes
Taste	Sour	Bitter, chalky
Feel	May sting	Slippery
Turns Litmus	Red	Blue
Turns Phenolphthalein	Colorless	Pink
Neutralization	Neutralize bases	Neutralize acids

SAMPLE PROBLEM 10.2 Acids and Bases

In each of the following equations, identify the reactant that is a Brønsted–Lowry acid and the reactant that is a Brønsted–Lowry base:

a. $HBr(aq) + H_2O(l) \longrightarrow H_3O^+(aq) + Br^-(aq)$
b. $H_2O(l) + HS^-(aq) \rightleftharpoons H_2S(aq) + OH^-(aq)$

SOLUTION
a. HBr, Brønsted–Lowry acid; H_2O, Brønsted–Lowry base
b. H_2O, Brønsted–Lowry acid; HS^-, Brønsted–Lowry base

STUDY CHECK 10.2

When HNO_3 reacts with water, water acts as a Brønsted–Lowry base. Write the equation for the reaction.

TUTORIAL
Identifying Conjugate Acid–Base Pairs

Conjugate Acid–Base Pairs

According to the Brønsted–Lowry theory, a **conjugate acid–base pair** consists of molecules or ions related by the loss of one H^+ by an acid, and the gain of one H^+ by a base. Every acid–base reaction contains two conjugate acid–base pairs because an H^+ is transferred in both the forward and reverse reactions. When the acid such as HF loses one H^+, its conjugate base, F^-, is formed. When the base H_2O gains an H^+, its conjugate acid, H_3O^+, is formed.

Because the overall reaction of HF is reversible, the conjugate acid H_3O^+ can donate H^+ to the conjugate base F^- and re-form the acid HF and the base H_2O. Using the relationship of loss and gain of one H^+, we can now identify the conjugate acid–base pairs as HF/F^- along with H_3O^+/H_2O.

Conjugate acid–base pair

HF   Donates H^+ F^-

Conjugate acid–base pair

H_2O Accepts H^+ H_3O^+

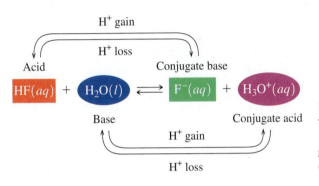

HF, an acid, loses one H^+ to form its conjugate base F^-. Water acts as a base by gaining one H^+ to form its conjugate acid H_3O^+.

In another reaction, the base ammonia, NH_3, accepts H^+ from H_2O to form its conjugate acid NH_4^+ and conjugate base OH^-. Each of these conjugate acid–base pairs, NH_4^+ and NH_3 as well as H_2O and OH^-, are related by the loss and gain of one H^+.

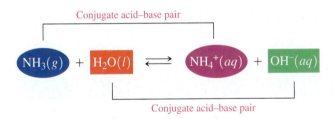

Ammonia, NH_3, acts as a base when it gains one H^+ to form its conjugate acid NH_4^+. Water acts as an acid by losing one H^+ to form its conjugate base OH^-.

In these two examples, we see that water can act as an acid when it donates H^+ or a base when it accepts H^+. Substances that can act as both acids and bases are **amphoteric** or *amphiprotic*. For water, the most common amphoteric substance, the acidic or basic behavior depends on the other reactant. Water donates H^+ when it reacts with a stronger base and accepts H^+ when it reacts with a stronger acid. Another example of an amphoteric substance is bicarbonate, HCO_3^-. With a base, HCO_3^- acts as an acid and donates one H^+ to give CO_3^{2-}. However, when HCO_3^- reacts with an acid, it acts as a base and accepts one H^+ to form H_2CO_3.

Amphoteric substances can act as both acids and bases.

CONCEPT CHECK 10.3   Conjugate Acid–Base Pairs

a. Write the formula for the conjugate base of $HClO_3$.
b. Write the conjugate acid of HS^-.

ANSWER

a. A conjugate base forms when a Brønsted–Lowry acid loses one H^+. When $HClO_3$ loses one H^+, it forms its conjugate base ClO_3^-.
b. A conjugate acid forms when a Brønsted–Lowry base gains one H^+. When HS^- gains one H^+, it forms its conjugate acid H_2S.

SAMPLE PROBLEM 10.3   Identifying Conjugate Acid–Base Pairs

Identify the conjugate acid–base pairs in the following equation:

$$HBr(aq) + NH_3(aq) \longrightarrow Br^-(aq) + NH_4^+(aq)$$

SOLUTION

Analyze the Problem

	Reactant	Product	H^+ Loss/Gain
Given	HBr	Br^-	1 H^+ lost
	NH_3	NH_4^+	1 H^+ gained
Need			
Conjugate Acid–Base Pair			
Conjugate Acid–Base Pair			

Acting as a Brønsted–Lowry acid, HBr loses one H^+ to form Br^-, which is its conjugate base. The NH_3, acting as a Brønsted–Lowry base, gains one H^+ to form its conjugate acid, NH_4^+. The conjugate acid–base pairs are HBr/Br^- and NH_4^+/NH_3.

STUDY CHECK 10.3

In the following reaction, identify the conjugate acid–base pairs:

$$HNO_2(aq) + SO_4^{2-}(aq) \rightleftharpoons NO_2^-(aq) + HSO_4^-(aq)$$

QUESTIONS AND PROBLEMS

10.1 Acids and Bases

LEARNING GOAL: *Describe and name Arrhenius and Brønsted–Lowry acids and bases; identify conjugate acid–base pairs.*

10.1 Indicate each of the following statements as a characteristic of an acid, base, or both:
   a. has a sour taste
   b. neutralizes bases
   c. produces H^+ ions in water
   d. is named potassium hydroxide
   e. is an electrolyte

10.2 Indicate each of the following statements as a characteristic of an acid, base, or both:
   a. neutralizes acids
   b. produces OH^- ions in water
   c. has a slippery feel
   d. conducts an electrical current
   e. turns litmus red

10.3 Name each of the following acids and bases:
   a. HCl   **b.** $Ca(OH)_2$ **c.** H_2CO_3
   d. HNO_3 **e.** H_2SO_3 **f.** $Fe(OH)_2$

10.4 Name each of the following acids and bases:
   a. $Al(OH)_3$ **b.** HBr   **c.** H_2SO_4
   d. KOH   **e.** HNO_2 **f.** $HBrO_2$

10.5 Write formulas for each of the following acids and bases:
   a. magnesium hydroxide   **b.** hydrofluoric acid
   c. phosphorus acid   **d.** lithium hydroxide
   e. copper(II) hydroxide

10.6 Write formulas for each of the following acids and bases:
   a. barium hydroxide   **b.** hydroiodic acid
   c. nitric acid   **d.** strontium hydroxide
   e. sodium hydroxide

10.7 Identify the reactant that is a Brønsted–Lowry acid and the reactant that is a Brønsted–Lowry base in each of the following:
   a. $HI(aq) + H_2O(l) \longrightarrow H_3O^+(aq) + I^-(aq)$
   b. $F^-(aq) + H_2O(l) \rightleftharpoons HF(aq) + OH^-(aq)$

10.8 Identify the reactant that is a Brønsted–Lowry acid and the reactant that is a Brønsted–Lowry base in each of the following:
a. $CO_3^{2-}(aq) + H_2O(l) \rightleftharpoons HCO_3^-(aq) + OH^-(aq)$
b. $H_2SO_4(aq) + H_2O(l) \longrightarrow H_3O^+(aq) + HSO_4^-(aq)$

10.9 Write the formula and name of the conjugate base for each of the following:
a. HF b. H_2O c. H_2CO_3 d. HSO_4^-

10.10 Write the formula and name of the conjugate base for each of the following:
a. HCO_3^- b. H_3O^+ c. HPO_4^{2-} d. HNO_2

10.11 Write the formula and name of the conjugate acid for each of the following:
a. CO_3^{2-} b. H_2O c. $H_2PO_4^-$ d. SO_3^{2-}

10.12 Write the formula and name of the conjugate acid for each of the following:
a. SO_4^{2-} b. BrO_2^- c. OH^- d. ClO^-

10.13 Identify the Brønsted–Lowry acid–base pairs in each of the following equations:
a. $H_2CO_3(aq) + H_2O(l) \rightleftharpoons H_3O^+(aq) + HCO_3^-(aq)$
b. $NH_4^+(aq) + H_2O(l) \rightleftharpoons H_3O^+(aq) + NH_3(aq)$
c. $HCN(aq) + NO_2^-(aq) \rightleftharpoons CN^-(aq) + HNO_2(aq)$

10.14 Identify the Brønsted–Lowry acid–base pairs in each of the following equations:
a. $H_3PO_4(aq) + H_2O(l) \rightleftharpoons H_3O^+(aq) + H_2PO_4^-(aq)$
b. $CO_3^{2-}(aq) + H_2O(l) \rightleftharpoons OH^-(aq) + HCO_3^-(aq)$
c. $H_3PO_4(aq) + NH_3(aq) \rightleftharpoons NH_4^+(aq) + H_2PO_4^-(aq)$

10.2 Strengths of Acids and Bases

LEARNING GOAL

Write equations for the dissociation of strong and weak acids; write the equilibrium expression for a weak acid.

In the process called **dissociation**, an acid or base separates into ions in water. The *strength* of acids is determined by the moles of H_3O^+ that are produced for each mole of acid that dissolves. The *strength* of bases is determined by the moles of OH^- that are produced for each mole of base that dissolves. Strong acids and strong bases dissociate completely in water, whereas weak acids and weak bases dissociate only slightly, leaving most of the initial acid or base undissociated.

Strong and Weak Acids

Strong acids are examples of strong electrolytes, which we discussed in Section 8.2. **Strong acids** donate hydrogen ions so easily that their dissociation in water is nearly complete. For example, when HCl, a strong acid, dissociates in water, H^+ is transferred to H_2O; the resulting solution contains only the ions H_3O^+ and Cl^-. Because strong acids completely dissociate, we consider the reaction of HCl in H_2O to go 100% to products. Thus, we use a single arrow when we write the equation for a strong acid.

$$HCl(g) + H_2O(l) \longrightarrow H_3O^+(aq) + Cl^-(aq)$$

There are only six common strong acids. All other acids are weak. Table 10.3 lists the strong acids along with some common weak acids, from strongest to weakest acid.

Weak acids are weak electrolytes, which we discussed in Section 8.2. **Weak acids** dissociate slightly in water, which means that only a small percentage of H^+ is transferred from a weak acid to H_2O, forming only a small amount of H_3O^+. In general, a weak acid sticks together rather than splitting apart. A weak acid has a strong conjugate base, which is why the reverse reaction is more prevalent. Even at high concentrations, weak acids produce low concentrations of H_3O^+ ions (see Figure 10.1).

Many of the products we use at home contain weak acids. For example, vinegar is a 5% solution of acetic acid, $HC_2H_3O_2$, a weak acid. In water, a few $HC_2H_3O_2$ molecules donate H^+ to H_2O to form H_3O^+ ions and acetate ions $C_2H_3O_2^-$. The formation of hydronium ions from vinegar is the reason we notice the sour taste of vinegar. In a weak acid, a reverse reaction also takes place, which converts the H_3O^+ ions and acetate ions $C_2H_3O_2^-$ back to reactants. This means that a weak acid such as acetic acid reaches equilibrium between the mostly undissociated acid and its ions. We write the equation for a weak acid in an aqueous solution with a double arrow to indicate that the forward and reverse reactions are at equilibrium.

$$HC_2H_3O_2(aq) + H_2O(l) \rightleftharpoons H_3O^+(aq) + C_2H_3O_2^-(aq)$$

Acetic acid   Acetate ion

Acids produce hydrogen ions in aqueous solutions.

Diprotic Acids

Some weak acids, such as carbonic acid, are *diprotic acids* that have two H^+, which dissociate one at a time. In carbonated soft drinks, for example, CO_2 dissolves in water to form carbonic acid, H_2CO_3. The weak acid H_2CO_3 reaches equilibrium between the undissociated H_2CO_3

TABLE 10.3 Some Conjugate Acid–Base Pairs

Acid		Conjugate Base	
Strong Acids			
Hydroiodic acid	HI	I^-	Iodide ion
Hydrobromic acid	HBr	Br^-	Bromide ion
Perchloric acid	$HClO_4$	ClO_4^-	Perchlorate ion
Hydrochloric acid	HCl	Cl^-	Chloride ion
Sulfuric acid	H_2SO_4	HSO_4^-	Hydrogen sulfate ion
Nitric acid	HNO_3	NO_3^-	Nitrate ion
Weak Acids			
Hydronium ion	H_3O^+	H_2O	Water
Hydrogen sulfate ion	HSO_4^-	SO_4^{2-}	Sulfate ion
Phosphoric acid	H_3PO_4	$H_2PO_4^-$	Dihydrogen phosphate ion
Hydrofluoric acid	HF	F^-	Fluoride ion
Nitrous acid	HNO_2	NO_2^-	Nitrite ion
Acetic acid	$HC_2H_3O_2$	$C_2H_3O_2^-$	Acetate ion
Carbonic acid	H_2CO_3	HCO_3^-	Bicarbonate ion
Hydrosulfuric acid	H_2S	HS^-	Hydrogen sulfide ion
Dihydrogen phosphate ion	$H_2PO_4^-$	HPO_4^{2-}	Hydrogen phosphate ion
Ammonium ion	NH_4^+	NH_3	Ammonia
Bicarbonate ion	HCO_3^-	CO_3^{2-}	Carbonate ion
Hydrogen sulfide ion	HS^-	S^{2-}	Sulfide ion
Water	H_2O	OH^-	Hydroxide ion

Increasing Acid Strength

Increasing Base Strength

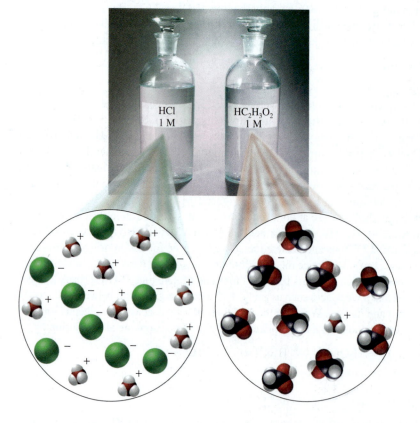

FIGURE 10.1 A strong acid such as HCl is completely dissociated (≈ 100%) in solution, whereas a solution of a weak acid such as $HC_2H_3O_2$ is only slightly ionized to form a weak acid solution that contains mostly molecules and a few ions.

Q What is the difference between a strong acid and a weak acid?

molecules and the ions H_3O^+ and HCO_3^-. Because HCO_3^- is also a weak acid, a second dissociation can take place to produce another hydronium ion and the carbonate ion, CO_3^{2-}.

$$H_2CO_3(aq) + H_2O(l) \rightleftharpoons H_3O^+(aq) + HCO_3^-(aq)$$
Carbonic acid   Bicarbonate ion (hydrogen carbonate)

$$HCO_3^-(aq) + H_2O(l) \rightleftharpoons H_3O^+(aq) + CO_3^{2-}(aq)$$
Bicarbonate ion   Carbonate ion

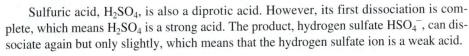

H_2CO_3 HCO_3^- CO_3^{2-}

Carbonic acid, a weak acid, loses one H^+ to form hydrogen carbonate ion, which loses a second H^+ to form carbonate ion.

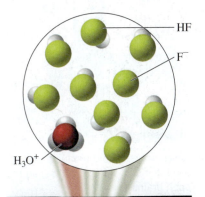

Sulfuric acid, H_2SO_4, is also a diprotic acid. However, its first dissociation is complete, which means H_2SO_4 is a strong acid. The product, hydrogen sulfate HSO_4^-, can dissociate again but only slightly, which means that the hydrogen sulfate ion is a weak acid.

$$H_2SO_4(aq) + H_2O(l) \longrightarrow H_3O^+(aq) + HSO_4^-(aq)$$
Sulfuric acid   Hydrogen sulfate ion

$$HSO_4^-(aq) + H_2O(l) \rightleftharpoons H_3O^+(aq) + SO_4^{2-}(aq)$$
Hydrogen sulfate ion   Sulfate ion

In summary, a strong acid such as HI in water dissociates completely to form an aqueous solution of the ions H_3O^+ and I^-. A weak acid such as HF dissociates only slightly in water to form an aqueous solution that consists mostly of undissociated HF molecules and only a few H_3O^+ and F^- ions (see Figure 10.2).

Strong acid: $HI(aq) + H_2O(l) \longrightarrow H_3O^+(aq) + I^-(aq)$ (completely dissociated)

Weak acid: $HF(aq) + H_2O(l) \rightleftharpoons H_3O^+(aq) + F^-(aq)$ (slightly dissociated)

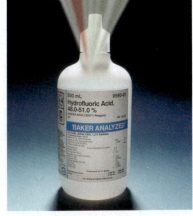

Hydrofluoric acid is the only halogen acid that is a weak acid.

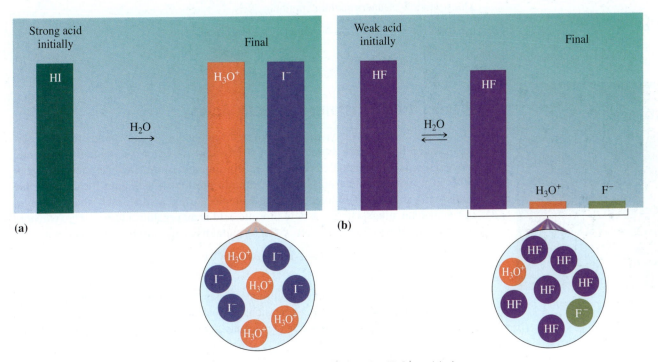

FIGURE 10.2 **(a)** A strong acid such as HI dissociates completely to give H_3O^+ and I^- ions. **(b)** A weak acid such as HF dissociates only slightly to form a solution containing a few H_3O^+ and F^- ions, and mostly undissociated HF molecules.

Q How does the height of the H_3O^+ in the bar diagram change for a strong acid as compared to a weak acid?

Bases in household products are used to clean, remove grease, and to open drains.

Bases in Household Products

Weak Bases

Window cleaner, ammonia, NH_3
Bleach, NaOCl
Laundry detergent, Na_2CO_3, Na_3PO_4
Toothpaste and baking soda, $NaHCO_3$
Baking powder, scouring powder, Na_2CO_3
Lime for lawns and agriculture, $CaCO_3$
Laxatives, antacids, $Mg(OH)_2$, $Al(OH)_3$

Strong Bases

Drain cleaner, oven cleaner, NaOH

TUTORIAL
Using Dissociation Constants

A red ant sting contains formic acid that irritates the skin.

Strong and Weak Bases

As strong electrolytes, **strong bases** dissociate completely in water. Because these strong bases are ionic compounds, they dissociate in water to give an aqueous solution of metal ions and hydroxide ions. The Group 1A (1) hydroxides are very soluble in water, which can give high concentrations of OH^- ions. A few bases are not very soluble in water, but what does dissolve dissociates completely as ions. For example, when KOH, a strong base, dissociates in water, the solution consists only of the ions K^+ and OH^-.

$$KOH(s) \xrightarrow{H_2O} K^+(aq) + OH^-(aq)$$

Strong Bases

Lithium hydroxide LiOH
Sodium hydroxide NaOH
Potassium hydroxide KOH
Strontium hydroxide $Sr(OH)_2$*
Calcium hydroxide $Ca(OH)_2$*
Barium hydroxide $Ba(OH)_2$*

*Low solubility, but they dissociate completely

Sodium hydroxide, NaOH (also known as lye), is used in household products to remove grease in ovens and to clean drains. Because high concentrations of hydroxide ions cause severe damage to the skin and eyes, directions must be followed carefully when such products are used in the home, and use in the chemistry laboratory should be carefully supervised. If you spill an acid or a base on your skin or get some in your eyes, be sure to flood the area immediately with water for at least 10 minutes and seek medical attention.

Weak bases are weak electrolytes because they produce very few ions in solution. In an aqueous solution of NH_3, only a few molecules react with H_2O to form NH_4^+ and OH^-. Many window cleaners contain ammonia, NH_3.

$$NH_3(g) + H_2O(l) \rightleftharpoons NH_4^+(aq) + OH^-(aq)$$
Ammonia   Ammonium hydroxide

Dissociation Constants for Weak Acids

As we have seen, acids have different strengths depending on how much they dissociate in water. Because the dissociation of strong acids in water is essentially complete, the reaction is not considered to be an equilibrium situation. However, because weak acids in water dissociate only slightly, the ion products reach equilibrium with the undissociated weak acid molecules. For example, formic acid $HCHO_2$, the acid found in bee and ant stings, is a weak acid. Formic acid is an organic acid or *carboxylic acid* in which the H written on the left of the formula dissociates to form formate ion.

$$HCHO_2(aq) + H_2O(l) \rightleftharpoons H_3O^+(aq) + CHO_2^-(aq)$$
Formic acid   Formate ion

In Section 9.3, we wrote the equilibrium constant expression for gases at equilibrium. We can also write an equilibrium expression for weak acids that gives the ratio of the concentrations of products to the weak acid reactants. As with other equilibrium constants, the molar concentration of the products is divided by the molar concentration of the reactants. We can write the equilibrium for formic acid as:

$$HCHO_2(aq) + H_2O(l) \rightleftharpoons H_3O^+(aq) + CHO_2^-(aq)$$

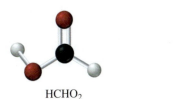

HCHO$_2$

CHO$_2^-$

Formic acid, a weak acid, loses one H$^+$ to form formate ion.

Because water is a pure liquid, its concentration, which is constant, is omitted from the equilibrium constant, called the **acid dissociation constant, K_a** (or acid ionization constant). The value of the K_a for formic acid at 25 °C is determined by experiment to be 1.8×10^{-4}. Thus, for the weak acid $HCHO_2$, the K_a is written

$$K_a = \frac{[H_3O^+][CHO_2^-]}{[HCHO_2]} = 1.8 \times 10^{-4} \quad \text{Acid dissociation constant}$$

The K_a measured for formic acid is small, which confirms that the equilibrium mixture of formic acid in water contains mostly reactants and only small amounts of the products. (Recall that the concentration units are omitted in the values given for equilibrium constants.) The smaller the K_a value, the weaker the acid. On the other hand, strong acids, which are essentially 100% dissociated, have very large K_a values, but these values are not usually given. Table 10.4 gives K_a values for selected weak acids.

TABLE 10.4 K_a **Values for Selected Weak Acids**

Acid	Formula	K_a
Phosphoric acid	H_3PO_4	7.5×10^{-3}
Hydrofluoric acid	HF	7.2×10^{-4}
Nitrous acid	HNO_2	4.5×10^{-4}
Formic acid	$HCHO_2$	1.8×10^{-4}
Acetic acid	$HC_2H_3O_2$	1.8×10^{-5}
Carbonic acid	H_2CO_3	4.3×10^{-7}
Hydrosulfuric acid	H_2S	9.1×10^{-8}
Dihydrogen phosphate	$H_2PO_4^-$	6.2×10^{-8}
Bicarbonate	HCO_3^-	5.6×10^{-11}
Hydrogen phosphate	HPO_4^{2-}	2.2×10^{-13}

We have described strong and weak acids in several ways. Table 10.5 summarizes the characteristics of acids in terms of strength and equilibrium position.

TABLE 10.5 **Characteristics of Acids**

Characteristic	Strong Acids	Weak Acids
Equilibrium Position	Toward products (ionized)	Toward reactants (nonionized)
K_a	Large	Small
$[H_3O^+]$ and $[A^-]$	100% of initial $[HA]$	Small percent of initial $[HA]$
Conjugate Bases	Weak	Strong

CONCEPT CHECK 10.4 Acid Dissociation Constants

Nitrous acid, HNO_2, has a K_a of 4.5×10^{-4} and hypochlorous acid, $HOCl$, has a K_a of 3.5×10^{-8}. If each acid has a 0.10 M concentration, which solution has the higher concentration of H_3O^+?

ANSWER

Nitrous acid has a larger K_a value than does hypochlorous acid. When nitrous acid dissolves in water, there is more dissociation of HNO_2, which gives a higher concentration of H_3O^+ in solution.

SAMPLE PROBLEM 10.4 Writing Acid Dissociation Constants

Write the expression for the acid dissociation constant for nitrous acid.

SOLUTION

The equation for the dissociation of nitrous acid is written:

$$HNO_2(aq) + H_2O(l) \rightleftharpoons H_3O^+(aq) + NO_2^-(aq)$$

The acid dissociation constant is written as the concentrations of the products divided by the concentration of the undissociated weak acid.

$$K_a = \frac{[H_3O^+][NO_2^-]}{[HNO_2]}$$

STUDY CHECK 10.4

Using Table 10.4, determine whether nitrous acid or carbonic acid is the stronger acid. Explain your answer.

QUESTIONS AND PROBLEMS

10.2 Strengths of Acids and Bases

LEARNING GOAL: *Write equations for the dissociation of strong and weak acids; write the equilibrium expression for a weak acid.*

10.15 What is meant by the phrase, "A strong acid has a weak conjugate base"?

10.16 What is meant by the phrase, "A weak acid has a strong conjugate base"?

10.17 Answer *true* or *false* for each of the following:
A strong acid
  a. is completely ionized in aqueous solution
  b. has a small value of K_a
  c. has a strong conjugate base
  d. has a weak conjugate base
  e. is slightly ionized in aqueous solution

10.18 Answer *true* or *false* for each of the following:
A weak acid
  a. is completely ionized in aqueous solution
  b. has a small value of K_a
  c. has a strong conjugate base
  d. has a weak conjugate base
  e. is slightly ionized in aqueous solution

10.19 Using Table 10.3, identify the stronger acid in each of the following pairs:
  a. HBr or HNO_2
  b. H_3PO_4 or HSO_4^-
  c. NH_4^+ or H_2CO_3

10.20 Using Table 10.3, identify the stronger acid in each of the following pairs:
  a. NH_4^+ or H_3O^+ **b.** HNO_2 or HCl **c.** H_2O or H_2CO_3

10.21 Using Table 10.3, identify the weaker acid in each of the following pairs:
  a. HCl or HSO_4^- **b.** HNO_2 or HF **c.** HCO_3^- or NH_4^+

10.22 Using Table 10.3, identify the weaker acid in each of the following pairs:
  a. HNO_3 or HCO_3^- **b.** HSO_4^- or H_2O **c.** H_2SO_4 or H_2CO_3

10.23 Using Table 10.3, predict whether each of the following reactions contains mostly reactants or products at equilibrium:
  a. $H_2CO_3(aq) + H_2O(l) \rightleftharpoons H_3O^+(aq) + HCO_3^-(aq)$
  b. $NH_4^+(aq) + H_2O(l) \rightleftharpoons H_3O^+(aq) + NH_3(aq)$
  c. $HNO_2(aq) + NH_3(aq) \rightleftharpoons NO_2^-(aq) + NH_4^+(aq)$

10.24 Using Table 10.3, predict whether each of the following reactions contains mostly reactants or products at equilibrium:
  a. $H_3PO_4(aq) + F^-(aq) \rightleftharpoons HF(aq) + H_2PO_4^-(aq)$
  b. $CO_3^{2-}(aq) + H_2O(l) \rightleftharpoons OH^-(aq) + HCO_3^-(aq)$
  c. $HS^-(aq) + H_2O(l) \rightleftharpoons H_3O^+(aq) + S^{2-}(aq)$

10.25 Consider the following acids and their dissociation constants:

$$H_2SO_3(aq) + H_2O(l) \rightleftharpoons H_3O^+(aq) + HSO_3^-(aq)$$
$$K_a = 1.2 \times 10^{-2}$$

$$HS^-(aq) + H_2O(l) \rightleftharpoons H_3O^+(aq) + S^{2-}(aq)$$
$$K_a = 1.3 \times 10^{-19}$$

  a. Which is the stronger acid, H_2SO_3 or HS^-?
  b. What is the conjugate base of H_2SO_3?
  c. Which acid has the weaker conjugate base?
  d. Which acid produces more ions?

10.26 Consider the following acids and their dissociation constants:

$$HPO_4^{2-}(aq) + H_2O(l) \rightleftharpoons H_3O^+(aq) + PO_4^{3-}(aq)$$
$$K_a = 2.2 \times 10^{-13}$$

$$HCHO_2(aq) + H_2O(l) \rightleftharpoons H_3O^+(aq) + CHO_2^-(aq)$$
$$K_a = 1.8 \times 10^{-4}$$

a. Which is the weaker acid, HPO_4^{2-} or $HCHO_2$?
b. What is the conjugate base of HPO_4^{2-}?
c. Which acid has the weaker conjugate base?
d. Which acid produces more ions?

10.27 Phosphoric acid reacts with water to form dihydrogen phosphate and hydronium ion. Write the equation for the dissociation of phosphoric acid and the expression for its acid dissociation constant (K_a).

10.28 Carbonic acid, a weak acid, reacts with water to form bicarbonate and hydronium ion. Write the equation for the dissociation of carbonic acid and the expression for its acid dissociation constant (K_a).

10.3 Ionization of Water

We have seen that in acid–base reactions, water is amphoteric, which means it can act either as an acid or as a base. In pure water, there is a forward reaction between two water molecules that transfers H^+ from one water molecule to the other. One molecule acts as an acid by losing H^+, and the water molecule that gains H^+ acts as a base. Every time H^+ is transferred between two water molecules, the products are one H_3O^+ and one OH^-, which react in the reverse direction to re-form two water molecules. Thus, equilibrium is reached between the conjugate acid–base pairs of water.

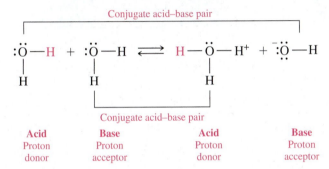

Writing the Ion Product Constant for Water, K_w

Using the equation for the reaction in water at equilibrium, we can write its equilibrium constant expression that shows the concentrations of the products divided by the concentrations of the reactants. Recall that square brackets around the symbols indicate their concentrations in moles per liter (M).

$$H_2O(l) + H_2O(l) \rightleftharpoons H_3O^+(aq) + OH^-(aq)$$

$$K_c = \frac{[H_3O^+][OH^-]}{[H_2O][H_2O]}$$

As we did for the acid dissociation constant expression, we omit the constant concentration of liquid water, which gives the **ion product constant for water, K_w**.

$$K_w = [H_3O^+][OH^-]$$

Experiments have determined that in pure water, the concentration of H_3O^+ at 25 °C is 1.0×10^{-7} M.

$$[H_3O^+] = 1.0 \times 10^{-7} \text{ M}$$

Because pure water contains equal number of OH^- ions and hydronium ions, the concentration of hydroxide ion must also be 1.0×10^{-7} M.

$$[H_3O^+] = [OH^-] = 1.0 \times 10^{-7} \text{ M} \quad \text{Pure water}$$

When we place the $[H_3O^+]$ and $[OH^-]$ into the K_w expression, we obtain the numerical value of K_w, which is 1.0×10^{-14} at 25 °C. As before, the concentration units are omitted in the K_w value.

$$K_w = [H_3O^+][OH^-]$$
$$= (1.0 \times 10^{-7} \text{ M})(1.0 \times 10^{-7} \text{ M}) = 1.0 \times 10^{-14}$$

Neutral, Acidic, and Basic Solutions

When the $[H_3O^+]$ and $[OH^-]$ in a solution are equal, the solution is **neutral**. However, most solutions are not neutral and have different concentrations of $[H_3O^+]$ and $[OH^-]$. If acid is added to water, there is an increase in $[H_3O^+]$ and a decrease in $[OH^-]$, which gives an acidic solution. If base is added, $[OH^-]$ increases and $[H_3O^+]$ decreases, which gives a basic solution (see Figure 10.3). However, for any aqueous solution, the product $[H_3O^+][OH^-]$ is always equal to K_w (1.0×10^{-14}) at 25 °C (see Table 10.6).

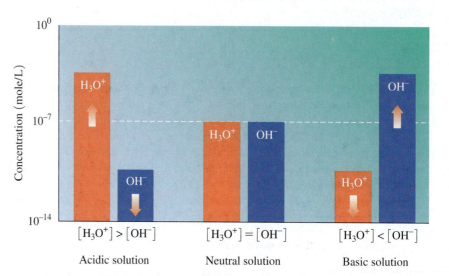

FIGURE 10.3 In a neutral solution, $[H_3O^+]$ and $[OH^-]$ are equal. In acidic solutions, the $[H_3O^+]$ is greater than the $[OH^-]$. In basic solutions, the $[OH^-]$ is greater than the $[H_3O^+]$.

Q Is a solution that has $[H_3O^+] = 1.0 \times 10^{-3}$ M acidic, basic, or neutral?

TABLE 10.6 Examples of $[H_3O^+]$ and $[OH^-]$ in Neutral, Acidic, and Basic Solutions

Type of Solution	$[H_3O^+]$	$[OH^-]$	K_w (25 °C)
Neutral	1.0×10^{-7} M	1.0×10^{-7} M	1.0×10^{-14}
Acidic	1.0×10^{-2} M	1.0×10^{-12} M	1.0×10^{-14}
Acidic	2.5×10^{-5} M	4.0×10^{-10} M	1.0×10^{-14}
Basic	1.0×10^{-8} M	1.0×10^{-6} M	1.0×10^{-14}
Basic	5.0×10^{-11} M	2.0×10^{-4} M	1.0×10^{-14}

Using the K_w to Calculate $[H_3O^+]$ and $[OH^-]$ in a Solution

If we know the $[OH^-]$ of a solution, we can use the K_w to calculate the $[H_3O^+]$. If we know the $[H_3O^+]$ of a solution, we can calculate the $[OH^-]$ from their relationship in the K_w, as shown in Sample Problem 10.5.

$$K_w = [H_3O^+][OH^-]$$

$$[OH^-] = \frac{K_w}{[H_3O^+]} \qquad [H_3O^+] = \frac{K_w}{[OH^-]}$$

SAMPLE PROBLEM 10.5 Calculating $[H_3O^+]$ and $[OH^-]$ in Solution

A vinegar solution has a $[H_3O^+] = 2.0 \times 10^{-3}$ M at 25 °C. What is the $[OH^-]$ of the vinegar solution? Is the solution acidic, basic, or neutral?

SOLUTION

Analyze the Problem

Solution Components	$[H_3O^+]$	$[OH^-]$	
Given	2.0×10^{-3} M		$K_w = 1.0 \times 10^{-14}$
Need		M (moles/L)	

Step 1   **Write the K_w for water.**

$$K_w = [H_3O^+][OH^-] = 1.0 \times 10^{-14}$$

Step 2   **Solve the K_w for the unknown $[H_3O^+]$ or $[OH^-]$.** Rearrange the ion product expression for $[OH^-]$ by dividing through by $[H_3O^+]$.

$$\frac{K_w}{[H_3O^+]} = \frac{[\cancel{H_3O^+}][OH^-]}{[\cancel{H_3O^+}]}$$

$$[OH^-] = \frac{1.0 \times 10^{-14}}{[H_3O^+]}$$

Step 3   **Substitute the known $[H_3O^+]$ or $[OH^-]$ into the equation and calculate.**

$$[OH^-] = \frac{1.0 \times 10^{-14}}{[2.0 \times 10^{-3}]} = 5.0 \times 10^{-12} \text{ M}$$

Because the $[H_3O^+]$ of 2.0×10^{-3} M is much larger than the $[OH^-]$ of 5.0×10^{-12} M, the solution is acidic.

STUDY CHECK 10.5

What is the $[H_3O^+]$ of an ammonia cleaning solution with $[OH^-] = 4.0 \times 10^{-4}$ M? Is the solution acidic, basic, or neutral?

Guide to Calculating $[H_3O^+]$ and $[OH^-]$ in Aqueous Solutions

1   Write the K_w for water.

2   Solve the K_w for the unknown $[H_3O^+]$ or $[OH^-]$.

3   Substitute the known $[H_3O^+]$ or $[OH^-]$ into the equation and calculate.

QUESTIONS AND PROBLEMS

10.3 Ionization of Water

LEARNING GOAL: *Use the ion product constant for water to calculate the $[H_3O^+]$ and $[OH^-]$ in an aqueous solution.*

10.29 Why are the concentrations of H_3O^+ and OH^- equal in pure water?

10.30 What is the meaning and value of K_w?

10.31 In an acidic solution, how does the concentration of H_3O^+ compare to the concentration of OH^-?

10.32 In a basic solution, how does the concentration of H_3O^+ compare to the concentration of OH^-?

10.33 Indicate whether each of the following is an acidic, basic, or neutral solution:
  a. $[H_3O^+] = 2.0 \times 10^{-5}$ M
  b. $[H_3O^+] = 1.4 \times 10^{-9}$ M
  c. $[OH^-] = 8.0 \times 10^{-3}$ M
  d. $[OH^-] = 3.5 \times 10^{-10}$ M

10.34 Indicate whether each of the following is an acidic, basic, or neutral solution:
  a. $[H_3O^+] = 6.0 \times 10^{-12}$ M
  b. $[H_3O^+] = 1.4 \times 10^{-4}$ M
  c. $[OH^-] = 5.0 \times 10^{-12}$ M
  d. $[OH^-] = 4.5 \times 10^{-2}$ M

10.35 Calculate the $[H_3O^+]$ of each aqueous solution with the following $[OH^-]$:
  a. coffee, 1.0×10^{-9} M
  b. soap, 1.0×10^{-6} M
  c. cleanser, 2.0×10^{-5} M
  d. lemon juice, 4.0×10^{-13} M

10.36 Calculate the $[H_3O^+]$ of each aqueous solution with the following $[OH^-]$:
  a. dishwashing detergent, 1.0×10^{-3} M
  b. milk of magnesia, 1.0×10^{-5} M
  c. aspirin, 1.8×10^{-11} M
  d. seawater, 2.5×10^{-6} M

10.37 Calculate the $[OH^-]$ of each aqueous solution with the following $[H_3O^+]$:
  a. vinegar, 1.0×10^{-3} M
  b. urine, 5.0×10^{-6} M
  c. ammonia solution, 1.8×10^{-12} M
  d. KOH solution, 4.0×10^{-13} M

10.38 Calculate the $[OH^-]$ of each aqueous solution with the following $[H_3O^+]$:
  a. baking soda, 1.0×10^{-8} M
  b. orange juice, 2.0×10^{-4} M
  c. milk, 5.0×10^{-7} M
  d. bleach, 4.8×10^{-12} M

10.4 The pH Scale

Many kinds of careers such as respiratory therapy, food processing, medicine, agriculture, spa and pool maintenance, and soap manufacturing require personnel to measure the $[H_3O^+]$ and $[OH^-]$ of solutions. The level of acidity is used to evaluate the functioning of the lungs and kidneys, to control bacterial growth in foods, and to prevent the growth of pests in food crops.

Although we have expressed the concentrations of H_3O^+ and OH^- as molarity, it is more convenient to describe the acidity of solutions using the *pH scale*. On this scale, a number between 0 and 14 represents the H_3O^+ concentration for common solutions. A neutral solution has a pH of 7.0 at 25 °C. An acidic solution has a pH less than 7.0; a basic solution has a pH greater than 7.0 (see Figure 10.4).

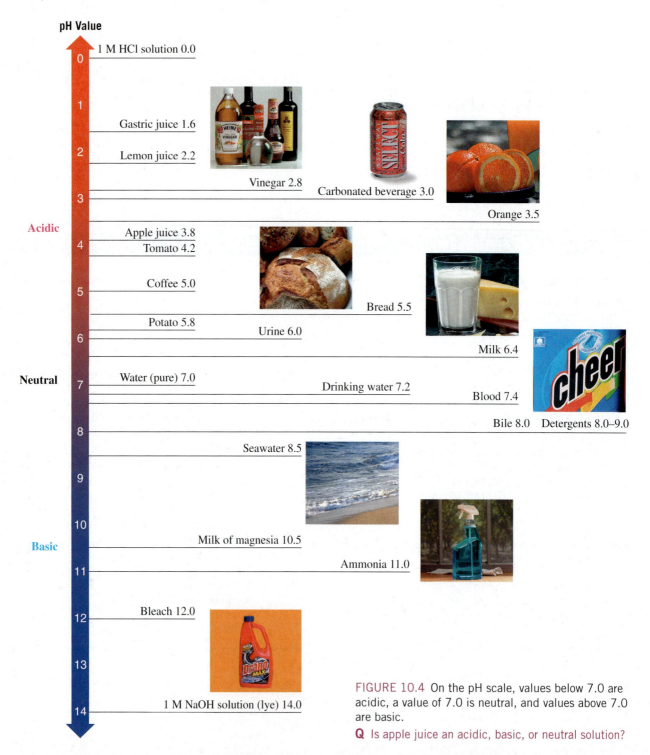

pH Value

0 — 1 M HCl solution 0.0

1

Gastric juice 1.6

2 — Lemon juice 2.2

Vinegar 2.8   Carbonated beverage 3.0

3 — Orange 3.5

Acidic

4 — Apple juice 3.8
Tomato 4.2

Coffee 5.0

5 — Bread 5.5

Potato 5.8   Urine 6.0

6 — Milk 6.4

Neutral 7 — Water (pure) 7.0   Drinking water 7.2   Blood 7.4

Bile 8.0   Detergents 8.0–9.0

8

Seawater 8.5

9

10

Basic   Milk of magnesia 10.5

Ammonia 11.0

11

Bleach 12.0

12

13

1 M NaOH solution (lye) 14.0

14

FIGURE 10.4 On the pH scale, values below 7.0 are acidic, a value of 7.0 is neutral, and values above 7.0 are basic.

Q Is apple juice an acidic, basic, or neutral solution?

- Acidic solution   pH < 7.0 $[H_3O^+] > 1.0 \times 10^{-7}$ M
- Neutral solution   pH = 7.0 $[H_3O^+] = 1.0 \times 10^{-7}$ M
- Basic solution   pH > 7.0 $[H_3O^+] < 1.0 \times 10^{-7}$ M

When we relate acidity and pH, we are using an inverse relationship, which is when one component increases while the other component decreases. When an acid is added to pure water, the $[H_3O^+]$ (acidity) of the solution increases but its pH decreases. When a base is added to pure water, it becomes more basic, which means its acidity decreases and the pH increases.

In the laboratory, a pH meter is commonly used to determine the pH of a solution. There are also various indicators and pH papers that turn specific colors when placed in solutions of different pH values. The pH is found by comparing the color on the test paper or the color of the solution to a color chart (see Figure 10.5).

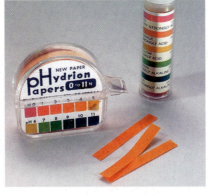
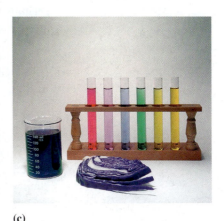

(a)   (b)   (c)

FIGURE 10.5 The pH of a solution can be determined using **(a)** a pH meter, **(b)** pH paper, and **(c)** indicators that turn different colors corresponding to different pH values.

Q If a pH meter reads 4.00, is the solution acidic, basic, or neutral?

CONCEPT CHECK 10.5   pH of Solutions

Consider the pH of the following items:

Item	pH
Root beer	5.8
Kitchen cleaner	10.9
Pickles	3.5
Glass cleaner	7.6
Cranberry juice	2.9

Cranberry juice has a pH of 2.9, which makes it acidic.

a. Place the pH values of the preceding items in order of most acidic to most basic.
b. Which item has the highest $[H_3O^+]$?
c. Which item has the highest $[OH^-]$?

ANSWER

a. The most acidic item is the one with the lowest pH, and the most basic is the item with the highest pH: cranberry juice (2.9), pickles (3.5), root beer (5.8), glass cleaner (7.6), kitchen cleaner (10.9).
b. The item with the highest $[H_3O^+]$ would have the lowest pH value, which is cranberry juice.
c. The item with the highest $[OH^-]$ would have the highest pH value, which is kitchen cleaner.

If soil is too acidic, nutrients are not absorbed by crops. Then lime ($CaCO_3$), which acts as a base, may be added to increase the soil pH.

TUTORIAL
Logarithms

TUTORIAL
The pH Scale

Calculating the pH of Solutions

The pH scale is a logarithmic scale that corresponds to the $[H_3O^+]$ of aqueous solutions. Mathematically, **pH** is the negative logarithm (base 10) of the $[H_3O^+]$.

$$pH = -\log[H_3O^+]$$

Essentially, the negative powers of 10 in the molar concentrations are converted to positive numbers. For example, a lemon juice solution with $[H_3O^+] = 1.0 \times 10^{-2}$ M has a pH of 2.00. This can be calculated using the pH equation.

$$pH = -\log[1.0 \times 10^{-2}]$$
$$pH = -(-2.00)$$
$$= 2.00$$

The number of *decimal places* in the pH value is the same as the number of significant figures in the $[H_3O^+]$. The number to the left of the decimal point in the pH value is the power of 10.

$$[H_3O^+] = \mathbf{1.0} \times 10^{-2} \qquad pH = \mathbf{2.00}$$

Two SFs   Two SFs

Because pH is a log scale, a change of one pH unit corresponds to a tenfold change in $[H_3O^+]$. It is important to note that the pH decreases as the $[H_3O^+]$ increases. For example, a solution with a pH of 2.00 has a $[H_3O^+]$ that is ten times greater than a solution with a pH of 3.00, and 100 times greater than a solution with a pH of 4.00.

CONCEPT CHECK 10.6   Calculating pH

Indicate if the pH values given for the following are correct or incorrect, and state why:

a. $[H_3O^+] = 1 \times 10^{-6}$ pH $= -6.0$
b. $[H_3O^+] = 1.0 \times 10^{-10}$ pH $= 10.0$
c. $[H_3O^+] = 1.0 \times 10^{-6}$ pH $= 6.00$

ANSWER

a. Incorrect. The pH of this solution is 6.0, which has a positive value, not negative.
b. Incorrect. This solution has a $[H_3O^+]$ of 1.0×10^{-10} M, which has a pH of 10.00. Two zeros are needed after the decimal point to match the two significant figures in the coefficient of the $[H_3O^+]$.
c. Correct. The pH has two zeros after the decimal point to match the two significant figures in the coefficient 1.0.

The pH of a solution is calculated using the *log* key and changing the sign as shown in Sample Problems 10.6 and 10.7.

SAMPLE PROBLEM 10.6 Calculating pH from [H₃O⁺]

Aspirin, which is acetylsalicylic acid, was the first nonsteroidal anti-inflammatory drug used to alleviate pain and fever. If a solution of aspirin has a $[H_3O^+] = 1.7 \times 10^{-3}$ M, what is the pH of the solution?

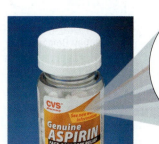

Acidic H that dissociates in aqueous solution

SOLUTION

Analyze the Problem

Solution Components	$[H_3O^+]$	pH
Given	1.7×10^{-3} M	
Need		pH

Aspirin, which is acetylsalicylic acid, is a weak acid with a K_a of 3.0×10^{-4}.

Step 1   Enter the [H₃O⁺].

Calculator Display

Enter 1.7 and press EE or EXP. 1.7^{00} or 1.700 or $1.7E00$

Enter 3 and press +/- to change the sign. 1.7^{-03} or $1.7-03$ or $1.7E-03$
(For calculators without a change sign key,
consult the instructions for the calculator.)

Step 2   Press the *log* key and change the sign.

log   +/- 2.769551079

The steps can be combined to give the calculator sequence as follows:

$$pH = -\log[1.7 \times 10^{-3}] = 1.7 \boxed{\text{EE or EXP}} 3 \boxed{+/-} \boxed{\text{log}} \boxed{+/-}$$
$$= 2.769551079$$

Be sure to check the instructions for your calculator. On some calculators, the log key is used first, followed by the concentration.

Step 3   Adjust the number of SFs on the *right* of the decimal point to equal the SFs in the coefficient. In a pH value, the number to the *left* of the decimal point is an *exact* number derived from the power of 10.

Guide to Calculating pH of an Aqueous Solution

1 Enter the $[H_3O^+]$.

2 Press the *log* key and change the sign.

3 Adjust the number of SFs on the *right* of the decimal point to equal the SFs in the coefficient.

Coefficient	Power of ten

$[H_3O^+] = \mathbf{1.7} \quad \times \quad 10^{-3}$ M $pH = -\log[1.7 \times 10^{-3}] = 2.\mathbf{77}$

Two SFs   Exact   Exact   Two SFs

STUDY CHECK 10.6

What is the pH of bleach with $[H_3O^+] = 4.2 \times 10^{-12}$ M?

When the $[OH^-]$ is given, we use the K_w to calculate $[H_3O^+]$, from which the pH of the solution can be calculated as shown in Sample Problem 10.7.

SAMPLE PROBLEM 10.7 Calculating pH from [OH⁻]

What is the pH of an ammonia solution at 25 °C with $[OH^-] = 3.7 \times 10^{-3}$ M?

SOLUTION

Analyze the Problem

Solution Components	$[OH^-]$	pH
Given	3.7×10^{-3} M	
Need		pH

Step 1 **Enter the $[H_3O^+]$.** Because $[OH^-]$ is given for the ammonia solution, we need to calculate $[H_3O^+]$. Using the ion product constant for water, K_w, we divide both sides by $[OH^-]$ to obtain $[H_3O^+]$.

$$\frac{K_w}{[OH^-]} = \frac{[H_3O^+]\,[\cancel{OH^-}]}{[\cancel{OH^-}]}$$

$$[H_3O^+] = \frac{1.0 \times 10^{-14}}{[3.7 \times 10^{-3}]} = 2.7 \times 10^{-12} \text{ M}$$

Calculator Display

2.7 [EE or EXP] 12 [+/−]   *2.7⁻¹² or 2.7−12 or 2.7E−12*

Step 2 **Press the *log* key and change the sign.**

[log] [+/−]   *11.56863624*

Step 3 **Adjust the number of SFs to the *right* of the decimal point to equal the SFs in the coefficient.**

2.7 × 10⁻¹² M   pH = 11.**57**

Two SFs   Exact   Exact   Two SFs

STUDY CHECK 10.7

Calculate the pH of a sample of acid rain that has $[OH^-] = 2 \times 10^{-10}$ M.

A comparison of $[H_3O^+]$, $[OH^-]$, and their corresponding pH values is given in Table 10.7.

TABLE 10.7 A Comparison of $[H_3O^+]$, $[OH^-]$, and Corresponding pH Values at 25 °C

$[H_3O^+]$	pH	$[OH^-]$	
10^0	0	10^{-14}	
10^{-1}	1	10^{-13}	
10^{-2}	2	10^{-12}	
10^{-3}	3	10^{-11}	Acidic
10^{-4}	4	10^{-10}	
10^{-5}	5	10^{-9}	
10^{-6}	6	10^{-8}	
10^{-7}	7	10^{-7}	Neutral
10^{-8}	8	10^{-6}	
10^{-9}	9	10^{-5}	
10^{-10}	10	10^{-4}	
10^{-11}	11	10^{-3}	Basic
10^{-12}	12	10^{-2}	
10^{-13}	13	10^{-1}	
10^{-14}	14	10^0	

Calculating $[H_3O^+]$ from pH

In another calculation, we are given the pH of a solution and asked to determine the $[H_3O^+]$. This is a reverse of the pH calculation.

$$[H_3O^+] = 10^{-pH}$$

For pH values that are whole numbers, the exponent in the power of 10 is the same as the pH.

pH

$$[H_3O^+] = 1 \times 10^{-3} \quad pH = 3.0$$
$$[H_3O^+] = 1 \times 10^{-9} \quad pH = 9.0$$

For pH values that are not whole numbers, the calculation requires the use of the 10^x key, which is usually a *2nd function* key. On some calculators, this operation is done by using the *inverse* key and then the *log* key.

SAMPLE PROBLEM 10.8 Calculating $[H_3O^+]$ from pH

Calculate $[H_3O^+]$ for a solution of baking soda with a pH of 8.25.

SOLUTION

Analyze the Problem

Solution Components	pH	$[H_3O^+]$
Given	8.25	
Need		M (moles/L)

Step 1 **Enter the pH value and change the sign.** This gives the negative value of the pH.

Calculator Display

8.25 [+/−]   *-8.25*

Step 2 **Convert –pH to concentration.** Press the *2nd function* key and then the 10^x key.

[2nd] [10ˣ]   *5.623413252⁻⁰⁹* or *5.623413252–09* or *5.623413252 E–09*

Or press the *inverse* key and then the *log* key.

[inv] [log]

Step 3 **Adjust the SFs in the coefficient.** Because the pH value of 8.25 has two SFs on the *right* of the decimal point, the coefficient for $[H_3O^+]$ is written with two SFs.

$$[H_3O^+] = 5.6 \times 10^{-9} \, M$$

STUDY CHECK 10.8

What are the $[H_3O^+]$ and $[OH^-]$ of a beer that has a pH of 4.7?

Guide to Calculating $[H_3O^+]$ from pH

1 Enter the pH value and change the sign.

2 Convert –pH to concentration.

3 Adjust the SFs in the coefficient.

Chemistry Link to Health

STOMACH ACID, HCl

Gastric acid, which contains HCl, is produced by parietal cells that line the stomach. When the stomach expands with the intake of food, the gastric glands begin to secrete a strongly acidic solution of HCl. In a single day, a person may secrete 2000 mL of gastric juice, which contains hydrochloric acid, mucins, and the enzymes pepsin and lipase.

The HCl in the gastric juice activates a digestive enzyme from the chief cells called *pepsinogen* to form *pepsin*, which breaks down proteins in food entering the stomach. The secretion of HCl continues until the stomach has a pH of about 2, which is the optimum pH for activating the digestive enzymes without ulcerating the stomach lining. In addition, the low pH is beneficial by destroying bacteria that reach the stomach. Normally, large quantities of viscous mucus are secreted within the stomach to protect its lining from acid and enzyme damage. In gastric reflux disease, the gastric acid solution from the stomach moves into the esophagus to cause symptoms such as heartburn or a hiatal hernia. Gastric acid may also form under conditions of stress when the nervous system activates the production of HCl.

As the contents of the stomach move into the small intestine, cells produce bicarbonate to neutralize the gastric acid to about a pH of 5.0.

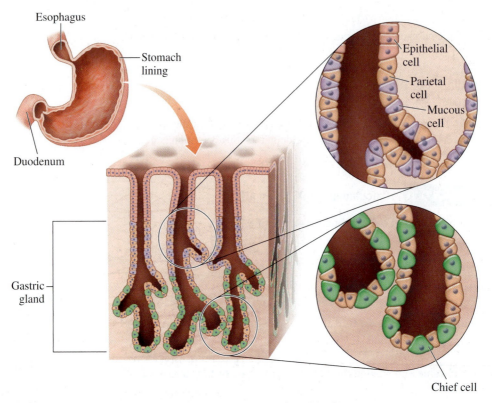

Parietal cells in the lining of the stomach secrete gastric acid HCl.

Explore Your World

USING VEGETABLES AND FLOWERS AS pH INDICATORS

Many flowers and vegetables with strong color, especially reds and purples, contain compounds that change color with changes in pH. Some examples are red cabbage, cranberry juice, and other highly colored drinks made from fruits or vegetables.

Materials Needed

Red cabbage or cranberry juice or drink, water, and a saucepan.

Several glasses or small glass containers and some tape and a pen or pencil to mark the containers.

Several colorless household solutions such as vinegar, lemon juice, other fruit juices, window cleaners, soaps, shampoos, detergents, and common household products such as baking soda, antacids, aspirin, salt, and sugar.

Procedure

1. Obtain a bottle of cranberry juice or cranberry drink, or use red cabbage to prepare the red cabbage pH indicator as follows: Tear up several red cabbage leaves, place them in a saucepan, and cover with water. Heat for about 5 minutes or until the juice is a dark purple. Cool and collect the purple solution. Alternatively,

place red cabbage leaves in a blender and cover with water. Blend until thoroughly mixed, remove, and pour off the liquid.

2. Place small amounts of each household solution into separate clear glass containers, and mark what each one is. If the sample is a solid or a thick liquid, add a small amount of water. Add some cranberry juice or some red cabbage indicator until you obtain a color.

3. Observe the colors of the various samples. The colors that indicate acidic solutions are the red and pink colors (pH 1–4) and the pink to lavender colors (pH 5–6). A neutral solution has about the same purple color as the indicator. Bases will give blue to green colors (pH 8–11) or a yellow color (pH 12–13).

4. Arrange your samples by color and pH. Classify each of the solutions as acidic (pH 1–6), neutral (pH 7), or basic (pH 8–13).

5. Try to make an indicator using other colorful fruits or flowers.

QUESTIONS

1. Which products that tested acidic listed an acid on their labels?
2. Which products that tested basic listed a base on their labels?
3. Which products were neutral?
4. Which flowers or vegetables behaved as indicators?

QUESTIONS AND PROBLEMS

10.4 The pH Scale

LEARNING GOAL: *Calculate pH from* $[H_3O^+]$; *given the pH, calculate the* $[H_3O^+]$ *and* $[OH^-]$ *of a solution.*

10.39 State whether each of the following is acidic, basic, or neutral:
  a. blood, pH 7.38
  b. vinegar, pH 2.8
  c. drain cleaner, pH 11.2
  d. coffee, pH 5.54
  e. tomatoes, pH 4.2
  f. chocolate cake, pH 7.6

10.40 State whether each of the following is acidic, basic, or neutral:
  a. soda, pH 3.22
  b. shampoo, pH 5.7
  c. laundry detergent, pH 9.4
  d. rain, pH 5.83
  e. honey, pH 3.9
  f. cheese, pH 5.2

10.41 Calculate the pH of each solution given the following $[H_3O^+]$ or $[OH^-]$ values:
  a. $[H_3O^+] = 1.0 \times 10^{-4}$ M
  b. $[H_3O^+] = 3.0 \times 10^{-9}$ M
  c. $[OH^-] = 1.0 \times 10^{-5}$ M
  d. $[OH^-] = 2.5 \times 10^{-11}$ M
  e. $[H_3O^+] = 6.7 \times 10^{-8}$ M
  f. $[OH^-] = 8.2 \times 10^{-4}$ M

10.42 Calculate the pH of each solution given the following $[H_3O^+]$ or $[OH^-]$ values:
  a. $[H_3O^+] = 1.0 \times 10^{-8}$ M
  b. $[H_3O^+] = 5.0 \times 10^{-6}$ M
  c. $[OH^-] = 4.0 \times 10^{-2}$ M
  d. $[OH^-] = 8.0 \times 10^{-3}$ M
  e. $[H_3O^+] = 4.7 \times 10^{-2}$ M
  f. $[OH^-] = 3.9 \times 10^{-6}$ M

10.43 Complete the following table:

$[H_3O^+]$	$[OH^-]$	pH	Acidic, Basic, or Neutral?
	1×10^{-6} M		
		3.00	
2.8×10^{-5} M			
		4.62	

10.44 Complete the following table:

$[H_3O^+]$	$[OH^-]$	pH	Acidic, Basic, or Neutral?
		10.00	
			Neutral
6.4×10^{-12} M			
		11.3	

10.5 Reactions of Acids and Bases

LEARNING GOAL

Write balanced equations for reactions of acids with metals, carbonates, and bases; calculate the molarity or volume of an acid from titration information.

Typical reactions of acids and bases include the reactions of acids with metals, bases, and carbonate or bicarbonate ions. For example, when you drop an antacid tablet in water, the bicarbonate ion and citric acid in the tablet react to produce carbon dioxide bubbles, a salt, and water. A *salt* is an ionic compound that does not have H^+ as the cation or OH^- as the anion.

Acids and Metals

Acids react with certain metals to produce a salt and hydrogen gas (H_2). Metals that react with acids include potassium, sodium, calcium, magnesium, aluminum, zinc, iron, and tin. In reactions that are single replacement reactions, the metal ion replaces the hydrogen in the acid.

$$Mg(s) + 2HCl(aq) \longrightarrow MgCl_2(aq) + H_2(g)$$
Metal   Acid   Salt   Hydrogen

$$Zn(s) + 2HNO_3(aq) \longrightarrow Zn(NO_3)_2(aq) + H_2(g)$$
Metal   Acid   Salt   Hydrogen

SELF-STUDY ACTIVITY
Nature of Acids and Bases

CONCEPT CHECK 10.7 **Equations for Metals and Acids**

Write a balanced equation for the reaction of $Al(s)$ with $HCl(aq)$ by completing the following:

a. Write the reactants and products using "salt."
b. Determine the formula of the salt.
c. Balance the equation.

Magnesium reacts rapidly with acid and forms a salt of magnesium and H_2 gas.

When sodium bicarbonate (baking soda) reacts with an acid (vinegar), the products are carbon dioxide gas, water, and a salt.

ANSWER

a. When a metal reacts with an acid, the products are a salt and hydrogen gas.

$$Al(s) + HCl(aq) \longrightarrow salt + H_2(g)$$

b. When the metal Al(s) reacts with HCl, it forms Al^{3+}, which is balanced by $3Cl^-$ from HCl to give $AlCl_3(aq)$. We can place this formula in the equation.

$$Al(s) + HCl(aq) \longrightarrow AlCl_3(aq) + H_2(g)$$

c. Now the equation can be balanced.

$$2Al(s) + 6HCl(aq) \longrightarrow 2AlCl_3(aq) + 3H_2(g)$$

Acids, Carbonates, and Bicarbonates

When an acid is added to a carbonate or bicarbonate (hydrogen carbonate), the products are carbon dioxide gas, water, and an ionic compound (salt). The acid reacts with CO_3^{2-} or HCO_3^- to produce carbonic acid, H_2CO_3, which breaks down rapidly to CO_2 and H_2O.

$$2HBr(aq) + Na_2CO_3(aq) \longrightarrow CO_2(g) + H_2O(l) + 2NaBr(aq)$$
Acid   Carbonate   Carbon dioxide   Water   Salt

$$HCl(aq) + NaHCO_3(aq) \longrightarrow CO_2(g) + H_2O(l) + NaCl(aq)$$
Acid   Bicarbonate   Carbon dioxide   Water   Salt

Chemistry Link to the Environment

ACID RAIN

Rain is slightly acidic, with a pH of 5.6. In the atmosphere, carbon dioxide combines with water to form carbonic acid, a weak acid, which dissociates to give hydronium ions and bicarbonate.

$$CO_2(g) + H_2O(l) \rightleftharpoons H_2CO_3(aq)$$
$$H_2CO_3(aq) + H_2O(l) \rightleftharpoons H_3O^+(aq) + HCO_3^-(aq)$$

However, in many parts of the world, rain has become considerably more acidic. *Acid rain* is a term given to precipitation such as rain, snow, hail, or fog in which the water has a pH that is less than 5.6. In the United States, pH values of rain in some areas have decreased to about 4–4.5. In some parts of the world, pH values have been reported as low as 2.6, which is about as acidic as lemon juice or vinegar. Because the calculation of pH involves powers of 10, a pH value of 2.6 would be 1000 times more acidic than natural rain.

Although natural sources such as volcanoes and forest fires release SO_2, the primary sources of acid rain today are from the burning of fossil fuels in automobiles and coal in industrial plants. When coal and oil are burned, the sulfur impurities combine with oxygen in the air to produce SO_2 and SO_3. The reaction of SO_3 with water forms sulfuric acid, H_2SO_4, a strong acid.

$$S(g) + O_2(g) \longrightarrow SO_2(g)$$
$$2SO_2(g) + O_2(g) \longrightarrow 2SO_3(g)$$
$$SO_3(g) + H_2O(l) \longrightarrow H_2SO_4(aq)$$

In an effort to decrease the formation of acid rain, legislation has required a reduction in SO_2 emissions. Coal-burning plants have installed equipment called "scrubbers" that absorb SO_2 before it is emitted. In a smokestack, "scrubbing" removes 95% of the SO_2 as the flue gases containing SO_2 pass through limestone ($CaCO_3$) and water. The end product, $CaSO_4$, also called "gypsum," is used in agriculture as a soil conditioner and fertilizer and to prepare cement products.

Nitrogen oxide forms at high temperatures in the engines of automobiles as air containing nitrogen and oxygen gases is burned. As nitrogen oxide is emitted into the air, it combines with more oxygen to form nitrogen dioxide, which is responsible for the brown color of smog. When nitrogen dioxide dissolves in water in the atmosphere, nitric acid, a strong acid, forms.

$$N_2(g) + O_2(g) \longrightarrow 2NO(g)$$
$$2NO(g) + O_2(g) \longrightarrow 2NO_2(g)$$
$$3NO_2(g) + H_2O(g) \longrightarrow 2HNO_3(aq) + NO(g)$$

Air currents in the atmosphere carry the sulfuric acid and nitric acid many thousands of kilometers before they precipitate in areas far away from the site of the initial contamination. The acids in acid rain have detrimental effects on marble and limestone structures, lakes, and forests. Throughout the world, monuments made of marble (a form of $CaCO_3$) are deteriorating as acid rain dissolves the marble.

$$CaCO_3(s) + H_2SO_4(aq) \longrightarrow CO_2(g) + H_2O(l) + CaSO_4(aq)$$

Acid rain is changing the pH of many lakes and streams in parts of the United States and Europe. When the pH of a lake falls below 4.5–5, most fish and plant life cannot survive. As the soil near a lake becomes more acidic, aluminum becomes more soluble. Increased levels of aluminum ion in lakes are toxic to fish and other water animals.

Trees and forests are susceptible to acid rain, too. Acid rain breaks down the protective waxy coating on leaves and interferes with photosynthesis. Tree growth is impaired as nutrients and minerals in the soil dissolve and wash away. In Eastern Europe, acid rain is causing an environmental disaster. Nearly 70% of the forests in the Czech Republic have been severely damaged, and some parts of the land are so acidic that crops will not grow.

A marble statue in Washington Square Park has been eroded by acid rain.

Acid rain has severely damaged forests in Eastern Europe.

Acids and Hydroxides: Neutralization

Neutralization is a reaction of a strong or weak acid with a strong base to produce a salt and water. The H^+ of an acid and the OH^- of the base combine to form water. The salt is the combination of the cation from the base and the anion from the acid. We can write the following equation for the neutralization reaction between HCl and NaOH:

$$HCl(aq) + NaOH(aq) \longrightarrow NaCl(aq) + H_2O(l)$$

Acid   Base   Salt   Water

When we write the strong acid HCl and the strong base NaOH as ions, we see that H^+ combines with OH^- to form water, leaving the ions Na^+ and Cl^- in solution.

$$H^+(aq) + Cl^-(aq) + Na^+(aq) + OH^-(aq) \longrightarrow Na^+(aq) + Cl^-(aq) + H_2O(l)$$

When we omit the spectator ions that do not change during the reaction (Na^+ and Cl^-), we see that the equation for the neutralization is the reaction of H^+ and OH^- to form H_2O.

$$H^+(aq) + \cancel{Cl^-(aq)} + \cancel{Na^+(aq)} + OH^-(aq) \longrightarrow \cancel{Na^+(aq)} + \cancel{Cl^-(aq)} + H_2O(l)$$
$$H^+(aq) + OH^-(aq) \longrightarrow H_2O(l)$$

Balancing Neutralization Equations

In a typical neutralization reaction, one H^+ always combines with one OH^-. Therefore, a neutralization equation may need coefficients to balance the H^+ from the acid with the OH^- from the base (see Sample Problem 10.9).

SAMPLE PROBLEM 10.9   Balancing a Neutralization Equation

Write the balanced equation for the neutralization of $HCl(aq)$ and $Ba(OH)_2(s)$.

SOLUTION

Step 1   **Write the reactants and products.**

$$HCl(aq) + Ba(OH)_2(s) \longrightarrow H_2O(l) + salt$$

Step 2   **Balance the H^+ in the acid with the OH^- in the base.** Placing a coefficient 2 in front of the HCl provides $2H^+$ for the $2OH^-$ from $Ba(OH)_2$.

$$2HCl(aq) + Ba(OH)_2(s) \longrightarrow H_2O(l) + salt$$

Step 3   **Balance the H_2O with the H^+ and the OH^-.** Use a coefficient of 2 in front of H_2O to balance $2H^+$ and $2OH^-$.

$$2HCl(aq) + Ba(OH)_2(s) \longrightarrow 2H_2O(l) + salt$$

Guide to Balancing an Equation for Neutralization

1 Write the reactants and products.

2 Balance the H^+ in the acid with the OH^- in the base.

3 Balance the H_2O with the H^+ and the OH^-.

4 Write the salt from the remaining ions.

Step 4 **Write the salt from the remaining ions.** Use the ions Ba^{2+} and $2Cl^-$ to write the formula for the salt as $BaCl_2$.

$$2HCl(aq) + Ba(OH)_2(s) \longrightarrow 2H_2O(l) + BaCl_2(aq)$$

STUDY CHECK 10.9

Write the balanced equation for the reaction between H_2SO_4 and LiOH.

TUTORIAL
Acid–Base Titrations

Acid–Base Titration

Suppose we need to find the molarity of a solution of HCl, which has an unknown concentration. We can do this by a laboratory procedure called **titration** in which we neutralize an acid sample with a known amount of base. In a titration, we place a measured volume of the acid in a flask and add a few drops of an *indicator* such as phenolphthalein. An indicator is a compound that dramatically changes color when the pH of the solution changes. In an acidic solution, phenolphthalein is colorless. Then we fill a buret with a NaOH solution of known molarity and carefully add NaOH solution to neutralize the acid in the flask (see Figure 10.6). When the moles of OH^- added becomes equal to the moles of H_3O^+ initially in the solution, the titration is complete. We know that the neutralization *endpoint* is reached when the phenolphthalein indicator changes from colorless to a faint, permanent pink color (see Figure 10.6). From the measured volume of the NaOH solution and its molarity, we calculate the number of moles of NaOH, the moles of acid, and the concentration of the acid.

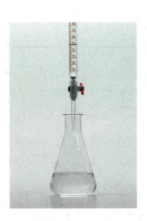
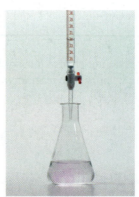

FIGURE 10.6 The titration of an acid. A known volume of an acid solution is placed in a flask with an indicator and titrated with a measured volume of a base solution, such as NaOH, to the neutralization endpoint.

Q What data is needed to determine the molarity of the acid in the flask?

Chemistry Link to Health

ANTACIDS

Antacids are substances used to neutralize excess stomach acid (HCl). Some antacids are mixtures of aluminum hydroxide and magnesium hydroxide. These hydroxides are not very soluble in water, so the levels of available OH^- are not damaging to the intestinal tract. However, aluminum hydroxide has the side effects of producing constipation and binding phosphate in the intestinal tract, which may cause weakness and loss of appetite. Magnesium hydroxide has a laxative effect. These side effects are less likely when a combination of the antacids is used.

$$Al(OH)_3(aq) + 3HCl(aq) \longrightarrow AlCl_3(aq) + 3H_2O(l)$$
$$Mg(OH)_2(s) + 2HCl(aq) \longrightarrow MgCl_2(aq) + 2H_2O(l)$$

Some antacids use calcium carbonate to neutralize excess stomach acid. About 10% of the calcium is absorbed into the bloodstream, where it

elevates the levels of serum calcium. Calcium carbonate is not recommended for patients who have peptic ulcers or a tendency to form kidney stones, which typically consist of an insoluble calcium salt.

$$CaCO_3(s) + 2HCl(aq) \longrightarrow CO_2(g) + H_2O(l) + CaCl_2(aq)$$

Still other antacids contain sodium bicarbonate. This type of antacid neutralizes excess gastric acid, increases blood pH, but also elevates sodium levels in the body fluids. It also is not recommended in the treatment of peptic ulcers.

$$NaHCO_3(s) + HCl(aq) \longrightarrow CO_2(g) + H_2O(l) + NaCl(aq)$$

The neutralizing substances in some antacid preparations are given in Table 10.8.

TABLE 10.8 Basic Compounds in Some Antacids

Antacid	Base(s)
Amphojel, Gaviscon, Mylanta	$Al(OH)_3$
Milk of magnesia	$Mg(OH)_2$
Mylanta, Maalox, Gelusil, Riopan, Equate, Maalox (liquid)	$Mg(OH)_2$, $Al(OH)_3$
Bisodol, Rolaids	$CaCO_3$, $Mg(OH)_2$
Titralac, Tums, Pepto-Bismol, Maalox (tablet)	$CaCO_3$
Alka-Seltzer	$NaHCO_3$, $KHCO_3$

Using too much antacid to reduce stomach acidity can interfere with the digestion of food and the absorption of iron, copper, the B vitamins, and some drugs. Too much antacid may also allow the growth of bacteria that would normally be destroyed by low pH of stomach acid.

Antacids neutralize excess stomach acid.

SAMPLE PROBLEM 10.10   Titration of an Acid

A 25.0-mL sample of an HCl solution is placed in a flask with a few drops of phenolphthalein (indicator). If 32.6 mL of a 0.185 M NaOH solution is needed to reach the endpoint, what is the concentration (M) of the HCl solution?

Guide to Calculations for an Acid–Base Titration

1 Write the balanced equation for the neutralization.

2 Write a plan to calculate the molarity or volume.

3 State equalities and conversion factors, including concentration.

4 Set up the problem to calculate the needed quantity.

Analyze the Problem

Solution Components	Acid Volume	Acid Molarity	Base Volume	Base Molarity
Given	25.0 mL (0.0250 L)		32.6 mL	0.185 M NaOH solution
Need		Molarity of HCl solution (moles/L)		
Neutralization Equation	$NaOH(aq) + HCl(aq) \longrightarrow NaCl(aq) + H_2O(l)$			

SOLUTION

Step 1   Write the balanced equation for the neutralization.

$$NaOH(aq) + HCl(aq) \longrightarrow NaCl(aq) + H_2O(l)$$

Step 2   Write a plan to calculate the molarity or volume.

mL of NaOH solution → [Metric factor] → L of NaOH solution → [Molarity] → moles of NaOH → [Mole–mole factor] → moles of HCl → [Divide by liters] → M HCl solution

Step 3   State equalities and conversion factors, including concentration.

1 L of NaOH solution = 1000 mL of NaOH solution

$$\frac{1\ L\ NaOH\ solution}{1000\ mL\ NaOH\ solution} \quad and \quad \frac{1000\ mL\ NaOH\ solution}{1\ L\ NaOH\ solution}$$

1 L of NaOH solution = 0.185 mole of NaOH

$$\frac{1\ L\ NaOH\ solution}{0.185\ mole\ NaOH} \quad and \quad \frac{0.185\ mole\ NaOH}{1\ L\ NaOH\ solution}$$

1 mole of HCl = 1 mole of NaOH

$$\frac{1\ mole\ HCl}{1\ mole\ NaOH} \quad and \quad \frac{1\ mole\ NaOH}{1\ mole\ HCl}$$

Step 4 Set up the problem to calculate the needed quantity.

$$32.6 \text{ mL NaOH solution} \times \frac{1 \text{ L NaOH solution}}{1000 \text{ mL NaOH solution}} \times \frac{0.185 \text{ mole NaOH}}{1 \text{ L solution}} \times \frac{1 \text{ mole HCl}}{1 \text{ mole NaOH}}$$

$$= 0.00603 \text{ mole of HCl}$$

$$\text{Molarity of HCl solution} = \frac{0.00603 \text{ mole HCl}}{0.0250 \text{ L solution}} = 0.241 \text{ M HCl solution}$$

STUDY CHECK 10.10

What is the molarity of an HCl solution if 28.6 mL of a 0.175 M NaOH solution is needed to neutralize a 25.0-mL sample of the HCl solution?

QUESTIONS AND PROBLEMS

10.5 Reactions of Acids and Bases

LEARNING GOAL: *Write balanced equations for reactions of acids with metals, carbonates, and bases; calculate the molarity or volume of an acid from titration information.*

10.45 Predict the products and write the balanced equation for the reaction of HCl with each of the following metals:
  a. Li **b.** Mg **c.** Sr

10.46 Predict the products and write the balanced equation for the reaction of HNO_3 with each of the following metals:
  a. Ca **b.** Zn **c.** Al

10.47 Predict the products and write the balanced equation for the reaction of HBr with each of the following carbonates or hydrogen carbonates:
  a. $LiHCO_3$
  b. $MgCO_3$
  c. $SrCO_3$

10.48 Predict the products and write the balanced equation for the reaction of H_2SO_4 with each of the following carbonates or hydrogen carbonates:
  a. $CaCO_3$
  b. Na_2CO_3
  c. $CsHCO_3$

10.49 Balance each of the following neutralization reactions:
  a. $HCl(aq) + Mg(OH)_2(s) \longrightarrow MgCl_2(aq) + H_2O(l)$
  b. $H_3PO_4(aq) + LiOH(aq) \longrightarrow Li_3PO_4(aq) + H_2O(l)$
  c. $H_2SO_4(aq) + Sr(OH)_2(s) \longrightarrow SrSO_4(aq) + H_2O(l)$

10.50 Balance each of the following neutralization reactions:
  a. $HNO_3(aq) + Ba(OH)_2(s) \longrightarrow Ba(NO_3)_2(aq) + H_2O(l)$
  b. $H_2SO_4(aq) + Al(OH)_3(s) \longrightarrow Al_2(SO_4)_3(aq) + H_2O(l)$
  c. $H_3PO_4(aq) + KOH(aq) \longrightarrow K_3PO_4(aq) + H_2O(l)$

10.51 Predict the products and write a balanced equation for the neutralization of each of the following:
  a. $H_2SO_4(aq)$ and $NaOH(aq) \longrightarrow$
  b. $HCl(aq)$ and $Fe(OH)_3(s) \longrightarrow$
  c. $H_2CO_3(aq)$ and $Mg(OH)_2(s) \longrightarrow$

10.52 Predict the products and write a balanced equation for the neutralization of each of the following:
  a. $H_3PO_4(aq)$ and $NaOH(aq) \longrightarrow$
  b. $HI(aq)$ and $LiOH(aq) \longrightarrow$
  c. $HNO_3(aq)$ and $Ca(OH)_2(s) \longrightarrow$

10.53 What is the molarity of an HCl solution if 5.00 mL of the HCl solution requires 28.6 mL of a 0.145 M NaOH solution to reach the endpoint?

$$HCl(aq) + NaOH(aq) \longrightarrow NaCl(aq) + H_2O(l)$$

10.54 If 29.7 mL of a 0.205 M KOH solution is required to completely neutralize 25.0 mL of an $HC_2H_3O_2$ solution, what is the molarity of the acetic acid solution?

$$HC_2H_3O_2(aq) + KOH(aq) \longrightarrow KC_2H_3O_2(aq) + H_2O(l)$$

10.55 If 38.2 mL of a 0.162 M KOH solution is required to neutralize completely 25.0 mL of an H_2SO_4 solution, what is the molarity of the acid solution?

$$H_2SO_4(aq) + 2KOH(aq) \longrightarrow K_2SO_4(aq) + 2H_2O(l)$$

10.56 A solution of 0.162 M NaOH is used to neutralize 25.0 mL of an H_2SO_4 solution. If 32.8 mL of the NaOH solution is required to reach the endpoint, what is the molarity of the H_2SO_4 solution?

$$H_2SO_4(aq) + 2NaOH(aq) \longrightarrow Na_2SO_4(aq) + 2H_2O(l)$$

10.57 A solution of 0.204 M NaOH is used to neutralize 50.0 mL of an H_3PO_4 solution. If 16.4 mL of the NaOH solution is required to reach the endpoint, what is the molarity of the H_3PO_4 solution?

$$H_3PO_4(aq) + 3NaOH(aq) \longrightarrow Na_3PO_4(aq) + 3H_2O(l)$$

10.58 A solution of 0.312 M KOH is used to neutralize 15.0 mL of an H_3PO_4 solution. If 28.3 mL of the KOH solution is required to reach the endpoint, what is the molarity of the H_3PO_4 solution?

$$H_3PO_4(aq) + 3KOH(aq) \longrightarrow K_3PO_4(aq) + 3H_2O(l)$$

10.6 Buffers

The pH of water and most solutions changes drastically when a small amount of acid or base is added. However, when acid or base is added to a *buffer solution*, there is very little change in pH. A **buffer solution** is a solution that maintains pH by neutralizing added acid or base. For example, blood contains buffers that maintain a consistent pH of about 7.4. If the pH of the blood goes slightly above or below 7.4, changes in our oxygen levels and our metabolic processes can be drastic enough to cause death. Even though we obtain acids and bases from foods and cellular reactions, the buffers in the body absorb those compounds so effectively that the pH of the blood remains essentially unchanged (see Figure 10.7).

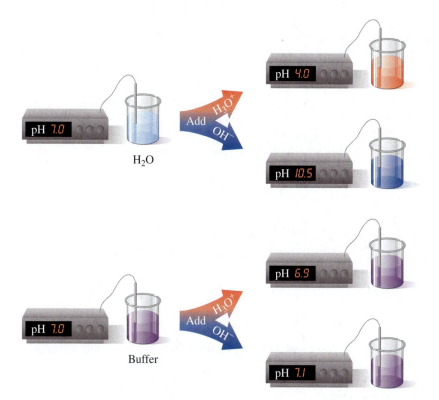

FIGURE 10.7 Adding an acid or a base to water changes the pH drastically, but a buffer resists pH change when small amounts of acid or base are added.

Q Why does the pH change several pH units when acid is added to water, but not when acid is added to a buffer?

In a buffer, an acid must be present to react with any OH^- that is added, and a base must be available to react with any added H_3O^+. However, that acid and base must not neutralize each other. Therefore, a combination of an acid–base conjugate pair is used in buffers. Most buffer solutions consist of nearly equal concentrations of a weak acid and a salt containing its conjugate base (see Figure 10.8). Buffers may also contain a weak base and the salt of the weak base, which contains its conjugate acid.

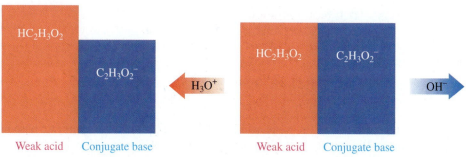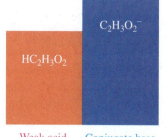

FIGURE 10.8 The buffer described here consists of about equal concentrations of acetic acid ($HC_2H_3O_2$) and its conjugate base, acetate ion ($C_2H_3O_2^-$). Adding H_3O^+ to the buffer uses up some $C_2H_3O_2^-$, whereas adding OH^- neutralizes $HC_2H_3O_2$. The pH of the solution is maintained as long as the added amounts of acid or base are small compared to the concentrations of the buffer components.

Q How does this acetic acid/acetate ion buffer maintain pH?

For example, a buffer can be made from the weak acid acetic acid ($HC_2H_3O_2$), and its salt, sodium acetate ($NaC_2H_3O_2$). As a weak acid, acetic acid dissociates slightly in water to form H_3O^+ and a very small amount of $C_2H_3O_2^-$. The addition of its salt, sodium acetate, provides a much larger concentration of acetate ion ($C_2H_3O_2^-$), which is necessary for its buffering capability.

$$HC_2H_3O_2(aq) + H_2O(l) \rightleftharpoons H_3O^+(aq) + C_2H_3O_2^-(aq)$$

Large amount   Large amount

We can now describe how this buffer solution maintains the $[H_3O^+]$. When a small amount of acid is added, it combines with the acetate ion, $C_2H_3O_2^-$, causing the equilibrium to shift in the direction of the reactants, acetic acid, and water. There will be a slight decrease in the $[C_2H_3O_2^-]$ and a slight increase in $[HC_2H_3O_2]$, but both the $[H_3O^+]$ and the pH of the solution are maintained.

$$HC_2H_3O_2(aq) + H_2O(l) \longleftarrow H_3O^+(aq) + C_2H_3O_2^-(aq)$$

Equilibrium shifts left

If a small amount of base is added to this buffer solution, it is neutralized by the acetic acid, $HC_2H_3O_2$, which shifts the equilibrium in the direction of the products acetate ion and water. The $[HC_2H_3O_2]$ decreases slightly, and the $[C_2H_3O_2^-]$ increases slightly, but again the $[H_3O^+]$ and thus the pH of the solution are maintained.

$$HC_2H_3O_2(aq) + OH^-(aq) \longrightarrow H_2O(l) + C_2H_3O_2^-(aq)$$

Equilibrium shifts left

CONCEPT CHECK 10.8   **Identifying Buffer Solutions**

Indicate whether each of the following would make a buffer solution:

a. HCl, a strong acid, and NaCl
b. H_3PO_4, a weak acid
c. HF, a weak acid, and NaF

ANSWER

a. No. A buffer requires a weak acid, not a strong acid, and a salt containing its conjugate base.
b. No. A weak acid is part of a buffer, but the salt containing the conjugate base of the weak acid is also needed.
c. Yes. This mixture would be a buffer because it contains a weak acid and its salt.

TUTORIAL
Calculating the pH of a Basic Buffer

TUTORIAL
Calculating the pH of an Acid Buffer

Calculating the pH of a Buffer

By rearranging the K_a expression to give $[H_3O^+]$, we can obtain the ratio of the acetic acid/acetate ion buffer:

$$K_a = \frac{[H_3O^+][C_2H_3O_2^-]}{[HC_2H_3O_2]}$$

Solving for $[H_3O^+]$ gives:

$$[H_3O^+] = K_a \times \frac{[HC_2H_3O_2]}{[C_2H_3O_2^-]} \quad\begin{array}{l}\longleftarrow \text{ Weak acid} \\ \longleftarrow \text{ Conjugate base}\end{array}$$

In this rearrangement of K_a, the weak acid is in the numerator and the conjugate base in the denominator. We can now calculate the $[H_3O^+]$ and pH for an acetic acid buffer as shown in Sample Problem 10.11.

SAMPLE PROBLEM 10.11   **pH of a Buffer**

The K_a for acetic acid, $HC_2H_3O_2$, is 1.8×10^{-5}. What is the pH of a buffer prepared with 1.0 M $HC_2H_3O_2$ and 1.0 M $C_2H_3O_2^-$ (its conjugate base from 1.0 M $NaC_2H_3O_2$)?

SOLUTION

Analyze the Problem

Solution Components	Acid Molarity	Anion Molarity	pH	K_a
Given	1.0 M $HC_2H_3O_2$	1.0 M $C_2H_3O_2^-$		1.8×10^{-5}
Need			pH	
Equation	$HC_2H_3O_2(aq) + H_2O(l) \rightleftharpoons H_3O^+(aq) + C_2H_3O_2^-(aq)$			

Step 1 **Write the K_a expression.**

$$K_a = \frac{[H_3O^+][C_2H_3O_2^-]}{[HC_2H_3O_2]}$$

Step 2 **Rearrange the K_a expression for $[H_3O^+]$.**

$$[H_3O^+] = K_a \times \frac{[HC_2H_3O_2]}{[C_2H_3O_2^-]}$$

Step 3 **Substitute $[HA]$ and $[A^-]$ into the K_a expression.** Substituting these values into the expression for $[H_3O^+]$ gives:

$$[H_3O^+] = (1.8 \times 10^{-5}) \times \frac{[1.0]}{[1.0]}$$
$$[H_3O^+] = 1.8 \times 10^{-5} \text{ M}$$

Step 4 **Use $[H_3O^+]$ to calculate pH.** Placing the $[H_3O^+]$ into the pH expression gives the pH of the buffer.

$$pH = -\log[1.8 \times 10^{-5}] = 4.74$$

STUDY CHECK 10.11

The acid–base pair in a buffer is $H_2PO_4^-/HPO_4^{2-}$, which has a K_a of 6.2×10^{-8}. What is the pH of a buffer that is made of 0.10 M $H_2PO_4^-$ and 0.50 M HPO_4^{2-}?

Guide to Calculating pH of a Buffer

1 Write the K_a expression.

2 Rearrange the K_a expression for $[H_3O^+]$.

3 Substitute $[HA]$ and $[A^-]$ into the K_a expression.

4 Use $[H_3O^+]$ to calculate pH.

Because K_a is a constant at a given temperature, the $[H_3O^+]$ is determined by the $[HC_2H_3O_2]/[C_2H_3O_2^-]$ ratio. As long as the addition of small amounts of either acid or base changes the ratio of $[HC_2H_3O_2]/[C_2H_3O_2^-]$ only slightly, the changes in $[H_3O^+]$ will be small and the pH will be maintained. If a large amount of acid or base is added, the *buffering capacity* of the system may be exceeded. Buffers can be prepared from conjugate acid–base pairs such as $H_2PO_4^-/HPO_4^{2-}$, HPO_4^{2-}/PO_4^{3-}, HCO_3^-/CO_3^{2-}, or NH_4^+/NH_3. The pH of the buffer solution will depend on the acid–base pair chosen.

Using a common phosphate buffer for biological specimens, we can look at the effect of using different ratios of $[H_2PO_4^-]/[HPO_4^{2-}]$ on the $[H_3O^+]$ and pH. The K_a of $H_2PO_4^-$ is 6.2×10^{-8}. The equation and the $[H_3O^+]$ are written as follows:

$$H_2PO_4^-(aq) + H_2O(l) \rightleftharpoons H_3O^+(aq) + HPO_4^{2-}(aq)$$

$$[H_3O^+] = K_a \times \frac{[H_2PO_4^-]}{[HPO_4^{2-}]}$$

K_a	$\dfrac{[\text{H}_2\text{PO}_4^-]}{[\text{HPO}_4^{2-}]}$	Ratio	$[\text{H}_3\text{O}^+]$	pH
6.2×10^{-8}	$\dfrac{1.0\text{ M}}{0.10\text{ M}}$	$\dfrac{10}{1}$	6.2×10^{-7}	6.21
6.2×10^{-8}	$\dfrac{1.0\text{ M}}{1.0\text{ M}}$	$\dfrac{1}{1}$	6.2×10^{-8}	7.21
6.2×10^{-8}	$\dfrac{0.10\text{ M}}{1.0\text{ M}}$	$\dfrac{1}{10}$	6.2×10^{-9}	8.21

To prepare a phosphate buffer with a pH close to the pH of a biological sample, 7.4, we would choose concentrations that are about equal, such as 1.0 M H_2PO_4^- and 1.0 M HPO_4^{2-}.

CONCEPT CHECK 10.9 Preparation of Buffers

A buffer solution is needed to maintain a pH of 3.5 to 3.8 in a urine sample. Which of the following buffers would you use if 0.1 M solutions of the weak acid and conjugate base are available?

Formic acid/formate $K_a = 1.8 \times 10^{-4}$

Carbonic acid/bicarbonate $K_a = 4.3 \times 10^{-7}$

Ammonium/ammonia $K_a = 5.6 \times 10^{-10}$

ANSWER

Because formic acid has a K_a of 1.8×10^{-4}, the pH of a formic acid/formate buffer would be around 4, whereas the carbonic acid/bicarbonate buffer would be around pH 7, and the ammonium/ammonia buffer would be around 10. Thus, we can calculate the $[\text{H}_3\text{O}^+]$ and pH of a formic acid/formate buffer that uses 0.1 M solutions of the weak acid and the conjugate base.

$$[\text{H}_3\text{O}^+] = K_a \times \frac{[\text{HCHO}_2]}{[\text{CHO}_2^-]}$$

$$[\text{H}_3\text{O}^+] = (1.8 \times 10^{-4}) \times \frac{[0.1]}{[0.1]} = 1.8 \times 10^{-4}\text{ M}$$

$$\text{pH} = -\log[1.8 \times 10^{-4}] = 3.74$$

Chemistry Link to Health

BUFFERS IN THE BLOOD

The arterial blood has a normal pH of 7.35–7.45. If changes in $[\text{H}_3\text{O}^+]$ lower the pH below 6.8 or raise it above 8.0, cells cannot function properly and death may result. In our cells, CO_2 is continually produced as an end product of cellular metabolism. Some CO_2 is carried to the lungs for elimination, and the rest dissolves in body fluids such as plasma and saliva, forming carbonic acid. As a weak acid, carbonic acid dissociates to give bicarbonate and H_3O^+. More of the anion HCO_3^- is supplied by the kidneys to give an important buffer system in the body fluid, the $\text{H}_2\text{CO}_3/\text{HCO}_3^-$ buffer.

$$\text{CO}_2 + \text{H}_2\text{O} \rightleftharpoons \text{H}_2\text{CO}_3 \rightleftharpoons \text{H}_3\text{O}^+ + \text{HCO}_3^-$$

Excess H_3O^+ entering the body fluids reacts with HCO_3^-, and excess OH^- reacts with the carbonic acid.

$$\text{H}_2\text{CO}_3(aq) + \text{H}_2\text{O}(l) \longleftarrow \text{H}_3\text{O}^+(aq) + \text{HCO}_3^-(aq)$$

Equilibrium shifts left

$$\text{H}_2\text{CO}_3(aq) + \text{OH}^-(aq) \longrightarrow \text{H}_2\text{O}(l) + \text{HCO}_3^-(aq)$$

Equilibrium shifts right

For the carbonic acid, we can write the equilibrium expression as:

$$K_a = \frac{[\text{H}_3\text{O}^+][\text{HCO}_3^-]}{[\text{H}_2\text{CO}_3]}$$

To maintain the normal blood pH (7.35–7.45), the ratio of $\text{H}_2\text{CO}_3/\text{HCO}_3^-$ needs to be about 1 to 10, which is obtained by typical concentrations in the blood of 0.0024 M H_2CO_3 and 0.024 M HCO_3^-.

$$[\text{H}_3\text{O}^+] = K_a \times \frac{[\text{H}_2\text{CO}_3]}{[\text{HCO}_3^-]} = (4.3 \times 10^{-7}) \times \frac{[0.0024]}{[0.024]}$$

$$= (4.3 \times 10^{-7}) \times 0.10 = 4.3 \times 10^{-8}\text{ M}$$

$$\text{pH} = -\log[4.3 \times 10^{-8}] = 7.37$$

In the body, the concentration of carbonic acid is closely associated with the partial pressure of CO_2. Table 10.9 lists the normal values for arterial blood. If the CO_2 level rises, producing more H_2CO_3, the equilibrium produces more H_3O^+, which lowers the pH. This condition is called *acidosis*. Difficulty with ventilation or gas diffusion can lead to respiratory acidosis, which can happen in emphysema or when an accident or depressive drugs affect the medulla of the brain.

A lowering of the CO_2 level leads to a high blood pH, a condition called *alkalosis*. Excitement, trauma, or a high temperature may cause a person to hyperventilate, which expels large amounts of CO_2. As the partial pressure of CO_2 in the blood falls below normal, the equilibrium shifts from H_2CO_3 to CO_2 and H_2O. This shift decreases the $\left[H_3O^+\right]$ and raises the pH. Table 10.10 lists some of the conditions that lead

to changes in the blood pH and some possible treatments. The kidneys also regulate H_3O^+ and HCO_3^- components, but they do so more slowly than the adjustment made by the lungs through ventilation.

TABLE 10.9 Normal Values for Blood Buffer in Arterial Blood

P_{CO_2}	40 mmHg
H_2CO_3	2.4 mmoles/L of plasma
HCO_3^-	24 mmoles/L of plasma
pH	7.35–7.45

TABLE 10.10 Acidosis and Alkalosis: Symptoms, Causes, and Treatments

Respiratory Acidosis: $CO_2 \uparrow$ pH $\downarrow$	**Metabolic Acidosis: $H^+ \uparrow$ pH $\downarrow$**
Symptoms: Failure to ventilae, suppression of breathing, disorientation, weakness, coma	**Symptoms:** Increased ventilation, fatigue, confusion
Causes: Lung disease blocking gas diffusion (e.g., emphysema, pneumonia, bronchitis, asthma); depression of the respiratory center by drugs, cardiopulmonary arrest, stroke, poliomyelitis, or nervous system disorders	**Causes:** Renal disease, including hepatitis and cirrhosis; increased acid production in diabetes mellitus, hyperthyroidism, alcoholism, and starvation; loss of alkali in diarrhea; acid retention in renal failure
Treatment: Correction of disorder, infusion of bicarbonate	**Treatment:** Sodium bicarbonate given orally, dialysis for renal failure, insulin treatment for diabetic ketosis
Respiratory Alkalosis: $CO_2 \downarrow$ pH $\uparrow$	**Metabolic Alkalosis: $H^+ \downarrow$ pH $\uparrow$**
Symptoms: Increased rate and depth of breathing, numbness, light-headedness, tetany	**Symptoms:** Depressed breathing, apathy, confusion
Causes: Hyperventilation due to anxiety, hysteria, fever, exercise; reaction to drugs such as salicylate, quinine, and antihistamines; conditions causing hypoxia (e.g., pneumonia, pulmonary edema, heart disease)	**Causes:** Vomiting, diseases of the adrenal glands, ingestion of excess alkali
Treatment: Elimination of anxiety-producing state, rebreathing into a paper bag	**Treatment:** Infusion of saline solution, treatment of underlying diseases

QUESTIONS AND PROBLEMS

10.6 Buffers

LEARNING GOAL: *Describe the role of buffers in maintaining the pH of a solution.*

10.59 Consider the following: (1) NaOH and NaCl, (2) H_2CO_3 and $NaHCO_3$, (3) HF and KF, (4) KCl and NaCl. Which of these represent a buffer system? Explain.

10.60 Consider the following: (1) $HClO_2$, (2) $NaNO_3$, (3) $HC_2H_3O_2$ and $NaC_2H_3O_2$, and (4) HCl and NaOH. Which of these represent a buffer system? Explain.

10.61 Consider the buffer system of hydrofluoric acid, HF, and its salt, NaF.

$$HF(aq) + H_2O(l) \rightleftharpoons H_3O^+(aq) + F^-(aq)$$

a. The purpose of the buffer system is to:
   1. maintain $\left[HF\right]$ **2.** maintain $\left[F^-\right]$ **3.** maintain pH
b. The salt of the weak acid is needed to:
   1. provide the conjugate base   **2.** neutralize added H_3O^+
   3. provide the conjugate acid
c. The addition of OH^- is neutralized by:
   1. the salt   **2.** H_2O **3.** H_3O^+

d. When H_3O^+ is added, the equilibrium shifts in the direction of the.
   1. reactants   **2.** products   **3.** does not change

10.62 Consider the buffer system of nitrous acid, HNO_2, and its salt, $NaNO_2$.

$$HNO_2(aq) + H_2O(l) \rightleftharpoons H_3O^+(aq) + NO_2^-(aq)$$

a. The purpose of the buffer system is to:
   1. maintain $\left[HNO_2\right]$
   2. maintain $\left[NO_2^-\right]$
   3. maintain pH
b. The weak acid is needed to:
   1. provide the conjugate base
   2. neutralize added OH^-
   3. provide the conjugate acid
c. The addition of H_3O^+ is neutralized by:
   1. the salt   **2.** H_2O **3.** OH^-
d. When OH^- is added, the equilibrium shifts in the direction of the:
   1. reactants   **2.** products   **3.** does not change

10.63 Nitrous acid has a K_a of 4.5×10^{-4}. What is the pH of a buffer solution containing 0.10 M HNO_2 and 0.10 M NO_2^-?

10.64 Acetic acid has a K_a of 1.8×10^{-5}. What is the pH of a buffer solution containing 0.15 M $HC_2H_3O_2$ (acetic acid) and 0.15 M $C_2H_3O_2^-$?

10.65 Using Table 10.4 for K_a values, compare the pH of an HF buffer that contains 0.10 M HF and 0.10 M NaF with another HF buffer that contains 0.060 M HF and 0.120 M NaF.

10.66 Using Table 10.4 for K_a values, compare the pH of an H_2CO_3 buffer that contains 0.10 M H_2CO_3 and 0.10 M $NaHCO_3$ with another H_2CO_3 buffer that contains 0.15 M H_2CO_3 and 0.050 M $NaHCO_3$.

CONCEPT MAP

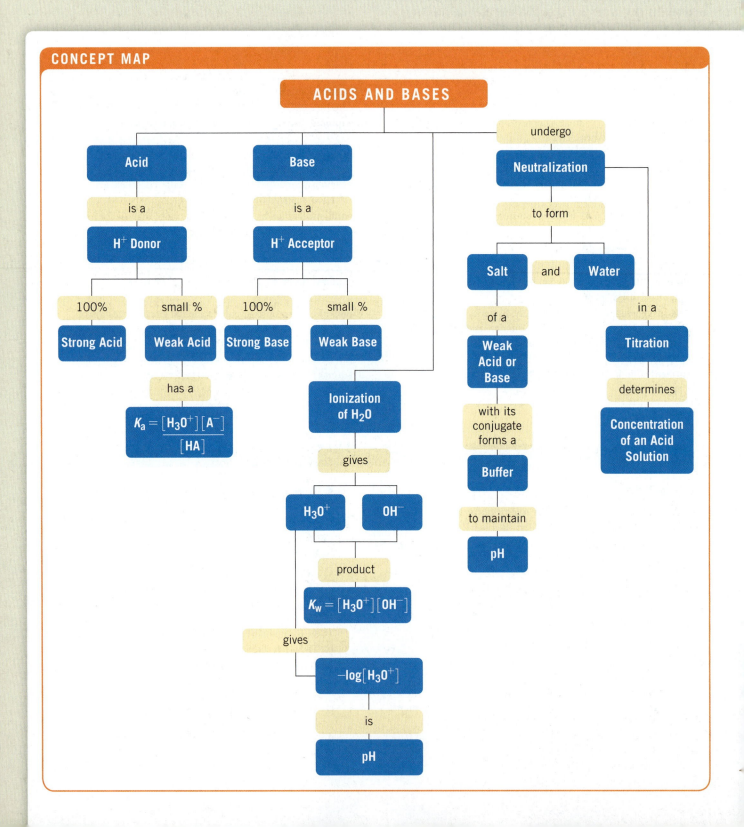

CHAPTER REVIEW

10.1 Acids and Bases

LEARNING GOAL: Describe and name Arrhenius and Brønsted–Lowry acids and bases; identify conjugate acid–base pairs.

NaOH(s)

OH⁻
Na⁺

Water

$NaOH(s) \xrightarrow{H_2O} Na^+(aq) + OH^-(aq)$
Ionic   Ionization   Hydroxide
compound   ion

- An Arrhenius acid produces H^+ and an Arrhenius base produces OH^- in aqueous solutions.
- Acids taste sour, may sting, and neutralize bases.
- Bases taste bitter, feel slippery, and neutralize acids.
- Acids containing a simple anion are named using a *hydro* prefix and an *ic acid* ending.
- Acids with oxygen-containing polyatomic anions are named as *ic* or *ous acids.*
- According to the Brønsted–Lowry theory, acids are H^+ donors and bases are H^+ acceptors.
- Each conjugate acid–base pair is related by the loss or gain of one H^+.

10.2 Strengths of Acids and Bases

LEARNING GOAL: Write equations for the dissociation of strong and weak acids; write the equilibrium expression for a weak acid.

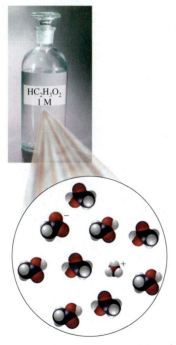

$HC_2H_3O_2$
1 M

- Strong acids dissociate completely in water and the H^+ is accepted by H_2O acting as a base.
- A weak acid dissociates slightly in water producing only a small percentage of H_3O^+.

- Strong bases are hydroxides of Groups 1A (1) and 2A (2) that dissociate completely in water.
- An important weak base is ammonia, NH_3.
- In water, weak acids and weak bases produce only a few ions when equilibrium is reached.
- The equilibrium of a weak acid and its products can be written as an acid dissociation expression, K_a.

10.3 Ionization of Water

LEARNING GOAL: Use the ion product constant for water to calculate the $[H_3O^+]$ and $[OH^-]$ in an aqueous solution.

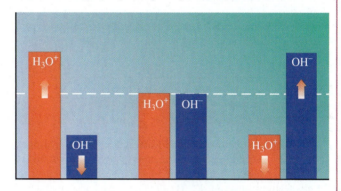

- In pure water, a few water molecules transfer H^+ to other water molecules, producing small but equal amounts of H_3O^+ and OH^-.
- In pure water, the concentrations of H_3O^+ and OH^- are each 1.0×10^{-7} mole/L.
- The ion product constant for water, K_w, $[H_3O^+][OH^-] = 1 \times 10^{-14}$ at 25 °C.
- In acidic solutions, the $[H_3O^+]$ is greater than the $[OH^-]$.
- In neutral solutions, the $[H_3O^+]$ is equal to the $[OH^-]$.
- In basic solutions, the $[OH^-]$ is greater than the $[H_3O^+]$.

10.4 The pH Scale

LEARNING GOAL: Calculate pH from $[H_3O^+]$; given the pH, calculate the $[H_3O^+]$ and $[OH^-]$ of a solution.

- The pH scale is a range of numbers, typically from 0 to 14, which represents the $[H_3O^+]$ of the solution.
- A neutral solution has a pH of 7.0. In acidic solutions, the pH is below 7.0; in basic solutions, the pH is above 7.0.
- Mathematically, pH is the negative logarithm of the hydronium ion concentration: $pH = -\log[H_3O^+]$.

10.5 Reactions of Acids and Bases

LEARNING GOAL: Write balanced equations for reactions of acids with metals, carbonates, and bases; calculate the molarity or volume of an acid from titration information.

- An acid reacts with a metal to produce hydrogen gas and a salt.
- The reaction of an acid with a carbonate or bicarbonate produces carbon dioxide, water, and a salt.
- In neutralization, an acid reacts with a base to produce a salt and water.
- In a titration, an acid sample is neutralized with a known amount of a base.
- From the volume and molarity of the base, the concentration of the acid is calculated.

10.6 Buffers

LEARNING GOAL: Describe the role of buffers in maintaining the pH of a solution.

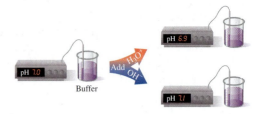

- A buffer solution resists changes in pH when small amounts of acid or base are added.
- A buffer contains either a weak acid and its salt, or a weak base and its salt.
- In a buffer, the weak acid reacts with added OH^-, and the anion of the salt reacts with added H_3O^+.
- Buffers are important in maintaining the pH of the blood.

KEY TERMS

acid A substance that dissolves in water and produces hydrogen ions (H^+), according to the Arrhenius theory. All acids are H^+ donors, according to the Brønsted–Lowry theory.

acid dissociation constant, K_a The product of the concentrations of the ions from the dissociation of a weak acid divided by the concentration of the weak acid.

amphoteric Substances that can act as either an acid or a base in water.

base A substance that dissolves in water and produces hydroxide ions (OH^-), according to the Arrhenius theory. All bases are H^+ acceptors, according to the Brønsted–Lowry theory.

Brønsted–Lowry acids and bases An acid is an H^+ donor; a base is an H^+ acceptor.

buffer solution A solution of a weak acid and its conjugate base, or a weak base and its conjugate acid, that maintains the pH by neutralizing added acid or base.

conjugate acid–base pair An acid and base that differ by one H^+. When an acid donates H^+, the product is its conjugate base, which is capable of accepting H^+ in the reverse reaction.

dissociation The separation of an acid or base into ions in water.

hydronium ion, H_3O^+ The ion, formed by the attraction of H^+ to a H_2O molecule, written as H_3O^+.

ion product constant for water, K_w The product of $[H_3O^+]$ and $[OH^-]$ in solution; $K_w = [H_3O^+][OH^-]$.

neutral The term that describes a solution with equal concentrations of H_3O^+ and OH^-.

neutralization A reaction between an acid and a base to form a salt and water.

pH A measure of the $[H_3O^+]$ in a solution; $pH = -\log[H_3O^+]$.

strong acid An acid that completely ionizes in water.

strong base A base that completely ionizes in water.

titration The addition of base to an acid sample to determine the concentration of the acid.

weak acid An acid that dissociates only slightly in water.

weak base A base that produces only a small number of ions in water.

UNDERSTANDING THE CONCEPTS

The chapter sections to review are shown in parentheses at the end of each question.

10.67 In each of the following diagrams of acid solutions, determine if each diagram represents a strong acid or a weak acid. The acid has the formula HX. (10.2)

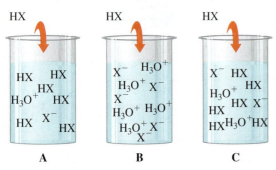

A   B   C

10.68 Adding a few drops of a strong acid to water will lower the pH appreciably. However, adding the same number of drops to a buffer does not appreciably alter the pH. Why? (10.6)

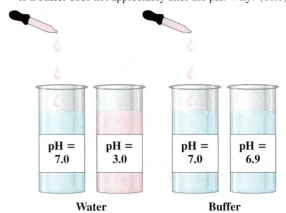

Water   Buffer

10.69 Sometimes, during stress or trauma, a person can start to hyperventilate. Then the person might breathe into a paper bag to avoid fainting. (10.6)

a. What changes occur in the blood pH during hyperventilation?

b. How does breathing into a paper bag help return the blood pH to normal?

Breathing into a paper bag can help a person who is hyperventilating.

10.70 In the blood plasma, pH is maintained by the carbonic acid–bicarbonate buffer system. (10.6)

a. Which component of the carbonic acid–bicarbonate buffer reacts when acid is added?

b. Which component of the carbonic acid–bicarbonate buffer reacts when base is added?

ADDITIONAL QUESTIONS AND PROBLEMS

For instructor-assigned homework, go to www.masteringchemistry.com.

10.71 Identify each of the following as an acid, base, or salt, and give its name: (10.1)

a. LiOH **b.** $Ca(NO_3)_2$ **c.** HBr
d. $Ba(OH)_2$ **e.** H_2CO_3 **f.** $HClO_2$

10.72 Identify each of the following as an acid, base, or salt, and give its name: (10.1)

a. H_3PO_4 **b.** $MgBr_2$ **c.** NH_3
d. H_2SO_4 **e.** NaCl **f.** KOH

10.73 Identify the conjugate acid–base pairs in each of the following equations and state whether the equilibrium mixture contains mostly products or mostly reactants: (10.5)

a. $NH_3(aq) + HNO_3(aq) \rightleftharpoons NH_4^+(aq) + NO_3^-(aq)$
b. $H_2O(l) + HBr(aq) \rightleftharpoons H_3O^+(aq) + Br^-(aq)$

10.74 Identify the conjugate acid–base pairs in each of the following equations and state whether the equilibrium mixture contains mostly products or mostly reactants: (10.5)

a. $HNO_2(aq) + HS^-(aq) \rightleftharpoons H_2S(g) + NO_2^-(aq)$
b. $Cl^-(aq) + H_2O(l) \rightleftharpoons OH^-(aq) + HCl(aq)$

10.75 Complete the following table: (10.1)

Acid	Conjugate Base
HI	
	Cl^-
NH_4^+	
	HS^-

10.76 Complete the following table: (10.1)

Base	Conjugate Acid
	HS^-
	$HC_2H_3O_2$
NH_3	
ClO_4^-	

10.77 Are each of the following solutions acidic, basic, or neutral? (10.4)

a. rain, pH 5.2 **b.** tears, pH 7.5
c. tea, pH 3.8 **d.** cola, pH 2.5
e. photo developer, pH 12.0

10.78 Are each of the following solutions acidic, basic, or neutral? (10.4)

a. saliva, pH 6.8 **b.** urine, pH 5.9
c. pancreatic juice, pH 8.0 **d.** bile, pH 8.4
e. blood, pH 7.45

10.79 Using Table 10.3, identify the stronger acid in each of the following pairs: (10.2)

a. HF or H_2S **b.** H_3O^+ or H_2CO_3
c. HNO_2 or $HC_2H_3O_2$ **d.** H_2O or HCO_3^-

10.80 Using Table 10.3, identify the stronger base in each of the following pairs: (10.2)

a. H_2O or Cl^- **b.** OH^- or H_2CO_3
c. SO_4^{2-} or NO_2^- **d.** CO_3^{2-} or H_2O

10.81 Determine the pH for the following solutions: (10.4)

a. $[H_3O^+] = 2.0 \times 10^{-8}$ M
b. $[H_3O^+] = 5.0 \times 10^{-2}$ M
c. $[OH^-] = 3.5 \times 10^{-4}$ M
d. $[OH^-] = 0.0054$ M

10.82 Determine the pH for the following solutions: (10.4)

a. $[OH^-] = 1.0 \times 10^{-7}$ M
b. $[H_3O^+] = 4.2 \times 10^{-3}$ M
c. $[H_3O^+] = 0.0001$ M
d. $[OH^-] = 8.5 \times 10^{-9}$ M

10.83 Are the solutions in Problem 10.81 acidic, basic, or neutral? (10.4)

10.84 Are the solutions in Problem 10.82 acidic, basic, or neutral? (10.4)

10.85 What are the $[H_3O^+]$ and $[OH^-]$ for a solution with each of the following pH values? (10.3, 10.4)

a. 3.00 **b.** 6.48
c. 8.85 **d.** 11.00

10.86 What are the $[H_3O^+]$ and $[OH^-]$ for a solution with each of the following pH values? (10.3, 10.4)

a. 10.0 **b.** 5.0
c. 7.00 **d.** 1.82

10.87 Sour milk (A) has a pH of 4.5, and maple syrup (B) has a pH of 6.7. (10.4)
  a. Which solution is more acidic?
  b. What is the $[H_3O^+]$ in each?
  c. What is the $[OH^-]$ in each?

10.88 A solution of borax (A) has a pH of 9.2, and human saliva (B) has a pH of 6.5. (10.4)
  a. Which solution is more acidic?
  b. What is the $[H_3O^+]$ in each?
  c. What is the $[OH^-]$ in each?

10.89 What is the $[OH^-]$ in a solution that contains 0.225 g of NaOH in 0.250 L of solution? (10.3)

10.90 What is the $[H_3O^+]$ in a solution that contains 1.54 g of HNO_3 in 0.500 L of solution? (10.3)

10.91 What is the pH of a solution prepared by dissolving 2.5 g of HCl in water to make 425 mL of solution? (10.4)

10.92 What is the pH of a solution prepared by dissolving 1.00 g of $Ca(OH)_2$ in water to make 875 mL of solution? (10.4)

10.93 a. Write the neutralization equation for KOH and H_3PO_4. (10.5)
  b. Calculate the volume (mL) of a 0.150 M KOH solution that will completely neutralize 10.0 mL of a 0.560 M H_3PO_4 solution.

10.94 a. Write the neutralization equation for NaOH and H_2SO_4. (10.5)
  b. How many milliliters of a 0.215 M NaOH solution are needed to completely neutralize 2.50 mL of a 0.825 M H_2SO_4 solution?

CHALLENGE QUESTIONS

10.95 For each of the following: (10.1, 10.2)
  1. H_2S **2.** H_3PO_4
  a. Write the formula for the conjugate base.
  b. Write the K_a expression.
  c. Which is the weaker acid?

10.96 For each of the following: (10.1, 10.2)
  1. HCO_3^- **2.** $HC_2H_3O_2$
  a. Write the formula for the conjugate base.
  b. Write the K_a expression.
  c. Which is the stronger acid?

10.97 A solution of 0.205 M NaOH is used to neutralize 20.0 mL of an H_2SO_4 solution. If 45.6 mL of the NaOH solution is required to reach the endpoint, what is the molarity of the H_2SO_4 solution? (10.5)

$$H_2SO_4(aq) + 2NaOH(aq) \longrightarrow Na_2SO_4(aq) + 2H_2O(l)$$

10.98 A 10.0-mL sample of vinegar, which is an aqueous solution of acetic acid, $HC_2H_3O_2$, requires 16.5 mL of a 0.500 M NaOH solution to reach the endpoint in a titration. What is the molarity of the acetic acid solution? (10.5)

$$HC_2H_3O_2(aq) + NaOH(aq) \longrightarrow NaC_2H_3O_2(aq) + H_2O(l)$$

10.99 A buffer is made by dissolving H_3PO_4 and NaH_2PO_4 in water. (10.6)
  a. Write an equation that shows how this buffer neutralizes added acid.
  b. Write an equation that shows how this buffer neutralizes added base.
  c. Calculate the pH of this buffer if it contains 0.10 M H_3PO_4 and 0.10 M $H_2PO_4^-$; the K_a for H_3PO_4 is 7.5×10^{-3}.
  d. Calculate the pH of this buffer if it contains 0.50 M H_3PO_4 and 0.20 M $H_2PO_4^-$; the K_a for H_3PO_4 is 7.5×10^{-3}.

10.100 A buffer is made by dissolving $HC_2H_3O_2$ and $NaC_2H_3O_2$ in water. (10.6)
  a. Write an equation that shows how this buffer neutralizes added acid.
  b. Write an equation that shows how this buffer neutralizes added base.
  c. Calculate the pH of this buffer if it contains 0.10 M $HC_2H_3O_2$ and 0.10 M $C_2H_3O_2^-$; the K_a for $HC_2H_3O_2$ is 1.8×10^{-5}.
  d. Calculate the pH of this buffer if it contains 0.20 M $HC_2H_3O_2$ and 0.40 M $C_2H_3O_2^-$; the K_a for $HC_2H_3O_2$ is 1.8×10^{-5}.

10.101 Determine each of the following for a 0.050 M KOH solution: (10.5)
  a. $[H_3O^+]$
  b. pH
  c. the balanced equation when reacted with H_2SO_4
  d. milliliters of KOH solution required to neutralize 40.0 mL of a 0.035 M H_2SO_4 solution

10.102 Determine each of the following for a 0.100 M HBr solution: (10.5)
  a. $[H_3O^+]$
  b. pH
  c. the balanced equation when reacted with LiOH
  d. milliliters of HBr solution required to neutralize 36.0 mL of a 0.250 M LiOH solution

10.103 One of the most acidic lakes in the United States is Little Echo Pond in the Adirondacks in New York. Recently, this lake had a pH of 4.2, well below the recommended pH of 6.5. (10.3, 10.4, 10.5)

A helicopter drops calcium carbonate on an acidic lake to increase its pH.

  a. What are the $[H_3O^+]$ and $[OH^-]$ of Little Echo Pond?
  b. What are the $[H_3O^+]$ and $[OH^-]$ of a lake that has a pH of 6.5?
  c. One way to raise the pH of an acidic lake (and restore aquatic life) is to add limestone ($CaCO_3$). How many grams of $CaCO_3$ are needed to neutralize 1.0 kL of the acidic water from Little Echo Pond if we assume all the acid is sulfuric acid?

$$H_2SO_4(aq) + CaCO_3(s) \longrightarrow CO_2(g) + H_2O(l) + CaSO_4(aq)$$

10.104 The daily output of stomach acid (gastric juice) is 1000 mL to 2000 mL. Prior to a meal, stomach acid (HCl) typically has a pH of 1.42. (10.3, 10.4, 10.5)
  a. What is the $[H_3O^+]$ of stomach acid?
  b. One chewable tablet of the antacid Maalox contains 600. mg of $CaCO_3$. Write the neutralization equation and calculate the milliliters of stomach acid neutralized by two tablets of Maalox.

  c. The antacid milk of magnesia contains 400. mg of $Mg(OH)_2$ per teaspoon. Write the neutralization equation and calculate the milliliters of stomach acid that are neutralized by 1 tablespoon of milk of magnesia (1 tablespoon = 3 teaspoons).

ANSWERS

Answers to Study Checks

10.1 a. acid; chloric acid
  b. $Fe(OH)_3$

10.2 $HNO_3(aq) + H_2O(l) \longrightarrow H_3O^+(aq) + NO_3^-(aq)$

10.3 The conjugate acid–base pairs are HNO_2/NO_2^- and HSO_4^-/SO_4^{2-}.

10.4 Nitrous acid has a larger K_a than carbonic acid; it dissociates more in H_2O, forms more $[H_3O^+]$, and is a stronger acid.

10.5 $[H_3O^+] = 2.5 \times 10^{-11}$ M; basic

10.6 11.38

10.7 4.3

10.8 $[H_3O^+] = 2 \times 10^{-5}$ M; $[OH^-] = 5 \times 10^{-10}$ M

10.9 $H_2SO_4(aq) + 2LiOH(aq) \longrightarrow Li_2SO_4(aq) + 2H_2O(l)$

10.10 0.200 M HCl solution

10.11 pH = 7.91

Answers to Selected Questions and Problems

10.1 a. acid **b.** acid **c.** acid
  d. base **e.** both

10.3 a. hydrochloric acid **b.** calcium hydroxide
  c. carbonic acid **d.** nitric acid
  e. sulfurous acid **f.** iron(II) hydroxide

10.5 a. $Mg(OH)_2$ **b.** HF **c.** H_3PO_3
  d. LiOH **e.** $Cu(OH)_2$

10.7 a. HI is the acid (H^+ donor) and H_2O is the base (H^+ acceptor).
  b. H_2O is the acid (H^+ donor) and F^- is the base (H^+ acceptor).

10.9 a. F^-, fluoride ion
  b. OH^-, hydroxide ion
  c. HCO_3^-, bicarbonate ion *or* hydrogen carbonate ion
  d. SO_4^{2-}, sulfate ion

10.11 a. HCO_3^-, bicarbonate ion *or* hydrogen carbonate ion
  b. H_3O^+, hydronium ion
  c. H_3PO_4, phosphoric acid
  d. HSO_3^-, bisulfite ion *or* hydrogen sulfite ion

10.13 a. acid H_2CO_3, conjugate base HCO_3^-; base H_2O, conjugate acid H_3O^+
  b. acid NH_4^+, conjugate base NH_3; base H_2O, conjugate acid H_3O^+
  c. acid HCN, conjugate base CN^-; base NO_2^-, conjugate acid HNO_2

10.15 A strong acid is a good H^+ donor, whereas its conjugate base is a poor H^+ acceptor.

10.17 a. true **b.** false **c.** false
  d. true **e.** false

10.19 a. HBr **b.** HSO_4^- **c.** H_2CO_3

10.21 a. HSO_4^- **b.** HNO_2 **c.** HCO_3^-

10.23 a. reactants **b.** reactants **c.** products

10.25 a. H_2SO_3 **b.** HSO_3^- **c.** H_2SO_3
  d. H_2SO_3

10.27 $H_3PO_4(aq) + H_2O(l) \rightleftharpoons H_3O^+(aq) + H_2PO_4^-(aq)$
$$K_a = \frac{[H_3O^+][H_2PO_4^-]}{[H_3PO_4]}$$

10.29 In pure water, $[H_3O^+] = [OH^-]$ because one of each is produced every time H^+ is transferred from one water molecule to another.

10.31 In an acidic solution, the $[H_3O^+]$ is greater than the $[OH^-]$.

10.33 a. acidic **b.** basic **c.** basic
  d. acidic

10.35 a. 1.0×10^{-5} M **b.** 1.0×10^{-8} M
  c. 5.0×10^{-10} M **d.** 2.5×10^{-2} M

10.37 a. 1.0×10^{-11} M **b.** 2.0×10^{-9} M
  c. 5.6×10^{-3} M **d.** 2.5×10^{-2} M

10.39 a. basic **b.** acidic **c.** basic
  d. acidic **e.** acidic **f.** basic

10.41 a. 4.00 **b.** 8.52 **c.** 9.00
  d. 3.40 **e.** 7.17 **f.** 10.92

10.43

$[H_3O^+]$	$[OH^-]$	pH	Acidic, Basic, or Neutral?
1×10^{-8} M	1×10^{-6} M	8.0	Basic
1.0×10^{-3} M	1.0×10^{-11} M	3.00	Acidic
2.8×10^{-5} M	3.6×10^{-10} M	4.55	Acidic
2.4×10^{-5} M	4.2×10^{-10} M	4.62	Acidic

10.45 a. products: $LiCl(aq)$ and $H_2(g)$
  balanced equation:
  $$2Li(s) + 2HCl(aq) \longrightarrow 2LiCl(aq) + H_2(g)$$

b. products: $MgCl_2(aq)$ and $H_2(g)$
balanced equation:

$$Mg(s) + 2HCl(aq) \longrightarrow MgCl_2(aq) + H_2(g)$$

c. products: $SrCl_2(aq)$ and $H_2(g)$
balanced equation:

$$Sr(s) + 2HCl(aq) \longrightarrow SrCl_2(aq) + H_2(g)$$

10.47 a. products: $LiBr(aq)$, $H_2O(l)$, and $CO_2(g)$
balanced equation:

$$HBr(aq) + LiHCO_3(s) \longrightarrow LiBr(aq) + H_2O(l) + CO_2(g)$$

b. products: $MgBr_2(aq)$, $H_2O(l)$, and $CO_2(g)$
balanced equation:

$$2HBr(aq) + MgCO_3(s) \longrightarrow MgBr_2(aq) + H_2O(l) + CO_2(g)$$

c. products: $SrBr_2(aq)$, $H_2O(l)$, and $CO_2(g)$
balanced equation:

$$2HBr(aq) + SrCO_3(s) \longrightarrow SrBr_2(aq) + H_2O(l) + CO_2(g)$$

10.49 a. $2HCl(aq) + Mg(OH)_2(s) \longrightarrow MgCl_2(aq) + 2H_2O(l)$
b. $H_3PO_4(aq) + 3LiOH(aq) \longrightarrow Li_3PO_4(aq) + 3H_2O(l)$
c. $H_2SO_4(aq) + Sr(OH)_2(s) \longrightarrow SrSO_4(aq) + 2H_2O(l)$

10.51 a. $H_2SO_4(aq) + 2NaOH(aq) \longrightarrow Na_2SO_4(aq) + 2H_2O(l)$
b. $3HCl(aq) + Fe(OH)_3(s) \longrightarrow FeCl_3(aq) + 3H_2O(l)$
c. $H_2CO_3(aq) + Mg(OH)_2(s) \longrightarrow MgCO_3(s) + 2H_2O(l)$

10.53 0.830 M HCl solution

10.55 0.124 M H_2SO_4 solution

10.57 0.0224 M H_3PO_4 solution

10.59 (2) and (3) are buffer systems. (2) contains the weak acid H_2CO_3 and its salt $NaHCO_3$. (3) contains HF, a weak acid, and its salt KF.

10.61 a. 3   **b.** 1, 2   **c.** 3   **d.** 1

10.63 pH = 3.35

10.65 The pH of the 0.10 M HF / 0.10 M NaF buffer is 3.14. The pH of the 0.060 M HF / 0.120 M NaF buffer is 3.44.

10.67 a. weak acid   **b.** strong acid   **c.** weak acid

10.69 a. Hyperventilation will lower the CO_2 level in the blood, which lowers the $[H_2CO_3]$ which decreases the $[H_3O^+]$ and increases the blood pH.
b. Breathing into a bag will increase the CO_2 level, increase the $[H_2CO_3]$, increase $[H_3O^+]$, and lower the blood pH.

10.71 a. base, lithium hydroxide   **b.** salt, calcium nitrate
c. acid, hydrobromic acid   **d.** base, barium hydroxide
e. acid, carbonic acid   **f.** acid, chlorous acid

10.73 a. NH_4^+/NH_3 and HNO_3/NO_3^-; mostly products
b. HBr/Br^- and H_3O^+/H_2O; mostly products

10.75

Acid	Conjugate Base
HI	I^-
HCl	Cl^-
NH_4^+	NH_3
H_2S	HS^-

10.77 a. acidic   **b.** basic   **c.** acidic
d. acidic   **e.** basic

10.79 a. HF   **b.** H_3O^+ **c.** HNO_2
d. HCO_3^-

10.81 a. pH 7.70   **b.** pH 1.30   **c.** pH 10.54
d. pH 11.72

10.83 a. basic   **b.** acidic   **c.** basic
d. basic

10.85 a. $[H_3O^+] = 1.0 \times 10^{-3}$ M; $[OH^-] = 1.0 \times 10^{-11}$ M
b. $[H_3O^+] = 3.3 \times 10^{-7}$ M; $[OH^-] = 3.0 \times 10^{-8}$ M
c. $[H_3O^+] = 1.4 \times 10^{-9}$ M; $[OH^-] = 7.1 \times 10^{-6}$ M
d. $[H_3O^+] = 1.0 \times 10^{-11}$ M; $[OH^-] = 1.0 \times 10^{-3}$ M

10.87 a. A
b. A, $[H_3O^+] = 3 \times 10^{-5}$ M   B, $[H_3O^+] = 2 \times 10^{-7}$ M
c. A, $[OH^-] = 3 \times 10^{-10}$ M   B, $[OH^-] = 5 \times 10^{-8}$ M

10.89 $[OH^-] = 0.0225$ M

10.91 pH = 0.80

10.93 a. $H_3PO_4(aq) + 3KOH(aq) \longrightarrow K_3PO_4(aq) + 3H_2O(l)$
b. 112 mL of KOH solution

10.95 a. 1. HS^- 2. $H_2PO_4^-$

b. 1. $\dfrac{[H_3O^+][HS^-]}{[H_2S]}$

    2. $\dfrac{[H_3O^+][H_2PO_4^-]}{[H_3PO_4]}$

c. H_2S

10.97 0.234 M H_2SO_4 solution

10.99 a. $H_2PO_4^-(aq) + H_3O^+(aq) \longrightarrow H_3PO_4(aq) + H_2O(l)$
b. $H_3PO_4(aq) + OH^-(aq) \longrightarrow H_2PO_4^-(aq) + H_2O(l)$
c. pH = 2.12
d. pH = 1.72

10.101 a. $[H_3O^+] = 2.0 \times 10^{-13}$ M
b. pH = 12.70
c. $2KOH(aq) + H_2SO_4(aq) \longrightarrow K_2SO_4(aq) + 2H_2O(l)$
d. 56 mL of KOH solution

10.103 a. $[H_3O^+] = 6 \times 10^{-5}$ M; $[OH^-] = 2 \times 10^{-10}$ M
b. $[H_3O^+] = 3 \times 10^{-7}$ M; $[OH^-] = 3 \times 10^{-8}$ M
c. 3 g of $CaCO_3$

Combining Ideas from Chapters 7 to 10

CI.17 Methane is a major component of purified natural gas used for heating and cooking. When 1.0 mole of methane gas burns with oxygen to produce carbon dioxide and water vapor, 883 kJ of heat is produced. At STP, methane gas has a density of 0.715 g/L. For transport, the natural gas is cooled to $-163\,°C$ to form liquefied natural gas (LNG) with a density of 0.45 g/mL. A tank on a ship can hold 7.0 million gallons of LNG. (1.10, 5.5, 6.1, 6.5, 6.6, 6.7, 6.9, 7.7)

An LNG carrier transports liquefied natural gas.

a. Draw the electron-dot formula for methane, which has the formula CH_4.
b. What is the mass, in kilograms, of LNG (assume that LNG is all methane) transported in one tank on a ship?
c. What is the volume, in liters, of methane gas when the LNG (methane) from one tank is converted to gas at STP?
d. Write the balanced equation for the combustion of methane in a gas burner, including the heat of reaction.

Methane is the fuel burned in a gas cooktop.

e. How many kilograms of oxygen are needed to react with all of the methane from one tank of LNG?
f. How much heat, in kilojoules, is released after burning all of the methane from one tank of LNG?

CI.18 Automobile exhaust is a major cause of air pollution. One pollutant is nitrogen oxide, which forms from nitrogen and oxygen gases in the air at the high temperatures in an automobile engine. Once emitted into the air, nitrogen oxide reacts with oxygen to produce nitrogen dioxide, a reddish-brown gas with a sharp, pungent odor that makes up smog. One component of gasoline is octane, C_8H_{18}, which has a density of 0.803 g/mL. In one year, a typical automobile uses 550 gal of gasoline and produces 41 lb of nitrogen oxide. (1.10, 6.1, 6.5, 6.6, 6.7, 7.7)

Two gases found in automobile exhaust are carbon dioxide and nitrogen oxide.

a. Write balanced equations for the production of nitrogen oxide and nitrogen dioxide.
b. If all the nitrogen oxide emitted by one automobile is converted to nitrogen dioxide in the atmosphere, how many kilograms of nitrogen dioxide are produced in one year by a single automobile?
c. Write a balanced equation for the combustion of octane.
d. How many moles of C_8H_{18} are present in 15.2 gal of octane?
e. How many liters of CO_2 at STP are produced in one year from the gasoline used by the typical automobile?

CI.19 A piece of magnesium with a mass of 0.121 g is added to 50.0 mL of a 1.00 M HCl solution at a temperature of 22.0 °C. When the magnesium dissolves, the solution reaches a temperature of 33.0 °C. (2.5, 6.5, 6.6, 6.7, 6.8, 7.8)

$$Mg(s) + 2HCl(aq) \longrightarrow MgCl_2(aq) + H_2(g)$$

Magnesium metal reacts rapidly with HCl.

a. What is the limiting reactant?
b. What volume, in liters, of hydrogen gas would be produced if the pressure is 750. mmHg and the temperature is 33.0 °C?
c. How many joules were released by the reaction of the magnesium? Assume the density and specific heat of the HCl solution are the same as for water.
d. What is the heat of reaction for magnesium in J/g? In kJ/mole?

CI.20 In wine making, glucose ($C_6H_{12}O_6$) from grapes undergoes fermentation in the absence of oxygen to produce ethanol and carbon dioxide. A bottle of vintage port wine has a volume of 750 mL and contains 135 mL of ethanol (C_2H_6O). Ethanol has a density of 0.789 g/mL. In 1.5 lb of grapes, there are 26 g of glucose. (1.9, 1.10, 6.1, 6.5, 6.6, 6.7, 8.4)

When the glucose in grapes is fermented, ethanol is produced.

Port is a type of fortified wine that is produced in Portugal.

a. Calculate the volume percent (v/v) of ethanol in the port wine.
b. What is the molarity (M) of ethanol in the port wine?
c. Write the balanced equation for the fermentation reaction of glucose.
d. How many grams of glucose are required to produce one bottle of port wine?
e. How many bottles of port wine can be produced from 1.0 ton of grapes? (1 ton = 2000 lb)

CI.21 Consider the following reaction at equilibrium:

$$2H_2(g) + S_2(g) \rightleftharpoons 2H_2S(g)$$

In a 10.0-L container, an equilibrium mixture contains 2.02 g of H_2, 10.3 g of S_2, and 68.2 g of H_2S. (9.2, 9.3, 9.4. 9.5)
a. What is the K_c value for this equilibrium mixture?
b. If more H_2 is added to the mixture, how will the equilibrium shift?
c. How will the equilibrium shift if the mixture is placed in a 5.00-L container with no change in temperature?
d. If a 5.00-L container has an equilibrium mixture of 0.300 mole of H_2 and 2.50 moles of H_2S, what is the $[S_2]$ if temperature is the same?

CI.22 A mixture of 25.0 g of CS_2 gas and 30.0 g of O_2 gas is placed in 10.0-L container and heated to 125 °C. The products of the reaction are carbon dioxide gas and sulfur dioxide gas. (6.1, 6.5, 6.6, 6.7, 6.8, 7.8, 7.9)
a. Write a balanced equation for the reaction.
b. How many grams of CO_2 are produced?
c. What is the partial pressure of the remaining reactant?
d. What is the final pressure in the container?

CI.23 A metal M with a mass of 0.420 g completely reacts with 34.8 mL of a 0.520 M HCl solution to form aqueous MCl_3 and H_2 gas. (6.1, 6.5, 6.6, 6.7, 7.8)

When a metal reacts with a strong acid, hydrogen gas forms.

a. Write a balanced equation for the reaction of the metal M(s) and HCl(aq).
b. What volume, in milliliters, of H_2 at 720. mmHg and 24 °C is produced?
c. How many moles of metal M reacted?
d. Use your results from part c to determine the molar mass and name of metal M.
e. Write the balanced equation for the reaction.

CI.24 In a teaspoon (5.0 mL) of a liquid antacid, there are 400. mg of $Mg(OH)_2$ and 400. mg of $Al(OH)_3$. A 0.080 M HCl solution, which is similar to stomach acid, is used to neutralize 5.0 mL of the liquid antacid. (6.5, 6.6, 6.7, 10.4, 10.5)

An antacid neutralizes stomach acid and raises the pH.

a. Write the equation for the neutralization of HCl and $Mg(OH)_2$.
b. Write the equation for the neutralization of HCl and $Al(OH)_3$.
c. What is the pH of the HCl solution?
d. How many milliliters of the HCl solution is needed to neutralize the $Mg(OH)_2$?
e. How many milliliters of the HCl solution is needed to neutralize the $Al(OH)_3$?

ANSWERS

CI.17 a. H:C:H   or   H—C—H (with H above, H below on both structures)

b. 1.2×10^7 kg of LNG (methane)
c. 1.7×10^{10} L of methane at STP
d. $CH_4(g) + 2O_2(g) \xrightarrow{\Delta} CO_2(g) + 2H_2O(g) + 883$ kJ
e. 4.8×10^7 kg of O_2
f. 6.6×10^{11} kJ

CI.19 a. Mg is the limiting reactant.
b. 0.127 L of H_2
c. 2.30×10^3 J
d. 1.90×10^4 J/g; 462 kJ/mole

CI.21 a. $K_c = 250$.
b. If more H_2 is added, the equilibrium will shift in the direction of the products.
c. If the volume of the container decreases, the equilibrium shifts in the direction of the products.
d. $[S_2] = 0.278$ mole/L

CI.23 a. $2M(s) + 6HCl(aq) \longrightarrow 2MCl_3(aq) + 3H_2(g)$
b. 233 mL of H_2
c. 6.03×10^{-3} mole of M
d. 69.7 g/mole; gallium
e. $2Ga(s) + 6HCl(aq) \longrightarrow 2GaCl_3(aq) + 3H_2(g)$

Introduction to Organic Chemistry: Alkanes

11

LOOKING AHEAD

Visit **www.masteringchemistry.com** for self-study materials and instructor-assigned homework.

A wildfire started near Rocky Mountain National Park from a lightning strike. Due to a lack of rain, there was considerable dry timber and grasses to provide fuel for the fire. The local firefighters decided to begin a backfire, which is deliberately set in the path of the wildfire as it consumes the dry timber and grasses, and thus, stops or confines the fire. Jack puts on his fire-resistant pants, jacket, and face protection. Jack then starts the backfire by using a drip torch containing a mixture of diesel and gasoline.

Gasoline and diesel consist of organic molecules called alkanes. Alkanes, or hydrocarbons, are chains of carbon and hydrogen atoms, and are considered to be the backbone of organic chemistry. The alkanes present in gasoline consist of a mixture of 5–10 carbon atoms in a chain, while diesel typically consists of a mixture of 11–20 carbon atoms. Because alkanes undergo combustion reactions, they can be used as a fuel source to start a backfire.

Career: Firefighter

Firefighters are first responders to fires, traffic accidents, and other emergency situations. They are required to have an emergency medical technician or paramedic certification in order to be able to treat seriously injured people.

By combining the skills of a firefighter and a paramedic, they increase the survival rates of the wounded. The physical demands of firefighters are extremely high as they fight, extinguish, and prevent fires while wearing heavy protective clothing and gear. They also train for and participate in firefighting drills, and maintain fire equipment so that it is always working and ready. Firefighters must also be knowledgeable about fire codes, arson, and the handling and disposal of hazardous materials. Since firefighters also provide emergency care for sick and injured people, they need to be aware of emergency medical and rescue procedures, as well as the proper methods for controlling the spread of infectious disease.

Organic chemistry is the chemistry of compounds that contain carbon and hydrogen. The element carbon has a special role in chemistry because it bonds with other carbon atoms to give a vast array of molecules. The variety of molecules is so great that we find organic compounds in many common products we use, such as gasoline, medicines, shampoos, plastic bottles, and perfumes. The food we eat is composed of different organic compounds that supply us with fuel for energy and the carbon atoms needed to build and repair the cells of our bodies.

Although many organic compounds occur in nature, chemists have synthesized even more. The cotton, wool, or silk in your clothes contains naturally occurring organic compounds, whereas materials such as polyester, nylon, or plastic have been synthesized through organic reactions. Sometimes it is convenient to synthesize a molecule in the lab even though that molecule is also found in nature. For example, vitamin C synthesized in a laboratory has the same structure as the vitamin C in oranges or lemons. Learning about the structures and reactions of organic molecules will provide you with a foundation for understanding the more complex molecules of biochemistry.

Foods in the diet provide energy and materials for the cells of the body.

11.1 Organic Compounds

At the beginning of the nineteenth century, scientists classified chemical compounds as inorganic and organic. An *inorganic compound* was a substance that was composed of minerals, and an *organic compound* was a substance that came from an organism, thus the origin of the word "organic." Early scientists thought that some type of "vital force," which could be found only in living cells, was required to synthesize an organic compound. This idea was shown to be incorrect in 1828 when the German chemist Friedrich Wöhler synthesized urea, a product of protein metabolism, by heating an inorganic compound, ammonium cyanate.

$$NH_4CNO \xrightarrow{\text{Heat}} H_2N-\overset{\overset{\displaystyle O}{\|}}{C}-NH_2$$

Ammonium cyanate (inorganic)   Urea (organic)

Organic chemistry is the study of carbon compounds. **Organic compounds** typically contain carbon (C) and hydrogen (H), and sometimes oxygen (O), sulfur (S), nitrogen (N), phosphorus (P), or a halogen (F, Cl, Br, and I). The formulas of organic compounds are written with carbon first, followed by hydrogen, and then any other elements.

Many organic compounds are nonpolar molecules with weak attractions between molecules. As a result, they typically have low melting and boiling points, are not soluble in water, and are less dense than water. For example, vegetable oil, which is a mixture of organic compounds, does not dissolve in water, but floats on top of it. A very typical reaction of organic compounds is that they burn vigorously in air.

In contrast, many of the inorganic compounds contain elements other than carbon and hydrogen. They are typically ionic with high melting and boiling points. Inorganic compounds that have ionic or polar covalent bonds are usually soluble in water and most

Vegetable oil, an organic compound, is not soluble in water.

do not burn in air. Table 11.1 contrasts some of the properties associated with organic compounds, such as propane (C_3H_8), and inorganic compounds, such as sodium chloride (NaCl) (see Figure 11.1).

TABLE 11.1 Some Typical Properties of Organic and Inorganic Compounds

Property	Organic	Example: C_3H_8	Inorganic	Example: NaCl
Elements	C and H, sometimes O, S, N, P, or Cl (F, Br, I)	C and H	Most metals and nonmetals	Na and Cl
Bonding	Mostly covalent	Covalent (4 bonds to each C)	Many are ionic, some covalent	Ionic
Polarity of Bonds	Nonpolar, unless a very electronegative atom is present	Nonpolar	Most are ionic or polar covalent, a few are nonpolar covalent	Ionic
Melting Point	Usually low	$-188\,°C$	Usually high	$801\,°C$
Boiling Point	Usually low	$-42\,°C$	Usually high	$1413\,°C$
Flammability	High	Burns in air	Low	Does not burn
Solubility in Water	Not soluble, unless a polar group is present	No	Most are soluble, unless nonpolar	Yes

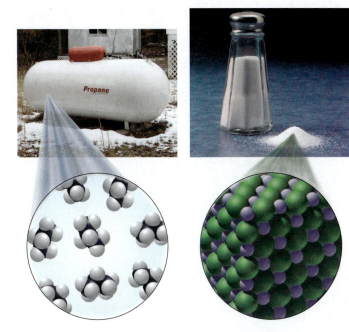

FIGURE 11.1 Propane, C_3H_8, is an organic compound, whereas sodium chloride, NaCl, is an inorganic compound.

Q Why is propane used as a fuel?

CONCEPT CHECK 11.1   Properties of Organic Compounds

Indicate whether the following properties are more typical of organic or inorganic compounds:

a. is not soluble in water
b. has a high melting point
c. burns in air

ANSWER

a. Many organic compounds are not soluble in water.
b. Inorganic compounds are more likely to have high melting points.
c. Organic compounds are more likely to burn in air.

Bonding in Organic Compounds

Hydrocarbons, as the name suggests, are organic compounds that consist of only carbon and hydrogen. In the simplest hydrocarbon, methane (CH_4), the carbon atom forms an octet by sharing its four valence electrons with the valence electrons of four hydrogen atoms. In the electron-dot formula, each shared pair of electrons represents a single covalent bond. In all organic molecules, every carbon atom has four bonds. A hydrocarbon is referred to as a *saturated hydrocarbon* when all of the bonds in the molecule are single bonds. We can draw an **expanded structural formula** for methane by showing the bonds between all of its atoms.

$$\cdot \overset{\cdot}{\underset{\cdot}{C}} \cdot \; + \; 4H\cdot \; \longrightarrow \; H\overset{H}{\underset{H}{:C:}}H \; = \; H-\overset{\overset{\displaystyle H}{|}}{\underset{\underset{\displaystyle H}{|}}{C}}-H$$

Methane

The Tetrahedral Structure of Carbon

The VSEPR theory, which we discussed in Section 5.8, predicts that a molecule with four atoms bonded to a central atom has a tetrahedral shape. Thus, for methane, CH_4, the covalent bonds from the carbon atom to the four hydrogen atoms are directed to the corners of a tetrahedron with bond angles of 109°. The various ways to represent the structure of methane are illustrated in Figure 11.2.

In ethane, C_2H_6, each carbon atom is bonded to another carbon and three hydrogen atoms. As in methane, each carbon atom retains its tetrahedral shape. The various ways to represent ethane are seen in Figure 11.3.

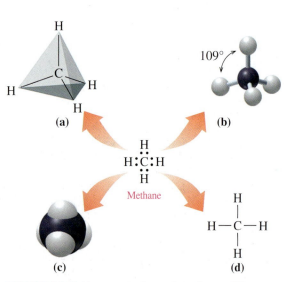

FIGURE 11.2 Representations of methane, CH_4: **(a)** tetrahedron, **(b)** ball-and-stick model, **(c)** space-filling model, **(d)** expanded structural formula.

Q Why does methane have a tetrahedral shape and not a flat shape?

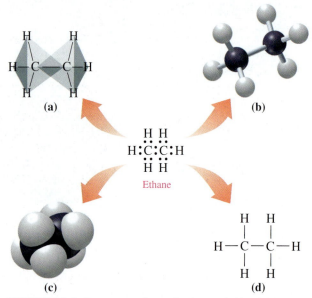

FIGURE 11.3 Representations of ethane, C_2H_6: **(a)** tetrahedral shape of each carbon, **(b)** ball-and-stick model, **(c)** space-filling model, **(d)** expanded structural formula.

Q How is the tetrahedral shape maintained by each carbon in a molecule with two carbon atoms?

QUESTIONS AND PROBLEMS

11.1 Organic Compounds

LEARNING GOAL: *Identify the characteristic properties of organic or inorganic compounds.*

11.1 Identify the following as formulas of organic or inorganic compounds:

    a. KCl   **b.** C_4H_{10} **c.** C_2H_6O

    d. H_2SO_4 **e.** $CaCl_2$ **f.** C_3H_7Cl

11.2 Identify the following as formulas of organic or inorganic compounds:

    a. $C_6H_{12}O_6$ **b.** K_3PO_4 **c.** I_2

    d. C_2H_6S **e.** $C_{10}H_{22}$ **f.** CH_4

11.3 Identify the following properties as more typical of organic or inorganic compounds:

    a. is soluble in water   **b.** has a low boiling point

    c. contains carbon and hydrogen

    d. contains ionic bonds

11.4 Identify the following properties as more typical of organic or inorganic compounds:

    a. contains Li and F   **b.** is a gas at room temperature

    c. contains covalent bonds **d.** is an electrolyte

11.5 Match the following physical and chemical properties with the compounds ethane, C_2H_6, or sodium bromide, NaBr:

    a. boils at $-89\,°C$ **b.** burns vigorously in air

    c. is a solid at $250\,°C$ **d.** dissolves in water

11.6 Match the following physical and chemical properties with the compounds cyclohexane, C_6H_{12}, or calcium nitrate, $Ca(NO_3)_2$:

    a. melts at $500\,°C$ **b.** is insoluble in water

    c. produces ions in water

    d. is a liquid at room temperature

11.7 How are the hydrogen atoms of methane, CH_4, arranged in space?

11.8 In a propane molecule with three carbon atoms, what is the shape around each carbon atom?

Propane

11.2 Alkanes

More than 90% of the compounds in the world are organic compounds. This large number of carbon compounds is possible because the covalent bond between carbon atoms $(C—C)$ is very strong, allowing carbon atoms to form long, stable chains. To help us study this large group of compounds, we organize them into classes that have similar structures and chemical properties.

The **alkanes** are a class of hydrocarbons in which the atoms are connected by single bonds. One of the most common uses of alkanes is as fuels. Methane, used in gas heaters and gas cooktops, is an alkane with one carbon atom. Ethane, propane, and butane contain two, three, and four carbon atoms, respectively, connected in a row or a *continuous chain*. As we can see, all the names for alkanes end in *ane*. Such names are part of the **IUPAC** (International Union of Pure and Applied Chemistry) **system** used by chemists to name organic compounds. Alkanes with five or more carbon atoms in a chain are named using Greek prefixes: *pent* (5), *hex* (6), *hept* (7), *oct* (8), *non* (9), and *dec* (10) (see Table 11.2).

LEARNING GOAL

Write the IUPAC names and draw the condensed structural formulas for alkanes.

TUTORIAL
IUPAC Naming of Alkanes

TABLE 11.2 IUPAC Names for the First Ten Alkanes

Number of Carbon Atoms	Prefix	Name	Molecular Formula	Condensed Structural Formula
1	Meth	Methane	CH_4	CH_4
2	Eth	Ethane	C_2H_6	$CH_3—CH_3$
3	Prop	Propane	C_3H_8	$CH_3—CH_2—CH_3$
4	But	Butane	C_4H_{10}	$CH_3—CH_2—CH_2—CH_3$
5	Pent	Pentane	C_5H_{12}	$CH_3—CH_2—CH_2—CH_2—CH_3$
6	Hex	Hexane	C_6H_{14}	$CH_3—CH_2—CH_2—CH_2—CH_2—CH_3$
7	Hept	Heptane	C_7H_{16}	$CH_3—CH_2—CH_2—CH_2—CH_2—CH_2—CH_3$
8	Oct	Octane	C_8H_{18}	$CH_3—CH_2—CH_2—CH_2—CH_2—CH_2—CH_2—CH_3$
9	Non	Nonane	C_9H_{20}	$CH_3—CH_2—CH_2—CH_2—CH_2—CH_2—CH_2—CH_2—CH_3$
10	Dec	Decane	$C_{10}H_{22}$	$CH_3—CH_2—CH_2—CH_2—CH_2—CH_2—CH_2—CH_2—CH_2—CH_3$

Alkane Name Hexane
Molecular Formula C_6H_{14}
Ball-and-Stick Model

Expanded Structural Formula

$$\begin{array}{cccccc} H & H & H & H & H & H \\ | & | & | & | & | & | \\ H-C-&C-&C-&C-&C-&C-H \\ | & | & | & | & | & | \\ H & H & H & H & H & H \end{array}$$

Condensed Structural Formulas

$$\begin{array}{ccc} CH_2 & CH_2 & CH_3 \\ \diagup & \diagdown \diagup & \diagdown \diagup \\ CH_3 & CH_2 & CH_2 \end{array}$$

$$CH_3-CH_2-CH_2-CH_2-CH_2-CH_3$$

Skeletal Formula

FIGURE 11.4 A hexane molecule can be represented in several ways: molecular formula, ball-and-stick model, expanded structural formula, condensed structural formula, and skeletal formula.

Q Why do the carbon atoms in hexane appear to be arranged in a zigzag chain?

CONCEPT CHECK 11.2 **Naming Alkanes**

Using Table 11.2, give the IUPAC name for each of the following:

a. $CH_3-CH_2-CH_3$
b. C_6H_{14}

ANSWER

a. A chain with three carbon atoms and eight hydrogen atoms is propane.
b. An alkane with six carbon atoms and 14 hydrogen atoms is hexane.

Condensed Structural Formulas

In a **condensed structural formula**, each carbon atom and its attached hydrogen atoms are written as a group. A subscript indicates the number of hydrogen atoms bonded to each carbon atom.

$$\begin{array}{c} H \\ | \\ H-C- \\ | \\ H \end{array} = CH_3- \qquad \begin{array}{c} H \\ | \\ -C- \\ | \\ H \end{array} = -CH_2-$$

Expanded   Condensed   Expanded   Condensed

By contrast, the *molecular formula* gives the total number of carbon atoms and hydrogen atoms but does not indicate their arrangement in the molecule.

When an organic molecule consists of a chain of three or more carbon atoms, the carbon atoms do not lie in a straight line. The tetrahedral shape of carbon arranges the carbon bonds in a zigzag pattern. A simplified structure called the **skeletal formula** is a carbon skeleton in which carbon atoms are represented as the end of each line or as corners in a zigzag line. The hydrogen atoms are not shown, but each carbon is understood to have bonds to four atoms, including hydrogen. In the skeletal formula for hexane, each line in the zigzag drawing represents a single bond. The carbon atoms on the ends would be bonded to three hydrogen atoms. However, the other carbon atoms in the middle of the carbon chain are each bonded to two carbons, and therefore, two hydrogen atoms. Figure 11.4 shows the molecular formula, ball-and-stick model, expanded structural formula, condensed structural formula, and skeletal formula for hexane.

Because an alkane has only C—C single bonds, the groups attached to each C are not in fixed positions. They can rotate freely about the bond connecting the carbon atoms. This motion is analogous to the independent rotation of the wheels of a toy car. Thus, different arrangements, known as *conformations*, occur during the rotation about a single bond.

Suppose we could look at butane, C_4H_{10}, as it rotates. Sometimes, the —CH_3 groups line up in front of each other, and at other times, they are opposite each other. As the —CH_3 groups turn around the single bond, the carbon chain in the condensed structural formula appears at different angles. The conformation with the methyl groups opposite each other has lower energy (more stable) because there is less repulsion between the methyl groups.

Butane can be drawn using a variety of two-dimensional condensed structural formulas, as shown in Table 11.3. All of these condensed structural formulas represent the same compound with four carbon atoms.

TABLE 11.3 Structural Representations for Butane, C₄H₁₀

Expanded Structural Formula

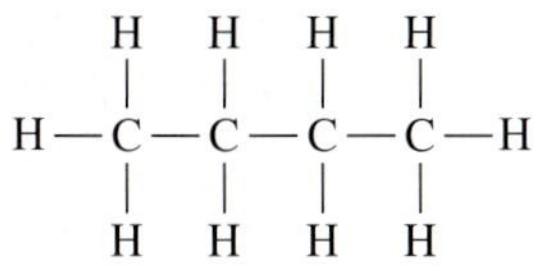

$$
\begin{array}{c}
\quad\;\; H \quad\; H \quad\; H \quad\; H \\
\quad\;\; | \quad\;\; | \quad\;\; | \quad\;\; | \\
H - C - C - C - C - H \\
\quad\;\; | \quad\;\; | \quad\;\; | \quad\;\; | \\
\quad\;\; H \quad\; H \quad\; H \quad\; H
\end{array}
$$

Condensed Structural Formulas

$CH_3 - CH_2 - CH_2 - CH_3$

$$
\begin{array}{cc}
CH_2 - CH_2 \\
| \quad\quad\; | \\
CH_3 \quad\; CH_3
\end{array}
$$

$$
\begin{array}{c}
CH_3 \\
| \\
CH_2 - CH_2 \\
\quad\quad\;\; | \\
\quad\quad\; CH_3
\end{array}
$$

$$
\begin{array}{c}
CH_3 \\
| \\
CH_2 \\
| \\
CH_2 \\
| \\
CH_3
\end{array}
$$

$$
\begin{array}{c}
CH_3 - CH_2 \\
\quad\quad\;\; | \\
\quad\; CH_2 - CH_3
\end{array}
$$

$$
\begin{array}{c}
CH_3 \\
| \\
CH_2 - CH_2 - CH_3
\end{array}
$$

$$
\begin{array}{ccc}
CH_3 & & CH_2 \\
\;\;\diagdown & & \diagup \quad\diagdown \\
& CH_2 & \quad CH_3
\end{array}
$$

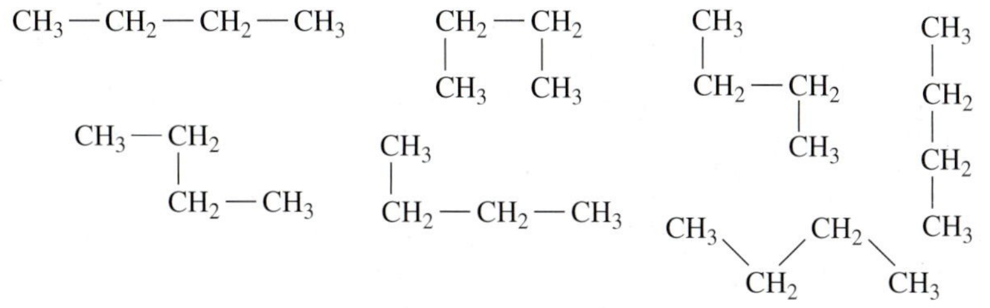

Skeletal Formulas

SAMPLE PROBLEM 11.1   **Drawing Structural Formulas for Alkanes**

Draw the expanded structural formula, condensed structural formula, and skeletal formula for pentane.

SOLUTION

A molecule of pentane, C_5H_{12}, has five carbon atoms in a row. In the expanded structural formula, the five carbon atoms are connected to each other and to hydrogen atoms with single bonds to give each carbon atom a total of four bonds. In the condensed structural formula, the carbon and hydrogen atoms on the ends are written as CH_3- and the carbon and hydrogen atoms in the middle are written $-CH_2-$. The skeletal formula shows the carbon skeleton as a zigzag line where the ends and corners represent C atoms.

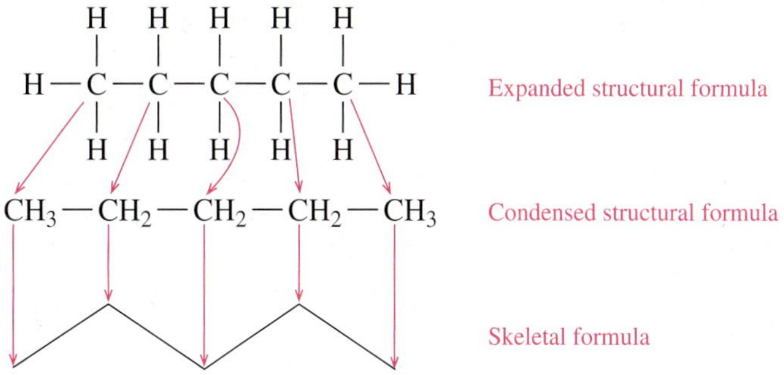

$$
\begin{array}{c}
\quad\; H \quad\; H \quad\; H \quad\; H \quad\; H \\
\quad\; | \quad\;\; | \quad\;\; | \quad\;\; | \quad\;\; | \\
H - C - C - C - C - C - H \\
\quad\; | \quad\;\; | \quad\;\; | \quad\;\; | \quad\;\; | \\
\quad\; H \quad\; H \quad\; H \quad\; H \quad\; H
\end{array}
$$
Expanded structural formula

$CH_3 - CH_2 - CH_2 - CH_2 - CH_3$ Condensed structural formula

Skeletal formula

STUDY CHECK 11.1

Draw the condensed structural formula and give the name for the following skeletal formula:

Cycloalkanes

Hydrocarbons can also form cyclic structures called **cycloalkanes**, which have two fewer hydrogen atoms than the corresponding alkanes. The simplest cycloalkane, cyclopropane, C_3H_6, has a ring of three carbon atoms bonded to six hydrogen atoms. Most often, a cycloalkane is drawn using its skeletal formula, which appears as a simple geometric figure. As seen for alkanes, each corner of the skeletal formula for a cycloalkane represents a carbon atom. A cycloalkane is named by adding the prefix *cyclo* to the name of the alkane with the same number of carbon atoms.

The ball-and-stick models, condensed structural formulas, and skeletal formulas for several cycloalkanes are shown in Table 11.4.

TABLE 11.4 Formulas of Some Common Cycloalkanes

Name

Cyclopropane	Cyclobutane	Cyclopentane	Cyclohexane

Ball-and-Stick Model

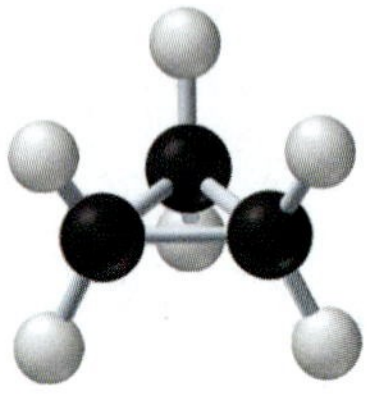

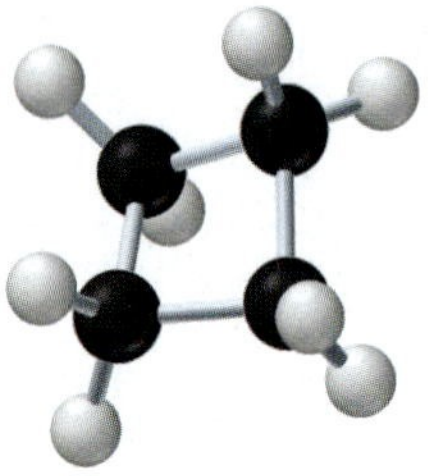

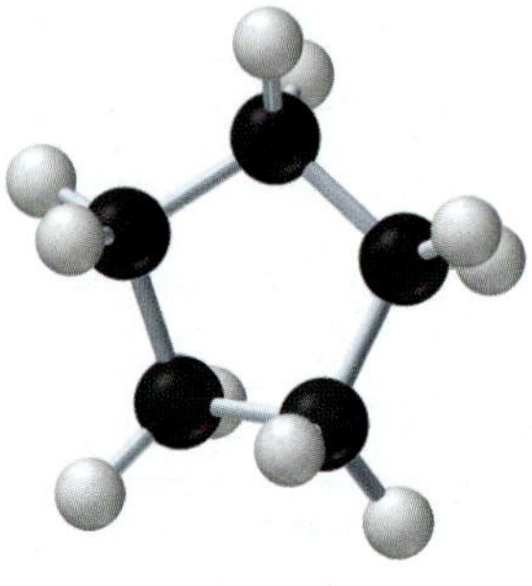

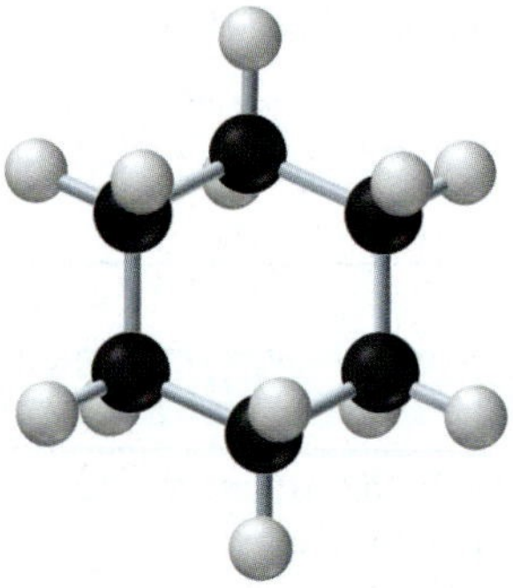

Condensed Structural Formula

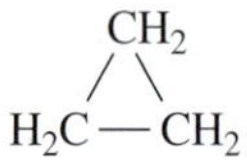

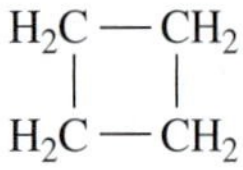

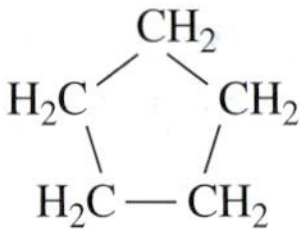

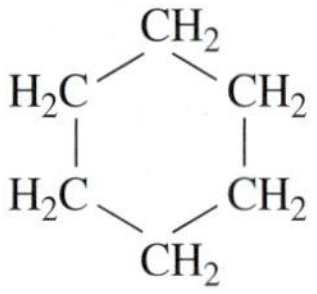

Skeletal Formula

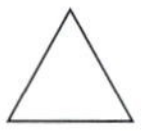

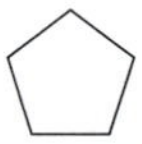

CONCEPT CHECK 11.3 **Identifying Cycloalkanes**

Name the cycloalkanes represented in the skeletal formula for cholesterol, an important steroid precursor in the body.

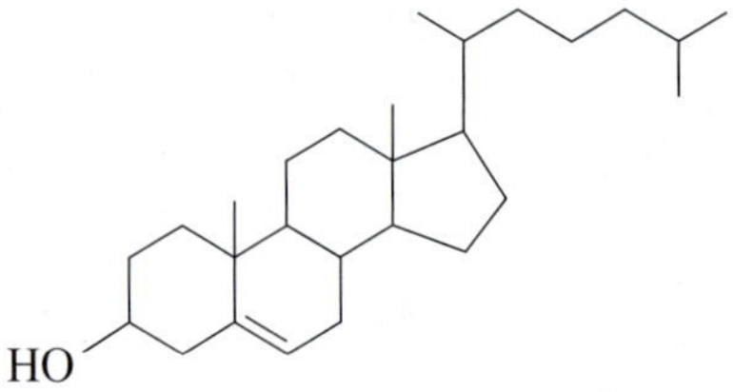

Cholesterol

ANSWER

Cholesterol contains the cycloalkanes cyclopentane and cyclohexane.

SAMPLE PROBLEM 11.2 Naming Alkanes

Give the IUPAC name for each of the following:

a. $CH_3-CH_2-CH_2-CH_2-CH_3$ **b.** ⬡   **c.** ⌁⌁⌁⌁

SOLUTION

a. A chain with five carbon atoms is pentane.
b. The ring of six carbon atoms is named cyclohexane.
c. This alkane is named octane because it has eight carbon atoms.

STUDY CHECK 11.2

What is the IUPAC name of the following compound?

QUESTIONS AND PROBLEMS

11.2 Alkanes

LEARNING GOAL: *Write the IUPAC names and draw the condensed structural formulas for alkanes.*

11.9 Draw the stated type of structural formula for each of the following:
   a. an expanded structural formula for propane
   b. the condensed structural formula for hexane
   c. the skeletal formula for pentane

11.10 Draw the stated type of structural formula for each of the following:
   a. an expanded structural formula for butane
   b. the condensed structural formula for octane
   c. the skeletal formula for decane

11.11 Give the IUPAC name for each of the following:

   a.
   $$CH_3$$
   $$|$$
   $$CH_2-CH_2-CH_2$$
   $$|$$
   $$CH_3$$
   $$CH_2-CH_3$$
   $$|$$
   $$CH_2$$
   $$|$$
   c. $CH_3-CH_2-CH_2$

   b. ⌁⌁⌁⌁

   d. ▢

11.12 Give the IUPAC name for each of the following:
   a. CH_4
   c.
   $$CH_3$$
   $$|$$
   $$CH_2$$
   $$|$$
   $$CH_3$$
   b. ⌁⌁⌁⌁
   d. ⬡

11.13 Draw the condensed structural formula for alkanes or the skeletal formula for cycloalkanes for each of the following:
   a. methane
   b. ethane
   c. pentane
   d. cyclopropane

11.14 Draw the condensed structural formula for alkanes or the skeletal formula for cycloalkanes for each of the following:
   a. propane
   b. hexane
   c. heptane
   d. cyclopentane

11.3 Alkanes with Substituents

When an alkane has four or more carbon atoms, the atoms can be arranged so that a side group called a **branch** or **substituent** is attached to a carbon chain. For example, there are two different ball-and-stick models for the molecular formula C_4H_{10}. One model is shown as a chain of four carbon atoms. In the other model, a carbon atom is attached as a branch or substituent to a carbon in a chain of three atoms (see Figure 11.5). An alkane with at least one branch is called a **branched alkane**. When two compounds have the same molecular formula but differ in the order in which the atoms are bonded, they are called **structural isomers**.

   In another example, we can draw three different structural isomers that have the molecular formula C_5H_{12}. One is the continuous or *straight* chain of five carbon atoms. The second one has a methyl group attached to a four-carbon chain. The third one has two

LEARNING GOAL

Write the IUPAC names and draw the condensed structural formulas and skeletal formulas for alkanes.

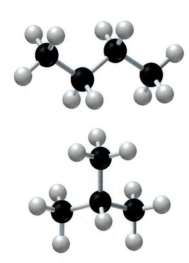

FIGURE 11.5 The structural isomers of C_4H_{10} have the same number and type of atoms but with a different order of bonding.

Q What makes these molecules structural isomers?

methyl groups attached to a three-carbon chain. Thus, three compounds with the same molecular formula can have the same atoms arranged in different bonding patterns.

Structural Isomers of C_5H_{12}

Alkane	Branched Alkanes	
$CH_3-CH_2-CH_2-CH_2-CH_3$	$CH_3-\overset{\overset{\displaystyle CH_3}{\vert}}{CH}-CH_2-CH_3$	$CH_3-\overset{\overset{\displaystyle CH_3}{\vert}}{\underset{\underset{\displaystyle CH_3}{\vert}}{C}}-CH_3$

The number of structural isomers of alkanes increases rapidly as the number of carbon atoms increases.

Number of Possible Structural Isomers for Alkanes with 1–10 Carbon Atoms

Number of Carbon Atoms	Numbers of Structural Isomers
1	1
2	1
3	1
4	2
5	3
6	5
7	9
8	18
9	35
10	75

CONCEPT CHECK 11.4 **Identifying Structural Isomers**

Identify each pair of condensed structural formulas as structural isomers or the same molecule.

a. $\overset{\overset{\displaystyle CH_3}{\vert}}{CH_2}-\overset{\overset{\displaystyle CH_3}{\vert}}{CH_2}$ and $\underset{\underset{\displaystyle CH_3}{\vert}}{CH_2}-CH_2-CH_3$

b. $CH_3-\overset{\overset{\displaystyle CH_3}{\vert}}{CH}-CH_2-CH_2-CH_3$ and $CH_3-\overset{\overset{\displaystyle CH_3}{\vert}}{CH}-\overset{\overset{\displaystyle CH_3}{\vert}}{CH}-CH_3$

ANSWER

a. When we add up the number of C atoms and H atoms, they give the same molecular formula, C_4H_{10}. We can then determine if they are structural isomers or the same molecule by looking at how the atoms are bonded to each other. The structural formula on the left consists of a chain of four C atoms. Even though the CH_3- ends are drawn pointing up, they are not branches on the chain but part of the four-carbon chain. The structural formula on the right also consists of a four-carbon chain even though one $-CH_3$ end is drawn pointing down. Thus, both condensed structural formulas consist of four-carbon chains with no substituents, which means they represent the same molecule and are not structural isomers.

b. When we add up the number of C atoms and H atoms, they give the same molecular formula, C_6H_{14}. We can then determine if they are structural isomers or the same molecule by looking at how the atoms are bonded to each other. The structural formula on the left consists of a five-carbon chain with a CH_3— branch on the second carbon of the chain. The structural formula on the right consists of a four-carbon chain with two CH_3— branches, one bonded to the second carbon and one bonded to the third carbon. The lengths of the longest carbon chains are different between the two molecules. This means that there is a different order of bonding of atoms in these two structural formulas. Thus, they represent a pair of structural isomers.

In the IUPAC names for alkanes, a carbon branch is named as an **alkyl group**, which is an alkane that is missing one hydrogen atom. The alkyl group is named by replacing the *ane* ending of the corresponding alkane name with *yl*. Alkyl groups cannot exist on their own; they must be attached to a carbon chain. When a halogen atom is attached to a carbon chain, it is named as a *halo* group: fluoro (F), chloro (Cl), bromo (Br), or iodo (I). Some of the common groups attached to carbon chains are illustrated in Table 11.5.

Rules for Naming Alkanes with Substituents

In the IUPAC system of naming, a carbon chain is numbered to give the location of one or more substituents. Let's take a look at how we use the IUPAC system to name the alkane shown in Sample Problem 11.3.

SELF-STUDY ACTIVITY
Isomers: Diversity in Molecules

TUTORIAL
Isomers

TUTORIAL
Naming Alkanes with Substituents

TABLE 11.5 Names and Formulas of Some Common Substituents

Substituent	Name
CH_3—	Methyl
CH_3—CH_2—	Ethyl
CH_3—CH_2—CH_2—	Propyl
CH_3—$\overset{\mid}{CH}$—CH_3	Isopropyl
F—, Cl—, Br—, I—	Fluoro, chloro, bromo, iodo

SAMPLE PROBLEM 11.3   **Naming a Branched Alkane**

Give the IUPAC name for the following alkane:

$$CH_3-\overset{\overset{\displaystyle CH_3}{\mid}}{CH}-CH_2-CH_2-CH_3$$

SOLUTION

Step 1   **Write the alkane name of the longest chain of carbon atoms.** In this alkane, the longest chain has five carbon atoms, which is *pentane*.

$$CH_3-\overset{\overset{\displaystyle CH_3}{\mid}}{CH}-CH_2-CH_2-CH_3 \qquad \text{pentane}$$

Step 2   **Number the carbon atoms starting from the end nearer a substituent.** Number the chain from 1 to 5 starting at the end nearer the branch of CH_3—. Once you start numbering, continue in that same direction.

$$\underset{1}{CH_3}-\underset{2}{\overset{\overset{\displaystyle CH_3}{\mid}}{CH}}-\underset{3}{CH_2}-\underset{4}{CH_2}-\underset{5}{CH_3} \qquad \text{pentane}$$

Step 3   **Give the location and name of each substituent (alphabetical order) as a prefix to the name of the main chain.** Place a hyphen between the number and the substituent name.

$$\underset{1}{CH_3}-\underset{2}{\overset{\overset{\displaystyle CH_3}{\mid}}{CH}}-\underset{3}{CH_2}-\underset{4}{CH_2}-\underset{5}{CH_3} \qquad \text{2-methylpentane}$$

Guide to Naming Alkanes

1 Write the alkane name of the longest chain of carbon atoms.

2 Number the carbon atoms starting from the end nearer a substituent.

3 Give the location and name of each substituent (alphabetical order) as a prefix to the name of the main chain.

STUDY CHECK 11.3

Give the IUPAC name for this structural isomer of the alkane in Sample Problem 11.3.

$$CH_3 - CH_2 - \overset{\overset{\displaystyle CH_3}{|}}{CH} - CH_2 - CH_3$$

Haloalkanes

In a **haloalkane**, halogen atoms replace hydrogen atoms in an alkane. The halogen substituents are numbered and arranged alphabetically, just as we did with the alkyl groups. Many times, chemists use the common, traditional name for these compounds rather than the systematic IUPAC name. Simple haloalkanes are commonly named as *alkyl halides*; the carbon group is named as an alkyl group followed by the halide name. For the IUPAC name, no number is necessary for a compound with one or two carbon atoms and one substituent.

$CH_3 - Br$	bromomethane
$CH_3 - CH_2 - Cl$	chloroethane

	$CH_3 - Cl$	$CH_3 - CH_2 - Br$	$CH_3 - \overset{\overset{\displaystyle F}{|}}{CH} - CH_3$
IUPAC Name	chloromethane	bromoethane	2-fluoropropane
Common Name	methyl chloride	ethyl bromide	isopropyl fluoride

CONCEPT CHECK 11.5 **Naming Haloalkanes**

Ethylene dibromide is the common name of a haloalkane used as a fumigant to treat wood for termites. It is toxic and is a carcinogen. What is its IUPAC name?

$$H - \overset{\overset{\displaystyle Br}{|}}{\underset{\underset{\displaystyle H}{|}}{C}} - \overset{\overset{\displaystyle Br}{|}}{\underset{\underset{\displaystyle H}{|}}{C}} - H \qquad \text{Ethylene dibromide}$$

ANSWER

The carbon chain consists of two carbons, which is ethane. There are two bromine atoms attached, one to carbon 1 and the other to carbon 2. Using the prefix *di* to indicate there are two Br atoms, we write the IUPAC name for this compound as 1,2,-dibromoethane.

TUTORIAL
Drawing Haloalkanes and Branched Alkanes

Chemistry Link to Health

COMMON USES OF HALOALKANES

Some common uses of haloalkanes include solvents and anesthetics. For many years, carbon tetrachloride, CCl_4, was widely used in dry cleaners and in home spot removers to take oils and grease out of clothes. However, its use was discontinued when carbon tetrachloride was found to be toxic to the liver, where it can cause cancer. Today, dry cleaners use other halogenated compounds such as dichloromethane; 1,1,1-trichloroethane; and 1,1,2-trichloro-1,2,2-trifluoroethane.

General anesthetics are compounds that are inhaled or injected to cause a loss of sensation and consciousness so that surgery or other procedures can be done without causing pain to the patient. As nonpolar compounds, anesthetics are soluble in the nonpolar nerve membranes, where they decrease the ability of the nerve cells to conduct the sensation of pain. Trichloromethane, commonly called chloroform, $CHCl_3$, was once used as an anesthetic, but it is toxic and may be carcinogenic. One of the most widely used general anesthetics is halothane (2-bromo-2-chloro-1,1,1-trifluoroethane), also called Fluothane. It has a pleasant odor, is nonexplosive, has few side effects, undergoes few reactions, and is eliminated quickly from the body.

CH_2Cl_2	$Cl_3C - CH_3$	$FCl_2C - CClF_2$
Dichloromethane	1,1,1-Trichloroethane	1,1,2-Trichloro-1,2,2-trifluoroethane

F   Cl
| |
F — C — C — Br   Halothane (Fluothane)
| |
F   H

For minor surgeries, a local anesthetic such as chloroethane (ethyl chloride), CH_3—CH_2—Cl, is applied to an area of the skin. Chloroethane evaporates quickly, which cools the skin and causes a loss of sensation.

Anesthetics, such as halothane, decrease the sensation of pain.

A local anesthetic evaporates quickly to reduce the sensation of pain.

SAMPLE PROBLEM 11.4   Writing IUPAC Names

Give the IUPAC name for the following:

$$CH_3 — CH — CH_2 — CH_2 — C — CH_3$$
with CH_3 above the second carbon, and Br above / CH_3 below the fifth carbon

SOLUTION

Step 1   **Write the alkane name of the longest chain of carbon atoms.** In this alkane, the longest chain has six carbon atoms, which is *hexane*.

$$CH_3 — CH — CH_2 — CH_2 — C — CH_3 \qquad hexane$$

Step 2   **Number the carbon atoms starting from the end nearer a substituent.** When there are two or more substituents, the main chain is numbered in the direction that gives the lower set of numbers. Carbon 1 on the chain will be the carbon closer to the two substituents, the Br atom and the methyl group (CH_3—).

$$CH_3 — CH — CH_2 — CH_2 — C — CH_3 \qquad hexane$$
     6   5   4   3   2   1

Step 3   **Give the location and name of each substituent (alphabetical order) as a prefix to the name of the main chain.** The substituents, which are bromo and methyl groups, are listed in alphabetical order (bromo first, then methyl). A hyphen is placed between the number on the carbon chain and the substituent name. When there are two or more of the same substituent, a prefix (*di*, *tri*, *tetra*) is used in front of the name. Then commas are used to separate the numbers that designate the locations of the same substituent.

$$CH_3 — CH — CH_2 — CH_2 — C — CH_3 \qquad \text{2-bromo-2,5-dimethylhexane}$$
     6   5   4   3   2   1

STUDY CHECK 11.4

Give the IUPAC name for the following compound:

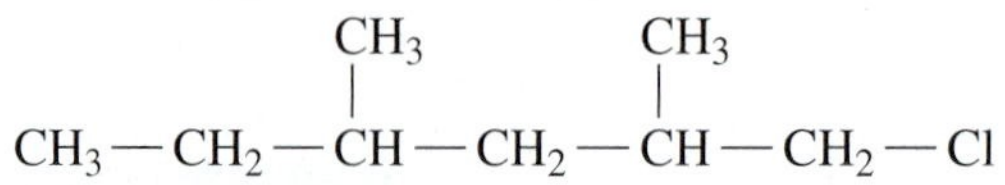

$$CH_3-CH_2-\underset{\underset{CH_3}{|}}{CH}-CH_2-\underset{\underset{CH_3}{|}}{CH}-CH_2-Cl$$

TUTORIAL
Naming Cycloalkanes

Naming Cycloalkanes with Substituents

When one substituent is attached to a carbon atom in a ring, the name of the substituent is placed in front of the cycloalkane name. No number is needed when a single alkyl group or halogen atom is attached to the cycloalkane. However, if two or more substituents are attached, the ring is numbered by assigning carbon 1 to the substituent that comes first alphabetically. Then we count the carbon atoms in the ring in the direction (clockwise or counterclockwise) that gives the lower numbers to the substituents.

Career Focus

GEOLOGIST

A geologist is interested in how the Earth was formed and its resources and uses chemistry to determine oil and reservoir formation. Other geologists map the surface of the Earth, study fossils and the age of rocks, and study the environmental impact of buildings and roads.

Methylcyclopentane

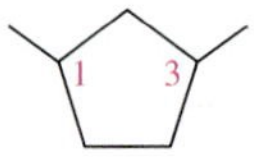

1,3-Dimethylcyclopentane

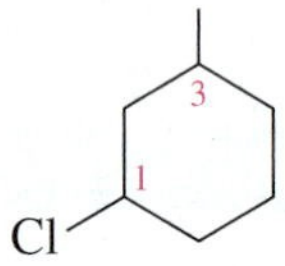

1-Chloro-3-methylcyclohexane

Drawing Structural Formulas for Alkanes

The IUPAC name gives all the information needed to draw the condensed structural formula for an alkane. Suppose you are asked to draw the condensed structural formula for 2,3-dimethylbutane. The alkane name gives the number of carbon atoms in the longest chain. The names in the beginning indicate the substituents and where they are attached. We can break down the name in the following way:

2,3-Dimethylbutane

2,3-	di	methyl	but	ane
Substituents on carbons 2 and 3	Two identical groups	CH_3— alkyl groups	4 carbon atoms in the main chain	C—C single bonds

Guide to Drawing Alkane Formulas

1 Draw the main chain of carbon atoms.

2 Number the chain and place the substituents on the carbons indicated by the numbers.

3 Add the correct number of hydrogen atoms to give four bonds to each C atom.

SAMPLE PROBLEM 11.5   **Drawing Condensed Structural and Skeletal Formulas from IUPAC Names**

Draw the condensed structural formula and skeletal formula for 2,3-dimethylbutane.

SOLUTION

Step 1   **Draw the main chain of carbon atoms.** For butane, we draw a chain of four carbon atoms. For the skeletal formula, show bond lines.

C—C—C—C

Step 2   **Number the chain and place the substituents on the carbons indicated by the numbers.** The first part of the name indicates two methyl groups (CH_3—), one on carbon 2 and one on carbon 3.

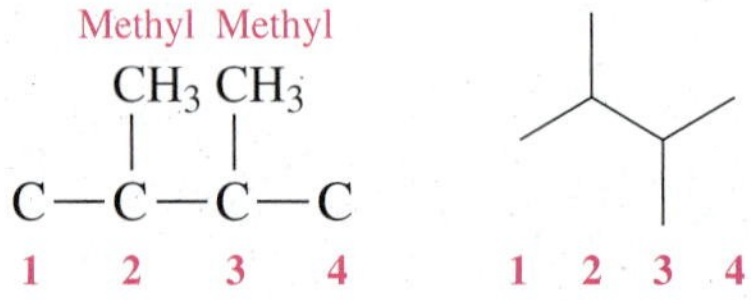

Methyl Methyl
$$\underset{1\quad\;2\quad\;3\quad\;4}{\overset{\overset{CH_3}{|}\;\overset{CH_3}{|}}{C-C-C-C}}$$

1 2 3 4

Step 3 **Add the correct number of hydrogen atoms to give fur bonds to each C atom.**

$$CH_3-CH-CH-CH_3$$

2,3-Dimethylbutane

STUDY CHECK 11.5

Draw the condensed structural formula and skeletal formula for 2-bromo-4-methylpentane.

Chemistry Link to the Environment

CFCS AND OZONE DEPLETION

The compounds called *chlorofluorocarbons* (CFCs) were used as propellants for hairsprays, underarm deodorants, and paints, and as refrigerants in home and car air conditioners. Two widely used CFCs, Freon 11 (CCl_3F) and Freon 12 (CCl_2F_2), were developed during the 1920s as nontoxic refrigerants, which were safer than the sulfur dioxide and ammonia used at the time.

Freon was used as a propellant for sprays.

Freon is added to the air conditioner unit in a car by a licensed automotive technician.

$$Cl-C-F$$
$$\quad\;\; Cl$$

Freon 11

$$F-C-F$$
$$\quad\;\; Cl$$

Freon 12

In the stratosphere, a layer of ozone (O_3) absorbs the ultraviolet (UV) radiation of the Sun and acts as a protective shield for plants and animals on Earth. Ozone is produced in the stratosphere when oxygen reacts with ultraviolet light and breaks into oxygen atoms that quickly combine with oxygen molecules to form ozone.

$$O_2 \xrightarrow{\text{UV light}} O + O$$
$$O_2 + O \longrightarrow O_3$$

During the 1970s, scientists became concerned that CFCs entering the atmosphere were accelerating the depletion of ozone and threatening the stability of the ozone layer. CFCs decompose in the upper atmosphere in the presence of UV light to produce highly reactive chlorine atoms.

$$CCl_3F \xrightarrow{\text{UV light}} CCl_2F + Cl$$

The reactive chlorine atoms catalyze the breakdown of ozone molecules.

$$Cl + O_3 \longrightarrow ClO + O_2$$
$$ClO + O_3 \longrightarrow Cl + 2O_2$$

It has been estimated that one chlorine atom, also called a *radical*, can destroy as many as 100 000 ozone molecules. Normally, there is a balance between the ozone and oxygen in the atmosphere, but the rapid destruction of ozone has upset that equilibrium. Reports of polar ozone depletion over Antarctica in March 1985 prompted scientists to call for a freeze on the production of CFCs. In some areas, as much as 50% of the ozone had been depleted, causing an ozone hole to appear at certain times of the year. There is evidence of thinning in the ozone layer over the Arctic as well, but to a somewhat lesser degree due to warmer temperatures. It is interesting that in the lower atmosphere, ozone is an automobile and industrial pollutant, but in the stratosphere, ozone is a life-protecting compound.

Today, the use of CFCs as a propellant has been phased out. However, it is still used in closed systems such as home and car air conditioning units. Then it is necessary that the CFCs are handled by a licensed technician. It is expected that ozone levels will remain low for several decades due to the stability of the current level of CFCs. Chemical companies are developing substitutes for CFCs that are not as damaging to the ozone layer. Replacement compounds such as hydrochlorofluorocarbons (HCFCs) contain chlorine atoms, but these compounds break down in the lower atmosphere, reducing the amount of chlorine that reaches the stratosphere. Hydrofluorocarbons

(HFCs), which contain no chlorine, are being considered as another replacement for CFCs. However, the potential effects of fluorine compounds on ozone destruction must still be determined.

The level of ozone, which protects life on Earth, is lowest over Antarctica. The seasonal decrease in the ozone layer above Antarctica allows increased amounts of UV light to reach Earth's surface. The size of the ozone hole or depleted ozone region was greatest in December 2000, but has retreated (closed up) in more recent years.

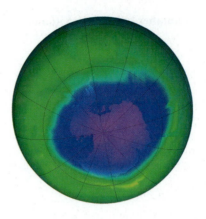

In the satellite image, the lowest levels of ozone, in blue, are over Antarctica.

QUESTIONS AND PROBLEMS

11.3 Alkanes with Substituents

LEARNING GOAL: *Write the IUPAC names and draw the condensed structural formulas and skeletal formulas for alkanes.*

11.15 Indicate whether each of the following pairs of condensed structural formulas represent structural isomers or the same molecule:

a. 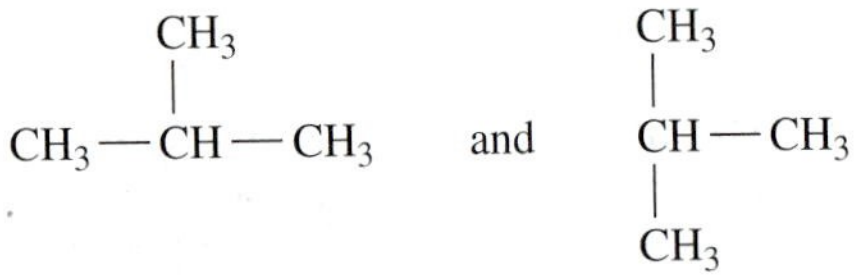 $CH_3-CH-CH_3$ (with CH_3 above CH) and $CH-CH_3$ (with CH_3 above and CH_3 below CH)

b. 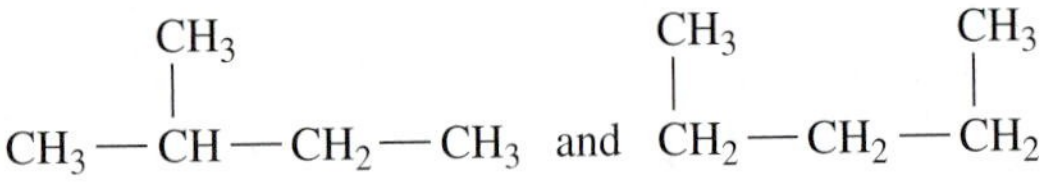 $CH_3-CH-CH_2-CH_3$ (with CH_3 above CH) and $CH_2-CH_2-CH_2$ (with CH_3 above)

c. 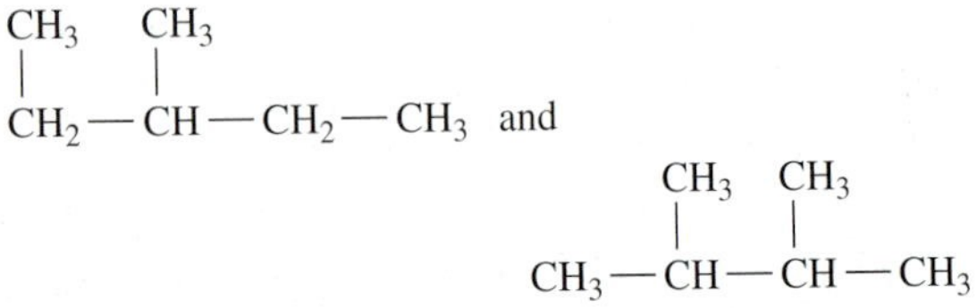 $CH_2-CH-CH_2-CH_3$ (with CH_3 above both CH groups) and

$CH_3-CH-CH-CH_3$ (with CH_3 above both CH groups)

11.16 Indicate whether each of the following pairs of condensed structural formulas represent structural isomers or the same molecule:

a. 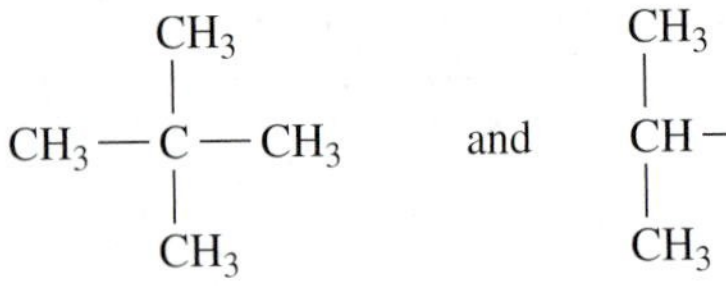 CH_3-C-CH_3 (with CH_3 above and CH_3 below C) and $CH-CH_2-CH_3$ (with CH_3 above and CH_3 below CH)

b. $CH_3-CH-CH-CH_2$ (with CH_3 above each) and

$CH_3-CH-CH_2-CH-CH_3$ (with CH_3 above the two CH groups)

c. $CH_3-CH-CH_2-CH_3$ (with CH_3 above CH) and

$CH_3-CH_2-CH-CH_3$ (with CH_3 above CH)

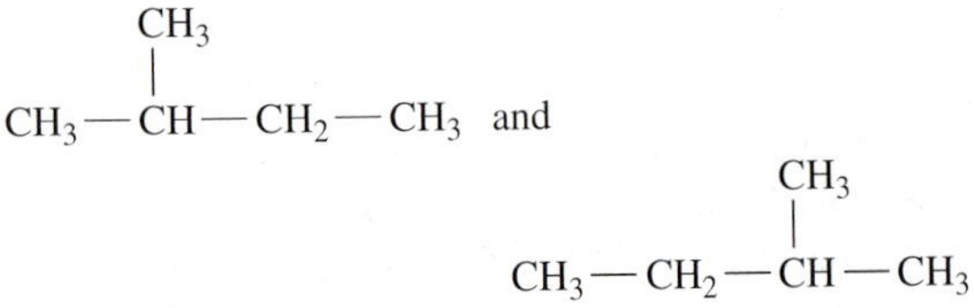

11.17 Give the IUPAC name for each of the following:

a. $CH_3-CH_2-CH_2-F$

b.

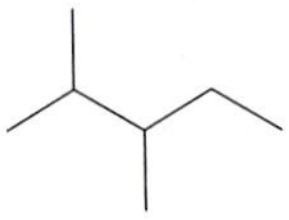

c. 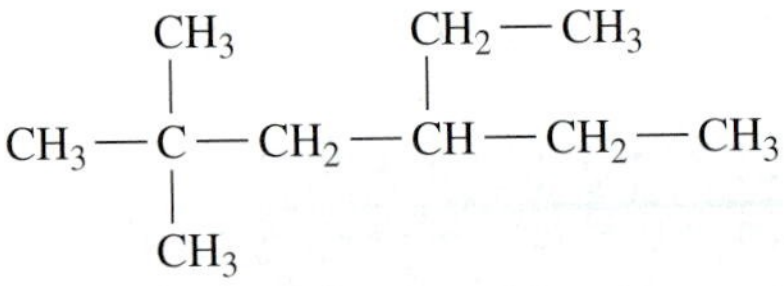 $CH_3-C-CH_2-CH-CH_2-CH_3$ (with CH_3 above and CH_3 below C; with CH_2-CH_3 above CH)

d.  [cyclopentane with Cl]

e. 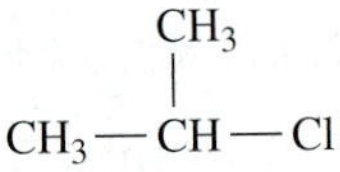 $CH_3-CH-Cl$ (with CH_3 above CH)

f. 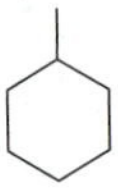 [cyclohexane]

11.18 Give the IUPAC name for each of the following:

a.

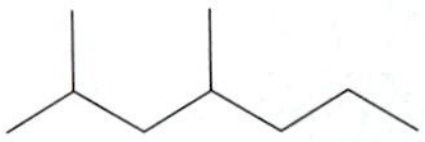

b. 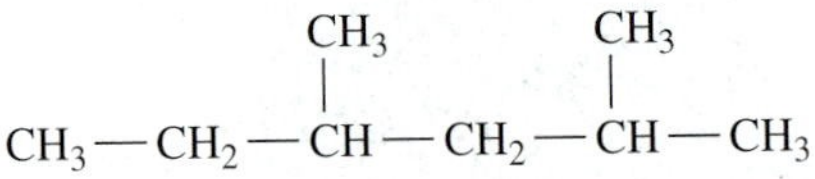 $CH_3-CH_2-CH-CH_2-CH-CH_3$ (with CH_3 above each CH)

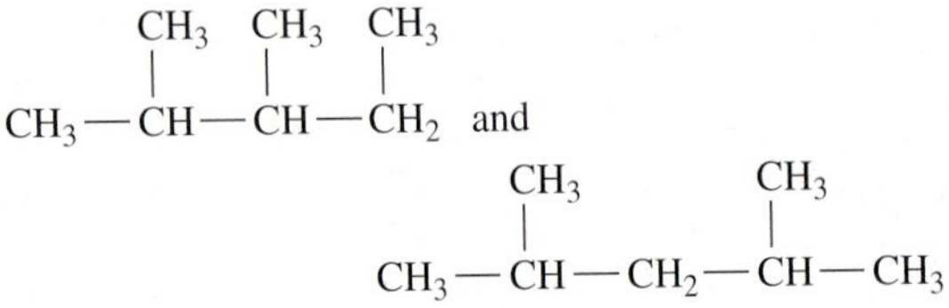

c. 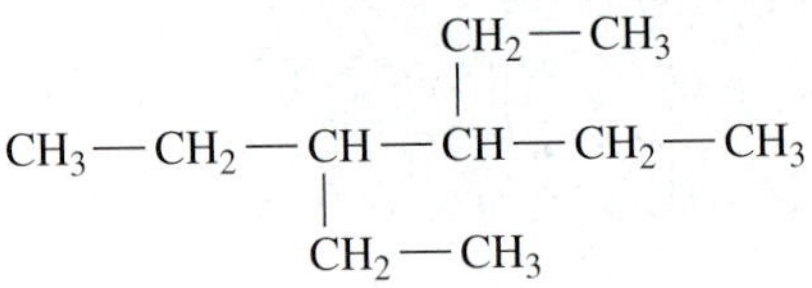 $CH_3-CH_2-CH-CH-CH_2-CH_3$ (with CH_2-CH_3 above the third carbon and CH_2-CH_3 below the fourth carbon)

d. 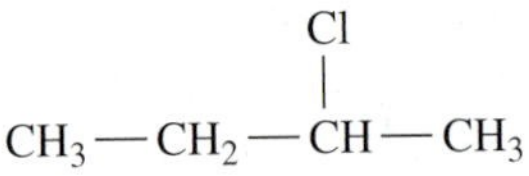 $CH_3-CH_2-CH-CH_3$ (with Cl above CH)

e. 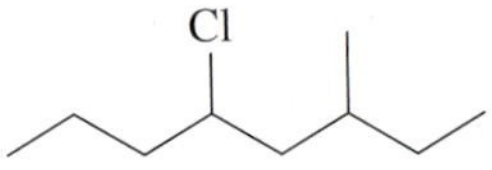 [skeletal structure with Cl]

f. 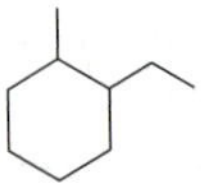 [cyclohexane with ethyl and methyl substituents]

11.19 Draw the condensed structural formula for each of the following:
  a. 1-bromo-3-chloropropane
  b. 3,3-dimethylpentane
  c. 2,3,5-trimethylhexane
  d. 3-ethyl-2,5-dimethyloctane
  e. 1,2-dibromoethane

11.20 Draw the condensed structural formula for each of the following:
  a. 3-ethylpentane
  b. 2,2,3,5-tetramethylhexane
  c. 4-ethyl-2,2-dimethyloctane
  d. 1,1,2,2-tetrabromopropane
  e. 2,3-dichloro-2-methylbutane

11.21 Draw the skeletal formula for each of the following:
  a. methylcyclopropane
  b. 2-chloro-2-methylhexane
  c. 2,3-dimethylheptane
  d. 1-bromo-2,3-dimethylcyclopentane
  e. 3-chloro-2-methylpentane

11.22 Draw the skeletal formula for each of the following:
  a. 1,5-dibromo-3-methylheptane
  b. ethylcyclohexane
  c. 1,2-dichlorocyclobutane
  d. 1,1,5-trichloropentane
  e. 2,2,3-trimethylheptane

11.4 Properties of Alkanes

LEARNING GOAL

Identify the properties of alkanes, and write chemical equations for combustion.

Many types of alkanes are the components of fuels that power our cars and oil that heats our homes. You may have used a mixture of hydrocarbons such as mineral oil as a laxative, or petrolatum (Vaseline) to soften your skin. The differences in uses of many of the alkanes result from their physical properties, including solubility, density, and boiling point.

Some Uses of Alkanes

The first four alkanes with 1 to 4 carbon atoms—methane, ethane, propane, and butane—are gases at room temperature and are widely used as heating fuels.

Alkanes having 5 to 8 carbon atoms (pentane, hexane, heptane, and octane) are liquids at room temperature. They are highly volatile, which makes them useful in fuels such as gasoline.

Liquid alkanes with 9 to 17 carbon atoms have higher boiling points and are found in kerosene, diesel, and jet fuels. Motor oil is a mixture of high-molecular-weight liquid hydrocarbons and is used to lubricate the internal components of engines. Mineral oil is a mixture of liquid hydrocarbons and is used as a laxative and a lubricant. Alkanes with 18 or more carbon atoms are waxy solids at room temperature. Larger alkanes, known as paraffins, are waxy solids used to coat fruits and vegetables to retain moisture, inhibit mold growth, and enhance appearance (see Figure 11.6). Petrolatum, or Vaseline, is a semisolid mixture of hydrocarbons with more than 25 carbon atoms used in ointments and cosmetics and as a lubricant and a solvent.

Solubility and Density

Alkanes are nonpolar, which makes them insoluble in water. However, they are soluble in nonpolar solvents such as other alkanes. Alkanes have densities from 0.62 g/mL to about 0.79 g/mL, which is less than the density of water (1.0 g/mL).

If there is an oil spill in the ocean, the alkanes in the oil, which do not mix with water, form a thin layer on the surface that spreads over a large area. In April 2010, an explosion on an oil-drilling rig in the Gulf of Mexico caused the largest oil spill in United States history. An estimated 10 million liters of oil was leaked every day, from April until July. Other major oil spills occurred in Queensland, Australia (2009), the coast of Wales (1996), the Shetland Islands (1993), and Alaska, from the *Exxon Valdez*, in 1989 (see Figure 11.7). If the crude oil reaches land, there can be considerable damage to beaches, shellfish, fish, birds, and wildlife habitats. When animals such as birds are covered with oil, they must be cleaned quickly because ingestion of the hydrocarbons when they try to clean themselves is fatal.

Cleanup of oil spills includes mechanical, chemical, and microbiological methods. A boom may be placed around the leaking oil to contain it until it can be removed. Boats

CASE STUDY
Hazardous Materials

FIGURE 11.6 The solid alkanes that make up waxy coatings on fruits and vegetables help retain moisture, inhibit mold, and enhance appearance.

Q Why does the waxy coating help the fruits and vegetables retain moisture?

FIGURE 11.7 In oil spills, large quantities of oil spread over the surface of the water.

Q What physical properties cause oil to remain on the surface of water?

called skimmers then scoop up the oil and place it in tanks. A chemical method involves a substance that attracts oil, which is then scraped into recovery tanks. Certain bacteria that ingest oil are used to break oil down into less harmful products.

Melting and Boiling Points

Alkanes have the lowest melting and boiling points of all the organic compounds. This occurs because alkanes contain only the nonpolar bonds of C—C and C—H. Therefore, the attractions that occur between alkane molecules in the solid and liquid states are due to relatively weak dispersion forces. As the number of carbon atoms increases, there is also an increase in the number of electrons, which increases the attraction due to dispersion forces. Thus, alkanes with higher masses have higher melting and boiling points.

CH_4 CH_3—CH_3 CH_3—CH_2—CH_3 CH_3—CH_2—CH_2—CH_3 CH_3—CH_2—CH_2—CH_2—CH_3

Methane   Ethane   Propane   Butane   Pentane

bp = −164 °C   bp = −89 °C   bp = −42 °C   bp = 0.5 °C   bp = 36 °C

Increase in Number of Carbon Atoms
Increase in Boiling Point

The boiling points of branched alkanes are generally lower than the straight-chain isomers. The branched-chain alkanes tend to be more compact, which reduces the points of contact between the molecules. In an analogy, we can think of the carbon chains of straight-chain alkanes as pieces of licorice in a package. Because they have linear shapes, they can line up very close to each other, which gives many points of contact between the surface of the molecules. In our analogy, we can also think of branched alkanes as tennis balls in a can that, because of their spherical shapes, have only a small area of contact. One tennis ball represents an entire molecule. Because branched alkanes have fewer attractions, they have lower melting and boiling points.

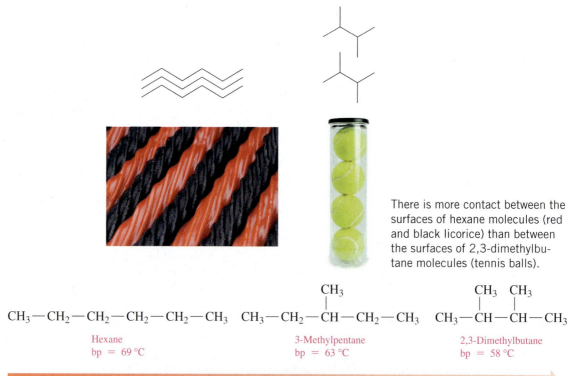

There is more contact between the surfaces of hexane molecules (red and black licorice) than between the surfaces of 2,3-dimethylbutane molecules (tennis balls).

CH_3—CH_2—CH_2—CH_2—CH_2—CH_3 CH_3—CH_2—$\overset{\displaystyle CH_3}{\underset{|}{CH}}$—$CH_2$—$CH_3$ CH_3—$\overset{\displaystyle CH_3}{\underset{|}{CH}}$—$\overset{\displaystyle CH_3}{\underset{|}{CH}}$—$CH_3$

Hexane   3-Methylpentane   2,3-Dimethylbutane

bp = 69 °C   bp = 63 °C   bp = 58 °C

Increase in Number of Branches
Decrease in Boiling Point

Cycloalkanes have higher boiling points than the straight-chain alkanes with the same number of carbon atoms. Because rotation of carbon bonds is restricted, cycloalkanes maintain a rigid structure. Cycloalkanes with their rigid structures can be stacked closely together, which gives them many points of contact and therefore many attractions to each other.

We can compare the boiling points of straight-chain alkanes, branched-chain alkanes, and cycloalkanes with five carbon atoms as shown in Table 11.6.

TABLE 11.6 Comparison of Boiling Points of Alkanes and Cycloalkanes with Five Carbons

Formula	Name	Boiling Point (°C)
Straight-Chain Alkane		
$CH_3-CH_2-CH_2-CH_2-CH_3$	Pentane	36
Branched-Chain Alkanes		
$CH_3-\overset{\overset{\displaystyle CH_3}{\mid}}{CH}-CH_2-CH_3$	2-Methylbutane	28
$CH_3-\overset{\overset{\displaystyle CH_3}{\mid}}{\underset{\underset{\displaystyle CH_3}{\mid}}{C}}-CH_3$	Dimethylpropane	10
Cycloalkane		
	Cyclopentane	49

TUTORIAL
Writing Balanced Equations for Combustion of Alkanes

CASE STUDY
Poison in the Home: Carbon Monoxide

Combustion of Alkanes

The carbon–carbon single bonds in alkanes are difficult to break, which makes them the least reactive family of organic compounds. However, alkanes burn readily in oxygen. As we discussed in Section 6.2, a carbon-containing compound, such as an alkane, undergoes **combustion** when it reacts completely with oxygen to produce carbon dioxide, water, and energy.

$$\text{Alkane}(g) + O_2(g) \xrightarrow{\Delta} CO_2(g) + H_2O(g) + \text{energy}$$

For example, methane is the gas we use to cook our food and heat our homes. The equation for the combustion of methane (CH_4) is written:

$$CH_4(g) + 2O_2(g) \xrightarrow{\Delta} CO_2(g) + 2H_2O(g) + \text{energy}$$
Methane

In another example, propane is the gas used in portable heaters and gas barbecues (see Figure 11.8). The equation for the combustion of propane (C_3H_8) is written:

$$C_3H_8(g) + 5O_2(g) \xrightarrow{\Delta} 3CO_2(g) + 4H_2O(g) + \text{energy}$$
Propane

In the cells of our bodies, energy is produced by the combustion of glucose. Although a series of reactions is involved, we can write the overall combustion of glucose in our cells as follows:

$$C_6H_{12}O_6(aq) + 6O_2(g) \xrightarrow{\text{Enzymes}} 6CO_2(g) + 6H_2O(l) + \text{energy}$$
Glucose

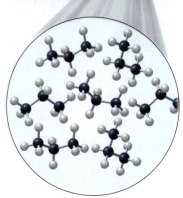

FIGURE 11.8 The propane fuel in the tank undergoes combustion, which provides energy.

Q What is the balanced equation for the combustion of propane?

Explore Your World

COMBUSTION

In this exploration, we will look at the behavior of the products of combustion. You will need one or two candles, a Pyrex glass such as a measuring cup, and some matches or wooden splints.

Hold a Pyrex cup upside down, and insert a burning match inside it. The match will continue to burn as long as oxygen is available. Light a candle and hold the inverted Pyrex cup above it for 15–20 seconds. Remove the cup from the candle and immediately insert a burning match inside it. The CO_2 accumulated from the combustion of the candle should extinguish the match.

Add some water and a lot of ice to the same Pyrex cup. It should become cold to the touch. Wipe the bottom of the cup and carefully hold the bottom of the Pyrex cup over a burning candle. Look for the formation of liquid water on the outside of the Pyrex cup.

QUESTIONS

1. What are the products of combustion of candle wax?
2. What was the evidence for the production of CO_2?
3. What observations gave evidence for the production of water during combustion?

CONCEPT CHECK 11.6 **Completing and Balancing Combustion Equations**

A portable burner is fueled with butane. Write the balanced equation for the complete combustion of butane.

ANSWER

Butane is an alkane with 4 C atoms and 10 H atoms, which gives a molecular formula of C_4H_{10}. In the combustion reaction, butane reacts with oxygen to form carbon dioxide, water, and energy. We write the unbalanced equation as:

$$C_4H_{10}(g) + O_2(g) \xrightarrow{\Delta} CO_2(g) + H_2O(g) + energy$$

We can begin by balancing the C atoms and H atoms in the products with the C_4H_{10}. However, we notice this gives an odd number (13) of O atoms.

$$C_4H_{10}(g) + O_2(g) \xrightarrow{\Delta} 4CO_2(g) + 5H_2O(g) + energy$$

Thus, we double the number of C_4H_{10} molecules, which gives the balanced equation for the combustion of butane.

$$2C_4H_{10}(g) + 13O_2(g) \xrightarrow{\Delta} 8CO_2(g) + 10H_2O(g) + energy$$

When camping, a butane cartridge provides fuel for a portable burner.

Chemistry Link to Health

TOXICITY OF CARBON MONOXIDE

When a propane heater, fireplace, or wood stove is used in a closed room, there must be adequate ventilation. If the supply of oxygen is limited, *incomplete combustion* from burning gas, oil, or wood produces carbon monoxide. The incomplete combustion of methane in natural gas is written as follows:

$$2CH_4(g) + 3O_2(g) \xrightarrow{\Delta} 2CO(g) + 4H_2O(g) + energy$$

Limited oxygen supply   Carbon monoxide

Carbon monoxide (CO) is a colorless, odorless, poisonous gas. When inhaled, CO passes into the bloodstream, where it binds to the iron in hemoglobin, which reduces the amount of oxygen (O_2) reaching the cells. As a result, a healthy person can experience a reduction in exercise capability, visual perception, and manual dexterity.

Hemoglobin is the protein that transports O_2 in the blood. When the amount of hemoglobin bound to CO (COHb) is about 10 percent, a person may experience shortness of breath, mild headache, and drowsiness. Heavy smokers can have levels of COHb in their blood as high as 9 percent. When as much as 30 percent of the hemoglobin is bound to CO, a person may experience more severe symptoms, including dizziness, mental confusion, severe headache, and nausea. If 50 percent or more of the hemoglobin is bound to CO, a person could become unconscious and die if not treated immediately with oxygen.

Chemistry Link to Industry

CRUDE OIL

Crude oil, or petroleum, contains a wide variety of hydrocarbons. At an oil refinery, the components in crude oil are separated by *fractional distillation*, a process that removes groups or fractions of hydrocarbons by continually heating the mixture to higher temperatures (see Table 11.7). Fractions containing alkanes with longer carbon chains require higher temperatures before they reach their boiling point and form gases. The gases are removed and passed through a distillation column where they cool and condense back to liquids. The major use of crude oil is to obtain gasoline, which makes up about 35 percent of crude oil. To increase the production of gasoline, larger alkanes are broken down using specialized catalysts to give the lower-weight alkanes.

TABLE 11.7 Typical Alkane Mixtures Obtained by Distillation of Crude Oil

Distillation Temperatures (°C)	Number of Carbon Atoms	Product
Below 30	1–4	Natural gas
30–200	5–12	Gasoline
200–250	12–16	Kerosene, jet fuel
250–350	16–18	Diesel fuel, heating oil
350–450	18–25	Lubricating oil
Nonvolatile residue	Over 25	Asphalt, tar

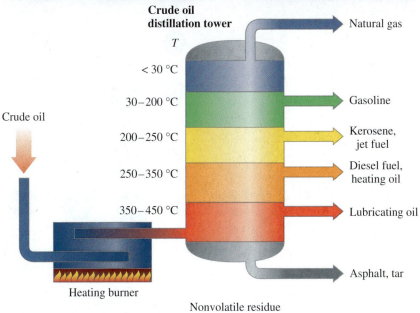

QUESTIONS AND PROBLEMS

11.4 Properties of Alkanes

LEARNING GOAL: *Identify the properties of alkanes, and write chemical equations for combustion.*

11.23 Heptane, used as a solvent for rubber cement, has a density of 0.68 g/mL and boils at 98 °C.
   a. Draw the condensed structural formula and skeletal formula for heptane.
   b. Is heptane a solid, liquid, or gas at room temperature?
   c. Is heptane soluble in water?
   d. Will heptane float or sink in water?
   e. Write the balanced chemical equation for the complete combustion of heptane.

11.24 Nonane has a density of 0.72 g/mL and boils at 151 °C.
   a. Draw the condensed structural formula and skeletal formula for nonane.
   b. Is nonane a solid, liquid, or gas at room temperature?
   c. Is nonane soluble in water?
   d. Will nonane float or sink in water?

   e. Write the balanced chemical equation for the complete combustion of nonane.

11.25 In each of the following pairs of hydrocarbons, which one would you expect to have the higher boiling point?
   a. pentane or heptane   **b.** propane or cyclopropane
   c. hexane or 2-methylpentane

11.26 In each of the following pairs of hydrocarbons, which one would you expect to have the higher boiling point?
   a. propane or butane   **b.** hexane or cyclohexane
   c. 2,2-dimethylpentane or heptane

11.27 Write the balanced equation for the complete combustion of each of the following compounds:
   a. ethane   **b.** octane   **c.** cyclohexane, C_6H_{12}

11.28 Write the balanced equation for the complete combustion of each of the following compounds:
   a. hexane   **b.** cyclopentane, C_5H_{10}
   c. 2-methylbutane

11.5 Functional Groups

In organic compounds, carbon atoms are most likely to bond with nonmetals such as hydrogen, oxygen, nitrogen, sulfur, phosphorus, and halogens. Table 11.8 lists the number of covalent bonds most often formed by these elements in order to achieve a complete set of valence electrons. Hydrogen and the halogens form one covalent bond, and carbon forms four covalent bonds. Nitrogen forms three covalent bonds, whereas oxygen and sulfur each form two covalent bonds.

TABLE 11.8 Covalent Bonds for Elements in Organic Compounds

Element	Group	Covalent Bonds	Structure of Atoms	Representation of Atoms
H	1A (1)	1	—H	H atom
C	4A (14)	4	$-\overset{\mid}{\underset{\mid}{C}}-$	C atom
N, P	5A (15)	3	$-\overset{\mid}{\underset{\cdot\cdot}{N}}-$ $-\overset{\mid}{\underset{\cdot\cdot}{P}}-$	N atom P atom
O, S	6A (16)	2	$-\overset{\cdot\cdot}{\underset{\cdot\cdot}{O}}-$ $-\overset{\cdot\cdot}{\underset{\cdot\cdot}{S}}-$	O atom S atom
F, Cl, Br, I	7A (17)	1	$-\overset{\cdot\cdot}{\underset{\cdot\cdot}{X}}:$ (X = F, Cl, Br, I)	F atom Cl atom Br atom I atom

Organic compounds number in the millions, and more are synthesized every day. We organize many of the organic compounds by their **functional groups**, which are groups of atoms bonded in a specific way. Compounds that contain the same functional

group have similar chemical and physical properties. The identification of functional groups allows us to classify organic compounds according to their structure, to name compounds within each family, and to predict their chemical reactions. We can predict the behavior of organic compounds from just their functional groups rather than the carbon chains to which they are attached. We will focus on recognizing the patterns of atoms that make up each of the functional groups, which we will discuss in more detail in the following chapters.

Alkenes, Alkynes, and Aromatic Compounds

In the hydrocarbon family, there are also *alkenes*, *alkynes*, and *aromatics*. An **alkene** contains one or more double bonds between carbon atoms; an **alkyne** contains a triple bond. Compounds that contain benzene are called **aromatic** compounds. Benzene is a molecule that has a ring of six carbon atoms with one hydrogen atom attached to each carbon. The benzene structure is represented as a hexagon with a circle in the center.

Alkene

Alkyne

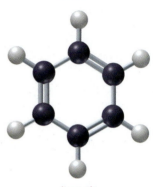

Aromatic

Functional Group	$\diagdown C{=}C \diagup$	$-C{\equiv}C-$
Condensed Structural Formula	$H_2C{=}CH_2$	$HC{\equiv}CH$
	Alkene	Alkyne

Aromatic (functional group hexagon)

Aromatic (condensed structural formula hexagon)

Alcohols, Thiols, and Ethers

The characteristic functional group in an **alcohol** is the *hydroxyl group* ($-OH$) bonded to a carbon atom of an alkane chain. The characteristic functional group found in a **thiol** is the *thiol group* ($-SH$) bonded to a carbon atom in an alkane chain. The characteristic structural feature of an **ether** is an oxygen atom ($-O-$) bonded to two carbon atoms of two alkyl groups.

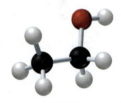

Alcohol

Functional Group	$-OH$	$-SH$	$-O-$
Condensed Structural Formula	CH_3-CH_2-OH	CH_3-CH_2-SH	CH_3-O-CH_3
	Alcohol	Thiol	Ether

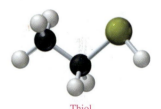

Thiol

Ether

Aldehydes and Ketones

Aldehydes and ketones are organic classes of compounds that contain a **carbonyl group** ($C{=}O$), which is made up of a carbon atom with a double bond to an oxygen atom. In an **aldehyde**, the functional group is the carbonyl group bonded to an H atom, which means the carbonyl group is always the first carbon. Only the simplest aldehyde, HCHO, has a carbonyl group attached to two hydrogen atoms. In a **ketone**, the functional group is the carbonyl bonded to the carbon atoms of two alkyl groups.

Aldehyde

Ketone

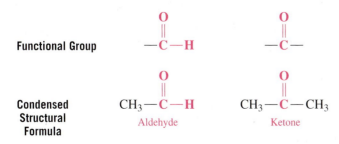

Functional Group	$\overset{\displaystyle O}{\underset{\parallel}{-C}}-H$	$\overset{\displaystyle O}{\underset{\parallel}{-C}}-$
Condensed Structural Formula	$\overset{\displaystyle O}{CH_3-\overset{\parallel}{C}-H}$	$\overset{\displaystyle O}{CH_3-\overset{\parallel}{C}-CH_3}$
	Aldehyde	Ketone

CONCEPT CHECK 11.7 Identifying Functional Groups

Highlight the functional group in each of the following and give the name of the class (family) of organic compounds that contains this functional group:

a. $CH_3-CH_2-CH_2-OH$

b. $CH_3-C\equiv C-CH_3$

c. $CH_3-CH_2-\overset{\overset{\displaystyle O}{\|}}{C}-CH_2-CH_3$

d. $CH_3-\overset{\overset{\displaystyle SH}{|}}{CH}-CH_3$

ANSWER

a. $CH_3-CH_2-CH_2-\boxed{OH}$

When the hydroxyl functional group (—OH), is attached to an alkane chain, the compound is classified as an alcohol.

b. $CH_3-\boxed{C\equiv C}-CH_3$

Because this compound contains a triple bond functional group, it is classified as an alkyne.

c. $CH_3-CH_2-\overset{\overset{\displaystyle O}{\|}}{\boxed{C}}-CH_2-CH_3$

Because the carbon atom of a carbonyl group (C=O) is attached to two alkyl groups, this compound is classified as a ketone.

d. $CH_3-\overset{\overset{\displaystyle \boxed{SH}}{|}}{CH}-CH_3$

Because the functional group —SH is attached to an alkane chain, this compound is classified as a thiol.

Carboxylic Acids and Esters

In the organic class of compounds known as **carboxylic acids**, the characteristic functional group is the *carboxyl group*, which is a combination of a carbonyl group (C=O) and a hydroxyl group (—OH). In a carboxylic acid, the first carbon atom in the chain is the carbon in the carboxyl group.

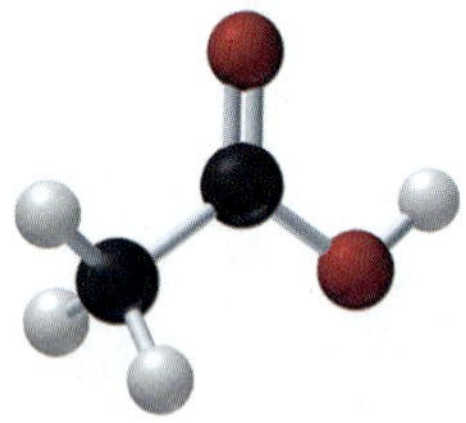

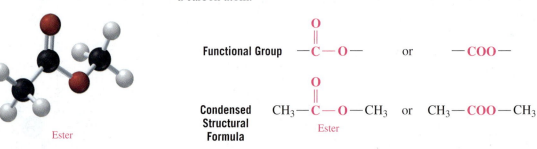

Functional Group $-\overset{\overset{\displaystyle O}{\|}}{C}-OH$ or $-COOH$

Condensed Structural Formula $CH_3-\overset{\overset{\displaystyle O}{\|}}{C}-OH$ or CH_3-COOH

Carboxylic acid

The organic group of compounds known as **esters** has a functional group that is similar to the carboxyl group in carboxylic acids, except that the carboxyl group is attached to a carbon atom.

Functional Group $-\overset{\overset{\displaystyle O}{\|}}{C}-O-$ or $-COO-$

Condensed Structural Formula $CH_3-\overset{\overset{\displaystyle O}{\|}}{C}-O-CH_3$ or $CH_3-COO-CH_3$

Ester

Carboxylic acid

Ester

Amines and Amides

In the class of organic compounds called **amines**, the characteristic functional group is a nitrogen atom bonded to one, two, or three alkyl groups.

Functional group $-\overset{|}{\underset{|}{N}}-$

Condensed Structural Formula CH_3-NH_2 $\quad CH_3-\underset{\displaystyle |\atop CH_3}{NH}$ $\quad CH_3-\underset{\displaystyle |\atop CH_3}{N}-CH_3$

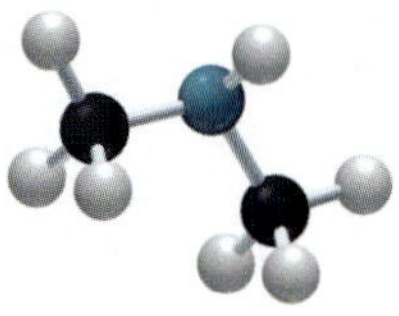

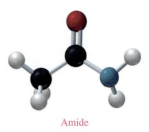

Amine

The organic class of compounds called **amides** is closely related to the amines. In an amide, the carbonyl group is attached to a nitrogen atom.

Functional Group $-\overset{\displaystyle O\atop \|}{C}-\overset{|}{N}-$

Condensed Structural Formula $CH_3-\overset{\displaystyle O\atop \|}{C}-NH_2$

Amide

Amide

CONCEPT CHECK 11.8 The Amine Functional Group

Describe the functional group found in amines.

ANSWER

The amine functional group has a nitrogen atom bonded to one, two, or three carbon atoms.

SAMPLE PROBLEM 11.6 Identifying Functional Groups

Classify the following organic compounds according to their functional groups:

a. $CH_3-CH_2-NH-CH_3$

b. $CH_3-\overset{\displaystyle O\atop \|}{C}-O-CH_2-CH_3$

c. $CH_3-CH_2-\overset{\displaystyle O\atop \|}{C}-OH$

SOLUTION

a. amine
b. ester
c. carboxylic acid

STUDY CHECK 11.6

Why is $CH_3-CH_2-O-CH_3$ an ether?

A list of the common functional groups in organic compounds is shown in Table 11.9.

TABLE 11.9 Classification of Organic Compounds

Class	Functional Group	Example
Alkene	$\diagdown C = C \diagup$	$H_2C = CH_2$
Alkyne	$-C \equiv C-$	$HC \equiv CH$
Aromatic	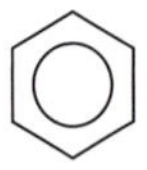 (benzene ring)	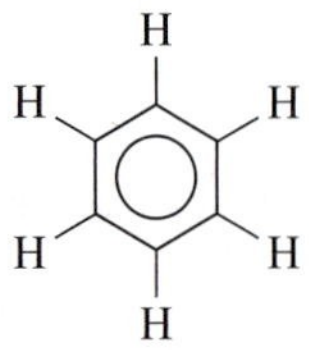 (benzene ring with H's)
Alcohol	$-OH$	CH_3-CH_2-OH
Thiol	$-SH$	CH_3-SH
Ether	$-O-$	CH_3-O-CH_3
Aldehyde	$\overset{O}{\overset{\|}{-C-H}}$	$CH_3-\overset{O}{\overset{\|}{C}}-H$
Ketone	$\overset{O}{\overset{\|}{-C-}}$	$CH_3-\overset{O}{\overset{\|}{C}}-CH_3$
Carboxylic acid	$\overset{O}{\overset{\|}{-C-OH}}$	$CH_3-\overset{O}{\overset{\|}{C}}-OH$
Ester	$\overset{O}{\overset{\|}{-C-O-}}$	$CH_3-\overset{O}{\overset{\|}{C}}-O-CH_3$
Amine	$-\overset{\|}{N}-$	CH_3-NH_2
Amide	$\overset{O}{\overset{\|}{-C-}}\overset{\|}{N}-$	$CH_3-\overset{O}{\overset{\|}{C}}-NH_2$

TUTORIAL
Drawing Organic Compounds with
Functional Groups

Chemistry Link to the Environment

FUNCTIONAL GROUPS IN FAMILIAR COMPOUNDS

The flavors and odors of foods and many household products can be attributed to the functional groups of organic compounds. As we discuss these familiar products, look for the functional groups we have described.

Ethyl alcohol is the alcohol found in alcoholic beverages. Isopropyl alcohol is another alcohol commonly used to disinfect skin before giving injections and to treat cuts.

$$CH_3-CH_2-OH \qquad CH_3-\overset{OH}{\overset{\|}{CH}}-CH_3$$

Ethyl alcohol   Isopropyl alcohol

Acetone, or dimethyl ketone, is produced in great amounts commercially. Acetone is used as an organic solvent because it dissolves a wide variety of organic substances. You may be familiar with acetone as fingernail polish remover.

$$CH_3-\overset{O}{\overset{\|}{C}}-CH_3$$

Acetone

Ketones and aldehydes are found in flavorings such as vanilla, cinnamon, and spearmint. When we buy a small bottle of liquid flavoring, the aldehyde or ketone is dissolved in alcohol because the compounds are not very soluble in water. Formaldehyde, HCHO, the simplest aldehyde, is a colorless gas with a pungent odor. Industrially, it is a reactant in the synthesis of polymers used to make fabrics, insulation materials, carpeting, pressed wood products such as plywood, and plastics for kitchen counters. An aqueous solution called formalin, which contains 40% formaldehyde, is used as a germicide and to preserve biological specimens. The aldehyde butyraldehyde adds a buttery taste to foods and margarine.

$$CH_3 - CH_2 - CH_2 - \overset{\displaystyle O}{\overset{\|}{C}} - H$$
Butyraldehyde (butter flavoring)

The sour tastes of vinegar and fruit juices and the pain from ant stings are all due to carboxylic acids. Acetic acid is the carboxylic acid that makes up vinegar and formic acid is the carboxylic acid in ant stings. Aspirin also contains a carboxylic acid group. Esters found in fruits produce the pleasant aromas and tastes of bananas, oranges, pears, and pineapples. Esters are also used as solvents in many household cleaners, polishes, and glues.

One of the characteristics of fish is their odor, which is due to amines like methylamine. Amines produced when proteins decay have a particularly pungent and offensive odor, thus the descriptive names putrescine and cadaverine.

$$H_2N - CH_2 - CH_2 - CH_2 - CH_2 - NH_2$$
Putrescine

$$H_2N - CH_2 - CH_2 - CH_2 - CH_2 - CH_2 - NH_2$$
Cadaverine

$$CH_3 - \overset{\displaystyle O}{\overset{\|}{C}} - OH$$
Acetic acid (in vinegar)

$$CH_3 - \overset{\displaystyle O}{\overset{\|}{C}} - O - CH_2 - CH_2 - CH_2$$
Propyl acetate (pears)

$$CH_3 - NH_2$$
Methylamine

$$CH_3 - \overset{\displaystyle O}{\overset{\|}{C}} - O - CH_2 - CH_2 - CH_2 - CH_2 - CH_3$$
Pentyl acetate (bananas)

QUESTIONS AND PROBLEMS

11.5 Functional Groups

LEARNING GOAL: *Classify organic molecules according to their functional groups.*

11.29 Identify the class of compounds that contains each of the following functional groups:
  a. a hydroxyl group attached to a carbon chain
  b. a carbon–carbon double bond
  c. a carbonyl group attached to a hydrogen atom
  d. a carboxyl group attached to two carbon atoms

11.30 Identify the class of compounds that contains each of the following functional groups:
  a. a nitrogen atom attached to one or more carbon atoms
  b. a carboxyl group
  c. an oxygen atom bonded to two carbon atoms
  d. a carbonyl group between two carbon atoms

11.31 Classify the following molecules according to their functional groups. The possibilities are alcohol, ether, ketone, carboxylic acid, or amine.
  a. $CH_3 - CH_2 - O - CH_2 - CH_3$

  b. $CH_3 - \overset{\displaystyle OH}{\overset{|}{CH}} - CH_3$

  c. $CH_3 - \overset{\displaystyle O}{\overset{\|}{C}} - CH_2 - CH_3$
  d. $CH_3 - CH_2 - CH_2 - COOH$
  e. $CH_3 - CH_2 - NH_2$

11.32 Classify the following molecules according to their functional groups. The possibilities are alkene, aldehyde, carboxylic acid, ester, or amide.
  a. $CH_3 - CH_2 - \overset{\displaystyle O}{\overset{\|}{C}} - O - CH_2 - CH_3$
  b. $CH_3 - \overset{\displaystyle O}{\overset{\|}{C}} - NH_2$
  c. $CH_3 - CH_2 - CH_2 - \overset{\displaystyle O}{\overset{\|}{C}} - H$
  d. $CH_3 - CH_2 - CH_2 - CH_2 - COOH$
  e. $CH_3 - CH = CH - CH_3$

CONCEPT MAP

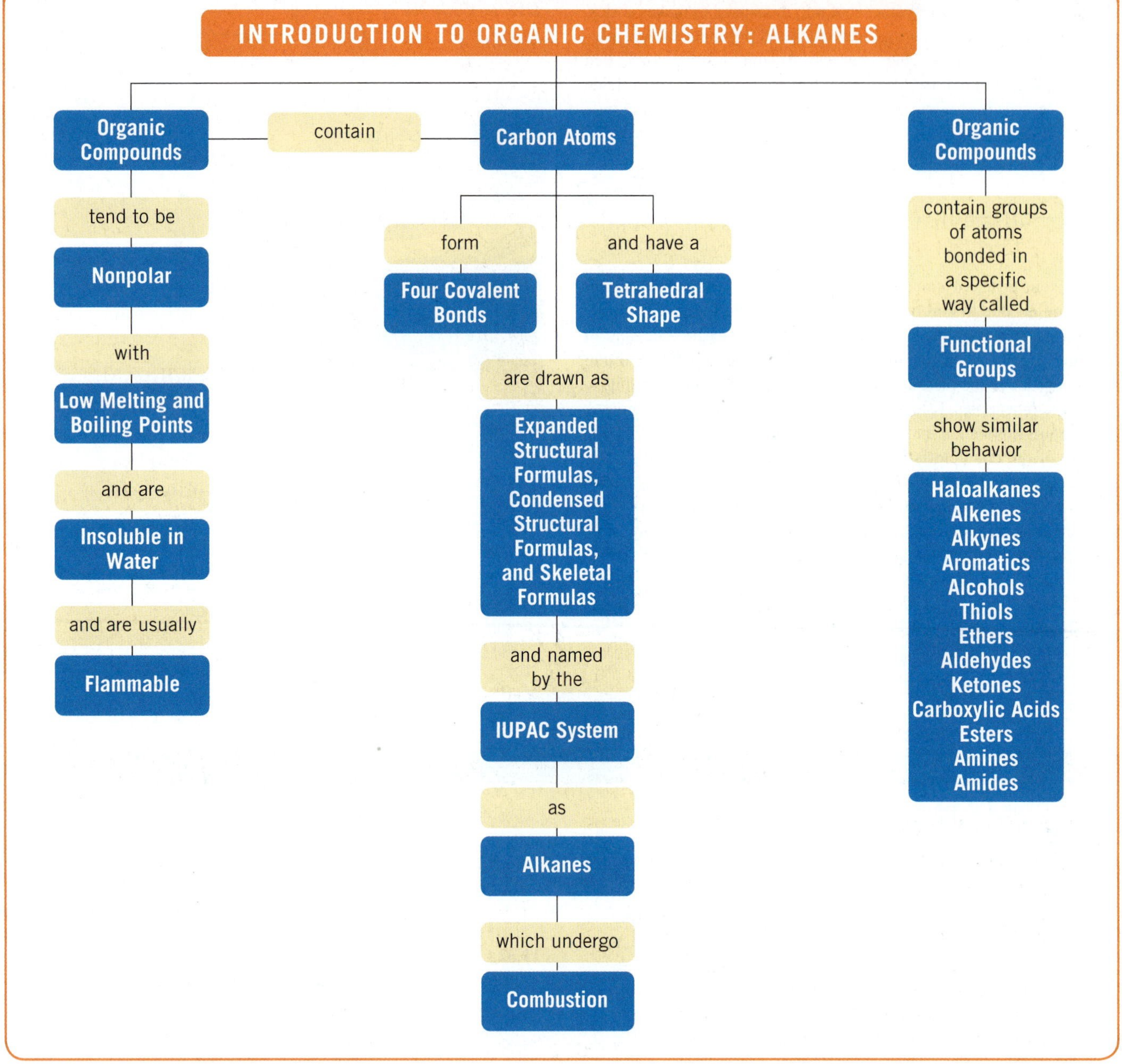

INTRODUCTION TO ORGANIC CHEMISTRY: ALKANES

Organic Compounds — contain — **Carbon Atoms**

Organic Compounds

Organic Compounds
tend to be
Nonpolar
with
Low Melting and Boiling Points
and are
Insoluble in Water
and are usually
Flammable

Carbon Atoms
form
Four Covalent Bonds
and have a
Tetrahedral Shape

are drawn as
Expanded Structural Formulas, Condensed Structural Formulas, and Skeletal Formulas
and named by the
IUPAC System
as
Alkanes
which undergo
Combustion

Organic Compounds
contain groups of atoms bonded in a specific way called
Functional Groups
show similar behavior
**Haloalkanes
Alkenes
Alkynes
Aromatics
Alcohols
Thiols
Ethers
Aldehydes
Ketones
Carboxylic Acids
Esters
Amines
Amides**

CHAPTER REVIEW

11.1 Organic Compounds

LEARNING GOAL: Identify the characteristic properties of organic or inorganic compounds.

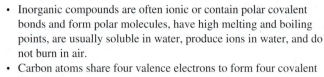

- Organic compounds have covalent bonds, mostly form nonpolar molecules, have low melting points and low boiling points, are not very soluble in water, produce molecules in solutions, and burn vigorously in air.

- Inorganic compounds are often ionic or contain polar covalent bonds and form polar molecules, have high melting and boiling points, are usually soluble in water, produce ions in water, and do not burn in air.
- Carbon atoms share four valence electrons to form four covalent bonds.
- In the simplest organic molecule, methane, CH_4, the C—H bonds that attach four hydrogen atoms to the carbon atom are directed to the corners of a tetrahedron with bond angles of 109°.

11.2 Alkanes

LEARNING GOAL: Write the IUPAC names and draw the condensed structural formulas for alkanes.

- Alkanes are hydrocarbons that have only C—C single bonds.
- In the expanded structural formula, a separate line is drawn for every bonded atom.
- A condensed structural formula depicts groups composed of each carbon atom and its attached hydrogen atoms.
- A skeletal formula represents the carbon skeleton as ends and corners of a zigzag line or geometric figure.
- The IUPAC system is used to name organic compounds by indicating the number of carbon atoms.
- The name of a cycloalkane is written by placing the prefix *cyclo* before the alkane name with the same number of carbon atoms.

11.3 Alkanes with Substituents

LEARNING GOAL: Write the IUPAC names and draw the condensed structural formulas and skeletal formulas for alkanes.

- Substituents, which are attached to an alkane chain, include alkyl groups and halogen atoms (F, Cl, Br, or I).
- In the IUPAC system, alkyl substituents have names such as methyl, ethyl, propyl, and isopropyl; halogen atoms are named as fluoro, chloro, bromo, or iodo.
- In the common names of some compounds, the name of the alkyl group precedes *halide*, for example, methyl chloride.

11.4 Properties of Alkanes

LEARNING GOAL: Identify the properties of alkanes, and write chemical equations for combustion.

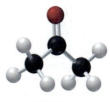

- Alkanes, which are nonpolar molecules, are not soluble in water, and are usually less dense than water.
- Alkanes are only weakly attracted to other molecules by dispersion forces, which gives them low melting and boiling points.
- For alkanes of similar mass, branched alkanes have lower boiling points and cycloalkanes have higher boiling points than their nonbranched structural isomers.
- Alkanes undergo combustion in which they react with oxygen to produce carbon dioxide, water, and energy.

11.5 Functional Groups

LEARNING GOAL: Classify organic molecules according to their functional groups.

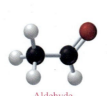

Aldehyde   Ketone

- An organic molecule contains a characteristic group of atoms called a *functional group* that determines the molecule's family name and chemical reactivity.
- Functional groups are used to classify organic compounds, act as reactive sites in the molecule, and provide a system of naming for organic compounds.
- Some common functional groups include the hydroxyl group (—OH) in alcohols, the carbonyl group (C=O) in aldehydes and ketones, a carboxyl group (—COOH) in carboxylic acids, and a nitrogen (N) atom in amines.

SUMMARY OF NAMING

Type	Example	Name
Alkane	$CH_3 - CH_2 - CH_3$	Propane
	$CH_3 - CH - CH_3$ with CH_3 above CH	Methylpropane
Haloalkane	$CH_3 - CH_2 - CH_2 - Cl$	1-Chloropropane
Cycloalkane	□	Cyclobutane

SUMMARY OF REACTIONS

Combustion

$$\text{Alkane}(g) + O_2(g) \xrightarrow{\Delta} CO_2(g) + H_2O(g) + \text{energy}$$

KEY TERMS

alcohol A class of organic compounds that contains the hydroxyl group (—OH) bonded to a carbon atom.

aldehyde A class of organic compounds that contains a carbonyl group (C=O) bonded to at least one hydrogen atom.

alkanes Hydrocarbons containing only single bonds between carbon atoms.

alkenes Hydrocarbons that contain carbon–carbon double bonds (C=C).

alkyl group An alkane minus one hydrogen atom. Alkyl groups are named like the alkanes except a *yl* ending replaces *ane*.

alkynes Hydrocarbons that contain carbon–carbon triple bonds (C≡C).

amide A class of organic compounds in which the hydroxyl group of a carboxylic acid is replaced by a nitrogen group.

amine A class of organic compounds that contains a nitrogen atom bonded to one or more carbon atoms.

aromatic A compound that contains benzene. Benzene has a six-carbon ring with only one hydrogen atom attached to each carbon.

branch A carbon group bonded to the main carbon chain.

branched alkane A single-bonded hydrocarbon containing a substituent bonded to the main chain.

carbonyl group A functional group that contains a double bond between a carbon atom and an oxygen atom (C=O).

carboxylic acid A class of organic compounds that contains the carboxyl functional group.

combustion A chemical reaction in which an alkane reacts with oxygen to produce CO_2, H_2O, and energy.

condensed structural formula A structural formula that shows the arrangement of the carbon atoms in a molecule, but groups each carbon atom with its bonded hydrogen atoms.

cycloalkane An alkane that has a ring or cyclic structure.

ester A class of organic compounds that contains a —COO— group with an oxygen atom bonded to carbon.

ether A class of organic compounds that contains an oxygen atom bonded to two carbon atoms (—O—).

expanded structural formula A type of structural formula that shows the arrangement of the atoms by showing each bond in the hydrocarbon as C—H, C—C, C=C, or C≡C.

functional group A group of atoms bonded in a specific way that determines the physical and chemical properties of organic compounds.

haloalkane A type of alkane that contains one or more halogen atoms.

hydrocarbons Organic compounds consisting of only carbon and hydrogen.

IUPAC system The system for naming organic compounds devised by the International Union of Pure and Applied Chemistry.

ketone A class of organic compounds in which a carbonyl group (C=O) is bonded to two carbon atoms.

organic compounds Compounds made of carbon that typically have covalent bonds, are nonpolar molecules, have low melting and boiling points, are insoluble in water, and are flammable.

skeletal formula A type of structural formula that shows only the bonds between carbon atoms represented as the end of a line or a corner.

structural isomers Organic compounds in which identical molecular formulas have different arrangements of atoms.

substituent Groups of atoms such as an alkyl group or a halogen bonded to the main chain or ring of carbon atoms.

thiol A class of organic molecules that contains the —SH functional group bonded to a carbon atom.

UNDERSTANDING THE CONCEPTS

The chapter sections to review are shown in parentheses at the end of each question.

11.33 Match the following physical and chemical properties with the compound butane, C_4H_{10}, or potassium chloride, KCl: (11.1)

a. melts at −138 °C **b.** burns vigorously in air
c. melts at 770 °C **d.** contains ionic bonds
e. is a gas at room temperature

11.34 Match the following physical and chemical properties with the compound octane, C_8H_{18}, or magnesium sulfate, $MgSO_4$: (11.1)
a. contains only covalent bonds
b. melts at 1124 °C
c. is insoluble in water
d. is a liquid at room temperature
e. is a strong electrolyte

11.35 Identify the compounds in each of the following pairs as structural isomers or not structural isomers: (11.3. 11.5)

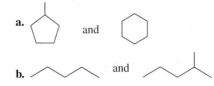

11.36 Identify the compounds in each of the following pairs as structural isomers or not structural isomers: (11.3. 11.5)

a.

$$CH_2—CH_2—CH_2$$
$$|\qquad\qquad|$$
$$CH_3\qquad CH_2—CH_3$$

and

$$CH_3\qquad\qquad CH_3$$
$$|\qquad\qquad\qquad|$$
$$CH_2—CH_2—CH_2—CH_2$$

b. and

11.37 Convert each of the following skeletal structures to condensed structural formulas and give the IUPAC name: (11.2)

a.

b.
Cl   Br

11.38 Convert each of the following skeletal structures to condensed structural formulas and give the IUPAC name: (11.2)

a.

b.

11.39 Match each of the descriptions (**a–f**) with a corresponding term in the following list: alkane, alkene, alkyne, alcohol, ether, aldehyde, ketone, carboxylic acid, ester, amine, functional group, structural isomer. (11.5)

  a. an organic compound that contains a hydroxyl group bonded to a carbon

  b. a hydrocarbon that contains one or more carbon–carbon double bonds

  c. an organic compound in which the carbon of a carbonyl group is bonded to a hydrogen

  d. a hydrocarbon that contains only carbon–carbon single bonds

  e. an organic compound in which the carbon of a carbonyl group is bonded to a hydroxyl group

  f. an organic compound that contains a nitrogen atom bonded to one or more carbon atoms

11.40 Match each of the descriptions (**a–f**) with a corresponding term in the following list: alkane, alkene, alkyne, alcohol, ether, aldehyde, ketone, carboxylic acid, ester, amine, functional group, structural isomer. (11.5)

  a. organic compounds with identical molecular formulas that differ only in the arrangement of atoms

  b. an organic compound in which the hydrogen atom of a carboxyl group is replaced by a carbon atom

  c. an organic compound that contains an oxygen atom bonded to two carbon atoms

  d. a hydrocarbon that contains a carbon–carbon triple bond

  e. a characteristic group of atoms that makes compounds behave and react in a particular way

  f. an organic compound in which the carbonyl group is bonded to two carbon atoms

11.41 Classify the following according to their functional groups: (11.5)

  a. $CH_3—NH_2$

  b. $CH_3—\overset{\overset{\displaystyle O}{\|}}{C}—CH_3$

  c. $CH_3—\overset{\overset{\displaystyle O}{\|}}{C}—O—CH_2—CH_3$

  d. $CH_3—CH_2—CH_2—OH$

11.42 Classify each of the following by their functional group: (11.5)

  a. $CH_3—C{\equiv}CH$

  b. $CH_3—CH_2—CH_2—SH$

  c. $CH_3—O—CH_2—CH_3$

  d. —CH_3

11.43 Identify the functional groups in each of the following: (11.5)

  a.

Almonds

  b.

Cinnamon sticks

  c. $CH_3—\overset{\overset{\displaystyle O}{\|}}{C}—\overset{\overset{\displaystyle O}{\|}}{C}—CH_3$

Butter

11.44 Identify the functional groups in each of the following: (11.5)

  a. BHA is an antioxidant used as a preservative in foods such as baked goods, butter, meats, and snack foods. Identify the functional groups in BHA.

Baked goods contain BHA as a preservative.

  b. Vanillin is a flavoring obtained from the seeds of the vanilla bean. Identify the functional groups in vanillin.

Vanilla extract is a solution containing the compound vanillin.

ADDITIONAL QUESTIONS AND PROBLEMS

For instructor-assigned homework, go to www.masteringchemistry.com.

11.45 Write the name of each of the following substituents: (11.3)
 a. CH_3—
 b. CH_3—CH_2—CH_2—
 c. Cl—

11.46 Write the name of each of the following substituents: (11.3)
 a. Br—
 b. CH_3—CH— (with CH_3 branch above the CH)
 c. CH_3—CH_2—

11.47 Give the IUPAC name for each of the following: (11.2, 11.3)

 a. (cyclopentane structure)

 b. Cl—CH_2—CH—CH_2—Br (with Br branch above the CH)

 c. CH_3—CH—CH—CH_3
  (with CH_3 above the first CH; and below the second CH: CH_2—CH_2—CH_3 chain)

 d. CH_3—CH_2—C—CH_2—CH_3
  (with Cl above the C; and below the C: CH_2—CH_3 chain)

11.48 Give the IUPAC name for each of the following: (11.2, 11.3)

 a. CH_3—CH_2—C—CH_3
  (with CH_3 above and CH_3 below the C)

 b. CH_3—CH_2—Cl

 c. CH_3—CH_2—CH—CH_2—CH—CH_3
  (with CH_3—CH_2 above the first CH; and Br above the second CH)

 d. (cyclohexane with two Br substituents)

11.49 Draw the condensed structural formulas for the four possible isomers that have four carbon atoms and one bromine atom, and give the IUPAC name for each. (11.3)

11.50 Draw the condensed structural formulas for the four possible isomers that have three carbon atoms and two chlorine atoms, and give the IUPAC name for each. (11.3)

11.51 Draw the skeletal formulas for three structural isomers that have the molecular formula C_7H_{14}, with two methyl groups attached to a ring, and give the IUPAC name for each. (11.3)

11.52 Draw the skeletal formulas for four structural isomers that have the molecular formula C_4H_9Br, and give the IUPAC name for each. (11.3)

11.53 Draw the condensed structural formula for each of the following molecules: (11.2, 11.3)
 a. 3-ethylhexane
 b. 1,3-dimethylcyclopentane
 c. 1,3-dichloro-3-methylheptane
 d. bromocyclobutane

11.54 Draw the condensed structural formula for each of the following molecules: (11.2, 11.3)
 a. ethylcyclopropane
 b. 2-methylhexane
 c. isopropylcyclopentane
 d. 1,1-dichloropentane

11.55 Draw the skeletal formula for each of the following molecules: (11.2, 11.3)
 a. pentane
 b. 2,3-dimethylhexane
 c. 2-bromo-4-methylheptane
 d. 1,4-dimethylcyclohexane

11.56 Draw the skeletal formula for each of the following molecules: (11.2, 11.3)
 a. butane
 b. 2,3,3-trimethylpentane
 c. 1,4-dichlorobutane
 d. 2-bromo-1-methylcyclopentane

11.57 Identify the compound in each of the following pairs that has the higher boiling point: (11.4)
 a. pentane or propane
 b. pentane or cyclopentane
 c. hexane or 2,2-dimethylbutane
 d. 2-methylbutane or 2,2-dimethylpropane

11.58 Identify the compound in each of the following pairs that has the higher boiling point: (11.4)
 a. butane or octane
 b. butane or cyclobutane
 c. pentane or 2-methylbutane
 d. hexane or 2,3-dimethylbutane

11.59 Write the balanced equation for the complete combustion of each of the following: (11.4)
 a. CH_3—CH=CH_2
 b. C_5H_{12}
 c. cyclobutane, C_4H_8

11.60 Write the balanced equation for the complete combustion of each of the following: (11.4)
 a. heptane
 b. HC≡C—CH_2—CH_3
 c. 2-methylpropane

11.61 A tank on an outdoor heater contains 2.8 kg of propane. (6.6, 6.7, 11.2, 11.4)
 a. Write the balanced equation for the complete combustion of propane.
 b. How many kilograms of CO_2 are produced by the complete combustion of the propane?

11.62 A butane fireplace lighter contains 56.0 g of butane. (6.6, 6.7, 11.2, 11.4)

   a. Write the balanced equation for the complete combustion of butane.

   b. How many grams of oxygen are needed for the complete combustion of the butane in the lighter?

11.63 Sunscreens contain compounds such as oxybenzone and 2-ethylhexyl-*p*-methoxycinnamate that absorb UV light. Identify the functional groups in each of the following UV-absorbing compounds used in suncreens: (11.5)

   a. oxybenzone

   b. 2-ethylhexyl-*p*-methoxycinnamate

11.64 Oxymetazoline is a vasoconstrictor used in nasal decongestant sprays such as Afrin.

What functional groups are in oxymetazoline? (11.5)

11.65 Decimemide is used as an anticonvulsant.

Identify the functional groups in decimemide. (11.5)

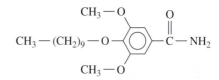

11.66 The odor and taste of pineapples is from ethyl butyrate.

What functional group is in ethyl butyrate? (11.5)

$$CH_3 - CH_2 - CH_2 - \overset{\overset{O}{\|}}{C} - O - CH_2 - CH_3$$

CHALLENGE QUESTIONS

11.67 In an automobile engine, "knocking" occurs when the combustion of gasoline occurs too rapidly. The octane number of gasoline represents the ability of a gasoline mixture to reduce knocking. A sample of gasoline is compared with heptane, rated 0, because it reacts with severe knocking, and 2,2,4-trimethylpentane, which has a rating of 100 because of its low knocking. (11.2, 11.3, 11.4)

   a. Draw the condensed structural formula for 2,2,4-trimethylpentane.

   b. Write the balanced equation for the complete combustion of 2,2,4-trimethylpentane.

11.68 Draw the condensed structural formula for each of the following halogenated compounds, used as refrigerants and propellants: (11.2, 11.3)

   a. Freon 14, tetrafluoromethane

   b. Freon 114, 1,2-dichloro-1,1,2,2-tetrafluoroethane

   c. Freon C318, octafluorocyclobutane

   d. Halon 2311, 2-bromo-2-chloro-1,1,1-trifluoroethane

11.69 Draw the condensed structural formulas for three structural isomers that have the molecular formula C_3H_8O and contain an alcohol or ether functional group. (11.3, 11.5)

11.70 Draw the condensed structural formulas for three structural isomers that have the molecular formula C_4H_8O and contain an aldehyde or ketone functional group. (11.3, 11.5)

11.71 Consider the compound propane. (6.6, 6.7, 7.7, 11.2, 11.3, 11.5)
a. Draw the condensed structural formula.
b. Write the balanced equation for the complete combustion of propane.
c. How many grams of O_2 are needed to react with 12.0 L of propane gas at STP?
d. How many grams of CO_2 would be produced from the reaction in part **c**?

11.72 Consider the compound ethylcyclopentane. (6.6, 6.7, 7.7, 11.2, 11.3, 11.5)
a. Draw the skeletal formula.
b. Write the balanced equation for the complete combustion of ethylcyclopentane.
c. How many grams of O_2 are required for the reaction of 25.0 g of ethylcyclopentane?
d. How many liters of CO_2 would be produced at STP from the reaction in part **c**?

ANSWERS

Answers to Study Checks

11.1 $CH_3—CH_2—CH_2—CH_2—CH_2—CH_2—CH_3$

heptane

11.2 cyclopropane

11.3 3-methylpentane

11.4 1-chloro-2,4-dimethylhexane

11.5 $CH_3—\overset{\overset{\displaystyle Br}{|}}{CH}—CH_2—\overset{\overset{\displaystyle CH_3}{|}}{CH}—CH_3$;

11.6 $CH_3—CH_2—O—CH_3$ contains the functional group $C—O—C$; it is an ether.

Answers to Selected Questions and Problems

11.1 a. inorganic   b. organic   c. organic
d. inorganic   e. inorganic   f. organic

11.3 a. inorganic   b. organic
c. organic   d. inorganic

11.5 a. ethane   b. ethane
c. NaBr   d. NaBr

11.7 VSEPR theory predicts that the four bonds in CH_4 will be as far apart as possible, which means that the hydrogen atoms are at the corners of a tetrahedron.

11.9 a. $H—\overset{\overset{\displaystyle H}{|}}{\underset{\underset{\displaystyle H}{|}}{C}}—\overset{\overset{\displaystyle H}{|}}{\underset{\underset{\displaystyle H}{|}}{C}}—\overset{\overset{\displaystyle H}{|}}{\underset{\underset{\displaystyle H}{|}}{C}}—H$

b. $CH_3—CH_2—CH_2—CH_2—CH_2—CH_3$
c.

11.11 a. pentane   b. heptane
c. hexane   d. cyclobutane

11.13 a. CH_4 b. $CH_3—CH_3$
c. $CH_3—CH_2—CH_2—CH_2—CH_3$ d.

11.15 a. same molecule
b. structural isomers of C_5H_{12}
c. structural isomers of C_6H_{14}

11.17 a. 1-fluoropropane
b. 2,3-dimethylpentane
c. 4-ethyl-2,2-dimethylhexane
d. chlorocyclopentane
e. 2-chloropropane
f. methylcyclohexane

11.19 a. $Br—CH_2—CH_2—CH_2—Cl$

b. $CH_3—CH_2—\overset{\overset{\displaystyle CH_3}{|}}{\underset{\underset{\displaystyle CH_3}{|}}{C}}—CH_2—CH_3$

c. $CH_3—\overset{\overset{\displaystyle CH_3}{|}}{CH}—\overset{\overset{\displaystyle CH_3}{|}}{CH}—CH_2—\overset{\overset{\displaystyle CH_3}{|}}{CH}—CH_3$

d. $CH_3—\overset{\overset{\displaystyle CH_3}{|}}{CH}—\overset{\overset{\displaystyle CH_2—CH_3}{|}}{CH}—CH_2—\overset{\overset{\displaystyle CH_3}{|}}{CH}—CH_2—CH_2—CH_3$

e. $Br—CH_2—CH_2—Br$

11.21 a.   b.   c.   d.   e.

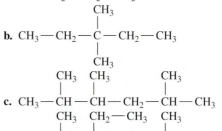

11.23 a. $CH_3—CH_2—CH_2—CH_2—CH_2—CH_2—CH_3$;

b. liquid
c. No, heptane is insoluble in water.
d. float
e. $C_7H_{16}(g) + 11O_2(g) \xrightarrow{\Delta} 7CO_2(g) + 8H_2O(g) + energy$

11.25 a. heptane   b. cyclopropane
c. hexane

11.27 a. $2C_2H_6(g) + 7O_2(g) \xrightarrow{\Delta} 4CO_2(g) + 6H_2O(g) + energy$
b. $2C_8H_{18}(g) + 25O_2(g) \xrightarrow{\Delta} 16CO_2(g) + 18H_2O(g) + energy$
c. $C_6H_{12}(g) + 9O_2(g) \xrightarrow{\Delta} 6CO_2(g) + 6H_2O(g) + energy$

11.29 a. alcohol **b.** alkene
c. aldehyde **d.** ester

11.31 a. ether **b.** alcohol
c. ketone **d.** carboxylic acid
e. amine

11.33 a. butane **b.** butane
c. potassium chloride **d.** potassium chloride
e. butane

11.35 a. structural isomers **b.** not structural isomers

11.37 a. $CH_3 - CH_2 - CH_2 - \overset{\overset{\displaystyle CH_3}{|}}{CH} - \overset{\overset{\displaystyle |}{|}}{\underset{\underset{\displaystyle CH_3}{|}}{CH}} - CH_3$

2,3-dimethylhexane

b. $CH_3 - \overset{\overset{\displaystyle Cl}{|}}{CH} - \overset{\overset{\displaystyle CH_3}{|}}{CH} - \overset{\overset{\displaystyle Br}{|}}{CH} - CH_2 - CH_3$

4-bromo-2-chloro-3-methylhexane

11.39 a. alcohol **b.** alkene
c. aldehyde **d.** alkane
e. carboxylic acid **f.** amine

11.41 a. amine **b.** ketone
c. ester **d.** alcohol

11.43 a. aromatic, aldehyde
b. aromatic, alkene, aldehyde
c. ketone

11.45 a. methyl
b. propyl
c. chloro

11.47 a. methylcyclopentane
b. 1,2-dibromo-3-chloropropane
c. 2,3-dimethylhexane
d. 3-chloro-3-ethylpentane

11.49 $CH_3 - CH_2 - CH_2 - CH_2 - Br$ $CH_3 - \overset{\overset{\displaystyle Br}{|}}{CH} - CH_2 - CH_3$
    1-bromobutane   2-bromobutane

$CH_3 - \overset{\overset{\displaystyle CH_3}{|}}{\underset{\underset{\displaystyle Br}{|}}{C}} - CH_3$ $CH_3 - \overset{\overset{\displaystyle CH_3}{|}}{CH} - CH_2 - Br$
    2-bromo-   1-bromo-
2-methylpropane   2-methylpropane

11.51

1,1-dimethylcyclopentane

1,2-dimethylcyclopentane   1,3-dimethylcyclopentane

11.53 a. $CH_3 - CH_2 - \overset{\overset{\displaystyle CH_2 - CH_3}{|}}{CH} - CH_2 - CH_2 - CH_3$

b.

c. $Cl - CH_2 - CH_2 - \overset{\overset{\displaystyle Cl}{|}}{\underset{\underset{\displaystyle CH_3}{|}}{C}} - CH_2 - CH_2 - CH_2 - CH_3$

d.

11.55 a.   **b.**

c.   **d.**

11.57 a. pentane **b.** cyclopentane
c. hexane **d.** 2-methylbutane

11.59 a. $2C_3H_6(g) + 9O_2(g) \xrightarrow{\Delta} 6CO_2(g) + 6H_2O(g) + \text{energy}$
b. $C_5H_{12}(g) + 8O_2(g) \xrightarrow{\Delta} 5CO_2(g) + 6H_2O(g) + \text{energy}$
c. $C_4H_8(g) + 6O_2(g) \xrightarrow{\Delta} 4CO_2(g) + 4H_2O(g) + \text{energy}$

11.61 a. $C_3H_8(g) + 5O_2(g) \xrightarrow{\Delta} 3CO_2(g) + 4H_2O(g) + \text{energy}$
b. 8.4 kg of CO_2

11.63 a. aromatic, ether, alcohol, ketone
b. aromatic, ether, alkene, ester

11.65 aromatic, ether, amide

11.67 a. $CH_3 - \overset{\overset{\displaystyle CH_3}{|}}{\underset{\underset{\displaystyle CH_3}{|}}{C}} - CH_2 - \overset{\overset{\displaystyle CH_3}{|}}{CH} - CH_3$

b. $2C_8H_{18}(g) + 25O_2(g) \xrightarrow{\Delta}$
    $16CO_2(g) + 18H_2O(g) + \text{energy}$

11.69 $CH_3 - CH_2 - CH_2 - OH$

$CH_3 - \overset{\overset{\displaystyle OH}{|}}{CH} - CH_3$ $CH_3 - CH_2 - O - CH_3$

11.71 a. $CH_3 - CH_2 - CH_3$
b. $C_3H_8(g) + 5O_2(g) \xrightarrow{\Delta} 3CO_2(g) + 4H_2O(g) + \text{energy}$
c. 85.7 g of O_2
d. 70.7 g of CO_2

12 Alkenes, Alkynes, and Aromatic Compounds

Mastering**CHEMISTRY**™

Visit **www.masteringchemistry.com** for self-study materials and instructor-assigned homework.

A shipment of unripe lemons, limes, and

bananas is arriving in the United States from Chile. Before the fruit can be delivered to the local supermarkets, Kevin, a food safety specialist, inspects the fruit. Then he begins the ripening process by exposing the fruit to ethylene gas, C_2H_4, which is a natural plant hormone. Ethylene binds to specific receptors on the surface of a fruit or vegetable, where it regulates the ripening. Most fruits and vegetables naturally produce small amounts of ethylene gas to allow them to ripen slowly. By increasing the concentration of ethylene, Kevin increases the rate of ripening.

Ethylene gas is the common name for ethene, which is an alkene. Alkenes contain at least one carbon–carbon double bond, which means that they are unsaturated. Ethene can be identified as an alkene by the "ene" at the end of its name. The carbon–carbon double bond makes alkenes planar or flat, and also quite reactive.

Career: Food Safety Specialist

Food safety specialists ensure the quality and safety of our food, which requires them to monitor cultivation, harvesting, processing, storage, delivery, packaging, labeling, and transportation of food. For instance, a food safety specialist checks that foods are kept at the correct temperatures to maintain freshness and prevent spoilage, and that expired foods are removed from the shelves and discarded. In doing this, they guarantee that all types of food sold in grocery stores are safe for the public. Food safety specialists also inspect locations that prepare food commercially, like restaurants, to enforce health and safety regulations. This involves inspecting equipment and identifying possible sources of contamination that may result in foodborne illnesses.

n Chapter 11, we looked primarily at alkanes that contain only single bonds. Now we will investigate hydrocarbons called alkenes, which contain double bonds, and alkynes, which have triple bonds between carbon atoms. One important alkene is ethene (ethylene), which is used to ripen fruit when ready for market. A common alkyne called ethyne (acetylene) burns at high temperatures that can be used in welding metals. When we cook with vegetable oils such as corn oil, safflower oil, or olive oil, we are using organic compounds that have long carbon chains containing one or more double bonds. Because of their double bonds, vegetable oils are liquids at room temperature. When hydrogen is added to the double bonds in vegetable oils, they are converted to solids such as margarine.

Commercially, small alkenes such as ethene are used as reactants in forming long carbon chains of polymers such as polyethylene.

12.1 Alkenes and Alkynes

Alkenes and alkynes are families of hydrocarbons that contain double and triple bonds, respectively. They are called *unsaturated hydrocarbons* because they do not contain the maximum number of hydrogen atoms that could be attached to each carbon atom, as do alkanes. These unsaturated hydrocarbons react with hydrogen gas to become alkanes, which are *saturated hydrocarbons*.

LEARNING GOAL

Write the IUPAC names for alkenes and alkynes; give common names for simple structures.

Identifying Alkenes and Alkynes

Alkenes contain one or more carbon–carbon double bond that forms when adjacent carbon atoms share two pairs of valence electrons. Recall that *a carbon atom always forms four covalent bonds*. In the simplest alkene, ethene, C_2H_4, two carbon atoms are connected by a double bond, and each is also attached to two H atoms. According to VSEPR theory (Section 5.8), each carbon atom in the double bond has a trigonal planar arrangement. There is a 120° angle between each carbon atom in the double bond and the two atoms to which carbon is bonded. As a result, the ethene molecule is flat because the carbon and hydrogen atoms all lie in the same plane. In an **alkyne**, a triple bond forms when two carbon atoms share three pairs of valence electrons. In a triple bond, each carbon atom is attached to two other atoms. According to VSEPR theory, each carbon atom in the triple bond has a linear arrangement with angles of 180° (see Figure 12.1). The atoms in the multiple bonds of alkene and alkyne molecules all lie in the same plane.

Ethene, commonly called ethylene, is an important plant hormone involved in promoting the ripening of fruit. Commercially grown fruit, such as avocados, bananas, and tomatoes, are often picked before they are ripe. Before the fruit is brought to market, it is exposed to ethylene to accelerate the ripening process. Ethylene also accelerates the breakdown of cellulose in plants, which causes flowers to wilt and leaves to fall from trees.

The simplest alkyne, ethyne (C_2H_2), commonly called acetylene, is used in welding, where it reacts with oxygen to produce flames with temperatures above 3300 °C.

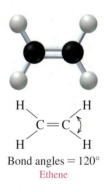

Bond angles = 120°
Ethene

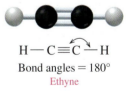

$H - C \equiv C - H$
Bond angles = 180°
Ethyne

FIGURE 12.1 Ball-and-stick models of ethene and ethyne show the functional groups of double or triple bonds and the bond angles.

Q Why are these compounds called unsaturated hydrocarbons?

CONCEPT CHECK 12.1   **Identifying Alkanes, Alkenes, and Alkynes**

Classify each of the following condensed structural or skeletal formulas as an alkane, an alkene, or an alkyne:

a. $CH_3 - C \equiv C - CH_3$ **b.** 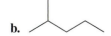   **c.**

Fruit is ripened with ethene, a plant hormone.

A mixture of acetylene and oxygen undergoes combustion during the welding of metals.

TUTORIAL
Naming Alkenes and Alkynes

Explore Your World

RIPENING FRUIT

Obtain two unripe (green) bananas. Place one in a plastic bag and seal the bag. Leave the banana and the banana in the plastic bag on the counter. Check the bananas twice a day for 2 or 3 days and observe any difference in the ripening process.

QUESTIONS

1. What compound helps ripen the bananas?
2. What are some possible reasons for any difference in the ripening rate?
3. If you wish to ripen an avocado, what procedure might you use?

ANSWER

a. A condensed structural formula with a triple bond is an alkyne.
b. A skeletal formula with only single bonds between carbon atoms is an alkane.
c. A skeletal formula with a double bond is an alkene.

Naming Alkenes and Alkynes

The IUPAC names for alkenes and alkynes are similar to those of alkanes. For alkenes or alkynes, the name is based on the longest carbon chain that contains the double or triple bonds (see Table 12.1).

TABLE 12.1 Comparison of Names for Alkanes, Alkenes, and Alkynes

Alkane	Alkene	Alkyne
CH_3-CH_3	$H_2C=CH_2$	$HC\equiv CH$
Ethane	Ethene (ethylene)	Ethyne (acetylene)
$CH_3-CH_2-CH_3$	$CH_3-CH=CH_2$	$CH_3-C\equiv CH$
Propane	Propene	Propyne

CONCEPT CHECK 12.2   Comparing Alkenes and Alkynes

Compare the condensed structural formulas of propane, propene, and propyne shown in Table 12.1.

ANSWER

Propane, propene, and propyne each contain three carbon atoms. Propane contains only single bonds, propene contains a double bond, and propyne contains a triple bond. Propane has eight hydrogen atoms, propene has six hydrogen atoms, and propyne has four hydrogen atoms.

Examples of naming an alkene and an alkyne are shown in Sample Problem 12.1.

SAMPLE PROBLEM 12.1   Naming Alkenes and Alkynes

Write the IUPAC name for each of the following:

$$\begin{array}{c} CH_3 \\ | \\ \text{a. } CH_3-CH-CH=CH-CH_3 \end{array}$$

b. $CH_3-CH_2-C\equiv C-CH_2-CH_3$

SOLUTION

a.   **Analyze the Problem**

Functional Group	Family	IUPAC Naming	IUPAC Name
Double bond	Alkene	Replace the *ane* of the alkane name with *ene*.	Alkene

Step 1   **Name the longest carbon chain that contains the double or triple bond.** There are five carbon atoms in the longest carbon chain containing the double bond. Replacing the corresponding alkane ending with *ene* gives pentene.

$$\begin{array}{c} CH_3 \\ | \\ CH_3-CH-CH=CH-CH_3 \end{array} \qquad \text{pentene}$$

Step 2 **Number the carbon chain from the end nearer the double or triple bond.** The number of the first carbon in the double bond is used to give the location of the double bond. Alkenes or alkynes with two or three carbons do not need numbers. For example, the double bond in ethene or propene must be between carbon 1 and carbon 2.

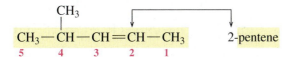

$$CH_3—CH—CH=CH—CH_3 \qquad \text{2-pentene}$$
$$54321$$

Step 3 **Give the location and name of each substituent (alphabetical order) as a prefix to the alkene or alkyne name.** The methyl group is located on carbon 4.

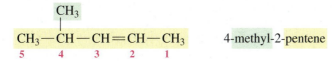

$$CH_3—CH—CH=CH—CH_3 \qquad \text{4-methyl-2-pentene}$$
$$54321$$

b. **Analyze the Problem**

Functional Group	Family	IUPAC Naming	IUPAC Name
Triple bond	Alkyne	Replace the *ane* of the alkane name with *yne*.	Alkyne

Step 1 **Name the longest carbon chain that contains the double or triple bond.** There are six carbon atoms in the longest chain containing the triple bond. Replacing the corresponding alkane ending with *yne* gives hexyne.

$$CH_3—CH_2—C≡C—CH_2—CH_3 \qquad \text{hexyne}$$

Step 2 **Number the main chain from the end nearer the double or triple bond.** The location of the triple bond is designated by the number of the first carbon in the triple bond.

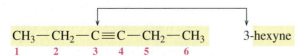

$$CH_3—CH_2—C≡C—CH_2—CH_3 \qquad \text{3-hexyne}$$
$$123456$$

Step 3 **Give the location and name of each substituent (alphabetical order) as a prefix to the alkene or alkyne name.** There are no substituents in this formula.

STUDY CHECK 12.1

Draw the condensed structural formula for each of the following:

a. 2-pentyne

b. 2-chloro-1-hexene

Naming Cycloalkenes

Some alkenes called *cycloalkenes* have a double bond within a ring structure. If there is no substituent, the double bond does not need a number. If there is a substituent, the carbons in the double bond are numbered as 1 and 2, and the ring is numbered from carbon 2 in the direction that will give the lower number to the substituent.

TUTORIAL
Drawing Alkenes and Alkynes

Cyclobutene   3-Methylcyclopentene

Chemistry Link to the Environment

FRAGRANT ALKENES

The odors you associate with lemons, oranges, roses, and lavender are due to volatile compounds that are synthesized by the plants. The pleasant flavors and fragrances of many fruits and flowers are often due to unsaturated compounds. They were some of the first kinds of compounds to be extracted from natural plant material. In ancient times, they were highly valued in their pure forms. Limonene and myrcene give the characteristic odors and flavors to lemons and bay leaves, respectively. Geraniol and citronellal give roses and lemongrass their distinct aromas. In the food and perfume industries, these compounds are extracted or synthesized and used as perfumes and flavorings.

The characteristic odor of a rose is due to geraniol, a 10-carbon alcohol with two double bonds.

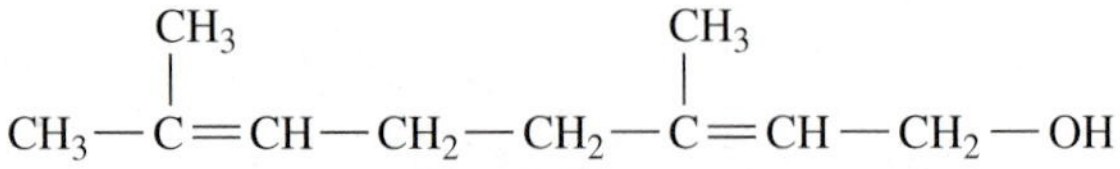

$$CH_3-\overset{\overset{\textstyle CH_3}{|}}{C}=CH-CH_2-CH_2-\overset{\overset{\textstyle CH_3}{|}}{C}=CH-CH_2-OH$$
Geraniol, roses

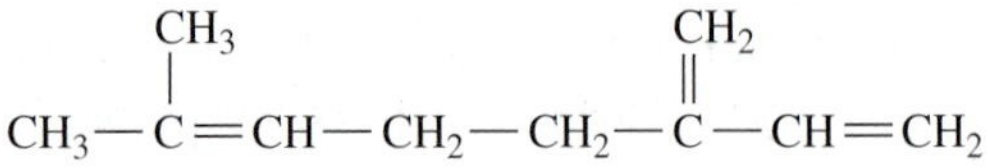

$$CH_3-\overset{\overset{\textstyle CH_3}{|}}{C}=CH-CH_2-CH_2-\overset{\overset{\textstyle CH_2}{||}}{C}-CH=CH_2$$
Myrcene, bay leaves

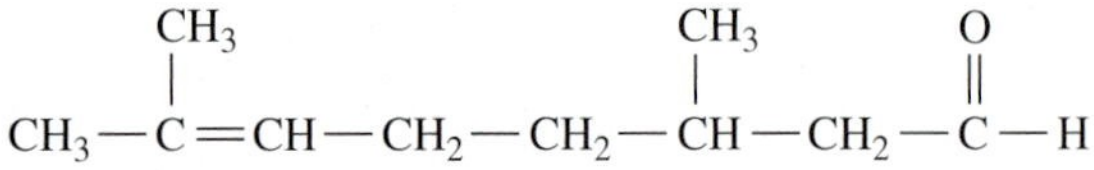

$$CH_3-\overset{\overset{\textstyle CH_3}{|}}{C}=CH-CH_2-CH_2-\overset{\overset{\textstyle CH_3}{|}}{CH}-CH_2-\overset{\overset{\textstyle O}{||}}{C}-H$$
Citronellal, lemongrass

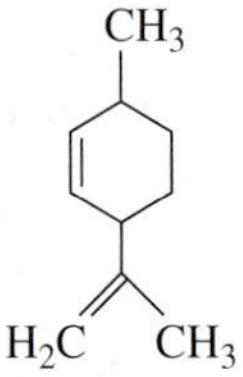

Limonene, lemons and oranges

QUESTIONS AND PROBLEMS

12.1 Alkenes and Alkynes

LEARNING GOAL: *Write the IUPAC names for alkenes and alkynes; give common names for simple structures.*

12.1 Identify each of the following as an alkene, a cycloalkene, or an alkyne:

a. 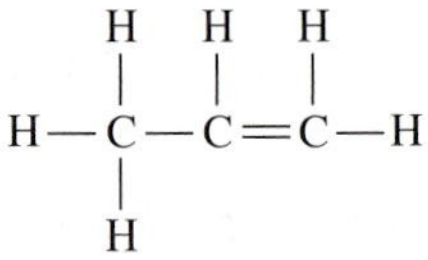 $H-\overset{\overset{\textstyle H}{|}}{\underset{\underset{\textstyle H}{|}}{C}}-\overset{\overset{\textstyle H}{|}}{C}=\overset{\overset{\textstyle H}{|}}{C}-H$ **b.** $CH_3-CH_2-C\equiv C-H$

c. 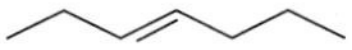 **d.**

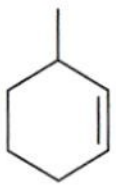

12.2 Identify each of the following as an alkene, a cycloalkene, or an alkyne:

a.  **b.**

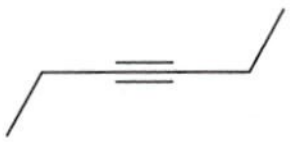

c. 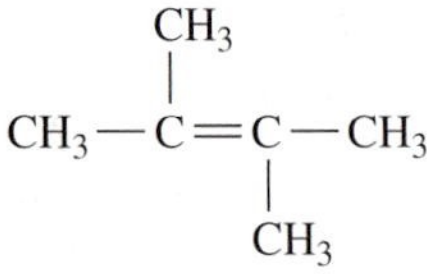 $CH_3-\overset{\overset{\textstyle CH_3}{|}}{\underset{\underset{\textstyle CH_3}{|}}{C}}=C-CH_3$ **d.** 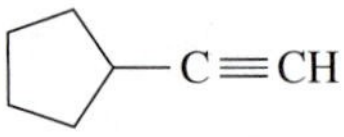 $-C\equiv CH$

12.3 Give the IUPAC name for each of the following:

a. 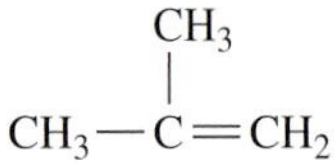 $CH_3-\overset{\overset{\textstyle CH_3}{|}}{C}=CH_2$ **b.** 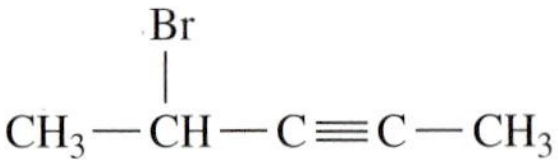 $CH_3-\overset{\overset{\textstyle Br}{|}}{CH}-C\equiv C-CH_3$

c. 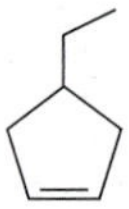 **d.**

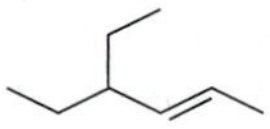

12.4 Give the IUPAC name for each of the following:

a. $H_2C=CH-CH_2-CH_2-CH_2-CH_3$

b. 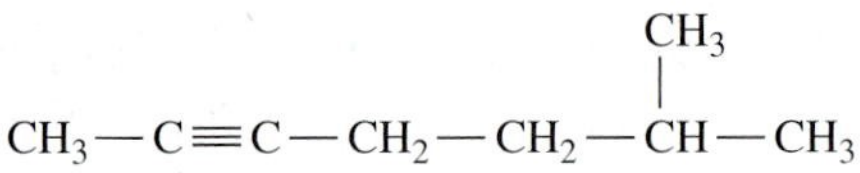 $CH_3-C\equiv C-CH_2-CH_2-\overset{\overset{\textstyle CH_3}{|}}{CH}-CH_3$

c.

d. 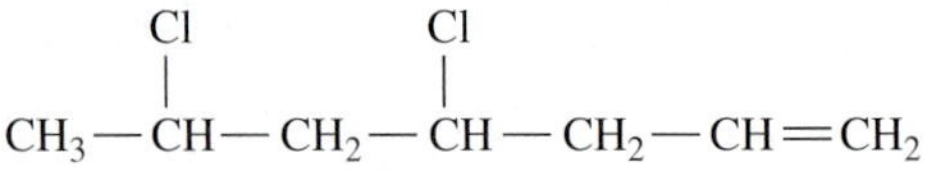 $CH_3-\overset{\overset{\textstyle Cl}{|}}{CH}-CH_2-\overset{\overset{\textstyle Cl}{|}}{CH}-CH_2-CH=CH_2$

12.5 Draw the condensed structural formula or skeletal formula, if cyclic, for each of the following:
  a. 1-pentene
  b. 2-methyl-1-butene
  c. 3-methylcyclohexene
  d. 4-chloro-2-pentyne

12.6 Draw the condensed structural formula or skeletal formula, if cyclic, for each of the following:
  a. 3-methyl-1-butyne
  b. 3,4-dimethyl-1-pentene
  c. 1,2-dichlorocyclopentene
  d. 2-methyl-2-hexene

12.2 Cis–Trans Isomers

LEARNING GOAL

Draw the condensed structural formulas and give the names for the cis–trans isomers of alkenes.

MC™

SELF-STUDY ACTIVITY
Geometric Isomers

TUTORIAL
Cis–Trans Isomers

In any alkene, the double bond is rigid, which means there is no rotation around the double bond as with single bonds (see *Explore Your World* "Modeling Cis–Trans Isomers"). As a result, atoms or groups can attach to the carbon atoms in the double bond on one side or the other, which gives two different structures or *cis–trans isomers*.

For example, the formula for 1,2-dichloroethene can be drawn as two different molecules, which are cis–trans isomers. In the expanded structural formulas, the atoms bonded to the carbon atoms in the double bond have bond angles of 120°. When we draw 1,2-dichloroethene, we add the prefix *cis* or *trans* to denote whether the atoms bonded to the carbon atoms are on the same side or opposite sides of the molecule. In the **cis isomer**, the chlorine atoms are on the same side of the double bond. In the **trans isomer**, the chlorine atoms are on opposite sides of the double bond. Trans means "across," as in transcontinental; cis means "on this side."

$$Cl-CH=CH-Cl$$
1,2-Dichloroethene

| Chlorine atoms are on the same side of the double bond. | | | Chlorine atoms are on opposite sides of the double bond. |

cis-1,2-Dichloroethene   *trans*-1,2-Dichloroethene

Another example of a cis–trans isomer is 2-butene. If we look closely at 2-butene, we find that each carbon in the double bond is bonded to a CH_3- group and a hydrogen atom. We can draw cis–trans isomers for 2-butene. In the *cis*-2-butene isomer, the CH_3- groups are attached on the same side of the double bond. In the *trans*-2-butene isomer, the CH_3- groups are attached to the double bond on opposite sides, as shown in their ball-and-stick-models (see Figure 12.2). As with any pair of cis–trans isomers, *cis*-2-butene and *trans*-2-butene are different compounds with different physical properties and chemical properties.

$$CH_3-CH=CH-CH_3$$
2-Butene

cis-2-Butene
(mp −139 °C; bp 3.7 °C)

trans-2-Butene
(mp −106 °C; bp 0.3 °C)

When the carbon atoms in the double bond are attached to two different atoms or groups of atoms, an alkene can have cis–trans isomers. For example, 3-hexene can be drawn with cis and trans isomers because there is one H atom and a CH_3-CH_2- group attached to each carbon atom in the double bond. When you are asked to draw the formula for an alkene, it is important to consider the possibility of cis and trans isomers.

$$CH_3-CH_2-CH=CH-CH_2-CH_3$$
3-Hexene

Same side   Opposite sides

cis-3-Hexene   *trans*-3-Hexene

However, some alkene formulas cannot be drawn with cis–trans isomers. If one carbon atom in the double bond is attached to two identical groups, there is only one

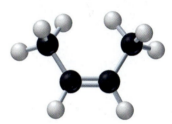

cis-2-Butene

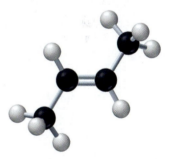

trans-2-Butene

FIGURE 12.2 Ball-and-stick models of the cis and trans isomers of 2-butene.

Q What feature in 2-butene accounts for the cis and trans isomers?

formula and no cis–trans isomers. For example, in 1-butene there are two hydrogen atoms on carbon 1. In 2-methylpropene, there are two identical groups (CH_3—) on carbon 2 and two hydrogen atoms on carbon 1.

Identical atoms

No cis–trans isomers

1-Butene

2-Methylpropene

Identical groups

No cis–trans isomers

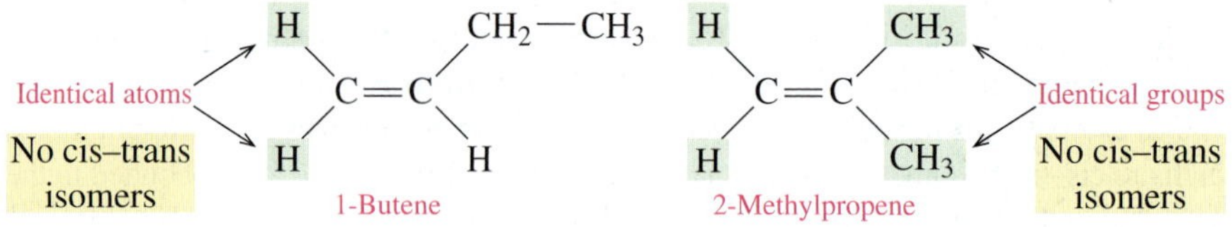

Alkynes do not have cis–trans isomers, because the carbons in the triple bond are each attached to only one group.

$$H—C\equiv C—CH_3 \qquad CH_3—C\equiv C—CH_2—CH_3$$

CONCEPT CHECK 12.3 Converting Formulas of Alkenes to Cis and Trans Isomers

Convert the condensed structural formula for each of the following to cis and trans isomers. If there are no cis and trans isomers, explain why.

a. 2-pentene **b.** 1-pentene

ANSWER

a. We start by drawing the condensed structural formula for 2-pentene:

$$CH_3—CH=CH—CH_2—CH_3$$

However, we can make it easier to see the atoms of groups attached to the double bond if we show the H atoms with a bond line. Now we can identify that one C atom of the double bond is attached to an H atom and a one-carbon group, and the other C atom of the double bond is attached to an H atom and a two-carbon group.

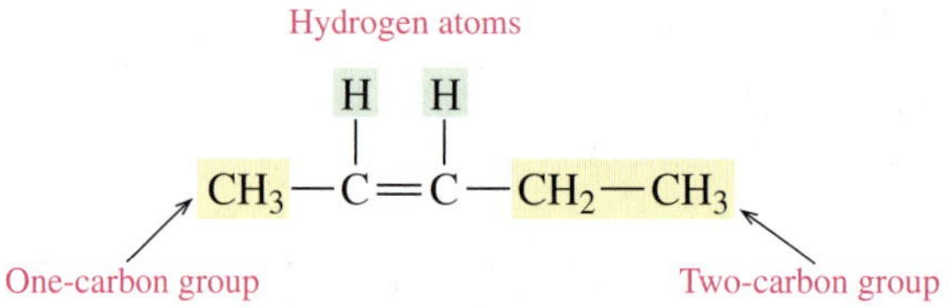

Hydrogen atoms

$$CH_3—\overset{\overset{\text{H}}{|}}{C}=\overset{\overset{\text{H}}{|}}{C}—CH_2—CH_3$$

One-carbon group   Two-carbon group

Because the groups attached to each carbon atom in the double bond are different, 2-pentene can be drawn as cis–trans isomers. The H atoms and the carbon groups can be drawn on the same side of the double bond to give the cis isomer. When the H atoms and the carbon groups are drawn on opposite sides of the double bond, it gives the trans isomer.

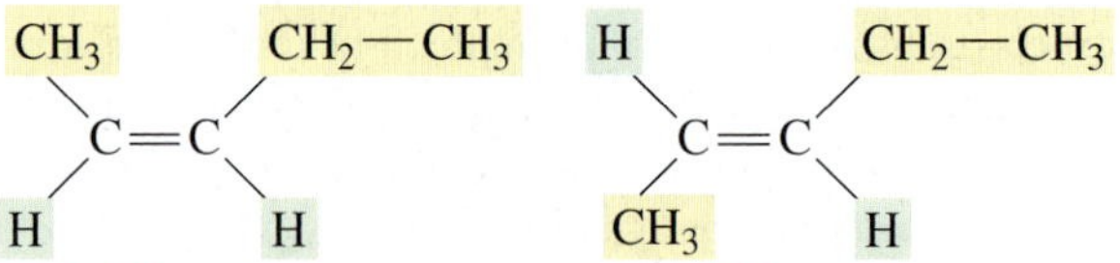

cis-2-Pentene   *trans*-2-Pentene

b. We start by drawing the condensed structural formula for 1-pentene.

$$H_2C=CH—CH_2—CH_2—CH_3$$

Now we make it easier to see the atoms of groups attached to the double bond if we show the H atoms with a bond line.

Identical H atoms

$$H—\overset{\overset{\text{H}}{|}}{C}=\overset{\overset{\text{H}}{|}}{C}—CH_2—CH_2—CH_3$$

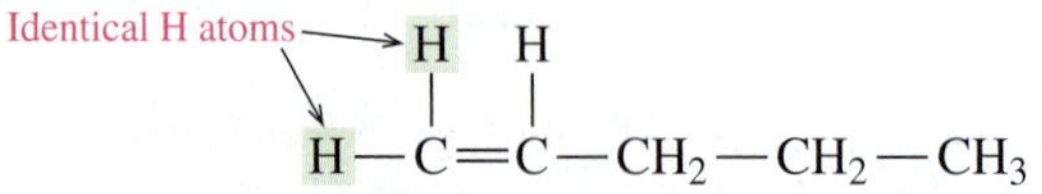

Because there are identical H atoms on the first carbon atom in the double bond, it is not possible to draw cis–trans isomers for 1-pentene. 1-Pentene does not have cis and trans isomers.

SAMPLE PROBLEM 12.2 **Naming Cis–Trans Isomers**

Identify each of the following as a cis or trans isomer and give its name:

a.

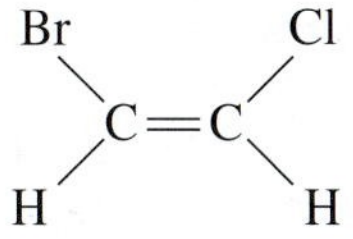

$$\underset{H}{\overset{Br}{\diagdown}} C = C \underset{H}{\overset{Cl}{\diagup}}$$

b.

$$\underset{H}{\overset{CH_3}{\diagdown}} C = C \underset{CH_2-CH_3}{\overset{H}{\diagup}}$$

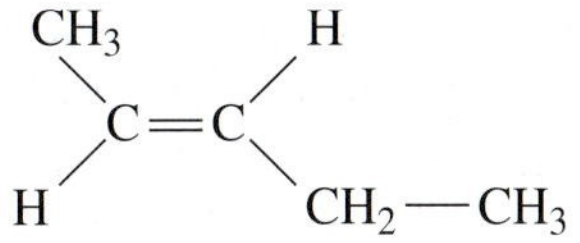

SOLUTION

a. This is a cis isomer because the two halogen atoms attached to the carbon atoms of the double bond are on the same side. The name of the two-carbon alkene, starting with the bromo group on carbon 1, is *cis*-1-bromo-2-chloroethene.

b. This is a trans isomer because the two alkyl groups attached to the carbon atoms of the double bond are on opposite sides of the double bond. This isomer of the five-carbon alkene, 2-pentene, is named *trans*-2-pentene.

STUDY CHECK 12.2

Give the name of the following compound, including cis or trans:

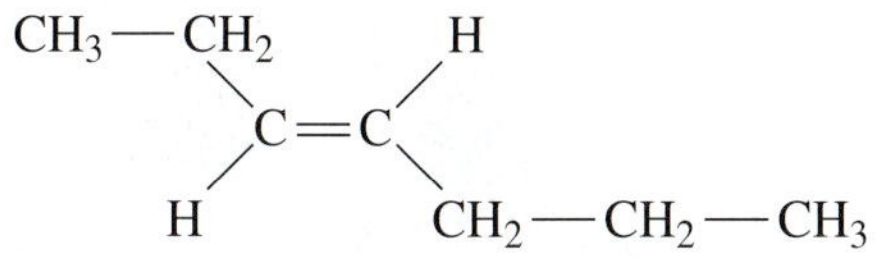

$$\underset{H}{\overset{CH_3-CH_2}{\diagdown}} C = C \underset{CH_2-CH_2-CH_3}{\overset{H}{\diagup}}$$

CONCEPT CHECK 12.4 **Double Bonds in Fatty Acids**

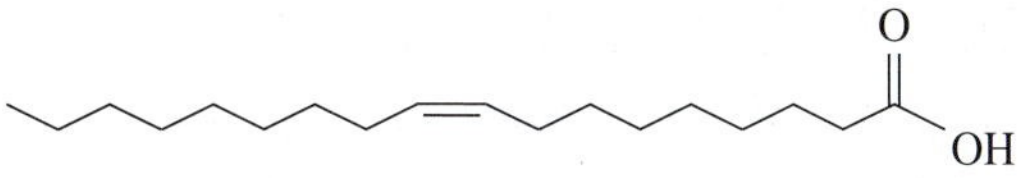

Olive oil has a high percentage of oleic acid, a fatty acid.

The formula of oleic acid, found in olive oil, is often drawn in its skeletal form.

a. Why is oleic acid an acid?
b. Is oleic acid an unsaturated or saturated fatty acid?
c. Is this skeletal structure for oleic acid drawn as the cis isomer or the trans isomer?

ANSWER

a. Oleic acid has a carboxyl functional group, which makes it a carboxylic acid.
b. Oleic acid contains one double bond, which makes it an unsaturated fatty acid.
c. This skeletal structure of oleic acid is drawn as the cis isomer.

 Explore Your World

MODELING CIS–TRANS ISOMERS

Because cis–trans isomerism is not easy to visualize, here are some things you can do to understand the difference in rotation around a single bond compared to a double bond, and how it affects groups that are attached to the carbon atoms in the double bond.

Put the fingertips of your index fingers together. This is a model of a single bond. Consider the index fingers as a pair of carbon atoms, and think of your thumbs and other fingers as other parts of a carbon chain. While your index fingers are touching, twist your hands and change the position of your thumbs relative to each other. Notice how the relationship of your other fingers changes.

Now place the tips of your index fingers and middle fingers together in a model of a double bond. As you did before, twist your hands to try to change the position of the thumbs. What happens? Can you change the location of your thumbs relative to each other without breaking the double bond? The difficulty of moving your hands with two fingers touching represents the lack of rotation about a double bond. You have made a model of a cis isomer when both thumbs are on the same side. If you turn one hand over so one thumb points down and the other thumb points up, you have made a model of a trans isomer.

Cis-hands (*cis*-thumbs/fingers)

Trans-hands (*trans*-thumbs/fingers)

Using Gumdrops and Toothpicks to Model Cis–Trans Isomers

Obtain some toothpicks and yellow, green, and black gumdrops. The black gumdrops represent C atoms, the yellow gumdrops represent H atoms, and the green gumdrops represent Cl atoms. Place a toothpick between two black gumdrops. Use three more toothpicks to attach two yellow gumdrops, and one green gumdrop to each black gumdrop (carbon atom). Rotate one of the gumdrop carbon atoms to show the conformations of the attached H and Cl atoms.

Remove a toothpick and yellow gumdrop from each black gumdrop. Place a second toothpick between the black gumdrops, which makes a double bond. Try to twist the double bond of toothpicks. Can you do it? When you observe the location of the green gumdrops, does the model you made represent a cis or a trans isomer? Why? If your model is a cis isomer, how would you change it to a trans isomer? If your model is a trans isomer, how would you change it to a cis isomer?

Models from gumdrops represent the cis and trans isomers.

Chemistry Link to the Environment

PHEROMONES IN INSECT COMMUNICATION

Many insects emit minute quantities of chemicals called *pheromones* to send messages to other individuals of the same species. Some pheromones warn of danger, while others call for defense, mark a trail, or attract the opposite sex. During the past 40 years, the structures of many pheromones have been chemically determined. One of the most studied is bombykol, the sex pheromone produced by the female silkworm moth. Even a few nanograms of bombykol will attract male silkworm moths from distances of over 1 kilometer. The bombykol molecule is a 16-carbon chain with one cis double bond, one trans double bond, and an alcohol group. The effectiveness of many of these pheromones depends on the cis or trans configuration of the double bonds in the molecules. A certain species will respond to one isomer but not the other.

Scientists are interested in synthesizing pheromones to use as nontoxic alternatives to pesticides. When placed in a trap, bombykol can be used to isolate male silkworm moths. When a synthetic pheromone is released in a field, the males cannot locate the females, which disrupts the reproductive cycle. This technique has been successful in controlling the oriental fruit moth, the grapevine moth, and the pink bollworm.

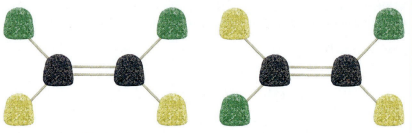

Bombykol, sex attractant for the silkworm moth

Pheromones allow insects to attract mates from a great distance.

Chemistry Link to Health

CIS–TRANS ISOMERS FOR NIGHT VISION

The retinas of the eyes consist of two types of cells: rods and cones. The rods on the edge of the retina allow us to see in dim light, and the cones, in the center, produce our vision in bright light. The rods contain a substance called *rhodopsin* that absorbs light. Rhodopsin is composed of *cis*-11-retinal, an unsaturated compound, attached to a protein. When rhodopsin absorbs light, the *cis*-11-retinal isomer is converted to its trans isomer, which changes its shape. The trans form no longer fits, and it separates from the protein. The change from the cis to trans isomer and the separation from the protein generate an electrical signal that the brain converts into an image.

An enzyme (isomerase) converts the trans isomer back to the *cis*-11-retinal isomer and the rhodopsin re-forms. If there is a deficiency of rhodopsin in the rods of the retina, nightblindness may occur. One common cause of night blindness is a lack of vitamin A in the diet. We obtain vitamin A from β-carotene, which is found in foods such as carrots, squash, and spinach. In the small intestine, β-carotene is converted to vitamin A, which can be converted to *cis*-11-retinal or stored in the liver for future use. Without a sufficient quantity of retinal, not enough rhodopsin is produced to enable us to see adequately in dim light.

Cis–Trans Isomers of Retinal

Cis double bond

Trans double bond

cis-11-Retinal

trans-11-Retinal

Light

QUESTIONS AND PROBLEMS

12.2 Cis–Trans Isomers

LEARNING GOAL: *Draw the condensed structural formulas and give the names for the cis–trans isomers of alkenes.*

12.7 Which of the following cannot have a cis–trans isomer? Explain.

  a. $H_2C = CH - CH_3$

  b. $CH_3 - CH_2 - CH = CH - CH_3$

  c.
$$CH_3 \quad\quad CH_2 - CH_3$$
$$C = C$$
$$CH_3 \quad\quad CH_2 - CH_3$$

12.8 Which of the following cannot have a cis–trans isomer? Explain.

  a.
$$H \quad\quad H$$
$$C = C$$
$$CH_3 - CH_2 \quad\quad CH_2 - CH_3$$

  b. $CH_3 - CH_2 - CH_2 - CH = CH_2$

  c.
$$CH_3$$
$$|$$
$$H_2C = CH - CH_2 - CH - CH_3$$

12.9 Write the IUPAC name for each of the following using *cis* or *trans* prefixes:

  a.
$$CH_3 \quad\quad CH_3$$
$$C = C$$
$$H \quad\quad H$$

  b.
$$CH_3 - CH_2 \quad\quad H$$
$$C = C$$
$$H \quad\quad CH_2 - CH_2 - CH_2 - CH_3$$

  c.
$$CH_3 - CH_2 - CH_2 \quad\quad CH_2 - CH_3$$
$$C = C$$
$$H \quad\quad H$$

12.10 Write the IUPAC name for each of the following using *cis* or *trans* prefixes:

  a.
$$CH_3 \quad\quad CH_2 - CH_3$$
$$C = C$$
$$H \quad\quad H$$

  b.
$$CH_3 \quad\quad H$$
$$C = C$$
$$H \quad\quad CH_2 - CH_2 - CH_2 - CH_3$$

  c.
$$CH_3 - CH_2 - CH_2 \quad\quad H$$
$$C = C$$
$$H \quad\quad CH_3$$

12.11 Draw the condensed structural formula for each of the following:

  a. *trans*-1-chloro-2-butene

  b. *cis*-2-pentene

  c. *trans*-3-heptene

12.12 Draw the condensed structural formula for each of the following:

  a. *cis*-1,2-difluoroethene

  b. *trans*-2-pentene

  c. *cis*-4-octene

12.3 Addition Reactions

The most characteristic reaction of alkenes and alkynes is the **addition** of atoms or groups of atoms to the carbons of the double or triple bond. Addition occurs because double and triple bonds are easily broken, providing electrons to form new single bonds. The general equation for the addition of a reactant A—B to an alkene can be written as follows:

$$\underset{\text{Alkene}}{\diagdown \text{C}=\text{C} \diagup} + \text{A}-\text{B} \xrightarrow{\text{Addition}} \overset{\overset{\text{A}}{|}}{-\text{C}}-\overset{\overset{\text{B}}{|}}{\underset{|}{\text{C}}}-$$

The addition reactions have different names that depend on the type of reactant we add to the alkene. For example, *hydrogenation* adds two hydrogen atoms to the double bond of an alkene to yield an alkane, and *halogenation* adds two chlorine or two bromine atoms to the double bond. A summary of types of addition reactions is shown in Table 12.2.

TABLE 12.2 Summary of Addition Reactions

Name of Addition Reaction	Reactants	Catalysts	Products
Hydrogenation	Alkene + H_2	Pt, Ni, or Pd	Alkane
	Alkyne + $2H_2$	Pt, Ni, or Pd	Alkane
Halogenation	Alkene + Cl_2 (Br_2)		Haloalkane
	Alkyne + $2Cl_2$ ($2Br_2$)		Haloalkane
Hydrohalogenation	Alkene + HCl (HBr)		Haloalkane
Hydration	Alkene + HOH	H^+ (strong acid)	Alcohol

Hydrogenation

In a reaction called **hydrogenation**, H atoms add to each of the carbons in a double bond or in the triple bond of an alkyne. During hydrogenation, the double or triple bonds are converted to single bonds in alkanes. The reaction usually takes place under high temperature and pressure, and a catalyst such as finely divided platinum (Pt), nickel (Ni), or palladium (Pd) is used to speed up the reaction. The general equation for hydrogenation of an alkene can be written as follows:

$$\underset{\text{Alkene}}{\diagdown \text{C}=\text{C} \diagup} + \text{H}-\text{H} \xrightarrow{\text{Catalyst}} \underset{\text{Alkane}}{\overset{\overset{\text{H} \quad \text{H}}{| \quad |}}{-\text{C}-\text{C}-}}$$

Some examples of the hydrogenation of alkenes follow:

$$\underset{\text{2-Butene}}{CH_3-CH=CH-CH_3} + \text{H}-\text{H} \xrightarrow{\text{Pt}} \underset{\text{Butane}}{CH_3-\overset{\overset{\text{H}}{|}}{\text{CH}}-\overset{\overset{\text{H}}{|}}{\text{CH}}-CH_3}$$

$$\underset{\text{Cyclohexene}}{\hexagon} + \text{H}-\text{H} \xrightarrow{\text{Ni}} \underset{\text{Cyclohexane}}{\hexagon}$$

The hydrogenation of an alkyne requires two molecules of hydrogen ($2H_2$) to form the alkane product.

$$\underset{\text{2-Butyne}}{CH_3-C \equiv C-CH_3} + 2\text{H}-\text{H} \xrightarrow{\text{Pt}} \underset{\text{Butane}}{CH_3-\overset{\overset{\text{H}}{|}}{\underset{\underset{\text{H}}{|}}{\text{C}}}-\overset{\overset{\text{H}}{|}}{\underset{\underset{\text{H}}{|}}{\text{C}}}-CH_3}$$

SAMPLE PROBLEM 12.3   **Products of Hydrogenation**

Draw the condensed structural formula or skeletal formula, if cyclic, for the product of each of the following hydrogenation reactions:

a. $CH_3—CH{=}CH_2 + H_2 \xrightarrow{Pt}$?

b.  $+ H_2 \xrightarrow{Pt}$?

c. $HC{\equiv}CH + 2H_2 \xrightarrow{Ni}$?

SOLUTION

Analyze the Problem

Reactant	Type of Reaction	Product
Alkene or alkyne	Hydrogenation (addition of H atoms to a double or triple bond)	Alkane

a. $CH_3—CH_2—CH_3$

b.

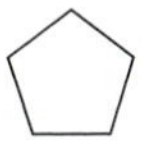

c. $CH_3—CH_3$

STUDY CHECK 12.3

Draw the condensed structural formula for the product of the hydrogenation of 2-methyl-1-butene using a platinum catalyst.

Explore Your World

UNSATURATION IN FATS AND OILS

Read the labels on containers of vegetable oils, margarine, peanut butter, and shortenings.

QUESTIONS

1. What terms on the label tell you that the compounds contain double bonds?
2. A label on a bottle of canola oil lists saturated, polyunsaturated, and monounsaturated fats. What do these terms tell you about the type of bonding in the fats?
3. A peanut butter label states that it contains partially hydrogenated vegetable oils or completely hydrogenated vegetable oils. What does this tell you about the type of reaction that took place in preparing the peanut butter?

Chemistry Link to Health

HYDROGENATION OF UNSATURATED FATS

Vegetable oils such as corn oil or safflower oil are unsaturated fats composed of fatty acids that contain double bonds. The process of hydrogenation is used commercially to convert the double bonds in the unsaturated fats in vegetable oils to all single bonds. This results in a saturated fat such as margarine, which is solid at room temperature, not liquid. Adjusting the amount of added hydrogen produces partially hydrogenated fats such as soft margarine, solid margarine in sticks, and shortenings, which are used in cooking. For example, oleic acid is a typical unsaturated fatty acid in olive oil and has a cis double bond at carbon 9. When oleic acid is hydrogenated, it is converted to stearic acid, a saturated fatty acid.

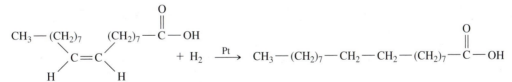

Oleic acid (found in olive oil and other unsaturated fats)

Stearic acid (found in saturated fats)

In commercial hydrogenation, nickel is used to catalyze the hydrogenation of unsaturated fats in vegetable oils to produce solid products containing saturated fats.

Halogenation

In the **halogenation** reactions of alkenes or alkynes, halogen atoms such as chlorine or bromine are added to a double or a triple bond. The reaction occurs readily, without the use of any catalyst, to produce a dihaloalkane from an alkene or a tetrahaloalkane from an alkyne. In the general equation for halogenation, the symbol X—X or X_2 is used for Cl_2 or Br_2.

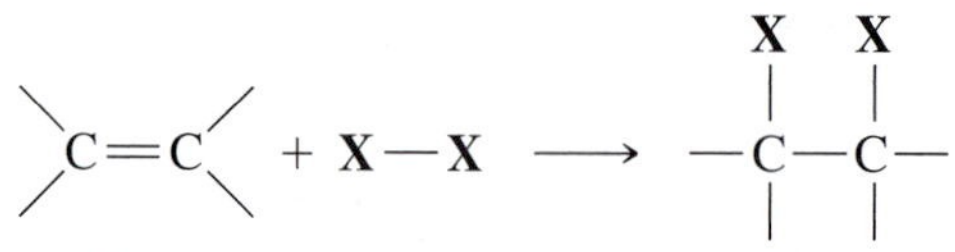

$$\text{\textbackslash}C{=}C\diagup + X{-}X \longrightarrow \overset{X\ \ X}{-\underset{|}{C}-\underset{|}{C}-}$$

Alkene   Dihaloalkane

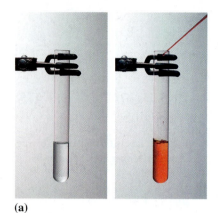

(a)

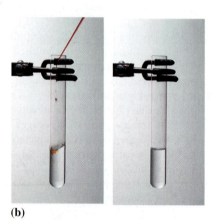

(b)

FIGURE 12.3 **(a)** When bromine is added to an alkane in the first test tube, the orange color of bromine remains because the alkane does not react or reacts slowly. **(b)** When bromine is added to an alkene in the second test tube, the orange color immediately disappears as the bromine atoms add to the double bond.

Q Will the orange color disappear when bromine is added to cyclohexane or cyclohexene?

Here are some examples of adding Cl_2 or Br_2 to alkenes and alkynes.

$$H_2C{=}CH_2 + Cl{-}Cl \longrightarrow \overset{Cl\ \ \ Cl}{CH_2{-}CH_2}$$

Ethene   1,2-Dichloroethane

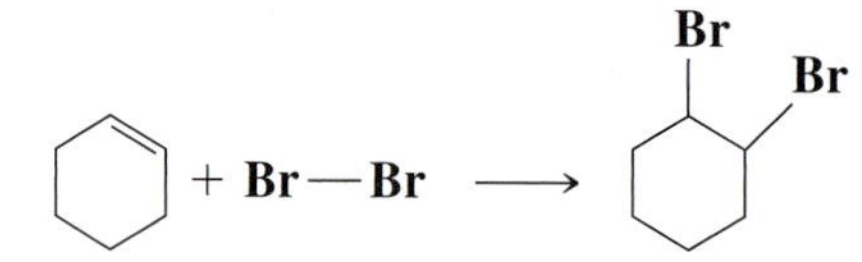

Cyclohexene + Br—Br ⟶ 1,2-Dibromocyclohexane

$$CH_3{-}C{\equiv}C{-}H + 2Cl{-}Cl \longrightarrow CH_3{-}\overset{Cl\ \ Cl}{\underset{Cl\ \ Cl}{C{-}C}}{-}H$$

Propyne   1,1,2,2-Tetrachloropropane

The addition reaction of bromine is used to test for the presence of double and triple bonds, as shown in Figure 12.3.

SAMPLE PROBLEM 12.4   **Drawing Products of Halogenation**

Draw the condensed structural formula for the product of the following reaction:

$$CH_3{-}\overset{CH_3}{\underset{}{C}}{=}CH_2 + Br_2 \longrightarrow$$

SOLUTION

Analyze the Problem

Reactant	Type of Reaction	Product
Alkene	Halogenation (addition of halogen atoms to a double bond)	Dihaloalkane

$$CH_3{-}\overset{CH_3}{\underset{Br\ \ Br}{C}}{-}CH_2$$

STUDY CHECK 12.4

What is the name of the product formed when chlorine is added to 1-butene?

Hydrohalogenation

In the reaction called **hydrohalogenation**, a hydrogen halide (HCl or HBr) adds to an alkene to yield a haloalkane. The reaction occurs without the use of a catalyst. The hydrogen atom adds to one carbon of the double bond, and the halogen atom adds to the other carbon. The general reaction, in which HX represents HCl or HBr, can be written as follows:

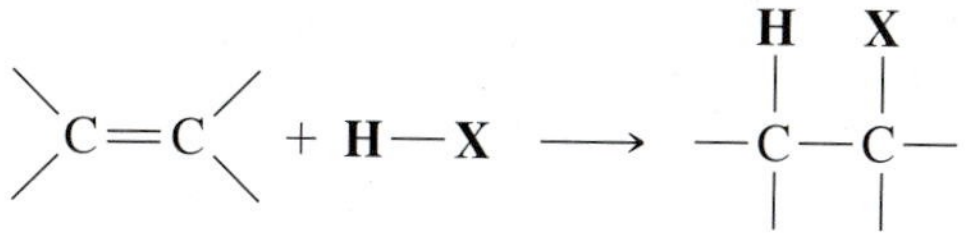

Alkene   Haloalkane (alkyl halide)

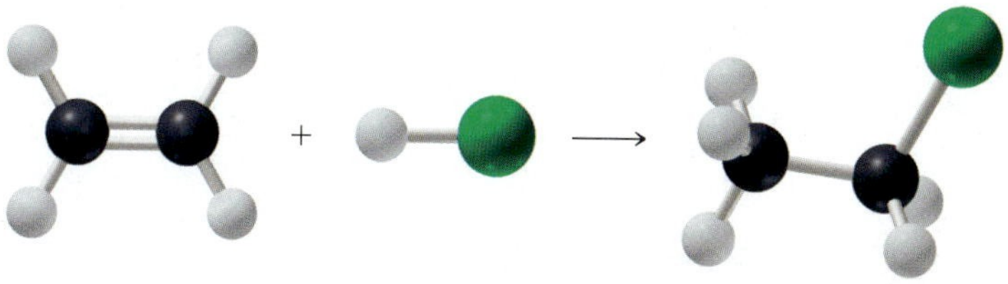

Two examples of hydrohalogenation follow:

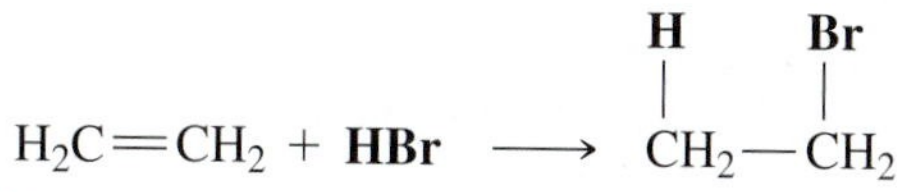

Ethene (ethylene)   Bromoethane (ethyl bromide)

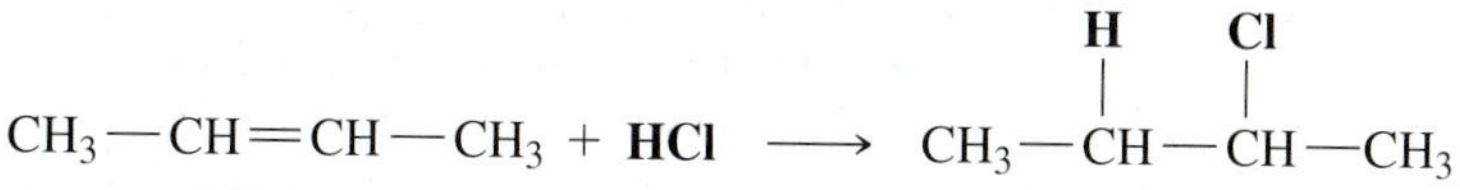

2-Butene   2-Chlorobutane

Steps in Addition Reactions of HX to Alkenes

We have seen that in the addition reaction of an alkene, two groups add to the carbons in the double bond to give a saturated compound. To understand how the addition of HX takes place, we can consider the two steps involved when HBr adds to ethene. First, a pair of electrons in the double bond reacts with a hydrogen ion (H^+) from the HBr, which is shown by a curved arrow. This reaction produces a **carbocation** (a carbon cation) with a positive charge. In the second step, a pair of electrons from the bromide ion Br^- reacts rapidly with the carbocation. A new covalent bond is formed by the bonding of bromine to carbon.

Step 1

Step 2

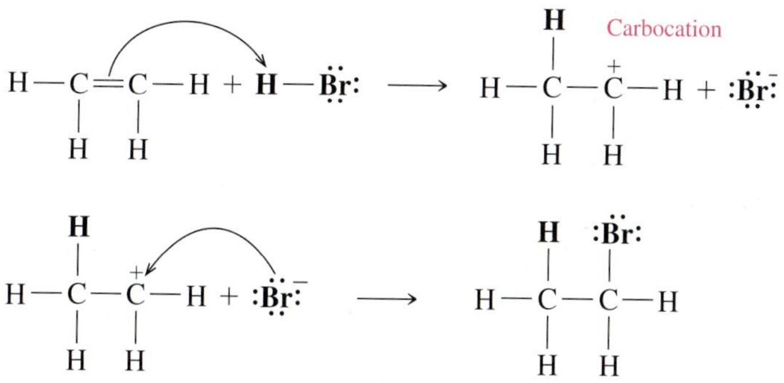

Bromoethane

Markovnikov's Rule

When HBr adds to a symmetrical alkene, such as ethene, a single product is formed. However, when HBr adds to a double bond in an unsymmetrical alkene, two products are possible. In 1870, Vladimir Markovnikov, a Russian chemist, observed that when HX adds to a double bond, the H attaches to the carbon that has more hydrogen atoms, and the X attaches to the carbon that has fewer hydrogen atoms. This observation is now called **Markovnikov's rule**.

When an unsymmetrical alkene forms a carbocation, the more stable form is the one where the C^+ is attached to the most alkyl groups. Therefore, in the initial step, the H^+ adds to the carbon that has fewer alkyl groups, which is the carbon in the double bond that has the greater number of hydrogen atoms. The Br^- bonds to the other carbon.

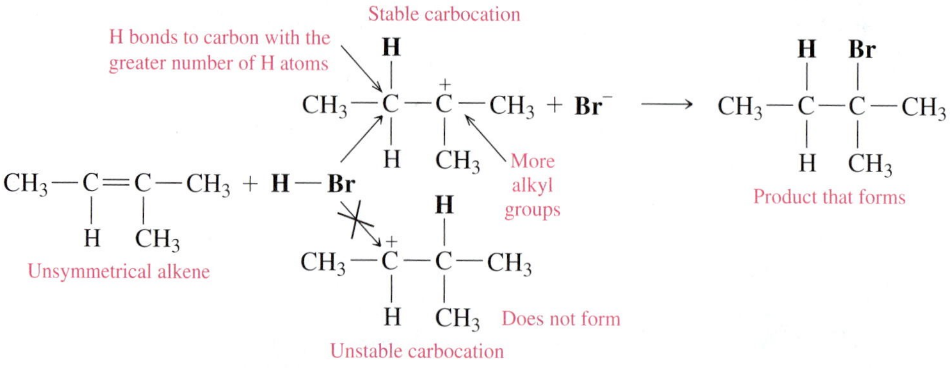

Career Focus

LABORATORY TECHNOLOGIST

Laboratory technologists analyze the components of body fluids for abnormal levels using automated machines that perform several tests simultaneously. The results are analyzed and passed on to doctors.

CONCEPT CHECK 12.5 **Markovnikov's Rule**

a. Why would you need to use Markovnikov's rule to determine the product for the addition of HBr to 1-hexene but not to 3-hexene?
b. What is the name of the product for the addition of HBr to 1-hexene?
c. What is the name of the product for the addition of HBr to 3-hexene?

ANSWER

a. Markovnikov's rule is used to determine the haloalkane product when HBr is added to 1-hexene because 1-hexene is unsymmetrical with a different number of alkyl groups attached to the carbon atoms in the double bond. Thus, the product is formed from the carbocation that has more alkyl groups attached. Markovnikov's rule is not needed when HBr is added to 3-hexene, because 3-hexene is symmetrical.
b. The H of HBr adds to carbon 1, which has more hydrogen atoms, and the Br adds to carbon 2 to form 2-bromohexane.
c. Since 3-hexene is symmetrical, addition of HBr gives 3-bromohexane.

SAMPLE PROBLEM 12.5 **Addition to Alkenes**

Draw the condensed structural formula for the product for each of the following reactions:

a. $CH_3-CH{=}CH-CH_3 + HBr \longrightarrow$

b. $CH_3-\overset{\displaystyle CH_3}{\underset{\displaystyle |}{C}}{=}CH-CH_3 + HCl \longrightarrow$

SOLUTION

Analyze the Problem

Reactant	Type of Reaction	Product
Alkene (symmetrical)	Hydrohalogenation (addition of a H atom and a halogen atom to a double bond)	Haloalkane
Alkene (unsymmetrical)	Markovnikov's rule applies	

a. This is a symmetrical alkene. The H attaches to one carbon in the double bond and the Br attaches to the other carbon of the double bond.

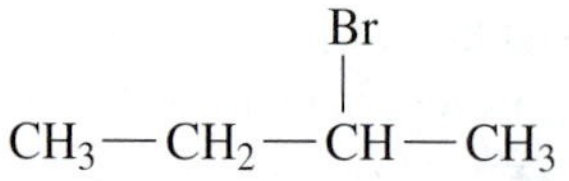

$$CH_3-CH_2-\overset{\displaystyle Br}{\underset{\displaystyle |}{C}}H-CH_3$$

b. This is an unsymmetrical alkene. Using Markovnikov's rule, the H from HCl adds to the carbon atom with the greater number of H atoms (carbon 3), and the Cl adds to the carbon with the fewer number of H atoms (carbon 2).

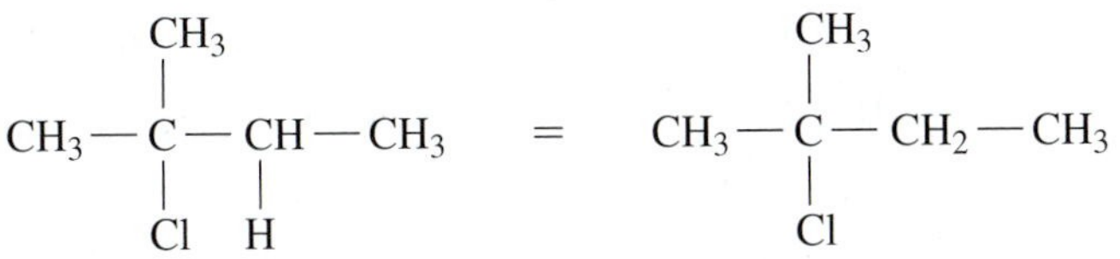

$$
\begin{array}{ccc}
& CH_3 & & CH_3 \\
& | & & | \\
CH_3\!-\!C\!-\!CH\!-\!CH_3 & = & CH_3\!-\!C\!-\!CH_2\!-\!CH_3 \\
& | \quad | & & | \\
& Cl \quad H & & Cl
\end{array}
$$

STUDY CHECK 12.5

Draw the skeletal formula and give the name of the product obtained when HBr adds to 1-methylcyclopentene.

Hydration

In **hydration**, alkenes react with water ($H\!-\!OH$). A hydrogen atom ($H\!-$) from water forms a bond with one carbon atom in the double bond, and the oxygen atom in $-OH$ forms a bond with the other carbon. The reaction is catalyzed by a strong acid such as H_2SO_4. Hydration is used to prepare alcohols, which have the hydroxyl functional group ($-OH$). In the general equation, water is written $H\!-\!OH$, and the acid catalyst is represented by H^+.

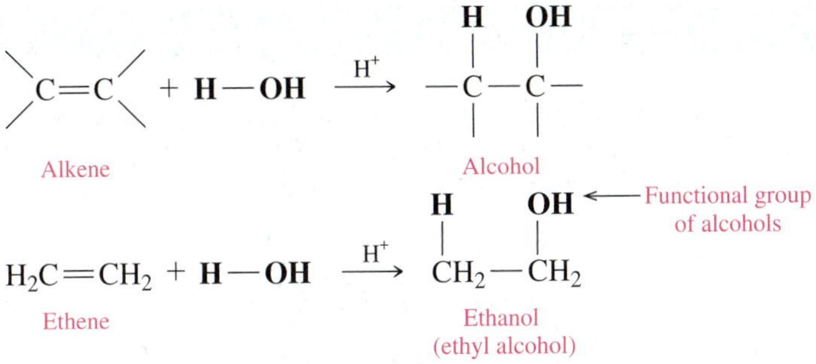

$$
\begin{array}{ccc}
& & H \quad OH \\
& & | \quad\quad | \\
\diagdown\!\!\!\diagup\!\!C\!=\!C\!\diagdown\!\!\!\diagup + H\!-\!OH \xrightarrow{\;H^+\;} & & -C\!-\!C- \\
& & | \quad\quad | \\
\text{Alkene} & & \text{Alcohol}
\end{array}
$$

$$
\begin{array}{cc}
& H \quad\quad OH \quad\longleftarrow \text{Functional group} \\
& | \quad\quad\quad | \quad\quad\quad\quad \text{of alcohols} \\
H_2C\!=\!CH_2 + H\!-\!OH \xrightarrow{\;H^+\;} & CH_2\!-\!CH_2 \\
\text{Ethene} & \text{Ethanol} \\
& \text{(ethyl alcohol)}
\end{array}
$$

When water adds to a double bond in which the carbon atoms are attached to different numbers of H atoms, the double bond is unsymmetrical. Markovnikov's rule also applies when HOH adds to an unsymmetrical alkene. Then the addition of water follows Markovnikov's rule: the $H\!-$ from HOH attaches to the carbon in the double bond that has the greater number of H atoms, and the $-OH$ attaches to the carbon with fewer H atoms.

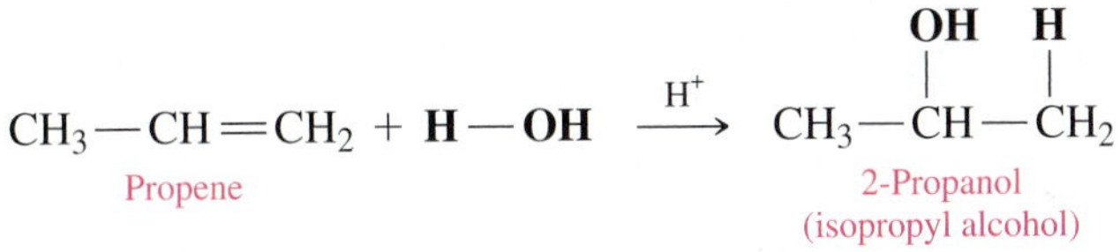

$$
\begin{array}{cc}
& OH \quad H \\
& | \quad\quad | \\
CH_3\!-\!CH\!=\!CH_2 + H\!-\!OH \xrightarrow{\;H^+\;} & CH_3\!-\!CH\!-\!CH_2 \\
\text{Propene} & \text{2-Propanol} \\
& \text{(isopropyl alcohol)}
\end{array}
$$

SAMPLE PROBLEM 12.6   **Drawing the Products of Hydration**

Draw the condensed structural formula or skeletal formula, if cyclic, for the product that forms in each of the following hydration reactions:

a. $CH_3\!-\!CH_2\!-\!CH_2\!-\!CH\!=\!CH_2 + HOH \xrightarrow{\;H^+\;}$ **b.** $\square\!\!\!|\; + HOH \xrightarrow{\;H^+\;}$

SOLUTION

Analyze the Problem

Reactant	Type of Reaction	Product
Alkene (unsymmetrical)	Markovnikov's rule applies	Alcohol
Alkene (symmetrical)	Hydration (addition of HOH to a double bond)	

a. Because the double bond is unsymmetrical, we use Markovnikov's rule. Then the H— adds to the carbon atom in the double bond that has the greater number of H atoms, and the —OH from water attaches to the carbon atom in the double bond with fewer H atoms.

$$CH_3-CH_2-CH_2-\overset{\overset{\displaystyle OH}{\downarrow}}{C}H=\overset{\overset{\displaystyle H}{\downarrow}}{C}H_2 \xrightarrow{H^+} CH_3-CH_2-CH_2-\overset{\overset{\displaystyle OH}{|}}{C}H-CH_3$$

b. Cyclobutene has a symmetrical double bond because each carbon atom in the double bond is attached to one H. Therefore, we do not need to use Markovnikov's rule. The H— from water adds to one carbon in the double bond, and the —OH group adds to the other carbon.

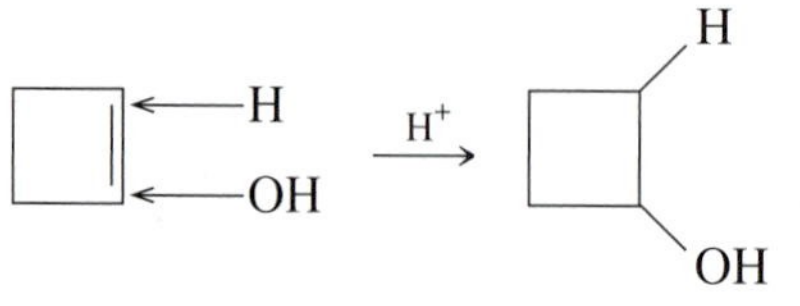

STUDY CHECK 12.6

Draw the condensed structural formula for the alcohol obtained by the hydration of 2-methyl-2-butene.

QUESTIONS AND PROBLEMS

12.3 Addition Reactions

LEARNING GOAL: *Draw the condensed structural formulas or skeletal formulas, if cyclic, and give the names for the organic products of addition reactions of alkenes and alkynes.*

12.13 Draw the condensed structural formula, or skeletal formula if cyclic, and give the name of the product in each of the following reactions:

a. $CH_3-CH_2-CH_2-CH=CH_2 + H_2 \xrightarrow{Pt}$

b. $H_2C=\overset{\overset{\displaystyle CH_3}{|}}{C}-CH_2-CH_3 + Cl_2 \longrightarrow$

c.  ☐‖ $+ Br_2 \longrightarrow$ **d.** cyclopentene $+ H_2 \xrightarrow{Pt}$

e. 2-methyl-2-butene $+ Cl_2 \longrightarrow$

f. 2-pentyne $+ 2H_2 \xrightarrow{Pd}$

12.14 Draw the condensed structural formula, or skeletal formula if cyclic, and give the name of the product in each of the following reactions:

a. $CH_3-CH_2-CH=CH_2 + Br_2 \longrightarrow$

b. cyclohexene $+ H_2 \xrightarrow{Pt}$

c. *cis*-2-butene $+ H_2 \xrightarrow{Pt}$

d. $CH_3-\overset{\overset{\displaystyle CH_3}{|}}{C}=CH-CH_2-CH_3 + Cl_2 \longrightarrow$

e. 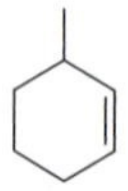 ⬡‖ $+ Br_2 \longrightarrow$

f. $CH_3-\overset{\overset{\displaystyle CH_3}{|}}{C}H-C\equiv CH + 2Cl_2 \longrightarrow$

12.15 Draw the condensed structural formula, or skeletal formula, if cyclic, for the product in each of the following reactions, using Markovnikov's rule when necessary:

a. $CH_3-CH=CH-CH_3 + HBr \longrightarrow$

b. cyclopentene $+ HOH \xrightarrow{H^+}$

c. $H_2C=CH-CH_2-CH_3 + HCl \longrightarrow$

d. $CH_3-\overset{\overset{\displaystyle CH_3}{|}}{C}=\overset{\underset{\displaystyle CH_3}{|}}{C}-CH_3 + HI \longrightarrow$

e. $CH_3-CH_2-\overset{\overset{\displaystyle CH_3}{|}}{C}=CH-CH_3 + HBr \longrightarrow$

f. 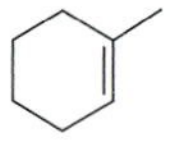 ⬡ $+ HOH \xrightarrow{H^+}$

12.16 Draw the condensed structural formula, or skeletal formula if cyclic, for the product in each of the following reactions, using Markovnikov's rule, when necessary:

a. $CH_3-\overset{\overset{\displaystyle CH_3}{|}}{C}=CH-CH_3 + HCl \longrightarrow$

b. $CH_3-CH_2-CH=CH-CH_2-CH_3 + HOH \xrightarrow{H^+}$

c. $CH_3-\overset{\overset{\displaystyle CH_3}{|}}{C}=CH_2 + HBr \longrightarrow$

d. 4-methylcyclopentene $+ HOH \xrightarrow{H^+}$

e.  ⬡‖ $+ HBr \longrightarrow$

f. $CH_3-C\equiv C-CH_3 + 2HCl \longrightarrow$

12.17 Write an equation, including any catalysts, for each of the following reactions:
   a. hydrogenation of methylpropene
   b. addition of hydrogen chloride to cyclopentene
   c. addition of bromine to 2-pentene
   d. hydration of propene
   e. addition of chlorine to 2-butyne

12.18 Write an equation, including any catalysts, for each of the following reactions:
   a. hydration of 1-methylcyclobutene
   b. hydrogenation of 3-hexene
   c. addition of hydrogen bromide to 2-methyl-2-butene
   d. addition of chlorine to 2,3-dimethyl-2-pentene
   e. addition of HCl to 1-methylcyclopentene

12.4 Polymers of Alkenes

LEARNING GOAL

Draw condensed structural formulas for monomers that form a polymer or a section of a polymer.

A **polymer** is a large molecule that consists of small repeating units called **monomers**. In the past hundred years, the plastics industry has made synthetic polymers that are in many of the materials we use every day, such as carpeting, plastic wrap, nonstick pans, plastic cups, and rain gear. In medicine, synthetic polymers are used to replace diseased or damaged body parts such as hip joints, teeth, heart valves, and blood vessels (see Figure 12.4). There are about 100 billion kg of plastics produced every year, which is about 15 kg for every person on Earth.

Many of the synthetic polymers are made by addition reactions of small alkene monomers. Many polymerization reactions require high temperature, a catalyst, and high pressure (over 1000 atm). In an addition reaction, a polymer grows longer as each monomer is added at the end of the chain. A polymer may contain as many as 1000 monomers. Polyethylene, a polymer made from ethylene monomers, is used in plastic bottles, film, and plastic dinnerware. More polyethylene is produced worldwide than any other polymer.

SELF-STUDY ACTIVITY
Polymers

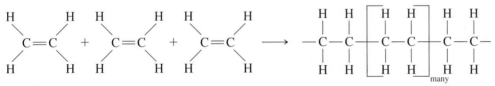

Ethene (ethylene) monomers → Polyethylene section

Monomer unit repeats

FIGURE 12.4 Synthetic polymers are used to replace diseased veins and arteries.

Q Why are the substances in these plastic devices called polymers?

Table 12.3 lists several alkene monomers that are used to produce common synthetic polymers, and Figure 12.5 shows examples of each. The alkane-like nature of these plastic

Polyethylene

Polyvinyl chloride

Polypropylene

Polytetrafluoroethylene (Teflon®)

Polydichloroethylene (Saran™)

Polystyrene

FIGURE 12.5 Synthetic polymers provide a wide variety of items that we use every day.

Q What are some alkenes used to make the polymers in these plastic items?

TABLE 12.3 **Some Alkenes and Their Polymers**

Monomer	Polymer Section	Common Uses
$H_2C=CH_2$ Ethene (ethylene)	Polyethylene	Plastic bottles, film, insulation materials
$H_2C=CH$ — Cl Chloroethene (vinyl chloride)	Polyvinyl chloride (PVC)	Plastic pipes and tubing, garden hoses, garbage bags
$H_2C=CH$ — CH_3 Propene (propylene)	Polypropylene	Ski and hiking clothing, carpets, artificial joints
$F-C=C-F$ (with F) Tetrafluoroethene	Polytetrafluoroethylene (Teflon®)	Nonstick coatings
$H_2C=C$ — Cl (with Cl) 1,1-Dichloroethene	Polydichloroethylene (Saran™)	Plastic film and wrap
$H_2C=CH$ — (phenyl) Phenylethene (styrene)	$-CH_2-CH-CH_2-CH-CH_2-CH-$ Polystyrene	Plastic coffee cups and cartons, insulation

TUTORIAL
Polymers

The recycling symbol indicates the type of polymer.

Tables, benches, and trash receptacles can be manufactured from recycled plastics.

synthetic polymers makes them unreactive. Thus, they do not decompose easily (they are not biodegradable). As a result, they have become significant contributors to pollution, on land and in the oceans. Efforts are being made to make them more degradable.

You can identify the type of polymer used to manufacture a plastic item by looking for the recycling symbol (arrows in a triangle) found on the label or on the bottom of the plastic container. For example, the number 5 or the letters PP inside the triangle is the code for a polypropylene plastic. There are now many cities that maintain recycling programs that reduce the amount of plastic materials that are transported to landfills.

1	2	3	4	5	6	7
PETE	HDPE	PVC	LDPE	PP	PS	O
Polyethylene terephthalate	High-density polyethylene	Polyvinyl chloride	Low-density polyethylene	Polypropylene	Polystyrene	Other

Today, products such as lumber, tables and benches, trash receptacles, and pipes used for irrigation systems are made from recycled plastics.

SAMPLE PROBLEM 12.7 Polymers

Give the name and draw the condensed structural formula for the starting monomers for each of the following polymers:

a. polypropylene

b. Saran

$$-C-C-C-C-C-C-$$

with H, Cl, H, Cl, H, Cl on top and H, Cl, H, Cl, H, Cl on bottom

SOLUTION

a. propene (propylene), $H_2C\!=\!CH$ with CH_3 above CH

b. 1,1-dichloroethene, $H_2C\!=\!C-Cl$ with Cl above C

STUDY CHECK 12.7

Draw the condensed structural formula for the monomer used in the manufacturing of PVC.

Explore Your World

POLYMERS AND RECYCLING PLASTICS

1. Make a list of the items you use or have in your room or home that are made of polymers.
2. Recycling information on the bottom or side of a plastic bottle includes a triangle with a code number that identifies the type of polymer used to make the plastic. Make a collection of several different kinds of plastic bottles. Try to find plastic items with each type of polymer.

QUESTIONS

1. What are the most common types of plastics among the plastic containers in your collection?
2. What are the monomers of some of the plastics you looked at?

QUESTIONS AND PROBLEMS

12.4 Polymers of Alkenes

LEARNING GOAL: Draw condensed structural formulas for monomers that form a polymer or a section of a polymer.

12.19 What is a polymer?

12.20 What is a monomer?

12.21 Write an equation that represents the formation of a portion of polypropylene from three of its monomers.

12.22 Write an equation that represents the formation of a portion of polystyrene from three of its monomers.

12.23 The plastic polyvinylidene difluoride, PVDF, is made from monomers of 1,1-difluoroethene. Draw the expanded structural formula for a portion of the polymer formed from three monomers of 1,1-difluoroethene.

12.24 The polymer polyacrylonitrile used in the fabric material Orlon is made from monomers of acrylonitrile. Draw the expanded structural formula for a portion of the polymer formed from three monomers of acrylonitrile.

Acrylonitrile $H_2C\!=\!CH$ with CN above CH

12.5 Aromatic Compounds

In 1825, Michael Faraday isolated a hydrocarbon called *benzene*, which had the molecular formula C_6H_6. A molecule of **benzene** consists of a ring of six carbon atoms with one hydrogen atom attached to each carbon. Because many compounds containing benzene had fragrant odors, the family of benzene compounds became known as **aromatic compounds**. Some common examples of aromatic compounds that we use for flavor are anisole from anise, estragole from tarragon, and thymol from thyme.

In benzene, each carbon atom uses three valence electrons to bond to the hydrogen atom and two adjacent carbons. That leaves one valence electron, which scientists first thought was shared in a double bond with an adjacent carbon. In 1865, August Kekulé proposed that the carbon atoms in benzene were arranged in a flat ring with alternating single and double bonds between the carbon atoms. There are two possible structural representations of benzene due to resonance in which the double bonds can form between two different carbon atoms (see Section 5.5).

However, scientists discovered that benzene behaved more like an alkane and not like an alkene because benzene does not undergo addition reactions. Today, we know that the six

LEARNING GOAL

Describe the bonding in benzene; name aromatic compounds, and draw their skeletal formulas.

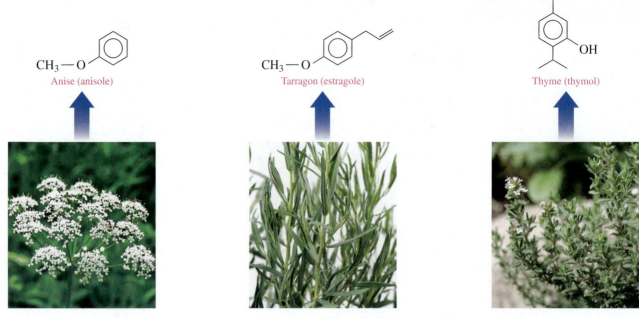

CH_3-O- Anise (anisole)

CH_3-O- Tarragon (estragole)

Thyme (thymol)

The aroma and flavor of the herbs anise, tarragon, and thyme are due to aromatic compounds.

electrons are shared equally among the six carbon atoms and that all the carbon–carbon bonds in benzene are identical due to resonance. This unique feature of benzene makes it especially stable. Benzene is most often represented as a skeletal formula, which shows a hexagon with a circle in the center. Some of the ways to represent benzene are shown as follows:

Structural representations for benzene

TUTORIAL
Naming Aromatic Compounds

Naming Aromatic Compounds

Many compounds containing benzene have been important in chemistry for many years and still use their common names. Names such as toluene, aniline, and phenol are allowed by IUPAC rules.

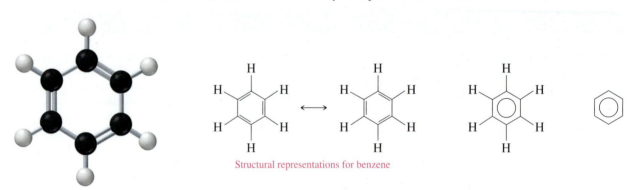

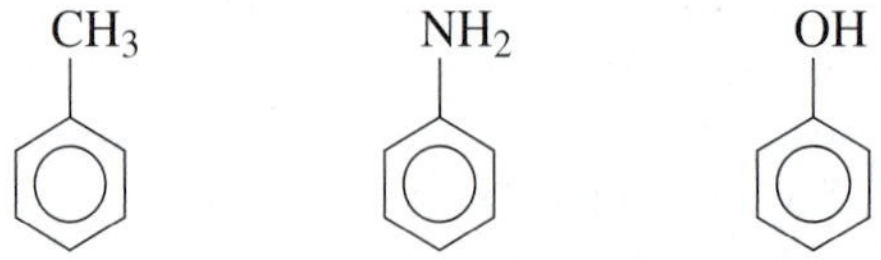

CH_3

Toluene
(methylbenzene)

NH_2

Aniline
(aminobenzene)

OH

Phenol
(hydroxybenzene)

When a benzene ring is a substituent, C_6H_5-, it is named as a phenyl group.

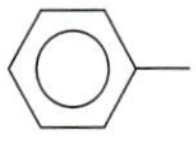

$CH_3-CH-CH=CH_2$

Phenyl group 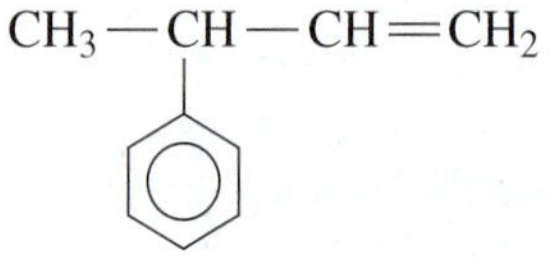   3-Phenyl-1-butene

When benzene has only one substituent, the ring is not numbered. When there are two substituents, the benzene ring is numbered to give the lowest numbers to the substituents. When a common name can be used such as toluene, phenol, or aniline, the carbon atom attached to the methyl, hydroxyl, or amine group is numbered as carbon 1. In a common name, there are prefixes that are used to show the position of two substituents. The prefix **ortho** (*o*) indicates a 1,2 arrangement, **meta** (*m*) is a 1,3 arrangement, and **para** (*p*) is used for 1,4 arrangements.

Chlorobenzene 1,2-Dichlorobenzene 1,3-Dichlorobenzene 1,4-Dichlorobenzene
 (*o*-dichlorobenzene) (*m*-dichlorobenzene) (*p*-dichlorobenzene)

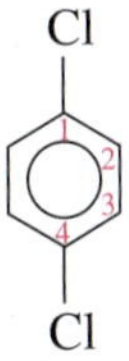

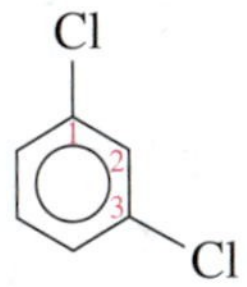

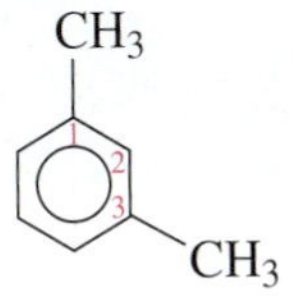

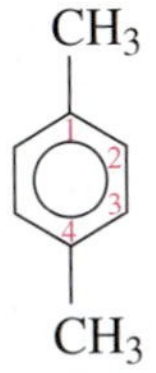

The common name xylene is used for the isomers of dimethylbenzene.

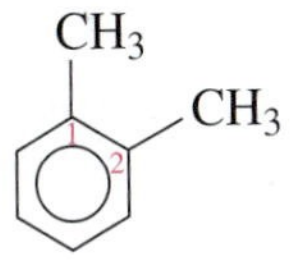

1,2-Dimethylbenzene 1,3-Dimethylbenzene 1,4-Dimethylbenzene
 (*o*-xylene) (*m*-xylene) (*p*-xylene)

When there are three or more substituents attached to the benzene ring, they are numbered in the direction to give the lowest set of numbers and then named alphabetically.

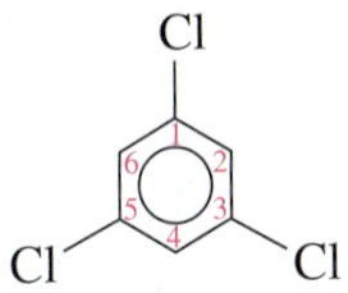

1,3,5-Trichlorobenzene 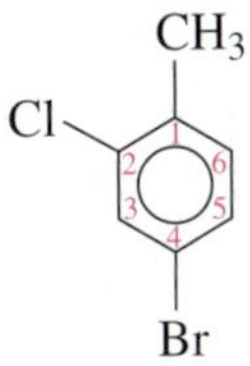 4-Bromo-2-chlorotoluene 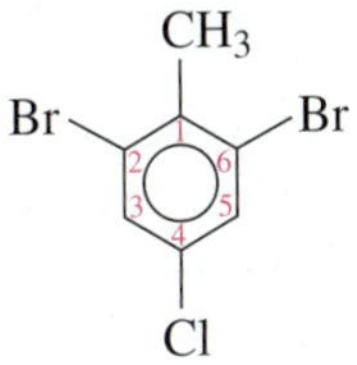 2,6-Dibromo-4-chlorotoluene

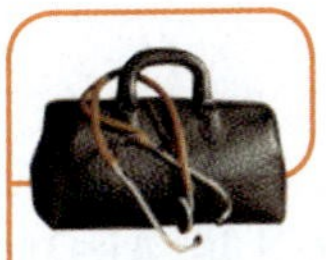

SAMPLE PROBLEM 12.8 **Naming Aromatic Compounds**

Give the IUPAC name and any common name for each of the following:

a. **b.** **c.**

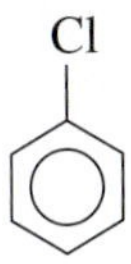

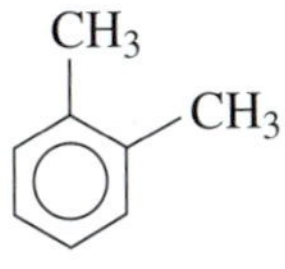

SOLUTION

a. chlorobenzene **b.** 4-bromo-3-chlorotoluene
c. 1,2-dimethylbenzene; *o*-xylene

STUDY CHECK 12.8

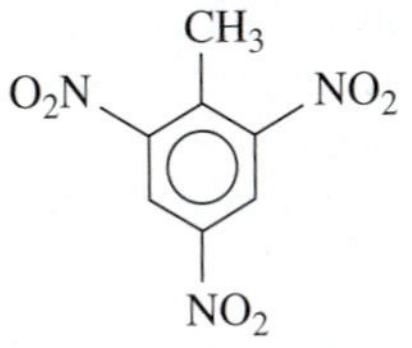

Name the following compound:

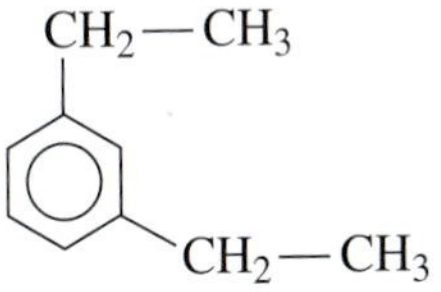

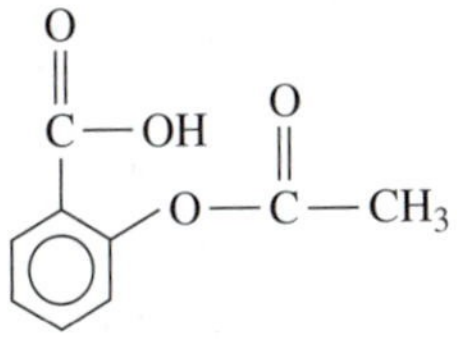

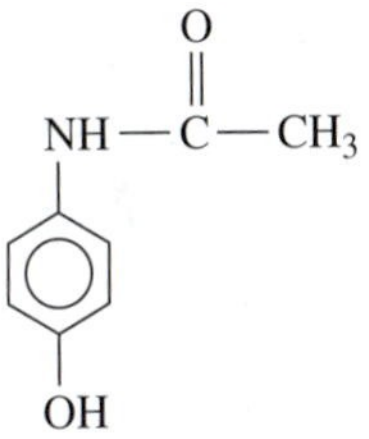

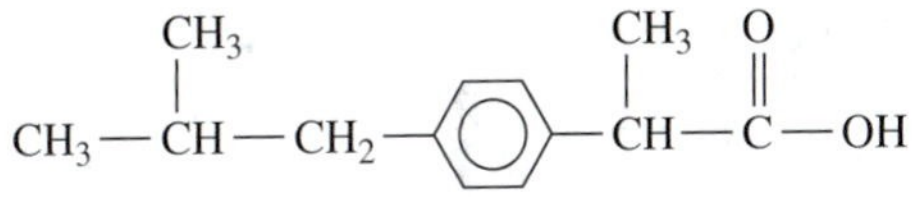

$CH_2 - CH_3$

$CH_2 - CH_3$

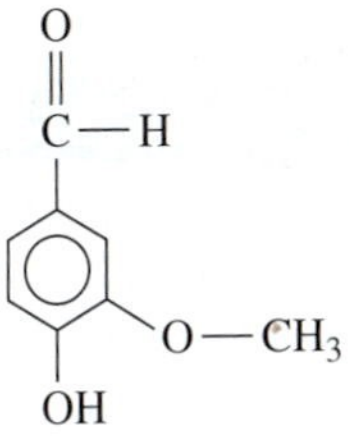

Chemistry Link to Health

POLYCYCLIC AROMATIC HYDROCARBONS (PAHs)

Large aromatic compounds known as *polycyclic aromatic hydrocarbons* are formed by fusing together two or more benzene rings edge to edge. In a fused-ring compound, neighboring benzene rings share two or more carbon atoms. Naphthalene, with two benzene rings, is known for its use in mothballs. Anthracene, with three rings, is used in the manufacture of dyes.

Naphthalene   Anthracene 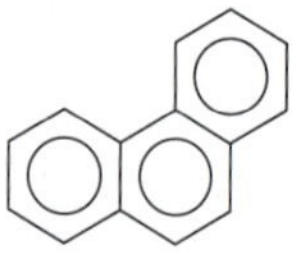   Phenanthrene

When a polycyclic compound contains the three fused rings of phenanthrene, it may act as a carcinogen, a substance known to cause cancer.

Compounds containing five or more fused benzene rings such as benz[*a*]pyrene are potent carcinogens. The molecules interact with the

DNA in the cells, causing abnormal cell growth and cancer. Increased exposure to carcinogens increases the chance of DNA alterations in the cells. Benz[*a*]pyrene, a product of combustion, has been identified in coal tar, tobacco smoke, barbecued meats, and automobile exhaust.

Benz[*a*]pyrene

Aromatic compounds such as benz[*a*]pyrene are strongly associated with lung cancers.

Properties of Aromatic Compounds

The flat symmetrical structure of benzene allows the individual cyclic structures to be very close together, which contributes to the higher melting points and boiling points of benzene and its derivatives. For example, hexane melts at −95 °C, while benzene melts at 6 °C. Among the disubstituted benzene compounds, the para isomers are more symmetric and have higher melting points than the ortho and meta isomers: *o*-xylene melts at −26 °C and *m*-xylene melts at −48 °C, while *p*-xylene melts at 13 °C.

Aromatic compounds are less dense than water, although they are somewhat denser than other hydrocarbons. Halogenated benzene compounds are denser than water. Aromatic hydrocarbons are insoluble in water and are used as solvents for other organic compounds. Only those aromatic compounds containing strongly polar functional groups such as —OH or —COOH will be somewhat soluble in water. Benzene and other aromatic compounds are resistant to reactions that break up the aromatic system, although they are flammable, as are other hydrocarbon compounds.

QUESTIONS AND PROBLEMS

12.5 Aromatic Compounds

LEARNING GOAL: *Describe the bonding in benzene; name aromatic compounds, and draw their skeletal formulas.*

12.25 Match the following statements with the compound cyclohexane or benzene:
  a. formula C_6H_{12}
  b. has one hydrogen atom bonded to each carbon
  c. contains only single bonds

12.26 Match the following statements with the compound cyclohexane or benzene:
  a. contains a stable aromatic system
  b. has two hydrogen atoms bonded to each carbon
  c. formula C_6H_6

12.27 Give the IUPAC name and any common name for each of the following:

a.
b.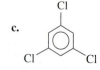
c.

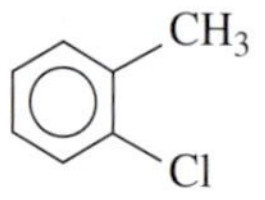

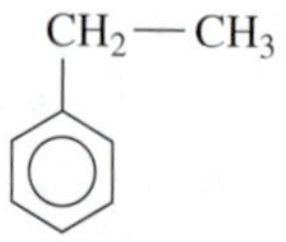

d.
e.
f.

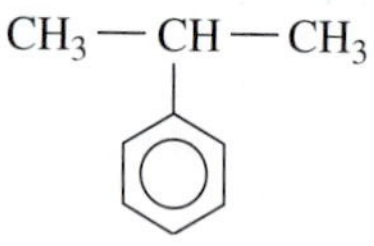

12.28 Give the IUPAC name and any common name for each of the following:

a.
b.
c.

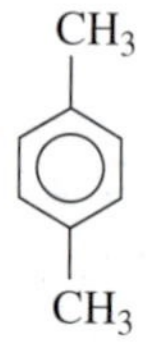

d.
e. 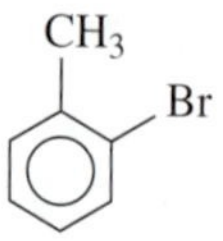
f.

12.29 Draw the skeletal formula for each of the following:
  a. methylbenzene
  b. 1-bromo-3-chlorobenzene
  c. 1-ethyl-4-methylbenzene
  d. *p*-chlorotoluene

12.30 Draw the skeletal formula for each of the following:
  a. *m*-dibromobenzene
  b. *o*-chloroethylbenzene
  c. propylbenzene
  d. 1,2,4-trichlorobenzene

CONCEPT MAP

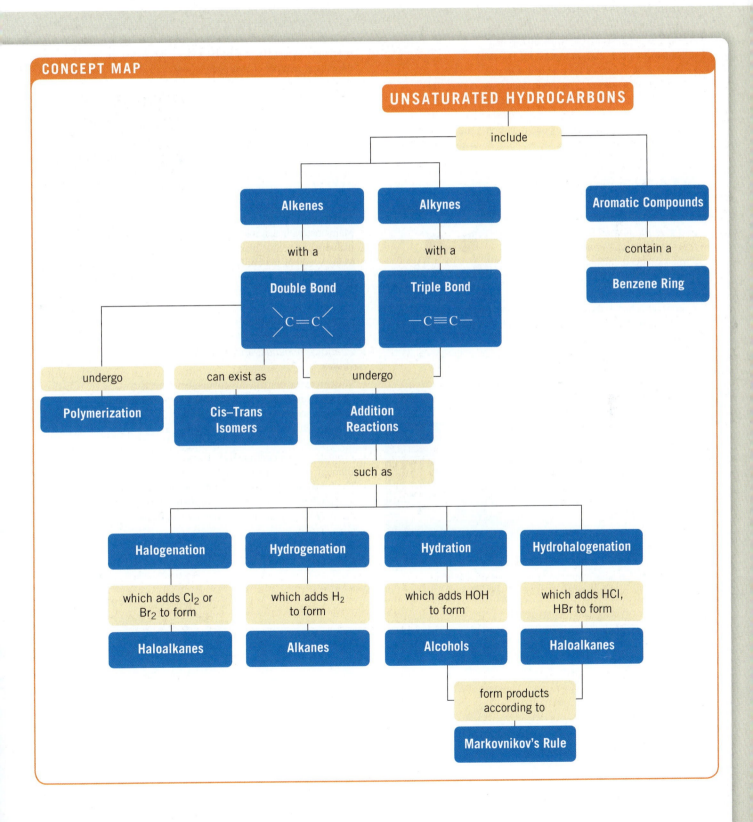

CHAPTER REVIEW

12.1 Alkenes and Alkynes

LEARNING GOAL: Write the IUPAC names for alkenes and alkynes; give common names for simple structures.

Bond angles = 120°

- Alkenes are unsaturated hydrocarbons that contain carbon–carbon double bonds (C=C).
- The IUPAC names of alkenes end with *ene*.
- Alkynes are unsaturated hydrocarbons that contain a carbon–carbon triple bond (C≡C).
- The IUPAC names of alkynes end with *yne*.
- To name substituents in an unsaturated hydrocarbon, the main chain is numbered from the end nearer the double or triple bond.
- In a cycloalkene, the double bond is carbon 1 and 2, and the ring is numbered to give the lowest numbers to any substituents, which are named alphabetically.

12.2 Cis–Trans Isomers

LEARNING GOAL: Draw the condensed structural formulas and give the names for the cis–trans isomers of alkenes.

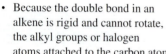

cis-2-Butene

- Because the double bond in an alkene is rigid and cannot rotate, the alkyl groups or halogen atoms attached to the carbon atoms in the double bond stay on one side or the other, giving the possibility of two cis–trans isomers.
- In the cis isomer, the alkyl groups or halogen atoms are on the same side of the double bond.
- In the trans isomer, the alkyl groups or halogen atoms are on opposite sides of the double bond.

12.3 Addition Reactions

LEARNING GOAL: Draw the condensed structural formulas or skeletal formulas, if cyclic, and give the names for the organic products of addition reactions of alkenes and alkynes.

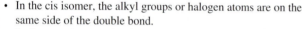

- The addition of small molecules to the double bond or triple bond is a characteristic reaction of alkenes and alkynes.
- Hydrogenation adds hydrogen atoms to the double bond of an alkene or the triple bond of an alkyne to yield an alkane.

- Halogenation adds bromine or chlorine atoms to the double bond of an alkene or the triple bond of an alkyne to produce di- or tetrahaloalkanes.
- Hydrohalogenation adds a hydrogen halide to a double bond of an alkene to give a haloalkane.
- Hydration adds water to a double bond of an alkene to form an alcohol.
- When a different number of hydrogen atoms are attached to the carbons in a double bond, Markovnikov's rule states that the H from the reactant (H—X or H—OH) adds to the carbon with the greater number of hydrogen atoms.

12.4 Polymers of Alkenes

LEARNING GOAL: Draw condensed structural formulas for monomers that form a polymer or a section of a polymer.

- Polymers are long-chain molecules that consist of many repeating units of smaller carbon molecules called monomers.
- Many materials that we use every day are synthetic polymers, including carpeting, plastic wrap, nonstick pans, and nylon.
- Many synthetic materials are made using addition reactions in which a catalyst links the carbon atoms from various kinds of alkene molecules (monomers).

12.5 Aromatic Compounds

LEARNING GOAL: Describe the bonding in benzene; name aromatic compounds, and draw their skeletal formulas.

- Most aromatic compounds contain benzene, a cyclic structure containing six carbon atoms and six hydrogen atoms.
- The structure of benzene is represented as a hexagon with a circle in the center.
- Aromatic compounds are named using the IUPAC name benzene, although common names such as toluene are retained.
- The benzene ring is numbered, and the substituents are listed in alphabetical order. For two substituents, the positions are often shown by the prefixes *ortho* (1,2-), *meta* (1,3-), and *para* (1,4-).

SUMMARY OF NAMING

Family	Example	Structure
Alkene	Propene (propylene)	$CH_3-CH=CH_2$
	cis-1,2-Dibromoethene	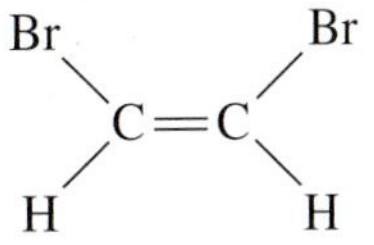
	trans-1,2-Dibromoethene	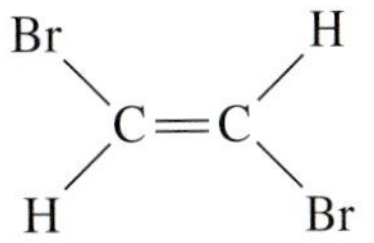
Cycloalkene	Cyclopropene	
Alkyne	Propyne	$CH_3-C\equiv CH$
Aromatic	Benzene	
	Methylbenzene; toluene	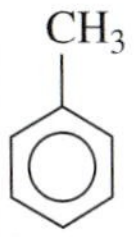
	1,4-Dichlorobenzene; p-dichlorobenzene	

SUMMARY OF REACTIONS

Hydrogenation

$$H_2C=CH-CH_3 + H_2 \xrightarrow{Pt} CH_2-CH_2-CH_3$$
Propene   Propane

$$CH_3-C\equiv CH + 2H_2 \xrightarrow{Pt} CH_3-CH_2-CH_3$$
Propyne   Propane

Halogenation

$$H_2C=CH-CH_3 + Cl_2 \longrightarrow \underset{\text{1,2-Dichloropropane}}{CH_2-CH-CH_3}$$
Propene
(Cl, Cl substituents)

Hydrohalogenation

Markovnikov's rule

$$H_2C=CH-CH_3 + HCl \longrightarrow \underset{\text{2-Chloropropane}}{CH_3-CH-CH_3}$$
Propene
(Cl substituent)

Hydration

Markovnikov's rule

$$H_2C=CH-CH_3 + HOH \xrightarrow{H^+} \underset{\text{2-Propanol}}{CH_3-CH-CH_3}$$
Propene
(OH substituent)

KEY TERMS

addition A reaction in which atoms or groups of atoms bond to a double bond. Addition reactions include the addition of hydrogen (hydrogenation), halogens (halogenation), hydrogen halides (hydrohalogenation), and water (hydration).

alkene A hydrocarbon containing a carbon–carbon double bond.
alkyne A hydrocarbon containing a carbon–carbon triple bond.
aromatic compounds Compounds that usually have fragrant odors and often contain the ring structure of benzene.

benzene A ring of six carbon atoms, each of which is attached to a hydrogen atom, C_6H_6.

carbocation A carbon cation that has only three bonds and a positive charge, and is formed during the addition reactions of hydration and hydrohalogenation.

cis isomer An isomer of an alkene in which large groups are attached to the same side of the double bond.

halogenation The addition of Cl_2 or Br_2 to an alkene or alkyne to form halogen-containing compounds.

hydration An addition reaction in which the components of water, H— and —OH, bond to the carbon–carbon double bond to form an alcohol.

hydrogenation The addition of hydrogen (H_2) to an alkene or alkyne to yield an alkane.

hydrohalogenation The addition of a hydrogen halide such as HCl or HBr to a double bond.

Markovnikov's rule When adding HX or HOH to alkenes with different numbers of groups attached to the double bonds, the H— adds to the carbon that has the greater number of hydrogen atoms.

meta A method of naming that indicates substituents at carbons 1 and 3 of a benzene ring.

monomer The small organic molecule that is repeated many times in a polymer.

ortho A method of naming that indicates substituents at carbons 1 and 2 of a benzene ring.

para A method of naming that indicates substituents at carbons 1 and 4 of a benzene ring.

polymer A very large molecule that is composed of many small, repeating structural units that are identical.

trans isomer An isomer of an alkene in which large groups are attached on opposite sides of the double bond.

UNDERSTANDING THE CONCEPTS

The chapter sections to review are shown in parentheses at the end of each question.

12.31 Draw a portion of the polymer of Teflon, which is made from 1,1,2,2-tetrafluoroethene (use four monomers). (12.4)

Teflon is used as a nonstick coating on cooking pans.

12.32 A garden hose is made of polyvinyl chloride (PVC) from chloroethene (vinyl chloride). Draw a portion of the polymer (use four monomers) for PVC. (12.4)

A garden hose is made of polyvinyl chloride (PVC).

ADDITIONAL QUESTIONS AND PROBLEMS

For instructor-assigned homework, go to www.masteringchemistry.com.

12.33 Give the number of carbon atoms and the types of carbon–carbon bonds for each of the following: (12.1)
  a. propane
  b. cyclopropane
  c. propene
  d. propyne

12.34 Give the number of carbon atoms and the types of carbon–carbon bonds for each of the following: (12.1)
  a. butane
  b. cyclobutane
  c. cyclobutene
  d. 2-butyne

12.35 Give the IUPAC name for each of the following compounds: (12.1, 12.2)

  a. H_2C=$\overset{\displaystyle CH_3}{\underset{\displaystyle |}{C}}$—$CH_2$—$CH_2$—$CH_3$

  b.

  c.

  d. CH_3—CH_2—C≡C—CH_3

12.36 Give the IUPAC name for each of the following compounds: (12.1, 12.2)

  a.

  b.

  c.

  d. HC≡C—$\overset{\displaystyle CH_3}{\underset{\displaystyle |}{CH}}$—$CH_3$

12.37 Draw the condensed structural formula or skeletal formula, if cyclic, for each of the following: (12.1, 12.2)
  a. 1,2-dibromocyclopentene
  b. 2-hexyne
  c. *cis*-2-heptene

12.38 Draw the condensed structural formula or skeletal formula, if cyclic, for each of the following: (12.1, 12.2)
  a. *trans*-3-hexene
  b. 2-bromo-3-chlorocyclohexene
  c. 3-chloro-1-butyne

12.39 Indicate if each of the following pairs represents structural isomers, cis–trans isomers, or identical compounds: (12.1, 12.2)

a.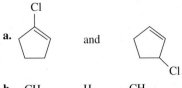

and

b. CH$_3$—C=C—H / H and CH$_3$—C=C—CH$_3$ / H (structures with C=C double bonds)

12.40 Indicate if each of the following pairs represents structural isomers, cis–trans isomers, or identical compounds: (12.1, 12.2)

a. H$_2$C=CH
   |
   CH$_2$—CH$_2$
          |
          CH$_3$
and CH$_3$—CH$_2$—CH$_2$—CH=CH$_2$

b. CH$_3$—CH—CH$_2$—C=CH$_2$
          | |
          CH$_3$ CH$_3$
and
   CH$_3$—CH$_2$—CH—CH$_2$—CH=CH$_2$
                     |
                     CH$_3$

12.41 Write the IUPAC name, including cis or trans, for each of the following: (12.1, 12.2)

a. CH$_3$—CH$_2$ CH$_2$—CH$_2$—CH$_3$
              \C=C/
              H   H

b. (skeletal structure)

c. CH$_3$ H
        \C=C/
        H   CH$_2$—CH$_2$—CH$_2$—CH$_3$

12.42 Write the IUPAC name, including cis or trans, for each of the following: (12.1, 12.2)

a. H   CH$_2$—CH—CH$_3$
         \C=C/ |
                      CH$_3$
   CH$_3$—CH$_2$ H

b. (skeletal structure)

c. CH$_3$—CH   H
             | \C=C/
             CH$_3$ CH$_2$—CH$_2$—CH$_2$—CH$_3$

12.43 Draw the condensed structural formulas for the cis and trans isomers for each of the following: (12.1, 12.2)
a. 2-pentene   **b.** 3-hexene

12.44 Draw the condensed structural formulas for the cis and trans isomers for each of the following: (12.1, 12.2)
a. 2-butene   **b.** 2-hexene

12.45 Give the name of the product from the complete hydrogenation of each of the following: (12.3)
a. 3-methyl-2-pentene   **b.** cyclohexene
c. 2-pentyne

12.46 Give the name of the product from the complete hydrogenation of each of the following: (12.3)
a. *cis*-3-hexene   **b.** 2-methyl-2-butene
c. propyne

12.47 Draw the condensed structural formula or skeletal formula, if cyclic, for the product for each of the following: (12.3)
a. CH$_3$—CH=CH—CH$_3$ + HBr ⟶
b. (cyclohexene) + HOH $\xrightarrow{H^+}$
c. CH$_3$—CH=CH—CH$_3$ + Cl$_2$ ⟶

12.48 Draw the condensed structural formula or skeletal formula, if cyclic, for the product for each of the following: (12.3)
a. CH$_3$—CH=CH—CH$_3$ + HOH $\xrightarrow{H^+}$
b. (cyclopentene) + HBr ⟶
c. CH$_3$—C=C—CH$_3$ + HCl ⟶
            | |
            CH$_3$ CH$_3$

12.49 Give the IUPAC name of the organic compound needed to react in each of the following: (12.3)
a. ? + H$_2$ $\xrightarrow{Ni}$ (cyclohexane)
b. ? + Br$_2$ ⟶ CH$_3$—CH—CH—CH$_2$—CH$_3$
                              | |
                              Br   Br

12.50 Give the IUPAC name of the organic compound needed to react in each of the following: (12.3)
a. ? + HCl ⟶ CH$_3$—CH—CH$_2$—CH$_3$
                          |
                          Cl
b. ? + HOH $\xrightarrow{H^+}$ (cyclopentane with OH)

12.51 Copolymers contain more than one type of monomer. One copolymer used in medicine is made of alternating units of styrene and acrylonitrile. Draw the expanded structural formula for a section of the copolymer that would have three each of these alternating units. (For structure of styrene, see Table 12.3.) (12.4)

CN
|
H$_2$C=CH

Acrylonitrile

12.52 Lucite, or Plexiglas, is a polymer of methylmethacrylate. Draw the expanded structural formula for a section of the polymer that is made from the addition of three of these monomers. (12.4)

CH$_3$ O
| ‖
H$_2$C=C—C—O—CH$_3$

Methylmethacrylate

12.53 Name each of the following aromatic compounds: (12.5)

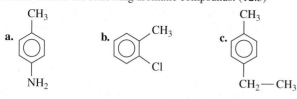

a. b. c.

12.54 Name each of the following aromatic compounds: (12.5)

a. 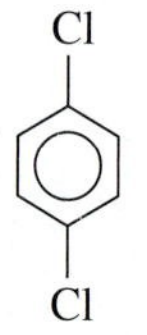 b. 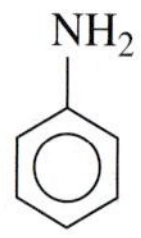 c.

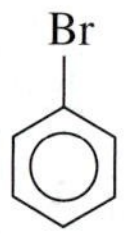

12.55 Draw the skeletal formula for each of the following: (12.5)
a. *p*-bromotoluene
b. 2,6-dimethylaniline
c. 1,4-dimethylbenzene

12.56 Draw the skeletal formula for each of the following: (12.5)
a. ethylbenzene
b. *m*-chloroaniline
c. 1,2,4-trimethylbenzene

CHALLENGE QUESTIONS

12.57 If a female silkworm moth secretes 50 ng of bombykol, a sex attractant, how many molecules did she secrete? (See Chemistry Link to the Environment "Pheromones in Insect Communication.") (6.4, 12.1)

12.58 How many grams of hydrogen are needed to hydrogenate 30.0 g of 2-butene? (12.3)

12.59 Draw the condensed structural formula for and give the name of all the possible alkenes with molecular formula C_5H_{10} that have a five-carbon chain, including those with cis and trans isomers. (12.1, 12.2)

12.60 Draw the condensed structural formula for and give the name of all the possible alkenes with molecular formula C_6H_{12} that have a six-carbon chain, including those with cis and trans isomers. (12.1, 12.2)

12.61 Explosives used in mining contain TNT or 2,4,6-trinitrotoluene. (12.5)

Explosives containing TNT are used in mining.

a. If the functional group *nitro* is $-NO_2$, what is the skeletal formula of 2,4,6-trinitrotoluene?
b. TNT is actually a mixture of structural isomers of trinitrotoluene. Draw the skeletal formula for two other possible structural isomers.

12.62 Margarine is produced from the hydrogenation of vegetable oils, which contain unsaturated fatty acids. How many grams of hydrogen are required to completely saturate 75.0 g of oleic acid, $C_{18}H_{34}O_2$, which has one double bond? (12.3)

Margarines are produced by the hydrogenation of unsaturated fats.

ANSWERS

Answers to Study Checks

12.1 a. $CH_3-C\equiv C-CH_2-CH_3$

b. $H_2C=C(-Cl)-CH_2-CH_2-CH_2-CH_3$

12.2 *trans*-3-heptene

12.3 $CH_3-CH(-CH_3)-CH_2-CH_3$

12.4 1,2-dichlorobutane

12.5 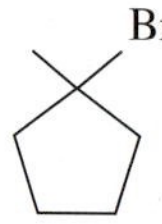 1-bromo-1-methylcyclopentane

12.6 $CH_3-C(-CH_3)(-OH)-CH_2-CH_3$

12.7 H C=C Cl H H H

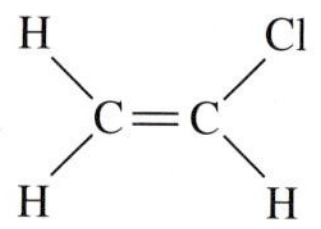

12.8 1,3-diethylbenzene; *m*-diethylbenzene

Answers to Selected Questions and Problems

12.1 a. alkene
b. alkyne
c. alkene
d. cycloalkene

12.3 a. 2-methylpropene
b. 4-bromo-2-pentyne
c. 4-ethylcyclopentene
d. 4-ethyl-2-hexene

12.5 a. $H_2C=CH-CH_2-CH_2-CH_3$

b. $H_2C=C(-CH_3)-CH_2-CH_3$
c.

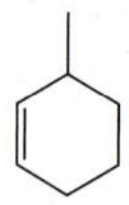

d. 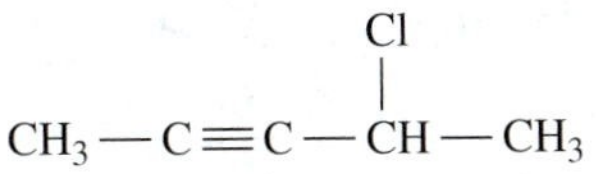 CH$_3$—C≡C—CH—CH$_3$ (with Cl on CH)

12.7 **a** and **c** cannot have cis–trans isomers because they each have two identical groups on at least one of the carbon atoms in the double bond.

12.9 a. *cis*-2-butene   **b.** *trans*-3-octene
c. *cis*-3-heptene

12.11 a.

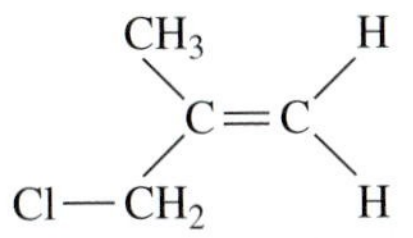

b.

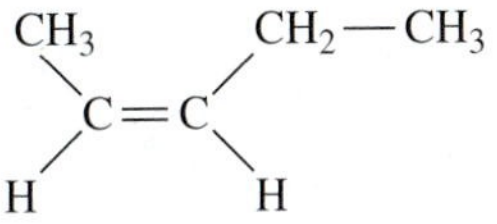

c.

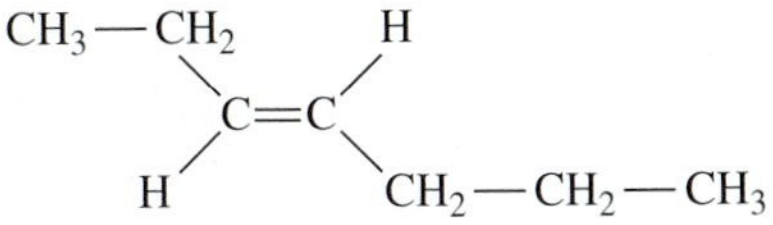

12.13 a. CH$_3$—CH$_2$—CH$_2$—CH$_2$—CH$_3$ Pentane

b. 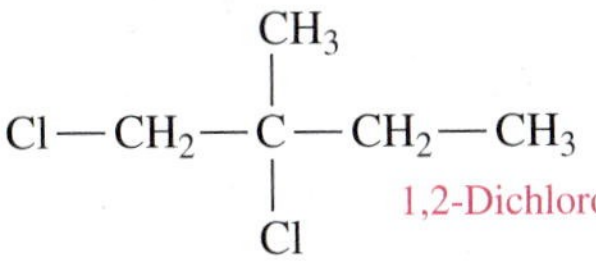 Cl—CH$_2$—C(CH$_3$)(Cl)—CH$_2$—CH$_3$ 1,2-Dichloro-2-methylbutane

c. 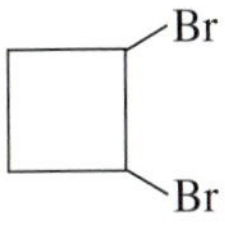 (cyclobutane with Br, Br)   1,2-Dibromocyclobutane

d. 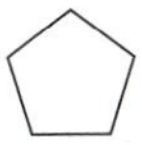 (cyclopentane)   Cyclopentane

e. 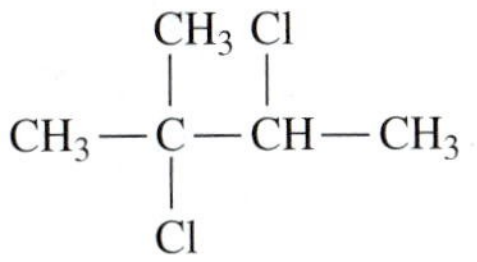 CH$_3$—C(CH$_3$)(Cl)—CH(Cl)—CH$_3$ 2,3-Dichloro-2-methylbutane

f. CH$_3$—CH$_2$—CH$_2$—CH$_2$—CH$_3$ Pentane

12.15 a. 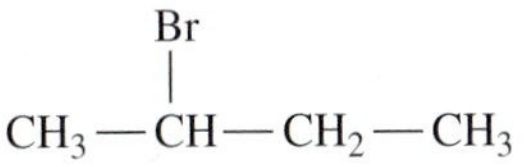 CH$_3$—CH(Br)—CH$_2$—CH$_3$ **b.**  (cyclopentane with OH)

c. 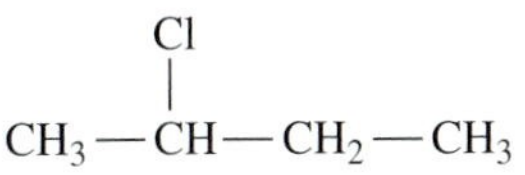 CH$_3$—CH(Cl)—CH$_2$—CH$_3$ **d.** 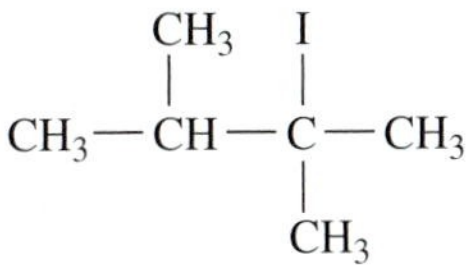 CH$_3$—CH(CH$_3$)—C(I)(CH$_3$)—CH$_3$

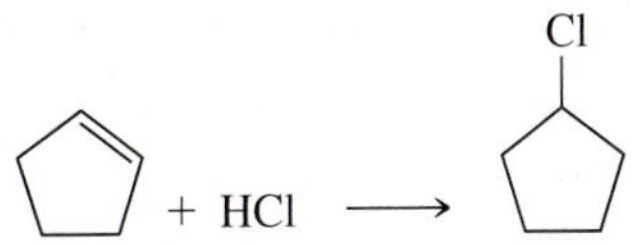

e. 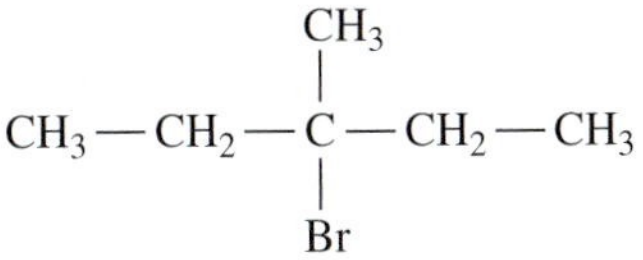 CH$_3$—CH$_2$—C(CH$_3$)(Br)—CH$_2$—CH$_3$

f. 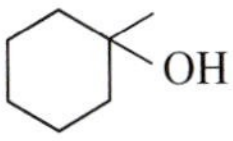 (cyclohexane with CH$_3$ and OH)

12.17 a. 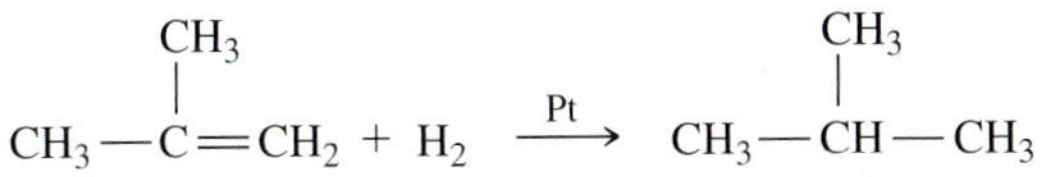 CH$_3$—C(CH$_3$)=CH$_2$ + H$_2$ $\xrightarrow{Pt}$ CH$_3$—CH(CH$_3$)—CH$_3$

b.

(cyclopentene) + HCl ⟶ (cyclopentane with Cl)

c. CH$_3$—CH=CH—CH$_2$—CH$_3$ + Br$_2$ ⟶

CH$_3$—CH(Br)—CH(Br)—CH$_2$—CH$_3$

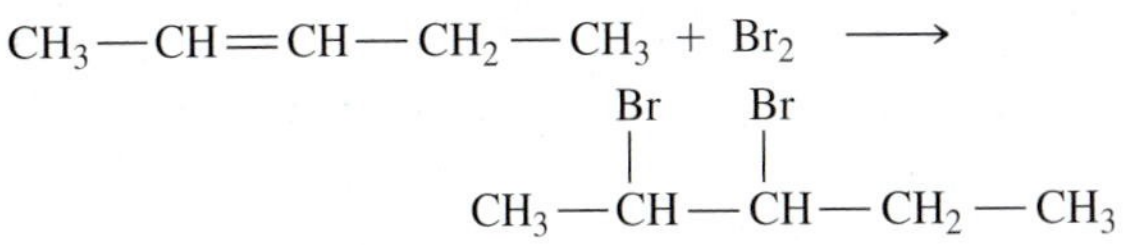

d. 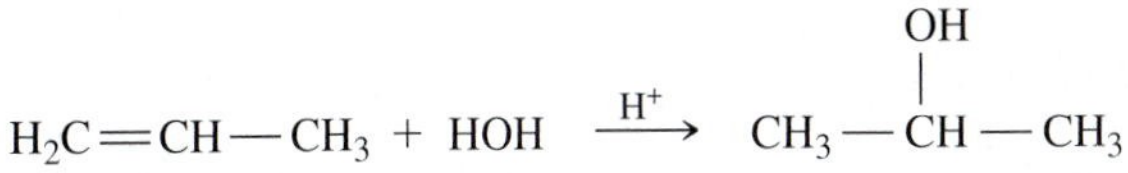 H$_2$C=CH—CH$_3$ + HOH $\xrightarrow{H^+}$ CH$_3$—CH(OH)—CH$_3$

e. 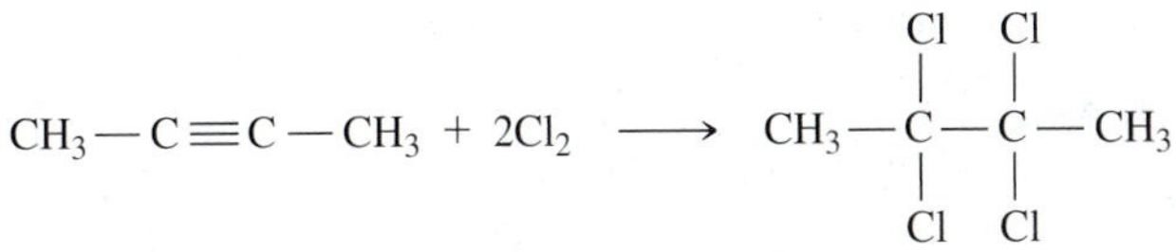 CH$_3$—C≡C—CH$_3$ + 2Cl$_2$ ⟶ CH$_3$—C(Cl)$_2$—C(Cl)$_2$—CH$_3$

12.19 A polymer is a very large molecule composed of small units (monomers) that are repeated many times.

12.21 3 H$_2$C=CH(CH$_3$) ⟶

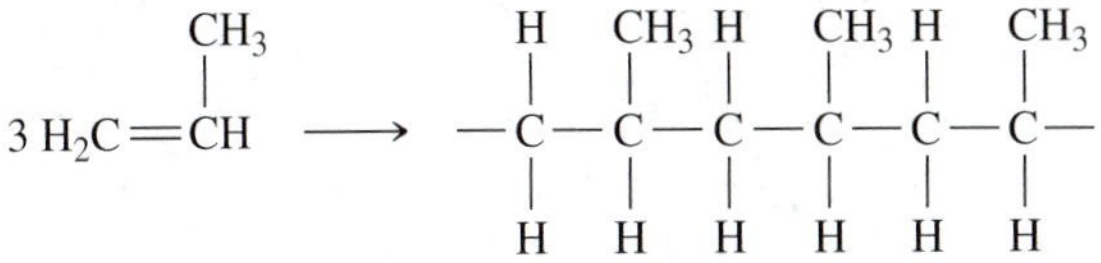

12.23

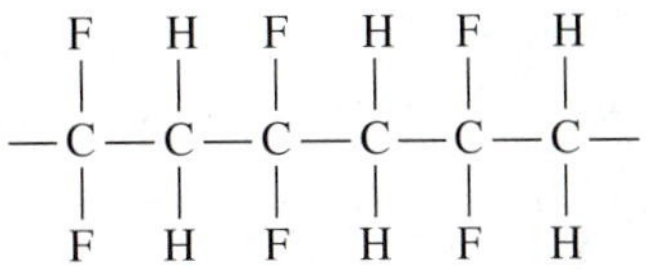

12.25 a. cyclohexane   **b.** benzene
c. cyclohexane

12.27 a. 1-chloro-2-methylbenzene, 2-chlorotoluene, *o*-chlorotoluene
b. ethylbenzene
c. 1,3,5-trichlorobenzene
d. 1,3-dimethylbenzene, 3-methyltoluene, *m*-xylene, *m*-dimethylbenzene, *m*-methyltoluene
e. 3-bromo-5-chlorotoluene, 3-bromo-5-chloro-1-methylbenzene
f. isopropylbenzene

12.29 a.  (toluene)   **b.** 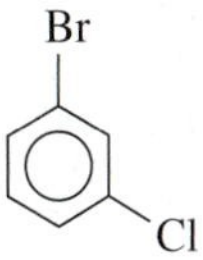 (3-bromochlorobenzene)   **c.** 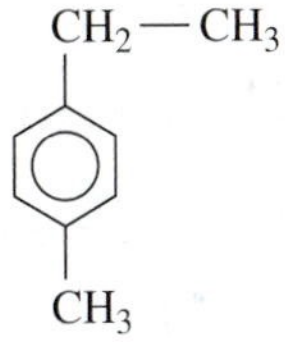 (4-ethyltoluene)   **d.**  (4-chlorotoluene)

12.31

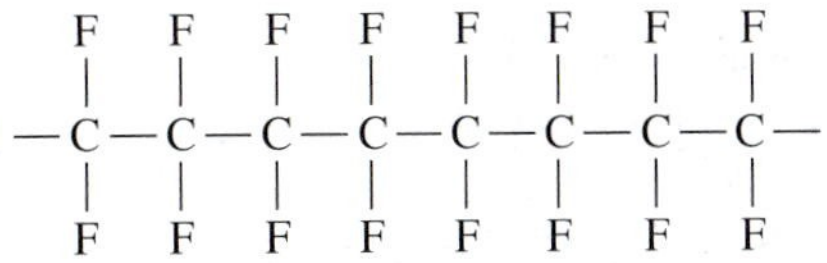

12.33 a. three carbon atoms; two carbon–carbon single bonds
b. three carbon atoms; three carbon–carbon single bonds in a ring
c. three carbon atoms; one carbon–carbon single bond; one carbon–carbon double bond
d. three carbon atoms; one carbon–carbon single bond; one carbon–carbon triple bond

12.35 a. 2-methyl-1-pentene   **b.** 4-bromo-5-methyl-1-hexene
c. cyclopentene   **d.** 2-pentyne

12.37 a.

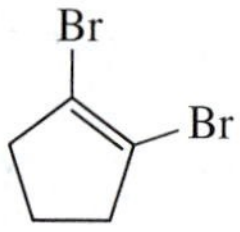

b. $CH_3 - C \equiv C - CH_2 - CH_2 - CH_3$

c.

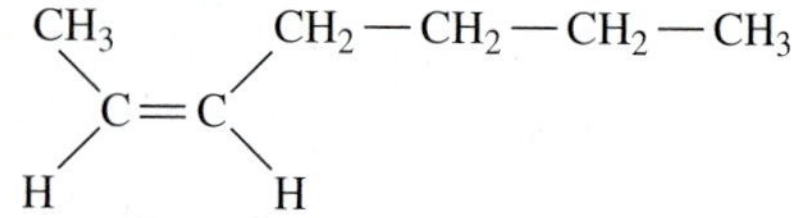

12.39 a. structural isomers   **b.** cis–trans isomers

12.41 a. *cis*-3-heptene   **b.** *trans*-2-methyl-3-hexene
   c. *trans*-2-heptene

12.43 a. 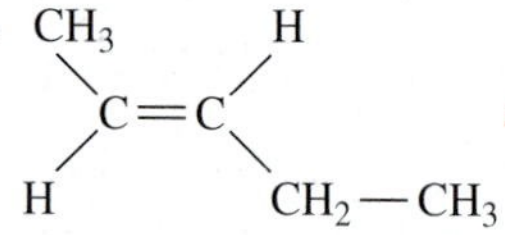   *trans*-2-Pentene

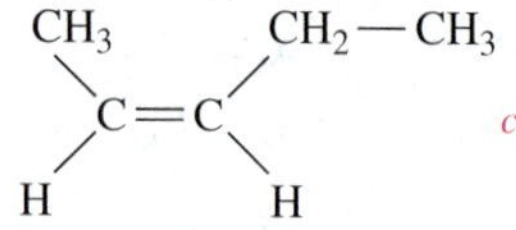

  cis-2-Pentene

b. 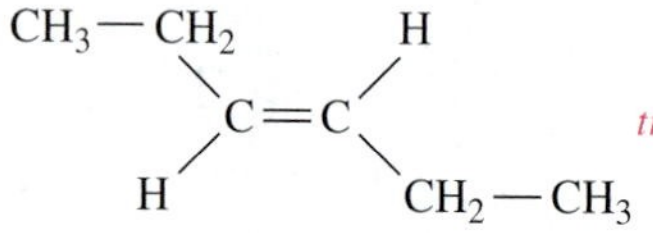   *trans*-3-Hexene

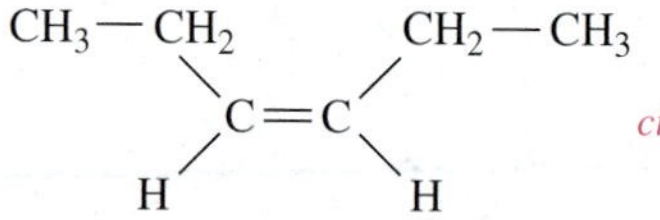

  cis-3-Hexene

12.45 a. 3-methylpentane   **b.** cyclohexane
   c. pentane

12.47 a. 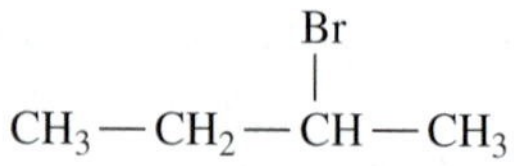   **b.**

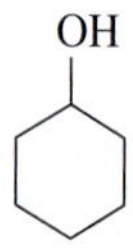

c.

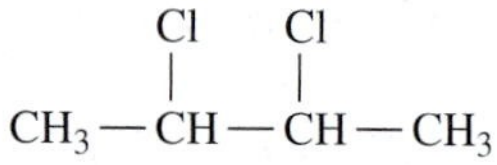

12.49 a. cyclohexene   **b.** 2-pentene

12.51

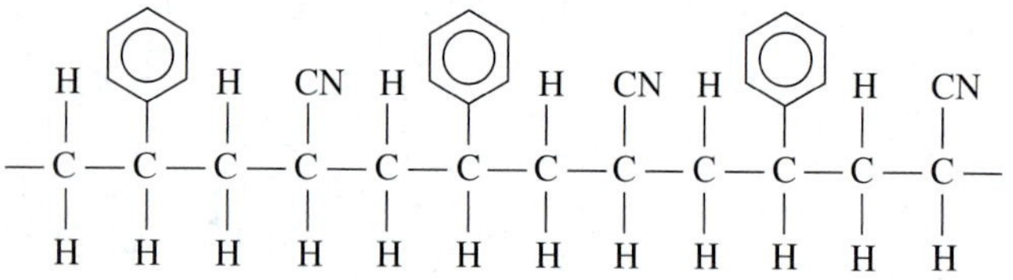

12.53 a. 3-methylaniline, *p*-methylaniline
   b. 1-chloro-2-methylbenzene, *o*-chlorotoluene,
     2-chlorotoluene
   c. 1-ethyl-4-methylbenzene, *p*-ethylmethylbenzene,
     p-ethyltoluene, 4-ethyltoluene

12.55 a. 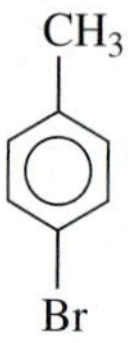   **b.**

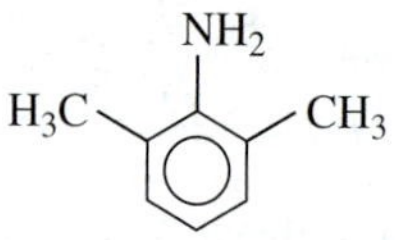

c.

12.57 1×10^{14} molecules of bombykol

12.59 $H_2C = CH - CH_2 - CH_2 - CH_3$ 1-Pentene

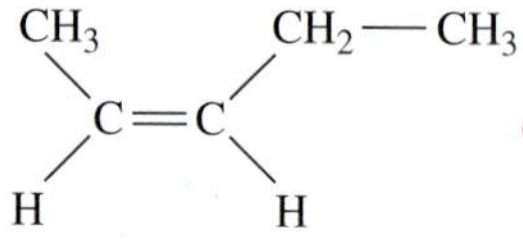

  cis-2-Pentene

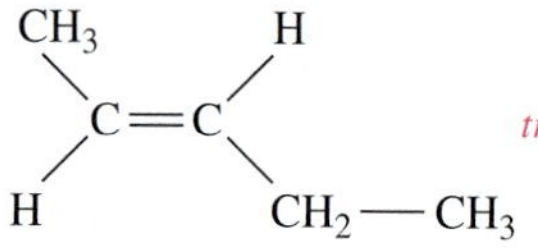

  trans-2-Pentene

12.61 a.

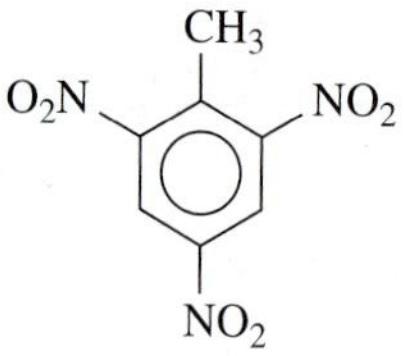

b.

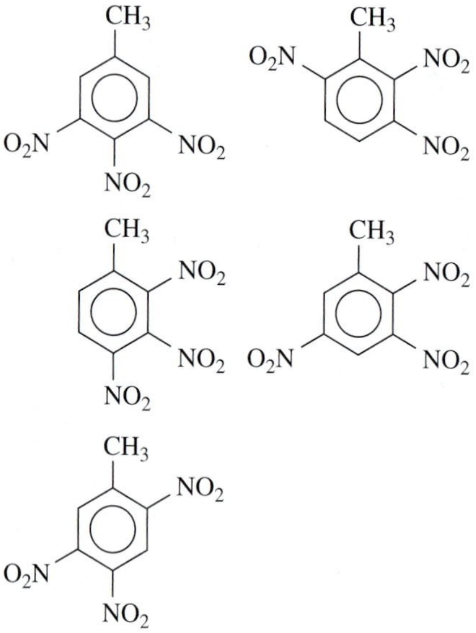

Alcohols, Phenols, Thiols, and Ethers

LOOKING AHEAD

Mastering**CHEMISTRY**™

Visit **www.masteringchemistry.com** for self-study materials and instructor-assigned homework.

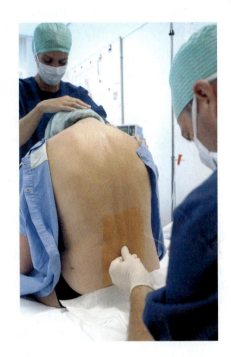

An epidural is a regional anesthesia that will provide pain relief for Janet during her labor and delivery by blocking pain in the lower half of her body. Tom, a nurse anesthetist, prepares the medication for the epidural injection, which consists of a local anesthetic, chloroprocaine, and a small amount of fentanyl, a common opioid. Tom administers the anesthetic through a catheter into Janet's lower spine and within moments, her pain subsides.

One of the earliest anesthetics used in medicine was diethyl ether, more commonly referred to as ether. Diethyl ether contains an ether functional group, which is an oxygen atom bonded by single bonds to two carbon groups. Today, ether is rarely used because it is extremely flammable, and produces undesirable side effects such as postanesthetic nausea and vomiting. Chloroprocaine, a more modern anesthetic that does not cause nausea and vomiting, contains an aromatic ring, a chlorine atom, and ester and amine functional groups.

Career: Nurse Anesthetist

More than 26 million people in the United States each year require anesthesia associated with a medical or dental procedure. Anesthesia is typically administered by a nurse anesthetist who provides care before, during, and after the procedure by giving medications to keep a patient asleep and pain-free while monitoring the patient's vital signs. A nurse anesthetist also obtains supplies, equipment, and an ample blood supply for a potential emergency, and interprets pre-surgical tests to determine how the anesthesia will affect the patient. A nurse anesthetist may also be required to insert artificial airways, administer oxygen, or work to prevent surgical shock during a procedure, working under the direction of the attending surgeon, dentist, or anesthesiologist.

$$CH_3-CH_2-O-CH_2-CH_3$$

Diethyl ether

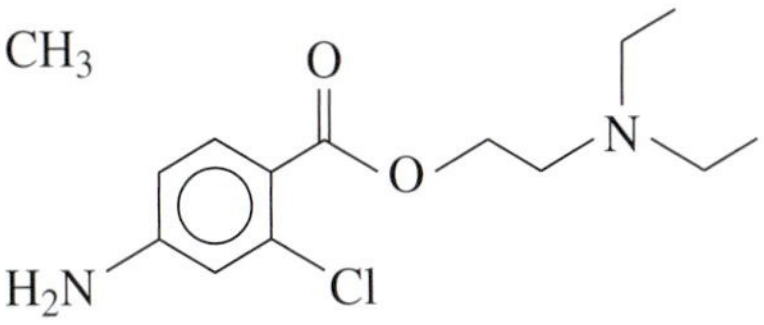

Chloroprocaine

n this chapter, we will look at organic compounds that contain functional groups with oxygen atoms or sulfur atoms. Alcohols, which contain the hydroxyl group (—OH), are commonly found in nature and are used in industry and at home. For centuries, grains, vegetables, and fruits have been fermented to produce the ethanol present in alcoholic beverages. The hydroxyl group is important in biomolecules, such as sugars and starches, as well as in steroids, such as cholesterol and estradiol. Menthol is a cyclic alcohol with a minty odor and flavor that is used in cough drops, shaving creams, and ointments. The phenols contain the hydroxyl group (—OH) attached to a benzene ring.

Ethers are compounds that contain an oxygen atom connected to two carbon atoms (—O—). Beginning in 1842, diethyl ether was used for about 100 years as a general anesthetic. Today, less flammable and more easily tolerated anesthetics are used. Thiols, which contain the —SH group, give the strong odors we associate with garlic and onions.

13.1 Alcohols, Phenols, and Thiols

As we learned in Section 11.5, alcohols are a class of organic compounds that contain an oxygen (O) atom, shown in red in the ball-and-stick models. Thiols contain a sulfur (S) atom, shown in yellow. In an **alcohol**, a hydroxyl group (—OH) is bonded to a hydrocarbon chain. In a **phenol**, the hydroxyl group is attached to a benzene ring. Molecules of alcohols and phenols have a bent shape around the oxygen atom.

Thiols are a family of sulfur-containing organic compounds that have a thiol group (—SH). Thiols have structures that are similar to those of alcohols except that the —SH group takes the place of the —OH group. In the models of thiols, the sulfur atom is yellow.

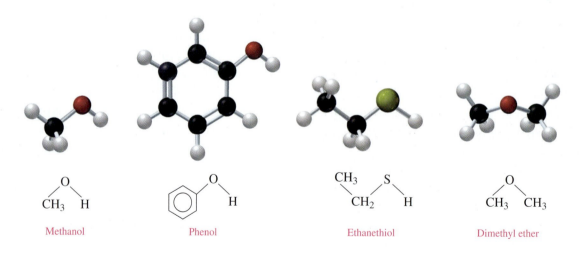

O	O	CH$_3$ S	O
CH$_3$ H	H	CH$_2$ H	CH$_3$ CH$_3$
Methanol	Phenol	Ethanethiol	Dimethyl ether

Naming Alcohols

In the IUPAC system, an alcohol is named by replacing the *e* of the corresponding alkane name with *ol*. The common name of a simple alcohol uses the name of the alkyl group followed by *alcohol*.

CH$_3$—OH   CH$_3$—CH$_2$—OH
Methanol   Ethanol
(methyl alcohol)   (ethyl alcohol)

Alcohols with one or two carbon atoms do not require a number for the hydroxyl group. When an alcohol consists of a chain with 3 or more carbon atoms, the chain is numbered to give the position of the —OH group and any substituents on the chain. An alcohol with two —OH groups is named as a *diol*, and an alcohol with three —OH groups is named as a *triol*.

$$CH_3-CH_2-CH_2-OH$$
3 2 1
1-Propanol
(propyl alcohol)

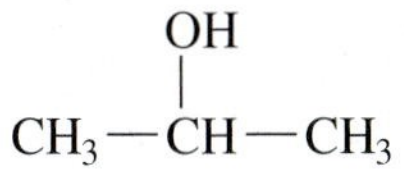

$$CH_3-\underset{|}{\overset{OH}{CH}}-CH_3$$
1 2 3
2-Propanol
(isopropyl alcohol)

We can also draw the skeletal formulas for alcohols as shown for 2-propanol and 2-butanol.

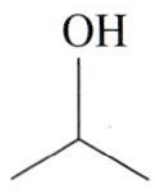

2-Propanol

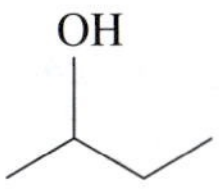

2-Butanol

A cyclic alcohol is named as a *cycloalkanol*. If there are substituents, the ring is numbered from carbon 1, which is the carbon attached to the OH group. Compounds with no substituents on the ring do not require a number for the hydroxyl group.

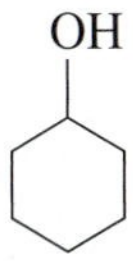

Cyclohexanol

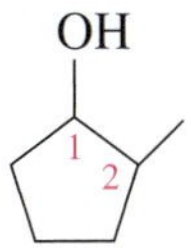

2-Methylcyclopentanol

Naming Phenols

The term *phenol* is the IUPAC name for a benzene ring bonded to a hydroxyl group (—OH), which is used in the name of the family of organic compounds derived from phenol. When there is a second substituent, the benzene ring is numbered starting from carbon 1, which is the carbon bonded to the —OH group. The terms *ortho*, *meta*, and *para* are used for the common names of simple phenols. Common names of *cresol* are also used for methylphenols.

Phenol

3-Chlorophenol
(*meta*-chlorophenol)

4-Ethylphenol
(*para*-ethylphenol)

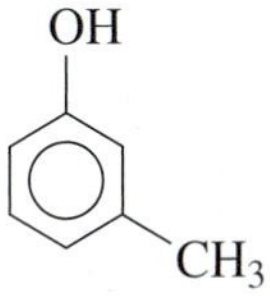

3-Methylphenol
(*meta*-cresol)

SAMPLE PROBLEM 13.1   Naming Alcohols

Give the IUPAC name for the following:

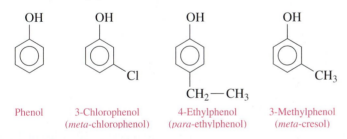

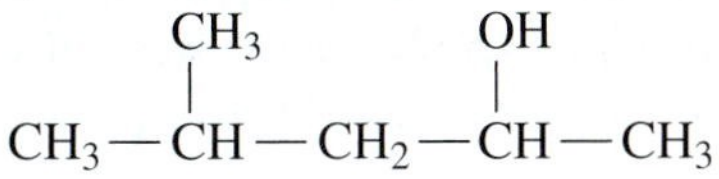

SOLUTION

Analyze the Problem

Functional Group	Family	IUPAC Naming	IUPAC Name
Hydroxyl group	Alcohol	Replace the *e* of the alkane name with *ol*.	Alkanol

Guide to Naming Alcohols

1 Name the longest carbon chain attached to the —OH group by replacing the *e* in the corresponding alkane name with *ol*. Name an aromatic alcohol as a *phenol*.

2 Number the chain starting at the end nearer to the —OH group.

3 Give the location and name of each substituent relative to the —OH group.

Explore Your World

ALCOHOLS IN HOUSEHOLD PRODUCTS

Read the labels on household products such as sanitizers, mouthwashes, cold remedies, rubbing alcohol, and flavoring extracts. Look for names of alcohols, such as ethyl alcohol, isopropyl alcohol, thymol, and menthol.

QUESTIONS

1. What part of the name tells you that it is an alcohol?
2. What alcohol is usually meant by the term "alcohol"?
3. What is the percentage of alcohol in the products?
4. Draw the condensed structural formulas for the alcohols you find listed on the labels. You may need to use the Internet or a reference book for some structures.

Step 1   **Name the longest carbon chain attached to the —OH group by replacing the *e* in the corresponding alkane name with *ol*.** Name an aromatic alcohol as a *phenol*.

$$CH_3-CH-CH_2-CH-CH_3 \qquad \text{pentanol}$$
(CH₃ on carbon 2, OH on carbon 4)

Step 2   **Number the chain starting at the end nearer to the —OH group.** This carbon chain is numbered from right to left to give the position of the —OH group as carbon 2, which is shown as a prefix in the name 2-pentanol.

$$\underset{5\quad4\quad3\quad2\quad1}{CH_3-CH-CH_2-CH-CH_3} \qquad \text{2-pentanol}$$

Step 3   **Give the location and name of each substituent relative to the —OH group.** With a methyl group on carbon 4, the compound is named 4-methyl-2-pentanol.

$$\underset{5\quad4\quad3\quad2\quad1}{CH_3-CH-CH_2-CH-CH_3} \qquad \text{4-methyl-2-pentanol}$$

STUDY CHECK 13.1

Give the IUPAC name for the following:

$$CH_3-CH-CH_2-CH_2-OH$$
(Cl on carbon 2)

SAMPLE PROBLEM 13.2   Naming Phenols

Give the IUPAC name for the following:

(benzene ring with Br and OH)

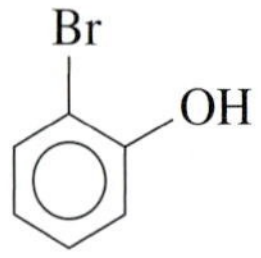

SOLUTION

Analyze the Problem

Functional Group	Family	IUPAC Naming	IUPAC Name
Hydroxyl group on a benzene ring	Phenol	Phenol with halogen substituent; number the ring to give lower numbers.	Halophenol

Step 1   **Name the longest carbon chain attached to the —OH group by replacing the *e* in the corresponding alkane name with *ol*.** Name an aromatic alcohol as a *phenol.* The compound is a *phenol* because it consists of a benzene attached to —OH.

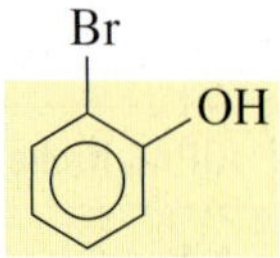

(benzene ring with Br and OH)   phenol

Step 2 **Number the chain starting at the end nearer to the —OH group.** For a phenol, the carbon atom attached to the —OH group is carbon 1. Then number the ring in the direction that gives the lower number to the bromine atom.

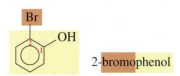

phenol

Step 3 **Give the location and name of each substituent relative to the —OH group.** The IUPAC name for the compound is 2-bromophenol.

2-bromophenol

STUDY CHECK 13.2

Give the IUPAC and common name for the following:

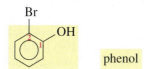

Chemistry Link to Health

SOME IMPORTANT ALCOHOLS AND PHENOLS

Methanol (*methyl alcohol*), the simplest alcohol, is found in many solvents and paint removers. If ingested, methanol is oxidized to formaldehyde, which can cause headaches, blindness, and death. Methanol is used to make plastics, medicines, and fuels. In car racing, it is used as a fuel because it is less flammable and has a higher octane rating than does gasoline.

Ethanol (*ethyl alcohol*) has been known since prehistoric times as an intoxicating product formed by the fermentation of grains, sugars, and starches.

$$C_6H_{12}O_6 \xrightarrow{\text{Fermentation}} 2CH_3-CH_2-OH + 2CO_2$$

Today, ethanol for commercial use is produced by reacting ethene and water at high temperatures and pressures, as we saw in Section 12.3. Ethanol is used as a solvent for perfumes, varnishes, and some medicines, such as tincture of iodine. Recent interest in alternative fuels has led to increased production of ethanol by the fermentation of sugars from grains such as corn, wheat, and rice. "Gasohol" is a mixture of ethanol and gasoline used as a fuel.

1,2,3-Propanetriol (*glycerol* or *glycerin*), a trihydroxy alcohol, is a viscous liquid obtained from oils and fats during the production of soaps. The presence of several polar —OH groups makes it strongly attracted to water, a feature that makes glycerin useful as a skin softener in products such as skin lotions, cosmetics, shaving creams, and liquid soaps.

$$HO-CH_2-\overset{\displaystyle OH}{\underset{\displaystyle |}{CH}}-CH_2-OH$$

1,2,3-Propanetriol
(glycerol)

1,2-Ethanediol (*ethylene glycol*) is used as an antifreeze in heating and cooling systems. It is also a solvent for paints, inks, and plastics, and it is used in the production of synthetic fibers such as Dacron. If ingested, it is extremely toxic. In the body, it is oxidized to oxalic acid, which forms insoluble salts in the kidneys that cause renal damage, convulsions, and death. Because its sweet taste is attractive to pets and children, ethylene glycol solutions must be carefully stored.

$$HO-CH_2-CH_2-OH \xrightarrow{[O]} HO-\overset{\displaystyle O}{\overset{\displaystyle ||}{C}}-\overset{\displaystyle O}{\overset{\displaystyle ||}{C}}-OH$$

1,2-Ethanediol
(ethylene glycol)

Oxalic acid

$$H_2C=CH_2 + H_2O \xrightarrow{\text{300 °C, 200 atm, H}^+} CH_3-CH_2-OH$$

An antifreeze raises the boiling point and decreases the freezing point of water in a radiator.

Phenols are found in several of the essential oils of plants, which produce the odor or flavor of the plant. Eugenol is found in cloves, vanillin in vanilla bean, isoeugenol in nutmeg, and thymol in thyme and mint. Thymol has a pleasant, minty taste and is used in mouthwashes and by dentists to disinfect a cavity before adding a filling compound.

Bisphenol A (*BPA*) is used to make polycarbonate, a clear plastic that is used to manufacture beverage bottles, including baby bottles. Washing polycarbonate bottles with certain detergents or at high temperatures disrupts the polymer, causing small amounts of BPA to leach from the bottles. Because BPA is an estrogen mimic, there are concerns about the harmful effects from low levels of BPA. In 2008, Canada banned the use of polycarbonate baby bottles, which are now labelled "BPA free". Plastic bottles and containers made of polycarbonate have the recycling symbol "7".

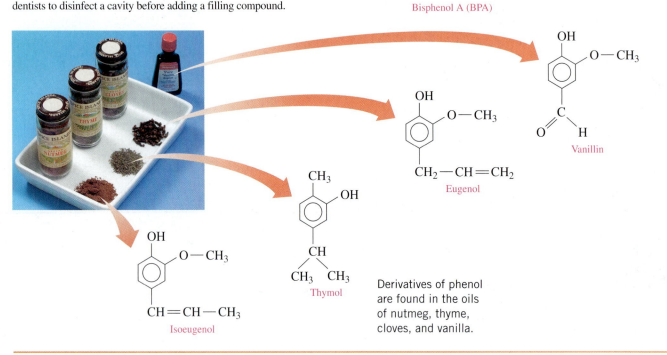

Bisphenol A (BPA)

Vanillin

Eugenol

Thymol

Isoeugenol

Derivatives of phenol are found in the oils of nutmeg, thyme, cloves, and vanilla.

Thiols

The spray of a skunk contains a mixture of thiols.

Thiols are a family of sulfur-containing organic compounds that have a *thiol* group ($-SH$). In the IUPAC system, thiols are named by adding *thiol* to the alkane name of the longest carbon chain and numbering the carbon chain from the end nearer the $-SH$ group.

$$CH_3-OH \qquad CH_3-SH \qquad CH_3-\overset{\overset{\displaystyle SH}{|}}{CH}-CH_2-CH_3 \qquad CH_3-CH_2-SH$$

Methanol   Methanethiol   2-Butanethiol   Ethanethiol

An important property of thiols is a strong, sometimes disagreeable, odor. To help us detect natural gas (methane) leaks, a small amount of ethanethiol is added to the gas supply, which is normally odorless. There are thiols such as *trans*-2-butene-1-thiol in the spray emitted when a skunk senses danger.

trans-2-Butene-1-thiol
(in skunk spray)

Methanethiol is the characteristic odor of oysters, cheddar cheese, onions, and garlic. Garlic also contains 2-propene-1-thiol. The odor of onions is due to 1-propanethiol, which is also a lachrymator, a substance that makes eyes tear (see Figure 13.1).

CH_3—SH
Methanethiol
Oysters and cheese

CH_3—CH_2—CH_2—SH
1-Propanethiol
Onions

H_2C=CH—CH_2—SH
2-Propene-1-thiol
Garlic

FIGURE 13.1 Thiols are sulfur-containing compounds with a —SH group, and often have strong odors.

Q How are the structures of thiols similar to alcohols?

QUESTIONS AND PROBLEMS

13.1 Alcohols, Phenols, and Thiols

LEARNING GOAL: *Give the IUPAC and common names for alcohols, phenols, and thiols; draw their condensed structural formulas or skeletal formulas.*

13.1 Give the IUPAC name for each of the following:

a. CH_3—CH_2—OH

b. CH_3—CH_2—$\overset{\displaystyle OH}{\underset{\displaystyle |}{CH}}$—$CH_3$

c. OH (skeletal structure)

d. OH (cyclohexanol with methyl)

e. OH phenyl with Br

13.2 Give the IUPAC name for each of the following:

a. cyclobutane—OH

b. CH_3—CH_2—$\overset{\displaystyle CH_3}{\underset{\displaystyle |}{CH}}$—$CH_2$—OH

c. skeletal structure with OH and methyl groups

d. OH phenol with CH_2—CH_3

e. CH_3—CH_2—$\overset{\displaystyle OH}{\underset{\displaystyle |}{CH}}$—$CH_2$—$CH_2$—$CH_3$

13.3 Draw the condensed structural formula or skeletal formula, if cyclic, for each of the following:
a. 1-propanol
b. 3-pentanol
c. 2-methyl-2-butanol
d. *p*-chlorophenol
e. 2-bromo-4-chlorophenol

13.4 Draw the condensed structural formula or skeletal formula, if cyclic, for each of the following:
a. 3-methyl-1-butanol
b. 2,4-dichlorocyclohexanol
c. 3-chloro-2-methyl-1-pentanol
d. *o*-bromophenol
e. 2,4-dimethylphenol

13.2 Ethers

An **ether** consists of an oxygen atom that is attached by single bonds to two carbon groups that are alkyl or aromatic groups.

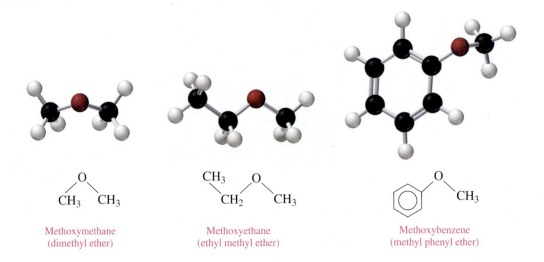

Methoxymethane
(dimethyl ether)

Methoxyethane
(ethyl methyl ether)

Methoxybenzene
(methyl phenyl ether)

TUTORIAL
Naming Ethers

TUTORIAL
Drawing Ethers

Naming Ethers

In the common name of an ether, the names of the alkyl or aromatic groups attached to the oxygen atom are written in alphabetical order, followed by the word *ether*.

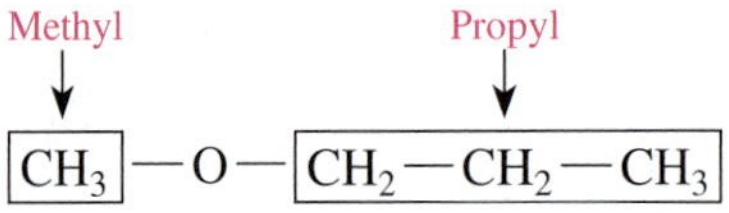

Methyl   Propyl

$$\boxed{CH_3}-O-\boxed{CH_2-CH_2-CH_3}$$ Common name: Methyl propyl ether

In the IUPAC system, an ether is named using an alkoxy group made up of the smaller alkyl group and the oxygen atom, followed by the alkane name of the longer carbon chain.

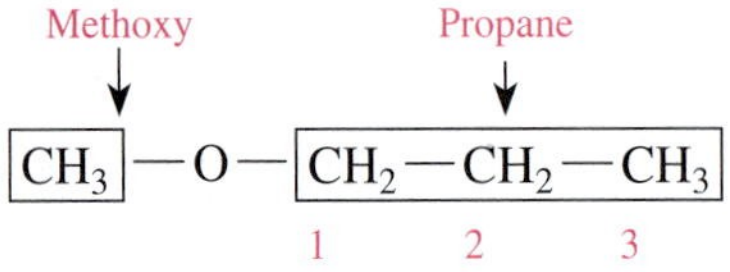

Methoxy   Propane

$$\boxed{CH_3}-O-\boxed{\underset{1\quad\ \ 2\quad\ \ 3}{CH_2-CH_2-CH_3}}$$ IUPAC name: 1-Methoxypropane

More examples of naming ethers with both IUPAC and common names follow:

$$CH_3-O-CH_3$$
Methoxymethane
(dimethyl ether)

$$CH_3-CH_2-O-CH_2-CH_3$$
Ethoxyethane
(diethyl ether)

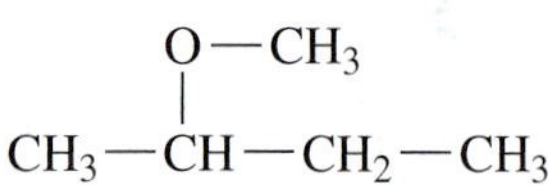

$$CH_3-\underset{\underset{\displaystyle O-CH_3}{|}}{CH}-CH_2-CH_3$$
2-Methoxybutane

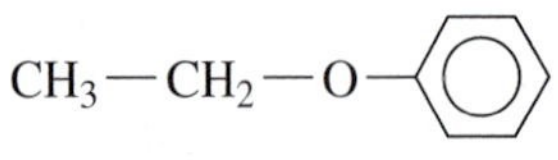

$$CH_3-CH_2-O-\langle\bigcirc\rangle$$
Ethoxybenzene
(ethyl phenyl ether)

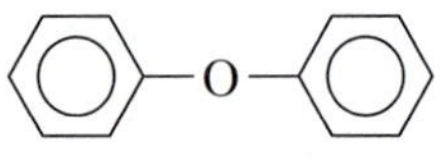

$$\langle\bigcirc\rangle-O-\langle\bigcirc\rangle$$
Phenoxybenzene
(diphenyl ether)

SAMPLE PROBLEM 13.3 Naming Ethers

Give the IUPAC name for the following:

$$CH_3-CH_2-O-CH_2-CH_2-CH_2-CH_3$$

SOLUTION

Analyze the Problem

Functional Group	Family	IUPAC Naming	IUPAC Name
Oxygen atom attached to two carbon groups	Ether	Name the shorter alkyl group and oxygen atom as *alkoxy*, followed by the alkane name of the longer carbon chain.	Alkoxyalkane

Guide to Naming Ethers

1 Write the alkane name of the longer carbon chain.

2 Name the oxygen and smaller alkyl group as an alkoxy group.

3 Number the longer carbon chain from the end nearer the alkoxy group and give its location.

Step 1 Write the alkane name of the longer carbon chain.

$$CH_3-CH_2-O-\underbrace{CH_2-CH_2-CH_2-CH_3}_{\text{Longer carbon chain}} \quad \text{butane}$$

Step 2 Name the oxygen and smaller alkyl group as an alkoxy group.

$$CH_3-CH_2-O - CH_2-CH_2-CH_2-CH_3 \quad \text{ethoxybutane}$$

Ethoxy group

Step 3 Number the longer carbon chain from the end nearer the alkoxy group and give its location.

$$CH_3-CH_2-O - \underset{1 \quad 2 \quad 3 \quad 4}{CH_2-CH_2-CH_2-CH_3} \quad \text{1-ethoxybutane}$$

STUDY CHECK 13.3

What is the IUPAC name of methyl phenyl ether?

Isomers of Alcohols and Ethers

Alcohols and ethers can have the same molecular formula. For example, we can draw condensed structural formulas for the isomers with the molecular formula C_2H_6O as follows:

$$CH_3-CH_2-OH \qquad CH_3-O-CH_3$$

Ethanol   Methoxymethane

CONCEPT CHECK 13.1 Isomers of Alcohols and Ethers

Why do the following condensed structural formulas represent a pair of structural isomers?

$$CH_3-CH_2-CH_2-OH \qquad CH_3-O-CH_2-CH_3$$

ANSWER

These two compounds, one an alcohol and the other an ether, have the same molecular formula, C_3H_8O, but their atoms are arranged in a different order, which makes them structural isomers.

Chemistry Link to Health

ETHERS AS ANESTHETICS

Anesthesia is the loss of all sensation and consciousness. A general anesthetic is a substance that blocks signals to the awareness centers in the brain, so the person has a loss of memory, a loss of feeling pain, and an artificial sleep. The term *ether* has been associated with anesthesia because diethyl ether was the most widely used anesthetic for more than a hundred years. Although it is easy to administer, ether is very volatile and highly flammable. A small spark in the operating room could cause an explosion. Since the 1950s, anesthetics such as Forane (isoflurane), Ethrane (enflurane), and Penthrane (methoxyflurane) have been developed that are not

as flammable. Most of these anesthetics retain the ether group, but the addition of many halogen atoms reduces the volatility and flammability of the ethers. More recently, they have been replaced by Fluothane (halothane) (2-bromo-2-chloro-1,1,1-trifluoroethane) because of the negative side effects of the ether-type inhalation anesthetics, such as toxicity to the liver and kidneys, and arrhythmia.

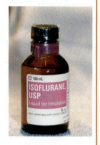

Isoflurane (Forane) is an inhaled anesthetic.

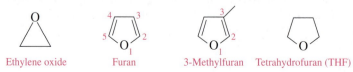

Forane® (isoflurane)   Ethrane® (enflurane)   Penthrane® (methoxyflurane)   Fluothane (halothane)

SAMPLE PROBLEM 13.4   Isomers of Alcohols and Ethers

Draw the condensed structural formulas and give the IUPAC and common names for two alcohols and one ether with a molecular formula of C_3H_8O.

SOLUTION

To draw the structural isomers for the alcohols, the hydroxyl group is bonded to two different atoms in a chain of three carbon atoms. For the ether, the oxygen atom is bonded to two alkyl groups.

$$CH_3 - CH_2 - CH_2 - OH \qquad CH_3 - \overset{\displaystyle OH}{\underset{\displaystyle |}{CH}} - CH_3 \qquad CH_3 - CH_2 - O - CH_3$$

1-Propanol (propyl alcohol)   2-Propanol (isopropyl alcohol)   Methoxyethane (ethyl methyl ether)

STUDY CHECK 13.4

Write the IUPAC names for two unbranched alcohols and two unbranched ethers that are structural isomers, all of which have the molecular formula $C_4H_{10}O$.

Cyclic Ethers

A **cyclic ether** consists of an oxygen atom within a carbon ring. Because one or more of the atoms in the ring are not carbon, they are known as *heterocyclic compounds*. Most often, the cyclic ethers are named using their common names. A heterocyclic ring of five atoms has a common name derived from *furan*. When there are substituents, the ring is numbered from the oxygen atom as 1.

Ethylene oxide   Furan   3-Methylfuran   Tetrahydrofuran (THF)

The name of a heterocyclic ether ring of six atoms is derived from *pyran*.

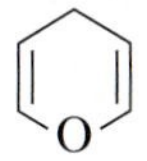

Pyran 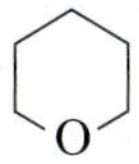   Tetrahydropyran (THP) 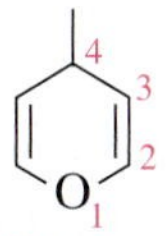   4-Methylpyran

A cyclic ether containing two oxygen atoms in a ring of six atoms is called *dioxane*. The oxygen atoms are numbered because they can take different positions in the ring. When a six-atom ring with two oxygen atoms contains two double bonds, the ether is called *dioxin*.

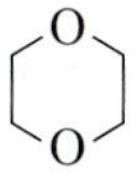

1,4-Dioxane 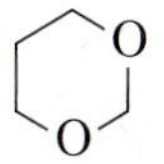   1,3-Dioxane 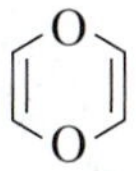   1,4-Dioxin

 ## Chemistry Link to the Environment

TOXIC ETHERS

The compounds known as *dioxins* are extremely toxic. One of the most toxic is 2,3,7,8-tetrachlorodibenzo-*p*-dioxin (TCDD), which is commonly called *dioxin*. It is classed as a carcinogen (cancer causing) because its structure interferes with DNA. TCDD is formed as a by-product of several industrial processes involving chlorine, such as pesticide manufacturing and pulp and paper bleaching with chlorine. The herbicide Agent Orange used in Vietnam was contaminated by TCDD, a by-product which formed during the synthesis of Agent Orange.

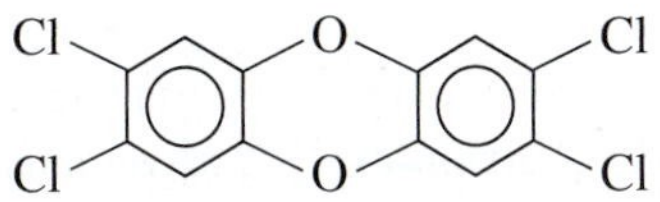

2,3,7,8-Tetrachlorodibenzo-*p*-dioxin
(TCDD, "dioxin")

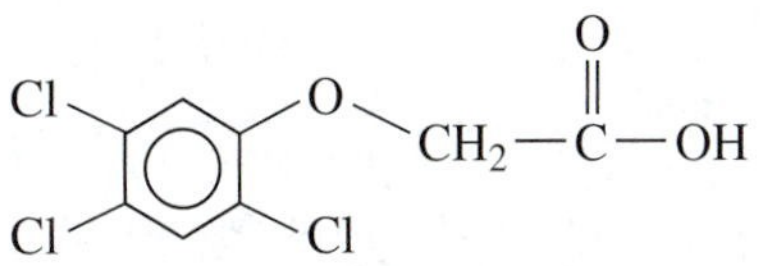

2,4,5-Trichlorophenoxyacetic acid
(2,4,5-T; Agent Orange)

CONCEPT CHECK 13.2   **Ethers**

Identify each of the following as a cyclic alcohol, ether, or cyclic ether:

a. 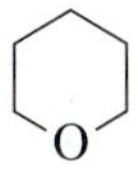   **b.** 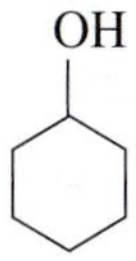   **c.**

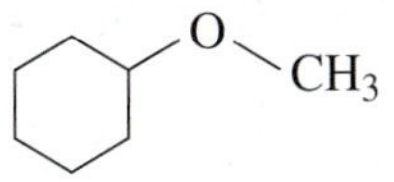

ANSWER
a. A cyclic ether has an oxygen atom in the ring.
b. A cyclic alcohol has a hydroxyl group bonded to a cycloalkane.
c. An ether has an oxygen atom that is bonded by single bonds to two carbon groups.

QUESTIONS AND PROBLEMS

13.2 Ethers

LEARNING GOAL: Give the IUPAC and common names for ethers; draw their condensed structural formulas or skeletal formulas.

13.5 Give the IUPAC name and any common name for each of the following ethers:

a. $CH_3-O-CH_2-CH_3$ **b.**

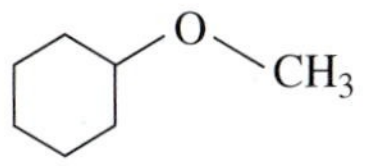

c.

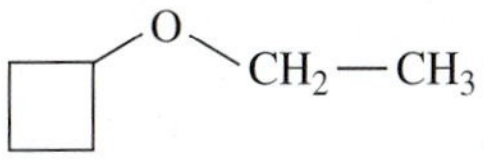

d. $CH_3-O-CH_2-CH_2-CH_3$

13.6 Give the IUPAC name and any common name for each of the following ethers:

a. $CH_3-CH_2-O-CH_2-CH_2-CH_3$

b.

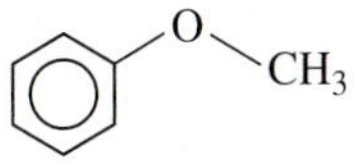

c.

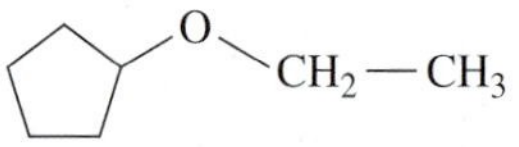

d. CH_3-O-CH_3

13.7 Draw the condensed structural formula or skeletal formula, if cyclic, for each of the following:
  a. ethyl propyl ether   **b.** cyclopropyl ethyl ether
  c. methoxycyclopentane
  d. 1-ethoxy-2-methylbutane
  e. 2,3-dimethoxypentane

13.8 Draw the condensed structural formula or skeletal formula, if cyclic, for each of the following:
  a. diethyl ether   **b.** diphenyl ether
  c. ethoxycyclohexane
  d. 2-methoxy-2,3-dimethylbutane
  e. 1,2-dimethoxybenzene

13.9 Indicate whether each of the following pairs represents structural isomers or not:
  a. 2-pentanol and 2-methoxybutane

  b. 2-butanol and cyclobutanol
  c. ethyl propyl ether and 2-methyl-1-butanol

13.10 Indicate whether each of the following pairs represents structural isomers or not:
  a. 2-methoxybutane and 3-methyl-2-butanol
  b. 1-hexanol and dipropyl ether
  c. 2-methyl-2-propanol and diethyl ether

13.11 Give the name for each of the following cyclic ethers:

  a.    **b.**   **c.**

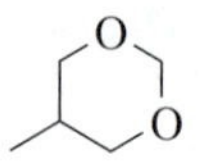

13.12 Give the name for each of the following cyclic ethers:

  a.    **b.** 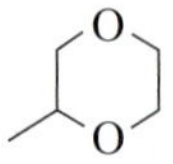   **c.**

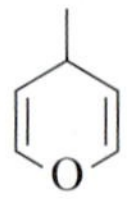

13.3 Physical Properties of Alcohols, Phenols, and Ethers

Alcohols are classified by the number of alkyl groups attached to the carbon atom bonded to the hydroxyl group ($-OH$). A **primary** (**1°**) **alcohol** has one alkyl group attached to the carbon atom bonded to the $-OH$ group. The simplest alcohol, methanol (CH_3OH), which has a carbon attached to three H atoms but no alkyl group, is considered a primary alcohol; a **secondary** (**2°**) **alcohol** has two alkyl groups, and a **tertiary** (**3°**) **alcohol** has three alkyl groups.

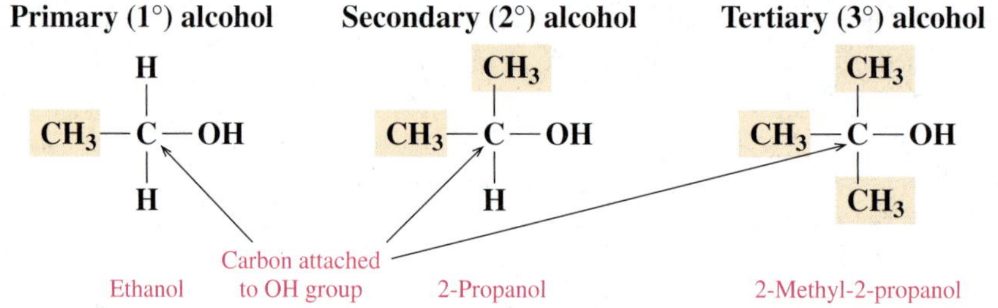

Primary (1°) alcohol	Secondary (2°) alcohol	Tertiary (3°) alcohol

Primary (1°) alcohol:

$$CH_3-\overset{\displaystyle H}{\underset{\displaystyle H}{C}}-OH$$

Ethanol

Secondary (2°) alcohol:

$$CH_3-\overset{\displaystyle CH_3}{\underset{\displaystyle H}{C}}-OH$$

2-Propanol

Tertiary (3°) alcohol:

$$CH_3-\overset{\displaystyle CH_3}{\underset{\displaystyle CH_3}{C}}-OH$$

2-Methyl-2-propanol

Carbon attached to OH group

CONCEPT CHECK 13.3   **Classifying Alcohols**

Classify each of the following alcohols as primary (1°), secondary (2°), or tertiary (3°):

a. $CH_3-CH_2-CH_2-OH$ **b.** 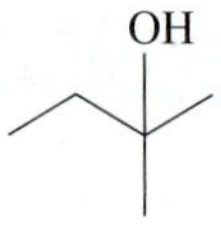   **c.**

ANSWER

a. The carbon atom bonded to the $-OH$ group is attached to one alkyl group, which makes this a primary (1°) alcohol.

b. The carbon atom bonded to the $-OH$ group is attached to three alkyl groups, which makes this a tertiary (3°) alcohol.

c. In a cyclic alcohol, the carbon atom in the ring bonded to the $-OH$ group is attached to two other carbon atoms, which makes this a secondary (2°) alcohol.

CONCEPT CHECK 13.4   Boiling Points of Alcohols and Ethers

Why does 1-propanol have a higher boiling point than its structural isomer, ethyl methyl ether?

ANSWER

Because many hydrogen bonds form between the polar —OH groups of molecules of 1-propanol, more energy and thus a higher temperature is required for 1-propanol to boil. Ethyl methyl ether does not form hydrogen bonds with other molecules of ethyl methyl ether, which means it boils at a lower temperature.

TUTORIAL
Physical Properties of Alcohols and Ethers

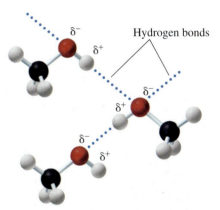

Methyl alcohol

Boiling Points

Because there is a large electronegativity difference between the oxygen and hydrogen atoms in the —OH group, the oxygen has a partially negative charge, and the hydrogen has a partially positive charge. As a result, hydrogen bonds form between the oxygen of one alcohol and hydrogen in the —OH of another alcohol. Hydrogen bonds cannot form between ether molecules because there are not any polar —OH groups.

Alcohols have higher boiling points than do ethers of the same mass because alcohols require higher temperatures to provide sufficient energy to break the many hydrogen bonds. The boiling points of ethers are similar to those of alkanes because neither can form hydrogen bonds.

No hydrogen bonds

Dimethyl ether

Hydrogen bonds can form between alcohol molecules but not between ether molecules.

Solubility of Alcohols and Ethers in Water

The electronegativity of the oxygen atom in both alcohols and ethers influences their solubility in water. In alcohols, the atoms in the —OH group can form hydrogen bonds with the H and O atoms of water. Alcohols with one to three carbon atoms are *miscible* in water, which means that any amount is completely soluble in water. However, the solubility provided by the polar —OH group decreases as the number of carbon atoms increases. Alcohols with four carbon atoms are slightly soluble, and alcohols with five or more carbon atoms are not soluble.

Nonpolar carbon chain ⟶ $\boxed{CH_3-CH_2}$—OH
Soluble in water

$\boxed{CH_3-CH_2-CH_2-CH_2-CH_2-CH_2-CH_2-CH_2}$—OH
Insoluble in water

Although ethers can form hydrogen bonds with water, they do not form as many hydrogen bonds with water as do the alcohols. Ethers containing up to four carbon atoms are slightly soluble in water. Table 13.1 compares the boiling points and the solubility in water of some alcohols and ethers of similar mass.

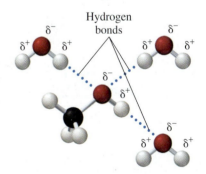

Methyl alcohol in water

Solubility and Boiling Point of Phenol

Phenol has a high boiling point (182 °C) because the —OH group allows phenol molecules to hydrogen bond with other phenol molecules. Phenol is slightly soluble in water because the —OH group can form hydrogen bonds with water molecules. In water, the —OH group of phenol ionizes slightly, which makes it a weak acid ($K_a = 1 \times 10^{-10}$). In fact, an early name for phenol was *carbolic acid*. Phenol is very corrosive and highly irritating to the skin; it can cause severe burns and ingestion can be fatal. At one time, dilute solutions of phenol were used in hospitals as antiseptics, but they have generally been replaced.

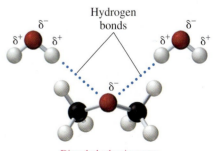

Dimethyl ether in water

OH ⬡ + H_2O ⇌ O⁻ ⬡ + H_3O^+

Phenol   Phenoxide ion

TABLE 13.1 Boiling Points and Solubility of Some Typical Alcohols and Ethers

Compound	Condensed Structural Formula	Family	Number of Carbon Atoms	Boiling Point (°C)	Solubility in Water
Methanol	CH_3-OH	Alcohol	1	65	Soluble
Ethanol	CH_3-CH_2-OH	Alcohol	2	78	Soluble
1-Propanol	$CH_3-CH_2-CH_2-OH$	Alcohol	3	97	Soluble
1-Butanol	$CH_3-CH_2-CH_2-CH_2-OH$	Alcohol	4	118	Slightly soluble
1-Pentanol	$CH_3-CH_2-CH_2-CH_2-CH_2-OH$	Alcohol	5	138	Insoluble
Dimethyl ether	CH_3-O-CH_3	Ether	2	−23	Slightly soluble
Ethyl methyl ether	$CH_3-O-CH_2-CH_3$	Ether	3	8	Slightly soluble
Diethyl ether	$CH_3-CH_2-O-CH_2-CH_3$	Ether	4	35	Slightly soluble
Ethyl propyl ether	$CH_3-CH_2-O-CH_2-CH_2-CH_3$	Ether	5	64	Insoluble

Chemistry Link to Health

HAND SANITIZERS AND ETHANOL

Hand sanitizers are used as an alternative to washing hands to kill most bacteria and viruses that spread colds and flu. As a gel or liquid solution, many hand sanitizers use ethanol as their active ingredient. While safe for most adults, supervision is recommended when used by children because there is some concern about their risk to the health of children. After using an ethanol- or isopropyl alcohol-based hand sanitizer, children might ingest enough alcohol to make them sick.

The amount of ethanol in an alcohol-containing sanitizer is typically 60% (v/v), but can be as high as 85% (v/v). The high volume of ethanol can make hand sanitizers a fire hazard in the home because they are highly flammable. When ethanol undergoes combustion, it produces a transparent blue flame. When using an ethanol-containing sanitizer, it is important to rub hands until they are completely dry. It is also recommended that sanitizers containing ethanol be placed in storage areas that are away from heat sources in the home.

Some sanitizers are alcohol-free, but often the active ingredient is triclosan, which contains aromatic, ether, and phenol functional groups. The Food and Drug Administration is considering banning triclosan in personal care products because when mixed with tap water for disposal, the triclosan that accumulates in the environment may promote the growth of antibiotic-resistant bacteria.

Hand sanitizers that contain ethanol are used to kill bacteria on the hands.

Triclosan is an antibacterial compound used in personal care products.

QUESTIONS AND PROBLEMS

13.3 Physical Properties of Alcohols, Phenols, and Ethers

LEARNING GOAL: Describe the classification, boiling points, and solubility of alcohols, phenols, and ethers.

13.13 Classify each of the following as a primary (1°), secondary (2°), or tertiary (3°) alcohol:

a. $CH_3-\underset{\underset{CH_3}{|}}{CH}-CH_2-CH_2-OH$

b. $CH_3-CH_2-CH_2-CH_2-OH$

c. $CH_3-\underset{\underset{CH_3}{|}}{\overset{\overset{OH}{|}}{C}}-CH_2-CH_3$ d.

13.14 Classify each of the following as a primary (1°), secondary (2°), or tertiary (3°) alcohol:

a.

b.

c.

d. $CH_3-CH_2-CH_2-\underset{\underset{CH_3}{|}}{\overset{\overset{CH_3}{|}}{C}}-OH$

13.15 Predict the compound with the higher boiling point in each of the following pairs:
   a. ethane or methanol   **b.** diethyl ether or 1-butanol
   c. 1-butanol or pentane

13.16 Predict the compound with the higher boiling point in each of the following pairs:
   a. 2-propanol and 2-butanol
   b. dimethyl ether or ethanol
   c. dimethyl ether or diethyl ether

13.17 Are each of the following soluble, slightly soluble, or insoluble in water? Explain.
   a. CH_3—CH_2—OH
   b. CH_3—O—CH_3
   c. CH_3—CH_2—CH_2—CH_2—CH_2—CH_2—OH

13.18 Are each of the following soluble, slightly soluble, or insoluble in water? Explain.
   a. CH_3—CH_2—CH_2—OH

b.

OH

c. CH_3—CH_2—O—CH_2—CH_3

13.19 Give an explanation for each of the following observations:
   a. Methanol is soluble in water, but ethane is not.
   b. 2-Propanol is soluble in water, but 1-butanol is only slightly soluble.
   c. 1-Propanol is soluble in water, but ethyl methyl ether is only slightly soluble.

13.20 Give an explanation for each of the following observations:
   a. Ethanol is soluble in water, but propane is not.
   b. Dimethyl ether is slightly soluble in water, but pentane is not.
   c. 1-Propanol is soluble in water, but 1-hexanol is not.

13.4 Reactions of Alcohols and Thiols

In Section 11.4, we learned that hydrocarbons undergo combustion in the presence of oxygen. Alcohols burn with oxygen, too. For example, in a restaurant, a flaming dessert may be prepared by pouring a liquor on fruit or ice cream and lighting it (see Figure 13.2). The combustion of the ethanol in the liquor proceeds as follows:

$$CH_3\text{—}CH_2\text{—}OH(g) + 3O_2(g) \xrightarrow{\Delta} 2CO_2(g) + 3H_2O(g) + \text{energy}$$

Dehydration of Alcohols to Form Alkenes

We have seen that alkenes can add water to yield alcohols. In a reverse reaction, alcohols lose a water molecule when they are heated at a high temperature (180 °C) with an acid catalyst such as H_2SO_4. During the **dehydration** of an alcohol, H— and —OH are removed from *adjacent carbon atoms of the same alcohol* to produce a water molecule. A double bond forms between the same two carbon atoms to produce an alkene product.

FIGURE 13.2 A flaming dessert is prepared using a liquor that undergoes combustion.

Q What is the equation for the complete combustion of the ethanol in the liquor?

Examples

TUTORIAL
Dehydration and Oxidation of Alcohols

The dehydration of a secondary alcohol can result in the formation of two products. **Saytzeff's rule** states that the major product is the one that forms by removing the hydrogen from the carbon atom that has the smaller number of hydrogen atoms. A hydrogen atom is easier to remove from the carbon atom adjacent to the carbon atom attached to the —OH group that has fewer hydrogen atoms.

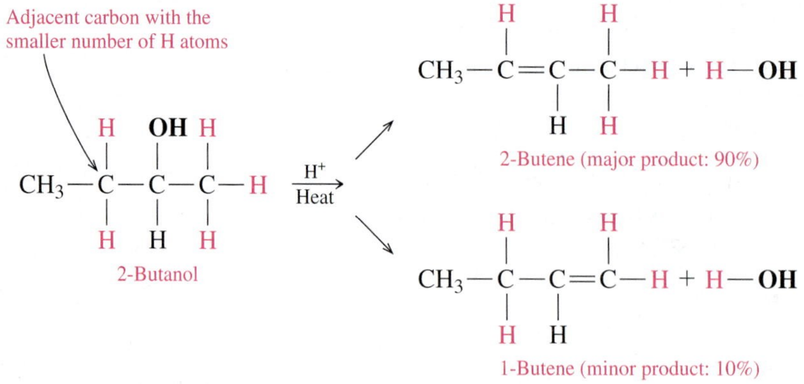

Adjacent carbon with the smaller number of H atoms

2-Butanol

$$CH_3-C=C-C-H + H-OH$$

2-Butene (major product: 90%)

$$CH_3-C-C=C-H + H-OH$$

1-Butene (minor product: 10%)

CONCEPT CHECK 13.5   Dehydration of Alcohols

Consider the dehydration of 1-pentanol and 2-pentanol.

a. Is Saytzeff's rule needed to determine the dehydration product from each alcohol?
b. What is the name of the major dehydration product from each alcohol?

ANSWER

a. Saytzeff's rule is used to determine the major product from the dehydration of 2-pentanol, but not from the dehydration of 1-pentanol. Carbon 2 in 2-pentanol is attached to adjacent carbon atoms with different numbers of hydrogen atoms.
b. The 1-pentanol loses the —OH from carbon 1 and a H— from carbon 2 to form 1-pentene. This is the only possible product. Using Saytzeff's rule, dehydration of 2-pentanol removes the —OH from carbon 2 and a H— from carbon 3, which has the smaller number of H atoms. The major product is 2-pentene.

SAMPLE PROBLEM 13.5   Dehydration of Alcohols

Draw the condensed structural formula or skeletal formula, if cyclic, for the alkene produced by the dehydration of each of the following alcohols:

a. $$CH_3-CH_2-CH-CH_2-CH_3 \xrightarrow[\text{Heat}]{H^+}$$ with OH on the CH

b. 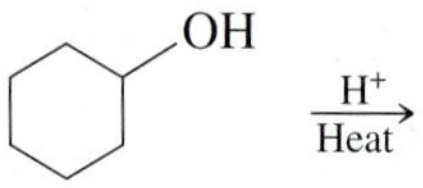 cyclohexanol with OH $\xrightarrow[\text{Heat}]{H^+}$

SOLUTION

a. Because the molecule is a symmetrical alcohol, the H— may be removed from either carbon adjacent to the carbon attached to the —OH group, which forms the following product:

$$CH_3-CH_2-CH=CH-CH_3$$

b. The —OH of this symmetrical alcohol is removed along with a H— from an adjacent carbon. Remember that the hydrogen atoms are not drawn in this type of skeletal structure:

STUDY CHECK 13.5

What is the name of the alkene produced by the dehydration of cyclopentanol?

SAMPLE PROBLEM 13.6   Predicting Reactants

Draw the condensed structural formula or skeletal formula, if cyclic, for the alcohol that reacts to give each of the following products:

a.

b. $$CH_3-C=CH-CH_3$$
with CH_3 below the C

SOLUTION

a. (cyclopentanol structure with OH)

b. $CH_3-\overset{\overset{\displaystyle OH}{|}}{\underset{\underset{\displaystyle CH_3}{|}}{C}}-CH_2-CH_3$ or $CH_3-\overset{\overset{\displaystyle OH}{|}}{CH}-\overset{\underset{\underset{\displaystyle CH_3}{|}}{}}{CH}-CH_3$

STUDY CHECK 13.6

What are the names of two alcohols that dehydrate to give 2-methylpropene?

Formation of Ethers

Ethers form when the dehydration of alcohols occurs at lower temperatures (130 °C) in the presence of an acid catalyst. Then the components of water are removed: H— from one alcohol and —OH from another. When the remaining portions of two separate alcohols join, an ether is produced.

$$CH_3-OH + HO-CH_3 \xrightarrow[\text{Heat}]{H^+} CH_3-O-CH_3 + H_2O$$

Methanol   Methanol   Dimethyl ether

Oxidation of Alcohols

As we discussed in Section 6.3, **oxidation** is a loss of hydrogen atoms or the addition of oxygen. When we compare the level of oxidation from alkanes to carboxylic acids, we find there is an increase in the number of carbon–oxygen bonds. When a compound is reduced, it forms a product with fewer carbon–oxygen bonds.

No bonds to O   1 bond to O   2 bonds to O   3 bonds to O

$$CH_3-CH_3 \underset{\text{Reduction}}{\overset{\text{Oxidation}}{\rightleftharpoons}} CH_3-\overset{\overset{\displaystyle OH}{|}}{CH_2} \underset{\text{Reduction}}{\overset{\text{Oxidation}}{\rightleftharpoons}} CH_3-\overset{\overset{\displaystyle O}{\|}}{C}-H \underset{\text{Reduction}}{\overset{\text{Oxidation}}{\rightleftharpoons}} CH_3-\overset{\overset{\displaystyle O}{\|}}{C}-OH$$

Alkane   Alcohol (1°)   Aldehyde   Carboxylic acid

No bonds to O   1 bond to O   2 bonds to O

$$CH_3-CH_2-CH_3 \underset{\text{Reduction}}{\overset{\text{Oxidation}}{\rightleftharpoons}} CH_3-\overset{\overset{\displaystyle OH}{|}}{\underset{\underset{\displaystyle H}{|}}{C}}-CH_3 \underset{\text{Reduction}}{\overset{\text{Oxidation}}{\rightleftharpoons}} CH_3-\overset{\overset{\displaystyle O}{\|}}{C}-CH_3$$

No further oxidation

Alkane   Alcohol (2°)   Ketone

An alcohol is more oxidized than an alkane; an aldehyde or ketone is more oxidized than an alcohol; a carboxylic acid is more oxidized than an aldehyde.

Oxidation of Primary and Secondary Alcohols

The oxidation of a primary alcohol produces an aldehyde, which contains a double bond between carbon and oxygen. The oxidation takes place when two hydrogen atoms are removed, one from the —OH group and another from the carbon that is bonded to the —OH group. The reaction is written with the symbol $[O]$ over the arrow to indicate that O is obtained from an oxidizing agent, such as $KMnO_4$ or $K_2Cr_2O_7$.

$$H-\overset{\overset{\displaystyle OH}{|}}{\underset{\underset{\displaystyle H}{|}}{C}}-H \xrightarrow{[O]} H-\overset{\overset{\displaystyle O}{\|}}{C}-H + H_2O \qquad CH_3-\overset{\overset{\displaystyle OH}{|}}{\underset{\underset{\displaystyle H}{|}}{C}}-H \xrightarrow{[O]} CH_3-\overset{\overset{\displaystyle O}{\|}}{C}-H + H_2O$$

Methanol   Methanal   Ethanol   Ethanal
(methyl alcohol)   (formaldehyde)   (ethyl alcohol)   (acetaldehyde)

Chemistry Link to Health

METHANOL POISONING

Methanol, or "wood alcohol," is a highly toxic alcohol present in products such as windshield-washer fluid, Sterno, and paint strippers. Methanol is rapidly absorbed in the gastrointestinal tract. In the liver, it is metabolized to formaldehyde and then formic acid, a substance that causes nausea, severe abdominal pain, and blurred vision. Blindness can occur because the intermediate products destroy the retina of the eye. As little as 4 mL of methanol can produce blindness. The formic acid, which is not readily eliminated from the body, lowers blood pH so severely that just 30 mL of methanol can lead to coma and death.

The treatment for methanol poisoning involves giving sodium bicarbonate to neutralize the formic acid in the blood. In some cases, ethanol is given intravenously to the patient. The enzymes in the liver pick up ethanol molecules to oxidize instead of methanol molecules. This process gives time for the methanol to be eliminated via the lungs without the formation of its dangerous oxidation products.

Aldehydes oxidize further by the addition of oxygen to form a carboxylic acid. This step occurs so readily that it is often difficult to isolate the aldehyde product during oxidation.

$$CH_3-\overset{\overset{\displaystyle O}{\|}}{C}-H \xrightarrow{[O]} CH_3-\overset{\overset{\displaystyle O}{\|}}{C}-OH$$

Ethanal (acetaldehyde) → Ethanoic acid (acetic acid)

We will learn more about carboxylic acids in Chapter 16.

In the oxidation of secondary alcohols, the products are ketones. One hydrogen is removed from the —OH and another from the carbon bonded to the —OH group. The result is a ketone that has the carbon–oxygen double bond attached to alkyl groups on both sides. There is no further oxidation of a ketone because there are no hydrogen atoms attached to the carbon of the ketone group.

$$CH_3-\overset{\overset{\displaystyle OH}{|}}{\underset{\underset{\displaystyle H}{|}}{C}}-CH_3 \xrightarrow{[O]} CH_3-\overset{\overset{\displaystyle O}{\|}}{C}-CH_3 + H_2O$$

2-Propanol (isopropyl alcohol) → Propanone (dimethyl ketone; acetone)

Tertiary alcohols do not oxidize readily, because there are no hydrogen atoms on the carbon bonded to the —OH group. Because C—C bonds are usually too strong to oxidize, tertiary alcohols resist oxidation.

No double bond forms No hydrogen on this carbon

$$CH_3-\overset{\overset{\displaystyle OH}{|}}{\underset{\underset{\displaystyle CH_3}{|}}{C}}-CH_3 \xrightarrow{[O]} \text{No oxidation product readily forms}$$

Alcohol (3°)

SAMPLE PROBLEM 13.7 Oxidation of Alcohols

Draw the condensed structural formula for the aldehyde or ketone formed by the oxidation of each of the following:

a. $CH_3-CH_2-\overset{\overset{\displaystyle OH}{|}}{CH}-CH_3$

b. $CH_3-CH_2-CH_2-OH$

SOLUTION

a. This is a secondary (2°) alcohol, which oxidizes to a ketone.

$$CH_3-CH_2-\overset{\overset{\displaystyle O}{\|}}{C}-CH_3$$

b. This is a primary (1°) alcohol, which oxidizes to an aldehyde.

$$CH_3-CH_2-\overset{\overset{\displaystyle O}{\|}}{C}-H$$

STUDY CHECK 13.7

Draw the condensed structural formula for the product formed by the oxidation of 2-pentanol.

During vigorous exercise, lactic acid accumulates in the muscles and causes fatigue. When the activity level is decreased, oxygen enters the muscles. The secondary —OH group in lactic acid is oxidized to a ketone group in pyruvic acid, which eventually is oxidized to CO_2 and H_2O. The muscles in highly trained athletes are capable of taking up greater quantities of oxygen so that vigorous exercise can be maintained for longer periods of time.

CASE STUDY
Alcohol Toxicity

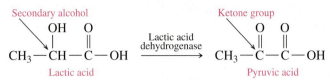

Chemistry Link to Health

OXIDATION OF ALCOHOL IN THE BODY

Ethanol is the most commonly abused drug in the United States. When ingested in small amounts, ethanol may produce a feeling of euphoria, despite the fact that it is a depressant. In the liver, enzymes such as alcohol dehydrogenase oxidize ethanol to acetaldehyde, a substance that impairs mental and physical coordination. If the blood alcohol concentration exceeds 0.4%, coma or death may occur. Table 13.2 gives some of the typical behaviors exhibited at various levels of blood alcohol.

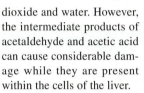

The acetaldehyde produced from ethanol in the liver is further oxidized to acetic acid, which is eventually converted to carbon

dioxide and water. However, the intermediate products of acetaldehyde and acetic acid can cause considerable damage while they are present within the cells of the liver.

A person weighing 150 lb requires about one hour to metabolize 10 oz of beer. However, the rate of metabolism of ethanol varies between nondrinkers and drinkers. Typically, nondrinkers and social drinkers can metabolize 12–15 mg of ethanol/dL of blood in one hour, but an alcoholic can metabolize as much as 30 mg of ethanol/dL in one hour. Some effects of alcohol metabolism include an increase in liver lipids (fatty liver), an increase in serum triglycerides, gastritis, pancreatitis, ketoacidosis, alcoholic hepatitis, and psychological disturbances.

When alcohol is present in the blood, it evaporates through the lungs. Thus, the percentage of alcohol in the lungs can be used to calculate the blood alcohol concentration (BAC). Several devices are used to measure the BAC. When a Breathalyzer is used, a suspected drunk driver exhales through a mouthpiece into a solution containing the orange Cr^{6+} ion. Any alcohol present in the exhaled air is oxidized, which reduces the orange Cr^{6+} to a green Cr^{3+}.

TABLE 13.2 Typical Behaviors Exhibited by a 150-lb Person Consuming Alcohol

Number of Beers (12 oz) or Glasses of Wine (5 oz) in 1 hour	Blood Alcohol Level (% m/v)	Typical Behavior
1	0.025	Slightly dizzy, talkative
2	0.05	Euphoria, loud talking and laughing
4	0.10	Loss of inhibition, loss of coordination, drowsiness, legally drunk in most states
8	0.20	Intoxicated, quick to anger, exaggerated emotions
12	0.30	Unconscious
16–20	0.40–0.50	Coma and death

$$CH_3-CH_2-OH + Cr^{6+} \xrightarrow{[O]} CH_3-\overset{O}{\overset{\|}{C}}-OH + Cr^{3+}$$
Ethanol   Orange   Acetic acid   Green

The Alcosensor uses the oxidation of alcohol in a fuel cell to generate an electric current that is measured. The Intoxilyzer measures the amount of light absorbed by the alcohol molecules.

Sometimes alcoholics are treated with a drug called Antabuse (disulfiram), which prevents the oxidation of acetaldehyde to acetic acid. As a result, acetaldehyde accumulates in the blood, which causes nausea, profuse sweating, headache, dizziness, vomiting, and respiratory difficulties. Because of these unpleasant side effects, the patient is less likely to use alcohol.

Oxidation of Thiols

Thiols also undergo oxidation by a loss of hydrogen atoms from the —SH groups. The oxidized product is called a **disulfide**.

$$CH_3-S-H + H-S-CH_3 \xrightarrow{[O]} CH_3-S-S-CH_3 + H_2O$$
Methanethiol   Dimethyl disulfide

TUTORIAL
Oxidation of Thiols

Much of the protein in the hair is cross-linked by disulfide bonds, which occur between the thiol groups of the amino acid cysteine:

Protein Chain—CH_2—SH + HS—CH_2—Protein Chain $\xrightarrow{[O]}$

Cysteine side groups

Protein Chain—CH_2—S—S—CH_2—Protein Chain + H_2O

Disulfide bond

When a person is given a "perm" ("permanent wave"), a reducing substance is used to break the disulfide bonds. While the hair is still wrapped around the curlers, an oxidizing substance is then applied that causes new disulfide bonds to form between different parts of the protein hair strands, which gives the hair a new shape.

QUESTIONS AND PROBLEMS

13.4 Reactions of Alcohols and Thiols

LEARNING GOAL: Write equations for the combustion, dehydration, and oxidation of alcohols and thiols.

13.21 Draw the condensed structural formula or skeletal formula, if cyclic, for the alkene that is the major product from each of the following dehydration reactions:

a. CH_3—CH_2—CH_2—CH_2—OH $\xrightarrow[\text{Heat}]{H^+}$

b. 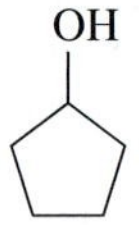 (cyclopentanol) $\xrightarrow[\text{Heat}]{H^+}$

c. 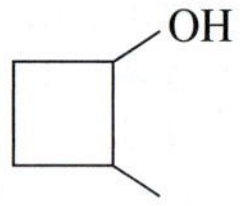 (methylcyclobutanol with OH) $\xrightarrow[\text{Heat}]{H^+}$

d. CH_3—CH_2—CH_2—$\underset{\underset{OH}{|}}{CH}$—$CH_3$ $\xrightarrow[\text{Heat}]{H^+}$

13.22 Draw the condensed structural formula or skeletal formula, if cyclic, for the alkene that is the major product from each of the following dehydration reactions:

a. CH_3—$\underset{\underset{CH_3}{|}}{CH}$—$CH_2$—OH $\xrightarrow[\text{Heat}]{H^+}$

b. CH_3—$\underset{\underset{OH}{|}}{CH}$—$\underset{\underset{CH_3}{|}}{CH}$—$CH_2$—$CH_3$ $\xrightarrow[\text{Heat}]{H^+}$

c. 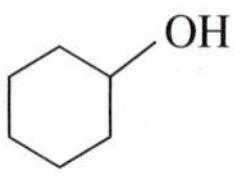 (cyclohexanol) $\xrightarrow[\text{Heat}]{H^+}$

d. 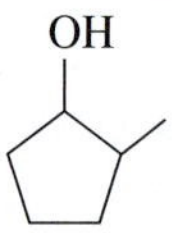 (cyclopentanol) $\xrightarrow[\text{Heat}]{H^+}$

13.23 Draw the condensed structural formula for the ether produced by each of the following reactions:

a. $2CH_3$—OH $\xrightarrow[\text{Heat}]{H^+}$

b. $2CH_3$—CH_2—CH_2—OH $\xrightarrow[\text{Heat}]{H^+}$

13.24 Draw the condensed structural formula for the ether produced by each of the following reactions:

a. $2CH_3$—CH_2—OH $\xrightarrow[\text{Heat}]{H^+}$

b. $2CH_3$—$\underset{\underset{CH_3}{|}}{CH}$—$CH_2$—OH $\xrightarrow[\text{Heat}]{H^+}$

13.25 What alcohol(s) could be used to produce each of the following compounds?

a. H_2C=CH_2 **b.** CH_3—O—CH_2—CH_3 **c.**  (cyclohexene)

13.26 What alcohol(s) could be used to produce each of the following compounds?

a. CH_3—CH_2—O—CH_2—CH_3

b. CH_3—CH_2—$\underset{\underset{CH_3}{|}}{C}$=$CH$—$CH_3$ **c.** 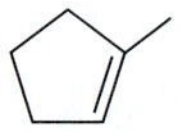 (methylcyclopentene)

13.27 Draw the condensed structural formula or skeletal formula, if cyclic, for the aldehyde or ketone produced when each of the following alcohols is oxidized $[O]$ (if no reaction, write *none*):

a. CH_3—CH_2—CH_2—CH_2—CH_2—OH

b. CH_3—CH_2—$\underset{\underset{OH}{|}}{CH}$—$CH_3$ **c.** 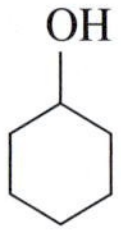 (cyclohexanol)

d. CH_3—$\underset{\underset{OH}{|}}{CH}$—$CH_2$—$\underset{\underset{CH_3}{|}}{CH}$—$CH_3$

e. CH_3—$\underset{\underset{CH_3}{|}}{CH}$—$CH_2$—$CH_2$—OH

13.28 Draw the condensed structural formula or skeletal formula, if cyclic, for the aldehyde or ketone produced when each of the following alcohols is oxidized $[O]$ (if no reaction, write *none*):

a. 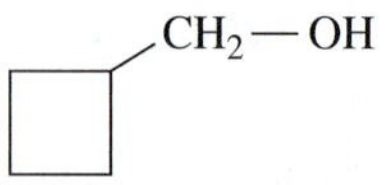 (cyclobutane with CH_2—OH)

b. CH_3—$\underset{\underset{CH_3}{|}}{CH}$—$CH_2$—$\underset{\underset{CH_3}{|}}{CH}$—OH

c. CH_3—CH_2—$\underset{\underset{CH_3}{\overset{OH}{|}}}{C}$—$CH_3$

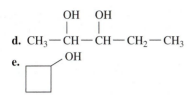

d. $CH_3-CH-CH-CH_2-CH_3$ (OH OH)

e. (cyclobutane with OH)

13.29 Draw the condensed structural formula or skeletal formula, if cyclic, for the alcohol needed to give each of the following oxidation products:

a. $H-\overset{O}{\overset{\|}{C}}-H$ **b.** (cyclopentanone)   **c.** $CH_3-\overset{O}{\overset{\|}{C}}-CH_2-CH_3$

d. (benzaldehyde)   **e.** (methylcyclohexanone)

13.30 Draw the condensed structural formula or skeletal formula, if cyclic, for the alcohol needed to give each of the following oxidation products:

a. $CH_3-\overset{O}{\overset{\|}{C}}-H$ **b.** $CH_3-\overset{O}{\overset{\|}{C}}-\overset{CH_3}{\overset{|}{CH}}-CH_3$ **c.** (cyclohexanone)

d. $CH_3-CH_2-\overset{O}{\overset{\|}{C}}-H$ **e.** $CH_3-\overset{CH_3}{\overset{|}{CH}}-CH_2-\overset{O}{\overset{\|}{C}}-H$

CONCEPT MAP

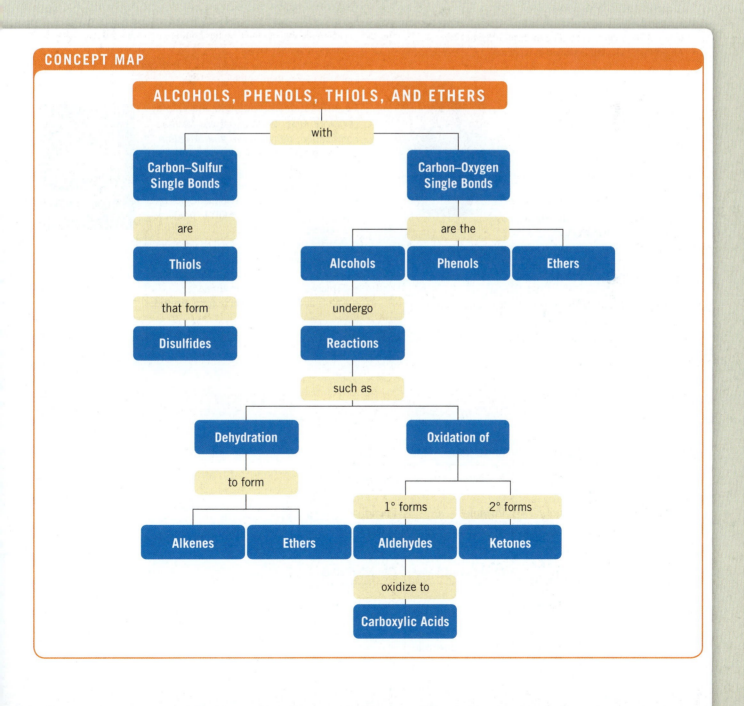

ALCOHOLS, PHENOLS, THIOLS, AND ETHERS

with

Carbon–Sulfur Single Bonds — are → **Thiols** — that form → **Disulfides**

Carbon–Oxygen Single Bonds — are the → **Alcohols**, **Phenols**, **Ethers**

Alcohols — undergo → **Reactions** — such as → **Dehydration**, **Oxidation of**

Dehydration — to form → **Alkenes**, **Ethers**

Oxidation of — 1° forms → **Aldehydes** — 2° forms → **Ketones**

Aldehydes — oxidize to → **Carboxylic Acids**

CHAPTER REVIEW

13.1 Alcohols, Phenols, and Thiols

LEARNING GOAL: Give the IUPAC and common names for alcohols, phenols, and thiols; draw their condensed structural formulas and skeletal formulas.

$CH_3 — CH_2 — CH_2 — SH$

1-Propanethiol
Onions

- The functional group of an alcohol is the hydroxyl group ($—OH$) bonded to a carbon chain.
- In a phenol, the hydroxyl group is bonded to an aromatic ring.
- In thiols, the functional group is $—SH$, which is analogous to the $—OH$ group of alcohols.
- In the IUPAC system, the names of alcohols have *ol* endings, and the location of the $—OH$ group is given by numbering the carbon chain.
- A cyclic alcohol is named as a cycloalkanol.
- Simple alcohols are generally named by their common names, with the alkyl name preceding the term *alcohol*.
- An aromatic alcohol is named as a phenol.

13.2 Ethers

LEARNING GOAL: Give the IUPAC and common names for ethers; draw their condensed structural formulas or skeletal formulas.

- In an ether, an oxygen atom is connected by single bonds to two alkyl or aromatic groups.
- In the common names of ethers, the alkyl groups are listed alphabetically, followed by the name *ether*.
- In the IUPAC name of an ether, the smaller alkyl group with the oxygen is named as an alkoxy group and is attached to the longer alkane chain, which is numbered to give the location of the alkoxy group.
- Some alcohols and ethers are isomers, which means that they have the same molecular formulas.

13.3 Physical Properties of Alcohols, Phenols, and Ethers

LEARNING GOAL: Describe the classification, boiling points, and solubility of alcohols, phenols, and ethers.

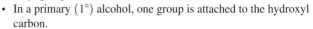
Hydrogen bonds

Methyl alcohol

- Alcohols are classified according to the number of alkyl groups bonded to the carbon that holds the $—OH$.
- In a primary (1°) alcohol, one group is attached to the hydroxyl carbon.
- In a secondary (2°) alcohol, two groups are attached.
- In a tertiary (3°) alcohol, there are three groups bonded to the hydroxyl carbon.
- The $—OH$ group allows alcohols to hydrogen bond, which causes alcohols to have higher boiling points than alkanes and ethers of similar mass.
- Short-chain alcohols and ethers can hydrogen bond with water, which makes them soluble.

13.4 Reactions of Alcohols and Thiols

LEARNING GOAL: Write equations for the combustion, dehydration, and oxidation of alcohols and thiols.

- At high temperatures, alcohols dehydrate in the presence of an acid to yield alkenes.
- At lower temperatures, two molecules of alcohol lose H$—$ and $—OH$ to produce an ether.
- Primary alcohols are oxidized to aldehydes, which can oxidize further to carboxylic acids.
- Secondary alcohols are oxidized to ketones.
- Tertiary alcohols do not oxidize.
- Thiols undergo oxidation to form disulfides.

SUMMARY OF NAMING

Structure	Family	IUPAC Name	Common Name
$CH_3—OH$	Alcohol	Methanol	Methyl alcohol
⬡$—OH$	Phenol	Phenol	Phenol
$CH_3—SH$	Thiol	Methanethiol	
$CH_3—O—CH_3$	Ether	Methoxymethane	Dimethyl ether
⬠O	Cyclic ether	Furan	
$CH_3—S—S—CH_3$	Disulfide	Dimethyldisulfide	

SUMMARY OF REACTIONS

Combustion of Alcohols

$$CH_3-CH_2-OH + 3O_2 \longrightarrow 2CO_2 + 3H_2O$$
Ethanol   Oxygen   Carbon   Water
                            dioxide

Dehydration of Alcohols to Form Alkenes

$$CH_3-CH_2-CH_2-OH \xrightarrow[Heat]{H^+}$$
1-Propanol

$$CH_3-CH=CH_2 + H_2O$$
Propene

Formation of Ethers

$$CH_3-OH + HO-CH_3 \xrightarrow[Heat]{H^+}$$
Methanol

$$CH_3-O-CH_3 + H_2O$$
Dimethyl ether

Oxidation of Primary Alcohols to Form Aldehydes

$$\underset{Ethanol}{CH_3-\overset{\overset{\displaystyle OH}{|}}{CH_2}} \xrightarrow{[O]} \underset{Ethanal}{CH_3-\overset{\overset{\displaystyle O}{\|}}{C}-H} + H_2O$$

Oxidation of Secondary Alcohols to Form Ketones

$$\underset{2\text{-Propanol}}{CH_3-\overset{\overset{\displaystyle OH}{|}}{CH}-CH_3} \xrightarrow{[O]} \underset{Propanone}{CH_3-\overset{\overset{\displaystyle O}{\|}}{C}-CH_3} + H_2O$$

Oxidation of Thiols to Form Disulfides

$$\underset{Methanethiol}{CH_3-S-H + H-S-CH_3} \xrightarrow{[O]}$$

$$CH_3-S-S-CH_3 + H_2O$$
Dimethyl disulfide

Oxidation of Aldehydes to Form Carboxylic Acids

$$\underset{Ethanal}{CH_3-\overset{\overset{\displaystyle O}{\|}}{C}-H} \xrightarrow{[O]} \underset{Ethanoic\ acid}{CH_3-\overset{\overset{\displaystyle O}{\|}}{C}-OH}$$

KEY TERMS

alcohol An organic compound that contains the hydroxyl functional group (—OH) attached to a carbon chain.

cyclic ether A compound that contains an oxygen atom in a carbon ring.

dehydration A reaction that removes water from an alcohol in the presence of an acid to form alkenes at high temperatures, or ethers at lower temperatures.

disulfide A compound formed from thiols; disulfides contain the —S—S— functional group.

ether An organic compound in which an oxygen atom is bonded to two carbon groups that are alkyl or aromatic.

oxidation The loss of two hydrogen atoms from a reactant to give a more oxidized compound: primary alcohols oxidize to aldehydes, secondary alcohols oxidize to ketones. An oxidation can

also be the addition of an oxygen atom, as in the oxidation of aldehydes to carboxylic acids.

phenol An organic compound that has a hydroxyl group (—OH) attached to a benzene ring.

primary (1°) alcohol An alcohol that has one alkyl group bonded to the alcohol's carbon atom.

Saytzeff's rule In the dehydration of an alcohol, hydrogen is removed from the carbon that already has the smaller number of hydrogen atoms to form an alkene.

secondary (2°) alcohol An alcohol that has two alkyl groups bonded to the carbon atom with the —OH group.

tertiary (3°) alcohol An alcohol that has three alkyl groups bonded to the carbon atom with the —OH group.

thiol An organic compound that contains a thiol group (—SH).

UNDERSTANDING THE CONCEPTS

The chapter sections to review are shown in parentheses at the end of each question.

13.31 Urushiol is a substance in poison ivy and poison oak that causes itching and blistering of the skin. Identify the functional groups in urushiol. (13.1, 13.2)

Poison ivy contains urushiol, which causes a rash and itching of the skin.

13.32 Menthol, which gives a peppermint taste and color, is used in candy and throat lozenges. Identify the functional groups in menthol. (13.1, 13.2)

Menthol gives the taste of peppermint in candy.

13.33 Identify each of the following as an alcohol, a phenol, an ether, a cyclic ether, or a thiol: (13.1, 13.2)

a.

$$\text{(cyclohexane ring with OH and Cl)}$$

b.

$$\text{(benzene ring)}-O-CH_3$$

c. $CH_3-\overset{\overset{\displaystyle SH}{|}}{CH}-CH_3$

d. $CH_3-\overset{\overset{\displaystyle OH}{|}}{\underset{\underset{\displaystyle CH_3}{|}}{C}}-CH_2-\overset{\overset{\displaystyle CH_3}{|}}{CH}-CH_3$

e. $CH_3-CH_2-CH_2-O-CH_3$

f.

$$\text{(furan ring)}$$

13.34 Identify each of the following as an alcohol, a phenol, an ether, a cyclic ether, or a thiol: (13.1, 13.2)

a.

$$\text{(benzene ring with OH and Cl)}$$

b. $CH_3-CH_2-CH_2-SH$

c. $\text{(cyclohexane ring)}-O-CH_2-CH_3$

d. $CH_3-\overset{\overset{\displaystyle SH}{|}}{\underset{\underset{\displaystyle CH_3}{|}}{C}}-CH_2-\overset{\overset{\displaystyle CH_3}{|}}{CH}-CH_3$

e. $CH_3-CH_2-\overset{\overset{\displaystyle O-CH_3}{|}}{CH}-CH_2-CH_3$

f.

$$\text{(1,4-dioxane ring)}$$

g.

$$\text{(cyclohexane ring with OH, Cl, Cl)}$$

h.

$$\text{(benzene ring with OH, CH}_3\text{, CH}_3\text{)}$$

13.35 Give the IUPAC and common names (if any) for each of the compounds in Problem 13.33. (13.1, 13.2)

13.36 Give the IUPAC and common names (if any) for each of the compounds in Problem 13.34. (13.1, 13.2)

ADDITIONAL QUESTIONS AND PROBLEMS

For instructor-assigned homework, go to www.masteringchemistry.com.

13.37 Draw the condensed structural formula or skeletal formula, if cyclic, for each for the following compounds: (13.1, 13.2)
a. 3-methylcyclopentanol   b. 4-chlorophenol
c. 2-methyl-3-pentanol   d. ethyl phenyl ether
e. 3-pentanethiol   f. *ortho*-cresol
g. 2,4-dibromophenol

13.38 Draw the condensed structural formula or skeletal formula, if cyclic, for each for the following compounds: (13.1, 13.2)
a. 3-methoxypentane   b. *meta*-chlorophenol
c. 2,3-pentanediol   d. methyl propyl ether
e. methanethiol   f. 3-methyl-2-butanol
g. 3,4-dichlorocyclohexanol

13.39 Draw the condensed structural formulas for all the alcohols with a molecular formula $C_4H_{10}O$. (13.1)

13.40 Draw the condensed structural formulas for all the ethers with a molecular formula $C_4H_{10}O$. (13.2)

13.41 Classify each of the following as a primary ($1°$), secondary ($2°$), or tertiary ($3°$) alcohol: (13.3)

a.

$$\text{(cyclohexane ring)}-OH$$

b.

$$\text{(cyclohexane ring)}-CH_2-OH$$

c. $CH_3-\overset{\overset{\displaystyle CH_3}{|}}{CH}-CH_2-OH$

d. $CH_3-\overset{\overset{\displaystyle CH_3}{|}}{\underset{\underset{\displaystyle CH_3}{|}}{C}}-CH_2-\overset{\overset{\displaystyle OH}{|}}{CH}-CH_3$

e. $HO-CH_2-CH_2-CH_3$

f.

$$\text{(cyclopentane ring)}-\overset{\overset{\displaystyle OH}{|}}{\underset{\underset{\displaystyle CH_3}{|}}{C}}-CH_3$$

13.33 and **13.34** g. $CH_3-\overset{\overset{\displaystyle Br}{|}}{CH}-CH_2-\overset{\overset{\displaystyle OH}{|}}{CH}-CH_3$

h.

$$\text{(benzene ring with OH and CH}_3\text{)}$$

13.42 Classify each of the following as a primary (1°), secondary (2°), or tertiary (3°) alcohol: (13.3)

a. HO $\overset{|}{\underset{|}{\diagdown}}$ (structure)

b. (structure with OH)

c. $\overset{CH_2-OH}{\underset{}{|}}$ $CH_3-CH-CH_2-CH_3$

d. $CH_3-\overset{OH}{\underset{CH_3}{\overset{|}{\underset{|}{C}}}}-CH_2-\overset{CH_3}{\underset{}{\overset{|}{CH}}}-CH_3$

e. $CH_3-CH_2-CH_2-CH_2-OH$

f. $\overset{CH_3}{\underset{}{\overset{|}{CH}}}-OH$ (cyclopentane ring)

13.43 Which compound in each of the following pairs would you expect to have the higher boiling point? Explain. (13.3)
a. butane or 1-propanol   b. 1-propanol or ethyl methyl ether
c. ethanol or 1-butanol

13.44 Which compound in each of the following pairs would you expect to have the higher boiling point? Explain. (13.3)
a. propane or ethyl alcohol   b. 2-propanol or 2-pentanol
c. methyl propyl ether or 1-butanol

13.45 Explain why each of the following compounds would be soluble or insoluble in water: (13.3)
a. 2-propanol   b. dipropyl ether   c. 1-hexanol

13.46 Explain why each of the following compounds would be soluble or insoluble in water: (13.3)
a. glycerol   b. butane   c. 1,3-hexanediol

13.47 Draw the condensed structural formula or skeletal formula, if cyclic, for the alkene (major product), aldehyde, ether, ketone, or *none* produced in each of the following: (13.4)

a. $CH_3-CH_2-CH_2-OH \xrightarrow[\text{Heat}]{H^+}$

b. $CH_3-CH_2-CH_2-OH \xrightarrow{[O]}$

c. $CH_3-CH_2-\overset{OH}{\underset{}{\overset{|}{CH}}}-CH_3 \xrightarrow[\text{Heat}]{H^+}$

d. (cyclohexanol, OH) $\xrightarrow[\text{Heat}]{H^+}$

e. (cyclohexanol with methyl, OH) $\xrightarrow{[O]}$

13.48 Draw the condensed structural formula or skeletal formula, if cyclic, for the alkene (major product), aldehyde, ether, ketone, or *none* produced in each of the following: (13.4)

a. $2CH_3-CH_2-\overset{CH_3}{\underset{}{\overset{|}{CH}}}-OH \xrightarrow{H^+}$

b. $CH_3-\overset{CH_3}{\underset{}{\overset{|}{CH}}}-\overset{OH}{\underset{}{\overset{|}{CH}}}-CH_3 \xrightarrow[\text{Heat}]{H^+}$

c. $CH_3-\overset{CH_3}{\underset{}{\overset{|}{CH}}}-\overset{OH}{\underset{}{\overset{|}{CH}}}-CH_3 \xrightarrow{[O]}$

d. (cyclopentanol with methyl, OH) $\xrightarrow{[O]}$

e. $CH_3-CH_2-CH_2-\overset{OH}{\underset{}{\overset{|}{CH}}}-CH_3 \xrightarrow[\text{Heat}]{H^+}$

13.49 Sometimes several steps are needed to prepare a compound. Using a combination of the reactions we have studied, indicate how you might prepare the following from the starting substance given. For example, 2-propanol could be prepared from 1-propanol by first dehydrating the alcohol to give propene and then hydrating it again to give 2-propanol according to Markovnikov's rule, as follows: (13.4)

$CH_3-CH_2-CH_2-OH \xrightarrow[\text{Heat}]{H^+} CH_3-CH=CH_2 + H_2O$
    1-Propanol   Propene

$\xrightarrow{H^+} CH_3-\overset{OH}{\underset{}{\overset{|}{CH}}}-CH_3$
          2-Propanol

a. prepare 2-chloropropane from 1-propanol
b. prepare 2-methylpropane from 2-methyl-2-propanol
c. prepare $CH_3-\overset{O}{\overset{||}{C}}-CH_3$ from 1-propanol

13.50 As in Problem 13.49, indicate how you might prepare the following from the starting substance given: (13.4)
a. prepare 1-pentene from 1-pentanol
b. prepare chlorocyclohexane from cyclohexanol
c. prepare 1,2-dibromobutane from 1-butanol

13.51 Identify the functional groups in the following: (13.1, 13.2)

Testosterone

13.52 Identify the functional groups in the following: (13.1, 13.2)

Tetrahydrocannabinol (THC)

13.53 Hexylresorcinol, an antiseptic ingredient used in mouthwashes and throat lozenges, has the IUPAC name of 4-hexyl-1,3-benzenediol. Draw its condensed structural formula. (13.1)

13.54 Menthol, which has a minty flavor, is used in throat sprays and lozenges. Thymol is used as a topical antiseptic to destroy mold.
a. For each, give their IUPAC names.
b. What is similar and what is different about their structures? (13.1)

      Menthol   Thymol

CHALLENGE QUESTIONS

13.55 Draw the condensed structural formula or skeletal formula, if cyclic, for each of the following naturally occurring compounds: (13.1, 13.2)
   a. 2,5-dichlorophenol, a defense pheromone of a grasshopper
   b. 3-methyl-1-butanethiol and *trans*-2-butene-1-thiol, a mixture that gives skunk scent its odor
   c. pentachlorophenol, a wood preservative

13.56 Dimethyl ether and ethyl alcohol both have the molecular formula C_2H_6O. One has a boiling point of $-24\ °C$, and the other, $79\ °C$. Draw the condensed structural formula for each compound. Decide which boiling point goes with which compound and explain. (13.1, 13.2, 13.3)

13.57 A compound with the formula C_4H_8O is synthesized from 2-methyl-1-propanol and oxidizes easily to give a carboxylic acid. Draw the condensed structural formula for the compound. (13.4)

13.58 Methyl *tert*-butyl ether (MTBE), or 2-methoxy-2-methylpropane, has been used as a fuel additive for gasoline to boost the octane rating and to reduce CO emissions. (1.1, 6.1, 6.5, 6.7, 7.7, 13.2)
   a. If fuel mixtures are required to contain 2.7% oxygen by mass, how many grams of MTBE must be present in each 100. g of gasoline?
   b. How many liters of MTBE would be in 1.0 L of fuel if the density of both gasoline and MTBE is 0.740 g/mL?
   c. Write the balanced equation for the complete combustion of MTBE.
   d. How many liters of air containing 21% (v/v) O_2 are required at STP to completely react (combust) 1.00 L of liquid MTBE?

ANSWERS

Answers to Study Checks

13.1 3-chloro-1-butanol

13.2 4-methylphenol; *p*-cresol

13.3 methoxybenzene

13.4 1-butanol, 2-butanol, 1-methoxypropane, ethoxyethane

13.5 cyclopentene

13.6 2-methyl-1-propanol, 2-methyl-2-propanol

13.7
$$CH_3-\overset{\overset{\displaystyle O}{\|}}{C}-CH_2-CH_2-CH_3$$

Answers to Selected Questions and Problems

13.1 a. ethanol
   b. 2-butanol
   c. 2-pentanol
   d. 4-methylcyclohexanol
   e. 3-bromophenol

13.3 a. $CH_3-CH_2-CH_2-OH$
   b. $CH_3-CH_2-\overset{\overset{\displaystyle OH}{|}}{CH}-CH_2-CH_3$
   c. $CH_3-\overset{\overset{\displaystyle OH}{|}}{\underset{\underset{\displaystyle CH_3}{|}}{C}}-CH_2-CH_3$
   d. *(4-chlorophenol skeletal structure with OH and Cl)*
   e. *(bromo-chloro-phenol skeletal structure with OH, Br, Cl)*

13.5 a. methoxyethane, ethyl methyl ether
   b. methoxycyclohexane, cyclohexyl methyl ether
   c. ethoxycyclobutane, cyclobutyl ethyl ether
   d. 1-methoxypropane, methyl propyl ether

13.7 a. $CH_3-CH_2-O-CH_2-CH_2-CH_3$
   b. $CH_3-CH_2-O-\triangleleft$
   c. *(cyclopentane with $O-CH_3$ substituent)*
   d. $CH_3-CH_2-O-CH_2-\overset{\overset{\displaystyle CH_3}{|}}{CH}-CH_2-CH_3$
   e. $CH_3-\overset{\overset{\displaystyle O-CH_3}{|}}{CH}-\overset{\overset{\displaystyle O-CH_3}{|}}{CH}-CH_2-CH_3$

13.9 a. structural isomers $(C_5H_{12}O)$ **b.** not structural isomers
   c. structural isomers $(C_5H_{12}O)$

13.11 a. tetrahydrofuran   **b.** 3-methylfuran
   c. 5-methyl-1,3-dioxane

13.13 a. 1°   **b.** 1°   **c.** 3°   **d.** 2°

13.15 a. methanol   **b.** 1-butanol
   c. 1-butanol

13.17 a. Soluble; ethanol with a short carbon chain is soluble because the hydroxyl group forms hydrogen bonds with water.
   b. Slightly soluble; ethers with up to four carbon atoms are slightly soluble in water because they can form a few hydrogen bonds with water.
   c. Insoluble; an alcohol with a carbon chain of five or more carbon atoms is not soluble in water.

13.19 a. Methanol can form hydrogen bonds with water, but ethane cannot.
  b. 2-Propanol is more soluble because it has a shorter carbon chain.
  c. 1-Propanol is more soluble because it can form more hydrogen bonds.

13.21 a. $CH_3-CH_2-CH=CH_2$
  b.
  c.
  d. $CH_3-CH_2-CH=CH-CH_3$

13.23 a. CH_3-O-CH_3
  b. $CH_3-CH_2-CH_2-O-CH_2-CH_2-CH_3$

13.25 a. CH_3-CH_2-OH
  b. $CH_3-OH + CH_3-CH_2-OH$
  c.

13.27 a. $CH_3-CH_2-CH_2-CH_2-\overset{O}{\overset{\|}{C}}-H$
  b. $CH_3-CH_2-\overset{O}{\overset{\|}{C}}-CH_3$
  c.
  d. $CH_3-\overset{O}{\overset{\|}{C}}-CH_2-\overset{CH_3}{\underset{|}{CH}}-CH_3$
  e. $CH_3-\overset{CH_3}{\underset{|}{CH}}-CH_2-\overset{O}{\overset{\|}{C}}-H$

13.29 a. CH_3-OH
  b.
  c. $CH_3-\overset{OH}{\underset{|}{CH}}-CH_2-CH_3$
  d.
  e.

13.31 phenol

13.33 a. alcohol **b.** ether **c.** thiol
  d. alcohol **e.** ether **f.** cyclic ether
  g. alcohol **h.** phenol

13.35 a. 2-chloro-4-methylcyclohexanol
  b. methoxybenzene, methyl phenyl ether
  c. 2-propanethiol
  d. 2,4-dimethyl-2-pentanol
  e. 1-methoxypropane, methyl propyl ether
  f. 2-methylfuran
  g. 4-bromo-2-pentanol
  h. *meta*-cresol, 3-methylphenol

13.37 a.
  b.
  c. $CH_3-\overset{CH_3}{\underset{|}{CH}}-\overset{OH}{\underset{|}{CH}}-CH_2-CH_3$
  d.
  e. $CH_3-CH_2-\overset{SH}{\underset{|}{CH}}-CH_2-CH_3$
  f.
  g.

13.39 $CH_3-CH_2-CH_2-CH_2-OH$

$CH_3-\overset{CH_3}{\underset{|}{CH}}-CH_2-OH$

$CH_3-\overset{OH}{\underset{|}{CH}}-CH_2-CH_3$

$CH_3-\overset{OH}{\underset{|}{\underset{|}{C}}}-CH_3$ with CH_3 below

13.41 a. 2° **b.** 1° **c.** 1°
d. 2° **e.** 1° **f.** 3°

13.43 a. 1-propanol, hydrogen bonding
b. 1-propanol, hydrogen bonding
c. 1-butanol, greater molar mass

13.45 a. soluble, hydrogen bonding
b. insoluble, long carbon chain diminishes effect of hydrogen bonding of water to —O—
c. insoluble, long carbon chain diminishes effect of polar —OH group on hydrogen bonding

13.47 a. $CH_3—CH=CH_2$

b. $CH_3—CH_2—\overset{\overset{\textstyle O}{\|}}{C}—H$

c. $CH_3—CH=CH—CH_3$

d.

e.

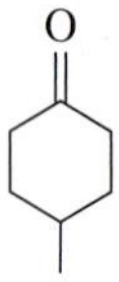

13.49 a. $CH_3—CH_2—CH_2—OH \xrightarrow[\text{Heat}]{H^+} CH_3—CH=CH_2 + HCl \longrightarrow CH_3—\underset{\underset{\textstyle Cl}{|}}{CH}—CH_3$

b. $CH_3—\underset{\underset{\textstyle CH_3}{|}}{\overset{\overset{\textstyle OH}{|}}{C}}—CH_3 \xrightarrow[\text{Heat}]{H^+} CH_3—\underset{\underset{\textstyle CH_3}{|}}{C}=CH_2 + H_2 \xrightarrow{Pt} CH_3—\underset{\underset{\textstyle CH_3}{|}}{CH}—CH_3$

c. $CH_3—CH_2—CH_2—OH \xrightarrow[\text{Heat}]{H^+} CH_3—CH=CH_2 + H_2O \xrightarrow[\text{Heat}]{H^+} CH_3—\underset{\underset{\textstyle CH_3}{|}}{\overset{\overset{\textstyle OH}{|}}{CH}} \xrightarrow{[O]} CH_3—\overset{\overset{\textstyle O}{\|}}{C}—CH_3$

13.51 cycloalkane, cycloalkene, ketone, alcohol

13.53

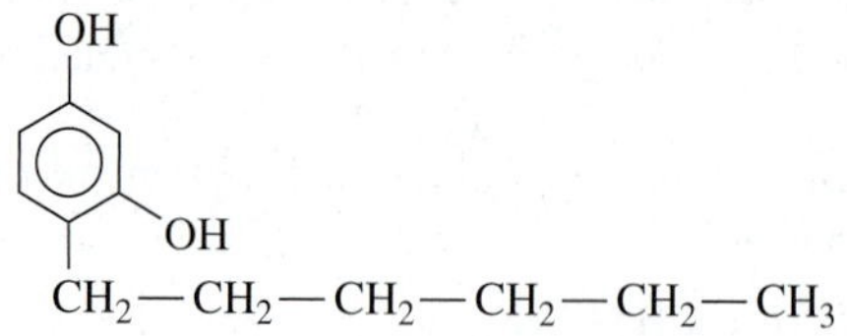

13.55 a.

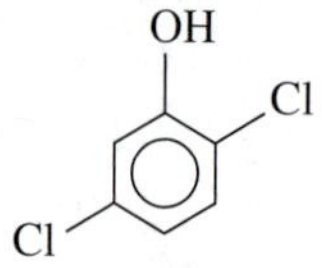

b. $CH_3—\underset{\underset{\textstyle CH_3}{|}}{CH}—CH_2—CH_2—SH$

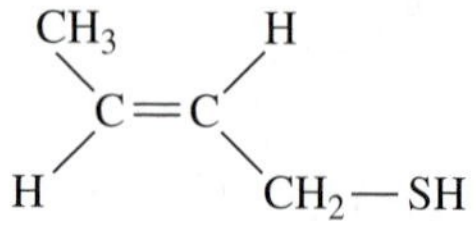

c.

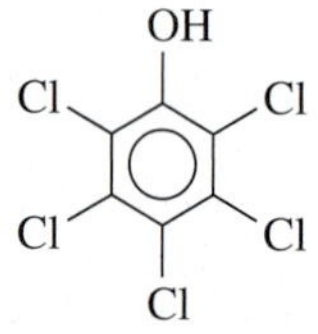

13.57 $CH_3—\underset{\underset{\textstyle CH_3}{|}}{CH}—\overset{\overset{\textstyle O}{\|}}{C}—H$

Aldehydes, Ketones, and Chiral Molecules

LOOKING AHEAD

14.1 Aldehydes and Ketones

14.2 Physical Properties of Aldehydes and Ketones

14.3 Oxidation and Reduction of Aldehydes and Ketones

14.4 Hemiacetals and Acetals

14.5 Chiral Molecules

Visit **www.masteringchemistry.com** for self-study materials and instructor-assigned homework.

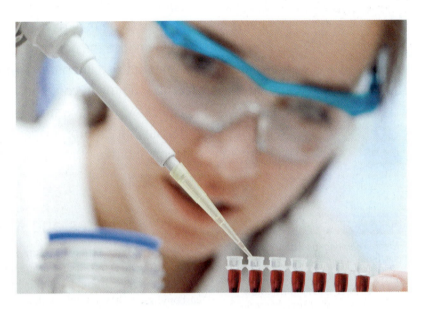

A female victim is found dead in her home.

The police suspect that she was murdered, so samples of her blood and stomach contents are sent to Diane, a forensic toxicologist. Using a variety of qualitative and quantitative tests, Diane finds traces of ethylene glycol. The qualitative tests identify the presence of ethylene glycol, while the quantitative tests indicate the amount of ethylene glycol ingested by the victim. Diane determines that the victim was poisoned when she ingested three tablespoons of ethylene glycol that were placed in an alcoholic beverage. Since initial symptoms of ethylene glycol poisoning are similar to being intoxicated, the victim was unaware of the poisoning.

Ethylene glycol is a diol, as it contains two alcohol functional groups. Alcohols undergo oxidation reactions to form aldehydes, which can be further oxidized to a carboxylic acid.

Initially, ethylene glycol is oxidized to glycoaldehyde, which is oxidized to glycolic acid. Glycoaldehyde and glycolic acid accumulate in the liver where they interfere with enzymes, which results in renal failure and severe metabolic acidosis. Metabolism of these molecules continues within the body and calcium oxalate is produced, which crystallizes in the kidneys, and is fatal.

Career: Forensic Toxicologist

Forensic toxicologists analyze bodily fluids and tissue samples, within a laboratory setting, that were collected by crime scene investigators. In analyzing these samples, a forensic toxicologist identifies the presence or absence of specific chemicals within the body to help solve criminal cases. Tests are conducted to detect various chemicals, including alcohol, illegal or prescription drugs, poisons, metals, and various gases like carbon monoxide. In order to identify these substances, a variety of chemical instrumentation and highly specified methodologies are used that require patience and exact documentation. A forensic toxicologist also analyzes samples for drug testing and gives the results of the tests to law enforcement officials, athletes, and employers. They also work on cases involving environmental contamination and animal samples for wildlife crimes.

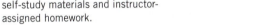

Ethylene glycol   Glycoaldehyde   Glycolic acid

In this chapter, we will study two families of organic compounds: aldehydes and ketones. Many of the odors that you associate with flavorings and perfumes are due to compounds containing a carbon–oxygen double bond called a *carbonyl group* (C=O). Important biomolecules such as carbohydrates, proteins, and nucleic acids also contain carbonyl groups, which influence their structure and function.

Aldehydes in foods and perfumes provide the odors and flavors of vanilla, almond, and cinnamon. In biology, you may have seen specimens preserved in a solution of formaldehyde. You probably notice the odor of a ketone if you use paint or nail polish remover. Aldehydes and ketones are also important compounds in industry, providing the solvents and reactants that make up many common materials we use in our lives. Finally, we will look at chiral molecules, which have structures that are mirror images of each other. We are interested in chirality and mirror images because these three-dimensional structures determine the function and role of many biologically active molecules.

LEARNING GOAL

Identify compounds with a carbonyl group as aldehydes and ketones. Give the IUPAC and common names for aldehydes and ketones; draw their condensed structural formulas or skeletal formulas, if cyclic.

SELF-STUDY ACTIVITY
Aldehydes and Ketones

TUTORIAL
Naming Aldehydes and Ketones

14.1 Aldehydes and Ketones

As we learned in Section 11.5, the carbonyl group (C=O) has a carbon–oxygen double bond with two groups of atoms attached to the carbon at angles of 120°. Because the oxygen atom in the carbonyl group is much more electronegative than the carbon atom, the carbonyl group has a dipole with a partial negative charge (δ^-) on the oxygen and a partial positive charge (δ^+) on the carbon. The polarity of the carbonyl group strongly influences the physical and chemical properties of aldehydes and ketones.

$$O^{\delta^-}$$
$$\|$$
$$C^{\delta^+}$$

In an **aldehyde**, the carbon of the carbonyl group is bonded to at least one hydrogen atom. That carbon may also be bonded to another hydrogen atom, a carbon of an alkyl group, or an aromatic ring (see Figure 14.1). In a **ketone**, the carbonyl group is bonded to two alkyl groups or aromatic rings.

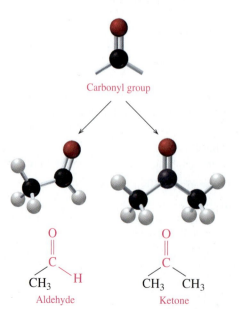

Carbonyl group

O
‖
C
CH₃   H

Aldehyde

O
‖
C
CH₃   CH₃

Ketone

FIGURE 14.1 The carbonyl group is found in aldehydes and ketones.

Q If aldehydes and ketones both contain a carbonyl group, how can you differentiate between compounds from each family?

There are several ways to draw the carbonyl group in the condensed structural formulas of aldehydes and ketones. In an aldehyde, the carbonyl group may be drawn as separate atoms, or it may be written as —CHO. It would not be written as —COH, which looks like a hydroxyl group. The carbonyl group in a ketone (C=O), which would be located somewhere in the middle of the carbon chain, may be written as CO. In the skeletal formulas for aldehydes and ketones, the carbonyl group is shown as a double bond to an oxygen atom.

TUTORIAL
Aldehyde or Ketone?

Representations of Structural and Skeletal Formulas for an Aldehyde and a Ketone of C_3H_6O

Aldehyde

$$CH_3-CH_2-\overset{\overset{\displaystyle O}{\|}}{C}-H \;=\; CH_3-CH_2-CHO \;=\;$$

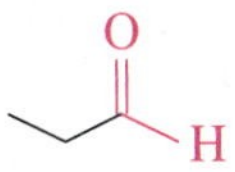

Ketone

$$CH_3-\overset{\overset{\displaystyle O}{\|}}{C}-CH_3 \;=\; CH_3-CO-CH_3 \;=\;$$

CONCEPT CHECK 14.1 **Identifying Aldehydes and Ketones**

Identify each of the following compounds as an aldehyde or ketone:

a.

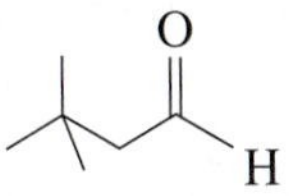

b.

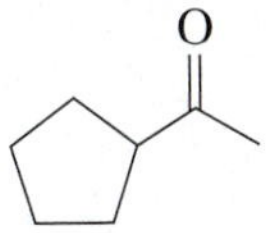

c.

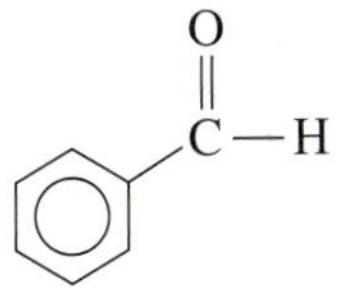

d.

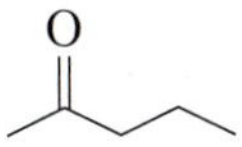

ANSWER

a. A carbonyl group (C=O) attached to a hydrogen atom at the end of the carbon chain makes this compound an aldehyde.
b. A carbonyl group (C=O) attached to two carbon atoms within the carbon chain makes this compound a ketone.
c. A carbonyl group (C=O) attached to a hydrogen atom at the end of the carbon chain makes this compound an aldehyde.
d. A carbonyl group (C=O) attached to two carbon atoms within the carbon chain makes this compound a ketone.

Naming Aldehydes

In the IUPAC system, an aldehyde is named by replacing the *e* of the corresponding alkane name with *al*. No number is needed for the aldehyde group because it always appears at the beginning of the chain. However, the aldehydes with carbon chains of one to four carbon atoms are often referred to by their common names, which end in *aldehyde*. The roots (*form*, *acet*, *propion*, and *butyr*) of these common names are derived from Latin or Greek words (see Figure 14.2).

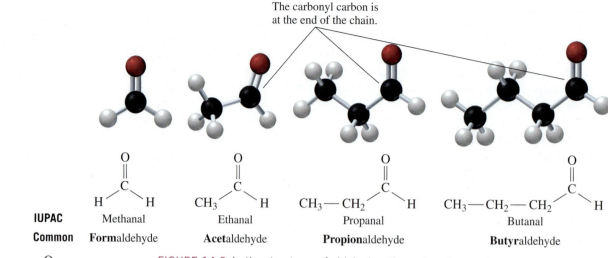

The carbonyl carbon is at the end of the chain.

$\overset{O}{\underset{H}{\overset{\|}{C}}}H$	$\overset{O}{\underset{H}{CH_3-\overset{\|}{C}}}$	$\overset{O}{\underset{H}{CH_3-CH_2-\overset{\|}{C}}}$	$\overset{O}{\underset{H}{CH_3-CH_2-CH_2-\overset{\|}{C}}}$
IUPAC Methanal	Ethanal	Propanal	Butanal
Common **Form**aldehyde	**Acet**aldehyde	**Propion**aldehyde	**Butyr**aldehyde

$\overset{O}{\underset{H}{\overset{\|}{C}}}$

Benzaldehyde

FIGURE 14.2 In the structures of aldehydes, the carbonyl group is always the end carbon.
Q Why is the carbon in the carbonyl group in aldehydes always at the end of the chain?

The aldehyde of benzene is named benzaldehyde.

SAMPLE PROBLEM 14.1 Naming Aldehydes

Give the IUPAC name for each of the following aldehydes:

a. $CH_3-CH_2-\overset{\overset{\displaystyle CH_3}{|}}{CH}-CH_2-\overset{\overset{\displaystyle O}{\|}}{C}-H$

b. $Cl-\langle\bigcirc\rangle-\overset{\overset{\displaystyle O}{\|}}{C}-H$

SOLUTION

Analyze the Problem

Family	IUPAC Naming	Name
Aldehyde	Change *e* to *al* and count from carbon 1 of the carbonyl group for the substituent.	Alkanal

Guide to Naming Aldehydes

1 Name the longest carbon chain by replacing the *e* in the alkane name with *al*.

2 Name and number the substituents by counting the carbonyl group as carbon 1.

a. Step 1 **Name the longest carbon chain by replacing the *e* in the alkane name with *al*.** The longest carbon chain containing the carbonyl group has five carbon atoms. It is named by replacing the *e* in the alkane name with *al* to give pentanal.

$CH_3-CH_2-\overset{\overset{\displaystyle CH_3}{|}}{CH}-CH_2-\overset{\overset{\displaystyle O}{\|}}{C}-H$ pentanal

Step 2 **Name and number the substituents by counting the carbonyl group as carbon 1.** The substituent, which is the $-CH_3$ group on carbon 3, is methyl. The IUPAC name for this compound is 3-methylpentanal.

$\underset{5}{CH_3}-\underset{4}{CH_2}-\underset{3}{\overset{\overset{\displaystyle CH_3}{|}}{CH}}-\underset{2}{CH_2}-\underset{1}{\overset{\overset{\displaystyle O}{\|}}{C}}-H$ 3-methylpentanal

Analyze the Problem

Family	IUPAC Naming	Name
Aldehyde	Benzaldehyde is the IUPAC name for the aldehyde of benzene.	Benzaldehyde

b. Step 1 **Name the longest carbon chain by replacing the *e* in the alkane name with *al*.** The longest carbon chain consists of a benzene ring attached to a carbonyl group, which is named benzaldehyde.

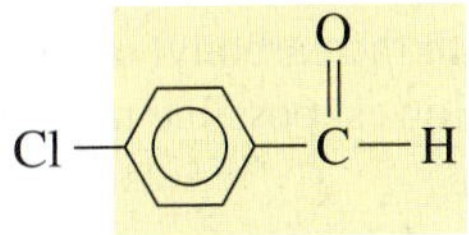

benzaldehyde

Step 2 **Name and number the substituents by counting the carbonyl group as carbon 1.** Counting from carbon 1 of the ring where the carbonyl group is attached, the chloro group is attached to carbon 4.

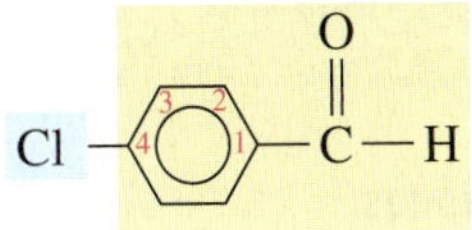

4-chlorobenzaldehyde

STUDY CHECK 14.1

What is the IUPAC name of the following compound?

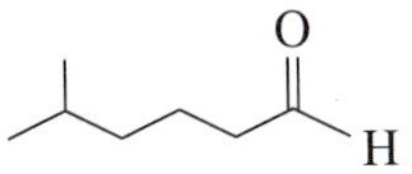

Chemistry Link to the Environment

VANILLA

Vanilla has been used as a flavoring for over a thousand years. After drinking a beverage made from powdered vanilla and cocoa beans with Emperor Montezuma in Mexico, the Spanish conquistador Hernán Cortés took vanilla back to Europe, where it became popular for flavoring and for scenting perfumes and tobacco. Thomas Jefferson introduced vanilla to the United States during the late 1700s. Today, much of the vanilla we use in the world is grown in Mexico, Madagascar, Réunion, Seychelles, Tahiti, Sri Lanka, Java, the Philippines, and Africa.

The vanilla plant is a member of the orchid family and thrives under tropical conditions. There are many species of *Vanilla*, but *Vanilla planifolia* (or *V. fragrans*) is considered to produce the best flavor. The vanilla plant is a vine that can grow to 100 feet in length. Its flowers are hand-pollinated to produce a green fruit that is picked in 8 or 9 months. The fruit is sun-dried so that it becomes a long, dark brown pod, which is called a "vanilla bean" because it looks like a string bean. The flavor and fragrance of the vanilla bean comes from the tiny black seeds found inside the dried bean.

The seeds and pod are used to flavor desserts such as custards and ice cream. The extract of vanilla is made by chopping up vanilla beans and mixing them with a 35% ethanol–water mixture. The liquid, which contains the aldehyde *vanillin*, is drained from the bean residue and used for flavoring.

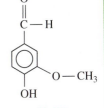

Vanillin
(vanilla)

The vanilla bean is the dried fruit of the vanilla plant.

Vanilla flavoring is prepared by soaking vanilla beans in ethanol and water.

Naming Ketones

Aldehydes and ketones are some of the most important classes of organic compounds and have played a major role in organic chemistry for more than a century. In the IUPAC system, the name of a ketone is obtained by replacing the *e* in the corresponding alkane name with *one*. However, the common names for unbranched ketones are still in use. Then the alkyl groups bonded on either side of the carbonyl group are listed alphabetically followed by *ketone*. The name of acetone, which is another name for propanone, has also been retained by the IUPAC system.

For cyclic ketones, the prefix *cyclo* is used in front of the ketone name. Any substituents are located by numbering the ring starting with the carbonyl carbon as carbon 1. The ring is numbered so that the substituents have the lowest possible number.

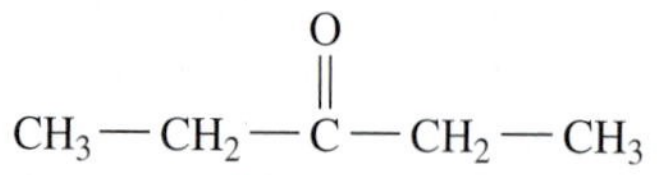

$$CH_3-CH_2-\overset{\overset{\displaystyle O}{\|}}{C}-CH_2-CH_3$$

3-Pentanone
(diethyl ketone)

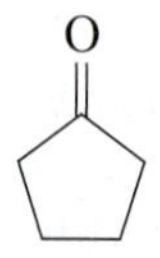

Cyclopentanone

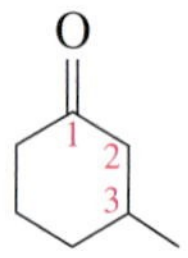

3-Methylcyclohexanone

SAMPLE PROBLEM 14.2 **Names of Ketones**

Give the IUPAC name for the following ketone:

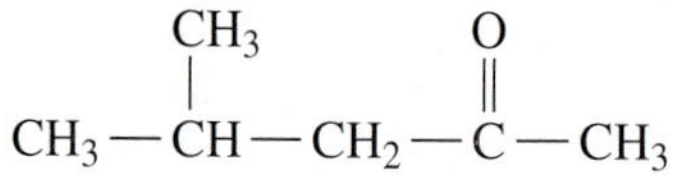

$$CH_3-\overset{\overset{\displaystyle CH_3}{|}}{CH}-CH_2-\overset{\overset{\displaystyle O}{\|}}{C}-CH_3$$

SOLUTION

Analyze the Problem

Family	IUPAC Naming	Name
Ketone	Change *e* to *one* and count from the end of the carbon chain nearer the carbonyl group to number the substituent.	Alkanone

Guide to Naming Ketones

1 Name the longest carbon chain by replacing the *e* in the alkane name with *one*.

2 Number the carbon chain from the end nearer the carbonyl group, and indicate its location.

3 Name and number any substituents on the carbon chain.

Step 1 **Name the longest carbon chain by replacing the *e* in the alkane name with *one*.**

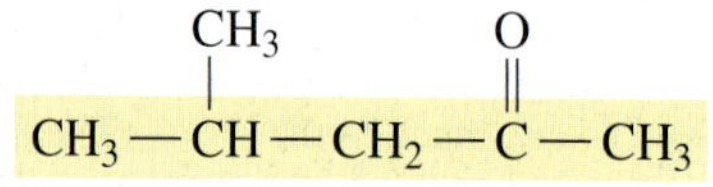

$$CH_3-\overset{\overset{\displaystyle CH_3}{|}}{CH}-CH_2-\overset{\overset{\displaystyle O}{\|}}{C}-CH_3 \qquad \text{pentanone}$$

Step 2 **Number the carbon chain from the end nearer the carbonyl group, and indicate its location.**

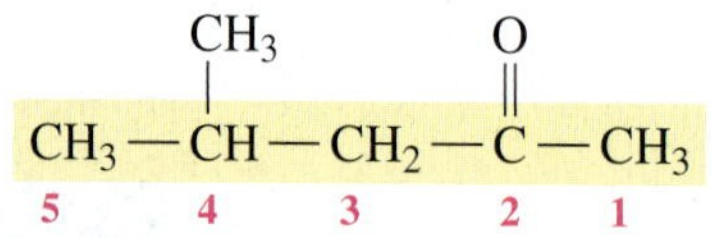

$$\underset{5}{CH_3}-\underset{4}{\overset{\overset{\displaystyle CH_3}{|}}{CH}}-\underset{3}{CH_2}-\underset{2}{\overset{\overset{\displaystyle O}{\|}}{C}}-\underset{1}{CH_3} \qquad \text{2-pentanone}$$

Step 3 **Name and number any substituents on the carbon chain.** Counting from the end nearer the carbonyl group places the methyl group on carbon 4.

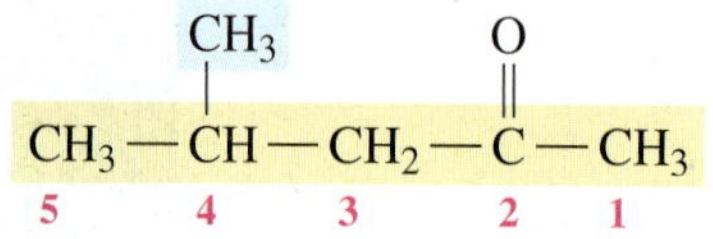

$$\underset{5}{CH_3}-\underset{4}{\overset{\overset{\displaystyle CH_3}{|}}{CH}}-\underset{3}{CH_2}-\underset{2}{\overset{\overset{\displaystyle O}{\|}}{C}}-\underset{1}{CH_3} \qquad \text{4-methyl-2-pentanone}$$

STUDY CHECK 14.2

What is the common name of 3-hexanone?

Chemistry Link to Health

SOME IMPORTANT ALDEHYDES AND KETONES

Formaldehyde, the simplest aldehyde, is a colorless gas with a pungent odor. Industrially, it is used as a reactant in the synthesis of fabrics, insulation materials, carpeting, pressed wood products such as plywood, and plastics for kitchen counters. An aqueous solution called formalin, which contains 40% formaldehyde, is used as a germicide and to preserve biological specimens. Exposure to formaldehyde fumes can irritate the eyes, nose, and upper respiratory tract and cause skin rashes, headaches, dizziness, and general fatigue. Formaldehyde is classified as a carcinogen.

Acetone, or propanone (dimethyl ketone), which is the simplest ketone, is a colorless liquid with a mild odor that is widely used as a solvent in cleaning fluids, paint and nail polish removers, and rubber cement. It is extremely flammable, and care must be taken when using acetone. Normal metabolic processes in humans and animals produce small amounts of acetone. Larger amounts of acetone may be produced in uncontrolled diabetes, during fasting and high-protein diets when large amounts of fats are metabolized for energy, and after consumption of large amounts of alcohol.

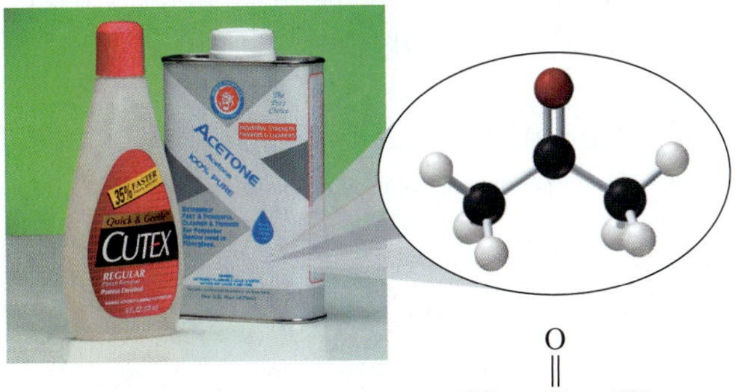

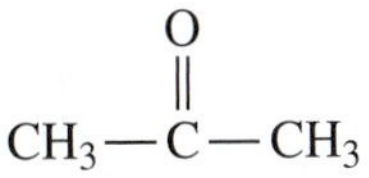

Muscone is used to make musk perfumes, and oil of spearmint contains carvone.

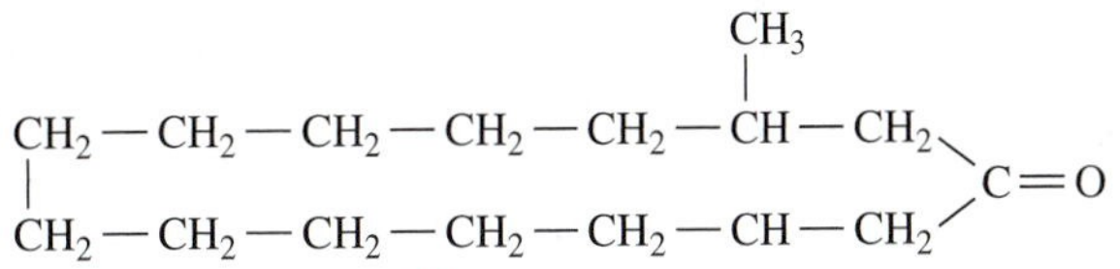

Muscone (musk)

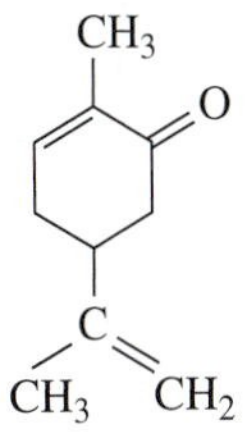

Carvone (spearmint oil)

Glucose, also known as blood sugar, is an important monosaccharide, which we obtain from fruits, vegetables, and honey. It consists of a six-carbon backbone with five hydroxyl groups (—OH) and an aldehyde group. Glucose is produced in plants during photosynthesis. In animals, starches from rice, wheat, and other grains are broken down during digestion to yield glucose, which is used by the body for energy.

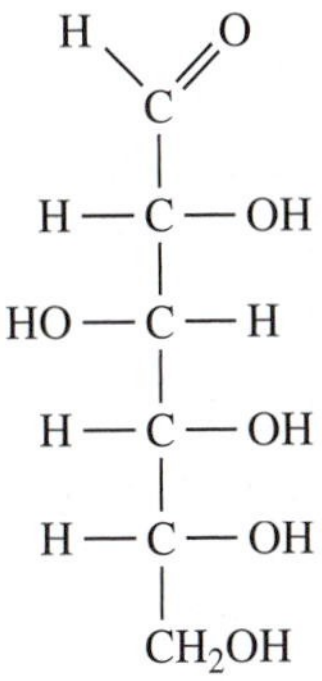

Foods containing starches are a source of glucose.

Propanone

Acetone (propanone) is used as a solvent in paint and nail polish.

Several naturally occurring aromatic aldehydes are used as food flavors and as fragrances in perfumes. Benzaldehyde is found in almonds, vanillin comes from vanilla beans, and cinnamaldehyde is found in cinnamon.

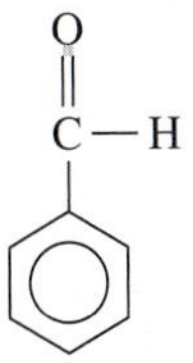

Benzaldehyde (almond)

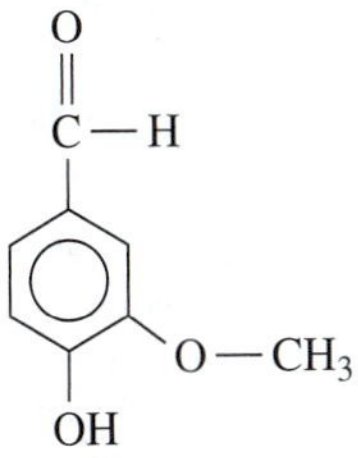

Vanillin (vanilla)

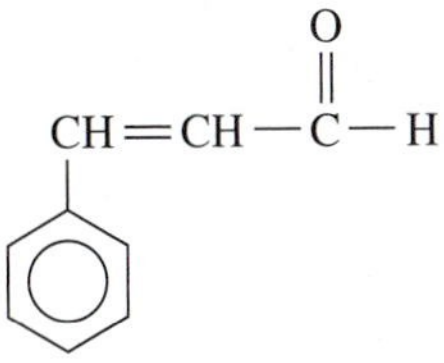

Cinnamaldehyde (cinnamon)

QUESTIONS AND PROBLEMS

14.1 Aldehydes and Ketones

LEARNING GOAL: *Identify compounds with a carbonyl group as aldehydes and ketones. Give the IUPAC and common names for aldehydes and ketones; draw their condensed structural formulas or skeletal formulas, if cyclic.*

14.1 Identify each of the following compounds as an aldehyde or a ketone:

a. $CH_3-CH_2-\overset{\overset{\text{O}}{\|}}{C}-CH_3$ b. (skeletal structure with aldehyde)

c. (cyclopentanone with methyl)   d. $\overset{\overset{\text{O}}{\|}}{C}-H$ (cyclohexyl)

14.2 Identify each of the following compounds as an aldehyde or a ketone:

a. (skeletal with CHO)   b. $CH_3-\overset{CH_3}{\underset{|}{CH}}-\overset{\overset{\text{O}}{\|}}{C}-H$

c. (skeletal ketone)   d. (cyclohexyl)$-\overset{\overset{\text{O}}{\|}}{C}-CH_2-CH_3$

14.3 Indicate if each of the following pairs represents structural isomers or not:

a. $CH_3-\overset{\overset{\text{O}}{\|}}{C}-CH_3$ and $CH_3-CH_2-\overset{\overset{\text{O}}{\|}}{C}-H$

b. (skeletal) and (skeletal)

c. $CH_3-\overset{\overset{\text{O}}{\|}}{C}-CH_2-CH_3$ and

$CH_3-\overset{\overset{\text{O}}{\|}}{C}-CH_2-CH_2-CH_3$

14.4 Indicate if each of the following pairs represents structural isomers or not:

a. $CH_3-CH_2-CH_2-\overset{\overset{\text{O}}{\|}}{C}-H$ and $\overset{\overset{\text{O}}{\|}}{C}-H$ (cyclobutyl)

b. (skeletal) and (skeletal)

c. (cyclohexenone) and (cyclohexenol OH)

14.5 Give the IUPAC name for each of the following compounds:

a. $CH_3-\overset{Br}{\underset{|}{CH}}-CH_2-\overset{\overset{\text{O}}{\|}}{C}-H$ b. (skeletal ketone)

c. (cyclopentanone with methyl)   d. $\overset{\overset{\text{O}}{\|}}{C}-H$ (benzaldehyde with Br)

14.6 Give the IUPAC name for each of the following compounds:

a. $CH_3-CH_2-CH_2-\overset{\overset{\text{O}}{\|}}{C}-H$ b. (branched ketone)

c. (cyclopentanone with 2 Cl)   d. (benzaldehyde with 2 Cl)

14.7 Give a common name for each of the following compounds:

a. $CH_3-\overset{\overset{\text{O}}{\|}}{C}-H$

b. $CH_3-\overset{\overset{\text{O}}{\|}}{C}-CH_2-CH_2-CH_3$

c. $H-\overset{\overset{\text{O}}{\|}}{C}-H$

14.8 Give the common name for each of the following compounds:

a. $CH_3-\overset{\overset{\text{O}}{\|}}{C}-CH_2-CH_3$

b. $CH_3-CH_2-\overset{\overset{\text{O}}{\|}}{C}-CH_2-CH_3$

c. $CH_3-CH_2-\overset{\overset{\text{O}}{\|}}{C}-H$

14.9 Draw the condensed structural formula for each of the following compounds:
   a. ethanal   b. 2-methyl-3-pentanone
   c. butyl methyl ketone   d. 3-methylhexanal

14.10 Draw the condensed structural formula for each of the following compounds:
   a. butyraldehyde   b. 3,4-dichloropentanal
   c. 4-bromobutanone   d. acetone

14.11 Anisaldehyde, from Korean mint or blue licorice, is a medicinal herb used in Chinese medicine. The IUPAC name of anisaldehyde is 4-methoxybenzaldehyde. Draw the skeletal formula for anisaldehyde.

14.12 The IUPAC name of ethyl vanillin, a synthetic compound used as a flavoring, is 3-ethoxy-4-hydroxybenzaldehyde. Draw the skeletal formula for ethyl vanillin.

14.2 Physical Properties of Aldehydes and Ketones

LEARNING GOAL

Describe the boiling points and solubility of aldehydes and ketones in water.

At room temperature, methanal (formaldehyde) and ethanal (acetaldehyde) are gases. Aldehydes and ketones containing 3 to 10 carbon atoms are liquids. The polar carbonyl group with a partially negative oxygen atom and a partially positive carbon atom has an influence on the boiling points and the solubility of aldehydes and ketones in water.

Boiling Points of Aldehydes and Ketones

TUTORIAL
Properties of Aldehydes and Ketones

The polar carbonyl group in aldehydes and ketones provides dipole–dipole attractions, which alkanes do not have. Thus, aldehydes and ketones have higher boiling points than alkanes. However, aldehydes and ketones cannot form hydrogen bonds with each other as do alcohols. Thus, alcohols have higher boiling points than aldehydes and ketones of similar molar mass.

Dipole–dipole attractions

$\overset{\backslash}{/}C^{\delta+}=O^{\delta-}\cdots\cdots\overset{\backslash}{/}C^{\delta+}=O^{\delta-}\cdots\cdots\overset{\backslash}{/}C^{\delta+}=O^{\delta-}$

	$CH_3-CH_2-CH_2-CH_3$	$CH_3-CH_2-\overset{O}{\overset{\|}{C}}-H$	$CH_3-\overset{O}{\overset{\|}{C}}-CH_3$	$CH_3-CH_2-CH_2-OH$
Name	Butane	Propanal	Propanone	1-Propanol
Molar Mass	58	58	58	60
Family	Alkane	Aldehyde	Ketone	Alcohol
bp	0 °C	49 °C	56 °C	97 °C

Increase in Boiling Point

For aldehydes and ketones, the boiling points increase as the number of carbon atoms in the chain increases. As the molecules become larger, there are more electrons and more temporary dipoles (dispersion forces), which give higher boiling points. Table 14.1 gives the boiling points and solubility of selected aldehydes and ketones.

TABLE 14.1 Boiling Points and Solubility of Selected Aldehydes and Ketones

Compound	Condensed Structural Formula	Number of Carbon Atoms	Boiling Point (°C)	Solubility in Water
Methanal (formaldehyde)	H—CHO	1	−21	Soluble
Ethanal (acetaldehyde)	CH_3—CHO	2	21	Soluble
Propanal (propionaldehyde)	CH_3—CH_2—CHO	3	49	Soluble
Propanone (acetone)	CH_3—CO—CH_3	3	56	Soluble
Butanal (butyraldehyde)	CH_3—CH_2—CH_2—CHO	4	75	Soluble
Butanone	CH_3—CO—CH_2—CH_3	4	80	Soluble
Pentanal	CH_3—CH_2—CH_2—CH_2—CHO	5	103	Slightly soluble
2-Pentanone	CH_3—CO—CH_2—CH_2—CH_3	5	102	Slightly soluble
Hexanal	CH_3—CH_2—CH_2—CH_2—CH_2—CHO	6	129	Not soluble
2-Hexanone	CH_3—CO—CH_2—CH_2—CH_2—CH_3	6	127	Not soluble

Solubility of Aldehydes and Ketones in Water

Although aldehydes and ketones do not hydrogen bond with each other, the electronegative oxygen atom does hydrogen bond with water molecules (see

Hydrogen bonds

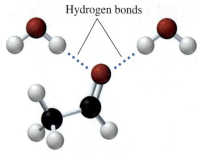

Acetaldehyde in water

Hydrogen bonds

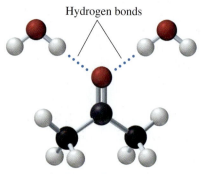

Acetone in water

FIGURE 14.3 Hydrogen bonding of acetaldehyde and acetone with water.

Q Would you expect propanal to be soluble in water?

Figure 14.3). Aldehydes and ketones with one to four carbons are very soluble in water. However, those with five or more carbon atoms are not very soluble, because the longer, nonpolar hydrocarbon chains diminish the solubility effect of the polar carbonyl group.

CONCEPT CHECK 14.2 **Boiling Point**

Would you expect ethanol (CH_3—CH_2—OH) to have a higher or lower boiling point than ethanal (CH_3—CHO)? Explain.

ANSWER

Ethanol would have a higher boiling point because its molecules can hydrogen bond with each other, whereas molecules of ethanal cannot.

SAMPLE PROBLEM 14.3 **Boiling Point and Solubility**

Arrange pentane, 2-butanol, and butanone, which have similar molar masses, in order of increasing boiling points. Explain.

SOLUTION

The only attractions between molecules of alkanes such as pentane are weak dispersion forces. With no dipole–dipole attractions or hydrogen bonds, pentane has the lowest boiling point of the three compounds. With a polar carbonyl group, butanone molecules form dipole–dipole attractions, but no hydrogen bonds. Butanone has a higher boiling point than pentane. Because molecules of 2-butanol can form hydrogen bonds with other butanol molecules, it has the highest boiling point of the three compounds. The actual boiling points are pentane (36 °C), butanone (80 °C), and 2-butanol (100 °C).

STUDY CHECK 14.3

If acetone molecules cannot hydrogen bond with each other, why is acetone soluble in water?

QUESTIONS AND PROBLEMS

14.2 Physical Properties of Aldehydes and Ketones

LEARNING GOAL: *Describe the boiling points and solubility of aldehydes and ketones in water.*

14.13 Which compound in each of the following pairs would have the higher boiling point? Explain.

a. CH_3—CH_2—CH_3 or CH_3—$\overset{\overset{\displaystyle O}{\|}}{C}$—H

b. propanal or pentanal

c. butanal or 1-butanol

14.14 Which compound in each of the following pairs would have the higher boiling point? Explain.

a. [structure with OH] or [structure with O]

b. pentane or butanone

c. propanone or pentanone

14.15 Which compound in each of the following pairs would be more soluble in water? Explain.

a. CH_3—$\overset{\overset{\displaystyle O}{\|}}{C}$—$CH_2$—$CH_2$—$CH_3$ or

CH_3—$\overset{\overset{\displaystyle O}{\|}}{C}$—$\overset{\overset{\displaystyle O}{\|}}{C}$—$CH_2$—$CH_3$

b. propanal or pentanal   **c.** acetone or 2-pentanone

14.16 Which compound in each of the following pairs would be more soluble in water? Explain.

a. CH_3—CH_2—CH_3 or CH_3—CH_2—CHO

b. propanone or 3-hexanone   **c.** propane or propanone

14.17 Would you expect an aldehyde with a formula of $C_8H_{16}O$ to be soluble in water? Explain.

14.18 Would you expect an aldehyde with a formula of C_3H_6O to be soluble in water? Explain.

14.3 Oxidation and Reduction of Aldehydes and Ketones

In Section 13.4, we described how aldehydes produced by the oxidation of primary alcohols oxidize readily to carboxylic acids. In fact, aldehydes oxidize readily to form carboxylic acids when they are exposed to the air. In contrast, ketones produced by the oxidation of secondary alcohols do not undergo further oxidation. Let's review examples of the oxidation reactions of primary and secondary alcohols that form aldehydes and ketones.

TUTORIAL
Oxidation–Reduction Reactions of Aldehydes and Ketones

$$CH_3{-}CH_2{-}OH \xrightarrow{\text{Oxidation}} CH_3{-}\overset{\displaystyle O}{\overset{\|}{C}}{-}H \xrightarrow[\text{oxidation}]{\text{Further}} CH_3{-}\overset{\displaystyle O}{\overset{\|}{C}}{-}OH$$

Ethanol (1°)   Ethanal   Ethanoic acid

$$CH_3{-}\overset{\displaystyle OH}{\overset{|}{CH}}{-}CH_3 \xrightarrow{\text{Oxidation}} CH_3{-}\overset{\displaystyle O}{\overset{\|}{C}}{-}CH_3 \xrightarrow[\text{oxidation}]{\text{Further}} \text{no reaction}$$

2-Propanol (2°)   Propanone

CONCEPT CHECK 14.3   Oxidation of Alcohols to Carboxylic Acids

Draw the condensed structural formulas for the aldehyde and carboxylic acid that form during the oxidation of 1-propanol.

ANSWER

The formulas of the oxidation products of 1-propanol show the oxidation of the functional group. When 1-propanol, a primary alcohol, is oxidized, the carbon attached to the —OH group is converted to an aldehyde (propanal), which is further oxidized to a carboxylic acid (propanoic acid).

$$CH_3{-}CH_2{-}CH_2{-}OH \xrightarrow{[O]} CH_3{-}CH_2{-}\overset{\displaystyle O}{\overset{\|}{C}}{-}H \xrightarrow{[O]} CH_3{-}CH_2{-}\overset{\displaystyle O}{\overset{\|}{C}}{-}OH$$

Alcohol (1°)   Aldehyde   Carboxylic acid

Tollens' Test

The ease of oxidation of aldehydes allows certain mild oxidizing agents to oxidize the aldehyde functional group without oxidizing other functional groups such as alcohols or ethers. In the laboratory, **Tollens' test** may be used to distinguish between aldehydes and ketones. Tollens' reagent, which is a solution of Ag^+ ($AgNO_3$) and ammonia, oxidizes aldehydes, but not ketones. The silver ion is reduced and forms a layer called a "silver mirror" on the inside of the container.

$$CH_3{-}\overset{\displaystyle O}{\overset{\|}{C}}{-}H + 2Ag^+ \xrightarrow{[O]} 2Ag(s) + CH_3{-}\overset{\displaystyle O}{\overset{\|}{C}}{-}OH$$

Ethanal   Tollens'   Silver mirror   Ethanoic acid
(acetaldehyde)   reagent   (acetic acid)

Commercially, a similar process is used to make mirrors by applying a solution of $AgNO_3$ and ammonia on glass with a spray gun (see Figure 14.4).

Another test, called **Benedict's test**, gives a positive test with compounds that have an aldehyde functional group and an adjacent hydroxyl group. When Benedict's solution containing Cu^{2+} ($CuSO_4$) ions is added to this type of aldehyde and heated, a brick-red

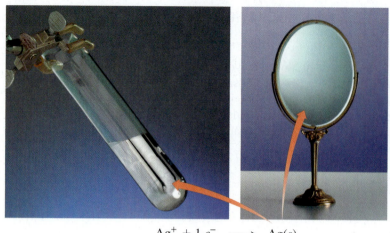

FIGURE 14.4 In Tollens' test, a "silver mirror" forms when the oxidation of an aldehyde reduces silver ions to metallic silver. The silvery surface of a mirror is formed in a similar way.

Q What is the product of the oxidation of an aldehyde?

$$Ag^+ + 1\,e^- \longrightarrow Ag(s)$$

solid of Cu_2O forms (see Figure 14.5). The test is negative with simple aldehydes and ketones.

$$
\underset{\text{2-Hydroxypropanal}}{CH_3-\overset{\overset{\displaystyle OH}{|}}{CH}-\overset{\overset{\displaystyle O}{\|}}{C}-H} + \underset{\substack{\text{Benedict's} \\ \text{reagent}}}{2Cu^{2+}} \longrightarrow \underset{\text{Brick-red solid}}{Cu_2O(s)} + \underset{\text{2-Hydroxypropanoic acid}}{CH_3-\overset{\overset{\displaystyle OH}{|}}{CH}-\overset{\overset{\displaystyle O}{\|}}{C}-OH}
$$

Because many sugars such as glucose contain this type of aldehyde grouping, Benedict's reagent can be used to determine the presence of glucose in blood or urine.

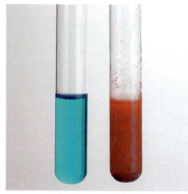

Cu^{2+} $\quad Cu_2O(s)$

FIGURE 14.5 The blue Cu^{2+} in Benedict's solution forms a brick-red solid of Cu_2O in a positive test for many sugars and aldehydes with adjacent hydroxyl groups.

Q Which test tube indicates that glucose is present?

D-Glucose + 2Cu²⁺ (Benedict's, blue) ⟶ D-Gluconic acid + Cu₂O(s) (brick red)

CONCEPT CHECK 14.4 **Oxidation**

Draw the condensed structural formula for the product, if any, when each of the following undergoes oxidation:

a. $CH_3-\overset{\overset{\displaystyle O}{\|}}{C}-CH_2-CH_3$

b. $CH_3-\overset{\overset{\displaystyle CH_3}{|}}{CH}-\overset{\overset{\displaystyle O}{\|}}{C}-H$

ANSWER

a. A ketone does not undergo further oxidation.

b. An aldehyde oxidizes to its corresponding carboxylic acid.

$$CH_3-\overset{\overset{\displaystyle CH_3}{|}}{CH}-\overset{\overset{\displaystyle O}{\|}}{C}-OH$$

SAMPLE PROBLEM 14.4 **Tollens' Test**

Draw the condensed structural formula for the product of oxidation, if any, when Tollens' reagent is added to each of the following compounds:

a. propanal **b.** propanone **c.** 2-methylbutanal

SOLUTION

Tollens' reagent will oxidize aldehydes but not ketones.

a. 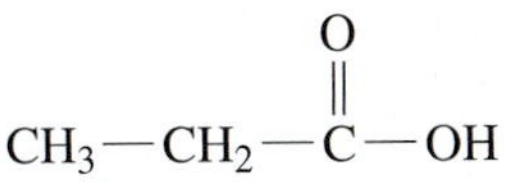 $CH_3-CH_2-\overset{\overset{\displaystyle O}{\|}}{C}-OH$ **b.** no reaction **c.** 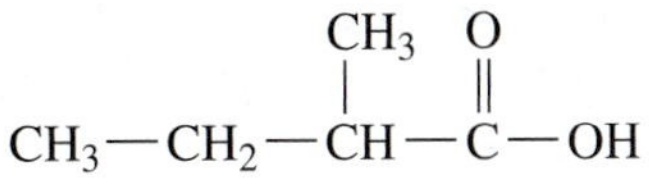 $CH_3-CH_2-\overset{\overset{\displaystyle CH_3}{|}}{CH}-\overset{\overset{\displaystyle O}{\|}}{C}-OH$

STUDY CHECK 14.4

Why does a silver mirror form when Tollens' reagent is added to a test tube containing benzaldehyde?

Reduction of Aldehydes and Ketones

Aldehydes and ketones are reduced by hydrogen (H_2) or sodium borohydride ($NaBH_4$). In the **reduction** of organic compounds, there is a decrease in the number of carbon–oxygen bonds. Aldehydes are reduced to primary alcohols, and ketones are reduced to secondary alcohols. A catalyst such as nickel, platinum, or palladium is needed for the addition of hydrogen.

Aldehydes Reduce to Primary Alcohols

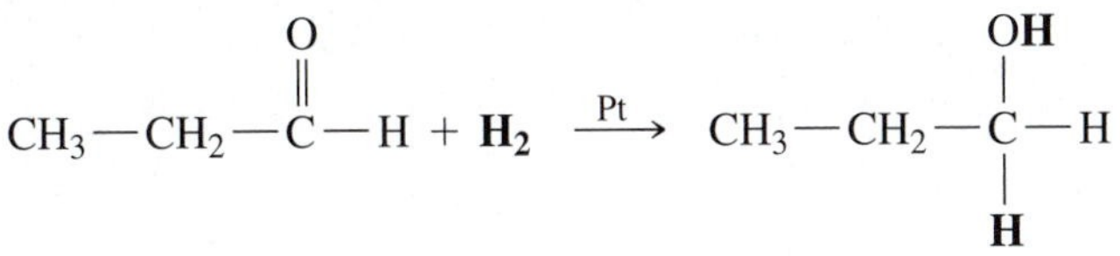

$$CH_3-CH_2-\overset{\overset{\displaystyle O}{\|}}{C}-H + H_2 \xrightarrow{Pt} CH_3-CH_2-\overset{\overset{\displaystyle OH}{|}}{\underset{\underset{\displaystyle H}{|}}{C}}-H$$

Propanal 1-Propanol (1° alcohol)
(propionaldehyde) (propyl alcohol)

Ketones Reduce to Secondary Alcohols

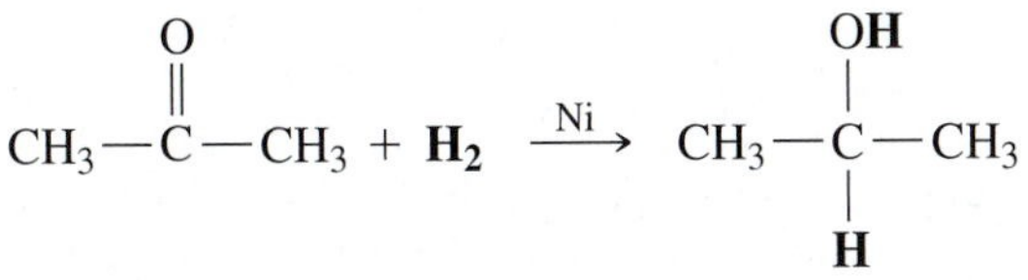

$$CH_3-\overset{\overset{\displaystyle O}{\|}}{C}-CH_3 + H_2 \xrightarrow{Ni} CH_3-\overset{\overset{\displaystyle OH}{|}}{\underset{\underset{\displaystyle H}{|}}{C}}-CH_3$$

Propanone 2-Propanol (2° alcohol)
(dimethyl ketone) (isopropyl alcohol)

SAMPLE PROBLEM 14.5 **Reduction of Carbonyl Groups**

Write the equation for the reduction of cyclopentanone using hydrogen in the presence of a nickel catalyst.

SOLUTION

The reacting molecule is a cyclic ketone that has five carbon atoms. During the reduction, hydrogen atoms add to the carbon and oxygen in the carbonyl group, which reduces the ketone to the corresponding secondary alcohol.

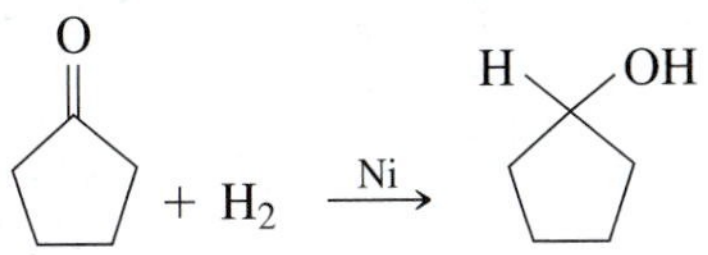

Cyclopentanone Cyclopentanol

STUDY CHECK 14.5

What is the name of the product obtained from the hydrogenation of 2-methylbutanal?

QUESTIONS AND PROBLEMS

14.3 Oxidation and Reduction of Aldehydes and Ketones

LEARNING GOAL: *Draw the condensed structural or skeletal formulas for the reactants and products in the oxidation or reduction of aldehydes and ketones.*

14.19 Draw the condensed structural formula, or skeletal formula, if cyclic, for the product of oxidation (if any) for each of the following compounds:
   a. methanal
   b. butanone
   c. benzaldehyde
   d. 3-methylcyclohexanone

14.20 Draw the condensed structural formula, or skeletal formula, if cyclic, for the product of oxidation (if any) for each of the following compounds:
   a. acetaldehyde
   b. 3-methylbutanone
   c. cyclohexanone
   d. 3-methylbutanal

14.21 Which of the following compounds would react with Tollens' reagent, Benedict's reagent, both, or neither?

   a. $CH_3-CH_2-CH_2-\overset{\displaystyle O}{\overset{\displaystyle \|}{C}}-H$

   b. $CH_3-\overset{\displaystyle O}{\overset{\displaystyle \|}{C}}-CH_3$

   c. $CH_3-\overset{\displaystyle OH}{\overset{\displaystyle |}{CH}}-\overset{\displaystyle O}{\overset{\displaystyle \|}{C}}-H$

14.22 Which of the following compounds would react with Tollens' reagent, Benedict's reagent, both, or neither?

   a. $CH_3-\overset{\displaystyle O}{\overset{\displaystyle \|}{C}}-\overset{\displaystyle CH_3}{\overset{\displaystyle |}{CH}}-CH_3$

   b. $CH_3-CH_2-\overset{\displaystyle OH}{\overset{\displaystyle |}{CH}}-\overset{\displaystyle O}{\overset{\displaystyle \|}{C}}-H$

   c. $CH_3-\overset{\displaystyle O}{\overset{\displaystyle \|}{C}}-H$

14.23 Draw the condensed structural formula for the product formed when each of the following is reduced by hydrogen in the presence of a nickel catalyst:
   a. butyraldehyde
   b. acetone
   c. 3-bromohexanal
   d. 2-methyl-3-pentanone

14.24 Draw the condensed structural formula for the product formed when each of the following is reduced by hydrogen in the presence of a nickel catalyst:
   a. ethyl propyl ketone
   b. formaldehyde
   c. 3-chloropentanal
   d. 2-pentanone

LEARNING GOAL

Draw the condensed structural formulas for the products of the addition of alcohols to aldehydes and ketones.

TUTORIAL
Addition of Polar Molecules to a Carbonyl Group

14.4 Hemiacetals and Acetals

We have seen that the carbonyl group $(C=O)$ is polar, which makes aldehydes and ketones very reactive. One of the most common reactions of aldehydes and ketones is the addition of one or two molecules of an alcohol to the carbonyl group.

Hemiacetal and Acetal Formation

When one alcohol adds to an aldehyde or ketone in the presence of an acid catalyst, the product is a **hemiacetal**, which contains two functional groups on the same C atom: a hydroxyl group $(-OH)$ and an alkoxy group $(-OR)$. However, hemiacetals are generally unstable and react with a second molecule of the alcohol to form a stable *acetal* and water. The **acetal** has two alkoxy groups $(-OR)$ attached to the same carbon atom. Commercially, compounds that are acetals are used to produce vitamins, dyes, pharmaceuticals, and perfumes.

$$\overset{O^{\delta-}}{\underset{}{\underset{\displaystyle C^{\delta+}}{\|}}} + ROH \underset{}{\overset{H^+}{\rightleftharpoons}} \overset{O-H}{\underset{}{\underset{\displaystyle C}{|}}}-OR + ROH \underset{}{\overset{H^+}{\rightleftharpoons}} \overset{OR}{\underset{}{\underset{\displaystyle C}{|}}}-OR + H-O-H$$

In general, aldehydes are more reactive than ketones because the carbonyl carbon is more positive in aldehydes. Also, the presence of two alkyl groups in ketones makes it more difficult for a molecule to form bonds with the carbon in the carbonyl group.

Examples of the formation of a hemiacetal and acetal from an aldehyde and a ketone follow:

Hemiacetal and Acetal Formation from an Aldehyde

$$CH_3-\overset{\overset{\displaystyle O}{\|}}{C}-H + HO-CH_3 \underset{}{\overset{H^+}{\rightleftharpoons}} CH_3-\overset{\overset{\displaystyle O-CH_3}{|}}{\underset{\underset{\displaystyle OH}{|}}{C}}-H + HO-CH_3 \underset{}{\overset{H^+}{\rightleftharpoons}} CH_3-\overset{\overset{\displaystyle O-CH_3}{|}}{\underset{\underset{\displaystyle O-CH_3}{|}}{C}}-H + H_2O$$

Ethanal   Methanol   Hemiacetal   Acetal

Hemiacetal and Acetal Formation from a Ketone

$$CH_3-\overset{\overset{\displaystyle O}{\|}}{C}-CH_3 + HO-CH_2-CH_3 \underset{}{\overset{H^+}{\rightleftharpoons}} CH_3-\overset{\overset{\displaystyle O-CH_2-CH_3}{|}}{\underset{\underset{\displaystyle OH}{|}}{C}}-CH_3 + HO-CH_2-CH_3 \underset{}{\overset{H^+}{\rightleftharpoons}} CH_3-\overset{\overset{\displaystyle O-CH_2-CH_3}{|}}{\underset{\underset{\displaystyle O-CH_2-CH_3}{|}}{C}}-CH_3 + H_2O$$

Propanone   Ethanol   Hemiacetal   Acetal

The reactions in the formation of hemiacetals and acetals are reversible. As predicted by Le Châtelier's principle, the forward reaction is favored by removing water from the reaction mixture. The reverse reaction, which is the hydrolysis of an acetal, is favored by adding water to drive the equilibrium in the direction of the ketone or aldehyde.

CONCEPT CHECK 14.5   **Hemiacetals and Acetals**

From the following descriptions, identify the compound as a hemiacetal or an acetal:

a. a molecule that contains a carbon atom attached to a hydroxyl group and an ethoxy group
b. a molecule that contains a carbon atom attached to two ethoxy groups
c. the intermediate that forms when one molecule of an alcohol adds to a ketone
d. the product that forms when two molecules of an alcohol add to an aldehyde

ANSWER

a. A hemiacetal contains a carbon atom attached to a hydroxyl group and an ethoxy group.
b. An acetal contains a carbon atom attached to two ethoxy groups.
c. A hemiacetal involves the addition of one molecule of an alcohol to a ketone.
d. An acetal involves the addition of two molecules of an alcohol to an aldehyde.

SAMPLE PROBLEM 14.6   **Hemiacetals and Acetals**

Draw the condensed structural formulas for the hemiacetal and acetal formed when methanol adds to propanal.

SOLUTION

To form the hemiacetal, the hydrogen from the methanol adds to the oxygen of the carbonyl group to form a new hydroxyl group. The remaining part of the methanol adds to the carbon atom in the carbonyl group. The acetal forms when a second molecule of methanol adds to the carbonyl carbon atom.

$$CH_3-CH_2-\overset{\overset{\displaystyle O}{\|}}{C}-H + CH_3-OH \underset{}{\overset{H^+}{\rightleftharpoons}} CH_3-CH_2-\overset{\overset{\displaystyle OH}{|}}{\underset{\underset{\displaystyle O-CH_3}{|}}{C}}-H + CH_3-OH \underset{}{\overset{H^+}{\rightleftharpoons}} CH_3-CH_2-\overset{\overset{\displaystyle O-CH_3}{|}}{\underset{\underset{\displaystyle O-CH_3}{|}}{C}}-H + H_2O$$

Propanal   Methanol   Hemiacetal   Methanol   Acetal

STUDY CHECK 14.6

Draw the condensed structural formula for the acetal formed when methanol adds to butanone.

Cyclic Hemiacetals

One very important type of hemiacetal that can be isolated is a *cyclic hemiacetal* that forms when the carbonyl group and the —OH group are in the *same* molecule.

Open chain   Cyclic hemiacetal

The five- and six-atom cyclic hemiacetals and acetals are more stable than their open-chain structures. The importance of understanding acetals is shown for glucose, a carbohydrate, which has both carbonyl and hydroxyl groups that can form acetal bonds. Glucose forms a cyclic hemiacetal when the hydroxyl group on carbon 5 bonds with the carbonyl group on carbon 1. The hemiacetal of glucose is so stable that almost all the glucose (99%) exists as the cyclic hemiacetal in aqueous solution. We will discuss carbohydrates and their structures in Chapter 15.

Glucose   Formation of cyclic hemiacetal   Hemiacetal of glucose

An alcohol can add to the cyclic hemiacetal to form a cyclic acetal. This reaction is also very important in carbohydrate chemistry. It is the linkage that bonds glucose molecules to other glucose molecules in the formation of disaccharides and polysaccharides.

Cyclic hemiacetal $+ CH_3—OH$ Cyclic acetal

Maltose is a disaccharide consisting of two glucose molecules, and is produced from the hydrolysis of starch from grains. In maltose, an acetal bond (shown in red) links two glucose molecules. One glucose retains the cyclic hemiacetal bond (shown in green).

Maltose, a disaccharide, is produced from the hydrolysis of the starches in grains, such as barley.

α-Maltose

QUESTIONS AND PROBLEMS

14.4 Hemiacetals and Acetals

LEARNING GOAL: *Draw the condensed structural formulas for the products of the addition of alcohols to aldehydes and ketones.*

14.25 Indicate whether each of the following is a hemiacetal, acetal, or neither:

a. $CH_3-CH_2-O-CH_2-OH$

b. $CH_3-CH_2-CH_2-\overset{\overset{\displaystyle O-CH_3}{|}}{\underset{\underset{\displaystyle OH}{|}}{C}}-H$

c. $CH_3-\overset{\overset{\displaystyle O-CH_2-CH_3}{|}}{\underset{\underset{\displaystyle O-CH_2-CH_3}{|}}{C}}-CH_2-CH_3$

d. (cyclohexane ring with) $\overset{OH}{\underset{O-CH_2-CH_3}{}}$

e. (cyclopentane ring with) $CH_3-O \quad O-CH_3$

14.26 Indicate whether each of the following is a hemiacetal, acetal, or neither:

a. $CH_3-CH_2-O-CH_2-CH_3$

b. $HO-CH_2-CH_2-O-CH_2-CH_2-O-CH_3$

c. $CH_3-\overset{\overset{\displaystyle O-CH_2-CH_3}{|}}{\underset{\underset{\displaystyle OH}{|}}{C}}-CH_3$

d. (cyclohexane ring with) $\overset{O-CH_3}{\underset{O-CH_3}{}}$

e. (cyclopentane ring with) $\overset{O-CH_3}{\underset{O-CH_3}{}}$

14.27 Draw the condensed structural formula for the hemiacetal formed by adding one methanol molecule to each of the following:

a. ethanal   **b.** propanone   **c.** butanal

14.28 Draw the condensed structural formula for the hemiacetal formed by adding one ethanol molecule to each of the following:

a. propanal   **b.** butanone   **c.** methanal

14.29 Draw the condensed structural formula for the acetal formed by adding a second methanol molecule to the compounds in Problem 14.27.

14.30 Draw the condensed structural formula for the acetal formed by adding a second ethanol molecule to the compounds in Problem 14.28.

14.5 Chiral Molecules

LEARNING GOAL

Identify chiral and achiral carbon atoms in an organic molecule.

In the preceding chapters, we identified structural isomers as molecules that have the same molecular formula, but different bonding arrangements of atoms.

Structural Isomers

C_2H_6O CH_3-CH_2-OH CH_3-O-CH_3
            Ethanol   Dimethyl ether

C_3H_6O $CH_3-CH_2-\overset{\overset{\displaystyle O}{\|}}{C}-H$ $CH_3-\overset{\overset{\displaystyle O}{\|}}{C}-CH_3$
            Propanal   Propanone

Another group of isomers called *stereoisomers* have identical molecular formulas, too, but they are not structural isomers. In **stereoisomers**, the atoms are bonded in the same sequence, but differ in the way they are arranged in space.

Chirality

Everything has a mirror image. If you hold your right hand up to a mirror, you see its mirror image, which matches your left hand (see Figure 14.6). If you turn your palms toward each other, one hand is the mirror image of the other. If you look at your hands with your palms facing up, your thumbs are on opposite sides. If you then place your right hand over your left hand, you cannot match up all the parts of the hands: palms, backs, thumbs, and little fingers. The thumbs and little fingers can be matched, but the palms and backs of your hands are still facing each other. Your hands are mirror images that cannot be superimposed on each other. Similarly, when the mirror images of organic molecules cannot be completely matched, they are *nonsuperimposable*.

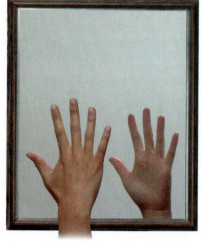

Left hand

Right hand

Mirror image of right hand

FIGURE 14.6 The left and right hands are mirror images that cannot be superimposed on each other.

Q Can your left and right shoes be superimposed on each other?

Objects such as hands that have nonsuperimposable mirror images are **chiral** (pronounced *'kai-rel*). Left and right shoes are chiral; left- and right-handed golf clubs are chiral. When we think of how difficult it is to put a left-hand glove on our right hand, put a right shoe on our left foot, or use left-handed scissors if we are right handed, we begin to realize that certain properties of mirror images are very different.

When the mirror image of an object is identical and can be superimposed on the original, it is **achiral**. For example, the mirror image of a plain drinking glass is identical to the glass, which means the mirror image can be superimposed on the glass (see Figure 14.7).

Chiral

Achiral

Achiral

Chiral

FIGURE 14.7 Everyday objects such as gloves and shoes are chiral, but an unmarked bat and a plain glass are achiral.

Q Why are some of the above objects chiral and others achiral?

Everyday Chiral Objects

Classify each of the following objects as chiral or achiral:

a. left ear
b. flip-flop beach sandal
c. plain golf ball

ANSWER

a. A left ear is chiral because it cannot be superimposed on the right ear.
b. The mirror image of a left flip-flop is the right flip-flop. They are chiral because they are not superimposable.
c. A golf ball is achiral because the mirror images are superimposable.

Chiral Carbon Atoms

An organic compound is chiral if it has at least one carbon atom bonded to *four different atoms or groups*. This type of carbon atom is called a **chiral carbon** because there are two different ways that it can bond to four atoms or groups of atoms. The resulting structures are nonsuperimposable mirror images. Let's look at the mirror images of a carbon bonded to four different atoms (see Figure 14.8). If we line up the hydrogen and iodine atoms in the mirror images, the bromine and chlorine atoms appear on opposite sides. No matter how we turn the models, we cannot superimpose all four atoms. When stereoisomers cannot be superimposed, they are called **enantiomers**.

If two or more atoms bonded to a particular carbon are the same, the atoms can be aligned (superimposed if rotated), and then the mirror images represent the same structure (see Figure 14.9).

TUTORIAL
Chiral Carbon Atoms

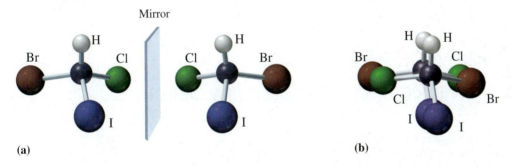

(a)   **(b)**

FIGURE 14.8 **(a)** The enantiomers of a chiral molecule are mirror images. **(b)** The enantiomers of a chiral molecule cannot be superimposed on each other.

Q Why is the carbon atom in this compound a chiral carbon?

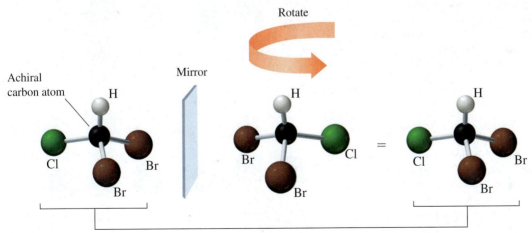

These are the same structures.

FIGURE 14.9 The mirror images of an achiral compound can be superimposed on each other.
Q Why can the mirror images of the compound be superimposed?

Molecules in nature also have mirror images, and often one stereoisomer has a different biological effect than the other one. For some compounds, one enantiomer has a certain odor, and the other enantiomer has a completely different odor. For example, the oils that give the scent of spearmint and caraway seeds are *both* composed of carvone. However, carvone has one chiral carbon in the carbon ring indicated by an asterisk, which gives carvone two enantiomers. Olfactory receptors in the nose detect these enantiomers as two different odors. One enantiomer of carvone that is produced by the spearmint plant smells and tastes like spearmint, whereas its mirror image, produced by the caraway plant, has the odor and taste of caraway in rye bread. Thus, our senses of smell and taste are responsive to the chirality of molecules.

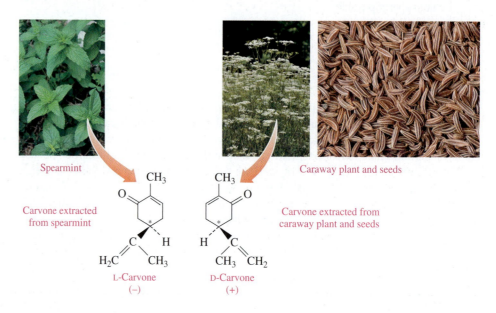

Spearmint

Caraway plant and seeds

Carvone extracted from spearmint

Carvone extracted from caraway plant and seeds

L-Carvone
(−)

D-Carvone
(+)

Explore Your World

USING GUMDROPS AND TOOTHPICKS TO MODEL CHIRAL OBJECTS

Part 1: Achiral Objects

Obtain some toothpicks and several orange, yellow, green, purple, and black gumdrops. Place four toothpicks into the black gumdrop, making the ends of toothpicks form a tetrahedron. Attach gumdrops to the ends of the four toothpicks: two orange, one green, and one yellow.

Using another black gumdrop, make a second model that is the mirror image of the original model. Now rotate one of the models, and try to superimpose it on the other model. Are the models superimposable? If achiral objects have superimposable mirror images, are these models chiral or achiral?

Part 2: Chiral Objects

Using one of the original models, replace one orange gumdrop with a purple gumdrop. Now there are four different colors of gumdrops attached to the black gumdrop. Make its mirror image by replacing one orange gumdrop with a purple one on the second model. Now rotate one of the models, and try to superimpose it on the other model. Are the models superimposable? If chiral objects have nonsuperimposable mirror images, are these models chiral or achiral?

SAMPLE PROBLEM 14.7   **Chiral Carbons**

For each of the following, indicate whether the carbon in red is chiral or achiral:

a. Glycerol, which is used to sweeten and preserve foods and as a lubricant in soaps, creams, and hair care products.

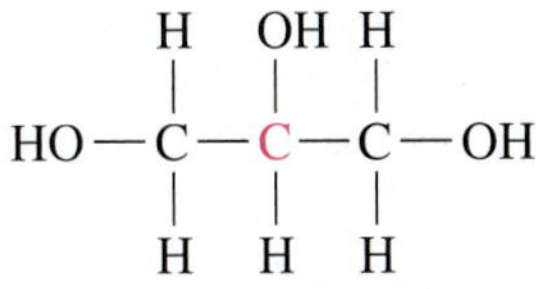

$$HO - \overset{\displaystyle H}{\underset{\displaystyle H}{C}} - \overset{\displaystyle OH}{\underset{\displaystyle H}{C}} - \overset{\displaystyle H}{\underset{\displaystyle H}{C}} - OH$$

Glycerol

b. Monosodium glutamate (MSG), which is the salt of the amino acid glutamic acid used as a flavor enhancer in foods.

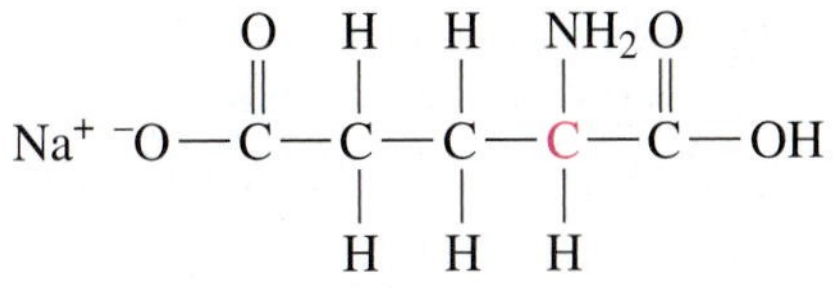

$$Na^+ \ {}^-O - \overset{\displaystyle O}{\overset{\|}{C}} - \overset{\displaystyle H}{\underset{\displaystyle H}{C}} - \overset{\displaystyle H}{\underset{\displaystyle H}{C}} - \overset{\displaystyle NH_2}{\underset{\displaystyle H}{C}} - \overset{\displaystyle O}{\overset{\|}{C}} - OH$$

Monosodium glutamate (MSG)

c. Ibuprofen, which is a nonsteroidal anti-inflammatory drug used to relieve fever and pain.

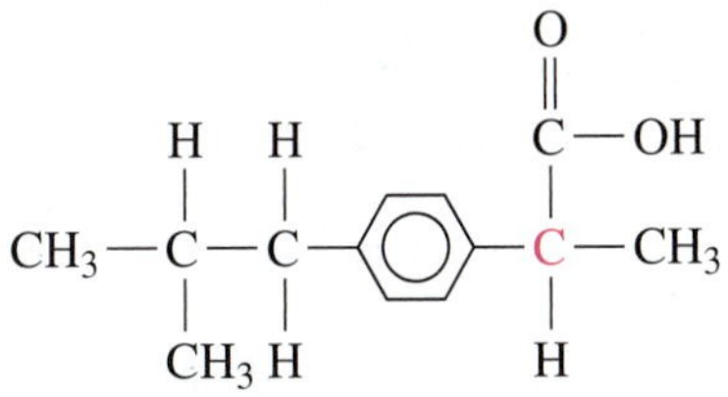

$$CH_3 - \overset{\displaystyle H}{\underset{\displaystyle CH_3}{C}} - \overset{\displaystyle H}{\underset{\displaystyle H}{C}} - \bigcirc\!\!\!\!\!\bigcirc - \overset{\overset{\displaystyle O}{\overset{\|}{C} - OH}}{\underset{\displaystyle H}{C}} - CH_3$$

Ibuprofen

SOLUTION

a. Achiral. Two of the substituents on the carbon in magenta are the same ($-CH_2OH$). A chiral carbon must be bonded to four different groups or atoms.
b. Chiral. The carbon in red is bonded to four different groups: $-COOH$, $-NH_2$, $-H$, and $-CH_2-CH_2-COO^- \ Na^+$.
c. Chiral. The carbon in red is bonded to four different groups: $-H$, $-CH_3$, $-COOH$, and

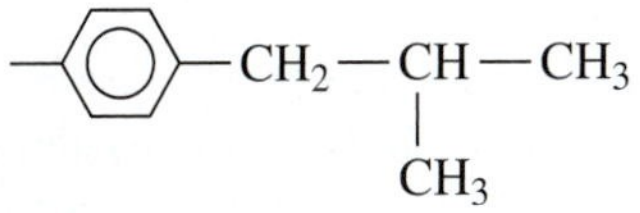

$$\bigcirc\!\!\!\!\!\bigcirc - CH_2 - \underset{\displaystyle CH_3}{CH} - CH_3$$

STUDY CHECK 14.7

Circle the chiral carbon of penicillamine, which is used in the treatment of rheumatoid arthritis.

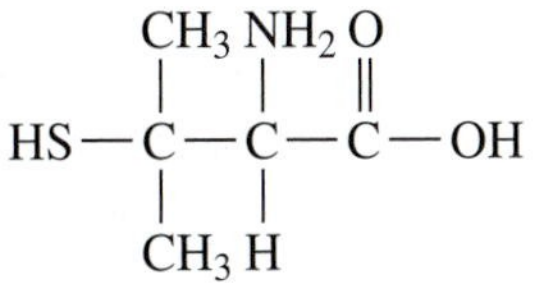

$$HS - \overset{\displaystyle CH_3}{\underset{\displaystyle CH_3}{C}} - \overset{\displaystyle NH_2}{\underset{\displaystyle H}{C}} - \overset{\displaystyle O}{\overset{\|}{C}} - OH$$

Drawing Fischer Projections

Emil Fischer devised a simplified system for drawing stereoisomers that shows the arrangements of the atoms around their chiral centers. Fischer received the Nobel Prize in Chemistry in 1902 for his contributions to carbohydrate and protein chemistry. Now we can use his model, called a **Fischer projection**, to represent a three-dimensional structure of enantiomers. Vertical lines represent bonds that project backward from a carbon atom and horizontal lines represent bonds that project forward. In this model, the most highly oxidized carbon is placed at the top and the intersections of vertical and horizontal lines to represent a carbon atom that is usually chiral.

For glyceraldehyde, the only chiral carbon in this molecule is the middle carbon. In the Fischer projection, the carbonyl group, which is the most highly oxidized group, is drawn at the top above the chiral carbon and the —CH_2OH group is drawn at the bottom. The —H and the —OH groups are drawn at each end of a horizontal line, but in two different ways. The stereoisomer that has the —OH group drawn to the left of the chiral atom is designated as the L isomer. The other stereoisomer with the —OH group drawn to the right of the chiral carbon represents the D isomer. Today, the "D- and L-" system is used to identify the enantiomers of carbohydrates and amino acids (see Figure 14.10).

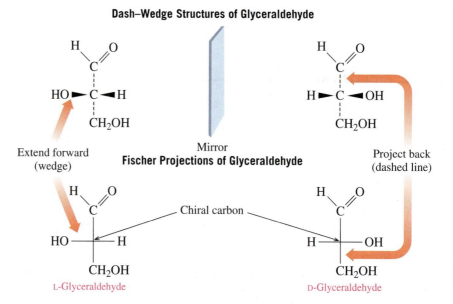

Dash–Wedge Structures of Glyceraldehyde

Extend forward (wedge)   Mirror   Project back (dashed line)

Fischer Projections of Glyceraldehyde

Chiral carbon

L-Glyceraldehyde   D-Glyceraldehyde

FIGURE 14.10 In a Fischer projection, the chiral carbon atom is at the center, with horizontal lines for bonds that extend toward the viewer and vertical lines for bonds that point away. The symbols D and L are used as prefixes to distinguish the two substances that constitute an enantiomeric pair.

Q Why does glyceraldehyde have only one chiral carbon atom?

Fischer projections can also be drawn for compounds that have two or more chiral carbons. For example, in the mirror images of erythrose, both of the carbon atoms at the intersections are chiral. To draw the mirror image for L-erythrose, we need to reverse the positions of *all* the —H and the —OH groups on the horizontal lines. For compounds with two or more chiral carbons, the designation as a D or L isomer is determined by the position of the —OH group attached to the chiral carbon *farthest from the carbonyl group*.

L-isomer   D-isomer

L-Erythrose   D-Erythrose

SAMPLE PROBLEM 14.8   Fischer Projections

Identify each of the following as the D or L isomer and draw its mirror image.

a. 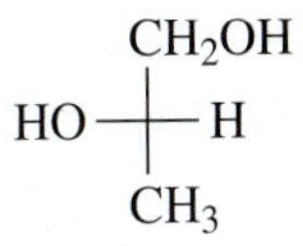
$$
\begin{array}{c}
CH_2OH \\
HO \!-\!\!\mid\!\!-\! H \\
CH_3
\end{array}
$$

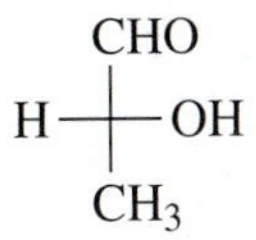

b.
$$
\begin{array}{c}
CHO \\
H \!-\!\!\mid\!\!-\! OH \\
CH_3
\end{array}
$$

c.
$$
\begin{array}{c}
CHO \\
HO \!-\!\!\mid\!\!-\! H \\
H \!-\!\!\mid\!\!-\! OH \\
CH_2OH
\end{array}
$$

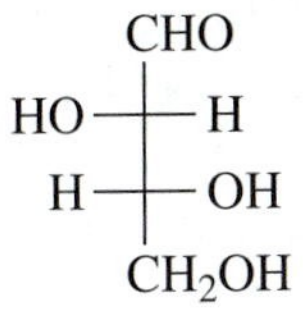

SOLUTION

a. When the —OH group is drawn to the left of the chiral carbon, it is the L isomer. Its mirror image is drawn by reversing the —H and —OH groups on the chiral carbon.

$$
\begin{array}{c}
CH_2OH \\
H \!-\!\!\mid\!\!-\! OH \\
CH_3
\end{array}
$$

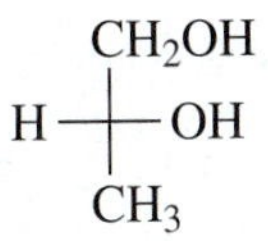

b. When the —OH group is drawn to the right of the chiral carbon, it is the D isomer. Its mirror image is drawn by reversing the —H and —OH groups on the chiral carbon.

$$
\begin{array}{c}
CHO \\
HO \!-\!\!\mid\!\!-\! H \\
CH_3
\end{array}
$$

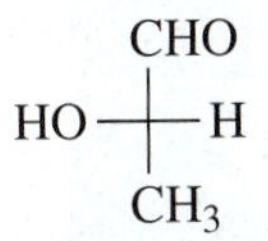

c. When the —OH group is drawn to the right of the chiral carbon farthest from the top of the Fischer projection, it is the D isomer. Its mirror image is drawn by reversing all the —H and —OH groups on both chiral carbons.

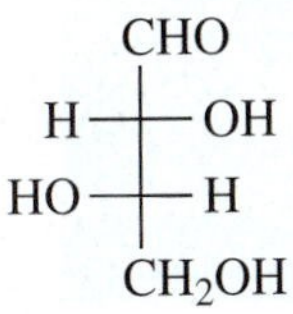

$$
\begin{array}{c}
CHO \\
H \!-\!\!\mid\!\!-\! OH \\
HO \!-\!\!\mid\!\!-\! H \\
CH_2OH
\end{array}
$$

STUDY CHECK 14.8

Draw the Fischer projections for the D and L stereoisomers of 2-hydroxypropanal and label the D and L isomers.

Chemistry Link to Health

ENANTIOMERS IN BIOLOGICAL SYSTEMS

Most compounds that are active in biological systems consist of only one enantiomer. Rarely are both enantiomers of biological molecules active. For example, there are D- and L-forms for all amino acids except glycine. But all proteins, from animals, plants, bacteria, and even viruses, are built entirely of L-amino acids. This happens because the enzymes and cell surface receptors on which metabolic reactions take place are themselves chiral. Thus, only one enantiomer interacts with its enzymes or receptors; the other is inactive. The chiral receptor fits the arrangement of the substituents in only one enantiomer; its mirror image does not fit properly (see Figure 14.11).

In the brain, one enantiomer of LSD affects the production of serotonin, affecting sensory perception and possibly leading to hallucinations. However, its enantiomer produces little effect in the brain. The behavior of nicotine and epinephrine (adrenaline) also depends upon only one of their enantiomers. For example,

one enantiomer of nicotine is more toxic than the other. Only one enantiomer of epinephrine is responsible for the constriction of blood vessels.

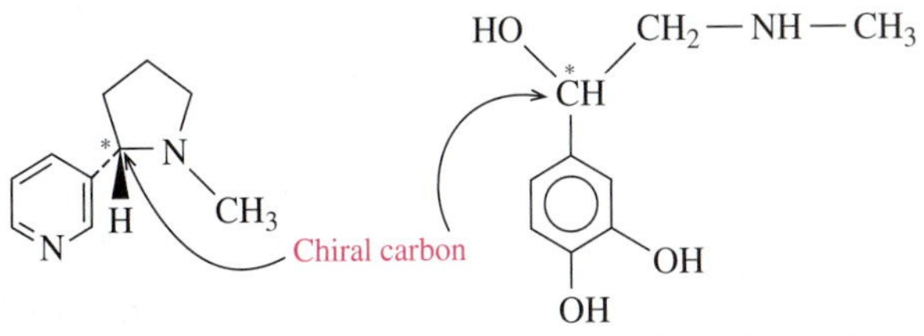

Nicotine

Epinephrine (adrenaline)

A substance used to treat Parkinson's disease is L-dopa, which is converted to dopamine in the brain, where it raises the serotonin level. However, the D-dopa enantiomer is not effective for the treatment of Parkinson's disease.

L-Dopa, anti-Parkinsonian drug

D-Dopa has no biological effect

Active form of naproxen

Mirror image of naproxen (inactive form)

For many drugs, only one of the enantiomers is biologically active. However, for many years, drugs have been produced that were mixtures of their enantiomers. Today, drug researchers are using *chiral technology* to produce the active enantiomers of chiral drugs. Chiral catalysts are being designed that direct the formation of just one enantiomer rather than both. The active forms of several enantiomers are now being produced such as L-dopa and naproxen. Naproxen is a nonsteroidal anti-inflammatory drug used to relieve pain, fever, and inflammation caused by osteoarthritis and tendinitis. The benefits of producing only the active enantiomer include using a lower dose, enhancing activity, reducing interactions with other drugs, and eliminating possible harmful side effects from the inactive enantiomer.

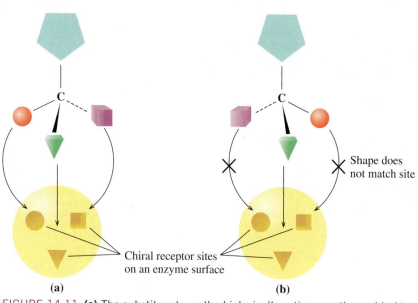

FIGURE 14.11 **(a)** The substituents on the biologically active enantiomer bind to all the sites on a chiral receptor; **(b)** its enantiomer does not bind properly and is not active biologically.

Q Why doesn't the mirror image of the active enantiomer fit into a chiral receptor site?

The active enantiomer of the popular analgesic ibuprofen used in Advil, Motrin, and Nuprin has been produced. However, recent research shows that humans have an enzyme called *isomerase* that converts the inactive enantiomer of ibuprofen to its active form. Due to the lower cost of preparation, most manufacturers prepare ibuprofen as a mixture of inactive and active forms.

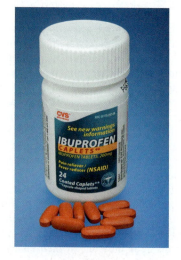

Active form of ibuprofen

Mirror image (inactive form)

QUESTIONS AND PROBLEMS

14.5 Chiral Molecules

LEARNING GOAL: *Identify chiral and achiral carbon atoms in an organic molecule.*

14.31 Identify each of the following structures as chiral or achiral. If chiral, indicate the chiral carbon.

a. $CH_3 - \overset{\overset{\displaystyle OH}{|}}{C}H - CH_3$

b. $CH_3 - \overset{\overset{\displaystyle Br}{|}}{C}H - CH_2 - CH_3$

c. $CH_3 - \overset{\overset{\displaystyle Br}{|}}{C}H - \overset{\overset{\displaystyle O}{||}}{C} - H$

d. $CH_3 - CH_2 - \overset{\overset{\displaystyle OH}{|}}{\underset{\underset{\displaystyle CH_3}{|}}{C}} - CH_3$

14.32 Identify each of the following structures as chiral or achiral. If chiral, indicate the chiral carbon.

a. $CH_3 - \overset{\overset{\displaystyle Cl}{|}}{\underset{\underset{\displaystyle CH_3}{|}}{C}} - CH_2 - \overset{\overset{\displaystyle Cl}{|}}{C}H - CH_3$

b. $CH_3 - \overset{\overset{\displaystyle Br}{|}}{C} = CH - CH_3$

c. $CH_3 - \overset{\overset{\displaystyle OH}{|}}{\underset{\underset{\displaystyle CH_3}{|}}{C}} - \overset{\overset{\displaystyle OH}{|}}{C}H - CH_3$

d. $Br - CH_2 - \overset{\overset{\displaystyle Cl}{|}}{C}H - CH_3$

14.33 Identify the chiral carbon in each of the following naturally occurring compounds:

a. citronellol, one enantiomer has the geranium odor

$CH_3 - \overset{\overset{\displaystyle CH_3}{|}}{C} = CH - CH_2 - CH_2 - \overset{\overset{\displaystyle CH_3}{|}}{C}H - CH_2 - CH_2 - OH$

b. alanine, an amino acid

$H_2N - \overset{\overset{\displaystyle CH_3}{|}}{C}H - \overset{\overset{\displaystyle O}{||}}{C} - OH$

14.34 Identify the chiral carbon in each of the following naturally occurring compounds:

a. amphetamine (Benzedrine), a stimulant and treatment for hyperactivity

(benzene ring) $- CH_2 - \overset{\overset{\displaystyle CH_3}{|}}{C}H - NH_2$

b. norepinephrine, which increases blood pressure and nerve transmission

(benzene ring with HO, HO) $\overset{\overset{\displaystyle OH}{|}}{C}H - CH_2 - NH_2$

14.35 Draw the Fischer projection for each of the following dash–wedge structures:

a. H, C, HO, Br, CH_3

b. CH_3, C, Cl, Br, OH

c. CHO, C, HO, H, CH_2CH_3

14.36 Draw the Fischer projection for each of the following dash–wedge structures:

a. CHO, C, HO, Br, CH_2OH

b. CHO, C, H, OH, CH_2OH

c. CHO, C, HO, H, CH_2OH

14.37 Indicate whether each pair of Fischer projections represents enantiomers or identical structures:

a. $\underset{CH_3}{\overset{CH_3}{Br - \!\!\!\!\!\mid\!\!\!\!\!- Cl}}$ and $\underset{CH_3}{\overset{CH_3}{Cl - \!\!\!\!\!\mid\!\!\!\!\!- Br}}$

b. $\underset{CH_3}{\overset{CHO}{HO - \!\!\!\!\!\mid\!\!\!\!\!- H}}$ and $\underset{CH_3}{\overset{CHO}{H - \!\!\!\!\!\mid\!\!\!\!\!- OH}}$

c. $\underset{H}{\overset{CH_3}{Cl - \!\!\!\!\!\mid\!\!\!\!\!- Br}}$ and $\underset{H}{\overset{CH_3}{Br - \!\!\!\!\!\mid\!\!\!\!\!- Cl}}$

d. $\underset{CH_3}{\overset{COOH}{H - \!\!\!\!\!\mid\!\!\!\!\!- OH}}$ and $\underset{CH_3}{\overset{COOH}{HO - \!\!\!\!\!\mid\!\!\!\!\!- H}}$

14.38 Indicate whether each pair of Fischer projections represents enantiomers or identical structures:

a. $\underset{CH_3}{\overset{CH_2OH}{Br - \!\!\!\!\!\mid\!\!\!\!\!- Cl}}$ and $\underset{CH_3}{\overset{CH_2OH}{Cl - \!\!\!\!\!\mid\!\!\!\!\!- Br}}$

b. $\underset{CH_3}{\overset{CHO}{H - \!\!\!\!\!\mid\!\!\!\!\!- H}}$ and $\underset{CH_3}{\overset{CHO}{H - \!\!\!\!\!\mid\!\!\!\!\!- H}}$

c. $\underset{CH_2CH_3}{\overset{CH_3}{H - \!\!\!\!\!\mid\!\!\!\!\!- OH}}$ and $\underset{CH_2CH_3}{\overset{CH_3}{HO - \!\!\!\!\!\mid\!\!\!\!\!- H}}$

d. $\underset{CH_3}{\overset{COOH}{H - \!\!\!\!\!\mid\!\!\!\!\!- NH_2}}$ and $\underset{CH_3}{\overset{COOH}{H_2N - \!\!\!\!\!\mid\!\!\!\!\!- H}}$

CONCEPT MAP

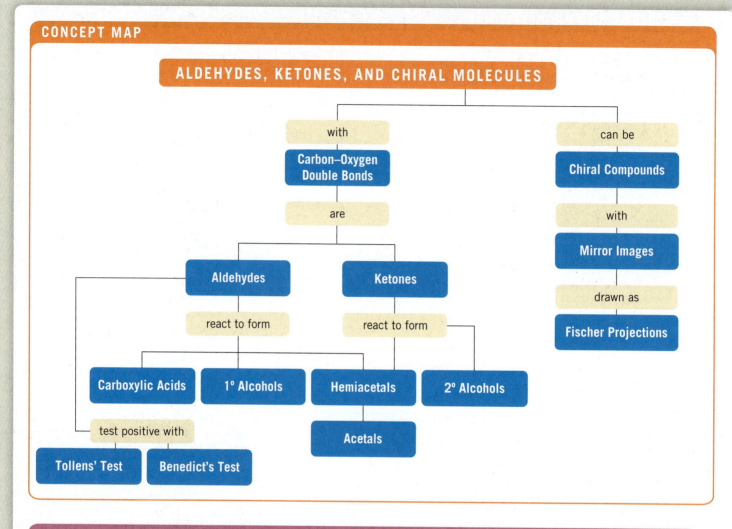

ALDEHYDES, KETONES, AND CHIRAL MOLECULES

with → **Carbon–Oxygen Double Bonds** → are

- **Aldehydes** → react to form → **Carboxylic Acids**, **1° Alcohols**
  - test positive with → **Tollens' Test**, **Benedict's Test**
- **Ketones** → react to form → **Hemiacetals**, **2° Alcohols**
  - **Hemiacetals** → **Acetals**

can be → **Chiral Compounds** → with → **Mirror Images** → drawn as → **Fischer Projections**

CHAPTER REVIEW

14.1 Aldehydes and Ketones

LEARNING GOAL: Identify compounds with a carbonyl group as aldehydes and ketones. Give the IUPAC and common names for aldehydes and ketones; draw their condensed structural formulas or skeletal formulas, if cyclic.

- Aldehydes and ketones contain a carbonyl group (C=O), which is strongly polar.
- In aldehydes, the carbonyl group appears at the end of carbon chains attached to at least one hydrogen atom.
- In ketones, the carbonyl group occurs between two alkyl or aromatic groups.
- In the IUPAC system, the *e* in the corresponding alkane is replaced with *al* for aldehydes and *one* for ketones. For ketones with more than four carbon atoms in the main chain, the carbonyl group is numbered to show its location.
- Many of the simple aldehydes and ketones use common names.
- Many aldehydes and ketones are found in biological systems, flavorings, and drugs.

Carbonyl group

CH_3—C—H Aldehyde

CH_3—C—CH_3 Ketone

14.2 Physical Properties of Aldehydes and Ketones

LEARNING GOAL: Describe the boiling points and solubility of aldehydes and ketones in water.

- The polar carbonyl group in aldehydes and ketones gives higher boiling points than alkanes.
- The boiling points of aldehydes and ketones are lower than alcohols because aldehydes and ketones cannot hydrogen bond with each other.
- Aldehydes and ketones form hydrogen bonds with water molecules, which makes carbonyl compounds with one to four carbon atoms soluble in water.

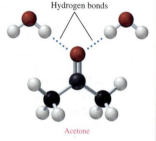

Hydrogen bonds

Acetone

14.3 Oxidation and Reduction of Aldehydes and Ketones

LEARNING GOAL: Draw the condensed structural or skeletal formulas for the reactants and products in the oxidation or reduction of aldehydes and ketones.

- Primary alcohols can be oxidized to aldehydes, whereas secondary alcohols can oxidize to ketones.
- Aldehydes are easily oxidized to carboxylic acids, but ketones do not oxidize further.
- Aldehydes, but not ketones, react with Tollens' reagent to give "silver mirrors."
- In Benedict's test, aldehydes with adjacent hydroxyl groups reduce blue Cu^{2+} to give a brick-red Cu_2O solid.
- The reduction of aldehydes with hydrogen produces primary alcohols, while ketones are reduced to secondary alcohols.

14.4 Hemiacetals and Acetals

LEARNING GOAL: Draw the condensed structural formulas for the products of the addition of alcohols to aldehydes and ketones.

- Alcohols can add to the carbonyl group of aldehydes and ketones.
- The addition of one alcohol molecule forms a hemiacetal, while the addition of two alcohol molecules forms an acetal.

- Hemiacetals are not usually stable, except for cyclic hemiacetals, which are the most common form of simple sugars such as glucose.

14.5 Chiral Molecules

LEARNING GOAL: Identify chiral and achiral carbon atoms in an organic molecule.

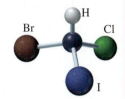

- Chiral molecules are molecules with mirror images that cannot be superimposed on each other. These types of stereoisomers are called enantiomers.
- A chiral molecule must have at least one chiral carbon, which is a carbon bonded to four different atoms or groups of atoms.
- The Fischer projection is a simplified way to draw the arrangements of atoms by placing the carbon atoms at the intersection of vertical and horizontal lines.
- The names of the mirror images are labeled D or L to differentiate between enantiomers of carbohydrates and amino acids.

SUMMARY OF NAMING

Structure	Family	IUPAC Name	Common Name
$H-\overset{\overset{\displaystyle O}{\|\|}}{C}-H$	Aldehyde	Methanal	Formaldehyde
$CH_3-\overset{\overset{\displaystyle O}{\|\|}}{C}-CH_3$	Ketone	Propanone	Acetone; dimethyl ketone

SUMMARY OF REACTIONS

Oxidation of Aldehydes to Form Carboxylic Acids

$$CH_3-\overset{\overset{\displaystyle O}{\|\|}}{C}-H \xrightarrow{[O]} CH_3-\overset{\overset{\displaystyle O}{\|\|}}{C}-OH$$

Acetaldehyde   Acetic acid

Reduction of Aldehydes to Form Primary Alcohols

$$CH_3-\overset{\overset{\displaystyle O}{\|\|}}{C}-H \ + \ H_2 \xrightarrow{Ni} CH_3-\overset{\overset{\displaystyle OH}{\|}}{C}H_2$$

Acetaldehyde   Ethanol

Reduction of Ketones to Form Secondary Alcohols

$$CH_3-\overset{\overset{\displaystyle O}{\|\|}}{C}-CH_3 \ + \ H_2 \xrightarrow{Ni} CH_3-\overset{\overset{\displaystyle OH}{\|}}{C}H-CH_3$$

Acetone   2-Propanol

Addition of Alcohols to Form Hemiacetals and Acetals

$$H-\overset{\overset{\displaystyle O}{\|}}{C}-H + CH_3-OH \xrightarrow{H^+} H-\overset{\overset{\displaystyle O-CH_3}{|}}{\underset{\underset{\displaystyle OH}{|}}{C}}-H + CH_3-OH \xrightarrow{H^+} H-\overset{\overset{\displaystyle O-CH_3}{|}}{\underset{\underset{\displaystyle O-CH_3}{|}}{C}}-H + H_2O$$

Formaldehyde   Methanol   Hemiacetal   Acetal

$$CH_3-\overset{\overset{\displaystyle O}{\|}}{C}-CH_3 + CH_3-OH \xrightarrow{H^+} CH_3-\overset{\overset{\displaystyle O-CH_3}{|}}{\underset{\underset{\displaystyle OH}{|}}{C}}-CH_3 + CH_3-OH \xrightarrow{H^+} CH_3-\overset{\overset{\displaystyle O-CH_3}{|}}{\underset{\underset{\displaystyle O-CH_3}{|}}{C}}-CH_3 + H_2O$$

Acetone   Methanol   Hemiacetal   Acetal

KEY TERMS

acetal The product of the addition of two alcohols to an aldehyde or ketone.

achiral Molecules with mirror images that are superimposable.

aldehyde An organic compound with a carbonyl functional group and at least one hydrogen attached to the carbon in the carbonyl group.

Benedict's test A test for aldehydes with adjacent hydroxyl groups in which Cu^{2+} ($CuSO_4$) ions in Benedict's reagent are reduced to a brick-red solid of Cu_2O.

chiral Objects or molecules that have nonsuperimposable mirror images.

chiral carbon A carbon atom that is bonded to four different atoms or groups.

enantiomers Stereoisomers that are mirror images that cannot be superimposed.

Fischer projection A system for drawing stereoisomers; an intersection of a vertical and horizontal line represents a carbon atom.

A vertical line represents bonds that project backwards from a carbon atom and a horizontal line represents bonds that project forward. The most highly oxidized carbon is at the top.

hemiacetal The product of the addition of one alcohol to the double bond of the carbonyl group in aldehydes and ketones.

ketone An organic compound in which the carbonyl functional group is bonded to two alkyl or aromatic groups.

reduction A decrease in the number of carbon–oxygen bonds by the addition of hydrogen to a carbonyl bond. Aldehydes are reduced to primary alcohols; ketones to secondary alcohols.

stereoisomers Isomers that have atoms bonded in the same order, but with different arrangements in space.

Tollens' test A test for aldehydes in which the Ag^+ in Tollens' reagent is reduced to metallic silver, which forms a "silver mirror" on the walls of the container.

UNDERSTANDING THE CONCEPTS

The chapter sections to review are shown in parentheses at the end of each question.

14.39 Why does the $C{=}O$ double bond have a dipole, whereas the $C{=}C$ double bond does not? (14.1)

14.40 Why are aldehydes and ketones with one to four carbon atoms soluble in water? (14.2)

14.41 Which of the following will give a positive Tollens' test? (14.3)

a. $CH_3-CH_2-\overset{\overset{\displaystyle O}{\|}}{C}-H$ **b.** $CH_3-\overset{\overset{\displaystyle CH_3}{|}}{CH}-\overset{\overset{\displaystyle O}{\|}}{C}-H$

c. $CH_3-O-CH_2-CH_3$

14.42 Which of the following will give a positive Tollens' test? (14.3)

a. $CH_3-CH_2-CH_2-OH$ **b.** $CH_3-\overset{\overset{\displaystyle OH}{|}}{CH}-CH_3$

c. $\overset{\overset{\displaystyle O}{\|}}{\underset{\displaystyle \triangle}{C-H}}$

14.43 Draw the condensed structural formula and the skeletal formula for each of the following: (14.1)

   a. *trans*-2-hexenal, alarm pheromone of ants
   b. 2,6-dimethyl-5-heptenal, communication pheromone of ants

14.44 Draw the condensed structural formula and the skeletal formula for each of the following: (14.1)

   a. 4-methyl-3-heptanone, ant trail pheromone
   b. 2-nonanone, moth sex attractant pheromone

ADDITIONAL QUESTIONS AND PROBLEMS

For instructor-assigned homework, go to www.masteringchemistry.com.

14.45 Give the IUPAC name for each of the following compounds: (14.1)

a.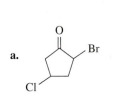

b.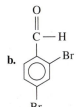

c. $Cl-CH_2-CH_2-\overset{\displaystyle O}{\overset{\|}{C}}-H$

d. $CH_3-CH_2-\overset{\displaystyle O}{\overset{\|}{C}}-CH_2-\overset{\displaystyle Cl}{\overset{|}{C}H}-CH_3$

e. (skeletal structure)

14.46 Give the IUPAC name for each of the following compounds: (14.1)

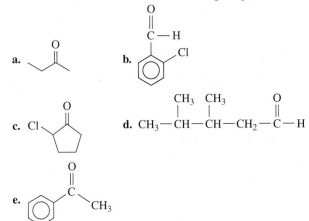

14.47 Draw the condensed structural formula or skeletal formula, if cyclic, for each of the following: (14.1)
- a. 3-methylcyclopentanone
- b. pentanal
- c. ethyl methyl ketone
- d. 4-methylhexanal

14.48 Draw the condensed structural formula or skeletal formula, if cyclic, for each of the following: (14.1)
- a. 2-chlorobutanal
- b. 2-methylcyclohexanone
- c. 3,5-dimethylhexanal
- d. 3-bromocyclopentanone

14.49 Which of the following aldehydes or ketones are soluble in water? (14.2)

a. $CH_3-CH_2-\overset{\displaystyle O}{\overset{\|}{C}}-H$ b. $CH_3-\overset{\displaystyle O}{\overset{\|}{C}}-CH_3$

c. $CH_3-CH_2-\overset{\displaystyle O}{\overset{\|}{C}}-CH_2-CH_2-CH_3$

14.50 Which of the following aldehydes or ketones are soluble in water? (14.2)

a. $CH_3-CH_2-\overset{\displaystyle O}{\overset{\|}{C}}-CH_3$ b. $CH_3-\overset{\displaystyle O}{\overset{\|}{C}}-H$

c. $CH_3-CH_2-\overset{\displaystyle CH_3}{\overset{|}{C}H}-CH_2-\overset{\displaystyle O}{\overset{\|}{C}}-H$

14.51 In each of the following pairs of compounds, select the compound with the higher boiling point: (14.2)

a. $CH_3-CH_2-CH_2-OH$ or $CH_3-\overset{\displaystyle O}{\overset{\|}{C}}-CH_3$

b. $CH_3-CH_2-CH_2-CH_3$ or $CH_3-CH_2-\overset{\displaystyle O}{\overset{\|}{C}}-H$

c. CH_3-CH_2-OH or $CH_3-\overset{\displaystyle O}{\overset{\|}{C}}-H$

14.52 In each of the following pairs of compounds, select the compound with the higher boiling point: (14.2)

a. $CH_3-\overset{\displaystyle O}{\overset{\|}{C}}-H$ or $CH_3-CH_2-CH_2-CH_2-\overset{\displaystyle O}{\overset{\|}{C}}-H$

b. $CH_3-CH_2-\overset{\displaystyle O}{\overset{\|}{C}}-H$ or $CH_3-\overset{\displaystyle OH}{\overset{|}{C}H}-CH_3$

c. $CH_3-CH_2-CH_2-CH_3$ or $CH_3-\overset{\displaystyle O}{\overset{\|}{C}}-CH_3$

14.53 Circle the chiral carbons, if any, in each of the following compounds: (14.5)

a. $H-\overset{\displaystyle Cl}{\underset{\displaystyle Cl}{\overset{|}{\underset{|}{C}}}}-\overset{\displaystyle Cl}{\underset{\displaystyle H}{\overset{|}{\underset{|}{C}}}}-OH$ b. $CH_3-\overset{\displaystyle H}{\overset{|}{C}}=\overset{\displaystyle CH_3}{\overset{|}{C}}-CH_3$

c. $HO-CH_2-\overset{\displaystyle OH}{\overset{|}{C}H}-CH_2-OH$ d. $CH_3-\overset{\displaystyle NH_2}{\overset{|}{C}H}-\overset{\displaystyle O}{\overset{\|}{C}}-H$

e. $CH_3-CH_2-\overset{\displaystyle Br}{\underset{\displaystyle OH}{\overset{|}{\underset{|}{C}}}H}-CH_2-CH_2-CH_3$

f. (cyclohexane skeletal structure)

14.54 Circle the chiral carbons, if any, in each of the following compounds: (14.5)

a. $CH_3-\overset{\displaystyle O-CH_3}{\overset{|}{C}H}-CH_3$ b. $CH_3-\overset{\displaystyle OH}{\overset{|}{C}H}-\overset{\displaystyle O}{\overset{\|}{C}}-CH_3$

c. $CH_3-\overset{\displaystyle OH}{\underset{\displaystyle OH}{\overset{|}{\underset{|}{C}}}}-H$ d. $CH_3-\overset{\displaystyle CH_3}{\overset{|}{C}H}-\overset{\displaystyle O}{\overset{\|}{C}}-CH_3$

e. $CH_3-\overset{\displaystyle Br}{\underset{\displaystyle OH}{\overset{|}{\underset{|}{C}}}}-CH_2-CH_3$ f. (cyclohexane with two Cl substituents skeletal structure)

14.55 Identify each of the following pairs of Fischer projections as enantiomers or identical compounds: (14.5)

a. (Fischer projection: CHO, H—OH, CH₂OH) and (Fischer projection: CHO, HO—H, CH₂OH)

b. 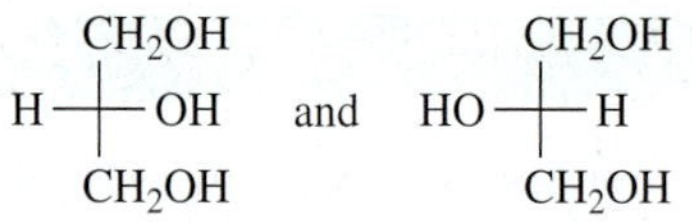 H⟶OH and HO⟶H (CH₂OH top / CH₂OH bottom) ...

b.
$$\text{CH}_2\text{OH} \quad\quad \text{CH}_2\text{OH}$$
H—|—OH   and   HO—|—H
$$\text{CH}_2\text{OH} \quad\quad \text{CH}_2\text{OH}$$

c. 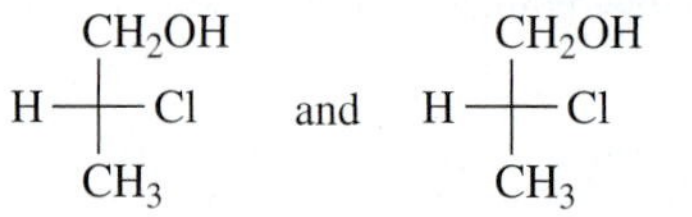
$$\text{CH}_2\text{OH} \quad\quad \text{CH}_2\text{OH}$$
H—|—Cl   and   H—|—Cl
$$\text{CH}_3 \quad\quad \text{CH}_3$$

d. 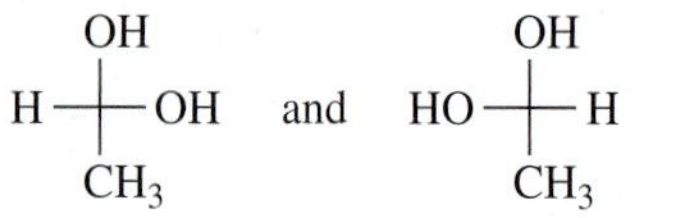
$$\text{OH} \quad\quad \text{OH}$$
H—|—OH   and   HO—|—H
$$\text{CH}_3 \quad\quad \text{CH}_3$$

14.56 Identify each of the following pairs of Fischer projections as enantiomers or identical compounds: (14.5)

a. 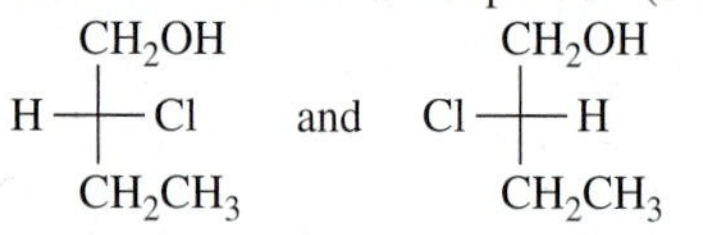
$$\text{CH}_2\text{OH} \quad\quad \text{CH}_2\text{OH}$$
H—|—Cl   and   Cl—|—H
$$\text{CH}_2\text{CH}_3 \quad\quad \text{CH}_2\text{CH}_3$$

b. 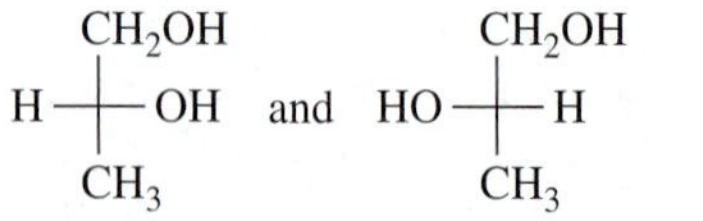
$$\text{CH}_2\text{OH} \quad\quad \text{CH}_2\text{OH}$$
H—|—OH   and   HO—|—H
$$\text{CH}_3 \quad\quad \text{CH}_3$$

c. 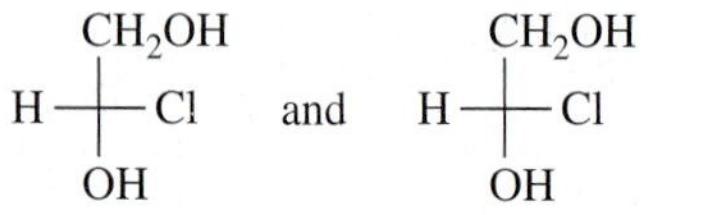
$$\text{CH}_2\text{OH} \quad\quad \text{CH}_2\text{OH}$$
H—|—Cl   and   H—|—Cl
$$\text{OH} \quad\quad \text{OH}$$

d. 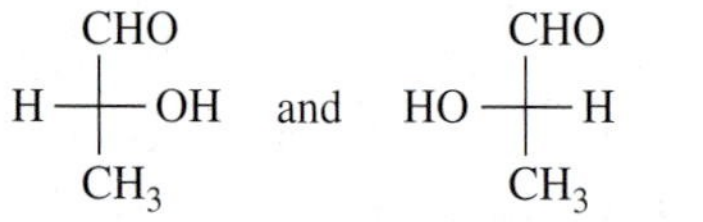
$$\text{CHO} \quad\quad \text{CHO}$$
H—|—OH   and   HO—|—H
$$\text{CH}_3 \quad\quad \text{CH}_3$$

14.57 Draw the condensed structural formula for the product when each of the following is oxidized: (14.3)

a. $CH_3—CH_2—CH_2—OH$

b. $CH_3—CH(OH)—CH_2—CH_2—CH_3$

c. $CH_3—CH_2—CH_2—C(=O)—H$

d. 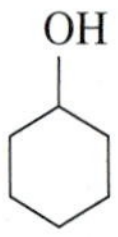 (cyclohexanol with OH)

14.58 Draw the condensed structural formula for the product when each of the following is oxidized: (14.3)

a. $CH_3—CH_2—CH_2—CH_2—OH$

b. $CH_3—CH_2—CH(OH)—CH_3$

c. $CH_3—CH(CH_3)—CH_2—C(=O)—H$

d. 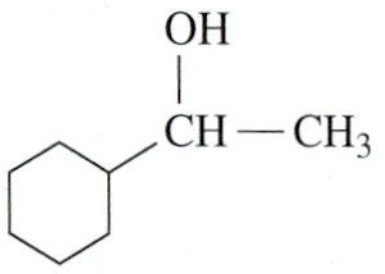 (cyclohexane with CH(OH)—CH₃)

14.59 Draw the condensed structural formula for the product when hydrogen and a nickel catalyst reduce each of the following: (14.3)

a. $CH_3—C(=O)—CH_3$

b. 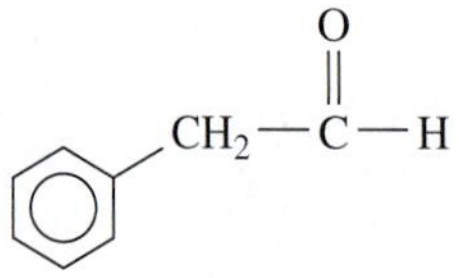 (benzene ring)—$CH_2—C(=O)—H$

c. $CH_3—CH(CH_3)—CH_2—C(=O)—CH_3$

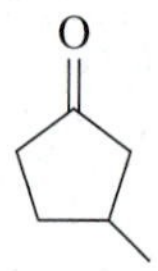

14.60 Draw the condensed structural formula for the product when $NaBH_4$ reduces each of the following: (14.3)

a. $CH_3—C(=O)—H$

b. (methylcyclopentanone with O)

c. $H—C(=O)—H$

14.61 Give the name of the alcohol, aldehyde, or ketone produced from each of the following reactions: (14.3, 14.4)
a. oxidation of 1-propanol
b. oxidation of 2-pentanol
c. reduction of butanone
d. oxidation of cyclohexanol

14.62 Give the name of the alcohol, aldehyde, or ketone produced from each of the following reactions: (14.3, 14.4)
a. reduction of butyraldehyde
b. oxidation of 3-methyl-2-pentanol
c. reduction of 4-methyl-2-hexanone
d. oxidation of 3-methylcyclopentanol

14.63 Identify the following as hemiacetals or acetals. Give the names of the carbonyl compounds and alcohols used in their synthesis. (14.4)

a.
$$\text{O—CH}_3$$
$CH_3—CH_2—C—H$
$$\text{O—CH}_3$$

b.
$$\text{O—CH}_2—\text{CH}_3$$
$CH_3—CH_2—C—CH_3$
$$\text{OH}$$

c. 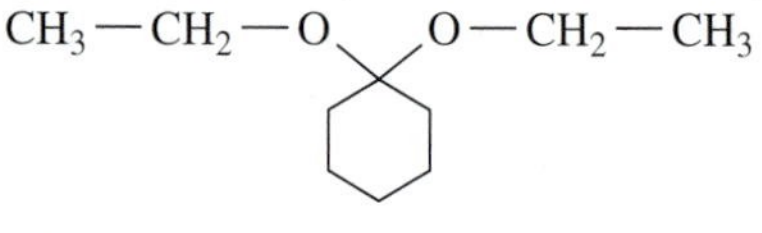 $CH_3—CH_2—O$, $O—CH_2—CH_3$ (cyclohexane ring)

14.64 Identify the following as hemiacetals or acetals. Give the names of the carbonyl compounds and alcohols used in their synthesis. (14.4)

a.
$$\text{O—CH}_3$$
$CH_3—CH_2—C—H$
$$\text{OH}$$

b. 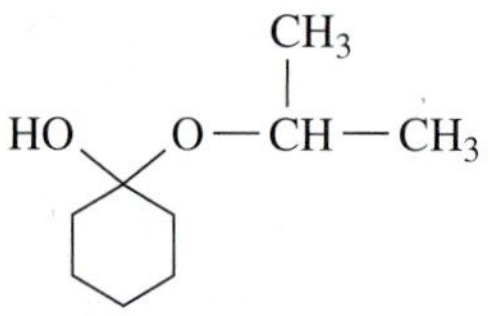
$$\text{CH}_3$$
HO , O—CH—CH₃ (cyclohexane ring)

c.
$$\text{O—CH}_2—\text{CH}_2—\text{CH}_3$$
$CH_3—C—H$
$$\text{O—CH}_2—\text{CH}_2—\text{CH}_3$$

CHALLENGE QUESTIONS

Use the following condensed structural and skeletal formulas **A** to **F** to answer Problems 14.65 and 14.66: (14.1, 14.5)

A CH$_3$—CH$_2$—C(=O)—CH$_2$—CH$_3$

B CH$_3$—CH$_2$—CH$_2$—C(=O)—CH$_3$

C CH$_3$—C(=O)—CH$_2$—CH$_2$—CH$_3$

D CH$_3$—CH$_2$—CH$_2$—CH$_2$—C(=O)—H

E (cyclopentanone skeletal structure)

F (cyclobutane with C(=O)—H skeletal structure)

14.65 True or False?
a. **A** and **B** are structural isomers.
b. **A** and **C** are the same compound.
c. **B** and **C** are the same compound.
d. **C** and **D** are structural isomers.

14.66 True or False?
a. **E** and **F** are structural isomers.
b. **A** is chiral.
c. **D** and **F** are aldehydes.
d. **B** and **E** are ketones.

14.67 A compound with the formula C_4H_8O is made by oxidation of 2-butanol and cannot be oxidized further. Draw the condensed structural formula and give the IUPAC name for the compound. (14.1, 14.3)

14.68 A compound with the formula C_4H_8O is made by oxidation of 2-methyl-1-propanol and oxidizes easily to give a carboxylic acid. Draw the condensed structural formula and give the IUPAC name for the compound. (14.1, 14.3)

14.69 Draw the condensed structural formulas and give the IUPAC names for all the aldehydes and ketones that have the molecular formula C_4H_8O. (14.1)

14.70 Draw the condensed structural formulas and give the IUPAC names for all the aldehydes and ketones that have the molecular formula $C_5H_{10}O$. (14.1)

14.71 Compound **A** is 1-propanol. When compound **A** is heated with a strong acid, it dehydrates to form compound **B** (C_3H_6). When compound **A** is oxidized, compound **C** (C_3H_6O) forms. Draw the condensed structural formulas and give the IUPAC names for compounds **A**, **B**, and **C**. (14.1, 14.3)

14.72 Compound **X** is 2-propanol. When compound **X** is heated with a strong acid, it dehydrates to form compound **Y** (C_3H_6). When compound **X** is oxidized, compound **Z** (C_3H_6O) forms, which cannot be oxidized further. Draw the condensed structural formulas and give the IUPAC names for compounds **X**, **Y**, and **Z**. (14.1, 14.3)

ANSWERS

Answers to Study Checks

14.1 5-methylhexanal

14.2 ethyl propyl ketone

14.3 The oxygen atom in the carbonyl group of acetone hydrogen bonds with water molecules.

14.4 The oxidation of benzaldehyde reduces Ag^+ to metallic silver, which forms a silvery coating on the walls of the test tube.

14.5 2-methyl-1-butanol

14.6 CH$_3$—C(O—CH$_3$)(O—CH$_3$)—CH$_2$—CH$_3$

14.7 HS—C(CH$_3$)—C(NH$_2$)(H)—C(=O)—OH

14.8
CHO with H—OH, CH$_3$ (D-2-Hydroxypropanal)
CHO with HO—H, CH$_3$ (L-2-Hydroxypropanal)

Answers to Selected Questions and Problems

14.1 a. ketone   b. aldehyde
c. ketone   d. aldehyde

14.3 a. structural isomers of C_3H_6O
b. structural isomers of $C_5H_{10}O$
c. not structural isomers

14.5 a. 3-bromobutanal   b. 2-pentanone
c. 2-methylcyclopentanone   d. 3-bromobenzaldehyde

14.7 a. acetaldehyde   b. methyl propyl ketone
c. formaldehyde

14.9 a. CH$_3$—C(=O)—H
b. CH$_3$—CH(CH$_3$)—C(=O)—CH$_2$—CH$_3$
c. CH$_3$—C(=O)—CH$_2$—CH$_2$—CH$_2$—CH$_3$
d. CH$_3$—CH$_2$—CH$_2$—CH(CH$_3$)—CH$_2$—C(=O)—H

14.11 (benzene ring with CHO at top and O—CH$_3$ at bottom)

14.13 a.

$$CH_3-\overset{\overset{\displaystyle O}{\|}}{C}-H$$

Ethanal has a higher boiling point than propane because the polar carbonyl group in ethanal forms dipole–dipole attractions.

b. Pentanal has a longer carbon chain, more electrons, and more dispersion forces, which give it a higher boiling point.

c. 1-Butanol has a higher boiling point because it can hydrogen bond with other 1-butanol molecules.

14.15 a.

$$CH_3-\overset{\overset{\displaystyle O}{\|}}{C}-\overset{\overset{\displaystyle O}{\|}}{C}-CH_2-CH_3 \text{ has two polar carbonyl}$$

groups and can form more hydrogen bonds with water.

b. Propanal has a shorter carbon chain than pentanal, in which the larger hydrocarbon chain reduces the impact on solubility of the polar carbonyl group.

c. Acetone has a shorter carbon chain than 2-pentanone, in which the larger hydrocarbon chain reduces the impact on solubility of the polar carbonyl group.

14.17 No. A hydrocarbon chain of eight carbon atoms reduces the impact on solubility of the polar carbonyl group.

14.19 a.

$$H-\overset{\overset{\displaystyle O}{\|}}{C}-OH$$

b. none

c.

$$\overset{\overset{\displaystyle O}{\|}}{\underset{\bigcirc}{C}}-OH$$

d. none

14.21 a. Tollens' reagent   **b.** neither   **c.** both

14.23 a. $CH_3-CH_2-CH_2-CH_2-OH$

b. $CH_3-\overset{\overset{\displaystyle OH}{|}}{CH}-CH_3$

c. $CH_3-CH_2-CH_2-\overset{\overset{\displaystyle Br}{|}}{CH}-CH_2-CH_2-OH$

d. $CH_3-\overset{\overset{\displaystyle CH_3}{|}}{CH}-\overset{\overset{\displaystyle OH}{|}}{CH}-CH_2-CH_3$

14.25 a. hemiacetal   **b.** hemiacetal   **c.** acetal
   d. hemiacetal   **e.** acetal

14.27 a. $CH_3-\overset{\overset{\displaystyle O-CH_3}{|}}{\underset{\underset{\displaystyle OH}{|}}{C}}-H$ **b.** $CH_3-\overset{\overset{\displaystyle O-CH_3}{|}}{\underset{\underset{\displaystyle OH}{|}}{C}}-CH_3$

c. $CH_3-CH_2-CH_2-\overset{\overset{\displaystyle O-CH_3}{|}}{\underset{\underset{\displaystyle OH}{|}}{C}}-H$

14.29 a. $CH_3-\overset{\overset{\displaystyle O-CH_3}{|}}{\underset{\underset{\displaystyle O-CH_3}{|}}{C}}-H$ **b.** $CH_3-\overset{\overset{\displaystyle O-CH_3}{|}}{\underset{\underset{\displaystyle O-CH_3}{|}}{C}}-CH_3$

c. $CH_3-CH_2-CH_2-\overset{\overset{\displaystyle O-CH_3}{|}}{\underset{\underset{\displaystyle O-CH_3}{|}}{C}}-H$

14.31 a. achiral
b. chiral

$$CH_3-\overset{\overset{\displaystyle Br}{|}\,\text{Chiral carbon}}{CH}-CH_2-CH_3$$

c. chiral

$$CH_3-\overset{\overset{\displaystyle Br}{|}}{CH}-\overset{\overset{\displaystyle O}{\|}}{C}-H \quad \text{Chiral carbon}$$

d. achiral

14.33 a.

$$CH_3-\overset{\overset{\displaystyle CH_3}{|}}{C}=CH-CH_2-CH_2-\overset{\overset{\displaystyle CH_3}{|}\,\text{Chiral carbon}}{CH}-CH_2-CH_2-OH$$

b.

$$H_2N-\overset{\overset{\displaystyle CH_3}{|}}{CH}-\overset{\overset{\displaystyle O}{\|}}{C}-OH$$

Chiral carbon

14.35 a.

$$HO-\!\!\!\overset{\displaystyle H}{\underset{\displaystyle CH_3}{\rule{2em}{0.4pt}}}\!\!\!-Br$$

b.

$$Cl-\!\!\!\overset{\displaystyle CH_3}{\underset{\displaystyle OH}{\rule{2em}{0.4pt}}}\!\!\!-Br$$

c.

$$HO-\!\!\!\overset{\displaystyle CHO}{\underset{\displaystyle CH_2CH_3}{\rule{2em}{0.4pt}}}\!\!\!-H$$

14.37 a. identical   **b.** enantiomers
    c. enantiomers   **d.** enantiomers

14.39 The $C=O$ double bond has a dipole because the oxygen atom is highly electronegative compared to the carbon atom. In the $C=C$ double bond, both atoms have the same electronegativity, and there is no dipole.

14.41 a and b

14.43

$$\overset{H}{\underset{CH_3-CH_2-CH_2}{}}C=C\overset{\overset{\displaystyle O}{\|}}{\underset{H}{\overset{}{}}}{C}-H$$

a. $CH_3-CH_2-CH_2$

b. $CH_3-\overset{\overset{\displaystyle CH_3}{|}}{C}=CH-CH_2-CH_2-\overset{\overset{\displaystyle CH_3}{|}}{CH}-\overset{\overset{\displaystyle O}{\|}}{C}-H$

14.45 a. 2-bromo-4-chlorocyclopentanone
b. 2,4-dibromobenzaldehyde
c. 3-chloropropanal
d. 5-chloro-3-hexanone
e. 2-chloro-3-pentanone

14.47 a.

b. $CH_3-CH_2-CH_2-CH_2-\overset{\displaystyle O}{\overset{\|}{C}}-H$

c. $CH_3-CH_2-\overset{\displaystyle O}{\overset{\|}{C}}-CH_3$

d. $CH_3-CH_2-\overset{\displaystyle CH_3}{\overset{|}{C}H}-CH_2-CH_2-\overset{\displaystyle O}{\overset{\|}{C}}-H$

14.49 a and **b**

14.51 a. $CH_3-CH_2-CH_2-OH$ **b.** $CH_3-CH_2-\overset{\displaystyle O}{\overset{\|}{C}}-H$
c. CH_3-CH_2-OH

14.53 a. $H-\overset{\displaystyle Cl}{\underset{\displaystyle Cl}{\overset{|}{\underset{|}{C}}}}-\overset{\displaystyle Cl}{\underset{\displaystyle H}{\overset{|}{\underset{|}{\textcircled{C}}}}}-OH$ **b.** none

c. none   **d.** $CH_3-\overset{\displaystyle NH_2}{\overset{|}{\textcircled{C}H}}-\overset{\displaystyle O}{\overset{\|}{C}}-H$

e. $CH_3-CH_2-\overset{\displaystyle Br}{\overset{|}{\textcircled{C}H}}-CH_2-CH_2-CH_3$
f. none

14.55 a. enantiomers   **b.** identical
c. identical   **d.** identical

14.57 a. $CH_3-CH_2-\overset{\displaystyle O}{\overset{\|}{C}}-H \xrightarrow[\text{oxidation}]{\text{Further}} CH_3-CH_2-\overset{\displaystyle O}{\overset{\|}{C}}-OH$

b. $CH_3-\overset{\displaystyle O}{\overset{\|}{C}}-CH_2-CH_2-CH_3$

c. $CH_3-CH_2-CH_2-\overset{\displaystyle O}{\overset{\|}{C}}-OH$ **d.**

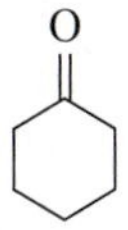

14.59 a. $CH_3-\overset{\displaystyle OH}{\overset{|}{C}H}-CH_3$

b.

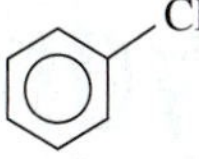

c. $CH_3-\overset{\displaystyle CH_3}{\overset{|}{C}H}-CH_2-\overset{\displaystyle OH}{\overset{|}{C}H}-CH_3$

14.61 a. propanal   **b.** 2-pentanone
c. 2-butanol   **d.** cyclohexanone

14.63 a. acetal; propanal and methanol
b. hemiacetal; butanone and ethanol
c. acetal; cyclohexanone and ethanol

14.65 a. true   **b.** false   **c.** true   **d.** true

14.67 $CH_3-\overset{\displaystyle O}{\overset{\|}{C}}-CH_2-CH_3$ Butanone

14.69 $CH_3-CH_2-CH_2-\overset{\displaystyle O}{\overset{\|}{C}}-H$ Butanal

$CH_3-\overset{\displaystyle CH_3}{\overset{|}{C}H}-\overset{\displaystyle O}{\overset{\|}{C}}-H$ 2-Methylpropanal

$CH_3-\overset{\displaystyle O}{\overset{\|}{C}}-CH_2-CH_3$ Butanone

14.71 A $CH_3-CH_2-CH_2-OH$ 1-propanol
B $CH_3-CH=CH_2$ propene
C $CH_3-CH_2-\overset{\displaystyle O}{\overset{\|}{C}}-H$ propanal

15

Carbohydrates

Visit **www.masteringchemistry.com** for self-study materials and instructor-assigned homework.

Kate and Paula proceed to plan several meals. Because a meal should contain about 45–60 grams of carbohydrates, they combine fruits and vegetables in the same meal that have high and low levels of carbohydrates, in order to stay within the recommended range. Kate and Paula also discuss the fact that complex carbohydrates in the body take longer to break down into glucose and, therefore, raise the blood sugar more gradually.

Career: Diabetes Nurse

Diabetes nurses teach patients about diabetes, so they can self-manage and control their condition. This includes education on proper diets and nutrition for both diabetic and pre-diabetic patients. Diabetes nurses help patients learn to monitor their medication, blood sugar levels, and to look for symptoms like diabetic nerve damage and vision loss. Diabetes nurses may also work with patients who have been hospitalized due to complications from their disease. This requires a thorough knowledge of the endocrine system, as this system is often involved with obesity and other diseases, resulting in some overlap between diabetes and endocrinology nursing. In fact, children with type I diabetes are the most common patient for endocrinology pediatric nurses.

Kate has recently been diagnosed as having type 2 diabetes. Her doctor recommends that she takes a series of educational courses taught by Paula, a diabetes nurse, who teaches Kate to test her blood glucose levels before and after a meal. Paula explains to Kate that her pre-meal number should be 110 mg/dL or less, and if it increases by more than 50 mg/dL, she needs to lower the amount of carbohydrates she consumes. Complex carbohydrates are long chains of glucose molecules that we obtain from ingesting breads and grains. They are broken down in the body into glucose, which is a simple carbohydrate or a monosaccharide.

Carbohydrates are the most abundant of all the organic compounds in nature. In plants, energy from the Sun converts carbon dioxide and water into the carbohydrate glucose. Many of the glucose molecules are made into long-chain polymers of starch that store energy or into cellulose to build the structural framework of the plant. About 65% of the foods in our diet consist of carbohydrates. Each day, we utilize carbohydrates, known as *starches*, in foods such as bread, pasta, potatoes, and rice.

Other carbohydrates called *disaccharides* include sucrose (table sugar) and lactose in milk. During digestion and cellular metabolism, carbohydrates are oxidized in our cells to provide our bodies with energy and to provide the cells with carbon atoms for building molecules of proteins, lipids, and nucleic acids. Cellulose from plants has other important uses, too. The wood in our furniture, the pages in this book, and the cotton in our clothing are made of cellulose.

Carbohydrates contained in foods such as pasta and bread provide energy for the body.

15.1 Carbohydrates

Carbohydrates such as table sugar, lactose, and cellulose are all made of carbon, hydrogen, and oxygen. Simple sugars, which have formulas of $C_n(H_2O)_n$, were once thought to be hydrates of carbon, thus the name *carbohydrate*. In a series of reactions in plant cells called *photosynthesis*, energy from the Sun is used to combine the carbon atoms from carbon dioxide (CO_2) and the hydrogen and oxygen atoms of water into the carbohydrate glucose.

$$6CO_2 + 6H_2O + energy \underset{\text{Respiration}}{\overset{\text{Photosynthesis}}{\rightleftharpoons}} \underset{\text{Glucose}}{C_6H_{12}O_6} + 6O_2$$

In the body, glucose is oxidized in a series of metabolic reactions known as *respiration*, which releases chemical energy to do work in the cells. Carbon dioxide and water are produced and returned to the atmosphere. The combination of photosynthesis and respiration is called the *carbon cycle*, in which energy from the Sun is stored in plants by photosynthesis and made available to us when the carbohydrates in our diets are metabolized (see Figure 15.1).

Types of Carbohydrates

The simplest carbohydrates are the **monosaccharides**. A monosaccharide cannot be split or hydrolyzed into smaller carbohydrates. One of the most common carbohydrates, glucose, $C_6H_{12}O_6$, is a monosaccharide. A **disaccharide** consists of two monosaccharide units joined together, which can be split into two monosaccharide units. For example, ordinary table sugar, sucrose, $C_{12}H_{22}O_{11}$, is a disaccharide that can be split by water (hydrolysis) in the presence of an acid or an enzyme to give one molecule of glucose and one molecule of another monosaccharide, fructose.

$$\underset{\text{Sucrose}}{C_{12}H_{22}O_{11}} + H_2O \xrightarrow{\text{H}^+ \text{ or enzyme}} \underset{\text{Glucose}}{C_6H_{12}O_6} + \underset{\text{Fructose}}{C_6H_{12}O_6}$$

LEARNING GOAL

Classify a monosaccharide as an aldose or ketose, and indicate the number of carbon atoms.

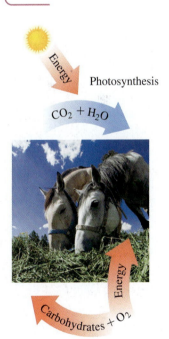

FIGURE 15.1 During photosynthesis, energy from the Sun combines CO_2 and H_2O to form glucose ($C_6H_{12}O_6$) and O_2. During respiration in the body, carbohydrates are oxidized to CO_2 and H_2O, while energy is produced.

Q What are the products of respiration?

SELF-STUDY ACTIVITY
Carbohydrates

TUTORIAL
Carbohydrates

Polysaccharides are carbohydrates that are naturally occurring polymers containing many monosaccharide units. In the presence of an acid or an enzyme, a polysaccharide can be completely hydrolyzed to yield many molecules of monosaccharide.

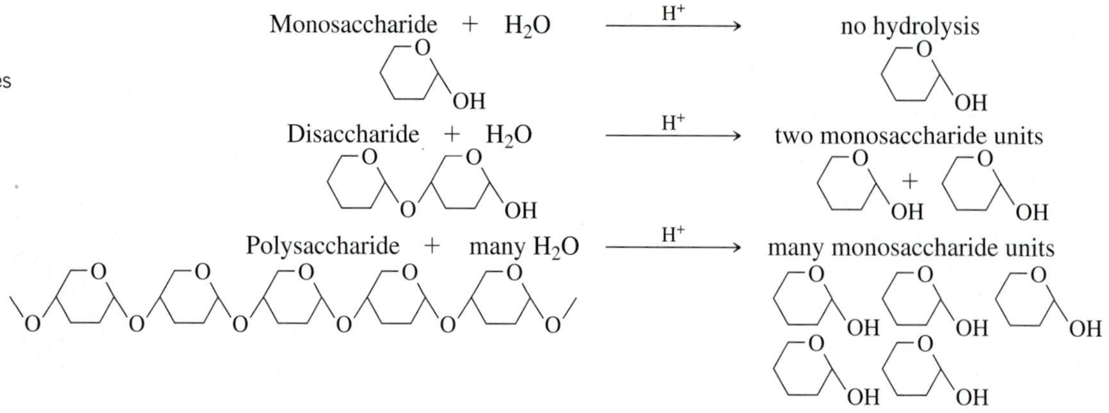

Monosaccharide + H_2O $\xrightarrow{H^+}$ no hydrolysis

Disaccharide + H_2O $\xrightarrow{H^+}$ two monosaccharide units

Polysaccharide + many H_2O $\xrightarrow{H^+}$ many monosaccharide units

TUTORIAL
Types of Carbohydrates

TUTORIAL
Carbonyls in Carbohydrates

Monosaccharides

Monosaccharides are sugars that have a chain of three to eight carbon atoms, one in a carbonyl group and the rest attached to hydroxyl groups. There are two types of monosaccharide structures. In an **aldose**, the carbonyl group is on the first carbon as an aldehyde, whereas a **ketose** contains the carbonyl group on the second carbon atom as a ketone.

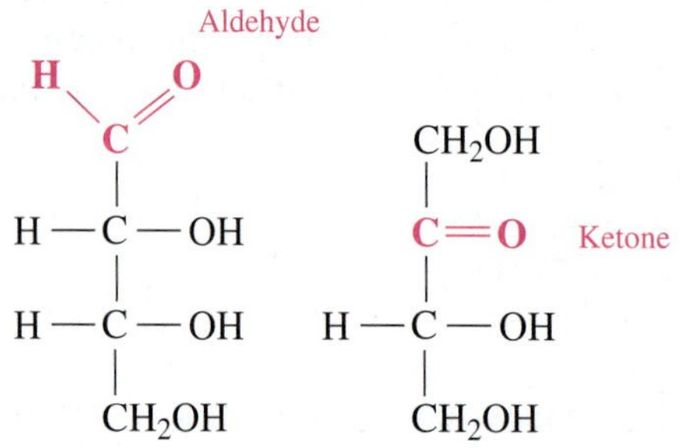

Erythrose, an aldose

Erythrulose, a ketose

A monosaccharide with three carbon atoms is a *triose*, one with four carbon atoms is a *tetrose*, a *pentose* has five carbons, and a *hexose* contains six carbons. We can use both classification systems to indicate the type of carbonyl group and the number of carbon atoms. An aldopentose is a five-carbon monosaccharide that is an aldehyde; a ketohexose would be a six-carbon monosaccharide that is a ketone.

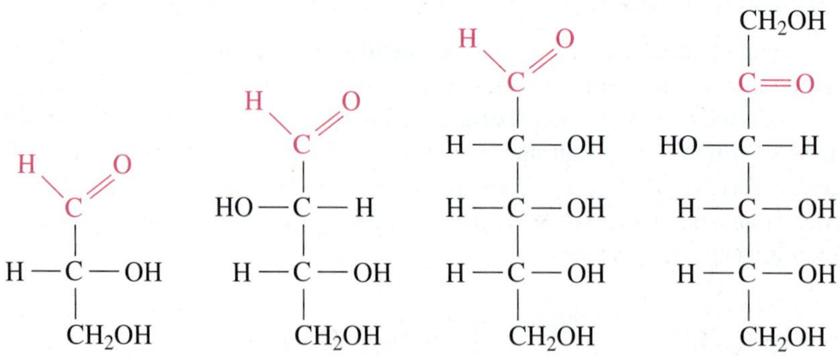

Glyceraldehyde (aldotriose)

Threose (aldotetrose)

Ribose (aldopentose)

Fructose (ketohexose)

CONCEPT CHECK 15.1   **Monosaccharides**

Classify each of the following monosaccharides as an aldopentose, aldohexose, keto-pentose, or ketohexose:

a. 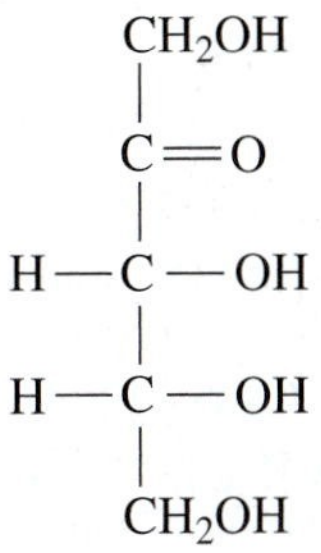
$$
\begin{array}{c}
CH_2OH \\
| \\
C{=}O \\
| \\
H{-}C{-}OH \\
| \\
H{-}C{-}OH \\
| \\
CH_2OH
\end{array}
$$
Ribulose

b. 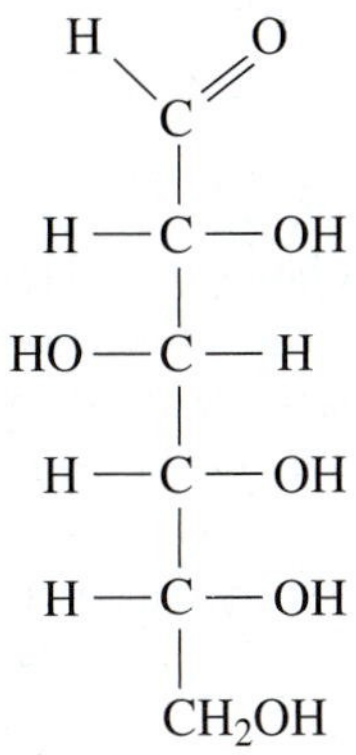
$$
\begin{array}{c}
H\!\diagdown\!{C}{\diagup}\!O \\
| \\
H{-}C{-}OH \\
| \\
HO{-}C{-}H \\
| \\
H{-}C{-}OH \\
| \\
H{-}C{-}OH \\
| \\
CH_2OH
\end{array}
$$
Glucose

ANSWER

a. Ribulose has five carbon atoms (pentose) and a ketone group; ribulose is a ketopentose.

b. Glucose has six carbon atoms (hexose) and an aldehyde group; glucose is an aldohexose.

QUESTIONS AND PROBLEMS

15.1 Carbohydrates

LEARNING GOAL: *Classify a monosaccharide as an aldose or ketose, and indicate the number of carbon atoms.*

15.1 What reactants are needed for photosynthesis and respiration?

15.2 What is the relationship between photosynthesis and respiration?

15.3 What is a monosaccharide? A disaccharide?

15.4 What is a polysaccharide?

15.5 What functional groups are found in all monosaccharides?

15.6 What is the difference between an aldose and a ketose?

15.7 What are the functional groups and number of carbons in a ketopentose?

15.8 What are the functional groups and number of carbons in an aldoheptose?

15.9 Classify each of the following monosaccharides as an aldopentose, aldohexose, ketopentose, or ketohexose:

a. 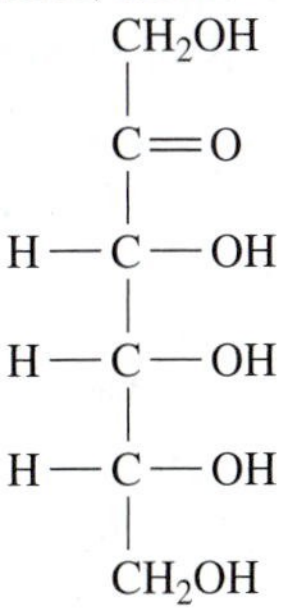
$$
\begin{array}{c}
CH_2OH \\
| \\
C{=}O \\
| \\
H{-}C{-}OH \\
| \\
H{-}C{-}OH \\
| \\
H{-}C{-}OH \\
| \\
CH_2OH
\end{array}
$$
Psicose

b. 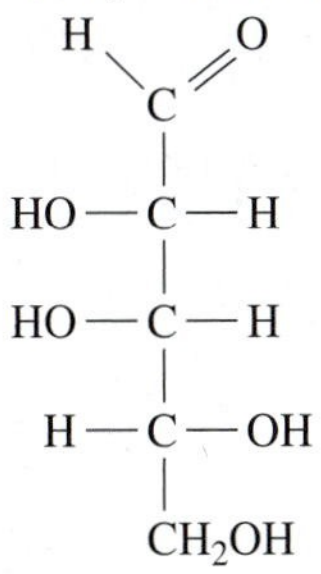
$$
\begin{array}{c}
H\!\diagdown\!{C}{\diagup}\!O \\
| \\
HO{-}C{-}H \\
| \\
HO{-}C{-}H \\
| \\
H{-}C{-}OH \\
| \\
CH_2OH
\end{array}
$$
Lyxose

15.10 Classify each of the following monosaccharides as an aldopentose, aldohexose, ketopentose, or ketohexose:

a. 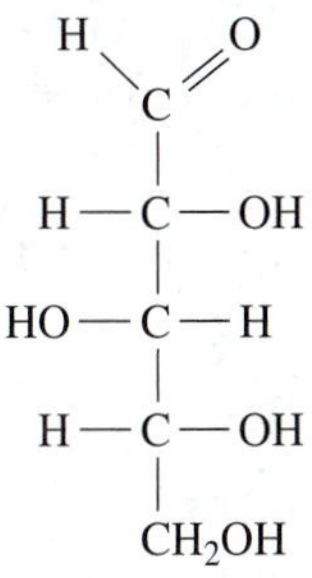
$$
\begin{array}{c}
H\!\diagdown\!{C}{\diagup}\!O \\
| \\
H{-}C{-}OH \\
| \\
HO{-}C{-}H \\
| \\
H{-}C{-}OH \\
| \\
CH_2OH
\end{array}
$$
Xylose

b. 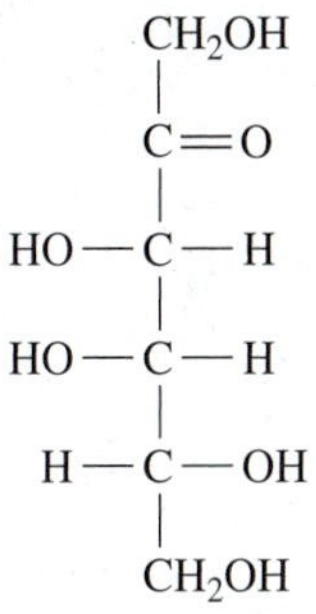
$$
\begin{array}{c}
CH_2OH \\
| \\
C{=}O \\
| \\
HO{-}C{-}H \\
| \\
HO{-}C{-}H \\
| \\
H{-}C{-}OH \\
| \\
CH_2OH
\end{array}
$$
Tagatose

LEARNING GOAL

Use Fischer projections to draw the D or L stereoisomers of glucose, galactose, and fructose.

SELF-STUDY ACTIVITY
Forms of Carbohydrates

TUTORIAL
Identifying D and L Sugars

TUTORIAL
Identifying Chiral Carbons in Monosaccharides

TUTORIAL
Drawing Fischer Projections of Monosaccharides

15.2 Fischer Projections of Monosaccharides

In Section 14.5, we learned that chiral compounds exist as mirror images that cannot be superimposed. Many monosaccharides exist as mirror images.

Fischer Projections

A Fischer projection for the simplest aldose, glyceraldehyde, is drawn with vertical and horizontal lines that represent the carbon chain. The aldehyde group (the most oxidized carbon) is placed at the top of the vertical line and the —H and —OH groups are on the horizontal intersecting line. In L-glyceraldehyde, the letter L is assigned to the stereoisomer with the —OH group on the left of the chiral carbon. In D-glyceraldehyde, the —OH group is on the right. The carbon atom in the $—CH_2OH$ group at the bottom of the Fischer projection is not chiral, because it does not have four different groups bonded to it.

L-Glyceraldehyde

D-Glyceraldehyde

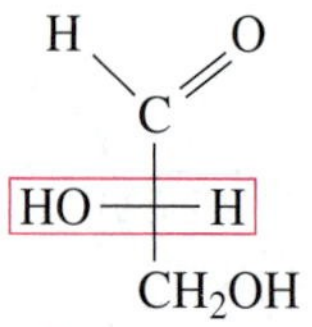

Most of the monosaccharides we will study have carbon chains consisting of five or six carbon atoms with several chiral carbons. As we discussed in Section 14.5, the —OH group on the chiral carbon *farthest* from the carbonyl group is used to determine the D or L stereoisomer. The following are the Fischer projections for the D and L stereoisomers of ribose, a five-carbon monosaccharide, and the D and L stereoisomers of glucose, a six-carbon monosaccharide. The vertical carbon chain is numbered starting from the top carbon.

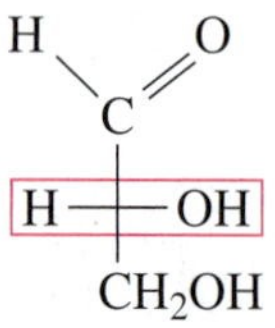

In each pair of mirror images, it is important to see that all of the —OH groups on chiral carbon atoms are reversed so that they appear on the opposite sides of the molecule. For example, in L-ribose, all of the —OH groups drawn on the left side of the vertical line are drawn on the right side in the mirror image of D-ribose.

L-Ribose D-Ribose L-Glucose D-Glucose

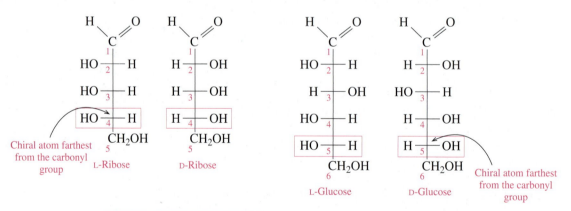

SAMPLE PROBLEM 15.1 **Identifying D and L Stereoisomers of Sugars**

Identify the Fischer projection of xylose as D- or L-xylose.

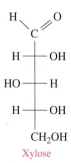

Xylose

SOLUTION

Analyze the Problem

Need to Identify	Procedure
Carbon Chain	Number the carbon chain starting at the top of the Fischer projection.
Chiral Carbon	Chiral carbon 4 has the highest number.
Position of —OH Group	The —OH group is drawn on the right of carbon 4, which makes it D-xylose.

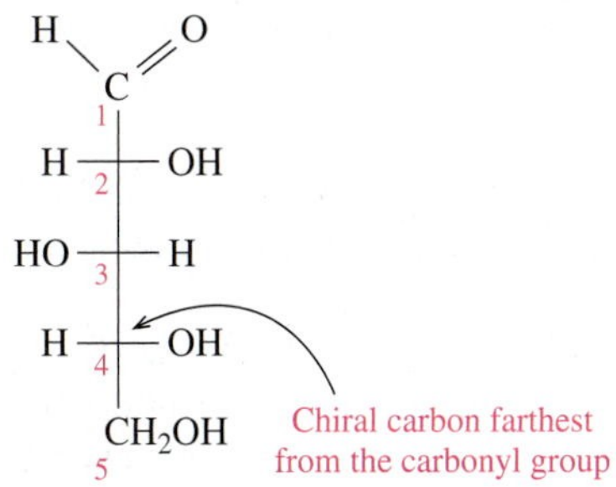

H–C=O
H–OH (2)
HO–H (3)
H–OH (4)
CH₂OH (5)

Chiral carbon farthest
from the carbonyl group

D-Xylose

STUDY CHECK 15.1

Draw the Fischer projection for L-xylose.

Some Important Monosaccharides

The hexoses glucose, galactose, and fructose are the most important monosaccharides. They are all hexoses with the molecular formula $C_6H_{12}O_6$ and are isomers of each other. Although we can draw Fischer projections for their D and L stereoisomers, the D stereoisomers are commonly found in nature and used in the cells of the body. The Fischer projections for the D stereoisomers are drawn as follows:

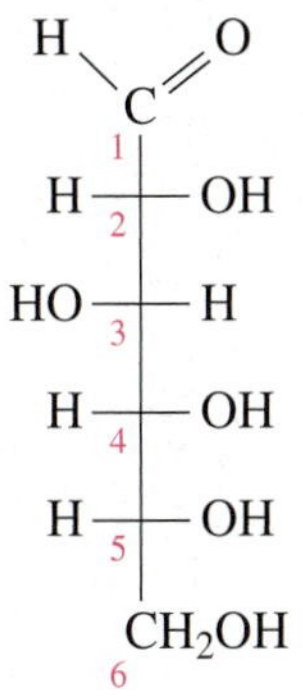

D-Glucose

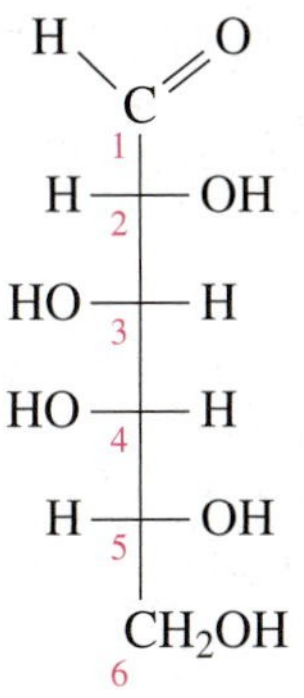

D-Galactose

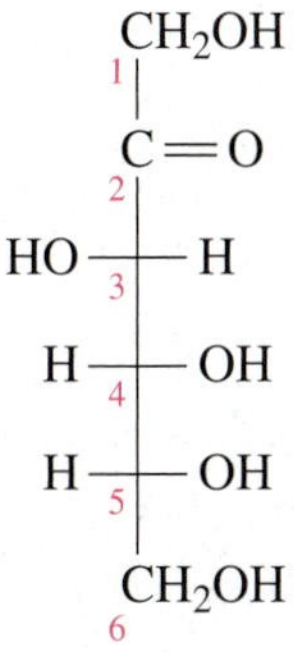

D-Fructose

The most common hexose, **D-glucose**, $C_6H_{12}O_6$, also known as dextrose and blood sugar, is found in fruits, vegetables, corn syrup, and honey. D-glucose is a building block of the disaccharides sucrose, lactose, and maltose, and polysaccharides such as amylose, cellulose, and glycogen.

In the body, glucose normally occurs at a concentration of 70–90 mg/dL (1 dL = 100 mL) of blood. Excess glucose is converted to glycogen and stored in the liver and muscle. When the amount of glucose exceeds what is needed for energy or glycogen, the excess glucose is converted to fat, which can be stored in unlimited amounts.

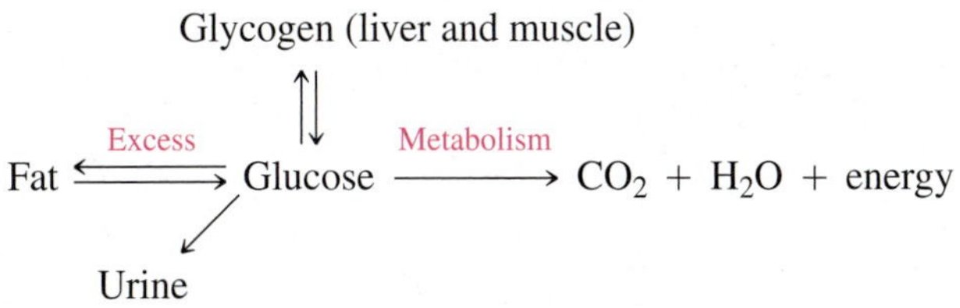

CASE STUDY
Diabetes and Blood Glucose

Glycogen (liver and muscle)

Fat ⇌ Glucose ⟶ $CO_2 + H_2O$ + energy

Excess   Metabolism

Urine

Galactose, $C_6H_{12}O_6$, is an aldohexose that is obtained from the disaccharide lactose, which is found in milk and milk products. Galactose is important in the cellular membranes of the brain and nervous system. The only difference in the Fischer projections of D-glucose and D-galactose is the arrangement of the —OH group on carbon 4.

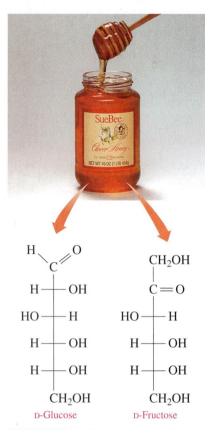

FIGURE 15.2 The sweet taste of honey is due to the monosaccharides D-glucose and D-fructose.

Q What are some differences in the Fischer projections of D-glucose and D-fructose?

In a condition called *galactosemia*, an enzyme needed to convert galactose to glucose is missing. The accumulation of galactose in the blood and tissues can lead to cataracts, mental retardation, failure to thrive, and liver disease. The treatment for galactosemia is the removal of all galactose-containing foods, mainly milk and milk products, from the diet. If this is done for an infant immediately after birth, the damaging effects of galactose accumulation can be avoided.

In contrast to glucose and galactose, **fructose**, $C_6H_{12}O_6$, is a ketohexose. The structure of fructose differs from glucose at carbons 1 and 2 by the location of the carbonyl group. Fructose is the sweetest of the carbohydrates, almost twice as sweet as sucrose (table sugar). This characteristic makes fructose popular with dieters because less fructose, and therefore fewer calories, is needed to provide a pleasant taste. Fructose, also called levulose and fruit sugar, is found in fruit juices and honey (see Figure 15.2).

Fructose is also obtained as one of the hydrolysis products of sucrose, the disaccharide known as table sugar. High-fructose corn syrup (HFCS) is a sweetener that is produced by using an enzyme to break down sucrose to glucose and fructose. An HFCS mixture containing about 50% fructose and 50% glucose is used in soft drinks and many foods, such as baked goods.

SAMPLE PROBLEM 15.2 Monosaccharides

Ribulose has the following Fischer projection:

$$
\begin{array}{c}
\text{CH}_2\text{OH} \\
|\\
\text{C}=\text{O} \\
\text{HO}-\!\!\!-\!\!\!-\text{H} \\
\text{H}-\!\!\!-\!\!\!-\text{OH} \\
|\\
\text{CH}_2\text{OH}
\end{array}
$$

a. Identify the compound as D- or L-ribulose.

b. Draw the Fischer projection of its mirror image.

SOLUTION

Analyze the Problem

Need to Identify	Procedure
Carbon Chain	Number the carbon chain starting at the top of the Fischer projection.
Chiral Carbon	Chiral carbon 4 has the highest number.
Position of —OH Group	The —OH group is drawn on the right side of carbon 4, which makes it D-ribulose.
Mirror Image	The —OH groups on the chiral carbons are drawn on the opposite side.

a. The compound is D-ribulose because the —OH group on the chiral carbon farthest from the carbonyl group is drawn on the right side.

$$
\begin{array}{c}
\overset{1}{\text{CH}_2\text{OH}} \\
|\\
\overset{2}{\text{C}}=\text{O} \\
\text{H}-\overset{3}{\underset{}{}}-\text{OH} \\
\text{H}-\overset{4}{\underset{}{}}-\text{OH} \\
\overset{5}{\text{CH}_2\text{OH}}
\end{array}
$$

D-Ribulose

b. To draw the mirror image, all the —OH groups on the chiral carbon atoms are drawn on the opposite side. L-Ribulose has the following Fischer projection:

$$
\begin{array}{c}
\text{CH}_2\text{OH} \\
| \\
\text{C}=\text{O} \\
\text{HO}\!-\!\!\!-\!\text{H} \\
\text{HO}\!-\!\!\!-\!\text{H} \\
\text{CH}_2\text{OH}
\end{array}
$$

L-Ribulose

STUDY CHECK 15.2

Classify ribulose as an aldopentose, aldohexose, or ketohexose.

Chemistry Link to Health

HYPERGLYCEMIA AND HYPOGLYCEMIA

A doctor may order a glucose tolerance test to evaluate the body's ability to return to normal glucose concentrations (70–90 mg/dL) in response to the ingestion of a specified amount of glucose. The patient fasts for 12 h and then drinks a solution containing glucose. A blood sample is taken immediately, followed by more blood samples each half-hour for 2 h, and then every hour for a total of 5 h. If the blood glucose exceeds 200 mg/dL in plasma and remains high, hyperglycemia may be indicated. The term *glyc* or *gluco* refers to "sugar." The prefix *hyper* means above or over, *hypo* means below or under, and the suffix *emia* means "in the blood." Thus, the blood sugar level in *hyperglycemia* is above normal and, in *hypoglycemia*, it is below normal.

An example of a disease that can cause hyperglycemia is diabetes mellitus, which occurs when the pancreas is unable to produce sufficient quantities of insulin. As a result, glucose levels in the body fluids can rise as high as 350 mg/dL of plasma. Symptoms of diabetes in people under the age of 40 include thirst, excessive urination, increased appetite, and weight loss. In older adults, diabetes is sometimes a consequence of excessive weight gain.

When a person is hypoglycemic, the blood glucose level rises and then decreases rapidly to levels as low as 40 mg/dL of plasma. In some cases, hypoglycemia is caused by overproduction of insulin by the pancreas. Low blood glucose can cause dizziness, general weakness, and muscle tremors. A diet may be prescribed that consists of several small meals high in protein and low in carbohydrate. Some hypoglycemic patients are finding success with diets that include more complex carbohydrates rather than simple sugars.

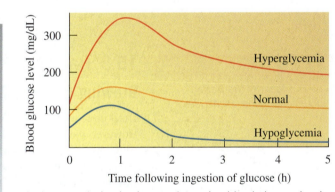

A glucose solution is given to determine blood glucose levels.

QUESTIONS AND PROBLEMS

15.2 Fischer Projections of Monosaccharides

LEARNING GOAL: *Use Fischer projections to draw the D or L stereoisomers of glucose, galactose, and fructose.*

15.11 How is a Fischer projection identified as a D or L stereoisomer?

15.12 Draw the Fischer projection for D-glyceraldehyde and L-glyceraldehyde.

15.13 Identify each of the following as the D or L stereoisomer:

a.
$$
\begin{array}{c}
\text{H}\!\diagdown\!\!\!\!\diagup\!\text{O} \\
\text{C} \\
\text{HO}\!-\!\!\!-\!\text{H} \\
\text{H}\!-\!\!\!-\!\text{OH} \\
\text{CH}_2\text{OH}
\end{array}
$$

Threose

b.
$$
\begin{array}{c}
\text{CH}_2\text{OH} \\
| \\
\text{C}=\text{O} \\
\text{HO}\!-\!\!\!-\!\text{H} \\
\text{H}\!-\!\!\!-\!\text{OH} \\
\text{CH}_2\text{OH}
\end{array}
$$

Xylulose

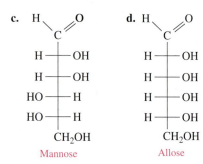

c. Mannose

d. Allose

15.14 Identify each of the following as the D or L stereoisomer:

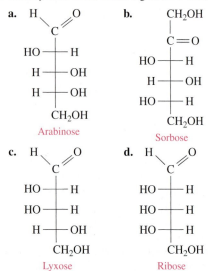

a. Arabinose

b. Sorbose

c. Lyxose

d. Ribose

15.15 Draw the Fischer projections for the mirror images of molecules **a** to **d** in Problem 15.13.

15.16 Draw the Fischer projections for the mirror images of molecules **a** to **d** in Problem 15.14.

15.17 Draw the Fischer projections for D-glucose and L-glucose.

15.18 Draw the Fischer projections for D-fructose and L-fructose.

15.19 How does the Fischer projection for D-galactose differ from that of D-glucose?

15.20 How does the Fischer projection for D-fructose differ from that of D-glucose?

15.21 Identify the monosaccharide that fits each of the following descriptions:
   a. is also called blood sugar
   b. is not metabolized in galactosemia
   c. is also called fruit sugar

15.22 Identify the monosaccharide that fits each of the following descriptions:
   a. high levels are found in the blood of diabetics
   b. is obtained as a hydrolysis product of lactose
   c. is the sweetest of the monosaccharides

15.3 Haworth Structures of Monosaccharides

Drawing Haworth Structures for Cyclic Forms

Until now, we have drawn the Fischer projections of monosaccharides as open chains. However, the most stable form of pentoses and hexoses are five- or six-atom rings. These rings, known as **Haworth structures**, are produced from the reaction of a carbonyl group and a hydroxyl group in the *same* molecule, which forms a *cyclic hemiacetal*. For example, the following diagram shows that the oxygen atom in the hydroxyl group on carbon 5 of an aldohexose bonds with carbon 1 in the carbonyl and produces a six-atom cyclic hemiacetal.

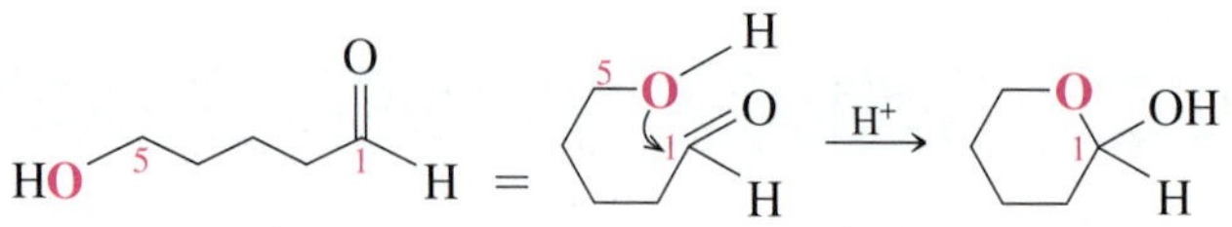

Open chain $\xrightarrow{\text{H}^+}$ Cyclic hemiacetal

We will now show how to draw the Haworth structure for D-glucose from its Fischer projection.

Step 1 **Turn the Fischer projection for D-glucose clockwise by 90°.** The —H and —OH groups on the right of the vertical carbon chain are now below the horizontal carbon chain. Those on the left of the vertical carbon chain are now above the horizontal carbon chain.

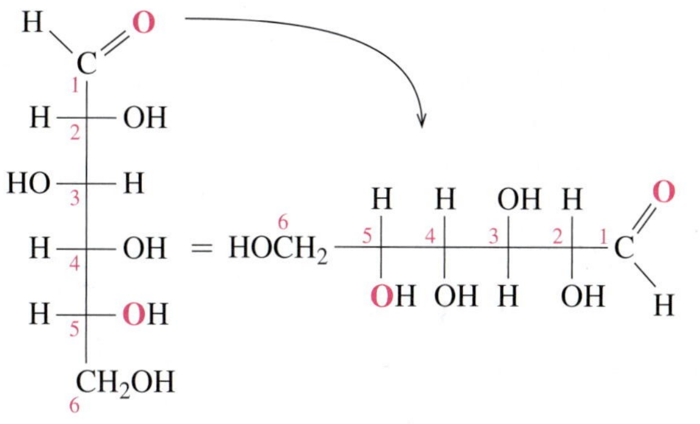

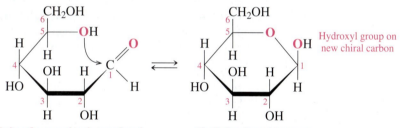

D-Glucose (open chain)

Step 2 **Fold the horizontal carbon chain into a hexagon and bond the O on carbon 5 to the carbonyl group to form the hemiacetal.** With carbons 2 and 3 as the base of the hexagon, move the remaining carbons upward. Draw the reacting —OH group on carbon 5 next to the carbonyl carbon 1. Draw carbon 6 in the —CH_2OH group above carbon 5. To complete the Haworth structure, draw a bond between the oxygen of the —OH group on carbon 5 to the carbonyl carbon.

Carbon-5 oxygen bonds to carbonyl   Cyclic hemiacetal structure

Hydroxyl group on new chiral carbon

Step 3 **Complete the Haworth structure by drawing the —OH group on carbon 1 below the ring to give the α anomer, or above the ring to give the β anomer.** Because the new —OH group can form above or below the plane of the Haworth structure, there are two stereoisomers of D-glucose called **anomers**, which differ only by the configurations of the —OH group at carbon 1. In one configuration called the α (alpha) anomer, the —OH group is drawn below the plane of the ring. In the other configuration called the β (beta) anomer, the —OH group is drawn above the plane of the ring. Carbon 1 in the hemiacetal is referred to as the *anomeric carbon*.

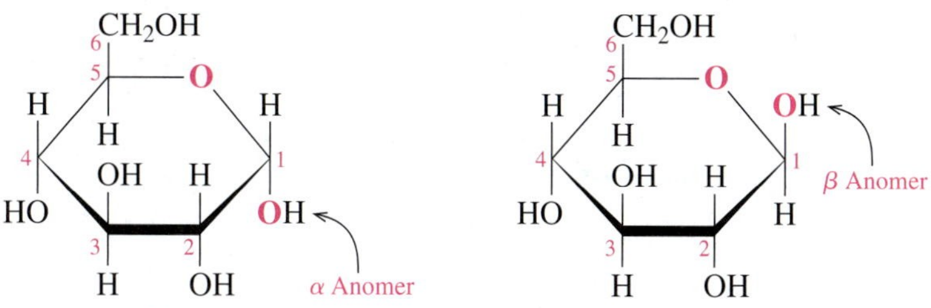

α Anomer

β Anomer

α-D-Glucose   β-D-Glucose

SAMPLE PROBLEM 15.3   **Drawing Haworth Structures for Sugars**

D-Mannose, a carbohydrate found in immunoglobulins, has the following Fischer projection. Draw the Haworth structure for β-D-mannose.

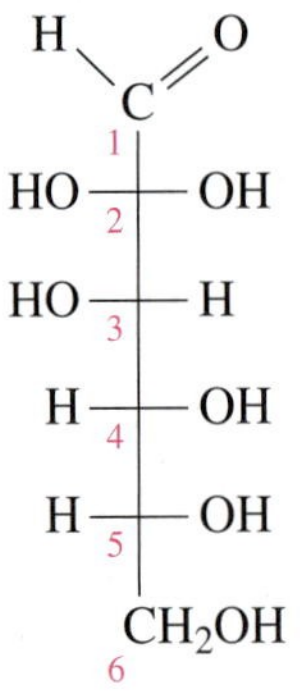

D-Mannose

Guide to Drawing Haworth Structures

1 Turn the Fischer projection clockwise by 90°.

2 Fold the horizontal carbon chain into a hexagon and bond the O on carbon 5 to the carbonyl group to form the hemiacetal.

3 Complete the Haworth structure by drawing the —OH group on carbon 1 below the ring to give the α anomer, or above the ring to give the β anomer.

SOLUTION

Step 1 Turn the Fischer projection clockwise by 90°.

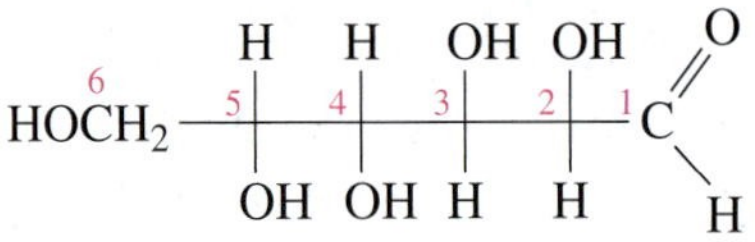

Step 2 **Fold the horizontal carbon chain into a hexagon and bond the O on carbon 5 to the carbonyl group to form the hemiacetal.** Draw the —CH$_2$OH group above carbon 5 and the —OH group next to the carbonyl. Draw a bond between the O of the —OH group (carbon 5) and carbon 1 of the carbonyl group, which forms the hemiacetal.

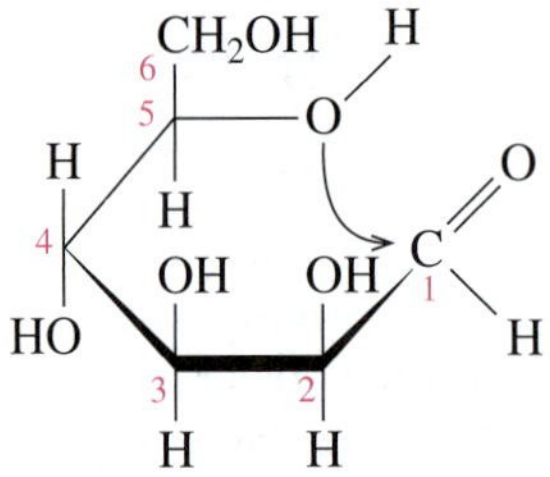

Step 3 **Complete the Haworth structure by drawing the —OH group on carbon 1 below the ring to give the α anomer, or above the ring to give the β anomer.** To draw the β anomer of mannose, we need to draw the —OH group on carbon 1 above the ring.

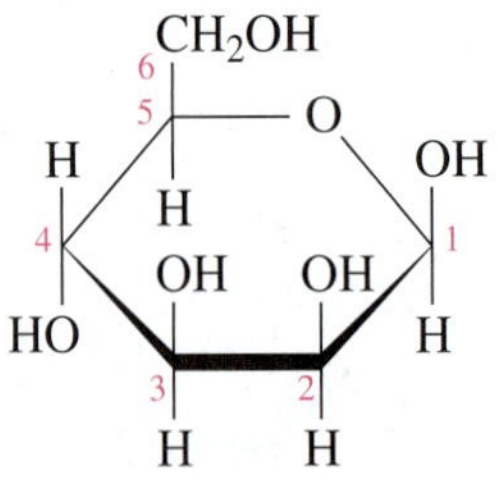

β-D-Mannose

STUDY CHECK 15.3

Draw the Haworth structure for α-D-mannose.

Mutarotation of α- and β-D-Glucose

In aqueous solution, the Haworth structure of α-D-glucose opens to give the open chain of D-glucose, which has an aldehyde group. However, the open chain can close because the carbonyl group reacts quickly to form the cyclic hemiacetal. As the ring opens and closes, the hydroxyl group (—OH) on carbon 1 can form either the α or the β anomer. This process, called **mutarotation**, continuously converts both anomers to the open chain and back to a cyclic hemiacetal. At equilibrium, a glucose solution contains a mixture of 36% of the α anomer and 64% of the β anomer. Although the open chain is an essential part of mutarotation, only a trace amount of the open chain is present at any given time.

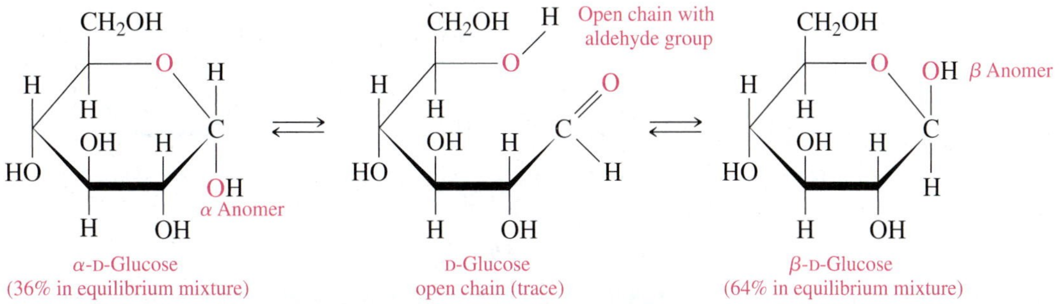

α-D-Glucose
(36% in equilibrium mixture)

D-Glucose
open chain (trace)

β-D-Glucose
(64% in equilibrium mixture)

Haworth Structures of Galactose

Galactose is an aldohexose that differs from glucose only in the arrangement of the —OH group on carbon 4. Thus, its Haworth structure is similar to glucose, except that in galactose, the —OH group on carbon 4 is above the plane of the ring. Similar to glucose, galactose also exists as α and β anomers because it undergoes mutarotation to produce an open chain with an aldehyde group in aqueous solution.

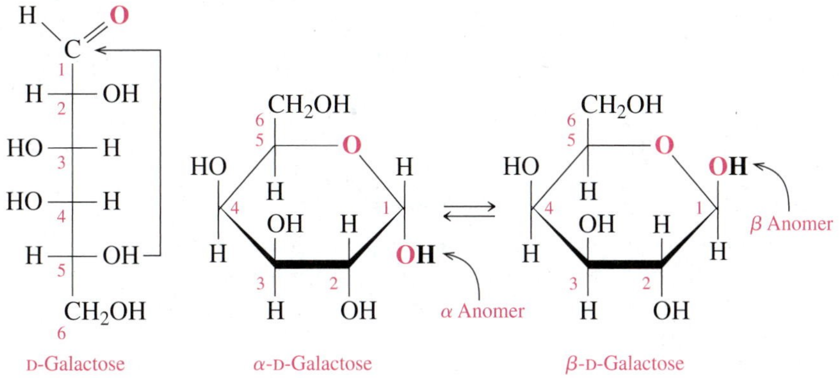

D-Galactose

α-D-Galactose

β-D-Galactose

CONCEPT CHECK 15.2   Anomers

a. Why is the Haworth structure of D-galactose a hemiacetal?
b. What is the difference between α and β anomers of D-galactose?

ANSWER

a. Galactose is a hemiacetal because it has both a hydroxyl group and an alkoxy group bonded to the same carbon, in this case, carbon 1.
b. When the hemiacetal forms, a free —OH group appears on carbon 1. Thus, two stereoisomers called *anomers* are possible because the —OH group can form above or below the ring. In the α anomer, the —OH group is drawn below the plane of the ring, and for the β anomer, the —OH group is drawn above the plane of the ring.

Haworth Structures of Fructose

In contrast to glucose and galactose, fructose is a ketohexose. Thus, the hemiacetal group for the Haworth structure of fructose forms between the —OH group on carbon 5 and carbon 2 of the ketone group to make a five-atom ring. In fructose, the anomeric carbon, which is carbon 2, is bonded to an —OH group and a $—CH_2OH$ group (carbon 1). The mutarotation of the hemiacetal (carbon 2) gives fructose α and β anomers. Note that the $—CH_2OH$ group (carbon 1) is drawn in the opposite direction of the —OH group in the anomers.

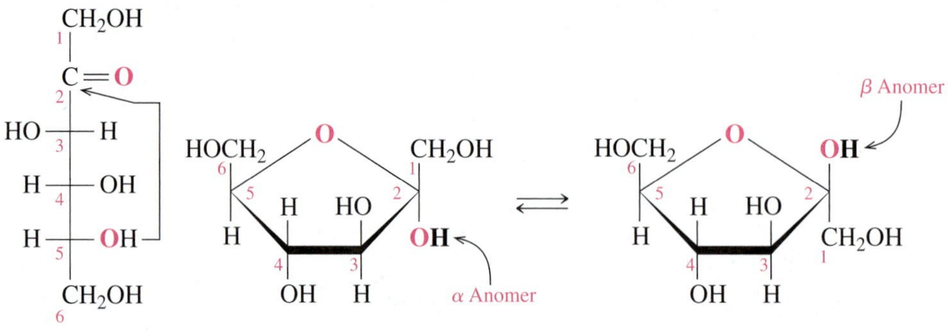

D-Fructose α-D-Fructose β-D-Fructose

QUESTIONS AND PROBLEMS

15.3 Haworth Structures of Monosaccharides

LEARNING GOAL: *Draw and identify the Haworth structures of monosaccharides.*

15.23 Name the kind and number of atoms in the ring portion of the Haworth structure of glucose.

15.24 Name the kind and number of atoms in the ring portion of the Haworth structure of fructose.

15.25 Draw the Haworth structures for the α and β anomers of D-glucose.

15.26 Draw the Haworth structures for the α and β anomers of D-fructose.

15.27 Identify each of the following Haworth structures as the α or β anomer:

a.

b.

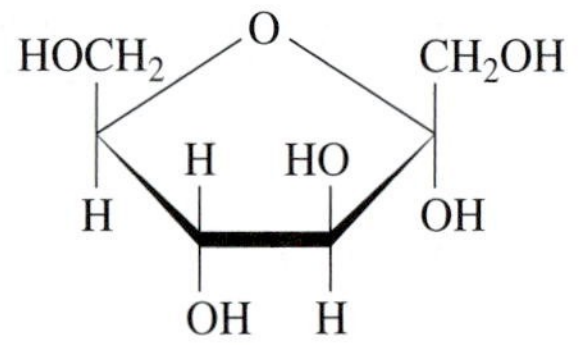

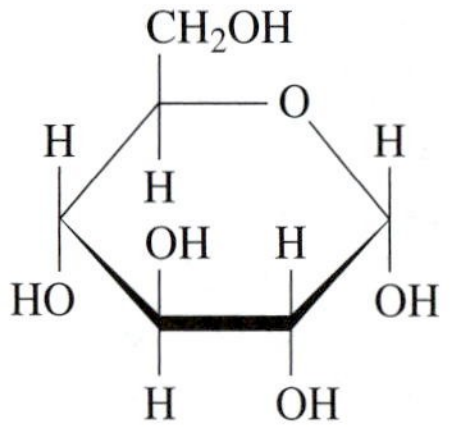

15.28 Identify each of the following Haworth structures as the α or β anomer:

a.

b.

LEARNING GOAL

Identify the products of oxidation or reduction of monosaccharides; determine whether a carbohydrate is a reducing sugar.

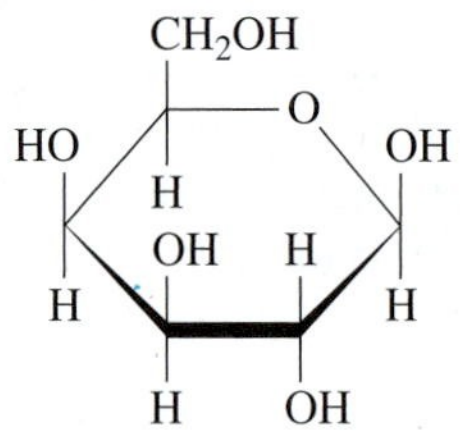

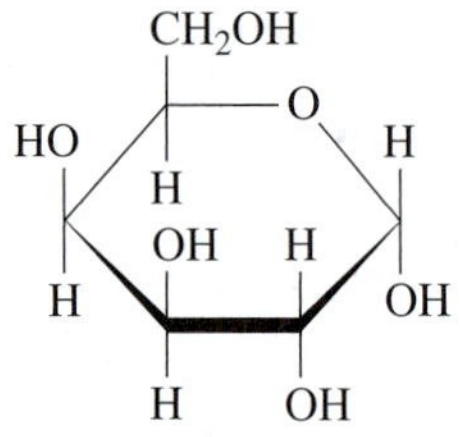

15.4 Chemical Properties of Monosaccharides

Monosaccharides contain functional groups that can undergo chemical reactions. In an aldose, the aldehyde group can be oxidized to a carboxylic acid. The carbonyl group in both an aldose and a ketose can be reduced to give a hydroxyl group. The hydroxyl groups can react with other compounds to form a variety of derivatives that are important in biological structures.

Oxidation of Monosaccharides

Although monosaccharides exist mostly as cyclic hemiacetals, a trace amount of the open-chain structure is always present, which provides an aldehyde group. As we discussed in Section 14.3, an aldehyde group with an adjacent hydroxyl group can be oxidized to a carboxylic acid by an oxidizing agent such as Benedict's reagent. The sugar acids are named by replacing the *ose* ending of the monosaccharide with *onic acid*. Then the Cu^{2+} is reduced to Cu^+, which forms a brick-red precipitate of Cu_2O. Monosaccharides that reduce another substance are called **reducing sugars**.

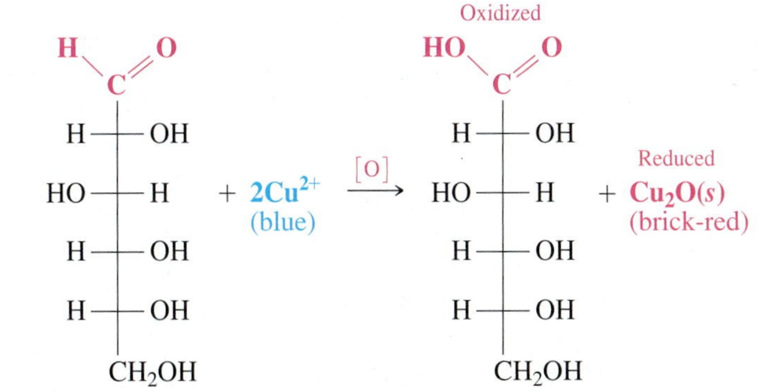

Open chain of D-glucose, a reducing sugar

D-Gluconic acid

Fructose, a ketohexose, is also a reducing sugar. Usually, a ketone cannot be oxidized. However, in a basic Benedict's solution, a rearrangement moves the carbonyl group from carbon 2 to carbon 1. As a result, this rearrangement converts fructose to glucose, which provides an aldehyde group that can be oxidized.

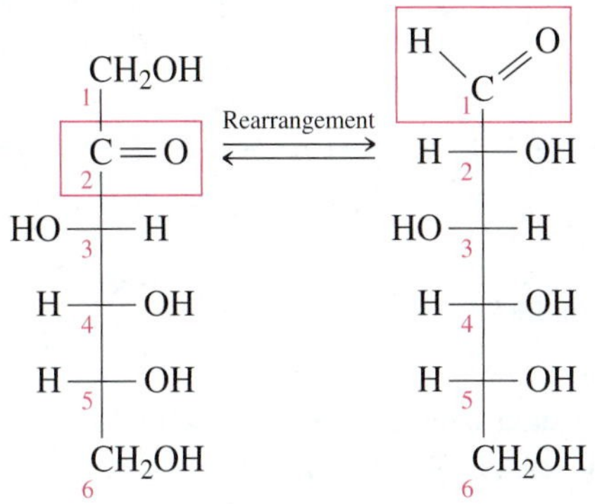

D-Fructose
(ketose)

D-Glucose
(aldose)

Reduction of Monosaccharides

The reduction of the aldehyde group in monosaccharides produces sugar alcohols, which are also called *alditols*. D-Glucose is reduced to D-glucitol, better known as *sorbitol*. The sugar alcohols are named by changing the *ose* ending of the monosaccharide to *itol*. Sugar alcohols such as sorbitol, xylitol from xylose, and mannitol from mannose are used as sweeteners in many sugar-free products such as diet drinks and sugarless gum, as well as products for people with diabetes. However, there are some side effects of these sugar substitutes. Some people experience discomfort, such as gas and diarrhea, from the ingestion of sugar alcohols. In diabetics, glucose accumulates in the lens of the eye where it is converted to sorbitol, which can lead to the development of cataracts.

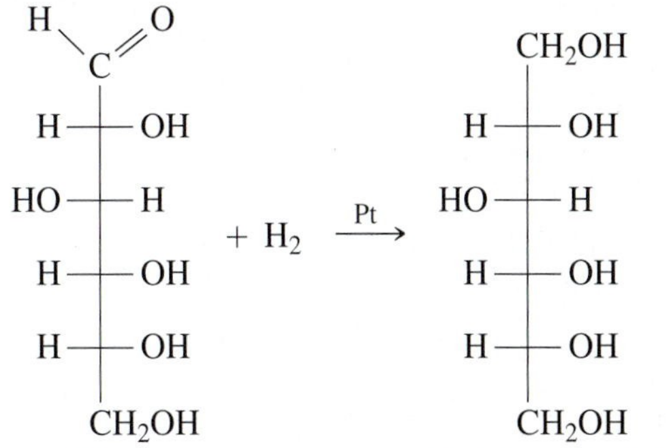

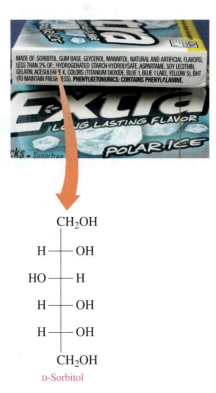

D-Glucose

D-Glucitol or D-Sorbitol

D-Sorbitol

Chemistry Link to Health

TESTING FOR GLUCOSE IN URINE

Normally, blood glucose flows through the kidneys and is reabsorbed into the bloodstream. However, if the blood level exceeds about 160 mg of glucose/dL of blood, the kidneys cannot reabsorb it all, and glucose spills over into the urine, a condition known as *glucosuria*. A symptom of diabetes mellitus is a high level of glucose in the urine.

Benedict's test can be used to determine the presence of glucose in urine. The amount of copper(I) oxide (Cu_2O) formed is proportional to the concentration of reducing sugar present in the urine. Low to moderate levels of reducing sugar turn the solution green; solutions with high glucose levels turn Benedict's solution yellow or brick-red. Table 15.1 lists some colors associated with the concentration of glucose in the urine.

In another clinical test that is more specific for glucose, the enzyme glucose oxidase is used. The oxidase enzyme converts glucose to gluconic acid and hydrogen peroxide (H_2O_2). The peroxide produced reacts with a dye in a test strip to produce different colors. The level of glucose present in the urine is found by matching the color produced to a color chart on the container.

The color of a test strip determines the glucose level in urine.

TABLE 15.1 Glucose Test Results

Color of Benedict's Test Solution	Glucose Present in Urine	
	% (m/v)	mg/dL
Blue	0	0
Blue-green	0.25	250
Green	0.50	500
Yellow	1.00	1000
Brick-red	2.00	2000

CONCEPT CHECK 15.3 **Reducing Sugars**

a. Why is D-glucose called a reducing sugar?
b. In a laboratory test using Benedict's reagent, a sample of urine turns brick-red. According to Table 15.1, what might this test result indicate?

ANSWER

a. The aldehyde in D-glucose with an adjacent hydroxyl group is easily oxidized because the carbonyl group is highly reactive and can reduce other substances. Thus, D-glucose is a reducing sugar.
b. This result indicates a high level of reducing sugar (probably glucose) in the urine. One common cause of this condition is diabetes mellitus.

QUESTIONS AND PROBLEMS

15.4 Chemical Properties of Monosaccharides

LEARNING GOAL: *Identify the products of oxidation or reduction of monosaccharides; determine whether a carbohydrate is a reducing sugar.*

15.29 Draw the Fischer projection for D-xylitol that is produced when D-xylose is reduced.

```
      H   O
       \ //
        C
   H ——|—— OH
  HO ——|—— H
   H ——|—— OH
       CH₂OH
```
D-Xylose

15.30 Draw the Fischer projection for D-mannitol that is produced when D-mannose is reduced.

```
      H   O
       \ //
        C
  HO ——|—— H
  HO ——|—— H
   H ——|—— OH
   H ——|—— OH
       CH₂OH
```
D-Mannose

15.31 Draw the Fischer projections for the oxidation and reduction products of D-arabinose. What are the names of the sugar acid and the sugar alcohol produced?

$$
\begin{array}{c}
H-C=O \\
HO-H \\
H-OH \\
H-OH \\
CH_2OH
\end{array}
$$

D-Arabinose

15.32 Draw the Fischer projections for the oxidation and reduction products of D-ribose. What are the names of the sugar acid and the sugar alcohol produced?

$$
\begin{array}{c}
H-C=O \\
H-OH \\
H-OH \\
H-OH \\
CH_2OH
\end{array}
$$

D-Ribose

15.5 Disaccharides

A disaccharide is composed of two monosaccharides linked together. The most common disaccharides are maltose, lactose, and sucrose. When two monosaccharides combine in a dehydration reaction, the product is an acetal and water as we discussed in Section 14.4. The reaction occurs between the anomeric hydroxyl group as a hemiacetal and one of the hydroxyl groups on a second monosaccharide as the alcohol.

Glucose + glucose $\xrightarrow{\text{Maltose synthase}}$ maltose + H_2O

Glucose + galactose $\xrightarrow{\text{Lactose synthase}}$ lactose + H_2O

Glucose + fructose $\xrightarrow{\text{Sucrose synthase}}$ sucrose + H_2O

Maltose, or malt sugar, used in cereals, candies, and the brewing of beverages, is a disaccharide. Maltose has a **glycosidic bond**, which is an acetal, between two glucose molecules. To form maltose, the —OH group on carbon 1 of the hemiacetal in the first glucose forms a bond with the —OH group on carbon 4 in a second glucose molecule, which results in a 1,4-glycosidic bond. Because the —OH group on carbon 1 of the hemiacetal of the first glucose is the α anomer, it is an α-1,4-glycosidic bond. For maltose, it is the free —OH group in the hemiacetal on carbon 1 of the second glucose molecule that determines if maltose is the α or β anomer.

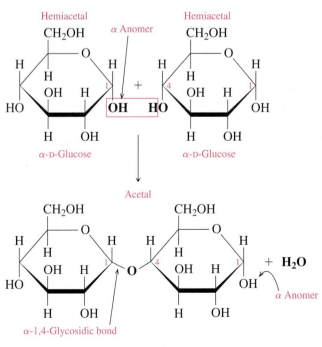

α-Maltose, a disaccharide

LEARNING GOAL

Describe the monosaccharide units and glycosidic bonds in disaccharides.

Explore
Your World

SUGAR AND SWEETENERS

Add a tablespoon of sugar to a glass of water and stir. Taste. Add more tablespoons of sugar, stir, and taste. If you have other carbohydrates such as fructose, honey, cornstarch, arrowroot, or flour, add some of each to separate glasses of water and stir. If you have some artificial sweeteners, add a few drops of the sweetener or a package, if solid, to a glass of water. Taste each.

QUESTIONS

1. Which substance is the most soluble in water?
2. Place the substances in order from the one that tastes least sweet to the sweetest.
3. How does your list compare to Table 15.2 on page 555?
4. How does the sweetness of sucrose compare with the artificial sweeteners?
5. Check the labels of food products in your kitchen. Look for sugars such as sucrose and fructose, or artificial sweeteners such as aspartame or sucralose on the label. How many grams of sugar are in a serving of the food?

Earlier in Section 15.3, we described how the hemiacetal of glucose forms an alde-hyde as it undergoes mutarotation between the α and β anomers. This also occurs with those disaccharides that have a free —OH group in the hemiacetal on carbon 1 in the second molecule. Thus, maltose is a reducing sugar because the free —OH group in the hemiacetal undergoes mutarotation, which gives an aldehyde group that can reduce other substances. When maltose from the starches in barley and other grains is hydrolyzed by yeast with an enzyme (maltase), two molecules of glucose are obtained, which can undergo fermentation to produce ethanol.

Lactose, milk sugar, is a disaccharide found in milk and milk products (see Figure 15.3). The acetal bond in lactose is a β-1,4-glycosidic bond because it is the —OH group of a β ano-mer of galactose that forms an acetal with the —OH group on carbon 4 of glucose. In lactose, the hemiacetal of glucose undergoes mutarotation, which gives α and β anomers. Therefore, lactose is a reducing sugar because the hemiacetal can open to give an aldehyde that can reduce other substances.

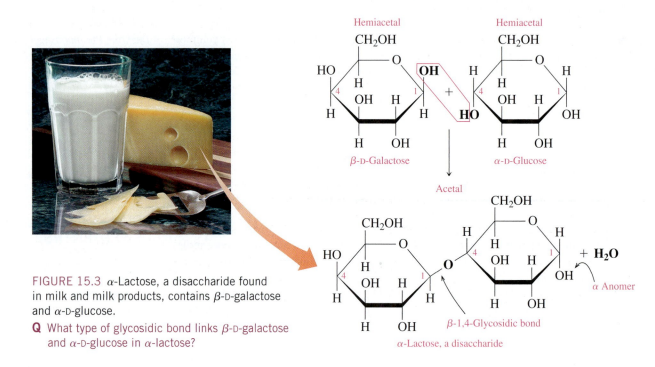

FIGURE 15.3 α-Lactose, a disaccharide found in milk and milk products, contains β-D-galactose and α-D-glucose.

Q What type of glycosidic bond links β-D-galactose and α-D-glucose in α-lactose?

Lactose makes up 6–8% of human milk and about 4–5% of cow's milk, and it is used in products that attempt to duplicate mother's milk. When a person does not pro-duce sufficient quantities of the enzyme lactase, which is needed to hydrolyze lactose, it remains undigested when it enters the colon. Then bacteria in the colon digest the lactose in a fermentation process that creates large amounts of gas including carbon dioxide and methane, which cause bloating and abdominal cramps. In some commercial milk prod-ucts, lactase has already been added to break down lactose.

Sucrose consists of an α-D-glucose and a β-D-fructose molecule joined by an α,β-1,2-glycosidic bond (see Figure 15.4). Unlike maltose and lactose, the glycosidic bond in sucrose forms between the —OH groups in the hemiacetals of glucose and fruc-tose. As a result, sucrose does not have any hemiacetals and cannot undergo mutarotation to an aldehyde. Thus, sucrose is not a reducing sugar.

The sugar we use to sweeten our cereal, coffee, and tea is sucrose. Most of the sucrose for table sugar comes from sugar cane (20% by mass) or sugar beets (15% by mass). Both the raw and refined forms of sugar are sucrose. Some estimates indicate that each person in the United States consumes an average of 68 kg (150 lb) of sucrose every year, either by itself or in a variety of food products. In the body, the enzyme sucrase hydrolyzes sucrose to glucose and fructose.

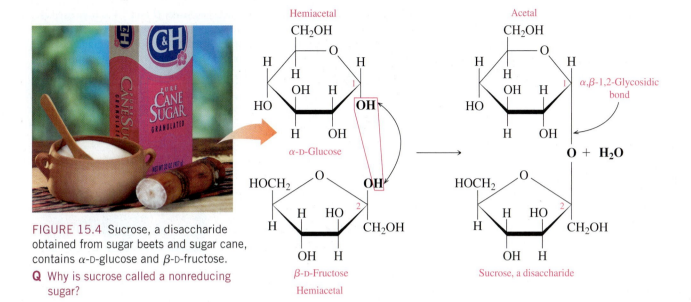

FIGURE 15.4 Sucrose, a disaccharide obtained from sugar beets and sugar cane, contains α-D-glucose and β-D-fructose.

Q Why is sucrose called a nonreducing sugar?

Chemistry Link to Health

HOW SWEET IS MY SWEETENER?

Although many of the monosaccharides and disaccharides taste sweet, they differ considerably in their degree of sweetness. Dietetic foods contain sweeteners that are noncarbohydrates, or carbohydrates that are sweeter than sucrose. Some examples of sweeteners compared with sucrose are shown in Table 15.2.

TABLE 15.2 Relative Sweetness of Sugars and Artificial Sweeteners

	Sweetness Relative to Sucrose (= 100)
Monosaccharides	
Galactose	30
Glucose	75
Fructose	175
Disaccharides	
Lactose	16
Maltose	33
Sucrose	100 = reference standard
Sugar Alcohols	
Sorbitol (Glucitol)	60
Maltitol	80
Xylitol	100
Artificial Sweeteners (Noncarbohydrate)	
Aspartame	18 000
Saccharin	45 000
Sucralose	60 000
Neotame	1 000 000

Sucralose is made from sucrose by replacing some of the hydroxyl groups with chlorine atoms.

Sucralose

Aspartame, which is marketed as NutraSweet and Equal®, is used in a large number of sugar-free products. It is a noncarbohydrate sweetener made of aspartic acid and a methyl ester of phenylalanine. It does have some caloric value, but it is so sweet that only a very small quantity is needed. However, phenylalanine, one of the breakdown products, poses a danger to anyone who cannot metabolize it properly, a condition called *phenylketonuria (PKU)*.

From aspartic acid   From phenylalanine
Aspartame (NutraSweet®)

Another artificial sweetener, Neotame, is a modification of the aspartame structure. The addition of a large alkyl group to the amine group prevents enzymes from breaking the amide bond between aspartic acid and phenylalanine. Thus, phenylalanine is not produced when Neotame is used as a sweetener. Very small amounts of Neotame are needed because it is about 10 000 times sweeter than sucrose.

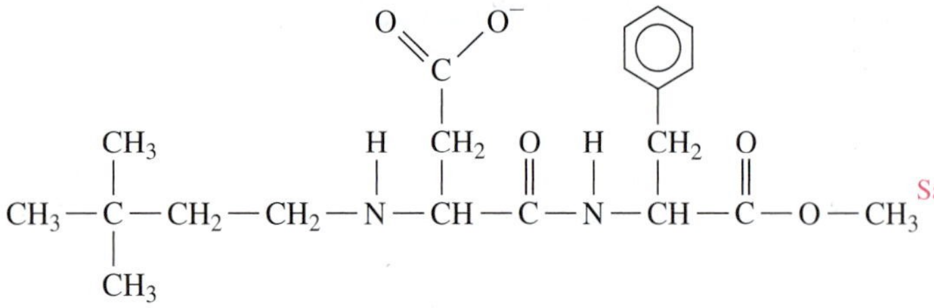

Saccharin, which is marketed as Sweet'N Low®, has been used as a noncarbohydrate artificial sweetener for the past 25 years. The use of saccharin has been banned in Canada because studies indicate that it may cause bladder tumors. However, it has still been approved by the FDA for use in the United States.

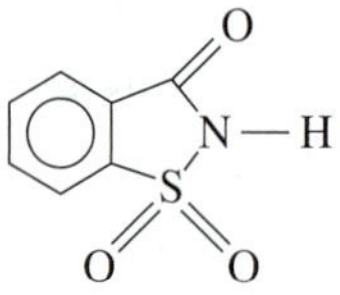

Saccharin (Sweet'N Low®)

Large alkyl group to modify Aspartame

Neotame

Artificial sweeteners are used as sugar substitutes.

Chemistry Link to Health

BLOOD TYPES AND CARBOHYDRATES

Every individual's blood can be typed as one of four blood groups: A, B, AB, and O. Although there is some variation among ethnic groups in the United States, the incidence of blood types in the general population is about 43% O, 40% A, 12% B, and 5% AB.

The blood types A, B, and O are determined by terminal saccharides attached to the surface of red blood cells. Blood type O has three terminal monosaccharides: *N*-acetylglucosamine, galactose, and fucose. Blood type A contains the same three monosaccharides, but in addition, a molecule of *N*-acetylgalactosamine is attached to galactose in the saccharide chain. Blood type B also contains the same three monosaccharides, but in addition, a second molecule of galactose is attached to the saccharide chain. Blood type AB consists of the same monosaccharides found in blood types A and B. The structures of these monosaccharides are as follows:

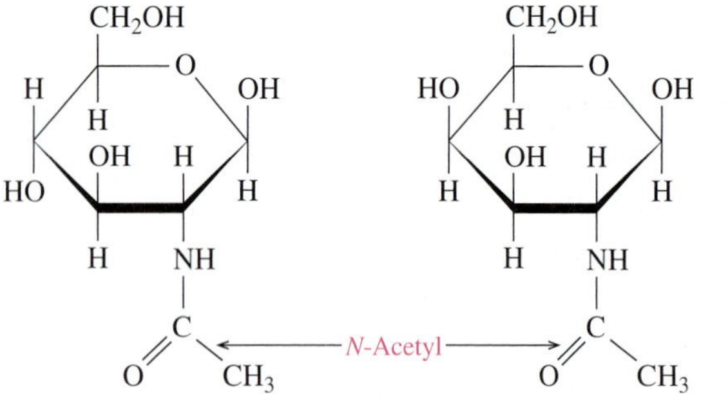

Because there is a different monosaccharide in type A blood than in type B blood, persons with type A blood produce antibodies against type B, and vice versa. For example, if a person with type A blood receives a transfusion of type B blood, the donor red blood cells are treated as if they are foreign invaders. An immune reaction occurs when the body sees the foreign saccharides on the red blood cells and makes antibodies against these donor red blood cells. The red blood cells will then clump together, or agglutinate, resulting in kidney failure, circulatory collapse, and death. The same thing will happen if a person with type B blood receives type A blood.

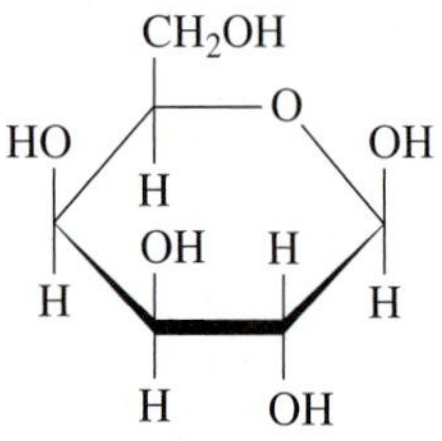

N-Acetylglucosamine (*N*-AcGlu)   *N*-Acetylgalactosamine (*N*-AcGal)

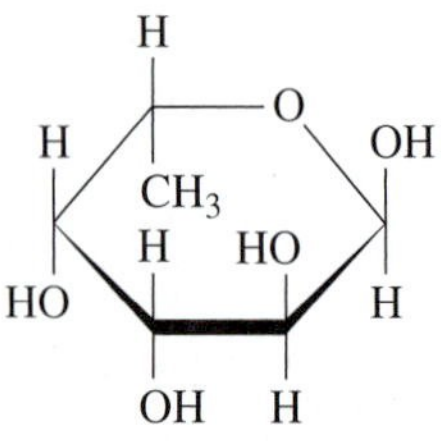

N-Acetyl

L-Fucose (Fuc)   D-Galactose (Gal)

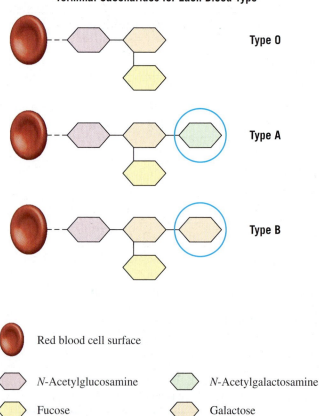

Terminal Saccharides for Each Blood Type

Type O

Type A

Type B

Red blood cell surface

N-Acetylglucosamine   *N*-Acetylgalactosamine

Fucose   Galactose

Because type O blood has only the three common terminal monosaccharides, a person with type O produces antibodies against blood types A, B, and AB. However, persons with blood types A, B, and AB can receive type O blood. Thus, persons with type O blood are *universal donors*. Because type AB blood contains all the terminal monosaccharides, a person with type AB blood produces no antibodies to type A, B, or O blood. Persons with type AB blood are *universal recipients*. Table 15.3 summarizes the compatibility of blood groups for transfusion.

TABLE 15.3 **Compatibility of Blood Groups**

Blood Type	Produce Antibodies Against	Can Receive
A	B, AB	A, O
B	A, AB	B, O
AB universal recipient	None	A, B, AB, O
O universal donor	A, B, AB	O

Blood from a donor is screened to make sure that there is an exact match with the blood type of the recipient.

CONCEPT CHECK 15.4 **Glycosidic Bonds**

Why is the glycosidic bond in maltose called an α-1,4-glycosidic bond, whereas in lactose it is called a β-1,4-glycosidic bond?

ANSWER

When the hydroxyl group from the α anomer of one glucose forms an acetal with the hydroxyl group on carbon 4 of another glucose, the glycosidic bond is an α-1,4-glycosidic bond. In lactose, a hydroxyl group from the β anomer of galactose forms an acetal with the hydroxyl group on carbon 4 of glucose. Then the glycosidic bond is a β-1,4-glycosidic bond.

SAMPLE PROBLEM 15.4 **Glycosidic Bonds in Disaccharides**

Melibiose is a disaccharide that is 30 times sweeter than sucrose.

a. What are the monosaccharide units in melibiose?
b. What type of glycosidic bond links the monosaccharides?
c. Identify the structure as α- or β-melibiose.

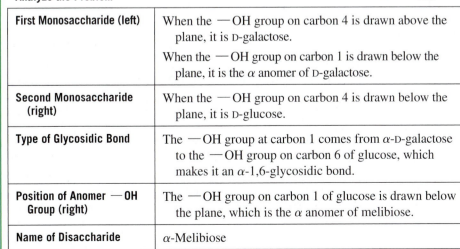

Melibiose

SOLUTION

Analyze the Problem

First Monosaccharide (left)	When the —OH group on carbon 4 is drawn above the plane, it is D-galactose.
	When the —OH group on carbon 1 is drawn below the plane, it is the α anomer of D-galactose.
Second Monosaccharide (right)	When the —OH group on carbon 4 is drawn below the plane, it is D-glucose.
Type of Glycosidic Bond	The —OH group at carbon 1 comes from α-D-galactose to the —OH group on carbon 6 of glucose, which makes it an α-1,6-glycosidic bond.
Position of Anomer —OH Group (right)	The —OH group on carbon 1 of glucose is drawn below the plane, which is the α anomer of melibiose.
Name of Disaccharide	α-Melibiose

Career Focus

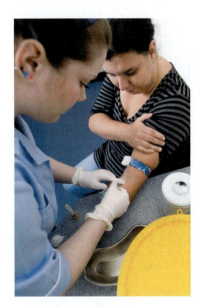

PHLEBOTOMIST

As part of the medical team, phlebotomists collect and process blood for laboratory tests. They work directly with patients, calming them if necessary before the collection of blood. Phlebotomists are trained to collect blood in a safe manner and provide patient care if fainting occurs. Blood is drawn through venipuncture methods such as syringe, vacutainer, and fingerstick. They also prepare patients for procedures such as glucose tolerance tests. In the preparation of specimens for analysis, a phlebotomist determines media, inoculation method, and reagents for culture setup.

a. α-D-galactose and α-D-glucose
b. α-1,6-glycosidic bond
c. α-melibiose

STUDY CHECK 15.4

Cellobiose is a disaccharide composed of two β-D-glucose molecules linked by a β-1,4-glycosidic linkage. Draw the Haworth structure for β-cellobiose.

QUESTIONS AND PROBLEMS

15.5 Disaccharides

LEARNING GOAL: Describe the monosaccharide units and glycosidic bonds in disaccharides.

15.33 For each of the following, state the monosaccharide units produced by hydrolysis, the type of glycosidic bond, and the name of the disaccharide, including the α or β anomer:

a.

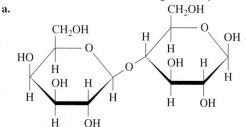

b.

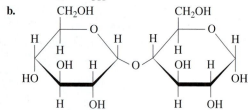

15.34 For each of the following, state the monosaccharide units produced by hydrolysis, the type of glycosidic bond, and the name of the disaccharide, including the α or β anomer:

a.

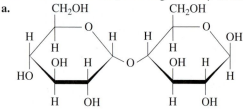

b.

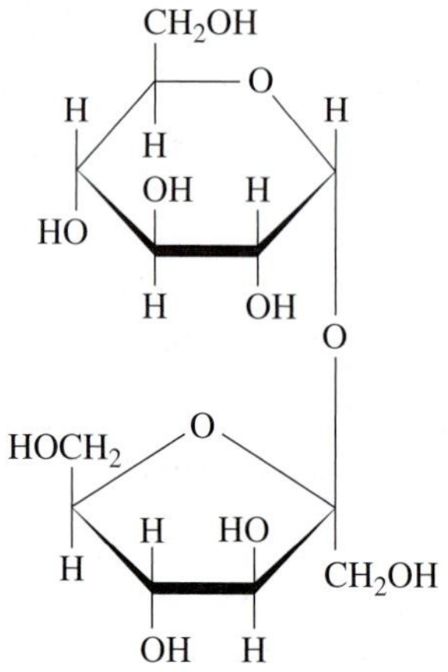

15.35 Indicate whether each disaccharide in Problem 15.33 is a reducing sugar or not.

15.36 Indicate whether each disaccharide in Problem 15.34 is a reducing sugar or not.

15.37 Identify the disaccharide that fits each of the following descriptions:
   a. ordinary table sugar
   b. found in milk and milk products
   c. also called malt sugar
   d. hydrolysis gives galactose and glucose

15.38 Identify the disaccharide that fits each of the following descriptions:
   a. not a reducing sugar
   b. composed of two glucose units
   c. also called milk sugar
   d. hydrolysis gives glucose and fructose

LEARNING GOAL

Describe the structural features of amylose, amylopectin, glycogen, and cellulose.

SELF-STUDY ACTIVITY
Polymers

15.6 Polysaccharides

A *polysaccharide* is a polymer of many monosaccharides joined together. Four biologically important polysaccharides—amylose, amylopectin, cellulose, and glycogen—are all polymers of D-glucose that differ only in the type of glycosidic bonds and the amount of branching in the molecule.

Starch, a storage form of glucose in plants, is found as insoluble granules in rice, wheat, potatoes, beans, and cereals. Starch is composed of two kinds of polysaccharides, *amylose* and *amylopectin*. **Amylose**, which makes up about 20% of starch, consists of 250 to 4000 α-D-glucose molecules connected by α-1,4-glycosidic bonds in a continuous chain. Sometimes called a straight-chain polymer, polymers of amylose are actually coiled in helical fashion.

Amylopectin, which makes up as much as 80% of plant starch, is a branched-chain polysaccharide. Like amylose, α-1,4-glycosidic bonds connect the glucose molecules.

However, at about every 25 glucose units, there is a branch of glucose molecules attached by an α-1,6-glycosidic bond between carbon 1 of the branch and carbon 6 in the main chain (see Figure 15.5).

Starches hydrolyze easily in water and acid to give shorter glucose chains called *dextrins*, which then hydrolyze to maltose and finally glucose. In our bodies, these complex carbohydrates are digested by the enzymes amylase (in saliva) and maltase (in the intestine). The glucose obtained usually provides about 50% of our nutritional calories.

$$\text{Amylose, amylopectin} \xrightarrow[\text{amylase}]{H^+ \text{ or}} \text{dextrins} \xrightarrow[\text{amylase}]{H^+ \text{ or}} \text{maltose} \xrightarrow[\text{maltase}]{H^+ \text{ or}} \text{many D-glucose units}$$

Glycogen, or animal starch, is a non-linear polymer of glucose that is stored in the liver and muscle of animals. It is hydrolyzed in our cells at a rate that maintains an adequate blood level of glucose and provides energy between meals. The structure of glycogen is very similar to that of amylopectin, found in plants, except that glycogen is more highly branched. In glycogen, α-1,4-glycosidic bonds join the glucose units, and branches occurring about every 10 to 15 glucose units are attached by α-1,6-glycosidic bonds.

Cellulose is the major structural material of wood and plants. Cotton is almost pure cellulose. In cellulose, glucose molecules form a long unbranched chain similar to that of

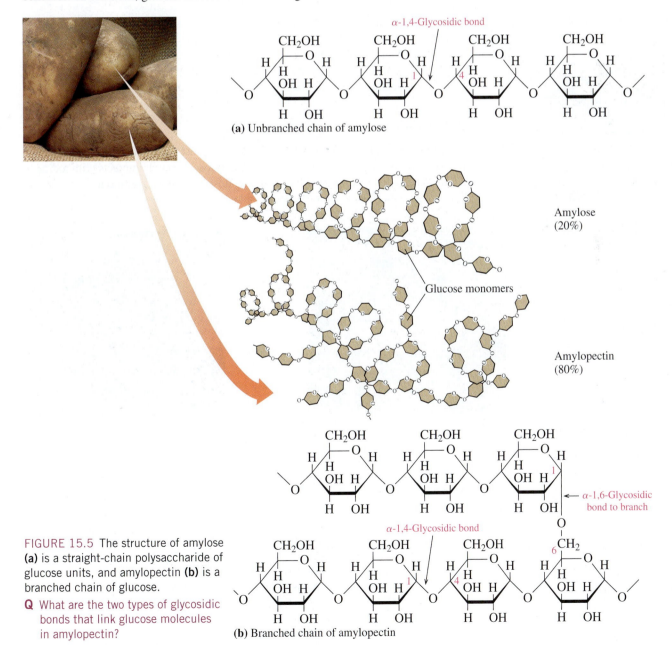

FIGURE 15.5 The structure of amylose **(a)** is a straight-chain polysaccharide of glucose units, and amylopectin **(b)** is a branched chain of glucose.

Q What are the two types of glycosidic bonds that link glucose molecules in amylopectin?

Explore Your World

POLYSACCHARIDES

Read the nutrition label on a box of crackers, cereal, bread, or chips. The major ingredient in crackers is flour, a starch. Chew on a single cracker for 4 or 5 minutes. Note how the taste changes as you chew the cracker. An enzyme (amylase) in your saliva breaks apart the bonds in starch.

QUESTIONS

1. How are carbohydrates listed on the label?

2. What other carbohydrates are listed?
3. How did the taste of the cracker change during the time that you chewed it?
4. What happened to the starches in the cracker as the amylase enzyme in your saliva reacted with the amylose and amylopectin?

When iodine (in the dropper) is added to a starch solution, the amylose turns the solution to a blue-black color.

amylose. However, the glucose units in cellulose are linked by β-1,4-glycosidic bonds. As a result, cellulose chains do not form coils like amylose, but are aligned in parallel rows that are held in place by hydrogen bonds between hydroxyl groups in adjacent chains. This arrangement makes cellulose insoluble in water and gives a rigid structure to the cell walls in wood and fiber that is more resistant to hydrolysis than the α-1,4-glycosidic bonds in starches (see Figure 15.6).

Humans have an enzyme called α-amylase in saliva and pancreatic juices that hydrolyzes the α-1,4-glycosidic bonds of the starches but not the β-1,4-glycosidic bonds of cellulose. Thus, humans cannot digest cellulose. Animals such as horses, cows, and goats can obtain glucose from cellulose because their digestive systems contain bacteria that provide enzymes such as cellulase to hydrolyze β-1,4-glycosidic bonds.

Iodine Test

In the **iodine test**, iodine (I_2) is used to test for the presence of amylose in starch. The unbranched helical shape of the polysaccharide amylose in starch interacts with iodine to form a deep blue-black color. Amylopectin, cellulose, glycogen, and mono- or disaccharides do not give this characteristic deep blue-black color.

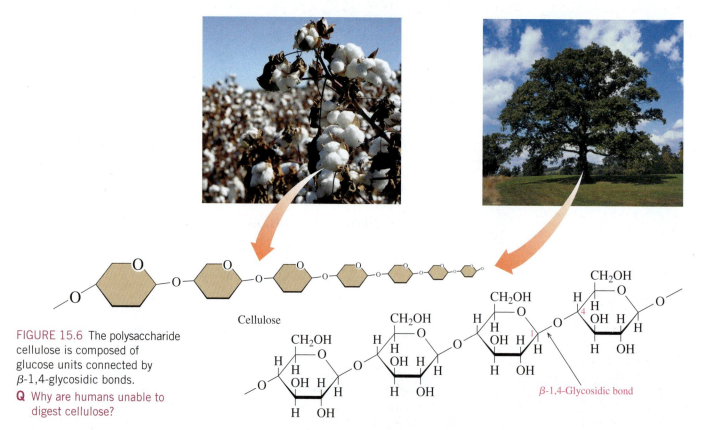

FIGURE 15.6 The polysaccharide cellulose is composed of glucose units connected by β-1,4-glycosidic bonds.

Q Why are humans unable to digest cellulose?

Cellulose

β-1,4-Glycosidic bond

SAMPLE PROBLEM 15.5   **Structures of Polysaccharides**

Identify the polysaccharide described by each of the following:

a. a polysaccharide that is stored in the liver and muscle tissues
b. an unbranched polysaccharide containing β-1,4-glycosidic bonds
c. a starch containing α-1,4- and α-1,6-glycosidic bonds

SOLUTION

a. glycogen   **b.** cellulose   **c.** amylopectin, glycogen

STUDY CHECK 15.5

Amylose and amylopectin are both glucose polymers. How do they differ?

QUESTIONS AND PROBLEMS

15.6 Polysaccharides

LEARNING GOAL: *Describe the structural features of amylose, amylopectin, glycogen, and cellulose.*

15.39 Describe the similarities and differences in the following:
  a. amylose and amylopectin   **b.** amylopectin and glycogen

15.40 Describe the similarities and differences in the following:
  a. amylose and cellulose   **b.** cellulose and glycogen

15.41 Give the name of one or more polysaccharides that matches each of the following descriptions:
  a. not digestible by humans
  b. the storage form of carbohydrates in plants
  c. contains only α-1,4-glycosidic bonds
  d. the most highly branched polysaccharide

15.42 Give the name of one or more polysaccharides that matches each of the following descriptions:
  a. the storage form of carbohydrates in animals
  b. contains only β-1,4-glycosidic bonds
  c. contains both α-1,4- and α-1,6-glycosidic bonds
  d. produces maltose during digestion

CONCEPT MAP

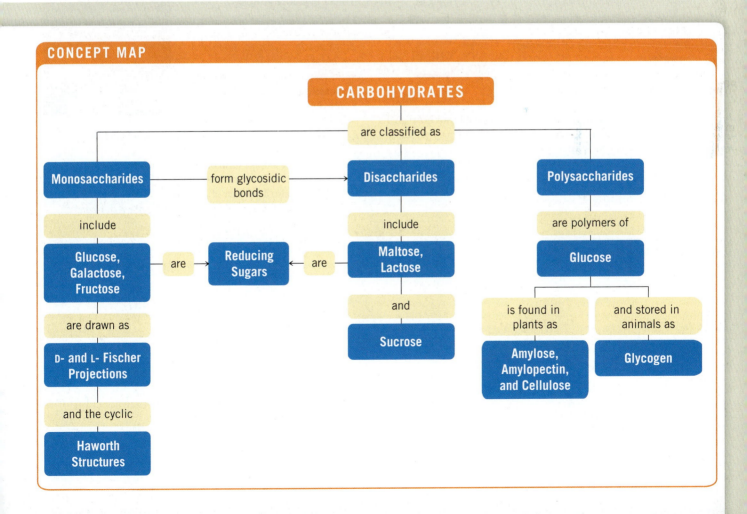

CHAPTER REVIEW

15.1 Carbohydrates

LEARNING GOAL: Classify a monosaccharide as an aldose or ketose, and indicate the number of carbon atoms.

- Carbohydrates are classified as monosaccharides (simple sugars), disaccharides (two monosaccharide units), or polysaccharides (many monosaccharide units).
- Monosaccharides are polyhydroxy aldehydes (*aldoses*) or ketones (*ketoses*).
- Monosaccharides are also classified by their number of carbon atoms: *triose*, *tetrose*, *pentose*, or *hexose*.

15.2 Fischer Projections of Monosaccharides

LEARNING GOAL: Use Fischer projections to draw the D or L stereoisomers of glucose, galactose, and fructose.

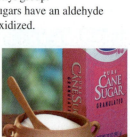

- Chiral molecules can exist in two different forms, which are mirror images of each other.
- In a Fischer projection (straight chain), the prefixes D- and L- are used to distinguish between the mirror images.
- In D stereoisomers, the —OH group is on the right of the chiral carbon farthest from the carbonyl carbon; it is on the left in L stereoisomers.
- Important monosaccharides are the aldohexoses, glucose and galactose, and the ketohexose, fructose.

15.3 Haworth Structures of Monosaccharides

LEARNING GOAL: Draw and identify the Haworth structures of monosaccharides.

- The predominant form of monosaccharides is the cyclic arrangement of five or six atoms.
- In hexoses, the cyclic structure of a hemiacetal forms between the carbon in the carbonyl group and the —OH group on carbon 5 within the same molecule.
- The mutarotation of the hydroxyl group on carbon 1 (or carbon 2 in ketoses like fructose) gives α and β anomers of the cyclic hemiacetal.

15.4 Chemical Properties of Monosaccharides

LEARNING GOAL: Identify the products of oxidation or reduction of monosaccharides; determine whether a carbohydrate is a reducing sugar.

- The aldehyde group in an aldose can be oxidized to a carboxylic acid, while the carbonyl group in an aldose or a ketose can be reduced to give a hydroxyl group.
- Monosaccharides that are reducing sugars have an aldehyde group in the open chain that can be oxidized.

15.5 Disaccharides

LEARNING GOAL: Describe the monosaccharide units and glycosidic bonds in disaccharides.

- Disaccharides are two monosaccharide units joined together by a glycosidic bond.
- In the common disaccharides maltose, lactose, and sucrose, there is at least one glucose unit.
- Maltose and lactose contain an acetal bond and a free —OH group in the hemiacetal, which gives α and β anomers.
- Sucrose contains an acetal bond, but is not a hemiacetal, and does not have α and β anomers and is not a reducing sugar.

15.6 Polysaccharides

LEARNING GOAL: Describe the structural features of amylose, amylopectin, glycogen, and cellulose.

- Polysaccharides are polymers of monosaccharide units.
- Amylose is an unbranched chain of glucose with α-1,4-glycosidic bonds, and amylopectin is a branched polymer of glucose with α-1,4- and α-1,6-glycosidic bonds.
- Glycogen, the storage form of glucose in animals, is similar to amylopectin but has more branching.
- Cellulose is also a polymer of glucose, but in cellulose, the glycosidic bonds are β-1,4-bonds rather than the α-1,4-bonds found in amylose.

SUMMARY OF CARBOHYDRATES

Carbohydrate	Food Sources	Monosaccharide Components
Monosaccharides		
Glucose	Fruit juices, honey, corn syrup	
Galactose	Lactose hydrolysis	
Fructose	Fruit juices, honey, sucrose hydrolysis	
Disaccharides		
Maltose	Germinating grains, starch hydrolysis	Glucose + glucose
Lactose	Milk, yogurt, ice cream	Glucose + galactose
Sucrose	Sugar cane, sugar beets	Glucose + fructose
Polysaccharides		
Amylose	Rice, wheat, grains, cereals	Unbranched polymer of glucose joined by α-1,4-glycosidic bonds
Amylopectin	Rice, wheat, grains, cereals	Branched polymer of glucose joined by α-1,4- and α-1,6-glycosidic bonds
Glycogen	Liver, muscles	Highly branched polymer of glucose joined by α-1,4- and α-1,6-glycosidic bonds
Cellulose	Plant fiber, bran, beans, celery	Unbranched polymer of glucose joined by β-1,4-glycosidic bonds

SUMMARY OF REACTIONS

Formation of Disaccharides

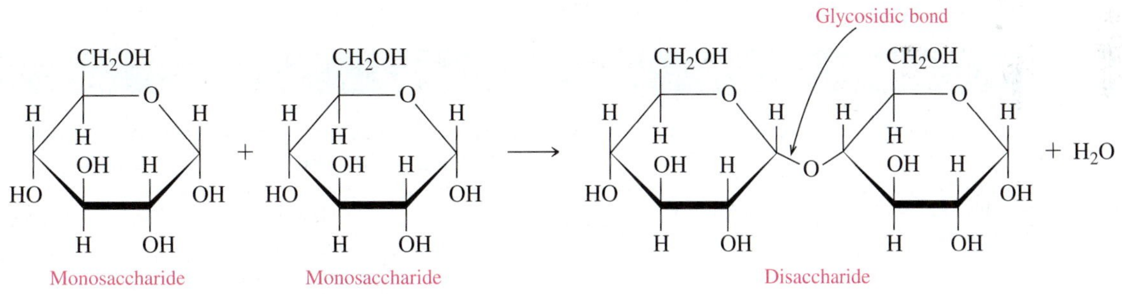

Monosaccharide + Monosaccharide → Disaccharide + H_2O

Glycosidic bond

Oxidation and Reduction of Monosaccharides

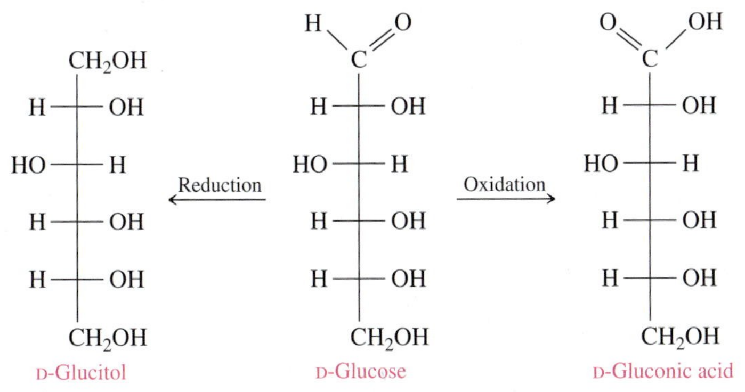

D-Glucitol ← Reduction — D-Glucose — Oxidation → D-Gluconic acid

Hydrolysis of Disaccharides

Maltose + H_2O $\xrightarrow{\text{H}^+ \text{ or maltase}}$ glucose + glucose

Lactose + H_2O $\xrightarrow{\text{H}^+ \text{ or lactase}}$ glucose + galactose

Sucrose + H_2O $\xrightarrow{\text{H}^+ \text{ or sucrase}}$ glucose + fructose

Hydrolysis of Polysaccharides

Amylose, amylopectin $\xrightarrow{\text{H}^+ \text{ or enzymes}}$ many D-glucose units

KEY TERMS

aldose A monosaccharide that contains an aldehyde group.

amylopectin A branched-chain polymer of starch composed of glucose units joined by α-1,4- and α-1,6-glycosidic bonds.

amylose An unbranched polymer of starch composed of glucose units joined by α-1,4-glycosidic bonds.

anomers The isomers of cyclic hemiacetals of monosaccharides that have a hydroxyl group on carbon 1 (or carbon 2). In the α anomer, the —OH group is drawn below the ring; in the β anomer, the —OH group is above the ring.

carbohydrate A simple or complex sugar composed of carbon, hydrogen, and oxygen.

cellulose An unbranched polysaccharide composed of glucose units linked by β-1,4-glycosidic bonds that cannot be hydrolyzed by the human digestive system.

disaccharide A carbohydrate composed of two monosaccharides joined by a glycosidic bond.

fructose A monosaccharide, also called levulose and fruit sugar, that is found in honey and fruit juices; when it combines with glucose, sucrose is formed.

galactose A monosaccharide; when it combines with glucose, lactose is formed.

glucose An aldohexose, which is the most prevalent monosaccharide in the diet, that is found in fruits, vegetables, corn syrup, and honey; it is also known as blood sugar and dextrose. Most polysaccharides are polymers of glucose.

glycogen A polysaccharide formed in the liver and muscles for the storage of glucose as an energy reserve. It is composed of

glucose in a highly branched polymer that is joined by α-1,4- and α-1,6-glycosidic bonds.

glycosidic bond The bond that forms when the —OH group in the hemiacetal of one monosaccharide reacts with the —OH group of another monosaccharide to form an acetal; it is the type of bond that links monosaccharide units in di- or polysaccharides.

Haworth structure The cyclic structure that represents the closed chain of a monosaccharide.

iodine test A test for amylose that shows a blue-black color after iodine is added to the sample.

ketose A monosaccharide that contains a ketone group.

lactose A disaccharide consisting of glucose and galactose; it is found in milk and milk products.

maltose A disaccharide consisting of two glucose units; it is obtained from the hydrolysis of starch and germinating grains.

monosaccharide A polyhydroxy compound that contains an aldehyde or ketone group.

mutarotation The conversion between α and β anomers via an open chain.

polysaccharide A polymer of many monosaccharide units, usually glucose. Polysaccharides differ in the types of glycosidic bonds and the amount of branching in the polymer.

reducing sugar A carbohydrate with an aldehyde group capable of reducing the Cu^{2+} in Benedict's reagent.

sucrose A disaccharide composed of glucose and fructose; a nonreducing sugar, commonly called table sugar or "sugar."

UNDERSTANDING THE CONCEPTS

The chapter sections to review are shown in parentheses at the end of each question.

15.43 Isomaltose, obtained from the breakdown of starch, has the following Haworth structure: (15.1, 15.3, 15.5)

Isomaltose

a. Is isomaltose a mono-, di-, or polysaccharide?
b. What are the monosaccharides in isomaltose?
c. What is the glycosidic link in isomaltose?
d. Is this the α or β anomer of isomaltose?
e. Would isomaltose be a reducing sugar?

15.44 Sophorose, a carbohydrate found in certain types of beans, has the following Haworth structure: (15.1, 15.3, 15.5)

Sophorose

a. Is sophorose a mono-, di-, or polysaccharide?
b. What are the monosaccharides in sophorose?
c. What is the glycosidic link in sophorose?
d. Is this the α or β anomer of sophorose?
e. Is sophorose a reducing sugar?

15.45 Melezitose, a carbohydrate secreted by insects, has the following Haworth structure: (15.1, 15.3, 15.5)

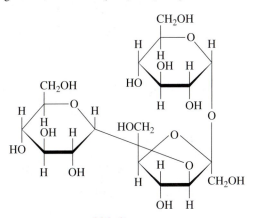

Melezitose

a. Is melezitose a mono-, di-, tri-, or polysaccharide?
b. What ketohexose and aldohexose are used to produce melezitose?
c. Is melezitose a reducing sugar?

15.46 What are the disaccharides and polysaccharides present in each of the following? (15.5, 15.6)

(a)   (b)

(c)   (d)

ADDITIONAL QUESTIONS AND PROBLEMS

For instructor-assigned homework, go to www.masteringchemistry.com.

15.47 What are the differences in the Fischer projections of D-fructose and D-galactose ? (15.2)

15.48 What are the differences in the Fischer projections of D-glucose and D-fructose ? (15.2)

15.49 What are the differences in the Fischer projections of D-galactose and L-galactose? (15.2)

15.50 What are the differences in the Haworth structures of α-D-glucose and β-D-glucose? (15.2)

15.51 The sugar D-gulose is a sweet-tasting syrup that has the following Fischer projection: (15.2, 15.3)

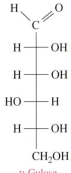

D-Gulose

a. Draw the Fischer projection for L-gulose.
b. Draw the Haworth structures for α- and β-D-gulose.

15.52 Consider the Fischer projection for D-gulose in Question 15.51. (15.4)

a. Draw the Fischer projection and give the name of the product formed by the reduction of D-gulose.
b. Draw the Fischer projection and give the name of the product formed by the oxidation of D-gulose.

15.53 D-Sorbitol, a sweetener found in seaweed and berries, contains only hydroxyl functional groups. When D-sorbitol is oxidized, it forms D-glucose. Draw the Fischer projection of D-sorbitol. (15.4)

15.54 Raffinose is a trisaccharide found in green vegetables such as cabbage, asparagus, and broccoli. It is composed of three different monosaccharides. Identify the monosaccharides in raffinose. (15.3, 15.4)

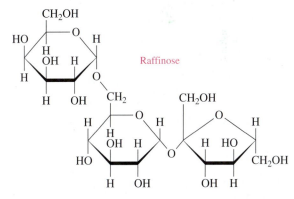

Raffinose

15.55 If α-galactose is dissolved in water, β-galactose is eventually present. Explain how this occurs. (15.4)

15.56 Why are lactose and maltose considered reducing sugars, but sucrose is not? (15.4)

CHALLENGE QUESTIONS

15.57 β-Cellobiose is a disaccharide obtained from the hydrolysis of cellulose. It is similar to maltose except it has a β-1,4-glycosidic bond. Draw the Haworth structure for β-cellobiose. (15.3)

15.58 The disaccharide trehalose found in mushrooms is composed of two α-D-glucose molecules joined by an α,α-1,1-glycosidic bond. Draw the Haworth structure for trehalose. (15.3, 15.5)

15.59 Gentiobiose, a carbohydrate found in saffron, contains two glucose molecules linked by a β-1,6-glycosidic bond. (15.3, 15.5)
   a. Draw the Haworth structure for α-gentiobiose.
   b. Is gentiobiose a reducing sugar? Explain.

15.60 Identify the open-chain formula **1** to **4** that matches each of the following: (15.2)
   a. L-mannose   **b.** a ketopentose
   c. an aldopentose   **d.** a ketohexose

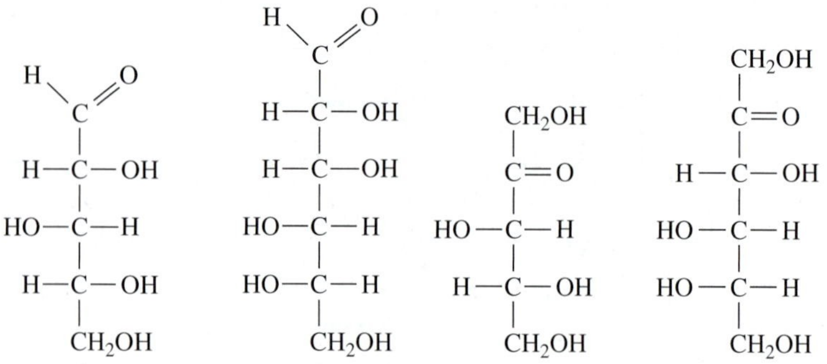

1   2   3   4

ANSWERS

Answers to Study Checks

15.1

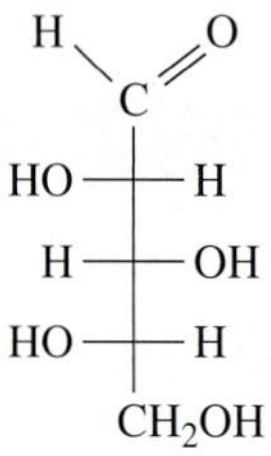

15.2 Ribulose is a ketopentose.

15.3

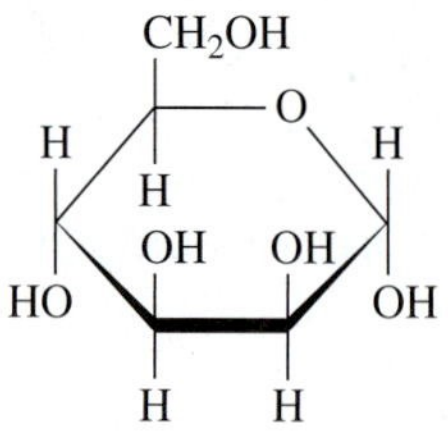

15.4

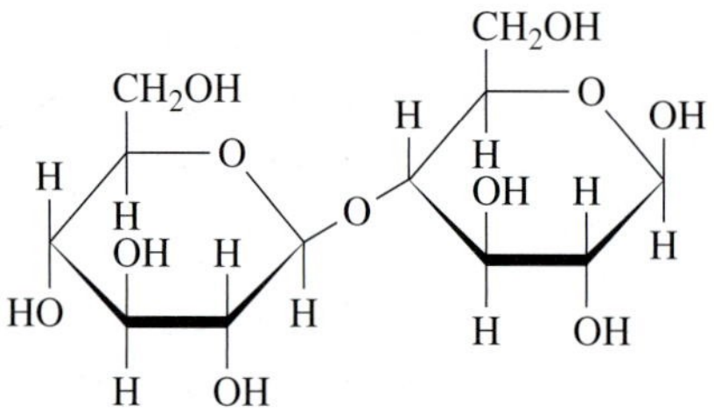

15.5 Both amylose and amylopectin contain glucose units connected by α-1,4-glycosidic bonds. However, in amylopectin, branches of glucose units are connected by α-1,6-glycosidic bonds about every 25 glucose units on the chain.

Answers to Selected Questions and Problems

15.1 Photosynthesis requires CO_2, H_2O, and the energy from the Sun. Respiration requires O_2 from the air and glucose from our foods.

15.3 Monosaccharides can be a chain of three to eight carbon atoms, one in a carbonyl group as an aldehyde or ketone, and the rest attached to hydroxyl groups. A monosaccharide cannot be split or hydrolyzed into smaller carbohydrates. A disaccharide consists of two monosaccharide units joined together that can be split.

15.5 Hydroxyl groups are found in all monosaccharides, along with a carbonyl on the first or second carbon that gives an aldehyde or ketone functional group.

15.7 A ketopentose contains hydroxyl and ketone functional groups, and has five carbon atoms.

15.9 a. ketohexose   **b.** aldopentose

15.11 In the D stereoisomer, the —OH group on the chiral carbon atom at the bottom of the chain is on the right side, whereas in the L stereoisomer, the —OH group appears on the left side.

15.13 a. D   **b.** D   **c.** L   **d.** D

15.15 a.

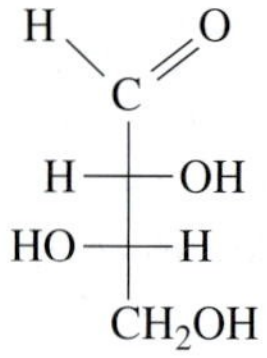

b.

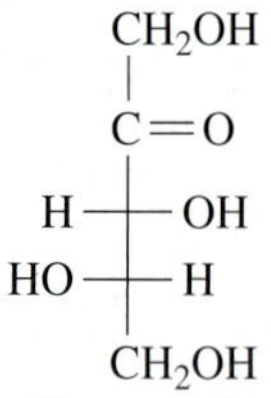

c.

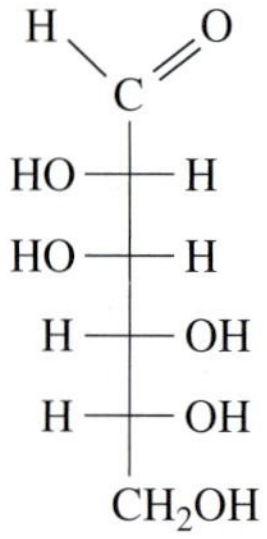

d.

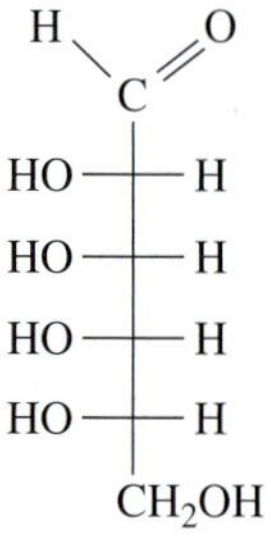

15.17

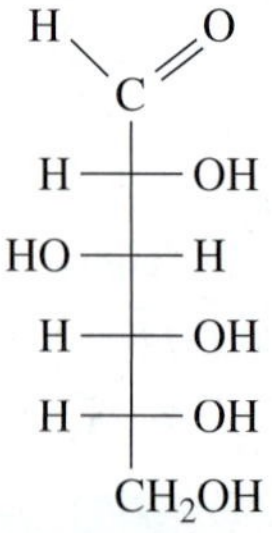

D-Glucose 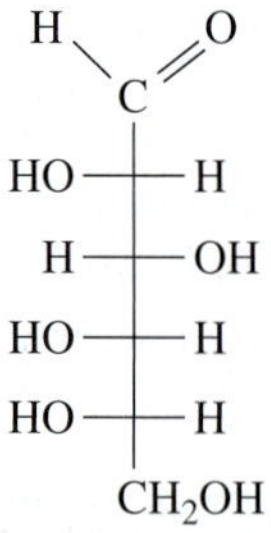   L-Glucose

15.19 In D-galactose, the hydroxyl group on carbon 4 extends to the left. In D-glucose, this hydroxyl group goes to the right.

15.21 a. glucose   **b.** galactose   **c.** fructose

15.23 In the cyclic structure of glucose, there are five carbon atoms and an oxygen atom.

15.25

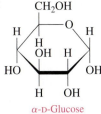

α-D-Glucose 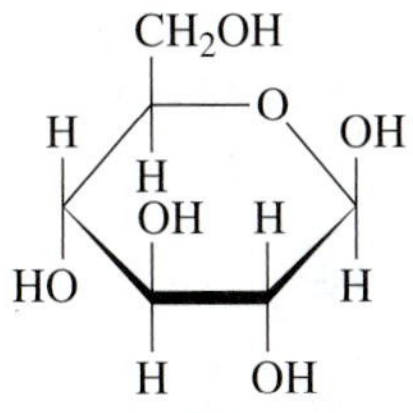   β-D-Glucose

15.27 a. α anomer   **b.** α anomer

15.29

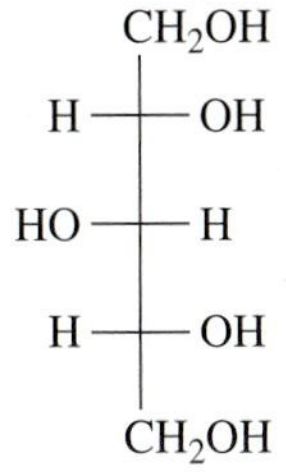

CH₂OH
H ——— OH
HO ——— H
H ——— OH
CH₂OH

D-Xylitol

15.31 Oxidation product: Reduction product (sugar alcohol):

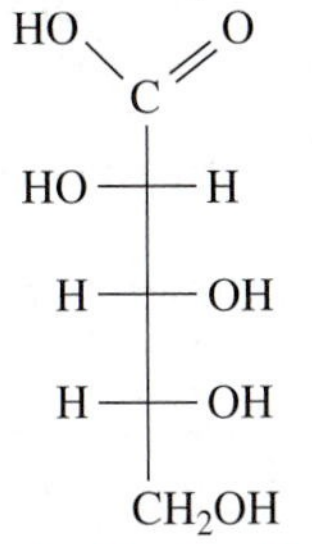

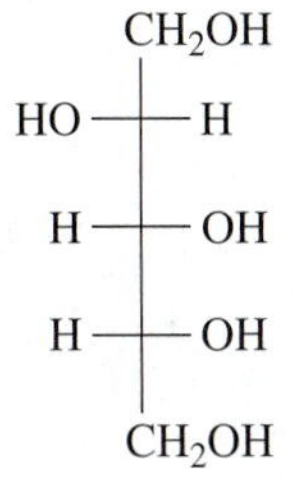

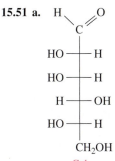

D-Arabinonic acid   D-Arabitol

15.33 a. galactose and glucose, β-1,4-glycosidic bond, β-lactose
b. glucose and glucose, α-1,4-glycosidic bond, α-maltose

15.35 a. reducing sugar   **b.** reducing sugar

15.37 a. sucrose   **b.** lactose
c. maltose   **d.** lactose

15.39 a. Amylose is an unbranched polymer of glucose units joined by α-1,4-glycosidic bonds; amylopectin is a branched polymer of glucose joined by α-1,4- and α-1,6-glycosidic bonds.
b. Amylopectin, which is produced in plants, is a branched polymer of glucose, joined by α-1,4- and α-1,6-glycosidic bonds. The branches in amylopectin occur about every 25 glucose units. Glycogen, which is produced in animals, is a highly branched polymer of glucose, joined by α-1,4- and α-1,6-glycosidic bonds. The branches in glycogen occur about every 10 to 15 glucose units.

15.41 a. cellulose   **b.** amylose, amylopectin
c. amylose   **d.** glycogen

15.43 a. disaccharide   **b.** α-D-glucose
c. α-1,6-glycosidic bond   **d.** α
e. yes

15.45 a. trisaccharide
b. two α-D-glucose and one β-D-fructose
c. Melezitose does not have a hemiacetal, therefore it cannot undergo mutarotation to form an aldehyde. Thus, melezitose is not a reducing sugar.

15.47 D-Fructose is a ketohexose, whereas D-galactose is an aldohexose. In the Fischer projection of galactose, the —OH group on carbon 4 is drawn on the left; in fructose, the —OH group is on the right.

15.49 D-Galactose is the mirror image of L-galactose. In the Fischer projection of D-galactose, the —OH groups on carbons 2 and 5 are drawn on the right side, but they are on the left for carbons 3 and 4. In L-galactose, the —OH groups are reversed; carbons 2 and 5 have —OH groups on the left, and carbons 3 and 4 have —OH groups on the right.

15.51 a.

H
  \\
   C ═ O
HO ——— H
HO ——— H
H ——— OH
HO ——— H
CH₂OH

L-Gulose

b.

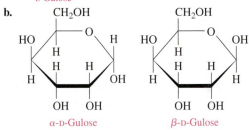

α-D-Gulose   β-D-Gulose

15.53

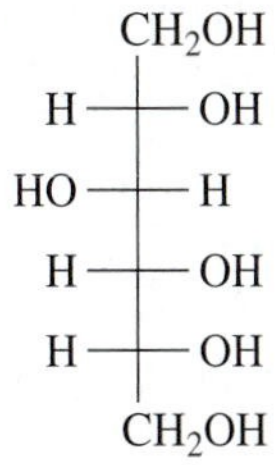

CH₂OH
H ——— OH
HO ——— H
H ——— OH
H ——— OH
CH₂OH

15.55 When the α-galactose forms an open chain in the water, it can close to form either α- or β-galactose.

15.57

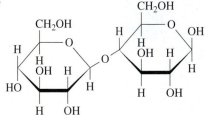

15.59 a.

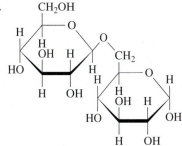

b. Yes. Gentiobiose is a reducing sugar. The ring containing the hemiacetal with the —OH group can open to form an aldehyde that can be oxidized.

Combining Ideas from Chapters 11 to 15

CI.25 A compound called butylated hydroxytoluene, or BHT, has been added to cereal and other foods since 1947 as an antioxidant. A common name for BHT is 2,6-di-*tertbutyl*-4-methylphenol. The alkyl group called *tertbutyl* has the following structure: (1.8, 6.5, 12.1, 13.1)

BHT is an antioxidant added to preserve foods such as cereal.

a. Draw the condensed structural formula for BHT.
b. BHT is produced from 4-methylphenol and 2-methylpropene. Draw the condensed structural formulas of these reactants.
c. What are the molecular formula and molar mass of BHT?
d. The FDA (Food and Drug Administration) allows a maximum of 50. ppm of BHT added to cereal. How many milligrams of BHT could be added to a box of cereal that contains 15 oz of dry cereal?

CI.26 Used in sunless tanning lotions, the compound 1,3-dihydroxy-2-propanone, or dihydroxyacetone (DHA), darkens the skin without exposure to sunlight. DHA reacts with amino acids in the outer surface of the skin. A typical drugstore lotion contains 4.0% (m/v) DHA. (8.4, 12.1, 13.1, 14.1)

A sunless tanning lotion contains DHA to darker the skin.

a. Draw the condensed structural formula for DHA.
b. What are the functional groups in DHA?
c. What are the molecular formula and molar mass of DHA?
d. Why is DHA called a ketotriose?
e. A bottle of sunless tanning lotion contains 177 mL of lotion. How many milligrams of DHA are in a bottle?

CI.27 Acetone (propanone), a clear liquid solvent with an acrid odor, is used to remove nail polish, paints, and resins. It has a low boiling point and is highly flammable. (6.5, 14.1, 14.3)

a. Draw the condensed structural formula for propanone.
b. What are the molecular formula and molar mass of propanone?
c. Draw the condensed structural formula for the alcohol that can be oxidized to produce propanone.

CI.28 Acetone (propanone) has a density of 0.786 g/mL and a heat of combustion of 428 kcal/mole. Use your answers to Problem CI.27 to solve the following: (6.1, 6.2, 6.6, 6.7, 6.9, 7.7)
a. Write the equation for the complete combustion of propanone.
b. How much heat, in kilojoules, is released if 2.58 g of propanone reacts with oxygen?
c. How many grams of oxygen gas are needed to react with 15.0 mL of propanone?
d. How many liters of carbon dioxide gas are produced at STP in part **c**?

CI.29 Panose is a trisaccharide that is being considered as a possible sweetener by the food industry. (15.1, 15.3, 15.4, 15.5)

Panose

a. What are the monosaccharide units, **A**, **B**, and **C**, in panose?
b. What type of glycosidic bond connects the monosaccharides **A** and **B**?
c. What type of glycosidic bond connects the monosaccharides **B** and **C**?
d. Is the anomer shown α- or β- panose?
e. Why would panose be a reducing sugar?

CI.30 Ionone is a compound that gives sweet violets their aroma. The small edible purple flowers of violets are used in salads and to make teas. An antioxidant called anthocyanin produces the blue and purple colors of violets. Liquid ionone has a density of 0.935 g/mL. (1.10, 6.1, 6.4, 6.5, 6.6, 6.7, 7.7, 11.5, 12.2, 14.4).

The aroma of violets is due to ionone.

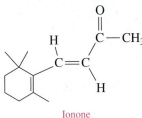

Ionone

a. What functional groups are present in ionone?
b. Is the double bond on the side chain cis or trans?
c. What are the molecular formula and molar mass of ionone?
d. How many moles are in 2.00 mL of ionone?
e. When ionone reacts with hydrogen in the presence of a platinum catalyst, hydrogen adds to the double bonds and converts the ketone group to an alcohol. What is the condensed structural formula and molecular formula for the product?
f. How many milliliters of hydrogen gas are needed at STP to completely react 5.0 mL of ionone?

CI.31 Butyraldehyde is a clear liquid solvent with an unpleasant odor. It has a low boiling point and is highly flammable. (14.1, 14.3)

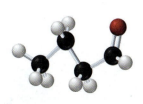

The unpleasant odor of old gym socks is due to butyraldehyde.

a. Draw the condensed structural formula for butyraldehyde.
b. Draw the skeletal formula for butyraldehyde.
c. What is the IUPAC name of butyraldehyde?
d. Draw the condensed structural formula for the alcohol that is produced when butyraldehyde is reduced.

CI.32 Butyraldehyde has a density of 0.802 g/mL and a heat of combustion of 1520 kJ/mole. Using your solutions for Problem CI.31, answer the following: (1.10, 6.1, 6.4, 6.5, 6.6, 6.7, 6.9, 7.7)
a. Write the balanced equation for the complete combustion of butyraldehyde.
b. How many grams of oxygen gas are needed to completely react 15.0 mL of butyraldehyde?
c. How many liters of carbon dioxide gas are produced at STP in part **b**?
d. Calculate the heat, in kilojoules, that is released from the combustion of butyraldehyde in part **b**.

ANSWERS

CI.25 a.

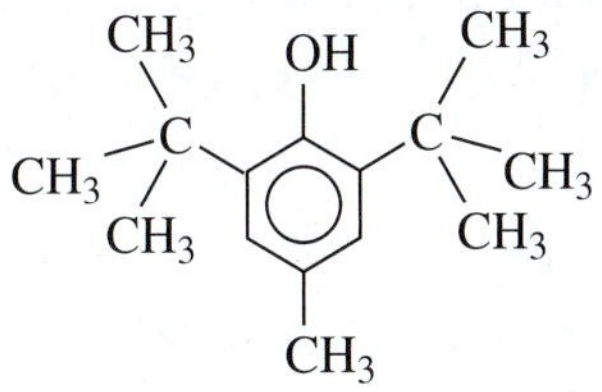

b.

4-Methylphenol   2-Methylpropene

c. $C_{15}H_{24}O$; 220. g/mole   **d.** 21 mg

CI.27 a. $CH_3-C(=O)-CH_3$

b. C_3H_6O; 58.1 g/mole
c. $CH_3-CH(OH)-CH_3$

CI.29 a. A, B, and C are all glucose.
b. An α-1,6-glycosidic bond links A and B.
c. An α-1,4-glycosidic bond links B and C.
d. β-panose
e. Panose is a reducing sugar because the anomeric carbon 1 of C is a hemiacetal that opens and closes during mutarotation to form the open-chain aldehyde.

CI.31 a. $CH_3-CH_2-CH_2-C(=O)-H$
b. 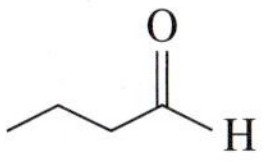
c. butanal
d. $CH_3-CH_2-CH_2-CH_2-OH$

16

Carboxylic Acids and Esters

Visit **www.masteringchemistry.com** for self-study materials and instructor-assigned homework.

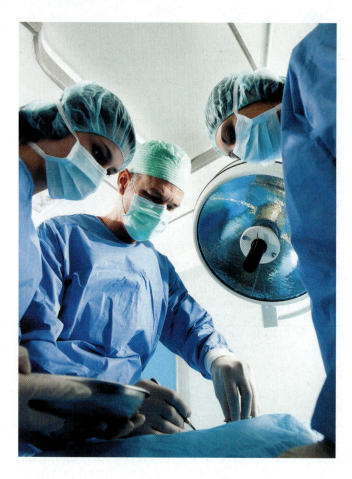

Maureen, a surgical technician, begins preparing for Robert's heart surgery. After Maureen places all of the surgical instruments into an autoclave for sterilization, she prepares the room by ensuring that all of the equipment is working properly. She also determines that the room is sterile, as this will minimize the chance of an infection. Right before surgery begins, Maureen shaves Robert's chest and disinfects the incision sites.

After the surgery, Maureen applies Indermil, which is a type of liquid bandage, to Robert's incision sites. Liquid bandages are tissue adhesives that seal surgical or wound incisions on a patient. Stitches and staples are not required and scarring is minimal. The polymer in a liquid bandage is typically dissolved in an alcohol-based solvent. The alcohol also acts as an antiseptic.

The polymer in Indermil is a cyano ester, as it consists of a cyano group ($C\equiv N$) and an ester functional group. Esters have a carbonyl group ($C=O$), which has a single bond to a carbon group on one side of the carbonyl and an oxygen atom on the other side. The oxygen atom is then bonded to a carbon group by a single bond. The cyano ester in Indermil is butyl cyanoacrylate, which is a derivative of the polymer in superglue. The "*ate*" in butyl cyanoacrylate indicates that an ester is present in the molecule, and the "*butyl*" indicates the four-carbon group that is bonded to the oxygen atom.

Career: Surgical Technician

Surgical technicians prepare the operating room by creating a sterile environment. This includes setting up surgical instruments and equipment, and ensuring that all of the equipment is working properly. A sterile environment is critical to the patient's recovery, as it helps lower the chance of an infection. They also prepare patients for surgery by washing, shaving, and disinfecting incision sites. During the surgery, a surgical technician provides the sterile instruments and supplies to the surgeons and surgical assistants.

Indermil

Carboxylic acids are similar to the weak acids we studied in Section 10.2. They have a sour or tart taste, produce hydronium ions in water, and neutralize bases. You encounter carboxylic acids when you taste the vinegar in a salad dressing, which is a solution of acetic acid and water, or experience the sour taste of citric acid in a grapefruit or lemon. When a carboxylic acid combines with an alcohol, an ester and water are produced. Fats and oils are esters of glycerol and fatty acids, which are long-chain carboxylic acids. Esters produce the pleasant aromas and flavors of many fruits, such as bananas, strawberries, and oranges.

16.1 Carboxylic Acids

LEARNING GOAL

Give the common names, IUPAC names, and draw the condensed structural formulas for carboxylic acids.

In Section 14.1, we described the carbonyl group (C=O) in aldehydes and ketones. We also described the oxidation of an aldehyde to produce a carboxylic acid. In a **carboxylic acid**, the carbon atom of a carbonyl group is attached to a hydroxyl group, which forms a **carboxyl group**. Some ways to represent the carboxyl group in propanoic acid are shown below.

Carbonyl group

Hydroxyl group

Carboxyl group

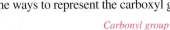

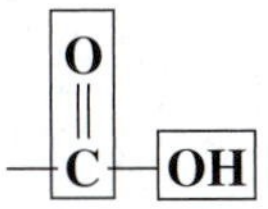

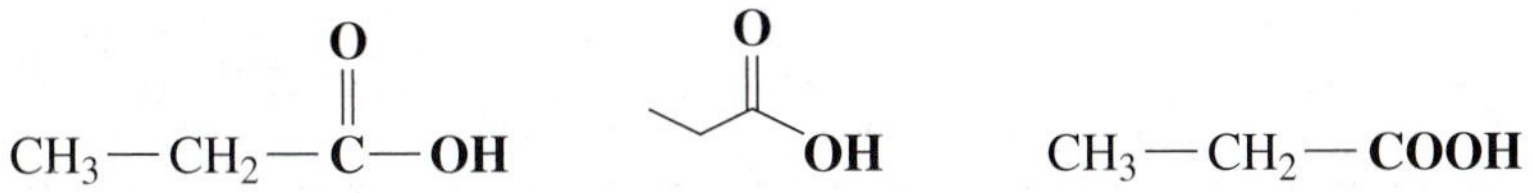

Propanoic acid
(propionic acid)

SELF-STUDY ACTIVITY
Carboxylic Acids

IUPAC Names of Carboxylic Acids

The IUPAC names of carboxylic acids replace the *e* of the corresponding alkane with *oic acid*. If there are substituents, the carbon chain is numbered beginning with the carboxyl carbon.

TUTORIAL
Naming and Drawing Carboxylic Acids

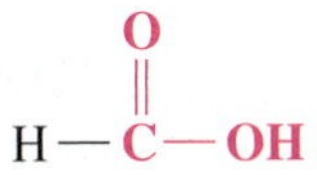

Methanoic acid

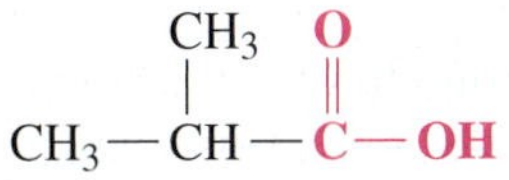

2-Methylpropanoic acid

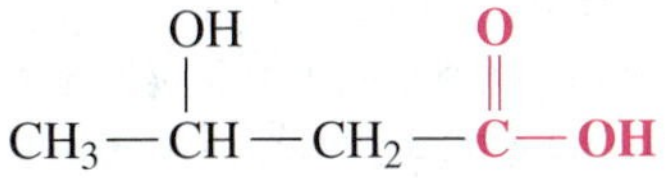

3-Hydroxybutanoic acid

The name of the carboxylic acid of benzene is benzoic acid. The carbon of the carboxyl group is bonded to carbon 1 in the ring and the ring is numbered to give the lowest possible numbers for any substituents. As before, the prefixes *ortho*, *meta*, and *para* may be used to show the position of one other substituent.

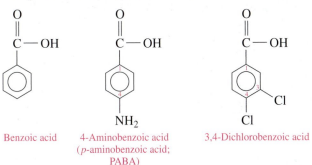

Benzoic acid

4-Aminobenzoic acid
(*p*-aminobenzoic acid; PABA)

3,4-Dichlorobenzoic acid

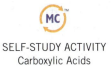

A red ant sting contains formic acid that irritates the skin.

Many carboxylic acids are still named by their common names, which use prefixes: *form, acet, propion, butyr*. When using the common names, the Greek letters alpha (α), beta (β), and gamma (γ) are assigned to the carbons adjacent to the carboxyl carbon.

$$CH_3-\overset{\overset{\displaystyle CH_3}{|}}{CH}-CH_2-\overset{\overset{\displaystyle O}{||}}{C}-OH$$

IUPAC	4	3	2	1
Common		γ	β	α

Formic acid is injected under the skin during bee or red ant stings and other insect bites. Acetic acid is the oxidation product of the ethanol in wines and apple cider. The resulting solution of acetic acid and water is known as vinegar. Propionic acid is obtained from the fats of dairy products. Butyric acid gives the foul odor to rancid butter (see Table 16.1).

TABLE 16.1 IUPAC and Common Names of Selected Carboxylic Acids

Condensed Structural Formula	IUPAC Name	Common Name	Ball-and-Stick Model
$H-\overset{\overset{\displaystyle O}{||}}{C}-OH$	Methanoic acid	Formic acid	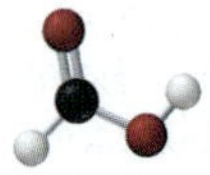
$CH_3-\overset{\overset{\displaystyle O}{||}}{C}-OH$	Ethanoic acid	Acetic acid	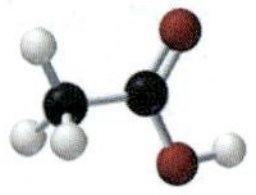
$CH_3-CH_2-\overset{\overset{\displaystyle O}{||}}{C}-OH$	Propanoic acid	Propionic acid	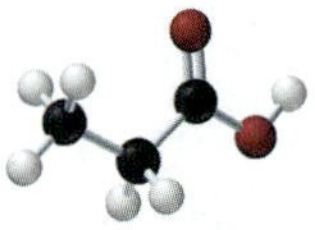
$CH_3-CH_2-CH_2-\overset{\overset{\displaystyle O}{||}}{C}-OH$	Butanoic acid	Butyric acid	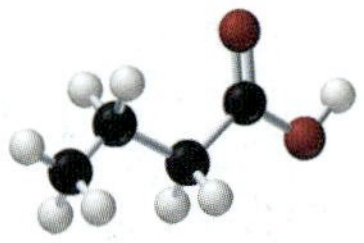

CONCEPT CHECK 16.1 **Naming Carboxylic Acids**

What is the IUPAC name of the following molecule?

$$CH_3-CH_2-CH_2-CH_2-\overset{\overset{\displaystyle O}{||}}{C}-OH$$

ANSWER

The carbon chain with the carboxyl group has five carbon atoms. In the IUPAC system, the *e* in pentane is replaced by *oic acid*, which gives the IUPAC name of pentanoic acid.

SAMPLE PROBLEM 16.1 **Naming Carboxylic Acids**

Give the IUPAC and common name, if any, for each of the following carboxylic acids:

a.

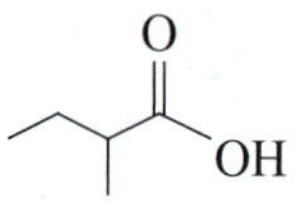

b.

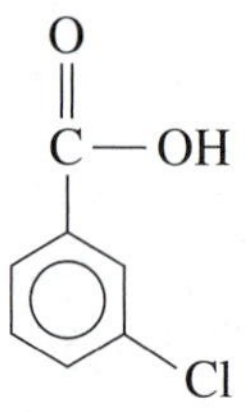

SOLUTION

Analyze the Problem

Family	IUPAC Naming	IUPAC Name
Carboxylic acid	Change the *e* of the alkane name to *oic acid* and count from carbon 1 of the carboxyl group for any substituents.	Alkanoic acid

a. **Step 1** **Identify the longest carbon chain and replace the *e* in the corresponding alkane name with *oic acid*.** A carboxylic acid with four carbon atoms is named butanoic acid; the common name is butyric acid.

butanoic acid

Step 2 **Give the location and name of each substituent by counting the carboxyl carbon as 1.** With a methyl group on the second carbon, the IUPAC name is 2-methylbutanoic acid. For the common name, the Greek letter α specifies the carbon atom next to the carboxyl carbon, α-methylbutyric acid.

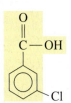

4 3 2 1
γ β α

2-methylbutanoic acid
α-methylbutyric acid

b. **Step 1** **Identify the longest carbon chain and replace the *e* in the corresponding alkane name with *oic acid*.** An aromatic carboxylic acid is named as benzoic acid.

benzoic acid

Step 2 **Give the location and name of each substituent by counting the carboxyl carbon as 1.** Counting from carbon 1 attached to the carboxyl group places the —Cl on carbon 3, which gives the IUPAC name of 3-chlorobenzoic acid. The common name is *meta*-chlorobenzoic acid or *m*-chlorobenzoic acid.

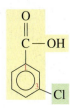

3-chlorobenzoic acid
meta-chlorobenzoic acid

STUDY CHECK 16.1

Draw the condensed structural formula for 3-phenylpropanoic acid.

Guide to Naming Carboxylic Acids

1 Identify the longest carbon chain and replace the *e* in the corresponding alkane name with *oic acid*.

2 Give the location and name of each substituent by counting the carboxyl carbon as 1.

Preparation of Carboxylic Acids

Carboxylic acids can be prepared from primary alcohols or aldehydes. As we discussed in Section 13.4, there is an increase in carbon–oxygen bonds as a primary alcohol is oxidized to an aldehyde. In Section 14.3, we learned that oxidation continues easily to

The sour taste of vinegar is due to ethanoic acid (acetic acid).

yield a carboxylic acid. For example, when ethyl alcohol in wine is exposed to oxygen in the air, vinegar is produced. The oxidation process converts the ethyl alcohol (1° alcohol) to acetaldehyde, and then to acetic acid, the carboxylic acid in vinegar.

$$CH_3-\overset{\overset{\displaystyle OH}{|}}{CH_2} \xrightarrow{[O]} CH_3-\overset{\overset{\displaystyle O}{\|}}{C}-H \xrightarrow{[O]} CH_3-\overset{\overset{\displaystyle O}{\|}}{C}-OH$$

Ethanol (ethyl alcohol)   Ethanal (acetaldehyde)   Ethanoic acid (acetic acid)

Chemistry Link to Health

ALPHA HYDROXY ACIDS

Alpha hydroxy acids (AHAs), found in fruits, milk, and sugar cane, are naturally occurring carboxylic acids with a hydroxyl group ($-OH$) on the carbon atom that is adjacent to the carboxyl group. Cleopatra, Queen of Egypt, reportedly bathed in sour milk to smooth her skin. Dermatologists have been using products with high concentrations (20–70%) of AHAs to remove acne scars and in skin peels to reduce irregular pigmentation and age spots. Lower concentrations (8–10%) of AHAs are added to skin care products for the purpose of smoothing fine lines, improving skin texture, and cleansing pores. Several different alpha hydroxy acids may be found in skin care products singly or in combination. Glycolic acid and lactic acid are most frequently used.

Recent studies indicate that products with AHAs increase sensitivity of the skin to sun and UV radiation. It is recommended that a sunscreen with a sun protection factor (SPF) of at least 15 be used when treating the skin with products that include AHAs. Products containing AHAs at concentrations under 10% and pH values greater than 3.5 are generally considered safe. However, the Food and Drug Administration (FDA) has received reports of AHAs causing skin irritation including blisters, rashes, and discoloration of the skin. The FDA does not require product safety reports from cosmetic manufacturers, although they are responsible for marketing safe products. The FDA advises that you test any product containing AHAs on a small area of skin before you use it on a large area.

Alpha Hydroxy Acid (Source)	Condensed Structural Formula
Glycolic acid (sugar cane)	$HO-CH_2-\overset{\overset{\displaystyle O}{\|}}{C}-OH$
Lactic acid (sour milk)	$CH_3-\overset{\overset{\displaystyle OH}{\|}}{CH}-\overset{\overset{\displaystyle O}{\|}}{C}-OH$
Tartaric acid (grapes)	$HO-\overset{\overset{\displaystyle O}{\|}}{C}-\overset{\overset{\displaystyle OH}{\|}}{CH}-\overset{\overset{\displaystyle OH}{\|}}{CH}-\overset{\overset{\displaystyle O}{\|}}{C}-OH$
Malic acid (apples)	$HO-\overset{\overset{\displaystyle O}{\|}}{C}-CH_2-\overset{\overset{\displaystyle OH}{\|}}{CH}-\overset{\overset{\displaystyle O}{\|}}{C}-OH$
Citric acid (citrus fruits)	$HO-\overset{\overset{\displaystyle CH_2-COOH}{\|}}{\underset{\underset{\displaystyle CH_2-COOH}{\|}}{C}}-COOH$

Alpha hydroxy carboxylic acids are used in many skin care products.

QUESTIONS AND PROBLEMS

16.1 Carboxylic Acids

LEARNING GOAL: *Give the common names, IUPAC names, and draw the condensed structural formulas for carboxylic acids.*

16.1 What carboxylic acid is responsible for the pain of an ant sting?

16.2 What carboxylic acid is found in vinegar?

16.3 Draw the condensed structural formula and give the IUPAC name for each of the following:
  a. a carboxylic acid that has the formula $C_4H_8O_2$, with no substituents
  b. a carboxylic acid that has the formula $C_4H_8O_2$, with one methyl substituent

16.4 Draw the condensed structural formula and give the IUPAC name for each of the following:
   a. a carboxylic acid that has the formula $C_5H_{10}O_2$, with no substituents
   b. a carboxylic acid that has the formula $C_5H_{10}O_2$, with two methyl substituents

16.5 Give the IUPAC and common name, if any, for each of the following carboxylic acids:

a. $CH_3-\overset{\overset{\displaystyle O}{\|}}{C}-OH$ **b.** (condensed structural formula with C=O and OH)

c. (condensed structural formula with branched chain and OH)   **d.** (aromatic ring structure with C=O, OH, and two Br substituents)

16.6 Give the IUPAC and common name, if any, for each of the following carboxylic acids:

a. $H-\overset{\overset{\displaystyle O}{\|}}{C}-OH$ **b.** (structure with OH and Br substituent)

c. (benzene ring with C=O, OH and Cl substituent)   **d.** $CH_3-CH_2-\overset{\overset{\displaystyle CH_3}{|}}{CH}-\overset{\overset{\displaystyle O}{\|}}{C}-OH$

16.7 Draw the condensed structural formula for each of the following carboxylic acids:
   a. 2-chloroethanoic acid   **b.** 3-hydroxypropanoic acid
   c. α-methylbutyric acid   **d.** 3,5-dibromoheptanoic acid

16.8 Draw the condensed structural formula for each of the following carboxylic acids:
   a. pentanoic acid   **b.** 3-ethylbenzoic acid
   c. α-hydroxyacetic acid   **d.** 2,4-dibromobutanoic acid

16.9 Draw the condensed structural formula for the carboxylic acid formed by the oxidation of each of the following:

a. CH_3-OH **b.** $CH_3-\overset{\overset{\displaystyle O}{\|}}{C}-H$

c. $CH_3-\overset{\overset{\displaystyle CH_3}{|}}{CH}-CH_2-CH_2-OH$

d. (cyclopentane ring)$-CH_2-CH_2-OH$

16.10 Draw the condensed structural formula for the carboxylic acid formed by the oxidation of each of the following:
   a. $CH_3-CH_2-CH_2-CH_2-CH_2-CH_2-OH$

b. $CH_3-CH_2-CH_2-CH_2-\overset{\overset{\displaystyle O}{\|}}{C}-H$

c. $CH_3-\overset{\overset{\displaystyle CH_3}{|}}{CH}-CH_2-\overset{\overset{\displaystyle O}{\|}}{C}-H$

d. (benzene ring)$-CH_2-CH_2-OH$

16.2 Properties of Carboxylic Acids

LEARNING GOAL

Describe the boiling points, solubility, and ionization of carboxylic acids in water.

Carboxylic acids are among the most polar organic compounds because their functional group consists of two polar groups: a hydroxyl group (—OH) and a carbonyl group (C=O). The —OH group is similar to the functional group in alcohols, and the C=O is similar to the functional group of aldehydes and ketones.

(Structures illustrating "Two polar groups" with δ− and δ+ charge labels on formic acid and propanoic acid)

TUTORIAL
Properties of Carboxylic Acids

Boiling Points

The polar carboxyl groups allow carboxylic acids to form several hydrogen bonds with other carboxylic acid molecules. This effect of hydrogen bonds gives carboxylic acids higher boiling points than alcohols, ketones, and aldehydes of similar molar mass.

	$CH_3-CH_2-\overset{\overset{\displaystyle O}{\|}}{C}-H$	$CH_3-CH_2-CH_2-OH$	$CH_3-\overset{\overset{\displaystyle O}{\|}}{C}-OH$
Name	Propanal	1-Propanol	Ethanoic acid
Molar Mass	58	60	60
Family	Aldehyde	Alcohol	Carboxylic acid
bp	49 °C	97 °C	118 °C

Increase in Boiling Point →

Two hydrogen bonds

A dimer of two ethanoic acid molecules

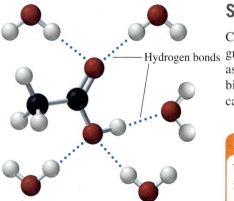

Acetic acid crystals form at a freezing point of 16.5 °C.

An important reason for the higher boiling points of carboxylic acids is that two carboxylic acids form hydrogen bonds between their carboxyl groups, resulting in a *dimer*. As a dimer, the mass of the carboxylic acid is effectively doubled, which means that a higher temperature is required to reach the boiling point. Table 16.2 lists the boiling points for some selected carboxylic acids.

SAMPLE PROBLEM 16.2 Boiling Points of Carboxylic Acids

Match each of the compounds 2-butanol, pentane, propanoic acid with a boiling point of 141 °C, 100 °C, or 36 °C. (They have about the same molar mass.)

SOLUTION

Analyze the Problem

Compound	Hydrogen Bonding
2-Butanol	Some
Pentane	None
Propanoic acid	Most (dimers)

The boiling point increases when the molecules of a compound can form hydrogen bonds or have dipole–dipole attractions. Pentane has the lowest boiling point, 36 °C, because alkanes cannot form hydrogen bonds or dipole–dipole attractions. 2-Butanol has a higher boiling point, 100 °C, than pentane because an alcohol can form hydrogen bonds. Propanoic acid has the highest boiling point, 141 °C, because carboxylic acids can form stable dimers through hydrogen bonding to increase their effective molar mass and therefore their boiling points.

STUDY CHECK 16.2

Why would methanoic acid (molar mass 46, bp 101 °C) have a higher boiling point than ethanol (molar mass 46, bp 78 °C)?

Solubility in Water

Carboxylic acids with one to five carbons are soluble in water because the carboxyl group forms hydrogen bonds with several water molecules (see Figure 16.1). However, as the length of the hydrocarbon chain increases, the nonpolar portion reduces the solubility of the carboxylic acid in water. Table 16.2 lists the solubility for some selected carboxylic acids.

Hydrogen bonds

FIGURE 16.1 Acetic acid forms hydrogen bonds with water molecules.

Q Why do the atoms in the carboxyl group form hydrogen bonds with water molecules?

CONCEPT CHECK 16.2 Solubility of Carboxylic Acids

Why is butanoic acid completely soluble in water, but 1-butanol is only slightly soluble in water?

ANSWER

Butanoic acid contains a carboxyl group, which contains a polar carbonyl group (C=O) as well as a polar hydroxyl group (—OH). These two polar groups make butanoic acid completely soluble in water. 1-Butanol is only slightly soluble in water because it has a four-carbon chain that reduces the solubility of a single —OH group.

Acidity of Carboxylic Acids

An important property of carboxylic acids is their ionization in water. When a carboxylic acid ionizes in water, H^+ is transferred to a water molecule to form a negatively charged **carboxylate ion** and a positively charged hydronium ion (H_3O^+). Carboxylic acids are weak acids

TABLE 16.2 Boiling Points, Solubilities, and Acid Dissociation Constants for Selected Carboxylic Acids

IUPAC Name	Condensed Structural Formula	Boiling Point (°C)	Solubility in Water	Acid Dissociation Constant (at 25 °C)
Methanoic acid	$H-\overset{\overset{O}{\|}}{C}-OH$	101	Soluble	1.8×10^{-4}
Ethanoic acid	$CH_3-\overset{\overset{O}{\|}}{C}-OH$	118	Soluble	1.8×10^{-5}
Propanoic acid	$CH_3-CH_2-\overset{\overset{O}{\|}}{C}-OH$	141	Soluble	1.3×10^{-5}
Butanoic acid	$CH_3-CH_2-CH_2-\overset{\overset{O}{\|}}{C}-OH$	164	Soluble	1.5×10^{-5}
Pentanoic acid	$CH_3-CH_2-CH_2-CH_2-\overset{\overset{O}{\|}}{C}-OH$	187	Soluble	1.5×10^{-5}
Hexanoic acid	$CH_3-CH_2-CH_2-CH_2-CH_2-\overset{\overset{O}{\|}}{C}-OH$	205	Slightly soluble	1.4×10^{-5}
Benzoic acid	$\overset{\overset{O}{\|}}{C}-OH$ (benzene ring)	250	Slightly soluble	6.4×10^{-5}

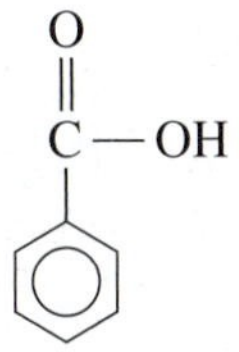

because only a small percentage ($\sim$1%) of the carboxylic acid molecules in a dilute solution is ionized. The acid dissociation constants of some carboxylic acids are given in Table 16.2.

Carboxylic Acid   **Carboxylate Ion**

$$CH_3-\overset{\overset{O}{\|}}{C}-OH + H_2O \rightleftharpoons CH_3-\overset{\overset{O}{\|}}{C}-O^- + H_3O^+$$

Ethanoic acid   Ethanoate ion   Hydronium
(acetic acid)   (acetate ion)   ion

SAMPLE PROBLEM 16.3   Ionization of Carboxylic Acids in Water

Write the equation for the ionization of propanoic acid in water.

SOLUTION

Analyze the Problem

Ionization of a Carboxylic Acid in Water	Reactants		Products	
General	Carboxylic acid	H_2O	Carboxylate ion	H_3O^+

$$CH_3-CH_2-\overset{\overset{O}{\|}}{C}-OH + H_2O \rightleftharpoons CH_3-CH_2-\overset{\overset{O}{\|}}{C}-O^- + H_3O^+$$

Propanoic acid   Propanoate ion

STUDY CHECK 16.3

Write the equation for the ionization of formic acid in water.

Neutralization of Carboxylic Acids

Because carboxylic acids are weak acids, they are completely neutralized by strong bases such as NaOH and KOH. The products are a **carboxylate salt** and water. The carboxylate ion is named by replacing the *ic acid* ending of the acid name with *ate*.

$$\text{H}-\overset{\overset{\displaystyle O}{\|}}{\text{C}}-\text{OH} + \textbf{NaOH} \longrightarrow \text{H}-\overset{\overset{\displaystyle O}{\|}}{\text{C}}-\text{O}^-\text{Na}^+ + \textbf{H}_2\textbf{O}$$

Methanoic acid (formic acid)　　　　Sodium methanoate (sodium formate)

Benzoic acid + KOH ⟶ Potassium benzoate + **H₂O**

FIGURE 16.2 Carboxylate salts are used as preservatives and flavor enhancers in soups and seasonings.

Q What is the carboxylate salt produced by the neutralization of butanoic acid and lithium hydroxide?

Another example of a carboxylate salt is sodium propionate, a preservative, which is added to bread, cheeses, and bakery items to inhibit the spoilage of the food by microorganisms. Sodium benzoate, an inhibitor of mold and bacteria, is added to juices, margarine, relishes, salads, and jams. Monosodium glutamate (MSG) is added to meats, fish, vegetables, and bakery items to enhance flavor, although it causes a headache in some people (see Figure 16.2).

$$\text{CH}_3-\text{CH}_2-\overset{\overset{\displaystyle O}{\|}}{\text{C}}-\text{O}^-\text{Na}^+$$

Sodium propanoate (sodium propionate)

Sodium benzoate

$$\text{HO}-\overset{\overset{\displaystyle O}{\|}}{\text{C}}-\overset{\overset{\displaystyle NH_2}{|}}{\text{CH}}-\text{CH}_2-\text{CH}_2-\overset{\overset{\displaystyle O}{\|}}{\text{C}}-\text{O}^-\text{Na}^+$$

Monosodium glutamate

Carboxylate salts are ionic compounds with strong attractions between positively charged metal ions such as Li^+, Na^+, and K^+ and the negatively charged carboxylate ion. Like most salts, the carboxylate salts are solids at room temperature, have high melting points, and are usually soluble in water.

SAMPLE PROBLEM 16.4　Neutralization of a Carboxylic Acid

Write the balanced equation for the neutralization of propanoic acid (propionic acid) with sodium hydroxide.

SOLUTION

Analyze the Problem

Neutralization of a Carboxylic Acid	Reactants		Products	
General	Carboxylic acid	Base	Carboxylate salt	H₂O

$$\text{CH}_3-\text{CH}_2-\overset{\overset{\displaystyle O}{\|}}{\text{C}}-\text{OH} + \text{NaOH} \longrightarrow \text{CH}_3-\text{CH}_2-\overset{\overset{\displaystyle O}{\|}}{\text{C}}-\text{O}^-\text{Na}^+ + \text{H}_2\text{O}$$

Propanoic acid (propionic acid)　Sodium hydroxide　　Sodium propanoate (sodium propionate)

STUDY CHECK 16.4

What carboxylic acid will give potassium butanoate (potassium butyrate) when it is neutralized by KOH?

Chemistry Link to Health

CARBOXYLIC ACIDS IN METABOLISM

Several carboxylic acids are part of the metabolic processes within our cells. For example, during glycolysis, a molecule of glucose is broken down into two molecules of pyruvic acid, or actually, its carboxylate ion, pyruvate. During strenuous exercise when oxygen levels are low (anaerobic), pyruvic acid is reduced to give lactic acid or the lactate ion.

$$CH_3 - \overset{\overset{\textstyle O}{\|}}{C} - \overset{\overset{\textstyle O}{\|}}{C} - OH \ + \ 2H \ \xrightarrow{\text{Reduction}} \ CH_3 - \overset{\overset{\textstyle OH}{|}}{CH} - \overset{\overset{\textstyle O}{\|}}{C} - OH$$

Pyruvic acid   Lactic acid

During exercise, pyruvic acid is converted to lactic acid in the muscles.

In the *citric acid cycle*, also called the Krebs cycle, di- and tricarboxylic acids are oxidized and decarboxylated (loss of CO_2) to produce energy for the cells of the body. These carboxylic acids are normally referred to by their common names. At the start of the citric acid cycle, citric acid with six carbons is converted to five-carbon α-ketoglutaric acid. Citric acid is also the acid that gives the sour taste to citrus fruits such as lemons and grapefruits.

$$\begin{array}{c} COOH \\ | \\ CH_2 \\ | \\ HO - C - COOH \\ | \\ CH_2 \\ | \\ COOH \end{array} \xrightarrow{[O]} \begin{array}{c} COOH \\ | \\ CH_2 \\ | \\ CH_2 \\ | \\ C = O \\ | \\ COOH \end{array} + CO_2$$

Citric acid α-Ketoglutaric acid

The citric acid cycle continues as α-ketoglutaric acid loses CO_2 to give a four-carbon succinic acid. Then a series of reactions converts succinic acid to oxaloacetic acid. We see that some of the functional groups we have studied, along with reactions such as hydration and oxidation, are part of the metabolic processes that take place in our cells.

$$\begin{array}{c} COOH \\ | \\ CH_2 \\ | \\ CH_2 \\ | \\ COOH \end{array} \xrightarrow{[O]} \begin{array}{c} COOH \\ | \\ C - H \\ \| \\ H - C \\ | \\ COOH \end{array} \xrightarrow{H_2O} \begin{array}{c} COOH \\ | \\ HO - C - H \\ | \\ CH_2 \\ | \\ COOH \end{array} \xrightarrow{[O]} \begin{array}{c} COOH \\ | \\ C = O \\ | \\ CH_2 \\ | \\ COOH \end{array}$$

Succinic acid   Fumaric acid   Malic acid   Oxaloacetic acid

At the pH of the aqueous environment in the cells, the carboxylic acids are ionized, which means it is actually the carboxylate ions that take part in the reactions of the citric acid cycle. For example, in water, succinic acid is in equilibrium with its carboxylate ion, succinate.

$$\begin{array}{c} COOH \\ | \\ CH_2 \\ | \\ CH_2 \\ | \\ COOH \end{array} + 2H_2O \ \rightleftharpoons \ \begin{array}{c} COO^- \\ | \\ CH_2 \\ | \\ CH_2 \\ | \\ COO^- \end{array} + 2H_3O^+$$

Succinic acid   Succinate ion

Citric acid gives the sour taste to citrus fruits.

QUESTIONS AND PROBLEMS

16.2 Properties of Carboxylic Acids

LEARNING GOAL: *Describe the boiling points, solubility, and ionization of carboxylic acids in water.*

16.11 Identify the compound in each of the following pairs that has the higher boiling point. Explain.
   a. ethanoic acid (acetic acid) or butanoic acid
   b. 1-propanol or propanoic acid
   c. butanone or butanoic acid

16.12 Identify the compound in each of the following pairs that has the higher boiling point. Explain.
   a. propanone (acetone) or propanoic acid
   b. propanoic acid or hexanoic acid
   c. ethanol or ethanoic acid (acetic acid)

16.13 Identify the compound in each of the following groups that is the most soluble in water. Explain.
   a. propanoic acid, hexanoic acid, benzoic acid
   b. pentane, 1-hexanol, propanoic acid

16.14 Identify the compound in each of the following groups that is the most soluble in water. Explain.
a. butanone, butanoic acid, butane
b. acetic acid, pentanoic acid, octanoic acid

16.15 Write the balanced equation for the ionization of each of the following carboxylic acids in water:
a. butanoic acid

b. $CH_3-CH_2-CH_2-CH_2-\overset{\displaystyle O}{\overset{\displaystyle \|}{C}}-OH$

16.16 Write the balanced equation for the ionization of each of the following carboxylic acids in water:

a. $CH_3-\overset{\displaystyle CH_3}{\overset{\displaystyle |}{C}H}-\overset{\displaystyle O}{\overset{\displaystyle \|}{C}}-OH$ **b.** α-hydroxyacetic acid

16.17 Write the balanced equation for the reaction of each of the following carboxylic acids with NaOH:
a. pentanoic acid
b. 2-chloropropanoic acid
c. benzoic acid

16.18 Write the balanced equation for the reaction of each of the following carboxylic acids with KOH:
a. hexanoic acid
b. 2-methylbutanoic acid
c. *p*-chlorobenzoic acid

16.19 Give the IUPAC and common names, if any, of the carboxylate salts produced in Problem 16.17.

16.20 Give the IUPAC and common names, if any, of the carboxylate salts produced in Problem 16.18.

LEARNING GOAL

Write a chemical equation for the formation of an ester.

TUTORIAL
Writing Esterification Equations

TUTORIAL
Formation of Esters from
Carboxylic Acids

16.3 Esters

A carboxylic acid reacts with an alcohol to form an **ester** and water. In an ester, the $-H$ of the carboxylic acid is replaced by an alkyl group. Fats and oils in our diets contain esters of long-chain carboxylic acids. The aromas and flavors of many fruits including bananas, oranges, and strawberries are due to esters.

Carboxylic Acid   **Ester**

$CH_3-\overset{\displaystyle O}{\overset{\displaystyle \|}{C}}-O-H$ $CH_3-\overset{\displaystyle O}{\overset{\displaystyle \|}{C}}-O-CH_3$
Ethanoic acid   Methyl ethanoate
(acetic acid)   (methyl acetate)

Esterification

In a reaction called **esterification**, an ester is produced when a carboxylic acid and an alcohol react in the presence of an acid catalyst (usually H_2SO_4) and heat. In esterification, the $-OH$ group from the carboxylic acid and the $-H$ from the alcohol are removed and combine to form water. An excess of the alcohol reactant is used to shift the equilibrium in the direction of the formation of the ester product.

$$CH_3-\overset{\displaystyle O}{\overset{\displaystyle \|}{C}}-O-H + H-O-CH_3 \underset{}{\overset{H^+,\ heat}{\rightleftharpoons}} CH_3-\overset{\displaystyle O}{\overset{\displaystyle \|}{C}}-O-CH_3 + H-O-H$$

Ethanoic acid   Methanol   Methyl ethanoate
(acetic acid)   (methyl alcohol)   (methyl acetate)

For example, the ester propyl acetate, which has the flavor and odor of pears, can be prepared using acetic acid and 1-propanol. The equation for this esterification is written as follows:

$$CH_3-\overset{\displaystyle O}{\overset{\displaystyle \|}{C}}-OH + H-O-CH_2-CH_2-CH_3 \underset{}{\overset{H^+,\ heat}{\rightleftharpoons}} CH_3-\overset{\displaystyle O}{\overset{\displaystyle \|}{C}}-O-CH_2-CH_2-CH_3 + H_2O$$

Ethanoic acid   1-Propanol   Propyl ethanoate
(acetic acid)   (propyl alcohol)   (propyl acetate)

SAMPLE PROBLEM 16.5   **Writing Esterification Equations**

The ester, methyl butyrate, which has the flavor and odor of pineapples, can be synthesized in the laboratory from butyric acid and methyl alcohol. What is the chemical equation for the formation of this ester?

SOLUTION

Analyze the Problem

Esterification	Reactants		Products	
General	Carboxylic acid	Alcohol	Ester	H₂O

$$CH_3-CH_2-CH_2-\overset{\overset{\textstyle O}{\|}}{C}-\textbf{OH} + \textbf{H}-O-CH_3 \underset{}{\overset{H^+, \text{ heat}}{\rightleftarrows}} CH_3-CH_2-CH_2-\overset{\overset{\textstyle O}{\|}}{C}-O-CH_3 + \textbf{H}_2\textbf{O}$$

Butanoic acid   Methanol   Methyl butanoate
(butyric acid)   (methyl alcohol)   (methyl butyrate)

STUDY CHECK 16.5

What are the IUPAC names of the carboxylic acid and alcohol that are needed to form the following ester, which has the odor of apples? (*Hint*: Separate the O and C=O of the ester group and add H— and —OH to give the original alcohol and carboxylic acid.)

$$CH_3-CH_2-\overset{\overset{\textstyle O}{\|}}{C}-O-CH_2-CH_2-CH_2-CH_2-CH_3$$

Chemistry Link to Health

SALICYLIC ACID FROM A WILLOW TREE

For many centuries, relief from pain and fever was obtained by chewing on the leaves or a piece of bark from the willow tree. By the 1800s, chemists discovered that salicin was the agent in the bark responsible for the relief of pain. However, the body converts salicin to salicylic acid, which has a carboxyl group and a hydroxyl group that irritates the stomach lining. In 1899, the Bayer chemical company in Germany produced an ester of salicylic acid and acetic acid, called acetylsalicylic acid (aspirin), which is less irritating. In some aspirin preparations, a buffer is added to neutralize the carboxylic acid group. Today, aspirin is used as an analgesic (pain reliever), antipyretic (fever reducer), and anti-inflammatory agent. Many people take a daily low-dose aspirin, which has been found to lower the risk of heart attack and stroke.

The discovery of salicin in the leaves and bark of the willow tree led to the development of aspirin.

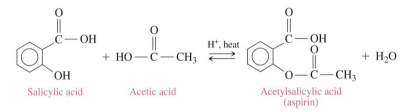

Salicylic acid   Acetic acid   Acetylsalicylic acid
(aspirin)

Oil of wintergreen, or methyl salicylate, has a pungent, minty odor and flavor. Because it can pass through the skin, methyl salicylate is used in skin ointments, where it acts as a counterirritant, producing heat to soothe sore muscles.

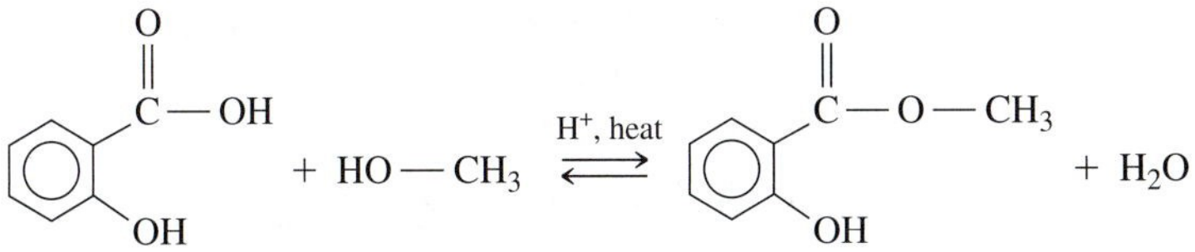

Salicylic acid   Methyl alcohol   Methyl salicylate
(oil of wintergreen)

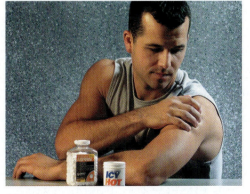

Ointments containing methyl salicylate are used to soothe sore muscles.

Chemistry Link to the Environment

PLASTICS

Terephthalic acid (an acid with two carboxyl groups) is produced in large quantities for the manufacture of polyesters such as Dacron. When terephthalic acid reacts with ethylene glycol, ester bonds form on both ends of the molecules, allowing many molecules to combine into a long polyester polymer.

Dacron, a synthetic material first produced by DuPont in the 1960s, is a polyester used to make permanent press fabrics, carpets, and clothes. Permanent press is a chemical process in which fabrics are permanently shaped and treated for wrinkle resistance. In medicine, artificial blood vessels and valves are made of Dacron, which is biologically inert and does not clot the blood. The polyester can also be made into a film called Mylar and a plastic known as PETE (**poly**ethylene**te**rephthalate). PETE is used for plastic soft drink and water bottles as well as for peanut butter jars, containers of salad dressings, shampoos, and dishwashing liquids.

Today, PETE (recycling symbol "1") is the most widely recycled of all the plastics. In 2008, more than 2.4×10^9 lb (1.1×10^9 kg)

of PETE was recycled. After PETE is separated from other plastics, it is used to make useful items, including polyester fabric for T-shirts and coats, carpets, fill for sleeping bags, doormats, and containers for tennis balls.

Dacron is a polyester used in permanent press clothing.

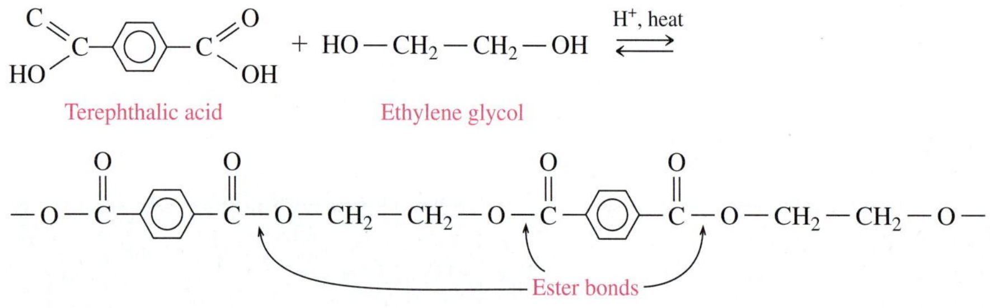

Polyester, in the form of the plastic PETE, is used to make soft drink bottles.

Terephthalic acid   +   Ethylene glycol   →   (H⁺, heat)

A section of the polyester Dacron — Ester bonds

QUESTIONS AND PROBLEMS

16.3 Esters

LEARNING GOAL: *Write a chemical equation for the formation of an ester.*

16.21 Identify each of the following as an aldehyde, a ketone, a carboxylic acid, or an ester:

a. $CH_3-C(=O)-H$

b. $CH_3-C(=O)-O-CH_3$

c. $CH_3-CH_2-C(=O)-CH_3$

d. $CH_3-CH_2-C(=O)-OH$

16.22 Identify each of the following as an aldehyde, a ketone, a carboxylic acid, or an ester:

a. $CH_3-C(=O)-OH$

b. $CH_3-C(=O)-O-CH_2-CH_3$

c. $CH_3-CH_2-C(=O)-H$

d. $CH_3-CH(CH_3)-C(=O)-O-CH_2-CH_3$

16.23 Draw the condensed structural formula for the ester formed when each of the following reacts with ethyl alcohol:
a. acetic acid
b. butyric acid
c. benzoic acid

16.24 Draw the condensed structural formula for the ester formed when each of the following reacts with methyl alcohol:
a. formic acid
b. propionic acid
c. 2-methylpentanoic acid

16.25 Draw the condensed structural formula for the ester formed in each of the following reactions:
a.
$$CH_3-CH_2-C(=O)-OH + HO-CH_2-CH_2-CH_3 \xrightarrow{H^+, heat}$$
b.
$$CH_3-CH_2-CH_2-CH_2-C(=O)-OH + HO-CH(CH_3)-CH_3 \xrightarrow{H^+, heat}$$

16.26 Draw the condensed structural formula for the ester formed in each of the following reactions:

a. 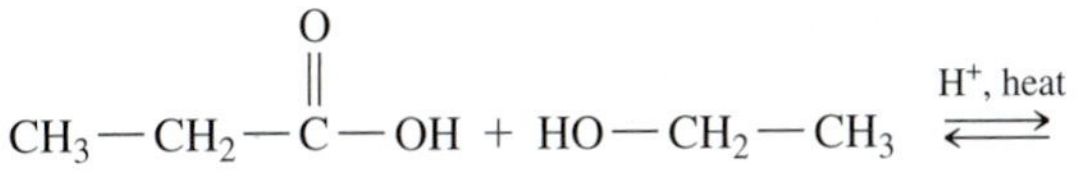 $CH_3-CH_2-\overset{\displaystyle O}{\overset{\|}{C}}-OH + HO-CH_2-CH_3 \underset{}{\overset{H^+,\ heat}{\rightleftharpoons}}$

b. 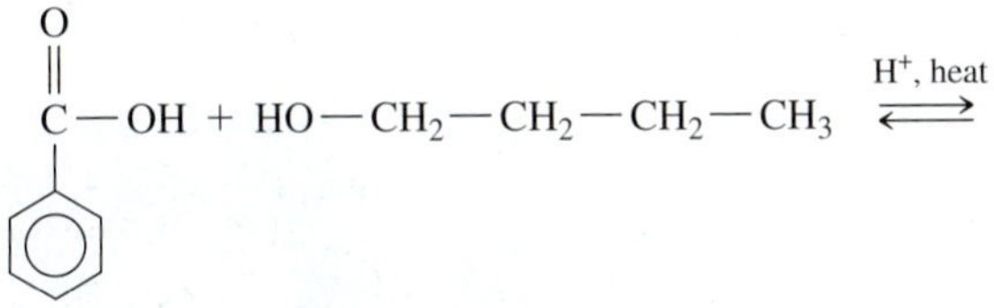 $\overset{\displaystyle O}{\overset{\|}{C}}-OH + HO-CH_2-CH_2-CH_2-CH_3 \underset{}{\overset{H^+,\ heat}{\rightleftharpoons}}$ (with benzene ring)

16.27 Give the IUPAC and common names, if any, of the carboxylic acid and alcohol needed to produce each of the following esters:

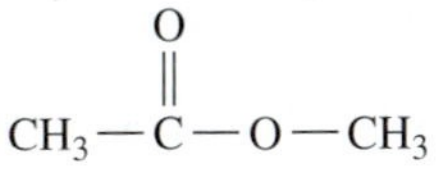

a. 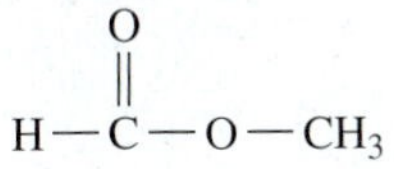 $H-\overset{\displaystyle O}{\overset{\|}{C}}-O-CH_3$ b. $CH_3-\overset{\displaystyle O}{\overset{\|}{C}}-O-CH_3$

c. $CH_3-CH_2-CH_2-\overset{\displaystyle O}{\overset{\|}{C}}-O-CH_3$

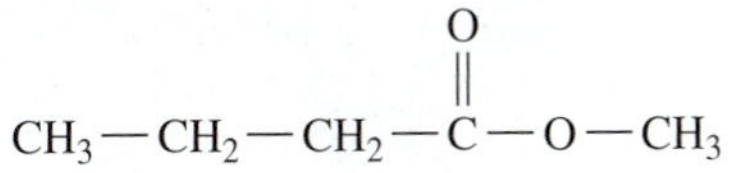

d. 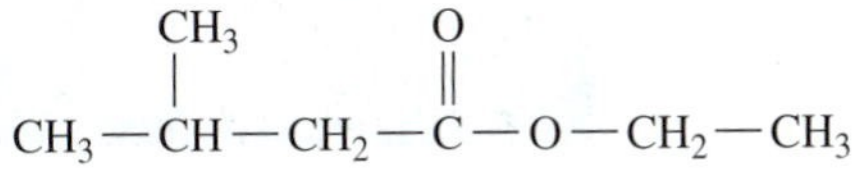 $CH_3-\overset{\displaystyle CH_3}{\overset{|}{CH}}-CH_2-\overset{\displaystyle O}{\overset{\|}{C}}-O-CH_2-CH_3$

16.28 Give the IUPAC and common names, if any, of the carboxylic acid and alcohol needed to produce each of the following esters:

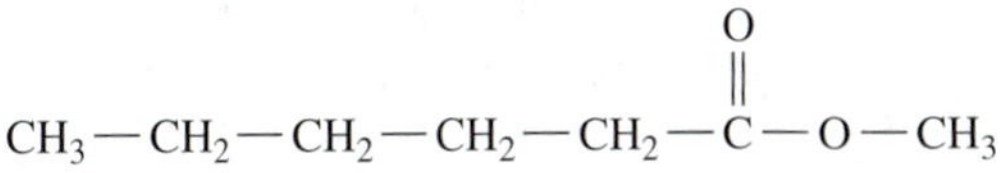

a. 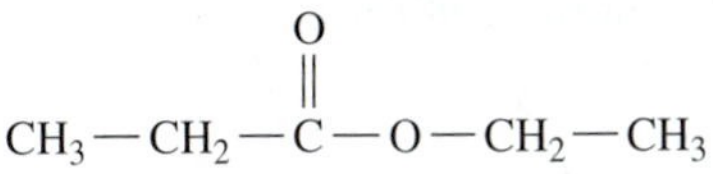 $CH_3-CH_2-\overset{\displaystyle O}{\overset{\|}{C}}-O-CH_2-CH_3$

b. $CH_3-CH_2-CH_2-CH_2-CH_2-\overset{\displaystyle O}{\overset{\|}{C}}-O-CH_3$

c. $CH_3-CH_2-\overset{\displaystyle O}{\underset{\displaystyle CH_3}{\overset{\|}{\underset{|}{CH}}}}-\overset{\displaystyle O}{\overset{\|}{C}}-O-CH_3$

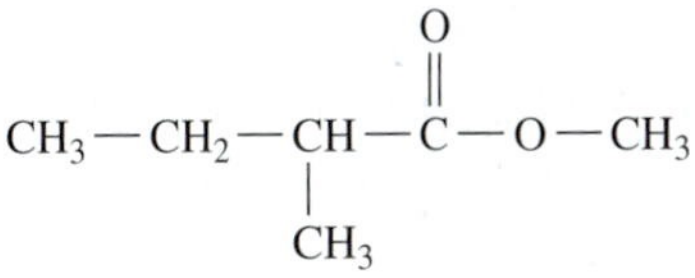

d. 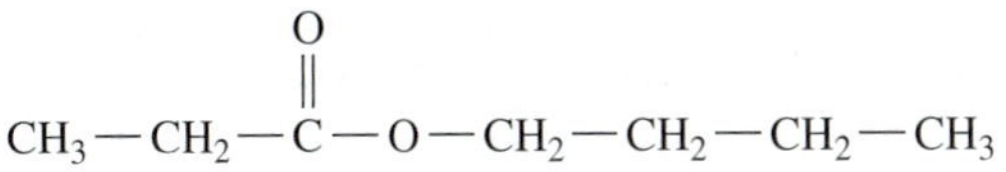 $CH_3-CH_2-\overset{\displaystyle O}{\overset{\|}{C}}-O-CH_2-CH_2-CH_2-CH_3$

16.4 Naming Esters

The name of an ester consists of two words that are derived from the names of the alcohol and the acid in that ester. The first word indicates the *alkyl* part from the alcohol. The second word is the *carboxylate* part from the carboxylic acid. The IUPAC names of esters use the IUPAC names for the carbon chain of the acid, while the common names of esters use the common names of the acids. Let's take a look at the following ester, which has a fruity odor. We start by separating the ester bond into two parts, which gives us the alkyl of the alcohol and the carboxylate of the acid. Then we name the ester as an alkyl carboxylate.

LEARNING GOAL

Write the IUPAC and common names for esters; draw condensed structural formulas.

TUTORIAL
Naming Esters

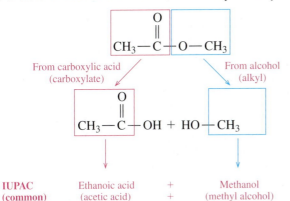

From carboxylic acid (carboxylate)   From alcohol (alkyl)

$CH_3-\overset{\displaystyle O}{\overset{\|}{C}}-OH + HO-CH_3$

| IUPAC | Ethanoic acid | + | Methanol | = Methyl ethanoate |
| (common) | (acetic acid) | + | (methyl alcohol) | = (methyl acetate) |

Ester name

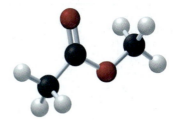

Methyl ethanoate
(methyl acetate)

The following examples of some typical esters show the IUPAC as well as the common names of esters:

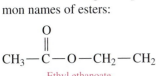

$CH_3-\overset{\displaystyle O}{\overset{\|}{C}}-O-CH_2-CH_2$
Ethyl ethanoate
(ethyl acetate)

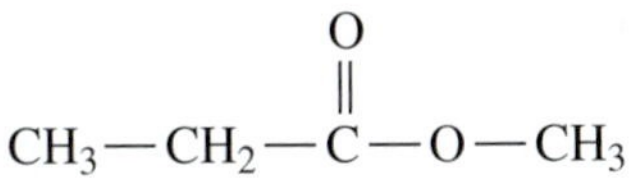

$CH_3-CH_2-\overset{\displaystyle O}{\overset{\|}{C}}-O-CH_3$
Methyl propanoate
(methyl propionate)

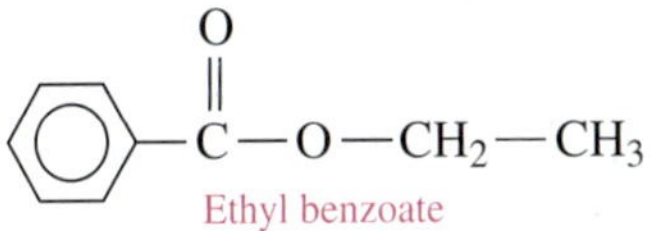

$\overset{\displaystyle O}{\overset{\|}{C}}-O-CH_2-CH_3$ (with benzene ring)
Ethyl benzoate

Many of the fragrances of perfumes and flowers, and the flavors of fruits are due to esters. Small esters are volatile so we can smell them and soluble in water so we can taste them. Several esters and their flavors and odor are listed in Table 16.3.

TABLE 16.3 Some Esters in Fruits and Flavorings

Condensed Structural Formula and Name	Flavor/Odor
$CH_3-\overset{\overset{\text{O}}{\|}}{C}-O-CH_2-CH_2-CH_3$ Propyl ethanoate (propyl acetate)	Pears
$CH_3-\overset{\overset{\text{O}}{\|}}{C}-O-CH_2-CH_2-CH_2-CH_2-CH_3$ Pentyl ethanoate (pentyl acetate)	Bananas
$CH_3-\overset{\overset{\text{O}}{\|}}{C}-O-CH_2-CH_2-CH_2-CH_2-CH_2-CH_2-CH_2-CH_3$ Octyl ethanoate (octyl acetate)	Oranges
$CH_3-CH_2-CH_2-\overset{\overset{\text{O}}{\|}}{C}-O-CH_2-CH_3$ Ethyl butanoate (ethyl butyrate)	Pineapples
$CH_3-CH_2-CH_2-\overset{\overset{\text{O}}{\|}}{C}-O-CH_2-CH_2-CH_2-CH_2-CH_3$ Pentyl butanoate (pentyl butyrate)	Apricots

Esters such as ethyl butanoate provide the odor and flavor of many fruits such as pineapples.

Guide to Naming Esters

1 Write the name of the carbon chain from the alcohol as an *alkyl* group.

2 Change the *ic acid* of the acid name to *ate*.

SAMPLE PROBLEM 16.6 Naming Esters

What are the IUPAC and common names of the following ester?

$$CH_3-CH_2-\overset{\overset{\text{O}}{\|}}{C}-O-CH_2-CH_2-CH_3$$

SOLUTION

Analyze the Problem

Family	IUPAC Naming	IUPAC Name
Ester	Write the alkyl name for the carbon chain of the alcohol, and change the *ic acid* in the acid name to *ate*.	Alkyl carboxylate

Step 1 **Write the name of the carbon chain from the alcohol as an *alkyl* group.** The alcohol that is used for the ester is propanol, which has a three-carbon chain named propyl.

$$CH_3-CH_2-\overset{\overset{\text{O}}{\|}}{C}-O-CH_2-CH_2-CH_3 \qquad propyl$$

Step 2 **Change the *ic acid* of the acid name to *ate*.** The carboxylic acid that is used for the ester is propanoic acid, which has three carbon atoms. Replacing the *ic acid* with *ate* gives propanoate. Thus, the IUPAC name is propyl propanoate.

Replacing the *ic acid* in the common name propionic acid with *ate* gives propionate. The common name for the ester is propyl propionate.

$$CH_3-CH_2-\overset{\overset{\displaystyle O}{\|}}{C}-O-CH_2-CH_2-CH_3$$

propyl propanoate

(propyl propionate)

The odor of grapes is due to ethyl heptanoate.

STUDY CHECK 16.6

Draw the condensed structural formula for ethyl heptanoate that gives odor and flavor to grapes.

QUESTIONS AND PROBLEMS

16.4 Naming Esters

LEARNING GOAL: *Write the IUPAC and common names for esters; draw condensed structural formulas.*

16.29 Give the IUPAC name and common name, if any, for each the following esters:

a. $H-\overset{\overset{\displaystyle O}{\|}}{C}-O-CH_3$ b. $CH_3-CH_2-\overset{\overset{\displaystyle O}{\|}}{C}-O-CH_2-CH_3$

c. $CH_3-CH_2-CH_2-\overset{\overset{\displaystyle O}{\|}}{C}-O-CH_3$

d. $CH_3-CH_2-CH_2-CH_2-\overset{\overset{\displaystyle O}{\|}}{C}-O-CH_2-\overset{\overset{\displaystyle CH_3}{|}}{CH}-CH_3$

16.30 Give the IUPAC name and common name, if any, for each of the following esters:

a. $CH_3-CH_2-CH_2-\overset{\overset{\displaystyle O}{\|}}{C}-O-CH_2-CH_3$

b. $CH_3-CH_2-CH_2-CH_2-CH_2-\overset{\overset{\displaystyle O}{\|}}{C}-O-CH_3$

c. $CH_3-\overset{\overset{\displaystyle CH_3}{|}}{CH}-CH_2-\overset{\overset{\displaystyle O}{\|}}{C}-O-CH_3$

d. $CH_3-CH_2-\overset{\overset{\displaystyle O}{\|}}{C}-O-CH_2-CH_2-CH_2-CH_3$

16.31 Draw the condensed structural formula for each of the following:
a. methyl acetate b. butyl formate
c. ethyl pentanoate d. 2-bromopropyl propanoate

16.32 Draw the condensed structural formula for each of the following:
a. hexyl acetate b. propyl propionate
c. ethyl 2-hydroxybutanoate d. methyl benzoate

16.33 What is the ester responsible for the flavor and odor of each of the following fruits?
a. banana b. orange
c. apricot

16.34 What flavor would you notice if you smelled or tasted each of the following?
a. ethyl butanoate b. propyl acetate
c. octyl acetate

16.5 Properties of Esters

LEARNING GOAL

Describe the boiling points and solubility of esters; draw the condensed structural formulas for the hydrolysis products.

Esters have boiling points higher than those of alkanes and ethers, but lower than those of alcohols and carboxylic acids of similar mass. Because ester molecules do not have hydroxyl groups, they cannot hydrogen bond to each other.

$CH_3-CH_2-CH_2-CH_3$	$H-\overset{\overset{\displaystyle O}{\|}}{C}-O-CH_3$	$CH_3-CH_2-CH_2-OH$	$CH_3-\overset{\overset{\displaystyle O}{\|}}{C}-OH$
Name Butane	Methyl methanoate	1-Propanol	Ethanoic acid
Molar Mass 58	60	60	60
Family Alkane	Ester	Alcohol	Carboxylic acid
bp 0 °C	32 °C	97 °C	118 °C

Increase in Boiling Points →

Solubility in Water

Esters with one to five carbon atoms are soluble in water. The partially negative oxygen of the carbonyl group forms hydrogen bonds with the partially positive hydrogen atoms of water molecules. The solubility of esters decreases as the number of carbon atoms increases.

TUTORIAL
Hydrolysis of Esters

Acid Hydrolysis of Esters

When esters react with water in the presence of a strong acid, usually H_2SO_4 or HCl, *hydrolysis* occurs. In **hydrolysis**, water reacts with an ester to form a carboxylic acid and an alcohol. Therefore, hydrolysis is the reverse of the esterification reaction. During hydrolysis, a water molecule provides —OH to convert the carbonyl group of the ester to a carboxyl group. According to Le Châtelier's principle, a large quantity of water will shift the equilibrium in the direction of the formation of the carboxylic acid and alcohol products. When hydrolysis of biological compounds occurs in the cells, an enzyme replaces the acid as the catalyst.

$$CH_3-\overset{\displaystyle O}{\overset{\|}{C}}-O-CH_3 + H-OH \underset{}{\overset{H^+, \text{ heat}}{\rightleftharpoons}} CH_3-\overset{\displaystyle O}{\overset{\|}{C}}-OH + CH_3-OH$$

Methyl ethanoate (methyl acetate) Water Ethanoic acid (acetic acid) Methanol (methyl alcohol)

SAMPLE PROBLEM 16.7   **Acid Hydrolysis of Esters**

Aspirin that has been stored for a long time may undergo hydrolysis in the presence of water and heat. What are the hydrolysis products of aspirin? Why does a bottle of old aspirin smell like vinegar?

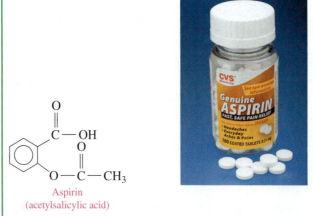

Aspirin
(acetylsalicylic acid)

Aspirin stored in a warm, humid place may undergo hydrolysis.

SOLUTION

Analyze the Problem

Hydrolysis	Reactants		Products	
General	Ester	H_2O	Carboxylic acid	Alcohol

To write the hydrolysis products, separate the compound at the ester bond. Complete the formula of the carboxylic acid by adding —OH (from water) to the carbonyl group and —H to complete the alcohol. The acetic acid in the products gives the odor of vinegar to a sample of aspirin that has hydrolyzed.

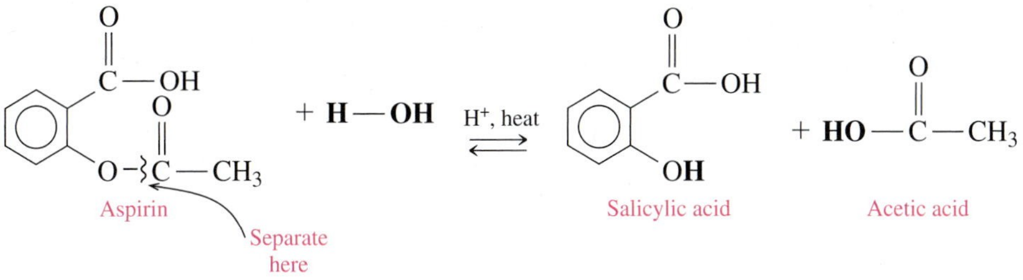

$$\underset{\text{Aspirin}}{} + \mathbf{H-OH} \xrightarrow[\text{H}^+,\text{ heat}]{} \underset{\text{Salicylic acid}}{} + \underset{\text{Acetic acid}}{\mathbf{HO-C-CH_3}}$$

Separate here

STUDY CHECK 16.7

What are the names of the products from the acid hydrolysis of ethyl propanoate (ethyl propionate)?

Base Hydrolysis of Esters (Saponification)

When an ester undergoes hydrolysis with a strong base such as NaOH or KOH, the products are the carboxylate salt and the corresponding alcohol. This hydrolysis in a basic environment is also called **saponification**, which refers to the reaction of a long-chain fatty acid with NaOH to make soap. Thus, a carboxylic acid, which is produced in acid hydrolysis, is converted to its carboxylate salt when neutralized by a strong base.

Ester   + Strong base ⟶ Carboxylate salt   +   Alcohol

$$\underset{\substack{\text{Methyl ethanoate}\\\text{(methyl acetate)}}}{CH_3-C\!-\!O-CH_3} + \underset{\text{Sodium hydroxide}}{NaOH} \xrightarrow{\text{Heat}} \underset{\substack{\text{Sodium ethanoate}\\\text{(sodium acetate)}}}{CH_3-C\!-\!O^-Na^+} + \underset{\substack{\text{Methanol}\\\text{(methyl alcohol)}}}{CH_3-OH}$$

CONCEPT CHECK 16.3   **Hydrolysis of Esters**

Ethyl methanoate is one of the esters responsible for the flavor of raspberries. Name the products of each of the following reactions of ethyl methanoate:

a. acid hydrolysis with HCl
b. saponification with KOH

ANSWER

a. The products of the acid hydrolysis of ethyl methanoate are the alcohol, ethanol, and the carboxylic acid, methanoic acid.
b. The products of the base hydrolysis (saponification) of ethyl methanoate with KOH are the alcohol, ethanol, and the carboxylate salt, potassium methanoate.

The flavor of raspberries is due to ethyl methanoate.

SAMPLE PROBLEM 16.8   **Base Hydrolysis of Esters**

Ethyl acetate is a solvent used in fingernail polish, plastics, and lacquers. Write the equation for the hydrolysis of ethyl acetate with NaOH.

SOLUTION

Analyze the Problem

Base Hydrolysis of an Ester	Reactants		Products	
General	Ester	Base	Carboxylate salt	Alcohol

Ethyl acetate is the solvent in fingernail polish.

$$CH_3 - \overset{\overset{\displaystyle O}{\|}}{C} - O - CH_2 - CH_3 \ + \ NaOH \ \xrightarrow{\text{Heat}} \ CH_3 - \overset{\overset{\displaystyle O}{\|}}{C} - O^- Na^+ \ + \ HO - CH_2 - CH_3$$

Ethyl ethanoate   Sodium ethanoate   Ethanol
(ethyl acetate)   (sodium acetate)   (ethyl alcohol)

STUDY CHECK 16.8

Draw the condensed structural formulas for the products from the hydrolysis of methyl benzoate with KOH.

Chemistry Link to the Environment

CLEANING ACTION OF SOAPS

For many centuries, soaps were made by heating a mixture of animal fats (tallow) with lye, a basic solution obtained by leaching wood ashes. In the soap-making process, fatty acids, which are long-chain carboxylic acids, undergo saponification with the strong base in lye.

$$CH_2 - O - \overset{\overset{\displaystyle O}{\|}}{C} - (CH_2)_{14} - CH_3$$
$$| \qquad\qquad \overset{\displaystyle O}{\|}$$
$$CH - O - \overset{}{C} - (CH_2)_{14} - CH_3 \ + \ \mathbf{3NaOH} \ \longrightarrow$$
$$| \qquad\qquad \overset{\displaystyle O}{\|}$$
$$CH_2 - O - \overset{}{C} - (CH_2)_{14} - CH_3$$

$$CH_2 - OH$$
$$|$$
$$CH - OH \ + \ \mathbf{3Na^+\,{}^-O} - \overset{\overset{\displaystyle O}{\|}}{C} - (CH_2)_{14} - CH_3$$
$$|$$
$$CH_2 - OH$$

Polar head (hydrophilic)

Nonpolar tail (hydrophobic)

| Fat | + | strong base | $\longrightarrow$ | glycerol | + | carboxylate salts (soaps) |

Soaps are typically prepared from fats such as coconut oil. Perfumes are added to give a pleasant-smelling product. We say that soap is the salt of a long-chain fatty acid because it has a long hydrocarbon-like chain with a carboxylate negative end, combined with a positive sodium or potassium ion. Soap has dual properties because parts of the soap molecule have different solubilities. The sodium or potassium carboxylate end is ionic and very soluble in water ("hydrophilic"), but it is not soluble in oils or grease. However, the long hydrocarbon end is not soluble in water ("hydrophobic"), but it is soluble in nonpolar substances such as oil or grease.

When soap is used, the hydrocarbon tails of the soap molecules dissolve in the nonpolar fats and oils that accompany dirt. The soap molecules coat the oil or grease, forming clusters called *micelles*, in which the water-loving salt ends of the soap molecules extend outside where they can dissolve in water. As a result, small globules of oil and fat coated with soap molecules are pulled into the water and rinsed away. One of the problems with using soaps is that the carboxylate end reacts with ions in water such as Ca^{2+} and Mg^{2+} and forms insoluble substances. This does not occur with detergents.

$$2CH_3(CH_2)_{16}COO^- \ + \ Mg^{2+} \ \longrightarrow \ [CH_3(CH_2)_{16}COO^-]_2Mg^{2+}$$

Stearate ion   Magnesium ion   Magnesium stearate (insoluble)

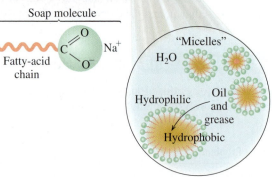

Soap molecule

Fatty-acid chain

"Micelles"
H_2O
Hydrophilic
Oil and grease
Hydrophobic

The hydrocarbon tails of soap molecules dissolve in grease and oil to form micelles, which are pulled by their ionic heads into the rinse water.

QUESTIONS AND PROBLEMS

16.5 Properties of Esters

LEARNING GOAL: *Describe the boiling points and solubility of esters; draw the condensed structural formulas for the hydrolysis products.*

16.35 For each of the following pairs of compounds, select the compound that has the higher boiling point:

a. $CH_3-\overset{\overset{\displaystyle O}{\|}}{C}-O-CH_3$ or $CH_3-CH_2-\overset{\overset{\displaystyle O}{\|}}{C}-OH$

b. $CH_3-\overset{\overset{\displaystyle O}{\|}}{C}-O-CH_3$ or $CH_3-CH_2-CH_2-CH_2-OH$

c. $CH_3-CH_2-CH_2-CH_2-CH_3$ or $CH_3-\overset{\overset{\displaystyle O}{\|}}{C}-O-CH_3$

16.36 For each of the following pairs of compounds, select the compound that has the higher boiling point:

a. $H-\overset{\overset{\displaystyle O}{\|}}{C}-O-CH_3$ or $CH_3-CH_2-CH_2-OH$

b. $CH_3-\overset{\overset{\displaystyle O}{\|}}{C}-O-CH_3$ or $CH_3-CH_2-\overset{\overset{\displaystyle O}{\|}}{C}-OH$

c. $CH_3-O-CH_2-CH_3$ or $H-\overset{\overset{\displaystyle O}{\|}}{C}-O-CH_3$

16.37 What are the products of the acid hydrolysis of an ester?

16.38 What are the products of the base hydrolysis of an ester?

16.39 Draw the condensed structural formulas for the products from the acid- or base-catalyzed hydrolysis of each of the following compounds:

a. $CH_3-CH_2-\overset{\overset{\displaystyle O}{\|}}{C}-O-CH_3 + NaOH \xrightarrow{\text{Heat}}$

b. $CH_3-\overset{\overset{\displaystyle O}{\|}}{C}-O-CH_2-CH_2-CH_3 + H_2O \underset{}{\overset{H^+, \text{heat}}{\rightleftarrows}}$

c. $CH_3-CH_2-CH_2-\overset{\overset{\displaystyle O}{\|}}{C}-O-CH_2-CH_3 + H_2O \underset{}{\overset{H^+, \text{heat}}{\rightleftarrows}}$

d. $\langle\bigcirc\rangle-\overset{\overset{\displaystyle O}{\|}}{C}-O-CH_2-CH_3 + H_2O \underset{}{\overset{H^+, \text{heat}}{\rightleftarrows}}$

e. $\langle\bigcirc\rangle-\overset{\overset{\displaystyle O}{\|}}{C}-O-CH_2-CH_3 + NaOH \xrightarrow{\text{Heat}}$

16.40 Draw the condensed structural formulas of the products from the acid- or base-catalyzed hydrolysis of each of the following compounds:

a. $CH_3-CH_2-\overset{\overset{\displaystyle O}{\|}}{C}-O-CH_2-CH_2-CH_2-CH_3 + H_2O \underset{}{\overset{H^+, \text{heat}}{\rightleftarrows}}$

b. $H-\overset{\overset{\displaystyle O}{\|}}{C}-O-CH_2-CH_2-CH_3 + NaOH \xrightarrow{\text{Heat}}$

c. $CH_3-CH_2-\overset{\overset{\displaystyle O}{\|}}{C}-O-CH_3 + H_2O \underset{}{\overset{H^+, \text{heat}}{\rightleftarrows}}$

d. $CH_3-CH_2-\overset{\overset{\displaystyle O}{\|}}{C}-O-\langle\bigcirc\rangle + H_2O \underset{}{\overset{H^+, \text{heat}}{\rightleftarrows}}$

e. $\langle\bigcirc\rangle-CH_2-\overset{\overset{\displaystyle O}{\|}}{C}-O-CH_2-CH_3 + NaOH \xrightarrow{\text{Heat}}$

CONCEPT MAP

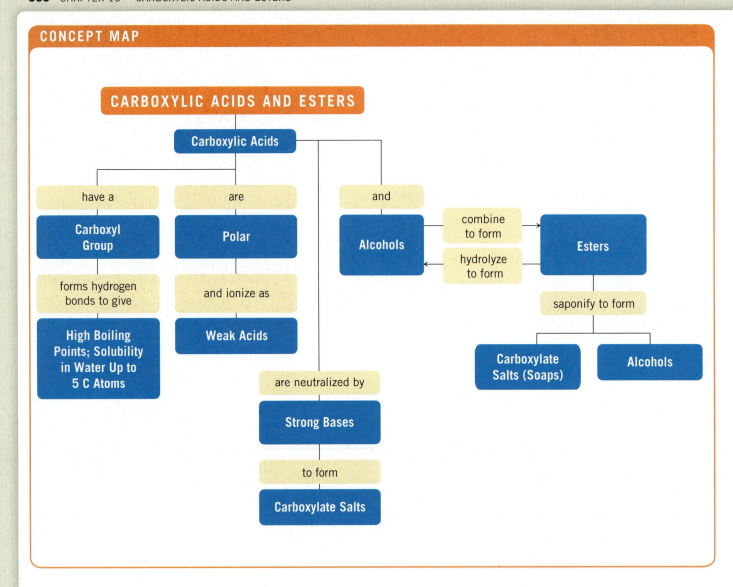

CARBOXYLIC ACIDS AND ESTERS

Carboxylic Acids

have a → **Carboxyl Group** → forms hydrogen bonds to give → **High Boiling Points; Solubility in Water Up to 5 C Atoms**

are → **Polar** → and ionize as → **Weak Acids**

are neutralized by → **Strong Bases** → to form → **Carboxylate Salts**

and → **Alcohols**

Alcohols — combine to form → **Esters**

Esters — hydrolyze to form → **Alcohols**

Esters → saponify to form → **Carboxylate Salts (Soaps)** and **Alcohols**

CHAPTER REVIEW

16.1 Carboxylic Acids

LEARNING GOAL: Give the common names, IUPAC names, and draw the condensed structural formulas for carboxylic acids.

- A carboxylic acid contains the carboxyl functional group, which is a hydroxyl group connected to a carbonyl group.
- The IUPAC name of a carboxylic acid is obtained by replacing the *e* in the alkane name with *oic acid*.
- The common names of carboxylic acids with one to four carbon atoms are: formic acid, acetic acid, propionic acid, and butyric acid.

16.2 Properties of Carboxylic Acids

LEARNING GOAL: Describe the boiling points, solubility, and ionization of carboxylic acids in water.

Hydrogen bonds

- The carboxyl group contains polar bonds of O—H and C=O, which makes a carboxylic acid with one to five carbon atoms soluble in water.
- As weak acids, carboxylic acids ionize slightly by donating a proton to water to form carboxylate and hydronium ions.
- Carboxylic acids are neutralized by base, producing a carboxylate salt and water.

16.3 Esters

LEARNING GOAL: Write a chemical equation for the formation of an ester.

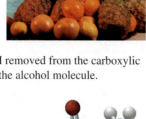

- In an ester, an alkyl or aromatic group replaces the H of the hydroxyl group of a carboxylic acid.
- In the presence of a strong acid, a carboxylic acid reacts with an alcohol to produce an ester and a molecule of water from the —OH removed from the carboxylic acid, and the —H removed from the alcohol molecule.

16.4 Naming Esters

LEARNING GOAL: Write the IUPAC and common names for esters; draw condensed structural formulas.

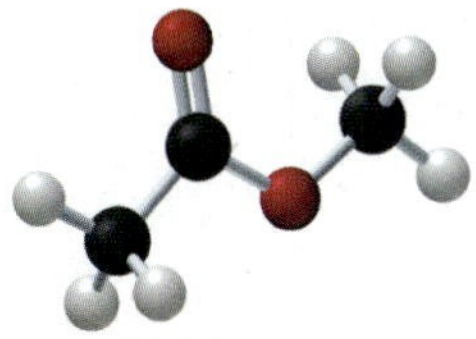

- The names of esters consist of two words: the alkyl group from the alcohol and the name of the carboxylate obtained by replacing *ic acid* with *ate*.

Methyl ethanoate
(methyl acetate)

16.5 Properties of Esters

LEARNING GOAL: Describe the boiling points and solubility of esters; draw the condensed structural formulas for the hydrolysis products.

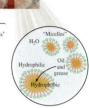

- Esters have boiling points that are lower than alcohols and carboxylic acids, but higher than alkanes.
- Esters with one to five carbon atoms are soluble in water.
- Esters undergo acid hydrolysis by adding water to yield the carboxylic acid and alcohol (or phenol).
- Base hydrolysis, or saponification, of an ester produces the carboxylate salt and an alcohol.

SUMMARY OF NAMING

Family	Condensed Structural Formula	IUPAC Name	Common Name
Carboxylic acid	$CH_3 - \overset{\overset{\textstyle O}{\|\|}}{C} - OH$	Ethanoic acid	Acetic acid
Carboxylate salt	$CH_3 - \overset{\overset{\textstyle O}{\|\|}}{C} - O^- Na^+$	Sodium ethanoate	Sodium acetate
Ester	$CH_3 - \overset{\overset{\textstyle O}{\|\|}}{C} - O - CH_3$	Methyl ethanoate	Methyl acetate

---

SUMMARY OF REACTIONS

Ionization of a Carboxylic Acid in Water

$$CH_3 - \overset{\overset{\textstyle O}{\|\|}}{C} - OH + H_2O \rightleftharpoons CH_3 - \overset{\overset{\textstyle O}{\|\|}}{C} - O^- + H_3O^+$$

Ethanoic acid (acetic acid)   Ethanoate ion (acetate ion)   Hydronium ion

Neutralization of a Carboxylic Acid

$$CH_3 - CH_2 - \overset{\overset{\textstyle O}{\|\|}}{C} - OH + NaOH \longrightarrow CH_3 - CH_2 - \overset{\overset{\textstyle O}{\|\|}}{C} - O^- Na^+ + H_2O$$

Propanoic acid (propionic acid)   Sodium hydroxide   Sodium propanoate (sodium propionate)

Esterification: Carboxylic Acid and an Alcohol

$$CH_3-\overset{\overset{\displaystyle O}{\|}}{C}-OH + HO-CH_3 \underset{}{\overset{H^+, \text{ heat}}{\rightleftharpoons}} CH_3-\overset{\overset{\displaystyle O}{\|}}{C}-O-CH_3 + H_2O$$

Ethanoic acid   Methanol   Methyl ethanoate
(acetic acid)   (methyl alcohol)   (methyl acetate)

Acid Hydrolysis of an Ester

$$CH_3-\overset{\overset{\displaystyle O}{\|}}{C}-O-CH_3 + H-OH \overset{H^+, \text{ heat}}{\rightleftharpoons} CH_3-\overset{\overset{\displaystyle O}{\|}}{C}-OH + HO-CH_3$$

Methyl ethanoate   Ethanoic acid   Methanol
(methyl acetate)   (acetic acid)   (methyl alcohol)

Base Hydrolysis of an Ester (Saponification)

$$CH_3-CH_2-\overset{\overset{\displaystyle O}{\|}}{C}-O-CH_3 + NaOH \overset{\text{Heat}}{\longrightarrow} CH_3-CH_2-\overset{\overset{\displaystyle O}{\|}}{C}-O^-Na^+ + HO-CH_3$$

Methyl propanoate   Sodium   Sodium propanoate   Methanol
(methyl propionate)   hydroxide   (sodium propionate)   (methyl alcohol)

KEY TERMS

carboxyl group A functional group found in carboxylic acids composed of carbonyl and hydroxyl groups.

$$-\overset{\overset{\displaystyle O}{\|}}{C}-OH$$

Carboxyl group

carboxylate ion The anion produced when a carboxylic acid donates a proton to water.

carboxylate salt The product of neutralization of a carboxylic acid, which is a carboxylate ion and a metal ion from the base.

carboxylic acid An organic compound containing the carboxyl group.

ester An organic compound in which an alkyl or aromatic group replaces the hydrogen atom in a carboxylic acid.

esterification The formation of an ester from a carboxylic acid and an alcohol with the elimination of a molecule of water in the presence of an acid catalyst.

hydrolysis The splitting of a molecule by the addition of water. Esters hydrolyze to produce a carboxylic acid and an alcohol.

saponification The hydrolysis of an ester with a strong base to produce a carboxylate salt and an alcohol.

UNDERSTANDING THE CONCEPTS

The chapter sections to review are shown in parentheses at the end of each question.

16.41 Draw the condensed structural formulas and give the IUPAC names of two structural isomers of the carboxylic acids that have the molecular formula $C_4H_8O_2$. (16.1)

16.42 Draw the condensed structural formulas and give the IUPAC names of four structural isomers of the esters that have the molecular formula $C_5H_{10}O_2$. (16.1)

16.43 Draw the condensed structural formulas and give the IUPAC names of two structural isomers of the esters that have the molecular formula $C_3H_6O_2$. (16.2, 16.3)

16.44 Draw the condensed structural formulas and give the IUPAC names of four structural isomers of the esters that have the molecular formula $C_4H_8O_2$. (16.2, 16.3)

16.45 The ester methyl butanoate has the odor and flavor of strawberries. (16.1, 16.2, 16.3, 16.5)

a. Draw the condensed structural formula for methyl butanoate.
b. Give the IUPAC name of the carboxylic acid and the alcohol used to prepare methyl butanoate.
c. Write a balanced equation for the acid hydrolysis of methyl butanoate.

16.46 The drug cocaine hydrochloride hydrolyzes in air to give methyl benzoate. Its odor, which smells like pineapple guava, is used to train drug-sniffing dogs. (16.1, 16.2, 16.3, 16.5)

a. Draw the condensed structural formula for methyl benzoate.
b. Give the name of the carboxylic acid and alcohol used to prepare methyl benzoate.
c. Write a balanced equation for the acid hydrolysis of methyl benzoate.

ADDITIONAL QUESTIONS AND PROBLEMS

For instructor-assigned homework, go to www.masteringchemistry.com.

16.47 Give the IUPAC and common names (if any) for each of the following compounds: (16.1, 16.4)

a.
$$CH_3-\overset{\overset{\displaystyle CH_3}{|}}{CH}-CH_2-\overset{\overset{\displaystyle O}{\|}}{C}-OH$$

b.
(benzene ring)—$\overset{\overset{\displaystyle O}{\|}}{C}-O-CH_2-CH_3$

c.
$$CH_3-CH_2-\overset{\overset{\displaystyle O}{\|}}{C}-O-CH_2-CH_3$$

d.
(benzene ring with COOH and Cl)

e.
$$CH_3-\overset{\overset{\displaystyle OH}{|}}{CH}-CH_2-CH_2-\overset{\overset{\displaystyle O}{\|}}{C}-OH$$

f.
$$CH_3-\overset{\overset{\displaystyle O}{\|}}{C}-O-\overset{\overset{\displaystyle CH_3}{|}}{CH}-CH_3$$

16.48 Give the IUPAC and common names (if any) for each of the following compounds: (16.1, 16.4)

a.
$$CH_3-\overset{\overset{\displaystyle CH_3}{|}}{CH}-CH_2-CH_2-\overset{\overset{\displaystyle O}{\|}}{C}-OH$$

b.
(benzene ring with C—OH and two Cl substituents)

c.
(benzene ring)—$\overset{\overset{\displaystyle O}{\|}}{C}-O-CH_3$

d.
$$CH_3-CH_2-CH_2-\overset{\overset{\displaystyle O}{\|}}{C}-O-CH_3$$

e.
$$CH_3-\overset{\overset{\displaystyle CH_3}{|}}{CH}-CH_2-\overset{\overset{\displaystyle O}{\|}}{C}-O-CH_2-CH_3$$

f.
$$CH_3-\overset{\overset{\displaystyle CH_3}{|}}{CH}-CH_2-\overset{\overset{\displaystyle OH}{|}}{CH}-\overset{\overset{\displaystyle O}{\|}}{C}-OH$$

16.49 Draw the condensed structural formulas for at least three carboxylic acids that have the molecular formula $C_5H_{10}O_2$. (16.1)

16.50 Draw the condensed structural formulas for the carboxylic acid and the ester that have the formula $C_2H_4O_2$. (16.1, 16.3, 16.4)

16.51 Draw the condensed structural formula for each of the following: (16.1, 16.3, 16.4)

a. methyl hexanoate
b. *p*-chlorobenzoic acid
c. β-chloropropionic acid
d. ethyl butanoate
e. 3-methylpentanoic acid
f. ethyl benzoate

16.52 Draw the condensed structural formula for each of the following: (16.1, 16.3, 16.4)

a. α-bromobutyric acid
b. ethyl butyrate
c. 2-methyloctanoic acid
d. 3,5-dimethylhexanoic acid
e. propyl acetate
f. 3,4-dibromobenzoic acid

16.53 For each of the following pairs, identify the compound that would have the higher boiling point. Explain. (16.5)

a. $CH_3-CH_2-CH_2-OH$ or $CH_3-\overset{\overset{\displaystyle O}{\|}}{C}-OH$

b. $CH_3-CH_2-CH_2-CH_3$ or $CH_3-\overset{\overset{\displaystyle O}{\|}}{C}-OH$

16.54 For each of the following pairs, identify the compound that would have the higher boiling point. Explain. (16.5)

a. $CH_3-\overset{\overset{\displaystyle OH}{|}}{CH}-CH_3$ or $H-\overset{\overset{\displaystyle O}{\|}}{C}-O-CH_3$

b. $H-\overset{\overset{\displaystyle O}{\|}}{C}-O-CH_3$ or $CH_3-CH_2-CH_2-CH_3$

16.55 Acetic acid, methyl formate and 1-propanol all have the same molar mass. The possible boiling points are 32 °C, 97 °C, and 118 °C. Match the compounds with the boiling points and explain your choice. (16.5)

16.56 Propionic acid, 1-butanol, and butyraldehyde all have the same molar mass. The possible boiling points are 76 °C, 118 °C, and 141 °C. Match the compounds with the boiling points and explain your choice. (16.5)

16.57 Which of the following compounds are soluble in water? (16.5)

a. $CH_3-CH_2-\overset{\overset{\displaystyle O}{\|}}{C}-O^-Na^+$

b. $CH_3-CH_2-\overset{\overset{\displaystyle O}{\|}}{C}-O-CH_2-CH_2-CH_3$

c. $CH_3-CH_2-CH_2-OH$

d. $CH_3-CH_2-\overset{\overset{\displaystyle O}{\|}}{C}-OH$

16.58 Which of the following compounds are soluble in water? (16.5)

a. $CH_3-CH_2-CH_2-\overset{\overset{\displaystyle O}{\|}}{C}-OH$

b. $CH_3-\overset{\overset{\displaystyle O}{\|}}{C}-O-CH_3$

c. $CH_3-CH_2-CH_2-CH_3$

d. (zigzag chain)—OH

16.59 Draw the condensed structural formulas for the products for each of the following reactions: (16.3, 16.5)

a. $CH_3-CH_2-\overset{\overset{\displaystyle O}{\|}}{C}-OH + H_2O \rightleftharpoons$

b. $CH_3-CH_2-\overset{\overset{\displaystyle O}{\|}}{C}-OH + KOH \longrightarrow$

c. $CH_3-CH_2-\overset{\overset{\displaystyle O}{\|}}{C}-OH + CH_3-OH \underset{}{\overset{H^+, \text{ heat}}{\rightleftharpoons}}$

d. [benzene ring]$-\overset{\overset{\displaystyle O}{\|}}{C}-OH + CH_3-CH_2-OH \underset{}{\overset{H^+, \text{ heat}}{\rightleftharpoons}}$

16.60 Draw the condensed structural formulas for the products for each of the following reactions: (16.3, 16.5)

a. $CH_3-\overset{\overset{\displaystyle O}{\|}}{C}-OH + NaOH \longrightarrow$

b. $CH_3-\overset{\overset{\displaystyle O}{\|}}{C}-OH + H_2O \rightleftharpoons$

c. $CH_3-\overset{\overset{\displaystyle CH_3}{|}}{CH}-\overset{\overset{\displaystyle O}{\|}}{C}-OH + KOH \longrightarrow$

d. $CH_3-\overset{\overset{\displaystyle CH_3}{|}}{CH}-\overset{\overset{\displaystyle O}{\|}}{C}-OH + CH_3-OH \underset{}{\overset{H^+, \text{ heat}}{\rightleftharpoons}}$

16.61 Give the IUPAC names of the carboxylic acid and alcohol needed to produce each of the following esters: (16.3)

a. $CH_3-\overset{\overset{\displaystyle CH_3}{|}}{CH}-CH_2-\overset{\overset{\displaystyle O}{\|}}{C}-O-CH_3$

b. [benzene ring with Cl substituent]$-\overset{\overset{\displaystyle O}{\|}}{C}-O-CH_2-CH_3$

c. $CH_3-CH_2-CH_2-CH_2-CH_2-\overset{\overset{\displaystyle O}{\|}}{C}-O-CH_2-CH_3$

16.62 Give the IUPAC names of the carboxylic acid and alcohol needed to produce each of the following esters: (16.3)

a. $CH_3-CH_2-CH_2-\overset{\overset{\displaystyle O}{\|}}{C}-O-CH_2-CH_3$

b. $CH_3-CH_2-\overset{\overset{\displaystyle O}{\|}}{C}-O-$[benzene ring with Cl]

c. $CH_3-\overset{\overset{\displaystyle CH_3}{|}}{CH}-\overset{\overset{\displaystyle CH_3}{|}}{CH}-\overset{\overset{\displaystyle O}{\|}}{C}-O-CH_3$

16.63 Draw the condensed structural formulas for the products for each of the following reactions: (16.5)

a. $CH_3-CH_2-\overset{\overset{\displaystyle O}{\|}}{C}-O-\overset{\overset{\displaystyle CH_3}{|}}{CH}-CH_3 + H_2O \underset{}{\overset{H^+, \text{ heat}}{\rightleftharpoons}}$

b. $CH_3-\overset{\overset{\displaystyle CH_3}{|}}{CH}-\overset{\overset{\displaystyle O}{\|}}{C}-O-CH_2-CH_2-CH_3 + NaOH \overset{\text{Heat}}{\longrightarrow}$

16.64 Draw the condensed structural formulas for the products for each of the following reactions: (16.5)

a. $CH_3-CH_2-\overset{\overset{\displaystyle O}{\|}}{C}-O-\overset{\overset{\displaystyle CH_3}{|}}{CH}-CH_3 + NaOH \overset{\text{Heat}}{\longrightarrow}$

b. $CH_3-\overset{\overset{\displaystyle CH_3}{|}}{CH}-\overset{\overset{\displaystyle O}{\|}}{C}-O-CH_2-CH_2-CH_3 + H_2O \underset{}{\overset{H^+, \text{ heat}}{\rightleftharpoons}}$

CHALLENGE QUESTIONS

16.65 Using the reactions we have studied, indicate how you might prepare the following from the starting substance given: (12.3, 16.1, 16.3)
a. acetic acid from ethene
b. butyric acid from 1-butanol

16.66 Using the reactions we have studied, indicate how you might prepare the following from the starting substance given: (12.3, 16.1, 16.3)
a. pentanoic acid from 1-pentanol
b. ethyl acetate from two molecules of ethanol

16.67 Methyl benzoate is not soluble in water; however, when it is heated with KOH, the ester forms soluble products. When HCl is added to neutralize the basic solution, a white solid forms. Draw the condensed structural formulas of the reactants and products when methyl benzoate and KOH react. Explain what happens. (16.4, 16.5)

16.68 Hexanoic acid is not soluble in water. However, when hexanoic acid is added to a NaOH solution, a soluble product forms. Draw the condensed structural formulas of the reactants and products when hexanoic acid and NaOH react. Explain what happens. (16.4, 16.5)

16.69 Propyl acetate is an ester that gives the odor and flavor of pears. (8.5, 16.3, 16.4, 16.5)

  a. Draw the condensed structural formula for propyl acetate.
  b. Write an equation for the formation of propyl acetate.
  c. Write an equation for the hydrolysis of propyl acetate with HCl.
  d. Write an equation for the hydrolysis of propyl acetate with NaOH.
  e. How many milliliters of a 0.208 M NaOH solution is needed to completely hydrolyze (saponify) 1.58 g of propyl acetate?

16.70 Ethyl octanoate is a flavor component of mangos. (8.5, 16.3, 16.4, 16.5)

  a. Draw the condensed structural formula for ethyl octanoate.
  b. Write an equation for the formation of ethyl octanoate.
  c. Write an equation for the hydrolysis of ethyl octanoate with HCl.
  d. Write an equation for the hydrolysis of ethyl octanoate with NaOH.
  e. How many milliliters of a 0.315 M NaOH solution is needed to completely hydrolyze (saponify) 2.84 g of ethyl octanoate?

ANSWERS

Answers to Study Checks

16.1

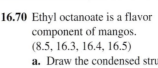

16.2 Two methanoic acid molecules form a dimer, which gives an effective molar mass that is double that of the single acid molecule. Thus, a higher boiling point is required than for ethanol.

16.3 H—C(=O)—OH + H$_2$O ⇌ H—C(=O)—O$^-$ + H$_3$O$^+$

16.4 butanoic acid (butyric acid)

16.5 propanoic acid and 1-pentanol

16.6 CH$_3$—CH$_2$—CH$_2$—CH$_2$—CH$_2$—CH$_2$—C(=O)—O—CH$_2$—CH$_3$

16.7 propanoic acid and ethanol

16.8 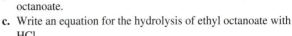 and CH$_3$—OH

Answers to Selected Questions and Problems

16.1 methanoic acid (formic acid)

16.3 a. CH$_3$—CH$_2$—CH$_2$—C(=O)—OH, butanoic acid
  b. CH$_3$—CH(CH$_3$)—C(=O)—OH, 2-methylpropanoic acid

16.5 a. ethanoic acid (acetic acid)   **b.** butanoic acid (butyric acid)
  c. 3-methylhexanoic acid   **d.** 3,4-dibromobenzoic acid

16.7 a. Cl—CH$_2$—C(=O)—OH
  b. HO—CH$_2$—CH$_2$—C(=O)—OH

16.9 a. H—C(=O)—OH   **b.** CH$_3$—C(=O)—OH
  c. CH$_3$—CH(CH$_3$)—CH$_2$—C(=O)—OH
  d. cyclopentyl-CH$_2$—C(=O)—OH

16.11 a. Butanoic acid has a greater molar mass and would have a higher boiling point.
  b. Propanoic acid can form dimers, effectively doubling the molar mass, which gives propanoic acid a higher boiling point.
  c. Butanoic acid can form dimers, effectively doubling the molar mass, which gives butanoic acid a higher boiling point.

16.13 a. Propanoic acid has the smallest alkyl group, which makes it most soluble.
  b. Propanoic acid forms more hydrogen bonds with water, which makes it most soluble.

16.15 a. CH$_3$—CH$_2$—CH$_2$—C(=O)—OH + H$_2$O ⇌ CH$_3$—CH$_2$—CH$_2$—C(=O)—O$^-$ + H$_3$O$^+$
  b. CH$_3$—CH$_2$—CH$_2$—CH$_2$—C(=O)—OH + H$_2$O ⇌ CH$_3$—CH$_2$—CH$_2$—CH$_2$—C(=O)—O$^-$ + H$_3$O$^+$

16.70c. CH$_3$—CH$_2$—CH(CH$_3$)—C(=O)—OH
d. CH$_3$—CH$_2$—CH(Br)—CH$_2$—CH(Br)—CH$_2$—C(=O)—OH

16.17 a.
$$CH_3-CH_2-CH_2-CH_2-\overset{\overset{\displaystyle O}{\|}}{C}-OH + NaOH \longrightarrow$$

$$CH_3-CH_2-CH_2-CH_2-\overset{\overset{\displaystyle O}{\|}}{C}-O^-Na^+ + H_2O$$

b.
$$CH_3-\overset{\overset{\displaystyle Cl}{|}}{CH}-\overset{\overset{\displaystyle O}{\|}}{C}-OH + NaOH \longrightarrow$$

$$CH_3-\overset{\overset{\displaystyle Cl}{|}}{CH}-\overset{\overset{\displaystyle O}{\|}}{C}-O^-Na^+ + H_2O$$

c.
phenyl−$\overset{\overset{\displaystyle O}{\|}}{C}$−OH + NaOH $\longrightarrow$ phenyl−$\overset{\overset{\displaystyle O}{\|}}{C}$−O$^-Na^+$ + H$_2$O

16.19 a. sodium pentanoate
b. sodium 2-chloropropanoate (sodium α-chloropropionate)
c. sodium benzoate

16.21 a. aldehyde   **b.** ester
c. ketone   **d.** carboxylic acid

16.23 a.
$$CH_3-\overset{\overset{\displaystyle O}{\|}}{C}-O-CH_2-CH_3$$

b.
$$CH_3-CH_2-CH_2-\overset{\overset{\displaystyle O}{\|}}{C}-O-CH_2-CH_3$$

c.
phenyl−$\overset{\overset{\displaystyle O}{\|}}{C}$−O−CH$_2$−CH$_3$

16.25 a.
$$CH_3-CH_2-\overset{\overset{\displaystyle O}{\|}}{C}-O-CH_2-CH_2-CH_3$$

b.
$$CH_3-CH_2-CH_2-CH_2-\overset{\overset{\displaystyle O}{\|}}{C}-O-\overset{\overset{\displaystyle CH_3}{|}}{CH}-CH_3$$

16.27 a. methanoic acid (formic acid) and methanol (methyl alcohol)
b. ethanoic acid (acetic acid) and methanol (methyl alcohol)
c. butanoic acid (butyric acid) and methanol (methyl alcohol)
d. 3-methylbutanoic acid (β-methylbutyric acid) and ethanol (ethyl alcohol)

16.29 a. methyl methanoate (methyl formate)
b. ethyl propanoate (ethyl propionate)
c. methyl butanoate (methyl butyrate)
d. 2-methylpropyl pentanoate

16.31 a.
$$CH_3-\overset{\overset{\displaystyle O}{\|}}{C}-O-CH_3$$

b.
$$H-\overset{\overset{\displaystyle O}{\|}}{C}-O-CH_2-CH_2-CH_2-CH_3$$

c.
$$CH_3-CH_2-CH_2-CH_2-\overset{\overset{\displaystyle O}{\|}}{C}-O-CH_2-CH_3$$

d.
$$CH_3-CH_2-\overset{\overset{\displaystyle O}{\|}}{C}-O-CH_2-\overset{\overset{\displaystyle Br}{|}}{CH}-CH_3$$

16.33 a. pentyl ethanoate (pentyl acetate)
b. octyl ethanoate (octyl acetate)
c. pentyl butanoate (pentyl butyrate)

16.35 a.
$$CH_3-CH_2-\overset{\overset{\displaystyle O}{\|}}{C}-OH$$

b. $CH_3-CH_2-CH_2-CH_2-OH$

c.
$$CH_3-\overset{\overset{\displaystyle O}{\|}}{C}-O-CH_3$$

16.37 The products of the acid hydrolysis of an ester are an alcohol and a carboxylic acid.

16.39 a. $CH_3-CH_2-\overset{\overset{\displaystyle O}{\|}}{C}-O^-Na^+$ and CH_3-OH

b. $CH_3-\overset{\overset{\displaystyle O}{\|}}{C}-OH$ and $CH_3-CH_2-CH_2-OH$

c. $CH_3-CH_2-CH_2-\overset{\overset{\displaystyle O}{\|}}{C}-OH$ and CH_3-CH_2-OH

d. phenyl−$\overset{\overset{\displaystyle O}{\|}}{C}$−OH and CH_3-CH_2-OH

e. phenyl−$\overset{\overset{\displaystyle O}{\|}}{C}$−O$^-Na^+$ and CH_3-CH_2-OH

16.41 $CH_3-CH_2-CH_2-\overset{\overset{\displaystyle O}{\|}}{C}-OH$ $CH_3-\overset{\overset{\displaystyle CH_3}{|}}{CH}-\overset{\overset{\displaystyle O}{\|}}{C}-OH$
butanoic acid   2-methylpropanoic acid

16.43 $CH_3-\overset{\overset{\displaystyle O}{\|}}{C}-O-CH_3$ $H-\overset{\overset{\displaystyle O}{\|}}{C}-O-CH_2-CH_3$
methyl ethanoate   ethyl methanoate

16.45 a.
$$CH_3-CH_2-CH_2-\overset{\overset{\displaystyle O}{\|}}{C}-O-CH_3$$

b. butanoic acid and methanol

c.
$$CH_3-CH_2-CH_2-\overset{\overset{\displaystyle O}{\|}}{C}-O-CH_3 + H_2O \overset{H^+, heat}{\rightleftharpoons}$$

$$CH_3-CH_2-CH_2-\overset{\overset{\displaystyle O}{\|}}{C}-OH + HO-CH_3$$

16.47 a. 3-methylbutanoic acid (β-methylbutyric acid)
  b. ethyl benzoate
  c. ethyl propanoate (ethyl propionate)
  d. 2-chlorobenzoic acid (*ortho*-chlorobenzoic acid)
  e. 4-hydroxypentanoic acid
  f. 2-propyl ethanoate (isopropyl acetate)

16.49

$$CH_3-CH_2-CH_2-CH_2-\overset{\overset{\displaystyle O}{\|}}{C}-OH \qquad CH_3-CH_2-\overset{\overset{\displaystyle CH_3}{|}}{CH}-\overset{\overset{\displaystyle O}{\|}}{C}-OH$$

$$CH_3-\overset{\overset{\displaystyle CH_3}{|}}{CH}-CH_2-\overset{\overset{\displaystyle O}{\|}}{C}-OH \qquad CH_3-\overset{\overset{\displaystyle CH_3}{|}}{\underset{\underset{\displaystyle CH_3}{|}}{C}}-\overset{\overset{\displaystyle O}{\|}}{C}-OH$$

16.51 a. $CH_3-CH_2-CH_2-CH_2-CH_2-\overset{\overset{\displaystyle O}{\|}}{C}-O-CH_3$

  b.
  COOH
  (benzene ring)
  Cl

  c. $Cl-CH_2-CH_2-\overset{\overset{\displaystyle O}{\|}}{C}-OH$

  d. $CH_3-CH_2-CH_2-\overset{\overset{\displaystyle O}{\|}}{C}-O-CH_2-CH_3$

  e. $CH_3-CH_2-\overset{\overset{\displaystyle CH_3}{|}}{CH}-CH_2-\overset{\overset{\displaystyle O}{\|}}{C}-OH$

  f. $\overset{\overset{\displaystyle O}{\|}}{C}-O-CH_2-CH_3$ (attached to benzene ring)

16.53 a. Ethanoic acid has a higher boiling point than 1-propanol because two molecules of ethanoic acid hydrogen bond to form a dimer, which effectively doubles the molar mass and requires a higher temperature to reach the boiling point.
  b. Ethanoic acid forms hydrogen bonds, but butane does not.

16.55 Of the three compounds, methyl formate would have the lowest boiling point since it only has dipole–dipole attractions. Both acetic acid and 1-propanol can form hydrogen bonds, but because acetic acid can form dimers and double the effective molar mass, it has the highest boiling point. Methyl formate, 32 °C; 1-propanol, 97 °C; acetic acid, 118 °C.

16.57 a, c, and **d** are soluble in water.

16.59 a. $CH_3-CH_2-\overset{\overset{\displaystyle O}{\|}}{C}-O^-$ and H_3O^+

  b. $CH_3-CH_2-\overset{\overset{\displaystyle O}{\|}}{C}-O^-K^+$ and H_2O

  c. $CH_3-CH_2-\overset{\overset{\displaystyle O}{\|}}{C}-O-CH_3$ and H_2O

d. $\overset{\overset{\displaystyle O}{\|}}{C}-O-CH_2-CH_3$ (attached to benzene ring) and H_2O

16.61 a. 3-methylbutanoic acid and methanol
  b. 3-chlorobenzoic acid and ethanol
  c. hexanoic acid and ethanol

16.63 a. $CH_3-CH_2-\overset{\overset{\displaystyle O}{\|}}{C}-OH$ and $HO-\overset{\overset{\displaystyle CH_3}{|}}{CH}-CH_3$

  b. $CH_3-\overset{\overset{\displaystyle CH_3}{|}}{CH}-\overset{\overset{\displaystyle O}{\|}}{C}-O^-Na^+$ and $HO-CH_2-CH_2-CH_3$

16.65 a. $H_2C{=}CH_2 + H_2O \xrightarrow{H^+}$

$$CH_3-CH_2-OH \xrightarrow{[O]} CH_3-\overset{\overset{\displaystyle O}{\|}}{C}-OH$$

  b. $CH_3-CH_2-CH_2-CH_2-OH \xrightarrow{[O]}$

$$CH_3-CH_2-CH_2-\overset{\overset{\displaystyle O}{\|}}{C}-OH$$

16.67 $\overset{\overset{\displaystyle O}{\|}}{C}-O-CH_3 + KOH \xrightarrow{\text{Heat}}$ (benzene ring attached)

$$\overset{\overset{\displaystyle O}{\|}}{C}-O^-K^+ + CH_3-OH \text{ (benzene ring attached)}$$

In KOH solution, the ester undergoes saponification to form the carboxylate salt, potassium benzoate, and methanol, which are soluble in water. When HCl is added, the salt is converted to benzoic acid, which is insoluble.

16.69 a. $CH_3-\overset{\overset{\displaystyle O}{\|}}{C}-O-CH_2-CH_2-CH_3$

  b. $CH_3-\overset{\overset{\displaystyle O}{\|}}{C}-OH + HO-CH_2-CH_2-CH_3 \underset{}{\overset{H^+, \text{heat}}{\rightleftharpoons}}$

$$CH_3-\overset{\overset{\displaystyle O}{\|}}{C}-O-CH_2-CH_2-CH_3 + H_2O$$

  c. $CH_3-\overset{\overset{\displaystyle O}{\|}}{C}-O-CH_2-CH_2-CH_3 + H_2O \underset{}{\overset{H^+, \text{heat}}{\rightleftharpoons}}$

$$CH_3-\overset{\overset{\displaystyle O}{\|}}{C}-OH + HO-CH_2-CH_2-CH_3$$

  d. $CH_3-\overset{\overset{\displaystyle O}{\|}}{C}-O-CH_2-CH_2-CH_3 + NaOH \xrightarrow{\text{Heat}}$

$$CH_3-\overset{\overset{\displaystyle O}{\|}}{C}-O^-Na^+ + HO-CH_2-CH_2-CH_3$$

  e. 74.4 mL of 0.208 M NaOH solution

17 Lipids

Mastering**CHEMISTRY**™

Visit **www.masteringchemistry.com** for self-study materials and instructor-assigned homework.

After eating, Bill, who is elderly, frequently has pain in his chest, some associated sweating and feels nauseous. His symptoms are similar to a heart attack, so he is taken to the ER. The emergency room doctor believes he may have acute gallbladder disease. The doctor orders several blood tests, including a lipid panel and an ultrasound of his abdomen. Meanwhile, they hospitalize Bill to monitor his condition.

Susan, a geriatric nurse, speaks with Bill about his results. She explains that the lipid panel measures the total cholesterol in his blood. This consists of the four types of fats or lipids in his blood: cholesterol, HDL, LDL, and triglycerides. HDL, or high-density lipoprotein cholesterol, is considered the "good" cholesterol as it helps to clear his arteries, while LDL, or low-density lipoprotein cholesterol, is the "bad" cholesterol because it deposits plaque in the arteries. The body stores excess calories by creating triglycerides, which are stored in fat cells. His levels are elevated, and the ultrasound confirms that his gallbladder is inflamed.

Susan and Bill discuss his treatment options and a number of changes he can make to his lifestyle to decrease his gallbladder attacks. This includes decreasing the amount of fats in his diet, exercising more, losing weight, and increasing his consumption of dietary fiber. If the attacks continue, Susan advises that Bill may want to have his gallbladder removed.

Career: Geriatric Nurse

Geriatric nurses provide care for elderly patients in hospitals, nursing homes, assisted living facilities, and in-home care. This includes conducting medical tests, administering medications, and working with the elderly patient to set personal health goals while promoting self-care. They focus on the creation and implementation of treatment plans for chronic illnesses, as well as educating and counseling patients' families. Geriatric nurses also assist physicians during exams, while providing care and compassion to their patients. Due to the age of the patient, geriatric nurses encounter patients with diminishing mental capacities, and often, death.

When we talk of fats and oils, waxes, steroids, cholesterol, and fat-soluble vitamins, we are discussing lipids. Lipids are naturally occurring compounds that vary considerably in structure, but share a common feature of being soluble in nonpolar solvents but not in water. Fats, which are one family of lipids, have many functions in the body, such as storing energy and protecting and insulating internal organs. Because lipids are not soluble in water, they are important in cellular membranes that function to separate the internal contents of cells from the external environment. Other types of lipids are found in nerve fibers and in hormones, which act as chemical messengers.

17.1 Lipids

Lipids are a family of biomolecules that have the common property of being soluble in organic solvents but not in water. The word "lipid" comes from the Greek word *lipos*, meaning "fat" or "lard." Typically, the lipid content of a cell can be extracted using a nonpolar solvent such as ether or chloroform. Lipids are an important feature in cell membranes, fat-soluble vitamins, and steroid hormones.

Types of Lipids

Within the lipid family, there are specific structures that distinguish the different types of lipids (see Figure 17.1). Lipids such as waxes, fats, oils, and glycerophospholipids are esters that can be hydrolyzed to give fatty acids along with other products, including an alcohol.

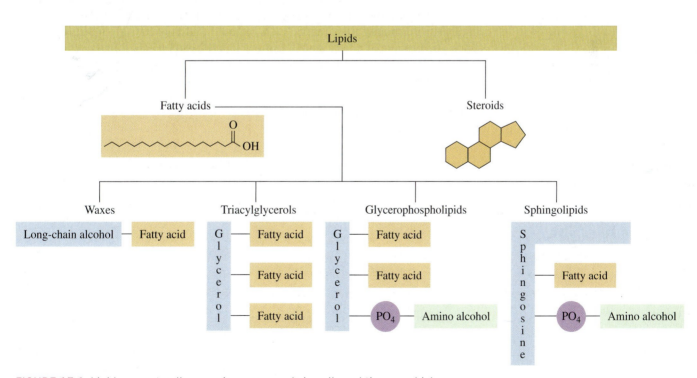

FIGURE 17.1 Lipids are naturally occurring compounds in cells and tissues, which are soluble in organic solvents and not in water.

Q What property do waxes, triacylglycerols, and steroids have in common?

Triacylglycerols and glycerophospholipids contain the alcohol *glycerol*, whereas sphingo-lipids contain an alcohol called *sphingosine*. Steroids, which have a completely different structure, do not contain fatty acids and cannot be hydrolyzed. Steroids are characterized by the *steroid nucleus* of four fused carbon rings.

> **CONCEPT CHECK 17.1** **Classes of Lipids**
>
> What type of lipid does not contain fatty acids?
>
> **ANSWER**
>
> The steroids are a group of lipids with no fatty acids.

QUESTIONS AND PROBLEMS

17.1 Lipids

LEARNING GOAL: *Describe the classes of lipids.*

17.1 What are some functions of lipids in the body?

17.2 What are some of the different kinds of lipids?

17.3 Lipids are not soluble in water. Are lipids polar or nonpolar molecules?

17.4 Which of the following solvents might be used to dissolve an oil stain?
   a. water
   b. CCl_4
   c. diethyl ether
   d. benzene
   e. NaCl solution

LEARNING GOAL

Draw the condensed structural formula for a fatty acid and identify it as saturated or unsaturated.

SELF-STUDY ACTIVITY
Fats

TUTORIAL
Lipids and Fatty Acids

17.2 Fatty Acids

The fatty acids are the simplest type of lipids, and are found as components in more complex lipids. A **fatty acid** contains a long hydrocarbon chain with a carboxylic acid group. Although the carboxylic acid part is hydrophilic, the long hydrophobic carbon chain makes fatty acids insoluble in water. Most naturally occurring fatty acids have an even number of carbon atoms, usually between 12 and 20. The most prevalent fatty acids in plants and animals are palmitic (C_{16}), oleic (C_{18}), linoleic (C_{18}), and stearic (C_{18}) acids. An example of a fatty acid is lauric acid, a 12-carbon acid found in coconut oil. A variety of condensed structural formulas, as well as the skeletal formula, can be drawn for a fatty acid as follows:

Drawing Formulas for Lauric Acid

$$CH_3-(CH_2)_{10}-\overset{\overset{\text{O}}{\|}}{C}-OH \qquad\qquad CH_3-(CH_2)_{10}-COOH$$

$$CH_3-CH_2-CH_2-CH_2-CH_2-CH_2-CH_2-CH_2-CH_2-CH_2-CH_2-C\overset{\nearrow O}{\searrow_{OH}}$$

Condensed structural formulas

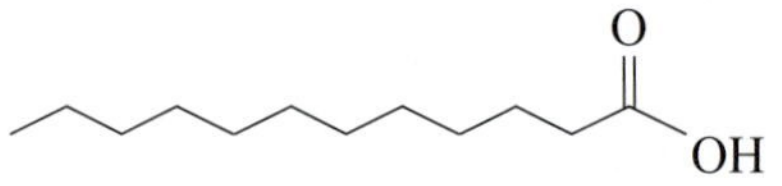

Skeletal formula

A **saturated fatty acid** contains only carbon–carbon single bonds, which makes the properties of a long-chain fatty acid similar to those of an alkane. An **unsaturated fatty acid** contains one or more carbon–carbon double bonds. In a **monounsaturated fatty acid**, the long carbon chain has one double bond, which makes its properties similar to those of an alkene. A **polyunsaturated fatty acid** has at least two carbon–carbon double bonds. Table 17.1 lists some of the typical fatty acids in lipids. In the lipids of plants and animals, about half of the fatty acids are saturated and half are unsaturated.

TABLE 17.1 **Structures and Melting Points of Common Fatty Acids**

Name	Carbon Atoms	Source	Melting Point (°C)	Structures
Saturated Fatty Acids				
Lauric acid	12	Coconut	44	$CH_3-(CH_2)_{10}-COOH$
Myristic acid	14	Nutmeg	55	$CH_3-(CH_2)_{12}-COOH$
Palmitic acid	16	Palm	63	$CH_3-(CH_2)_{14}-COOH$
Stearic acid	18	Animal fat	69	$CH_3-(CH_2)_{16}-COOH$
Monounsaturated Fatty Acids				
Palmitoleic acid	16	Butter	0	$CH_3-(CH_2)_5-CH{=}CH-(CH_2)_7-COOH$
Oleic acid	18	Olive, pecan, grapeseed	14	$CH_3-(CH_2)_7-CH{=}CH-(CH_2)_7-COOH$
Polyunsaturated Fatty Acids				
Linoleic acid	18	Soybeans, sunflowers	−5	$CH_3-(CH_2)_4-CH{=}CH-CH_2-CH{=}CH-(CH_2)_7-COOH$
Linolenic acid	18	Corn	−11	$CH_3-(CH_2-CH{=}CH)_3-(CH_2)_7-COOH$
Arachidonic acid	20	Meat, eggs, fish	−50	$CH_3-(CH_2)_3-(CH_2-CH{=}CH)_4-(CH_2)_3-COOH$

Cis and Trans Isomers of Unsaturated Fatty Acids

Unsaturated fatty acids can be drawn as cis and trans isomers in the same way as the cis and trans alkene structures we drew in Section 12.2. For example, oleic acid, a monounsaturated fatty acid, has one double bond at carbon 9. We can draw its cis and trans structures using its skeletal formula. However, the cis structure is found in almost all naturally occurring unsaturated fatty acids. In the cis isomer, the carbon chain has a "kink" at the double bond site. As we will see, the cis bond has a major impact on the properties of unsaturated fatty acids.

The human body is capable of synthesizing most fatty acids from carbohydrates or other fatty acids. However, humans do not synthesize sufficient amounts of polyunsaturated fatty acids, such as linoleic acid, linolenic acid, and arachidonic acid. Because these fatty acids must be obtained from the diet, they are known as *essential fatty acids*.

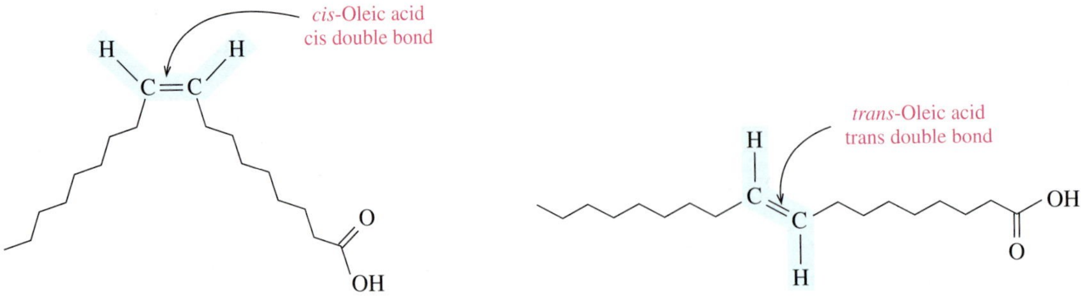

cis-Oleic acid
cis double bond

trans-Oleic acid
trans double bond

Almost all naturally occurring unsaturated fatty acids have one or more cis double bonds.

In infants, a deficiency of essential fatty acids can cause skin dermatitis. However, the role of fatty acids in adult nutrition is not well understood. Adults do not usually have a deficiency of essential fatty acids.

Properties of Fatty Acids

Saturated fatty acids fit closely together in a regular pattern, which allows many dispersion forces between the carbon chains. These normally weak intermolecular forces of attraction can be significant when molecules are close together. As a result, a significant amount of energy and high temperatures are required to separate the fatty acids and melt the fat. As the length of the carbon chain increases, more dispersion forces occur between the carbon chains, which results in higher melting points. Saturated fatty acids are usually solids at room temperature.

In unsaturated fatty acids, the cis double bonds cause the carbon chain to bend or "kink," which gives the molecules an irregular shape. As a result, cis fatty acids cannot stack as closely as saturated fatty acids, and thus have fewer dispersion forces between their carbon chains. We might think of saturated fatty acids as potato chips with regular shapes that stack closely together in a container. Similarly, irregularly shaped chips would be like unsaturated fatty acids that do not pack closely together. Thus, less energy is required to separate the fatty acid molecules, which makes the melting points of unsaturated fats lower than those of saturated fats (see Figure 17.2). Most unsaturated fats are oils at room temperature.

CONCEPT CHECK 17.2   Fatty Acids

1. Using Table 17.1, identify the following:
   a. an 18-carbon fatty acid that is saturated
   b. a monounsaturated fatty acid found in olives
   c. an 18-carbon fatty acid with three double bonds
2. List the fatty acids in part 1 in order of increasing melting points. Explain.

ANSWER

1. a. Stearic acid is a saturated 18-carbon fatty acid.
   b. Oleic acid is a monounsaturated fatty acid found in olives, having one double bond.
   c. Linolenic acid is a polyunsaturated 18-carbon fatty acid with three double bonds.
2. Saturated fatty acids have carbon chains with only single bonds that allow them to pack closely together and form molecular attractions. Unsaturated fats contain cis double bonds that place a "kink" in the carbon chain that does not allow the fatty acids to pack closely together. Thus, unsaturated fats have lower melting points than saturated fats. The order of increasing melting points for the fatty acids in part 1 are linolenic acid with three double bonds ($-11\ °C$), oleic acid with one double bond ($14\ °C$), and stearic acid with only single bonds ($69\ °C$).

Explore Your World

SOLUBILITY OF FATS AND OILS

Place some water in a small bowl. Add a drop of a vegetable oil. Then add a few more drops of the oil. Record your observations. Now add a few drops of liquid soap and mix. Record your observations.

Place a small amount of fat such as margarine, butter, shortening, or vegetable oil on a dish or plate. Run water over it. Record your observations. Mix some soap with the fat substance and run water over it again. Record your observations.

QUESTIONS

1. Do the drops of oil in the water separate or do they come together? Explain.
2. How does the soap affect the oil layer?
3. Why don't the fats on the dish or plate wash off with water?
4. In general, what is the solubility of lipids in water?
5. Why does soap help to wash the fats off the plate?

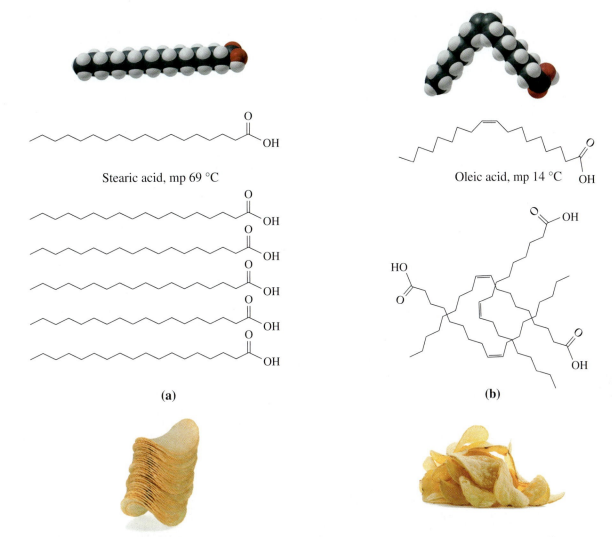

Stearic acid, mp 69 °C

Oleic acid, mp 14 °C

(a)

(b)

FIGURE 17.2 **(a)** In saturated fatty acids, the molecules fit closely together to give high melting points. **(b)** In unsaturated fatty acids, molecules cannot pack closely together, resulting in lower melting points.

Q Why does the cis double bond affect the melting points of unsaturated fatty acids?

SAMPLE PROBLEM 17.1   **Structures and Properties of Fatty Acids**

Consider the condensed structural formula for oleic acid:

$$CH_3-(CH_2)_7-CH{=}CH-(CH_2)_7-\overset{\overset{\displaystyle O}{\|}}{C}-OH$$

a. Why is this substance an acid?
b. How many carbon atoms are in oleic acid?
c. Is the fatty acid saturated, monounsaturated, or polyunsaturated?
d. Is it most likely to be solid or liquid at room temperature?
e. Would it be soluble in water?

SOLUTION

a. Oleic acid contains a carboxylic acid group.
b. It contains 18 carbon atoms.
c. It is a monounsaturated fatty acid.

TUTORIAL
Structures and Properties of Fatty Acids

d. It is liquid at room temperature.
e. No. Its long hydrocarbon chain makes it insoluble in water.

STUDY CHECK 17.1

Palmitoleic acid is a fatty acid with the following condensed structural formula:

$$CH_3-(CH_2)_5-CH=CH-(CH_2)_7-\overset{\overset{\displaystyle O}{\|}}{C}-OH$$

a. How many carbon atoms are in palmitoleic acid?
b. Is the fatty acid saturated, monounsaturated, or polyunsaturated?
c. Is it most likely to be solid or liquid at room temperature?

Prostaglandins

Prostaglandins (**PGs**) are fatty acids that are produced in low amounts in most cells of the body. The prostaglandins, also known as *eicosanoids*, are formed from arachidonic acid, the polyunsaturated fatty acid with 20 carbon atoms (*eicos* is the Greek word for 20). Swedish chemists first discovered prostaglandins and named them "prostaglandin E" (soluble in ether) and "prostaglandin F" (soluble in phosphate buffer, or *fosfat* in Swedish). The various kinds of prostaglandins differ by the substituents attached to the five-carbon ring. Prostaglandin E (PGE) has a ketone group on carbon 9, whereas prostaglandin F (PGF) has a hydroxyl group on carbon 9. In the notations for the different prostaglandins, the number of double bonds is shown as subscript 1 or 2.

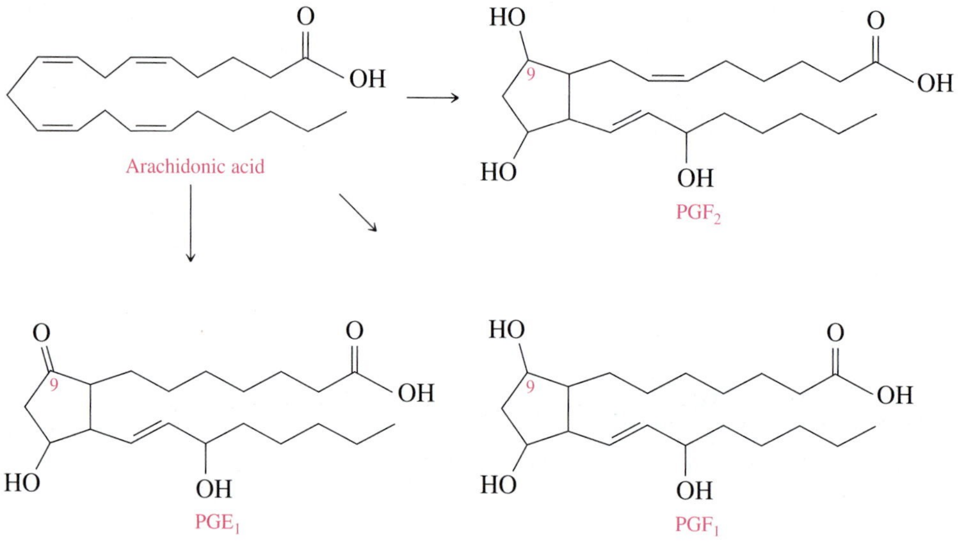

Although prostaglandins are broken down quickly, they have potent physiological effects. Some prostaglandins increase blood pressure, and others lower blood pressure. Other prostaglandins stimulate contraction and relaxation in the smooth muscle of the uterus during the birth process and the monthly menstrual cycle. When tissues are injured, arachidonic acid present in the blood is converted to prostaglandins such as PGE_1 and PGF_2 that produce inflammation and pain in the area.

The treatment of pain, fever, and inflammation is based on inhibiting the enzymes that convert arachidonic acid to prostaglandins. Several nonsteroidal anti-inflammatory drugs (NSAIDs), such as aspirin, block the production of prostaglandins, and in doing so, decrease pain (analgesics) and inflammation, and reduce fever (antipyretics). Ibuprofen has similar anti-inflammatory and analgesic effects. Other NSAIDs include naproxen (Aleve

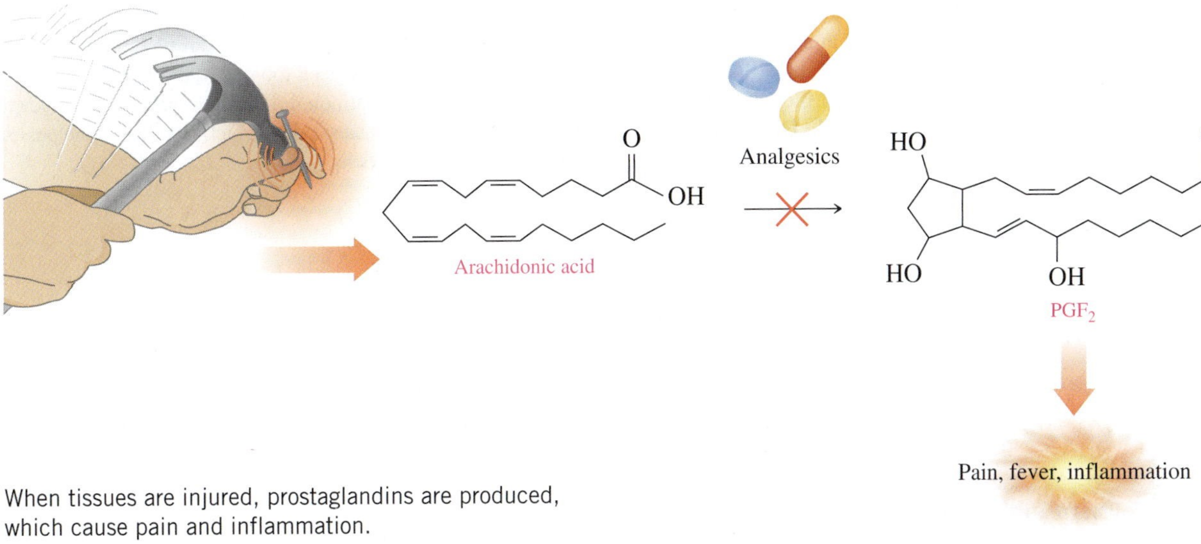

Arachidonic acid

Analgesics

PGF$_2$

Pain, fever, inflammation

When tissues are injured, prostaglandins are produced, which cause pain and inflammation.

and Naprosyn), ketoprofen (Actron), and nabumetone (Relafen). Although NSAIDs are helpful, their long-term use can result in liver, kidney, and gastrointestinal damage.

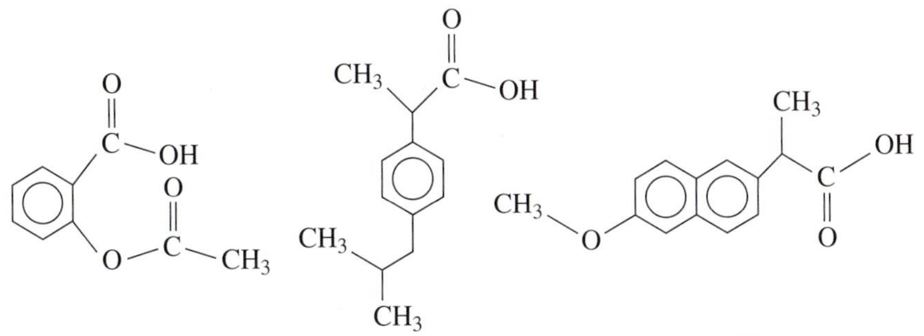

Aspirin (acetylsalicylic acid)   Ibuprofen (Advil, Motrin)   Naproxen (Aleve, Naprosyn)

Chemistry Link to Health

OMEGA-3 FATTY ACIDS IN FISH OILS

Because unsaturated fats are now recognized as being more beneficial to health than saturated fats, American diets have changed to include more unsaturated fats and less saturated fatty acids. This change is a response to research that indicates that atherosclerosis and heart disease are associated with high levels of fats in the diet. However, the Inuit people of Alaska have a diet with high levels of unsaturated fats as well as high levels of blood cholesterol, but a very low occurrence of atherosclerosis and heart attacks. The fats in the Inuit diet are primarily unsaturated fats from fish, rather than from land animals.

Both fish and vegetable oils have high levels of unsaturated fats. The fatty acids in vegetable oils are *omega-6 acids*, in which the first double bond occurs at carbon 6 counting from the methyl end of the carbon chain. Omega is the last letter in the Greek alphabet is used to denote the end. Two common omega-6 acids are linoleic acid (LA) and arachidonic acid (AA). However, the fatty acids in fish oils are mostly the omega-3 type, in which the first double bond occurs at the third carbon counting from the methyl group. Three common *omega-3 fatty acids* in fish are linolenic acid (ALA), eicosapentaenoic acid (EPA), and docosahexaenoic acid (DHA).

Cold water fish are a good source of omega-3 fatty acids.

In atherosclerosis and heart disease, cholesterol forms plaques that adhere to the walls of the blood vessels. Blood pressure rises as blood has to squeeze through a smaller opening in the blood vessel. As more plaque forms, there is also a possibility of blood clots blocking the blood vessels and causing a heart attack. Omega-3 fatty acids lower the tendency of blood platelets to stick together, thereby reducing the possibility of blood clots. However, high levels of omega-3 fatty acids can increase bleeding if the ability of the platelets to form blood clots is reduced too much. It does seem that a diet that includes fish such as salmon, tuna, and herring can provide higher amounts of the omega-3 fatty acids, which help lessen the possibility of developing heart disease.

Omega-6 Fatty Acids

Omega-6 fatty acid

Linoleic acid (LA)

Arachidonic acid (AA)

Omega-3 Fatty Acids

Omega-3 fatty acid

Linolenic acid (ALA)

Eicosapentaenoic acid (EPA)

Docosahexaenoic acid (DHA)

QUESTIONS AND PROBLEMS

17.2 Fatty Acids

LEARNING GOAL: Draw the condensed structural formula for a fatty acid and identify it as saturated or unsaturated.

17.5 Describe some similarities and differences in the structures of a saturated fatty acid and an unsaturated fatty acid.

17.6 Stearic acid and linoleic acid each have 18 carbon atoms. Why does stearic acid melt at 69 °C, but linoleic acid melts at −5 °C?

17.7 Draw the skeletal formula for each of the following fatty acids:
  a. palmitic acid   **b.** oleic acid

17.8 Draw the skeletal formula for each of the following fatty acids:
  a. stearic acid   **b.** linoleic acid

17.9 Classify each of the following fatty acids as saturated, monounsaturated, or polyunsaturated:
  a. lauric acid   **b.** linolenic acid
  c. palmitoleic acid   **d.** stearic acid

17.10 Classify each of the following fatty acids as saturated, monounsaturated, or polyunsaturated:
  a. linoleic acid   **b.** palmitic acid
  c. myristic acid   **d.** oleic acid

17.11 How does the structure of a fatty acid with a cis double bond differ from the structure of a fatty acid with a trans double bond?

17.12 How does the double bond influence the dispersion forces that can form between hydrocarbon chains of fatty acids?

17.13 What is the difference in the location of the first double bond in an omega-3 and an omega-6 fatty acid (see Chemistry Link to Health "Omega-3 Fatty Acids in Fish Oils")?

17.14 a. What are some sources of omega-3 and omega-6 fatty acids (see Chemistry Link to Health "Omega-3 Fatty Acids in Fish Oils")?
  b. How may omega-3 fatty acids help in lowering the risk of heart disease?

17.15 Compare the structures and functional groups of arachidonic acid and prostaglandin PGE_1.

17.16 Compare the structures and functional groups of prostaglandins PGF_1 and PGF_2.

17.17 What are some effects of prostaglandins in the body?

17.18 How do nonsteroidal anti-inflammatory drugs reduce inflammation caused by prostaglandins?

17.3 Waxes and Triacylglycerols

Waxes are found in many plants and animals. Natural waxes are found on the surface of fruits, and on the leaves and stems of plants where they help prevent loss of water and damage from pests. Waxes on the skin, fur, and feathers of animals and birds provide a waterproof coating. A wax is an ester of a saturated fatty acid and a long-chain alcohol, each containing from 14 to 30 carbon atoms.

The formulas of some common waxes are given in Table 17.2. Beeswax obtained from honeycombs and carnauba wax from palm trees are used to give a protective coating to furniture, cars, and floors. Jojoba wax is used in making candles and cosmetics such as lipstick. Lanolin, a mixture of waxes obtained from wool, is used in hand and facial lotions to aid retention of water, which softens the skin.

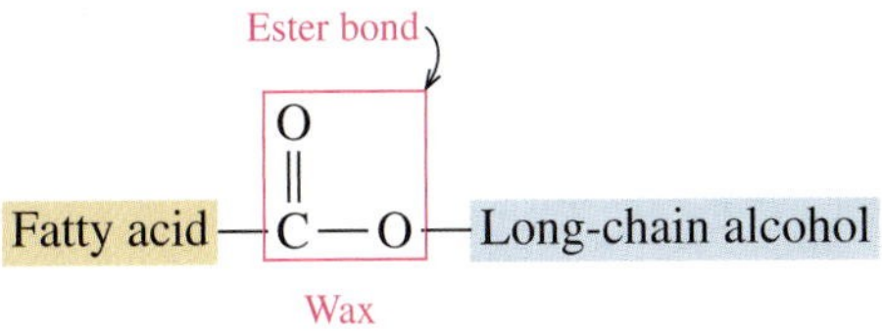

LEARNING GOAL

Draw the condensed structural formula for a wax or triacylglycerol produced by the reaction of a fatty acid and an alcohol or glycerol.

TABLE 17.2 Some Typical Waxes

Type	Condensed Structural Formula	Source	Uses
Beeswax	$CH_3-(CH_2)_{14}-\overset{\displaystyle O}{\overset{\displaystyle \|}{C}}-O-(CH_2)_{29}-CH_3$	Honeycomb	Candles, shoe polish, wax paper
Carnauba wax	$CH_3-(CH_2)_{24}-\overset{\displaystyle O}{\overset{\displaystyle \|}{C}}-O-(CH_2)_{29}-CH_3$	Brazilian palm tree	Waxes for furniture, cars, floors, shoes
Jojoba wax	$CH_3-(CH_2)_{18}-\overset{\displaystyle O}{\overset{\displaystyle \|}{C}}-O-(CH_2)_{19}-CH_3$	Jojoba bush	Candles, soaps, cosmetics

SELF-STUDY ACTIVITY
Triacylglycerols

SELF-STUDY ACTIVITY
Fats

Fats and Oils: Triacylglycerols

In the body, fatty acids are stored as fats and oils known as **triacylglycerols**. These substances, also called *triglycerides*, are triesters of glycerol (a trihydroxy alcohol) and fatty acids. The general formula for a triacylglycerol follows:

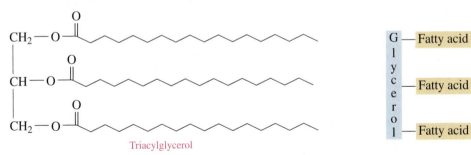

Triacylglycerol

In Section 16.3, we saw that esters are produced from the esterification reaction between a carboxylic acid and an alcohol. In a triacylglycerol, three hydroxyl groups on glycerol form ester bonds with the carboxyl groups of three fatty acids. For example, glycerol and three molecules of stearic acid form a triacylglycerol. In the name, glycerol is named *glyceryl* and the fatty acids are named as carboxylates. For example, stearic acid is named as stearate, which gives the name glyceryl tristearate. The common name of this compound is tristearin.

Tristearin consists of glycerol with three ester bonds to stearic acid molecules.

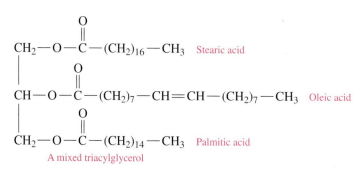

$$
\begin{array}{c}
\underset{\text{Glycerol}}{\left.\begin{array}{l}
CH_2-O-H + HO-\overset{\overset{O}{\parallel}}{C}-(CH_2)_{16}-CH_3 \\
CH-O-H + HO-\overset{\overset{O}{\parallel}}{C}-(CH_2)_{16}-CH_3 \\
CH_2-O-H + HO-\overset{\overset{O}{\parallel}}{C}-(CH_2)_{16}-CH_3
\end{array}\right.} \longrightarrow
\underset{\substack{\text{Glyceryl tristearate}\\ \text{(tristearin, a fat)}}}{\left.\begin{array}{l}
CH_2-O-\overset{\overset{O}{\parallel}}{C}-(CH_2)_{16}-CH_3 \\
CH-O-\overset{\overset{O}{\parallel}}{C}-(CH_2)_{16}-CH_3 \\
CH_2-O-\overset{\overset{O}{\parallel}}{C}-(CH_2)_{16}-CH_3
\end{array}\right.} + 3H_2O
\end{array}
$$

3 Stearic acid molecules — Ester bond

Most naturally occurring fats and oils are mixed triacylglycerols that contain glycerol bonded by ester bonds to two or three different fatty acids, typically palmitic acid, oleic acid, linoleic acid, and stearic acid. For example, a mixed triacylglycerol might be made from stearic acid, oleic acid, and palmitic acid. One possible structure for the mixed triacylglycerol follows:

$$
\begin{array}{l}
CH_2-O-\overset{\overset{O}{\parallel}}{C}-(CH_2)_{16}-CH_3 \quad \text{Stearic acid} \\
CH-O-\overset{\overset{O}{\parallel}}{C}-(CH_2)_7-CH=CH-(CH_2)_7-CH_3 \quad \text{Oleic acid} \\
CH_2-O-\overset{\overset{O}{\parallel}}{C}-(CH_2)_{14}-CH_3 \quad \text{Palmitic acid}
\end{array}
$$

A mixed triacylglycerol

Prior to hibernation, a polar bear eats food with a high content of fats and oils.

Triacylglycerols are the major form of energy storage for animals. Animals that hibernate eat large quantities of plants, seeds, and nuts that contain high levels of fats and oils. Prior to hibernation, these animals, such as polar bears, gain as much as 14 kilograms a week. As the external temperature drops, the animal goes into hibernation. The body temperature drops to nearly freezing, and cellular activity, respiration, and heart rate are drastically reduced. Animals that live in extremely cold climates will hibernate for 4 to 7 months. During this time, stored fat is their only source of energy.

CONCEPT CHECK 17.3 Triacylglycerols

The following triacylglycerol is used in creams and lotions as a thickening agent:

$$
\begin{array}{l}
CH_2-O-\overset{\overset{O}{\parallel}}{C}-CH_2-CH_2-CH_2-CH_2-CH_2-CH_2-CH_2-CH_2-CH_2-CH_2-CH_3 \\
CH-O-\overset{\overset{O}{\parallel}}{C}-CH_2-CH_2-CH_2-CH_2-CH_2-CH_2-CH_2-CH_2-CH_2-CH_2-CH_3 \\
CH_2-O-\overset{\overset{O}{\parallel}}{C}-CH_2-CH_2-CH_2-CH_2-CH_2-CH_2-CH_2-CH_2-CH_2-CH_2-CH_3
\end{array}
$$

Triacylglycerols are used to thicken creams and lotions.

a. Give the name of the alcohol and fatty acid.
b. Give the name of the triacylglycerol, including the common name.

ANSWER

a. The alcohol is glycerol, and the saturated fatty acid with 12 carbon atoms is lauric acid.
b. The triacylglycerol is named glyceryl trilaurate or trilaurin (common).

SAMPLE PROBLEM 17.2   **Drawing Structures for a Triacylglycerol**

Draw the condensed structural formula for glyceryl tripalmitoleate (tripalmitolein).

SOLUTION

Analyze the Problem

Name of Lipid	Type of Lipid	Type of Alcohol	Fatty Acids	Type of Bonds
Glyceryl tripalmitoleate (tripalmitolein)	Triacylglycerol	Glycerol	Three palmitoleic acids	Ester

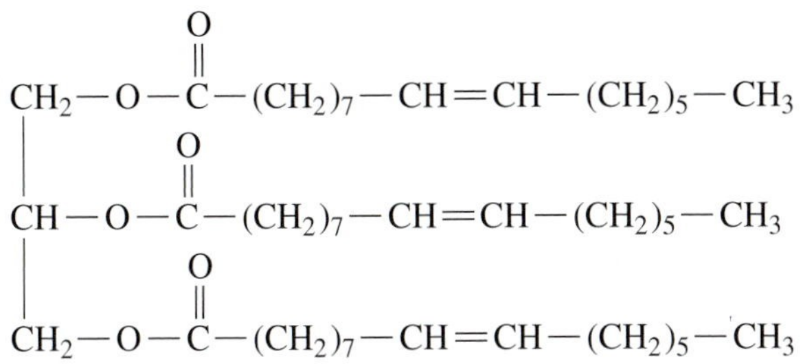

$$
\begin{array}{l}
\quad\quad\quad\quad O \\
\quad\quad\quad\quad \| \\
CH_2-O-C-(CH_2)_7-CH=CH-(CH_2)_5-CH_3 \\
|\quad\quad\quad O \\
|\quad\quad\quad \| \\
CH-O-C-(CH_2)_7-CH=CH-(CH_2)_5-CH_3 \\
|\quad\quad\quad O \\
|\quad\quad\quad \| \\
CH_2-O-C-(CH_2)_7-CH=CH-(CH_2)_5-CH_3
\end{array}
$$

Glyceryl tripalmitoleate (tripalmitolein)

STUDY CHECK 17.2

Draw the condensed structural formula for the triacylglycerol containing three molecules of myristic acid.

Melting Points of Fats and Oils

A **fat** is a triacylglycerol that is solid at room temperature and usually comes from animal sources such as meat, whole milk, butter, and cheese.

An **oil** is a triacylglycerol that is usually a liquid at room temperature and is obtained from a plant source. Olive oil and peanut oil are monounsaturated because they contain large amounts of oleic acid. Oils from corn, cottonseed, safflower seed, and sunflower seed are polyunsaturated because they contain large amounts of fatty acids with two or more double bonds (see Figure 17.3).

Palm oil and coconut oil are solids at room temperature because they consist mostly of saturated fatty acids. Although coconut oil is 92% saturated fat, about half is lauric acid, which contains 12 carbon atoms rather than the 18 carbon atoms found in stearic acid from animal sources. Thus, coconut oil has a melting point that is higher than typical vegetable oils, but not as high as fats from animal sources that contain stearic acid. The amounts of saturated, monounsaturated, and polyunsaturated fatty acids in some typical fats and oils are shown in Figure 17.4.

Saturated fatty acids have higher melting points than unsaturated fatty acids because they pack together more tightly. Animal fats usually contain more saturated fatty acids than do vegetable oils. Therefore, the melting points of animal fats are higher than those of vegetable oils.

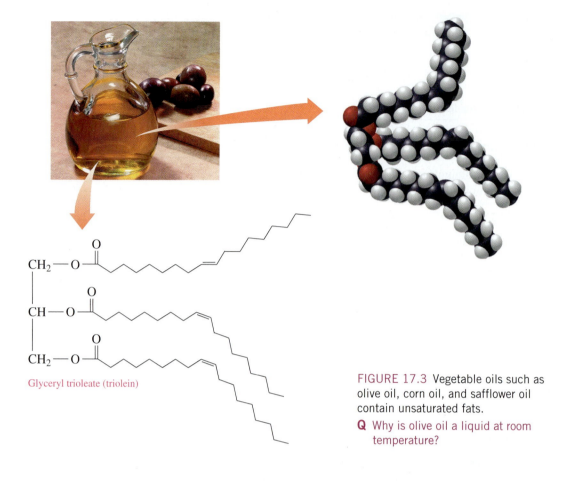

CH₂—O—C(=O)— ...

Glyceryl trioleate (triolein)

FIGURE 17.3 Vegetable oils such as olive oil, corn oil, and safflower oil contain unsaturated fats.

Q Why is olive oil a liquid at room temperature?

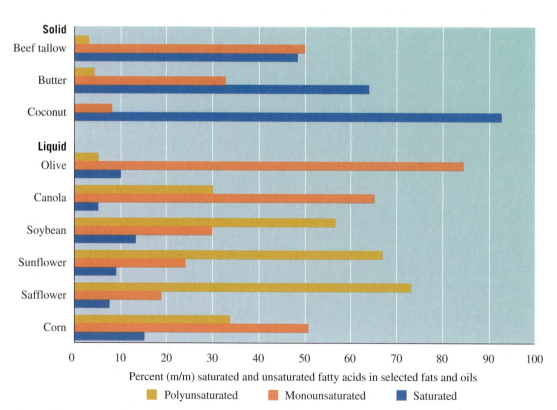

Percent (m/m) saturated and unsaturated fatty acids in selected fats and oils

■ Polyunsaturated ■ Monounsaturated ■ Saturated

FIGURE 17.4 Vegetable oils are liquids at room temperature because they have a higher percentage of unsaturated fatty acids than do animal fats.

Q Why is butter a solid at room temperature, whereas canola oil is a liquid?

Chemistry Link to Health

OLESTRA: A FAT SUBSTITUTE

In 1968, food scientists designed an artificial fat called *olestra* as an intended source of nutrition for premature babies. However, olestra could not be digested and was never used for that purpose. Later, scientists realized that olestra had the flavor and texture of a fat without the calories.

Olestra (also known by the brand name Olean) is manufactured by obtaining the fatty acids from the fats in cottonseed or soybean oils and bonding the fatty acids with the hydroxyl groups on sucrose. Chemically, olestra is composed of six to eight long-chain fatty acids attached by ester links to a sucrose molecule rather than to a glycerol molecule. This structure makes olestra a very large molecule that cannot be absorbed through the intestinal walls. The enzymes and bacteria in the intestinal tract are unable to break down the olestra molecule, and it travels through the intestinal tract undigested.

The large molecule of olestra also combines with fat-soluble vitamins (A, D, E, and K) before they can be absorbed through the intestinal wall. Once the olestra combines with these molecules, they pass through the intestinal tract without being absorbed. The FDA now requires manufacturers to add the four vitamins to olestra products. There have been reports of some adverse reactions, including diarrhea, abdominal cramps, and anal leakage, indicating that olestra may act as a laxative in some people. However, the manufacturers contend there is no direct proof that olestra is the cause of those effects.

Snack foods made with olestra, such as potato chips, tortilla chips, crackers, and fried snacks, are found in supermarkets nationwide. It remains to be seen whether olestra will have any significant effect on reducing the problem of obesity.

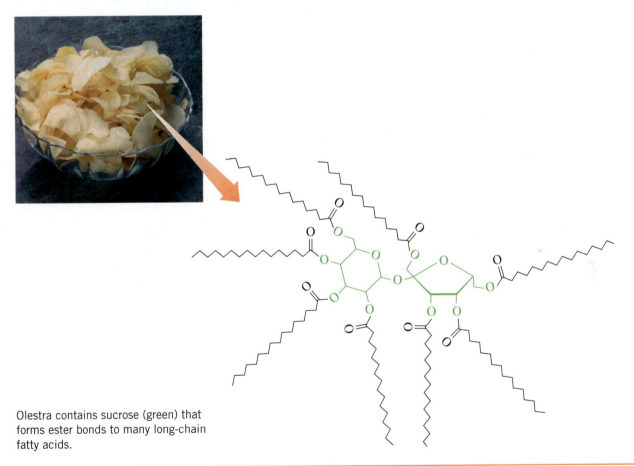

Olestra contains sucrose (green) that forms ester bonds to many long-chain fatty acids.

QUESTIONS AND PROBLEMS

17.3 Waxes and Triacylglycerols

LEARNING GOAL: *Draw the condensed structural formula for a wax or triacylglycerol produced by the reaction of a fatty acid and an alcohol or glycerol.*

17.19 Draw the condensed structural formula for the ester in beeswax that is formed from myricyl alcohol, $CH_3 — (CH_2)_{29} — OH$, and palmitic acid.

17.20 Draw the condensed structural formula for the ester in jojoba wax that is formed from arachidic acid, a 20-carbon saturated fatty acid, and 1-docosanol, $CH_3 — (CH_2)_{21} — OH$.

17.21 Draw the condensed structural formula for a triacylglycerol that contains stearic acid and glycerol.

17.22 Draw the condensed structural formula for a mixed triacyl-glycerol that contains two palmitic acid molecules and one oleic acid molecule on the second carbon (center carbon) of glycerol.

17.23 Draw the condensed structural formula for glyceryl tripalmi-tate (tripalmitin).

17.24 Draw the condensed structural formula for glyceryl trioleate (triolein).

17.25 Draw the condensed structural formula for glyceryl tricaprylate (tricaprylin). Caprylic acid is an 8-carbon saturated fatty acid.

17.26 Draw the condensed structural formula for glyceryl trilinole-ate (trilinolein).

17.27 Why would safflower oil have a lower melting point than olive oil?

17.28 Why does olive oil have a lower melting point than butterfat?

17.29 Why does coconut oil have a melting point that is similar to fats from animal sources?

17.30 A label on a bottle of 100% sunflower seed oil states that it is lower in saturated fats than all the leading oils.
   a. How does the percentage of saturated fats in sunflower seed oil compare to that of safflower, corn, and canola oil (see Figure 17.4)?
   b. Is the claim valid?

LEARNING GOAL

Draw the condensed structural formula for the product of a triacylglycerol that undergoes hydrogenation, hydrolysis, or saponification.

TUTORIAL
Hydrogenation and Hydrolysis of Triacylglycerols

17.4 Chemical Properties of Triacylglycerols

The chemical reactions of triacylglycerols (fats and oils) are the same as those we discussed for alkenes (Section 12.3) and esters (Section 16.5).

Hydrogenation

In the **hydrogenation** of an unsaturated fat, hydrogen is added to one or more carbon–carbon double bonds to form carbon–carbon single bonds. The hydrogen gas is bubbled through the heated oil, typically in the presence of a nickel, platinum, or palladium catalyst.

$$-CH=CH- + H_2 \xrightarrow{Ni} \begin{array}{c} H \quad H \\ | \quad | \\ -C-C- \\ | \quad | \\ H \quad H \end{array}$$

For example, when hydrogen adds to all of the double bonds of glyceryl trioleate (triolein), the product is the saturated fat glyceryl tristearate (tristearin).

$$
\begin{array}{l}
CH_2-O-\overset{O}{\overset{\|}{C}}-(CH_2)_7-CH=CH-(CH_2)_7-CH_3 \\[4pt]
CH-O-\overset{O}{\overset{\|}{C}}-(CH_2)_7-CH=CH-(CH_2)_7-CH_3 \quad + \quad 3H_2 \\[4pt]
CH_2-O-\overset{O}{\overset{\|}{C}}-(CH_2)_7-CH=CH-(CH_2)_7-CH_3
\end{array}
\xrightarrow{Ni}
\begin{array}{l}
CH_2-O-\overset{O}{\overset{\|}{C}}-(CH_2)_{16}-CH_3 \\[4pt]
CH-O-\overset{O}{\overset{\|}{C}}-(CH_2)_{16}-CH_3 \\[4pt]
CH_2-O-\overset{O}{\overset{\|}{C}}-(CH_2)_{16}-CH_3
\end{array}
$$

Glyceryl trioleate (triolein)   Glyceryl tristearate (tristearin)

In commercial hydrogenation, the addition of hydrogen is stopped before all the double bonds in a liquid vegetable oil become completely saturated. Complete hydrogenation gives a very brittle product, whereas the partial hydrogenation of a liquid vegetable oil changes it to a soft, semisolid fat. As the semisolid fat becomes more saturated, the melting point increases, and the substance becomes more solid at room temperature. By controlling the amount of hydrogen, manufacturers can produce the various types of products on the market today, such as soft margarines, solid stick margarines, and solid shortenings (see Figure 17.5). Although these products now contain more saturated fatty acids than the original oils, they contain no cholesterol, unlike similar products from animal sources, such as butter and lard.

FIGURE 17.5 Many soft margarines, stick margarines, and shortenings are produced by the partial hydrogenation of vegetable oils.

Q How does hydrogenation change the structure of the fatty acids in the vegetable oils?

Chemistry Link to Health

CONVERTING UNSATURATED FATS TO SATURATED FATS: HYDROGENATION AND INTERESTERIFICATION

During the early 1900s, margarine became a popular replacement for highly saturated fats such as butter and lard. Margarine is produced by partially hydrogenating the unsaturated fats in vegetable oils such as safflower oil, corn oil, canola oil, cottonseed oil, and sunflower oil.

Hydrogenation and Trans Fats

In vegetable oils, the unsaturated fats usually contain cis double bonds. As hydrogenation occurs, double bonds are converted to single bonds. However, a small amount of the cis double bonds are converted to trans double bonds because they are more stable, which causes a change in the overall structure of the fatty acids. If the label on a product states that the oils have been "partially hydrogenated," that product will also contain trans fatty acids. In the United States, it is estimated that 2–4% of our total calories comes from trans fatty acids.

The concern about trans fatty acids is that their altered structure may make them behave like saturated fatty acids in the body.

Several studies reported that trans fatty acids raise the levels of LDL-cholesterol and lower the levels of HDL-cholesterol. (LDLs and HDLs are described in Section 17.6.)

Foods containing a naturally-occurring trans fat include milk, beef, and eggs. Foods that contain trans fatty acids from the hydrogenation process include deep-fried foods, bread, baked goods, cookies, crackers, chips, stick and soft margarines, and vegetable shortening. The American Heart Association recommends that margarine should have no more than 2 grams of saturated fat per tablespoon, and a liquid vegetable oil should be the first ingredient. They also recommend the use of soft margarine, which is only slightly hydrogenated and therefore has fewer trans fatty acids. Currently, the amount of trans fats is included on the Nutritional Facts label on food products. In the United States, a food label for a product that has less than 0.5 g of trans fat in one serving can read "0 g of trans fat."

cis-Oleic acid

H_2/Ni

Ni catalyst

H_2 → Isomerization

Undesired side product (*trans*-oleic acid)

Addition of H_2

Desired saturated product (stearic acid)

The best advice may be to reduce total fat in the diet by using fats and oils sparingly, cooking with little or no fat, substituting olive oil or canola oil for other oils, and limiting the use of coconut oil and palm oil, which are high in saturated fatty acids.

Interesterification

Interesterification is a newer process used to change unsaturated vegetable oils into products that have the properties of solid and semisolid saturated fats. During the process of interesterification, lipase enzymes are used to hydrolyze ester bonds in triacylglycerols of vegetable oils so that glycerol and fatty acids are formed. Then the saturated fatty acids recombine with glycerol. For example, an unsaturated oleic acid in a vegetable oil could be replaced by a saturated stearic acid, which results in a more saturated fat with a higher melting point. The saturated products in the mixture are separated by differences in melting points. As a result of bypassing the hydrogenation process of converting double bonds to single bonds, there are no trans fatty acids present in the solid or semisolid fats products. Such products may have a label that reads "no trans fats."

Simplified Example of Interesterification

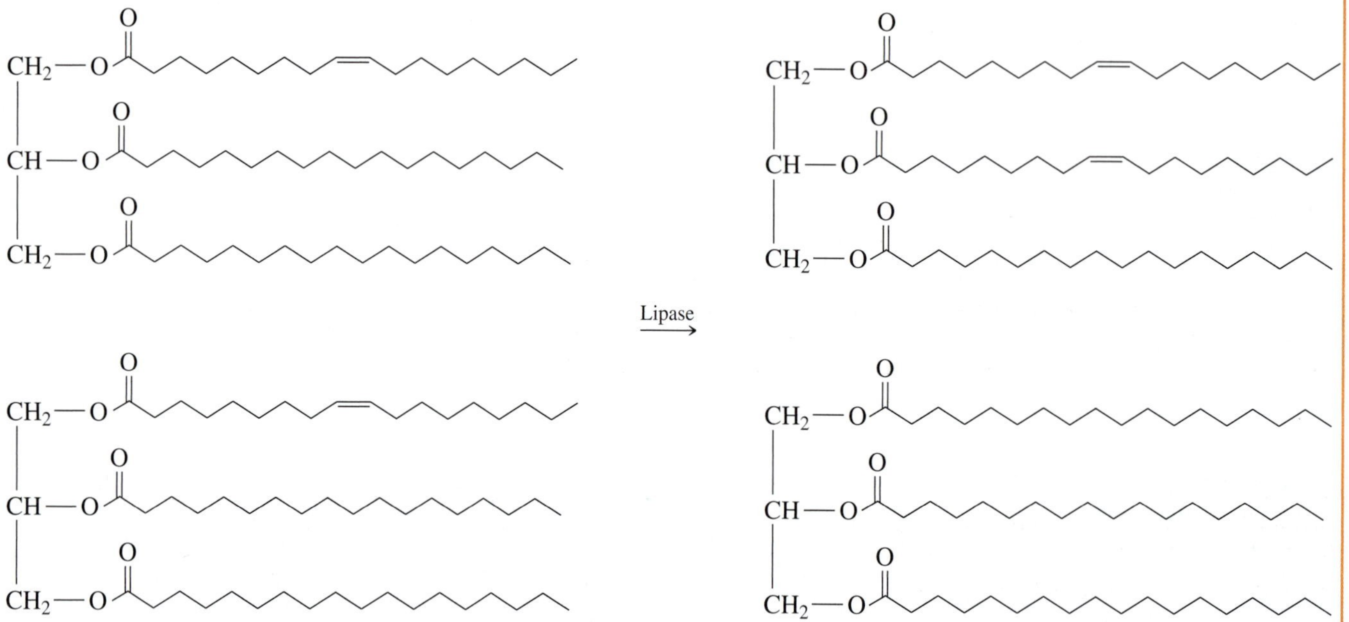

Mixed triacylglycerols are unsaturated and have lower melting points.

A new mixture of triacylglycerols includes saturated triacylglycerols with higher melting points, as well as unsaturated triacylglycerols.

Hydrolysis

Triacylglycerols are hydrolyzed (split by water) in the presence of strong acids such as HCl or H_2SO_4, or digestive enzymes called *lipases*. The products of hydrolysis of the ester bonds are glycerol and three fatty acids. The polar glycerol is soluble in water, but the fatty acids with their long hydrocarbon chains are not.

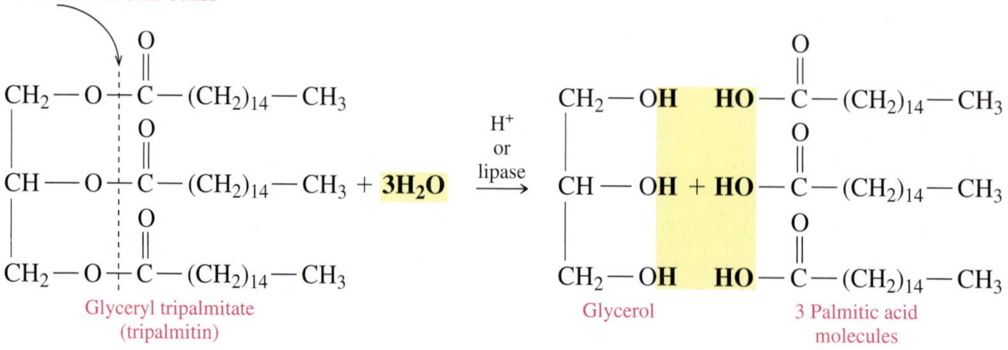

Glyceryl tripalmitate (tripalmitin)

Glycerol

3 Palmitic acid molecules

Saponification

Saponification occurs when a fat is heated with a strong base such as sodium hydroxide to give glycerol and the sodium salts of the fatty acids, which is soap. When NaOH is used, a solid soap is produced that can be molded into a desired shape; KOH produces a softer, liquid soap. Polyunsaturated oils produce softer soaps. Names like "coconut" or "avocado shampoo" tell you the sources of the oil used in the reaction.

Fat or oil   +   strong base $\longrightarrow$ glycerol   +   salts of fatty acids (soap)

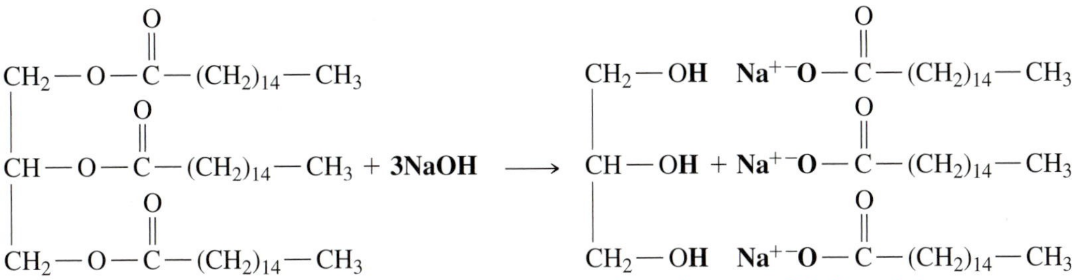

$$CH_2-O-\overset{\displaystyle O}{\overset{\|}{C}}-(CH_2)_{14}-CH_3$$

$$CH-O-\overset{\displaystyle O}{\overset{\|}{C}}-(CH_2)_{14}-CH_3 + 3NaOH \longrightarrow$$

$$CH_2-O-\overset{\displaystyle O}{\overset{\|}{C}}-(CH_2)_{14}-CH_3$$

Glyceryl tripalmitate
(tripalmitin)

$$CH_2-OH \quad Na^+ {}^-O-\overset{\displaystyle O}{\overset{\|}{C}}-(CH_2)_{14}-CH_3$$

$$CH-OH + Na^+ {}^-O-\overset{\displaystyle O}{\overset{\|}{C}}-(CH_2)_{14}-CH_3$$

$$CH_2-OH \quad Na^+ {}^-O-\overset{\displaystyle O}{\overset{\|}{C}}-(CH_2)_{14}-CH_3$$

Glycerol   3 Sodium palmitate
(soap)

The reactions we have discussed for fatty acids and triacylglycerols are similar to the hydrogenation reactions of alkenes (Section 12.3), the esterification of carboxylic acids and alcohols (Section 16.3), and the hydrolysis and saponification of esters (Section 16.5). A comparison of these organic reactions and their corresponding lipid reactions is given in Table 17.3.

TABLE 17.3 **Summary of Organic and Lipid Reactions**

Reaction	Organic Reactants and Products	Lipid Reactants and Products
Esterification	Carboxylic acid + alcohol $\xrightarrow{H^+, heat}$ ester + water	3 Fatty acids + glycerol $\xrightarrow{enzyme}$ triacylglycerol (fat) + 3 water
Hydrogenation	Alkene (double bond) + hydrogen $\xrightarrow{Pt}$ alkane (single bonds)	Unsaturated fat (double bond) + hydrogen $\xrightarrow{Pt}$ saturated fat (single bonds)
Hydrolysis	Ester + water $\xrightarrow{H^+, heat}$ carboxylic acid + alcohol	Triacylglycerol (fat) + 3 water $\xrightarrow{enzyme}$ 3 fatty acids + glycerol
Saponification	Ester + sodium hydroxide $\longrightarrow$ sodium salt of carboxylic acid + alcohol	Triacylglycerol (fat) + 3 sodium hydroxide $\longrightarrow$ 3 sodium salts of fatty acid (soap) + glycerol

CONCEPT CHECK 17.4 **Hydrogenation, Hydrolysis, and Saponification**

Identify each of the following processes as hydrogenation, hydrolysis, or saponification and identify the products:

a. the reaction of palm oil with KOH
b. the reaction of glyceryl trilinoleate from safflower oil with water and HCl
c. the reaction of corn oil and hydrogen (H_2) with a nickel catalyst

ANSWER

a. The reaction of palm oil with KOH is saponification, and the products are glycerol and the potassium salts of the fatty acids, which is soap.
b. In acid hydrolysis, glyceryl trilinoleate reacts with water, which splits the ester bonds to produce glycerol and three molecules of linoleic acid.
c. In hydrogenation, H_2 adds to double bonds in corn oil, which produces a more saturated, and thus more solid, fat.

SAMPLE PROBLEM 17.3   **Reactions of Lipids**

Write the equation for the reaction catalyzed by a lipase enzyme that completely hydro-lyzes glyceryl trilaurate (trilaurin).

SOLUTION

Analyze the Problem

Name of Lipid	Reactants	Reaction	Products
Glyceryl trilaurate (trilaurin)	Triacylglycerol and three water molecules	Hydrolysis	Glycerol and three lauric acids

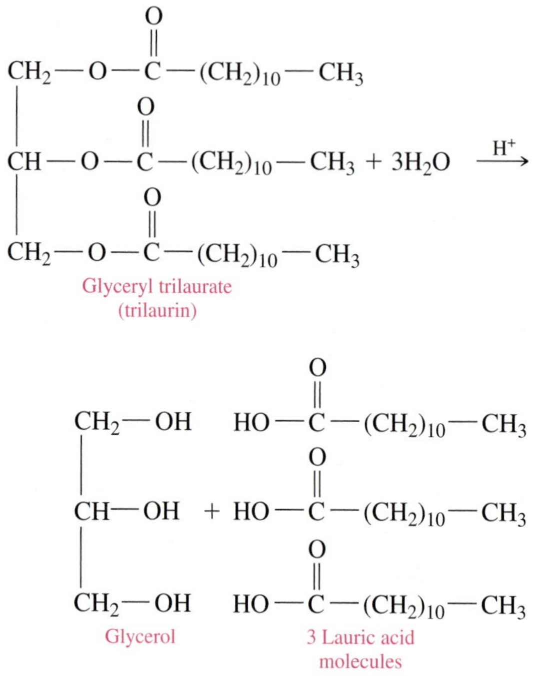

$$
\begin{array}{l}
CH_2-O-\overset{\displaystyle O}{\overset{\|}{C}}-(CH_2)_{10}-CH_3 \\[4pt]
\;|\qquad\quad \overset{\displaystyle O}{} \\
CH-O-\overset{\displaystyle O}{\overset{\|}{C}}-(CH_2)_{10}-CH_3 \;+\; 3H_2O \;\xrightarrow{\;H^+\;} \\[4pt]
\;|\qquad\quad \overset{\displaystyle O}{} \\
CH_2-O-\overset{\displaystyle O}{\overset{\|}{C}}-(CH_2)_{10}-CH_3
\end{array}
$$

Glyceryl trilaurate
(trilaurin)

$$
\begin{array}{ll}
CH_2-OH & HO-\overset{\displaystyle O}{\overset{\|}{C}}-(CH_2)_{10}-CH_3 \\[4pt]
\;| & \qquad\quad \overset{\displaystyle O}{} \\
CH-OH \;+\; & HO-\overset{\displaystyle O}{\overset{\|}{C}}-(CH_2)_{10}-CH_3 \\[4pt]
\;| & \qquad\quad \overset{\displaystyle O}{} \\
CH_2-OH & HO-\overset{\displaystyle O}{\overset{\|}{C}}-(CH_2)_{10}-CH_3
\end{array}
$$

Glycerol   3 Lauric acid
molecules

STUDY CHECK 17.3

What is the name of the product formed when a triacylglycerol containing oleic acid and linoleic acid is completely hydrogenated?

Explore Your World

TYPES OF FATS

Read the labels on food products that contain fats, such as butter, margarine, vegetable oils, peanut butter, and potato chips. Look for terms such as saturated, monounsaturated, polyunsaturated, and par-tially or fully hydrogenated.

QUESTIONS

1. What type(s) of fats or oils are in the product?
2. How many grams of saturated, monounsaturated, and polyunsatu-rated fat are in one serving of the product?
3. What percent of the total fat is saturated fat? Unsaturated fat?
4. If the product is a vegetable oil, what information is given about how to store it? Why?

5. The label on a container of peanut butter states that the cottonseed and canola oils used to make the peanut butter have been fully hydrogenated. What are the typical products that would form when hydrogen is added?
6. For each packaged food, determine the following:
   a. How many grams of fat are in one serving of the food?
   b. Using the caloric value for fat (9 kcal/gram of fat), how many Calories (kilocalories) come from the fat in one serving?
   c. What is the percentage of fat in one serving?

Chemistry Link to the Environment

BIODIESEL AS AN ALTERNATIVE FUEL

Biodiesel is a name of a nonpetroleum fuel that can be used in place of diesel fuel. Biodiesel is produced from renewable biological resources such as vegetable oils (primarily soybean), waste vegetable oils from restaurants, and some animal fats. Biodiesel is nontoxic and biodegradable.

Biodiesel is prepared from triacylglycerols and alcohols (usually ethanol) to form ethyl esters and glycerol. The glycerol that separates from the fat is used in soaps and other products. The reaction of triacylglycerols is catalyzed by a base such as NaOH or KOH at low temperatures.

Triacylglycerol + 3 ethanol $\longrightarrow$
                                  3 ethyl esters (biodiesel) + glycerol

Compared to diesel fuel from petroleum, biodiesel burns in an engine to produce much lower levels of carbon dioxide emissions, particulates, unburned hydrocarbons, and aromatic hydrocarbons that cause lung cancer. Because biodiesel has extremely low sulfur content, it does not contribute to the formation of the sulfur oxides that produce acid rain. The energy output from the combustion of biodiesel is almost the same as energy produced by the combustion of petroleum diesel.

In many cases, diesel engines need only slight modification to use biodiesel. Manufacturers of diesel cars, trucks, boats, and tractors have different suggestions for the percentage of biodiesel to use, ranging from 2% (B2) blended with standard diesel fuel to using 100% pure biodiesel (B100). For example, B20 is 20% biodiesel by volume, blended with 80% petroleum diesel by volume. In 2006, 9.8×10^{14} liters of biodiesel were used in the United States. Fuel stations in Europe and the United States are now stocking biodiesel fuel.

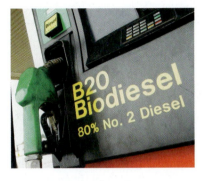

Biodiesel 20 contains 20% ethyl esters and 80% standard diesel fuel.

$$\begin{array}{l}
CH_2{-}O{-}\overset{\overset{\displaystyle O}{\|}}{C}{-}(CH_2)_{12}{-}CH_3 \\[4pt]
CH{-}O{-}\overset{\overset{\displaystyle O}{\|}}{C}{-}(CH_2)_7{-}CH{=}CH{-}(CH_2)_7{-}CH_3 \; + \; 3CH_3{-}CH_2{-}OH \\[4pt]
CH_2{-}O{-}\overset{\overset{\displaystyle O}{\|}}{C}{-}(CH_2)_{16}{-}CH_3
\end{array} \quad \xrightarrow[\text{catalyst}]{\text{NaOH}}$$

Triacylglycerol from vegetable oil   Ethanol

$$\begin{array}{ll}
CH_2{-}OH & CH_3{-}CH_2{-}O{-}\overset{\overset{\displaystyle O}{\|}}{C}{-}(CH_2)_{12}{-}CH_3 \\[4pt]
CH{-}OH \;\; + & CH_3{-}CH_2{-}O{-}\overset{\overset{\displaystyle O}{\|}}{C}{-}(CH_2)_7{-}CH{=}CH{-}(CH_2)_7{-}CH_3 \\[4pt]
CH_2{-}OH & CH_3{-}CH_2{-}O{-}\overset{\overset{\displaystyle O}{\|}}{C}{-}(CH_2)_{16}{-}CH_3
\end{array}$$

Glycerol   Ethyl esters used for biodiesel

QUESTIONS AND PROBLEMS

17.4 Chemical Properties of Triacylglycerols

LEARNING GOAL: *Draw the condensed structural formula for the product of a triacylglycerol that undergoes hydrogenation, hydrolysis, or saponification.*

17.31 Write an equation for the hydrogenation of glyceryl trioleate, a fat formed from glycerol and three oleic acid molecules.

17.32 Write an equation for the hydrogenation of glyceryl trilinolenate, a fat formed from glycerol and three linolenic acid molecules.

17.33 Write an equation for the acid hydrolysis of glyceryl trimyristate (trimyristin).

17.34 Write an equation for the acid hydrolysis of glyceryl trioleate (triolein).

17.35 Write an equation for the NaOH saponification of glyceryl trimyristate (trimyristin).

17.36 Write an equation for the NaOH saponification of glyceryl trioleate (triolein).

17.37 Compare the structure of a triacylglycerol to the structure of olestra.

17.38 How are trans fats formed during the hydrogenation of vegetable oils?

17.39 Draw the condensed structural formula for the hydrogenation product of the following triacylglycerol:

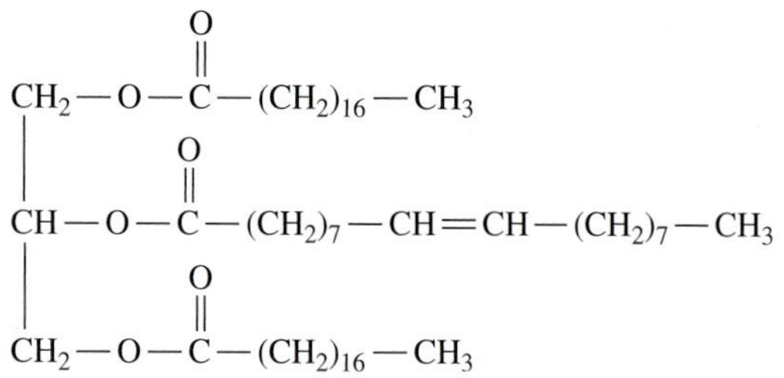

$$
\begin{array}{l}
\overset{\displaystyle O}{\underset{\displaystyle \|}{}} \\
CH_2\!-\!O\!-\!C\!-\!(CH_2)_{16}\!-\!CH_3 \\[2pt]
\hspace{1.3cm}\overset{\displaystyle O}{\underset{\displaystyle \|}{}} \\
CH\!-\!O\!-\!C\!-\!(CH_2)_7\!-\!CH\!=\!CH\!-\!(CH_2)_7\!-\!CH_3 \\[2pt]
\hspace{1.3cm}\overset{\displaystyle O}{\underset{\displaystyle \|}{}} \\
CH_2\!-\!O\!-\!C\!-\!(CH_2)_{16}\!-\!CH_3
\end{array}
$$

17.40 Draw the condensed structural formulas for all the products obtained when the triacylglycerol in Problem 17.39 undergoes complete acid hydrolysis.

LEARNING GOAL

Describe the structure of a phospholipid containing glycerol or sphingosine.

17.5 Phospholipids

The **phospholipids** are a family of lipids similar in structure to triacylglycerols; they include glycerophospholipids and sphingomyelin. In a **glycerophospholipid**, two fatty acids form ester bonds with the first and second hydroxyl group of glycerol. The third hydroxyl group forms an ester with phosphoric acid, which forms another phosphoester bond with an amino alcohol. In a *sphingomyelin*, sphingosine replaces glycerol. We can compare the general structures of a triacylglycerol, a glycerophospholipid, and a sphingolipid as follows:

MC
SELF-STUDY ACTIVITY
Phospholipids

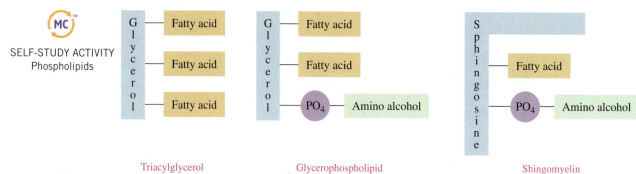

Triacylglycerol   Glycerophospholipid   Shingomyelin

MC
TUTORIAL
The Split Personality of
Glycerophospholipids

Amino Alcohols

Three amino alcohols found in glycerophospholipids are choline, serine, and ethanolamine. In the body, at a physiological pH of 7.4, these amino alcohols are ionized.

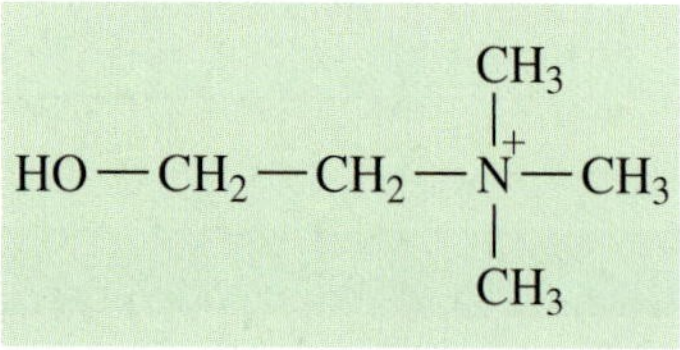

$$
HO\!-\!CH_2\!-\!CH_2\!-\!\overset{\displaystyle +}{N}\!\!\overset{\displaystyle CH_3}{\underset{\displaystyle CH_3}{|}}\!\!-\!CH_3
$$

Choline

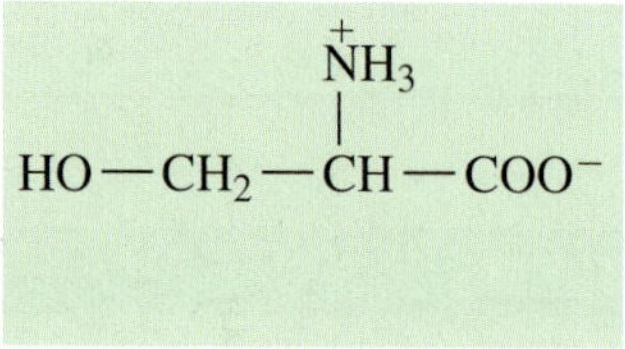

$$
HO\!-\!CH_2\!-\!\overset{\displaystyle \overset{+}{N}H_3}{\underset{\displaystyle |}{C}H}\!-\!COO^-
$$

Serine

$$
HO\!-\!CH_2\!-\!CH_2\!-\!\overset{\displaystyle +}{N}H_3
$$

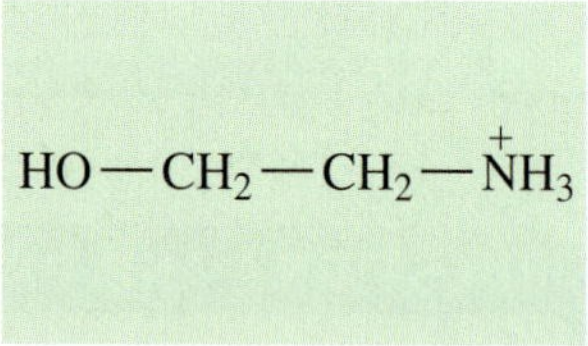

Ethanolamine

Lecithins and **cephalins** are two types of glycerophospholipids that are particularly abundant in brain and nerve tissues as well as in egg yolks, wheat germ, and yeast. Lecithins contain choline, and cephalins usually contain ethanolamine and sometimes serine. In the following structural formulas, the fatty acid that is used as an example is palmitic acid:

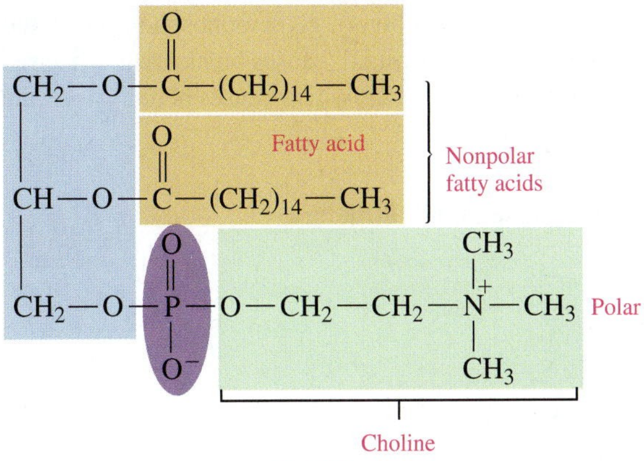

CH$_2$—O—C(=O)—(CH$_2$)$_{14}$—CH$_3$

CH—O—C(=O)—(CH$_2$)$_{14}$—CH$_3$ Fatty acid   Nonpolar fatty acids

CH$_2$—O—P(=O)(O$^-$)—O—CH$_2$—CH$_2$—N$^+$(CH$_3$)(CH$_3$)—CH$_3$ Polar

Choline

A lecithin

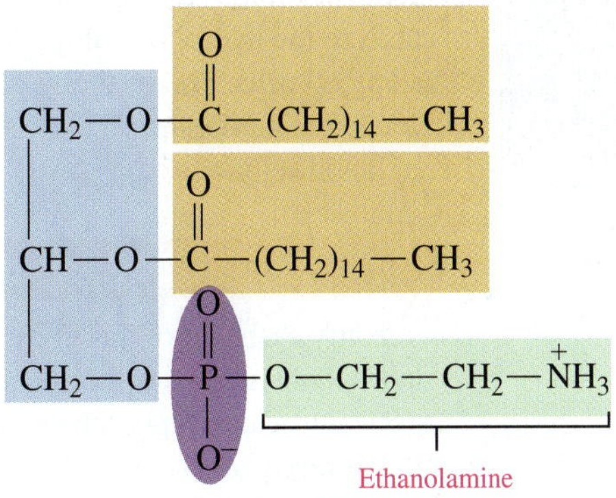

CH$_2$—O—C(=O)—(CH$_2$)$_{14}$—CH$_3$

CH—O—C(=O)—(CH$_2$)$_{14}$—CH$_3$

CH$_2$—O—P(=O)(O$^-$)—O—CH$_2$—CH$_2$—N$^+$H$_3$

Ethanolamine

A cephalin

Glycerophospholipids contain both polar and nonpolar regions, which allow them to interact with both polar and nonpolar substances. The ionized amino alcohol and phosphate portion, called "the head," is polar and strongly attracted to water (see Figure 17.6). The hydrocarbon chains of the two fatty acids are the nonpolar "tails" of the glycerophospholipid, which are only soluble in other nonpolar substances, mostly lipids.

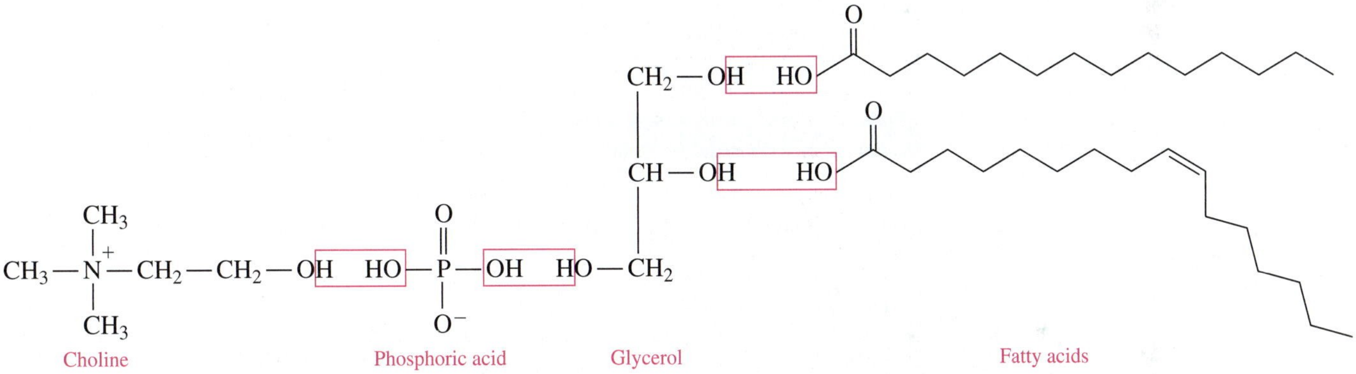

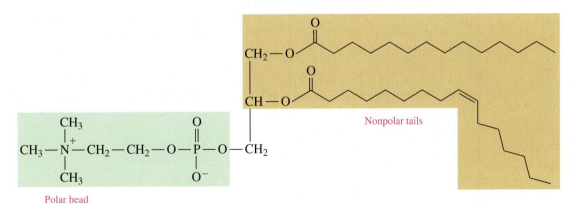

Choline   Phosphoric acid   Glycerol   Fatty acids

(a) Components of a typical glycerophospholipid

(b) Glycerophospholipid

Polar head   Nonpolar tails

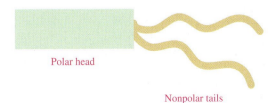

Polar head

Nonpolar tails

(c) Simplified way to draw a glycerophospholipid

FIGURE 17.6 **(a)** The components of a typical glycerophospholipid: an amino alcohol, phosphoric acid, glycerol, and two fatty acids. **(b)** In a glycerophospholipid, a polar "head" contains the ionized amino alcohol and phosphate, while the hydrocarbon chains of two fatty acids make up the nonpolar "tails." **(c)** A simplified drawing indicates the polar region and the nonpolar region.

Q Why are glycerophospholipids polar?

Poisonous snake venom contains phospholipases that hydrolyze phospholipids in red blood cells.

Snake venom is produced by the modified saliva glands of poisonous snakes. When a snake bites, venom is ejected through the fang of the snake. The venom of the eastern diamondback rattlesnake and the Indian cobra contains *phospholipases*, which are enzymes that catalyze the hydrolysis of the fatty acid on the center carbon of glycerophospholipids in the red blood cells. The resulting product, called lysophospholipid, causes breakdown of the red blood cell membranes. This makes them permeable to water, which causes hemolysis of the red blood cells.

CONCEPT CHECK 17.5 **Glycerophospholipid Structure**

Identify each part of this glycerophospholipid as (A) glycerol, (B) fatty acid, (C) phosphate, or (D) ionized amino alcohol:

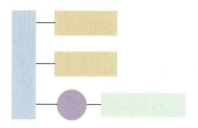

ANSWER

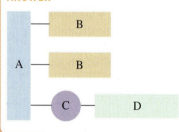

SAMPLE PROBLEM 17.4 **Drawing Glycerophospholipid Structures**

Draw the condensed structural formula for the cephalin that contains two stearic acids on the 1st and 2nd carbon atoms, with serine as the ionized amino alcohol.

SOLUTION

Analyze the Problem

Name of Lipid	Type of Lipid	Type of Alcohol	Fatty Acids	Other Components	Type of Bonds
Cephalin	Glycerophospholipid	Glycerol	Two stearic acids	Phosphate and serine as an ionized amino alcohol	Ester bonds to fatty acids; phosphoester bonds to glycerol and to serine

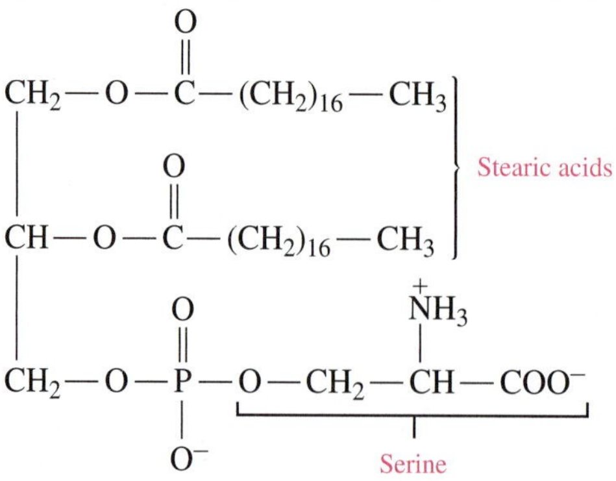

$$CH_2-O-\overset{\overset{\displaystyle O}{\|}}{C}-(CH_2)_{16}-CH_3$$
$$CH-O-\overset{\overset{\displaystyle O}{\|}}{C}-(CH_2)_{16}-CH_3$$

Stearic acids

$$CH_2-O-\overset{\overset{\displaystyle O}{\|}}{\underset{\underset{\displaystyle O^-}{|}}{P}}-O-CH_2-\overset{\overset{\displaystyle \overset{+}{N}H_3}{|}}{CH}-COO^-$$

Serine

STUDY CHECK 17.4

Draw the condensed structural formula for a lecithin, using myristic acid for the fatty acids and choline as the ionized amino alcohol.

Sphingosine, found in sphingomyelins, is a long-chain amino alcohol.

$$HO-CH-CH=CH-(CH_2)_{12}-CH_3$$
$$CH-NH_2$$
$$CH_2-OH$$

Shingosine

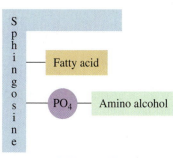

Sphingomyelin

In a **sphingomyelin**, the amine group of sphingosine forms an amide bond to a fatty acid and the hydroxyl group forms an ester bond with phosphate, which forms another phosphoester bond to choline or ethanolamine. The sphingomyelins are abundant in the white matter of the myelin sheath, a coating surrounding the nerve cells that increases the speed of nerve impulses and insulates and protects the nerve cells.

In multiple sclerosis, sphingomyelin is lost from the myelin sheath, which protects the neurons in the brain and spinal cord. As the disease progresses, the myelin sheath deteriorates. Scars form on the neurons and impair the transmission of nerve signals. The symptoms of multiple sclerosis include various levels of muscle weakness with loss of coordination and vision, depending on the amount of damage. The cause of multiple sclerosis is not yet known, although some researchers suggest that a virus is involved. Several studies also suggest that adequate levels of vitamin D may lessen the severity or lower the risk of developing multiple sclerosis.

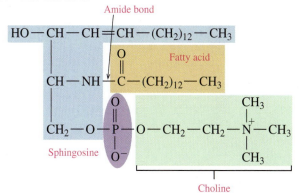

A sphingomyelin containing myristic acid and choline

SAMPLE PROBLEM 17.5   Sphingomyelin

The 16-carbon saturated fatty acid palmitic acid is the most common fatty acid found along with the ionized amino alcohol choline in the sphingomyelin of eggs. Draw the condensed structural formula for this sphingomyelin.

SOLUTION

Analyze the Problem

Name of Lipid	Type of Lipid	Type of Alcohol	Fatty Acid	Other Components	Type of Bonds
Sphingomyelin	Sphingolipid	Sphingosine	Palmitic acid (16 C)	Phosphate and choline as an ionized amino alcohol	Amide bond to palmitic acid; phosphoester bond to sphingosine and to choline

$$HO-CH-CH=CH-(CH_2)_{12}-CH_3$$
$$CH-\overset{H}{N}-\overset{O}{\overset{\|}{C}}-(CH_2)_{14}-CH_3 \text{ Palmitic acid}$$
$$CH_2-O-\overset{O}{\overset{\|}{\underset{O^-}{P}}}-O-CH_2-CH_2-\overset{CH_3}{\overset{|}{\underset{CH_3}{N^+}}}-CH_3$$

Choline

STUDY CHECK 17.5

Stearic acid is found in sphingomyelin in the brain. Draw the condensed structural formula for this sphingomyelin using ethanolamine as the ionized amino alcohol.

Chemistry Link to Health

INFANT RESPIRATORY DISTRESS SYNDROME (IRDS)

When an infant is born, an important key to its survival is proper lung function. In the lungs, there are many tiny air sacs called *alveoli*, where the exchange of O_2 and CO_2 takes place. Upon birth of a mature infant, surfactant is released into the lung tissues where it lowers the surface tension in the alveoli, which helps the air sacs inflate. The production of a

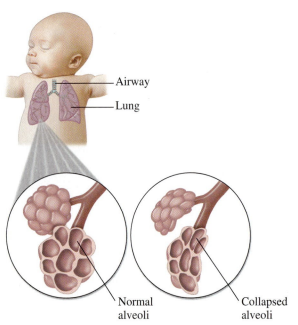

Without sufficient surfactant in the lungs of a premature infant, the alveoli collapse, which decreases pulmonary function.

pulmonary surfactant, which is a mixture of phospholipids including lecithin and sphingomyelin produced by specific lung cells, occurs in a fetus after 24–28 weeks of pregnancy. If an infant is born prematurely before 28 weeks of gestation, the low level of surfactant and immature lung development lead to a high risk of *Infant Respiratory Distress Syndrome* (*IRDS*). Without sufficient surfactant, the air sacs collapse and have to reopen with each breath. As a result, alveoli cells are damaged, less oxygen is taken in, and more carbon dioxide is retained, which can lead to hypoxia and acidosis.

One way to determine the maturity of the lungs of a fetus is to measure the *lecithin–sphingomyelin* (*L/S*) *ratio*. A ratio of 2.5 indicates mature fetal lung function, an L/S ratio of 2.4–1.6 indicates a low risk, and a ratio of less than 1.5 indicates a high risk of IRDS. Before the initiation of an early delivery, the L/S ratio of the amniotic fluid is measured. If the L/S ratio is low, steroids may be given to the mother to assist the lung development and production of surfactant in the fetus. Once a premature infant is born, treatment includes the use of steroids to help maturation of the lungs, the application of surfactants, and the administration of supplemental oxygen with ventilation to help minimize damage to the lungs.

A premature infant with respiratory distress is treated with a surfactant and oxygen.

QUESTIONS AND PROBLEMS

17.5 Phospholipids

LEARNING GOAL: *Describe the structure of a phospholipid containing glycerol or sphingosine.*

17.41 Describe the similarities and differences between triacylglycerols and glycerophospholipids.

17.42 Describe the similarities and differences between lecithins and cephalins.

17.43 Draw the condensed structural formula for the glycerophospholipid cephalin that contains two molecules of palmitic acid and the ionized amino alcohol ethanolamine.

17.44 Draw the condensed structural formula for the glycerophospholipid lecithin that contains two molecules of palmitic acid and the ionized amino alcohol choline.

17.45 Identify the following glycerophospholipid as a lecithin or cephalin and list its components:

17.46 Identify the following glycerophospholipid as a lecithin or cephalin and list its components:

17.6 **Steroids**

Steroids are compounds containing the *steroid nucleus*, which consists of three cyclohexane rings and one cyclopentane ring fused together. Although they are large molecules, steroids do not hydrolyze to give fatty acids and alcohols. The four rings in the steroid nucleus are designated A, B, C, and D. The carbon atoms are numbered beginning with the carbons in ring A and ending with the two methyl groups.

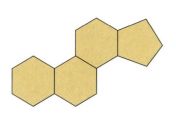

Steroid nucleus

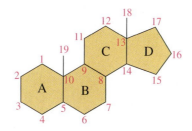

Steroid numbering system

TUTORIAL
Cholesterol

TUTORIAL
Characteristics of Cholesterol

Cholesterol

Attaching other atoms and groups of atoms to the steroid nucleus forms a wide variety of steroid compounds. **Cholesterol**, which is one of the most important and abundant steroids in the body, is a *sterol* because it contains an oxygen atom as a hydroxyl group (—OH) on carbon 3. Like many steroids, cholesterol has a double bond between carbon 5 and carbon 6, methyl groups at carbon 10 and carbon 13, and a carbon chain at carbon 17. In other steroids, the oxygen atom typically at carbon 3 forms a carbonyl group (C=O).

HO

Cholesterol

Cholesterol is a component of cellular membranes, myelin sheaths, and brain and nerve tissues. It is also found in the liver and bile salts; large quantities of it are found in the skin, and some of it becomes vitamin D when the skin is exposed to direct sunlight. In the adrenal gland, cholesterol is used to synthesize steroid hormones. The liver synthesizes sufficient cholesterol for the body from fats, carbohydrates, and proteins. Additional cholesterol is obtained from meat, milk, and eggs in the diet. There is no cholesterol in vegetable and plant products.

Cholesterol in the Body

If a diet is high in cholesterol, the liver produces less cholesterol. A typical daily American diet includes 400–500 mg of cholesterol, one of the highest in the world. The American Heart Association has recommended that we consume no more than 300 mg of cholesterol a day. The cholesterol content of some typical foods are listed in Table 17.4.

Researchers suggest that saturated fats and cholesterol are associated with diseases such as diabetes; cancers of the breast, pancreas, and colon; and atherosclerosis. In atherosclerosis, deposits of a protein–lipid complex (plaque) accumulate in the coronary blood vessels, restricting the flow of blood to the tissue and causing necrosis (death) of the tissue (see Figure 17.7). In the heart, plaque accumulation could result in a *myocardial infarction* (heart attack).

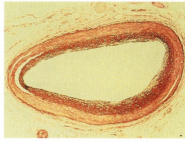

(a)

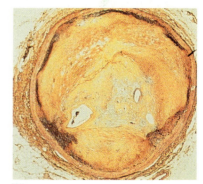

(b)

FIGURE 17.7 Excess cholesterol forms plaque that can block an artery, resulting in a heart attack. **(a)** A cross section of a normal, open artery shows no buildup of plaque. **(b)** A cross section of an artery that is almost completely clogged by atherosclerotic plaque.

Q What property of cholesterol would cause it to form deposits along the coronary arteries?

TABLE 17.4 Cholesterol Content of Some Foods

Food	Serving Size	Cholesterol (mg)
Liver (beef)	3 oz	370
Large egg	1	200
Lobster	3 oz	175
Fried chicken	$3\frac{1}{2}$ oz	130
Hamburger	3 oz	85
Chicken (no skin)	3 oz	75
Fish (salmon)	3 oz	40
Butter	1 tablespoon	30
Whole milk	1 cup	35
Skim milk	1 cup	5
Margarine	1 tablespoon	0

Clinically, cholesterol levels are considered elevated if the total plasma cholesterol level exceeds 200 mg/dL. A diet that is low in foods containing cholesterol and saturated fats appears to be helpful in reducing the serum cholesterol level. The American Institute for Cancer Research (AICR) has recommended that our diet contain more fiber and starch by adding more vegetables, fruits, whole grains, and moderate amounts of foods with low levels of fat and cholesterol such as fish, poultry, lean meats, and low-fat dairy products. AICR also suggests that we limit our intake of foods high in fat and cholesterol such as eggs, nuts, French fries, fatty or organ meats, cheeses, butter, and coconut and palm oil.

Saturated fats in the diet may stimulate the production of cholesterol by the liver. A diet that is low in foods containing cholesterol and saturated fats appears to be helpful in reducing the serum cholesterol level. Other factors that may also increase the risk of heart disease are family history, lack of exercise, smoking, obesity, diabetes, gender, and age.

SAMPLE PROBLEM 17.6   Cholesterol

Refer to the structure of cholesterol for the following questions:

a. What part of cholesterol is the steroid nucleus?
b. What features have been added to the steroid nucleus in cholesterol?
c. What classifies cholesterol as a sterol?

SOLUTION

a. The four fused rings form the steroid nucleus.
b. The cholesterol molecule contains a hydroxyl group (—OH) on the first ring, methyl groups on carbons 10 and 13, one double bond in the second ring, and a branched carbon chain on the fourth ring.
c. The hydroxyl group determines the sterol classification.

STUDY CHECK 17.6

Why is cholesterol in the lipid family?

Bile Salts

The *bile salts* in the body are produced from cholesterol in the liver and stored in the gallbladder. When bile is secreted into the small intestine, the bile salts mix with the water-insoluble fats and oils in our diets. The bile salts with their nonpolar and polar regions act much like soap, breaking down large globules of fat into smaller droplets. By decreasing their size, the droplets containing fat have a larger surface area to react with lipases, which are the enzymes that digest fat. Bile salts also help in the absorption of cholesterol into the intestinal mucosa.

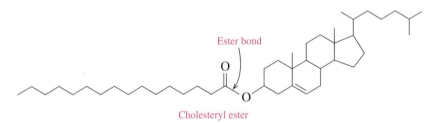

Sodium glycocholate (a bile salt)

When large amounts of cholesterol accumulate in the gallbladder, cholesterol can become solid, which forms gallstones (see Figure 17.8). Gallstones are composed of almost 100% cholesterol, with some calcium salts, fatty acids, and glycerophospholipids. Normally, small stones can pass through the bile duct into the duodenum, the first part of the small intestine immediately beyond the stomach. If a large stone passes into the bile duct, it can get stuck, and the pain can be severe. If the gallstone obstructs the duct, bile cannot be excreted. Then bile pigments known as bilirubin will not be able to pass through the bile duct into the duodenum. They will back up into the liver and be excreted via the blood, causing jaundice (*hyperbilirubinemia*), which gives a yellow color to the skin and the whites of the eyes.

FIGURE 17.8 Gallstones form in the gallbladder when cholesterol levels are high.

Q What type of steroid is stored in the gallbladder?

Lipoproteins: Transporting Lipids

In the body, lipids must move through the bloodstream to tissues where they are stored, used for energy, or used to make hormones. However, most lipids are nonpolar and insoluble in the aqueous environment of blood. They are made more soluble by combining them with glycerophospholipids and proteins to form water-soluble complexes called **lipoproteins**. In general, lipoproteins are spherical particles with an outer surface of polar proteins and glycerophospholipids that surround hundreds of nonpolar molecules of triacylglycerols and cholesteryl esters (see Figure 17.9). Cholesteryl esters are the prevalent form of cholesterol in the blood. They are formed by the esterification of the hydroxyl group in cholesterol with a fatty acid.

Ester bond

Cholesteryl ester

There are a variety of lipoproteins, which differ in density, lipid composition, and function. They include chylomicrons, very-low-density lipoprotein (VLDL), low-density lipoprotein (LDL), and high-density lipoprotein (HDL). The density of the lipoproteins increases as the percentage of protein increases (see Table 17.5).

Two important lipoproteins are the LDLs and HDLs, which transport cholesterol. The LDLs carry cholesterol to the tissues where it can be used for the synthesis of cell membranes and steroid hormones. When the LDLs exceed the amount of cholesterol needed by the tissues, the LDLs deposit cholesterol in the arteries (plaque), which can restrict blood flow and increase the risk of developing heart disease and/or myocardial

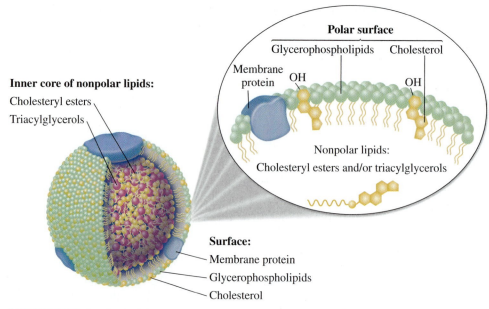

Inner core of nonpolar lipids:
Cholesteryl esters
Triacylglycerols

Polar surface
Glycerophospholipids Cholesterol
Membrane protein OH OH
Nonpolar lipids:
Cholesteryl esters and/or triacylglycerols

Surface:
Membrane protein
Glycerophospholipids
Cholesterol

FIGURE 17.9 A spherical lipoprotein particle surrounds nonpolar lipids with polar lipids and protein for transport to body cells.

Q Why are the polar components on the surface of a lipoprotein particle and the nonpolar components at the center?

TABLE 17.5 Composition and Properties of Plasma Lipoproteins

	Chylomicron	VLDL	LDL	HDL
Density (g/mL)	0.940	0.950–1.006	1.006–1.063	1.063–1.210
	Composition (% by mass)			
Type of Lipid				
Triacylglycerols	86	55	6	4
Phospholipids	7	18	22	24
Cholesterol	2	7	8	2
Cholesteryl esters	3	12	42	15
Protein	2	8	22	55

infarctions (heart attacks). This is why LDLs are called "bad" cholesterol. The HDLs pick up cholesterol from the tissues and carry it to the liver, where it can be converted to bile salts, which are eliminated from the body. This is why HDLs are called "good" cholesterol. Other lipoproteins include chylomicrons that carry triacylglycerols from the intestines to the liver, muscle, and adipose tissues, and VLDLs that carry the triacylglycerols synthesized in the liver to the adipose tissues for storage (see Figure 17.10).

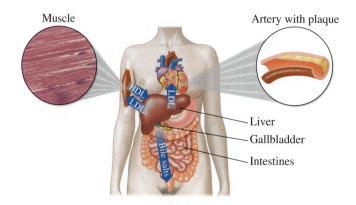

Muscle

Artery with plaque

Liver
Gallbladder
Intestines

FIGURE 17.10 HDL and LDL lipoproteins transport cholesterol between the tissues and the liver.

Q What type of lipoprotein transports cholesterol to the liver?

Because high cholesterol levels are associated with the onset of atherosclerosis and heart disease, a doctor may order a *lipid panel* as part of a health examination. A lipid panel is a blood test that measures serum lipid levels including cholesterol, triglycerides, high-density lipoprotein (HDL), and low-density lipoprotein (LDL). The results of a lipid panel are used to evaluate a patient's risk of heart disease and to help a doctor determine the type of treatment needed.

Lipid Panel	Recommended Level	Greater Risk of Heart Disease
Total Cholesterol	Less than 200 mg/dL	Greater than 240 mg/dL
Triglycerides (triacylglycerols)	Less than 150 mg/dL	Greater than 200 mg/dL
HDL ("good" cholesterol)	Greater than 60 mg/dL	Less than 40 mg/dL
LDL ("bad" cholesterol)	Less than 100 mg/dL	Greater than 160 mg/dL
Cholesterol/HDL Ratio	Less than 4	Greater than 7

Steroid Hormones

The word *hormone* comes from the Greek "to arouse" or "to excite." Hormones are chemical messengers that serve as a communication system from one part of the body to another. The *steroid* hormones, which include the sex hormones and the adrenocortical hormones, are closely related in structure to cholesterol and depend on cholesterol for their synthesis.

Two of the male sex hormones, *testosterone* and *androsterone*, promote the growth of muscle and facial hair, and the maturation of the male sex organs and of sperm.

The *estrogens*, a group of female sex hormones, direct the development of female sexual characteristics: the uterus increases in size, fat is deposited in the breasts, and the pelvis broadens. *Progesterone* prepares the uterus for the implantation of a fertilized egg. If an egg is not fertilized, the levels of progesterone and estrogen drop sharply, and menstruation follows. Synthetic forms of the female sex hormones are used in birth control pills. As with other kinds of steroids, side effects include weight gain and a greater risk of forming blood clots. The structures of some steroid hormones follow:

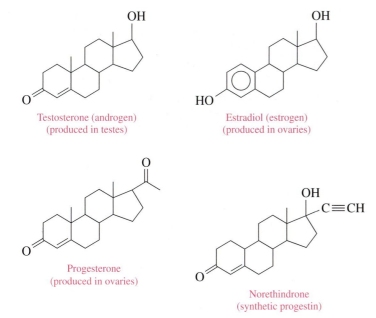

Testosterone (androgen)
(produced in testes)

Estradiol (estrogen)
(produced in ovaries)

Progesterone
(produced in ovaries)

Norethindrone
(synthetic progestin)

Chemistry Link to Health

ANABOLIC STEROIDS

Some of the physiological effects of testosterone are to increase muscle mass and decrease body fat. Derivatives of testosterone called *anabolic steroids* that enhance these effects have been synthesized. Although they have some medical uses, anabolic steroids have been used in rather high dosages by some athletes in an effort to increase muscle mass. Such use is banned by most sports organizations.

Use of anabolic steroids in attempting to improve athletic strength can cause numerous side effects: in males—a reduction in testicle size, low sperm count and infertility, male pattern baldness, and breast development; in females—facial hair, deepening of the voice, male pattern baldness, breast atrophy, and menstrual dysfunction. Possible long-term consequences of anabolic steroid use in both men and women include liver disease and tumors, depression, and heart complications, with an increased risk of prostate cancer for men.

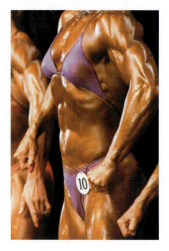

Some Anabolic Steroids

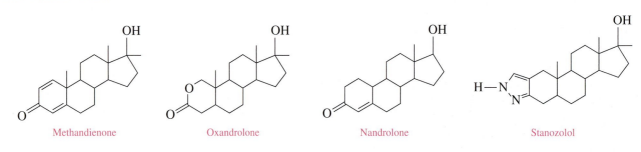

Methandienone   Oxandrolone   Nandrolone   Stanozolol

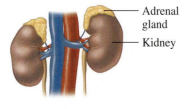

Adrenal gland
Kidney

Adrenal Corticosteroids

The adrenal glands, located on the top of each kidney, produce a large number of compounds known as the *corticosteroids*. *Cortisone* increases the blood glucose level and stimulates the synthesis of glycogen in the liver. *Aldosterone* is responsible for the regulation of electrolytes and water balance by the kidneys. *Cortisol* is released under stress to increase blood sugar and regulate carbohydrate, fat, and protein metabolism.

Synthetic corticosteroid drugs such as *prednisone* are derived from cortisone and used medically for reducing inflammation and treating asthma and rheumatoid arthritis, although health problems can result from long-term use.

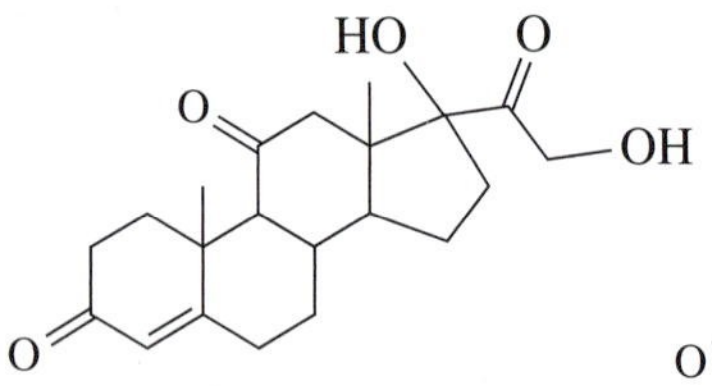

Cortisone 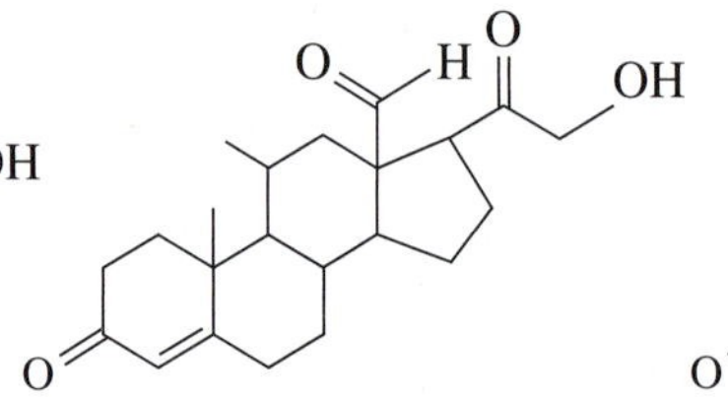   Aldosterone (mineralocorticoid) 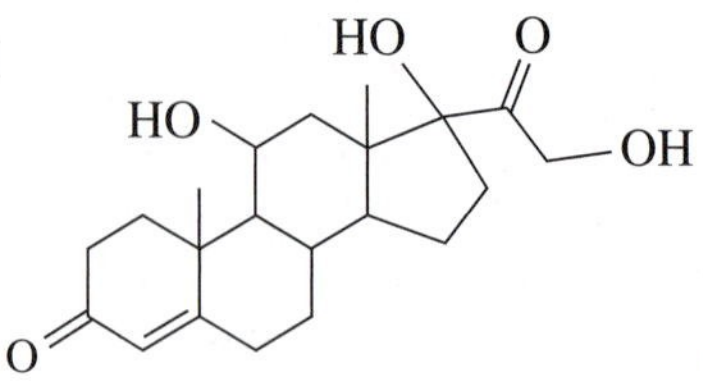   Cortisol 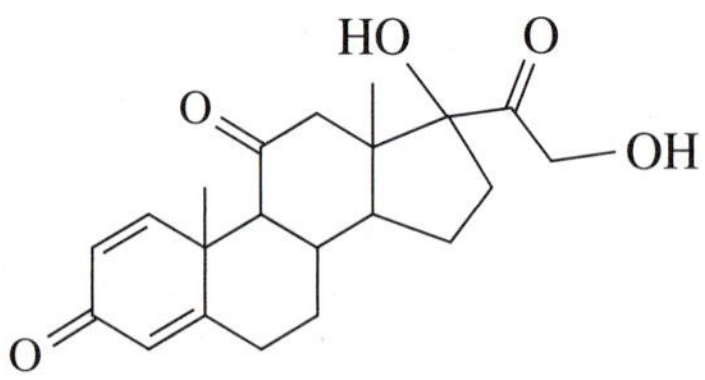   Prednisone

CONCEPT CHECK 17.6 Steroid Hormones

CONCEPT CHECK 17.6 Steroid Hormones

What are the similarities and differences in the structures of testosterone and the anabolic steroid nandrolone (see Chemistry Link to Health "Anabolic Steroids").

ANSWER

Testosterone and nandrolone both contain a steroid nucleus with one double bond and a ketone group in the first ring, and a methyl and a hydroxyl group on the five-carbon ring. They differ because nandrolone does not have a methyl group where the first and second rings join.

QUESTIONS AND PROBLEMS

17.6 Steroids

LEARNING GOAL: *Describe the structures of steroids.*

17.47 Draw the structure for the steroid nucleus.

17.48 Which of the following compounds are derived from cholesterol?
- **a.** glyceryl tristearate
- **b.** cortisone
- **c.** bile salts
- **d.** testosterone
- **e.** estradiol

17.49 What is the function of bile salts in digestion?

17.50 Why are gallstones composed of cholesterol?

17.51 What is the general structure of lipoproteins?

17.52 Why are lipoproteins needed to transport lipids in the bloodstream?

17.53 How do chylomicrons differ from very-low-density lipoproteins?

17.54 How do LDLs differ from HDLs?

17.55 Why are LDLs called "bad" cholesterol?

17.56 Why are HDLs called "good" cholesterol?

17.57 What are the similarities and differences between the hormones progesterone and testosterone?

17.58 What are the similarities and differences between the adrenal hormone cortisone and the synthetic corticoid prednisone?

17.59 Which of the following are steroid hormones?
- **a.** cholesterol
- **b.** cortisol
- **c.** estrogen
- **d.** testosterone

17.60 Which of the following are adrenal corticosteroids?
- **a.** nandrolone
- **b.** cortisone
- **c.** progesterone
- **d.** aldosterone

17.7 Cell Membranes

The membrane of a cell separates the contents of the cell from the external fluids. It is *semipermeable* so that nutrients can enter the cell and waste products can leave. The main components of a cell membrane are glycerophospholipids and sphingolipids. Earlier in this chapter, we saw that glycerophospholipids consist of a nonpolar region or hydrocarbon "tail" with two long-chain fatty acids, and a polar region or ionic "head" of phosphate and an ionized amino alcohol.

In a cell (plasma) membrane, two layers of glycerophospholipids are arranged with their hydrophilic heads at the outer and inner surfaces of the membrane, and their hydrophobic tails in the center. This double layer arrangement of glycerophospholipids is called a **lipid bilayer** (see Figure 17.11). The outer layer of glycerophospholipids is in contact with the external fluids, and the inner layer is in contact with the internal contents of the cell.

Most of the glycerophospholipids in the lipid bilayer contain unsaturated fatty acids. Because of the kinks in the carbon chains at the cis double bonds, the glycerophospholipids do not fit closely together. As a result, the lipid bilayer is not a rigid, fixed structure, but one that is dynamic and fluid-like. This liquid-like bilayer also contains proteins, carbohydrates, and cholesterol molecules. For this reason, the model of biological membranes is referred to as the **fluid mosaic model** of membranes.

LEARNING GOAL

Describe the composition and function of the lipid bilayer in cell membranes.

TUTORIAL
Phospholipids and the Cell Membrane

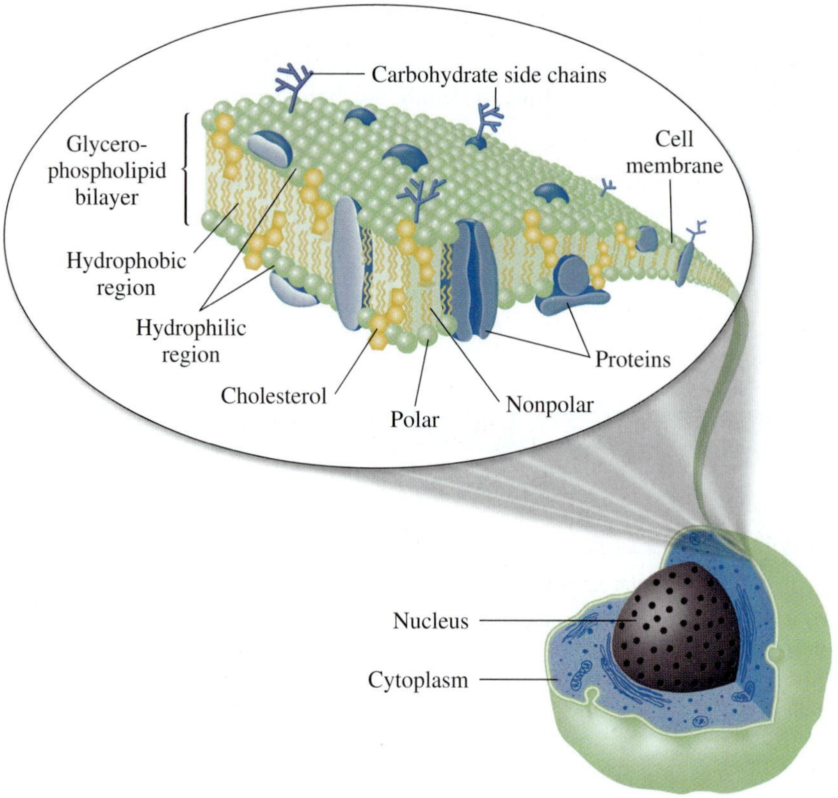

Carbohydrate side chains

Glycero-
phospholipid
bilayer

Cell
membrane

Hydrophobic
region

Hydrophilic
region

Cholesterol

Polar

Nonpolar

Proteins

Nucleus

Cytoplasm

FIGURE 17.11 In the fluid mosaic model of a cell membrane, proteins and cholesterol are embedded in a lipid bilayer of glycerophospholipids. The bilayer forms a membrane-type barrier, with polar heads at the membrane surfaces and the nonpolar tails in the center away from the water.

Q What types of fatty acids are found in the glycerophospholipids of the lipid bilayer?

SELF-STUDY ACTIVITY
Active Transport

In the fluid mosaic model, peripheral proteins emerge on just one of the surfaces, outer or inner. Integral proteins extend through the entire lipid bilayer and appear on both surfaces of the membrane. Some proteins and lipids on the outer surface of the cell membrane are attached to carbohydrates to form glycoproteins and glycosphingolipids. These carbohydrate chains project into the surrounding fluid environment, where they are responsible for cell recognition and communication with chemical messengers such as hormones and neurotransmitters. In animals, cholesterol molecules embedded among the glycerophospholipids make up 20–25% of the lipid bilayer. Because cholesterol molecules are large and rigid, they reduce the flexibility of the lipid bilayer and add strength to the cell membrane.

Transport Through Cell Membranes

Although a nonpolar membrane separates aqueous solutions, it is necessary that certain substances can enter and leave the cell.

The main function of a cell membrane is to allow the movement (transport) of ions and molecules on one side of the membrane to the other side. This transport of materials into and out of a cell is accomplished in several ways.

Diffusion (passive) transport In the simplest transport mechanism called *diffusion* or *passive transport*, molecules can diffuse from a higher concentration to a lower concentration. For example, small molecules such as O_2, CO_2, urea, and water diffuse via passive transport through cell membranes. If their concentrations are greater outside the cell than inside, they diffuse into the cell. If their concentrations are higher within the cell, they diffuse out of the cell. The diffusion of water is the process of osmosis discussed in Section 8.6.

Facilitated transport In *facilitated transport*, proteins that extend from one side of the bilayer membrane to the other provide a channel through which certain substances can diffuse more rapidly than by passive diffusion to meet cellular needs. These protein channels allow transport of chloride ion (Cl^-), bicarbonate ion (HCO_3^-), and glucose molecules in and out of the cell.

Active transport Certain ions, such as H^+, Na^+, K^+, Cl^-, and Ca^{2+}, move across a cell membrane *against* their concentration gradients. For example, the K^+ concentration is greater inside a cell, and the Na^+ concentration is greater outside. However, in the conduction of nerve impulses and contraction of muscles, K^+ moves into the cell, and Na^+ moves out by a process known as *active transport*. To move an ion from a lower to a higher concentration requires energy. The energy to move Na^+ and K^+ against their concentration gradients is obtained when a protein complex called a Na^+/K^+ pump breaks down adenosine triphosphate (ATP) to adenosine diphosphate (ADP), which releases energy (see Figure 17.12).

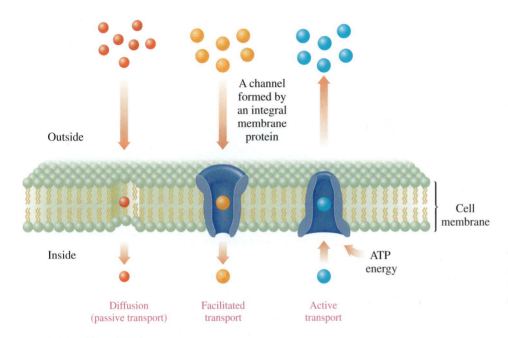

FIGURE 17.12 Substances are transported across a cell membrane by either diffusion, facilitated transport, or active transport.

Q What is the difference between diffusion and facilitated transport?

SAMPLE PROBLEM 17.7   **Lipid Bilayer in the Cell Membranes**

Describe the role of glycerophospholipids in the lipid bilayer.

SOLUTION

Glycerophospholipids consist of polar and nonpolar parts. In a cell membrane, an alignment of the nonpolar sections toward the center with the polar sections on the outside produces a barrier that prevents the contents of a cell from mixing with the fluids on the outside of the cell.

STUDY CHECK 17.7

Why are protein channels needed in the lipid bilayer?

QUESTIONS AND PROBLEMS

17.7 Cell Membranes

LEARNING GOAL: *Describe the composition and function of the lipid bilayer in cell membranes.*

17.61 What types of lipids are found in cell membranes?

17.62 Describe the structure of a lipid bilayer.

17.63 What is the function of the lipid bilayer in a cell membrane?

17.64 How do the unsaturated fatty acids in the glycerophospholipids affect the structure of cell membranes?

17.65 What is the difference between peripheral and integral proteins?

17.66 What components are attached to carbohydrates on the outer surface of a cell membrane?

17.67 What is the function of the carbohydrates on a cell membrane surface?

17.68 Describe how a cell membrane is semipermeable.

17.69 What are some ways that substances move in and out of cells?

17.70 Identify the type of transport described by each of the following:
  a. A molecule moves through a protein channel.
  b. O_2 moves into the cell from a higher concentration outside the cell.
  c. An ion moves from low to high concentration in the cell.

CONCEPT MAP

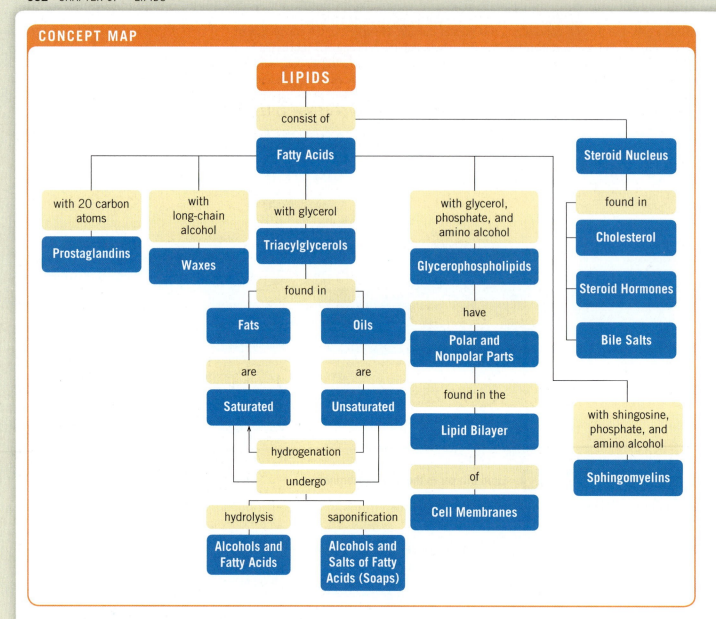

LIPIDS

consist of

Fatty Acids

with 20 carbon atoms → **Prostaglandins**

with long-chain alcohol → **Waxes**

with glycerol → **Triacylglycerols**

found in → **Fats** / **Oils**

Fats are **Saturated**

Oils are **Unsaturated**

hydrogenation

undergo

hydrolysis → **Alcohols and Fatty Acids**

saponification → **Alcohols and Salts of Fatty Acids (Soaps)**

with glycerol, phosphate, and amino alcohol → **Glycerophospholipids**

have **Polar and Nonpolar Parts**

found in the **Lipid Bilayer**

of **Cell Membranes**

Steroid Nucleus

found in **Cholesterol**, **Steroid Hormones**, **Bile Salts**

with shingosine, phosphate, and amino alcohol → **Sphingomyelins**

CHAPTER REVIEW

17.1 Lipids

LEARNING GOAL: Describe the classes of lipids.

- Lipids are nonpolar compounds that are not soluble in water.
- Classes of lipids include waxes, fats and oils, glycerophospholipids, and steroids.

17.2 Fatty Acids

LEARNING GOAL: Draw the condensed structural formula for a fatty acid and identify it as saturated or unsaturated.

- Fatty acids are unbranched carboxylic acids that typically contain an even number (12–20) of carbon atoms.

- Fatty acids may be saturated, monounsaturated with one double bond, or polyunsaturated with two or more double bonds.
- The double bonds in unsaturated fatty acids are almost always cis.

17.3 Waxes and Triacylglycerols

LEARNING GOAL: Draw the condensed structural formula for a wax or triacylglycerol produced by the reaction of a fatty acid and an alcohol or glycerol.

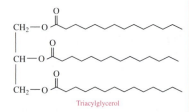

Triacylglycerol

- A wax is an ester of a long-chain fatty acid and a long-chain alcohol.
- The triacylglycerols of fats and oils are esters of glycerol with three long-chain fatty acids.
- Fats contain more saturated fatty acids and have higher melting points than most vegetable oils.

17.4 Chemical Properties of Triacylglycerols

LEARNING GOAL: Draw the condensed structural formula for the product of a triacylglycerol that undergoes hydrogenation, hydrolysis, or saponification.

Vegetable oils (liquids) — Tub (soft) margarine — Stick margarine (soft and solid) — Shortening (solid)

- The hydrogenation of unsaturated fatty acids converts double bonds to single bonds.
- The hydrolysis of the ester bonds in fats or oils produces glycerol and fatty acids.
- In saponification, a fat heated with a strong base produces glycerol and the salts of the fatty acids (soap).

17.5 Phospholipids

LEARNING GOAL: Describe the structure of a phospholipid containing glycerol or sphingosine.

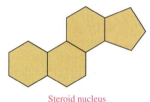

Glycerophospholipid

- Glycerophospholipids are esters of glycerol with two fatty acids and a phosphate group attached to an ionized amino alcohol.
- In sphingomyelin, the amino alcohol sphingosine forms an amide bond with a fatty acid, and phosphoester bonds to phosphate and an ionized amino alcohol.

17.6 Steroids

LEARNING GOAL: Describe the structures of steroids.

- Steroids are lipids containing the steroid nucleus, which is a fused structure of four rings.

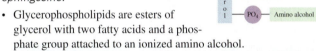

Steroid nucleus

- Steroids include cholesterol, bile salts, and vitamin D.
- Lipids, which are nonpolar, are transported through the aqueous environment of the blood by forming lipoproteins.
- Bile salts, synthesized from cholesterol, mix with water-insoluble fats and break them apart during digestion.
- Lipoproteins, such as chylomicrons and LDL, transport triacylglycerols from the intestines and the liver to fat cells and muscles for storage and energy.
- HDLs transport cholesterol from the tissues to the liver for elimination.
- The steroid hormones are closely related in structure to cholesterol and depend on cholesterol for their synthesis.
- The sex hormones, such as estrogen and testosterone, are responsible for sexual characteristics and reproduction.
- The adrenal corticosteroids, such as aldosterone and cortisone, regulate water balance and glucose levels in the cells, respectively.

17.7 Cell Membranes

LEARNING GOAL: Describe the composition and function of the lipid bilayer in cell membranes.

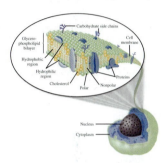

- All animal cells are surrounded by a semipermeable membrane that separates the cellular contents from the external fluids.
- The membrane is composed of two rows of glycerophospholipids in a lipid bilayer.
- Proteins and cholesterol are embedded in the lipid bilayer, and carbohydrates are attached to its surface.
- Nutrients and waste products move through the cell membrane using passive transport (diffusion), facilitated transport, or active transport.

SUMMARY OF REACTIONS

Esterification

Glycerol + 3 fatty acid molecules $\longrightarrow$ triacylglycerol + $3H_2O$

Hydrogenation of Triacylglycerols

Triacylglycerol (unsaturated) + H_2 $\xrightarrow{\text{Ni (Pd, Pt)}}$ triacylglycerol (saturated)

Hydrolysis of Triacylglycerols

Triacylglycerol + $3H_2O$ $\xrightarrow{\text{H}^+ \text{ or lipase}}$ glycerol + 3 fatty acid molecules

Saponification of Triacylglycerols

Triacylglycerol + 3NaOH $\longrightarrow$ glycerol + 3 sodium salts of fatty acids (soap)

KEY TERMS

cephalin A glycerophospholipid found in brain and nerve tissues that incorporates the amino alcohol serine or ethanolamine.

cholesterol The most prevalent of the steroid compounds; needed for cellular membranes and the synthesis of vitamin D, hormones, and bile salts.

fat A triacylglycerol that is solid at room temperature and usually comes from animal sources.

fatty acid A long-chain carboxylic acid found in many lipids.

fluid mosaic model The concept that cell membranes are lipid bilayer structures that contain an assortment of polar lipids and proteins in a dynamic, fluid arrangement.

glycerophospholipid A polar lipid of glycerol attached to two fatty acids and a phosphate group connected to an ionized amino alcohol such as choline, serine, or ethanolamine.

hydrogenation The addition of hydrogen to unsaturated fats.

lecithins Glycerophospholipids containing choline as the amino alcohol.

lipid bilayer A model of a cell membrane in which glycerophospholipids are arranged in two rows.

lipids A family of compounds that is nonpolar in nature and not soluble in water; includes fats, waxes, glycerophospholipids, and steroids.

lipoprotein A polar complex composed of a combination of nonpolar lipids, glycerophospholipids, and proteins that can be transported through body fluids.

monounsaturated fatty acid A fatty acid with one double bond.

oil A triacylglycerol that is usually a liquid at room temperature and is obtained from a plant source.

phospholipid A type of lipid found in cell membranes that is a glycerophospholipid or a sphingomyelin.

polyunsaturated fatty acid A fatty acid that contains two or more double bonds.

prostaglandins (PGs) A number of compounds derived from arachidonic acid that regulate several physiological processes.

saturated fatty acids Fatty acids that have no double bonds, which have higher melting points than unsaturated fatty acids, and are usually solids at room temperature.

sphingomyelin A sphingolipid that consists of sphingosine attached by an amide bond to a fatty acid and by an ester bond to phosphate, which is bonded by a phosphoester ester bond to choline, an ionized amino alcohol.

steroids Types of lipids that are constructed using a multicyclic ring system.

triacylglycerols A family of lipids composed of three fatty acids bonded through ester bonds to glycerol, a trihydroxy alcohol.

unsaturated fatty acids Fatty acids that have one or more double bonds, which have lower melting points than saturated fatty acids, and are usually liquids at room temperature.

wax The ester of a long-chain alcohol and a long-chain saturated fatty acid.

UNDERSTANDING THE CONCEPTS

The chapter sections to review are shown in parentheses at the end of each question.

17.71 Palmitic acid is obtained from palm oil as glyceryl tripalmitate. Draw the condensed structural formula for glyceryl tripalmitate. (17.3)

Palm fruit from palm trees are a source of palm oil.

17.72 Jojoba wax in candles consists of an 18-carbon saturated fatty acid and a 22-carbon saturated alcohol. Draw the condensed structural formula for jojoba wax. (17.3)

Candles contain jojoba wax.

17.73 Sunflower oil can be used to make margarine. A triacylglycerol in sunflower oil contains two linoleic acids and one oleic acid. (17.3, 17.4)
  a. Draw the condensed structural formulas for two isomers of the triacylglycerol in sunflower oil.
  b. Using one of the isomers, write the reaction that would be used when sunflower oil is used to make solid margarine.

Sunflower oil is obtained from the seeds of the sunflower.

17.74 Identify each of the following as a saturated, monounsaturated, polyunsaturated, omega-3, or omega-6 fatty acid: (17.2)
  a. $CH_3-(CH_2)_4-CH=CH-CH_2-CH=CH-(CH_2)_7-COOH$
  b. linolenic acid
  c. $CH_3-(CH_2)_{14}-COOH$
  d. $CH_3-(CH_2)_7-CH=CH-(CH_2)_7-COOH$

Salmon is a good source of omega-3 unsaturated fatty acids.

ADDITIONAL QUESTIONS AND PROBLEMS

For instructor-assigned homework, go to www.masteringchemistry.com.

17.75 Among the ingredients in lipstick are carnauba wax, hydrogenated vegetable oils, and glyceryl tricaprate (tricaprin). (17.1, 17.2, 17.3)
   a. What types of lipids have been used?
   b. Draw the condensed structural formula for glyceryl tricaprate (tricaprin). Capric acid is a saturated 10-carbon fatty acid.

17.76 Because peanut oil floats on the top of peanut butter, the peanut oil in many brands of peanut butter is hydrogenated and the solid is mixed into the peanut butter to give a solid product that does not separate. If a triacylglycerol in peanut oil that contains one oleic acid and two linoleic acids is completely hydrogenated, draw the condensed structural formula for the product. (17.3, 17.4)

17.77 Trans fats are produced during the hydrogenation of polyunsaturated oils. (17.2)
   a. What is the typical configuration of the double bond in a monounsaturated fatty acid?
   b. How does a trans fatty acid differ from a cis fatty acid?
   c. Draw the condensed structural formula for *trans*-oleic acid.

17.78 One mole of glyceryl trioleate (triolein) is completely hydrogenated. (6.1, 6.4, 6.5, 6.6, 6.7, 7.7, 17.3, 17.4)
   a. Draw the condensed structural formula for the product.
   b. How many moles of hydrogen are required?
   c. How many grams of hydrogen are required?
   d. How many liters of hydrogen gas are needed if the reaction is run at STP?

17.79 The total kilocalories and grams of fat for some typical meals at fast-food restaurants are listed here. Calculate the number of kilocalories from fat and the percentage of total kilocalories due to fat (1 gram of fat = 9 kcal). Round answers to the tens place. Would you expect the fats to be mostly saturated or unsaturated? Why? (17.2, 17.3)
   a. a chicken dinner, 830 kcal, 46 g of fat
   b. a quarter-pound cheeseburger, 520 kcal, 29 g of fat
   c. a pepperoni pizza (three slices), 560 kcal, 18 g of fat

17.80 The total kilocalories and grams of fat for some typical meals at fast-food restaurants are listed here. Calculate the number of kilocalories from fat and the percentage of total kilocalories due to fat (1 gram of fat = 9 kcal). Round answers to the tens place. Would you expect the fats to be mostly saturated or unsaturated? Why? (17.2, 17.3)
   a. a beef burrito, 470 kcal, 21 g of fat
   b. deep-fried fish (three pieces), 480 kcal, 28 g of fat
   c. a jumbo hot dog, 180 kcal, 18 g of fat

17.81 Identify each of the following as a fatty acid, soap, triacylglycerol, wax, glycerophospholipid, sphingolipid, or steroid: (17.1, 17.2, 17.3, 17.5, 17.6)
   a. beeswax   **b.** cholesterol
   c. lecithin   **d.** glyceryl tripalmitate (tripalmitin)
   e. sodium stearate   **f.** safflower oil

17.82 Identify each of the following as a fatty acid, soap, triacylglycerol, wax, glycerophospholipid, sphingolipid, or steroid: (17.1, 17.2, 17.3, 17.5, 17.6)
   a. sphingomyelin   **b.** whale blubber
   c. adipose tissue   **d.** progesterone
   e. cortisone   **f.** stearic acid

17.83 Identify the components (**1–6**) contained in each of the following lipids (**a–d**): (17.1, 17.2, 17.3, 17.5, 17.6)
   1. glycerol   **2.** fatty acid
   3. phosphate   **4.** amino alcohol
   5. steroid nucleus   **6.** sphingosine

   a. estrogen   **b.** cephalin
   c. wax   **d.** triacylglycerol

17.84 Identify the components (**1–6**) contained in each of the following lipids (**a–d**): (17.1, 17.2, 17.3, 17.5, 17.6)
   1. glycerol   **2.** fatty acid
   3. phosphate   **4.** amino alcohol
   5. steroid nucleus   **6.** sphingosine

   a. glycerophospholipid **b.** sphingomyelin
   c. aldosterone   **d.** linoleic acid

CHALLENGE QUESTIONS

17.85 Match the lipoprotein (**1–4**) with its description (**a–d**). (17.6)
   1. chylomicron   **2.** VLDL   **3.** LDL   **4.** HDL

   a. "good" cholesterol
   b. transports most of the cholesterol to the cells
   c. carries triacylglycerols from the intestine to the fat cells
   d. transports cholesterol to the liver

17.86 Match the lipoprotein (**1–4**) with its description (**a–d**). (17.6)
   1. chylomicron   **2.** VLDL   **3.** LDL   **4.** HDL

   a. has the greatest abundance of protein
   b. "bad" cholesterol
   c. carries triacylglycerols synthesized in the liver to the muscles
   d. has the lowest density

17.87 A sink drain can become clogged with solid fat such as glyceryl tristearate (tristearin). (6.1, 6.4, 6.5, 6.6, 6.7, 8.4, 8.5, 17.3, 17.4)
   a. How would adding lye (NaOH) to the sink drain remove the blockage?

A sink drain can become clogged with saturated fats.

   b. Write an equation for the reaction that occurs.
   c. How many milliliters of a 0.500 M NaOH solution are needed to completely saponify 10.0 g of glyceryl tristearate (tristearin)?

17.88 Olive oil contains glyceryl tripalmitoleate (tripalmitolein). (6.1, 6.4, 6.5, 6.6, 6.7, 7.7, 8.4, 8.5, 17.3, 17.4)
   a. Draw the condensed structural formula for glyceryl tripalmitoleate (tripalmitolein).
   b. How many liters of H_2 gas at STP are needed to completely react with all the double bonds in 100. g of glyceryl tripalmitoleate (tripalmitolein)?
   c. How many milliliters of a 0.250 M NaOH solution are needed to completely saponify 100. g of glyceryl tripalmitoleate (tripalmitolein)?

One of the triacylglycerols in olive oil is glyceryl tripalmitoleate (tripalmitolein).

ANSWERS

Answers to Study Checks

17.1 a. 16   **b.** monounsaturated   **c.** liquid

17.2

$$CH_2-O-\overset{\displaystyle O}{\overset{\displaystyle \|}{C}}-(CH_2)_{12}-CH_3$$
$$CH-O-\overset{\displaystyle O}{\overset{\displaystyle \|}{C}}-(CH_2)_{12}-CH_3$$
$$CH_2-O-\overset{\displaystyle O}{\overset{\displaystyle \|}{C}}-(CH_2)_{12}-CH_3$$

17.3 glyceryl tristearate (tristearin)

17.4

$$CH_2-O-\overset{\displaystyle O}{\overset{\displaystyle \|}{C}}-(CH_2)_{12}-CH_3$$
$$CH-O-\overset{\displaystyle O}{\overset{\displaystyle \|}{C}}-(CH_2)_{12}-CH_3$$
$$CH_2-O-\overset{\displaystyle O}{\overset{\displaystyle \|}{P}}-O-CH_2-CH_2-\overset{\displaystyle CH_3}{\overset{\displaystyle +}{N}}-CH_3$$
$$\underset{\displaystyle O^-}{\quad} \qquad \underset{\displaystyle CH_3}{\quad}$$

17.5

$$HO-CH-CH=CH-(CH_2)_{12}-CH_3$$
$$CH-N-\overset{\displaystyle O}{\overset{\displaystyle \|}{C}}-(CH_2)_{16}-CH_3$$
$$\quad\; H$$
$$CH_2-O-\overset{\displaystyle O}{\overset{\displaystyle \|}{P}}-O-CH_2-CH_2-\overset{\displaystyle +}{N}H_3$$
$$\underset{\displaystyle O^-}{\quad}$$

17.6 Cholesterol is not soluble in water; it is classified with the lipid family.

17.7 Protein channels allow ions and polar molecules to flow in and out of the cell through the lipid bilayer.

Answers to Selected Questions and Problems

17.1 Lipids provide energy, protection, and insulation for the organs in the body. Lipids are also an important part of cell membranes.

17.3 Because lipids are not soluble in water, a polar solvent, they are nonpolar molecules.

17.5 All fatty acids contain a long chain of carbon atoms with a carboxylic acid group. Saturated fatty acids contain only carbon–carbon single bonds; unsaturated fatty acids contain one or more double bonds.

17.7 a. palmitic acid

b. oleic acid

17.9 a. saturated   **b.** polyunsaturated
  c. monounsaturated   **d.** saturated

17.11 In a cis fatty acid, the hydrogen atoms are on the same side of the double bond, which produces a bend in the carbon chain. In a trans fatty acid, the hydrogen atoms are on opposite sides of the double bond, which gives a carbon chain without any bend.

17.13 In an omega-3 fatty acid, there is a double bond on carbon 3 counting from the methyl group, whereas in an omega-6 fatty acid, there is a double bond beginning at carbon 6 counting from the methyl group.

17.15 Arachidonic acid and PGE$_1$ are both carboxylic acids with 20 carbon atoms. The differences are that arachidonic acid has four cis double bonds and no other functional groups, whereas PGE$_1$ has one trans double bond, one ketone functional group, and two hydroxyl functional groups. In addition, a part of the PGE$_1$ chain forms cyclopentane.

17.17 Prostaglandins raise or lower blood pressure, stimulate contraction and relaxation of smooth muscle, and may cause inflammation and pain.

17.19

$$CH_3-(CH_2)_{14}-\overset{\displaystyle O}{\overset{\displaystyle \|}{C}}-O-(CH_2)_{29}-CH_3$$

17.21

$$CH_2-O-\overset{\displaystyle O}{\overset{\displaystyle \|}{C}}-(CH_2)_{16}-CH_3$$
$$CH-O-\overset{\displaystyle O}{\overset{\displaystyle \|}{C}}-(CH_2)_{16}-CH_3$$
$$CH_2-O-\overset{\displaystyle O}{\overset{\displaystyle \|}{C}}-(CH_2)_{16}-CH_3$$

17.23

$$CH_2-O-\overset{\displaystyle O}{\overset{\displaystyle \|}{C}}-(CH_2)_{14}-CH_3$$
$$CH-O-\overset{\displaystyle O}{\overset{\displaystyle \|}{C}}-(CH_2)_{14}-CH_3$$
$$CH_2-O-\overset{\displaystyle O}{\overset{\displaystyle \|}{C}}-(CH_2)_{14}-CH_3$$

17.25

$$CH_2-O-\overset{\displaystyle O}{\overset{\displaystyle \|}{C}}-(CH_2)_6-CH_3$$
$$CH-O-\overset{\displaystyle O}{\overset{\displaystyle \|}{C}}-(CH_2)_6-CH_3$$
$$CH_2-O-\overset{\displaystyle O}{\overset{\displaystyle \|}{C}}-(CH_2)_6-CH_3$$

17.27 Safflower oil has a lower melting point because it contains mostly polyunsaturated fatty acids, whereas olive oil contains a large amount of monounsaturated oleic acid. A polyunsaturated fatty acid has two or more kinks in its carbon chain, which means it does not have as many dispersion forces compared to the hydrocarbon chains in olive oil.

17.29 Although coconut oil comes from a plant source, it contains large amounts of saturated fatty acids and small amounts of unsaturated fatty acids.

17.31

$$CH_2-O-\overset{\overset{\displaystyle O}{\|}}{C}-(CH_2)_7-CH=CH-(CH_2)_7-CH_3$$
$$CH-O-\overset{\overset{\displaystyle O}{\|}}{C}-(CH_2)_7-CH=CH-(CH_2)_7-CH_3 + 3H_2 \xrightarrow{Ni}$$
$$CH_2-O-\overset{\overset{\displaystyle O}{\|}}{C}-(CH_2)_7-CH=CH-(CH_2)_7-CH_3$$

$$CH_2-O-\overset{\overset{\displaystyle O}{\|}}{C}-(CH_2)_{16}-CH_3$$
$$CH-O-\overset{\overset{\displaystyle O}{\|}}{C}-(CH_2)_{16}-CH_3$$
$$CH_2-O-\overset{\overset{\displaystyle O}{\|}}{C}-(CH_2)_{16}-CH_3$$

17.33

$$CH_2-O-\overset{\overset{\displaystyle O}{\|}}{C}-(CH_2)_{12}-CH_3$$
$$CH-O-\overset{\overset{\displaystyle O}{\|}}{C}-(CH_2)_{12}-CH_3 + 3H_2O \xrightarrow{H^+}$$
$$CH_2-O-\overset{\overset{\displaystyle O}{\|}}{C}-(CH_2)_{12}-CH_3$$

$$CH_2-OH$$
$$CH-OH + 3HO-\overset{\overset{\displaystyle O}{\|}}{C}-(CH_2)_{12}-CH_3$$
$$CH_2-OH$$

17.35

$$CH_2-O-\overset{\overset{\displaystyle O}{\|}}{C}-(CH_2)_{12}-CH_3$$
$$CH-O-\overset{\overset{\displaystyle O}{\|}}{C}-(CH_2)_{12}-CH_3 + 3NaOH \longrightarrow$$
$$CH_2-O-\overset{\overset{\displaystyle O}{\|}}{C}-(CH_2)_{12}-CH_3$$

$$CH_2-OH$$
$$CH-OH + 3Na^{+-}O-\overset{\overset{\displaystyle O}{\|}}{C}-(CH_2)_{12}-CH_3$$
$$CH_2-OH$$

17.37 A triacylglycerol is composed of glycerol with three hydroxyl groups that form ester links with three long-chain fatty acids. In olestra, six to eight long-chain fatty acids form ester links with the hydroxyl groups on sucrose, a sugar. The olestra cannot be digested because our pancreatic lipase enzyme cannot break down the large olestra molecule.

17.39

$$CH_2-O-\overset{\overset{\displaystyle O}{\|}}{C}-(CH_2)_{16}-CH_3$$
$$CH-O-\overset{\overset{\displaystyle O}{\|}}{C}-(CH_2)_{16}-CH_3$$
$$CH_2-O-\overset{\overset{\displaystyle O}{\|}}{C}-(CH_2)_{16}-CH_3$$

17.41 A triacylglycerol consists of glycerol and three fatty acids. A glycerophospholipid also contains glycerol, but has only two fatty acids. The hydroxyl group on the 3rd carbon is attached by a phosphoester bond to an ionized amino alcohol.

17.43

$$CH_2-O-\overset{\overset{\displaystyle O}{\|}}{C}-(CH_2)_{14}-CH_3$$
$$CH-O-\overset{\overset{\displaystyle O}{\|}}{C}-(CH_2)_{14}-CH_3$$
$$CH_2-O-\overset{\overset{\displaystyle O}{\|}}{\underset{\underset{\displaystyle O^-}{|}}{P}}-O-CH_2-CH_2-\overset{+}{N}H_3$$

17.45 This glycerophospholipid is a cephalin. It contains glycerol, oleic acid, stearic acid, a phosphate group, and ethanolamine.

17.47

17.49 Bile salts act to emulsify fat globules, allowing the fat to be more easily digested.

17.51 Lipoproteins are large, spherically shaped structures that transport lipids in the bloodstream. They consist of an outside layer of glycerophospholipids and proteins surrounding an inner core of hundreds of nonpolar lipids and cholesteryl esters.

17.53 Chylomicrons have a lower density than VLDLs. They pick up triacylglycerols from the intestine, whereas VLDLs transport triacylglycerols synthesized in the liver.

17.55 "Bad" cholesterol is the cholesterol carried by LDLs that can form deposits called plaque in the arteries, which narrow the arteries.

17.57 Both progesterone and testosterone contain the steroid nucleus, a ketone group, a double bond, and two methyl groups. Testosterone has a hydroxyl group on ring D, whereas progesterone has an acetyl group on ring D.

17.59 Cortisol (**b**), estrogen (**c**), and testosterone (**d**) are steroid hormones.

17.61 The lipids in a cell membrane are glycerophospholipids with smaller amounts of sphingolipids and cholesterol.

17.63 The lipid bilayer in a cell membrane surrounds the cell and separates the contents of the cell from the external fluids.

17.65 The peripheral proteins in the membrane emerge on the inner or outer surface only, whereas the integral proteins extend through the membrane to both surfaces.

17.67 The carbohydrates (glycoproteins and glycosphingolipids) on the surface of cells act as receptors for cell recognition and chemical messengers, such as neurotransmitters.

17.69 Substances move through cell membranes by passive transport (diffusion), facilitated transport, and active transport.

17.71

$$CH_2-O-\overset{\overset{\displaystyle O}{\|}}{C}-(CH_2)_{14}-CH_3$$
$$CH-O-\overset{\overset{\displaystyle O}{\|}}{C}-(CH_2)_{14}-CH_3$$
$$CH_2-O-\overset{\overset{\displaystyle O}{\|}}{C}-(CH_2)_{14}-CH_3$$

17.73 a.

$$CH_2-O-\overset{\overset{\displaystyle O}{\|}}{C}-(CH_2)_7-CH=CH-CH_2-CH=CH-(CH_2)_4-CH_3$$
$$|$$
$$CH-O-\overset{\overset{\displaystyle O}{\|}}{C}-(CH_2)_7-CH=CH-CH_2-CH=CH-(CH_2)_4-CH_3$$
$$|$$
$$CH_2-O-\overset{\overset{\displaystyle O}{\|}}{C}-(CH_2)_7-CH=CH-(CH_2)_7-CH_3$$

$$CH_2-O-\overset{\overset{\displaystyle O}{\|}}{C}-(CH_2)_7-CH=CH-CH_2-CH=CH-(CH_2)_4-CH_3$$
$$|$$
$$CH-O-\overset{\overset{\displaystyle O}{\|}}{C}-(CH_2)_7-CH=CH-(CH_2)_7-CH_3$$
$$|$$
$$CH_2-O-\overset{\overset{\displaystyle O}{\|}}{C}-(CH_2)_7-CH=CH-CH_2-CH=CH-(CH_2)_4-CH_3$$

b.

$$CH_2-O-\overset{\overset{\displaystyle O}{\|}}{C}-(CH_2)_7-CH=CH-CH_2-CH=CH-(CH_2)_4-CH_3$$
$$|$$
$$CH-O-\overset{\overset{\displaystyle O}{\|}}{C}-(CH_2)_7-CH=CH-(CH_2)_7-CH_3 + 5H_2 \xrightarrow{Ni}$$
$$|$$
$$CH_2-O-\overset{\overset{\displaystyle O}{\|}}{C}-(CH_2)_7-CH=CH-CH_2-CH=CH-(CH_2)_4-CH_3$$

$$CH_2-O-\overset{\overset{\displaystyle O}{\|}}{C}-(CH_2)_{16}-CH_3$$
$$|$$
$$CH-O-\overset{\overset{\displaystyle O}{\|}}{C}-(CH_2)_{16}-CH_3$$
$$|$$
$$CH_2-O-\overset{\overset{\displaystyle O}{\|}}{C}-(CH_2)_{16}-CH_3$$

17.75 a. Carnauba is a wax. Vegetable oil and glyceryl tricaprate (tricaprin) are triacylglycerols.

b.
$$CH_2-O-\overset{\overset{\displaystyle O}{\|}}{C}-(CH_2)_8-CH_3$$
$$|$$
$$CH-O-\overset{\overset{\displaystyle O}{\|}}{C}-(CH_2)_8-CH_3$$
$$|$$
$$CH_2-O-\overset{\overset{\displaystyle O}{\|}}{C}-(CH_2)_8-CH_3$$

Glyceryl tricaprate (tricaprin)

17.77 a. A typical unsaturated fatty acid has a cis double bond.
b. A cis unsaturated fatty acid contains hydrogen atoms on the same side of each double bond. A trans unsaturated fatty acid has hydrogen atoms on opposite sides of the double bond that forms during hydrogenation.

c.
$$CH_3-(CH_2)_6-CH_2 \quad \overset{H}{\underset{}{}} \overset{}{\underset{}{}} CH_2-(CH_2)_6-\overset{\overset{\displaystyle O}{\|}}{C}-OH$$

(structure: $CH_3-(CH_2)_6-CH_2$ and $CH_2-(CH_2)_6-C(=O)-OH$ attached across a $C=C$ with H on opposite sides)

17.79 a. 410 kcal from fat; 49% fat
b. 260 kcal from fat; 50.% fat
c. 160 kcal from fat; 29% fat

17.81 a. Beeswax is a wax.
b. Cholesterol is a steroid.
c. Lecithin is a glycerophospholipid.
d. Glyceryl tripalmitate is a triacylglycerol.
e. Sodium stearate is a soap.
f. Safflower oil is a triacylglycerol.

17.83 a. 5 **b.** 1, 2, 3, 4
c. 2 **d.** 1, 2

17.85 a. (**4**) HDL **b.** (**3**) LDL
c. (**1**) chylomicron **d.** (**4**) HDL

17.87 a. Adding NaOH would saponify lipids such as glyceryl tristearate (tristearin), forming glycerol and salts of the fatty acids that are soluble in water and would wash down the drain.

b.
$$CH_2-O-\overset{\overset{\displaystyle O}{\|}}{C}-(CH_2)_{16}-CH_3$$
$$|$$
$$CH-O-\overset{\overset{\displaystyle O}{\|}}{C}-(CH_2)_{16}-CH_3 + 3NaOH \longrightarrow$$
$$|$$
$$CH_2-O-\overset{\overset{\displaystyle O}{\|}}{C}-(CH_2)_{16}-CH_3$$

$$CH_2-OH$$
$$|$$
$$CH-OH + 3Na^{+-}O-\overset{\overset{\displaystyle O}{\|}}{C}-(CH_2)_{16}-CH_3$$
$$|$$
$$CH_2-OH$$

Glycerol   Salts of stearic acid

c. 67.3 mL of a 0.500 M NaOH solution

Amines and Amides

Visit **www.masteringchemistry.com** for self-study materials and instructor-assigned homework.

Lance, an environmental health practitioner, is collecting soil and water samples at a nearby farm to test for the presence and concentration of any pesticides and pharmaceuticals. Farmers use pesticides to increase food production and pharmaceuticals to treat and prevent animal-related diseases. Due to the common use of these chemicals, they may pass into the soil and water supply, potentially contaminating the environment and causing health problems.

Recently, the farmer's sheep were treated with a pharmaceutical dewormer, fenbendazole, to destroy any gastrointestinal worms. Fenbendazole contains several functional groups: aromatic rings, an ester, an amine, and imidazole, and a heterocyclic amine. Heterocyclic amines are carbon-based rings where one or more of the carbon atoms have been replaced by a nitrogen atom. Imidazole is a five-atom ring that contains two nitrogen atoms.

Lance detects small amounts of fenbendazole in the soil. He advises the farmer to decrease the dosage he administers to his sheep in order to reduce the amounts currently being detected in the soil. Lance then indicates he will be back in a month to re-test the soil and water.

Career: Environmental Health Practitioner

Environmental health practitioners (EHPs) monitor environmental pollution to protect the health of the public. By using specialized equipment, EHPs measure pollution levels in soil, air, and water, as well as noise and radiation levels. EHPs can specialize in a specific area, such as air quality or hazardous and solid waste. For instance, air quality experts monitor indoor air for allergens, mold, and toxins; they measure outdoor air pollutants created by businesses, vehicles, and agriculture. Since EHPs obtain samples with potentially hazardous materials, they must be knowledgeable about safety protocols and wear personal protective equipment. EHPs also recommend methods to diminish various pollutants, and may assist in cleanup and remediation efforts.

Amines and amides are organic compounds that contain nitrogen. Many nitrogen-containing compounds are important to life as components of amino acids, proteins, and nucleic acids (DNA and RNA). Many amines that exhibit strong physiological activity are used in medicine as decongestants, anesthetics, and sedatives. Examples include dopamine, histamine, epinephrine, and amphetamine.

Alkaloids such as caffeine, nicotine, cocaine, and digitalis, which demonstrate powerful physiological activity, are naturally occurring amines obtained from plants. In amides, the functional group consists of a carbonyl group attached to an amine. In biochemistry, the amide bond that links amino acids in a protein is called a peptide bond. Some medically important amides include acetaminophen (Tylenol) used to reduce fever; phenobarbital, a sedative and anticonvulsant medication; and penicillin, an antibiotic.

TUTORIAL
Drawing Amines

18.1 Amines

Amines are derivatives of ammonia (NH_3) in which the nitrogen atom, which has one lone pair of electrons, has three bonds to hydrogen atoms. In an amine, the nitrogen atom is bonded to one, two, or three alkyl or aromatic groups.

Naming Amines

In the IUPAC names for amines, the *e* in the corresponding alkane name is replaced with *amine*.

CH_4 $CH_3—NH_2$ $CH_3—CH_3$ $CH_3—CH_2—NH_2$
Methane   Methan**amine**   Ethane   Ethan**amine**

When the amine has a chain of three or more carbon atoms, it is numbered to show the position of the —NH_2 group and any other substituents.

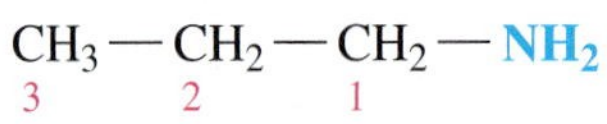

$$CH_3 — CH_2 — CH_2 — NH_2$$
$$3 \qquad 2 \qquad 1$$
1-Propan**amine**

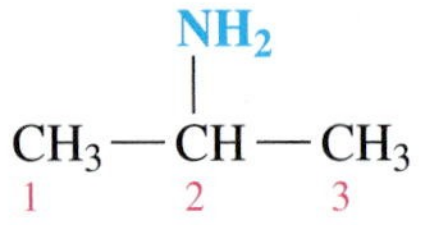

$$CH_3 — \overset{\overset{\displaystyle NH_2}{|}}{CH} — CH_3$$
$$1 \qquad 2 \qquad 3$$
2-Propan**amine**

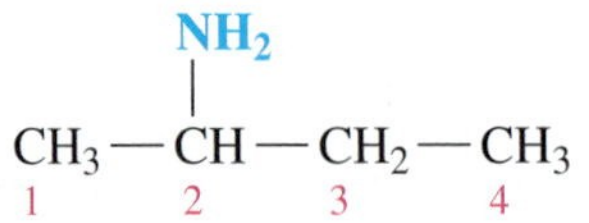

$$CH_3 — \overset{\overset{\displaystyle NH_2}{|}}{CH} — CH_2 — CH_3$$
$$1 \qquad 2 \qquad 3 \qquad 4$$
2-Butan**amine**

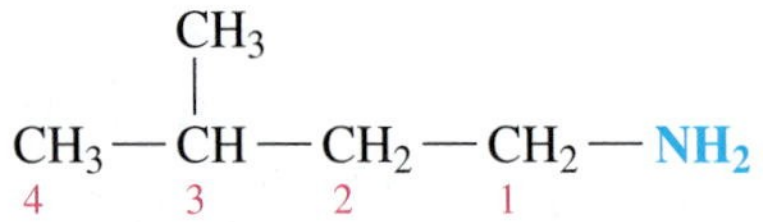

$$CH_3 — \overset{\overset{\displaystyle CH_3}{|}}{CH} — CH_2 — CH_2 — NH_2$$
$$4 \qquad 3 \qquad 2 \qquad 1$$
3-Methyl-1-butan**amine**

If there is an alkyl group attached to the nitrogen atom, the prefix *N*- and the alkyl name are placed in front of the amine name. If there are two alkyl groups bonded to the N atom, the prefix *N*- is used for each and they are listed alphabetically.

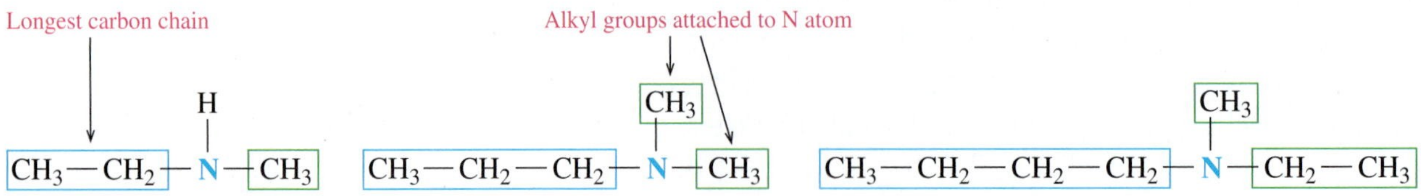

Longest carbon chain

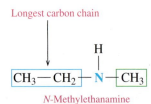

N-Methylethanamine

Alkyl groups attached to N atom

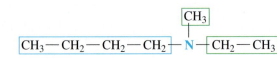

N,*N*-Dimethyl-1-propanamine   *N*-Ethyl-*N*-methyl-1-butanamine

CONCEPT CHECK 18.1   **IUPAC Names of Amines with Substituents**

An amine has the name *N*-methyl-1-hexanamine.

a. How many carbon atoms are in the carbon chain attached to the N atom?
b. What is indicated by the "1" in the 1-hexanamine part of the name?
c. What is indicated by the "*N*-methyl" part of the name?
d. Draw the condensed structural formula for this amine.

ANSWER

a. In a hexanamine, the carbon chain attached to the N atom has six carbon atoms.
b. The number 1 in 1-hexanamine indicates that the N atom is attached to carbon 1 of the chain.
c. The *N*-methyl part of the name indicates that a methyl group ($-CH_3$) is attached to the N atom.
d. The condensed structural formula for *N*-methyl-1-hexanamine is drawn as follows:

$$CH_3-CH_2-CH_2-CH_2-CH_2-CH_2-\underset{\underset{H}{|}}{N}-CH_3$$

SAMPLE PROBLEM 18.1   **IUPAC Names for Amines**

Give the IUPAC name for the following amine:

$$CH_3-CH_2-CH_2-CH_2-\underset{\underset{H}{|}}{N}-CH_3$$

SOLUTION

Guide to the IUPAC Naming of Amines

Step 1 Name the longest carbon chain bonded to the N atom by replacing the *e* of its alkane name with *amine*. The longest carbon chain bonded to the N atom has four carbon atoms, which is named by replacing the *e* in the alkane name with *amine* to give butanamine.

1 Name the longest carbon chain bonded to the N atom by replacing the *e* of its alkane name with *amine*.

$$CH_3-CH_2-CH_2-CH_2-\underset{\underset{H}{|}}{N}-CH_3 \quad \text{butanamine}$$

Step 2 Number the carbon chain to show the position of the amine group and other substituents. The N atom in the amine group is attached to carbon 1 of butanamine.

2 Number the carbon chain to show the position of the amine group and other substituents.

$$\underset{4}{CH_3}-\underset{3}{CH_2}-\underset{2}{CH_2}-\underset{1}{CH_2}-\underset{\underset{H}{|}}{N}-CH_3 \quad \text{1-butanamine}$$

Step 3 Any alkyl group attached to the nitrogen atom is indicated by the prefix *N*- and the alkyl name, which is placed in front of the amine name. Alkyl groups attached to the N atom are listed alphabetically.

3 Any alkyl group attached to the nitrogen atom is indicated by the prefix *N*- and the alkyl name, which is placed in front of the amine name.

$$\underset{4}{CH_3}-\underset{3}{CH_2}-\underset{2}{CH_2}-\underset{1}{CH_2}-\underset{\underset{H}{|}}{N}-CH_3 \quad \text{\textit{N}-methyl-1-butanamine}$$

STUDY CHECK 18.1

Draw the condensed structural formula for *N*-ethyl-1-propanamine.

Common Names of Amines

The common names of amines are often used when the alkyl groups are not branched. The alkyl groups bonded to the nitrogen atom are listed in alphabetical order. The prefixes *di* and *tri* are used to indicate two and three identical groups.

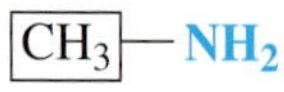

CH_3—NH_2 CH_3—$\overset{\overset{\displaystyle H}{|}}{N}$—$CH_3$ CH_3—CH_2—CH_2—$\overset{\overset{\displaystyle CH_3}{|}}{N}$—$CH_2$—$CH_3$

Methylamine 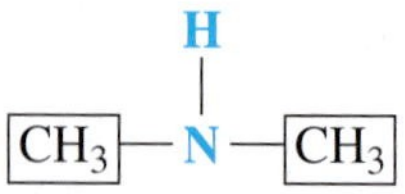   Dimethylamine 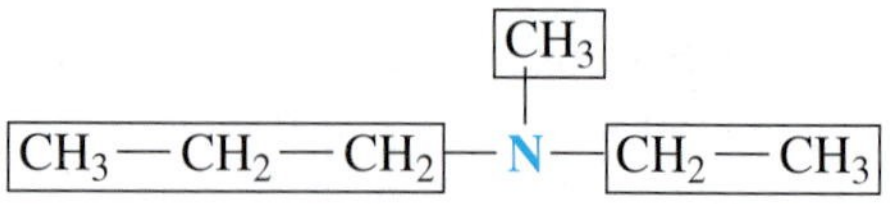   Ethylmethylpropylamine

---

CONCEPT CHECK 18.2   **Common Names of Amines**

Give a common name for each of the following amines:

a. CH_3—CH_2—NH_2 **b.** CH_3—$\overset{\overset{\displaystyle CH_3}{|}}{N}$—$CH_3$

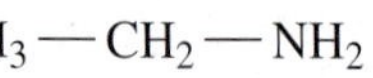

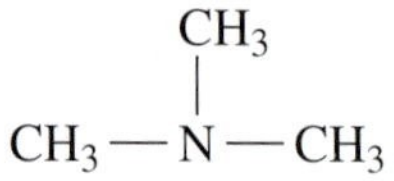

ANSWER

a. This amine has one ethyl group attached to the nitrogen atom; its name is ethylamine.

b. The common name for an amine with three methyl groups attached to the nitrogen atom is trimethylamine.

Naming Compounds with Two Functional Groups

When a compound contains more than one functional group, we need to identify which group is used as the name of the compound and which group is named as a substituent. According to IUPAC rules for nomenclature, an oxygen-containing group will take priority over an —NH_2 group. Therefore, the —NH_2 group is named as the substituent, *amino*. Table 18.1 lists the priorities for the major functional groups we have studied, and the names of the functional groups as substituents. The functional group that is highest on the list is named as the compound, and any group lower on the list is named as a substituent. Examples are given for naming an alcohol, ketone, and carboxylic acid that also contain an amine group.

CH_3—$\overset{\overset{\displaystyle NH_2}{|}}{CH}$—$CH_2$—$OH$ CH_3—$\overset{\overset{\displaystyle NH_2}{|}}{CH}$—$CH_2$—$\overset{\overset{\displaystyle O}{||}}{C}$—$CH_3$ CH_3—$\overset{\overset{\displaystyle NH_2}{|}}{CH}$—$CH_2$—$\overset{\overset{\displaystyle O}{||}}{C}$—$OH$

2-Amino-1-propanol 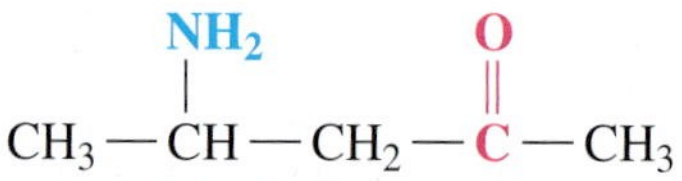   4-Amino-2-pentanone 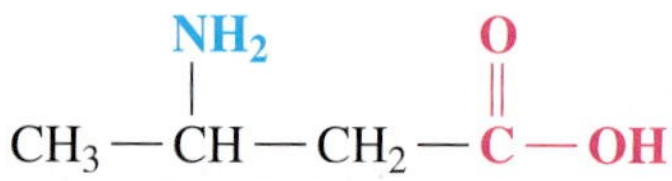   3-Aminobutanoic acid

TABLE 18.1 Priority of Functional Groups in IUPAC Names

	Functional Group	Name of Compound	Name as a Substituent
Highest Priority	carboxylic acid	oic acid	
	ester	oate	
	amide	amide	amido
	aldehyde	al	formyl
	ketone	one	oxo
	alcohol	ol	hydroxy
	amine	amine	amino
	alkane	ane	alkyl
Lowest Priority	halide		halo

SAMPLE PROBLEM 18.2   **IUPAC Names for Compounds with Two Functional Groups**

Give the IUPAC name of the following compound, which is used in the production of methadone:

$$\begin{array}{c} \text{OH} \\ | \\ \text{CH}_3\text{—CH—CH}_2\text{—NH}_2 \end{array}$$

SOLUTION

Step 1   **Identify the functional group with the highest priority and use the longest carbon chain to give the compound name.** Because the hydroxyl group has a higher priority than the amine group, the compound is named as an alcohol.

$$\begin{array}{c} \text{OH} \\ | \\ \text{CH}_3\text{—CH—CH}_2\text{—NH}_2 \end{array} \qquad \boxed{\text{propanol}}$$

Step 2   **Number the carbon chain, and give the position and name of the main group and the substituent group on the carbon chain.**

$$\begin{array}{c} \text{OH} \\ | \\ \text{CH}_3\text{—CH—CH}_2\text{—NH}_2 \\ \scriptstyle 3 \quad\; 2 \quad\;\; 1 \end{array} \qquad \text{1-amino-2-propanol}$$

STUDY CHECK 18.2

Draw the condensed structural formula for 3-aminopentanal.

Guide to Naming Compounds with Two Functional Groups

1 Identify the functional group with the highest priority and use the longest carbon chain to give the compound name.

2 Number the carbon chain, and give the position and name of the main group and the substituent group on the carbon chain.

Aromatic Amines

The aromatic amines use the name *aniline*, which is approved by IUPAC. Aniline is the simplest aromatic amine; it is used to make many industrial chemicals. Aniline was discovered in 1826 when it was first isolated from indigo plants. Then it was used to make synthetic dyes.

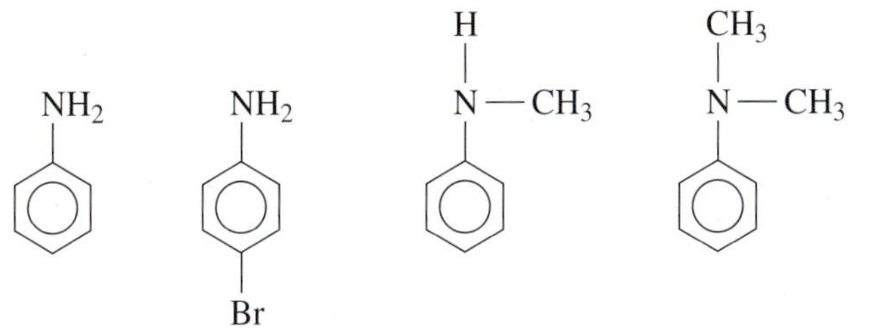

Aniline   4-Bromoaniline   *N*-Methylaniline   *N,N*-Dimethylaniline
           (*p*-bromoaniline)

Aniline is used to make many dyes, which give color to wool, cotton, and silk fibers, as well as blue jeans. It is also used to make the polymer polyurethane and in the synthesis of the pain reliever acetaminophen.

Indigo

Indigo used in blue dyes can be obtained from tropical plants such as *Indigofera tinctoria*.

Classification of Amines

Amines are classified by counting the number of carbon atoms directly bonded to the nitrogen atom. In a *primary* (*1°*) *amine*, the nitrogen atom is bonded to one alkyl group. In a *secondary* (*2°*) *amine*, the nitrogen atom is bonded to two alkyl groups. In a *tertiary* (*3°*) *amine*, the nitrogen atom is bonded to three alkyl groups. In each of the following models of ammonia and amines, the atoms are arranged around the nitrogen atom (blue) in a trigonal pyramidal shape:

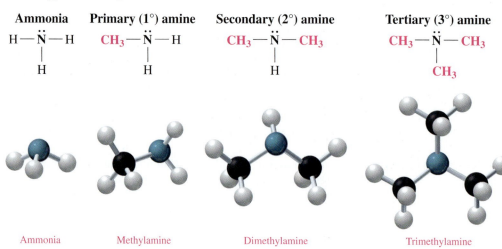

Ammonia	Primary (1°) amine	Secondary (2°) amine	Tertiary (3°) amine

| Ammonia | Methylamine | Dimethylamine | Trimethylamine |

Skeletal Formulas for Amines

We can draw skeletal formulas for amines just as we have for other organic compounds. In the skeletal formula for an amine, we show the hydrogen atoms bonded to the N atom. For example, we can draw the following skeletal formulas and classify each:

Primary amine (1°)   Secondary amine (2°)   Tertiary amine (3°)

SAMPLE PROBLEM 18.3 **Classifying Amines**

Classify the following amines as primary (1°), secondary (2°), or tertiary (3°):

a.

b. $CH_3 - \overset{\overset{\displaystyle CH_3}{|}}{N} - CH_2 - CH_3$

c.

d.

SOLUTION

a. This is a primary (1°) amine because there is one alkyl group (cyclohexyl) attached to the nitrogen atom.

b. This is a tertiary (3°) amine. There are three alkyl groups (two methyls and one ethyl) attached to the nitrogen atom.

c. This is a secondary (2°) amine with two carbon groups, methyl and phenyl, bonded to the nitrogen atom.

d. The nitrogen atom in this skeletal formula is bonded to two alkyl groups, which makes it a secondary (2°) amine.

STUDY CHECK 18.3

Classify the following amine as primary (1°), secondary (2°), or tertiary (3°):

$$CH_3-CH_2-\underset{\underset{CH_3}{|}}{N}-CH_2-CH_2-CH_3$$

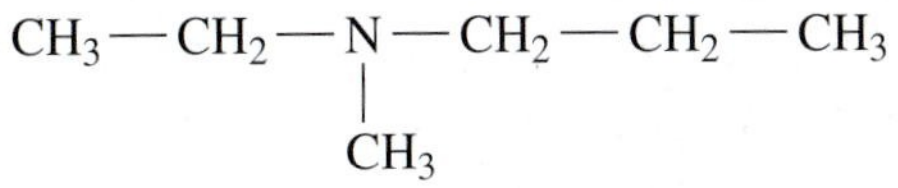

QUESTIONS AND PROBLEMS

18.1 Amines

LEARNING GOAL: *Name amines using IUPAC and common names; draw the condensed structural formulas given the names. Classify amines as primary (1°), secondary (2°), or tertiary (3°).*

18.1 What is a primary amine?

18.2 What is a tertiary amine?

18.3 Classify each of the following amines as primary (1°), secondary (2°), or tertiary (3°):

a. $CH_3-CH_2-CH_2-NH_2$ **b.** 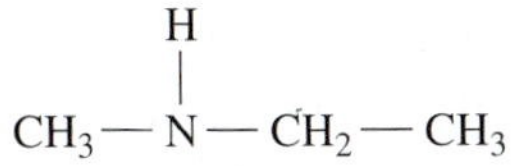 $CH_3-\underset{\underset{CH_3}{|}}{\overset{\overset{H}{|}}{N}}-CH_2-CH_3$

c. 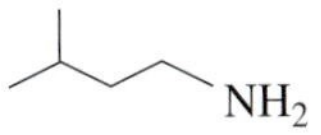 (isopentyl with NH_2)

d. 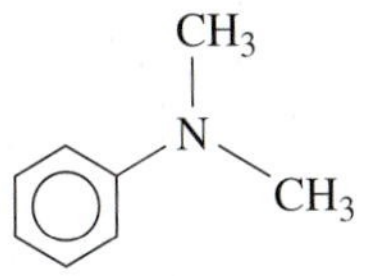 (phenyl-N with CH_3 and CH_3)

e. 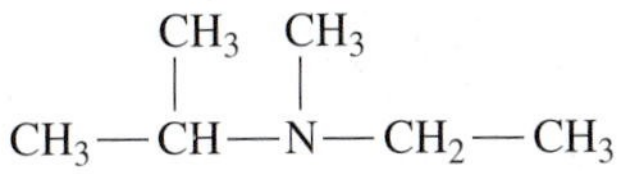 $CH_3-\underset{\underset{}{\overset{\overset{CH_3}{|}}{CH}}}-\underset{\underset{}{\overset{\overset{CH_3}{|}}{N}}}-CH_2-CH_3$

18.4 Classify each of the following amines as primary (1°), secondary (2°), or tertiary (3°):

a. 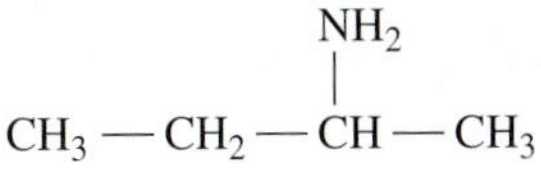 $CH_3-CH_2-\underset{\underset{NH_2}{|}}{CH}-CH_3$

b. 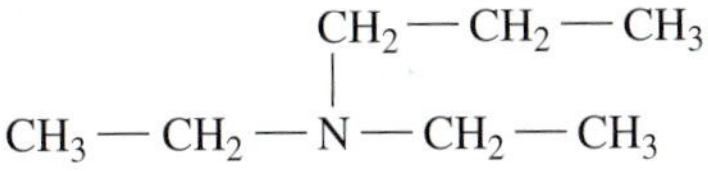 $CH_3-CH_2-\underset{\underset{CH_2-CH_3}{|}}{\overset{\overset{CH_2-CH_2-CH_3}{|}}{N}}-CH_2-CH_3$

c. 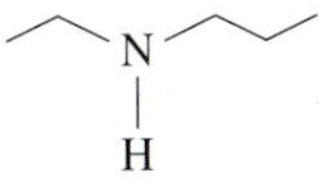 (ethyl-N(H)-propyl)

d. 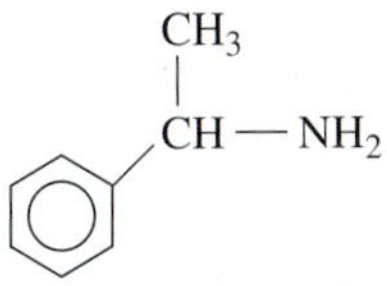 (phenyl-CH(CH_3)-NH_2)

e. 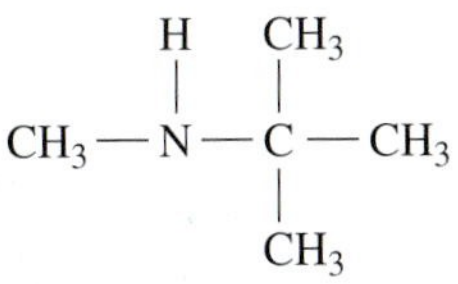 $CH_3-\underset{\underset{H}{|}}{N}-\underset{\underset{CH_3}{|}}{\overset{\overset{CH_3}{|}}{C}}-CH_3$

18.5 Write the IUPAC and common names for each of the following:

a. $CH_3-CH_2-NH_2$

b. $CH_3-NH-CH_2-CH_2-CH_3$

c. 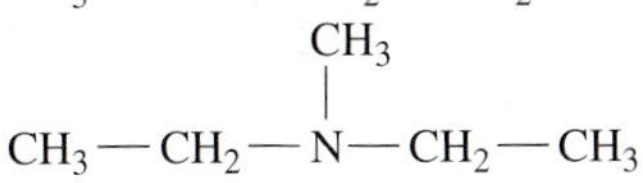 $CH_3-CH_2-\underset{\underset{}{\overset{\overset{CH_3}{|}}{N}}}-CH_2-CH_3$

d. 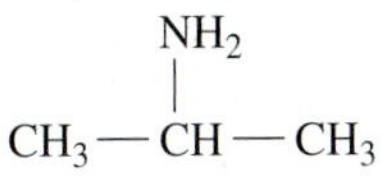 $CH_3-\underset{\underset{NH_2}{|}}{CH}-CH_3$

18.6 Write the IUPAC and common names for each of the following:

a. $CH_3-CH_2-CH_2-NH_2$

b. 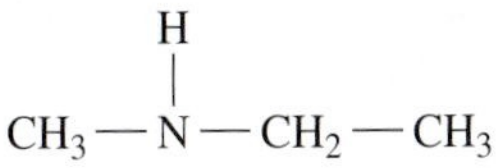 $CH_3-\underset{\underset{}{\overset{\overset{H}{|}}{N}}}-CH_2-CH_3$

c. $CH_3-CH_2-CH_2-CH_2-NH_2$

d. 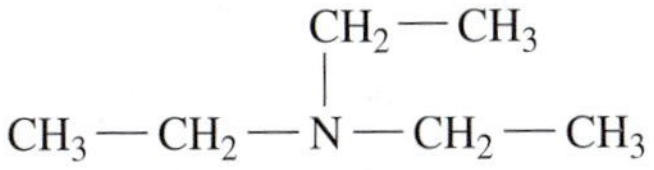 $CH_3-CH_2-\underset{\underset{}{\overset{\overset{CH_2-CH_3}{|}}{N}}}-CH_2-CH_3$

18.7 Write the IUPAC name for each of the following molecules that have two functional groups:

a. 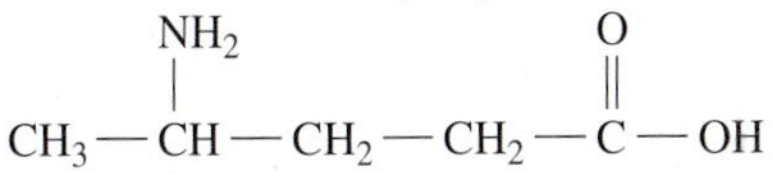 $CH_3-\underset{\underset{NH_2}{|}}{CH}-CH_2-CH_2-\overset{\overset{O}{||}}{C}-OH$

b. (benzene ring with NH_2 and Cl)

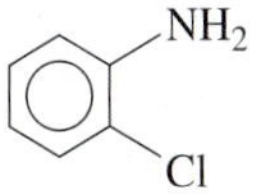

c. $H_2N-CH_2-CH_2-\overset{\overset{O}{||}}{C}-H$

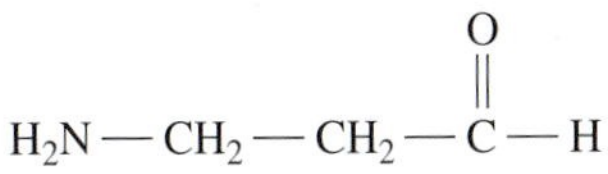

d. 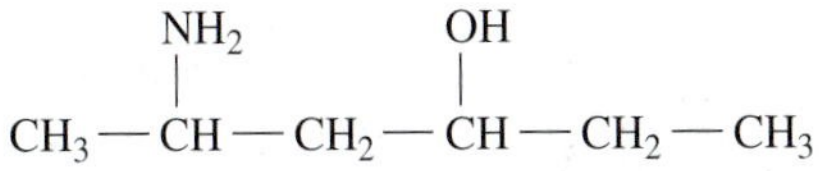 $CH_3-\underset{\underset{NH_2}{|}}{CH}-CH_2-\underset{\underset{OH}{|}}{CH}-CH_2-CH_3$

18.8 Write the IUPAC name for each of the following molecules that have two functional groups:

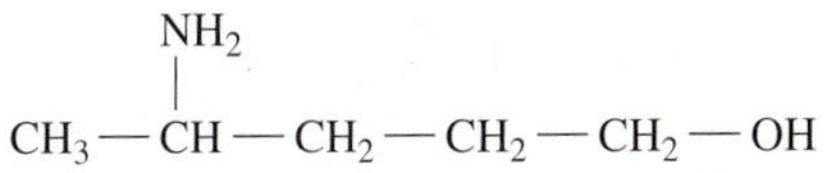

a. 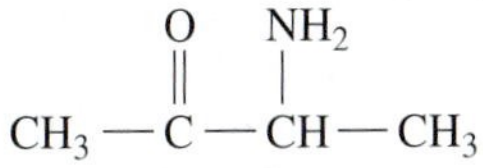 $CH_3-\overset{\overset{O}{||}}{C}-\underset{\underset{NH_2}{|}}{CH}-CH_3$

b. $CH_3-\underset{\underset{NH_2}{|}}{CH}-CH_2-CH_2-CH_2-OH$

c. (benzene ring with $NH-CH_3$ and Br)

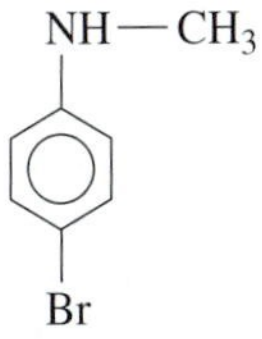

d. 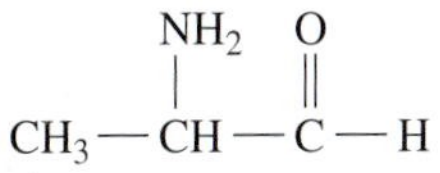 $CH_3-\underset{\underset{NH_2}{|}}{CH}-\overset{\overset{O}{||}}{C}-H$

18.9 Draw the condensed structural formula for each of the following amines:
a. 2-chloroethanamine **b.** *N*-methylaniline
c. butylpropylamine **d.** 2-aminobutanal

18.10 Draw the condensed structural formula for each of the following amines:
a. dimethylamine **b.** *p*-chloroaniline
c. *N,N*-diethylaniline **d.** 1-amino-3-pentanone

18.2 Properties of Amines

Amines contain polar N—H bonds, which allow primary and secondary amines to form hydrogen bonds with each other, while all amines can form hydrogen bonds with water. However, nitrogen is not as electronegative as oxygen, which means that the hydrogen bonds in amines are weaker than the hydrogen bonds in alcohols.

Most hydrogen bonds

No hydrogen bonds

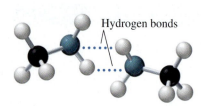

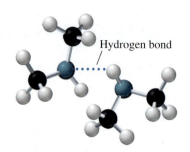

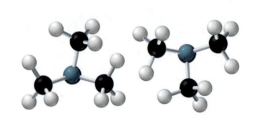

Boiling Points of Amines

Amines have boiling points that are higher than alkanes but lower than alcohols. Primary (1°) amines, with two N—H bonds, can form more hydrogen bonds, and thus have higher boiling points than secondary (2°) amines of the same mass. It is not possible for tertiary (3°) amines to hydrogen bond with each other since they have no N—H bonds. Tertiary amines have lower boiling points than primary or secondary amines of the same mass.

$$CH_3-CH_2-CH_2-NH_2 \qquad CH_3-CH_2-NH-CH_3 \qquad \overset{\displaystyle CH_3}{\underset{\displaystyle }{CH_3-\overset{|}{N}-CH_3}}$$

Propylamine (1°)   Ethylmethylamine (2°)   Trimethylamine (3°)
bp 48 °C   bp 36 °C   bp 3 °C

Solubility in Water

Amines with one to six carbon atoms, including tertiary amines, are soluble because they form several hydrogen bonds with water (see Figure 18.1). Generally, the primary amines are most soluble, and tertiary amines are least soluble. As the number of carbon atoms in an amine increases in the nonpolar alkyl portions, the effect of hydrogen bonding is diminished.

Most hydrogen bonds   **Fewest hydrogen bonds**

Primary amine   Secondary amine   Tertiary amine

FIGURE 18.1 Primary, secondary and tertiary amines form hydrogen bonds with water molecules, but primary amines form the most and tertiary amines form the least.

Q Why do tertiary (3°) amines form fewer hydrogen bonds with water than primary amines?

CONCEPT CHECK 18.3 **Boiling Points and Solubility of Amines**

a. The compounds trimethylamine and ethylmethylamine have the same molar mass. Why is the boiling point of trimethylamine (3 °C) lower than that of ethylmethylamine (37 °C)?

b. Why is $CH_3—CH_2—NH—CH_2—CH_3$ more soluble in water than $CH_3—CH_2—CH_2—CH_2—NH—CH_2—CH_2—CH_3$?

ANSWER

a. With polar N—H bonds, ethylmethylamine molecules form hydrogen bonds with each other. Thus, a higher temperature is required to break the hydrogen bonds and form a gas. However, trimethylamine, which is a tertiary amine, does not have N—H bonds and cannot hydrogen bond with other trimethylamine molecules. It does not need as high a temperature to form a gas.

b. Hydrogen bonding makes amines with six or fewer carbon atoms soluble in water. When there are seven or more carbon atoms in the alkyl portions of an amine, it is not very soluble in water because the nonpolar hydrocarbon groups have a greater effect on solubility than the amine group.

Amines React as Bases in Water

In Section 10.1, we described how ammonia (NH_3) acts as a Brønsted–Lowry base by accepting a proton (H^+) from water to produce an ammonium ion (NH_4^+) and a hydroxide ion (OH^-).

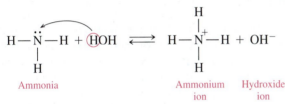

Ammonia   Ammonium   Hydroxide
ion   ion

TUTORIAL
Reactions of Amines

All of the amines we have discussed in this chapter are also Brønsted–Lowry bases because the lone pair of electrons on the nitrogen atom accepts a proton from water. In the reaction of an amine with water, the products are a positively charged alkyl ammonium ion and a negatively charged hydroxide ion. The organic product is named by adding *ammonium ion* to the name of its alkyl group.

SELF-STUDY ACTIVITY
Amines as Bases

Reaction of a Primary Amine with Water

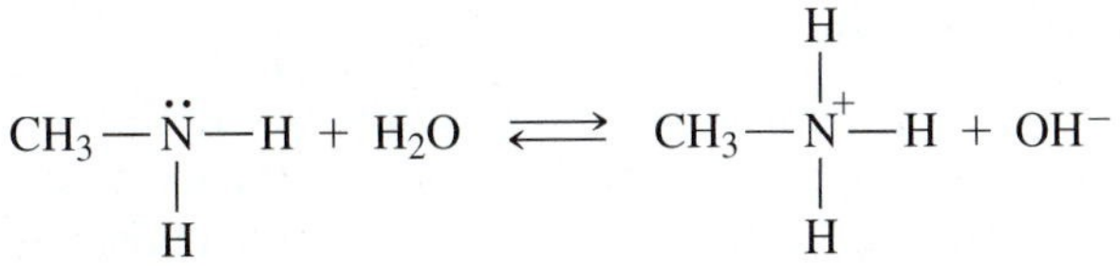

$$CH_3—\overset{..}{N}—H + H_2O \rightleftharpoons CH_3—\overset{\overset{H}{|}}{\underset{\underset{H}{|}}{N}}{}^+—H + OH^-$$

Methylamine   Methylammonium ion

Reaction of a Secondary Amine with Water

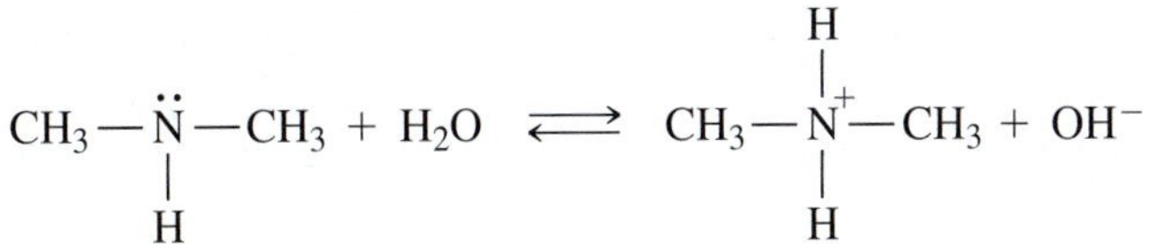

$$CH_3—\overset{..}{N}—CH_3 + H_2O \rightleftharpoons CH_3—\overset{\overset{H}{|}}{\underset{\underset{H}{|}}{N}}{}^+—CH_3 + OH^-$$

Dimethylamine   Dimethylammonium ion

Reaction of a Tertiary Amine with Water

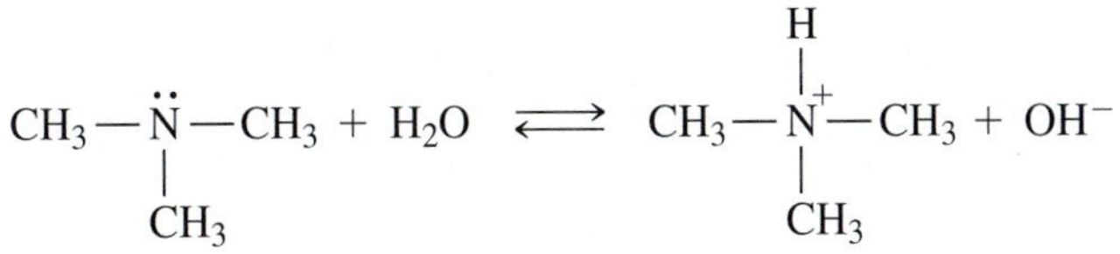

$$CH_3—\overset{..}{N}—CH_3 + H_2O \rightleftharpoons CH_3—\overset{\overset{H}{|}}{\underset{\underset{CH_3}{|}}{N}}{}^+—CH_3 + OH^-$$

Trimethylamine   Trimethylammonium ion

Ammonium Salts

The amines in fish react with the acid in lemon to neutralize the "fishy" odor.

When you squeeze lemon juice on fish, the "fishy" odor is removed by converting the amines to their ammonium salts. In a *neutralization reaction*, an amine acts as a base and reacts with an acid to form an **ammonium salt**. The lone pair of electrons on the nitrogen atom accepts a proton (H^+) from an acid to give an ammonium salt; no water is formed. An ammonium salt is named by using its alkyl ammonium ion name followed by the name of the negative ion.

Neutralization of an Amine

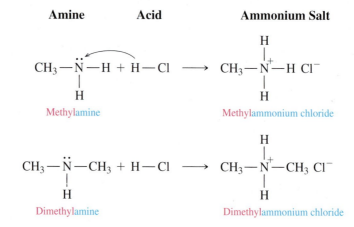

Quaternary Ammonium Salts

TUTORIAL
Properties of Amines and Amine Salts

In a **quaternary ammonium salt**, a nitrogen atom is bonded to four carbon groups, which classifies it as a 4° amine. As in other ammonium salts, the nitrogen atom has a positive charge. Choline, an amino alcohol we described in Section 17.5 as a component of glycerophospholipids, is a quaternary ammonium ion. The quaternary salts differ from other ammonium salts because the nitrogen atom is not bonded to an H atom.

Properties of Ammonium Salts

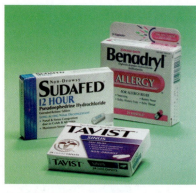

FIGURE 18.2 Decongestants and products that relieve itchy skin can contain ammonium salts.

Q Why are ammonium salts used in drugs rather than the biologically active amines?

Ammonium salts are ionic compounds with strong attractions between the positively charged ammonium ion and an anion, usually chloride. Like most salts, ammonium salts are solid at room temperature, odorless, and soluble in water and body fluids. For this reason, amines that are large molecules that are intended to be used as drugs are converted to their ammonium salts, which are soluble in water and body fluids. The ammonium salt of ephedrine is used as a bronchodilator and in decongestant products such as Sudafed®. The ammonium salt of diphenhydramine is used in products such as Benadryl® for relief of itching and pain from skin irritations and rashes (see Figure 18.2). In pharmaceuticals, the naming of the ammonium salt follows an older method of giving the amine name followed by the name of the acid.

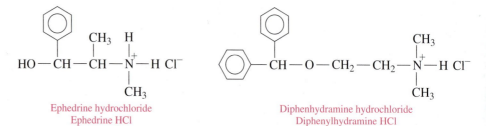

When an ammonium salt reacts with a strong base such as NaOH, it is converted back to the amine, which is also called the free amine or free base.

$$CH_3 - \overset{+}{N}H_3\ Cl^- + NaOH \longrightarrow CH_3 - NH_2 + NaCl + H_2O$$

The narcotic cocaine is typically extracted from coca leaves using an acidic solution to give a white, solid ammonium salt, which is cocaine hydrochloride. It is the salt of cocaine (cocaine hydrochloride) that is smuggled and used illegally on the street. "Crack cocaine" is the free amine or free base of the amine obtained by treating the cocaine hydrochloride with NaOH and ether, a process known as "free-basing." The solid product is known as "crack cocaine" because it makes a cracking noise when heated. The free amine is rapidly absorbed when smoked and gives stronger highs than the cocaine hydrochloride, which makes crack cocaine more addictive.

Coca leaves are a source of cocaine.

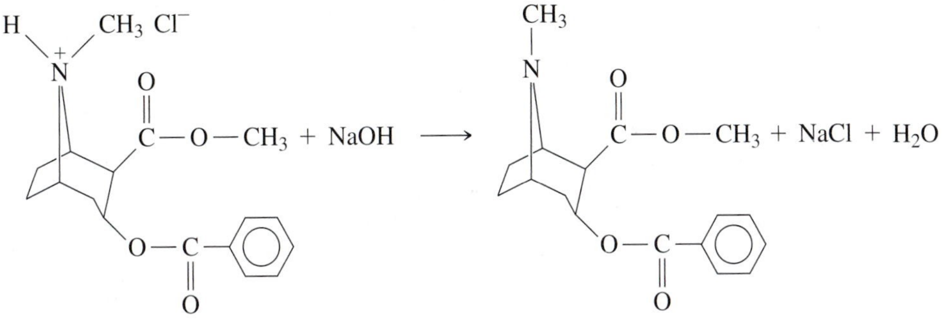

Cocaine hydrochloride + NaOH $\longrightarrow$ Cocaine ("free base"; crack cocaine) + NaCl + H_2O

CONCEPT CHECK 18.4 Reacting an Amine with HCl

Consider the reaction of dimethylamine with HCl.

a. What type of reaction takes place?
b. What type of product forms?
c. What is the name of the product that forms?

ANSWER

a. The reaction of an amine acting as a base and an acid is neutralization.
b. The product that forms is an ammonium salt.
c. The product is dimethylammonium chloride.

SAMPLE PROBLEM 18.4 Reactions of Amines

Write an equation that shows ethylamine:

a. acting as a weak base in water
b. neutralized by HCl

SOLUTION

a. $CH_3 - CH_2 - NH_2 + H_2O \rightleftharpoons CH_3 - CH_2 - \overset{+}{N}H_3 + OH^-$

b. $CH_3 - CH_2 - NH_2 + HCl \longrightarrow CH_3 - CH_2 - \overset{+}{N}H_3\ Cl^-$

STUDY CHECK 18.4

What is the condensed structural formula for the salt formed by the reaction of trimethylamine and HCl?

QUESTIONS AND PROBLEMS

18.2 Properties of Amines

LEARNING GOAL: Describe the boiling points and solubility of amines; write equations for the ionization and neutralization of amines.

18.11 Identify the compound in each pair that has the higher boiling point. Explain.
   a. $CH_3-CH_2-NH_2$ or CH_3-CH_2-OH
   b. CH_3-NH_2 or $CH_3-CH_2-CH_2-NH_2$
   c. $CH_3-\overset{\overset{\displaystyle CH_3}{|}}{N}-CH_3$ or $CH_3-CH_2-CH_2-NH_2$

18.12 Identify the compound in each pair that has the higher boiling point. Explain.
   a. $CH_3-CH_2-CH_2-CH_3$ or $CH_3-CH_2-CH_2-NH_2$
   b. CH_3-NH_2 or $CH_3-CH_2-NH_2$
   c. $CH_3-CH_2-CH_2-OH$ or $CH_3-\overset{\overset{\displaystyle NH_2}{|}}{CH}-CH_3$

18.13 Propylamine (59 g/mole) has a boiling point of 48 °C, and ethylmethylamine (59 g/mole) has a boiling point of 37 °C. Butane (58 g/mole) has a much lower boiling point of −1 °C. Explain.

18.14 Assign the boiling point of 3 °C, 48 °C, or 97 °C to the appropriate compound: 1-propanol, propylamine, and trimethylamine.

18.15 Indicate if each of the following is soluble in water. Explain.
   a. $CH_3-CH_2-NH_2$
   b. $CH_3-NH-CH_3$
   c. $CH_3-CH_2-CH_2-\overset{\overset{\displaystyle CH_2-CH_2-CH_3}{|}}{N}-CH_2-CH_2-CH_3$
   d. $CH_3-\overset{\overset{\displaystyle NH_2}{|}}{CH}-CH_2-CH_3$

18.16 Indicate if each of the following is soluble in water. Explain.
   a. $CH_3-CH_2-CH_2-NH_2$
   b. $CH_3-CH_2-CH_2-NH-CH_2-CH_3$
   c. $CH_3-\overset{\overset{\displaystyle NH_2}{|}}{CH}-CH_3$
   d.

18.17 Write an equation for the ionization of each of the following amines in water:
   a. methylamine   **b.** dimethylamine
   c. aniline

18.18 Write an equation for the ionization of each of the following amines in water:
   a. diethylamine   **b.** propylamine
   c. *N*-methylaniline

18.19 Draw the condensed structural formula for the ammonium salt obtained when each of the amines in Problem 18.17 reacts with HCl.

18.20 Draw the condensed structural formula for the ammonium salt obtained when each of the amines in Problem 18.18 reacts with HCl.

18.21 Novocain, a local anesthetic, is the ammonium salt of procaine.

$$H_2N-\langle\bigcirc\rangle-\overset{\overset{\displaystyle O}{||}}{C}-O-CH_2-CH_2-N\overset{\displaystyle CH_2-CH_3}{\underset{\displaystyle CH_2-CH_3}{<}}$$

Procaine

   a. Draw the condensed structural formula for the ammonium salt (procaine hydrochloride) formed when procaine reacts with HCl. (*Hint*: The tertiary amine reacts with HCl.)
   b. Why is procaine hydrochloride used rather than procaine?

18.22 Lidocaine (Xylocaine®) is used as a local anesthetic and cardiac depressant.

$$\overset{\displaystyle CH_3}{\underset{\displaystyle CH_3}{\langle\bigcirc\rangle}}-NH-\overset{\overset{\displaystyle O}{||}}{C}-CH_2-N\overset{\displaystyle CH_2-CH_3}{\underset{\displaystyle CH_2-CH_3}{<}}$$

Lidocaine (xylocaine)

   a. Draw the condensed structural formula for the ammonium salt formed when lidocaine reacts with HCl.
   b. Why is the ammonium salt of lidocaine used rather than the amine?

LEARNING GOAL

Identify heterocyclic amines; distinguish between the types of heterocyclic amines.

(MC)
TUTORIAL
Identifying Types of Heterocyclic Amines

18.3 Heterocyclic Amines

A **heterocyclic amine** is a cyclic organic compound that consists of a ring of five or six atoms, of which one or two are nitrogen atoms. Of the five-atom rings, the simplest one is pyrrolidine, which is a ring of four carbon atoms and one nitrogen atom, all with single bonds. Pyrrole is a five-atom ring with one nitrogen atom and two double bonds. Imidazole is a five-atom ring that contains two nitrogen atoms. Piperidine is a six-atom heterocyclic ring with a nitrogen atom. Some of the pungent aroma and taste of black pepper that we use to season our food is due to piperidine. Purine and pyrimidine rings are found in DNA and RNA. In purine, the structures of 6-atom pyrimidine and 5-atom imidazole are combined. Heterocyclic amines with two or three double bonds have aromatic properties similar to benzene.

5-Atom Heterocyclic Amines

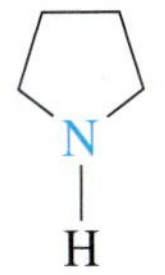

Pyrrolidine

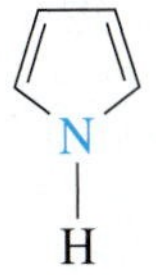

Pyrrole

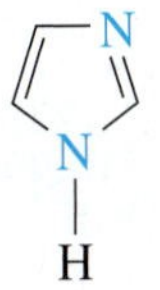

Imidazole

6-Atom Heterocyclic Amines

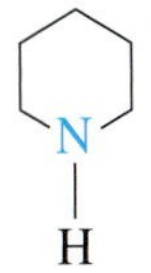

Piperidine

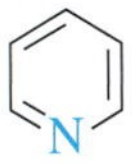

Pyridine

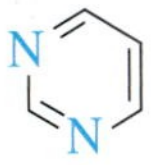

Pyrimidine

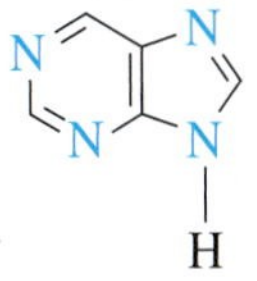

Purine

The aroma of pepper is due to piperidine, a heterocyclic amine.

CASE STUDY
Death by Chocolate?

CONCEPT CHECK 18.5   **Heterocyclic Amines**

Identify the heterocyclic amines that are part of the structure of nicotine.

Nicotine

ANSWER

Nicotine contains two heterocyclic rings. The 6-atom ring with one N atom and three double bonds is pyridine, and the 5-atom ring with one N atom and no double bonds is pyrrolidine. The N atom in the pyrrolidine ring is bonded to a methyl group ($-CH_3$).

Pyrrolidine

Pyridine

Alkaloids: Amines in Plants

Alkaloids are physiologically active nitrogen-containing compounds produced by plants. The term *alkaloid* refers to the "alkali-like" or basic characteristics we have seen for amines. Certain alkaloids are used in anesthetics, in antidepressants, and as stimulants, and many are habit forming.

As a stimulant, nicotine increases the level of adrenaline in the blood, which increases the heart rate and blood pressure. Nicotine is addictive because it activates pleasure centers in the brain. Nicotine has a simple alkaloid structure that includes a pyrrolidine ring. Coniine, which is obtained from hemlock, is an extremely toxic alkaloid that contains a piperidine ring.

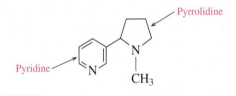

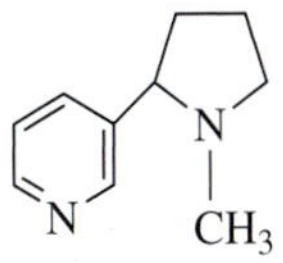

Nicotine

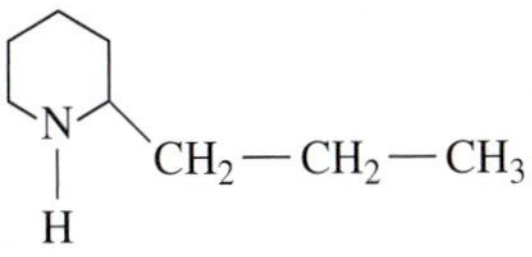

Coniine

Caffeine is a purine that is a central nervous system stimulant. Present in coffee, tea, soft drinks, energy drinks, chocolate, and cocoa, caffeine increases alertness, but it may cause nervousness and insomnia. Caffeine is also used in certain pain relievers to counteract the drowsiness caused by an antihistamine (see Figure 18.3).

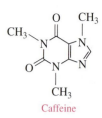

Caffeine

FIGURE 18.3 Caffeine is a stimulant found in coffee, tea, energy drinks, and chocolate.
Q Why is caffeine an alkaloid?

Several alkaloids are used in medicine. Quinine, obtained from the bark of the cinchona tree, has been used to treat malaria since the 1600s. Atropine from nightshade (belladonna) is used in low concentrations to accelerate slow heart rates and to dilate the eyes during eye examinations.

Quinine

Atropine

For many centuries, morphine and codeine, alkaloids found in the opium poppy plant, have been used as effective painkillers (see Figure 18.4). Codeine, which is structurally similar to morphine, is used in some prescription painkillers and cough syrups. Heroin, obtained by a chemical modification of morphine, is strongly addictive and is not used medically. The structure of the prescription drug OxyContin® (oxycodone) used to relieve severe pain is similar to heroin. Today, there are an increasing number of deaths from OxyContin® abuse because its physiological effects are also similar to those of heroin.

FIGURE 18.4 The green, unripe poppy seed capsule contains a milky sap (opium) that is the source of the alkaloids morphine and codeine.

Q Where is the piperidine ring in the structures of morphine and codeine?

Morphine

Codeine

Heroin

OxyContin®

What are the condensed structural formulas for the carboxylic acid and amine needed to prepare the following amide? (*Hint*: Separate the N and C=O of the amide group, and add —H and —OH to give the original amine and carboxylic acid.)

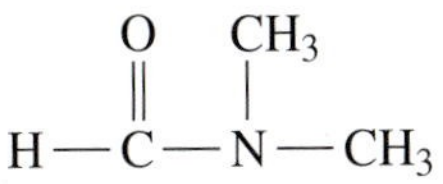

$$H-\overset{\displaystyle O}{\overset{\|}{C}}-\overset{\displaystyle CH_3}{\overset{|}{N}}-CH_3$$

Naming Amides

TUTORIAL
Naming Carboxylic Acid Derivatives

In both the IUPAC and common names, amides are named by dropping the *ic acid* or *oic acid* from the carboxylic acid name (IUPAC or common), and adding the suffix *amide*. We can diagram the name of an amide in the following way:

From butanoic acid (butyric acid)

From ammonia

$$CH_3-CH_2-CH_2-\overset{\displaystyle O}{\overset{\|}{C}}-NH_2$$

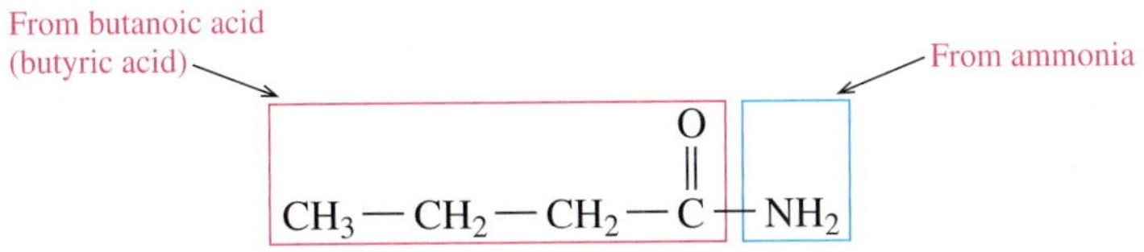

IUPAC   Butanamide
Common   Butyramide

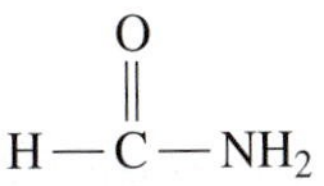

$$H-\overset{\displaystyle O}{\overset{\|}{C}}-NH_2 \qquad CH_3-\overset{\displaystyle O}{\overset{\|}{C}}-NH_2$$

Methanamide   Ethanamide
(formamide)   (acetamide)

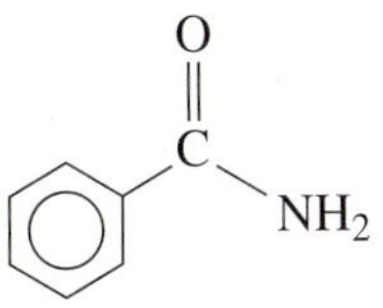

Benzamide

When alkyl groups are attached to the nitrogen atom, the prefix *N*- or *N,N*- precedes the name of the amide, depending on whether there are one or two groups. We can diagram the name of a substituted amide in the following way:

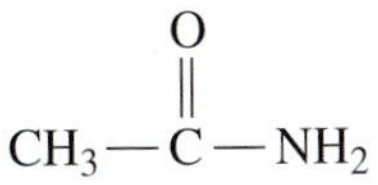

From butanoic acid (butyric acid)

From *N,N*-Dimethylamine

$$CH_3-CH_2-CH_2-\overset{\displaystyle O}{\overset{\|}{C}}-\overset{\displaystyle CH_3}{\overset{|}{N}}-CH_3$$

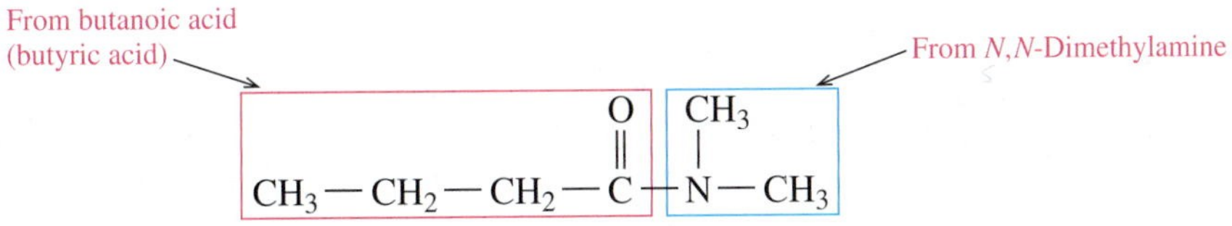

IUPAC   *N,N*-Dimethylbutanamide
Common   *N,N*-Dimethylbutyramide

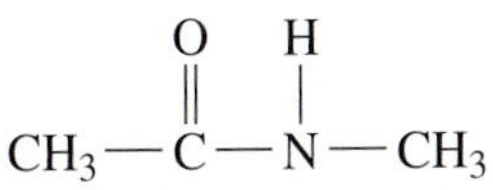

$$CH_3-\overset{\displaystyle O}{\overset{\|}{C}}-\overset{\displaystyle H}{\overset{|}{N}}-CH_3 \qquad CH_3-CH_2-\overset{\displaystyle O}{\overset{\|}{C}}-\overset{\displaystyle CH_3}{\overset{|}{N}}-CH_3$$

N-Methylethanamide   *N,N*-Dimethylpropanamide
(*N*-methylacetamide)   (*N,N*-dimethylpropionamide)

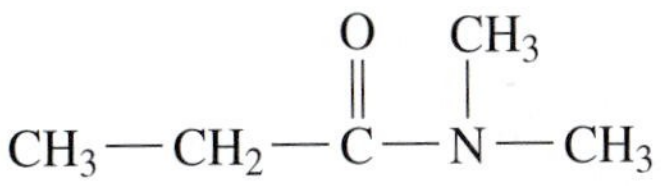

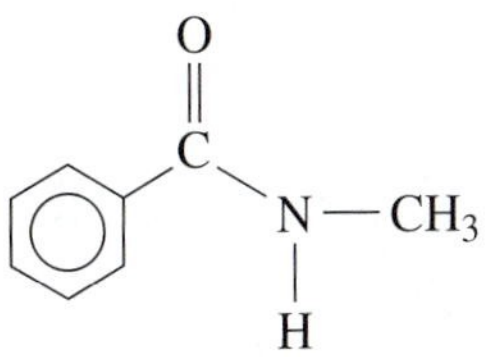

N-Methylbenzamide

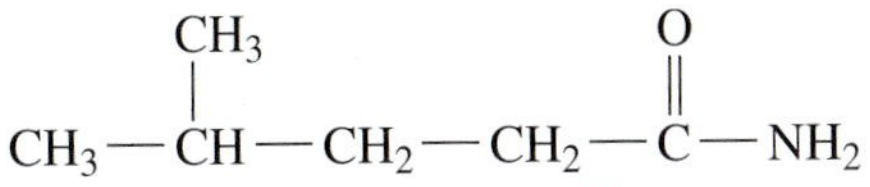

$$CH_3-\overset{\displaystyle CH_3}{\overset{|}{CH}}-CH_2-CH_2-\overset{\displaystyle O}{\overset{\|}{C}}-NH_2$$

4-Methylpentanamide

CONCEPT CHECK 18.6 **IUPAC Names of Amides**

An amide has the name *N*-ethylpentanamide.

a. What is the IUPAC name of the carboxylic acid used in the amidation reaction to form this amide?

b. What is indicated by the *N*-ethyl part of the name?

ANSWER

a. Pentanamide indicates that there are five carbon atoms. The corresponding carboxylic acid used in the amidation reaction would be pentanoic acid.

b. The *N*-ethyl part of the name indicates that an ethyl group is attached to the N atom.

SAMPLE PROBLEM 18.6 **Naming Amides**

Give the IUPAC name for the following amide:

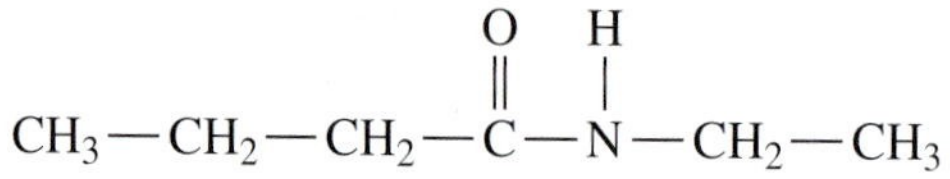

$$CH_3-CH_2-CH_2-\overset{\overset{O}{\|}}{C}-\overset{\overset{H}{|}}{N}-CH_2-CH_3$$

SOLUTION

Analyze the Problem

Functional Group	Amide	*N*-Substituent
Amide	Replace the *e* in the alkane name of the carboxyl portion with *amide*.	Ethyl

Guide to Naming Amides

1 Determine the alkane name of the carbon chain in the carboxyl portion and replace *e* with *amide*.

2 Name each substituent on the N atom using the prefix *N*- and the alkyl name.

Step 1 **Determine the alkane name of the carbon chain in the carboxyl portion and replace *e* with *amide*.**

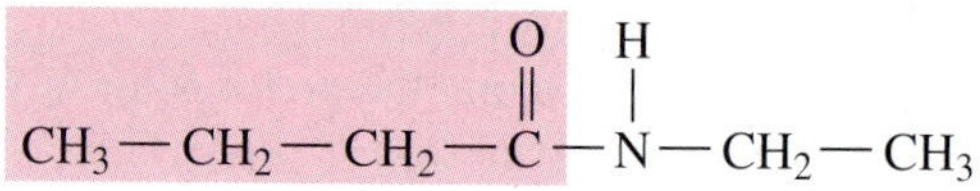

$$CH_3-CH_2-CH_2-\overset{\overset{O}{\|}}{C}-\overset{\overset{H}{|}}{N}-CH_2-CH_3$$ butanamide

Step 2 **Name each substituent on the N atom using the prefix *N*- and the alkyl name.**

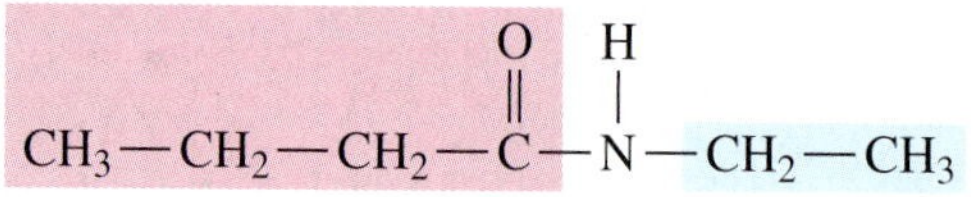

$$CH_3-CH_2-CH_2-\overset{\overset{O}{\|}}{C}-\overset{\overset{H}{|}}{N}-CH_2-CH_3$$ *N*-ethyl butanamide

STUDY CHECK 18.6

Draw the condensed structural formula for *N*,*N*-dimethylbenzamide.

Physical Properties of Amides

The amides do not have the properties of bases that we saw for the amines. Only methanamide is a liquid at room temperature, while the other amides are solids. For primary amides, the $-NH_2$ group can form more hydrogen bonds, which gives primary amides the highest melting points. The melting points of the secondary amides are lower because they form fewer hydrogen bonds. Because tertiary amides cannot form hydrogen bonds, they have the lowest melting points (see Table 18.2).

TABLE 18.2 **Melting Points of Selected Amides**		
Primary	**Secondary**	**Tertiary**
Methanamide 3 °C	*N*-methylmethanamide −3 °C	*N,N*-dimethylmethanamide −61 °C
Ethanamide 82 °C	*N*-methylethanamide 28 °C	*N,N*-dimethylethanamide −20 °C

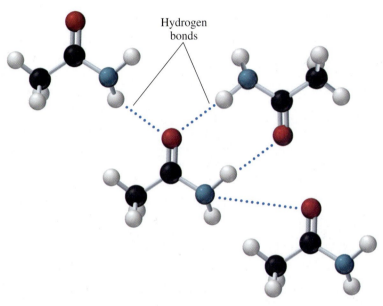

Hydrogen bonding between molecules of a primary amide.

The amides with one to five carbon atoms are soluble in water because they can hydrogen bond with water molecules.

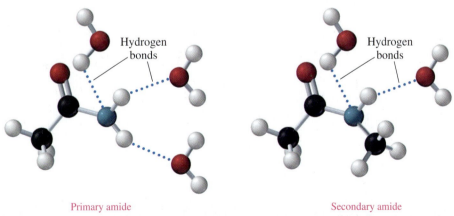

Primary amide   Secondary amide

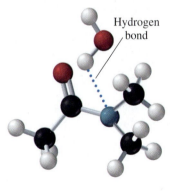

Tertiary amide

In water, primary amides form more hydrogen bonds than secondary and tertiary amides.

Chemistry Link to Health

AMIDES IN HEALTH AND MEDICINE

The simplest natural amide is urea, an end product of protein metabolism in the body. The kidneys remove urea from the blood and excrete it in urine. If the kidneys malfunction, urea is not removed and builds to a toxic level, a condition called *uremia*. Urea is also used as a component of fertilizer to increase nitrogen in the soil.

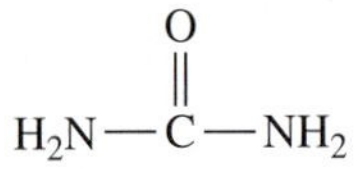

$$H_2N-\overset{\overset{\textstyle O}{\|}}{C}-NH_2$$
Urea

Synthetic amides are used as substitutes for sugar. Saccharin is a very powerful sweetener and is used as a sugar substitute. The sweetener aspartame is made from two amino acids, aspartic acid and phenylalanine, joined by an amide bond.

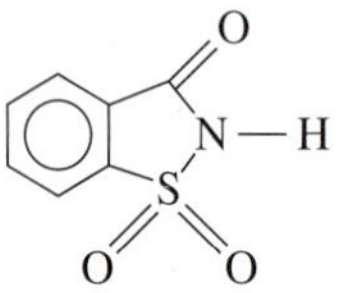

Saccharin

Amides are found in synthetic sweeteners, such as aspartame, and pain relievers, such as acetaminophen.

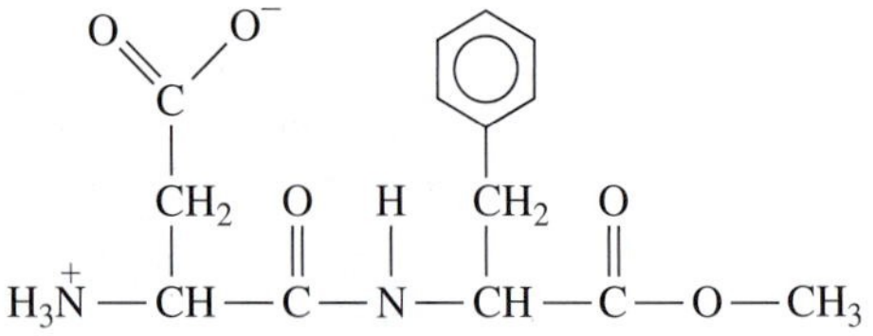

The compounds phenacetin and acetaminophen, which is used in Tylenol, reduce fever and pain, but they have little anti-inflammatory effect.

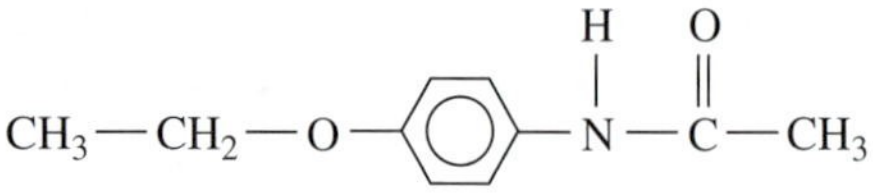

Phenacetin

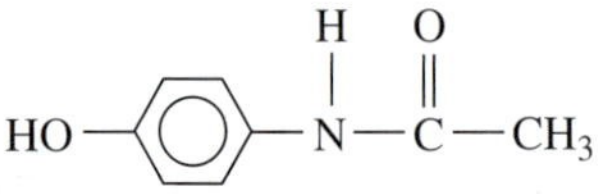

Acetaminophen

Many barbiturates are cyclic amides of barbituric acid that act as sedatives in small dosages or sleep inducers in larger dosages. They are often habit forming. Barbiturate drugs include phenobarbital (Luminal), pentobarbital (Nembutal), and secobarbital (Seconal). Other amides, such as meprobamate and diazepam, act as sedatives and tranquilizers.

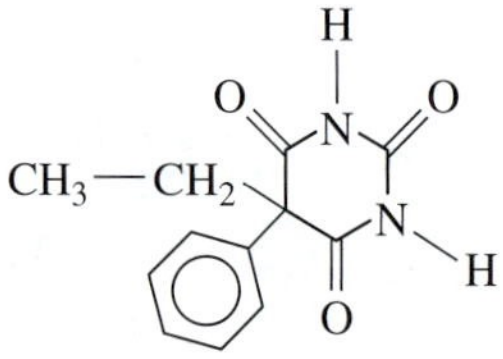

Phenobarbital 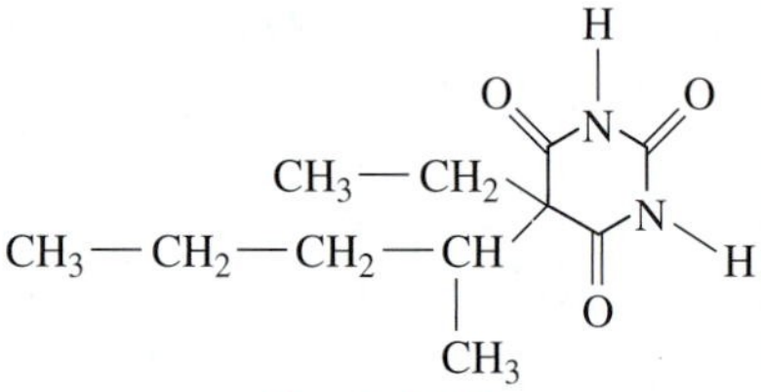   Pentobarbital

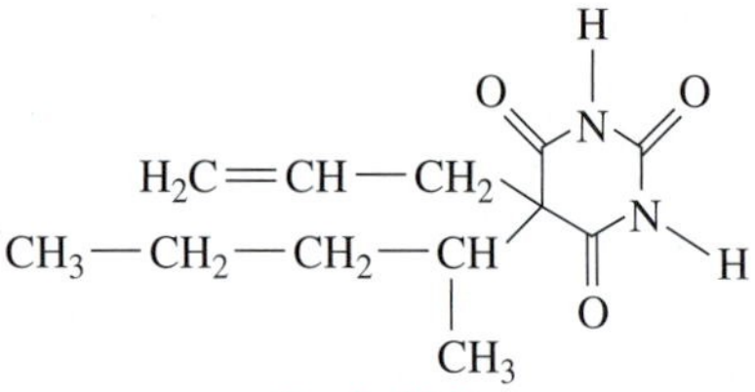

Secobarbital

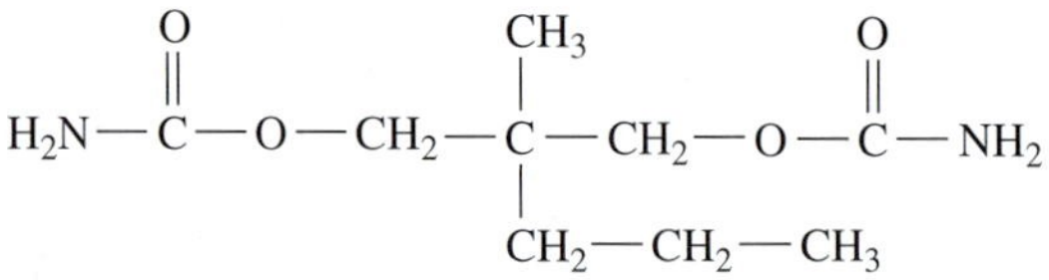

Aspartic acid   Phenylalanine   Methyl ester
Aspartame

Meprobamate

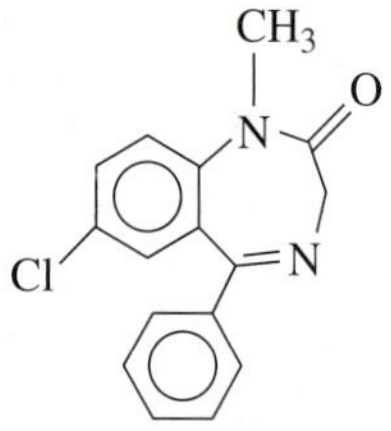

Diazepam

QUESTIONS AND PROBLEMS

18.4 Amides

LEARNING GOAL: *Write the amide products for amidation, and give their IUPAC and common names.*

18.29 Draw the condensed structural formula for the amide formed in each of the following reactions:

a. 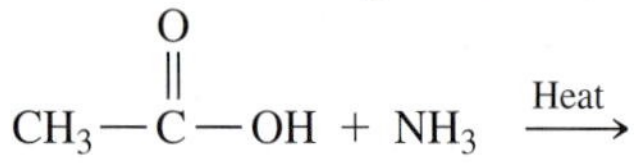 $CH_3-\overset{\overset{\textstyle O}{\|}}{C}-OH + NH_3 \xrightarrow{\text{Heat}}$

b. $CH_3-\overset{\overset{\textstyle O}{\|}}{C}-OH + H_2N-CH_2-CH_3 \xrightarrow{\text{Heat}}$

c. $\overset{\overset{\textstyle O}{\|}}{C}-OH + H_2N-CH_2-CH_2-CH_3 \xrightarrow{\text{Heat}}$

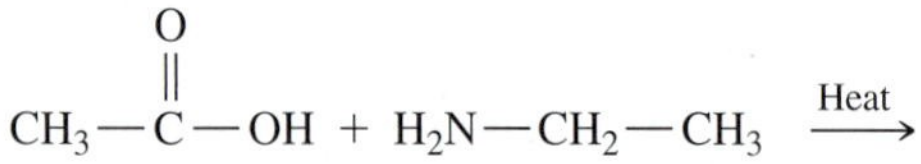

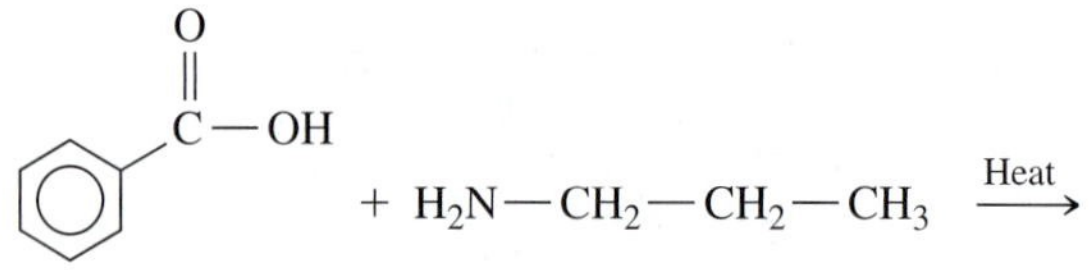

18.30 Draw the condensed structural formula for the amide formed in each of the following reactions:

a. $CH_3-CH_2-CH_2-CH_2-\overset{\overset{O}{\|}}{C}-OH + NH_3 \xrightarrow{\text{Heat}}$

b. $CH_3-\overset{\overset{CH_3}{|}}{CH}-\overset{\overset{O}{\|}}{C}-OH + H_2N-CH_2-CH_3 \xrightarrow{\text{Heat}}$

c. 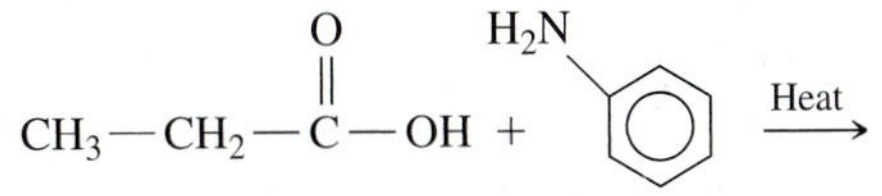 $CH_3-CH_2-\overset{\overset{O}{\|}}{C}-OH + \overset{H_2N}{\underset{}{\bigcirc}} \xrightarrow{\text{Heat}}$

18.31 Give the IUPAC and common names (if any) for each of the following amides:

a. $CH_3-\overset{\overset{O}{\|}}{C}-\overset{\overset{H}{|}}{N}-CH_3$

b. $CH_3-CH_2-CH_2-\overset{\overset{O}{\|}}{C}-NH_2$

c. $H-\overset{\overset{O}{\|}}{C}-NH_2$

d. 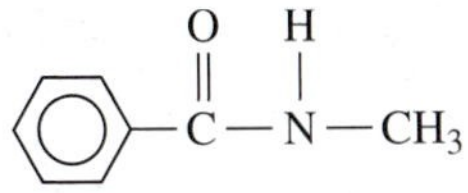 $\bigcirc-\overset{\overset{O}{\|}}{C}-\overset{\overset{H}{|}}{N}-CH_3$

18.32 Give the IUPAC and common names (if any) for the following amides:

a. $CH_3-CH_2-\overset{\overset{O}{\|}}{C}-\overset{\overset{H}{|}}{N}-CH_2-CH_3$

b. $CH_3-CH_2-CH_2-CH_2-CH_2-\overset{\overset{O}{\|}}{C}-NH_2$

c. $CH_3-\overset{\overset{O}{\|}}{C}-\overset{\overset{CH_3}{|}}{N}-CH_2-CH_2-CH_3$

d. 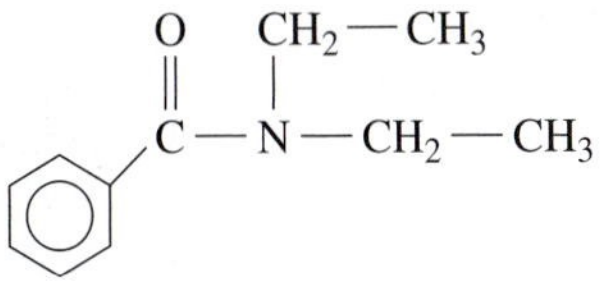 $\bigcirc-\overset{\overset{O}{\|}}{C}-\overset{\overset{CH_2-CH_3}{|}}{N}-CH_2-CH_3$

18.33 Draw the condensed structural formula for each of the following amides:
a. propionamide   **b.** pentanamide
c. N-ethylbenzamide   **d.** N-ethylbutyramide

18.34 Draw the condensed structural formula for each of the following amides:
a. N-ethyl-N-methylbenzamide   **b.** 3-methylbutanamide
c. hexanamide   **d.** N-propylpentanamide

18.35 For each of the following pairs, identify the compound that has the higher melting point. Explain.
a. ethanamide or N-methylethanamide
b. butane or propionamide
c. N,N-dimethylpropanamide or N-methylpropanamide

18.36 For each of the following pairs, identify the compound that has the higher melting point. Explain.
a. propane or ethanamide
b. N-methylethanamide or propanamide
c. N-ethylethanamide or N,N-dimethylethanamide

18.5 Hydrolysis of Amides

In a reverse reaction of amidation, **hydrolysis** occurs when water reacts with an amide in the presence of an acid, or a base reacts with an amide. In the acid hydrolysis of an amide, the products are the carboxylic acid and the ammonium salt. In the base hydrolysis, the products are the carboxylate salt and the amine or ammonia.

LEARNING GOAL

Write equations for the hydrolysis of amides.

TUTORIAL
Hydrolysis of Amides

Acid Hydrolysis of Amides

| Amide | | Carboxylic Acid | Ammonium Salt |

$\boxed{CH_3-\overset{\overset{O}{\|}}{C}}\boxed{\overset{\overset{H}{|}}{N}-H} + HOH + HCl \xrightarrow{\text{Heat}} \boxed{CH_3-\overset{\overset{O}{\|}}{C}-OH} + \boxed{H-\overset{\overset{H}{|}}{\underset{\underset{H}{|}}{\overset{+}{N}}}-H}\;Cl^-$

Ethanamide   Ethanoic acid   Ammonium
(acetamide)   (acetic acid)   chloride

Base Hydrolysis of Amides

| Amide | Carboxylate Salt | Amine |

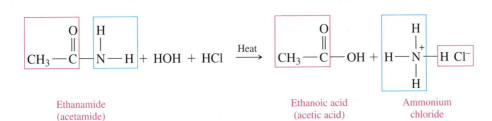

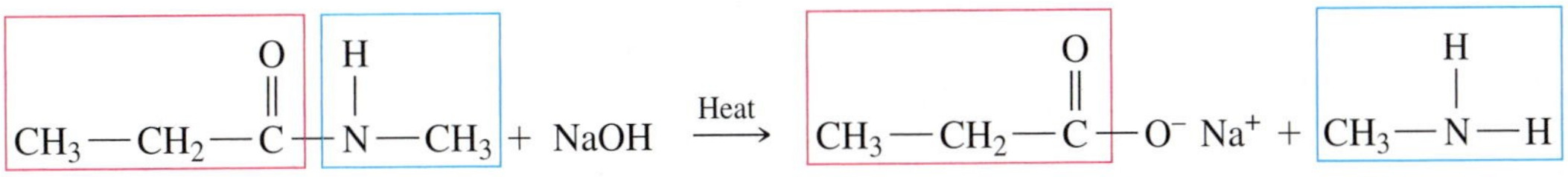

$\boxed{CH_3-CH_2-\overset{\overset{O}{\|}}{C}}\boxed{\overset{\overset{H}{|}}{N}-CH_3} + NaOH \xrightarrow{\text{Heat}} \boxed{CH_3-CH_2-\overset{\overset{O}{\|}}{C}-O^-\;Na^+} + \boxed{CH_3-\overset{\overset{H}{|}}{N}-H}$

N-Methylpropanamide   Sodium propanoate, a salt   Methanamine
(N-methylpropionamide)   (sodium propionate)   (methylamine)

CONCEPT CHECK 18.7 **Acid and Base Hydrolysis of Amides**

Give the names of the products that form when *N*-ethylpropanamide undergoes each of the following:

a. hydrolysis with HCl

b. hydrolysis with KOH

ANSWER

a. In acid (HCl) hydrolysis, the products are the corresponding carboxylic acid and the alkylammonium salt. The acid hydrolysis of *N*-ethylpropanamide with HCl forms propanoic acid (propionic acid) and ethylammonium chloride.

b. In base (KOH) hydrolysis, the products are the corresponding carboxylate salt and the amine. The base hydrolysis of *N*-ethylpropanamide with KOH forms potassium propanoate (potassium propionate) and ethanamine (ethylamine).

SAMPLE PROBLEM 18.7 **Hydrolysis of Amides**

Draw the condensed structural formulas and give the IUPAC names for the products of the hydrolysis of *N*-methylpentanamide with NaOH.

SOLUTION

In the hydrolysis of the amide, the amide bond is broken between the carboxyl carbon atom and the nitrogen atom. When a base such as NaOH is used, the products are the carboxylate salt and an amine.

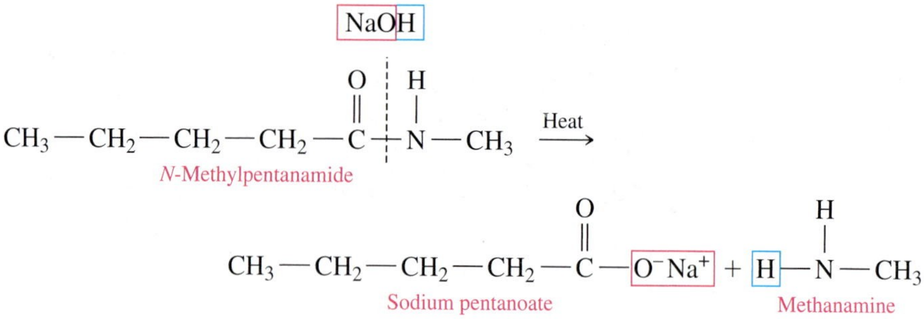

$$\text{NaOH}$$

$$\underset{\textit{N-Methylpentanamide}}{CH_3-CH_2-CH_2-CH_2-\overset{O}{\overset{\|}{C}}+\overset{H}{\underset{|}{N}}-CH_3} \xrightarrow{\text{Heat}}$$

$$CH_3-CH_2-CH_2-CH_2-\overset{O}{\overset{\|}{C}}-O^-Na^+ + H-\overset{H}{\underset{|}{N}}-CH_3$$

Sodium pentanoate   Methanamine

STUDY CHECK 18.7

Draw the condensed structural formulas for the products obtained from the hydrolysis of *N*-methylbutyramide with HBr.

QUESTIONS AND PROBLEMS

18.5 Hydrolysis of Amides

LEARNING GOAL: Write equations for the hydrolysis of amides.

18.37 Draw the condensed structural formulas for the products of the acid hydrolysis of each of the following with HCl:

a. 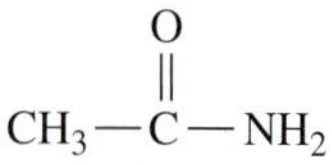 $CH_3-\overset{O}{\overset{\|}{C}}-NH_2$

b. $CH_3-CH_2-\overset{O}{\overset{\|}{C}}-NH_2$

c. $CH_3-CH_2-CH_2-\overset{O}{\overset{\|}{C}}-\overset{H}{\underset{|}{N}}-CH_3$

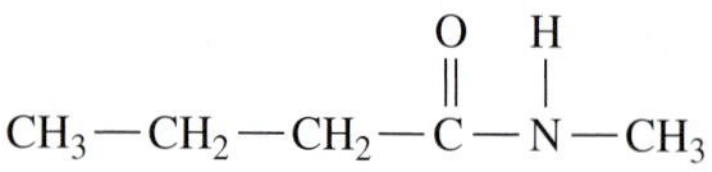

d. 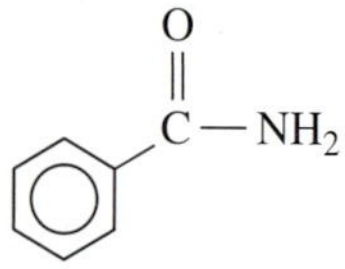 [benzene ring]$-\overset{O}{\overset{\|}{C}}-NH_2$

18.38 Draw the condensed structural formulas for the products of the base hydrolysis of each of the following with NaOH:

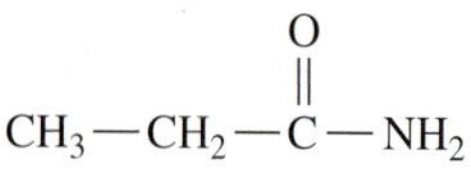

a. 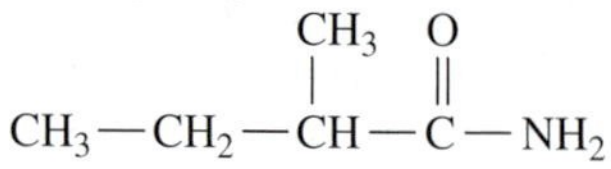 $CH_3-CH_2-\overset{CH_3}{\underset{|}{CH}}-\overset{O}{\overset{\|}{C}}-NH_2$

b. $CH_3-CH_2-CH_2-\overset{O}{\overset{\|}{C}}-\overset{CH_2-CH_3}{\underset{|}{N}}-CH_2-CH_3$

c. [benzene ring]$-\overset{O}{\overset{\|}{C}}-\overset{CH_3}{\underset{|}{N}}-CH_2-CH_2-CH_2-CH_3$

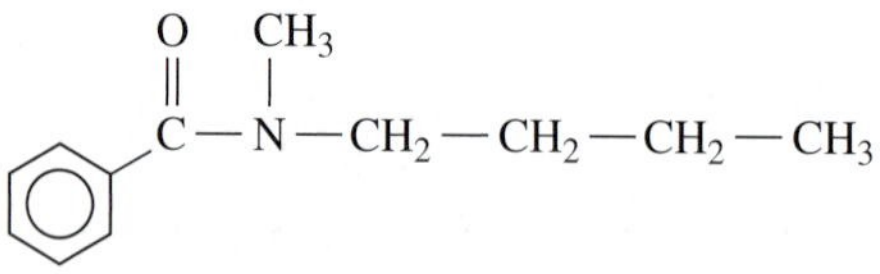

d. 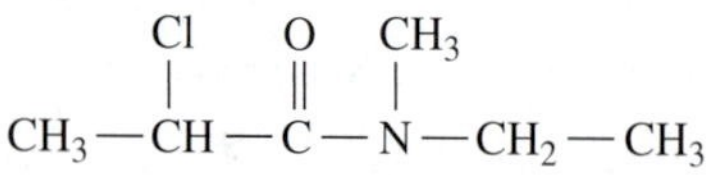 $CH_3-\overset{Cl}{\underset{|}{CH}}-\overset{O}{\overset{\|}{C}}-\overset{CH_3}{\underset{|}{N}}-CH_2-CH_3$

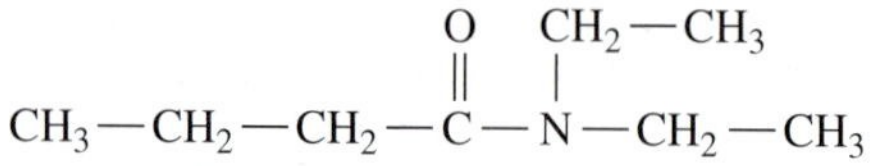

18.6 Neurotransmitters

A **neurotransmitter** is a chemical compound that transmits an impulse from a nerve cell (neuron) to a target cell such as another nerve cell, a muscle cell, or a gland cell. A typical neuron consists of a cell body and numerous filaments called *dendrites* at one end, and an axon that ends at the *axon terminal* at the opposite end. The axon terminals and the dendrites of other nerve cells form junctions called *synapses*. When an electrical signal reaches the axon terminal of a nerve cell, neurotransmitters are released into the synapse, which are taken up by the dendrites in nearby nerve cells. Thus, an alternating series of electrical impulses and chemical transmitters move information through a network of nerve cells in a very short period of time.

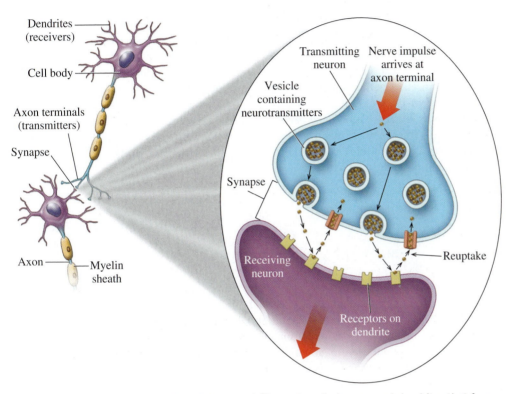

A nerve cell (neuron) consists of a cell body and filaments called axons and dendrites that form junctions (synapses) with nearby nerve cells to transmit nerve impulses.

Neurotransmitters at the Synapse

TUTORIAL
Neurotransmitters and How They Work

Within a nerve cell, a neurotransmitter is synthesized and stored in vesicles at the end of the axon terminal. There are many vesicles in a single filament, and each vesicle may contain several thousand molecules of a neurotransmitter. When a nerve impulse arrives at the nerve cell, it stimulates the vesicles to release the neurotransmitter into the synapse. The neurotransmitter molecules diffuse across the synapse to their receptor sites on the dendrites of another nerve cell. Neurotransmitters can be *excitatory*, which means they stimulate the receptors to send more nerve impulses, or *inhibitory*, which means they decrease the activity of the receptors. The binding of an excitatory neurotransmitter opens ion channels in nearby nerve cells. A flow of positive ions creates new electrical impulses that stimulate additional nerve cells to release the neurotransmitter from their vesicles into the synapse.

Termination of Neurotransmitter Action

Between nerve impulses, the neurotransmitters bound to the receptors are quickly removed to allow new signals to come from the adjacent nerve cells. The removal of neurotransmitters from the receptors can be done in different ways.

1. The neurotransmitter diffuses away from the synapse.
2. Enzymes in the receptors break down the neurotransmitter.
3. Reuptake returns the neurotransmitter to the vesicles where it is stored.

Amine Neurotransmitters

Neurotransmitters contain nitrogen atoms as amines and alkyl ammonium ions. Most are synthesized in a few steps from compounds such as amino acids obtained from our diets. The amino groups are usually ionized to form ammonium cations, and carboxyl groups are ionized to form carboxylate anions. In this section, we will draw these groups in their ionized form. Important amine neurotransmitters include acetylcholine, dopamine, norepinephrine (noradrenaline), epinephrine (adrenaline), serotonin, histamine, glutamate, and GABA.

TUTORIAL
The Role of Neurotransmitters in Health

Acetylcholine

Acetylcholine, the first neurotransmitter to be identified, communicates between the nervous system and the muscle, where it is involved in regulating muscle activation as well as learning and short-term memory. It is synthesized by forming an ester between choline and acetate, and is stored in the vesicles. When stimulated, acetylcholine is released into the synapse where it binds to receptors on the muscle cells and causes the muscles to contract. To enable continual nerve transmission, acetylcholine is quickly degraded by enzymes in the receptors that hydrolyze the ester bond. The loss of the acetylcholine at the receptors causes muscle cells to relax. The resulting choline and acetate are reconverted to acetylcholine and stored in the vesicles.

In older adults, a decrease in acetylcholine produces gaps in short-term memory. In Alzheimer's disease, the levels of acetylcholine may decrease by 90%, which causes severe loss of reasoning and motor function. Medications that are cholinesterase inhibitors such as Aricept are used to slow the enzymatic breakdown of acetylcholine in order to elevate the acetylcholine levels in the brain. Nicotine binds to the acetylcholine receptors, which enhances its effects.

Donepezil hydrochloride (Aricept)

Cholinesterase inhibitors slow the enzymatic breakdown of acetylcholine.

Nerve poisons such as Sarin, Soman, and Parathion bind to the acetylcholine esterase enzyme and inhibit its action. As a result, acetylcholine remains in the synapse and nerve transmissions stop. Because acetylcholine cannot be released, the muscles in the body cannot relax, and convulsions and respiratory failure soon occur.

Catecholamines

The word catecholamine refers to the catechol part (3,4-dihydroxyphenyl group) of these aromatic amines. The most important catecholamine neurotransmitters are dopamine, norepinephrine, and epinephrine, which are closely related in structure and all are synthesized from the amino acid tyrosine. In the diet, tyrosine is found in meats, nuts, eggs, and cheese.

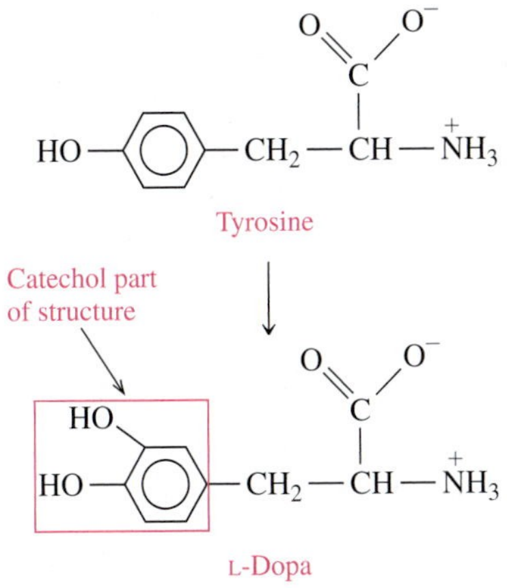

Tyrosine

Catechol part
of structure

L-Dopa

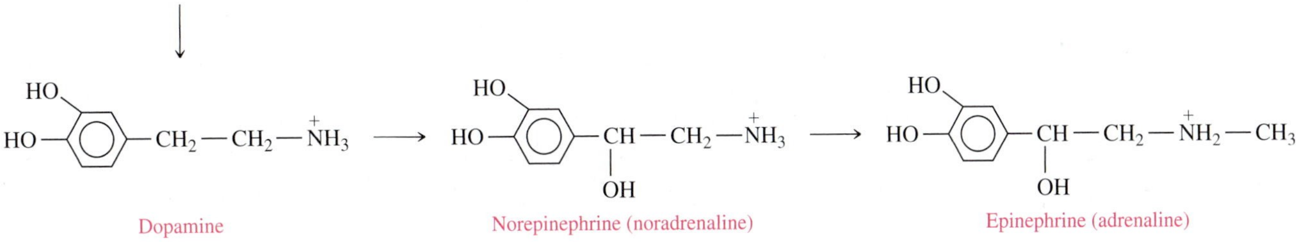

Neurotransmitters dopamine, norepinephrine, and epinephrine are synthesized from the amino acid tyrosine after it is converted to L-dopa.

Dopamine

Norepinephrine (noradrenaline)

Epinephrine (adrenaline)

Dopamine

Dopamine, which is produced in the nerve cells of the midbrain, works as a natural stimulant, to give us energy and feelings of enjoyment. It plays a role in controlling muscle movement, regulation of the sleep–wake cycle, and helps to improve cognition, attention, memory, and learning. High levels of dopamine may be involved in addictive behavior and schizophrenia. Cocaine and amphetamine block the reuptake of dopamine into the vesicles of the nerve cell. As a result, dopamine remains in the synapse longer. The addiction to cocaine may be a result of the extended exposure to high levels of dopamine in the synapses.

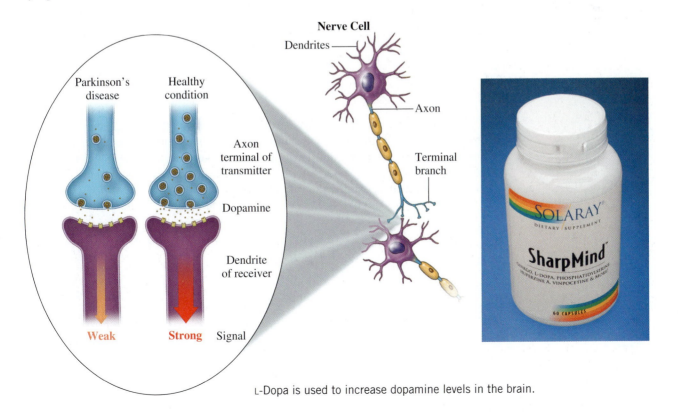

L-Dopa is used to increase dopamine levels in the brain.

In persons with Parkinson's disease, the midbrain nerve cells lose their ability to produce dopamine. As dopamine levels drop, there is a decrease in motor coordination, resulting in a slowing of movement and shuffling, rigidity of muscle, loss of cognition, and dementia. Although dopamine cannot cross the blood–brain barrier, persons with Parkinson's disease are given L-dopa, the precursor of dopamine, which does cross the blood–brain barrier.

TUTORIAL
How Epinephrine Delivers Its Message

Norepinephrine and Epinephrine

Norepinephrine (noradrenaline) and epinephrine (adrenaline) are hormonal neurotransmitters that play a role in sleep, attention and focus, and alertness. Epinephrine is synthesized from norepinephrine by the addition of a methyl group to the amine group. Norepinephrine (noradrenaline) and epinephrine (adrenaline) are normally produced in the adrenal glands, and are produced in large quantities when the stress of physical threat causes the fight-or-flight response. Then they cause an increase in blood pressure and heart rate, constrict blood vessels, dilate airways, and stimulate the breakdown of glycogen, which provides glucose and energy for the body. Because of its physiological effects, epinephrine is administered during cardiac arrest, and used as a bronchodilator during allergy or asthma attacks. As a neurotransmitter, low levels of norepinephrine as well as dopamine contribute to *attention deficit disorder (ADD)*. Medications such as Ritalin or Dexedrine may be prescribed to increases levels of norepinephrine and dopamine.

Serotonin

Serotonin (5-hydroxytryptamine) helps us to relax, sleep deeply and peacefully, think rationally, and gives us a feeling of well-being and calmness. Serotonin is synthesized from the amino acid tryptophan, which can cross the blood–brain barrier. A diet which contains foods such as eggs, fish, cheese, turkey, chicken, and beef, which have high levels of tryptophan, will increase serotonin levels. Foods with a low level of tryptophan, such as whole wheat, will lower serotonin levels. Psychedelic drugs such as LSD and mescaline stimulate the action of serotonin at its receptors.

Tryptophan (amino acid)   Serotonin $+ CO_2$

Low levels of serotonin in the brain may be associated with depression, anxiety disorders, obsessive-compulsive disorder, and eating disorders. Many antidepressant drugs, such as fluoxetine (Prozac) and paroxetine (Paxil), are selective serotonin reuptake inhibitors (SSRIs). When the reuptake of serotonin is slowed, it remains longer at the receptors, where it continues its action; the net effect is as if additional quantities of serotonin were taken.

Fluoxetine hydrochloride (Prozac)   Paroxetine hydrochloride (Paxil)

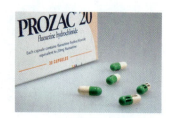

Prozac is one of the selective serotonin reuptake inhibitors (SSRIs) used to slow the reuptake of serotonin.

Histamine

Histamine is synthesized in the nerve cells in the hypothalamus from the amino acid histidine, when a carboxylate group is converted to CO_2. Histamine is produced by the immune system in response to pathogens and invaders, or injury. When histamine combines with histamine receptors, it causes allergic reactions, which may include inflammation, watery eyes, itchy skin, and hay fever. Histamine can also cause smooth muscle constriction, such as the closing of the trachea in persons allergic to shellfish. Histamine is also stored and released in the cells of the stomach, where it stimulates acid production. Antihistamines, such as Benadryl®, Zantac®, and Tagamet®, are used to block the histamine receptors and stop the allergic reactions.

Histidine $\xrightarrow{\text{Histidine decarboxylase}}$ Histamine $+\ CO_2$

Amino Acid Neurotransmitters

Glutamate is the most abundant neurotransmitter in the nervous system, where it is used to stimulate over 90% of the synapses. When glutamate binds to its receptor cells, it stimulates the synthesis of nitrogen oxide (NO), also a neurotransmitter in the brain. As NO reaches the transmitting nerve cells, more glutamate is released. Glutamate and NO are thought to be involved in learning and memory. Glutamate is used in many fast excitatory synapses in the brain and spinal cord. The reuptake of glutamate out of the synapse and back into the nerve cell occurs rapidly, which keeps glutamate levels low. If the reuptake of glutamate does not take place fast enough, a condition called *excitotoxicity* occurs in which excess glutamate at the receptors can destroy brain cells. In Lou Gehrig's disease (ALS), the production of an excessive amount of glutamate causes the degeneration of nerve cells in the spinal cord. As a result, a person with Lou Gehrig's disease suffers increasing weakness and muscular atrophy. When the reuptake of glutamate is too rapid, the levels of glutamate fall too low in the synapse, which may result in mental illness such as schizophrenia.

Glutamate $\longrightarrow$ Gamma (γ)-aminobutyric acid (GABA) $+\ CO_2$

Gamma(γ)-Aminobutyric Acid or GABA

Gamma(γ)-aminobutyric acid or GABA, which is produced from glutamate, is the most common inhibitory neurotransmitter in the brain. GABA produces a calming effect and reduces anxiety by inhibiting the ability of nerve cells to send electrical signals to nearby nerve cells. It is involved in the regulation of muscle tone, sleep, and anxiety. GABA can be obtained as a nutritional supplement. Medications such as benzodiazepines, and barbiturates such as phenobarbital, are used to increase GABA levels at the GABA receptors. Alcohol, sedatives, and tranquilizers increase the inhibitory effects of GABA. Caffeine

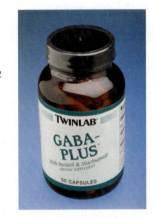

Glutamate is the major excitatory neurotransmitter, whereas GABA is the major inhibitory neurotransmitter.

decreases the GABA levels in the synapses, leading to conditions of anxiety and sleep problems.

Table 18.3 summarizes the properties and functions of selected neurotransmitters we have discussed.

TABLE 18.3 Selected Neurotransmitters

Amine Transmitters	Synthesized from	Site of Synthesis	Function	Effect Enhanced by
Acetylcholine	Acetyl-CoA and choline	Central nervous system	Excitatory: regulates muscle activation, learning, and short-term memory	Nicotine
Dopamine	Tyrosine	Central nervous system	Excitatory and inhibitory: regulates muscle movement, cognition, sleep, mood, and learning; deficiency leads to Parkinson's disease and schizophrenia	L-dopa, amphetamines, cocaine
Norepinephrine	Tyrosine	Central nervous system	Excitatory and inhibitory: sleep, focus, and alertness	Ritalin, Dexedrine
Epinephrine	Tyrosine	Adrenal glands	Excitatory: plays a role in sleep and being alert, and is involved the fight-or-flight response	Ritalin, Dexedrine
Serotonin	Tryptophan	Central nervous system	Inhibitory: regulates anxiety, eating, mood, sleep, learning, and memory	LSD; Prozac and Paxil blocks its action to relieve anxiety
Histamine	Histidine	Central nervous system: hypothalamus	Inhibitory: involved in allergic reactions, inflammation, and hay fever	Antihistamines
Amino Acid Transmitters				
Glutamate		Central nervous system: spinal cord	Excitatory: involved in learning and memory; main excitatory neurotransmitter in brain	Alcohol
GABA	Glutamate	Central nervous system: brain, hypothalamus	Inhibitory: regulates muscle tone, sleep, and anxiety	Alcohol, sedatives, tranquilizers; synthesis blocked by antianxiety drugs (benzodiazepines); caffeine decreases GABA levels in synapse

QUESTIONS AND PROBLEMS

18.6 Neurotransmitters

LEARNING GOAL: *Describe the role of amines as neurotransmitters.*

18.39 What is a neurotransmitter?

18.40 Where are the neurotransmitters stored in a neuron?

18.41 When is a neurotransmitter released into the synapse?

18.42 What happens to a neurotransmitter once it is in the synapse?

18.43 Why is it important to remove a neurotransmitter from its receptor?

18.44 What are three ways in which a neurotransmitter can be separated from a receptor?

18.45 What is the role of acetylcholine?

18.46 What are some physiological effects of low levels of acetylcholine?

18.47 What is the function of dopamine in the body?

18.48 What are some physiological effects of low levels of dopamine?

18.49 What is the function of serotonin in the body?

18.50 What are the physiological effects of low serotonin?

18.51 What is the function of histamine in the body?

18.52 How do antihistamines stop the action of histamine?

18.53 Why is it important that the levels of glutamate in the synapse remain low?

18.54 What happens if there is an excess of glutamate in the synapse?

18.55 What is the function of GABA in the body?

18.56 What is the effect of caffeine on GABA levels?

CONCEPT MAP

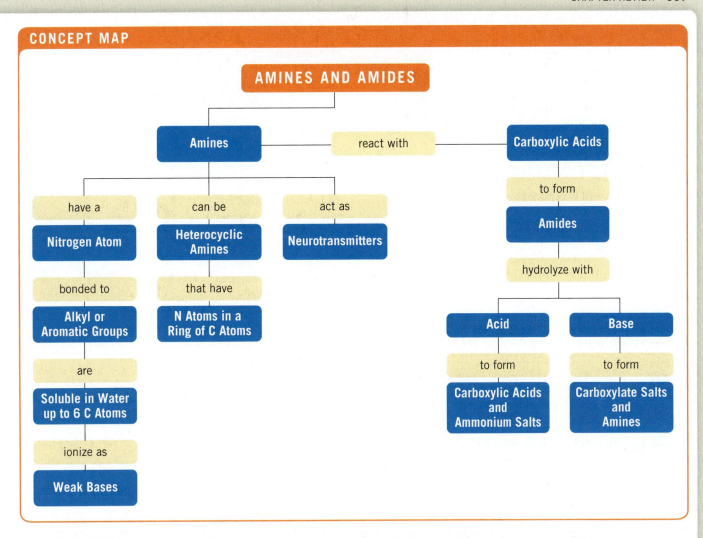

AMINES AND AMIDES

- **Amines** — react with — **Carboxylic Acids**

Amines:
- **have a** → **Nitrogen Atom** → bonded to → **Alkyl or Aromatic Groups** → are → **Soluble in Water up to 6 C Atoms** → ionize as → **Weak Bases**
- **can be** → **Heterocyclic Amines** → that have → **N Atoms in a Ring of C Atoms**
- **act as** → **Neurotransmitters**

Carboxylic Acids:
- to form → **Amides** → hydrolyze with → **Acid** / **Base**
  - Acid → to form → **Carboxylic Acids and Ammonium Salts**
  - Base → to form → **Carboxylate Salts and Amines**

CHAPTER REVIEW

18.1 Amines

LEARNING GOAL: Name amines using IUPAC and common names; draw the condensed structural formulas given the names. Classify amines as primary (1°), secondary (2°), or tertiary (3°).

Dimethylamine

- In the IUPAC system, the *amine* suffix is added to the alkane name (after dropping the *e*) of the longer carbon chain. Groups attached to the nitrogen atom use the *N-* prefix.
- When other functional groups are present, the —NH₂ is named as an amino group.
- In the common names of simple amines, the alkyl groups are listed alphabetically followed by the suffix *amine*.
- A nitrogen atom attached to one, two, or three alkyl or aromatic groups forms a primary (1°), secondary (2°), or tertiary (3°) amine.

18.2 Properties of Amines

LEARNING GOAL: Describe the boiling points and solubility of amines; write equations for the ionization and neutralization of amines.

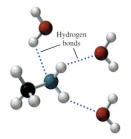

Hydrogen bonds

- Primary and secondary amines form hydrogen bonds, which make their

boiling points higher than those of alkanes of similar mass, but lower than those of alcohols.
- Amines with up to six carbon atoms are soluble in water.
- In water, amines act as weak bases because the nitrogen atom accepts a proton from water to produce ammonium and hydroxide ions.
- When amines react with acids, they form ammonium salts. As ionic compounds, ammonium salts are solids, soluble in water, and odorless.
- Quaternary (4°) ammonium salts contain four carbon groups bonded to the nitrogen atom.

18.3 Heterocyclic Amines

LEARNING GOAL: Identify heterocyclic amines; distinguish between the types of heterocyclic amines.

- Heterocyclic amines are cyclic organic compounds that contain one or more nitrogen atoms in the ring.
- Heterocyclic amines typically consist of five or six atoms and one or more nitrogen atoms.
- Many heterocyclic compounds are known for their physiological activity.
- Alkaloids such as caffeine and nicotine are physiologically active amines derived from plants.

18.4 Amides

LEARNING GOAL: *Write the amide products for amidation, and give their IUPAC and common names.*

- Amides are derivatives of carboxylic acids in which the hydroxyl group is replaced by $-NH_2$ or a primary or secondary amine group.
- Amides are formed when carboxylic acids react with ammonia or primary or secondary amines in the presence of heat.
- Amides are named by replacing the *ic acid* or *oic acid* from the carboxylic acid name with *amide*. Any carbon group attached to the nitrogen atom is named using the *N-* prefix.

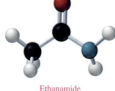
Ethanamide
(acetamide)

18.5 Hydrolysis of Amides

LEARNING GOAL: *Write equations for the hydrolysis of amides.*

$$CH_3-\overset{\overset{\displaystyle O}{\|}}{C}-NH_2 + HOH + HCl \longrightarrow CH_3-\overset{\overset{\displaystyle O}{\|}}{C}-OH + NH_4{}^+Cl^-$$

Ethanamide   Ethanoic acid   Ammonium
(acetamide)   (acetic acid)   chloride

- Hydrolysis of an amide by an acid produces a carboxylic acid and an ammonium salt.
- Hydrolysis of an amide by a base produces the carboxylate salt and an amine.

18.6 Neurotransmitters

LEARNING GOAL: *Describe the role of amines as neurotransmitters.*

- Neurotransmitters are chemicals that transfer a signal between nerve cells.

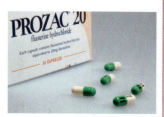

SUMMARY OF NAMING

Family	Condensed Structural Formula	IUPAC Name	Common Name
Amine	$CH_3-CH_2-NH_2$	Ethanamine	Ethylamine
	$CH_3-CH_2-NH-CH_3$	*N*-Methylethanamine	Ethylmethylamine
Ammonium salt	$CH_3-CH_2-\overset{+}{N}H_3\ Cl^-$	Ethylammonium chloride	Ethylammonium chloride
Amide	$CH_3-\overset{\overset{\displaystyle O}{\|}}{C}-NH_2$	Ethanamide	Acetamide

---

SUMMARY OF REACTIONS

Ionization of Amines in Water

$$CH_3-\overset{\overset{\displaystyle H}{|}}{\underset{\underset{\displaystyle H}{|}}{N}} + HOH \rightleftharpoons CH_3-\overset{\overset{\displaystyle H}{|}}{\underset{\underset{\displaystyle H}{|}}{\overset{+}{N}}}-H + OH^-$$

Methylamine   Methylammonium   Hydroxide
                             ion   ion

Formation of Ammonium Salts

$$CH_3-\overset{\overset{\displaystyle H}{|}}{\underset{\underset{\displaystyle H}{|}}{N}} + HCl \longrightarrow CH_3-\overset{\overset{\displaystyle H}{|}}{\underset{\underset{\displaystyle H}{|}}{\overset{+}{N}}}-H\ Cl^-$$

Methylamine   Methylammonium chloride

Formation of Amides

$$CH_3-CH_2-\overset{\overset{\displaystyle O}{\|}}{C}-OH + H-\overset{\overset{\displaystyle H}{|}}{N}-H \xrightarrow{\text{Heat}} CH_3-CH_2-\overset{\overset{\displaystyle O}{\|}}{C}-\overset{\overset{\displaystyle H}{|}}{N}-H + H_2O$$

Propanoic acid   Ammonia   Propanamide
(propionic acid)   (propionamide)

$$CH_3-CH_2-\overset{\overset{\displaystyle O}{\|}}{C}-OH + H-\overset{\overset{\displaystyle H}{|}}{N}-CH_3 \xrightarrow{\text{Heat}} CH_3-CH_2-\overset{\overset{\displaystyle O}{\|}}{C}-\overset{\overset{\displaystyle H}{|}}{N}-CH_3 + H_2O$$

Propanoic acid   Methanamine   *N*-Methylpropanamide
(propionic acid)   (methylamine)   (*N*-methylpropionamide)

Acid Hydrolysis of Amides

$$CH_3 - \overset{\overset{\displaystyle O}{\|}}{C} - NH_2 + HOH + HCl \xrightarrow{\text{Heat}} CH_3 - \overset{\overset{\displaystyle O}{\|}}{C} - OH + NH_4^+ \ Cl^-$$

Ethanamide   Ethanoic acid   Ammonium
(acetamide)   (acetic acid)   chloride

Base Hydrolysis of Amides

$$CH_3 - CH_2 - \overset{\overset{\displaystyle O}{\|}}{C} - \overset{\overset{\displaystyle H}{|}}{N} - CH_3 + NaOH \xrightarrow{\text{Heat}} CH_3 - CH_2 - \overset{\overset{\displaystyle O}{\|}}{C} - O^- \ Na^+ + H_2N - CH_3$$

N-Methylpropanamide   Sodium propanoate   Methanamine
(*N*-methylpropionamide)   (sodium propionate)   (methylamine)

KEY TERMS

alkaloid An amine having physiological activity that is produced in plants.

amidation The formation of an amide from a carboxylic acid and ammonia or an amine.

amide An organic compound containing the carbonyl group attached to an amino group or a substituted nitrogen atom.

amine An organic compound containing a nitrogen atom attached to one, two, or three alkyl or aromatic groups.

ammonium salt An ionic compound produced from an amine and an acid.

heterocyclic amine A cyclic organic compound that contains one or more nitrogen atoms in the ring.

hydrolysis The splitting of a molecule by the addition of water. Amides yield the corresponding carboxylic acid and amine, or their salts.

neurotransmitter A chemical compound that transmits an impulse from a nerve cell (neuron) to a target cell such as another nerve cell, a muscle cell, or a gland cell.

quaternary ammonium salt An ammonium salt in which the nitrogen atom is bonded to four carbon groups.

UNDERSTANDING THE CONCEPTS

The chapter sections to review are shown in parentheses at the end of each question.

18.57 The sweetener aspartame is made from two amino acids: aspartic acid and phenylalanine. Identify the functional groups in aspartame. (11.5, 18.2, 18.4)

Aspartame

18.58 Some aspirin substitutes contain phenacetin to reduce fever. Identify the functional groups in phenacetin. (11.5, 18.4)

$$CH_3 - CH_2 - O - \overset{}{\bigcirc} - NH - \overset{\overset{\displaystyle O}{\|}}{C} - CH_3$$

Phenacetin

18.59 Neo-Synephrine is the active ingredient in some nose sprays used to reduce the swelling of nasal membranes. Identify the functional groups in Neo-Synephrine. (11.5, 18.2)

Neo-Synephrine

18.60 Melatonin is a naturally occurring compound in plants and animals, where it regulates the biological time clock. Melatonin is sometimes used to counteract jet lag. Identify the functional groups in melatonin. (11.5, 18.2)

Melatonin

18.61 The insect repellent DEET can be formed from the amidation of 3-methylbenzoic acid by *N,N*-diethylamine. Draw the condensed structural formula for DEET. (16.1, 18.1, 18.4)

18.62 Nylon 66 is a polymer used to make shirts and jackets. The condensed structural formula for one unit of Nylon 66 is shown below. Draw the condensed structural formulas for the carboxylic acid and amine that are polymerized to make Nylon 66. (16.1, 18.1, 18.4)

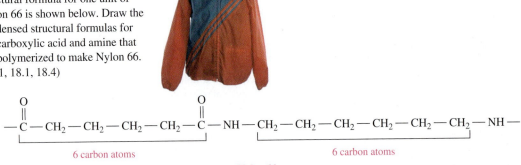

6 carbon atoms   6 carbon atoms

Nylon 66

18.63 What is an excitatory neurotransmitter? (18.6)

18.64 What is an inhibitory neurotransmitter? (18.6)

18.65 Identify the structural components that are the same in dopamine, norepinephrine, and epinephrine. (18.6)

18.66 Identify the structural components that are different in dopamine, norepinephrine, and epinephrine. (18.6)

ADDITIONAL QUESTIONS AND PROBLEMS

For instructor-assigned homework, go to www.masteringchemistry.com.

18.67 Give the IUPAC and common names (if any) and classify each of the following compounds as a primary (1°), secondary (2°), tertiary (3°) amine, or as a quaternary (4°) ammonium salt: (18.1, 18.2)

a. 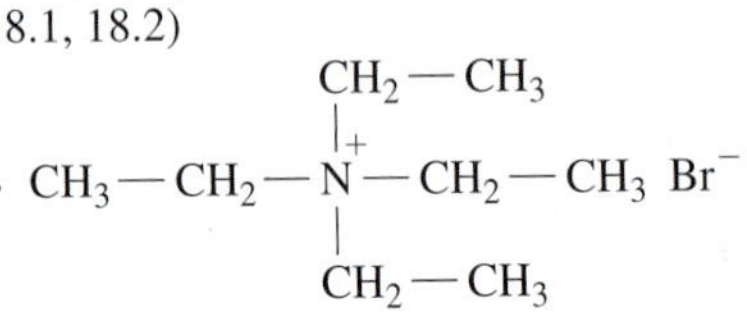 $CH_3-CH_2-\overset{\overset{\displaystyle CH_2-CH_3}{|+}}{\underset{\underset{\displaystyle CH_2-CH_3}{|}}{N}}-CH_2-CH_3 \ Br^-$

b. $CH_3-CH_2-CH_2-CH_2-CH_2-NH_2$

c. $CH_3-CH_2-CH_2-NH-CH_2-CH_3$

18.68 Give the IUPAC and common names (if any) and classify each of the following compounds as a primary (1°), secondary (2°), tertiary (3°) amine, or as a quaternary (4°) ammonium salt: (18.1, 18.2)

a. 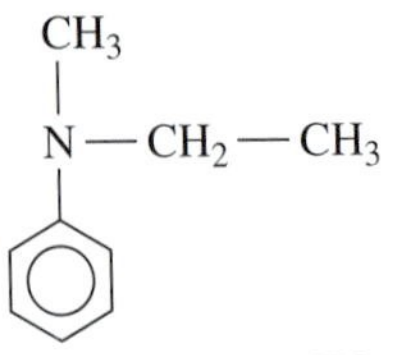 $\underset{\bigcirc}{\overset{\overset{\displaystyle CH_3}{|}}{N}}-CH_2-CH_3$

b. 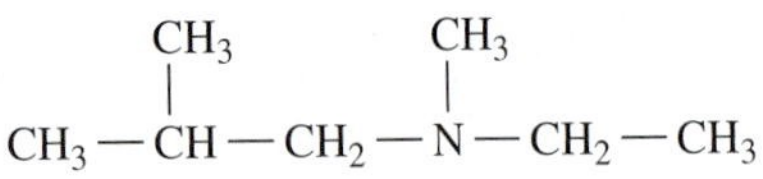 $CH_3-\overset{\overset{\displaystyle CH_3}{|}}{CH}-CH_2-\overset{\overset{\displaystyle CH_3}{|}}{N}-CH_2-CH_3$

c. 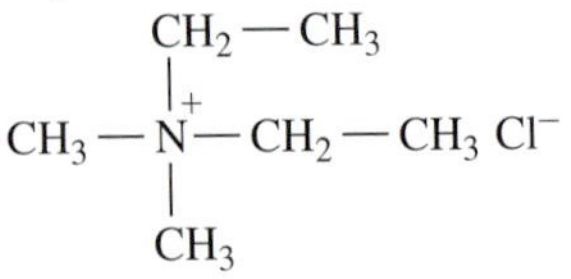 $CH_3-\overset{\overset{\displaystyle CH_2-CH_3}{|+}}{\underset{\underset{\displaystyle CH_3}{|}}{N}}-CH_2-CH_3 \ Cl^-$

18.69 Draw the condensed structural formula for each of the following compounds: (18.1, 18.2)
a. 3-pentanamine
b. cyclohexylamine
c. dimethylammonium chloride
d. triethylamine

18.70 Draw the condensed structural formula for each of the following compounds: (18.1, 18.2)
a. 3-amino-2-hexanol
b. tetramethylammonium bromide
c. *N,N*-dimethylaniline
d. butylethylmethylamine

18.71 In each of the following pairs, indicate the compound that has the higher boiling point. Explain. (18.1, 18.3)
a. 1-butanol or butanamine
b. ethylamine or dimethylamine

18.72 In each of the following pairs, indicate the compound that has the higher boiling point. Explain. (18.1, 18.3)
a. butylamine or diethylamine
b. butane or propylamine

18.73 In each of the following pairs, indicate the compound that is more soluble in water. Explain. (18.1, 18.3)
a. ethylamine or dibutylamine
b. trimethylamine or *N*-ethylcyclohexylamine

18.74 In each of the following pairs, indicate the compound that is more soluble in water. Explain. (18.1, 18.3)
a. butylamine or pentane **b.** butyramide or hexane

18.75 Give the IUPAC name for each of the following amides: (18.4)

a. 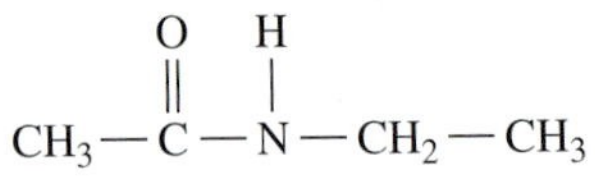 $CH_3-\overset{\overset{\displaystyle O}{||}}{C}-\overset{\overset{\displaystyle H}{|}}{N}-CH_2-CH_3$

b. $CH_3-CH_2-\overset{\overset{\displaystyle O}{||}}{C}-NH_2$

c. $CH_3-\overset{\overset{\displaystyle CH_3}{|}}{CH}-CH_2-\overset{\overset{\displaystyle O}{||}}{C}-NH_2$

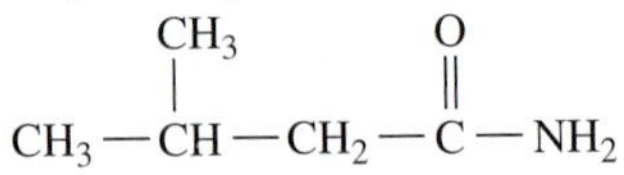

18.76 Give the IUPAC name for each of the following amides: (18.4)

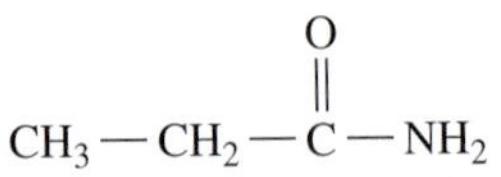

a. 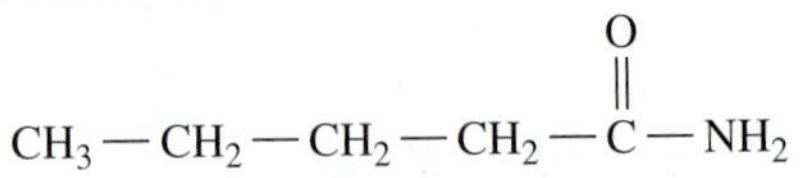 $CH_3-CH_2-CH_2-CH_2-\overset{\overset{\displaystyle O}{||}}{C}-NH_2$

b. $CH_3-\overset{\overset{\displaystyle O}{||}}{C}-\overset{\overset{\displaystyle CH_3}{|}}{N}-CH_2-CH_2-CH_2-CH_3$

c. $CH_3-\overset{\overset{\displaystyle O}{||}}{C}-\overset{\overset{\displaystyle CH_3}{|}}{N}-CH_3$

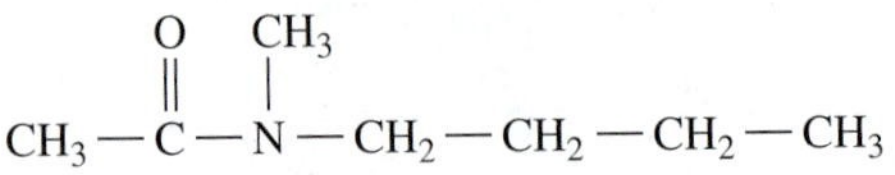

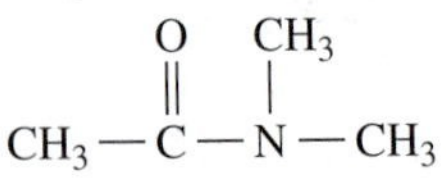

18.77 Give the name of the alkaloid described in each of the following: (18.3)
  a. from the bark of the cinchona tree and used in malaria treatment
  b. found in tobacco
  c. found in coffee and tea
  d. a painkiller found in the opium poppy plant

18.78 Identify the heterocyclic amine(s) in each of the following: (18.3)
  a. caffeine
  b. Demerol (meperidine)
  c. coniine
  d. quinine

18.79 Draw the condensed structural formulas for the products of the following reactions: (18.2)

  a. $CH_3-CH_2-\overset{\overset{\displaystyle CH_3}{|}}{\underset{+}{N}H_2}\ Cl^- + NaOH \longrightarrow$

  b. $CH_3-CH_2-NH-CH_3 + H_2O \rightleftharpoons$

18.80 Draw the condensed structural formulas for the products of the following reactions: (18.2)
  a. $CH_3-CH_2-NH-CH_3 + HCl \longrightarrow$
  b. $CH_3-CH_2-CH_2-\overset{+}{N}H_3Cl^- + NaOH \longrightarrow$

18.81 Voltaren (diclofenac) is indicated for acute and chronic treatment of the symptoms of rheumatoid arthritis. Name the functional groups in the voltaren molecule. (11.5, 18.2, 18.4)

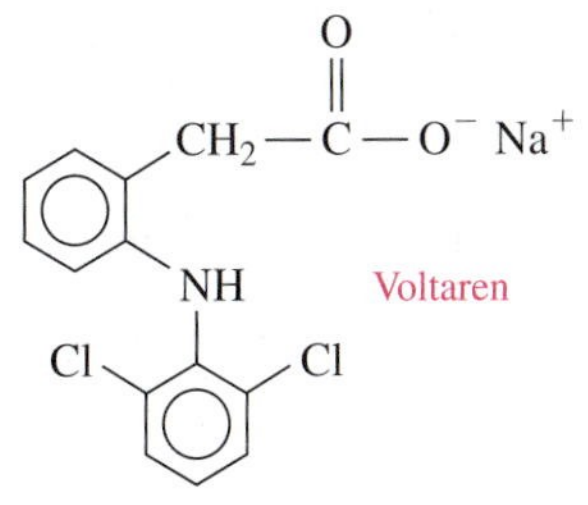

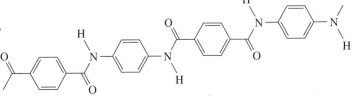

Voltaren

18.82 Toradol (ketorolac) is used in dentistry to relieve pain. Name the functional groups in toradol. (11.5, 18.2, 18.4)

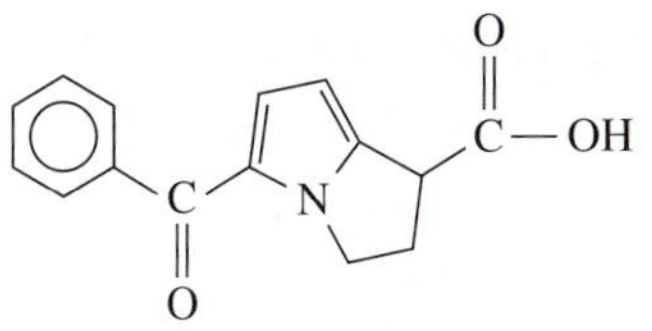

Toradol

18.83 What is the structural difference between tryptophan and serotonin? (18.6)

18.84 What is the structural difference between histidine and histamine? (18.6)

18.85 What does the abbreviation SSRI signify? (18.6)

18.86 Give an example of an SSRI and its role in treating depression. (18.6)

CHALLENGE QUESTIONS

18.87 There are four amine isomers with the molecular formula C_3H_9N. Draw their condensed structural formulas. Give the common name and classify each as a primary (1°), secondary (2°), or tertiary (3°) amine. (18.1)

18.88 There are four amide isomers with the molecular formula C_3H_7NO. Draw their condensed structural formulas. (18.4)

18.89 Use the Internet or a reference book such as the *Merck Index* or *Physicians' Desk Reference* to look up the structural formula for the following medicinal drugs. List the functional groups in each compound. (11.5, 18.2, 18.4)
  a. Keflex, an antibiotic (cefalexin)
  b. Inderal, a β-channel blocker used to treat heart irregularities (propranolol)
  c. Ibuprofen, an anti-inflammatory agent
  d. Aldomet (methyldopa)
  e. OxyContin (oxycodone), a narcotic pain reliever
  f. Triamterene, a diuretic

18.90 Kevlar is a lightweight polymer used in tires and bullet-proof vests. Part of the strength of Kevlar is due to hydrogen bonds between polymer chains. The polymer chain is: (16.1, 18.1, 18.4)

Poly-paraphenylene terephthalamide (Kevlar)

  a. Draw the condensed structural formulas for the carboxylic acid and amine that polymerize to make Kevlar.
  b. What feature of Kevlar will give the hydrogen bonds between the polymer chains?

18.91 Why is L-dopa, not dopamine, given to persons with low dopamine levels? (18.6)

18.92 How does cocaine increase the dopamine levels in the synapse? (18.6)

ANSWERS

Answers to Study Checks

18.1 $CH_3-CH_2-CH_2-\overset{\overset{\displaystyle H}{|}}{N}-CH_2-CH_3$

18.2 $CH_3-CH_2-\overset{\overset{\displaystyle NH_2}{|}}{CH}-CH_2-\overset{\overset{\displaystyle O}{||}}{C}-H$

18.3 tertiary (3°)

18.4 $CH_3-\overset{\overset{\displaystyle CH_3}{|}}{\underset{\underset{\displaystyle CH_3}{|}}{\overset{+}{N}}}-H\ Cl^-$

18.5 H—C(=O)—OH   and   H—N(CH$_3$)—CH$_3$

18.6 (phenyl)—C(=O)—N(CH$_3$)—CH$_3$

18.7 CH$_3$—CH$_2$—CH$_2$—C(=O)—OH   and   CH$_3$—$\overset{+}{N}$H$_3$ Br$^-$

Answers to Selected Questions and Problems

18.1 In a primary amine, there is one alkyl group (and two hydrogens) attached to a nitrogen atom.

18.3 **a.** primary (1°)
b. secondary (2°)
c. primary (1°)
d. tertiary (3°)
e. tertiary (3°)

18.5 **a.** ethanamine, ethylamine
b. N-methyl-1-propanamine, methylpropylamine
c. N-ethyl-N-methylethanamine, diethylmethylamine
d. 2-propanamine, isopropylamine

18.7 **a.** 4-aminopentanoic acid
b. 2-chloroaniline
c. 3-aminopropanal
d. 5-amino-3-hexanol

18.9 **a.** Cl—CH$_2$—CH$_2$—NH$_2$
b. (phenyl with N—CH$_3$ and H)
b. CH$_3$—CH$_2$—CH$_2$—CH$_2$—N—CH$_2$—CH$_2$—CH$_3$
c. CH$_3$—CH$_2$—CH(NH$_2$)—C(=O)—H

18.11 **a.** CH$_3$—CH$_2$—OH has a higher boiling point because the —OH group forms stronger hydrogen bonds than the —NH$_2$ group.
b. CH$_3$—CH$_2$—CH$_2$—NH$_2$ has the higher boiling point because it has a greater molar mass.
c. CH$_3$—CH$_2$—CH$_2$—NH$_2$ has the higher boiling point because it is a primary amine that forms hydrogen bonds. A tertiary amine cannot form hydrogen bonds with other tertiary amines.

18.13 As a primary amine, propylamine can form two hydrogen bonds, which gives it the highest boiling point. Ethylmethylamine, a secondary amine, can form one hydrogen bond, and butane cannot form hydrogen bonds. Thus, butane has the lowest boiling point of the three compounds.

18.15 **a.** Yes, amines with fewer than seven carbon atoms are soluble in water.
b. Yes, amines with fewer than seven carbon atoms are soluble in water.
c. No, an amine with nine carbon atoms is not soluble in water.
d. Yes, amines with fewer than seven carbon atoms are soluble in water.

18.17 **a.** CH$_3$—NH$_2$ + H$_2$O $\rightleftharpoons$ CH$_3$—$\overset{+}{N}$H$_3$ + OH$^-$
b. CH$_3$—NH—CH$_3$ + H$_2$O $\rightleftharpoons$ CH$_3$—$\overset{+}{N}$H$_2$—CH$_3$ + OH$^-$

c. (aniline, NH$_2$) + H$_2$O $\rightleftharpoons$ (anilinium, $\overset{+}{N}$H$_3$) + OH$^-$

18.19 **a.** CH$_3$—$\overset{+}{N}$H$_3$ Cl$^-$
b. CH$_3$—$\overset{+}{N}$H$_2$—CH$_3$ Cl$^-$
c. (phenyl with $\overset{+}{N}$H$_3$ Cl$^-$)

18.21 **a.** H$_2$N—(phenyl)—C(=O)—O—CH$_2$—CH$_2$—$\overset{+}{N}$H(CH$_2$—CH$_3$)(CH$_2$—CH$_3$) Cl$^-$
b. The ammonium salt (Novocain) is more soluble in aqueous body fluids than procaine.

18.23 **a.** piperidine   **b.** pyrimidine   **c.** pyrrole

18.25 piperidine

18.27 pyrrole

18.29 **a.** CH$_3$—C(=O)—NH$_2$
b. CH$_3$—C(=O)—N(H)—CH$_2$—CH$_3$
c. (phenyl)—C(=O)—N(H)—CH$_2$—CH$_2$—CH$_3$

18.31 **a.** N-methylethanamide (N-methylacetamide)
b. butanamide (butyramide)
c. methanamide (formamide)
d. N-methylbenzamide

18.33 **a.** CH$_3$—CH$_2$—C(=O)—NH$_2$
b. CH$_3$—CH$_2$—CH$_2$—CH$_2$—C(=O)—NH$_2$
c. (phenyl)—C(=O)—N(H)—CH$_2$—CH$_3$
d. CH$_3$—CH$_2$—CH$_2$—C(=O)—N(H)—CH$_2$—CH$_3$

18.35 **a.** Ethanamide has the higher melting point because it forms more hydrogen bonds as a primary amide than N-methylethanamide, which is a secondary amide.
b. Propionamide has the higher melting point because it forms hydrogen bonds, but butane does not.
c. N-methylpropanamide, a secondary amide, has a higher melting point because it can form hydrogen bonds, whereas N,N-dimethylpropanamide, a tertiary amide, cannot form hydrogen bonds.

18.37 a. $CH_3-\overset{\overset{\displaystyle O}{\|}}{C}-OH + NH_4^+\ Cl^-$

b. $CH_3-CH_2-\overset{\overset{\displaystyle O}{\|}}{C}-OH + NH_4^+\ Cl^-$

c. $CH_3-CH_2-CH_2-\overset{\overset{\displaystyle O}{\|}}{C}-OH + CH_3-\overset{+}{N}H_3\ Cl^-$

d. $\langle\bigcirc\rangle-\overset{\overset{\displaystyle O}{\|}}{C}-OH + NH_4^+\ Cl^-$

18.39 A neurotransmitter is a chemical compound that transmits an impulse from a nerve cell to a target cell.

18.41 When a nerve impulse reaches the axon terminal, it stimulates the release of neurotransmitters into the synapse.

18.43 A neurotransmitter must be removed from its receptor so that new signals can come from the nerve cells.

18.45 Acetylcholine is a neurotransmitter that communicates between the nervous system and muscle cells.

18.47 Dopamine is a neurotransmitter that controls muscle movement, regulates the sleep–wake cycle, and helps to improve cognition, attention, memory, and learning.

18.49 Serotonin is a neurotransmitter that helps to decrease anxiety, improve mood, learning, and memory; it also reduces appetite, and induces sleep.

18.51 Histamine is a neurotransmitter that causes allergic reactions, which may include inflammation, watery eyes, itchy skin, and hay fever.

18.53 Excess glutamate in the synapse can lead to destruction of brain cells.

18.55 GABA is a neurotransmitter that regulates muscle tone, sleep, and anxiety.

18.57 amine, carboxylic acid, amide, aromatic, ester

18.59 amine, aromatic, alcohol, phenol

18.61

$$\langle\bigcirc\rangle-\overset{\overset{\displaystyle O}{\|}}{C}-N\overset{\displaystyle CH_2-CH_3}{\underset{\displaystyle CH_2-CH_3}{}}$$
CH_3

18.63 Excitatory neurotransmitters open ion channels and stimulate the receptors to send more signals.

18.65 Dopamine, norepinephrine, and epinephrine all have catechol (3,4-dihydroxyphenyl) and amine components.

18.67 a. tetraethylammonium bromide; quaternary salt (4°)
b. 1-pentanamine; pentylamine; primary (1°)
c. N-ethyl-1-propanamine; ethylpropylamine secondary (2°)

18.69 a. $CH_3-CH_2-\overset{\overset{\displaystyle NH_2}{|}}{CH}-CH_2-CH_3$

b. (cyclohexane with NH_2)

c. $CH_3-\overset{+}{N}H_2\ Cl^-$

d. $CH_3-CH_2-\overset{\overset{\displaystyle CH_2-CH_3}{|}}{N}-CH_2-CH_3$

18.71 a. An alcohol with an —OH group such as 1-butanol forms stronger hydrogen bonds than an amine, and has a higher boiling point than an amine.
b. Ethylamine, a primary amine, forms more hydrogen bonds and has a higher boiling point than dimethylamine, which forms fewer hydrogen bonds as a secondary amine.

18.73 a. Ethylamine is a small amine that is soluble because it forms hydrogen bonds with water. Dibutylamine has two large nonpolar alkyl groups that decrease its solubility in water.
b. Trimethylamine is a small tertiary amine that is soluble because it hydrogen bonds with water. N-ethylcyclohexyl-amine has a large nonpolar cycloalkyl group that decreases its solubility in water.

18.75 a. N-ethylethanamide   **b.** propanamide
c. 3-methylbutanamide

18.77 a. quinine   **b.** nicotine
c. caffeine   **d.** morphine, codeine

18.79 a. $CH_3-CH_2-\overset{\overset{\displaystyle CH_3}{|}}{N}H + NaCl + H_2O$

b. $CH_3-CH_2-\overset{+}{N}H_2-CH_3 + OH^-$

18.81 carboxylate salt, aromatic, amine

18.83 Tryptophan contains a carboxylic acid group that is not present in serotonin. Serotonin has a hydroxyl group (—OH) on the aromatic ring that is not present in tryptophan.

18.85 SSRI stands for selective serotonin reuptake inhibitor.

18.87 $CH_3-CH_2-CH_2-NH_2$
Propylamine (1°)

$$CH_3-CH_2-\overset{\overset{\displaystyle H}{|}}{N}-CH_3$$
Ethylmethylamine (2°)

$$CH_3-\overset{\overset{\displaystyle CH_3}{|}}{N}-CH_3$$
Trimethylamine (3°)

$$CH_3-\overset{\overset{\displaystyle CH_3}{|}}{CH}-NH_2$$
Isopropylamine (1°)

18.89 a. aromatic, amine, amide, carboxylic acid, cycloalkene
b. aromatic, ether, alcohol, amine
c. aromatic, carboxylic acid
d. phenol, amine, carboxylic acid
e. aromatic, ether, alcohol, amine, ketone
f. aromatic, amine

18.91 Dopamine is needed in the brain, where it is important in controlling muscle movement. Since dopamine cannot cross the blood–brain barrier, persons with low levels of dopamine are given L-dopa, which can cross the blood–brain barrier, where it is converted to dopamine.

19

Amino Acids and Proteins

A burglary was being committed when

a young couple, Aaron and Debra, arrived home. Aaron was shot in the leg, the criminals fled, and Debra called 911. Aaron was taken to the hospital and luckily, he survived. The police arrived to investigate the crime and file a report, while a crime scene investigator collected evidence that included several strands of hair. The hair samples were sent to a crime lab, where Ron, a forensic scientist, begins the process of analyzing the samples.

Ron examines the hair samples under a microscope to determine if they are human, or if the hair came from a pet such as a dog or cat. Ron concludes that the hair is human and then begins to determine what part of the body the hair came from and if it could specify the person's race, whether it was dyed, and if the hair fell out or was pulled out. After this analysis, Ron extracts the hair DNA to build a DNA profile, which will help identify the criminals while strengthening the evidence for a potential court case.

Hair is a structural protein that is comprised of long strings of amino acids called polypeptides. Amino acids are the building blocks of all proteins, and there are 20 common amino acids. Each of these amino acids has a similar structure except for a unique side chain called an R group. The R group identifies each of the 20 amino acids. DNA codes for the exact sequence of the amino acids in the protein, and if there is a different DNA sequence, there will be a different protein.

Career: Forensic Scientist

Forensic scientists perform two main roles: the first is to examine and analyze evidence associated with a criminal investigation. The evidence varies depending upon the crime, as it may involve trace evidence such as gunshot residue, paint residue, illicit drugs, bullet casings, firearms, bodily fluids, hair or fiber samples, fingerprints, footprints, or any documents associated with the crime. This analysis requires forensic scientists to use a variety of sophisticated instruments to perform measurements and tests, carefully record the findings, and preserve the criminal evidence. The second role requires a forensic scientist to prepare detailed reports of his or her findings, and to testify as an expert witness in trials or hearings. Their work is critical in apprehending and convicting criminals.

The word "protein" is derived from the Greek word *proteios*, meaning "first." Made of amino acids, proteins provide structure in membranes, build cartilage and connective tissue, transport oxygen in blood and muscle, direct biological reactions as enzymes, defend the body against infection, and control metabolic processes as hormones. Proteins can even be a source of energy.

All of these different functions depend on the structures and chemical behavior of amino acids, the building blocks of proteins. We will see how peptide bonds link amino acids and how the sequence of the amino acids in these protein polymers directs the formation of unique three-dimensional structures.

19.1 Proteins and Amino Acids

Protein molecules, compared with many of the compounds we have studied, can be gigantic. Insulin has a molar mass of 5800, and hemoglobin has a molar mass of about 67 000. Some virus proteins are even larger, having molar masses of more than 40 million. Even though proteins can be huge, they all contain the same 20 amino acids. Every protein is a polymer built from these 20 different amino acid building blocks, repeated numerous times, with the specific sequence of the amino acids determining the characteristics of the protein and its biological action.

The many kinds of proteins perform different functions in the body. Some proteins form structural components such as cartilage, muscles, hair, and nails. Wool, silk, feathers, and horns in animals are made of proteins (see Figure 19.1). Proteins that function as enzymes regulate biological reactions such as digestion and cellular metabolism. Other proteins, such as hemoglobin and myoglobin, transport oxygen in the blood and muscle. Table 19.1 gives examples of proteins that are classified by their functions in biological systems.

LEARNING GOAL

Classify proteins by their functions. Give the name and abbreviations for an amino acid and draw its ionized structure.

FIGURE 19.1 The horns of animals are made of proteins.

Q What class of protein would be in horns?

TABLE 19.1 Classification of Proteins and Their Functions

Class of Protein	Function	Examples
Structural	Provide structural components	*Collagen* is in tendons and cartilage. *Keratin* is in hair, skin, wool, and nails.
Contractile	Make muscles move	*Myosin* and *actin* contract muscle fibers.
Transport	Carry essential substances throughout the body	*Hemoglobin* transports oxygen. *Lipoproteins* transport lipids.
Storage	Store nutrients	*Casein* stores protein in milk. *Ferritin* contains iron and is stored in the spleen and liver.
Hormonal	Regulate body metabolism and the nervous system	*Insulin* regulates the blood glucose level. *Growth hormone* regulates body growth.
Enzyme	Catalyze biochemical reactions in the cells	*Sucrase* catalyzes the hydrolysis of sucrose. *Trypsin* catalyzes the hydrolysis of proteins.
Protection	Recognize and destroy foreign substances	*Immunoglobulins* stimulate immune responses.

TUTORIAL
Protein Building Blocks

TUTORIAL
Proteins "R" Us

SELF-STUDY ACTIVITY
Functions of Proteins

CONCEPT CHECK 19.1   **Classifying Proteins by Function**

Give the class of protein that would perform each of the following functions:

a. catalyzes metabolic reactions of lipids
b. carries oxygen in the bloodstream
c. stores amino acids in milk

ANSWER

a. Enzymes catalyze metabolic reactions.
b. Transport proteins carry substances such as oxygen through the bloodstream.
c. Storage proteins store nutrients such as amino acids in milk.

Amino Acids

Proteins are composed of molecular building blocks called *amino acids*. However, there are only 20 amino acids commonly found in human proteins. Every **amino acid** has a central carbon atom called the α-carbon, bonded to two functional groups: an *amino* group ($-NH_2$) and a *carboxylic acid* group ($-COOH$). The α-carbon is also bonded to a hydrogen atom ($-H$), and a side chain called an R group. It is the R group, which differs in each of the 20 common α-amino acids, that provides unique characteristics to each type of amino acid. For example, alanine has a methyl, $-CH_3$, as its R group, whereas serine has $-CH_2OH$ as its R group.

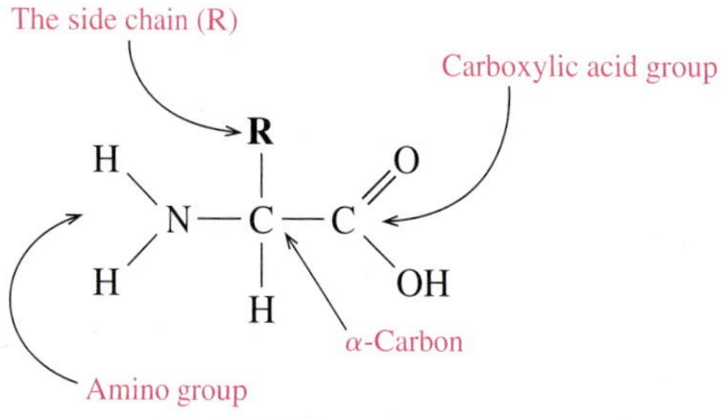

The side chain (R) · Carboxylic acid group · Methyl group · Carboxylic acid group

α-Carbon · Amino group · α-Amino acid · Amino group · α-Carbon · Alanine, an amino acid

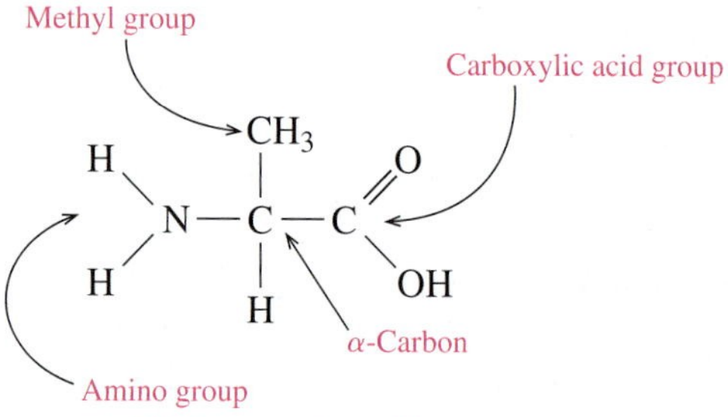

Ionization of Amino Acids

At the pH of most body fluids, amino acids are ionized. The carboxylic acid group ($-COOH$) donates H^+ to the amino group ($-NH_2$), which gives a carboxylate ($-COO^-$), and an ammonium group ($-NH_3^+$). In this ionized form called a **zwitterion**, the carboxylate and ammonium groups have charge balance, which means that *a zwitterion has an overall zero charge*. All zwitterions exist at specific pH values known as their **isoelectric points (pI)**. As zwitterions, amino acids are similar to salts, which have high melting points and are soluble in water, but not in nonpolar solvents.

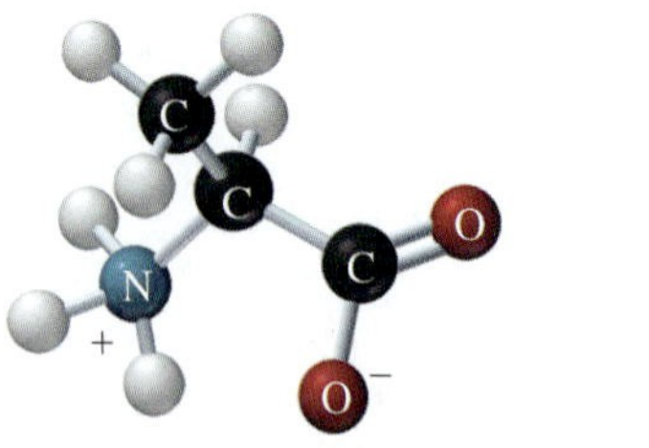

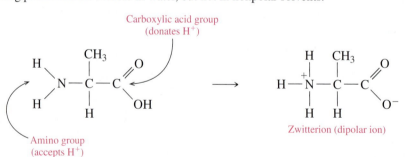

Carboxylic acid group (donates H^+)

Amino group (accepts H^+)

Zwitterion (dipolar ion)

Ball-and-stick model of the zwitterion of alanine at its pI 6.0.

Classification of Amino Acids

We classify amino acids according to their R groups, which determine their properties in aqueous solution. The **nonpolar amino acids** have hydrogen, alkyl, or aromatic R groups, which make them *hydrophobic* ("water fearing"). When an amino acid has a *polar* R group, it interacts with water because it is *hydrophilic* ("water loving"). **Neutral polar amino acids** contain hydroxyl ($-OH$), thiol ($-SH$), or amide ($-CONH_2$) groups. The **acidic polar amino acids** contain a carboxylate group ($-COO^-$). The **basic polar amino acids** have amine R groups. The ionized structures and common names of the 20 α-amino acids commonly found in proteins with their R groups highlighted in yellow, their three-letter and one-letter abbreviations, and pI values, are listed in Table 19.2.

A summary of the classification of amino acids follows:

Type of Amino Acid	Type of R Groups	Polarity	Water
Nonpolar	Nonpolar	Nonpolar	Hydrophobic
Polar, neutral	Contain O and S atoms, but no charge	Polar	Hydrophilic
Polar, acidic	Contain carboxyl groups, negative charge	Polar	Hydrophilic
Polar, basic	Contain amino groups, positive charge	Polar	Hydrophilic

SAMPLE PROBLEM 19.1   Structural Formulas of Amino Acids

Draw the zwitterion for each of the following amino acids, and write the three-letter and one-letter abbreviations:

a. serine   **b.** aspartic acid

SOLUTION

Analyze the Problem

The zwitterion of any amino acid has an α-carbon atom that is attached to three components common to all zwitterions, which are $-NH_3^+$, $-COO^-$, and $-H$. The fourth component is a specific R group that differs for each particular amino acid (see Table 19.2). Abbreviations are three letters or one letter derived from the name, or is specifically assigned.

Amino Acid	Common Components	R Group	Abbreviations
Serine	$-NH_3^+$, $-COO^-$, and $-H$	OH | CH_2 |	Ser, S
Aspartic acid	$-NH_3^+$, $-COO^-$, and $-H$	O=C(O⁻) | CH_2 |	Asp, D

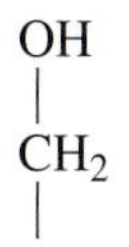

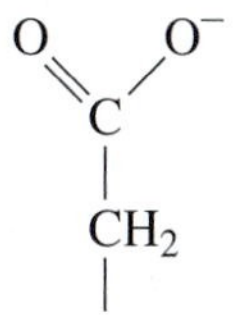

a.

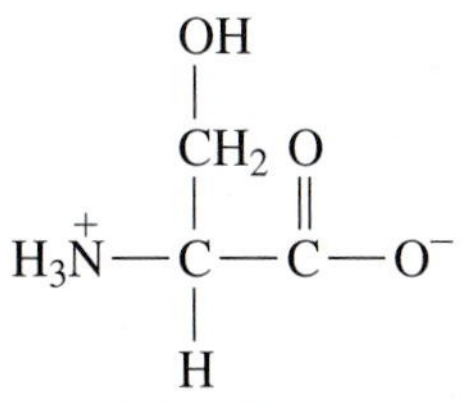

Serine (Ser, S)

b.

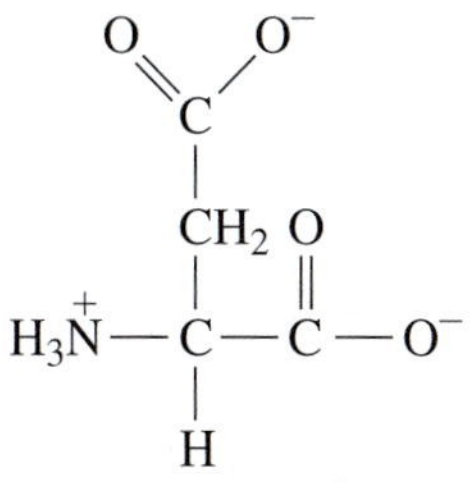

Aspartic acid (Asp, D)

STUDY CHECK 19.1

Classify the amino acids in Sample Problem 19.1 as polar or nonpolar. If polar, indicate if the R group is neutral, acidic, or basic.

TABLE 19.2 Structures, Names, Abbreviations, and Isoelectric Points (pI) of 20 Common Amino Acids at Physiological pH (7.4)

Nonpolar Amino Acids (Hydrophobic)

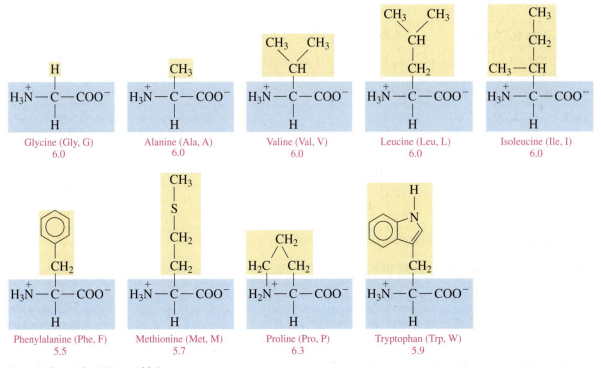

Glycine (Gly, G)
6.0

Alanine (Ala, A)
6.0

Valine (Val, V)
6.0

Leucine (Leu, L)
6.0

Isoleucine (Ile, I)
6.0

Phenylalanine (Phe, F)
5.5

Methionine (Met, M)
5.7

Proline (Pro, P)
6.3

Tryptophan (Trp, W)
5.9

Polar Amino Acids (Hydrophilic)

Amino Acids with Neutral R Groups

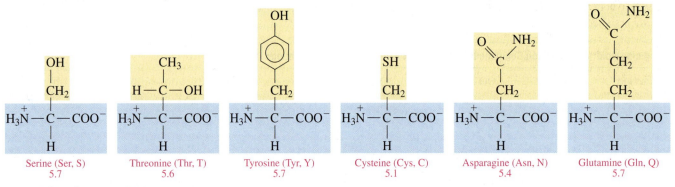

Serine (Ser, S)
5.7

Threonine (Thr, T)
5.6

Tyrosine (Tyr, Y)
5.7

Cysteine (Cys, C)
5.1

Asparagine (Asn, N)
5.4

Glutamine (Gln, Q)
5.7

Amino Acids with Charged R Groups

Acidic (negative charge)   Basic (positive charge)

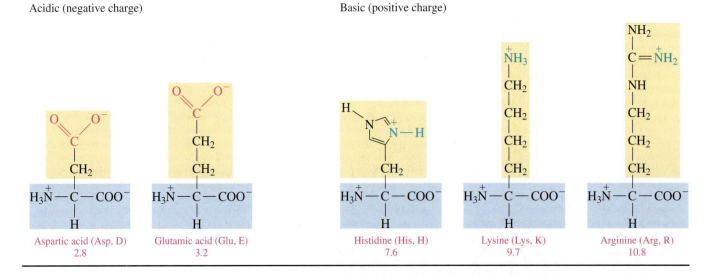

Aspartic acid (Asp, D)
2.8

Glutamic acid (Glu, E)
3.2

Histidine (His, H)
7.6

Lysine (Lys, K)
9.7

Arginine (Arg, R)
10.8

CONCEPT CHECK 19.2 **Polarity of Amino Acids**

Classify each of the following amino acids as nonpolar or polar. If polar, indicate if the R group is neutral, acidic, or basic. Indicate if each would be hydrophobic or hydrophilic.

a. valine   **b.** asparagine   **c.** histidine

ANSWER

a. The R group in valine consists of several C atoms and H atoms, which makes valine a nonpolar amino acid that is hydrophobic.
b. The R group in asparagine contains C atoms, H atoms, and an amide group, which makes asparagine a polar amino acid that is neutral and hydrophilic.
c. The R group in histidine contains C atoms, H atoms, and a heterocyclic ring with a N⁺, which makes histidine a polar amino acid that is basic and hydrophilic.

Amino Acid Stereoisomers

All of the α-amino acids except for glycine are chiral because the α-carbon is attached to four different groups. Thus, amino acids can exist as D and L enantiomers. We can draw Fischer projections for α-amino acids as we did in Section 14.5 for the chiral forms of glyceraldehyde by placing the carboxylate group at the top and the R group at the bottom. In the D enantiomer of an amino acid, the $-NH_3^+$ group is on the right, and in the L enantiomer, the $-NH_3^+$ group is on the left. In biological systems, the only amino acids incorporated into proteins are the L enantiomers. There are D amino acids found in nature, but not in proteins. Let's look at the enantiomers for L- and D-glyceraldehyde, a carbohydrate, and two amino acids, L- and D-alanine, and L- and D-cysteine.

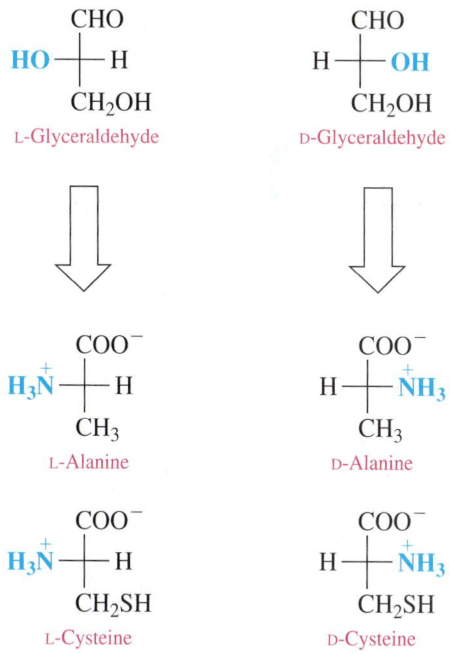

SAMPLE PROBLEM 19.2 **Chiral Amino Acids**

Draw the Fischer projection for L-serine.

SOLUTION

Analyze the Problem

In the Fischer projection of any amino acid, the oxidized $-COO^-$ group is drawn at the top, and the R group is drawn at the bottom. The L enantiomer has the $-NH_3^+$ on the left and $-H$ on the right of the intersection, whereas the D enantiomer has the $-NH_3^+$ on the right and $-H$ on the left. For L-serine, the R group is $-CH_2OH$, and the $-NH_3^+$ is drawn on the left and the $-H$ is drawn on the right of the intersection.

$$
\begin{array}{c}
\text{COO}^- \\
\text{H}_3\overset{+}{\text{N}} \!\!-\!\!\!+\!\!\!-\!\! \text{H} \\
\text{CH}_2\text{OH}
\end{array}
$$

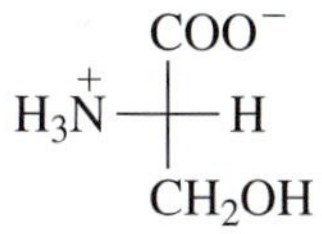

L-Serine

STUDY CHECK 19.2

How does the Fischer projection for D-serine differ from that of L-serine?

CHO
HO —+— H
CH₂OH
L-Glyceraldehyde

CHO
H —+— OH
CH₂OH
D-Glyceraldehyde

COO⁻
H₃N⁺ —+— H
CH₃
L-Alanine

COO⁻
H —+— N⁺H₃
CH₃
D-Alanine

COO⁻
H₃N⁺ —+— H
CH₂SH
L-Cysteine

COO⁻
H —+— N⁺H₃
CH₂SH
D-Cysteine

In amino acids, the $-NH_3^+$ group appears on the left or right of the chiral carbon to give L or D enantiomers.

Chemistry Link to Health

ESSENTIAL AMINO ACIDS

Of the 20 amino acids typically used to build proteins in the body, only 11 can be synthesized in the body. The other 9 amino acids, listed in Table 19.3, are called the **essential amino acids** because they must be obtained from the diet. In addition to the essential amino acids required by adults, infants and growing children also require arginine, cysteine and tyrosine.

Complete proteins, which contain all of the essential amino acids, are found in most animal products, such as eggs, milk, meat, fish, and poultry. However, gelatin and plant proteins such as grains, beans, and nuts are *incomplete proteins* because they are deficient in one or more of the essential amino acids. Diets that rely on plant foods for protein must contain a variety of protein sources to obtain all the essential amino acids. For example, a diet of rice and beans contains all the essential amino acids because they are *complementary protein* sources. Rice contains the methionine and tryptophan that are deficient in beans, while beans contain the lysine that is lacking in rice (see Table 19.4).

Complete proteins such as eggs, milk, meat, and fish contain all of the essential amino acids. Incomplete proteins from plants such as grains, beans, and nuts are deficient in one or more essential amino acids.

TABLE 19.3 Essential Amino Acids for Adults

Histidine (His)	Phenylalanine (Phe)
Isoleucine (Ile)	Threonine (Thr)
Leucine (Leu)	Tryptophan (Trp)
Lysine (Lys)	Valine (Val)
Methionine (Met)	

TABLE 19.4 Amino Acid Deficiencies in Selected Vegetables and Grains

Food Source	Amino Acid(s) Missing
Eggs, milk, meat, fish, poultry	None
Wheat, rice, oats	Lysine
Corn	Lysine, tryptophan
Beans	Methionine, tryptophan
Peas	Methionine
Almonds, walnuts	Lysine, tryptophan
Soy	Low in methionine

QUESTIONS AND PROBLEMS

19.1 Proteins and Amino Acids

LEARNING GOAL: *Classify proteins by their functions. Give the name and abbreviations for an amino acid and draw its ionized structure.*

19.1 Classify each of the following proteins according to its function:
    a. hemoglobin, oxygen carrier in the blood
    b. collagen, a major component of tendons and cartilage
    c. keratin, a protein found in hair
    d. amylases that catalyze the hydrolysis of starch

19.2 Classify each of the following proteins according to its function:
    a. insulin, a hormone needed for glucose utilization
    b. antibodies, disable foreign proteins
    c. casein, milk protein
    d. lipases that catalyze the hydrolysis of lipids

19.3 What functional groups are found in all α-amino acids?

19.4 How does the polarity of the R group in leucine compare to the polarity of the R group in serine?

19.5 Draw the ionized form for each of the following amino acids:
    a. isoleucine   **b.** glutamine
    c. glutamic acid   **d.** proline

19.6 Draw the ionized form for each of the following amino acids:
    a. lysine   **b.** arginine
    c. leucine   **d.** tyrosine

19.7 Classify each of the amino acids in Problem 19.5 as polar or nonpolar. If polar, indicate if the R group is neutral, acidic, or basic. Indicate if each is hydrophobic or hydrophilic.

19.8 Classify each of the amino acids in Problem 19.6 as polar or nonpolar. If polar, indicate if the R group is neutral, acidic, or basic. Indicate if each is hydrophobic or hydrophilic.

19.9 Give the name of the amino acid represented by each of the following abbreviations:
    a. Ala   **b.** V   **c.** Lys   **d.** Cys

19.10 Give the name of the amino acid represented by each of the following abbreviations:
    a. Trp   **b.** M   **c.** Pro   **d.** G

19.11 Draw the Fischer projection for each of the following amino acids:
    a. L-valine   **b.** D-cysteine

19.12 Draw the Fischer projection for each of the following amino acids:
    a. L-threonine   **b.** D-valine

LEARNING GOAL

Draw the zwitterion for an amino acid at its isoelectric point, and its ionized structure at pH values above or below its isoelectric point.

19.2 Amino Acids as Zwitterions

The pI values for nonpolar and polar neutral amino acids are from pH 5.1 to 6.3. As we have seen, alanine exists as a zwitterion at its pI of 6.0 with a carboxylate anion ($-COO^-$) and an ammonium cation ($-NH_3^+$), which give it an overall charge of zero. However, the charge balance changes when alanine is placed in a solution that has a pH that is more acidic or more basic than the pI. In a solution that is more acidic, with a lower pH than its pI (pH < 6.0), the

TUTORIAL
pH, pI, and Amino Acid Ionization

—COO$^-$ group of alanine gains H$^+$, which forms its carboxylic acid (—COOH). Because the —NH$_3^+$ group retains a charge of 1+, alanine has an overall positive charge (1+) at a pH lower than 6.0.

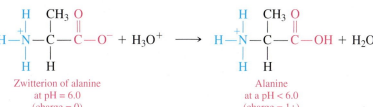

When alanine is placed in a solution that is more basic, with a higher pH than its pI (pH > 6.0), the —NH$_3^+$ group of alanine loses H$^+$ and forms an amino group (—NH$_2$), which has no charge. Because the carboxylate group (—COO$^-$) has a charge of 1−, alanine has an overall negative charge (1−) at a pH higher than 6.0. The charges on the carboxylate and ammonium groups for amino acids in solutions with pH below pI, at the pI, or above pI, are summarized in Table 19.5.

TABLE 19.5 Ionized Forms of Nonpolar and Polar Neutral Amino Acids

Solution	pH < pI (acidic)	pH = pI	pH > pI (basic)
Change in H$^+$	[H$^+$] increases	No change	[H$^+$] decreases
Carboxylic Acid/Carboxylate	—COOH	—COO$^-$	—COO$^-$
Ammonium/Amino	—NH$_3^+$	—NH$_3^+$	—NH$_2$
Overall Charge	1+	0	1−

Ionized Forms of Polar Acidic and Polar Basic Amino Acids

The pI values of the polar acidic amino acids (aspartic acid, glutamic acid) are around 3. In these zwitterions, at pH values of 3, the carboxylic acid group in the R group is not ionized. At a pH of 2.8, aspartic acid has a zero charge. However, in a solution that is more acidic than its pI (pH < 2.8), the —COO$^-$ group on the α-carbon of aspartic acid gains H$^+$ to form a carboxylic acid (—COOH) group. Because the —NH$_3^+$ group retains a charge of 1+, aspartic acid has an overall positive charge (1+) at a pH lower than 2.8.

When aspartic acid is placed in a solution that is more basic (for example, a pH = 7) than its pI, the carboxylic acid in the R group loses H$^+$ to become a carboxylate group (—COO$^-$). With two carboxylate groups and one ammonium group, aspartic acid has an overall charge of 1− at pH 7. When the solution becomes even more basic (pH > 10), the —NH$_3^+$ group on aspartic acid loses H$^+$ to form an amino group (—NH$_2$). With two carboxylate groups ($-COO^-$) and one amine group ($-NH_2$), aspartic acid has an overall charge of 2$-$ in a very basic solution.

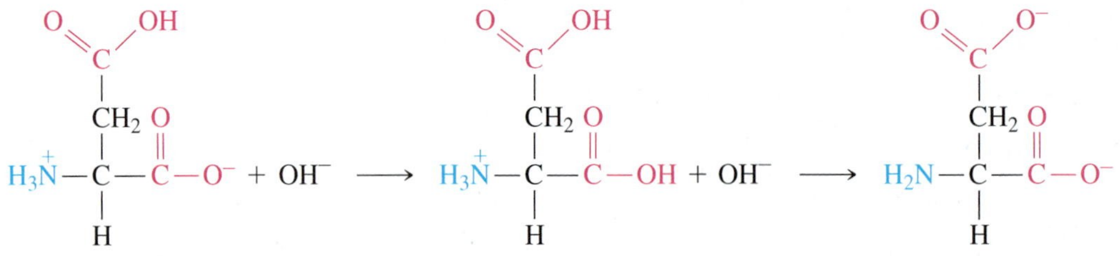

Zwitterion of aspartic acid	Aspartic acid	Aspartic acid
at pH = 2.8	at pH = 7	at a pH > 10
(charge = 0)	(charge = 1−)	(charge = 2−)

The pI values of the polar basic amino acids (lysine, arginine, and histidine) are from pH 8 to 11. In these zwitterions, at pH values of 8 to 11, the amines in the R groups are not ionized, which gives an overall charge of zero. At lower pH values, the amines ($-NH_2$) in the R groups gain H^+ to form ammonium groups ($-NH_3^+$). With one carboxylate group ($-COO^-$), and two ammonium groups ($-NH_3^+$), the basic amino acids have an overall 1+ charge at pH values below their pIs. When the pH is lowered further, the α-carboxylate group ($-COO^-$) gains H^+. With a carboxylic acid group ($-COOH$) and two ammonium groups ($-NH_3^+$), the basic amino acids at very low pH values have an overall charge of 2+.

CONCEPT CHECK 19.3 Zwitterions of Amino Acids

Consider the amino acid cysteine.

a. What is the pI of cysteine, and what does it mean?
b. At a pH of 2.0, how does the zwitterion change?

ANSWER

a. From Table 19.2, the pI of cysteine is 5.1. This means that at a pH of 5.1, cysteine exists as a zwitterion with a net charge of zero.
b. From Table 19.2, a pH of 2.0 is more acidic and below the pI of cysteine. Then the $-COO^-$ group accepts H^+ to give $-COOH$. The charge on the $-NH_3^+$ group gives cysteine an overall positive charge (1+).

SAMPLE PROBLEM 19.3 Amino Acids at Different pH Values

Draw the condensed structural formula for leucine at the following pH values and give the overall charge for each (see Table 19.2 for the pI of leucine):

a. 6.0 **b.** 10.0

SOLUTION

Analyze the Problem

An amino acid exists as a zwitterion, with $-NH_3^+$ and $-COO^-$ groups, when the pH is the same as its pI. In a more acidic solution than the pI, the $-COO^-$ group accepts H^+ to give a $-COOH$ group, which results in an overall charge of 1+. In a more basic solution than the pI, the $-NH_3^+$ group loses H^+ to give a $-NH_2$ group, which results in an overall charge of 1−.

Ionized Components (pI)	pH Change	Ionized Components	Overall Charge
$-NH_3^+$, $-COO^-$	none, pH = pI	$-NH_3^+$, $-COO^-$	0
$-NH_3^+$, $-COO^-$	More acidic, pH < pI	$-NH_3^+$	1+
$-NH_3^+$, $-COO^-$	More basic, pH > pI	$-COO^-$	1−

a. Leucine exists as a zwitterion at pH 6.0, which is equal to its pI of 6.0. It has a positively-charged ammonium group and a negatively-charged carboxylate group. Leucine has an overall charge of zero (0) at a pH of 6.0.

$$CH_3 \ CH_3$$
$$\backslash \ /$$
$$CH$$
$$|$$
$$CH_2 \ O$$
$$| \quad \parallel$$
$$\overset{+}{H_3N} - C - C - O^-$$
$$|$$
$$H$$

b. A pH of 10.0 is more basic than the pI of leucine. In a solution with a pH > 6.0, the ammonium group loses H^+ to give a $-NH_2$ group. With a negatively-charged carboxylate group, leucine has an overall charge of 1− at a pH of 10.0.

$$CH_3 \ CH_3$$
$$\backslash \ /$$
$$CH$$
$$|$$
$$CH_2 \ O$$
$$| \quad \parallel$$
$$H_2N - C - C - O^-$$
$$|$$
$$H$$

STUDY CHECK 19.3

Draw the condensed structural formula for leucine at a pH of 4.0.

Electrophoresis

A mixture of amino acids that have different pI values can be separated using a laboratory method called **electrophoresis**. The amino acid mixture, which is buffered to a particular pH, is applied to a gel on a thin plate or piece of filter paper that is connected to two electrodes. A voltage applied to the electrodes causes a positively-charged amino acid to move toward the negative electrode, and a negatively-charged amino acid to move toward the positive electrode. If an amino acid has a pI equal to the pH of the solution, that amino acid has an overall charge of zero and would not move. After sufficient separation has occurred, the electricity is turned off and then the plate or filter paper is removed from the electrophoresis apparatus. The gel is sprayed with a dye, such as ninhydrin, to make the amino acids visible. They are identified by their direction and rate of migration toward the electrodes. Electrophoresis is a method used in medicine to screen for the sickle-cell trait in newborn infants.

Suppose we have a mixture of valine (pI 6.0), aspartic acid (pI 2.8), and lysine (pI 9.7) in a buffer of pH 6.0. When the mixture is placed between two electrodes at a high voltage, the aspartic acid, which has a negative charge at pH 6.0, moves toward the positive electrode (anode). The lysine, which has a positive charge at a pH of 6.0, moves toward the negative electrode (cathode). Valine, which is at its pI and has an overall charge of zero, does not move in the presence of an electric field at pH 6.0 (see Figure 19.2).

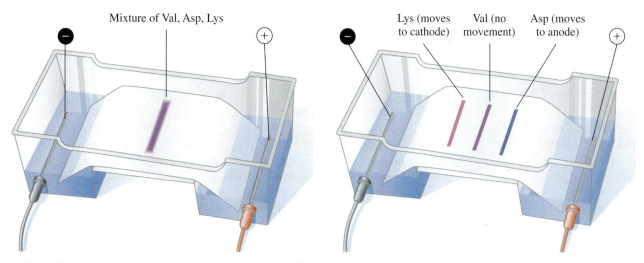

FIGURE 19.2 A positively-charged amino acid (pH < pI) moves toward the negative electrode; a negatively-charged amino acid (pH > pI) moves toward the positive electrode; an amino acid with no net charge (pH = pI) does not migrate.

Q How would the three amino acids migrate if the mixture were buffered to pH 9.7, the pI of lysine?

CONCEPT CHECK 19.4   Ionized Forms of Amino Acids

Explain each of the following:

a. Glutamic acid moves toward the positive electrode during electrophoresis at a pH of 7.0.
b. The pI of lysine is much higher than the pI of phenylalanine.

ANSWER

a. A pH of 7.0 is higher (more basic) than the pI of 3.2 for glutamic acid. At a pH of 7.0, glutamic acid would have two negatively-charged —COO^- groups and one —NH_3^+ group, which gives an overall charge of $1-$. The glutamic acid, with a negative charge, is attracted to the positive electrode.
b. At a pH of 5.5, the nonpolar phenylalanine forms a zwitterion with a zero net charge. However, lysine is a basic amino acid with two —NH_3^+ groups and one —COO^-. To form the zwitterion of lysine, a more basic environment is needed so that an —NH_3^+ group donates H^+ to give —NH_2 and a zwitterion with a net charge of zero. Thus, lysine has a higher pI because it requires a higher pH to form the zwitterion.

QUESTIONS AND PROBLEMS

19.2 Amino Acids as Zwitterions

LEARNING GOAL: *Draw the zwitterion for an amino acid at its isoelectric point, and its ionized structure at pH values above or below its isoelectric point.*

19.13 Draw the zwitterion for each of the following amino acids:
    a. Gly   **b.** C
    c. threonine   **d.** A

19.14 Draw the zwitterion for each of the following amino acids:
    a. phenylalanine   **b.** methionine
    c. I   **d.** Asn

19.15 Draw the ionized form for each of the amino acids in Problem 19.13 at a pH below 1.0.

19.16 Draw the ionized form for each of the amino acids in Problem 19.14 at a pH above 12.0.

19.17 Would each of the following ions of valine exist at a pH above, below, or at its pI?

             CH₃ CH₃
               \ /
                CH
                |
a. 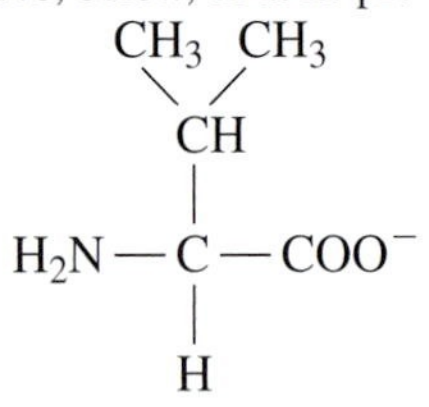 H_2N — C — COO^- **b.** $H_3\overset{+}{N}$ — C — COOH
               |
               H

             CH₃ CH₃
               \ /
                CH
                |
c. $H_3\overset{+}{N}$ — C — COO^-
               |
               H

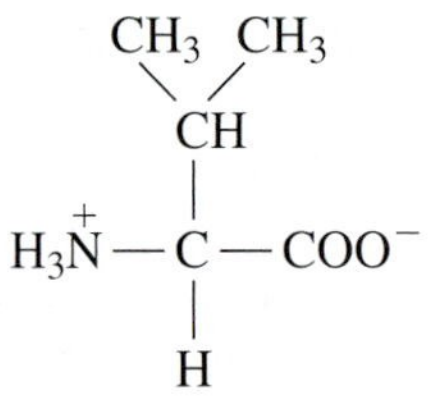

19.18 Would each of the following ions of serine exist at a pH above, below, or at its pI?

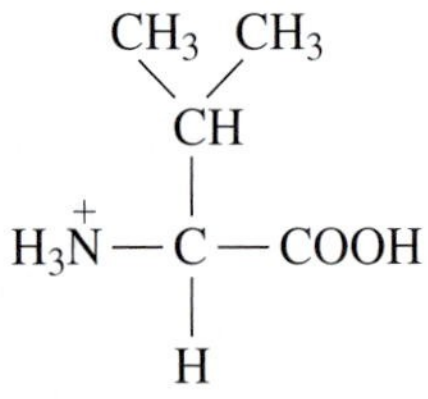

        OH   OH
        | |
        CH₂   CH₂
        | |
a. 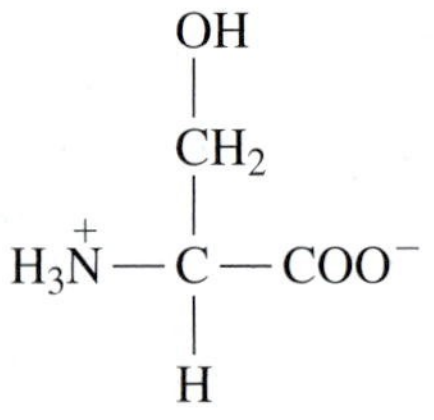 $H_3\overset{+}{N}$ — C — COO^- **b.** $H_3\overset{+}{N}$ — C — COOH
        | |
        H   H

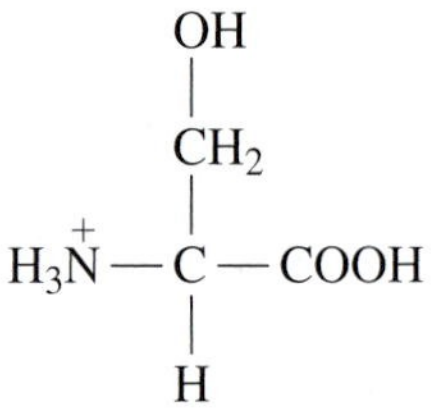

        OH
        |
        CH₂
        |
c. H_2N — C — COO^-
        |
        H

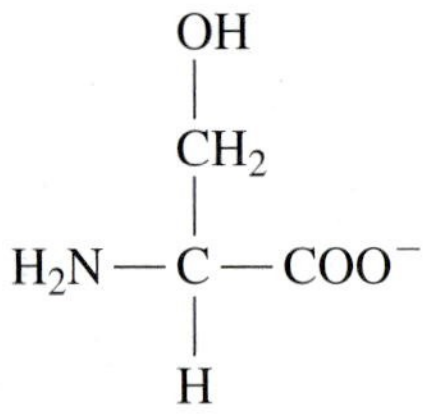

LEARNING GOAL

Draw the condensed structural formula for a dipeptide.

TUTORIAL
Peptide Bonds: Acid Meets Amino

19.3 Formation of Peptides

A **peptide bond** is an amide bond that forms when the —COO^- group of one amino acid reacts with the —NH_3^+ group of the next amino acid. The linking of two or more amino acids by peptide bonds forms a **peptide**. An O atom is removed from the carboxylate end of the first amino acid, and two H atoms are removed from the ammonium end of the second amino acid, which produces water. Two amino acids form a *dipeptide*, three amino acids form a *tripeptide*, and four amino acids form a *tetrapeptide*. A chain of five amino acids is a *pentapeptide*, and longer chains of amino acids form *polypeptides*.

As an example, we will write the formation of the dipeptide glycylalanine (Gly-Ala) between the zwitterions of glycine and alanine (see Figure 19.3). In a peptide, the amino acid written on the left, glycine, has a free —NH_3^+ group, which makes it the

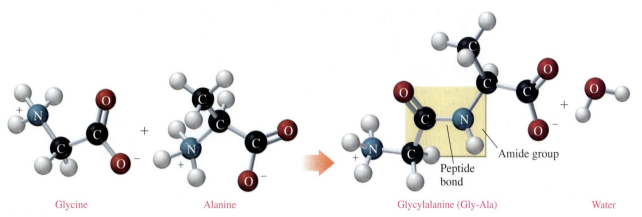

Glycine   Alanine   Glycylalanine (Gly-Ala)   Water

FIGURE 19.3 A peptide bond between glycine and alanine as zwitterions forms the dipeptide glycylalanine.
Q What functional groups in glycine and alanine form the peptide bond?

N-terminal amino acid. The amino acid written on the right, alanine, has a free $-COO^-$ group, which makes it the **C-terminal amino acid**. Any peptide is always written with the N-terminal amino acid on the left, and the C-terminal amino acid on the right.

Naming Peptides

In the name of a peptide, each amino acid beginning from the N-terminal end has the *ine* (or *ic acid*) replaced by *yl*. The last amino acid at the C-terminal end of the peptide has its full name. For example, a tripeptide consisting of alanine, glycine, and serine is named as alanylglycylserine. For convenience, the order of amino acids in the peptide is often written as the sequence of three-letter or one-letter abbreviations.

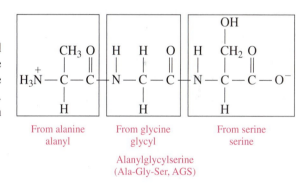

From alanine   From glycine   From serine
alanyl   glycyl   serine

Alanylglycylserine
(Ala-Gly-Ser, AGS)

CONCEPT CHECK 19.5   **Structures and Names of Peptides**

Answer each of the following for the dipeptide Val-Thr, VT:

a. What amino acid is the N-terminal amino acid?
b. What amino acid is the C-terminal amino acid?
c. How are the amino acids connected?
d. Give the name of the dipeptide.

ANSWER

a. Valine, the first amino acid in the peptide name, would be the N-terminal amino acid written on the left, which gives a free $-NH_3^+$ group.
b. Threonine, the last amino acid in the peptide name, would be the C-terminal amino acid and written on the right, which gives a free $-COO^-$ group.
c. The O is removed from the carboxylate group of valine and two H atoms are removed from the ammonium ion in threonine to form water. The $C=O$ part of valine and the $N-H$ part of threonine are joined, which gives a peptide (amide) bond in the dipeptide.
d. In the name of a peptide, the ending *ine* of valine is changed to *yl*, which is *valyl*. The last amino acid, threonine, which is the C-terminal amino acid, keeps its name *threonine*. Thus, the dipeptide is named valylthreonine.

SAMPLE PROBLEM 19.4 Drawing a Peptide

Draw the condensed structural formula for the tripeptide Gly-Ser-Met, GSM.

SOLUTION

Analyze the Problem

The name Gly-Ser-Met gives the order of the amino acids. The N-terminal amino acid drawn on the left is glycine, the middle amino acid is serine, and the C-terminal amino acid drawn on the right is methionine. We can obtain the R groups from Table 19.2.

Guide to Drawing a Peptide

1. Draw the structures for each amino acid in the peptide, starting with the N-terminal amino acid on the left.
2. Remove the O atom from the carboxylate group of the N-terminal amino acid and two H atoms from the adjacent amino acid. Repeat this process until the C-terminal amino acid is reached.
3. Connect the remaining parts of the amino acids by forming amide (peptide) bonds.

Step 1 **Draw the structures for each amino acid in the peptide, starting with the N-terminal amino acid on the left.**

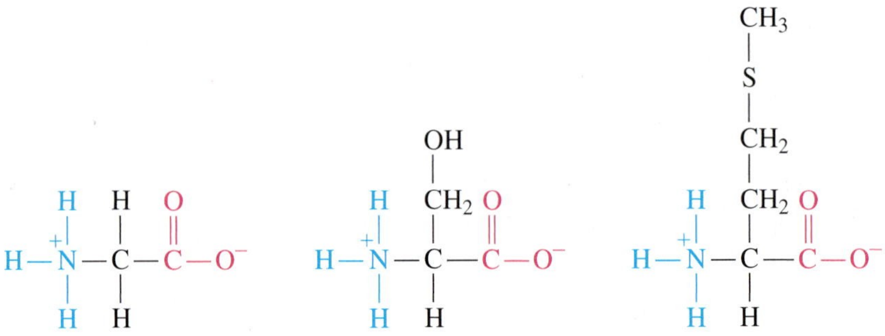

Gly, G N-terminal end — Ser, S — Met, M C-terminal end

Step 2 **Remove the O atom from the carboxylate group of the N-terminal amino acid and two H atoms from the adjacent amino acid. Repeat this process until the C-terminal amino acid is reached.**

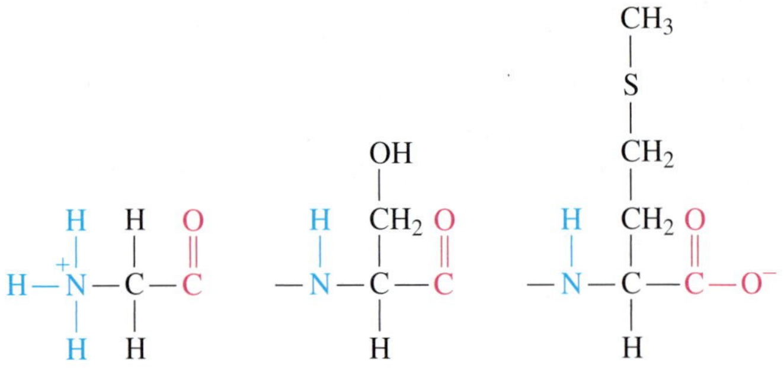

Gly, G N-terminal end — Ser, S — Met, M C-terminal end

Step 3 **Connect the remaining parts of the amino acids by forming amide (peptide) bonds.**

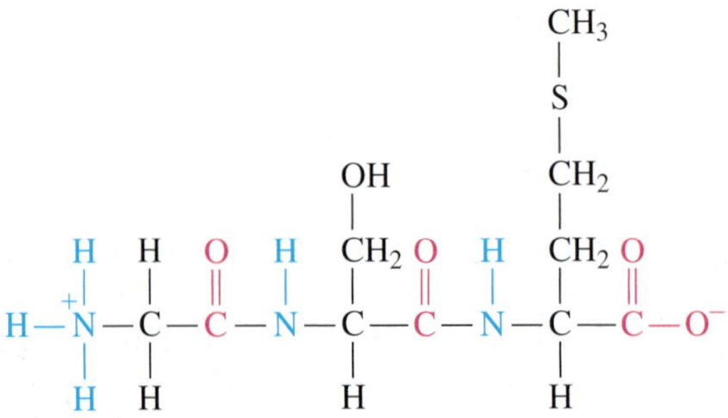

N-terminal end — C-terminal end

STUDY CHECK 19.4

Draw the condensed structural formula for the dipeptide Phe-Thr, part of the peptide glucagon, which increases blood glucose levels.

Identifying a Tripeptide

Answer each of the following questions for the tripeptide that is shown:

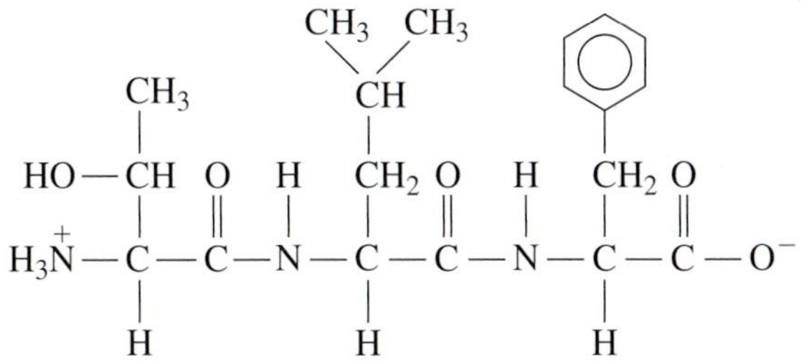

CH₃   CH₃

CH₃   CH

HO—CH O   H   CH₂ O   H   CH₂ O

H₃N⁺—C—C—N—C—C—N—C—C—O⁻

H   H   H

a. What is the N-terminal amino acid? What is the C-terminal amino acid?
b. Use the three-letter and one-letter abbreviations to give the amino acid order in the tripeptide.
c. What is the name of the tripeptide?

SOLUTION

a. Threonine is the N-terminal amino acid; phenylalanine is the C-terminal amino acid.
b. Thr-Leu-Phe; TLF
c. Beginning at the N-terminal end, the amino acids in the tripeptide are threonine, leucine, and phenylalanine. Changing the *ine* endings of the amino acids preceding the C-terminal amino acid (whose name does not change) gives the name threonylleucylphenylalanine.

STUDY CHECK 19.5

What is the name of the pentapeptide called met-enkephalin, a natural painkiller produced in the body, if it has the abbreviation Tyr-Gly-Gly-Phe-Met?

QUESTIONS AND PROBLEMS

19.3 Formation of Peptides

LEARNING GOAL: *Draw the condensed structural formula for a dipeptide.*

19.19 Draw the condensed structural formula for each of the following peptides, and give the three-letter and one-letter abbreviations for their names:
   a. alanylcysteine   **b.** serylphenylalanine
   c. glycylalanylvaline   **d.** valylisoleucyltryptophan

19.20 Draw the condensed structural formula for each of the following peptides, and give the three-letter and one-letter abbreviations for their names:
   a. methionylaspartic acid
   b. threonyltryptophan
   c. methionylglutaminyllysine
   d. histidylglycylglutamylisoleucine

19.4 Protein Structure: Primary and Secondary Levels

A **protein** is a polypeptide of 50 or more amino acids that has biological activity. Each protein in our cells has a unique sequence of amino acids that determines its three-dimensional structure and biological function.

Primary Structure

The **primary structure** of a protein is the particular sequence of amino acids held together by peptide bonds. For example, a hormone that stimulates the thyroid to release thyroxine is a tripeptide with the amino acid sequence Glu-His-Pro, EHP.

LEARNING GOAL

Describe the primary and secondary structures of a protein.

TUTORIAL
Peptides Are Chains of Amino Acids

SELF-STUDY ACTIVITY
Primary and Secondary Structure

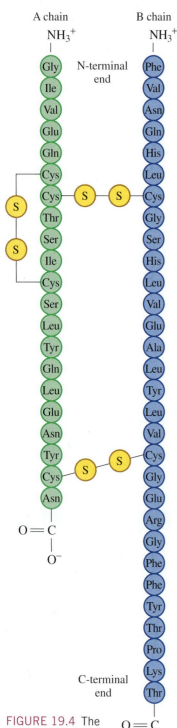

FIGURE 19.4 The sequence of amino acids in human insulin is the primary structure.

Q What kinds of bonds occur in the primary structure of a protein?

TUTORIAL
Levels of Structure in Proteins

Although five other sequences of the same three amino acids are possible, such as His-Pro-Glu or Pro-His-Glu, they do not produce hormonal activity. Thus, the biological function of peptides and proteins depends on the specific sequence of the amino acids.

The first protein to have its primary structure determined was insulin, which was accomplished by Frederick Sanger in 1953. Since that time, scientists have determined the amino acid sequences of thousands of proteins. Insulin is a hormone that regulates the glucose level in the blood. In the primary structure of human insulin, there are two polypeptide chains. In chain A, there are 21 amino acids, and in chain B there are 30 amino acids. The polypeptide chains are held together by *disulfide bonds* formed by the thiol groups of the cysteine amino acids in each of the chains (see Figure 19.4). Today, human insulin with this exact same structure is produced in large quantities through genetic engineering for the treatment of diabetes.

CONCEPT CHECK 19.6   Primary Structure

What are the three-letter and one-letter abbreviations of the possible tetrapeptides containing two valines, one proline, and one histidine if the C-terminal amino acid is proline?

ANSWER

The C-terminal amino acid of proline in the possible tetrapeptides would be preceded by three different sequences of two valines and one histidine: Val-Val-His-Pro (VVHP), Val-His-Val-Pro (VHVP), and His-Val-Val-Pro (HVVP).

Secondary Structures

The **secondary structure** of a protein describes the type of structure that forms when amino acids form hydrogen bonds within a single polypeptide chain or between polypeptide chains. The three most common types of secondary structures are the *alpha helix*, the *beta-pleated sheet*, and the *triple helix*.

Alpha Helix

In an **alpha helix** (**α helix**), hydrogen bonds form between the hydrogen atoms of the N—H groups in the amide bonds, and the oxygen atoms in the C=O groups of amide bonds that are four amino acids away in the next turn of the α helix (see Figure 19.5). All the R groups of the different amino acids in the polypeptide extend to the outside of the helix. The formation of many hydrogen bonds along the polypeptide chain gives the characteristic corkscrew or coiled shape of an alpha helix.

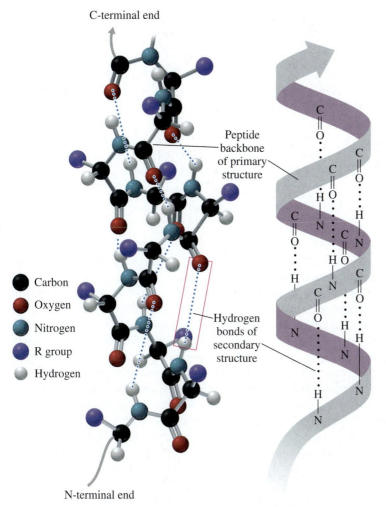

C-terminal end

Peptide
backbone
of primary
structure

- Carbon
- Oxygen
- Nitrogen
- R group
- Hydrogen

Hydrogen
bonds of
secondary
structure

N-terminal end

The shape of an alpha helix is similar to that of a spiral staircase.

SELF-STUDY ACTIVITY
Structure of Proteins

FIGURE 19.5 The α helix acquires a coiled shape from the hydrogen bonds between the hydrogen of the N—H group in one turn of the polypeptide, and the oxygen in the C=O group in the next turn.

Q What are the partial charges of the H in N—H and the O in C=O that permits hydrogen bonds to form?

Chemistry Link to Health

POLYPEPTIDES IN THE BODY

Enkephalins and endorphins are natural painkillers produced in the body. They are polypeptides that bind to receptors in the brain to give relief from pain. This effect appears to be responsible for the runner's high and the temporary loss of pain when severe injury occurs and with labor pains at childbirth.

The *enkephalins*, which are found in the thalamus and the spinal cord, are pentapeptides, the smallest molecules with opiate activity. The short amino acid sequence of met(methionine)-

enkephalin is incorporated into the longer amino acid sequence of the endorphins.

Four groups of *endorphins* have been identified: α-endorphin contains 16 amino acids, β-endorphin contains 31 amino acids, γ-endorphin has 17 amino acids, and δ-endorphin has 27 amino acids. Endorphins may produce their sedating effects by preventing the release of substance P, a polypeptide with 11 amino acids, which has been found to transmit pain impulses to the brain.

met-Enkephalin

When cells are damaged, a polypeptide called bradykinin is released, which stimulates the release of prostaglandins.

Arg—Pro—Pro—Gly—Phe—Ser—Pro—Phe—Arg
Bradykinin

Two hormones produced by the pituitary gland are the nonapeptides (peptides with nine amino acids) oxytocin and vasopressin. Oxytocin stimulates uterine contractions in labor, and vasopressin is an antidiuretic hormone that regulates blood pressure by adjusting the amount of water reabsorbed by the kidneys. The structures of these nonapeptides are very similar. Only the amino acids in positions 3 and 8 are different. However, the difference of two amino acids greatly affects how the two hormones function in the body.

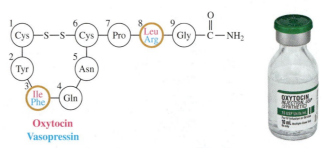

Oxytocin
Vasopressin

Oxytocin, a nonapeptide used to initiate labor, was the first hormone to be synthesized in the laboratory.

TUTORIAL
The Shapes of Protein Chains:
Helices and Sheets

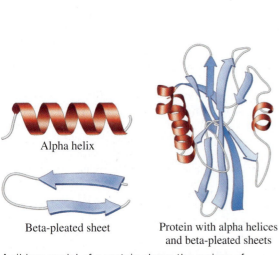

The secondary structure in silk is a beta-pleated sheet.

Beta-Pleated Sheet

Another type of secondary structure found in proteins is the **beta-pleated sheet** (**β-pleated sheet**). In a β-pleated sheet, polypeptide chains are held together side by side by hydrogen bonds that form between oxygen atoms of the carbonyl group ($C=O$) in one section of the polypeptide chain, and the hydrogen atoms in the N—H groups of the amide bonds in a nearby section of the polypeptide chain. A beta-pleated sheet can form between adjacent polypeptide chains or within the same polypeptide chain when the rigid structure of the amino acid proline causes a bend in the polypeptide chain. The tendency to form various kinds of secondary structures depends on the amino acids in a particular segment of the polypeptide chain. Typically, beta-pleated sheets contain mostly amino acids with small R groups such as glycine, valine, alanine, and serine, which extend above and below the beta-pleated sheet. The α-helical regions in a protein have higher amounts of amino acids with large R groups such as histidine, leucine, and methionine.

The hydrogen bonds holding the β-pleated sheets tightly in place account for the strength and durability of fibrous proteins such as silk (see Figure 19.6).

Alpha helix

Beta-pleated sheet

Protein with alpha helices and beta-pleated sheets

A ribbon model of a protein shows the regions of alpha helices and beta-pleated sheets.

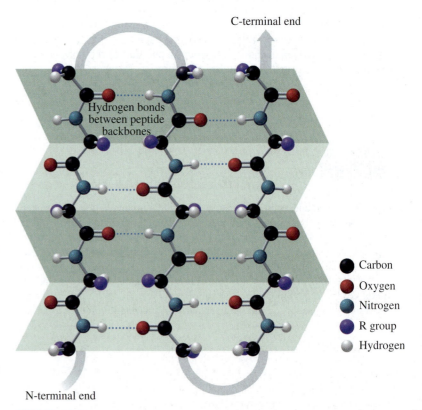

C-terminal end

Hydrogen bonds between peptide backbones

● Carbon
● Oxygen
● Nitrogen
● R group
● Hydrogen

N-terminal end

FIGURE 19.6 In the secondary structure of a β-pleated sheet, hydrogen bonds form between the peptide chains.

Q How do the hydrogen bonds differ between a β-pleated sheet and an α helix?

In some proteins, the polypeptide chain consists mostly of α helices, whereas other proteins consist mostly of β-pleated sheets. However, in some proteins, there are sections of both α helices and β-pleated sheets. Some sections of the polypeptide chain with no definite secondary structure exist as random coils.

The regions of the α helices and β-pleated sheets are shown in a ribbon model in which the coiled portions represent the α helices, and the long arrows that look like a piece of fettuccine represent the β-pleated sheets. Regions that are not α helices or β-pleated sheets are random regions indicated by thick lines.

Collagen

Collagen, which is the most abundant protein in the body, makes up 25–35% of all protein in vertebrates. It is found in connective tissue, blood vessels, skin, tendons, ligaments, the cornea of the eye, and cartilage. The strong structure of collagen is a result of three α helices woven together like a braid to form a **triple helix** (see Figure 19.7).

Collagen has a high content of glycine (33%), proline (22%), and alanine (12%), and smaller amounts of hydroxyproline and hydroxylysine, which are modified forms of proline and lysine. The —OH groups on these modified amino acids provide additional hydrogen bonds between the peptide chains to give strength to the collagen triple helix. When several triple helices wrap together as a braid, they form the fibrils that make up connective tissues and tendons. When a diet is deficient in vitamin C, collagen fibrils are weakened because the enzymes needed to form hydroxyproline and hydroxylysine require vitamin C. Collagen becomes less elastic as a person ages because additional bonds form between the fibrils. Bones, cartilage, and tendons become more brittle, and wrinkles are seen as the skin loses elasticity.

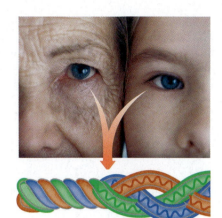

Triple helix   3 α Helix peptide chains

FIGURE 19.7 Collagen fibers are triple helices of polypeptide chains held together by hydrogen bonds.

Q What are some of the amino acids in collagen that form hydrogen bonds between the polypeptide chains?

CONCEPT CHECK 19.7 Identifying Secondary Structures

Indicate the secondary structure (α helix, β-pleated sheet, or triple helix) described in each of the following statements:

a. a structure that has hydrogen bonds between adjacent polypeptide chains
b. three α helical polypeptides woven together
c. a peptide chain with a coiled or corkscrew shape that is held in place by hydrogen bonds

ANSWER

a. β-pleated sheet
b. triple helix
c. α helix

Hydroxyproline and hydroxylysine provide additional hydrogen bonds in the triple alpha helices of collagen.

Chemistry Link to Health

PRIONS AND MAD COW DISEASE

Until recently, researchers thought that only viruses or bacteria were responsible for transmitting diseases. Now a group of diseases has been found in which the infectious agents are proteins called *prions*, a word coined in 1982 by Stanley B. Prusiner, who won the Nobel Prize in Physiology or Medicine in 1997 for his research into prions. *Bovine spongiform encephalopathy* (*BSE*), or "mad cow disease," is a fatal brain disease of cattle in which the brain fills with cavities, resembling a sponge. In the noninfectious form of the prion PrP^c, the N-terminal portion is a random coil. Although the noninfectious form may be ingested from meat products, its structure can change to what is known as PrP^s, or *prion-related protein scrapie*. In this infectious form, the end of the peptide chain folds into a β-pleated sheet, which has disastrous effects on the brain and spinal cord. The conditions that cause this structural change are not yet known.

Mad-cow disease was diagnosed in Great Britain in 1986. The protein is present in nerve tissue of animals, but it is not found in their meat. Cattle are normally herbivores, but when they were fed a bone meal that comes from cattle with mad-cow disease, the infectious agent, now known to be prions, can spread to other cattle. Control measures that exclude the brain and spinal cord from animal feed are now in place to reduce the incidence of BSE.

The human variant of this disease is called *Creutzfeldt-Jakob disease* (*CJD*). Around 1955, Dr. Carleton Gajdusek was studying the Fore people of Papua New Guinea, where many tribe members were dying of the neurological disease known as "kuru." Among the Fore, it was a custom to cannibalize members of the tribe upon their death. Gajdusek who received the Nobel Prize in Physiology or Medicine in 1976, eventually determined that this practice was responsible for transmitting the infectious agent from one tribe member to another.

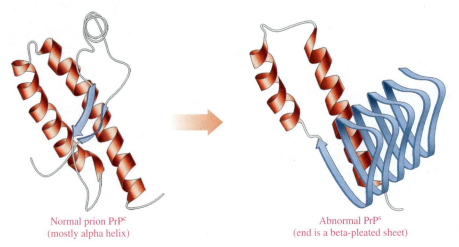

Normal prion PrP^c
(mostly alpha helix)

Abnormal PrP^s
(end is a beta-pleated sheet)

Prions are proteins that cause infections such as "mad cow disease."

QUESTIONS AND PROBLEMS

19.4 Protein Structure: Primary and Secondary Levels

LEARNING GOAL: Describe the primary and secondary structures of a protein.

19.21 What type of bonding occurs in the primary structure of a protein?

19.22 How can two proteins with exactly the same number and type of amino acids have different primary structures?

19.23 Two peptides each contain one molecule of valine and two molecules of methionine. What are their possible primary structures?

19.24 What are three different types of secondary protein structure?

19.25 What happens to the primary structure of a protein when a protein forms a secondary structure?

19.26 In an α helix, how does bonding occur between the amino acids in the polypeptide chain?

19.27 What is the difference in bonding between an α helix and a β-pleated sheet?

19.28 How is the secondary structure of a β-pleated sheet different from that of a triple helix?

LEARNING GOAL

Describe the tertiary and quaternary structures of a protein.

SELF-STUDY ACTIVITY
Tertiary and Quaternary Structure

19.5 Protein Structure: Tertiary and Quaternary Levels

The **tertiary structure** of a protein involves attractions and repulsions between the R groups of the amino acids in the polypeptide chain. As interactions occur between different parts of the peptide chain, segments of the chain twist and bend until the protein acquires a specific three-dimensional shape.

Interactions Between R Groups in Tertiary Structures

The tertiary structure of a protein is stabilized by interactions between the R groups of the amino acids in one region of the polypeptide chain and the R groups of amino acids in other regions of the protein (see Figure 19.8). The stabilizing interactions of tertiary structures are detailed as follows:

1. **Hydrophobic interactions** are interactions between amino acids that have nonpolar R groups. Within a protein, the amino acids with nonpolar R groups are pushed away from the aqueous environment, which forms a hydrophobic center at the interior of the protein.
2. **Hydrophilic interactions** are attractions between the external aqueous environment and the R groups of polar amino acids. The polar R groups are pulled to the outer surface of proteins where they interact with the polar water molecules.
3. **Salt bridges** are ionic bonds between the ionized R groups of basic and acidic amino acids. For example, the ionized R group of arginine, which has a positive charge, can form a salt bridge (ionic bond) with the R group in aspartic acid, which has a negative charge.
4. **Hydrogen bonds** form between the H of a polar R group and the O or N of a second polar amino acid. For example, a hydrogen bond can occur between the —OH groups of two serines or between the —OH of serine and the —NH$_2$ in the R group of glutamine.
5. **Disulfide bonds** (—S—S—) are covalent bonds that form between the —SH groups of two cysteines in the polypeptide chain. In some proteins, there may be several disulfide bonds between the R groups of cysteines in the polypeptide chain.

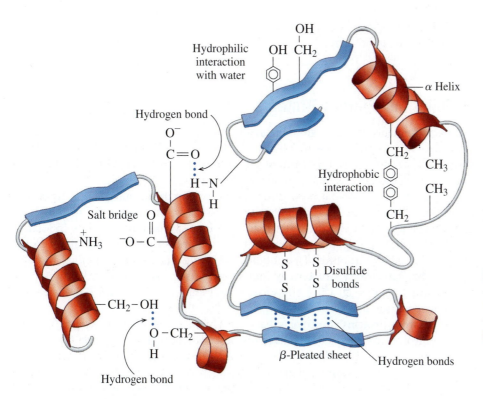

FIGURE 19.8 Interactions between amino acid R groups fold a polypeptide into a specific three-dimensional shape called its tertiary structure.

Q Why would one section of the polypeptide chain be pushed to the center while another section would be pulled to the surface?

SAMPLE PROBLEM 19.6 **Interactions Between R Groups in Tertiary Structures**

What type of interaction would you expect between the R groups of the following amino acids in a tertiary structure?

a. cysteine and cysteine
b. aspartic acid and lysine
c. tyrosine and water

TUTORIAL
Levels of Structure in Proteins

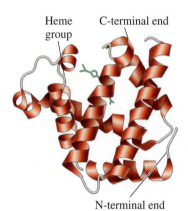

Heme group   C-terminal end

N-terminal end

FIGURE 19.9 The ribbon model represents the tertiary structure of the polypeptide chain of myoglobin, which is a globular protein that contains a heme group that binds oxygen.

Q Would hydrophilic amino acids be found on the outside or inside of the myoglobin structure?

α Helix

α-Keratin

FIGURE 19.10 The fibrous proteins of *α*-keratin wrap together to form fibrils of hair and wool.

Q Why does hair have a large amount of cysteine amino acids?

Analyze the Problem

To determine the interaction between the R groups of two amino acids or a polar R group and water, we need to identify each R group (see Table 19.2). Then we can determine what type of interaction will occur as follows:

Types of R Groups	Type of Interaction
Nonpolar and nonpolar	hydrophobic
Polar (neutral) and water	hydrophilic
Polar (basic) —NH_3^+ and polar (acidic) —COO^-	salt bridges
Polar (neutral) and polar (neutral) —OH and —NH— or —NH_2	hydrogen bonds
—SH and —SH	disulfide bonds

a. Two cysteines, each with an R group containing —SH, will form a disulfide bond.
b. The interaction of the —COO^- in the R group of aspartic acid and the —NH_3^+ in the R group of lysine will form an ionic bond called a salt bridge.
c. The R group in tyrosine has an —OH group that is attracted to water by hydrophilic interactions.

STUDY CHECK 19.6

In a protein, would you expect to find valine and leucine on the outside or the inside of the tertiary structure? Why?

Globular and Fibrous Proteins

A group of proteins known as **globular proteins** have compact, spherical shapes because sections of the polypeptide chain fold over on top of each other due to the various interactions between R groups. It is the globular proteins that carry out the work of the cells: functions such as synthesis, transport, and metabolism.

Myoglobin is a globular protein that stores oxygen in skeletal muscle. High concentrations of myoglobin are found in the muscles of sea mammals, such as seals and whales that stay under the water for a long time. Myoglobin contains 153 amino acids in a single polypeptide chain with about three-fourths of the chain in the *α* helix secondary structure. The polypeptide chain, including its helical regions, forms a compact tertiary structure by folding upon itself (see Figure 19.9). Within the tertiary structure, oxygen (O_2) binds to a heme group, which is a large, organic compound with an iron ion in the center.

The **fibrous proteins** are proteins that consist of long, thin, fiber-like shapes. They are typically involved in the structure of cells and tissues. Two types of fibrous protein are the *α*- and *β*-keratins. The *α*-keratins are the proteins that make up hair, wool, skin, and nails. In hair, three *α* helices coil together like a braid to form a fibril. Within the fibril, the *α* helices are held together by disulfide (—S—S—) linkages between the R groups of the many cysteine amino acids in hair. Several fibrils bind together to form a strand of hair (see Figure 19.10). The *β*-keratins are the type of proteins found in the feathers of birds and scales of reptiles. In *β*-keratins, the proteins consist of large amounts of *β*-pleated sheet structure.

Quaternary Structure: Hemoglobin

While many proteins are biologically active as tertiary structures, some proteins require two or more tertiary structures to be biologically active. When several polypeptide chains called *subunits* bind to form a larger complex, it is referred to as a **quaternary structure**. Hemoglobin, a globular protein that transports oxygen in blood, consists of four polypeptide chains: two α-chains with 141 amino acids, and two β-chains with 146 amino acids. Although the α-chains and β-chains have different sequences of amino acids, they both form similar tertiary structures with similar shapes.

In the quaternary structure, the subunits are held together by the same interactions that stabilize their tertiary structures, such as hydrogen bonds and salt bridges between R groups, disulfide bonds, and hydrophobic interactions (see Figure 19.11). Each subunit of hemoglobin is a globular protein with an embedded heme group, which contains one iron atom that can bind an oxygen molecule. In the hemoglobin molecule in adults, there must be four subunits, two of α and two of β, in order for hemoglobin to properly function as an oxygen carrier. Therefore, the complete quaternary structure of hemoglobin can bind and transport up to four molecules of oxygen.

Hemoglobin and myoglobin have similar biological functions. Hemoglobin carries oxygen in the blood, whereas myoglobin carries oxygen in muscle. Myoglobin, a single polypeptide chain with a molar mass of 17 000, has about one-fourth the molar mass of hemoglobin (67 000). The tertiary structure of the single polypeptide myoglobin is almost identical to the tertiary structure of each of the subunits of hemoglobin. Myoglobin stores just one molecule of oxygen, just as each subunit of hemoglobin carries one oxygen molecule. The similarity in tertiary structures allows each protein to bind and release oxygen in a similar manner. Table 19.6 and Figure 19.12 summarize the structural levels of proteins.

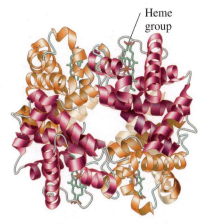

Heme group

FIGURE 19.11 In the ribbon model of hemoglobin, the quaternary structure is made up of four polypeptide subunits—two (orange) are α-chains and two (red) are β-chains. The heme groups (green) in the four subunits bind oxygen.

Q What is the difference between a tertiary structure and a quaternary structure?

TABLE 19.6 Summary of Structural Levels in Proteins

Structural Level	Characteristics
Primary	Peptide bonds join amino acids in a specific sequence in a polypeptide.
Secondary	The α helix, β-pleated sheet, or triple helix forms by hydrogen bonding between the atoms in the peptide bonds along the chain.
Tertiary	A polypeptide folds into a compact, three-dimensional shape stabilized by interactions between R groups of amino acids to form a biologically active protein.
Quaternary	Two or more protein subunits combine to form a biologically active protein.

CONCEPT CHECK 19.8   Structural Levels of Proteins

Match the level of protein structure (**a–d**) with the correct descriptions (**1–4**). Explain.

a. primary structure
b. secondary structure
c. tertiary structure
d. quaternary structure

1. hydrogen bonds that occur between sections of a peptide to form an α helix or a β-pleated sheet
2. association of four polypeptide chains
3. interactions between polar R groups in a single polypeptide
4. a sequence of amino acids held together by peptide bonds

ANSWER

a. (**4**) The sequence of amino acids determines the primary structure.
b. (**1**) Hydrogen bonds between two sections of a polypeptide occur in the secondary structures of an α helix and a β-pleated sheet.
c. (**3**) Interactions between two polar R groups occur in the tertiary structure of a single polypeptide.
d. (**2**) The association of four polypeptide chains occurs in the quaternary structures of proteins.

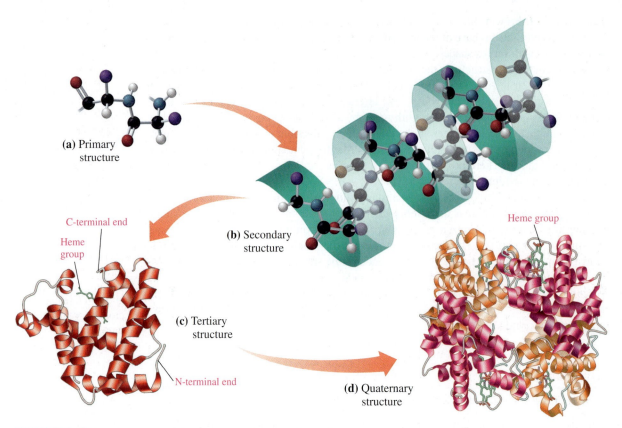

(a) Primary structure

(b) Secondary structure

C-terminal end

Heme group

(c) Tertiary structure

N-terminal end

Heme group

(d) Quaternary structure

FIGURE 19.12 Proteins consist of **(a)** primary, **(b)** secondary, **(c)** tertiary, and sometimes **(d)** quaternary structural levels.
Q What is the difference between a primary structure and a tertiary structure?

Chemistry Link to Health

SICKLE CELL ANEMIA

Sickle cell anemia is a disease caused by an abnormality in the shape of one of the subunits of the hemoglobin protein. In the β-chain, the sixth amino acid, glutamic acid, which is polar acidic, is replaced by valine, a nonpolar amino acid.

Because valine has a nonpolar R group, it is attracted to the nonpolar regions within the beta hemoglobin chains. The affected red blood cells (RBC) change from a rounded shape to a crescent shape, which interferes with their ability to transport adequate quantities of oxygen. Hydrophobic interactions also cause sickle-cell hemoglobin molecules to stick together. They form insoluble fibers of sickle-cell hemoglobin that clog capillaries, where they cause inflammation, pain, and organ damage. Critically low oxygen levels may occur in the affected tissues.

In sickle-cell anemia, both genes for the altered hemoglobin must be inherited. However, a few sickled cells are found in persons who carry one gene for sickle-cell hemoglobin, a condition that is also known to provide some resistance to malaria.

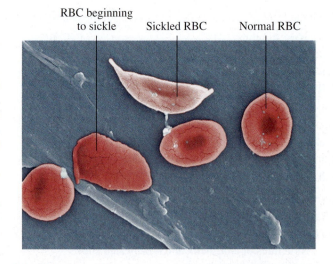

RBC beginning to sickle   Sickled RBC   Normal RBC

Normal β-chain: Val—His—Leu—Thr—Pro—|Glu|—Glu—Lys—   ← Polar acidic amino acid
Sickled β-chain: Val—His—Leu—Thr—Pro—|Val|—Glu—Lys—   ← Nonpolar amino acid

SAMPLE PROBLEM 19.7 Identifying Protein Structure

Indicate whether the following are responsible for primary, secondary, tertiary, or quaternary protein structures:

a. Disulfide bonds that form between sections of a protein chain.
b. Peptide bonds that form a chain of amino acids.
c. Hydrogen bonds between the H of a peptide bond and the O of a peptide bond four amino acids away.

SOLUTION

Analyze the Problem

The level of protein structure is identified from the characteristics of the protein structure.

Structural Level	Characteristics
Primary	Peptide bonds join amino acids in a specific sequence in a polypeptide.
Secondary	The α helix, β-pleated sheet, or triple helix forms by hydrogen bonding between peptide bonds along the chain.
Tertiary	A polypeptide folds into a compact, three-dimensional shape stabilized by interactions between R groups of amino acids to form a biologically active protein.
Quaternary	Two or more protein subunits combine to form a biologically active protein.

a. Disulfide bonds are a type of interaction found in the tertiary and quaternary levels of protein structure.
b. The sequence of amino acids in a polypeptide is the primary level of protein structure.
c. Hydrogen bonding between peptide bonds forms the secondary level of protein structure.

STUDY CHECK 19.7

What structural level is represented by the interaction of the two subunits in insulin?

QUESTIONS AND PROBLEMS

19.5 Protein Structure: Tertiary and Quaternary Levels

LEARNING GOAL: *Describe the tertiary and quaternary structures of a protein.*

19.29 What type of interaction would you expect between the following groups in a tertiary structure?
    a. two cysteines   **b.** glutamic acid and lysine
    c. serine and aspartic acid   **d.** two leucines

19.30 What type of interaction would you expect between the following groups in a tertiary structure?
    a. phenylalanine and isoleucine   **b.** aspartic acid and histidine
    c. asparagine and tyrosine   **d.** alanine and proline

19.31 A portion of a polypeptide chain contains the following sequence of amino acids:

    -Leu-Val-Cys-Asp-

    a. Which amino acid can form a disulfide bond?
    b. Which amino acids are likely to be found on the inside of the protein structure? Why?
    c. Which amino acids would be found on the outside of the protein? Why?
    d. How does the primary structure of a protein affect its tertiary structure?

19.32 About one-half of the 153 amino acids in myoglobin have nonpolar R groups.
    a. Where would you expect those amino acids to be located in the tertiary structure?
    b. Where would you expect the polar R groups to be?
    c. Why is myoglobin more soluble in water than silk or wool?

19.33 Indicate whether the following statements describe the primary, secondary, tertiary, or quaternary protein structure:
    a. R groups interact to form disulfide bonds or ionic bonds.
    b. Peptide bonds join the amino acids in a polypeptide chain.
    c. Several polypeptides in a β-pleated sheet are held together by hydrogen bonds between adjacent chains.
    d. Hydrogen bonding between amino acids in the same polypeptide gives a coiled shape to the protein.

19.34 Indicate whether the following statements describe the primary, secondary, tertiary, or quaternary protein structure:
    a. Hydrophobic R groups seeking a nonpolar environment move toward the inside of the folded protein.
    b. Protein chains of collagen form a triple helix.
    c. An active protein contains four tertiary subunits.
    d. In sickle-cell anemia, valine replaces glutamic acid in the β-chain.

TUTORIAL
Protein Demolition

Explore Your World

DENATURATION OF MILK PROTEIN

Pour some milk in each of five glasses. Add the following to the milk samples in glasses 1–4. The fifth glass of milk is a reference sample.

1. Vinegar, drop by drop. Stir.
2. One-half teaspoon of meat tenderizer. Stir.
3. One teaspoon of fresh pineapple juice. (Canned juice has been heated and cannot be used.)
4. One teaspoon of fresh pineapple juice after the juice is heated to boiling.

QUESTIONS

1. How did the appearance of the milk change in each of the samples?
2. What enzyme is listed on the package label of the tenderizer?
3. How does the effect of the heated pineapple juice compare with that of the fresh juice? Explain.
4. Why is cooked pineapple used when making gelatin (a protein) desserts?

TUTORIAL
Understanding Protein Degradation

19.6 Protein Hydrolysis and Denaturation

Peptide bonds can be hydrolyzed to give individual amino acids. This process occurs in the stomach when enzymes such as pepsin or trypsin catalyze the hydrolysis of proteins to give amino acids. This hydrolysis disrupts the primary structure by breaking the covalent amide bonds that link the amino acids. In the digestion of proteins, the amino acids are absorbed through the intestinal walls and carried to the cells, where they can be used to synthesize new proteins.

Alanylglycylserine (Ala-Gly-Ser, AGS)

Alanine (Ala, A) + Glycine (Gly, G) + Serine (Ser, S)

Denaturation of Proteins

Denaturation of a protein occurs when there is a disruption of the interactions between R groups that stabilize the secondary, tertiary, or quaternary structure. However, the covalent amide bonds of the primary structure are not affected.

The loss of secondary and tertiary structures occurs when conditions change, such as increasing the temperature or making the pH very acidic or basic. If the pH changes, the basic and acidic R groups lose their ionic charges and cannot form salt bridges, which causes a change in the shape of the protein. Denaturation can also occur by adding certain organic compounds or heavy metal ions, or through mechanical agitation. When there is a disruption of the interactions between the R groups of a globular protein, it unfolds like a loose piece of cooked spaghetti. With the loss of its overall shape (tertiary structure), the protein is no longer biologically active (see Figure 19.13).

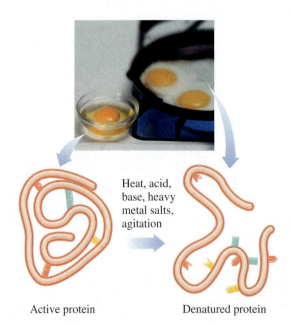

Active protein → Heat, acid, base, heavy metal salts, agitation → Denatured protein

FIGURE 19.13 Denaturation of a protein occurs when the interactions of R groups that stabilize tertiary or quaternary structures are disrupted, which destroys the shape and renders the protein biologically inactive.

Q What are some ways in which proteins are denatured?

Heat

Heat denatures proteins by breaking apart hydrogen bonds and the hydrophobic inter-actions between nonpolar R groups. Few proteins can remain biologically active above 50 °C. Whenever you cook food, you are using heat to denature protein. The nutritional value of the proteins in food is not changed, but they are made more digestible. High temperatures are also used to disinfect surgical instruments and gowns by denaturing the proteins of any bacteria present.

Acids and Bases

When an acid or a base is added to a protein, the change in pH breaks down hydro-gen bonds and disrupts the ionic bonds (salt bridges). In the preparation of yogurt and cheese, bacteria that produce lactic acid are added to denature the milk protein and produce solid casein. Tannic acid, a weak acid used in burn ointments, is used to coagulate proteins at the site of the burn, forming a protective cover and preventing further loss of fluid from the burn.

Organic Compounds

Ethanol and isopropyl alcohol act as disinfectants by forming their own hydrogen bonds with a protein and disrupting the side chain intramolecular hydrogen bonding. An alcohol swab is used to clean wounds or to prepare the skin for an injection because the alcohol passes through the cell walls and coagulates the proteins inside the bacteria.

Heavy Metal Ions

Heavy metal ions such as Ag^+, Pb^{2+}, and Hg^{2+} denature protein by forming bonds with ionic R groups or reacting with disulfide ($-S-S-$) bonds. In hospitals, a dilute (1%) solution of $AgNO_3$ is placed in the eyes of newborn babies to destroy the bacteria that cause gonorrhea. If heavy metals are ingested, they act as poisons by severely denaturing body proteins and disrupting metabolic reactions. An antidote is a high-protein food such as milk, eggs, or cheese that combines with the heavy metal ions until the stomach can be pumped.

Agitation

The whipping of cream and the beating of egg whites are examples of using mechanical agitation to denature protein. The whipping action stretches the polypeptide chains until the stabilizing interactions are disrupted. Table 19.7 summarizes protein denaturation.

TABLE 19.7 **Protein Denaturation**		
Denaturing Agent	**Bonds Disrupted**	**Examples**
Heat Above 50 °C	Hydrogen bonds; hydrophobic interactions between nonpolar R groups	Cooking food and autoclaving surgical items
Acids and Bases	Hydrogen bonds between polar R groups; salt bridges	Lactic acid from bacteria, which denatures milk protein in the preparation of yogurt and cheese
Organic Compounds	Hydrophobic interactions	Ethanol and isopropyl alcohol, which disinfect wounds and prepare the skin for injections
Heavy Metal Ions Ag^+, Pb^{2+}, and Hg^{2+}	Disulfide bonds in proteins by forming ionic bonds	Mercury and lead poisoning
Agitation	Hydrogen bonds and hydrophobic interactions by stretching polypeptide chains and disrupting stabilizing interactions	Whipped cream, meringue made from egg whites

CONCEPT CHECK 19.9   Denaturation of Proteins

Describe the denaturation process in each of the following:

a. An appetizer known as ceviche is prepared without heat by placing slices of raw fish in a solution of lemon or lime juice. After 3 or 4 hours, the fish appears to be "cooked."
b. When baking scalloped potatoes, the added milk curdles (forms solids).

ANSWER

a. The acids in lemon or lime juice break down the hydrogen bonds between polar R groups and disrupt salt bridges, which denature the proteins of the fish.
b. The heat during baking breaks apart hydrogen bonds and hydrophobic interactions between nonpolar R groups in the milk. When the milk denatures, the proteins become insoluble and form solids called curds.

SAMPLE PROBLEM 19.8   Effects of Denaturation

What happens to the tertiary structure of a globular protein when it is placed in an acidic solution?

SOLUTION

An acid causes denaturation by disrupting the hydrogen bonds and the ionic bonds between the R groups. A loss in interactions causes the tertiary structure to lose stability. As the protein unfolds, both the shape and biological function are lost.

STUDY CHECK 19.8

Why is a dilute solution of $AgNO_3$ used to disinfect the eyes of newborn infants?

QUESTIONS AND PROBLEMS

19.6 Protein Hydrolysis and Denaturation

LEARNING GOAL: *Describe the hydrolysis and denaturation of proteins.*

19.35 What products would result from the complete hydrolysis of Gly-Ala-Ser?

19.36 Would the hydrolysis products of the tripeptide Ala-Ser-Gly be the same or different from the products in Problem 19.35? Explain.

19.37 What dipeptides could be produced from the partial hydrolysis of His-Met-Gly-Val?

19.38 What tripeptides could be produced from the partial hydrolysis of Ser-Leu-Gly-Gly-Ala?

19.39 What structural level of a protein is affected by hydrolysis?

19.40 What structural level of a protein is affected by denaturation?

19.41 Indicate the changes in the secondary and tertiary structural levels of proteins for each of the following:
a. An egg placed in water at 100 °C is soft-boiled after 3 minutes.
b. Prior to giving an injection, the skin is wiped with an alcohol swab.
c. Surgical instruments are placed in a 120 °C autoclave.
d. During surgery, a wound is closed by cauterization (heat).

19.42 Indicate the changes in the secondary and tertiary structural levels of proteins for each of the following:
a. Tannic acid is placed on a burn.
b. Milk is heated to 60 °C to make yogurt.
c. To avoid spoilage, seeds are treated with a solution of $HgCl_2$.
d. Hamburger is cooked at high temperatures to destroy *E. coli* bacteria that may cause intestinal illness.

CONCEPT MAP

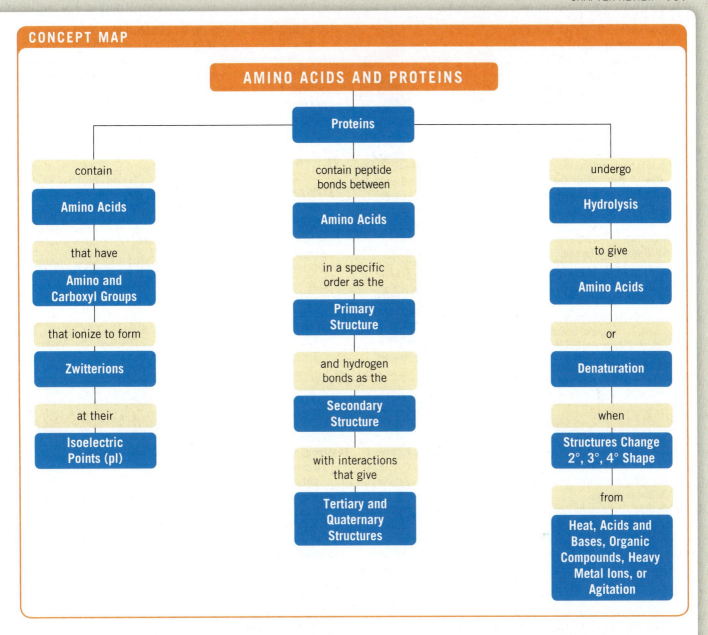

AMINO ACIDS AND PROTEINS

Proteins

contain → **Amino Acids** that have → **Amino and Carboxyl Groups** that ionize to form → **Zwitterions** at their → **Isoelectric Points (pI)**

contain peptide bonds between → **Amino Acids** in a specific order as the → **Primary Structure** and hydrogen bonds as the → **Secondary Structure** with interactions that give → **Tertiary and Quaternary Structures**

undergo → **Hydrolysis** to give → **Amino Acids** or → **Denaturation** when → **Structures Change 2°, 3°, 4° Shape** from → **Heat, Acids and Bases, Organic Compounds, Heavy Metal Ions, or Agitation**

CHAPTER REVIEW

19.1 Proteins and Amino Acids

LEARNING GOAL: Classify proteins by their functions. Give the name and abbreviations for an amino acid and draw its ionized structure.

- Some proteins are enzymes or hormones, whereas others are important in structure, transport, protection, storage, and muscle contraction.
- A group of 20 amino acids provides the molecular building blocks of proteins.
- Attached to the central alpha carbon of each amino acid are an ammonium group, a carboxylate group, and a unique R group.
- The R group gives an amino acid the property of being nonpolar, polar, acidic, or basic.

19.2 Amino Acids as Zwitterions

LEARNING GOAL: Draw the zwitterion for an amino acid at its isoelectric point, and its ionized structure at pH values above or below its isoelectric point.

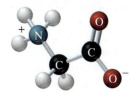

- Amino acids exist as dipolar ions called zwitterions, as positive ions at low pH, and as negative ions at high pH levels.
- At the isoelectric point, zwitterions have a net charge of zero.

19.3 Formation of Peptides

LEARNING GOAL: Draw the condensed structural formula for a dipeptide.

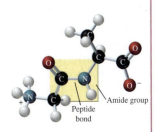

Peptide bond

Amide group

- Peptides form when an amide bond links the carboxylate group of one amino acid and the ammonium group of a second amino acid.

19.4 Protein Structure: Primary and Secondary Levels

LEARNING GOAL: Describe the primary and secondary structures of a protein.

- Long chains of amino acids that are biologically active are called proteins.
- The primary structure of a protein is its sequence of amino acids.
- In the secondary structure, hydrogen bonds between peptide groups produce a characteristic shape such as an α helix, β-pleated sheet, or a triple helix.

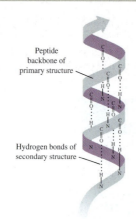

Peptide backbone of primary structure

Hydrogen bonds of secondary structure

19.5 Protein Structure: Tertiary and Quaternary Levels

LEARNING GOAL: Describe the tertiary and quaternary structures of a protein.

- In globular proteins, the polypeptide chain, including α-helical and β-pleated sheet regions, folds upon itself to form a tertiary structure.

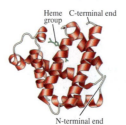

Heme group   C-terminal end

N-terminal end

- A tertiary structure is stabilized by interactions that push amino acids with hydrophobic R groups to the center and pull amino acid with hydrophilic R groups to the surface, and by interactions between amino acids with R groups that form hydrogen bonds, disulfide bonds, and salt bridges.
- In a quaternary structure, two or more tertiary subunits are joined together for biological activity, held by the same interactions found in tertiary structures.

19.6 Protein Hydrolysis and Denaturation

LEARNING GOAL: Describe the hydrolysis and denaturation of proteins.

- Denaturation of a protein occurs when heat or other denaturing agents destroy the structure of the protein (but not the primary structure) until biological activity is lost.

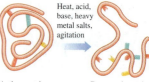

Active protein   Denatured protein

Heat, acid, base, heavy metal salts, agitation

KEY TERMS

alpha helix A secondary level of protein structure, in which hydrogen bonds connect the N—H of one peptide bond with the C=O of a peptide bond farther down the chain to form a coiled or corkscrew structure.

amino acid The building block of proteins, consisting of an ammonium group, a carboxylate group, and a unique R group attached to a carbon.

beta-pleated sheet A secondary level of protein structure that consists of hydrogen bonds between peptide links in parallel polypeptide chains.

C-terminal amino acid The end amino acid in a peptide chain with a free carboxylate group ($-COO^-$).

collagen The most abundant form of protein in the body, which is composed of fibrils of triple helices that are hydrogen-bonded together between $-OH$ groups of hydroxyproline and hydroxylysine.

denaturation The loss of secondary, tertiary, and quaternary protein structure caused by heat, acids, bases, organic compounds, heavy metals, and/or agitation.

disulfide bonds Covalent $-S-S-$ bonds that form between the $-SH$ groups of two cysteines in a protein, which stabilize tertiary and quaternary structures.

electrophoresis The use of electrical current to separate proteins or other charged molecules with different isoelectric points.

essential amino acids Amino acids that must be supplied by the diet because they are not synthesized by the body.

fibrous proteins Proteins that are insoluble in water; consisting of polypeptide chains with α helices or β-pleated sheets, and comprising the fibers of hair, wool, skin, nails, and silk.

globular proteins Proteins that acquire a compact shape from attractions between the R groups of the amino acids in the protein.

hydrogen bonds The interactions between water and the polar R groups such as $-OH$, $-NH_3^+$, and $-COO^-$ on the outside surface of a polypeptide chain.

hydrophilic interactions The attractions between polar R groups on the protein surface and water.

hydrophobic interactions The attractions between nonpolar R groups on the inside of a globular protein.

isoelectric point (pI) The pH at which an amino acid exists as a zwitterion with a net charge of zero.

N-terminal amino acid The end amino acid in a peptide with a free $-NH_3^+$ group.

nonpolar amino acids Amino acids with nonpolar R groups containing only C and H atoms.

peptide The combination of two or more amino acids joined by peptide bonds; dipeptide, tripeptide, and so on.

peptide bond The amide bond in peptides that joins the carboxylate group of one amino acid with the ammonium group in the next amino acid.

polar amino acid (acidic) An amino acid that has an R group with a carboxylate group ($-COO^-$).

polar amino acid (basic) An amino acid that contains an amine R group.

polar amino acids (neutral) Amino acids with polar R groups.

primary structure The specific sequence of the amino acids in a protein.

protein Polypeptides containing many amino acids linked together by peptide bonds that have biological activity.

quaternary structure A protein structure in which two or more protein subunits form an active protein.

salt bridge The attraction between the ionized R groups of basic and acidic amino acids in the tertiary structure of a protein.

secondary structure The formation of an α helix, β-pleated sheet, or triple helix.

tertiary structure The folding of the secondary structure of a protein into a compact structure that is stabilized by the interactions of R groups such as ionic and disulfide bonds.

triple helix The protein structure found in collagen consisting of three alpha-helical polypeptide chains woven together like a braid.

zwitterion The dipolar form of an amino acid consisting of two oppositely charged ionic regions, $-NH_3^+$ and $-COO^-$.

UNDERSTANDING THE CONCEPTS

The chapter sections to review are shown in parentheses at the end of each question.

19.43 Seeds and vegetables are often deficient in one or more essential amino acids. The table below shows which essential amino acids are present in each food. (19.1)

Source	Lysine	Tryptophan	Methionine
Oatmeal	No	Yes	Yes
Rice	No	Yes	Yes
Garbanzo beans	Yes	No	Yes
Lima beans	Yes	No	No
Cornmeal	No	No	Yes

Use the table to decide if each food combination provides the essential amino acids lysine, tryptophan, and methionine.
a. rice and garbanzo beans
b. lima beans and cornmeal
c. a salad of garbanzo beans and lima beans

19.44 Use the table in Problem 19.43 to decide if each food combination provides the essential amino acids lysine, tryptophan, and methionine. (19.1)

Oatmeal is deficient in the essential amino acid lysine.

a. rice and lima beans
b. rice and oatmeal
c. oatmeal and lima beans

Use the following condensed structural formulas of cysteine (**1–4**) to answer Problems 19.45 and 19.46:

$$\begin{array}{cc}
CH_2-SH & CH_2-SH \\
| & | \\
H_2N-C-COO^- & H_3\overset{+}{N}-C-COOH \\
| & | \\
H & H \\
(1) & (2)
\end{array}$$

$$\begin{array}{cc}
CH_2-SH & CH_2-SH \\
| & | \\
H_3\overset{+}{N}-C-COO^- & H_2N-C-COOH \\
| & | \\
H & H \\
(3) & (4)
\end{array}$$

19.45 If cysteine, an amino acid prevalent in hair, has a pI of 5.1, which condensed structural formula would it have in solutions with each the following pH values? (19.2)
a. pH = 10.5
b. pH = 5.1
c. pH = 1.8

The proteins in hair contain many cysteine R groups that form disulfide bonds.

19.46 If cysteine, an amino acid prevalent in hair, has a pI of 5.1, which condensed structural formula would it have in solutions with each of the following pH values? (19.2)
a. pH = 2.0
b. pH = 3.5
c. pH = 9.1

19.47 Each of three peptides contains one molecule of valine and two molecules of serine. Use their three-letter and one-letter abbreviations to write the three possible peptides. (19.3, 19.4)

19.48 Each of three peptides contains one molecule of glycine, one molecule of alanine, and two molecules of isoleucine. In this peptide, the N-terminal end is glycine. Use their three-letter and one-letter abbreviations to write the three possible peptides. (19.3, 19.4)

19.49 Identify the amino acids and the type of interaction that occurs between the following amino acids and R groups in a tertiary protein structure: (19.5)

$$\begin{array}{l}
\qquad\qquad\quad O \\
\qquad\qquad\quad \| \\
\textbf{a. } -CH_2-C-NH_2 \quad \text{and} \quad HO-CH_2- \\
\textbf{b. } -CH_2-SH \quad \text{and} \quad HS-CH_2- \\
\qquad\qquad\quad CH_3 \\
\qquad\qquad\quad | \\
\textbf{c. } -CH_2-CH-CH_3 \quad \text{and} \quad CH_3-
\end{array}$$

19.50 What type of interaction would you expect between the R groups of the following amino acids in a tertiary structure? (19.2, 19.5)
a. threonine and glutamine
b. valine and alanine
c. arginine and glutamic acid

ADDITIONAL QUESTIONS AND PROBLEMS

For instructor-assigned homework, go to www.masteringchemistry.com.

19.51 Draw the condensed structural formula for each of the following amino acids at pH 4: (19.1, 19.2)
   a. serine   **b.** alanine   **c.** lysine

19.52 Draw the condensed structural formula for each of the following amino acids at pH 11: (19.1, 19.2)
   a. cysteine   **b.** aspartic acid   **c.** valine

19.53 **a.** Draw the condensed structural formula for Ser-Lys-Asp. (19.3, 19.4, 19.5)
   b. Would you expect to find this segment at the center or at the surface of a globular protein? Why?

19.54 **a.** Draw the condensed structural formula for Val-Ala-Leu. (19.3, 19.4, 19.5)
   b. Would you expect to find this segment at the center or at the surface of a globular protein? Why?

19.55 **a.** Where in the body is collagen found? (19.4)
   b. What type of secondary structure is used to form collagen?

19.56 **a.** What are some functions of collagen? (19.4)
   b. What amino acids give strength to collagen?

19.57 Would you expect a polypeptide with a high content of His, Met, and Leu to have more α-helical sections or β-pleated sheet sections? (19.4)

19.58 Would you expect a polypeptide with a high content of Val, Pro, and Ser to have more α-helical sections or β-pleated sheet sections? (19.4)

19.59 If serine was replaced by valine in a protein, how would the tertiary structure be affected? (19.5)

19.60 If glycine was replaced by alanine in a protein, how would the tertiary structure be affected? (19.5)

19.61 The amino acids lysine, proline, and glutamic acid are found in a protein. Which of these amino acids would: (19.5)
   a. be found in hydrophobic regions?
   b. be found in hydrophilic regions?
   c. form salt bridges?

19.62 The amino acids histidine, phenylalanine, and serine are found in a protein. Which of these amino acids would: (19.5)
   a. be found in hydrophobic regions?
   b. be found in hydrophilic regions?
   c. form hydrogen bonds?

19.63 Aspartame, which is used in artificial sweeteners, contains the following dipeptide: (19.3)

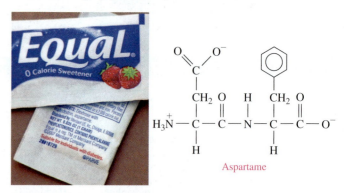

Aspartame

Aspartame is an artificial sweetener.

   a. What are the amino acids in aspartame?
   b. How would you name the dipeptide in aspartame?
   c. Give the three-letter and one-letter abbreviations for the dipeptide in aspartame.

19.64 GHK-Cu is a tripeptide that has a strong attraction for Cu^{2+} and is present in human blood and saliva. It has the following structure:

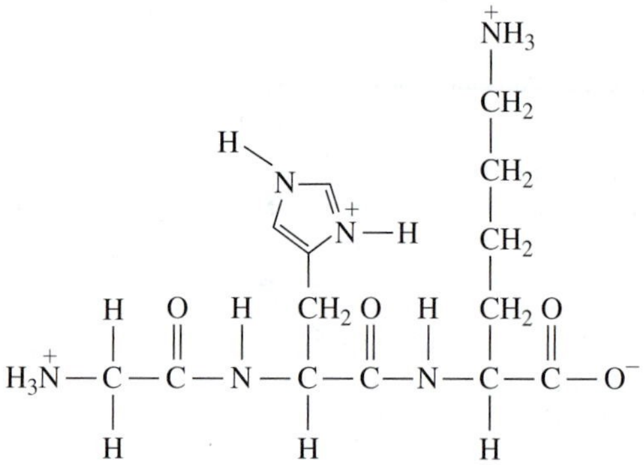

GHK-Cu

   a. What are the amino acids in GHK-Cu?
   b. How would you name this tripeptide, GHK-Cu?
   c. Give the three-letter and one-letter abbreviations for the tripeptide GHK-Cu.

19.65 In the preparation of meringue for a pie, a few drops of lemon juice are added and the egg whites are whipped. What causes the meringue to form? (19.6)

19.66 How does denaturation of a protein differ from its hydrolysis? (19.6)

CHALLENGE QUESTIONS

19.67 Indicate the overall charge of each amino acid at the following pH values as 0, 1+, or 1−: (19.1, 19.2)
   a. serine at pH 5.7
   b. threonine at pH 2.0
   c. isoleucine at pH 3.0
   d. leucine at pH 9.0

19.68 Indicate the overall charge of each amino acid at the following pH values as 0, 1+, or 1−: (19.1, 19.2)
   a. tyrosine at pH 3.0
   b. glycine at pH 10.0
   c. phenylalanine at pH 8.5
   d. methionine at pH 5.7

Use the following diagram for Problems 19.69 and 19.70:

Mixture of
amino acids

⊖   ⊕

19.69 A mixture of the amino acids arginine, leucine, and glutamic acid at pH 6.0 is subjected to an electric voltage. (19.2, 19.3, 19.4)

  a. Which amino acid will migrate toward the positive electrode?

  b. Which amino acid will migrate toward the negative electrode?

  c. Which amino acid will remain at the same place it was originally placed?

  d. If the mixture is the result of hydrolyzing a tripeptide, what are the possible sequences if one unit of each amino acid is present?

19.70 A mixture of the amino acids cysteine, glutamic acid, and histidine at pH 5.1 is subjected to an electric voltage. (19.2, 19.3, 19.4)

  a. Which amino acid will migrate toward the positive electrode?

b. Which amino acid will migrate toward the negative electrode?

c. Which amino acid will remain at the same place it was originally placed?

d. If the mixture is the result of hydrolyzing a tripeptide, what are the possible sequences if one unit of each amino acid is present?

19.71 What are some differences between each of the following? (19.1, 19.2, 19.3, 19.4, 19.5)

  a. secondary and tertiary protein structures

  b. essential and nonessential amino acids

  c. polar and nonpolar amino acids

  d. dipeptides and tripeptides

19.72 What are some differences between each of the following? (19.1, 19.2, 19.3, 19.4, 19.5)

  a. an ionic bond (salt bridge) and a disulfide bond

  b. fibrous and globular proteins

  c. α helix and β-pleated sheet

  d. tertiary and quaternary structures of proteins

ANSWERS

Answers to Study Checks

19.1 a. polar, neutral   **b.** polar, acidic

19.2 In the Fischer projection of D-serine, the $-NH_3^+$ group is on the right side; in L-serine, the $-NH_3^+$ group is on the left side.

19.3

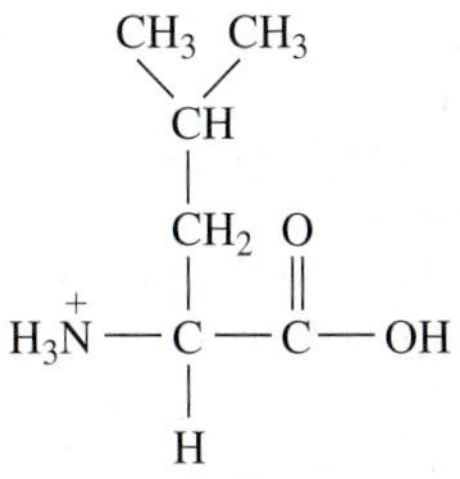

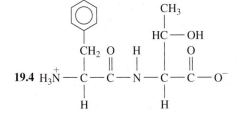

19.4

$$\overset{+}{H_3N} - \underset{H}{\overset{CH_2}{\underset{|}{\overset{|}{C}}}} - \overset{O}{\overset{||}{C}} - \underset{H}{\overset{H}{\underset{|}{\overset{|}{N}}}} - \underset{\substack{HC-OH \\ |}}{\overset{\substack{CH_3 \\ |}}{\underset{|}{C}}} - \overset{O}{\overset{||}{C}} - O^-$$

19.5 tyrosylglycylglycylphenylalanylmethionine

19.6 Both valine and leucine have nonpolar R groups and would be found on the inside of the tertiary structure.

19.7 quaternary

19.8 The heavy metal Ag^+ denatures the proteins in bacteria that cause gonorrhea.

Answers to Selected Questions and Problems

19.1 a. transport

  b. structural

  c. structural

  d. enzyme

19.3 All amino acids contain a carboxylate group and an ammonium group on the α-carbon.

19.5 a.

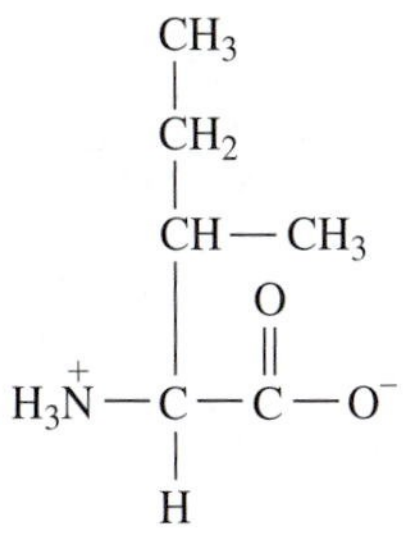

  b. (structure shown)

  c.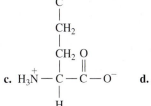

  d.

19.7 a. nonpolar; hydrophobic
  b. polar, neutral; hydrophilic
  c. polar, acidic; hydrophilic
  d. nonpolar; hydrophobic

19.9 a. alanine
  b. valine
  c. lysine
  d. cysteine

19.11 a. 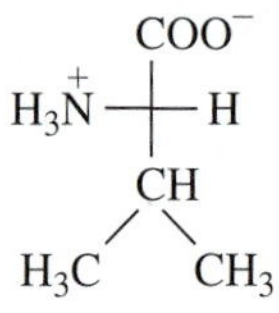 **b.**

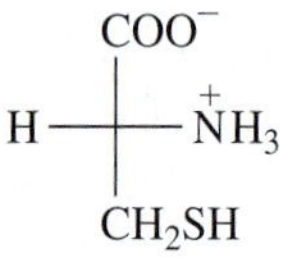

19.13 a. 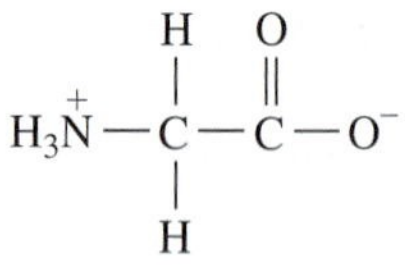 **b.** 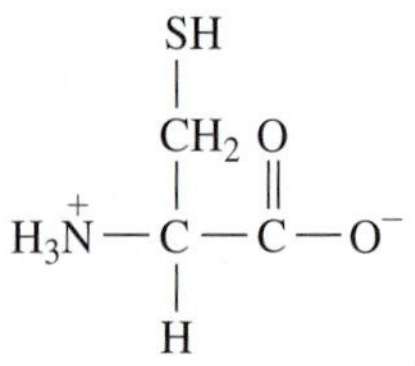
  c. 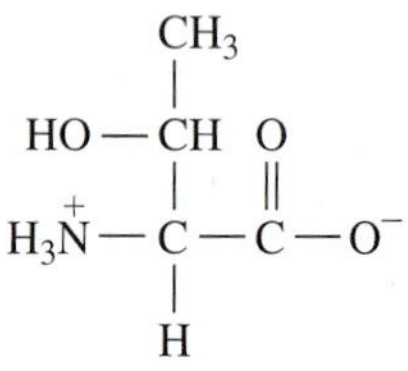 **d.**

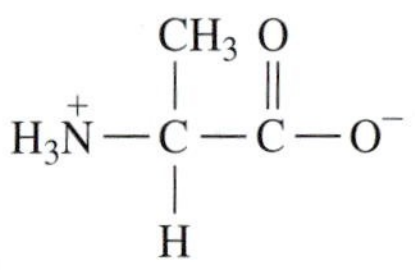

19.15 a. 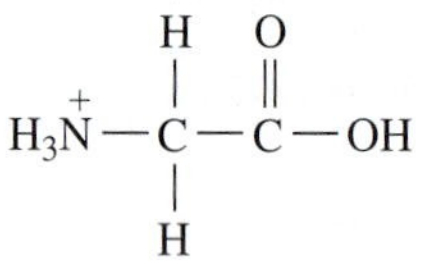 **b.** 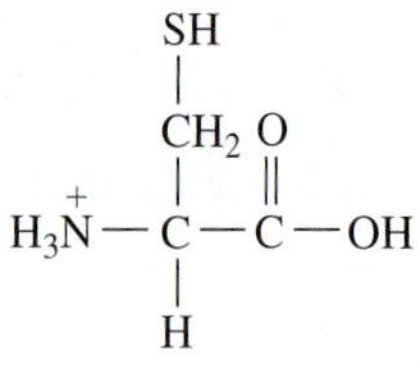
  c. 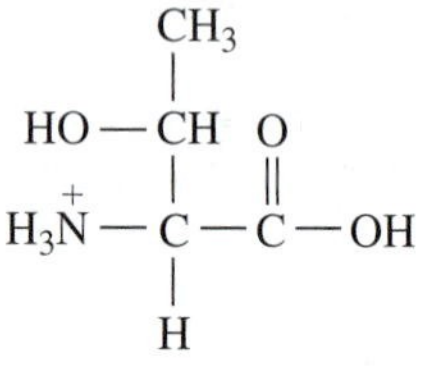 **d.**

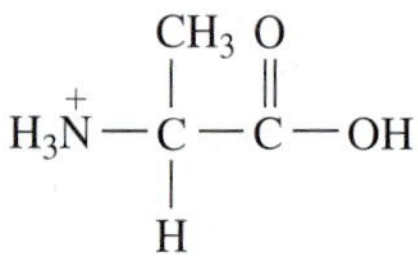

19.17 a. above its pI **b.** below its pI **c.** at its pI

19.19 a.

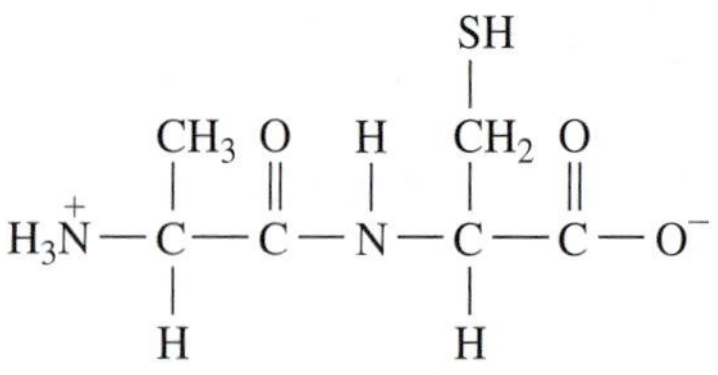

Ala-Cys, AC

  b.

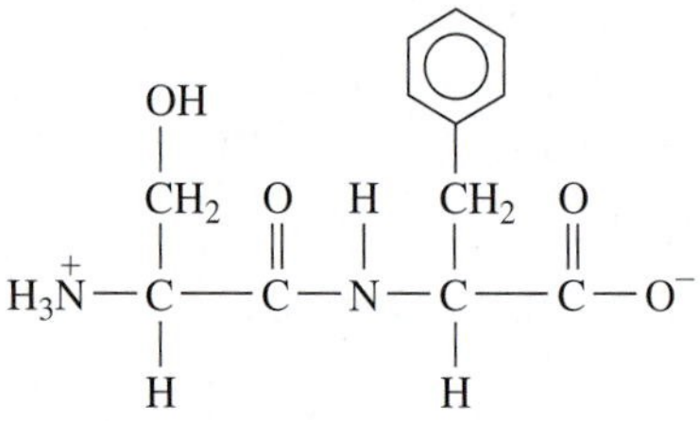

Ser-Phe, SF

c.

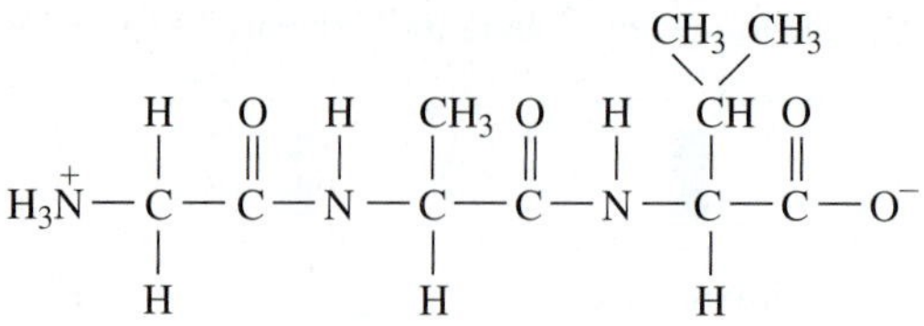

Gly-Ala-Val, GAV

d.

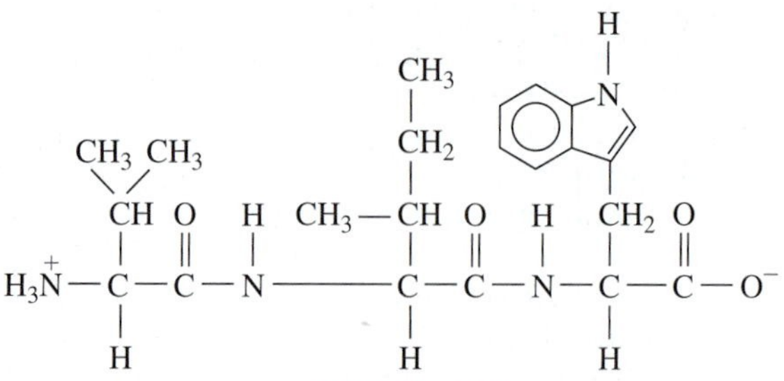

Val-Ile-Trp, VIW

19.21 Amide bonds form to connect the amino acids that make up the protein.

19.23 Val-Met-Met, VMM; Met-Val-Met, MVM; Met-Met-Val, MMV

19.25 The primary structure remains unchanged and intact as hydrogen bonds form between carbonyl oxygen atoms and amino hydrogen atoms in the secondary structure.

19.27 In the α helix, hydrogen bonds form between the carbonyl oxygen atom and the amino hydrogen atom in the next turn of the helix. In the β-pleated sheet, hydrogen bonds occur between parallel peptides or sections of a long polypeptide chain.

19.29 a. disulfide bond
  b. salt bridge
  c. hydrogen bond
  d. hydrophobic interaction

19.31 a. cysteine
  b. Leucine and valine will be found on the inside of the protein because they are hydrophobic.
  c. The cysteine and aspartic acid would be on the outside of the protein because they are polar.
  d. The order of the amino acids (the primary structure) provides the R groups whose interactions determine the tertiary structure of the protein.

19.33 a. tertiary and quaternary **b.** primary
  c. secondary **d.** secondary

19.35 The products would be the amino acids glycine, alanine, and serine.

19.37 His-Met, Met-Gly, Gly-Val

19.39 Hydrolysis splits the amide linkages in the primary structure.

19.41 a. Placing an egg in boiling water coagulates the proteins of the egg because the heat disrupts hydrogen bonds and hydrophobic interactions.
  b. The alcohol on the swab coagulates the proteins of any bacteria present by forming hydrogen bonds and disrupting hydrophobic interactions.

c. The heat from an autoclave will coagulate the proteins of any bacteria on the surgical instruments by disrupting hydrogen bonds and hydrophobic interactions.

d. Heat will coagulate the surrounding proteins to close the wound by disrupting hydrogen bonds and hydrophobic interactions.

19.43 a. yes   **b.** no   **c.** no

19.45 a. (1)   **b.** (3)   **c.** (2)

19.47 Val-Ser-Ser (VSS), Ser-Ser-Val (SSV), Ser-Val-Ser (SVS)

19.49 a. asparagine and serine, hydrogen bond
b. cysteine and cysteine, disulfide bond
c. leucine and alanine, hydrophobic interaction

19.51 a.

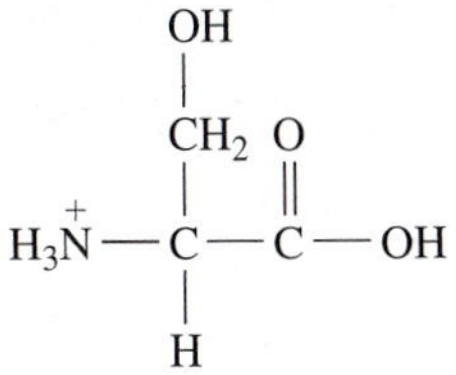

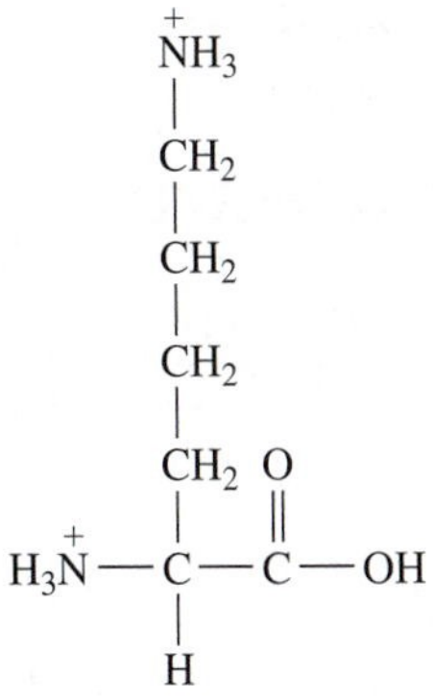

19.53 a.

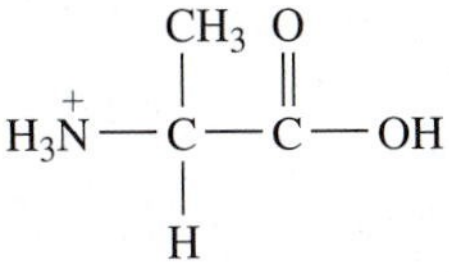

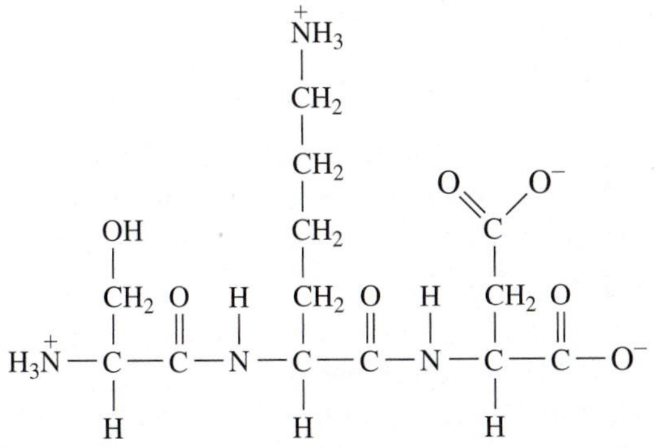

b. This segment contains polar R groups, which would be found on the surface of a globular protein where they hydrogen bond with water.

19.55 a. Collagen is found in connective tissue, blood vessels, skin, tendons, ligaments, the cornea of the eye, and cartilage.
b. A triple helix is the secondary structure found in collagen.

19.57 α helix

19.59 Serine is a polar amino acid, whereas valine is a nonpolar amino acid. Serine would move to the outside surface of the protein where it can form hydrogen bonds with water. However, valine, which is nonpolar, would be pushed to the center of the tertiary structure where it is stabilized by forming hydrophobic interactions.

19.61 a. proline
b. lysine, glutamic acid
c. lysine, glutamic acid

19.63 a. aspartic acid and phenylalanine
b. aspartylphenylalanine
c. Asp-Phe, DF

19.65 The acid from the lemon juice and the mechanical whipping (agitation) denature the proteins of the egg white which turn into solids as meringue.

19.67 a. 0   **b.** 1+   **c.** 1+   **d.** 1−

19.69 a. Glutamic acid will migrate to the positive electrode.
b. Arginine will migrate to the negative electrode.
c. Leucine will remain where it was placed.
d. Arg-Leu-Glu, Arg-Glu-Leu, Leu-Glu-Arg, Leu-Arg-Glu, Glu-Leu-Arg, Glu-Arg-Leu

19.71 a. In the secondary structure of proteins, hydrogen bonds form a helix or a pleated sheet; the tertiary structure is determined by hydrogen bonds as well as by disulfide bonds and salt bridges.
b. Nonessential amino acids can be synthesized by the body; essential amino acids must be supplied by the diet.
c. Polar amino acids have hydrophilic R groups, whereas nonpolar amino acids have hydrophobic R groups.
d. A dipeptide contains two amino acids, but a tripeptide contains three amino acids.

20 Enzymes and Vitamins

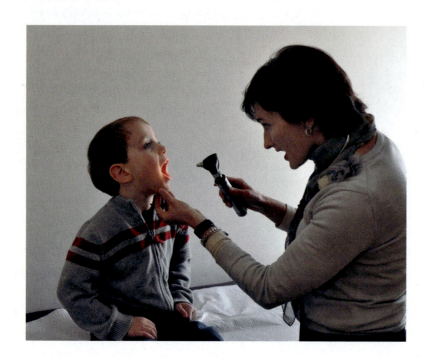

Visit **www.masteringchemistry.com** for self-study materials and instructor-assigned homework.

Noah, a 4-year-old boy, is having severe diarrhea, abdominal pain, and intestinal growling two hours after he eats. Noah is also underweight for his age. His mother makes an appointment for Noah to see Emma, his physician assistant. Emma immediately suspects that Noah may be lactose intolerant, which occurs due to an enzyme deficiency.

Emma orders a hydrogen breath test for Noah after confirming that he has not eaten for eight hours. The hydrogen breath test involves breathing into a balloon-type container, drinking a solution containing lactose, and then collecting additional breathing samples. Due to the presence of hydrogen in Noah's breath, they confirm he is lactose intolerant, as hydrogen is only present when undigested lactose is fermented in the colon by bacteria. Emma advises Noah and his mother to limit dairy products and use lactase when Noah consumes a milk-based product.

Lactase is an enzyme, or a biological catalyst, that is also a protein. Enzymes significantly increase the rate of a reaction, and since they are not consumed in the reaction, they can be re-used. Lactose is the substrate, or the reacting molecule, that is broken down by lactase. Lactose has a structure or shape that is specific to the active site of the lactase enzyme. The active site is a region in an enzyme where the reaction occurs.

Career: Physician Assistant

A physician assistant, commonly referred to as a PA, helps a doctor by examining and treating patients, as well as prescribing medications. Many physician assistants take on the role of the primary caregiver. Their duties would also include obtaining patient medical records and histories, diagnosing illnesses, educating and counseling patients, and referring the patient, when needed, to a specialist. Due to this diversity, physician assistants must be knowledgeable about a variety of medical conditions. Physician assistants may also help the doctor during major surgery. Physician assistants can work in clinics, hospitals, health maintenance organizations, private practices, or take on a more administrative role that involves hiring new PAs and acting as the go-between for the hospital and patient or their family.

Every second, thousands of chemical reactions occur in the cells of our body. For example, many reactions occur to digest the food we eat, convert the products to chemical energy, and synthesize proteins and other macromolecules in our cells. In the laboratory, we can carry out reactions that hydrolyze polysaccharides, fats, or proteins, but we must use a strong acid or base, high temperatures, and long reaction times. In the cells of our body, these reactions must take place at much faster rates that meet our physiological and metabolic needs. To make this happen, enzymes catalyze the chemical reactions in our cells, with a different enzyme for each reaction. Digestive enzymes in the mouth, stomach, and small intestine catalyze the hydrolysis of carbohydrate, fats, and proteins. Enzymes in the mitochondria extract energy from biomolecules to give us energy.

Every enzyme responds to what comes into the cells and to what the cells need. Enzymes keep reactions going when our cells need certain products, and turn off reactions when they don't need those products.

Many enzymes require cofactors to function properly. Cofactors are inorganic metal ions (minerals) or organic compounds such as vitamins. We obtain minerals such as zinc (Zn^{2+}) and iron (Fe^{3+}) and vitamins from our diets. A lack of minerals and vitamins can lead to certain nutritional diseases. For example, rickets is a deficiency of vitamin D, and scurvy occurs when a diet is low in vitamin C.

20.1 Enzymes and Enzyme Action

Biological catalysts known as **enzymes** catalyze nearly all the chemical reactions that take place in the body. As we discussed in Section 9.1, a *catalyst* increases the rate of a reaction by changing the way a reaction takes place; the enzyme itself is not changed. An uncatalyzed reaction in a cell may take place eventually, but not at a rate fast enough for survival. For example, the hydrolysis of proteins in our diet would eventually occur without a catalyst, but the reactions would not occur fast enough to meet the body's requirements for amino acids. The chemical reactions in our cells occur at incredibly fast rates under mild conditions, near pH 7.4 and a body temperature of 37 °C. Enzymes permit cells to use energy and materials efficiently while responding to cellular needs.

As catalysts, enzymes lower the activation energy for a chemical reaction (see Figure 20.1). Less energy is required to convert reactant molecules to products, which increases the rate of a biochemical reaction compared to the rate of the uncatalyzed reaction. The rates of enzyme-catalyzed reactions are much faster than the rates of the uncatalyzed reactions. Some enzymes can increase the rate of a biological reaction by a factor of a billion, a trillion, or even a hundred million trillion compared to the rate of the uncatalyzed reaction. For example, an enzyme in the blood called carbonic anhydrase catalyzes the rapid interconversion of carbon dioxide and water to bicarbonate and H^+. In one second, one molecule of carbonic anhydrase can catalyze the reaction of about one million molecules of carbon dioxide. Carbonic anhydrase also catalyzes the reverse reaction, converting bicarbonate and H^+ to carbon dioxide and water.

$$CO_2 + H_2O \underset{\text{Carbonic anhydrase}}{\rightleftharpoons} HCO_3^- + H^+$$

LEARNING GOAL

Describe enzymes and their role in enzyme-catalyzed reactions.

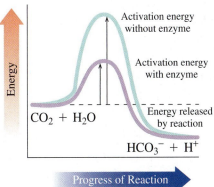

FIGURE 20.1 The enzyme carbonic anhydrase lowers the activation energy for the reversible reaction that converts CO_2 and H_2O to bicarbonate and H^+.

Q Why are enzymes needed in biological reactions?

TUTORIAL
Enzymes and Activation Energy

SELF-STUDY ACTIVITY
How Enzymes Work

Enzymes and Active Sites

Nearly all enzymes are globular proteins. Each has a unique three-dimensional shape that recognizes and binds a small group of reacting molecules, which are called **substrates**. The tertiary structure of an enzyme plays an important role in how that enzyme catalyzes reactions.

In a catalyzed reaction, an enzyme must bind to a substrate in a way that favors catalysis. A typical enzyme is much larger than its substrate. However, within the enzyme's tertiary structure is a region called the **active site**, in which the substrate or substrates are held while the reaction takes place (see Figure 20.2). The active site is often a small pocket within the larger tertiary structure that closely fits the substrate. Within the active site of an enzyme, R groups of specific amino acids interact with functional groups of the substrate to form hydrogen bonds, salt bridges, and hydrophobic interactions. Because the active site of an enzyme accommodates a particular type of substrate, enzymes generally catalyze only specific types of reactions.

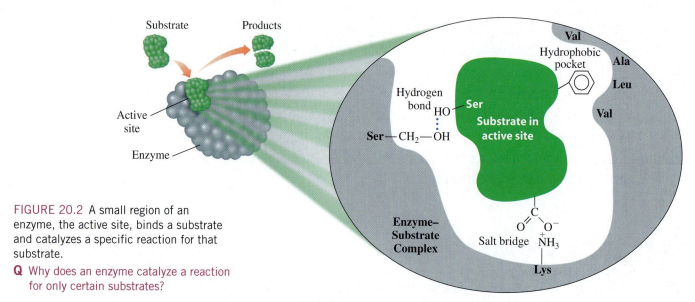

FIGURE 20.2 A small region of an enzyme, the active site, binds a substrate and catalyzes a specific reaction for that substrate.

Q Why does an enzyme catalyze a reaction for only certain substrates?

CONCEPT CHECK 20.1 The Enzyme Active Site

What is the function of the active site in an enzyme?

ANSWER

The R groups of amino acids within the active site of an enzyme bind the substrate by forming hydrogen bonds, salt bridges, and hydrophobic interactions with the substrate and catalyze the reaction.

Specificity of Enzymes

Some enzymes show absolute specificity by catalyzing only one reaction for one specific substrate. Other enzymes catalyze a reaction for two or more substrates. Still other enzymes catalyze a reaction for a specific type of bond. Types of enzyme specificity are listed in Table 20.1.

TABLE 20.1 Types of Enzyme Specificity

Type	Reaction Type	Example
Absolute	Catalyzes one type of reaction for one substrate	Urease catalyzes only the hydrolysis of urea.
Group	Catalyzes one type of reaction for similar substrates	Hexokinase adds a phosphate group to hexoses.
Linkage	Catalyzes one type of reaction for a specific type of bond	Chymotrypsin catalyzes the hydrolysis of peptide bonds.

Enzyme-Catalyzed Reaction

The combination of an enzyme and a substrate forms an **enzyme–substrate (ES) complex** that provides an alternative pathway for the reaction with lower activation energy. Within the active site, amino acid side chains catalyze the reaction to give an *enzyme–product complex*. Then the products are released and the enzyme is available to bind to another substrate molecule.

$$\textbf{E + S} \quad \rightleftharpoons \quad \textbf{ES complex} \quad \longrightarrow \quad \textbf{EP complex} \quad \longrightarrow \quad \textbf{E + P}$$

Enzyme and Substrate   Enzyme–Substrate Complex   Enzyme–Product Complex   Enzyme and Product

In the hydrolysis of the disaccharide sucrose by the enzyme sucrase, a molecule of sucrose binds to the active site of sucrase. In this ES complex, the glycosidic bond of sucrose is in a position that is favorable for hydrolysis, which is the splitting by water of a large molecule into smaller parts. The R groups on the amino acid in the active site then catalyze the hydrolysis of sucrose, which produces the monosaccharides glucose and fructose. Because the structures of the products are no longer attracted to the active site, they are released, which allows sucrase to react with another sucrose (see Figure 20.3).

$$\textbf{E + S} \quad \rightleftharpoons \quad \textbf{ES complex} \quad \longrightarrow \quad \textbf{EP complex} \quad \longrightarrow \quad \textbf{E + P}$$

Sucrase + Sucrose ⇌ Sucrase–Sucrose Complex ⟶ Sucrase–Glucose–Fructose Complex ⟶ Sucrase + Glucose + Fructose

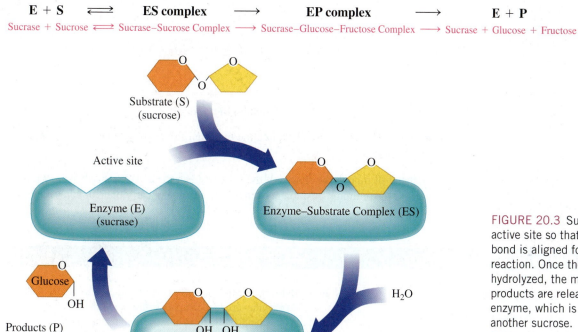

FIGURE 20.3 Sucrose binds to the active site so that the glycosidic bond is aligned for the hydrolysis reaction. Once the disaccharide is hydrolyzed, the monosaccharide products are released from the enzyme, which is ready to bind another sucrose.

Q Why does the enzyme-catalyzed hydrolysis of sucrose go faster than the hydrolysis of sucrose in the chemistry laboratory?

Models of Enzyme Action

An early theory of enzyme action, called the *lock-and-key model*, described the active site as having a rigid, inflexible shape. According to the lock-and-key model, the shape of the active site was analogous to a lock, and its substrate was the key that specifically fit that lock. However, this model was a static one that did not include the flexibility of the tertiary shape of an enzyme and the way we now know that the active site can adjust to the shape of a substrate.

In the dynamic model of enzyme action, called the **induced-fit model**, the flexibility of the active site allows it to adapt to the shape of the substrate. At the same time, the shape of the substrate is modified to better fit the geometry of the active site. As a result, the fit of both the active site and the substrate provides the best alignment for the catalysis of the reaction of the substrate. In the induced-fit model, substrate and enzyme work together to acquire a geometrical arrangement that lowers the activation energy (see Figure 20.4).

TUTORIAL
Enzymes and the Lock-and-Key Model

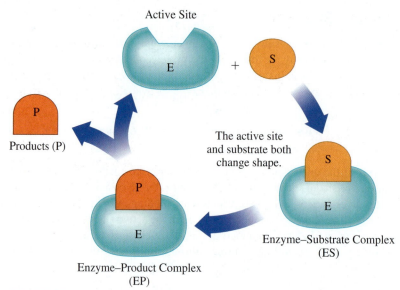

Active Site

FIGURE 20.4 In the induced-fit model, a flexible active site and substrate both adjust to provide the best fit for the reaction.

Q How does the induced-fit model provide the proper alignment of substrate and active site?

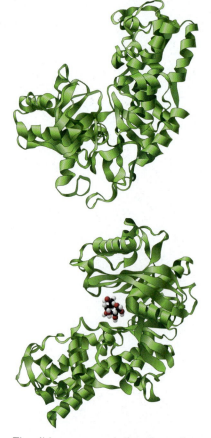

The ribbon representation shows the change in the shape of the enzyme hexokinase as the glucose molecule binds to its active site.

CONCEPT CHECK 20.2 **The Induced-Fit Model**

How does the induced-fit model explain the binding of the substrate at the active site?

ANSWER

In the induced-fit model, the shapes of the substrate and the active site adjust so that the substrate is in the optimum position needed for the enzyme to carry out reaction catalysis.

QUESTIONS AND PROBLEMS

20.1 Enzymes and Enzyme Action

LEARNING GOAL: *Describe enzymes and their role in enzyme-catalyzed reactions.*

20.1 Why do chemical reactions in the body require enzymes?

20.2 How do enzymes make chemical reactions in the body proceed at faster rates?

20.3 Match the terms, (1) enzyme–substrate complex, (2) enzyme, and (3) substrate, with each of the following:
   a. has a tertiary structure that recognizes the substrate
   b. the combination of an enzyme with the substrate
   c. has a structure that fits the active site of an enzyme

20.4 Match the terms, (1) active site, (2) induced-fit model, and (3) enzyme–product complex with each of the following:
   a. the combination of an enzyme with the product
   b. the portion of an enzyme where catalytic activity occurs
   c. an active site that adapts to the shape of a substrate

20.5 **a.** Write an equation that represents an enzyme-catalyzed reaction.
   b. How is the active site different from the whole enzyme structure?

20.6 **a.** How does an enzyme speed up the reaction of a substrate?
   b. After the products have formed, what happens to the enzyme?

20.2 Classification of Enzymes

LEARNING GOAL

Classify enzymes and give their names.

The name of an enzyme describes the compound or the reaction that is catalyzed. The actual names of enzymes are derived by replacing the end of the name of the reaction or reacting compound with the suffix *ase*. For example, an *oxidase* is an enzyme that catalyzes an oxidation reaction, and a *dehydrogenase* is an enzyme that is involved in the removal or addition of hydrogen atoms. These enzymes are classified as *oxidoreductases* because they catalyze the loss or gain of hydrogen or oxygen. The enzyme *sucrase* is a catalyst in the hydrolysis of sucrose, and *lipase* catalyzes reactions that hydrolyze lipids. Some enzymes use names that end in the suffix *in*, such as *papain* found in papaya; *rennin* found in milk; and *pepsin* and *trypsin*, enzymes that catalyze the hydrolysis of proteins. These enzymes including sucrase and lipase are classified as *hydrolases* because they use water to split large molecules into smaller ones.

The International Commission on Enzymes has classified enzymes according to the six general types of reactions they catalyze (see Table 20.2).

TABLE 20.2 Classification of Enzymes

Class	Examples
1. Oxidoreductases	
Catalyze oxidation–reduction reactions	*Oxidases* catalyze the oxidation of a compound.
	Dehydrogenases catalyze the removal or addition of two H atoms.

$$CH_3-CH_2-OH + NAD^+ \xrightarrow{\text{Alcohol dehydrogenase}} CH_3-\overset{\displaystyle O}{\overset{\|}{C}}-H + NADH + H^+$$

Ethanol   Coenzyme   Ethanal   Coenzyme

2. Transferases	
Catalyze the transfer of a functional group between two compounds	*Transaminases* catalyze the transfer of an amino group from one compound to another.
	Kinases catalyze the transfer of phosphate groups.

$$CH_3-\overset{\overset{\displaystyle +}{NH_3}}{\overset{|}{C}H}-COO^- + {}^-OOC-\overset{\displaystyle O}{\overset{\|}{C}}-CH_2-CH_2-COO^- \underset{\xleftarrow{}}{\xrightarrow{\text{Alanine transaminase}}} CH_3-\overset{\displaystyle O}{\overset{\|}{C}}-COO^- + {}^-OOC-\overset{\overset{\displaystyle +}{NH_3}}{\overset{|}{C}H}-CH_2-CH_2-COO^-$$

Alanine   α-Ketoglutarate   Pyruvate   Glutamate

3. Hydrolases	
Catalyze hydrolysis (add H_2O) reactions that split a compound into two products	*Peptidases* catalyze the hydrolysis of peptide bonds.
	Lipases catalyze the hydrolysis of ester bonds in lipids.

$$-\overset{H}{\overset{|}{N}}-\overset{R}{\overset{|}{C}H}-\overset{O}{\overset{\|}{C}}-\overset{H}{\overset{|}{N}}-\overset{R}{\overset{|}{C}H}-COO^- + H_2O \xrightarrow{\text{Peptidase}} -\overset{H}{\overset{|}{N}}-\overset{R}{\overset{|}{C}H}-\overset{O}{\overset{\|}{C}}-O^- + H_3\overset{+}{N}-\overset{R}{\overset{|}{C}H}-COO^-$$

Polypeptide C-terminal end   Shorter polypeptide   Amino acid from C-terminal end

4. Lyases	
Catalyze the addition or removal of a group without hydrolysis	*Decarboxylases* catalyze the removal of CO_2.
	Deaminases catalyze the removal of NH_3.

$$CH_3-\overset{\displaystyle O}{\overset{\|}{C}}-COO^- + H^+ \xrightarrow{\text{Pyruvate decarboxylase}} CH_3-\overset{\displaystyle O}{\overset{\|}{C}}-H + CO_2$$

Pyruvate   Ethanal   Carbon dioxide

5. Isomerases	
Catalyze the rearrangement of atoms within a molecule to form an isomer	*Isomerases* catalyze the conversion between cis to trans bonds.
	Epimerases catalyze the conversion of D and L isomers.

$$\overset{{}^-OOC}{\underset{H}{}}C=C\overset{COO^-}{\underset{H}{}} \underset{\xleftarrow{}}{\xrightarrow{\text{Maleate isomerase}}} \overset{{}^-OOC}{\underset{H}{}}C=C\overset{H}{\underset{COO^-}{}}$$

Maleate   Fumarate

6. Ligases	
Catalyze the joining of two molecules using ATP energy (see Section 22.2)	*Synthetases* catalyze the combination of two molecules.
	Carboxylases catalyze the addition of CO_2.

$$^-OOC-\overset{\displaystyle O}{\overset{\|}{C}}-CH_3 + CO_2 + ATP \xrightarrow{\text{Pyruvate carboxylase}} {}^-OOC-\overset{\displaystyle O}{\overset{\|}{C}}-CH_2-COO^- + ADP + P_i + H^+$$

Pyruvate   Oxaloacetate

CONCEPT CHECK 20.3 **Classes of Enzymes**

Identify the general class of enzymes that catalyzes each of the following reactions:

a. a phosphate group is moved from one substrate to another
b. a peptide bond in a protein is hydrolyzed
c. a C atom is removed as CO_2 from a substrate

ANSWER

a. A transferase catalyzes the transfer of a phosphate group from one substrate to another.
b. A hydrolase catalyzes the hydrolysis of a peptide bond in a protein.
c. A lyase catalyzes the removal of a C atom as CO_2 from a substrate.

SAMPLE PROBLEM 20.1 **Classifying Enzymes**

What is the classification of the enzyme that catalyzes each of the following?

a. the transfer of an amino group
b. the removal of hydrogen from lactate

SOLUTION

a. The class of enzymes called transferases includes enzymes that catalyze the transfer of an amino group from one reactant to another.
b. The class of enzymes called oxidoreductases includes enzymes that catalyze the removal of hydrogen from lactate.

STUDY CHECK 20.1

What is the classification of the enzyme lipase that catalyzes the hydrolysis of ester bonds in triglycerides?

Chemistry Link to Health

ISOENZYMES AS DIAGNOSTIC TOOLS

Isoenzymes are different forms of an enzyme that catalyze the same reaction in different cells or tissues of the body. Isoenzymes consist of quaternary structures with slight variations in the amino acids of the polypeptide subunits. For example, there are five isoenzymes of *lactate dehydrogenase (LDH)* that catalyze the conversion between lactate and pyruvate.

$$CH_3-\underset{\underset{\text{Lactate}}{|}}{\overset{\overset{OH}{|}}{CH}}-COO^- + NAD^+ \underset{\xleftarrow{\hspace{1cm}}}{\overset{\text{Lactate}}{\overset{\text{dehydrogenase}}{\xrightarrow{\hspace{1cm}}}}}$$

$$CH_3-\underset{\underset{\text{Pyruvate}}{}}{\overset{\overset{O}{\|}}{C}}-COO^- + NADH + H^+$$

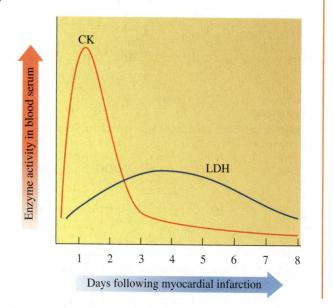

Each LDH isoenzyme contains a mix of two polypeptide subunits, M and H. In the liver and muscle, lactate is converted to pyruvate by the LDH_5 isoenzyme with four M subunits, designated M_4. In the heart, the same reaction is catalyzed by the LDH_1 isoenzyme called H_4, containing four H subunits. Different combinations of the M and H subunits are found in the LDH isoenzymes of the brain, red blood cells, kidney, and white blood cells.

Forms of Isoenzymes

The different forms of an enzyme allow a medical diagnosis of damage or disease to a particular organ or tissue. In healthy tissues, isoenzymes function within the cells. However, when a disease damages a particular organ, cells die, which releases the isoenzymes into the blood. Measurements of the elevated levels of specific isoenzymes in the blood serum help to identify the disease and its location in the body. For example, an elevation in the serum of LDH_5 (M_4) indicates liver damage. When a *myocardial infarction (MI)*, or heart attack, damages the cells in heart muscle, an increase in the level of LDH_1 (H_4) isoenzyme is detected in the blood serum (see Table 20.3).

TABLE 20.3 Isoenzymes of Lactate Dehydrogenase and Creatine Kinase

Isoenzyme	Abundant in	Subunits
Lactate Dehydrogenase (LDH)		
LDH_1	Heart, kidneys	H_4
LDH_2	Red blood cells, heart, kidney, brain	H_3M
LDH_3	Brain, lung, white blood cells	H_2M_2
LDH_4	Lung, skeletal muscle	HM_3
LDH_5	Skeletal muscle, liver	M_4
Creatine Kinase (CK)		
CK_1	Brain, lung	BB
CK_2	Heart	MB
CK_3	Skeletal muscle, red blood cells	MM

Another isoenzyme used diagnostically is creatine kinase (CK), which consists of two types of polypeptide subunits. Subunit B is prevalent in the brain, and subunit M predominates in muscle. Normally, only CK_3 (subunits MM) is present in low amounts in the blood serum. However, in a patient who has suffered a myocardial infarction (MI), the level of CK_2 (subunits MB) is elevated within 4–6 hours and reaches a peak in about 24 hours. Table 20.4 lists some enzymes used to diagnose tissue damage and diseases of certain organs.

Isoenzymes of Lactate Dehydrogenase	Highest Levels Found in the Following:
H M	
H_4 (LDH_1)	Heart, kidneys
H_3M (LDH_2)	Red blood cells, heart, kidney, brain
H_2M_2 (LDH_3)	Brain, lung, white blood cells
HM_3 (LDH_4)	Lung, skeletal muscle
M_4 (LDH_5)	Skeletal muscle, liver

TABLE 20.4 Serum Enzymes Used in the Diagnosis of Tissue Damage

Condition	Diagnostic Enzymes Elevated
Heart attack or liver disease (cirrhosis, hepatitis)	Lactate dehydrogenase (LDH) Aspartate transaminase (AST)
Heart attack	Creatine kinase (CK)
Hepatitis	Alanine transaminase (ALT)
Liver carcinoma or bone disease (rickets)	Alkaline phosphatase (ALP)
Pancreatic disease	Pancreatic amylase (PA), cholinesterase (CE), lipase (LPS)
Prostate carcinoma	Acid phosphatase (ACP) Prostate-specific antigen (PSA)

QUESTIONS AND PROBLEMS

20.2 Classification of Enzymes

LEARNING GOAL: Classify enzymes and give their names.

20.7 What type of reaction is catalyzed by each of the following classes of enzymes?
   a. oxidoreductases   **b.** transferases   **c.** hydrolases

20.8 What type of reaction is catalyzed by each of the following classes of enzymes?
   a. lyases
   b. isomerases
   c. ligases

20.9 What is the name of the class of enzymes that catalyzes each of the following reactions?
  a. hydrolysis of sucrose
  b. converting glucose ($C_6H_{12}O_6$) to fructose ($C_6H_{12}O_6$)
  c. moving an amino group from one molecule to another

20.10 What is the name of the class of enzymes that catalyzes each of the following reactions?
  a. joining of glucose and fructose using ATP energy
  b. removal of hydrogen atoms
  c. removal of CO_2 from pyruvate

20.11 Identify the class of enzymes that catalyzes each of the following reactions:

  a. $CH_3 - \overset{\overset{\displaystyle O}{\|}}{C} - COO^- + H^+ \longrightarrow CH_3 - \overset{\overset{\displaystyle O}{\|}}{C} - H + CO_2$

  b. $CH_3 - \overset{\overset{\displaystyle +}{\underset{\displaystyle |}{NH_3}}}{CH} - COO^- + {}^-OOC - \overset{\overset{\displaystyle O}{\|}}{C} - CH_2 - CH_3 \rightleftharpoons$

  $CH_3 - \overset{\overset{\displaystyle O}{\|}}{C} - COO^- + {}^-OOC - \overset{\overset{\displaystyle +}{\underset{\displaystyle |}{NH_3}}}{CH} - CH_2 - CH_3$

20.12 Identify the class of enzymes that catalyzes each of the following reactions:

  a. $CH_3 - \overset{\overset{\displaystyle O}{\|}}{C} - COO^- + CO_2 + ATP \longrightarrow$

  ${}^-OOC - CH_2 - \overset{\overset{\displaystyle O}{\|}}{C} - COO^- + ADP + P_i + H^+$

b. $CH_3 - CH_2 - OH + NAD^+ \longrightarrow$

  $CH_3 - \overset{\overset{\displaystyle O}{\|}}{C} - H + NADH + H^+$

20.13 Name the enzyme that catalyzes each of the following reactions:
  a. oxidation of succinate
  b. combination of glutamate and ammonia to form glutamine
  c. removal of 2H from an alcohol

20.14 Name the enzyme that catalyzes each of the following reactions:
  a. hydrolysis of sucrose
  b. transfer of an amino group from aspartate
  c. removal of a carboxylate group from pyruvate

20.15 What are isoenzymes?

20.16 How is the LDH isoenzyme in the heart different from the LDH isoenzyme in the liver?

20.17 A patient arrives in the emergency room complaining of chest pains. What enzymes might be present in the patient's blood serum?

20.18 A patient who is an alcoholic has elevated levels of LDH and AST. What condition might be indicated?

Describe the effect of temperature, pH, concentration of enzyme, and concentration of substrate on enzyme activity.

20.3 Factors Affecting Enzyme Activity

The **activity** of an enzyme describes how fast an enzyme catalyzes the reaction that converts a substrate to product. This activity is strongly affected by reaction conditions, which include the temperature, pH, concentration of the enzyme, and concentration of the substrate (see Section 19.6 to review protein denaturation).

Temperature

Enzymes are very sensitive to temperature. At low temperatures, most enzymes show little activity because there is not a sufficient amount of energy for the catalyzed reaction to take place. At higher temperatures, enzyme activity increases as reacting molecules move faster to cause more collisions with enzymes. Enzymes are most active at **optimum temperature**, which is 37 °C, or body temperature, for most enzymes (see Figure 20.5). At temperatures above 50 °C, the tertiary structure, and thus the shape of most proteins, is destroyed, which causes a loss in enzyme activity. For this reason, equipment in hospitals and laboratories is sterilized in autoclaves where the high temperatures denature the enzymes in harmful bacteria. A high fever in the body may be helpful in denaturing enzymes in bacteria that cause infection.

Certain organisms, known as thermophiles, live in environments where temperatures range from 50 °C to 120 °C. In order to survive in these extreme conditions, thermophiles must have enzymes with tertiary structures that are not destroyed by such high temperatures. Some research shows that their enzymes are very similar to ordinary enzymes except they contain more arginine and tyrosine. These slight changes allow the enzymes in thermophiles to form more hydrogen bonds and salt bridges that stabilize their tertiary structures at high temperatures, and resist unfolding and the loss of enzymatic activity.

Thermophiles survive in the high temperatures (50 °C to 120 °C) of a hot spring.

pH

Enzymes are most active at their **optimum pH**, the pH that maintains the proper tertiary structure of the protein (see Figure 20.6). If a pH value is above or below the optimum pH, the R group interactions are disrupted, which destroys the tertiary structure and the active site. As a result, the enzyme can no longer bind to a substrate properly, and no reaction occurs. If a small change in pH is reversed, an enzyme may regain its structure and activity. However, large variations from optimum pH permanently destroy the structure of the enzyme.

Enzymes in most cells have optimum pH values at physiological pH around 7.4. However, enzymes in the stomach have a low optimum pH because they hydrolyze proteins at the acidic pH in the stomach. For example, pepsin, a digestive enzyme in the stomach, has an optimum pH of 1.5–2.0. Between meals, the pH in the stomach is 4 or 5, and pepsin shows little or no digestive activity. When food enters the stomach, the secretion of HCl lowers the pH to about 2, which activates pepsin. Table 20.5 lists the optimum pH values for selected enzymes.

TABLE 20.5 Optimum pH for Selected Enzymes

Enzyme	Location	Substrate	Optimum pH
Pepsin	Stomach	Peptide bonds	1.5–2.0
Sucrase	Small intestine	Sucrose	6.2
Amylase	Pancreas	Amylose	6.7–7.0
Urease	Liver	Urea	7.0
Trypsin	Small intestine	Peptide bonds	7.7–8.0
Lipase	Pancreas	Lipid (ester bonds)	8.0
Arginase	Liver	Arginine	9.7

Enzyme and Substrate Concentration

In any catalyzed reaction, the substrate must first bind with the enzyme to form the enzyme–substrate complex. For a particular substrate concentration, an increase in enzyme concentration increases the rate of the catalyzed reaction. At higher enzyme concentrations, more molecules are available to bind substrate and catalyze the reaction. As long as the substrate concentration is greater than the enzyme concentration, there is a direct relationship between the enzyme concentration and enzyme activity (see Figure 20.7a). In most enzyme-catalyzed reactions, the concentration of the substrate is much greater than the concentration of the enzyme.

When the enzyme concentration is kept constant, the addition of more substrate will increase the rate of the reaction. If the substrate concentration is high, it can saturate all of the enzyme molecules. Then the rate of the reaction reaches its maximum, and the addition of more substrate does not increase the rate further (see Figure 20.7b).

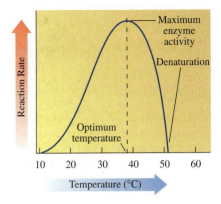

FIGURE 20.5 An enzyme attains maximum activity at its optimum temperature, usually 37 °C. Lower temperatures slow the rate of reaction, and temperatures above 50 °C denature most enzymes, resulting in a loss of catalytic activity.

Q Why is 37 °C the optimum temperature for many enzymes?

TUTORIAL
Denaturation and Enzyme Activity

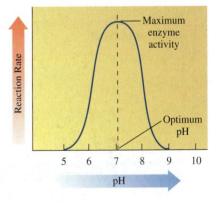

FIGURE 20.6 Enzymes are most active at their optimum pH. At a higher or lower pH, denaturation of the enzyme causes a loss of catalytic activity.

Q Why does the digestive enzyme pepsin have an optimum pH of 2.0?

TUTORIAL
Enzyme and Substrate Concentrations

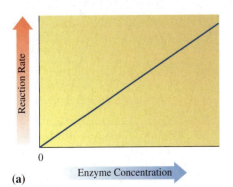

(a)

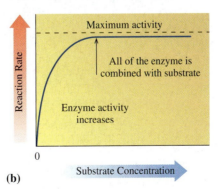

(b)

FIGURE 20.7 (a) Increasing the enzyme concentration increases the rate of reaction. **(b)** Increasing the substrate concentration increases the rate of reaction until the enzyme molecules are saturated with substrate.

Q What happens to the rate of reaction when substrate saturates the enzyme?

Explore Your World

ENZYME ACTIVITY

The enzymes on the surface of a freshly cut apple, avocado, or banana react with oxygen in the air to turn the surface brown. An antioxidant, such as vitamin C in lemon juice, prevents the oxidation reaction. Cut an apple, an avocado, or a banana into several slices. Place one slice in a plastic zipper bag, squeeze out all the air, and close the zipper lock. Dip another slice in lemon juice. Sprinkle another slice with a crushed vitamin C tablet. Leave another slice alone as a control. Observe the surface of each of your samples. Record your observations immediately, then every hour for 6 hours or longer.

QUESTIONS

1. Which slice(s) shows the most oxidation (a brown color)?
2. Which slice(s) shows little or no oxidation?
3. How was the oxidation reaction on each slice affected by treatment with an antioxidant?

CONCEPT CHECK 20.4 Enzyme Activity

Describe how each of the following affects the activity of an enzyme:
a. decreasing the pH from the optimum pH
b. increasing the temperature above the optimum temperature
c. increasing the substrate concentration at constant temperature and pH

ANSWER

a. A more acidic environment disrupts the hydrogen bonds and salt bridges of the tertiary structure, which causes a loss of enzyme activity.
b. When the temperature is greater than the optimum temperature, the tertiary structure breaks down (denaturation), the shape of the active site deteriorates, and enzyme activity is lost.
c. An increase in a substrate concentration increases the rate of reaction until all the enzyme molecules are combined with substrate. Then the reaction rate is constant.

SAMPLE PROBLEM 20.2 Factors Affecting Enzymatic Activity

Describe the effect each of the following changes would have on the rate of the reaction that is catalyzed by urease:

$$H_2N-\overset{\overset{\displaystyle O}{\|}}{C}-NH_2 + H_2O \xrightarrow{\text{Urease}} 2NH_3 + CO_2$$

Urea

a. increasing the urea concentration
b. lowering the temperature to 10 °C

SOLUTION

a. An increase in urea concentration will increase the rate of reaction until all the enzyme molecules bind to urea. Then no further increase in rate occurs.
b. Because 10 °C is lower than the optimum temperature of 37 °C, there is a decrease in the rate of the reaction.

STUDY CHECK 20.2

If urease has an optimum pH of 7.0, what is the effect of lowering the pH to 3.0?

QUESTIONS AND PROBLEMS

20.3 Factors Affecting Enzyme Activity

LEARNING GOAL: *Describe the effect of temperature, pH, concentration of enzyme, and concentration of substrate on enzyme activity.*

20.19 Trypsin, a peptidase that catalyzes the hydrolysis of proteins, functions in the small intestine at an optimum pH of 7.7–8.0. How would each of the following affect the trypsin-catalyzed reaction?
   a. lowering the concentration of polypeptides
   b. changing the pH to 3.0
   c. running the reaction at 75 °C
   d. adding more trypsin

20.20 Pepsin, a peptidase that catalyzes the hydrolysis of proteins, functions in the stomach at an optimum pH of 1.5–2.0. How would each of the following affect the pepsin-catalyzed reaction?
   a. increasing the concentration of proteins
   b. changing the pH to 5.0
   c. running the reaction at 0 °C
   d. using less pepsin

20.21 The following graph shows activity/pH curves for pepsin, sucrase, and trypsin. Estimate the optimum pH for each.

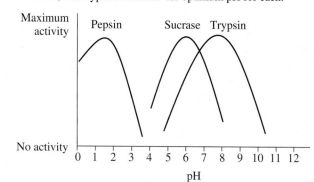

20.22 Refer to the graph in Problem 20.21 to determine if the reaction rate at each of the following pH readings will be at the optimum rate or not:
   a. trypsin, pH 5.0
   b. sucrase, pH 5.0
   c. pepsin, pH 4.0
   d. trypsin, pH 8.0
   e. pepsin, pH 2.0

20.4 Enzyme Inhibition

Many kinds of molecules called **inhibitors** cause enzymes to lose catalytic activity. Although inhibitors act differently, they all prevent the active site from binding with a substrate. An enzyme with a *reversible inhibitor* can regain enzymatic activity, but an enzyme attached to an *irreversible inhibitor* loses enzymatic activity permanently.

Reversible Inhibition

In **reversible inhibition**, an inhibitor causes a loss of enzymatic activity that can be reversed. A reversible inhibitor can act in different ways but does not form covalent bonds with the enzyme. Reversible inhibition can be competitive or noncompetitive. In *competitive inhibition*, an inhibitor competes for the active site, whereas in *noncompetitive inhibition*, the inhibitor acts on another site that is not the active site.

TUTORIAL
Enzyme Inhibition

Competitive Inhibitors

A **competitive inhibitor** has a chemical structure and polarity that is similar to that of the substrate. Thus, a competitive inhibitor competes with the substrate for the active site. When the inhibitor occupies the active site, the substrate cannot bind to the enzyme and no reaction can occur (see Figure 20.8). Enzymatic activity is lost. However, the effect of a competitive inhibitor can be reversed by adding more substrate. Then the competitive inhibitor is displaced from the active site so that more enzyme–substrate complex (ES) forms and enzymatic activity is regained.

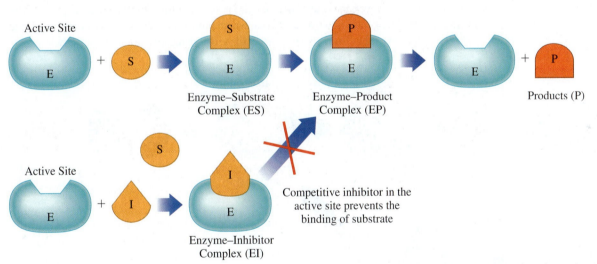

FIGURE 20.8 A competitive inhibitor, which has a structure similar to the substrate, also fits the active site and competes with the substrate.

Q Why does increasing the substrate concentration reverse the inhibition by a competitive inhibitor?

Malonate, which has a structure and polarity similar to that of succinate, competes for the active site on the enzyme succinate dehydrogenase. As long as malonate, a competitive inhibitor, occupies the active site, no reaction occurs. When more of the substrate succinate is added, malonate is displaced from the active site, and the inhibition is reversed.

SELF-STUDY ACTIVITY
Enzyme Inhibition

Some bacterial infections are treated with competitive inhibitors called *antimetabolites*. Sulfanilamide, one of the first sulfa drugs, competes with *p*-aminobenzoic acid (PABA), which is an essential substance (metabolite) in the growth cycle of bacteria.

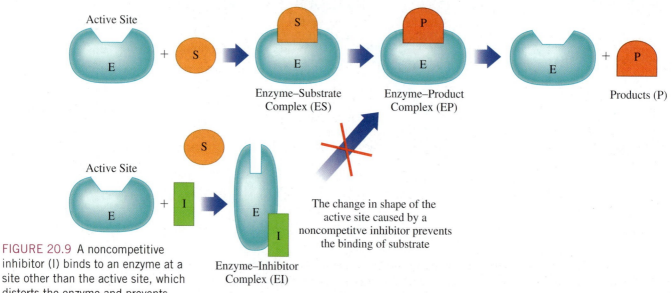

Noncompetitive Inhibitors

The structure of a **noncompetitive inhibitor** does not resemble the substrate and does not compete for the active site. Instead, a noncompetitive inhibitor binds to an enzyme not at the active site, but at a different location. The effect of a noncompetitive inhibitor is to distort the shape of the enzyme, which prevents the substrate from binding at the active site (see Figure 20.9). Examples of noncompetitive inhibitors are the heavy metal ions Pb^{2+}, Ag^+, and Hg^{2+} that bond with amino acid side groups such as $-COO^-$ or $-OH$. Unlike competitive inhibition, the addition of more substrate does not reverse the effect of a metallic noncompetitive inhibitor. However, the effect of a metallic noncompetitive inhibitor can be reversed by using chemical reagents known as *chelators*, which bind toxic metals, such as Pb^{2+}, Ag^+, and Hg^{2+}, and remove them from the body. Then the enzyme regains biological activity.

FIGURE 20.9 A noncompetitive inhibitor (I) binds to an enzyme at a site other than the active site, which distorts the enzyme and prevents the proper binding and catalysis of the substrate at the active site.

Q Does an increase in the substrate concentration reverse the inhibition by a noncompetitive inhibitor?

Irreversible Inhibitors

An **irreversible inhibitor** forms a covalent bond with the R group of an amino acid that may be near or away from the active site. The effect of the irreversible inhibitor changes the shape of the enzyme, which prevents the substrate from entering the active site. Unlike other inhibitors, an irreversible inhibitor cannot be removed, which results in a permanent loss of enzymatic activity.

Insecticides and nerve gases act as irreversible inhibitors of acetylcholinesterase, an enzyme needed for nerve conduction. The compound diisopropyl fluorophosphate (DFP) forms a covalent bond with the —CH₂—OH group of a serine in the active site. When acetylcholinesterase is inhibited, the transmission of nerve impulses is blocked, and paralysis occurs.

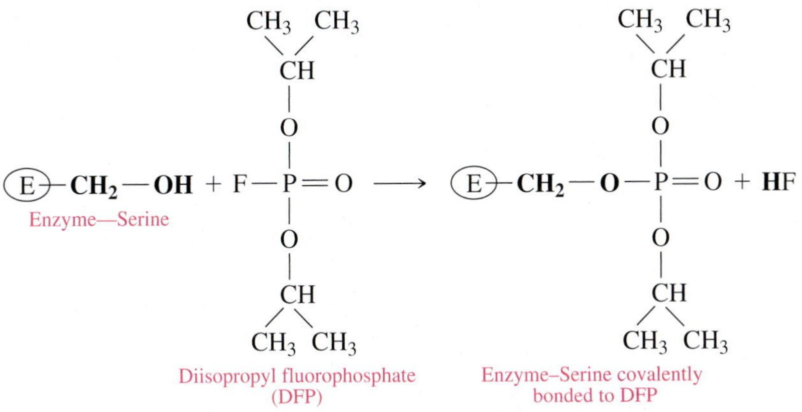

Diisopropyl fluorophosphate (DFP)   Enzyme–Serine covalently bonded to DFP

The compound DFP forms a covalent bond with the R group of serine in the enzyme acetylcholinesterase, causing permanent loss of enzymatic activity.

Antibiotics produced by bacteria, mold, or yeast are irreversible inhibitors used to inhibit bacterial growth. For example, penicillin inhibits a transpeptidase enzyme needed to catalyze a step in the formation of cell walls in bacteria but not human cell membranes. Penicillin, an irreversible inhibitor, forms a covalent bond with the —CH₂—OH group of a serine in the active site of transpeptidase that is stable and cannot be hydrolyzed. The resulting enzyme-inhibitor complex is inactive.

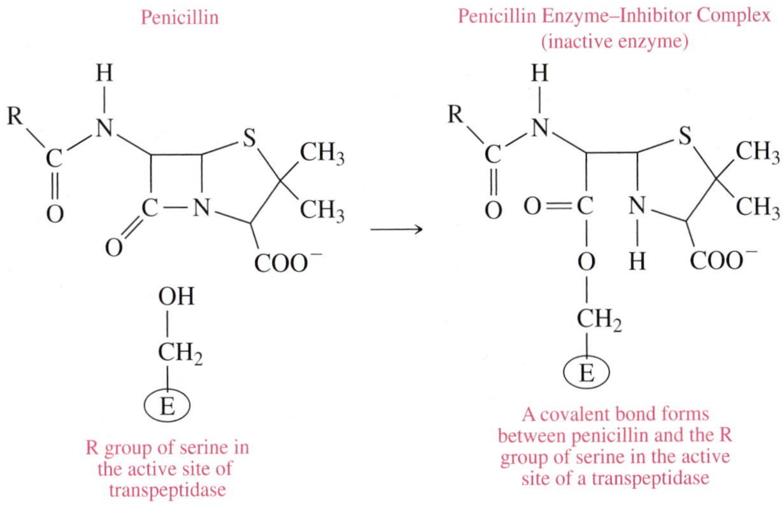

Penicillin   Penicillin Enzyme–Inhibitor Complex (inactive enzyme)

R group of serine in the active site of transpeptidase

A covalent bond forms between penicillin and the R group of serine in the active site of a transpeptidase

Without a complete cell wall, bacteria cannot survive, and the infection is stopped. However, some bacteria are resistant to penicillin because they produce penicillinase, an enzyme that breaks down penicillin. The penicillinase hydrolyzes the four-atom ring converting penicillin to penicillinoic acid, which is inactive. Over the years, derivatives of

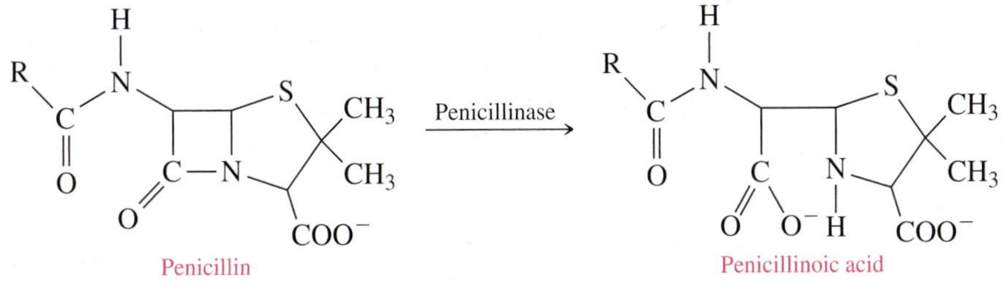

Penicillin   Penicillinoic acid

penicillin to which bacteria have not yet become resistant have been produced. Examples of some irreversible enzyme inhibitors are listed in Table 20.6.

TABLE 20.6 Examples of Irreversible Enzyme Inhibitors

Name	Structure	Source	Inhibitory Action
Cyanide	CN^-	Bitter almonds	Bonds to metal ions in enzymes involved in electron transport
Sarin	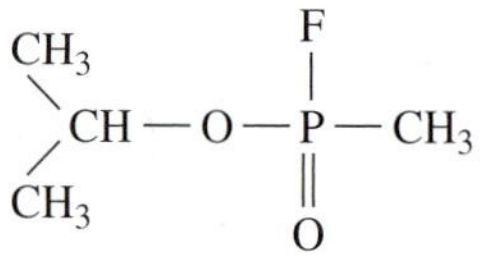	Nerve gas	Inhibits cholinesterase from breaking down acetylcholine, resulting in continual nerve transmission
Parathion	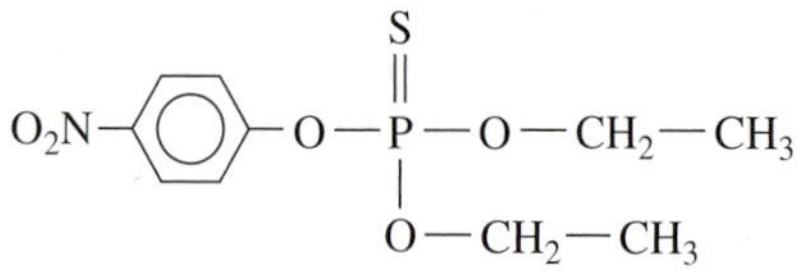	Insecticide	Inhibits cholinesterase from breaking down acetylcholine, resulting in continual nerve transmission
Penicillin	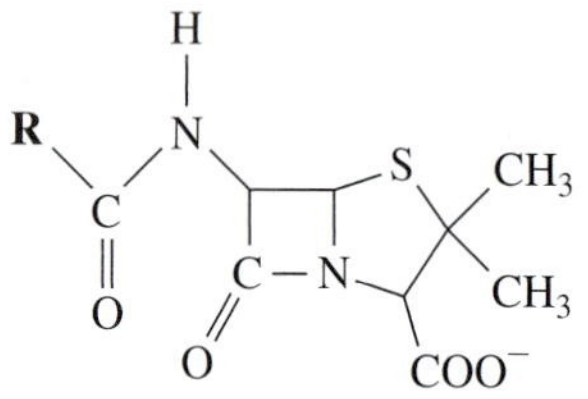	*Penicillium* fungus	Inhibits enzymes that build cell walls in bacteria

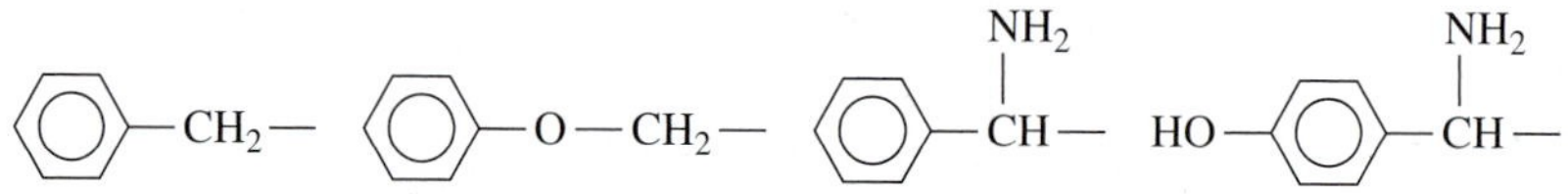

R Groups for Penicillin Derivatives

Penicillin G   Penicillin V   Ampicillin   Amoxicillin

SAMPLE PROBLEM 20.3 Enzyme Inhibition

Describe the type of inhibition described by each of the following:

a. an inhibitor that has a structure similar to that of the substrate
b. an inhibitor that binds to the surface of the enzyme, somewhere other than the active site, and changes its shape

SOLUTION

Analyze the Problem

Characteristics	Competitive	Noncompetitive	Irreversible
Shape of Inhibitor	similar shape to the substrate	does not have a similar shape to the substrate	does not have a similar shape to substrate
Binding to Enzyme	competes for and binds at the active site	binds away from the active site to change the shape of the enzyme and its activity	forms a covalent bond with the enzyme
Reversibility	adding more substrate reverses the inhibition	not reversed by adding more substrate, but by a chemical change that removes the inhibitor	permanent, not reversible

a. When an inhibitor has a structure similar to that of the substrate, it competes with the substrate for the active site. This type of inhibition is competitive inhibition, which is reversed by increasing the concentration of the substrate.
b. When an inhibitor binds to the surface of the enzyme, it changes the shape of the enzyme and the active site. This type of inhibition is noncompetitive inhibition because the inhibitor does not have a similar shape to the substrate and does not compete with the substrate for the active site.

STUDY CHECK 20.3

What type of inhibition occurs when Sarin, a nerve gas, forms a covalent bond with the R group of serine in the active site of acetylcholinesterase?

QUESTIONS AND PROBLEMS

20.4 Enzyme Inhibition

LEARNING GOAL: *Describe competitive and noncompetitive inhibition, and reversible and irreversible inhibition.*

20.23 Indicate whether each of the following describes a competitive or a noncompetitive enzyme inhibitor:
  a. The inhibitor has a structure similar to the substrate.
  b. The effect of the inhibitor cannot be reversed by adding more substrate.
  c. The inhibitor competes with the substrate for the active site.
  d. The structure of the inhibitor is not similar to the substrate.
  e. The addition of more substrate reverses the inhibition.

20.24 Oxaloacetate is an inhibitor of succinate dehydrogenase.

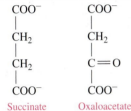

Succinate   Oxaloacetate

  a. Would you expect oxaloacetate to be a competitive or a noncompetitive inhibitor? Why?

  b. Would oxaloacetate bind to the active site or elsewhere on the enzyme?
  c. How would you reverse the effect of the inhibitor?

20.25 Methanol and ethanol are oxidized by alcohol dehydrogenase. When ethanol is oxidized, it becomes acetaldehyde, which can be converted to acetic acid in the liver. However, when methanol is oxidized, it forms formaldehyde. In methanol poisoning, ethanol is given intravenously to prevent the formation of formaldehyde that has toxic effects.
  a. Draw the condensed structural formulas for methanol and ethanol.
  b. Would ethanol compete for the active site or bind to a different site on the enzyme?
  c. Would ethanol be a competitive or noncompetitive inhibitor of methanol oxidation?

20.26 In humans, the antibiotic amoxicillin (a type of penicillin) is used to treat certain bacterial infections.
  a. Does the antibiotic inhibit human enzymes?
  b. Why does the antibiotic kill bacteria but not humans?
  c. Is amoxicillin a reversible or irreversible inhibitor?

20.5 Regulation of Enzyme Activity

LEARNING GOAL

Describe the role of zymogens, feedback control, and allosteric enzymes in regulating enzyme activity.

In enzyme-catalyzed reactions, products are produced in the amounts and at the times they are needed. This means that the rate of a catalyzed reaction must be controlled so it is activated when more product is needed, and inactivated when the amount of that product is sufficient for the cell.

TUTORIAL
Regulating Enzyme Action

Zymogens

Many enzymes are active as soon as they are synthesized and acquire their tertiary structure. However, **zymogens**, or *proenzymes*, are produced as an inactive form and stored for later use. Examples of zymogens include protein hormones, such as insulin, digestive enzymes, and blood clotting enzymes (see Table 20.7). For example, proteases, which are digestive enzymes that hydrolyze protein, are produced as larger, inactive forms. Once a zymogen is formed, it can be transported to the part of the body where the active form is needed. Then the zymogen is converted to its active form by a chemical change, such as the removal of a polypeptide section, which uncovers its active site. The pancreatic zymogens are stored in *zymogen granules*, which have cellular membranes that are resistant to most enzymatic digestion. If zymogen activation should occur when the zymogen is in the storage organ, the proteins within the tissue of the pancreas would undergo digestion, which would cause inflammation and could result in a painful condition called *pancreatitis*.

TABLE 20.7 Examples of Zymogens and Their Active Forms

Zymogen (Inactive Enzyme)	Produced in	Activated in	Enzyme (Active)
Proinsulin	Pancreas	Pancreas	Insulin
Chymotrypsinogen	Pancreas	Small intestine	Chymotrypsin
Pepsinogen	Chief cells	Stomach	Pepsin
Trypsinogen	Pancreas	Small intestine	Trypsin
Fibrinogen	Blood	Damaged tissues	Fibrin
Prothrombin	Blood	Damaged tissues	Thrombin

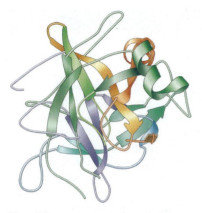

The ribbon representation of chymotrypsin, which is an enzyme that hydrolyzes peptide bonds.

The proteases *trypsinogen* and *chymotrypsinogen* are produced as zymogens and stored in the pancreas. After food is ingested and enters the small intestine, hormones trigger the release of the zymogens of digestive enzymes from the pancreas. In the small intestine, the zymogens are converted into active digestive enzymes by proteases that remove peptide sections from their protein chains. For example, a hexapeptide from the zymogen trypsinogen is removed by a peptidase to form the active digestive enzyme trypsin. As more trypsin forms, it in turn also removes more peptide sections to activate trypsinogen.

Trypsin also activates the zymogen chymotrypsinogen, which consists of 245 amino acids, by removing two dipeptides to give the active enzyme chymotrypsin, which has three peptide sections connected by disulfide bonds.

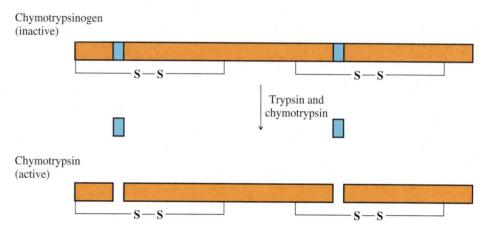

The activation of trypsinogen and chymotrypsinogen are shown in the following diagram:

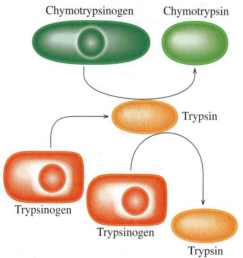

Once formed, trypsin catalyzes the removal of peptides from chymotrypsinogen and trypsinogen to give the active proteases chymotrypsin and trypsin.

The protein hormone insulin is initially synthesized in the pancreas as a zymogen called proinsulin (see Table 20.7). When the polypeptide chain of 33 amino acids is removed by peptidases, insulin becomes biologically active.

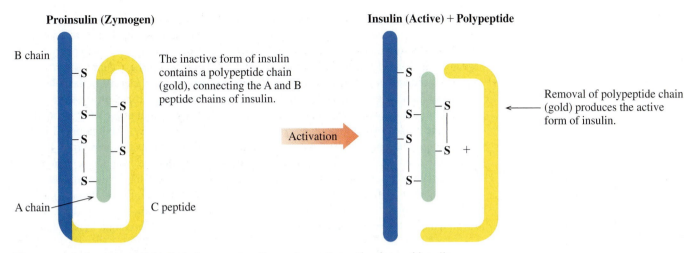

Proinsulin (Zymogen)

B chain

The inactive form of insulin contains a polypeptide chain (gold), connecting the A and B peptide chains of insulin.

Activation

A chain

C peptide

Insulin (Active) + Polypeptide

Removal of polypeptide chain (gold) produces the active form of insulin.

The removal of a polypeptide chain from proinsulin produces the active form of insulin.

Feedback Control

Certain enzymes known as **allosteric enzymes** are capable of binding a regulator molecule that is different from the substrate. The binding of a regulator causes a change in the shape of the enzyme, and therefore, a change in the active site. There are both positive and negative regulators. A *positive regulator* speeds up a reaction by causing a change in the shape of the active site that permits the substrate to bind more effectively. A *negative regulator* slows down the rate of catalysis by preventing the proper binding of the substrate. In **feedback control**, the end product of a series of reactions acts as a negative regulator (see Figure 20.10). When the end product is present in sufficient amounts for the cell, some of the end product molecules bind to the first enzyme (E_1) in the reaction series, which is an allosteric enzyme. By inhibiting the allosteric enzyme in the beginning of the reaction series, the production of all the intermediate compounds in the reaction sequence stops. The entire enzyme-catalyzed reaction sequence shuts down.

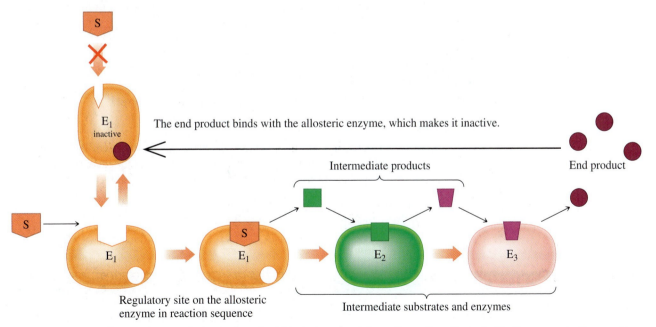

FIGURE 20.10 In feedback control, the end product binds to a regulatory site on the allosteric (first) enzyme in the reaction sequence, which prevents the formation of all intermediate compounds needed in the synthesis of the end product.

Q Do the intermediate enzymes in a reaction sequence have regulatory sites?

When the level of end product is low, the regulator dissociates from the allosteric enzyme (E_1), which unblocks the active site. The enzyme is activated and can bind with the initial substrate once again. Feedback control allows the reaction series to operate only when the end product is needed by the cell. This control prevents the accumulation of intermediate products as well as end product, thereby conserving the materials in the cell.

Let's look at feedback control for the reaction sequence that converts the amino acid threonine to isoleucine. When the level of isoleucine is high in the cell, some of the isoleucine binds to the allosteric enzyme, threonine deaminase, E_1. The binding of isoleucine changes the shape of the threonine deaminase, which prevents threonine from binding to its active site. As a result, the entire reaction sequence does not function. None of the intermediate products formed by the remaining enzymes can inhibit the allosteric enzyme. As isoleucine is utilized in the cell and its concentration decreases, the inhibitor is released from the threonine deaminase. The tertiary shape of the deaminase returns to its active form, which allows the reaction sequence to once again convert threonine to isoleucine.

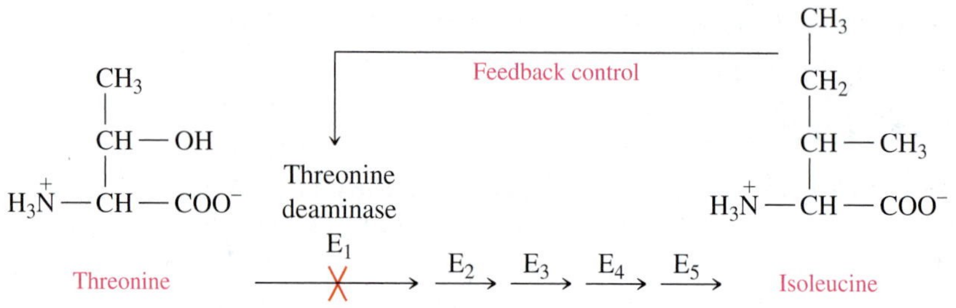

CONCEPT CHECK 20.5   Regulation of Enzyme Activity

Why are the enzymes trypsin and chymotrypsin produced as zymogens in the pancreas rather than as active enzymes?

ANSWER

Trypsin and chymotrypsin are digestive enzymes that break down proteins. If they were produced as active enzymes in the pancreas, they would digest the proteins within the tissue of the pancreas. They are produced as zymogens, transported to the site where they are needed, and activated to start digestion.

SAMPLE PROBLEM 20.4   Enzyme Regulation

How is the rate of a reaction sequence regulated in feedback control?

SOLUTION

When the end product of a reaction sequence is produced at sufficient levels for the cell, some product molecules bind to the first enzyme in the sequence, which shuts down all the reactions that follow and stops the synthesis of end product.

STUDY CHECK 20.4

Why is pepsin, a digestive enzyme, produced as a zymogen?

QUESTIONS AND PROBLEMS

20.5 Regulation of Enzyme Activity

LEARNING GOAL: *Describe the role of zymogens, feedback control, and allosteric enzymes in regulating enzyme activity.*

20.27 Why are many of the enzymes that act on proteins synthesized as zymogens?

20.28 The zymogen trypsinogen produced in the pancreas is activated in the small intestine, where it catalyzes the digestion and hydrolysis of proteins. Explain how the activation of the zymogen while still in the pancreas can lead to an inflammation of the pancreas called pancreatitis.

20.29 In feedback control, how does the end product of a reaction sequence regulate enzyme activity?

20.30 Why are the second or third enzymes in a reaction sequence not used as regulatory enzymes?

20.31 How does an allosteric enzyme function as a regulatory enzyme?

20.32 What is the difference between a negative regulator and a positive regulator?

20.33 Indicate if the following statements describe (1) a zymogen, (2) a positive regulator, (3) a negative regulator, or (4) an allosteric enzyme:
  a. It slows down a reaction, but its shape is different from that of the substrate.

  b. An enzyme that binds a regulator molecule that differs from the substrate.

  c. It is produced as an inactive enzyme.

20.34 Indicate if the following statements describe (1) a zymogen, (2) a positive regulator, (3) a negative regulator, or (4) an allosteric enzyme:
  a. It is activated when a peptide section is removed from its protein chain.

  b. It speeds up a reaction, but it is not the substrate.

  c. When it binds to end product, it stops the formation of more end product.

20.6 Enzyme Cofactors and Vitamins

For many enzymes, their polypeptide chains are biologically active. However, there are also enzymes in which the polypeptide chain is inactive and cannot catalyze a reaction. An inactive enzyme becomes active when it combines with a **cofactor**, which is a nonprotein component such as a vitamin or a metal ion. If the cofactor is an organic molecule, it is known as a **coenzyme**. A cofactor binds to an enzyme in a way that prepares the active site to take part in the catalysis of its substrate.

Metal Ions as Cofactors

The metal ions from the minerals that we obtain from foods in our diet have various functions in enzyme catalysis. Metal ion cofactors such as Fe^{2+} and Cu^{2+} are required by enzymes involved in the loss or gain of electrons. Other metal ions such as Zn^{2+} stabilize the R groups of amino acids in the active site of hydrolases. Some of the metal ion cofactors that are required by enzymes are listed in Table 20.8.

The enzyme carboxypeptidase is produced in the pancreas and moves into the small intestine where it catalyzes the hydrolysis of the C-terminal amino acid with an aromatic R group in a protein (see Figure 20.11).

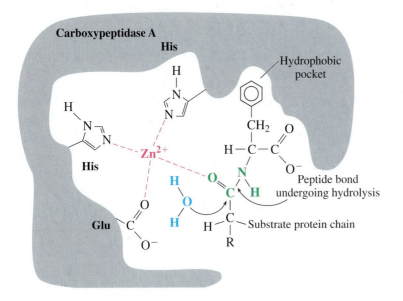

LEARNING GOAL

Describe the types of cofactors found in enzymes.

TUTORIAL
Enzyme Cofactors and Vitamins

TABLE 20.8 Enzymes and the Metal Ions Required as Cofactors

Metal Ion	Enzymes Requiring Metal Ion Cofactors
Cu^{2+}/Cu^+	Cytochrome oxidase
Fe^{2+}/Fe^{3+}	Catalase
	Cytochrome oxidase
Zn^{2+}	Alcohol dehydrogenase
	Carbonic anhydrase
	Carboxypeptidase A
Mg^{2+}	Glucose-6-phosphatase
	Hexokinase
Mn^{2+}	Arginase
Ni^{2+}	Urease

FIGURE 20.11 Carboxypeptidase requires a Zn^{2+} cofactor for the hydrolysis of the peptide bond of a C-terminal aromatic amino acid.

Q Why is Zn^{2+} a cofactor for carboxypeptidase?

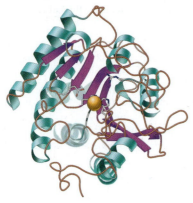

The ribbon representation of carboxypeptidase shows a Zn^{2+} cofactor (orange sphere) in the center of the active site, held in place by R groups in the active site.

The active site includes a pocket that fits the bulky hydrophobic R group on a protein substrate. In the center of the active site, a Zn^{2+} cofactor is bonded to the nitrogen atom in each of two histidine R groups, and an oxygen atom in the R group of glutamic acid. The Zn^{2+} promotes the hydrolysis of the peptide bond by stabilizing the partial negative charge of the oxygen in the carbonyl group of the C-terminal amino acid. The hydrolysis reaction takes place between water and the carbonyl carbon, which breaks the peptide bond to the C-terminal amino acid.

SAMPLE PROBLEM 20.5 Cofactors

Indicate whether each of the following enzymes is active with or without a cofactor:

a. an enzyme that needs Mg^{2+} for catalytic activity
b. a polypeptide chain that is biologically active
c. an enzyme that binds to vitamin B_6 to become active

SOLUTION

a. The enzyme would be active with the metal ion Mg^{2+} cofactor.
b. An active enzyme that is only a polypeptide chain does not require a cofactor.
c. An enzyme that requires vitamin B_6 is active with a cofactor.

STUDY CHECK 20.5

Which cofactor for the enzymes in Sample Problem 20.5 would be called a coenzyme?

Vitamins and Coenzymes

Vitamins are organic molecules that are essential for normal health and growth. They are required in trace amounts and need to be obtained from the diet because sufficient amounts are not synthesized in the body. Before vitamins were discovered, it was known that lime juice prevented the disease scurvy in sailors, and that cod liver oil could prevent rickets. In 1912, scientists found that in addition to carbohydrates, fats, and proteins, certain other factors called vitamins must be obtained from the diet. Vitamin B_1 (thiamine) was the first B vitamin to be identified, thus the abbreviation B_1.

Vitamins are classified into two groups by solubility: water-soluble and fat-soluble. **Water-soluble vitamins** have polar groups such as —OH and —COOH, which make them soluble in the aqueous environment of the cells. The **fat-soluble vitamins** are nonpolar compounds, which are soluble in the fat (lipid) components of the body such as fat deposits and cell membranes.

$$CH_2OH$$
$$CHOH$$

Vitamin C (ascorbic acid)

FIGURE 20.12 Oranges, lemons, peppers, and tomatoes contain vitamin C (ascorbic acid).

Q What happens to the excess vitamin C that may be consumed in one day?

Water-Soluble Vitamins

Because water-soluble vitamins cannot be stored in the body, any excess amounts are excreted in the urine each day. Therefore, the water-soluble vitamins must be in the foods of our daily diets (see Figure 20.12). Because many water-soluble vitamins are easily destroyed by heat, oxygen, and ultraviolet light, care must be taken in food preparation, processing, and storage. Because refining grains such as wheat causes a loss of vitamins, during the 1940s, the Committee on Food and Nutrition of the National Research Council began to recommend dietary enrichment of cereal grains. Vitamin B_1 (thiamine), vitamin B_2 (riboflavin), and iron were in the first group of added nutrients recommended. The Recommended Daily Allowance (RDA) for many vitamins and minerals appears on food product labels.

Many of the water-soluble vitamins are precursors of cofactors required by many enzymes to carry out certain aspects of catalytic action (see Table 20.9). The coenzymes do not remain bonded to a particular enzyme, but are used repeatedly by different enzyme molecules to facilitate an enzyme-catalyzed reaction (see Figure 20.13). Thus, only small amounts of coenzymes are required in the cells. Table 20.10 gives the structures of the water-soluble vitamins.

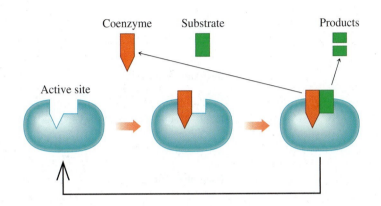

FIGURE 20.13 A coenzyme is required so that an enzyme can become active.

Q What is the function of water-soluble vitamins in enzymes?

TABLE 20.9 Water-Soluble Vitamins, Coenzymes, Functions, Sources and RDA, and Deficiency Symptoms

Vitamin	Coenzyme	Transfer Function	Sources and RDA (Adults)	Deficiency Symptoms
B_1 (Thiamine)	Thiamine pyrophosphate (TPP)	Aldehyde groups	Liver, yeast, whole grain bread, cereals, milk (1.2 mg)	Beriberi: fatigue, poor appetite, weight loss
B_2 (Riboflavin)	Flavin adenine dinucleotide (FAD); flavin mononucleotide (FMN)	Electrons	Beef, liver, chicken, eggs, green leafy vegetables, dairy foods, peanuts, whole grains (1.2–1.8 mg)	Dermatitis; dry skin; red, sore tongue; cataracts
B_3 (Niacin)	Nicotinamide adenine dinucleotide (NAD^+); nicotinamide adenine dinucleotide phosphate ($NADP^+$)	Electrons	Brewer's yeast, chicken, beef, fish, liver, brown rice, whole grains (14–18 mg)	Pellagra: dermatitis, muscle fatigue, loss of appetite, diarrhea, mouth sores
B_5 (Pantothenic acid)	Coenzyme A	Acetyl groups	Salmon, beef, liver, eggs, brewer's yeast, whole grains, fresh vegetables (5 mg)	Fatigue, retarded growth, muscle cramps, anemia
B_6 (Pyridoxine)	Pyridoxal 5′-phosphate (PLP)	Amino groups	Meat, liver, fish, nuts, whole grains, spinach (1.3–2.0 mg)	Dermatitis, fatigue, anemia, retarded growth
B_9 (Folic acid)	Tetrahydrofolate (THF)	Methyl groups	Green leafy vegetables, beans, meat, seafood, yeast, asparagus, whole grains enriched with folic acid (400 μg)	Abnormal red blood cells, anemia, intestinal tract disturbances, loss of hair, growth impairment, depression
B_{12} (Cobalamin)	Methylcobalamin	Methyl groups, hydrogen	Liver, beef, kidney, chicken, fish, milk products (2.0–2.6 μg)	Pernicious anemia, malformed red blood cells, nerve damage
C	Ascorbic acid	Electrons	Blueberries, citrus fruits, strawberries, cantaloupe, tomatoes, peppers, broccoli, cabbage, spinach (75–90 mg)	Scurvy: bleeding gums, weakened connective tissues, slow-healing wounds, anemia
H (Biotin)	Biocytin	Carbon dioxide	Liver, yeast, nuts, eggs (30 μg)	Dermatitis, loss of hair, fatigue, anemia, depression

TABLE 20.10 Structures of Water Soluble Vitamins

B₁ (Thiamine)

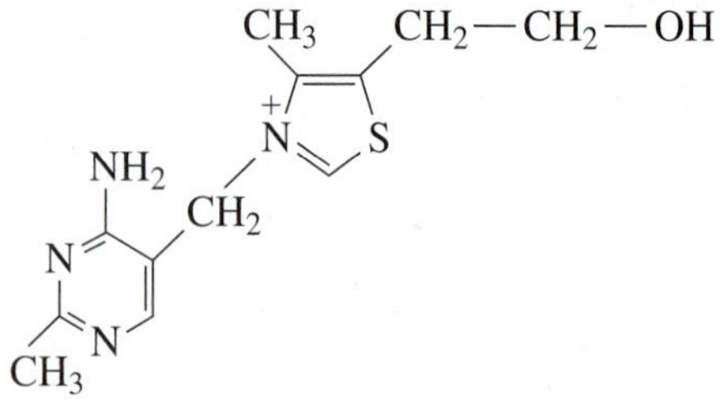

B₂ (Riboflavin)

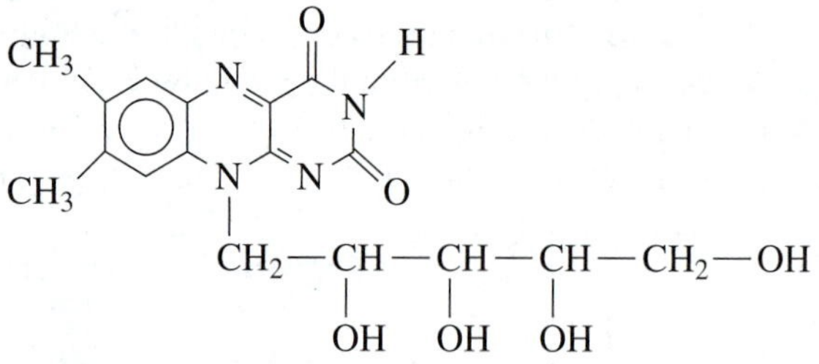

B₃ (Niacin)

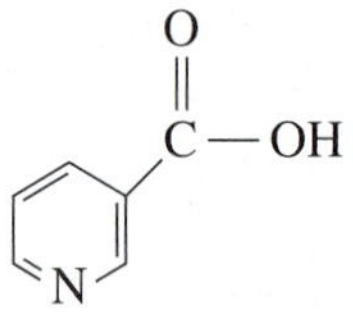

B₅ (Pantothenic acid)

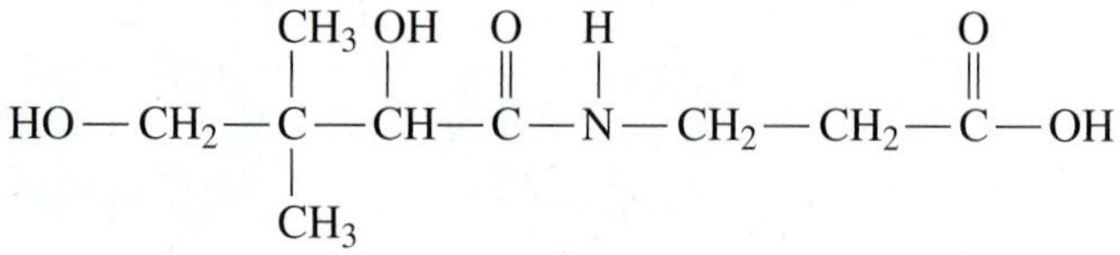

B₆ (Pyridoxine)

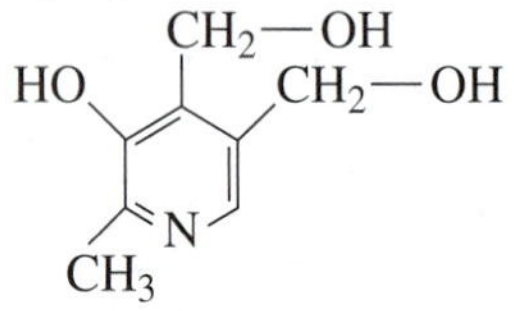

B₁₂ (Cobalamin)

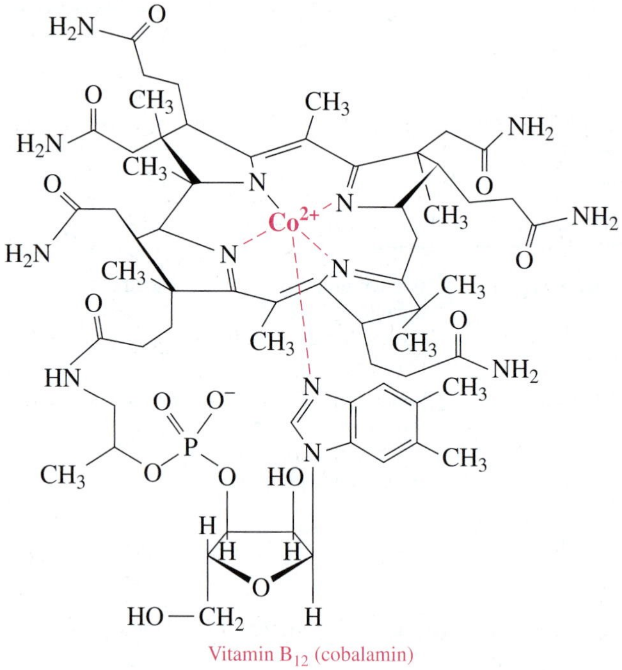

C (Ascorbic acid)

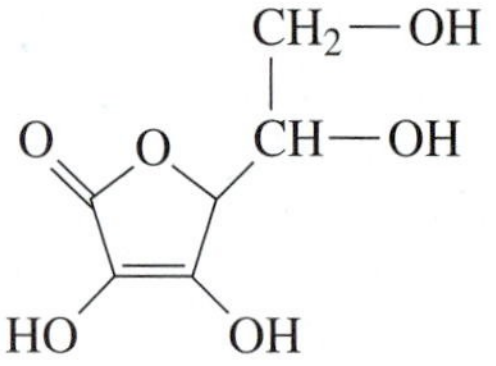

H (Biotin)

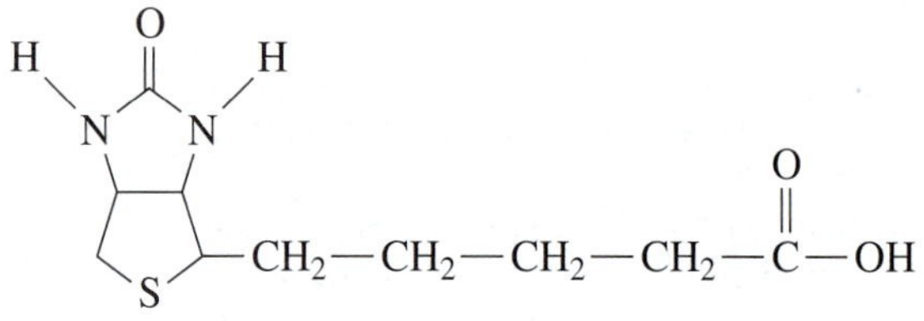

Vitamin B₁₂ (cobalamin)

B₉ (Folic acid)

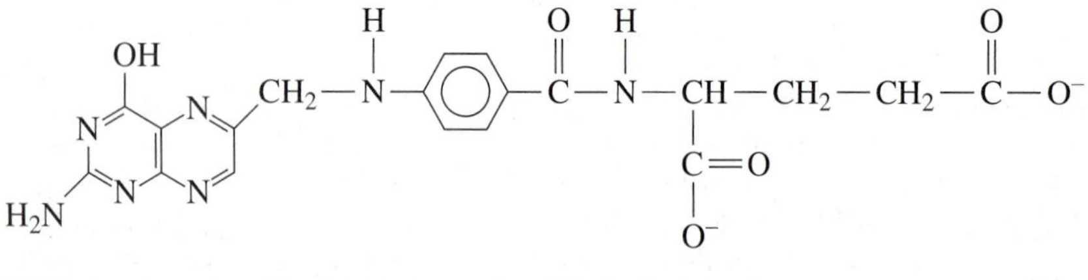

For example, one of the lyases we described in Section 20.1 is carbonic anhydrase, which catalyzes the reaction from carbon dioxide and water to bicarbonate and H^+. The reaction, which is reversible, maintains the proper pH in the blood and tissues. The active form of the anhydrase requires a Zn^{2+} cofactor, which is bonded to three histidine R groups and a water molecule within the active site. After the water molecule loses H^+, the remaining OH^- remains bound to the Zn^{2+} cofactor. A CO_2 molecule is held in the active site close to the Zn^{2+} where it can react with the OH^- group to form HCO_3^-, which is then released from the active site.

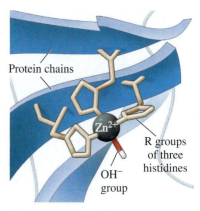

Protein chains

Zn^{2+}

R groups of three histidines

OH^- group

The enzyme carbonic anhydrase needs a Zn^{2+} cofactor to be biologically active.

Fat-Soluble Vitamins

The fat-soluble vitamins—A, D, E, and K—are not involved as coenzymes in catalytic reactions, but they are important in processes such as vision, formation of bone, protection from oxidation, and proper blood clotting (see Table 20.11). Because the fat-soluble vitamins are stored in the body, and not eliminated, it is possible to take too much, which could be toxic primarily in the liver and fatty tissues. Table 20.12 gives the structures of the fat-soluble vitamins.

TABLE 20.11 Function, Sources and RDA, and Deficiency Symptoms of Fat-Soluble Vitamins

Vitamin	Function	Sources and RDA (Adults)	Deficiency Symptoms
A (Retinol)	Formation of visual pigments, synthesis of RNA	Yellow and green fruits and vegetables ($800\ \mu g$)	Night blindness, immune system repression, slowed growth, rickets
D (Cholecalciferol)	Regulation of absorption of P and Ca during bone growth	Sunlight, cod liver oil, enriched milk, eggs ($5–10\ \mu g$)	Rickets, weak bone structure, osteomalacia
E (Tocopherol)	Antioxidant; prevents oxidation of vitamin A and unsaturated fatty acids	Meats, whole grains, vegetables (15 mg)	Hemolysis, anemia
K (Menaquinone)	Synthesis of zymogen prothrombin for blood clotting	Liver, spinach, cauliflower ($90–120\ \mu g$)	Prolonged bleeding time, bruising

TABLE 20.12 Structures of Fat Soluble Vitamins

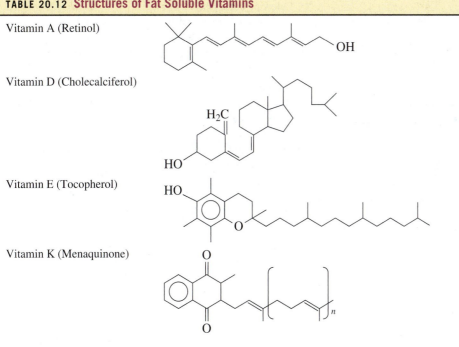

Vitamin A (Retinol)

OH

Vitamin D (Cholecalciferol)

H_2C

HO

Vitamin E (Tocopherol)

HO

O

Vitamin K (Menaquinone)

O

O

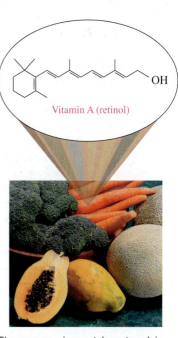

Vitamin A (retinol)

OH

The orange pigment (carotene) in carrots is used to synthesize vitamin A (retinol) in the body.

CONCEPT CHECK 20.6 **Vitamins**

Identify the vitamin(s) described by each of the following:

a. is synthesized in the skin by sunlight
b. contains a Co^{2+} ion
c. is fat soluble
d. can lead to scurvy and slow-healing wounds if deficient in the diet

ANSWER

a. Vitamin D_3 (cholecalciferol) is synthesized in the skin by sunlight.
b. Vitamin B_{12} (cobalamin) contains a Co^{2+} ion.
c. Vitamins A (retinol), D (cholecalciferol), E (tocopherol), and K (menaquinone) are fat soluble.
d. Vitamin C (ascorbic acid) deficiency can lead to scurvy and slow-healing wounds.

SAMPLE PROBLEM 20.6 **Vitamins**

Why do you need a certain amount of thiamine and riboflavin in your diet every day, but not vitamins A or D?

SOLUTION

Water-soluble vitamins like vitamin B_1 (thiamine) and vitamin B_2 (riboflavin) are not stored in the body, whereas fat-soluble vitamins such as vitamin A (retinol) and vitamin D (cholecalciferol) are stored in the liver and body fat. Any excess of thiamine or riboflavin is eliminated in the urine and must be replenished each day from the diet.

STUDY CHECK 20.6

Why are fresh fruits rather than cooked fruits recommended as a source of vitamin C?

QUESTIONS AND PROBLEMS

20.6 Enzyme Cofactors and Vitamins

LEARNING GOAL: Describe the types of cofactors found in enzymes.

20.35 Is the enzyme described in each of the following statements active with or without a cofactor?
   a. requires vitamin B_1 (thiamine)
   b. needs Zn^{2+} for catalytic activity
   c. its active form consists of two polypeptide chains

20.36 Is the enzyme described in each of the following statements active with or without a cofactor?
   a. requires vitamin B_2 (riboflavin)
   b. its active form is composed of 155 amino acids
   c. uses Cu^{2+} during catalysis

20.37 Identify the vitamin that is a component of each of the following coenzymes:
   a. coenzyme A   b. tetrahydrofolate (THF)   c. NAD^+

20.38 Identify the vitamin that is a component of each of the following coenzymes:
   a. thiamine pyrophosphate   b. FAD
   c. pyridoxal 5'-phosphate

20.39 What vitamin may be deficient in the following conditions?
   a. rickets   b. scurvy
   c. pellagra

20.40 What vitamin may be deficient in the following conditions?
   a. poor night vision   b. pernicious anemia
   c. beriberi

20.41 The RDA for vitamin B_6 (pyridoxine) is 2 mg. Why will it not improve your nutrition to take 100 mg of pyridoxine daily?

20.42 The RDA for vitamin C (ascorbic acid) is 75–90 mg. If you take 1000 mg of vitamin C daily, what happens to the vitamin C you do not need?

CONCEPT MAP

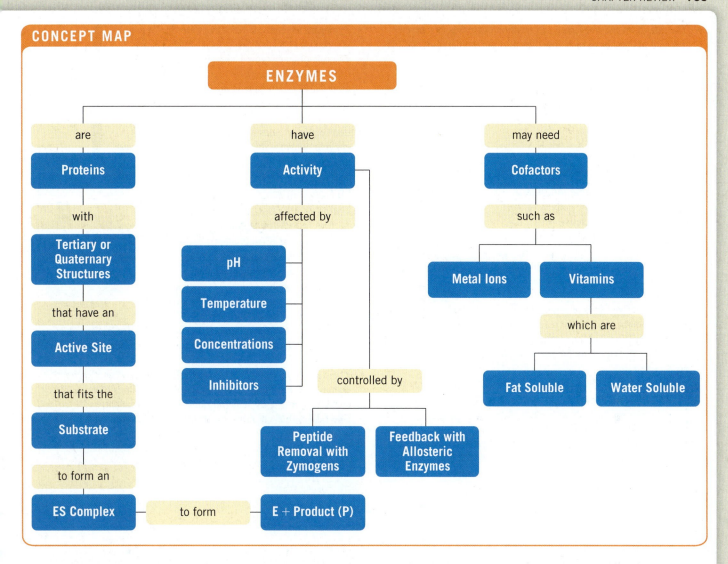

ENZYMES

are → **Proteins** with → **Tertiary or Quaternary Structures** that have an → **Active Site** that fits the → **Substrate** to form an → **ES Complex** — to form — **E + Product (P)**

have → **Activity** affected by → **pH**, **Temperature**, **Concentrations**, **Inhibitors**

controlled by → **Peptide Removal with Zymogens**, **Feedback with Allosteric Enzymes**

may need → **Cofactors** such as → **Metal Ions**, **Vitamins** which are → **Fat Soluble**, **Water Soluble**

CHAPTER REVIEW

20.1 Enzymes and Enzyme Action

LEARNING GOAL: Describe enzymes and their role in enzyme-catalyzed reactions.

- Enzymes are globular proteins that act as biological catalysts by lowering activation energy and accelerating the rate of cellular reactions.
- Within the tertiary structure of an enzyme, a small pocket called the active site binds the substrate.
- In the lock-and-key model, a substrate precisely fits the shape of the active site.
- In the induced-fit model, both the active site and the substrate undergo changes in their shapes to give the best fit for efficient catalysis.
- In the enzyme–substrate complex, catalysis takes place when amino acid R groups in the active site of an enzyme react with a substrate.
- When the products of catalysis are released, the enzyme can bind to another substrate molecule.

Substrate → Products

Active site

Enzyme

20.2 Classification of Enzymes

LEARNING GOAL: Classify enzymes and give their names.

- The names of most enzymes ending in *ase* describe the compound or reaction catalyzed by the enzyme.
- Enzymes are classified by the main type of reaction they catalyze, such as oxidoreductase, transferase, or isomerase.

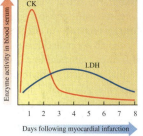

20.3 Factors Affecting Enzyme Activity

LEARNING GOAL: Describe the effect of temperature, pH, concentration of enzyme, and concentration of substrate on enzyme activity.

- The optimum temperature at which most enzymes are effective is usually 37 °C, and the optimum pH is usually 7.4.

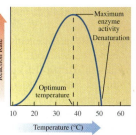

- The rate of an enzyme-catalyzed reaction decreases as temperature and pH go above or below the optimum temperature and pH values.
- An increase in substrate concentration increases the reaction rate of an enzyme-catalyzed reaction, but a maximum rate is reached when all of the enzyme molecules are combined with substrate.

20.4 Enzyme Inhibition

LEARNING GOAL: Describe competitive and noncompetitive inhibition, and reversible and irreversible inhibition.

Enzyme–Substrate Complex

- An inhibitor reduces the activity of an enzyme or makes it inactive.
- An inhibitor can be reversible or irreversible.
- A competitive inhibitor has a structure similar to the substrate and competes for the active site.
- When the active site is occupied, the enzyme cannot catalyze the reaction of the substrate.

Enzyme–Inhibitor Complex

- A noncompetitive inhibitor attaches to the enzyme away from the active site, changing the shape of both the enzyme and its active site.
- An irreversible inhibitor forms a covalent bond within the active site that permanently prevents catalytic activity.

20.5 Regulation of Enzyme Activity

LEARNING GOAL: Describe the role of zymogens, feedback control, and allosteric enzymes in regulating enzyme activity.

- Insulin and most digestive enzymes are produced as inactive forms called zymogens.

- Zymogens are converted to active forms by the removal of a peptide chain that covers their active sites.
- The rate of an enzyme-catalyzed reaction can be increased or decreased by regulator molecules that bind to a regulator site on an allosteric enzyme, which is the first enzyme in a reaction sequence.
- In feedback control, the end product of a reaction sequence binds to a regulator site on the first enzyme, which is an allosteric enzyme, to decrease product formation.

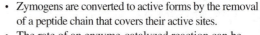

20.6 Enzyme Cofactors and Vitamins

LEARNING GOAL: Describe the types of cofactors found in enzymes.

Coenzyme   Products

- Some enzymes are biologically active as protein only, whereas other enzymes require a nonprotein component called a cofactor.
- A cofactor may be a metal ion, such as Cu^{2+} or Fe^{2+}, or an organic molecule or a vitamin called a coenzyme.
- A vitamin is a small organic molecule needed for health and normal growth that is obtained in small amounts from the diet.
- The water-soluble vitamins are B and C, and they function as coenzymes. Vitamin B is essential for the workings of certain enzymes in the body, and vitamin C is an antioxidant.
- The fat-soluble vitamins are A, D, E, and K. Vitamin A is important in vision, vitamin D for proper bone growth, vitamin E is an antioxidant, and vitamin K is required for proper blood clotting.

KEY TERMS

active site A pocket in a part of the tertiary enzyme structure that binds to a substrate and catalyzes a reaction.

activity The rate at which an enzyme catalyzes the reaction that converts a substrate to a product.

allosteric enzyme An enzyme that regulates the rate of a reaction when a regulator molecule attaches to a site other than the active site.

antibiotics Substances usually produced by bacteria, mold, or yeast that inhibit the growth of bacteria.

coenzyme An organic molecule, usually a vitamin, required as a cofactor in enzyme action.

cofactor A metal ion or an organic molecule that is necessary for a biologically functional enzyme.

competitive inhibitor A molecule that has a structure similar to a substrate, and that inhibits enzyme action by competing for the active site.

enzymes Globular proteins, sometimes with cofactors, that catalyze biological reactions.

enzyme–substrate (ES) complex An intermediate consisting of an enzyme that binds to a substrate in an enzyme-catalyzed reaction.

fat-soluble vitamins Vitamins that are not soluble in water and can be stored in the liver and body fat.

feedback control A type of inhibition in which an end product inhibits the first enzyme in a sequence of enzyme-catalyzed reactions.

induced-fit model A model of enzyme action in which the shape of a substrate and the active site of the enzyme adjust to give an optimal fit.

inhibitors Substances that make an enzyme inactive by interfering with its ability to react with a substrate.

irreversible inhibitor A compound or metal ion that causes the loss of enzymatic activity by forming a covalent bond near or at the active site.

noncompetitive inhibitor An inhibitor that does not resemble the substrate, and attaches to the enzyme away from the active site to prevent the binding of the substrate.

optimum pH The pH at which an enzyme is most active.

optimum temperature The temperature at which an enzyme is most active.

reversible inhibition The loss of enzymatic activity by an inhibitor whose effect can be reversed.

substrate The molecule that reacts in the active site in an enzyme-catalyzed reaction.

vitamins Organic molecules that are essential for normal health and growth, and are obtained in small amounts from the diet.

water-soluble vitamins Vitamins that are soluble in water; they cannot be stored in the body; are easily destroyed by heat, ultraviolet light, and oxygen; and function as coenzymes.

zymogen An inactive form of an enzyme that is activated by the removal of a peptide portion from one end of the protein.

UNDERSTANDING THE CONCEPTS

The chapter sections to review are shown in parentheses at the end of each question.

20.43 Ethylene glycol ($HO-CH_2-CH_2-OH$) is a major component of antifreeze. If ingested, in the body, it is first converted to $HOOC-CHO$ (oxoethanoic acid) and then to $HOOC-COOH$ (oxalic acid), which is toxic. (20.1, 20.4)
  a. What class of enzyme catalyzes both of the reactions of ethylene glycol?
  b. The treatment for the ingestion of ethylene glycol is an intravenous solution of ethanol. How might this help prevent toxic levels of oxalic acid in the body?

Ethylene glycol is added to a radiator to prevent freezing and boiling.

20.44 Adults who are lactose intolerant cannot break down the disaccharide in milk products. To help digest dairy food, a product known as Lactaid can be added to milk. The milk is then refrigerated for 24 h. (20.1, 20.3)
  a. What is the name of the enzyme present in Lactaid, and what is the major class of this enzyme?
  b. What might happen to the enzyme if the digestion product were stored in a warm area?

The disaccharide lactose is present in milk products.

20.45 Fresh pineapple contains the enzyme bromelain that degrades proteins. (20.3)
  a. The directions on a gelatin (protein) package say not to add fresh pineapple. However, canned pineapple that has been heated to high temperatures can be added. Why?
  b. Fresh pineapple can be used as a marinade to tenderize tough meat. Why?

Fresh pineapple contains the enzyme bromelain.

20.46 Beano contains an enzyme that breaks down polysaccharides into smaller, more digestible sugars, which diminishes the intestinal gas formation that can occur after eating foods such as vegetables and beans. (20.1, 20.3, 20.4)
  a. The label says "contains alpha-galactosidase." What class of enzyme is this?
  b. What is the substrate for the enzyme?
  c. The directions indicate you should not cook with or heat Beano. Why?

Beano contains an enzyme that breaks down carbohydrates.

ADDITIONAL QUESTIONS AND PROBLEMS

For instructor-assigned homework, go to www.masteringchemistry.com.

20.47 Why do the cells in the body have so many enzymes? (20.1)

20.48 Are all the possible enzymes present at the same time in a cell? (20.1)

20.49 How are enzymes different from the catalysts used in chemistry laboratories? (20.1)

20.50 Why do enzymes function only under mild conditions? (20.1)

20.51 How does an enzyme change the activation energy for a reaction in a cell? (20.1)

20.52 Why do most enzyme-catalyzed reactions go fast? (20.1)

20.53 Indicate whether each of the following would be a substrate (S) or an enzyme (E): (20.1)
  a. lactose   **b.** lactase   **c.** lipase
  d. trypsin   **e.** pyruvate   **f.** transaminase

20.54 Indicate whether each of the following would be a substrate (S) or an enzyme (E): (20.1)
  a. glucose   **b.** hydrolase   **c.** maleate isomerase
  d. alanine   **e.** amylose   **f.** amylase

20.55 Give the substrate for each of the following enzymes: (20.1)
  a. urease   **b.** succinate dehydrogenase
  c. aspartate transaminase   **d.** phenylalanine hydroxylase

20.56 Give the substrate for each of the following enzymes: (20.1)
  a. maltase   **b.** fructose oxidase
  c. phenolase   **d.** sucrase

20.57 Predict the major class for each of the following enzymes: (20.1)
  a. acyltransferase   **b.** oxidase
  c. lipase   **d.** decarboxylase

20.58 Predict the major class for each of the following enzymes: (20.1)
  a. cis–trans isomerase   **b.** reductase
  c. carboxylase   **d.** peptidase

20.59 How does the lock-and-key model explain the binding of a substrate at the active site? (20.2)

20.60 How does the induced-fit model of enzyme action explain the binding of a substrate at the active site? (20.2)

20.61 If a blood test indicates a high level of LDH and CK, what could be the cause? (20.2)

20.62 If a blood test indicates a high level of ALT, what could be the cause? (20.2)

20.63 What is meant by the optimum temperature for an enzyme? (20.3)

20.64 What is meant by the optimum pH for an enzyme? (20.3)

20.65 Indicate how each of the following will affect an enzyme-catalyzed reaction if the enzyme has an optimum temperature of 37 °C and an optimum pH of 7: (20.3)
  a. heating the reaction mixture to 100 °C
  b. placing the reaction mixture in ice
  c. adjusting the pH of the reaction mixture to pH 2

20.66 Indicate how each of the following will affect an enzyme-catalyzed reaction if the enzyme has an optimum temperature of 37 °C and an optimum pH of 8: (20.3)
  a. decreasing the temperature of the reaction mixture from 37 °C to 15 °C
  b. adjusting the pH of the reaction mixture to pH 5
  c. adjusting the pH of the reaction mixture to pH 10

20.67 Indicate whether an enzyme is saturated or unsaturated in each of the following conditions: (20.3)
  a. adding more substrate does not increase the rate of reaction
  b. doubling the substrate concentration doubles the rate of reaction

20.68 Indicate whether each of the following enzymes would be functional: (20.3)
  a. pepsin, a digestive enzyme, at pH 2
  b. an enzyme at 37 °C, if the enzyme is from a type of thermophilic bacteria that has an optimum temperature of 100 °C

20.69 How does reversible inhibition differ from irreversible inhibition? (20.4)

20.70 How does competitive reversible inhibition differ from noncompetitive reversible inhibition? (20.4)

20.71 Match the type of inhibitor (**1–3**) with the following statements (**a–d**): (20.4)
  1. competitive inhibitor
  2. noncompetitive inhibitor
  3. irreversible inhibitor
  a. forms a covalent bond with an R group in the active site
  b. has a structure similar to the substrate
  c. the addition of more substrate reverses the inhibition
  d. bonds to the surface of the enzyme, causing a change in the shape of the enzyme and active site

20.72 Match the type of inhibitor (**1–3**) with the following statements (**a–d**): (20.4)
  1. competitive inhibitor
  2. noncompetitive inhibitor
  3. irreversible inhibitor
  a. has a structure that is not similar to the substrate
  b. the addition of more substrate does not reverse the inhibition, but the removal of the inhibitor by chemical reaction can return activity to the enzyme
  c. the inhibition is permanent, and it cannot be reversed
  d. competes with the substrate for the active site

20.73 **a.** What type of an inhibitor is the antibiotic amoxicillin? (20.4)
  b. Why is amoxicillin used to treat bacterial infections?

20.74 **a.** A gardener using Parathion develops a headache, dizziness, nausea, blurred vision, excessive salivation, and muscle twitching. (20.4)
  a. What might be happening to the gardener?
  b. Why must humans be careful when using insecticides?

20.75 The zymogen pepsinogen is produced in the gastric chief cells of the stomach. (20.5)
  a. How and where does pepsinogen become the active form, pepsin?
  b. Why are proteases such as pepsin produced in inactive forms?

20.76 Thrombin is an enzyme that helps produce blood clotting when an injury and bleeding occur. (20.5)
  a. What would be the name of the zymogen of thrombin?
  b. Why would the active form of thrombin be produced only when an injury to tissue occurs?

20.77 What is an allosteric enzyme? (20.5)

20.78 Why can some regulator molecules speed up a reaction, while others slow it down? (20.5)

20.79 In feedback control, what type of regulator slows down the catalytic activity of the reaction series? (20.5)

20.80 Why aren't the intermediate products in a reaction sequence used in feedback control? (20.5)

20.81 Which of the following statements describe an enzyme that requires a cofactor? (20.6)
  a. contains Mg^{2+} in the active site
  b. has catalytic activity as a tertiary protein structure
  c. requires folic acid for catalytic activity

20.82 Which of the following statements describes an enzyme that requires a cofactor? (20.6)
  a. contains riboflavin (vitamin B_2)
  b. has four subunits of polypeptide chains
  c. requires Fe^{3+} in the active site for catalytic activity

20.83 Match the following coenzymes (**1–3**) with their vitamins (**a–c**): (20.6)
  1. NAD^+ **2.** thiamine pyrophosphate (TPP)
  3. coenzyme A
  a. pantothenic acid (B_5)   **b.** niacin (B_3)
  c. thiamine (B_1)

20.84 Match the following coenzymes (**1–3**) with their vitamins (**a–c**): (20.6)
  1. pyridoxal 5'-phosphate   **2.** tetrahydrofolate (THF)
  3. FAD
  a. folate   **b.** riboflavin (B_2)   **c.** pyridoxine

20.85 Why are only small amounts of vitamins needed in the cells when there are several enzymes that require coenzymes? (20.6)

20.86 Why is there a daily requirement for vitamins? (20.6)

20.87 Match each of the following symptoms or conditions (**1–3**) with a vitamin deficiency (**a–c**): (20.6)
  1. night blindness   **2.** weak bone structure   **3.** pellagra
  a. niacin   **b.** vitamin A   **c.** vitamin D

20.88 Match each of the following symptoms or conditions (**1–3**) with a vitamin deficiency (**a–c**): (20.6)
  1. bleeding   **2.** anemia   **3.** scurvy
  a. cobalamin   **b.** vitamin C   **c.** vitamin K

CHALLENGE QUESTIONS

20.89 Lactase is an enzyme that hydrolyzes lactose to glucose and galactose. (20.1, 20.2)
   a. What are the reactants and products of the reaction?
   b. Draw an energy diagram for the reaction with and without lactase.
   c. How does lactase make the reaction go faster?

20.90 Maltase is an enzyme that hydrolyzes maltose into two glucose molecules. (20.1, 20.2)
   a. What are the reactants and products of the reaction?
   b. Draw an energy diagram for the reaction with and without maltase.
   c. How does maltase make the reaction go faster?

20.91 What is the class of the enzyme that would catalyze each of the following reactions? (20.1)

a. $CH_3-\overset{\overset{\displaystyle O}{\|}}{C}-H \longrightarrow CH_3-\overset{\overset{\displaystyle O}{\|}}{C}-OH$

b. $\overset{+}{H_3N}-CH_2-\overset{\overset{\displaystyle O}{\|}}{C}-\overset{\overset{\displaystyle H}{|}}{N}-\overset{\overset{\displaystyle CH_3}{|}}{CH}-\overset{\overset{\displaystyle O}{\|}}{C}-O^- + H_2O \longrightarrow$

$\overset{+}{H_3N}-CH_2-\overset{\overset{\displaystyle O}{\|}}{C}-O^- + \overset{+}{H_3N}-\overset{\overset{\displaystyle CH_3}{|}}{CH}-\overset{\overset{\displaystyle O}{\|}}{C}-O^-$

c. $CH_3-CH{=}CH-CH_3 + H_2O \longrightarrow$

$CH_3-CH_2-\overset{\overset{\displaystyle OH}{|}}{CH}-CH_3$

20.92 What is the class of the enzyme that would catalyze each of the following reactions? (20.1)

a. $CH_3-\overset{\overset{\displaystyle O}{\|}}{C}-\overset{\overset{\displaystyle O}{\|}}{C}-OH \longrightarrow$

$CH_3-\overset{\overset{\displaystyle O}{\|}}{C}-OH + CO_2$

b. $CH_3-\overset{\overset{\displaystyle O}{\|}}{C}-\overset{\overset{\displaystyle O}{\|}}{C}-OH + CO_2 + ATP \longrightarrow$

$HO-\overset{\overset{\displaystyle O}{\|}}{C}-CH_2-\overset{\overset{\displaystyle O}{\|}}{C}-\overset{\overset{\displaystyle O}{\|}}{C}-OH + ADP + P_i$

c. glucose-6-phosphate $\longrightarrow$ fructose-6-phosphate

ANSWERS

Answers to Study Checks

20.1 hydrolase

20.2 At a pH lower than the optimum pH, the hydrogen bonds and salt bridges of urease will be disrupted, resulting in the denaturation of the enzyme and a decrease in its activity.

20.3 Because Sarin forms a covalent bond with an R group in the active site of the enzyme, the inhibition by Sarin is irreversible.

20.4 Pepsin hydrolyzes proteins in the foods we ingest. It is synthesized as a zymogen, pepsinogen, to prevent its digestion of the proteins that make up the organs in the body.

20.5 vitamin B_6

20.6 Water-soluble vitamins such as vitamin C are easily destroyed by heat.

Answers to Selected Questions and Problems

20.1 Chemical reactions can occur without enzymes, but the rates are too slow. Catalyzed reactions, which are many times faster, provide the amounts of products needed by the cell at a particular time.

20.3 a. (2) enzyme   **b.** (1) enzyme–substrate complex
   c. (3) substrate

20.5 a. $E + S \rightleftharpoons ES \longrightarrow EP \longrightarrow E + P$
   b. The active site is a region or pocket within the tertiary structure of an enzyme that accepts the substrate, aligns the substrate for reaction, and catalyzes the reaction.

20.7 a. oxidation–reduction
   b. transfer of a group from one substance to another
   c. hydrolysis (splitting) of molecules with the addition of water

20.9 a. hydrolase   **b.** isomerase   **c.** transferase

20.11 a. lyase   **b.** transferase

20.13 a. succinate oxidase   **b.** glutamine synthetase
   c. alcohol dehydrogenase

20.15 Isoenzymes are slightly different forms of an enzyme that catalyze the same reaction in different organs and tissues of the body.

20.17 A doctor might run tests for the enzymes CK and LDH to determine if the patient had a heart attack.

20.19 a. The reaction will be slower.
   b. The reaction will slow or stop because the enzyme will be denatured at low pH.
   c. The reaction will slow or stop because the high temperature will denature the enzyme.
   d. The reaction will go faster as long as there are polypeptides to react.

20.21 pepsin, pH 2; sucrase, pH 6; trypsin, pH 8

20.23 a. competitive   **b.** noncompetitive   **c.** competitive
   d. noncompetitive   **e.** competitive

20.25 a. methanol, CH_3-OH; ethanol, CH_3-CH_2-OH
   b. Ethanol has a similar structure to methanol and could compete for the active site.
   c. Ethanol is a competitive inhibitor of methanol oxidation.

20.27 Enzymes that act on proteins are proteases, and would digest the proteins of the organ where they are produced if they were active immediately upon synthesis. Therefore, digestive enzymes are produced in one organ and transported to the site of digestion where they are activated.

20.29 In feedback control, the product binds to the first enzyme in a series and changes the shape of the active site. If the active site can no longer bind the substrate effectively, the reaction will stop.

20.31 When a regulator molecule binds to an allosteric site, the shape of the enzyme is altered, which makes the active site more reactive or less reactive, and thereby increases or decreases the rate of the reaction.

20.33 a. (3) negative regulator
b. (4) allosteric enzyme
c. (1) zymogen

20.35 a. active with a cofactor
b. active with a cofactor
c. does not require a cofactor

20.37 a. pantothenic acid (vitamin B_5)
b. folic acid
c. niacin (vitamin B_3)

20.39 a. vitamin D (cholescalciferol)
b. vitamin C (ascorbic acid)
c. vitamin B_3 (niacin)

20.41 Vitamin B_6 is a water-soluble vitamin, which means that each day any excess of vitamin B_6 is eliminated from the body.

20.43 a. oxidoreductase
b. Ethanol would act as a competitive inhibitor of ethylene glycol, saturate the alcohol dehydrogenase enzyme, and allow ethylene glycol to be removed from the body without producing oxalic acid.

20.45 a. Fresh pineapple contains an enzyme that breaks down protein, which means that the gelatin dessert would not turn solid upon cooking. The high temperatures used to prepare canned pineapple denature the enzyme so it no longer can break down protein.
b. The enzyme in fresh pineapple juice can be used to tenderize tough meat because the enzyme breaks down proteins.

20.47 The many different reactions that take place in cells require different enzymes because enzymes react with only a certain type of substrate.

20.49 Enzymes are catalysts that are proteins and function only at mild temperature and pH. Catalysts used in chemistry laboratories are usually inorganic materials that can function at high temperatures and in strongly acidic or basic conditions.

20.51 An enzyme lowers the activation energy for a reaction.

20.53 a. S **b.** E **c.** E
d. E **e.** S **f.** E

20.55 a. urea **b.** succinate
c. aspartate **d.** phenylalanine

20.57 a. transferase **b.** oxidoreductase
c. hydrolase **d.** lyase

20.59 In the lock-and-key model, a substrate fits the exact shape of the active site.

20.61 A heart attack may be the cause.

20.63 The optimum temperature for an enzyme is the temperature at which the enzyme is fully active and most effective.

20.65 a. The rate of catalysis will slow and stop as a high temperature denatures the enzyme.
b. The rate of the catalyzed reaction will slow as temperature is lowered.
c. The enzyme will not be functional at pH 2.

20.67 a. saturated **b.** unsaturated

20.69 In reversible inhibition, the inhibitor can dissociate from the enzyme, whereas in irreversible inhibition, the inhibitor forms a strong covalent bond with the enzyme and does not dissociate. Irreversible inhibitors act as poisons to enzymes.

20.71 a. (3) irreversible inhibitor
b. (1) competitive inhibitor
c. (1) competitive inhibitor
d. (2) noncompetitive inhibitor

20.73 a. Antibiotics such as amoxicillin are irreversible inhibitors.
b. Antibiotics inhibit enzymes needed to form cell walls in bacteria, not humans.

20.75 a. When pepsinogen enters the stomach, the low pH cleaves a peptide from its protein chain to form pepsin.
b. An active protease would digest the proteins of the stomach rather than the proteins in foods.

20.77 An allosteric enzyme contains sites for regulators that alter the enzyme and speed up or slow down the rate of the catalyzed reaction.

20.79 In feedback control, a negative regulator slows down the catalytic activity.

20.81 a. requires a cofactor
b. does not require a cofactor
c. requires a cofactor (coenzyme)

20.83 a. (3) coenzyme A
b. (1) NAD^+
c. (2) thiamine pyrophosphate (TPP)

20.85 A vitamin combines with an enzyme only when the enzyme and coenzyme are needed to catalyze a reaction. When the enzyme is not needed, the vitamin dissociates for use by other enzymes in the cell.

20.87 a. niacin, (3) pellagra
b. vitamin A, (1) night blindness
c. vitamin D, (2) weak bone structure

20.89 a. The reactants are lactose and water and the products are glucose and galactose.
b.

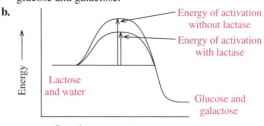

c. By lowering the energy of activation, the enzyme furnishes a lower energy pathway by which the reaction can take place.

20.91 a. oxidoreductase **b.** hydrolase **c.** lyase

Combining Ideas from Chapters 16 to 20

CI.31 The plastic known as PETE (**p**oly**e**thylene**te**rephthalate) is a polymer of terephthalic acid and ethylene glycol. PETE is used to make plastic soft drink bottles and containers for salad dressing, shampoos, and dishwashing liquids. Today, PETE is the most widely recycled of all the plastics; in a single year, 2.4×10^9 lb of PETE are recycled. After PETE is separated from other plastics, it is recycled and used to make polyester fabric, door mats, tennis ball containers, and fill for sleeping bags. The density of PETE is 1.38 g/mL. (1.7, 1.8, 1.9, 1.10, 16.3)

Terephthalic acid   Ethylene glycol

Plastic bottles made of PETE are ready to be recycled.

a. Draw the condensed structural formula for the ester formed from one molecule of terephthalic acid and one molecule of ethylene glycol.
b. Draw the condensed structural formula for the product formed when a second molecule of ethylene glycol reacts with the ester you drew in part **a**.
c. How many kilograms of PETE are recycled in one year?
d. What volume, in liters, of PETE is recycled in one year?
e. Suppose a landfill holds 2.7×10^7 L of recycled PETE. If all of the PETE that is recycled in a year were placed in landfills, how many would it fill?

CI.32 Using the Internet or a reference book such as the *Merck Index* or *Physicians' Desk Reference*, look up the condensed structural formulas for the following medicinal drugs and list the functional groups in the compounds. You may need to refer to the cross-index of names at the back of the reference book. (11.5, 16.1, 16.3, 18.1, 18.4)
a. baclofen, a muscle relaxant
b. anethole, a licorice flavoring agent in anise and fennel
c. alibendol, an antispasmodic drug
d. pargyline, an antihypertensive drug
e. naproxen, a nonsteroidal anti-inflammatory drug

CI.33 Epibatidine is one of the alkaloids that the Ecuadorian poison dart frog (*Epipedobates tricolor*) secretes through its skin. Natives of the rainforest prepare poison darts by rubbing the tips on the skin of the poison dart frogs. The effect of a very small amount of the poison can paralyze or kill an animal. As a pain reliever, epibatidine is 200 times more effective than morphine. Although a therapeutic dose has been calculated as $2.5\,\mu g/kg$, epibatidine has adverse effects. It is expected that more research to chemically modify the epibatidine molecule will produce an important pain reliever. (6.4, 6.5, 18.3)

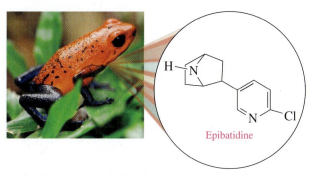

Epibatidine

Natives in the South American rainforests obtain poison for blow darts from the alkaloids secreted by poison dart frogs.

a. What two heterocyclic amines are in the structure of epibatidine?
b. What is the molecular formula of epibatidine?
c. What is the molar mass of epibatidine?
d. How many grams of epibatidine would be given to a 60. kg person if the dose is 2.5 $\mu g/kg$?
e. How many molecules of epibatidine would be given to a 60. kg person for the dose in part **d**?

CI.34 Glyceryl trimyristate (trimyristin) is found in the seeds of nutmeg (*Myristica fragrans*). Trimyristin is used as a lubricant and fragrance in soaps and shaving creams. Isopropyl myristate is used to increase absorption of skin creams. Draw the condensed structural formula for each of the following: (16.3, 16.4, 16.5, 17.2, 17.3)

Nutmeg contains high levels of glyceryl trimyristate.

a. myristic acid
b. glyceryl trimyristate (trimyristin)
c. isopropyl myristate
d. products of the hydrolysis of glyceryl trimyristate with an acid catalyst
e. products of the saponification of glyceryl trimyristate with KOH
f. reactant and product for oxidation of myristyl alcohol to myristic acid

CI.35 Hyaluronic acid (HA), a polymer of about 25 000 disaccharide units, is a natural component of eye and joint fluid, as well as of skin and cartilage. Due to the ability of HA to absorb water, it is used in skin care products and injections to smooth wrinkles, and for treatment of arthritis. The disaccharide units in HA consist of D-gluconic acid and N-acetyl-D-glucosamine.

Hyaluronic acid

D-Glucosamine has an amino group ($-NH_2$) in place of the hydroxyl group on carbon 2 of D-glucose. N-acetyl-D-glucosamine is the amide formed from acetic acid and D-glucosamine. Another natural polymer called chitin is found in the shells of lobsters and crabs. Chitin is made of repeating units of N-acetyl-D-glucosamine connected by β-1,4-glycosidic bonds. (13.4, 15.3, 15.5, 15.6, 18.4)

a. Draw the Haworth structure for the product of the oxidation reaction of the hydroxyl group on carbon 6 in β-D-glucose to form β-D-gluconic acid.

b. Draw the Haworth structure for β-D-glucosamine.

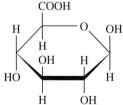

The shells of crabs and lobsters contain chitin.

c. Draw the Haworth structure for N-acetyl-beta-D-glucosamine.

d. What are the two types of glycosidic bonds that link the monosaccharides in hyaluronic acid?

e. Draw the structure for a section of chitin with two N-acetyl-beta-D-glucosamine units linked by β-1,4-glycosidic bonds.

CI.36 In response to signals from the nervous system, the hypothalamus secretes a polypeptide hormone known as gonadotropin-releasing factor (GnRF), which stimulates the pituitary gland to release other hormones into the bloodstream. Two of these hormones are luteinizing hormone (LH) and follicle-stimulating hormone (FSH). GnRF is a decapeptide with the following primary structure:

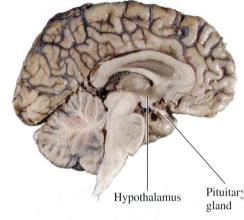

The hypothalamus secretes GnRF.

Glu—His—Tyr—Ser—Tyr—Gly—Leu—Arg—Pro—Gly. (19.1, 19.2, 19.3, 19.4, 20.5)

a. What is the N-terminal amino acid in GnRF?

b. What is the C-terminal amino acid in GnRF?

c. Which amino acids in GnRF are nonpolar or polar neutral?

d. Draw the condensed structural formulas for the acidic or basic amino acids at physiological pH.

e. Draw the primary structure for the first three amino acids of GnRF, starting from the N-terminal amino acid at physiological pH.

f. When the level of LH or FSH is high in the bloodstream, the hypothalamus stops secreting GnRF. What type of regulation of proteins does this represent?

ANSWERS

CI.31 a. HO—C(=O)—⟨⟩—C(=O)—O—CH_2—CH_2—OH

b.
HO—CH_2—CH_2—O—C(=O)—⟨⟩—C(=O)—O—CH_2—CH_2—OH

c. 1.1×10^9 kg of PETE

d. 8.0×10^8 L of PETE

e. 30 landfills

CI.33 a. pyridine and pyrrolidine

b. $C_{11}H_{13}N_2Cl$

c. 209 g/mole

d. 1.5×10^{-4} g of epibatidine

e. 4.3×10^{17} molecules of epibatidine

CI.35 a.

COOH structure (Haworth)

b.

CH_2OH structure (Haworth)

c.

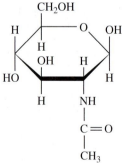

d. They are β-1,4- and β-1,3-glycosidic bonds.

e.

N-acetyl-glucosamine disaccharide structure (Haworth)

Nucleic Acids and Protein Synthesis

21

Mastering**CHEMISTRY**™

Visit **www.masteringchemistry.com** for self-study materials and instructor-assigned homework.

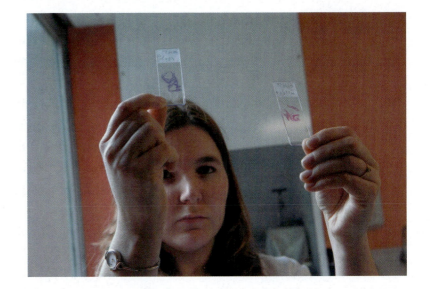

Daniel has been diagnosed with basal cell

carcinoma, the most common form of skin cancer. He has an appointment to undergo Mohs surgery, a specialized procedure to remove the cancerous growth found on his shoulder. The surgeon begins the process by removing the abnormal growth, in addition to a thin layer of surrounding (margin) tissue, which he sends to Lisa, a histologist. Lisa prepares the tissue sample to be viewed by a pathologist. Tissue preparation requires Lisa to cut the tissue into a very thin section (normally 4/10,000 of an inch), which is then mounted onto a microscope slide. Lisa then treats the tissue with a dye to stain the cells, as this enables the pathologist to view any abnormal cells more easily. The pathologist examines the tissue sample and reports back to the surgeon that no abnormal cells were present in the margin tissue, and Daniel's tumor has been completely removed. No further tissue removal is necessary.

DNA, or deoxyribonucleic acid, contains all of a person's genetic information such as skin and eye color. This information is copied every time a cell divides through a process called replication. However, changes can occur in the DNA sequence during replication, which result in a mutation. Mutations can lead to cancer.

Career: Histologist

Histologists study the microscopic make-up of tissues, cells, and bodily fluids with the purpose of detecting and identifying the presence of a specific disease. They determine blood types and the concentrations of drugs and other substances in the blood. Histologists also help establish a rationale for why a patient may not be responding to his or her treatment. Sample preparation is a critical component of a histologist's job, as they prepare tissue samples from humans, animals, and plants. The tissue samples are cut, using specialized equipment, into extremely thin sections which are then mounted, and stained using various chemical dyes. The dyes provide contrast for the cells to be viewed and help highlight any abnormalities that may exist. Utilization of various dyes requires the histologist to be familiar with solution preparation and the handling of potentially hazardous chemicals.

Nucleic acids are large molecules found in the nuclei of cells that store information and direct activities for cellular growth and reproduction. Deoxyribonucleic acid (DNA), the genetic material in the nucleus of a cell, contains all the information needed for the development of a complete living organism. The way you grow, your hair, your eyes, your physical appearance, and all the activities of all the cells in your body are determined by a set of directions contained within the DNA of your cells.

All of the genetic information in the cell is called the *genome*. Every time a cell divides, the information in the genome is copied and passed on to the new cells. This replication process must duplicate the genetic instructions exactly. Some sections of DNA called *genes* contain the information to make a particular protein.

When a cell requires protein, another type of nucleic acid, ribonucleic acid (RNA), translates the genetic information in DNA and carries that information to the ribosomes, where the synthesis of protein takes place. However, mistakes may occur that lead to mutations that affect the synthesis of a certain protein.

21.1 Components of Nucleic Acids

There are two closely related types of nucleic acids: *deoxyribonucleic acid* (**DNA**) and *ribonucleic acid* (**RNA**). Both are unbranched polymers of repeating monomer units known as *nucleotides*. Each nucleotide has three components: a base, a five-carbon sugar, and a phosphate group (see Figure 21.1). A DNA molecule may contain several million nucleotides; smaller RNA molecules may contain up to several thousand.

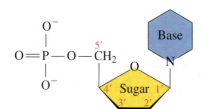

FIGURE 21.1 The general structure of a nucleotide includes a nitrogen-containing base, a sugar, and a phosphate group.

Q In a nucleotide, what types of groups are bonded to a five-carbon sugar?

Bases

The nitrogen-containing **bases** in nucleic acids are derivatives of the heterocyclic amines *pyrimidine* or *purine*, which we discussed in Section 18.3.

Pyrimidine   Purine

In DNA, the purine bases with double rings are adenine (A) and guanine (G), and the pyrimidine bases with single rings are cytosine (C) and thymine (T). RNA contains the same bases, except thymine (5-methyluracil) is replaced by uracil (U) (see Figure 21.2).

Pyrimidines

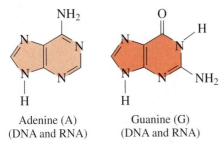

Cytosine (C)
(DNA and RNA)

Thymine (T)
(DNA only)

Uracil (U)
(RNA only)

Purines

Adenine (A)
(DNA and RNA)

Guanine (G)
(DNA and RNA)

FIGURE 21.2 DNA contains the bases A, G, C, and T; RNA contains A, G, C, and U.
Q Which bases are found in DNA?

CONCEPT CHECK 21.1 **Components of Nucleic Acids**

Identify each of the following bases as a purine or pyrimidine. Indicate if each base is found in DNA, RNA, or both.

a.

b.

ANSWER

a. Guanine is a purine found in both RNA and DNA.
b. Uracil is a pyrimidine found only in RNA.

Pentose sugars in RNA and DNA

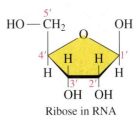

Ribose in RNA

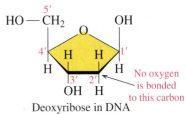

Deoxyribose in DNA

The five-carbon pentose sugar found in RNA is ribose and in DNA, deoxyribose.

Pentose Sugars

In RNA, the five-carbon sugar is *ribose*, which gives the letter R in the abbreviation RNA. The atoms in the pentose sugars are numbered with primes ($1'$, $2'$, $3'$, $4'$, and $5'$) to differentiate them from the atoms in the bases. In DNA, the five-carbon sugar is *deoxyribose*, which is similar to ribose except that there is no hydroxyl group (—OH) on C2'. The *deoxy* prefix means "without oxygen" and provides the letter D in DNA.

Nucleosides and Nucleotides

A **nucleoside** is produced when a pyrimidine or a purine forms a glycosidic bond to C1′ of a sugar, either ribose or deoxyribose. For example, adenine, a purine, and ribose form a nucleoside called adenosine.

A base forms an *N*-glycosidic bond with ribose or deoxyribose to form a nucleoside.

Nucleotides are nucleosides in which a phosphate group bonds to the —OH group on carbon 5 (C5′) of ribose or deoxyribose. The product is a *phosphoester*. Other hydroxyl groups on ribose can also form phosphoesters, but only 5′-monophosphate nucleotides are found in RNA and DNA. All the nucleotides in RNA and DNA are shown in Figure 21.3.

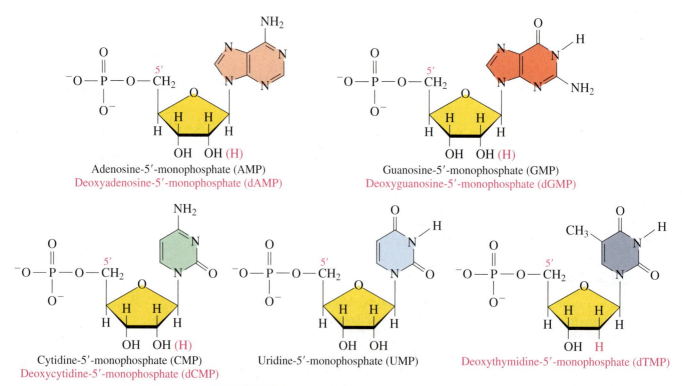

Adenosine-5′-monophosphate (AMP)
Deoxyadenosine-5′-monophosphate (dAMP)

Guanosine-5′-monophosphate (GMP)
Deoxyguanosine-5′-monophosphate (dGMP)

Cytidine-5′-monophosphate (CMP)
Deoxycytidine-5′-monophosphate (dCMP)

Uridine-5′-monophosphate (UMP)

Deoxythymidine-5′-monophosphate (dTMP)

FIGURE 21.3 The nucleotides of RNA are similar to those of DNA, except in DNA (shown in magenta) the sugar is deoxyribose and deoxythymidine replaces uridine.

Q What are two differences in the nucleotides of RNA and DNA?

Table 21.1 summarizes the components in DNA and RNA.

TABLE 21.1 Components in DNA and RNA

Component	DNA	RNA
Bases	A, G, C, and T	A, G, C, and U
Sugar	Deoxyribose	Ribose
Nucleoside	Base + deoxyribose	Base + ribose
Nucleotide	Base + deoxyribose + phosphate	Base + ribose + phosphate
Nucleic Acid	Polymer of deoxyribose nucleotides	Polymer of ribose nucleotides

Naming Nucleosides and Nucleotides

The name of a nucleoside that contains a purine ends with *osine*, whereas a nucleoside that contains a pyrimidine ends with *idine*. The names of nucleosides of DNA add *deoxy* to the beginning of their names. The corresponding nucleotides in RNA and DNA are named by adding 5′-*monophosphate*. Although the letters A, G, C, U, and T represent the bases, they are often used in the abbreviations of the respective nucleosides and nucleotides. The names of the bases, nucleosides, and nucleotides in DNA and RNA and their abbreviations are listed in Table 21.2.

TABLE 21.2 Nucleosides and Nucleotides in DNA and RNA

Base	Nucleosides	Nucleotides
DNA		
Adenine (A)	Deoxyadenosine (A)	Deoxyadenosine-5′-monophosphate (dAMP)
Guanine (G)	Deoxyguanosine (G)	Deoxyguanosine-5′-monophosphate (dGMP)
Cytosine (C)	Deoxycytidine (C)	Deoxycytidine-5′-monophosphate (dCMP)
Thymine (T)	Deoxythymidine (T)	Deoxythymidine-5′-monophosphate (dTMP)
RNA		
Adenine (A)	Adenosine (A)	Adenosine-5′-monophosphate (AMP)
Guanine (G)	Guanosine (G)	Guanosine-5′-monophosphate (GMP)
Cytosine (C)	Cytidine (C)	Cytidine-5′-monophosphate (CMP)
Uracil (U)	Uridine (U)	Uridine-5′-monophosphate (UMP)

CONCEPT CHECK 21.2 **Components of Nucleic Acid**

Identify each of the following as a pentose sugar, base, nucleoside, nucleotide, or nucleic acid and specify if it is found in DNA, RNA, or both:

a. guanine
b. deoxyadenosine-5′-monophosphate (dAMP)
c. ribose
d. cytidine

ANSWER

a. Guanine is one of the bases found in both DNA and RNA.
b. Deoxyadenosine-5′-monophosphate is a nucleotide (*tides* have phosphate) that is found in DNA.
c. Ribose is the pentose sugar found in RNA.
d. Cytidine is a nucleoside found in RNA.

Formation of Nucleoside Di- and Triphosphates

The phosphate group in any nucleoside 5′-monophosphate can bond to one or two additional phosphate groups to form di- and triphosphates. For example, adding one phosphate group to AMP gives ADP (*adenosine-5′-diphosphate*). Adding another phosphate group to ADP gives ATP (*adenosine-5′-triphosphate*) (see Figure 21.4). Of the triphosphates, ATP is of particular interest because it is the major source of energy for most energy-requiring activities in the cell. In other examples, phosphate is added to GMP to yield GDP and GTP, which is part of the citric acid cycle.

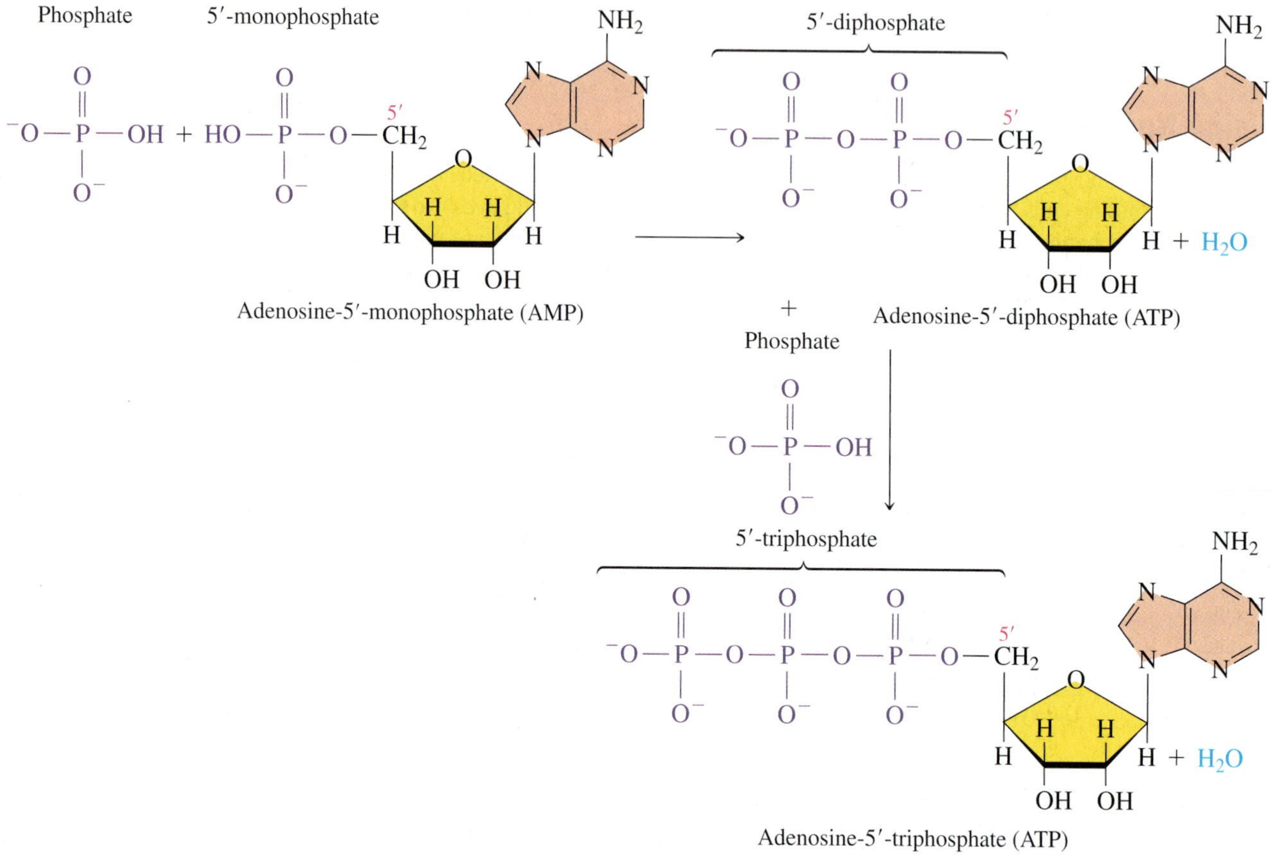

FIGURE 21.4 The addition of one or two phosphate groups to AMP forms adenosine-5′-diphosphate (ADP) and adenosine-5′-triphosphate (ATP).

Q How does the structure of deoxyguanosine-5′-triphosphate (dGTP) differ from ATP?

SAMPLE PROBLEM 21.1 Nucleotides

For each of the following nucleotides, identify the components and whether the nucleotide is found in DNA, RNA, or both:

a. deoxyguanosine-5′-monophosphate (dGMP)
b. adenosine-5′-monophosphate (AMP)

SOLUTION

a. This nucleotide of deoxyribose, guanine, and a phosphate group is found in DNA.
b. This nucleotide of ribose, adenine, and a phosphate group is found in RNA.

STUDY CHECK 21.1

What is the name and abbreviation of the DNA nucleotide of cytosine?

QUESTIONS AND PROBLEMS

21.1 Components of Nucleic Acids

LEARNING GOAL: *Describe the bases and ribose sugars that make up the nucleic acids DNA and RNA.*

21.1 Identify each of the following bases as a purine or pyrimidine:
   a. thymine
   b. NH₂

21.2 Identify each of the following bases as a purine or pyrimidine:
   a. guanine
   b. NH₂

21.3 Identify each of the bases in Problem 21.1 as a component of DNA, RNA, or both.

21.4 Identify each of the bases in Problem 21.2 as component of DNA, RNA, or both.

21.5 What are the names and abbreviations of the four nucleotides in DNA?

21.6 What are the names and abbreviations of the four nucleotides in RNA?

21.7 Identify each of the following as a nucleoside or nucleotide:
   a. adenosine   **b.** deoxycytidine
   c. uridine   **d.** cytidine-5′-monophosphate

21.8 Identify each of the following as a nucleoside or nucleotide:
   a. deoxythymidine   **b.** guanosine
   c. deoxyadenosine-5′-monophosphate
   d. uridine-5′-monophosphate

21.9 Draw the condensed structural formula for deoxyadenosine-5′-monophosphate (dAMP).

21.10 Draw the condensed structural formula for uridine-5′-monophosphate (UMP).

21.2 Primary Structure of Nucleic Acids

LEARNING GOAL

Describe the primary structures of RNA and DNA.

SELF-STUDY ACTIVITY
DNA and RNA Structure

The **nucleic acids** are polymers of many nucleotides in which the 3′-hydroxyl group of the sugar in one nucleotide bonds to the phosphate group on the 5′-carbon atom in the sugar of the next nucleotide. This link between the sugars in adjacent nucleotides is referred to as a **phosphodiester bond**. As more nucleotides are added using phosphodiester bonds, a backbone forms that consists of alternating sugar and phosphate groups. The bases, which are attached to each sugar, extend out from the sugar–phosphate backbone.

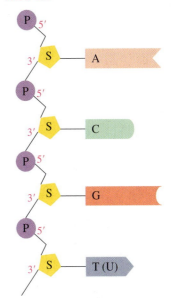

A phosphodiester bond forms between the 3′-hydroxyl group in the sugar of one nucleotide and the phosphate group on the 5′-carbon atom in the sugar of the next nucleotide.

Each nucleic acid has its own unique sequence of bases, which is known as its **primary structure**. It is this sequence of bases that carries the genetic information from one cell to the next. In any nucleic acid, the sugar at one end has an unreacted or free 5′-phosphate terminal end, and the sugar at the other end has an unreacted or free 3′-hydroxyl group.

A nucleic acid sequence is read from the sugar with the free 5′-phosphate to the sugar with the free 3′-hydroxyl group. The order of nucleotides is often written using only the letters of the bases. For example, the nucleotide sequence starting with adenine (free 5′-phosphate end) in the section of RNA shown in Figure 21.5 is 5′—A C G U—3′.

In the primary structure of nucleic acids, each sugar in a sugar–phosphate backbone is attached to a base.

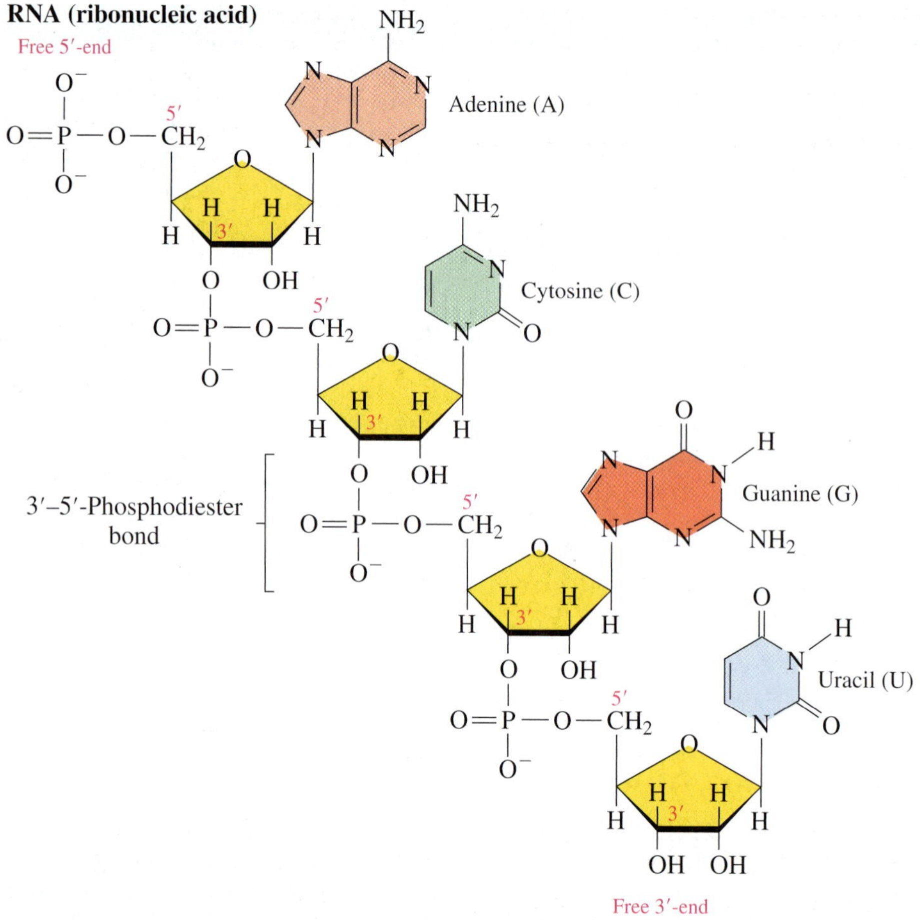

RNA (ribonucleic acid)

FIGURE 21.5 In the primary structure of RNA, A, C, G, and U are linked by 3′–5′-phosphodiester bonds.

Q Where are the free 5′-phosphate and 3′-hydroxyl groups?

SAMPLE PROBLEM 21.2   Bonding of Nucleotides

Draw the condensed structural formula for an RNA dinucleotide formed by two cytidine-5′-monophosphates.

SOLUTION

The dinucleotide is drawn by connecting the 3′-hydroxyl group on the first cytidine-5′-monophosphate with the 5′-phosphate group on the second cytidine-5′-monophosphate.

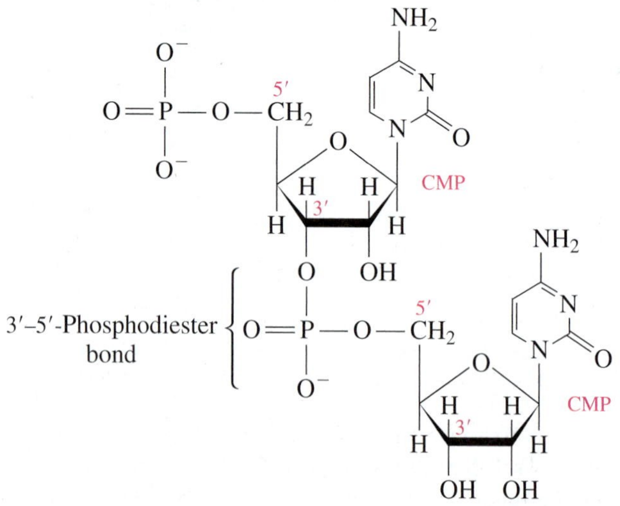

STUDY CHECK 21.2

In the dinucleotide of cytidine shown in the solution to Sample Problem 21.2, identify the free 5′-phosphate group and the free 3′-hydroxyl group.

21.3 DNA Double Helix

During the 1940s, scientists determined that DNA in a variety of organisms had a specific relationship: the amount of adenine (A) was equal to the amount of thymine (T), and the amount of guanine (G) was equal to the amount of cytosine (C) (see Table 21.3). Eventually, scientists determined that adenine is paired (1:1) with thymine, and guanine is paired (1:1) with cytosine. This relationship, known as *Chargaff's rules*, can be summarized as follows:

Number of purine molecules = Number of pyrimidine molecules
Adenine (A) = Thymine (T)
Guanine (G) = Cytosine (C)

TABLE 21.3 Percentages of Bases in the DNAs of Selected Organisms

Organism	%A	%T	%G	%C
Human	30	30	20	20
Chicken	28	28	22	22
Salmon	28	28	22	22
Corn (maize)	27	27	23	23
Neurospora	23	23	27	27

In 1953, James Watson and Francis Crick, using images of DNA by Rosalind Franklin, proposed that DNA was a **double helix** that consisted of two polynucleotide strands winding about each other like a spiral staircase (see Figure 21.6). The sugar–phosphate backbones are analogous to the outside railings of the stairs, with the bases arranged like steps along the inside. One strand goes from the 5′ to 3′ direction, and the other strand goes in the 3′ to 5′ direction.

Complementary Base Pairs

Each of the bases along one polynucleotide strand forms hydrogen bonds to only one specific base on the opposite DNA strand. Adenine forms hydrogen bonds to thymine only, and guanine bonds to cytosine only (see Figure 21.7). The pairs AT and GC are called **complementary base pairs**. Because of structural limitations, there are only two kinds of stable base pairs—bases that bind utilizing two hydrogen bonds, such as the pairing of adenine and thymine, and bases that bind utilizing three hydrogen bonds, such as the pairing of cytosine and guanine. *No other stable base pairs occur.* For example, adenine does not form hydrogen bonds with cytosine or guanine; cytosine does not form hydrogen bonds with adenine or thymine. This explains why DNA has equal amounts of A and T bases and equal amounts of G and C.

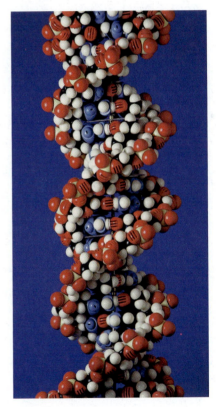

FIGURE 21.6 An atomic model of a DNA molecule shows the double helix as the characteristic shape of DNA molecules.

Q What is meant by the term *double helix*?

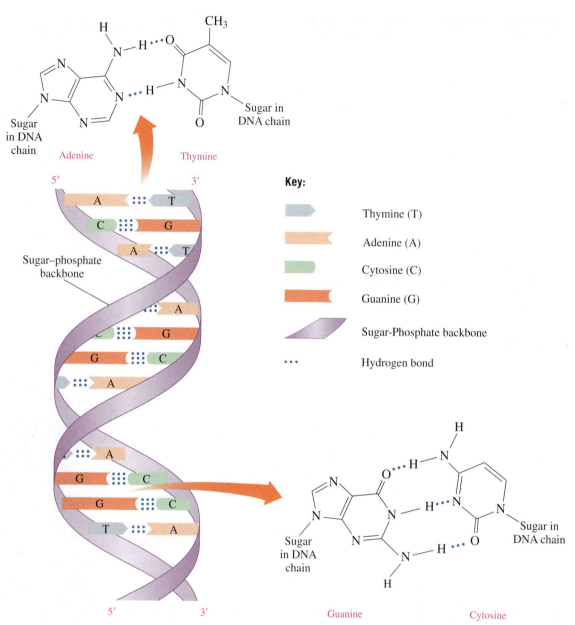

FIGURE 21.7 Hydrogen bonds between complementary base pairs hold together the polynucleotide strands in the double helix of DNA.

Q Why are GC base pairs more stable than AT base pairs?

SAMPLE PROBLEM 21.3 Complementary Base Pairs

Write the complementary base sequence for the following segment of a strand of DNA:

5′—A C G A T C T—3′

SOLUTION

Analyze the Problem

Base in Original DNA Strand	Complementary Base
A	T
T	A
C	G
G	C

Original segment of DNA: 5′—A C G A T C T—3′

⋮ ⋮ ⋮ ⋮ ⋮ ⋮ ⋮

Complementary segment: 3′—T G C T A G A—5′

STUDY CHECK 21.3

What sequence of bases is complementary to a DNA segment with a base sequence of 5′—G G T T A A C C—3′?

QUESTIONS AND PROBLEMS

21.3 DNA Double Helix

LEARNING GOAL: *Describe the double helix of DNA.*

21.15 How are the two strands of nucleic acid in DNA held together?

21.16 What is meant by complementary base pairing?

21.17 Write the base sequence in a new DNA segment if the original segment has the following base sequence:
a. 5′—A A A A A A —3′
b. 5′—G G G G G G—3′
c. 5′—A G T C C A G G T—3′
d. 5′—C T G T A T A C G T T A—3′

21.18 Write the base sequence in a new DNA segment if the original segment has the following base sequence:
a. 5′—T T T T T T—3′
b. 5′—C C C C C C C C C—3′
c. 5′—A T G G C A—3′
d. 5′—A T A T G C G C T A A A—3′

21.4 DNA Replication

LEARNING GOAL

Describe the process of DNA replication.

The function of DNA in the cells of animals and plants is to preserve genetic information. As cells divide, copied strands of DNA are transferred to the new cells, which receive the genetic information of the parent cell contained in the new strands.

Replication and Energy

MC

TUTORIAL
DNA Replication

SELF-STUDY ACTIVITY
DNA Replication

In DNA **replication**, the strands in the original or *parent* DNA molecule separate to allow the synthesis of complementary DNA strands. The process begins when an enzyme called *helicase* catalyzes the unwinding of a portion of the double helix by breaking the hydrogen bonds between the complementary bases. The resulting single strands act as templates for the synthesis of new complementary strands of DNA (see Figure 21.8).

As the complementary base pairs come together, *DNA polymerase* catalyzes the formation of phosphodiester bonds between the nucleotides. Eventually the entire double helix of the parent DNA is copied. In each new DNA molecule, one strand of the double helix is from the original DNA, and one is a newly synthesized strand. This process produces two new DNAs called *daughter DNAs* that are identical to each other and exact copies of the original parent DNA. In the process of DNA replication, complementary base pairing ensures the correct placements of bases in the new DNA strands.

Within the nucleus, nucleoside triphosphates of each base are available so that each exposed base on the template strand can form hydrogen bonds with its complementary base

CONCEPT CHECK 21.3 **DNA Replication**

In an original DNA strand, a segment has the base sequence 5′—G C A A T C—3′. What is the sequence of nucleotides in the daughter DNA strand that is complementary to this sequence?

ANSWER

Only one possible nucleotide can pair with each base in the original sequence. Thymine pairs only with adenine and cytosine pairs only with guanine to give the complementary base sequence of 3′—C G T T A G—5′ in the daughter strand.

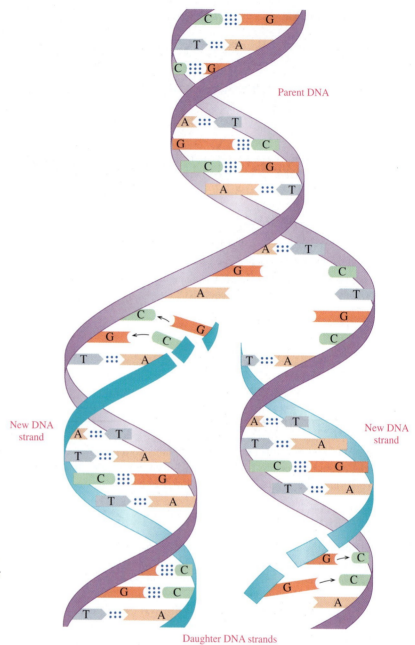

FIGURE 21.8 In DNA replication, the separate strands of the parent DNA are the templates for the synthesis of complementary strands, which produce two exact copies of DNA.

Q How many strands of the parent DNA are contained in each of the daughter DNAs?

in the nucleoside triphosphate. For example, T in the template strand or parent DNA strand hydrogen bonds with A in dATP, and G on the template strand hydrogen bonds with dCTP. As the hydrogen bonds form the base pairs, *DNA polymerase* catalyzes the formation of phosphodiester bonds between the nucleotides. The hydrolysis of pyrophosphate (PP$_i$) by DNA polymerase provides energy for the new bonds. In this way, energy is provided to join each new nucleotide to the backbone of a growing DNA strand (see Figure 21.9).

Direction of Replication

Now that we have seen the overall process, we can take a look at some of the details that are important in understanding DNA replication. The unwinding of DNA by *helicase* occurs simultaneously in several sections along the parent DNA molecule. As a result, *DNA polymerase* can catalyze the replication process at each of these open DNA sections called **replication forks**. However, DNA polymerase only moves in the 5′ to 3′ direction, which means it catalyzes the formation of phosphodiester bonds between the hydroxyl group at the end of the growing nucleic acid and the phosphate group of a nucleoside triphosphate. The new DNA strand that grows in the 5′ to 3′ direction, the *leading strand*, is synthesized continuously.

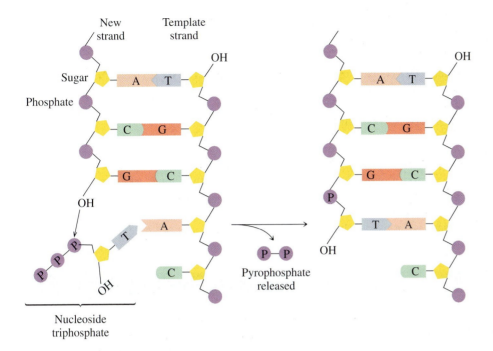

FIGURE 21.9 Energy for the formation of a bond between thymidine-5′-triphosphate and the 3′—OH group of the preceding sugar is provided by the removal of two phosphates (as pyrophosphate).

Q Why are nucleoside triphosphates used to provide complementary bases instead of nucleoside monophosphates?

The other new DNA, the *lagging strand*, is synthesized in the opposite direction, which is in the reverse 3′ to 5′ direction. In this lagging strand, short sections called **Okazaki fragments** are synthesized at the same time by several *DNA polymerases* and connected to form a continuous strand by *DNA ligases* to give a single 3′ to 5′ DNA strand. The reason why DNA polymerase has to synthesize the DNA in installments is because it is moving *away* from the direction of the unraveling and opening up of the replication fork (see Figure 21.10).

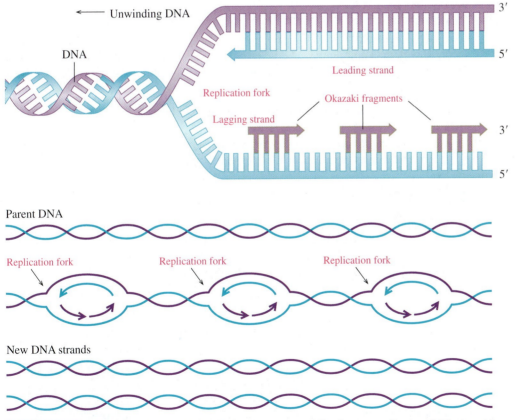

FIGURE 21.10 At each replication fork, DNA polymerase synthesizes a continuous DNA strand in the 5′ to 3′ direction. In the new 3′ to 5′ DNA strand, small Okazaki fragments are produced that are joined by DNA ligase.

Q Why is only one of the new DNA strands synthesized in a continuous direction?

CONCEPT CHECK 21.4   **Direction of DNA Replication**

In an original DNA strand, a segment has the base sequence 5′—A G T—3′.

a. What is the sequence of nucleotides in the daughter DNA strand that is complementary to this segment?

b. Why would the complementary sequence in the daughter DNA strand be synthesized as Okazaki fragments that require a DNA ligase?

ANSWER

a. Only one possible nucleotide can pair with each base in the original segment. Thymine will pair only with adenine, cytosine only with guanine, and adenine only with thymine to give the complementary base sequence: 3′—T C A—5′.

b. The DNA produced in the 3′ to 5′ direction, called the lagging strand, is synthesized as short sections, which are joined by DNA ligase.

QUESTIONS AND PROBLEMS

21.4 DNA Replication

LEARNING GOAL: *Describe the process of DNA replication.*

21.19 What is the function of the enzyme helicase in DNA replication?

21.20 What is the function of the enzyme DNA polymerase in DNA replication?

21.21 What process ensures that the replication of DNA produces identical copies?

21.22 Why are Okazaki fragments formed in the synthesis of the lagging strand?

21.5 RNA and Transcription

Ribonucleic acid, RNA, which makes up most of the nucleic acid found in the cell, is involved with transmitting the genetic information needed to operate the cell. Similar to DNA, RNA molecules are unbranched polymers of nucleotides. However, RNA differs from DNA in several important ways:

1. The sugar in RNA is ribose rather than the deoxyribose found in DNA.
2. In RNA, the base uracil replaces thymine.
3. RNA molecules are single stranded, not double stranded.
4. RNA molecules are much smaller than DNA molecules.

TUTORIAL
Types of RNA

Types of RNA

There are three major types of RNA in the cells: *messenger RNA*, *ribosomal RNA*, and *transfer RNA*. Ribosomal RNA (**rRNA**), the most abundant type of RNA, is combined with proteins to form ribosomes. Ribosomes, which are the sites within the cells where protein synthesis occurs, consist of two subunits: a large subunit and a small subunit (see Figure 21.11). Cells that synthesize large numbers of proteins have thousands of ribosomes.

FIGURE 21.11 A typical ribosome consists of a small subunit and a large subunit.

Q Why would there be many thousands of ribosomes in a cell?

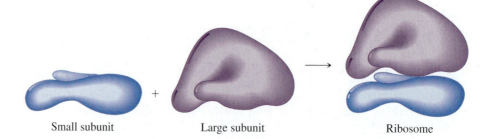

Small subunit   +   Large subunit   →   Ribosome

Messenger RNA (**mRNA**) carries genetic information from the DNA, located in the nucleus of the cell, to the ribosomes, located in the *cytoplasm*, the liquid within the cell. A gene segment of DNA will produce a specific mRNA for a particular protein that is needed in the cell. The size of an mRNA depends on the number of nucleotides in that gene.

Transfer RNA (**tRNA**), the smallest of the RNA molecules, interprets the genetic information in mRNA and brings specific amino acids to the ribosome for protein synthesis. Only tRNA can translate the genetic information into the amino acids that will be made into proteins. There can be more than one tRNA for each of the 20 amino acids. The structures of all of the transfer RNAs are similar, consisting of 70–90 nucleotides. Hydrogen bonds between some complementary bases in the strand produce loops that give some double-stranded regions. The types of RNA molecules in humans are summarized in Table 21.4.

TABLE 21.4 Types of RNA Molecules in Humans

Type	Abbreviation	Percentage of Total RNA	Function in the Cell
Ribosomal RNA	rRNA	80	Major component of the ribosomes; protein synthesis
Messenger RNA	mRNA	5	Carries information for protein synthesis from the DNA in the nucleus to the ribosomes
Transfer RNA	tRNA	15	Brings amino acids to the ribosomes for protein synthesis

Although the structure of tRNA is complex, we draw tRNA as a cloverleaf to illustrate its features. All tRNA molecules have a 3′-end with the nucleotide sequence ACC, which is known as the *acceptor stem*. An enzyme attaches an amino acid by forming an ester bond with the free —OH group of the acceptor stem. Each tRNA contains an **anticodon**, which is a series of three bases that complements three bases on mRNA (see Figure 21.12).

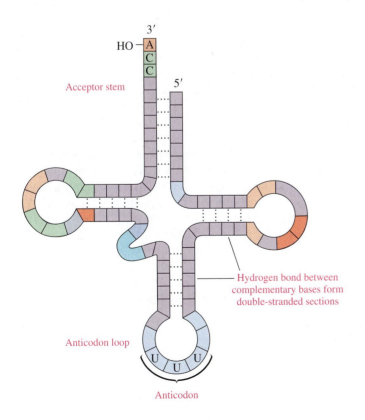

Acceptor stem

Hydrogen bond between complementary bases form double-stranded sections

Anticodon loop

Anticodon

FIGURE 21.12 A typical tRNA molecule has an acceptor stem that attaches to an amino acid and an anticodon loop that complements a codon on mRNA.

Q Why will different tRNAs have different bases in the anticodon loop?

CONCEPT CHECK 21.5 **Types of RNA**

a. What is the function of mRNA in a cell?
b. What is the function of tRNA in a cell?

ANSWER

a. mRNA carries the instructions for the synthesis of a protein from the DNA in the nucleus to the ribosomes in the cytoplasm.
b. Each type of tRNA brings specific amino acids to the ribosome for protein synthesis.

RNA and Protein Synthesis

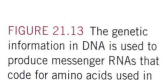

SELF-STUDY ACTIVITY
Transcription

We now look at the overall processes involved in transferring genetic information encoded in the DNA so that proteins can be produced. In the nucleus, the genetic information for the synthesis of a protein is copied from a gene in DNA to make a messenger RNA (mRNA), a process called **transcription**. The mRNA molecules move out of the nucleus into the cytoplasm, where they bind with the ribosomes. Then in a process called **translation**, tRNA molecules convert the mRNA information into amino acids, which are placed in the proper sequence to synthesize a protein (see Figure 21.13).

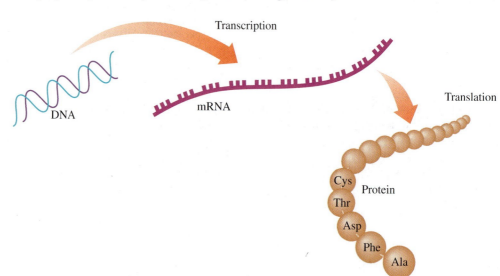

FIGURE 21.13 The genetic information in DNA is used to produce messenger RNAs that code for amino acids used in protein synthesis.

Q What is the difference between transcription and translation?

Transcription: Synthesis of mRNA

Transcription begins when the section of a DNA molecule that contains the gene to be copied unwinds. Within this unwound portion of DNA called a *transcription bubble*, RNA polymerase uses the strand in a 3′ to 5′ direction as a template. The mRNA forms with bases that are complementary to the DNA template: C and G form pairs, T (in DNA) pairs with A (in mRNA), and A (in DNA) pairs with U (in mRNA). When the RNA polymerase reaches the termination site, transcription ends, and the new mRNA is released. The unwound portion of the DNA returns to its double helix structure (see Figure 21.14).

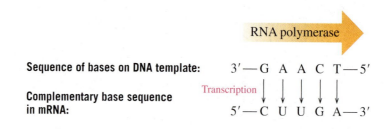

RNA polymerase

Sequence of bases on DNA template: 3′—G A A C T—5′

Transcription

Complementary base sequence in mRNA: 5′—C U U G A—3′

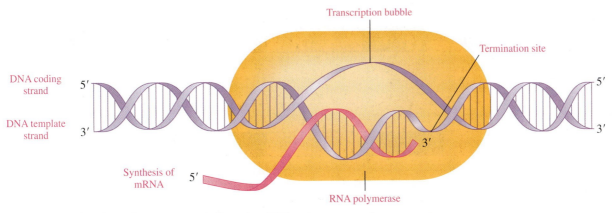

Transcription bubble

Termination site

DNA coding strand 5′

DNA template strand 3′

Synthesis of mRNA 5′

3′

5′

3′

RNA polymerase

FIGURE 21.14 DNA undergoes transcription when RNA polymerase makes a complementary copy of a gene using the 3′ to 5′ strand as the template.
Q Why is the mRNA connected in a 5′ to 3′ direction?

SAMPLE PROBLEM 21.4 **RNA Synthesis**

The sequence of bases in a part of the DNA template strand is 3′—C G A T C A—5′. What corresponding mRNA is produced?

SOLUTION

To form the mRNA, the bases in the DNA template are paired with their complementary bases: G with C, C with G, T with A, and A with U.

DNA template: 3′—C G A T C A—5′

Transcription: ↓ ↓ ↓ ↓ ↓ ↓

Complementary bases in mRNA: 5′—G C U A G U—3′

STUDY CHECK 21.4

What is the DNA template that codes for the mRNA segment with the nucleotide sequence 5′—G G G U U U A A A—3′?

Processing of mRNA

The DNA in eukaryotes—organisms including plants and animals—contains sections known as *exons* and *introns*. **Exons**, which code for proteins, are mixed in with sections called **introns** that do not code for proteins. A newly formed mRNA called a *pre-mRNA* is a copy of the entire DNA template, including the noncoding introns. Before the pre-mRNA leaves the nucleus, the introns must be removed. This processing of pre-mRNA produces a functional mRNA that leaves the nucleus to deliver the genetic information to the ribosomes for the synthesis of protein (see Figure 21.15).

Regulation of Transcription

The synthesis of mRNA occurs when cells require a particular protein; it does not occur randomly. The regulation of mRNA synthesis takes place at the transcription level, where the absence or presence of end products determines which mRNAs are needed for specific proteins. For example, *E. coli* bacteria that grow on lactose need β-galactosidase to hydrolyze lactose to glucose and galactose. When the lactose level is low, β-galactosidase is not needed; the transcription of its mRNA is turned off. When lactose enters the cell and β-galactosidase is required, lactose initiates the synthesis of mRNA for the enzyme. This process, known as **enzyme induction**, occurs when high levels of a substrate turn on the transcription of the genes that produce the mRNAs that code for specific enzymes.

Within a gene, sections of DNA called **operons** regulate the synthesis of related proteins. Each operon has a **control site** followed by the **structural genes** that produce the mRNAs for specific proteins (see Figure 21.16).

SELF-STUDY ACTIVITY
The Lactose Operon in *E. coli*

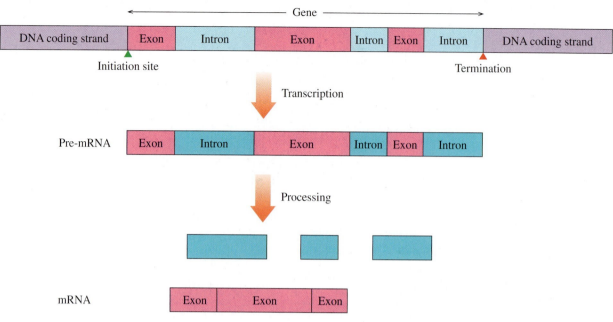

FIGURE 21.15 A pre-mRNA, containing copies of the exons and introns from the gene, is processed to remove the introns to form the mRNA that codes for a protein.

Q What is the difference between exons and introns?

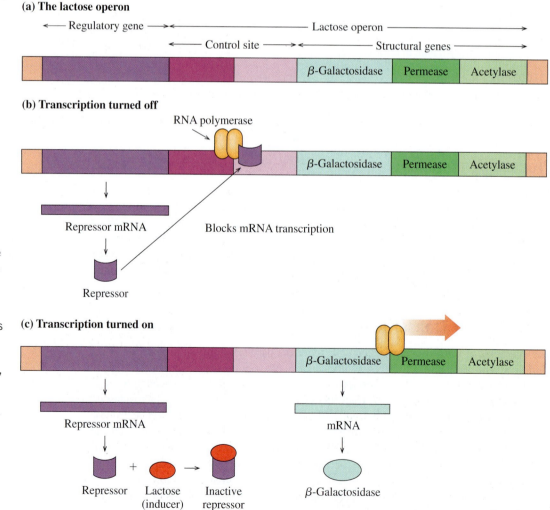

FIGURE 21.16 **(a)** The lactose operon consists of a control site and structural genes.
(b) Without lactose, a repressor protein blocks the transcription of enzymes for lactose.
(c) Lactose, an inducer, removes the repressor to allow the transcription of enzymes for lactose hydrolysis.

Q Why is transcription blocked when no lactose is present in the cell?

(a) The lactose operon

(b) Transcription turned off

(c) Transcription turned on

In front of the lactose operon, there is a **regulatory gene** that produces an mRNA for the synthesis of a **repressor** protein that binds to the control site and blocks the synthesis of β-galactosidase by RNA polymerase. When lactose enters the cell, it combines with the repressor and removes it from the control site. Without a repressor, RNA polymerase proceeds to the structural genes, which now produce the mRNA needed for the synthesis of the lactose enzymes.

TUTORIAL
Activating and Inhibiting Genes

CONCEPT CHECK 21.6 **Transcription**

Describe why transcription will or will not take place in each of the following conditions:

a. A repressor binds to the control site.
b. An inducer binds to the repressor protein.

ANSWER

a. Transcription will not take place as long as a repressor is attached to the control site, which blocks the synthesis of mRNA by RNA polymerase.
b. Transcription will take place when an inducer attaches to the repressor, which removes it from the control site.

QUESTIONS AND PROBLEMS

21.5 RNA and Transcription

LEARNING GOAL: *Identify the different types of RNA; describe the synthesis of mRNA.*

21.23 What are the three different types of RNA?

21.24 What is the function of each type of RNA?

21.25 What is the composition of a ribosome?

21.26 What is the smallest RNA?

21.27 What is meant by the term "transcription"?

21.28 What bases in mRNA are used to complement the bases A, T, G, and C in DNA?

21.29 Write the corresponding section of mRNA produced from the following section of DNA template strand:

$$3'—CCGAAGGTTCAC—5'$$

21.30 Write the corresponding section of mRNA produced from the following section of DNA template strand:

$$3'—TACGGCAAGCTA—5'$$

21.31 What are introns and exons?

21.32 What kind of processing do mRNA molecules undergo before they leave the nucleus?

21.33 What is an operon?

21.34 Why does the operon model control protein synthesis at the transcription level?

21.35 How is the lactose operon turned off in *E. coli* that grows on lactose?

21.36 How is the lactose operon activated in *E. coli* that grows on lactose?

21.6 The Genetic Code

The overall function of the different types of RNA in the cell is to facilitate the task of synthesizing proteins. After the genetic information encoded in DNA is transcribed into mRNA molecules, the mRNAs move out of the nucleus to the ribosomes in the cytoplasm. At the ribosomes, the genetic information in the mRNAs is converted into a sequence of amino acids in protein.

LEARNING GOAL

Describe the function of the codons in the genetic code.

TUTORIAL
Genetic Code

Codons

The **genetic code** consists of a series of three nucleotides (triplets) in mRNA called **codons** that specify the amino acids and their sequence in a protein. Early work on protein synthesis showed that repeating triplets of uracil (UUU) produced a polypeptide that contained only phenylalanine. Therefore, a sequence of $5'—UUU\ UUU\ UUU—3'$ codes for three phenylalanines.

Codons in mRNA $5'—UUU\ \ UUU\ \ UUU—3'$

Translation

Amino acid sequence —Phe—Phe—Phe—

Codons have been determined for all 20 amino acids. A total of 64 codons are possible from the triplet combinations of A, G, C, and U (see Table 21.5). Three of these, UGA, UAA, and UAG, are stop signals that code for the termination of protein synthesis. All the other three-base codons specify amino acids; one amino acid can have several codons. For example, glycine has four codons: GGU, GGC, GGA, and GGG. The triplet AUG has two roles in protein synthesis. At the beginning of an mRNA, the codon AUG signals the start of protein synthesis. In the middle of a series of codons, the AUG codon specifies the amino acid methionine.

TABLE 21.5 mRNA Codons: The Genetic Code for Amino Acids

First Base	Second Base				Third Base
	U	**C**	**A**	**G**	
U	UUU } Phe UUC	UCU } UCC } Ser	UAU } Tyr UAC	UGU } Cys UGC	U C
	UUA } Leu UUG	UCA } UCG	UAA STOP[b] UAG STOP[b]	UGA STOP[b] UGG Trp	A G
C	CUU CUC } Leu CUA CUG	CCU CCC } Pro CCA CCG	CAU } His CAC CAA } Gln CAG	CGU CGC } Arg CGA CGG	U C A G
A	AUU AUC } Ile AUA AUG START[a]/Met	ACU ACC } Thr ACA ACG	AAU } Asn AAC AAA } Lys AAG	AGU } Ser AGC AGA } Arg AGG	U C A G
G	GUU GUC } Val GUA GUG	GCU GCC } Ala GCA GCG	GAU } Asp GAC GAA } Glu GAG	GGU GGC } Gly GGA GGG	U C A G

START[a] codon signals the initiation of a peptide chain.
STOP[b] codons signal the end of a peptide chain.

CONCEPT CHECK 21.7 **The Genetic Code**

Indicate the nucleotides in mRNA that code for the following:

a. the amino acid phenylalanine
b. the amino acid proline
c. the start of polypeptide synthesis

ANSWER

a. In mRNA, the codons for the amino acid phenylalanine (Phe) are UUU and UUC.
b. In mRNA, the codons for the amino acid proline (Pro) are CCU, CCC, CCA, and CCG.
c. In mRNA, the codon AUG signals the start of polypeptide synthesis.

SAMPLE PROBLEM 21.5 **Codons**

What is the sequence of amino acids specified by the following codons in mRNA?

5′—GUC AGC CCA—3′

SOLUTION

Analyze the Problem

Codon (Three-Base Sequence) (refer to Table 21.5)	Amino Acid
GUC	Valine (Val)
AGC	Serine (Ser)
CCA	Proline (Pro)

The sequence 5′—GUC AGC CCA—3′ codes for the amino acids —Val—Ser—Pro—.

STUDY CHECK 21.5

Write the amino acid sequence produced by the following codons in mRNA (see Table 21.5).

5′—AAU GCU UGU—3′

QUESTIONS AND PROBLEMS

21.6 The Genetic Code

LEARNING GOAL: *Describe the function of the codons in the genetic code.*

21.37 What is a codon?

21.38 What is the genetic code?

21.39 What amino acid is produced by each of the following mRNA codons?
  a. CUU **b.** UCA **c.** GGU **d.** AGG

21.40 What amino acid is produced by each of the following mRNA codons?
  a. AAA **b.** UUC **c.** CGG **d.** GCA

21.41 When does the codon AUG signal the start of a protein? When does it code for the amino acid methionine?

21.42 The codons UGA, UAA, and UAG do not code for amino acids. What is their role as codons in mRNA?

21.7 Protein Synthesis: Translation

Once an mRNA is synthesized, it migrates out of the nucleus into the cytoplasm to the ribosomes. In the *translation* process, tRNA molecules, amino acids, and enzymes convert the mRNA codons into amino acids to build a protein.

Activation of tRNA

Each tRNA molecule contains a loop called the *anticodon*, which is a triplet of bases that complements a codon in mRNA. An amino acid is attached to the acceptor stem of each tRNA by an enzyme called *aminoacyl–tRNA synthetase*. Each amino acid has a different synthetase (see Figure 21.17). Activation of tRNA occurs when aminoacyl–tRNA synthetase forms an ester bond between the carboxylate group of its amino acid and the hydroxyl group on the acceptor stem. Each synthetase then checks the tRNA–amino acid combination and hydrolyzes any incorrect combinations.

Initiation and Chain Elongation

Protein synthesis begins when mRNA binds to a ribosome. The first codon in an mRNA is a *start* codon, AUG, which forms hydrogen bonds with methionine–tRNA. Another tRNA hydrogen bonds to the next codon, placing a second amino acid adjacent to methionine. A peptide bond forms between the C terminal of methionine and the N terminal of the second amino acid (see Figure 21.18). Then the initial tRNA detaches from the ribosome, which shifts to the next available codon, a process called *translocation*. During *chain elongation*, the ribosome moves along the mRNA from codon to codon so that the tRNAs can attach new amino acids to the growing polypeptide chain. Sometimes several ribosomes, called a polysome, translate the same strand of mRNA to produce several copies of the polypeptide at the same time.

LEARNING GOAL

Describe the process of protein synthesis from mRNA.

MC

SELF-STUDY ACTIVITY
Translation

SELF-STUDY ACTIVITY
Overview of Protein Synthesis

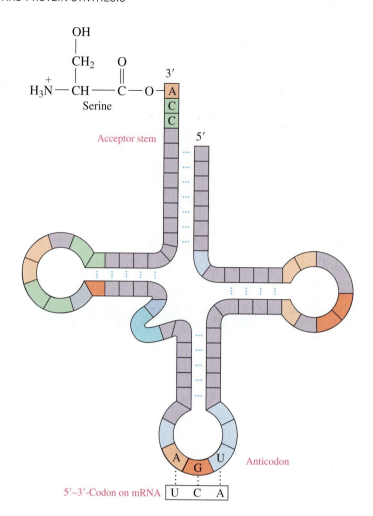

FIGURE 21.17 An activated tRNA with anticodon AGU bonds to serine at the acceptor stem.

Q What is the codon for serine for this tRNA?

TUTORIAL
Following the Instructions in DNA

Chain Termination

Eventually, a ribosome encounters a codon—UAA, UGA, or UAG—that has no corresponding tRNAs. These are stop codons, which signal the termination of polypeptide synthesis and the release of the polypeptide chain from the ribosome. The initial amino acid, methionine, is usually removed from the beginning of the polypeptide chain. The R groups of the amino acids in the new polypeptide chain form hydrogen bonds to give the secondary structures of α helices, β-pleated sheets, or triple helices and form interactions such as salt bridges and disulfide bonds to produce tertiary and quaternary structures, which make it a biologically active protein.

Table 21.6 summarizes the steps in protein synthesis.

TABLE 21.6 Steps in Protein Synthesis

Step	Site: Materials	Process
1. DNA Transcription	Nucleus: nucleotides, RNA polymerase	A DNA template is used to produce mRNA.
2. Activation of tRNA	Cytoplasm: amino acids, tRNAs, aminoacyl–tRNA synthetase	Molecules of tRNA pick up specific amino acids according to their anticodons.
3. Initiation and Chain Elongation	Ribosome: Met-tRNA, mRNA, aminoacyl–tRNAs	A start codon binds the first tRNA carrying the amino acid methionine to the mRNA. Successive tRNAs bind to and detach from the ribosome as they add an amino acid to the polypeptide.
4. Chain Termination	Ribosome: stop codon on mRNA	A polypeptide is released from the ribosome.

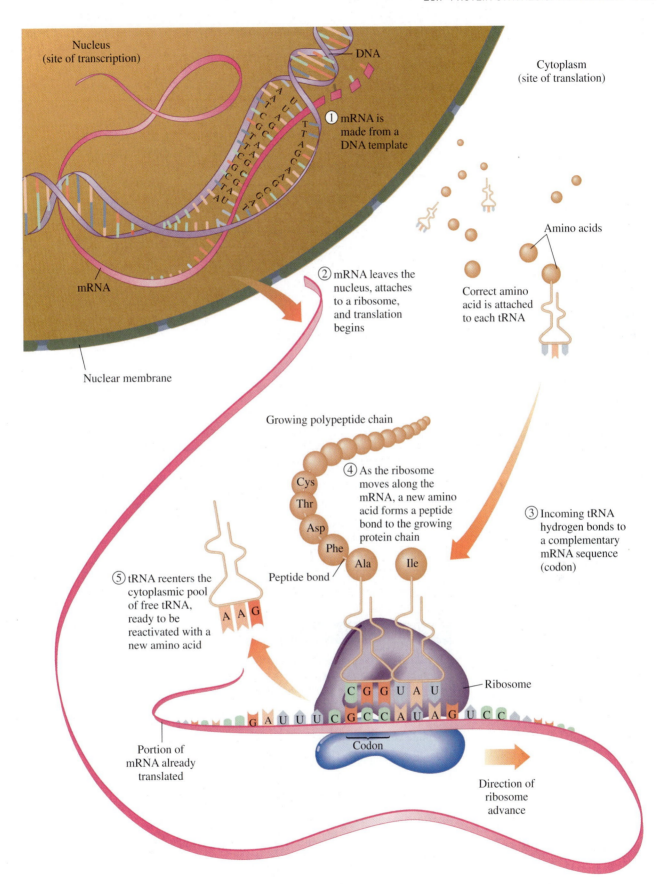

FIGURE 21.18 In the translation process, the mRNA synthesized by transcription attaches to a ribosome, and tRNAs pick up their amino acids, bind to the appropriate codon, and place them in a growing peptide chain.

Q How is the correct amino acid placed in the peptide chain?

Table 21.7 uses an example to summarize the nucleotide and amino acid sequences in protein synthesis.

TABLE 21.7 Complementary Sequences in DNA, mRNA, tRNA, and Peptides

Nucleus	
DNA coding strand	5′—GCG AGT GGA TAC—3′
DNA template strand	3′—CGC TCA CCT ATG—5′
Ribosome (cytoplasm)	
mRNA	5′—GCG AGU GGA UAC—3′
tRNA anticodons	3′—CGC UCA CCU AUG—5′
Polypeptide amino acids	—Ala—Ser—Gly—Tyr—

Chemistry Link to Health

MANY ANTIBIOTICS INHIBIT PROTEIN SYNTHESIS

Several antibiotics stop bacterial infections by interfering with the synthesis of proteins needed by the bacteria. Some antibiotics act only on bacterial cells, binding to the ribosomes in bacteria but not those in human cells. A description of some of these antibiotics is given in Table 21.8.

TABLE 21.8 Antibiotics That Inhibit Protein Synthesis in Bacterial Cells

Antibiotic	Effect on Ribosomes to Inhibit Protein Synthesis
Chloramphenicol	Inhibits peptide bond formation and prevents the binding of tRNA
Erythromycin	Inhibits peptide chain growth by preventing the translocation of the ribosome along the mRNA
Puromycin	Causes release of an incomplete protein by ending the growth of the polypeptide early
Streptomycin	Prevents the proper attachment of the initial tRNA
Tetracycline	Prevents the binding of tRNAs

SAMPLE PROBLEM 21.6 **Protein Synthesis: Translation**

What order of amino acids would you expect in a peptide for the mRNA sequence of 5′—UCA AAA GCC CUU—3′?

SOLUTION

Each of the codons specifies a particular amino acid. Using Table 21.5, we write a peptide with the following amino acid sequence:

mRNA codons: 5′—UCA AAA GCC CUU—3′
                          ↓   ↓   ↓   ↓
Amino acid sequence: —Ser—Lys—Ala—Leu—

STUDY CHECK 21.6

Where would protein synthesis stop in the following series of bases in an mRNA?

5′—GGG AGC AGU UAG GUU—3′

QUESTIONS AND PROBLEMS

21.7 Protein Synthesis: Translation

LEARNING GOAL: *Describe the process of protein synthesis from mRNA.*

21.43 What is the difference between a *codon* and an *anticodon*?

21.44 Why are there at least 20 different tRNAs?

21.45 What are the three steps of translation?

21.46 Where does protein synthesis take place?

21.47 What amino acid sequence would you expect from each of the following mRNA segments?
  a. 5′—ACC ACA ACU—3′
  b. 5′—UUU CCG UUC CCA—3′
  c. 5′—UAC GGG AGA UGU—3′

21.48 What amino acid sequence would you expect from each of the following mRNA segments?
  a. 5′—AAA CCC UUG GCC—3′
  b. 5′—CCU CGC AGC CCA UGA—3′
  c. 5′—AUG CAC AAG GAA GUA CUG—3′

21.49 How is a peptide chain extended?

21.50 What is meant by "translocation"?

21.51 The following sequence is a portion of the DNA template strand:

  3′—GCT TTT CAA AAA—5′

  a. What is the corresponding mRNA section?
  b. What are the anticodons of the tRNAs?
  c. What amino acids will be placed in the peptide chain?

21.52 The following sequence is a portion of the DNA template strand:

  3′—TGT GGG GTT ATT—5′

  a. What is the corresponding mRNA section?
  b. What are the anticodons of the tRNAs?
  c. What amino acids will be placed in the peptide chain?

21.8 Genetic Mutations

A **mutation** is a change in the nucleotide sequence of DNA. Such a change may alter the sequence of amino acids, affecting the structure and function of a protein in a cell. Mutations result from X-rays, overexposure to sun (ultraviolet or UV light), chemicals called *mutagens*, and possibly some viruses. If a mutation occurs in a somatic cell (a cell other than a reproductive cell), the altered DNA is limited to that cell and its daughter cells. If the mutation causes uncontrolled growth, cancer could result. If a mutation occurs in a germ cell (egg or sperm), then all DNA produced will contain the same genetic change. When a mutation severely alters proteins or enzymes, the new cells may not survive or the person may exhibit a disease or condition that is a result of a genetic defect.

Types of Mutations

Consider a triplet of bases CCG in the template strand of DNA, which produces the codon GGC in mRNA. At the ribosome, tRNA would place the amino acid glycine in the peptide chain (see Figure 21.19a). Now, suppose that T replaces the first C in the DNA triplet, which gives TCG as the triplet. Then the codon produced in the mRNA is AGC, which brings the tRNA with the amino acid serine to add to the peptide chain. The replacement of one base in the template strand of DNA with another is called a **substitution mutation**. When there is a change of a nucleotide in the codon, a different amino acid may be inserted into the polypeptide. However, if a substitution gives a codon for the same amino acid, there is no change in the amino acid sequence in the protein. This type of substitution is a *silent mutation*. Substitution is the most common way in which mutations occur (see Figure 21.19b).

In a **frameshift mutation**, a base is inserted into or deleted from the normal order of bases in the template strand of DNA (see Figure 21.19c). Suppose now an A is deleted from the triplet AAA, which gives a new triplet of AAC. The next triplet becomes CGA rather than CCG, and so on. All the triplets shift over by one base, which changes all the codons that follow and leads to a different sequence of amino acids from that point.

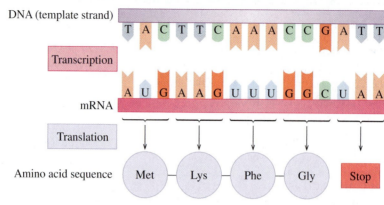

(a) Normal DNA and protein synthesis

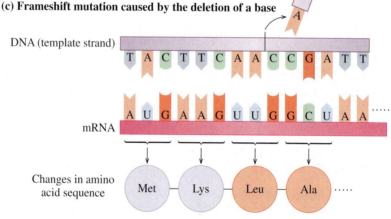

(b) Substitution of one base

(c) Frameshift mutation caused by the deletion of a base

FIGURE 21.19 An alteration in the DNA template strand produces a change in the sequence of amino acids in the protein, which may result in a mutation. **(a)** A normal DNA leads to the correct amino acid order in a protein. **(b)** The substitution of a base in DNA leads to a change in the mRNA codon and a change in an amino acid. **(c)** The deletion of a base causes a frameshift mutation, which changes the mRNA codons that follow the mutation and produces a different amino acid sequence.

Q When would a substitution mutation cause protein synthesis to stop?

Explore Your World

A MODEL FOR DNA REPLICATION AND MUTATION

1. Cut out 16 rectangular pieces of paper. Using 8 rectangular pieces for DNA strand 1, write two each of the following nucleotide symbols: A⚌, T⚌, G≡, and C≡.
2. Using the other 8 rectangular pieces for DNA strand 2, write two of each of the following nucleotide symbols: ⚌A, ⚌T, ≡G, and ≡C.
3. Place the pieces for strand 1 in random order.
4. Using the DNA segment strand 1 you made in part 3, select the correct bases to build the complementary segment of DNA strand 2.
5. Using the rectangular pieces for nucleotides, put together a DNA segment using a template strand of —ATTGCC—. What is the mRNA that would form from this segment of DNA? What is the dipeptide that would form from this mRNA?
6. In the DNA segment of part 5, change the G to an A. What is the mRNA that would form from this segment of DNA? What is the dipeptide that forms? How could this change in codons lead to a mutation?

Effect of Mutations

Some mutations do not cause a significant change in the primary structure of a protein and the protein is able to maintain biological activity. However, when a mutation causes a drastic change in the amino acid sequence, the structure of the resulting protein may be altered so that it loses biological activity. If the protein is an enzyme, it may no longer bind to its substrate or react with the substrate at the active site. When an altered enzyme cannot catalyze a reaction, certain substances may accumulate until they act as poisons in the cell, or substances vital to survival may not be synthesized. If a defective enzyme occurs in a major metabolic pathway or is involved in the building of a cell membrane, the mutation can be lethal. When a protein deficiency is hereditary, the condition is called a **genetic disease**.

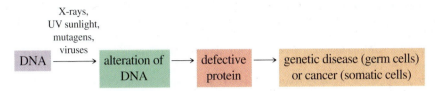

SAMPLE PROBLEM 21.7   Mutations

An mRNA has the sequence of codons 5′—CCC AGA GCC—3′. If a base substitution in the DNA changes the mRNA codon of AGA to GGA, how is the amino acid sequence affected in the resulting protein?

SOLUTION

The mRNA sequence 5′—CCC AGA GCC—3′ codes for the following amino acids: proline, arginine, and alanine. When the mutation occurs, the new sequence of the mRNA codons is 5′—CCC GGA GCC—3′, which now codes for proline, glycine, and alanine. The basic amino acid arginine is replaced by the nonpolar amino acid glycine.

	Normal	After Mutation
mRNA codons	5′—CCC AGA GCC—3′	5′—CCC GGA GCC—3′
Amino acids	—Pro—Arg—Ala—	—Pro—Gly—Ala—

STUDY CHECK 21.7

How might the protein made from this mRNA be affected by this mutation?

Genetic Diseases

A genetic disease is the result of a defective enzyme caused by a mutation in its genetic code. For example, *phenylketonuria (PKU)* results when DNA cannot direct the synthesis of the enzyme phenylalanine hydroxylase, required for the conversion of phenylalanine to tyrosine. In an attempt to break down the phenylalanine, other enzymes in the cells convert it to phenylpyruvate. If phenylalanine and phenylpyruvate accumulate in the blood of an infant, it can lead to severe brain damage and mental retardation. If PKU is detected in a newborn baby, a diet is prescribed that eliminates all foods that contain phenylalanine. Preventing the buildup of phenylpyruvate ensures normal growth and development.

The amino acid tyrosine is needed in the formation of melanin, the pigment that gives the color to our skin and hair. If the enzyme that converts tyrosine to melanin is defective, no melanin is produced, a genetic disease known as *albinism*. Persons and animals with no melanin have no skin, eye, or hair pigment (see Figure 21.20). Table 21.9 lists some other common genetic diseases and the type of metabolism or area affected.

FIGURE 21.20 A peacock with albinism does not produce the melanin needed to make bright colors for its feathers.

Q Why are traits such as albinism related to the gene?

TABLE 21.9 Some Genetic Diseases

Genetic Disease	Result
Galactosemia	In galactosemia, the transferase enzyme required for the metabolism of galactose-1-phosphate is absent, resulting in the accumulation of galactose-1-phosphate, which leads to cataracts and mental retardation. Galactosemia occurs in about 1 in every 50 000 births.
Cystic fibrosis (CF)	Cystic fibrosis is one of the most common inherited diseases in children. Thick mucus secretions make breathing difficult and block pancreatic function.
Down syndrome	Down syndrome is the leading cause of mental retardation, occurring in about 1 of every 800 live births; the mother's age strongly influences its occurrence. Mental and physical problems, including heart and eye defects, are the result of the formation of three chromosomes, usually chromosome 21, instead of a pair.
Familial hypercholesterolemia	Familial hypercholesterolemia occurs when there is a mutation of a gene on chromosome 19, which produces high cholesterol levels that lead to early coronary heart disease in people 30–40 years old.
Muscular dystrophy (MD) (Duchenne)	Muscular dystrophy, Duchenne form, is caused by a mutation in the X chromosome. This muscle-destroying disease appears at about age 5, with death by age 20, and occurs in about 1 of 10 000 males.
Huntington's disease (HD)	Huntington's disease affects the nervous system, leading to total physical impairment. It is the result of a mutation in a gene on chromosome 4, which can now be mapped to test people in families with a history of HD. There are about 30 000 people with Huntington's disease in the United States.
Sickle cell anemia	Sickle cell anemia is caused by a defective form of hemoglobin resulting from a mutation in a gene on chromosome 11. It decreases the oxygen-carrying ability of red blood cells, which take on a sickled shape, causing anemia and plugged capillaries from red blood cell aggregation. In the United States, about 72 000 people are affected by sickle cell anemia.
Hemophilia	Hemophilia is the result of one or more defective blood-clotting factors that lead to poor coagulation, excessive bleeding, and internal hemorrhages. There are about 20 000 hemophilia patients in the United States.
Tay-Sachs disease	Tay-Sachs disease is the result of a defective hexosaminidase A, which causes an accumulation of gangliosides and leads to mental retardation, loss of motor control, and early death.

QUESTIONS AND PROBLEMS

21.8 Genetic Mutations

LEARNING GOAL: *Describe some ways in which DNA is altered to cause mutations.*

21.53 What is a substitution mutation?

21.54 How does a substitution mutation in the genetic code for an enzyme affect the order of amino acids in that protein?

21.55 What is the effect of a frameshift mutation on the amino acid sequence of a polypeptide?

21.56 How can a mutation decrease the activity of a protein?

21.57 How is protein synthesis affected if the normal base sequence TTT in the DNA template strand is changed to TTC?

21.58 How is protein synthesis affected if the normal base sequence CCC in the DNA template strand is changed to ACC?

21.59 Consider the following segment of mRNA produced by the normal order of DNA nucleotides:

$5'$ — ACA UCA CGG GUA — $3'$

a. What is the amino acid order produced from this mRNA?
b. What is the amino acid order if a mutation changes UCA to ACA?
c. What is the amino acid order if a mutation changes CGG to GGG?
d. What happens to protein synthesis if a mutation changes UCA to UAA?
e. What happens if a G is added to the beginning of the mRNA segment?
f. What happens if the A is removed from the beginning of the mRNA segment?

21.60 Consider the following portion of mRNA produced by the normal order of DNA nucleotides:

$5'$ — CUU AAA CGA GUU — $3'$

a. What is the amino acid order produced from this mRNA?
b. What is the amino acid order if a mutation changes CUU to CCU?
c. What is the amino acid order if a mutation changes CGA to AGA?
d. What happens to protein synthesis if a mutation changes AAA to UAA?
e. What happens if a G is added to the beginning of the mRNA segment?
f. What happens if the C is removed from the beginning of the mRNA segment?

21.61 a. A base substitution changes a codon in the mRNA for an enzyme from GCC to GCA. Why is there no change in this amino acid in the protein?
b. In sickle cell anemia, a base substitution in hemoglobin results in the replacement of glutamic acid (a polar acidic amino acid) with valine. Why does the replacement of one amino acid cause such a drastic change in biological function?

21.62 a. A base substitution in the mRNA for an enzyme results in the replacement of leucine (a nonpolar amino acid) with alanine. Why does this change in amino acids have little effect on the biological activity of the enzyme?
b. A base substitution in mRNA replaces cytosine in the codon UCA with adenine. How would this substitution affect the amino acids in the protein?

21.9 Recombinant DNA

Techniques in the field of genetic engineering permit scientists to cut and recombine DNA fragments to form **recombinant DNA**. The technology of recombinant DNA is used to produce human insulin for diabetics, the antiviral substance interferon, blood clotting factor VIII, and human growth hormone.

Preparing Recombinant DNA

Most of the work with recombinant DNA is done with *Escherichia coli* (*E. coli*) bacteria. The DNA in bacterial cells exists as small, circular double-stranded DNA structures called *plasmids*, which are easy to isolate and capable of replication. Initially, *E. coli* cells are soaked in a detergent solution to disrupt the plasma membrane releasing the plasmids. A *restriction enzyme* is used to cut the double strands of DNA between specific bases in the DNA sequence (see Figure 21.21). For example, the restriction enzyme EcoR1 recognizes the base sequences GAATTC on both strands, and cuts both DNA strands between the G and A.

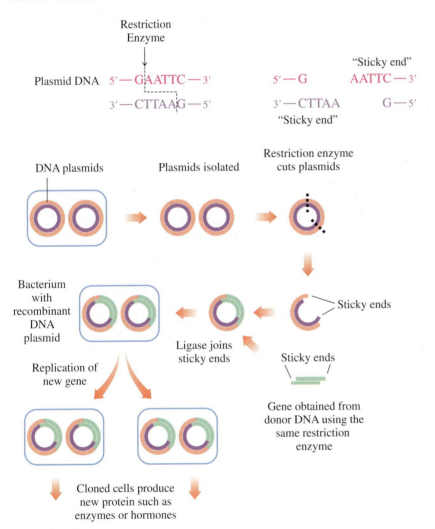

FIGURE 21.21 Recombinant DNA is formed by placing a gene from another organism in a plasmid DNA of the bacterium, which causes the bacterium to produce a nonbacterial protein such as insulin or growth hormone.

Q How can recombinant DNA help a person with a genetic disease?

The same restriction enzymes are used to cut a piece of DNA called donor DNA from a gene of a different organism, such as the gene that produces insulin or growth hormone. When the donor DNA is mixed with the cut plasmids, the nucleotides in their "sticky ends" join by forming complementary base pairs to make *recombinant DNA*.

Plasmid DNA	**Donor DNA**	**Recombinant DNA**
5′—G	AATTC—3′ ⟶	5′—GAATTC—3′
3′—CTTAA	G—5′ ⟶	3′—CTTAAG—5′

SELF-STUDY ACTIVITY
DNA

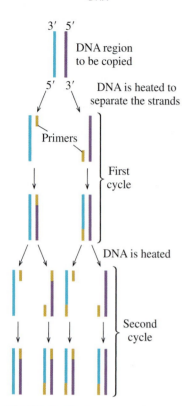

FIGURE 21.22 Each cycle of the polymerase chain reaction doubles the number of copies of the DNA section.

Q Why are the DNA strands heated at the start of each cycle?

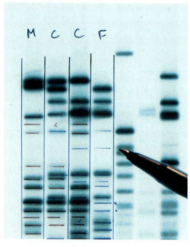

FIGURE 21.23 Dark and light bands on X-ray film represent DNA fingerprints that can be used to identify a person involved in a crime.

Q What causes DNA fragments to appear on X-ray film?

The resulting altered plasmids containing the recombinant DNA are placed in a fresh culture of *E. coli* bacteria, where they are reabsorbed into bacterial cells. The recombinant DNA inserted in the plasmids is now copied as the *E. coli* cells start to replicate. In a single day, one *E. coli* bacterium is capable of producing a million copies of itself including the recombinant DNA, a process known as *gene cloning*. If the inserted DNA codes for the human insulin protein, the altered plasmids begin to synthesize human insulin. Bacterial cells with the recombinant DNA can produce large quantities of the insulin protein, which is then collected and purified. Table 21.10 lists some of the products developed through recombinant DNA technology that are now used therapeutically.

TABLE 21.10 Therapeutic Products of Recombinant DNA

Product	Therapeutic Use
Human insulin	Treat diabetes
Erythropoietin (EPO)	Treat anemia; stimulate production of erythrocytes
Human growth hormone (HGH)	Stimulate growth
Interferon	Treat cancer and viral disease
Tumor necrosis factor (TNF)	Destroy tumor cells
Monoclonal antibodies	Transport drugs needed to treat cancer and transplant rejection
Epidermal growth factor (EGF)	Stimulate healing of wounds and burns
Human blood clotting factor VIII	Treat hemophilia; allows blood to clot normally
Interleukins	Stimulate immune system; treat cancer
Prourokinase	Destroy blood clots; treat myocardial infarctions
Influenza vaccine	Prevent influenza
Hepatitis B virus (HBV) vaccine	Prevent viral hepatitis

Polymerase Chain Reaction

The process of gene cloning using recombinant DNA requires living cells such as *E. coli*. In 1987, a process called the **polymerase chain reaction (PCR)** made it possible to produce multiple copies (amplify) of the DNA in a short time. In the PCR technique, a sequence of a DNA molecule is selected to copy, and the DNA is heated to separate the strands. Primers are used that are complementary to a small group of nucleotides on each strand end of the sequence to be copied. The DNA strands with their primers are mixed with a heat-stable DNA polymerase and a mixture of deoxyribonucleotides, and undergo repeated cycles of heating and cooling to produce complementary strands for the DNA section. Then the process is repeated with the new batch of DNA. After several cycles of the PCR process, millions of copies of the initial DNA section are produced (see Figure 21.22).

DNA Fingerprinting

In a process called *DNA fingerprinting* or *DNA profiling*, a small sample of DNA is obtained from blood, skin, saliva, or semen. The amount of DNA is amplified using the polymerase chain reaction method. Then restriction enzymes are used to cut the DNA into smaller fragments, which are placed on a gel and separated by size using electrophoresis. A radioactive probe is added that adheres to specific DNA sequences. When a piece of X-ray film is placed over the gel, the radiation from the probe bound to specific sequences creates a pattern of dark and light bands. This pattern on the film is known as a *DNA fingerprint* (see Figure 21.23). Scientists estimate that the odds of two people who are not identical twins producing the same DNA fingerprint are less than one in a billion.

One application of DNA fingerprinting is in forensic science, where DNA samples from blood, hair, or semen are used to connect a suspect with a crime. Recently, DNA fingerprinting has been used to gain the release of individuals who were wrongly convicted. Other applications of DNA fingerprinting are determining the biological parents of a child, establishing the identity of a deceased person, and matching recipients with organ donors.

Human Genome Project

The Human Genome Project, which began in 1990 and ended in 2003, was a project sponsored by the U.S. Department of Energy and the National Institutes of Health with contributions from Japan, France, Germany, United Kingdom, and other countries. The goals of the project were to identify about 25 000 genes in human DNA, to determine the base pair sequences in human DNA, and to store this information in databases accessible on the Internet. During that time, scientists used restriction enzymes to locate the genes within the DNA of the genome, which contains all the hereditary information.

Scientists determined that most of the human genome is not functional and has perhaps been carried from generation to generation for millions of years. Large blocks of genes are replicated, even though they do not code for needed proteins. Thus, the coding portions of the genes seem to make up only about 1% of the total genome. The results of the genome project will help us identify defective genes that lead to genetic disease. Today, DNA fingerprinting is used to screen for genes responsible for genetic diseases such as sickle cell anemia, cystic fibrosis, breast cancer, colon cancer, Huntington's disease, and Lou Gehrig's disease.

SELF-STUDY ACTIVITY
The Human Genome Project: Human Chromosome 17

QUESTIONS AND PROBLEMS

21.9 Recombinant DNA

LEARNING GOAL: *Describe the preparation and uses of recombinant DNA.*

21.63 Why are *E. coli* bacteria used in recombinant DNA procedures?

21.64 What is a plasmid?

21.65 How are plasmids obtained from *E. coli*?

21.66 Why are restriction enzymes mixed with the plasmids?

21.67 How is a gene for a particular protein inserted into a plasmid?

21.68 Why is DNA polymerase useful in criminal investigations?

21.69 What is a DNA fingerprint?

21.70 What beneficial proteins are produced from recombinant DNA technology?

21.10 Viruses

Viruses are small particles of 3 to 200 genes that cannot replicate without a host cell. A typical virus contains a nucleic acid, DNA or RNA, but not both, inside a protein coat. A virus does not have the necessary materials such as nucleotides and enzymes to synthesize proteins and to grow. The only way a virus can replicate (make additional copies of itself) is to invade a host cell and take over the mechanisms necessary for RNA, DNA, and protein synthesis. Some infections caused by viruses invading human cells are listed in Table 21.11. There are also viruses that attack bacteria, plants, and animals.

A viral infection begins when an enzyme in the protein coat of the virus makes a hole in the outside of the host cell, allowing the viral nucleic acid to enter and mix with the materials in the host cell (see Figure 21.24). If the virus contains DNA, the host cell begins to replicate the viral DNA in the same way it would replicate normal DNA. Viral DNA produces viral RNA, and a protease processes proteins to produce a protein coat to form a viral particle that leaves the cell. The cell synthesizes so many virus particles that they are eventually released so they can infect more cells.

Vaccines are inactive forms of viruses that boost the immune response by causing the body to produce antibodies to the virus. Several childhood diseases, such as polio, mumps, chicken pox, and measles, can be prevented through the use of vaccines.

LEARNING GOAL

Describe the methods by which a virus infects a cell.

TABLE 21.11 Some Diseases Caused by Viral Infection

Disease	Virus
Common cold	Coronavirus (over 100 types), rhinovirus (over 110 types)
Influenza	Orthomyxovirus
Warts	Papovavirus
Herpes	Herpesvirus
HPV	Human papilloma virus
Leukemia, cancers, AIDS	Retrovirus
Hepatitis	Hepatitis A virus (HAV), hepatitis B virus (HBV), hepatitis C virus (HCV)
Mumps	Paramyxovirus
Mononucleosis	Epstein–Barr virus (EBV)
Chicken pox (shingles)	*Varicella zoster* virus (VZV)

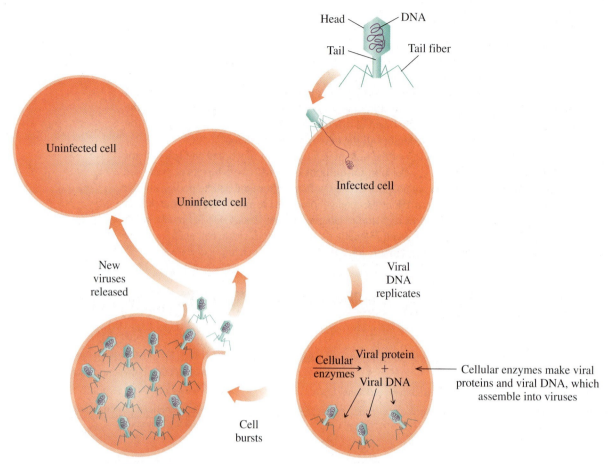

FIGURE 21.24 After a virus attaches to the host cell, it injects its viral DNA and uses the host cell's machinery and materials to synthesize viral RNA, protein, and enzymes. When the cell wall opens, the new viruses are released to infect other cells.

Q Why does a virus need a host cell for replication?

Reverse Transcription

A virus that contains RNA as its genetic material is a **retrovirus**. Once inside the host cell, the retrovirus must first make viral DNA using a process known as *reverse transcription*. A retrovirus contains a polymerase enzyme called *reverse transcriptase* that uses the viral RNA template to synthesize complementary strands of DNA. Once produced, the single DNA strands form double-stranded DNA using the nucleotides present in the host cell. This newly formed viral DNA, called a *provirus*, integrates with the DNA of the host cell (see Figure 21.25).

FIGURE 21.25 After a retrovirus injects its viral RNA into a cell, it forms a DNA strand by reverse transcription. The single-stranded DNA forms a double-stranded DNA called a provirus, which is incorporated into the host cell DNA. When the cell replicates, the provirus produces the viral RNA needed to produce more virus particles.

Q What is reverse transcription?

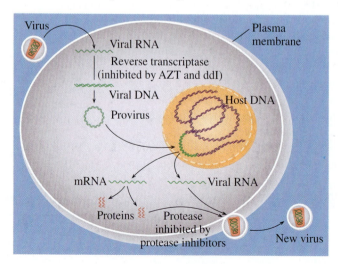

AIDS

During the early 1980s, a disease called *acquired immune deficiency syndrome*, commonly known as AIDS, began to claim an alarming number of lives. We now know that the HIV virus (human immunodeficiency virus) causes the disease (see Figure 21.26). HIV is a retrovirus that infects and destroys T4 lymphocyte cells, which are involved in the immune response. After the HIV binds to receptors on the surface of a T4 cell, the virus injects viral RNA into the host cell. As a retrovirus, the genes of the viral RNA direct the formation of viral DNA, which is then incorporated into the host's genome so it can replicate as part of the host cell's DNA. The gradual depletion of T4 cells reduces the ability of the immune system to destroy harmful organisms. The AIDS syndrome is characterized by opportunistic infections such as *Pneumocystis carinii*, which causes pneumonia, and *Kaposi's sarcoma*, a skin cancer.

Treatment for AIDS is based on attacking the HIV at different points in its life cycle, including reverse transcription and protein synthesis. Nucleoside analogs mimic the structures of the nucleosides used for DNA synthesis, and are able to successfully inhibit the reverse transcriptase enzyme. For example, the drug AZT (3′-azido-3′-deoxythymidine) is similar to thymidine, and ddI (2′,3′-dideoxyinosine) is similar to guanosine. Two other drugs are 2′,3′-dideoxycytidine (ddC) and 2′,3′-didehydro-2′,3′-dideoxythymidine (d4T). Such compounds are found in the "cocktails" that are providing extended remission of HIV infections. When a nucleoside analog is incorporated into viral DNA, the lack of a hydroxyl group on the 3′-carbon in the sugar prevents the formation of the sugar–phosphate bonds and stops the replication of the virus.

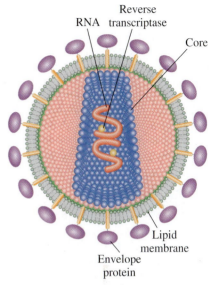

FIGURE 21.26 The HIV virus causes AIDS, which destroys the immune system in the body.

Q Is HIV a DNA virus or an RNA retrovirus?

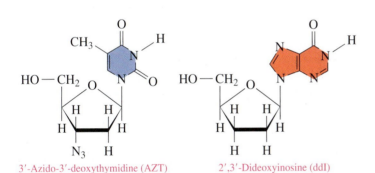

3′-Azido-3′-deoxythymidine (AZT)

2′,3′-Dideoxyinosine (ddI)

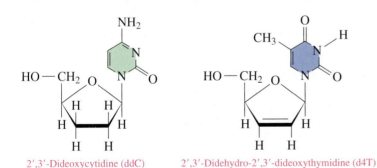

2′,3′-Dideoxycytidine (ddC)

2′,3′-Didehydro-2′,3′-dideoxythymidine (d4T)

Treatment of AIDS often combines reverse transcriptase inhibitors with protease inhibitors such as saquinavir (Invirase), indinavir (Crixivan), fosamprenavir (Lexiva), nelfinavir (Viracept), and ritonavir (Norvir). The inhibition of a protease enzyme prevents the proper cutting and formation of proteins used by viruses to make more copies. Researchers are not yet certain how long protease inhibitors will be beneficial for a person with AIDS.

Lexiva metabolizes slowly to provide amprenavir, an HIV-protease inhibitor.

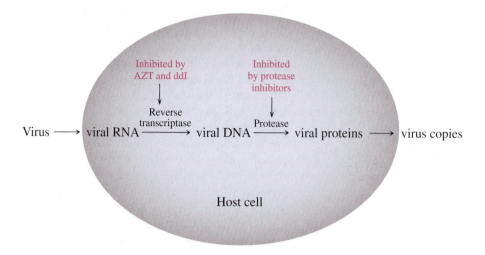

Chemistry Link to Health

CANCER

Normally, somatic cells undergo an orderly and controlled cell division. When cells in the body begin to grow and multiply uncontrollably, they are called a tumor. If the effect of these tumors is limited, they are benign. When they invade other tissues and interfere with normal functions of the body, the tumors are cancerous. Cancer can be caused by chemical and environmental substances, by radiation, or by *oncogenic viruses*, which are viruses associated with human cancers (see Table 21.12).

TABLE 21.12 Human Cancers Caused by Oncogenic Viruses

Virus	Disease
RNA Viruses	
Human T-cell lymphotropic virus-type I (HTLV-I)	Leukemia
DNA Viruses	
Epstein–Barr virus (EBV)	Burkitt's lymphoma (cancer of B lymphocytes)
	Nasopharyngeal carcinoma
	Hodgkin's disease
Hepatitis B virus (HBV)	Liver cancer
Herpes simplex virus (HSV type 2)	Cervical and uterine cancer
Papilloma virus	Cervical and colon cancer, genital warts

Some reports estimate that chemical and environmental substances initiate 70–80% of all human cancers. A *carcinogen* is any substance that increases the chance of inducing a tumor. Known carcinogens include dyes, cigarette smoke, and asbestos. More than 90% of all

persons with lung cancer are smokers. A carcinogen causes cancer by reacting with the DNA molecules in a cell, and altering the growth of that cell. Some known carcinogens are listed in Table 21.13.

TABLE 21.13 Some Chemical and Environmental Carcinogens

Carcinogen	Tumor Site
Aflatoxin	Liver
Aniline dyes	Bladder
Arsenic	Skin, lung
Asbestos	Lung, respiratory tract
Cadmium	Prostate, kidneys
Chromium	Lung
Nickel	Lung, sinuses
Nitrites	Stomach
Vinyl chloride	Liver

Radiant energy from sunlight or medical radiation is another type of environmental factor. Skin cancer has become one of the most prevalent forms of cancer. The DNA damage in the exposed areas of the skin may eventually cause mutations. The cells lose their ability to control protein synthesis. This type of uncontrolled cell division becomes skin cancer. The incidence of *malignant melanoma*, one of the most serious skin cancers, has been rapidly increasing. Some possible factors for this increase may be the popularity of sun tanning as well as the reduction of the ozone layer, which absorbs much of the harmful UVB radiation from sunlight.

Certain cancers such as retinoblastoma and breast cancer appear to occur more frequently in some families. Research indicates that a missing or defective gene is responsible.

CONCEPT CHECK 21.8 **Viruses**

Why are viruses unable to replicate on their own?

ANSWER

Viruses contain only packets of DNA or RNA, but not the necessary replication machinery that includes enzymes and nucleosides.

QUESTIONS AND PROBLEMS

21.10 Viruses

LEARNING GOAL: *Describe the methods by which a virus infects a cell.*

21.71 What type of genetic information is found in a virus?

21.72 Why do viruses need to invade a host cell?

21.73 A specific virus contains RNA as its genetic material.
  a. Why would reverse transcription be used in the life cycle of this type of virus?
  b. What is the name of this type of virus?

21.74 What is the purpose of a vaccine?

21.75 How do nucleoside analogs disrupt the life cycle of the HIV-1 virus?

21.76 How do protease inhibitors disrupt the life cycle of the HIV-1 virus?

CONCEPT MAP

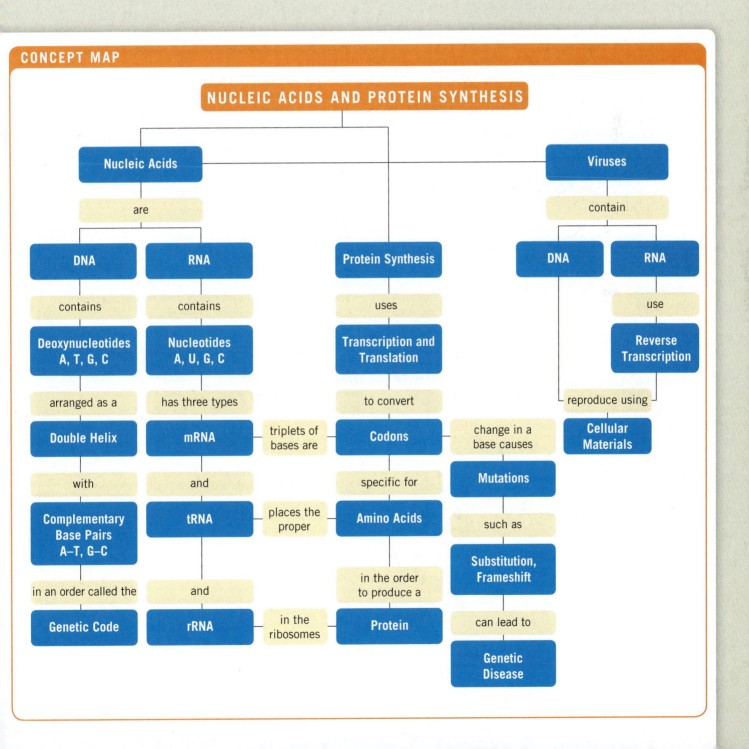

NUCLEIC ACIDS AND PROTEIN SYNTHESIS

- **Nucleic Acids**
  - are
    - **DNA**
      - contains **Deoxynucleotides A, T, G, C**
        - arranged as a **Double Helix**
          - with **Complementary Base Pairs A–T, G–C**
            - in an order called the **Genetic Code**
    - **RNA**
      - contains **Nucleotides A, U, G, C**
        - has three types **mRNA** — triplets of bases are
          - and **tRNA** — places the proper
            - and **rRNA** — in the ribosomes

- **Protein Synthesis**
  - uses **Transcription and Translation**
    - to convert **Codons**
      - specific for **Amino Acids**
        - in the order to produce a **Protein**

- change in a base causes **Mutations**
  - such as **Substitution, Frameshift**
    - can lead to **Genetic Disease**

- **Viruses**
  - contain
    - **DNA**
      - reproduce using **Cellular Materials**
    - **RNA**
      - use **Reverse Transcription**

CHAPTER REVIEW

21.1 Components of Nucleic Acids

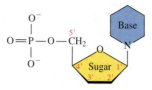

LEARNING GOAL: *Describe the bases and ribose sugars that make up the nucleic acids DNA and RNA.*

- Nucleic acids, such as deoxyribonucleic acid (DNA) and ribonucleic acid (RNA), are polymers of nucleotides.
- A nucleoside is a combination of a pentose sugar and a base.
- A nucleotide is composed of three parts: a pentose sugar, a base, and a phosphate group.
- In DNA, the sugar is deoxyribose and the base can be adenine, thymine, guanine, or cytosine.
- In RNA, the sugar is ribose, and uracil replaces thymine.

21.2 Primary Structure of Nucleic Acids

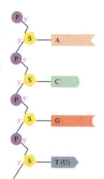

LEARNING GOAL: *Describe the primary structures of RNA and DNA.*

- Each nucleic acid has its own unique sequence of bases known as its primary structure.
- In a nucleic acid polymer, the 3′—OH group of each ribose in RNA or deoxyribose in DNA forms a phosphodiester bond to the phosphate group of the 5′-carbon atom of the sugar in the next nucleotide to give a backbone of alternating sugar and phosphate groups.
- There is a free 5′-phosphate at one end of the polymer and a free 3′—OH group at the other end.

21.3 DNA Double Helix

LEARNING GOAL: *Describe the double helix of DNA.*

- A DNA molecule consists of two strands of nucleotides that are wound around each other like a spiral staircase.
- The two strands are held together by hydrogen bonds between complementary base pairs, A with T, and G with C.

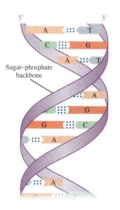

21.4 DNA Replication

LEARNING GOAL: *Describe the process of DNA replication.*

- During DNA replication, DNA polymerase makes new DNA strands along each of the original DNA strands that serve as templates.
- Complementary base pairing ensures the correct pairing of bases to give identical copies of the original DNA.

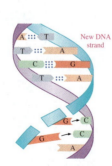

21.5 RNA and Transcription

LEARNING GOAL: *Identify the different types of RNA; describe the synthesis of mRNA.*

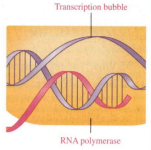

- The three types of RNA differ by function in the cell: ribosomal RNA makes up most of the structure of the ribosomes, messenger RNA carries genetic information from the DNA to the ribosomes, and transfer RNA places the correct amino acids in a growing peptide chain.
- Transcription is the process by which RNA polymerase produces mRNA from one strand of DNA.
- The bases in the mRNA are complementary to the DNA, except A in DNA is paired with U in RNA.
- The production of mRNA occurs when certain proteins are needed in the cell.
- In enzyme induction, the appearance of a substrate in a cell removes a repressor from the control site, which allows RNA polymerase to produce mRNA from structural genes.

21.6 The Genetic Code

LEARNING GOAL: *Describe the function of the codons in the genetic code.*

U	C
UUU ⎫ Phe UUC ⎭	UCU ⎫ UCC ⎪ Ser UCA ⎪ UCG ⎭
UUA ⎫ Leu UUG ⎭	
CUU ⎫ CUC ⎪ Leu CUA ⎪ CUG ⎭	CCU ⎫ CCC ⎪ Pro CCA ⎪ CCG ⎭

- The genetic code consists of a series of codons, which are sequences of three bases that specify the order for the amino acids in a protein.
- There are 64 codons for the 20 amino acids, which means there are multiple codons for most amino acids.
- The codon AUG signals the start of transcription, and codons UAG, UGA, and UAA signal it to stop.

21.7 Protein Synthesis: Translation

LEARNING GOAL: *Describe the process of protein synthesis from mRNA.*

- Proteins are synthesized at the ribosomes in a translation process that includes three steps: initiation, chain elongation, and termination.
- During translation, tRNAs bring the appropriate amino acids to the ribosome, and peptide bonds form to join the amino acids in a peptide chain.
- When the polypeptide is released, it takes on its secondary and tertiary structures and becomes a functional protein in the cell.

21.8 Genetic Mutations

LEARNING GOAL: Describe some ways in which DNA is altered to cause mutations.

- A genetic mutation is a change of one or more bases in the DNA sequence that alters the structure and ability of the resulting protein to function properly.
- In a substitution, one codon is altered, and a frameshift mutation inserts or deletes a base, which changes all the codons after the base change.

21.9 Recombinant DNA

LEARNING GOAL: Describe the preparation and uses of recombinant DNA.

- A recombinant DNA is prepared by inserting a DNA segment—a gene—into plasmid DNA present in *E. coli* bacteria.

- As the altered bacterial cells replicate, the protein expressed by the foreign DNA segment is produced.
- In criminal investigation, large quantities of DNA are obtained from smaller amounts by the polymerase chain reaction.

21.10 Viruses

LEARNING GOAL: Describe the methods by which a virus infects a cell.

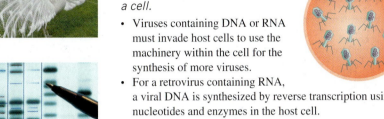

- Viruses containing DNA or RNA must invade host cells to use the machinery within the cell for the synthesis of more viruses.
- For a retrovirus containing RNA, a viral DNA is synthesized by reverse transcription using the nucleotides and enzymes in the host cell.
- In the treatment of AIDS, nucleoside analogs inhibit the reverse transcriptase of the HIV-1 virus, and protease inhibitors disrupt the catalytic activity of protease needed to produce proteins for the synthesis of more viruses.

KEY TERMS

anticodon The triplet of bases in the center loop of tRNA that is complementary to a codon on mRNA.

bases Nitrogen-containing compounds found in DNA and RNA: adenine (A), thymine (T), cytosine (C), guanine (G), and uracil (U).

codon A sequence of three bases in mRNA that specifies a certain amino acid to be placed in a protein. A few codons signal the start or stop of protein synthesis.

complementary base pairs In DNA, adenine is always paired with thymine (A and T or T and A), and guanine is always paired with cytosine (G and C or C and G). In forming RNA, adenine is always paired with uracil (A and U or U and A).

control site A section of DNA that regulates protein synthesis.

DNA Deoxyribonucleic acid; the genetic material of all cells containing nucleotides with deoxyribose, phosphate, and the four bases: adenine, thymine, guanine, and cytosine.

double helix The helical shape of the double chain of DNA that is like a spiral staircase with a sugar–phosphate backbone on the outside and base pairs like stair steps on the inside.

enzyme induction A model of cellular regulation in which protein synthesis is induced by a substrate.

exons The sections in a DNA template that code for proteins.

frameshift mutation A mutation that inserts or deletes a base in a DNA sequence.

genetic code The sequence of codons in mRNA that specifies the amino acid order for the synthesis of protein.

genetic disease A physical malformation or metabolic dysfunction caused by a mutation in the base sequence of DNA.

introns The sections in DNA that do not code for proteins.

mRNA Messenger RNA; produced in the nucleus from DNA to carry the genetic information to the ribosomes for the construction of a protein.

mutation A change in the DNA base sequence that alters the formation of a protein in the cell.

nucleic acids Large molecules composed of nucleotides; found as a double helix in DNA and as the single strands of RNA.

nucleoside The combination of a pentose sugar and a base.

nucleotides Building blocks of a nucleic acid consisting of a base, a pentose sugar (ribose or deoxyribose), and a phosphate group.

Okazaki fragments The short segments formed by DNA polymerase in the daughter DNA strand that runs in the 3′ to 5′ direction.

operon A group of genes, including a control site and structural genes, whose transcription is controlled by the same regulatory gene.

phosphodiester bond The phosphate link that joins the 3′-hydroxyl group in one nucleotide to the phosphate group on the 5′-carbon atom in the next nucleotide.

polymerase chain reaction (PCR) A procedure in which a strand of DNA is copied many times by mixing it with primers, DNA polymerase and a mixture of deoxyribonucleotides and subjecting it to repeated cycles of heating and cooling.

primary structure The sequence of nucleotides in nucleic acids.

recombinant DNA DNA combined from different organisms to form new, synthetic DNA.

regulatory gene A gene in front of the control site that produces a repressor.

replication The process of duplicating DNA by pairing the bases on each parent strand with their complementary bases.

replication forks The open sections in unwound DNA strands where DNA polymerase begins the replication process.

repressor A protein that interacts with the control site in an operon to prevent the transcription of mRNA.

retrovirus A virus that contains RNA as its genetic material and that synthesizes a complementary DNA strand inside a cell.

RNA Ribonucleic acid; a type of nucleic acid that is a single strand of nucleotides containing ribose, phosphate, and the four bases: adenine, cytosine, guanine, and uracil.

rRNA Ribosomal RNA; the most prevalent type of RNA and a major component of the ribosomes.

structural genes The sections of DNA that code for the synthesis of proteins.

substitution mutation A mutation that replaces one base in a DNA with a different base.

transcription The transfer of genetic information from DNA by the formation of mRNA.

translation The interpretation of the codons in mRNA as amino acids in a peptide.

tRNA Transfer RNA; an RNA that places a specific amino acid into a peptide chain at the ribosome so that a protein can be made. There is one or more tRNA for each of the 20 different amino acids.

virus Small particles containing DNA or RNA in a protein coat that require a host cell for replication.

UNDERSTANDING THE CONCEPTS

The chapter sections to review are given in parentheses at the end of each question.

21.77 Answer the following questions for the given section of DNA: (21.4, 21.5, 21.6, 21.7)

a. Complete the bases in the parent and new strands.

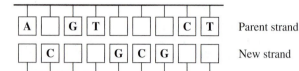

Parent strand

New strand

b. Using the new strand as a template, write the mRNA sequence.

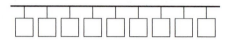

c. Write the 3-letter symbols of the amino acids that would go into the peptide from the mRNA you wrote in part **b**.

21.78 Suppose a mutation occurs in the DNA section in Problem 21.77, and the first base in the parent chain, adenine, is replaced by guanine. (21.4, 21.5, 21.6, 21.7, 21.8)

a. What type of mutation has occurred?

b. Using the new strand that results from this mutation, write the order of bases in the altered mRNA.

c. Write the 3-letter symbols of the amino acids that would go into the peptide from the mRNA you wrote in part **b**.

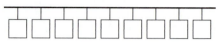

d. What effect, if any, might this mutation have on the structure and/or function of the resulting protein?

ADDITIONAL QUESTIONS AND PROBLEMS

For instructor-assigned homework, go to www.masteringchemistry.com.

21.79 Identify each of the following bases as a pyrimidine or a purine: (21.1)
  a. cytosine   **b.** adenine
  c. uracil

21.80 Indicate if each of the bases in Problem 21.79 is found in DNA only, RNA only, or both DNA and RNA. (21.1)

21.81 Identify the base and sugar in each of the following nucleosides: (21.1)
  a. deoxythymidine   **b.** adenosine
  c. cytidine   **d.** deoxyguanosine

21.82 Identify the base and sugar in each of the following nucleotides: (21.1)
  a. CMP   **b.** dAMP
  c. dTMP   **d.** UMP

21.83 How do the bases thymine and uracil differ? (21.1)

21.84 How do the bases cytosine and uracil differ? (21.1)

21.85 Draw the condensed structural formula for CMP. (21.1)

21.86 Draw the condensed structural formula for dGMP. (21.1)

21.87 What is similar about the primary structure of RNA and DNA? (21.2)

21.88 What is different about the primary structure of RNA and DNA? (21.2)

21.89 If the DNA double helix in salmon contains 28% adenine, what is the percentage of thymine, guanine, and cytosine? (21.3)

21.90 If the DNA double helix in humans contains 20% cytosine, what is the percentage of guanine, adenine, and thymine? (21.3)

21.91 In DNA, how many hydrogen bonds form between adenine and thymine? (21.3)

21.92 In DNA, how many hydrogen bonds are formed between guanine and cytosine? (21.3)

21.93 Write the complementary base sequence for each of the following DNA segments: (21.4)
  a. 5′—G A C T T A G G C—3′
  b. 3′—T G C A A A C T A G C T—5′
  c. 5′—A T C G A T C G A T C G—3′

21.94 Write the complementary base sequence for each of the following DNA segments: (21.4)
  a. 5′—T T A C G G A C C G C—3′
  b. 5′—A T A G C C C T T A C T G G—3′
  c. 3′—G G C C T A C C T T A A C G A C G—5′

21.95 In DNA replication, what is the difference between the synthesis of the leading strand and the synthesis of the lagging strand? (21.4)

21.96 How are the Okazaki fragments joined to the growing DNA strand? (21.4)

21.97 After the replication of a DNA, where are the original DNA strands located in the daughter DNA molecules? (21.4)

21.98 How can replication occur at several places along a DNA double helix? (21.4)

21.99 Match the following statements with rRNA, mRNA, or tRNA: (21.5)
  a. is the smallest type of RNA
  b. makes up the highest percentage of RNA in the cell
  c. carries genetic information from the nucleus to the ribosomes

21.100 Match the following statements with rRNA, mRNA, or tRNA: (21.5)
  a. combines with proteins to form ribosomes
  b. brings amino acids to the ribosomes for protein synthesis
  c. acts as a template for protein synthesis

21.101 What are the possible codons for each of the following amino acids? (21.6)
  a. threonine   **b.** serine   **c.** cysteine

21.102 What are the possible codons for each of the following amino acids? (21.6)
  a. valine   **b.** arginine   **c.** histidine

21.103 What is the amino acid for each of the following codons? (21.6)
  a. AAG   **b.** AUU   **c.** CGA

21.104 What is the amino acid for each of the following codons? (21.6)
  a. CAA   **b.** GGC   **c.** AAC

21.105 Endorphins are polypeptides that reduce pain. What is the amino acid order for the endorphin leucine enkephalin (leu-enkephalin), which has the following mRNA? (21.5, 21.6, 21.7, 21.8)

  5′ — AUG UAC GGU GGA UUU CUA UAA — 3′

21.106 Endorphins are polypeptides that reduce pain. What is the amino acid order for the endorphin methionine enkephalin (met-enkephalin), which has the following mRNA? (21.5, 21.6, 21.7, 21.8)

  5′ — AUG UAC GGU GGA UUU AUG UAA — 3′

21.107 What is the anticodon on tRNA for each of the following codons in an mRNA? (21.7)
  a. AGC   **b.** UAU   **c.** CCA

21.108 What is the anticodon on tRNA for each of the following codons in an mRNA? (21.7)
  a. GUG   **b.** CCC   **c.** GAA

CHALLENGE QUESTIONS

21.109 Oxytocin is a peptide that contains nine amino acids. How many nucleotides would be found in the mRNA for this protein? (21.6, 21.7)

21.110 A protein contains 36 amino acids. How many nucleotides would be found in the mRNA for this protein? (21.6, 21.7)

21.111 What is the difference between a DNA virus and a retrovirus? (21.10)

21.112 Why are there no base pairs in DNA between adenine and guanine or thymine and cytosine? (21.3)

ANSWERS

Answers to Study Checks

21.1 deoxycytidine-5′-monophosphate (dCMP)

21.2

21.3 3′ — C C A A T T G G — 5′

21.4 3′ — C C C A A A T T T — 5′

21.5 — Asn — Ala — Cys —

21.6 at UAG

21.7 Because the base substitution replaces a polar basic amino acid with a nonpolar neutral amino acid, the tertiary structure may be altered enough to cause the resulting protein to be less effective or nonfunctional.

Answers to Selected Questions and Problems

21.1 **a.** pyrimidine
  b. pyrimidine

21.3 **a.** DNA
  b. both DNA and RNA

21.5 deoxyadenosine-5′-monophosphate (dAMP), deoxythymidine-5′-monophosphate (dTMP), deoxycytidine-5′-monophosphate (dCMP), and deoxyguanosine-5′-monophosphate (dGMP)

21.7 **a.** nucleoside
  b. nucleoside
  c. nucleoside
  d. nucleotide

21.9

21.11 The nucleotides in nucleic acids are held together by phosphodiester bonds between the 3′ — OH group of a sugar (ribose or deoxyribose) and a phosphate group on the 5′-carbon of another sugar.

21.13

Guanosine (G)

Cytidine (C)

21.15 The two DNA strands are held together by hydrogen bonds between the complementary bases in each strand.

21.17
a. 3′—TTTTTT—5′
b. 3′—CCCCCC—5′
c. 3′—TCAGGTCCA—5′
d. 3′—GACATATGCAAT—5′

21.19 The enzyme helicase unwinds the DNA helix so that the parent DNA strands can be replicated into daughter DNA strands.

21.21 Once the DNA strands separate, the DNA polymerase pairs each of the bases with its complementary base and produces two exact copies of the original DNA.

21.23 ribosomal RNA, messenger RNA, and transfer RNA

21.25 A ribosome consists of a small subunit and a large subunit that contain rRNA combined with proteins.

21.27 In transcription, the sequence of nucleotides on a DNA template (one strand) is used to produce the base sequence of a messenger RNA.

21.29 5′—GGCUUCCAAGUG—3′

21.31 In eukaryotic cells, genes contain sections called exons that code for proteins and sections called introns that do not code for proteins.

21.33 An operon is a section of DNA that regulates the synthesis of one or more proteins.

21.35 When the lactose level is low in *E. coli*, a repressor produced by the mRNA from a regulatory gene binds to the control site, which blocks the synthesis of mRNA from a gene and prevents the synthesis of protein.

21.37 A codon is a three-base sequence in mRNA that codes for a specific amino acid in a protein.

21.39
a. leucine (Leu)
b. serine (Ser)
c. glycine (Gly)
d. arginine (Arg)

21.41 When AUG is the first codon, it signals the start of protein synthesis. Thereafter, AUG codes for methionine.

21.43 A codon is a base triplet in the mRNA. An anticodon is the complementary triplet on a tRNA for a specific amino acid.

21.45 initiation, chain elongation, and termination

21.47
a. —Thr—Thr—Thr—
b. —Phe—Pro—Phe—Pro—
c. —Tyr—Gly—Arg—Cys—

21.49 The new amino acid is joined by a peptide bond to the growing peptide chain. The ribosome moves to the next codon, which attaches to a tRNA carrying the next amino acid.

21.51
a. 5′—CGA—AAA—GUU—UUU—3′
b. GCU, UUU, CAA, AAA
c. —Arg—Lys—Val—Phe—

21.53 In a substitution mutation, a base in DNA is replaced by a different base.

21.55 In a frameshift mutation caused by a deletion or an addition, all the codons from the mutation onward are changed, which changes the order of amino acids in the rest of the polypeptide chain.

21.57 The normal triplet TTT forms a codon AAA, which codes for lysine. The mutation TTC forms a codon AAG, which also codes for lysine. There is no effect on the amino acid sequence.

21.59
a. —Thr—Ser—Arg—Val—
b. —Thr—Thr—Arg—Val—
c. —Thr—Ser—Gly—Val—
d. —Thr—STOP. Protein synthesis would terminate early. If this occurs early in the formation of the polypeptide, the resulting protein will probably be nonfunctional.
e. The new protein will contain the sequence —Asp—Ile—Thr—Gly—.
f. The new protein will contain the sequence —His—His—Gly—.

21.61
a. GCC and GCA both code for alanine.
b. A vital ionic cross-link in the tertiary structure of hemoglobin cannot be formed when the polar glutamic acid is replaced by valine, which is nonpolar. The resulting hemoglobin is malformed and less capable of carrying oxygen.

21.63 *E. coli* bacterial cells contain several small circular plasmids of DNA that can be isolated easily. After the recombinant DNA is formed, *E. coli* multiply rapidly, producing many copies of the recombinant DNA in a relatively short time.

21.65 *E. coli* are soaked in a detergent solution that disrupts the plasma membrane and releases the cell contents, including the plasmids, which are collected.

21.67 When a gene has been obtained using a restriction enzyme, it is mixed with plasmids that have been cut by the same enzyme. When mixed together, the sticky ends of the DNA fragments bond with the sticky ends of the plasmid DNA to form a recombinant DNA.

21.69 In DNA fingerprinting, restriction enzymes cut a sample DNA into fragments, which are sorted by size using gel electrophoresis. A radioactive probe that adheres to specific DNA sequences exposes an X-ray film and creates a pattern of dark and light bands called a DNA fingerprint.

21.71 DNA or RNA, but not both

21.73 a. A viral RNA is used to synthesize a viral DNA to produce the proteins for the protein coat, which allows the virus to replicate and leave the cell.
b. retrovirus

21.75 Nucleoside analogs such as AZT and ddI are similar to the nucleosides required to make viral DNA in reverse transcription. However, they interfere with the ability of the DNA to form and thereby disrupt the life cycle of the HIV-1 virus.

21.77 a.

| A | G | G | T | C | G | C | C | T | Parent strand |

b.

| T | C | C | A | G | C | G | G | A | New strand |

| A | G | G | U | C | G | C | C | U |

c. Arg — Ser — Pro

21.79 a. pyrimidine
b. purine
c. pyrimidine

21.81 a. thymine and deoxyribose
b. adenine and ribose
c. cytosine and ribose
d. guanine and deoxyribose

21.83 They are both pyrimidines, but thymine has a methyl group.

21.85

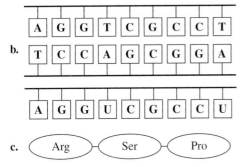

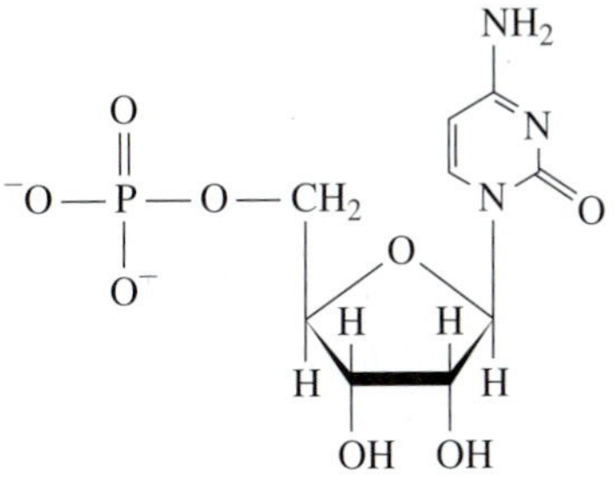

21.87 They are both polymers of nucleotides connected through phosphodiester bonds between alternating sugar and phosphate groups, with bases extending out from each sugar.

21.89 28% T, 22% G, and 22% C

21.91 two

21.93 a. 3′—C T G A A T C C G—5′
b. 5′—A C G T T T G A T C G A—3′
c. 3′—T A G C T A G C T A G C—5′

21.95 DNA polymerase synthesizes the leading strand continuously in the 5′ to 3′ direction. The lagging strand is synthesized in small segments called Okazaki fragments because it must grow in the 3′ to 5′ direction and DNA polymerase can only work in the 5′ to 3′ direction.

21.97 One strand of the parent DNA is found in each of the two copies of the daughter DNA molecule.

21.99 a. tRNA
b. rRNA
c. mRNA

21.101 a. ACU, ACC, ACA, and ACG
b. UCU, UCC, UCA, UCG, AGU, and AGC
c. UGU and UGC

21.103 a. lysine
b. isoleucine
c. arginine

21.105 START—Tyr—Gly—Gly—Phe—Leu—STOP

21.107 a. UCG
b. AUA
c. GGU

21.109 Three nucleotides are needed to code for each amino acid, plus the start and stop codons consisting of three nucleotides each, which makes a minimum total of 33 nucleotides.

21.111 A DNA virus attaches to a cell and injects viral DNA that uses the host cell to produce copies of the DNA to make viral RNA. A retrovirus injects viral RNA from which complementary DNA is produced by reverse transcription.

22 Metabolic Pathways for Carbohydrates

Visit **www.masteringchemistry.com** for self-study materials and instructor-assigned homework.

Max, a six-year-old dog, has an appointment in a few days for a dental cleaning with anesthesia. Before that, he is brought to his veterinarian for a blood chemistry profile and a urinalysis. Sean, a veterinary assistant, measures Max's weight and obtains the blood and urine samples needed for the pre-surgery diagnostics. The blood chemistry profile determines the overall health and condition of Max's liver and kidneys, detects any metabolic disorders, and measures the concentration of electrolytes.

The overall condition of Max's metabolism is determined by the concentration of glucose and several enzymes. Metabolism includes all of the chemical reactions in the body involving the breakdown of molecules to produce energy or the synthesis of complex molecules for cellular growth. These reactions frequently occur in a series and require multiple enzymes. The oxidation of glucose involves several of these metabolic pathways including glycolysis, the citric acid cycle, and electron transport.

On the day of the cleaning, Sean records Max's weight and eating habits for the past 24 hours. He prepares the surgical room to ensure it is clean and sterilized. Sean then shaves an area on Max's front leg and helps administer the anesthesia. After the cleaning, Sean monitors the heart rate and blood pressure as Max recovers from anesthesia.

Career: Veterinary Assistant

Veterinary assistants, or veterinary technicians, assist in the care of domesticated pets, and farm animals under the direct supervision of a veterinarian. Veterinary assistants are typically the first person an owner interacts with as they record the animal's symptoms and medical history. This includes dietary intake, medications, eating habits, weight, and any clinical signs. Veterinary assistants perform laboratory tests on animals including a complete blood count (CBC) and urinalysis. They also obtain tissue and blood samples, expose and develop X-rays, and assist with vaccinations. In addition, they assist with surgical procedures such as neutering and spaying, dental cleanings, removing tumors, and euthanizing animals.

When we eat food such as a tuna fish sandwich, the polysaccharides, lipids, and proteins are digested to smaller molecules that are absorbed into the cells of our bodies. As glucose, fatty acids, and amino acids are broken down further, energy is released. This energy is used in the cells to synthesize high-energy compounds such as adenosine triphosphate (ATP). Our cells utilize ATP energy when they do work such as contracting muscles, synthesizing large molecules, sending nerve impulses, and moving substances across cell membranes.

All the chemical reactions that take place in living cells to break down or build molecules are known as *metabolism*. In a metabolic pathway, reactions are linked together in a series, each catalyzed by a specific enzyme to produce an end product. In this and the following chapters, we will look at these pathways and the ways they produce energy and cellular compounds.

22.1 Metabolism and Cell Structure

LEARNING GOAL

Describe three stages of metabolism.

The term **metabolism** refers to all the chemical reactions that provide energy and the substances required for continued cell growth. There are two types of metabolic reactions: catabolic and anabolic. In **catabolic reactions**, complex molecules are broken down to simpler ones with an accompanying release of energy. **Anabolic reactions** utilize energy available in the cell to build large molecules from simple ones. We can think of the catabolic processes in metabolism as consisting of three stages (see Figure 22.1).

Stage 1 Catabolism begins with the processes of **digestion** in which enzymes in the digestive tract break down large molecules into smaller ones. The polysaccharides break down to monosaccharides, fats break down to glycerol and fatty acids, and the proteins yield amino acids. These digestion products diffuse into the bloodstream for transport to cells.

Stage 2 Within the cells, catabolic reactions continue as the digestion products are broken down further to yield three-carbon compounds such as pyruvate. Under aerobic conditions, pyruvate is degraded to a two-carbon acetyl group that is activated when combined with coenzyme A to give acetyl-CoA.

Stage 3 The major production of energy takes place in the mitochondria, as the two-carbon acetyl-CoA is oxidized in the citric acid cycle, which produces reduced coenzymes NADH and $FADH_2$. As long as the cells have oxygen, the hydrogen ions and electrons from the reduced coenzymes can enter electron transport to synthesize ATP.

Cell Structure for Metabolism

TUTORIAL
Metabolism and Cell Structure

To understand the relationships among metabolic reactions, we need to look at where these metabolic reactions take place in the cells of plants and animals. The cells in plants and animals are *eukaryotic* cells, which have a nucleus that contains DNA (see Figure 22.2). Single-celled organisms such as bacteria are *prokaryotic* cells, which have no nucleus.

In animals, a *cell membrane* separates the materials inside the cell from the aqueous environment surrounding the cell. In addition, the outer surface of the cell membrane contains structures that allow cells to communicate with each other. The *nucleus* contains the genes that control DNA replication and protein synthesis within the cell. The **cytoplasm** consists of all the materials between the nucleus and the cell membrane. The **cytosol**, the fluid part of the cytoplasm, is an aqueous solution of electrolytes and enzymes that catalyze many of the cell's chemical reactions.

Within the cytoplasm, specialized structures called *organelles* carry out specific functions in the cell. We have already seen (Section 21.5) that the *ribosomes* are the sites of

Stages of Metabolism

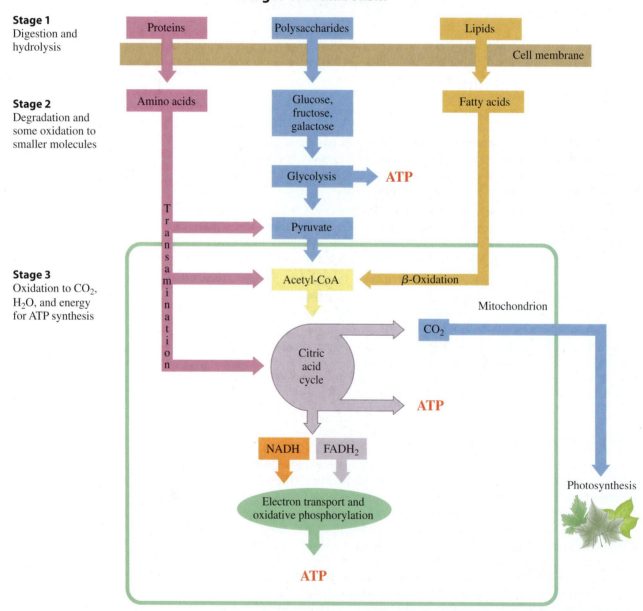

Stage 1
Digestion and hydrolysis

Stage 2
Degradation and some oxidation to smaller molecules

Stage 3
Oxidation to CO_2, H_2O, and energy for ATP synthesis

Proteins · Polysaccharides · Lipids

Cell membrane

Amino acids · Glucose, fructose, galactose · Fatty acids

Glycolysis → **ATP**

Pyruvate

Transamination

Acetyl-CoA ← β-Oxidation

Mitochondrion

Citric acid cycle → CO_2

ATP

NADH · FADH$_2$

Electron transport and oxidative phosphorylation

ATP

Photosynthesis

FIGURE 22.1 In the three stages of catabolism, large molecules from foods are digested and degraded to give smaller molecules that can be oxidized to produce energy.

Q Where is most of the ATP energy produced in the cells?

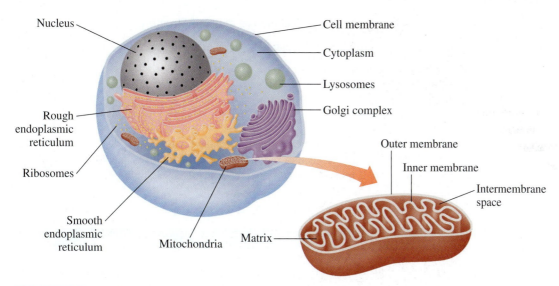

FIGURE 22.2 The diagram illustrates the major components of a typical animal cell.
Q What is the cytoplasm in a cell?

protein synthesis. The *endoplasmic reticulum* consists of two forms: a rough endoplasmic reticulum where proteins are processed for secretion and phospholipids are synthesized, and a smooth endoplasmic reticulum where fats and steroids are synthesized. The *Golgi complex* modifies proteins it receives from the rough endoplasmic reticulum, secretes these modified proteins into fluid surrounding the cell, and forms glycoproteins and cell membranes. *Lysosomes* contain enzymes that break down recyclable cellular structures that are no longer needed by the cell. The **mitochondria** are the energy-producing factories of the cells. A mitochondrion has an outer membrane and an inner membrane, with an intermembrane space between them. The fluid section surrounded by the inner membrane is called the *matrix*. Enzymes located in the matrix and along the inner membrane catalyze the oxidation of carbohydrates, fats, and amino acids. All of these oxidation pathways eventually produce CO_2, H_2O, and energy, which are used to form energy-rich compounds. Table 22.1 summarizes some of the functions of the cellular components in animal cells.

TABLE 22.1 Locations and Functions of Components in Animal Cells

Component	Description and Function
Cell membrane	Separates the contents of a cell from the external environment and contains structures that communicate with other cells
Cytoplasm	Consists of all of the cellular contents between the cell membrane and nucleus
Cytosol	Is the fluid part of the cytoplasm that contains enzymes for many of the cell's chemical reactions including glycolysis, and glucose and fatty acid synthesis
Endoplasmic reticulum	Rough type processes proteins for secretion and synthesizes phospholipids; smooth type synthesizes fats and steroids
Golgi complex	Modifies and secretes proteins from the endoplasmic reticulum and synthesizes cell membranes
Lysosome	Contains hydrolytic enzymes that digest and recycle old cell structures
Mitochondrion	Contains the structures for the synthesis of ATP from energy-producing reactions
Nucleus	Contains genetic information for the replication of DNA and the synthesis of protein
Ribosome	Is the site of protein synthesis using mRNA templates

CONCEPT CHECK 22.1 **Metabolism and Cell Structure**

Identify each of the following as a catabolic or an anabolic reaction:

a. digestion of polysaccharides
b. synthesis of proteins
c. oxidation of glucose to CO_2 and H_2O

ANSWER

a. The breakdown of large molecules involves catabolic reactions.
b. The synthesis of large molecules requires energy and involves anabolic reactions.
c. The breakdown of monomers such as glucose involves catabolic reactions.

QUESTIONS AND PROBLEMS

22.1 Metabolism and Cell Structure

LEARNING GOAL: Describe three stages of metabolism.

22.1 What stage of metabolism involves the digestion of polysaccharides?

22.2 What stage of metabolism involves the conversion of small molecules to CO_2, H_2O, and energy for the synthesis of ATP?

22.3 What is meant by a catabolic reaction in metabolism?

22.4 What is meant by an anabolic reaction in metabolism?

22.5 Match each of the following with its function in the cell: (1) lysosome, (2) Golgi complex, (3) smooth endoplasmic reticulum.
a. synthesis of fats and steroids
b. contains hydrolytic enzymes
c. modifies products from rough endoplasmic reticulum

22.6 Match each of the following with its function in the cell: (1) mitochondria, (2) rough endoplasmic reticulum, (3) cell membrane.
a. separates cell contents from external environment
b. sites of energy production
c. synthesizes proteins for secretion

22.2 ATP and Energy

In our cells, the energy released from the oxidation of the food we eat is stored in the form of a "high-energy" compound called *adenosine triphosphate* (abbreviated as ATP). As we saw in Section 21.1, the **ATP** molecule is composed of the base adenine, a ribose sugar, and three phosphate groups (see Figure 22.3).

TUTORIAL
ATP: Energy Storage

SELF-STUDY ACTIVITY
ATP

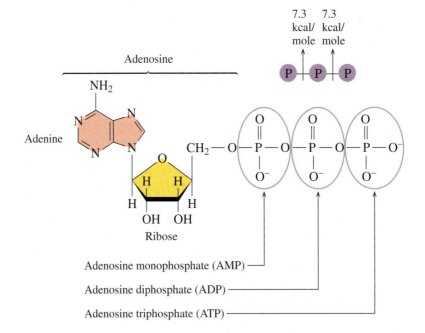

FIGURE 22.3 Adenosine triphosphate (ATP) hydrolyzes to form ADP and AMP, along with a release of energy.

Q How much energy is released when a phosphate group is cleaved from one mole of ATP?

Hydrolysis of ATP Yields Energy

One of the most important "high-energy" compounds is ATP, which undergoes hydrolysis to provide energy and the products adenosine diphosphate (**ADP**) and HPO_4^{2-}, an inorganic phosphate group abbreviated as P_i. One mole of ATP can provide 7.3 kcal/mole of ATP (31 kJ/mole of ATP).

$$ATP^{4-} + H_2O \longrightarrow ADP^{3-} + HPO_4^{2-} + H^+ + 7.3 \text{ kcal/mole (31 kJ/mole)}$$

However, in this text, we often write this equation in an abbreviated form.

$$ATP \longrightarrow ADP + P_i + 7.3 \text{ kcal/mole (31 kJ/mole)}$$

The ADP can also hydrolyze to form adenosine monophosphate (AMP) and an inorganic phosphate (P_i). The abbreviated equation is written as follows:

$$ADP \longrightarrow AMP + P_i + 7.3 \text{ kcal/mole (31 kJ/mole)}$$

Every time we contract muscles, move substances across cellular membranes, send nerve signals, or synthesize an enzyme, we use energy from the hydrolysis of ATP. In a cell that is doing work (anabolic processes), 1–2 million ATP molecules may be hydrolyzed in one second. The amount of ATP hydrolyzed in one day can be as much as our body mass, even though only about 1 gram of ATP is present in all our cells at any given time.

When we take in food, the resulting catabolic reactions provide energy to regenerate ATP in our cells. Then 7.3 kcal/mole (31 kJ/mole) is used to make ATP from ADP and P_i (see Figure 22.4).

$$ADP + P_i + 7.3 \text{ kcal/mole (31 kJ/mole)} \longrightarrow ATP$$

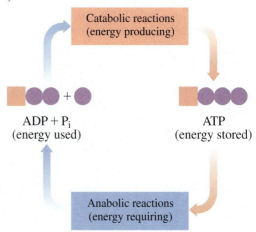

FIGURE 22.4 ATP, the energy-storage molecule, links energy-producing reactions with energy-requiring reactions in the cells.

Q What type of reaction provides energy for ATP synthesis?

ATP Drives Reactions

The pairing of a reaction that requires energy with a reaction that supplies energy is a very important concept in biochemistry. Many of the reactions essential to a cell do not proceed spontaneously, but they can be made to proceed by pairing them with a reaction that releases energy for their use.

ATP and other energy-rich compounds are often paired with energy-requiring reactions. For example, the glucose obtained from carbohydrates must add a phosphate group to start its breakdown in the cell. However, the energy needed to add a phosphate group to glucose is 3.3 kcal/mole (14 kJ/mole), which means that the reaction does not occur spontaneously. When the energy-requiring reaction is paired with the hydrolysis of ATP, sufficient energy is available to make the energy-requiring reaction take place.

ATP	$\longrightarrow$ ADP + P_i + 7.3 kcal/mole (31 kJ/mole)	Provides energy
Glucose + P_i + 3.3 kcal/mole (14 kJ/mole)	$\longrightarrow$ glucose-6-phosphate	Requires energy
ATP + Glucose	$\longrightarrow$ ADP + glucose-6-phosphate + 4.0 kcal/mole (17 kJ/mole)	

Chemistry Link to Health

ATP ENERGY AND Ca^{2+} NEEDED TO CONTRACT MUSCLES

Our muscles consist of thousands of parallel fibers. Within these muscle fibers are filaments composed of two kinds of proteins, myosin and actin. Arranged in alternating rows, the thick filaments of the protein myosin overlap the thin filaments containing the protein actin. During a muscle contraction, the thin filaments (actin) slide inward over the thick filaments (myosin), which shortens the muscle fibers.

Calcium ion (Ca^{2+}) and ATP play an important role in muscle contraction. An increase in the Ca^{2+} concentration in the muscle fibers causes the filaments to slide, while a decrease stops the process. In a relaxed muscle, the Ca^{2+} concentration is low. When a nerve impulse reaches the muscle, the calcium channels in the membrane open to allow Ca^{2+} to flow into the fluid surrounding the muscle filaments. The muscle contracts as myosin binds to actin and pulls the filaments inward. The energy for the contraction is provided by the hydrolysis of ATP to ADP + P_i.

Muscle contraction continues as long as both ATP and Ca^{2+} levels are high around the filaments. When the nerve impulse ends, the calcium channels close. The Ca^{2+} concentration decreases as energy from ATP pumps the remaining Ca^{2+} out of the filaments, which causes the muscle to relax. In rigor mortis, Ca^{2+} concentration remains high within the muscle fibers, causing a continued state of rigidity. After approximately 72 hours, Ca^{2+} decreases due to cellular deterioration, and the muscles relax.

Muscle contraction uses the energy from the breakdown of ATP.

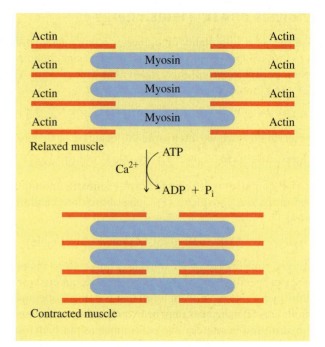

Muscles contract when myosin binds to actin.

QUESTIONS AND PROBLEMS

22.2 ATP and Energy

LEARNING GOAL: *Describe the structure of ATP and its role in catabolic and anabolic reactions.*

22.7 Why is ATP considered an energy-rich compound?

22.8 What is meant when we say that the hydrolysis of ATP is used to "drive" a reaction?

22.9 Phosphoenolpyruvate (PEP) is a high-energy compound that releases 14.8 kcal/mole of energy when it hydrolyzes to pyruvate and P_i. This reaction can be combined with the synthesis of ATP from ADP and P_i.
  a. Write an equation for the energy-releasing reaction of PEP.
  b. Write an equation for the energy-requiring reaction that forms ATP.
  c. Write the overall equation for the combined reaction including the net energy change.

22.10 The phosphorylation of glycerol to glycerol-3-phosphate requires 2.2 kcal/mole and is driven by the hydrolysis of ATP.
  a. Write an equation for the energy-releasing reaction of ATP.
  b. Write an equation for the energy-requiring reaction that forms glycerol-3-phosphate.
  c. Write the overall equation for the combined reaction including the net energy change.

22.3 Important Coenzymes in Metabolic Pathways

The metabolic reactions that extract energy from our food involve oxidation and reduction reactions. Therefore, we will review several important coenzymes in their oxidized and reduced forms. As we discussed in Section 6.3, an *oxidation* reaction involves the loss of hydrogen or electrons by a substance, or an increase in the number of bonds to oxygen. When an enzyme catalyzes an oxidation reaction, hydrogen atoms are removed from a substrate as hydrogen ions, $2H^+$, and electrons, $2\,e^-$.

$$\text{2H atoms (removed in oxidation)} \longrightarrow 2H^+ + 2\,e^-$$

Reduction is the gain of hydrogen ions and electrons or a decrease in the number of bonds to oxygen. When hydrogen ions and electrons are picked up by a coenzyme, it is reduced. Table 22.2 summarizes the characteristics of oxidation and reduction.

Oxidation: Loss of H, loss of e^-, or increase in number of bonds to O

$$CH_3-CH_3 \xrightarrow{[O]} CH_3-CH_2-OH \xrightarrow{[O]} CH_3-\overset{\overset{\displaystyle O}{\|}}{C}-H \xrightarrow{[O]} CH_3-\overset{\overset{\displaystyle O}{\|}}{C}-OH$$

Alkane   Alcohol (1°)   Aldehyde   Carboxylic acid

$$CH_3-CH_2-CH_3 \xrightarrow{[O]} CH_3-\overset{\overset{\displaystyle OH}{|}}{CH}-CH_3 \xrightarrow{[O]} CH_3-\overset{\overset{\displaystyle O}{\|}}{C}-CH_3$$

Alkane   Alcohol (2°)   Ketone

Reduction: Gain of H, gain of e^-, or decrease in number of bonds to O

TABLE 22.2 Characteristics of Oxidation and Reduction in Metabolic Pathways

Oxidation	Reduction
Loss of electrons	Gain of electrons
Loss of hydrogen	Gain of hydrogen
Gain of oxygen	Loss of oxygen
Increase number of bonds to oxygen	Decrease in number of bonds to oxygen

NAD^+

NAD^+ (nicotinamide adenine dinucleotide) is an important coenzyme in which the vitamin *niacin* provides the *nicotinamide* group, which is bonded to ribose and adenosine diphosphate (ADP) (see Figure 22.5). The oxidized form of NAD^+ undergoes reduction when a carbon in the nicotinamide ring reacts with one hydrogen ion and two electrons, leaving one H^+.

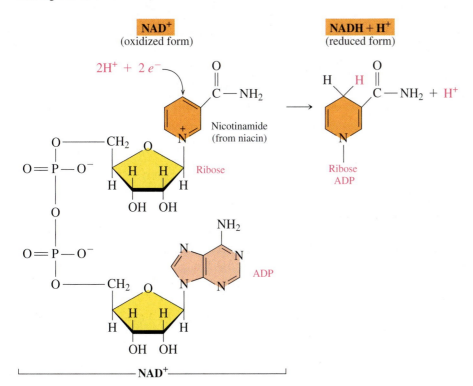

FIGURE 22.5 The coenzyme NAD^+ (nicotinamide adenine dinucleotide), which consists of adenosine diphosphate, nicotinamide from the vitamin niacin, and ribose, is reduced to NADH + H^+.

Q Why is the conversion of NAD^+ to NADH and H^+ called a reduction?

The NAD$^+$ coenzyme is required for reactions that produce carbon–oxygen (C=O) double bonds, such as the oxidation of alcohols to aldehydes and ketones. An example of an oxidation–reduction reaction that utilizes NAD$^+$ is the oxidation of ethanol in the liver to ethanal and NADH.

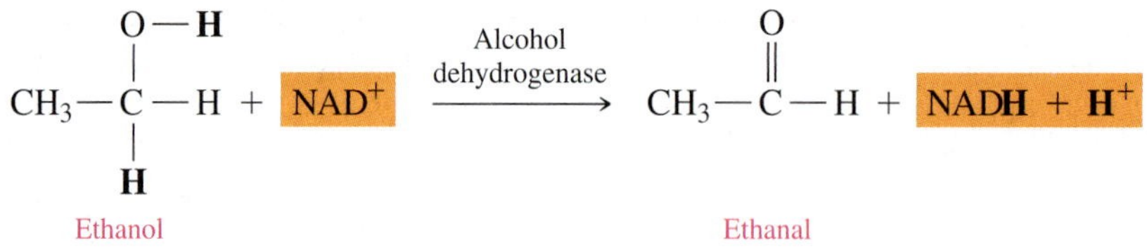

Ethanol   Ethanal

FAD

FAD (flavin adenine dinucleotide) is a coenzyme that contains adenosine diphosphate (ADP) and riboflavin. Riboflavin, also known as vitamin B$_2$, consists of ribitol (a sugar alcohol) and flavin. The oxidized form of FAD undergoes reduction when the two nitrogen atoms in the flavin part of the FAD coenzyme react with two hydrogen atoms, reducing FAD to FADH$_2$ (see Figure 22.6).

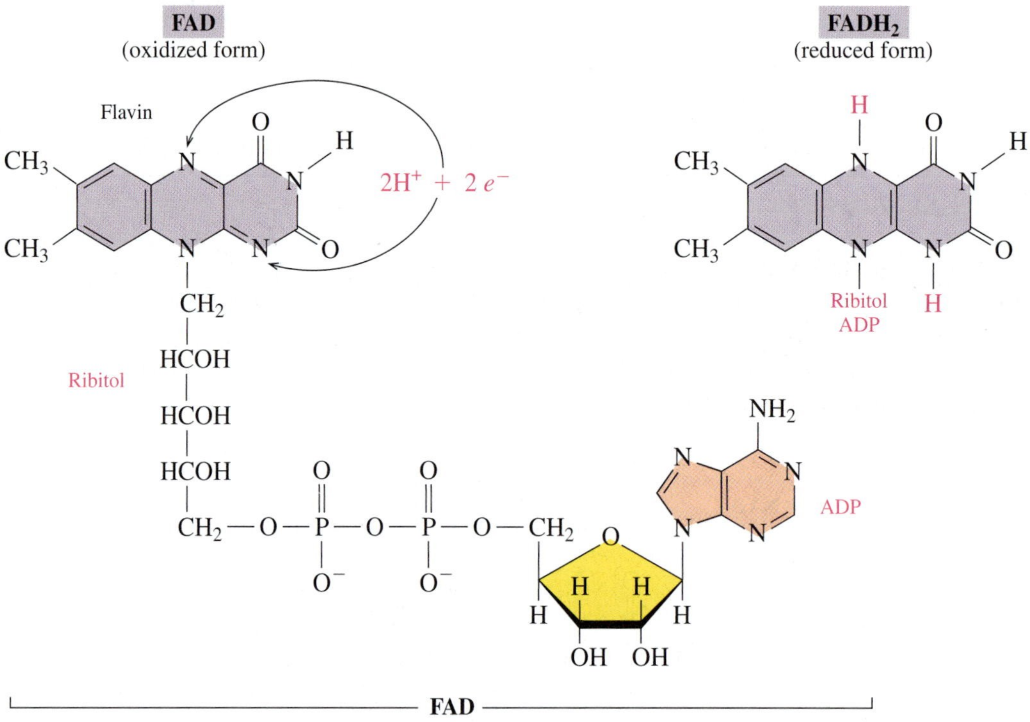

FIGURE 22.6 The coenzyme FAD (flavin adenine dinucleotide) made from riboflavin (vitamin B$_2$) and adenosine diphosphate is reduced to FADH$_2$.

Q What is the type of reaction in which FAD accepts hydrogen?

FAD is used as a coenzyme when a dehydrogenation reaction converts a carbon–carbon single bond to a carbon–carbon (C=C) double bond. An example of a reaction in the citric acid cycle that utilizes FAD is the conversion of the carbon–carbon single bond in succinate to a double bond in fumarate and FADH$_2$.

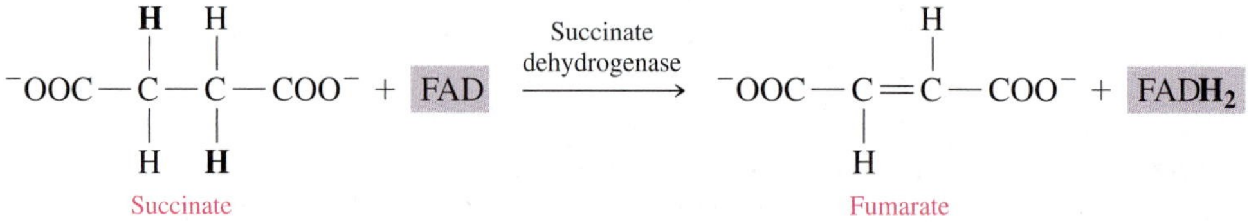

Succinate   Fumarate

Coenzyme A

Coenzyme A (CoA) is made up of several components: pantothenic acid (vitamin B_5), phosphorylated ADP, and aminoethanethiol (see Figure 22.7). An important function of coenzyme A is to prepare small acyl groups (represented by the letter A), such as acetyl, for reactions with enzymes. The reactive feature of coenzyme A is the thiol group ($-SH$), which bonds to a two-carbon acetyl group to produce the energy-rich thioester **acetyl-CoA**.

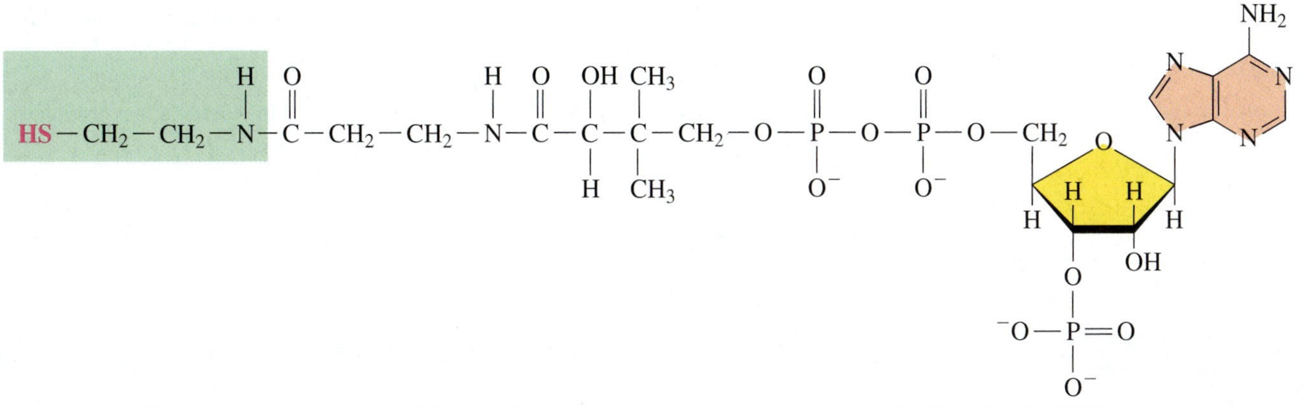

FIGURE 22.7 Coenzyme A is derived from a phosphorylated ADP and pantothenic acid bonded by an amide bond to aminoethanethiol, which contains the —SH reactive part of the molecule.
Q What part of coenzyme A reacts with a two-carbon acetyl group?

In biochemistry, several abbreviations are used for coenzyme A and the ester acetyl-coenzyme A. For discussions in this text, we will use CoA for coenzyme A and acetyl-CoA when the acetyl group is attached to the sulfur atom ($-S-$) in coenzyme A. In equations, we will show the $-SH$ group in coenzyme A as HS$-$CoA.

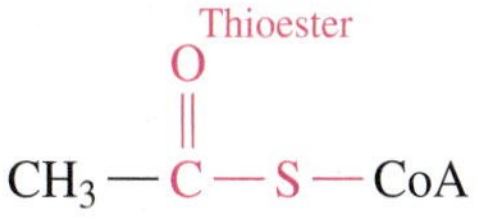

Types of Metabolic Reactions

Many reactions within the cells are similar to the types of reactions we looked at in organic chemistry such as hydration, dehydration, hydrogenation, oxidation, and reduction. Organic reactions typically require strong acids (low pH), high temperatures, and/or metallic catalysts. However, metabolic reactions take place at body temperature and physiological pH, which requires enzymes and often their coenzymes. Using the enzymes and coenzymes discussed in Sections 20.1, 20.2, and 20.6, we can summarize their association with metabolic reactions (see Table 22.3).

TABLE 22.3 Enzymes and Coenzymes in Metabolic Reactions

Reaction	Enzyme	Coenzyme
Oxidation	Dehydrogenase	NAD^+, FAD
Reduction	Dehydrogenase	$NADH + H^+$, $FADH_2$
Hydration	Hydrase	
Dehydration	Dehydrase	
Rearrangement	Isomerase	
Transfer of phosphate group	Transferase, kinase	ATP, GDP, ADP
Transfer of acetyl group	Acetyl-CoA transferase	CoA
Decarboxylation	Decarboxylase	
Hydrolysis	Hydrolase, protease, lipase	

SAMPLE PROBLEM 22.1 **Coenzymes**

Describe the reactive part of each of the following coenzymes and the way each participates in metabolic pathways:

a. FAD
b. NAD$^+$

ANSWER

a. When two nitrogen atoms in the flavin accept 2H$^+$ and 2 e^-, FAD is reduced to FADH$_2$. FAD is the coenzyme in oxidation reactions that produce a carbon–carbon (C=C) double bond.
b. When a carbon atom in the pyridine ring of nicotinamide accepts H$^+$ and 2 e^-, NAD$^+$ is reduced to NADH. The NAD$^+$ coenzyme participates in reactions that produce a carbon–oxygen (C=O) double bond.

STUDY CHECK 22.1

Describe the reactive part of coenzyme A and how it participates in metabolic reactions.

QUESTIONS AND PROBLEMS

22.3 Important Coenzymes in Metabolic Pathways

LEARNING GOAL: Describe the components and functions of the coenzymes FAD, NAD$^+$, and coenzyme A.

22.11 Identify one or more coenzymes with each of the following components:
  a. pantothenic acid
  b. niacin
  c. ribitol

22.12 Identify one or more coenzymes with each of the following components:
  a. riboflavin
  b. adenine
  c. aminoethanethiol

22.13 Give the abbreviation for each of the following:
  a. the reduced form of NAD$^+$
  b. the oxidized form of FADH$_2$

22.14 Give the abbreviation for each of the following:
  a. the reduced form of FAD
  b. the oxidized form of NADH

22.15 What coenzyme picks up hydrogen when a carbon–carbon double bond is formed?

22.16 What coenzyme picks up hydrogen when a carbon–oxygen double bond is formed?

LEARNING GOAL

Give the sites and products of the digestion of carbohydrates.

TUTORIAL
Breakdown of Carbohydrates

22.4 Digestion of Carbohydrates

In stage 1 of catabolism, foods undergo *digestion*, a process that converts large molecules to smaller ones that can be absorbed by the body.

Digestion of Carbohydrates

We begin the digestion of carbohydrates as soon as we chew food. Enzymes produced in the salivary glands hydrolyze some of the α-glycosidic bonds in amylose and amylopectin, producing maltose, glucose, and smaller polysaccharides called dextrins, which contain three to eight glucose units. After swallowing, the partially digested starches enter the acidic environment of the stomach, where the low pH soon stops further carbohydrate digestion (see Figure 22.8).

Mouth

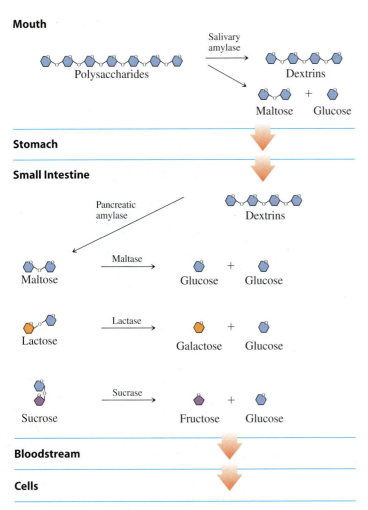

Stomach

Small Intestine

Bloodstream

Cells

FIGURE 22.8 In stage 1 of catabolic metabolism, the digestion of carbohydrates begins in the mouth and is completed in the small intestine.

Q Why is there little or no digestion of carbohydrates in the stomach?

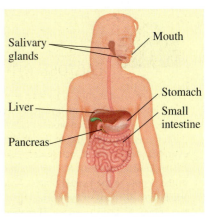

Carbohydrates begin digestion in the mouth, proteins in the stomach, and lipids in the small intestine.

Explore Your World

CARBOHYDRATE DIGESTION

1. Obtain a cracker or small piece of bread and chew it for 2–3 minutes. During that time observe any change in the taste.
2. Some milk products contain Lactaid, which is the lactase enzyme that digests lactose. Look for the brands of milk and ice cream that contain Lactaid or lactase enzyme.

QUESTIONS

1. **a.** How does the taste of the cracker or bread change after you have chewed it for 2–3 minutes? What could be an explanation for this change?
   b. What part of carbohydrate digestion occurs in the mouth?
2. **a.** Write an equation for the digestion of lactose.
   b. Where does lactose undergo digestion?

In the small intestine, which has a pH of about 8, enzymes produced in the pancreas hydrolyze the remaining dextrins to maltose and glucose. Then, enzymes produced in the mucosal cells that line the small intestine hydrolyze maltose, lactose, and sucrose. The resulting monosaccharides are absorbed through the intestinal wall into the bloodstream.

SAMPLE PROBLEM 22.2   **Digestion of Carbohydrates**

Indicate the carbohydrate that undergoes digestion in each of the following sites:

a. mouth
b. stomach
c. small intestine

SOLUTION

a. starches amylose and amylopectin (α-1,4-glycosidic bonds only)
b. essentially no digestion of carbohydrates
c. dextrins, maltose, sucrose, and lactose

STUDY CHECK 22.2

Describe the digestion of amylose, a polymer of glucose molecules joined by α-glycosidic bonds.

Chemistry Link to Health

LACTOSE INTOLERANCE

The disaccharide in milk is lactose, which is broken down by lactase in the intestinal tract to monosaccharides that are a source of energy. Infants and small children produce lactase to break down the lactose in milk. It is rare for an infant to lack the ability to produce lactase. However, the production of lactase decreases as many people age, which causes *lactose intolerance*. This condition affects approximately 25% of the people in the United States. A deficiency of lactase occurs in adults in many parts of the world, but in the United States, it is prevalent among African-American, Hispanic, and Asian populations.

When lactose is not broken down into glucose and galactose, it cannot be absorbed through the intestinal wall and remains in the intestinal tract. In the intestines, the lactose undergoes fermentation to products that include lactic acid and gases such as methane (CH_4) and CO_2. Symptoms of lactose intolerance, which appear approximately $\frac{1}{2}$ to 1 hour after ingesting milk or milk products, include nausea, abdominal cramps, and diarrhea. The severity of the symptoms depends on how much lactose is present in the food and how much lactase a person produces.

Treatment of Lactose Intolerance

One way to reduce the reaction to lactose is to avoid products that contain lactose, including milk and milk products such as cheese, butter, and ice cream. However, it is important to consume foods that provide the body with calcium. Many people with lactose intolerance seem to tolerate yogurt, which is a good source of calcium. Although there is lactose in yogurt, the bacteria in yogurt may produce some lactase, which helps to digest the lactose. A person who is lactose intolerant should also know that some foods that are not dairy

Lactaid contains an enzyme that aids the digestion of lactose.

products contain lactose. For example, baked goods, cereals, breakfast drinks, salad dressings, and even lunchmeat can contain lactose in their ingredients. You must read food labels carefully to see if the ingredients include "milk" or "lactose."

The enzyme lactase is now available in many forms, such as tablets that are taken with meals, drops that are added to milk, or as additives in many dairy products such as milk. When lactase is added to milk that is left in the refrigerator for 24 hours, the lactose level is reduced by 70–90%. Lactase pills or chewable tablets are taken when a person begins to eat a meal that contains dairy foods. If taken too far ahead of the meal, the lactase will be degraded by stomach acid. If taken following a meal, the lactose will have already entered the lower intestine.

QUESTIONS AND PROBLEMS

22.4 Digestion of Carbohydrates

LEARNING GOAL: *Give the sites and products of the digestion of carbohydrates.*

22.17 What is the general type of reaction that occurs during the digestion of carbohydrates?

22.18 Why is α-amylase produced in the salivary glands and in the pancreas?

22.19 Complete the following equations by filling in the missing words:
  a. _____ + H_2O ⟶ galactose + glucose
  b. Sucrose + H_2O ⟶ _____ + _____
  c. Maltose + H_2O ⟶ glucose + _____

22.20 Give the site and the enzyme for each of the reactions in Problem 22.19.

LEARNING GOAL

Describe the conversion of glucose to pyruvate in glycolysis.

22.5 Glycolysis: Oxidation of Glucose

The major source of energy for the body is the glucose produced when we digest the carbohydrates in our food or from glycogen, a polysaccharide stored in the liver and skeletal muscle. Glucose in the bloodstream enters our cells where it undergoes further degradation in a pathway called *glycolysis*. Early organisms used glycolysis to produce energy from simple nutrients long before there was any oxygen in Earth's atmosphere. Glycolysis is an **anaerobic** process; no oxygen is required.

In **glycolysis**, a six-carbon glucose molecule is broken down to yield two molecules of three-carbon pyruvate (see Figure 22.9). All the reactions in glycolysis take place in the cytoplasm of the cell where the enzymes for glycolysis are located. In the first five reactions (1–5), called the *energy-investing phase*, energy is obtained from the hydrolysis of two ATPs, which is needed to form sugar phosphates (see Figure 22.10). In reactions 4 and 5, a six-carbon sugar phosphate is split to yield two molecules of three-carbon sugar phosphate. In the last five reactions (6–10), called the *energy-generating phase*, energy is obtained from the hydrolysis of the energy-rich phosphate compounds and used to synthesize four ATPs.

SELF-STUDY ACTIVITY
Glycolysis

TUTORIAL
The Glycolysis Pathway

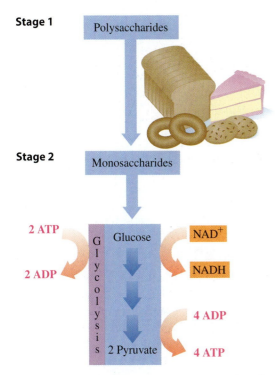

FIGURE 22.9 Glucose obtained from the digestion of polysaccharides is degraded in glycolysis to give pyruvate.

Q What is the end product of glycolysis?

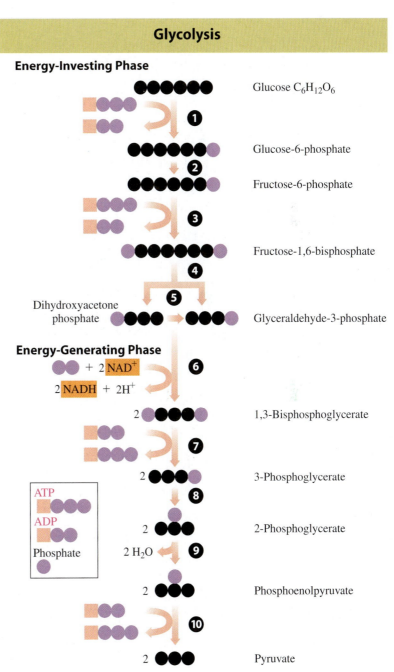

FIGURE 22.10 In glycolysis, the six-carbon glucose molecule is degraded to yield two three-carbon pyruvate molecules. A net of two ATPs are produced along with two NADHs.

Q Where in the glycolysis pathway is glucose cleaved to yield two three-carbon compounds?

Energy-Investing Reactions: 1–5

Reaction 1 Phosphorylation

In the initial reaction, a phosphate group from ATP is added to glucose to form glucose-6-phosphate and ADP.

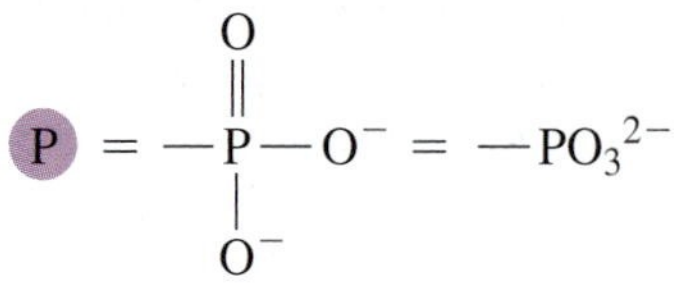

$$P = -\overset{\overset{\displaystyle O}{\|}}{\underset{\underset{\displaystyle O^-}{|}}{P}} - O^- = -PO_3^{2-}$$

Glucose

ATP
Hexokinase ❶
ADP

Glucose-6-phosphate
$+ \, H^+$

Reaction 2 Isomerization

The glucose-6-phosphate, the aldose from reaction 1, undergoes isomerization to fructose-6-phosphate, which is a ketose.

Phosphoglucose isomerase ❷

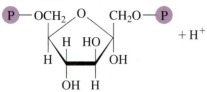

Fructose-6-phosphate

ATP
Phosphofructokinase ❸
ADP

Reaction 3 Phosphorylation

The hydrolysis of another ATP provides a second phosphate group, which converts fructose-6-phosphate to fructose-1,6-bisphosphate. The word *bisphosphate* is used to show that the two phosphate groups are on different carbons in fructose and not connected to each other.

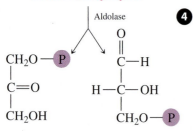

Fructose-1,6-bisphosphate
$+ \, H^+$

Aldolase ❹

Reaction 4 Cleavage

Fructose-1,6-bisphosphate is split into two three-carbon phosphate isomers: dihydroxyacetone phosphate and glyceraldehyde-3-phosphate.

Dihydroxyacetone phosphate   Glyceraldehyde-3-phosphate

Triose phosphate isomerase ❺

Reaction 5 Isomerization

Because dihydroxyacetone phosphate is a ketone, it cannot react further. However, it undergoes isomerization to provide a second molecule of glyceraldehyde-3-phosphate, which can be oxidized. Now all six carbon atoms from glucose are contained in two identical triose phosphates.

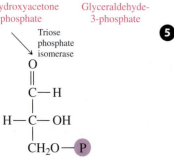

Glyceraldehyde-3-phosphate

Energy-Generating Reactions: 6–10

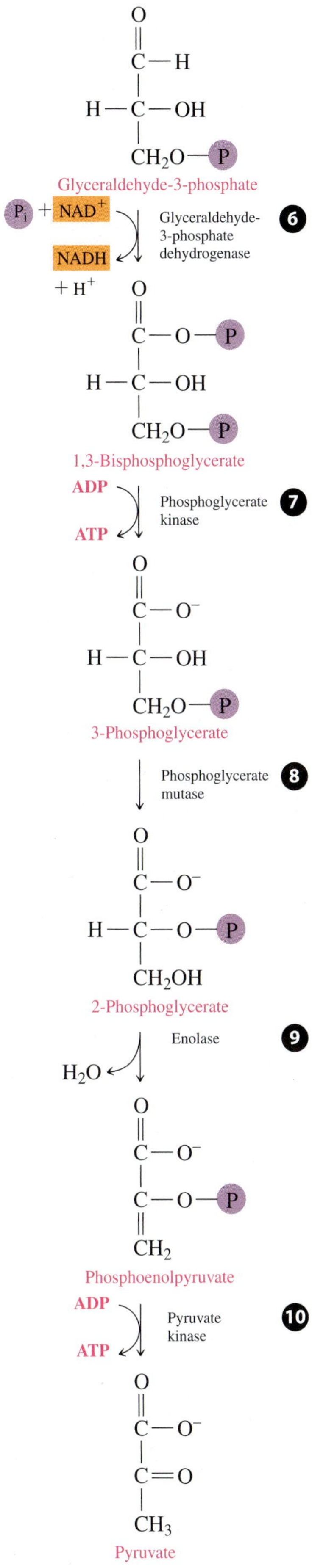

Reaction 6 Oxidation and Phosphorylation

The aldehyde group of each glyceraldehyde-3-phosphate is oxidized to a carboxyl group by the coenzyme NAD$^+$, which is reduced to NADH and H$^+$. A phosphate group adds to the new carboxyl groups to form two molecules of the high-energy compound, 1,3-bisphosphoglycerate.

Reaction 7 Phosphate Transfer

A phosphorylation transfers a phosphate group from each 1,3-bisphosphoglycerate to ADP to produce two molecules of the high-energy compound ATP. At this point in glycolysis, two ATPs are produced, which balance the two ATPs consumed in reactions 1 and 3.

Reaction 8 Isomerization

Two 3-phosphoglycerate molecules undergo isomerization, which moves the phosphate group from carbon 3 to carbon 2, yielding two molecules of 2-phosphoglycerate.

Reaction 9 Dehydration

Each of the phosphoglycerate molecules undergoes dehydration (loss of water) to give two high-energy molecules of phosphoenolpyruvate.

Reaction 10 Phosphate Transfer

In a second direct substrate phosphorylation, phosphate groups from two phosphoenol-pyruvates are transferred to two ADPs to form two pyruvates and two ATPs.

Other Hexoses Enter Glycolysis

Other monosaccharides such as fructose and galactose can enter glycolysis, but first they must be converted to intermediates that can enter into the pathway. In the muscles and kidneys, fructose is phosphorylated to fructose-6-phosphate, which enters glycolysis in reaction 3. In the liver, fructose is converted to glyceraldehyde-3-phosphate, which enters glycolysis at reaction 6. Galactose reacts with ATP to yield galactose-1-phosphate, which is converted to glucose-6-phosphate, which can enter glycolysis at reaction 2.

Summary of Glycolysis

In the glycolysis pathway, a six-carbon glucose molecule is converted to two three-carbon pyruvates. Initially, two ATPs are required to form fructose-1,6-bisphosphate. In later reactions (7 and 10), phosphate transfers produce a total of four ATPs. Overall, glycolysis yields two ATPs and two NADHs when a glucose molecule is converted to two pyruvates.

$$C_6H_{12}O_6 + 2NAD^+ \xrightarrow{\quad 2ADP + 2P_i \quad 2ATP \quad} 2CH_3-\overset{\overset{\displaystyle O}{\|}}{C}-COO^- + 2NADH + 4H^+$$

Glucose   Pyruvate

It appears right now that glycolysis does a lot of work to produce only two ATPs, two NADHs, and two pyruvates. However, under aerobic conditions, stage 3 operates to reoxidize NADH to produce more ATP, and pyruvate is converted to acetyl-CoA, which enters the citric acid cycle where it generates considerably more energy. We will look at the oxidative pathways of stage 3 in Chapter 23.

CONCEPT CHECK 22.2   **Glycolysis**

What are the reactions in glycolysis that generate ATP?

ANSWER

ATP is produced when phosphate groups are transferred directly to ADP from 1,3-bisphosphoglycerate (reaction 7) and from phosphoenolpyruvate (reaction 10).

SAMPLE PROBLEM 22.3   **Reactions in Glycolysis**

Identify each of the following reactions as an isomerization, phosphorylation, dehydration, or cleavage:

a. a phosphate group is transferred to ADP to form ATP
b. 3-phosphoglycerate is converted to 2-phosphoglycerate
c. water is lost from 2-phosphoglycerate

SOLUTION

a. Phosphorylation involves the transfer of a phosphate group to ADP to form ATP.
b. The change in location of a phosphate group on a carbon chain is isomerization.
c. The loss of water is dehydration.

STUDY CHECK 22.3

Identify the reaction in which fructose-1,6-bisphosphate splits to form two three-carbon compounds as an isomerization, phosphorylation, dehydration, or cleavage.

Regulation of Glycolysis

Metabolic pathways such as glycolysis do not run at the same rates all the time. The amount of glucose that is broken down is controlled by the requirements in the cells for pyruvate, ATP, and other intermediates of glycolysis. Within the glycolysis sequence, three enzymes respond to the levels of ATP and other products.

Reaction 1 Hexokinase

The amount of glucose entering the glycolysis pathway decreases when high levels of glucose-6-phosphate are present in the cell. This phosphorylation product inhibits hexokinase, which prevents glucose from reacting with ATP. This inhibition of the first enzyme in a pathway is an example of feedback control, which is a type of enzyme regulation we discussed in Chapter 20.

Reaction 3 Phosphofructokinase

The reaction catalyzed by phosphofructokinase is a very important control point for glycolysis. Once fructose-1,6-bisphosphate is formed, it must continue through the remaining reactions to pyruvate. As an allosteric enzyme, phosphofructokinase is inhibited by high levels of ATP and activated by high levels of ADP and AMP. High levels of ADP and AMP indicate that the cell has used up much of its ATP. As a regulator, phosphofructokinase increases the rate of pyruvate production for ATP synthesis when the cell needs to replenish ATP, and slows or stops the reaction when ATP is plentiful.

Reaction 10 Pyruvate Kinase

In the last reaction of glycolysis, high levels of ATP as well as acetyl-CoA inhibit pyruvate kinase, which is another allosteric enzyme.

Summary of Regulation

Reactions 1, 3, and 10 are examples of how metabolic pathways shut off enzymes to stop the production of molecules that are not needed. Pyruvate, which can be used to synthesize ATP, responds to ATP levels in the cell. When ATP levels are high, enzymes in glycolysis slow or stop the synthesis of pyruvate. With phosphofructokinase and pyruvate kinase inhibited by ATP, glucose-6-phosphate accumulates and inhibits reaction 1, and glucose does not enter the glycolysis pathway. The glycolysis pathway is shut down until ATP is once again needed in the cell. When ATP levels are low or AMP/ADP levels are high, these enzymes are activated and pyruvate production starts again.

CONCEPT CHECK 22.3   **Regulation of Glycolysis**

How is glycolysis regulated by each of the following enzymes?

a. hexokinase   **b.** phosphofructokinase   **c.** pyruvate kinase

ANSWER

a. High levels of glucose-6-phosphate inhibit hexokinase, which stops the addition of a phosphate group to glucose in reaction 1.

b. Phosphofructokinase, which catalyzes the formation of fructose-1,6-bisphosphate, is inhibited by high levels of ATP, and activated by high levels of ADP and AMP.

c. High levels of ATP or acetyl-CoA inhibit pyruvate kinase, which stops the formation of pyruvate in reaction 10.

QUESTIONS AND PROBLEMS

22.5 Glycolysis: Oxidation of Glucose

LEARNING GOAL: *Describe the conversion of glucose to pyruvate in glycolysis.*

22.21 What is the starting compound of glycolysis?

22.22 What is the three-carbon product of glycolysis?

22.23 How is ATP used in the initial steps of glycolysis?

22.24 How many ATP molecules are used in the initial steps of glycolysis?

22.25 What three-carbon intermediates are obtained when fructose-1,6-bisphosphate splits?

22.26 Why does one of the three-carbon intermediates undergo isomerization?

22.27 How does substrate phosphorylation account for the production of ATP in glycolysis?

22.28 Why are there two ATP molecules formed for one molecule of glucose?

22.29 Indicate the enzyme(s) that catalyze(s) each of the following reactions in glycolysis:
  a. phosphorylation
  b. direct transfer of a phosphate group

22.30 Indicate the enzyme(s) that catalyze(s) each of the following reactions in glycolysis:
  a. isomerization
  b. formation of a three-carbon ketone and a three-carbon aldehyde

22.31 How many ATP or NADH are produced (or required) in each of the following steps in glycolysis?
  a. glucose to glucose-6-phosphate
  b. glyceraldehyde-3-phosphate to 1,3-bisphosphoglycerate
  c. glucose to pyruvate

22.32 How many ATP or NADH are produced (or required) in each of the following steps in glycolysis?
  a. 1,3-bisphosphoglycerate to 3-phosphoglycerate
  b. fructose-6-phosphate to fructose-1,6-bisphosphate
  c. phosphoenolpyruvate to pyruvate

22.33 Which step(s) in glycolysis involve(s) the following?
  a. The first ATP molecule is hydrolyzed.
  b. Direct substrate phosphorylation occurs.
  c. Six-carbon sugar splits into two three-carbon molecules.

22.34 Which step(s) in glycolysis involve(s) the following?
  a. Isomerization takes place.
  b. NAD^+ is reduced.
  c. A second ATP molecule is synthesized.

22.35 How do galactose and fructose, obtained from the digestion of carbohydrates, enter glycolysis?

22.36 What are three enzymes that regulate glycolysis?

22.37 Indicate whether each of the following would activate or inhibit phosphofructokinase:
  a. low levels of ATP   **b.** high levels of ATP

22.38 Indicate whether each of the following would activate or inhibit pyruvate kinase:
  a. low levels of ATP   **b.** high levels of ATP

22.6 Pathways for Pyruvate

The pyruvate produced from glucose can now enter pathways that continue to extract energy. The available pathway depends on whether there is sufficient oxygen in the cell. During **aerobic** conditions, oxygen is available to convert pyruvate to acetyl-coenzyme A (acetyl-CoA). When oxygen levels are low, pyruvate is reduced to lactate. In yeast cells, which are anaerobic, pyruvate is converted to ethanol.

Aerobic Conditions

In glycolysis, two ATP molecules were generated when one glucose molecule was converted to two pyruvates. However, much more energy is obtained from glucose when oxygen levels are high in the cells. Under these aerobic conditions, pyruvate moves from the cytoplasm into the mitochondria to be oxidized further. In a complex reaction, pyruvate is oxidized, and a carbon atom is removed from pyruvate as CO_2. The coenzyme NAD^+ is reduced during the oxidation. The resulting two-carbon acetyl compound is attached to CoA, producing acetyl-CoA, an important intermediate in many metabolic pathways (see Figure 22.11).

$$CH_3-\overset{\overset{O}{\|}}{C}-\overset{\overset{O}{\|}}{C}-O^- + HS-CoA + \boxed{NAD^+} \xrightarrow{\text{Pyruvate dehydrogenase}} CH_3-\overset{\overset{O}{\|}}{C}-S-CoA + CO_2 + \boxed{NADH}$$

Pyruvate   Acetyl-CoA

Anaerobic Conditions

When we engage in strenuous exercise, the oxygen stored in our muscle cells is quickly depleted. Under anaerobic conditions, pyruvate remains in the cytoplasm where it is reduced to lactate. NAD^+ is produced and used to oxidize more glyceraldehyde-3-phosphate in the glycolysis pathway, which produces a small but needed amount of ATP.

$$CH_3-\overset{\overset{O}{\|}}{C}-\overset{\overset{O}{\|}}{C}-O^- \underset{\text{Lactate dehydrogenase}}{\overset{\boxed{NADH} + H^+ \quad \boxed{NAD^+}}{\rightleftharpoons}} CH_3-\overset{\overset{OH}{|}}{\underset{\underset{H}{|}}{C}}-\overset{\overset{O}{\|}}{C}-O^-$$

Pyruvate   Lactate
(oxidized)   (reduced)

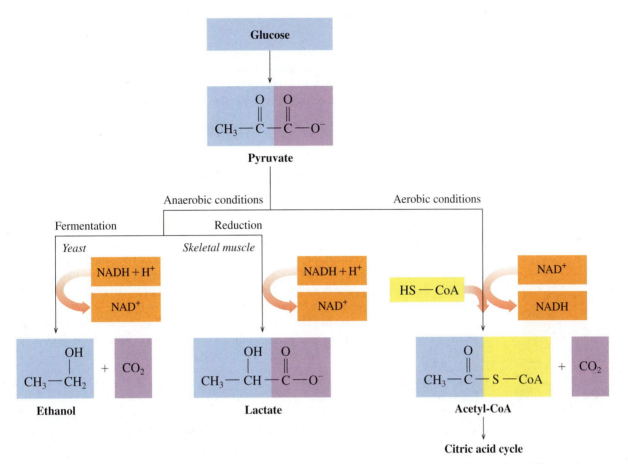

FIGURE 22.11 Pyruvate is converted to acetyl-CoA under aerobic conditions and to lactate or ethanol (in certain microorganisms) under anaerobic conditions.

Q During vigorous exercise, why does lactate accumulate in the muscles?

The accumulation of lactate causes the muscles to tire rapidly and become sore. After exercise, a person continues to breathe rapidly to repay the *oxygen debt* incurred during exercise. Most of the lactate is transported to the liver, where it is converted back into pyruvate. Under anaerobic conditions, the only ATP production in glycolysis occurs during the steps that phosphorylate ADP directly, giving a net gain of only two ATP molecules.

$$C_6H_{12}O_6 + 2ADP + 2P_i \longrightarrow 2CH_3-\overset{\overset{\displaystyle OH}{|}}{CH}-COO^- + 2ATP$$

Glucose   Lactate

Bacteria also convert pyruvate to lactate under anaerobic conditions. In the preparation of kimchee and sauerkraut, cabbage is covered with salt brine. The glucose obtained from the starches in the cabbage is converted to lactate. This acid environment acts as a preservative that prevents the growth of other bacteria. The pickling of olives and cucumbers gives similar products. When cultures of bacteria that produce lactate are added to milk, the acid denatures the milk proteins to give sour cream and yogurt.

After vigorous exercise, rapid breathing helps to repay the oxygen debt.

CONCEPT CHECK 22.4   **Pathways for Pyruvate**

When is pyruvate converted to each of the following?

a. acetyl-CoA   **b.** lactate

ANSWER

a. Pyruvate is converted to acetyl-CoA and NADH under aerobic conditions. The NADH must be oxidized back to NAD$^+$ to allow glycolysis to continue.

b. Pyruvate is converted to lactate and NAD$^+$ under anaerobic conditions, which provides NAD$^+$ for glycolysis.

Fermentation

Some microorganisms, particularly yeast, convert sugars to ethanol under anaerobic conditions by a process called **fermentation**. After pyruvate is formed in glycolysis, a carbon atom is removed in the form of CO_2 (**decarboxylation**). The NAD^+ for continued glycolysis is regenerated when the ethanal is reduced to ethanol.

$$CH_3-\overset{O}{\underset{}{C}}-\overset{O}{\underset{}{C}}-O^- + H^+ \xrightarrow[\text{decarboxylase}]{\text{Pyruvate}} CH_3-\overset{O}{\underset{}{C}}-H \xrightarrow[\text{Alcohol dehydrogenase}]{NADH + H^+ \quad NAD^+} CH_3-\overset{H}{\underset{H}{C}}-OH$$

Pyruvate CO_2 Ethanal   Ethanol

Beer is produced by the fermentation of pyruvate from barley malt, which gives carbon dioxide and ethanol.

The process of fermentation by yeast is one of the oldest known chemical reactions. Enzymes in the yeast convert the sugars in a variety of carbohydrate sources to glucose and then to ethanol. The evolution of CO_2 gas produces bubbles in beer, sparkling wines, and champagne. The type of carbohydrate used determines the taste associated with a particular alcoholic beverage. Beer is made from the fermentation of barley malt, wine and champagne from the sugars in grapes, vodka from potatoes or grain, sake from rice, and whiskeys from corn or rye. Fermentation produces solutions up to about 15% alcohol by volume. At this concentration, the alcohol kills the yeast, and fermentation stops.

SAMPLE PROBLEM 22.4   Fermentation of Pyruvate

In the production of wine, the fermentation process converts pyruvate to acetaldehyde (ethanal), which is converted to ethanol using NADH and H^+. Using pyruvate $(C_3H_3O_3^-) + H^+$ as the starting reactants, write the balanced chemical equations. How does fermentation supply NAD^+?

SOLUTION

Fermentation takes place under anaerobic conditions. Pyruvate $(C_3H_3O_3^-)$ undergoes decarboxylation to acetaldehyde (ethanal) (C_2H_4O), which is reduced by NADH and H^+ to ethanol (C_2H_6O) and NAD^+.

$$C_3H_3O_3^- + H^+ \longrightarrow C_2H_4O + CO_2$$
$$C_2H_4O + NADH + H^+ \longrightarrow C_2H_6O + NAD^+$$

In fermentation, NAD^+ is supplied when NADH and H^+ reduce the $C{=}O$ in acetaldehyde.

STUDY CHECK 22.4

After strenuous exercise, some lactate is oxidized back to pyruvate by lactate dehydrogenase using NAD^+. Write an equation to show this reaction.

QUESTIONS AND PROBLEMS

22.6 Pathways for Pyruvate

LEARNING GOAL: *Give the conditions for the conversion of pyruvate to lactate, ethanol, and acetyl-coenzyme A.*

22.39 What condition is needed in the cell to convert pyruvate to acetyl-CoA?

22.40 What coenzymes are needed for the oxidation of pyruvate to acetyl-CoA?

22.41 Write the overall equation for the conversion of pyruvate to acetyl-CoA.

22.42 What are the possible products of pyruvate under anaerobic conditions?

22.43 How does the formation of lactate permit glycolysis to continue under anaerobic conditions?

22.44 After running a marathon, a runner has muscle pain and cramping. What might have occurred in the muscle cells to cause this?

22.45 In fermentation, a carbon atom is removed from pyruvate. What is the compound formed with that carbon atom?

22.46 Some students decided to make some wine by placing yeast and grape juice in a container with a tight lid. A few weeks later, the container exploded. What reaction could account for the explosion?

22.7 Glycogen Metabolism

We have just eaten a large meal that has supplied us with all the glucose we need to produce pyruvate and ATP by glycolysis. Then we use excess glucose to replenish our energy reserves by synthesizing glycogen that is stored in limited amounts in our skeletal muscle and liver. When glycogen stores are full, any remaining glucose is converted to triacylglycerols and stored as body fat, as we will see in Chapter 24. When our diet does not supply sufficient glucose or we have utilized our blood glucose, we degrade the stored glycogen and release glucose.

Glycogenesis

Glycogen is a polymer of glucose with α-1,4-glycosidic bonds and multiple branches attached by α-1,6-glycosidic bonds, as seen in Chapter 15. **Glycogenesis** is the synthesis of glycogen from glucose molecules, which occurs when the digestion of polysaccharides produces high levels of glucose. The synthesis of glycogen starts with the glucose-6-phosphate obtained from the first reaction in glycolysis (see Figure 22.12).

Reaction 1 Isomerization
Glucose-6-phosphate is converted to the isomer glucose-1-phosphate.

Reaction 2 Activation
Before glucose-1-phosphate can be added to the glycogen chain, it is activated by the energy from the hydrolysis of high-energy UTP (uridine triphosphate) to form UDP-glucose (uridine diphosphate-glucose).

Reaction 3 Glycogen Synthesis
When the phosphate bond to glucose in UDP-glucose is broken, the glucose that is released forms an α-1,4-glycosidic bond with the end of the glycogen chain and uridine diphosphate (UDP) is released. UTP is regenerated by reacting UDP with ATP.

$$UDP + ATP \longrightarrow UTP + ADP$$

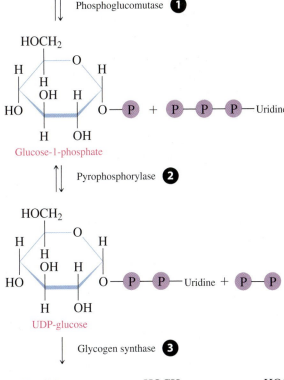

FIGURE 22.12 In glycogenesis, glucose is used to synthesize glycogen.

Q What is the function of UTP in glycogen synthesis?

TUTORIAL
Glycogen Metabolism

Glycogenolysis

Glycogen is a highly branched polysaccharide of glucose monomers with both α-1,4- and α-1,6-glycosidic bonds. Glucose is the primary energy source for muscle contractions, red blood cells, and the brain. When blood glucose is depleted, the glycogen stored in the muscle and liver is converted to glucose molecules in a process called **glycogenolysis**.

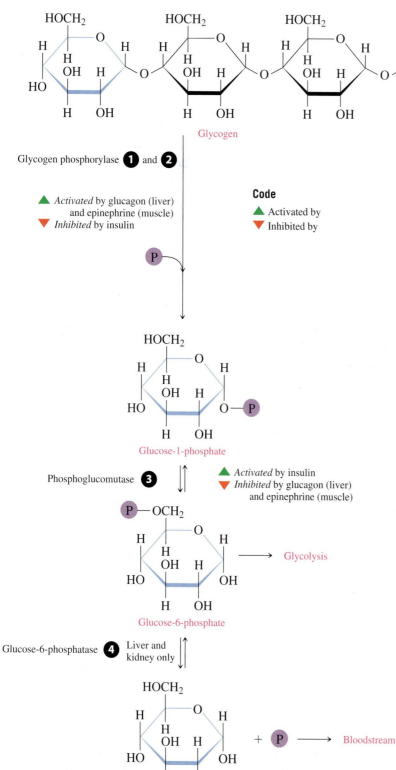

Glycogen

Glycogen phosphorylase **1** and **2**

▲ *Activated* by glucagon (liver) and epinephrine (muscle)
▼ *Inhibited* by insulin

Code
▲ Activated by
▼ Inhibited by

Glucose-1-phosphate

Phosphoglucomutase **3**

▲ *Activated* by insulin
▼ *Inhibited* by glucagon (liver) and epinephrine (muscle)

Glucose-6-phosphate

→ Glycolysis

Glucose-6-phosphatase **4** Liver and kidney only

+ P → Bloodstream

Glucose

Reaction 1 Phosphorolysis

Glucose molecules are removed one by one from the ends of the glycogen chain and phosphorylated to yield glucose-1-phosphate.

Reaction 2 Hydrolysis (α-1,6)

Glycogen phosphorylase continues to cleave α-1,4-links until one glucose remains bonded to the main chain by an α-1,6-glycosidic bond.

A debranching enzyme (α-1,6-glycosidase) breaks α-1,6-glycosidic bonds so that branches of glucose molecules can be hydrolyzed by reaction 1.

Reaction 3 Isomerization

The glucose-1-phosphate molecules are converted to glucose-6-phosphate molecules, which enter the glycolysis pathway at reaction 2.

Reaction 4 Dephosphorylation

Free glucose is needed for energy by the brain and muscle. While glucose can diffuse across cell membranes, glucose phosphates cannot. Only cells in the liver and kidneys have a glucose-6-phosphatase that hydrolyzes the glucose-6-phosphate to yield free glucose.

Regulation of Glycogen Metabolism

The brain, skeletal muscles, and red blood cells require large amounts of glucose every day to function properly. To protect the brain, hormones with opposing actions control blood glucose levels. When glucose is low, *glucagon*, a hormone produced in the pancreas, is secreted into the bloodstream. In the liver, glucagon accelerates the rate of glycogenolysis, which raises blood glucose levels. At the same time, glucagon inhibits the synthesis of glycogen.

Glycogen in skeletal muscle is broken down quickly when the body requires a "burst of energy," often referred to as "fight or flight." *Epinephrine* released from the adrenal glands converts glycogen phosphorylase from an inactive to an active form. The secretion of only a few molecules of epinephrine results in the breakdown of a huge number of glycogen molecules.

Soon after we have eaten and digested a meal, our blood glucose level rises, which stimulates the pancreas to secrete the hormone insulin into our bloodstream. Insulin promotes the use of glucose in the cells by accelerating glycogen synthesis, as well as degradation reactions such as glycolysis. At the same time, insulin inhibits the synthesis of glucose, which we will discuss in the next section.

CONCEPT CHECK 22.5 **Glycogen Metabolism**

What are the conditions and hormones that promote each of the following?

a. glycogenesis **b.** glycogenolysis

ANSWER

a. Glycogenesis occurs when glucose levels are high, particularly after the digestion of carbohydrates. High glucose levels stimulate the pancreas to secrete insulin, which accelerates the synthesis of glycogen.

b. Glycogenolysis occurs when blood glucose levels are depleted and glucose is needed for energy by muscle and the brain. The secretion of the hormone glucagon by the pancreas accelerates the breakdown of glycogen in the liver to glucose. In "fight or flight" situations, epinephrine from the adrenal glands accelerates glycogenolysis in muscle to raise the blood glucose level quickly.

SAMPLE PROBLEM 22.5 **Glycogen Metabolism**

Identify each of the following as part of the reaction pathways of glycolysis, glycogenolysis, or glycogenesis:

a. Glucose-1-phosphate is converted to glucose-6-phosphate.
b. Glucose-1-phosphate forms UDP-glucose.
c. An isomerase converts glucose-6-phosphate to fructose-6-phosphate.

SOLUTION

a. glycogenolysis **b.** glycogenesis **c.** glycolysis

STUDY CHECK 22.5

Why do cells in the liver and kidneys provide glucose to raise blood glucose levels, but cells in skeletal muscle do not?

QUESTIONS AND PROBLEMS

22.7 Glycogen Metabolism

LEARNING GOAL: *Describe the synthesis and breakdown of glycogen.*

22.47 What is meant by the term *glycogenesis*?

22.48 What is meant by the term *glycogenolysis*?

22.49 How do muscle cells use glycogen to provide energy?

22.50 How does the liver raise blood glucose levels?

22.51 What is the function of glycogen phosphorylase?

22.52 Why is the enzyme phosphoglucomutase used in both glycogenolysis and glycogenesis?

MC

TUTORIAL
Gluconeogenesis

22.8 Gluconeogenesis: Glucose Synthesis

Glycogen stored in our liver and muscles can supply us with about one day's requirement of glucose. However, glycogen stores are quickly depleted if we fast for more than one day or participate in heavy exercise. Then glucose is synthesized from carbon atoms obtained from noncarbohydrate compounds in a process called **gluconeogenesis**. Most glucose is synthesized in the cytosol of liver cells (see Figure 22.13).

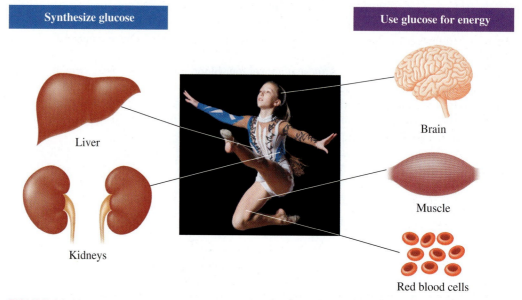

FIGURE 22.13 Glucose is synthesized in the tissues of the liver and kidneys. Tissues that use glucose as their main energy source are the brain, skeletal muscles, and red blood cells.

Q Why does the body need a pathway for the synthesis of glucose from noncarbohydrate sources?

Carbon atoms for glucose can be obtained from food sources, such as amino acids, and glycerol from fats. Each is converted to pyruvate or an intermediate for the synthesis of glucose. Most of the reactions in gluconeogenesis are the reverse of glycolysis and are catalyzed by the same enzymes. However, three of the glycolysis reactions are not reversible: the ones catalyzed by hexokinase, phosphofructokinase, and pyruvate kinase—glycolysis reactions 1, 3, and 10, respectively. Different enzymes are used to replace them, but all the other reactions simply reverse glycolysis and use the same enzymes. We will now look at these three reactions in gluconeogenesis that differ from the reactions of glycolysis.

Converting Pyruvate to Phosphoenolpyruvate (10)

To start the synthesis of glucose, two steps are needed. The first step converts pyruvate to oxaloacetate, and the second step converts oxaloacetate to phosphoenolpyruvate. The hydrolysis of ATP and GTP are used to drive the reactions. Molecules of phosphoenolpyruvate now enter the next five reverse reactions in glycolysis using the same enzymes to form fructose-1,6-bisphosphate.

$$CH_3-\overset{\overset{O}{\|}}{C}-COO^- + CO_2 + ATP + H_2O \xrightarrow{\text{Pyruvate carboxylase}} {}^-OOC-CH_2-\overset{\overset{O}{\|}}{C}-COO^- + ADP + P_i$$

Pyruvate
Oxaloacetate

$$^-OOC-CH_2-\overset{\overset{O}{\|}}{C}-COO^- + GTP \xrightarrow{\text{Phosphoenolpyruvate carboxykinase}} H_2C=\overset{\overset{O-P}{\|}}{C}-COO^- + CO_2 + GDP$$

Oxaloacetate
Phosphoenolpyruvate

Converting Fructose-1,6-Bisphosphate to Fructose-6-Phosphate (3)

The second irreversible reaction in glycolysis is bypassed when a phosphate group is cleaved from fructose-1,6-bisphosphate by hydrolysis with water. Then fructose-6-phosphate undergoes a reversible reaction to yield glucose-6-phosphate.

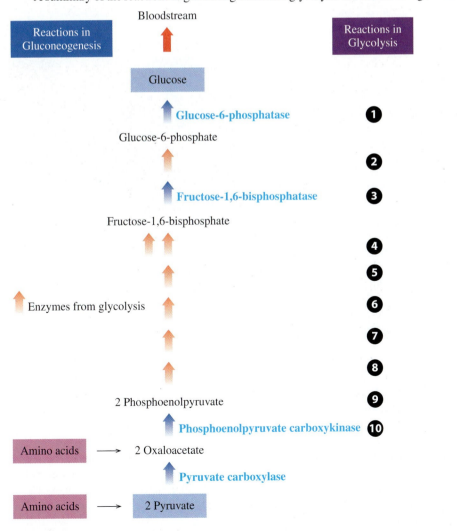

Fructose-1,6-bisphosphate + H_2O →(Fructose-1,6-bisphosphatase)→ Fructose-6-phosphate + P

Converting Glucose-6-Phosphate to Glucose (1)

In the final irreversible reaction, glucose-6-phosphate is hydrolyzed to glucose by a different enzyme than that used in glycolysis.

Glucose-6-phosphate + H_2O →(Glucose-6-phosphatase)→ Glucose + P

A summary of the reactions in gluconeogenesis and glycolysis are shown in Figure 22.14.

Bloodstream

Reactions in Gluconeogenesis

Reactions in Glycolysis

Glucose

 ↑ **Glucose-6-phosphatase** ❶

Glucose-6-phosphate

 ↑ ❷

 ↑ **Fructose-1,6-bisphosphatase** ❸

Fructose-1,6-bisphosphate

 ↑↑ ❹

 ↑ ❺

Enzymes from glycolysis ↑ ❻

 ↑ ❼

 ↑ ❽

2 Phosphoenolpyruvate ❾

 ↑ **Phosphoenolpyruvate carboxykinase** ❿

Amino acids → 2 Oxaloacetate

 ↑ **Pyruvate carboxylase**

Amino acids → 2 Pyruvate

FIGURE 22.14 In gluconeogenesis, three irreversible reactions of glycolysis are bypassed using four different enzymes.

Q Why are 11 enzymes required for gluconeogenesis and only 10 for glycolysis?

Energy Cost of Gluconeogenesis

The pathway of gluconeogenesis consists of seven reversible reactions of glycolysis and four new reactions that replace the three irreversible reactions. Overall, this synthesis of glucose requires four ATPs, two GTPs, and two NADHs. If all the reactions were simply the reverse of glycolysis, the synthesis of glucose would not be energetically favorable. By using energy resources and substituting four new reactions for the three irreversible and energy-requiring reactions, gluconeogenesis becomes favorable in terms of energy. The overall equation for gluconeogenesis is written as follows:

$$2\,\text{Pyruvate} + 4\,\text{ATP} + 2\,\text{GTP} + 2\,\text{NADH} + 2\text{H}^+ + 6\text{H}_2\text{O} \longrightarrow \text{glucose} + 4\,\text{ADP} + 2\,\text{GDP} + 6\text{P}_i + 2\,\text{NAD}^+$$

Lactate and the Cori Cycle

When a person exercises vigorously, anaerobic conditions cause the reduction of pyruvate to lactate, which accumulates in the muscle. This reaction is necessary to oxidize NADH to NAD$^+$, which allows glycolysis to continue to produce a small amount of ATP. Lactate is an important source of carbon for gluconeogenesis. Lactate is transported to the liver where it is oxidized to pyruvate, which is used to synthesize glucose. Glucose enters the bloodstream and returns to the muscle to rebuild glycogen stores. This flow of lactate and glucose between the muscle and liver, known as the **Cori cycle**, is very active when a person has just completed a period of vigorous exercise (see Figure 22.15).

FIGURE 22.15 Different pathways connect the utilization and synthesis of glucose.

Q Why is lactate formed in the muscle converted to glucose in the liver?

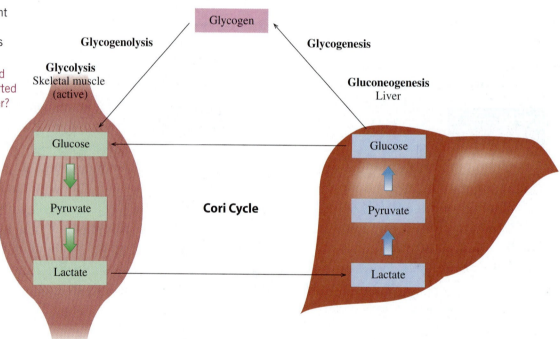

The relationship between the metabolic reactions of glucose for stage 1 and stage 2 are summarized in Figure 22.16.

Regulation of Gluconeogenesis

Gluconeogenesis is a pathway that protects the brain and nervous system from experiencing a loss of glucose, which causes impairment of function. It is also a pathway that is utilized when vigorous activity depletes blood glucose and glycogen stores. Thus, the level of carbohydrate available from the diet controls gluconeogenesis. When a diet is high in carbohydrate, the gluconeogenesis pathway is not utilized. However, when a diet is low in carbohydrate, the pathway is very active.

As long as conditions in a cell favor glycolysis, there is no synthesis of glucose. But when the cell requires the synthesis of glucose, glycolysis is turned off. The same three reactions that control glycolysis also control gluconeogenesis, but with different enzymes. Let's look at how high levels of certain compounds activate or inhibit the two processes (see Table 22.4).

Summary of Metabolic Reactions for Glucose in Stage 1 and Stage 2

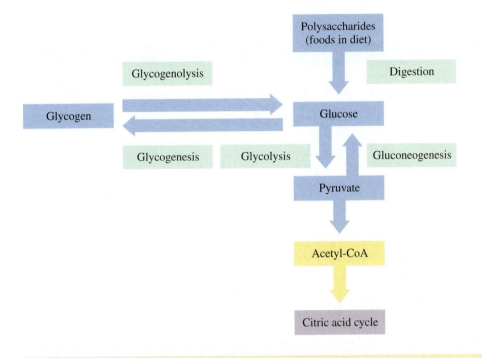

FIGURE 22.16 Glycogenolysis and glycogenesis involve the breakdown and synthesis of glycogen. Glycolysis involves the breakdown of glucose, and gluconeogenesis involves the synthesis of glucose.

Q Why does glycogenesis occur after the digestion of a meal high in carbohydrates?

TABLE 22.4 Regulation of Glycolysis and Gluconeogenesis

	Glycolysis	Gluconeogenesis
Enzyme	Hexokinase	Glucose-6-phosphatase
Activated by	High glucose levels, insulin, epinephrine	Low glucose levels, glucose-6-phosphate
Inhibited by	Glucose-6-phosphate	
Enzyme	Phosphofructokinase	Fructose-1,6-bisphosphatase
Activated by	AMP	Low glucose levels, glucagon
Inhibited by	ATP	AMP, insulin
Enzyme	Pyruvate kinase	Pyruvate carboxylase
Activated by	Fructose-1,6-bisphosphate	Low glucose levels, glucagon
Inhibited by	ATP, acetyl-CoA	Insulin

CONCEPT CHECK 22.6 Gluconeogenesis

Under what conditions does gluconeogenesis operate in a cell?

ANSWER

Gluconeogenesis operates when glycogen in the liver is depleted and the blood glucose level is extremely low. If the diet is not providing sufficient glucose for energy, glucose is produced from carbon atoms in noncarbohydrate sources, including amino acids, fatty acids, glycerol, and lactate.

SAMPLE PROBLEM 22.6 Gluconeogenesis

The conversion of fructose-1,6-bisphosphate to fructose-6-phosphate is an irreversible reaction using a glycolytic enzyme. How does gluconeogenesis make this reaction happen?

SOLUTION

This reverse reaction is catalyzed by a different enzyme, fructose-1,6-bisphosphatase, which cleaves a phosphate group using a hydrolysis reaction, a reaction that is energetically favorable.

QUESTIONS AND PROBLEMS

22.8 Gluconeogenesis: Glucose Synthesis

LEARNING GOAL: *Describe how glucose is synthesized from noncarbohydrate molecules.*

22.53 What is the function of gluconeogenesis in the body?

22.54 What enzymes in glycolysis are not used in gluconeogenesis?

22.55 What enzymes in glycolysis are used in gluconeogenesis?

22.56 How is the lactate produced in skeletal muscle used for glucose synthesis?

22.57 Indicate whether each of the following activates or inhibits gluconeogenesis:
   a. low glucose levels   **b.** glucagon
   c. insulin

22.58 Indicate whether each of the following activates or inhibits glycolysis:
   a. low glucose levels   **b.** insulin
   c. glucagon

CONCEPT MAP

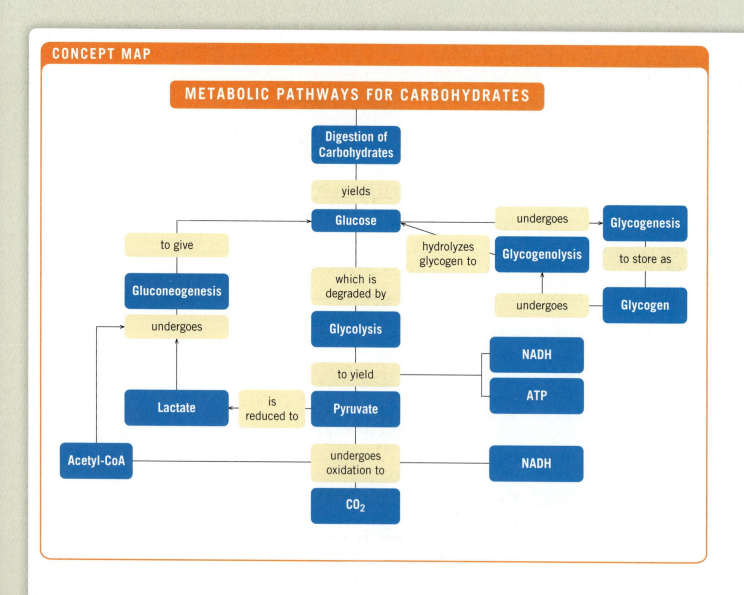

CHAPTER REVIEW

22.1 Metabolism and Cell Structure

LEARNING GOAL: Describe three stages of metabolism.

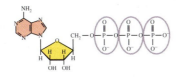

- Metabolism includes all the catabolic and anabolic reactions that occur in the cells.
- Catabolic reactions degrade large molecules into smaller ones with an accompanying release of energy.
- Anabolic reactions require energy to synthesize larger molecules from smaller ones.
- The three stages of metabolism are digestion of food, degradation of monomers such as glucose to pyruvate, and the extraction of energy from the two- and three-carbon compounds from stage 2.
- Many of the metabolic enzymes are present in the cytosol of the cell where metabolic reactions take place.

22.2 ATP and Energy

LEARNING GOAL: Describe the structure of ATP and its role in catabolic and anabolic reactions.

- Energy obtained from catabolic reactions is stored primarily in adenosine triphosphate (ATP), a high-energy compound.
- ATP is hydrolyzed when energy is required by anabolic reactions in the cells.

22.3 Important Coenzymes in Metabolic Pathways

LEARNING GOAL: Describe the components and functions of the coenzymes FAD, NAD+, and coenzyme A.

- FAD and NAD+ are the oxidized forms of coenzymes that participate in oxidation–reduction reactions.
- When FAD and NAD+ pick up hydrogen ions and electrons, they are reduced to $FADH_2$ and $NADH + H^+$.
- Coenzyme A contains a thiol group (—SH) that usually bonds with a two-carbon acetyl group (acetyl-CoA).

22.4 Digestion of Carbohydrates

LEARNING GOAL: Give the sites and products of the digestion of carbohydrates.

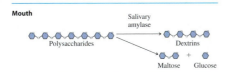

- The digestion of carbohydrates is a series of reactions that breaks down polysaccharides into hexose monomers such as glucose, galactose, and fructose.

- The hexose monomers are absorbed through the intestinal wall into the bloodstream to be carried to cells where they provide energy and carbon atoms for the synthesis of new molecules.

22.5 Glycolysis: Oxidation of Glucose

LEARNING GOAL: Describe the conversion of glucose to pyruvate in glycolysis.

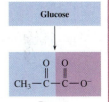

- Glycolysis, which occurs in the cytosol, consists of ten reactions that degrade glucose (six carbons) to two pyruvate molecules (three carbons each).
- The overall series of reactions yields two molecules of the reduced coenzyme NADH and two ATPs.

22.6 Pathways for Pyruvate

LEARNING GOAL: Give the conditions for the conversion of pyruvate to lactate, ethanol, and acetyl-coenzyme A.

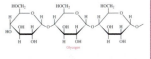

- Under aerobic conditions, pyruvate is oxidized in the mitochondria to acetyl-CoA.
- In the absence of oxygen, pyruvate is reduced to lactate and NAD+ is regenerated for the continuation of glycolysis, while microorganisms such as yeast reduce pyruvate to ethanol, a process known as fermentation.

22.7 Glycogen Metabolism

LEARNING GOAL: Describe the synthesis and breakdown of glycogen.

- When blood glucose levels are high, glycogenesis converts glucose to glycogen, which is stored in the liver.
- Glycogenolysis breaks down glycogen to glucose when glucose and ATP levels are low.

22.8 Gluconeogenesis: Glucose Synthesis

LEARNING GOAL: Describe how glucose is synthesized from noncarbohydrate molecules.

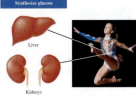

- When blood glucose levels are low and glycogen stores in the liver are depleted, glucose is synthesized from compounds such as pyruvate and lactate.

SUMMARY OF KEY REACTIONS

Hydrolysis of ATP

$$\text{ATP} \longrightarrow \text{ADP} + P_i + 7.3 \text{ kcal/mole (31 kJ/mole)}$$

Hydrolysis of ADP

$$\text{ADP} \longrightarrow \text{AMP} + P_i + 7.3 \text{ kcal/mole (31 kJ/mole)}$$

Formation of ATP

$$\text{ADP} + P_i + 7.3 \text{ kcal/mole (31 kJ/mole)} \longrightarrow \text{ATP}$$

Reduction of FAD and NAD$^+$

$$\text{FAD} + 2H^+ + 2\,e^- \longrightarrow \text{FADH}_2$$

$$\text{NAD}^+ + 2H^+ + 2\,e^- \longrightarrow \text{NADH} + H^+$$

Glycolysis

$$\text{C}_6\text{H}_{12}\text{O}_6 + 2\text{ADP} + 2P_i + 2\text{NAD}^+ \longrightarrow$$
Glucose

$$2\text{CH}_3 - \overset{\displaystyle O}{\overset{\|}{\text{C}}} - \text{COO}^- + 2\text{ATP} + 2\text{NADH} + 4H^+$$
Pyruvate

Oxidation of Pyruvate to Acetyl-CoA

$$\text{CH}_3 - \overset{\displaystyle O}{\overset{\|}{\text{C}}} - \text{COO}^- + \text{NAD}^+ + \text{HS} - \text{CoA}$$
Pyruvate

$$\xrightarrow[\text{dehydrogenase}]{\text{Pyruvate}} \text{CH}_3 - \overset{\displaystyle O}{\overset{\|}{\text{C}}} - \text{S} - \text{CoA} + \text{NADH} + \text{CO}_2$$
Acetyl-CoA

Reduction of Pyruvate to Lactate

$$\text{CH}_3 - \overset{\displaystyle O}{\overset{\|}{\text{C}}} - \text{COO}^- + \text{NADH} + H^+ \longrightarrow$$
Pyruvate

$$\text{CH}_3 - \overset{\displaystyle OH}{\overset{|}{\text{CH}}} - \text{COO}^- + \text{NAD}^+$$
Lactate

Oxidation of Glucose to Lactate

$$\text{Glucose} + 2\text{ADP} + 2P_i \longrightarrow 2\text{lactate} + 2\text{ATP}$$

Reduction of Pyruvate to Ethanol

$$\text{CH}_3 - \overset{\displaystyle O}{\overset{\|}{\text{C}}} - \text{COO}^- + \text{NADH} + 2H^+ \longrightarrow$$
Pyruvate

$$\text{CH}_3 - \text{CH}_2 - \text{OH} + \text{NAD}^+ + \text{CO}_2$$
Ethanol

Glycogenesis

$$\text{Glucose} \longrightarrow \text{glycogen}$$

Glycogenolysis

$$\text{Glycogen} \longrightarrow \text{glucose}$$

Gluconeogenesis

$$\text{Pyruvate (or lactate)} \longrightarrow \text{glucose}$$

$$2\text{Pyruvate} + 4\text{ATP} + 2\text{GTP} + 2\text{NADH} + 2H^+ + 6\text{H}_2\text{O} \longrightarrow$$
$$\text{glucose} + 4\text{ADP} + 2\text{GDP} + 6P_i + 2\text{NAD}^+$$

KEY TERMS

acetyl-CoA The compound that forms when a two-carbon acetyl unit bonds to coenzyme A.

ADP Adenosine diphosphate, formed by the hydrolysis of ATP; consists of adenine, a ribose sugar, and two phosphate groups.

aerobic An oxygen-containing environment in the cells.

anabolic reaction A metabolic reaction that requires energy to build large molecules from small molecules.

anaerobic A condition in cells when there is no oxygen.

ATP Adenosine triphosphate, a high-energy compound that stores energy in the cells; consists of adenine, a ribose sugar, and three phosphate groups.

catabolic reaction A metabolic reaction that produces energy for the cell by the degradation and oxidation of glucose and other molecules.

coenzyme A (CoA) A coenzyme that transports acyl and acetyl groups.

Cori cycle A cyclic process in which lactate produced in muscle is transferred to the liver to be converted to glucose, which can be used again by muscle.

cytoplasm The material in eukaryotic cells between the nucleus and the cell membrane.

cytosol The fluid of the cytoplasm, which is an aqueous solution of electrolytes and enzymes.

decarboxylation The loss of a carbon atom in the form of CO_2.

digestion The processes in the gastrointestinal tract that break down large food molecules to smaller ones that pass through the intestinal membrane into the bloodstream.

FAD A coenzyme (flavin adenine dinucleotide) for dehydrogenase enzymes that form carbon–carbon double bonds.

fermentation The anaerobic conversion of glucose by enzymes in yeast to yield alcohol and CO_2.

gluconeogenesis The synthesis of glucose from noncarbohydrate compounds.

glycogenesis The synthesis of glycogen from glucose molecules.

glycogenolysis The breakdown of glycogen into glucose molecules.

glycolysis The ten oxidation reactions of glucose that yield two pyruvate molecules.

metabolism All the chemical reactions in living cells that carry out molecular and energy transformations.

mitochondria The organelle of cells where energy-producing reactions take place.

NAD$^+$ The hydrogen acceptor used in oxidation reactions that form carbon–oxygen double bonds.

UNDERSTANDING THE CONCEPTS

The chapter sections to review are given in parentheses at the end of each question.

22.59 On a hike, you expend 350 kcal per hour. How many moles of ATP will you use if you hike for 2.5 h? (22.2)

Vigorous hiking can expend 350 kcal per hour.

22.60 Identify each of the following as a six-carbon or a three-carbon compound and arrange them in the order in which they occur in glycolysis: (22.5)
a. 3-phosphoglycerate
b. pyruvate
c. glucose-6-phosphate
d. glucose
e. fructose-1,6-bisphosphate

ADDITIONAL QUESTIONS AND PROBLEMS

For instructor-assigned homework, go to www.masteringchemistry.com.

22.61 What is meant by the term *metabolism*? (22.1)

22.62 How do catabolic reactions differ from anabolic reactions? (22.1)

22.63 What stage of metabolism involves the digestion of large food polymers? (22.1)

22.64 What stage of metabolism degrades monomers such as glucose into smaller molecules? (22.1)

22.65 What type of cell has a nucleus? (22.1)

22.66 What is the function of each of the following cell components? (22.1)
a. cell membrane   **b.** mitochondria
c. cytoplasm

22.67 What is the full name of ATP? (22.2)

22.68 What is the full name of ADP? (22.2)

22.69 Write an abbreviated equation for the hydrolysis of ATP to ADP. (22.2)

22.70 Write the abbreviated equation for the hydrolysis of ADP to AMP. (22.2)

22.71 What is the full name of FAD? (22.3)

22.72 What type of reaction uses FAD as the coenzyme? (22.3)

22.73 What is the full name of NAD^+? (22.3)

22.74 What type of reaction uses NAD^+ as the coenzyme? (22.3)

22.75 Write the abbreviation for the reduced form of each of the following: (22.3)
a. FAD   **b.** NAD^+

22.76 What is the name of the vitamin in the structure of each of the following? (22.3)
a. FAD   **b.** NAD^+
c. coenzyme A

22.77 How and where does lactose undergo digestion in the body? What are the products? (22.4)

22.78 How and where does sucrose undergo digestion in the body? What are the products? (22.4)

22.79 What are the reactant and product of glycolysis? (22.5)

22.80 What is the coenzyme used in glycolysis? (22.5)

22.81 **a.** In glycolysis, which reactions involve phosphorylation?
b. Which reactions involve a direct substrate phosphorylation to generate ATP? (22.5)

22.82 How do ADP and ATP regulate the glycolysis pathway? (22.5)

22.83 What reaction and enzyme in glycolysis convert a hexose bisphosphate into two three-carbon intermediates? (22.5)

22.84 How does the investment and generation of ATP give a net gain of ATP for glycolysis? (22.5)

22.85 What compound is converted to fructose-6-phosphate by phosphoglucose isomerase? (22.5)

22.86 What product forms when glyceraldehyde-3-phosphate adds a phosphate group? (22.5)

22.87 When is pyruvate converted to lactate in the body? (22.6)

22.88 When pyruvate is used to form acetyl-CoA or ethanol in fermentation, the product has only two carbon atoms. What happened to the third carbon? (22.6)

22.89 How does phosphofructokinase regulate the rate of glycolysis? (22.5)

22.90 How does pyruvate kinase regulate the rate of glycolysis? (22.5)

22.91 When does the rate of glycogenolysis increase in the cells? (22.5)

22.92 If glucose-1-phosphate is the product from glycogen breakdown, how does it enter glycolysis? (22.5)

22.93 What is the end product of glycogenolysis in the liver? (22.7)

22.94 What is the end product of glycogenolysis in skeletal muscle? (22.7)

22.95 Indicate whether each of the following conditions would increase or decrease the rate of glycogenolysis in the liver: (22.7)
 a. low blood glucose level **b.** secretion of insulin
 c. secretion of glucagon **d.** high levels of ATP

22.96 Indicate whether each of the following conditions would increase or decrease the rate of glycogenesis in the liver: (22.7)
 a. low blood glucose level **b.** secretion of insulin
 c. secretion of glucagon **d.** high levels of ATP

22.97 Indicate whether each of the following conditions would increase or decrease the rate of gluconeogenesis: (22.7)
 a. high blood glucose level **b.** secretion of insulin
 c. secretion of glucagon **d.** high levels of ATP

22.98 Indicate whether each of the following conditions would increase or decrease the rate of glycolysis: (22.7)
 a. high blood glucose level **b.** secretion of insulin
 c. secretion of glucagon **d.** high levels of ATP

CHALLENGE QUESTIONS

22.99 Why is glucose provided by glycogenolysis in the liver but not in skeletal muscle? (22.7)

22.100 When does the rate of glycogenesis increase in the cells? (22.7)

22.101 How do the hormones insulin and glucagon affect the rates of glycogenesis, glycogenolysis, and glycolysis? (22.5, 22.7)

22.102 What is the function of gluconeogenesis? (22.8)

22.103 Where does the Cori cycle operate? (22.8)

22.104 Identify each of the following as part of glycolysis, glycogenolysis, glycogenesis, or gluconeogenesis: (22.5, 22.7, 22.8)
 a. Glycogen is broken down to glucose in the liver.
 b. Glucose is synthesized from noncarbohydrate sources.

 c. Glucose is degraded to pyruvate.
 d. Glycogen is synthesized from glucose.

22.105 One cell at work may break down 2 million (2 000 000) ATP molecules in 1 second. Researchers estimate that the human body has about 10^{13} cells. (22.2)
 a. How much energy, in kcal, could be produced by the cells in the body in 24 hours?
 b. If ATP has a molar mass of 507 g/mole, how many grams of ATP are hydrolyzed in 24 hours?

ANSWERS

Answers to Study Checks

22.1 The thiol group (—SH) of aminoethanethiol in coenzyme A combines with an acetyl group to form acetyl-coenzyme A. The CoA participates in the transfer of acyl groups, usually acetyl groups.

22.2 The digestion of amylose begins in the mouth when salivary amylase hydrolyzes some of the glycosidic bonds. In the small intestine, pancreatic amylase hydrolyzes more glycosidic bonds, and finally maltose is hydrolyzed by maltase to yield glucose.

22.3 The splitting of fructose-1,6-bisphosphate is cleavage.

22.4
$$CH_3-\underset{\underset{OH}{|}}{CH}-\underset{\underset{O}{\|}}{C}-O^- + NAD^+ \xrightarrow{\text{Lactate dehydrogenase}}$$
$$CH_3-\underset{\underset{O}{\|}}{C}-\underset{\underset{O}{\|}}{C}-O^- + NADH + H^+$$

22.5 Only cells in the liver and kidneys have a glucose-6-phosphatase that hydrolyzes the glucose-6-phosphate to yield free glucose.

22.6 The reaction catalyzed by hexokinase in glycolysis is irreversible.

Answers to Selected Questions and Problems

22.1 The digestion of polysaccharides takes place in stage 1.

22.3 In metabolism, a catabolic reaction breaks apart large molecules, releasing energy.

22.5 **a.** (3) smooth endoplasmic reticulum
 b. (1) lysosome
 c. (2) Golgi complex

22.7 When a phosphate group is cleaved from ATP, sufficient energy is released for energy-requiring processes in the cell.

22.9 **a.** PEP $\longrightarrow$ pyruvate + P_i + 14.8 kcal/mole
 b. ADP + P_i + 7.3 kcal/mole $\longrightarrow$ ATP
 c. PEP + ADP $\longrightarrow$ ATP + pyruvate + 7.5 kcal/mole

22.11 **a.** coenzyme A **b.** NAD$^+$
 c. FAD

22.13 **a.** NADH **b.** FAD

22.15 FAD

22.17 Hydrolysis is the main reaction involved in the digestion of carbohydrates.

22.19 **a.** lactose **b.** glucose and fructose
 c. glucose

22.21 glucose

22.23 ATP is required in phosphorylation reactions.

22.25 glyceraldehyde-3-phosphate and dihydroxyacetone phosphate

22.27 ATP is produced in glycolysis by transferring a phosphate group from 1,3-bisphosphoglycerate and from phosphoenolpyruvate directly to ADP.

22.29 **a.** hexokinase; phosphofructokinase
 b. phosphoglycerate kinase; pyruvate kinase

22.31 **a.** 1 ATP required
b. 1 NADH produced
c. 2 ATP and 2 NADH produced

22.33 **a.** In reaction 1, a hexokinase uses ATP to phosphorylate glucose.
b. In reactions 7 and 10, phosphate groups are transferred from 1,3-bisphosphoglycerate and phosphoenolpyruvate directly to ADP to produce ATP.
c. In reaction 4, the six-carbon molecule fructose-1,6-bisphosphate is split into two three-carbon molecules, glyceraldehyde-3-phosphate and dihydroxyacetone phosphate.

22.35 Galactose reacts with ATP to yield galactose-1-phosphate, which is converted to glucose-6-phosphate, an intermediate in glycolysis. Fructose reacts with ATP to yield fructose-1-phosphate, which is cleaved to give dihydroxyacetone phosphate and glyceraldehyde. Dihydroxyacetone phosphate isomerizes to glyceraldehyde-3-phosphate, and glyceraldehyde is phosphorylated to glyceraldehyde-3-phosphate, which is an intermediate in glycolysis.

22.37 **a.** activate **b.** inhibit

22.39 Aerobic (oxygen) conditions are needed.

22.41 The oxidation of pyruvate converts NAD^+ to NADH and produces acetyl-CoA and CO_2.

Pyruvate $+ NAD^+ + CoA \longrightarrow$ Acetyl-CoA $+ CO_2 +$ NADH

22.43 When pyruvate is reduced to lactate, the NAD^+ is used to oxidize glyceraldehyde-3-phosphate, which allows glycolysis to continue, producing a small but needed amount of ATP.

22.45 carbon dioxide, CO_2

22.47 Glycogenesis is the synthesis of glycogen from glucose molecules.

22.49 Muscle cells break down glycogen to glucose-6-phosphate, which enters glycolysis.

22.51 Glycogen phosphorylase cleaves the glycosidic bonds at the ends of glycogen chains to remove glucose as glucose-1-phosphate.

22.53 When there are no glycogen stores remaining in the liver, gluconeogenesis synthesizes glucose from noncarbohydrate compounds such as pyruvate and lactate.

22.55 phosphoglucose isomerase, aldolase, triose phosphate isomerase, glyceraldehyde-3-phosphate dehydrogenase, phosphoglycerate kinase, phosphoglycerate mutase, and enolase

22.57 **a.** activates **b.** activates
c. inhibits

22.59 120 moles of ATP

22.61 Metabolism includes all the reactions in cells that provide energy and material for cell growth.

22.63 stage 1

22.65 eukaryotic cell

22.67 adenosine triphosphate

22.69 ATP $\longrightarrow$ ADP $+ P_i + 7.3$ kcal/mole (31 kJ/mole)

22.71 flavin adenine dinucleotide

22.73 nicotinamide adenine dinucleotide

22.75 **a.** $FADH_2$ **b.** NADH $+ H^+$

22.77 Lactose undergoes digestion in the small intestine to yield galactose and glucose.

22.79 Glucose is the reactant and pyruvate is the product of glycolysis.

22.81 **a.** Reactions 1 and 3 involve phosphorylation of hexoses with ATP.
b. Reactions 7 and 10 involve direct substrate phosphorylation that generates ATP.

22.83 Reaction 4, which converts fructose-1,6-bisphosphate into two three-carbon intermediates, is catalyzed by aldolase.

22.85 glucose-6-phosphate

22.87 Pyruvate is converted to lactate when oxygen is not present in the cell (anaerobic conditions) to regenerate NAD^+ for glycolysis.

22.89 Phosphofructokinase is an allosteric enzyme that is activated by high levels of AMP and ADP because the cell needs to produce more ATP. When ATP levels are high due to a decrease in energy needs, ATP inhibits phosphofructokinase, which reduces its catalysis of fructose-6-phosphate.

22.91 The rate of glycogenolysis increases when blood glucose levels are low and glucagon has been secreted, which accelerates the breakdown of glycogen.

22.93 glucose

22.95 **a.** increase **b.** decrease
c. increase **d.** decrease

22.97 **a.** decrease **b.** decrease
c. increase **d.** decrease

22.99 The cells in the liver, but not skeletal muscle, contain a phosphatase enzyme needed to convert glucose-6-phosphate to free glucose that can diffuse through cell membranes into the bloodstream. Glucose-6-phosphate, which is the end product of glycogenolysis in muscle cells, cannot diffuse easily across cell membranes.

22.101 Insulin increases the rate of glycogenesis and glycolysis and decreases the rate of glycogenolysis. Glucagon decreases the rate of glycogenesis and glycolysis and increases the rate of glycogenolysis.

22.103 The Cori cycle is a cyclic process that involves the transfer of lactate from muscle to the liver where glucose is synthesized, which can be used again by the muscle.

22.105 **a.** 21 kcal **b.** 1500 g of ATP

23 Metabolism and Energy Production

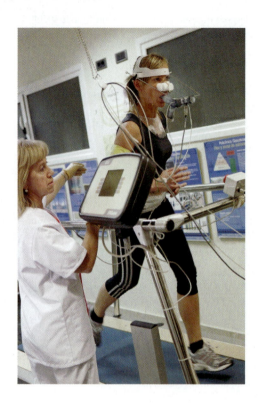

Visit **www.masteringchemistry.com** for self-study materials and instructor-assigned homework.

Natalie was recently diagnosed with mild emphysema due to secondhand cigarette smoke from her parents. She has been referred to Angela, an exercise physiologist, who begins to assess Natalie's condition by connecting her to an EKG, a pulse oximeter, and a blood pressure cuff. The EKG tracks Natalie's heart rate and rhythm, the pulse oximeter tracks the oxygen levels in her blood, while the blood pressure cuff determines the pressure exerted by the heart in pumping her blood. Natalie is then required to walk on a treadmill, to determine her overall physical condition.

Based on Natalie's results, Angela creates a workout regime. They begin with low-intensity exercises that utilize smaller muscles instead of larger muscles, which require more O_2 and can deplete a significant amount of the O_2 in her blood. During the exercises, Angela continues to monitor Natalie's heart rate, blood O_2 level, and blood pressure to ensure that Natalie is exercising at a level that will enable her to become stronger without breaking down muscle due to a lack of oxygen.

Oxygen is necessary for metabolism and the production of ATP. In the mitochondria, O_2 is required for the final step in electron transport as it reacts with hydrogen ions to form water. These reactions associated with electron transport are coupled with oxidative phosphorylation to produce ATP.

Career: Exercise Physiologist

Exercise physiologists work with athletes as well as patients who have been diagnosed with diabetes, heart disease, pulmonary (lung) disease, or any other chronic disability or disease. Patients who have been diagnosed with one of these diseases are often prescribed exercise as a form of treatment, and they are referred to an exercise physiologist. The exercise physiologist evaluates the patient's overall health and then creates a customized exercise program for that individual. The program for an athlete might focus on reducing the number of injuries, while a program for a cardiac patient would focus on strengthening the heart muscles. The exercise physiologist also monitors the patient for improvement and notes if the exercise is reducing or reversing the progression of the disease.

n Sections 22.4, 22.5, and 22.6, we described the digestion of carbohydrates to glucose and the degradation of glucose to pyruvate during glycolysis. We saw that pyruvate is converted to acetyl-CoA when oxygen is plentiful in the cell and to lactate when oxygen levels are low. Although glycolysis produces a small amount of ATP, most of the ATP in the cells is produced in stage 3 of metabolism during the conversion of pyruvate, when oxygen is available in the cell. In a process known as *respiration*, oxygen is required to complete the oxidation of glucose to CO_2 and H_2O.

In the *citric acid cycle*, a series of metabolic reactions in the mitochondria oxidizes the two carbon atoms in the acetyl component of acetyl-CoA to two molecules of carbon dioxide. The reduced coenzymes NADH and $FADH_2$ enter *electron transport*, or the *respiratory chain*, where they provide hydrogen ions and electrons that combine with oxygen (O_2) to form H_2O. The energy released during electron transport is used to synthesize ATP from ADP.

23.1 The Citric Acid Cycle

The **citric acid cycle** is a central pathway in metabolism that uses the two-carbon acetyl group from acetyl-CoA to produce CO_2, NADH + H^+, and $FADH_2$ (see Figure 23.1). The citric acid cycle connects the intermediate acetyl-CoA from stages 1 and 2 with electron transport and the synthesis of ATP in stage 3.

The citric acid cycle is named for the citrate ion from citric acid ($C_6H_8O_7$), a tricarboxylic acid, which forms in the first reaction. The citric acid cycle is also known as the *tricarboxylic acid (TCA) cycle* or the *Krebs cycle*, named for H. A. Krebs, who recognized it in 1937 as the major pathway for the production of energy.

Overview of the Citric Acid Cycle

There are a total of eight reactions and eight enzymes in the citric acid cycle (see Figure 23.2). Initially, an acetyl group (2C) from acetyl-CoA bonds with oxaloacetate (4C) to yield citrate (6C). Then, two decarboxylation reactions remove carbon atoms as CO_2 to give succinyl-CoA (4C). Finally, a series of reactions converts four-carbon succinyl-CoA to oxaloacetate, which combines with another acetyl-CoA, and the citric acid cycle starts all over. In one turn of the citric acid cycle, four oxidation reactions provide hydrogen ions and electrons, which are used to reduce FAD and NAD^+ coenzymes (see Figure 23.3).

We can now look at the details of the eight reactions that take place in the citric acid cycle. Most of the reactions, such as dehydration, hydration, oxidation, reduction, and hydrolysis, have already been discussed in previous chapters.

Reaction 1 Formation of Citrate

In the first reaction, *citrate synthase* hydrolyzes the thioester bond in acetyl-CoA and bonds the resulting acetyl group (2C) with oxaloacetate (4C) to yield citrate (6C) and coenzyme A.

LEARNING GOAL

Describe the oxidation of acetyl-CoA in the citric acid cycle.

SELF-STUDY ACTIVITY
Krebs Cycle

TUTORIAL
Citric Acid Cycle

$$CH_3-\overset{\overset{\displaystyle O}{\|}}{C}-S-CoA \ + \ \underset{\underset{\displaystyle COO^-}{|}}{\overset{\overset{\displaystyle COO^-}{|}}{\underset{\underset{\displaystyle CH_2}{|}}{C}}}=O \ + \ H_2O \ \xrightarrow[\text{synthase}]{\text{Citrate}} \ HO-\underset{\underset{\displaystyle COO^-}{|}}{\overset{\overset{\displaystyle COO^-}{|}}{\underset{\underset{\displaystyle CH_2}{|}}{\overset{\overset{\displaystyle CH_2}{|}}{C}}}}-COO^- \ + \ HS-CoA \ + \ H^+$$

| Acetyl-CoA | Oxaloacetate | | Citrate |

Stages of Metabolism

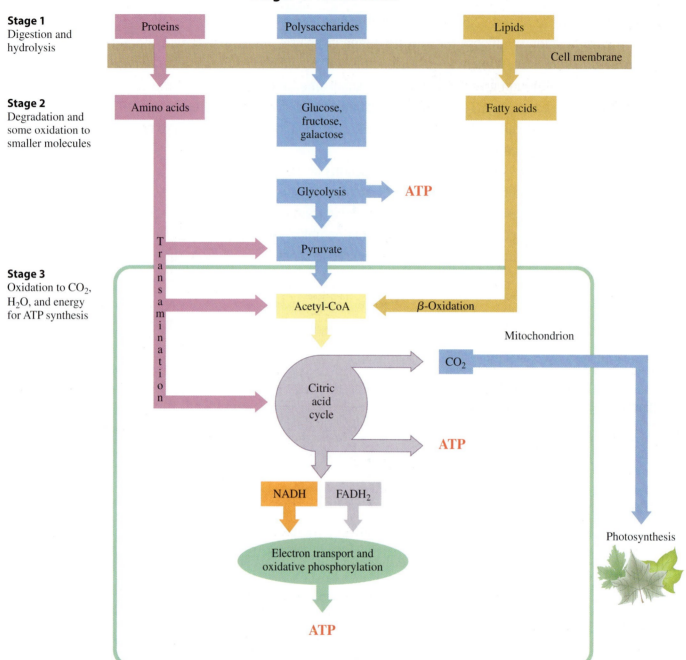

Stage 1
Digestion and
hydrolysis

Stage 2
Degradation and
some oxidation to
smaller molecules

Stage 3
Oxidation to CO_2,
H_2O, and energy
for ATP synthesis

FIGURE 23.1 The citric acid cycle connects the catabolic pathways that begin with the digestion and degradation of foods in stages 1 and 2 with the oxidation of substrates in stage 3 that generates most of the energy for ATP synthesis.

Q Why is the citric acid cycle called a central metabolic pathway?

Reaction 2   Isomerization

The citrate from reaction 1 contains a tertiary alcohol group that cannot be oxidized further. In reaction 2, citrate is converted to an isomer isocitrate that can be oxidized. Initially, *aconitase* catalyzes the dehydration of citrate to yield *cis*-aconitate, which is followed by a hydration that forms isocitrate. The combination of these two steps converts the tertiary hydroxyl group (—OH) in citrate to a secondary hydroxyl group (isocitrate) that is oxidized in the next reaction.

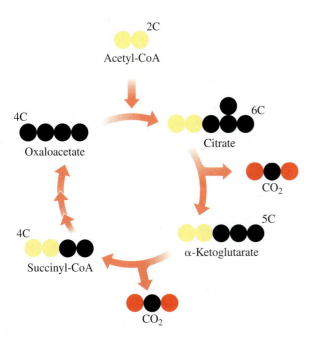

FIGURE 23.2 In the citric acid cycle, two carbon atoms are removed as CO_2 from six-carbon citrate to give four-carbon succinyl-CoA, which is converted to four-carbon oxaloacetate.

Q How many carbon atoms are removed in one turn of the citric acid cycle?

Reaction 3   Oxidation and Decarboxylation

In reaction 3, both an oxidation and a decarboxylation take place for the first time in the citric acid cycle. The alcohol group in isocitrate (6C) is oxidized to a ketone by *isocitrate dehydrogenase* and a **decarboxylation** removes one carbon by converting a carboxylate group (COO^-) to a CO_2 molecule. The ketone product is α-ketoglutarate (5C). The oxidation reaction also produces hydrogen ions and electrons that reduce NAD^+ to NADH and H^+. This reduced coenzyme NADH will be important in the energy-producing reactions we will discuss in electron transport.

$$
\begin{array}{ccc}
COO^- & & COO^- \\
| & & | \\
CH_2 & & CH_2 \\
| & \xrightarrow[\text{dehydrogenase}]{\text{Isocitrate}} & | \\
H-C-COO^- + NAD^+ & & H-C-H + CO_2 + NADH + H^+ \\
| & & | \\
HO-C-H & & C=O \\
| & & | \\
COO^- & & COO^- \\
\text{Isocitrate} & & \alpha\text{-Ketoglutarate}
\end{array}
$$

Reaction 4   Decarboxylation and Oxidation

In a reaction catalyzed by *α-ketoglutarate dehydrogenase*, α-ketoglutarate (5C) undergoes decarboxylation, and the four-carbon product combines with coenzyme A to yield succinyl-CoA (4C). The oxidation of the thiol group ($-SH$) provides hydrogen that reduces NAD^+ to NADH and H^+. This forms another reduced NADH that will be important in the energy-producing reactions.

$$
\begin{array}{ccc}
COO^- & & COO^- \\
| & & | \\
CH_2 & & CH_2 \\
| & \xrightarrow[\text{dehydrogenase}]{\alpha\text{-Ketoglutarate}} & | \\
CH_2 + NAD^+ + HS-CoA & & CH_2 + CO_2 + NADH + H^+ \\
| & & | \\
C=O & & C=O \\
| & & | \\
COO^- & & S-CoA \\
\alpha\text{-Ketoglutarate} & & \text{Succinyl-CoA}
\end{array}
$$

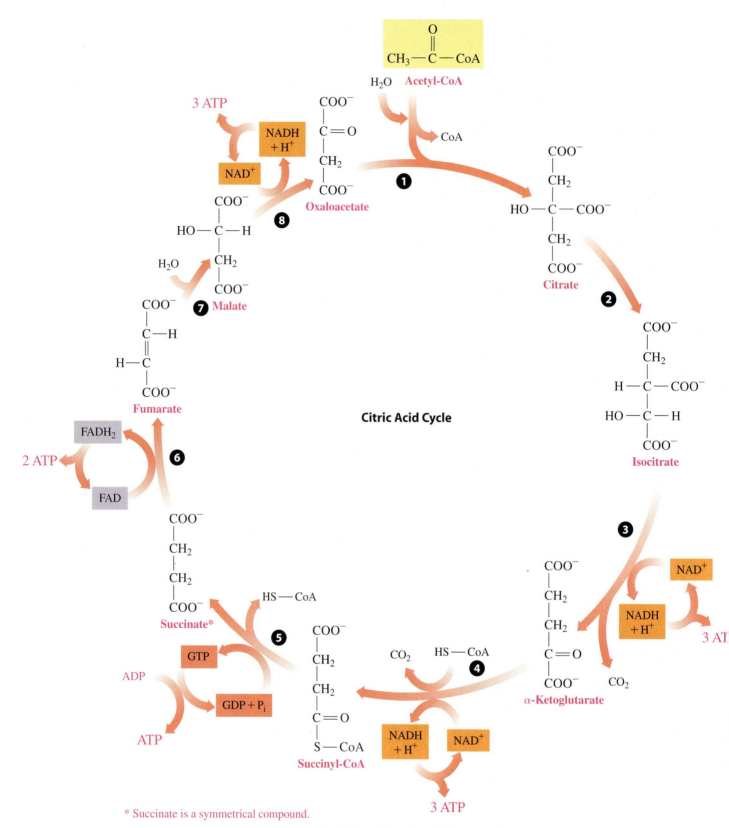

Citric Acid Cycle

* Succinate is a symmetrical compound.

FIGURE 23.3 In the citric acid cycle, oxidation reactions produce two CO_2 and reduced coenzymes NADH and $FADH_2$, and regenerate oxaloacetate.

Q How many reactions in the citric acid cycle produce a reduced coenzyme?

Reaction 5   Hydrolysis

In reaction 5, *succinyl-CoA synthetase* catalyses the hydrolysis of the thioester bond in succinyl-CoA to yield succinate and CoA. The energy released is used to add a phosphate group to GDP (guanosine diphosphate) to form GTP, a high-energy compound similar to ATP.

$$\begin{array}{l} COO^- \\ | \\ CH_2 \\ | \\ CH_2 \;+\; \textbf{GDP} + \textbf{P}_i + \textbf{H}^+ \\ | \\ C{=}O \\ | \\ \textbf{S}{-}\textbf{CoA} \end{array} \quad \xrightarrow[\text{synthetase}]{\text{Succinyl-CoA}} \quad \begin{array}{l} COO^- \\ | \\ CH_2 \\ | \\ CH_2 \;+\; \textbf{GTP} + \textbf{HS}{-}\textbf{CoA} \\ | \\ COO^- \end{array}$$

Succinyl-CoA   Succinate

Eventually, the GTP undergoes hydrolysis with a release of energy that is used to add a phosphate group to ADP to form ATP. This reaction is the only time in the citric acid cycle that ATP is produced by a direct transfer of a phosphate group. The reaction between GTP and ADP regenerates GDP that can be used again in the citric acid cycle.

$$GTP + ADP \longrightarrow GDP + ATP$$

Reaction 6   Oxidation

In reaction 6, *succinate dehydrogenase* catalyzes the oxidation of succinate to yield fumarate, a compound with a trans double bond. The formation of a carbon–carbon ($C{=}C$) double bond produces 2H that are used to reduce the coenzyme FAD to $FADH_2$. This reaction is the only time in the citric acid cycle that FAD is reduced to $FADH_2$. This reduced coenzyme $FADH_2$ is important in the energy-producing reactions we will discuss in electron transport.

$$\begin{array}{l} COO^- \\ | \\ CH_2 \\ | \\ CH_2 \;+\; \textbf{FAD} \\ | \\ COO^- \end{array} \quad \xrightarrow[\text{dehydrogenase}]{\text{Succinate}} \quad \begin{array}{c} {}^-OOC \qquad H \\ \diagdown \quad / \\ C \\ \| \\ C \qquad +\; \textbf{FADH}_2 \\ / \quad \diagdown \\ H \qquad COO^- \end{array}$$

Succinate   Fumarate

Reaction 7   Hydration

In reaction 7, a hydration catalyzed by *fumarase* adds water to the double bond of fumarate to yield malate, which is a secondary alcohol.

$$\begin{array}{c} {}^-OOC \qquad H \\ \diagdown \quad / \\ C \\ \| \\ C \;+\; \textbf{H}_2\textbf{O} \\ / \quad \diagdown \\ H \qquad COO^- \end{array} \quad \xrightarrow{\text{Fumarase}} \quad \begin{array}{l} COO^- \\ | \\ HO{-}C{-}H \\ | \\ H{-}C{-}H \\ | \\ COO^- \end{array}$$

Fumarate   Malate

Reaction 8   Oxidation

In reaction 8, the last step of the citric acid cycle, *malate dehydrogenase* catalyzes the oxidation of the hydroxyl group ($-OH$) in malate to yield oxaloacetate. For the third time in the citric acid cycle, an oxidation provides hydrogen ions and electrons for the reduction of NAD^+ to NADH and H^+.

$$\begin{array}{l} COO^- \\ | \\ HO{-}C{-}H \\ | \\ CH_2 \;+\; \textbf{NAD}^+ \\ | \\ COO^- \end{array} \quad \xrightarrow[\text{dehydrogenase}]{\text{Malate}} \quad \begin{array}{l} COO^- \\ | \\ C{=}O \\ | \\ CH_2 \;+\; \textbf{NADH} + \textbf{H}^+ \\ | \\ COO^- \end{array}$$

Malate   Oxaloacetate

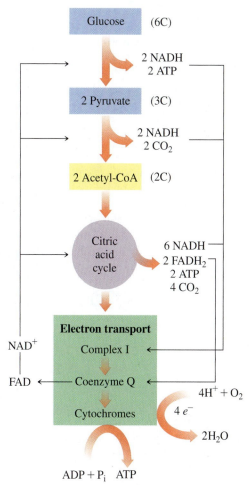

The reduced coenzymes NADH and $FADH_2$ that provide hydrogen ions and electrons in electron transport are regenerated as NAD^+ and FAD.

a. What happens to acetyl-CoA in reaction 1 of the citric acid cycle?
b. Why is citrate isomerized in reaction 2?
c. Where is ATP produced by a direct phosphate transfer in the citric acid cycle?
d. Where is oxaloacetate generated in the citric acid cycle?

ANSWER

a. In reaction 1 of the citric acid cycle, acetyl-CoA is hydrolyzed and the acetyl group (2C) combines with oxaloacetate (4C) to yield citrate (6C).
b. As a tertiary alcohol, citrate cannot be oxidized. In reaction 2, it is isomerized to isocitrate, which has a secondary alcohol group that can be oxidized.
c. Reaction 5 in the citric acid cycle produces GTP, which transfers a phosphate group to ADP to give ATP.
d. In reaction 8, malate is oxidized to generate oxaloacetate.

Summary of Products from the Citric Acid Cycle

We have seen that the citric acid cycle begins when a two-carbon acetyl group from acetyl-CoA combines with oxaloacetate to form citrate. Through oxidation and decarboxylation, two carbon atoms are removed to yield two CO_2 and a four-carbon compound that undergoes reactions to regenerate oxaloacetate.

In the four oxidation reactions of one turn of the citric acid cycle, three NAD^+s and one FAD are reduced to three NADHs and one $FADH_2$. One GDP is converted to one GTP, which is used to convert one ADP to ATP. We can write an overall chemical equation for one complete turn of the citric acid cycle as follows:

$$\text{Acetyl-CoA} + 3NAD^+ + FAD + GDP + P_i + 2H_2O \longrightarrow$$
$$2CO_2 + 3NADH + 3H^+ + FADH_2 + GTP + CoA$$

Regulation of the Citric Acid Cycle

The primary function of the citric acid cycle is to produce high-energy compounds for ATP synthesis. When the cell needs energy, low levels of ATP stimulate the conversion of pyruvate to acetyl-CoA, the fuel for the citric acid cycle. When ATP and NADH levels are high, there is a decrease in the production of acetyl-CoA from pyruvate.

In the citric acid cycle, the enzymes that catalyze reactions 3 and 4 respond to allosteric activation and inhibition (see Section 20.5). In reaction 3, isocitrate dehydrogenase is activated by high levels of ADP and inhibited by high levels of ATP and NADH. In reaction 4, α-ketoglutarate dehydrogenase is activated by high levels of ADP and inhibited by high levels of NADH and succinyl-CoA (see Figure 23.4).

When one acetyl-CoA completes the citric acid cycle, how many of each of the following is produced?

a. NADH   **b.** ketone group   **c.** CO_2

SOLUTION

a. One turn of the citric acid cycle produces three molecules of NADH.
b. Two ketone groups form when the secondary alcohol groups in isocitrate and malate are oxidized by NAD^+.
c. Two molecules of CO_2 are produced by the decarboxylation of isocitrate and α-ketoglutarate.

STUDY CHECK 23.1

What compound is a substrate in the first reaction of the citric acid cycle and a product in the last reaction?

Products from One Turn of the Citric Acid Cycle

2 CO_2
3 NADH and $3H^+$
1 $FADH_2$
1 GTP (1 ATP)
1 CoA

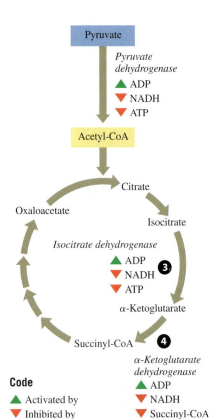

Code

▲ Activated by
▼ Inhibited by

FIGURE 23.4 High levels of ADP activate enzymes for the production of acetyl-CoA and the citric acid cycle, whereas high levels of ATP, NADH, and succinyl-CoA inhibit enzymes in the citric acid cycle.

Q How do high levels of ATP affect the rate of the citric acid cycle?

QUESTIONS AND PROBLEMS

23.1 The Citric Acid Cycle

LEARNING GOAL: *Describe the oxidation of acetyl-CoA in the citric acid cycle.*

23.1 What other names are used for the citric acid cycle?

23.2 What compounds are needed to start the citric acid cycle?

23.3 What are the products from one turn of the citric acid cycle?

23.4 What compound is regenerated in each turn of the citric acid cycle?

23.5 Which reaction(s) of the citric acid cycle involve(s) oxidation and decarboxylation?

23.6 Which reaction(s) of the citric acid cycle involve(s) a dehydration reaction?

23.7 Which reaction(s) of the citric acid cycle reduce(s) NAD^+?

23.8 Which reaction(s) of the citric acid cycle reduce(s) FAD?

23.9 Which reaction(s) in the citric acid cycle involve(s) a direct phosphate transfer?

23.10 What is the total NADH and total $FADH_2$ produced in one turn of the citric acid cycle?

23.11 Refer to the diagram of the citric acid cycle to answer each of the following:
  a. What are the six-carbon compounds?
  b. How is the number of carbon atoms decreased?
  c. What is the five-carbon compound?
  d. Which reactions are oxidation reactions?
  e. In which reactions are secondary alcohols oxidized?

23.12 Refer to the diagram of the citric acid cycle to answer each of the following:
  a. What is the yield of CO_2 molecules?
  b. What are the four-carbon compounds?

  c. What is the yield of GTP molecules?
  d. What are the decarboxylation reactions?
  e. Where does a hydration occur?

23.13 Indicate the name of the enzyme that catalyzes each of the following reactions in the citric acid cycle:
  a. joins acetyl-CoA to oxaloacetate
  b. forms a carbon–carbon double bond
  c. adds water to fumarate

23.14 Indicate the name of the enzyme that catalyzes each of the following reactions in the citric acid cycle:
  a. isomerizes citrate
  b. oxidizes and decarboxylates α-ketoglutarate
  c. hydrolyzes succinyl-CoA and adds P_i to GDP

23.15 Indicate the reactant that accepts a hydrogen or a phosphate group in each of the following:
  a. isocitrate $\longrightarrow$ α-ketoglutarate
  b. succinyl-CoA $\longrightarrow$ succinate

23.16 Indicate the reactant that accepts a hydrogen or a phosphate group in each of the following:
  a. malate $\longrightarrow$ oxaloacetate
  b. α-ketoglutarate $\longrightarrow$ succinyl-CoA

23.17 What enzymes in the citric acid cycle are allosteric enzymes?

23.18 Why does the rate of the oxidation of pyruvate affect the rate of the citric acid cycle?

23.19 How do high levels of ADP affect the rate of the citric acid cycle?

23.20 How do high levels of NADH affect the rate of the citric acid cycle?

23.2 Electron Transport

At this point in stage 3, for each glucose molecule that completes glycolysis, the oxidation of two pyruvates, and the citric acid cycle, four ATPs, ten NADHs, and two $FADH_2$s are produced.

LEARNING GOAL

Describe how hydrogen and electrons are transferred during electron transport.

From Glucose	ATP	Reduced Coenzymes	
Glycolysis	2	2 NADH	
Oxidation of 2 pyruvate		2 NADH	
Citric acid cycle with 2 acetyl-CoA	2	6 NADH	2 FADH$_2$
Total for one glucose	**4**	**10 NADH**	**2 FADH$_2$**

Now we will discuss the importance of the reduced coenzymes NADH and $FADH_2$, when they are oxidized to provide the energy for the synthesis of considerably more ATP. In **electron transport**, or the *respiratory chain*, hydrogen ions and electrons from NADH and $FADH_2$ are passed from one electron acceptor or electron carrier to the next until they combine with oxygen to form H_2O. The energy released during electron transport is used to synthesize ATP from ADP and P_i, a process called *oxidative phosphorylation* (see Section 23.3). As long as oxygen is available for the mitochondria in the cell, electron

transport and oxidative phosphorylation function to produce most of the ATP energy manufactured in the cell.

In Section 22.1, we saw that a mitochondrion contains an inner and outer membrane. Along the highly folded inner membrane are the enzymes and electron carriers required for electron transport. Within these membranes are four distinct protein complexes, complex I, II, III, and IV. Two electron carriers, coenzyme Q and cytochrome *c*, are not firmly attached to the membrane. They function as mobile carriers shuttling electrons between the protein complexes that are bound to the inner membrane (see Figure 23.5).

Intermembrane Space

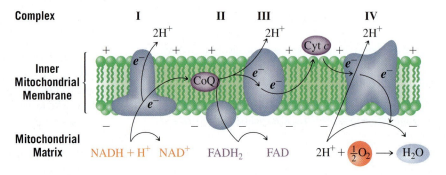

FIGURE 23.5 In electron transport, oxidation of NADH and FADH$_2$ provides hydrogen ions and electrons that react with oxygen to form water.

Q What is the major source of NADH for electron transport?

Complex I

Electron transport begins when hydrogen ions and two electrons are transferred from NADH to complex I and then to the mobile electron carrier **coenzyme Q (CoQ)**. Coenzyme Q is reduced to CoQH$_2$, which carries electrons from complex I and II to complex III (see Figure 23.6). The loss of hydrogen from NADH regenerates NAD$^+$, which becomes available again to oxidize more substrates in oxidative pathways such as the citric acid cycle. The hydrogen ions from NADH diffuse into the intermembrane space, where they produce a *proton gradient*. The overall reaction sequence in complex I is written as follows:

$$\text{NADH} + \text{H}^+ + \text{CoQ} \longrightarrow \text{CoQH}_2 + \text{NAD}^+$$

Quinone

CH$_3$O— ... —(CH$_2$—CH=C—CH$_2$)$_{10}$H $\rightleftharpoons$ CH$_3$O— ... —(CH$_2$—CH=C—CH$_2$)$_{10}$H

$2\text{H}^+ + 2\,e^-$

Oxidized coenzyme Q (CoQ)   **Reduced coenzyme Q (CoQH$_2$)**

FIGURE 23.6 The electron carrier coenzyme Q is reduced to CoQH$_2$ when it accepts 2H$^+$ and 2 e^- from NADH + H$^+$ or FADH$_2$.

Q How does reduced coenzyme Q compare to the oxidized form?

Complex II

In complex II, CoQ also obtains hydrogen ions and electrons from FADH$_2$, generated by the conversion of succinate to fumarate in the citric acid cycle, which yields CoQH$_2$ and the oxidized coenzyme FAD. The overall reaction sequence in complex II is written as follows:

$$\text{FADH}_2 + \text{CoQ} \longrightarrow \text{FAD} + \text{CoQH}_2$$

Complex III

In complex III, two electrons are transferred from the mobile carrier $CoQH_2$ to a series of iron-containing proteins called **cytochromes** and eventually to cytochrome c, which is a mobile electron carrier. The iron ion within the cytochromes is oxidized (Fe^{3+}) and reduced (Fe^{2+}) as electrons are lost and gained. The hydrogen ions released from $CoQH_2$ to yield CoQ diffuse into the intermembrane space, where they produce a proton gradient.

$$CoQH_2 + \underset{\text{Oxidized}}{2cyt\ c\ (Fe^{3+})} \longrightarrow CoQ + \underset{\text{Reduced}}{2cyt\ c\ (Fe^{2+})} + 2H^+$$

Complex IV

At complex IV, four electrons from four cytochrome c combine with hydrogen ions and oxygen (O_2) to form two molecules of water.

$$4cyt\ c\ (Fe^{2+}) + 4H^+ + O_2 \longrightarrow 4cyt\ c\ (Fe^{3+}) + 2H_2O$$

In a simplified form, we can write the reaction of hydrogen ions and electrons from NADH and $FADH_2$ with oxygen to form water as:

$$4\ e^- + 4H^+ + O_2 \longrightarrow 2H_2O$$

Overall, the reduced coenzymes NADH and $FADH_2$ from the citric acid cycle enter electron transport to provide hydrogen ions and electrons that react with oxygen, producing water and the oxidized coenzymes NAD^+ and FAD.

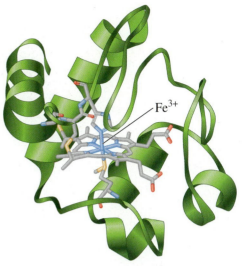

Fe^{3+}

In the mobile electron carrier cytochrome c, a covalent bond between cysteine (yellow) R groups forms between the heme (blue) portion and a protein (green) component. Oxygen atoms are shown in red.

Chemistry Link to Health

TOXINS: INHIBITORS OF ELECTRON TRANSPORT

Several substances can inhibit the electron carriers in the different complexes of electron transport. Rotenone, a product from a plant root used as an insecticide, and the painkillers Amytal and Demerol block electron transport between complex I and coenzyme Q. Another inhibitor is the antibiotic antimycin A, which blocks the flow of electrons between complex III and cytochrome c. Another group of compounds, including cyanide (CN^-) and carbon monoxide, block the flow of electrons between cytochrome c and complex IV.

The toxic nature of these compounds makes it clear that organisms rely heavily on the process of electron transport.

When an inhibitor blocks a step in electron transport, the carriers preceding that step are unable to transfer electrons, and remain in their reduced forms. All the carriers after the blocked step remain oxidized without a source of electrons. Thus, any of these inhibitors can shut down electron transport. Consequently, respiration stops, and the cells die.

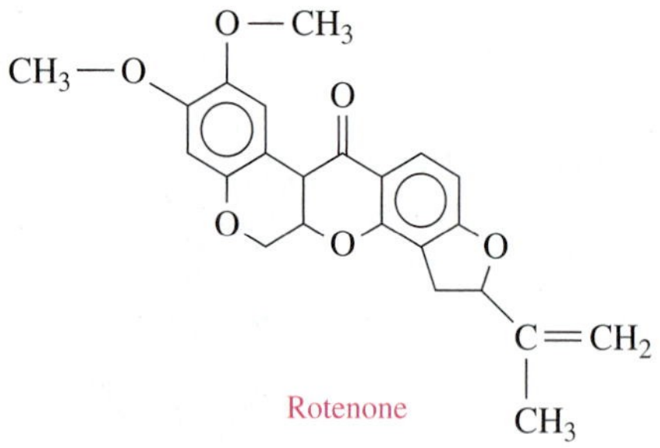

Rotenone

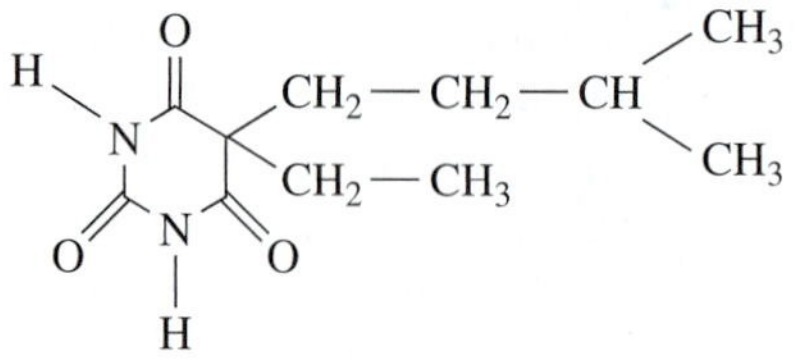

Amytal

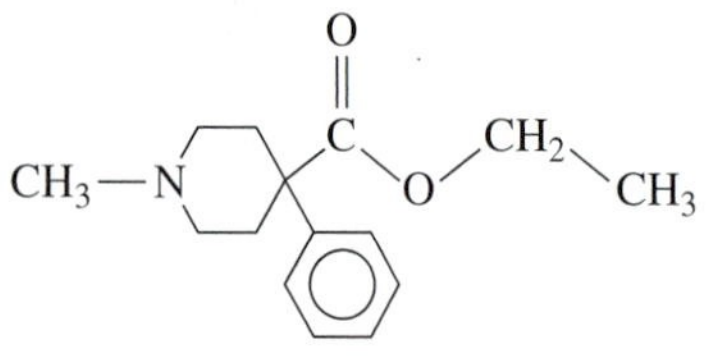

Demerol

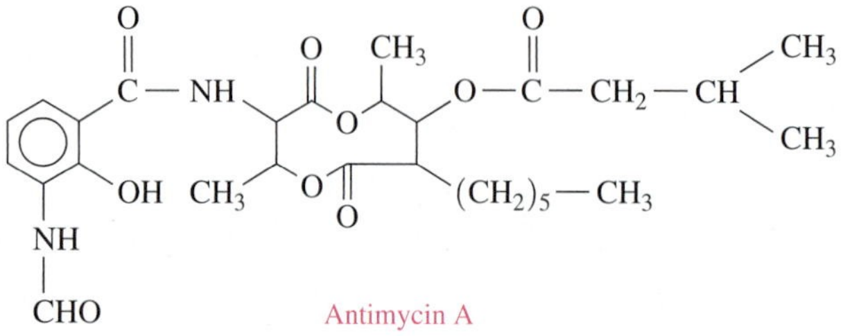

Antimycin A

QUESTIONS AND PROBLEMS

23.2 Electron Transport

LEARNING GOAL: *Describe how hydrogen and electrons are transferred during electron transport.*

23.21   Is cyt c (Fe^{3+}) the abbreviation for the oxidized or reduced form of cytochrome c?

23.22   Is $FADH_2$ the abbreviation for the oxidized or reduced form of flavin adenine dinucleotide?

23.23   Identify each of the following as oxidation or reduction:
   a. $NADH \longrightarrow NAD^+ + H^+ + 2\,e^-$
   b. $CoQ + 2H^+ + 2\,e^- \longrightarrow CoQH_2$

23.24   Identify each of the following as oxidation or reduction:
   a.   cyt c (Fe^{2+}) $\longrightarrow$ cyt c (Fe^{3+}) $+ e^-$
   b. $FAD + 2H^+ + 2\,e^- \longrightarrow FADH_2$

23.25   What reduced coenzyme provides the hydrogen ions and electrons for electron transport at complex I?

23.26   What reduced coenzyme provides the hydrogen ions and electrons for electron transport at complex II?

23.27   Arrange the following in the order in which they appear in electron transport: cytochrome c (Fe^{3+}), $FADH_2$, and CoQ.

23.28   Arrange the following in the order in which they appear in electron transport: O_2, NAD^+, and FAD.

23.29   How are electrons carried from complex I to complex III?

23.30   How are electrons carried from complex III to complex IV?

23.31   How is NADH oxidized in electron transport?

23.32   How is $FADH_2$ oxidized in electron transport?

23.33   Complete each of the following reactions in electron transport:
   a. $NADH + H^+ + \underline{\hspace{1cm}} \longrightarrow \underline{\hspace{1cm}} + CoQH_2$
   b. $CoQH_2 + 2cyt\ c\ (Fe^{3+}) \longrightarrow CoQ + \underline{\hspace{1cm}} + \underline{\hspace{1cm}}$

23.34   Complete each of the following reactions in electron transport:
   a. $CoQ + \underline{\hspace{1cm}} \longrightarrow \underline{\hspace{1cm}} + FAD$
   b. $4cyt\ c\ (Fe^{3+}) + 4H^+ + O_2 \longrightarrow$
               $4cyt\ c\ (Fe^{2+}) + \underline{\hspace{1cm}}$

LEARNING GOAL

Describe the process of oxidative phosphorylation in ATP synthesis.

TUTORIAL
The Chemiosmotic Model

SELF-STUDY ACTIVITY
Electron Transport

23.3 Oxidative Phosphorylation and ATP

We have seen that energy is generated when electrons from the oxidation of substrates flow through electron transport. Now we will look at how that energy is coupled with the production of ATP in the process called **oxidative phosphorylation**.

The Chemiosmotic Model

In 1978, Peter Mitchell received the Nobel Prize in chemistry for his theory called the **chemiosmotic model**, which links the energy from electron transport to a proton gradient that drives the synthesis of ATP. Three of the protein complexes (I, III, and IV) extend through the inner mitochondrial membrane, with one end of each complex in the matrix and the other end in the intermembrane space. In the chemiosmotic model, each of these complexes acts as a **proton pump** by pushing protons (H^+) out of the matrix and into the intermembrane space. This increase in protons in the intermembrane space lowers the pH and creates a proton gradient. Because protons are positively charged, the lower pH and the electrical charge of the proton gradient produce an *electrochemical gradient* (see Figure 23.7).

Intermembrane Space

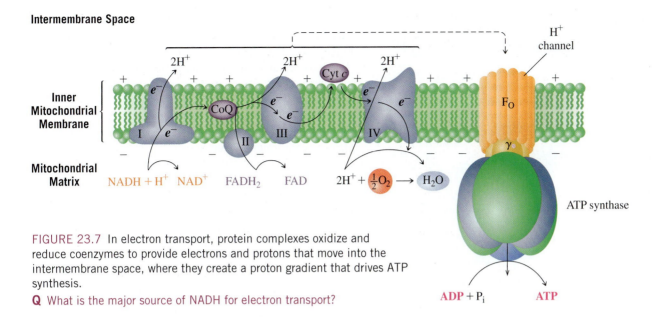

FIGURE 23.7 In electron transport, protein complexes oxidize and reduce coenzymes to provide electrons and protons that move into the intermembrane space, where they create a proton gradient that drives ATP synthesis.

Q What is the major source of NADH for electron transport?

To equalize the pH and the electrical charge between the intermembrane space and the matrix, protons return to the matrix by passing through the enzyme **ATP synthase**. As the protons flow through ATP synthase, the energy generated by the proton gradient is used to combine ADP and P_i to form ATP. Thus, the process of oxidative phosphorylation couples the energy from electron transport to the synthesis of ATP from ADP and P_i.

$$ADP + P_i + energy \xrightarrow{\text{ATP synthase}} ATP$$

CONCEPT CHECK 23.2 **The Chemiosmotic Model**

Consider the process of proton pumping in the chemiosmotic model.

a. What changes in pH take place in the mitochondrial matrix and in the intermembrane space?
b. How do the protons return to the matrix to rebalance the pH?
c. How is energy obtained for the synthesis of ATP?

ANSWER

a. The process of proton pumping "pushes" protons (H^+) out of the mitochondrial matrix, which increases the pH. At the same time, protons (H^+) are added to the intermembrane space, which decreases its pH.
b. Protons return to the matrix to rebalance the pH by passing through ATP synthase.
c. The energy from protons flowing through ATP synthase is used to synthesize ATP.

Details of ATP Synthase

ATP synthase consists of two sections (see Figure 23.8). The F_O section, which is in the inner membrane, contains the channel for the return of protons to the matrix. The F_1 section consists of a center subunit gamma (γ) that is surrounded by three groups of protein subunits. These protein subunits each contain active sites that change to three different shapes or conformations known as loose (L), tight (T), and open (O). As the protons flow through the F_O channel, the energy released turns the center subunit (γ). We might think of the flow of protons as a stream or river that turns a water wheel. As the center unit supplies energy to the three active sites, their shapes change.

ATP synthesis begins when the substrates ADP and P_i enter an open (O) active site. As the conformation of the active site changes to loose (L), ADP and P_i are bound to

MC

TUTORIAL
Power from Protons: ATP Synthase

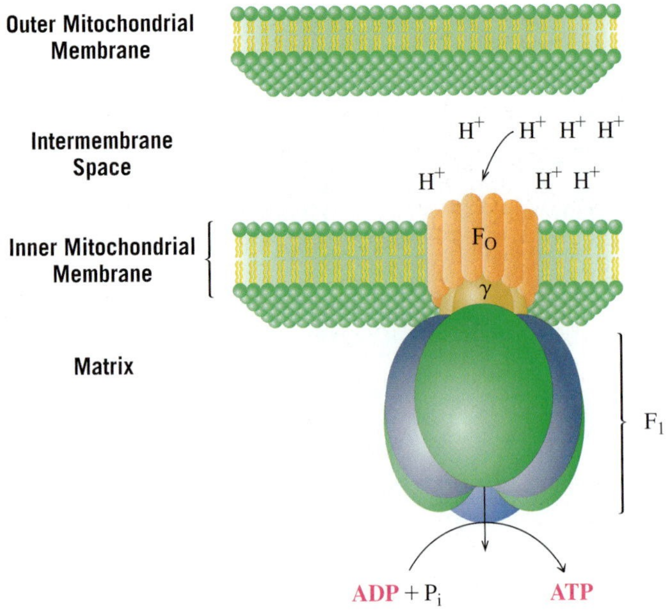

Outer Mitochondrial Membrane

Intermembrane Space

Inner Mitochondrial Membrane

Matrix

H^+ H^+ H^+ H^+
H^+ H^+ H^+

F_O

γ

F_1

$ADP + P_i$ → ATP

FIGURE 23.8 ATP synthase consists of two protein complexes. An F_O section contains the channel for proton flow, and an F_1 section uses the energy from the proton gradient to drive the synthesis of ATP.

Q What are the functions of the F_O and F_1 sections of ATP synthase?

FIGURE 23.9 In the F_1 ATP synthase, ATP is formed when the loose (L) active site containing ADP and P_i converts to a tight (T) conformation. When energy from the proton flow through F_O changes its active site to the open (O) conformation, ATP is released.

Q What shape of an active site in F_1 ATP synthase accepts the substrates, and which shape releases the ATP?

the ATP synthase enzyme. When the active site converts to a tight (T) conformation, ATP is formed, and it remains bound in the tight (T) conformation. As more protons flow through the proton channel and provide energy, the tight (T) conformation changes to an open (O) site, and ATP is released (see Figure 23.9).

In summary, the energy from protons flowing through F_O turns the center γ unit in F_1. The shape of each active site changes conformation from loose (L), which binds ADP and P_i, to tight (T), where ATP forms, and then to open (O), which releases ATP and accepts another $ADP + P_i$. This process of oxidative phosphorylation continues as long as energy from the electron transport system is generated, which pumps the protons into the intermembrane space and produces the proton gradient to fuel ATP synthase.

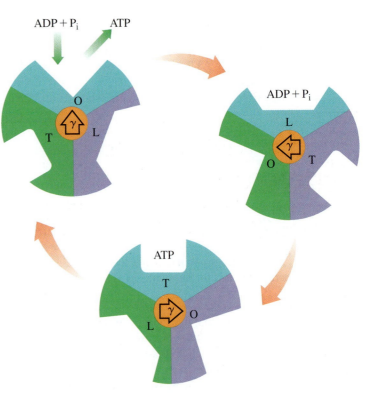

$ADP + P_i$ ATP

$ADP + P_i$

ATP

Electron Transport and ATP Synthesis

When NADH enters electron transport at complex I, the energy released from its oxidation is used to synthesize three ATP molecules. However, $FADH_2$ enters electron transport at complex II, which is at a lower energy level, and provides energy for the synthesis of only two ATPs. Recent measurements indicate that the oxidation of NADH has an energy yield closer to 2.5 ATPs and that one $FADH_2$ has an energy yield closer to 1.5 ATPs. Because there are still disagreements about the actual values for ATP yield, we will use the traditional values of 3 ATPs for NADH and 2 ATPs for $FADH_2$. The overall equation for the oxidation of NADH and $FADH_2$ can be written as follows:

$$\text{NADH} + \text{H}^+ + \tfrac{1}{2}O_2 + 3ADP + 3P_i \longrightarrow \text{NAD}^+ + H_2O + \textbf{3ATP}$$

$$\textbf{FADH}_2 + \tfrac{1}{2}O_2 + 2ADP + 2P_i \longrightarrow \text{FAD} + H_2O + \textbf{2ATP}$$

Regulation of Electron Transport and Oxidative Phosphorylation

Electron transport is regulated by the availability of ADP, P_i, oxygen (O_2), and NADH. Low levels of any of these compounds will decrease the activity of electron transport and the formation of ATP. When a cell is active and ATP is consumed rapidly, the elevated levels of ADP will activate the synthesis of ATP. Therefore, the activity of electron transport is strongly dependent on the levels of ADP for ATP synthesis.

SAMPLE PROBLEM 23.3   **ATP Synthesis**

Why does the oxidation of NADH provide energy for the formation of three ATPs molecules, whereas $FADH_2$ produces two ATPs?

SOLUTION

The oxidation of NADH occurs at complex I of electron transport so that protons can be pumped from the matrix into the intermembrane space through three complexes: I, III, and IV, which provides enough energy for the synthesis of three ATPs. However, $FADH_2$ is oxidized at complex II, so that protons are pumped through complexes III and IV into the intermembrane space. Thus, $FADH_2$ provides energy for the synthesis of only two ATPs.

STUDY CHECK 23.3

How do protons return to the matrix?

Chemistry Link to Health

UNCOUPLERS OF ATP SYNTHASE

Some types of compounds called *uncouplers* separate the electron transport system from ATP synthase. They do this by providing an alternate route for protons to return to the matrix without passing through ATP synthase and without synthesizing ATP.

Uncouplers transport protons through the inner mitochondrial membrane, which is normally impermeable to protons. Compounds such as 2,4-dinitrophenol (DNP) are hydrophobic and bind with protons and carry them across the inner membrane. By removing protons from the intermembrane space, there is no proton flow through the F_O channel to generate energy for ATP synthesis.

2,4-Dinitrophenol (DNP)

Animals that are adapted to cold climates have developed their own uncoupling system, which allows them to use electron transport energy for heat production. These animals have large amounts of a tissue called *brown fat*, which contains a high concentration of mitochondria. This tissue is brown because of the color of iron in the cytochromes of the mitochondria. The proton pumps still operate in brown fat, but a protein called thermogenin, present in the inner membrane of brown adipose tissues, provides an alternative route for protons to flow back to the matrix. Heat rather than ATP is produced. The brown fat deposits are located near major blood vessels,

Brown fat helps babies to keep warm.

which carry the warmed blood throughout the body. Newborn babies have a much higher percentage of brown fat than do adults because newborns have a small mass but large surface area, and they need to produce more heat than do adults. Most adults have little or no brown fat, although someone who works outdoors for long periods in a cold climate will develop some brown fat deposits.

Plants also use uncouplers. Some plants use uncoupling agents to volatize fragrant compounds that attract insects to pollinate the plants. Skunk cabbage uses this system. In other plants, heat is used to warm early shoots of plants under the snow, which helps them melt the snow around the plants.

QUESTIONS AND PROBLEMS

23.3 Oxidative Phosphorylation and ATP

LEARNING GOAL: Describe the process of oxidative phosphorylation in ATP synthesis.

23.35 What is meant by the term oxidative phosphorylation?

23.36 How is the proton gradient established?

23.37 According to the chemiosmotic model, how does the proton gradient provide energy to synthesize ATP?

23.38 How does the phosphorylation of ADP occur?

23.39 How are glycolysis and the citric acid cycle linked to the production of ATP by electron transport?

23.40 Why does FADH$_2$ have a yield of two ATPs via electron transport, whereas NADH yields three ATPs?

23.41 What are the components of ATP synthase?

23.42 What is the role of each section of ATP synthase in ATP synthesis?

23.43 Which conformation of the active site in ATP synthase binds ADP and P$_i$?

23.44 How is the ATP released from ATP synthase?

TUTORIAL
ATP Energy from Glucose

23.4 ATP Energy from Glucose

The total ATP for the complete oxidation of glucose under aerobic conditions is calculated by combining the ATP produced from glycolysis, the oxidation of pyruvate, the citric acid cycle, and electron transport.

ATP from Glycolysis

In glycolysis, the oxidation of glucose stores energy in two NADH molecules, as well as two ATP molecules from direct phosphate transfer. However, glycolysis occurs in the cytoplasm, and the NADH produced cannot pass through the mitochondrial membrane.

Therefore, the hydrogen ions and electrons from NADH in the cytoplasm are transferred to compounds that can enter the mitochondria. In this shuttle system, dihydroxyacetone phosphate produced in glycolysis is reduced to glycerol-3-phosphate using NADH + H$^+$, which regenerates NAD$^+$ for glycolysis. Glycerol-3-phosphate, which can cross the mitochondrial membrane, provides hydrogen ions and electrons that are transferred to FAD. FADH$_2$ is produced along with dihydroxyacetone phosphate, which returns to the cytoplasm. The overall reaction for the glycerol-3-phosphate shuttle is:

$$\text{NADH} + \text{H}^+ + \text{FAD} \longrightarrow \text{NAD}^+ + \text{FADH}_2$$
In cytoplasm   In mitochondria

Therefore, the transfer of electrons from NADH in the cytoplasm to FADH$_2$ produces two ATPs, rather than three. In glycolysis, glucose yields six ATPs: four ATPs from two NADHs, and two ATPs from direct phosphate transfer.

$$\text{Glucose} \longrightarrow 2\,\text{pyruvate} + 2\,\text{ATP} + 2\,\text{NADH}\,(\longrightarrow 2\,\text{FADH}_2)$$
$$\text{Glucose} \longrightarrow 2\,\text{pyruvate} + 6\,\text{ATP}$$

ATP from the Oxidation of Two Pyruvates

Under aerobic conditions, pyruvate enters the mitochondria, where it is oxidized to give acetyl-CoA, CO$_2$, and NADH. Because glucose yields two pyruvates, two NADHs enter electron transport, where the oxidation of two pyruvates leads to the production of six ATP molecules.

$$2\,\text{Pyruvate} \longrightarrow 2\,\text{acetyl-CoA} + 6\,\text{ATP}$$

ATP from the Citric Acid Cycle

One turn of the citric acid cycle produces two CO$_2$, three NADHs, one FADH$_2$, and one ATP by direct phosphate transfer. When the NADH and FADH$_2$ enter electron transport, three NADHs produce nine ATP molecules, and one FADH$_2$ produces two more ATPs. Thus, one turn of the citric acid cycle generates energy for the synthesis of a total of 12 ATP molecules.

$$
\begin{array}{lcl}
3\,\text{NADH} \times 3\,\text{ATP/NADH} & = & 9\,\text{ATP} \\
1\,\text{FADH}_2 \times 2\,\text{ATP/FADH}_2 & = & 2\,\text{ATP} \\
\underline{1\,\text{GTP} \quad\;\, \times 1\,\text{ATP/GTP}} & \underline{=} & \underline{1\,\text{ATP}} \\
\text{Total (one turn)} & = & 12\,\text{ATP}
\end{array}
$$

Every glucose molecule that enters glycolysis produces two acetyl-CoA molecules, and one glucose provides two turns of the citric acid cycle and produces a total of 24 ATPs.

Acetyl-CoA $\longrightarrow$ 2CO$_2$ + 12 ATP (one turn of the citric acid cycle)

2 Acetyl-CoA $\longrightarrow$ 4CO$_2$ + 24 ATP (two turns of the citric acid cycle)

ATP from the Complete Oxidation of Glucose

The total ATP production for the complete oxidation of glucose is calculated by combining the ATP produced from glycolysis plus the oxidation of pyruvate plus the citric acid cycle (see Figure 23.10). The ATP produced for these reactions is given in Table 23.1.

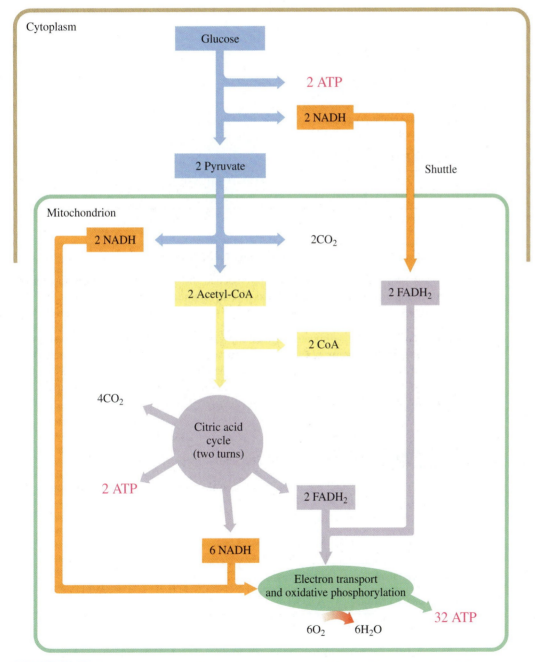

FIGURE 23.10 The complete oxidation of glucose to CO$_2$ and H$_2$O yields a total of 36 ATPs.

Q What metabolic pathway produces most of the ATP from the oxidation of glucose?

TABLE 23.1 ATP Produced by the Complete Oxidation of Glucose

Reaction	
ATP from Glycolysis	**ATP for 1 Glucose**
Activation of glucose	−2 ATP
Oxidation of glyceraldehyde-3-phosphate (2 NADH)	6 ATP
Conversion of 2 NADH $\longrightarrow$ 2 FADH$_2$	−2 ATP
Direct ADP phosphorylation (two triose phosphate)	4 ATP
Summary: C$_6$H$_{12}$O$_6$ $\longrightarrow$ 2 pyruvate + 2H$_2$O	6 ATP
Glucose	
ATP from Pyruvate	
2 pyruvate $\longrightarrow$ 2 acetyl-CoA (2 NADH)	6 ATP
ATP from the Citric Acid Cycle	
Oxidation of 2 isocitrate (2 NADH)	6 ATP
Oxidation of 2 α-ketoglutarate (2 NADH)	6 ATP
2 direct phosphate transfers (2 GTP)	2 ATP
Oxidation of 2 succinate (2 FADH$_2$)	4 ATP
Oxidation of 2 malate (2 NADH)	6 ATP
Summary: 2 acetyl-CoA $\longrightarrow$ 4CO$_2$ + 2H$_2$O	24 ATP
Overall ATP Production for 1 Glucose	
C$_6$H$_{12}$O$_6$ + 6O$_2$ + 36 ADP + 36 P$_i$ $\longrightarrow$ 6CO$_2$ + 6H$_2$O + 36 ATP	
Glucose	

CONCEPT CHECK 23.3 **ATP Production from Glucose**

How many turns of the citric acid cycle are needed for ATP production from the intermediate products formed from glucose in glycolysis under aerobic conditions?

ANSWER

When glucose with six carbons is degraded in glycolysis, two pyruvates (3C) are produced. The decarboxylation of two pyruvates gives two acetyl-CoAs (2C) that enter the citric acid cycle under aerobic conditions. In one turn of the citric acid cycle, two carbon atoms from the acetyl group are oxidized to two CO$_2$. For two acetyl groups from two acetyl-CoA molecules, two turns of the citric acid cycle are needed.

SAMPLE PROBLEM 23.4 **ATP Production**

Indicate the amount of ATP produced by each of the following oxidation reactions:

a. pyruvate to acetyl-CoA　　　　　**b.** glucose to acetyl-CoA

SOLUTION

Analyze the Problem

Substrate/Product	Coenzymes	Phosphate Transfer
a. Pyruvate/acetyl-CoA	NADH	
b. Glucose/acetyl-CoA	6 NADH, 2 FADH$_2$	2 GTP

a. The oxidation of pyruvate to acetyl-CoA produces one NADH, which yields three ATPs. We calculate this as:

$$1\,\text{NADH} \times 3\,\text{ATP/NADH} = 3\,\text{ATP}$$

b. Six ATPs are produced from the oxidation of glucose to two pyruvate molecules. Six more ATPs result from the oxidation of two pyruvate molecules to two acetyl-CoA molecules. Thus, a total of 12 ATPs are produced when glucose is oxidized to yield two acetyl-CoAs.

$$6 \text{ NADH } \times 3 \text{ ATP/NADH } = 18 \text{ ATP}$$
$$2 \text{ FADH}_2 \times 2 \text{ ATP/FADH}_2 = 4 \text{ ATP}$$
$$\underline{2 \text{ GTP } \times 1 \text{ ATP/GTP } = 2 \text{ ATP}}$$
$$\text{TOTAL} \quad 24 \text{ ATP}$$

STUDY CHECK 23.4

What are the sources of ATP in the citric acid cycle?

Chemistry Link to Health

EFFICIENCY OF ATP PRODUCTION

In a laboratory, a calorimeter is used to measure the heat energy from the combustion of glucose. In a calorimeter, 1 mole of glucose produces 680 kcal.

$$C_6H_{12}O_6 + 6O_2 \longrightarrow 6CO_2 + 6H_2O + 680 \text{ kcal}$$

We can compare the amount of energy produced from 1 mole of glucose in a calorimeter with the ATP energy produced in the mitochondria from glucose. We use the energy of the hydrolysis of ATP (7.3 kcal/mole of ATP). Because 1 mole of glucose generates energy for 36 moles of ATP, the total energy from the oxidation of 1 mole of glucose in the cells would be 260 kcal/mole.

$$\frac{36 \text{ moles ATP}}{1 \text{ mole glucose}} \times \frac{7.3 \text{ kcal}}{1 \text{ mole ATP}} = 260 \text{ kcal/1 mole of glucose}$$

Compared to the energy produced by burning glucose in a calorimeter, our cells are about 38% efficient in converting the total available chemical energy in glucose to ATP.

$$\frac{260 \text{ kcal (cells)}}{680 \text{ kcal (calorimeter)}} \times 100\% = 38\%$$

The rest of the energy from glucose produced during the oxidation of glucose in our cells is lost as heat.

Calorimeter	Cells
Energy produced by 1 mole of glucose (680 kcal)	Stored as ATP (260 kcal)
	Lost as heat (420 kcal)

QUESTIONS AND PROBLEMS

23.4 ATP Energy from Glucose

LEARNING GOAL: *Account for the ATP produced by the complete oxidation of glucose.*

23.45 Why does the NADH produced in glycolysis yield only two ATPs?

23.46 Under aerobic conditions, what is the maximum number of ATP molecules that can be produced from one glucose molecule?

23.47 What is the energy yield in ATP molecules associated with each of the following?
 a. NADH $\longrightarrow$ NAD$^+$ **b.** glucose $\longrightarrow$ 2 pyruvate
 c. 2 pyruvate $\longrightarrow$ 2 acetyl-CoA + 2CO$_2$

23.48 What is the energy yield in ATP molecules associated with each of the following?
 a. FADH$_2$ $\longrightarrow$ FAD
 b. glucose + 6O$_2$ $\longrightarrow$ 6CO$_2$ + 6H$_2$O
 c. acetyl-CoA $\longrightarrow$ 2CO$_2$

CONCEPT MAP

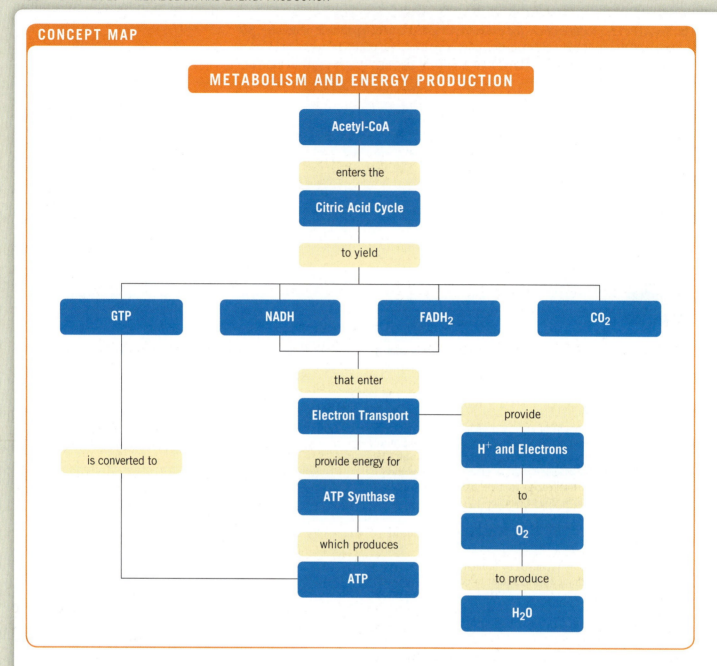

METABOLISM AND ENERGY PRODUCTION

Acetyl-CoA

enters the

Citric Acid Cycle

to yield

GTP   NADH   FADH₂   CO₂

is converted to

that enter

Electron Transport   provide

provide energy for   H⁺ and Electrons

ATP Synthase   to

which produces   O₂

ATP   to produce

H₂O

CHAPTER REVIEW

23.1 The Citric Acid Cycle

LEARNING GOAL: *Describe the oxidation of acetyl-CoA in the citric acid cycle.*

- In a sequence of reactions called the citric acid cycle, an acetyl group is combined with oxaloacetate to yield citrate.
- Citrate undergoes oxidation and decarboxylation to yield two CO_2, GTP, three NADHs, and FADH₂ with the regeneration of oxaloacetate.
- The direct phosphate transfer of ADP by GTP yields ATP.

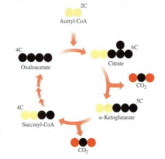

23.2 Electron Transport

LEARNING GOAL: *Describe how hydrogen and electrons are transferred during electron transport.*

- The reduced coenzymes NADH and FADH₂ from various metabolic pathways are oxidized to NAD^+ and FAD when their protons and electrons are transferred to the electron transport system.
- The energy released is used to synthesize ATP from ADP and P_i.
- The final acceptor, O_2, combines with protons and electrons to yield H_2O.

23.3 Oxidative Phosphorylation and ATP

LEARNING GOAL: *Describe the process of oxidative phosphorylation in ATP synthesis.*

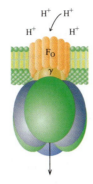

- The protein complexes in electron transport act as proton pumps to move protons into the intermembrane space, which produces a proton gradient.
- As the protons return to the matrix by way of ATP synthase, energy is generated.
- This energy is used to drive the synthesis of ATP in a process known as oxidative phosphorylation.
- The available ADP and ATP levels in the cells control the activity of electron transport.

23.4 ATP Energy from Glucose

LEARNING GOAL: *Account for the ATP produced by the complete oxidation of glucose.*

Calorimeter	Cells
Energy produced by 1 mole of glucose (680 kcal)	Stored as ATP (260 kcal)
	Lost as heat (420 kcal)

- With the exception of the NADH produced from glycolysis, the oxidation of NADH yields three ATP molecules, and $FADH_2$ yields two ATPs.
- The energy from the NADH produced in the cytoplasm is used to form $FADH_2$.
- Under aerobic conditions, the complete oxidation of glucose yields a total of 36 ATP from the oxidation of the reduced coenzymes NADH and $FADH_2$ by electron transport, oxidative phosphorylation, and from some direct phosphate transfer.

SUMMARY OF KEY REACTIONS

Citric Acid Cycle

$$\text{Acetyl-CoA} + 3\,NAD^+ + FAD + GDP + P_i + 2H_2O \longrightarrow 2CO_2 + 3\,NADH + 3H^+ + FADH_2 + HS—CoA + GTP$$

Electron Transport

$$NADH + H^+ + 3\,ADP + 3\,P_i + \tfrac{1}{2}O_2 \longrightarrow NAD^+ + 3\,ATP + H_2O$$

$$FADH_2 + 2\,ADP + 2\,P_i + \tfrac{1}{2}O_2 \longrightarrow FAD + 2\,ATP + H_2O$$

Phosphorylation of ADP

$$ADP + P_i \longrightarrow ATP + H_2O$$

Complete Oxidation of Glucose

$$C_6H_{12}O_6 + 6O_2 + 36\,ADP + 36\,P_i \longrightarrow 6CO_2 + 6H_2O + 36\,ATP$$

KEY TERMS

ATP synthase An enzyme complex that links the energy released by protons returning to the matrix with the synthesis of ATP from ADP and P_i. The F_O section contains the channel for proton flow, and the F_1 section uses the energy from the proton flow to drive the synthesis of ATP.

chemiosmotic model The conservation of energy from the transfer of electrons in electron transport that results from pumping protons into the intermembrane space to produce a proton gradient that provides the energy to synthesize ATP.

citric acid cycle A series of oxidation reactions in the mitochondria that converts acetyl-CoA to CO_2 and yields NADH and $FADH_2$. It is also called the tricarboxylic acid cycle or the Krebs cycle.

coenzyme Q (CoQ) A mobile carrier that transfers electrons from NADH and $FADH_2$ to complex III.

cytochromes (cyt) Iron-containing proteins that transfer electrons from $CoQH_2$ to oxygen.

decarboxylation A reaction in which a CO_2 molecule is produced.

electron transport A series of reactions in the mitochondria that transfer electrons from NADH and $FADH_2$ to electron carriers, and finally to O_2, which produces H_2O. Energy changes during three of these transfers provide energy for ATP synthesis.

oxidative phosphorylation The synthesis of ATP from ADP and P_i using energy generated by the oxidation reactions in electron transport.

proton pumps The enzyme complexes I, III, and IV that move protons from the matrix into the intermembrane space, creating a proton gradient.

UNDERSTANDING THE CONCEPTS

The chapter sections to review are given in parentheses at the end of each question.

23.49 Identify each of the following as a substance that is part of the citric acid cycle, electron transport, or both: (23.1, 23.2)
  a. succinate
  b. $CoQH_2$
  c. FAD
  d. cyt c (Fe^{2+})
  e. citrate

23.50 Identify each of the following as a substance that is part of the citric acid cycle, electron transport, or both: (23.1, 23.2)
  a. succinyl-CoA
  b. acetyl-CoA
  c. malate
  d. NAD^+
  e. α-ketoglutarate

23.51 Complete the names of the missing compounds in the citric acid cycle: (23.1)
- **a.** citrate $\longrightarrow$ _____
- **b.** succinyl-CoA $\longrightarrow$ _____
- **c.** malate $\longrightarrow$ _____

23.52 Complete the names of the missing compounds in the citric acid cycle: (23.1)
- **a.** oxaloacetate $\longrightarrow$ _____
- **b.** fumarate $\longrightarrow$ _____
- **c.** isocitrate $\longrightarrow$ _____

23.53 Identify the reactant and product for each of the following enzymes in the citric acid cycle: (23.1)
- **a.** aconitase
- **b.** succinate dehydrogenase
- **c.** fumarase

23.54 Identify the reactant and product for each of the following enzymes in the citric acid cycle: (23.1)
- **a.** isocitrate dehydrogenase
- **b.** succinyl-CoA synthetase
- **c.** malate dehydrogenase

23.55 For each of the given enzymes (**a–c**), indicate which of the following are needed: NAD^+, H_2O, FAD, GDP. (23.1)
- **a.** aconitase
- **b.** succinate dehydrogenase
- **c.** isocitrate dehydrogenase

23.56 For each of the given enzymes (**a–c**), indicate which of the following are needed: NAD^+, H_2O, FAD, GDP. (23.1)
- **a.** fumarase
- **b.** succinyl-CoA synthetase
- **c.** malate dehydrogenase

23.57 Identify the type(s) of reaction(s)—(1) oxidation, (2) decarboxylation, (3) hydrolysis, (4) hydration—catalyzed by each of the following enzymes (**a–c**): (23.1)
- **a.** aconitase
- **b.** succinate dehydrogenase
- **c.** isocitrate dehydrogenase

23.58 Identify the type(s) of reaction(s)—(1) oxidation, (2) decarboxylation, (3) hydrolysis, (4) hydration—catalyzed by each of the following enzymes (**a–c**): (23.1)
- **a.** fumarase
- **b.** α-ketoglutarate dehydrogenase
- **c.** malate dehydrogenase

ADDITIONAL QUESTIONS AND PROBLEMS

For instructor-assigned homework, go to www.masteringchemistry.com.

23.59 What is the main function of the citric acid cycle in energy production? (23.1)

23.60 Most metabolic pathways are not considered cycles. Why is the citric acid cycle considered a metabolic cycle? (23.1)

23.61 If there are no reactions in the citric acid cycle that use oxygen, O_2, why does the cycle operate only in aerobic conditions? (23.1)

23.62 What products of the citric acid cycle are needed for electron transport? (23.1)

23.63 Identify the compounds in the citric acid cycle that have the following: (23.1)
- **a.** six carbon atoms
- **b.** five carbon atoms
- **c.** a keto group

23.64 Identify the compounds in the citric acid cycle that have the following: (23.1)
- **a.** four carbon atoms
- **b.** a hydroxyl group
- **c.** a carbon–carbon double bond

23.65 In which reaction of the citric acid cycle does each of the following occur? (23.1)
- **a.** A five-carbon keto acid is decarboxylated.
- **b.** A carbon–carbon double bond is hydrated.
- **c.** NAD^+ is reduced.
- **d.** A secondary hydroxyl group is oxidized.

23.66 In which reaction of the citric acid cycle does each of the following occur? (23.1)
- **a.** FAD is reduced.
- **b.** A six-carbon keto acid is decarboxylated.
- **c.** A carbon–carbon double bond is formed.
- **d.** GDP undergoes direct phosphate transfer.

23.67 Indicate the coenzyme(s) for each of the following reactions: (23.1)
- **a.** isocitrate $\longrightarrow$ α-ketoglutarate
- **b.** α-ketoglutarate $\longrightarrow$ succinyl-CoA

23.68 Indicate the coenzyme(s) for each of the following reactions: (23.1)
- **a.** succinate $\longrightarrow$ fumarate
- **b.** malate $\longrightarrow$ oxaloacetate

23.69 How does each of the following regulate the citric acid cycle? (23.1)
- **a.** high levels of NADH
- **b.** high levels of ATP

23.70 How does each of the following regulate the citric acid cycle? (23.1)
- **a.** high levels of ADP
- **b.** low levels of NADH

23.71 At which complexes in the electron transport system are protons pumped into the intermembrane space? (23.2)

23.72 What is the effect of proton accumulation in the intermembrane space? (23.2)

23.73 Which complex in electron transport is inhibited by each of the following? (23.2)
- **a.** amytal and rotenone
- **b.** antimycin A
- **c.** cyanide and carbon monoxide

23.74 **a.** When an inhibitor blocks electron transport, how are the coenzymes that precede the blocked site affected? (23.2)
- **b.** When an inhibitor blocks electron transport, how are the coenzymes that follow the blocked site affected?

23.75 In the chemiosmotic model, how is energy provided to synthesize ATP? (23.3)

23.76 Where does the synthesis of ATP take place in electron transport? (23.2, 23.3)

23.77 Why do protons tend to leave the intermembrane space and return to the matrix within a mitochondrion? (23.3)

23.78 Why do the enzyme complexes that pump protons extend across the mitochondrial membrane from the matrix to the intermembrane space? (23.3)

23.79 How many ATP molecules are produced by energy generated when electrons flow from $FADH_2$ to oxygen (O_2)? (23.3)

23.80 How many ATP molecules are produced by energy generated when electrons flow from NADH to oxygen (O_2)? (23.3)

23.81 How many ATP molecules are produced when glucose is oxidized to pyruvate compared to when glucose is oxidized to CO_2 and H_2O? (23.4)

23.82 Why do the two NADHs produced in glycolysis provide a net of two ATPs and not three? (23.3)

23.83 Where is ATP synthase for oxidative phosphorylation located in the cell? (23.3)

23.84 Considering the efficiency of ATP synthesis, how many kilocalories of energy would be conserved from the complete oxidation of 4.0 moles of glucose? (23.4)

23.85 How is the energy from the proton gradient utilized by ATP synthase? (23.3)

23.86 In electron transport, would the solution in the space between the outer and inner mitochondrial membrane be more or less acidic than the solution in the matrix? (23.3)

23.87 Why would a bear that is hibernating have more brown fat than one that is active? (23.3)

23.88 How do the active sites on F_1 ATP synthase change during ATP production? (23.3)

CHALLENGE QUESTIONS

23.89 Using the value 7.3 kcal/mole for ATP, how many kilocalories can be produced from the ATP provided by the reaction of 1 mole of glucose in each of the following? (23.1, 23.4)
  a. glycolysis
  b. oxidation of pyruvate to acetyl-CoA
  c. citric acid cycle
  d. complete oxidation to CO_2 and H_2O

23.90 In a calorimeter, the combustion of 1 mole of glucose produces 680 kcal. What percentage of ATP energy is produced from 1 mole of glucose by each of the reactions in Problem 23.89 **a–d**? (23.1, 23.4)

23.91 What does it mean to say that the cell is 38% efficient in storing the energy from the complete combustion of glucose? (23.4)

23.92 A student is considering using 2,4-dinitrophenol, which is an uncoupler, to lose weight. (23.2)
  a. Explain how the uncoupler will affect the body temperature of the student.
  b. Why would DNP not be recommended for weight loss?

23.93 If acetyl-CoA has a molar mass of 809 g/mole, how many moles of ATP are produced when 1.0 μg of acetyl-CoA completes the citric acid cycle? (23.4)

ANSWERS

Answers to Study Checks

23.1 oxaloacetate

23.2 Oxygen (O_2) is the final substance that accepts electrons.

23.3 Protons return to the matrix by passing through ATP synthase.

23.4 Three NADHs provide nine ATPs, one $FADH_2$ provides two ATPs, and one direct phosphate transfer provides one ATP.

Answers to Selected Questions and Problems

23.1 Krebs cycle and tricarboxylic acid cycle

23.3 $2CO_2$, 3 NADH + $3H^+$, $FADH_2$, GTP (ATP), and HS—CoA

23.5 Two reactions, reactions 3 and 4, involve oxidation and decarboxylation.

23.7 NAD^+ is reduced in reactions 3, 4, and 8 of the citric acid cycle.

23.9 In reaction 5, GDP undergoes a direct phosphate transfer.

23.11 a. citrate and isocitrate
  b. A carbon atom is lost as CO_2 in decarboxylation.
  c. α-ketoglutarate
  d. isocitrate $\longrightarrow$ α-ketoglutarate;
    α-ketoglutarate $\longrightarrow$ succinyl-CoA;
    succinate $\longrightarrow$ fumarate;
    malate $\longrightarrow$ oxaloacetate
  e. reactions 3 and 8

23.13 a. citrate synthase
  b. succinate dehydrogenase and aconitase
  c. fumarase

23.15 a. NAD^+ **b.** GDP

23.17 Isocitrate dehydrogenase and α-ketoglutarate dehydrogenase are allosteric enzymes.

23.19 High levels of ADP increase the rate of the citric acid cycle.

23.21 oxidized

23.23 a. oxidation   **b.** reduction

23.25 NADH

23.27 $FADH_2$, CoQ, cytochrome c (Fe^{3+})

23.29 The mobile carrier CoQ transfers electrons from complex I to complex III.

23.31 NADH transfers electrons to complex I to give NAD^+.

23.33 a. $NADH + H^+ + CoQ \longrightarrow NAD^+ + CoQH_2$
b. $CoQH_2 + 2cyt\ c\ (Fe^{3+}) \longrightarrow CoQ + 2cyt\ c\ (Fe^{2+}) + 2H^+$

23.35 In oxidative phosphorylation, the energy from the oxidation reactions in electron transport is used to drive ATP synthesis.

23.37 As protons return to the lower energy environment in the matrix, they pass through ATP synthase where they release energy to drive the synthesis of ATP.

23.39 Glycolysis and the citric acid cycle produce reduced coenzymes NADH and $FADH_2$, which enter electron transport and release hydrogen ions and electrons that are used to generate energy for the synthesis of ATP.

23.41 ATP synthase consists of two protein complexes, F_O and F_1.

23.43 The loose (L) site in ATP synthase binds ADP and P_i.

23.45 Glycolysis takes place in the cytoplasm, not in the mitochondria. Because NADH cannot cross the mitochondrial membrane, the hydrogen ions and electrons from NADH are used to form glycerol-3-phosphate, which crosses the mitochondrial membrane. Then the hydrogen ions and electrons are transferred to FAD to form $FADH_2$. The resulting $FADH_2$ produces only two ATPs for each NADH produced in glycolysis.

23.47 a. 3 ATP   **b.** 6 ATP   **c.** 6 ATP

23.49 a. citric acid cycle   **b.** electron transport
c. both   **d.** electron transport
e. citric acid cycle

23.51 a. isocitrate   **b.** succinate   **c.** oxaloacetate

23.53 a. citrate, isocitrate   **b.** succinate, fumarate
c. fumarate, malate

23.55 a. Aconitase uses H_2O.
b. Succinate dehydrogenase uses FAD.
c. Isocitrate dehydrogenase uses NAD^+.

23.57 a. (4) hydration reaction   **b.** (1) oxidation reaction
c. (1) oxidation and (2) decarboxylation reaction

23.59 The oxidation reactions of the citric acid cycle produce a source of reduced coenzymes for electron transport and ATP synthesis.

23.61 The oxidized coenzymes NAD^+ and FAD needed for the citric acid cycle are regenerated by electron transport, which requires oxygen.

23.63 a. citrate, isocitrate   **b.** α-ketoglutarate
c. α-ketoglutarate, succinyl-CoA, oxaloacetate

23.65 a. In reaction 4, α-ketoglutarate, a five-carbon keto acid, is decarboxylated.
b. In reactions 2 and 7, double bonds in aconitate and fumarate are hydrated.
c. NAD^+ is reduced in reactions 3, 4, and 8.
d. In reactions 3 and 8, a secondary hydroxyl group in isocitrate and malate is oxidized.

23.67 a. NAD^+ **b.** NAD^+ and CoA

23.69 a. High levels of NADH inhibit isocitrate dehydrogenase and α-ketoglutarate dehydrogenase to slow the rate of the citric acid cycle.
b. High levels of ATP inhibit isocitrate dehydrogenase to slow the rate of the citric acid cycle.

23.71 complex I, III, and IV

23.73 a. electron flow from complex I to CoQ
b. electron flow from complex III to cyt c
c. electron flow from cytochrome c to complex IV

23.75 Energy is released as protons flow through ATP synthase back to the matrix and is utilized for the synthesis of ATP.

23.77 Protons flow into the matrix where the H^+ concentration is lower.

23.79 Two ATP molecules are produced from $FADH_2$.

23.81 The oxidation of glucose to pyruvate produces 6 ATP, whereas the oxidation of glucose to CO_2 and H_2O produces 36 ATP.

23.83 The ATP synthase extends through the inner mitochondrial membrane with the F_O section in contact with the proton gradient in the intermembrane space, while the F_1 complex is in the matrix.

23.85 As protons from the proton gradient move through the ATP synthase to return to the matrix, energy is released and used to drive ATP synthesis at the F_1 ATP synthase.

23.87 A hibernating bear has more brown fat because it can be used during the winter for heat rather than ATP energy.

23.89 a. 44 kcal   **b.** 44 kcal
c. 180 kcal   **d.** 260 kcal

23.91 If the combustion of glucose produces 680 kcal, but only 260 kcal (from 36 ATP) in cells, the efficiency of glucose use in the cells is 260 kcal/680 kcal or 38%.

23.93 1.5×10^{-8} mole of ATP

Metabolic Pathways for Lipids and Amino Acids

24

Mastering**CHEMISTRY**™

Visit **www.masteringchemistry.com** for self-study materials and instructor-assigned homework.

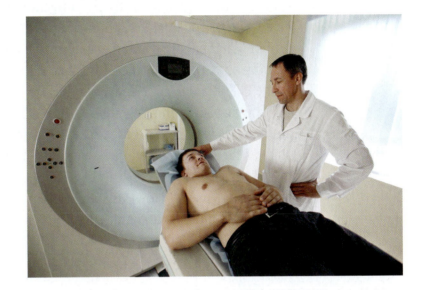

Luke has been experiencing weight loss,

loss of appetite, vomiting and some abdominal pain. Luke visits his doctor, who suspects a problem with his liver. The doctor orders blood work to be completed, and also refers Luke to a radiation technologist for a CT scan with contrast. Computed tomography, more commonly known as CT, uses X-rays to obtain a series of two-dimensional images and is commonly used for the diagnosis of abdominal diseases.

Fred, a radiation technologist, begins by explaining the procedure for the CT scan to Luke and asking him if he has any known allergies. Luke indicates that he has none and Fred places an IV port in Luke's arm. Fred then positions Luke into the scanner and an initial scan of Luke's liver is taken. Fred then injects the first dose of contrast into Luke's bloodstream and another scan is taken. Fred then repeats this process. From the CT scans, it is clear that a change in the liver tissue has occurred, possibly due to hepatitis or an infection.

The liver has many functions and is critical to metabolism. The liver produces bile, consisting of bile salts and other chemicals, which is required for the digestion of lipids. The liver is also responsible for the conversion of waste products from protein metabolism into urea, which is eliminated in the urine.

Career: Radiation Technologist

Radiation technologists, referred to as radiographers, produce X-ray films of specific body parts for use in diagnosing medical problems. With additional education, they are also able to specialize in specific techniques like computed tomography (CT), magnetic resonance imaging (MRI), and mammography. Radiation technologists prepare a patient by explaining the procedure, removing any items that would prevent the image from being obtained, and properly positioning the patient and the scanner so the correct area of the body is exposed as dictated by the physician. Radiographers must be knowledgeable about radiation exposure to limit the amount of radiation the patients are exposed to, as well as themselves. They may also prepare a contrast solution for a patient to drink, and maintain patient records and equipment.

n previous chapters, we focused on carbohydrates because glucose is the primary fuel for the synthesis of ATP. However, lipids and proteins also play an important role in metabolism and energy production. In this chapter, we will look at how the digestion of lipids produces fatty acids and glycerol and how the digestion of proteins gives amino acids. When our caloric intake exceeds the metabolic needs of our bodies, excess carbohydrates and fatty acids are converted to triacylglycerols and added to our fat cells. Almost all of our energy is stored in the form of triacylglycerols in the fat cells of adipose tissue. Many people go on diets after they discover that adipose tissue can store unlimited quantities of fat. This fact has become quite apparent in the large number of people in the U.S. that are considered obese.

The digestion and degradation of dietary proteins as well as body proteins provide amino acids, which are needed to synthesize nitrogen-containing compounds in our cells, such as new proteins and nucleic acids. Although amino acids are not considered a primary source of fuel, energy can be extracted from amino acids if glycogen and fat reserves have been depleted. However, when a person is fasting or starving, the breakdown of the body's own proteins eventually destroys essential body tissues, particularly muscles.

24.1 Digestion of Triacylglycerols

Our adipose tissue is made of fat cells called *adipocytes*, which store triacylglycerols (see Figure 24.1). Let's compare the amount of energy stored in the fat cells to the energy from glucose, glycogen, and protein. A typical 70-kg (150-lb) person has about 135 000 kcal of energy stored as fat, 24 000 kcal as protein, 720 kcal as glycogen reserves, and 80 kcal as blood glucose. Therefore, the energy available from stored fats is about 85% of the total energy available in the body. Thus, body fat is our major source of stored energy.

Digestion of Dietary Fats

The digestion of dietary fats begins in the small intestine, where hydrophobic fat globules mix with bile salts released from the gallbladder (see Sections 17.1, 17.3, and 17.6 to review lipids, triacylglycerols, and bile salts). In a process called *emulsification*, the bile

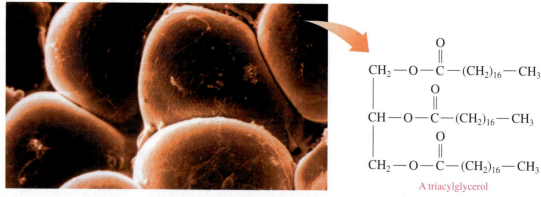

A triacylglycerol

FIGURE 24.1 The fat cells (adipocytes) that make up adipose tissue are capable of storing unlimited quantities of triacylglycerols.

Q What are some sources of fats in our diet?

salts break the fat globules into smaller droplets called *micelles*. Then, *pancreatic lipases* released from the pancreas hydrolyze the triacylglycerols to yield monoacylglycerols and fatty acids, which are absorbed into the intestinal lining, where they recombine to form triacylglycerols. These nonpolar compounds are then coated with proteins to form lipoproteins called *chylomicrons*, which are polar and soluble in the aqueous environment of the lymph and bloodstream (see Figure 24.2).

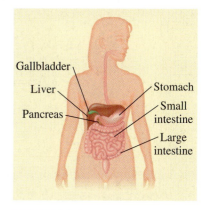

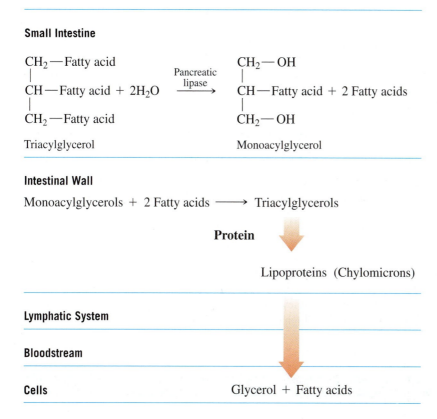

FIGURE 24.2 The digestion of fats begins in the small intestine when bile salts emulsify fats that undergo hydrolysis to glycerol and fatty acids.

Q What kinds of enzymes are secreted from the pancreas into the small intestine to hydrolyze triacylglycerols?

In the cells, enzymes hydrolyze the triacylglycerols to yield glycerol and free fatty acids, which can be used for energy production. Fatty acids, which are the preferred fuel of the heart, are oxidized to acetyl-CoA molecules for ATP synthesis. However, the brain and red blood cells cannot utilize fatty acids. Fatty acids cannot diffuse across the blood–brain barrier, and red blood cells have no mitochondria, which are where fatty acids are oxidized. Therefore, glucose and glycogen are the primary sources of energy for the brain and red blood cells.

Utilization of Fat Stores

When blood glucose is depleted and glycogen stores are low, the process of fat utilization breaks down triacylglycerols in adipose tissue to fatty acids and glycerol. The process is stimulated when the hormone *glucagon* or *epinephrine* is secreted into the bloodstream, where it binds to receptors on the membrane of adipose cells. Enzymes within the fat cells catalyze the hydrolysis of triacylglycerols to yield glycerol and free fatty acids, which diffuse into the bloodstream and bind with plasma proteins (albumin) to be transported to the tissues. Most of the glycerol goes into the liver, where it is converted to glucose.

Metabolism of Glycerol

Enzymes in the liver convert glycerol to dihydroxyacetone phosphate in two steps. In the first step, glycerol is phosphorylated using ATP to yield glycerol-3-phosphate. In the second step, the secondary hydroxyl group is oxidized to yield dihydroxyacetone phosphate,

Explore Your World

DIGESTION OF FATS

Place some water and several drops of vegetable oil in a container with a top. Cap the container and shake. Observe. Add a few drops of liquid soap or detergent to the oil and water, cap the container again, and shake. Observe.

QUESTIONS

1. Why does the oil separate from the water?
2. How does the appearance of the oil change after soap is added?
3. How is soap like the bile salts in the digestion of fats?
4. Where does fat digestion occur in the body?
5. Many people with gallbladder problems take supplemental lipase. Why is this necessary?

which is an intermediate in several metabolic pathways, including glycolysis and gluconeogenesis (see Section 22.5 and 22.8).

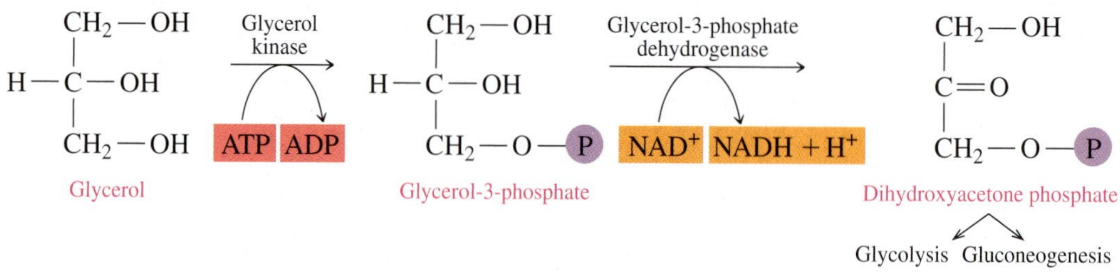

$$CH_2-OH$$
$$H-C-OH$$
$$CH_2-OH$$
Glycerol

Glycerol kinase

ATP ADP

$$CH_2-OH$$
$$H-C-OH$$
$$CH_2-O-P$$
Glycerol-3-phosphate

Glycerol-3-phosphate dehydrogenase

NAD⁺ NADH + H⁺

$$CH_2-OH$$
$$C=O$$
$$CH_2-O-P$$
Dihydroxyacetone phosphate

Glycolysis Gluconeogenesis

The overall reaction for the metabolism of glycerol is written as follows:

Glycerol + ATP + NAD⁺ $\longrightarrow$ dihydroxyacetone phosphate + ADP + NADH + H⁺

CONCEPT CHECK 24.1 **Fats and Digestion**

Answer each of the following for the digestion of triacylglycerols:

a. What are the sites, enzymes, and products of the digestion of triacylglycerols?
b. What happens to the products from the digestion of triacylglycerols in the membrane of the small intestine?

ANSWER

a. The digestion of triacylglycerols takes place in the small intestine where pancreatic lipase catalyzes their hydrolysis to monoacylglycerols and fatty acids.
b. Monoacylglycerols and fatty acids recombine in the membrane of the small intestine to form triacylglycerols. The triacylglycerols combine with proteins to form chylomicrons for transport to the lymphatic system and the bloodstream.

QUESTIONS AND PROBLEMS

24.1 Digestion of Triacylglycerols

LEARNING GOAL: *Describe the sites and products obtained from the digestion of triacylglycerols.*

24.1 What is the role of bile salts in lipid digestion?

24.2 How are insoluble triacylglycerols transported to the tissues?

24.3 When are fats released from fat stores?

24.4 What happens to the glycerol produced from the hydrolysis of triacylglycerols in adipose tissues?

24.5 How is glycerol converted to an intermediate of glycolysis?

24.6 How can glycerol be used to synthesize glucose?

LEARNING GOAL

Describe the metabolic pathway of β-oxidation.

24.2 Oxidation of Fatty Acids

A large amount of energy is obtained when fatty acids undergo oxidation in the mitochondria to yield acetyl-CoA. In fat metabolism, fatty acids undergo **beta-oxidation (β-oxidation)**, which removes two-carbon segments, one at a time, from a fatty acid.

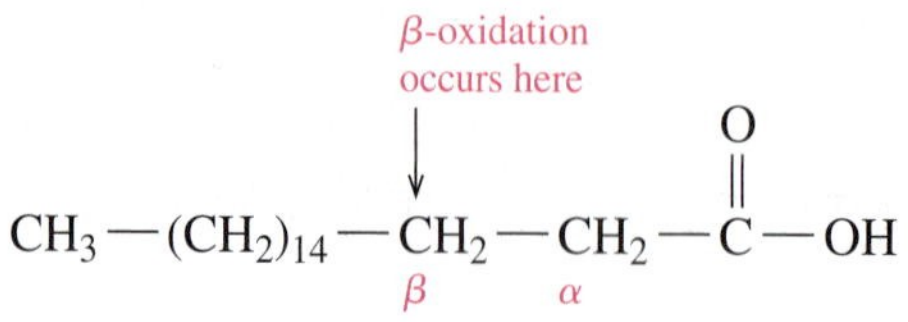

β-oxidation occurs here

$$CH_3-(CH_2)_{14}-\underset{\beta}{CH_2}-\underset{\alpha}{CH_2}-\overset{\displaystyle O}{\overset{\|}{C}}-OH$$

Stearic acid

TUTORIAL
Oxidation of Fatty Acids

Transport of Fatty Acids

The fatty acids, which are in the cytosol outside the mitochondria, must be moved through the inner membrane of the mitochondria before they can undergo oxidation in the mitochondrial matrix. In an *activation* process in the cytosol, a fatty acid is combined with coenzyme A to yield acyl-CoA. The energy released by the hydrolysis of ATP is used to drive the reaction. The products are AMP and two inorganic phosphates $(2P_i)$.

$$CH_3-(CH_2)_n-CH_2-CH_2-\overset{\overset{O}{\|}}{C}-OH + ATP + HS-CoA \xrightarrow{\text{Acyl-CoA synthetase}}$$

Fatty acid

$$CH_3-(CH_2)_n-CH_2-CH_2-\overset{\overset{O}{\|}}{C}-S-CoA + AMP + 2P_i + H_2O$$

Acyl-CoA

The long hydrocarbon chain in the acyl-CoA molecule prevents it from crossing into the matrix of the mitochondria. Thus, a transport molecule is formed by combining the acyl group with a charged carrier called *carnitine*. The reaction yields acyl-carnitine, which transports the acyl group into the matrix.

$$CH_3-(CH_2)_n-CH_2-CH_2-\overset{\overset{O}{\|}}{C}-S-CoA + H-\overset{\overset{\overset{+}{N(CH_3)_3}}{|}\overset{|}{CH_2}}{\underset{\overset{|}{CH_2}\overset{|}{COO^-}}{C}}-OH \xrightleftharpoons{\text{Carnitine acyltransferase}}$$

Acyl-CoA   Carnitine

$$H-\overset{\overset{\overset{+}{N(CH_3)_3}}{|}\overset{|}{CH_2}}{\underset{\overset{|}{CH_2}\overset{|}{COO^-}}{C}}-O-\overset{\overset{O}{\|}}{C}-CH_2-CH_2-(CH_2)_n-CH_3 + HS-CoA$$

Acyl-carnitine

In the matrix, the acyl group recombines with coenzyme A to form acyl-CoA and releases carnitine. While this may seem complicated, this transport system provides a way to regulate degradation (oxidation) and synthesis of fatty acids. When fatty acids are being synthesized in the cytosol, the transport of acyl-CoA into the matrix is blocked, which prevents their degradation (see Figure 24.3).

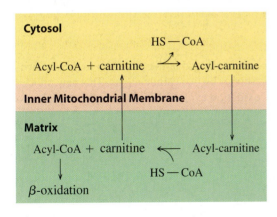

FIGURE 24.3 Fatty acids are activated and transported by carnitine through the inner mitochondrial membrane into the matrix.

Q Why is carnitine used to transport a fatty acid into the matrix?

Reactions of β-Oxidation Cycle

In the mitochondrial matrix, acyl-CoA molecules undergo β-oxidation, which is a cycle of four reactions that convert the —CH_2— of the β-carbon to a β-keto group. Once the β-keto group is formed, a two-carbon acetyl group can be split from the chain, which shortens the acyl group.

Reaction 1   Oxidation

In the first reaction of β-oxidation, the FAD coenzyme removes hydrogen atoms from the α- and β-carbons of the activated fatty acid to form a trans carbon–carbon double bond and $FADH_2$.

$$CH_3-(CH_2)_n-\underset{\beta}{CH_2}-\underset{\alpha}{CH_2}-\overset{\displaystyle O}{\overset{\|}{C}}-S-CoA + \boxed{FAD} \xrightarrow[\text{dehydrogenase}]{\text{Acyl-CoA}} CH_3-(CH_2)_n-\underset{\underset{H}{|}}{\overset{H}{\underset{\beta}{C}}}=\underset{\alpha}{C}-\overset{\displaystyle O}{\overset{\|}{C}}-S-CoA + \boxed{FADH_2}$$

Acyl-CoA   *trans*-Enoyl-CoA

Reaction 2   Hydration

A hydration reaction adds the components of water to the trans double bond, which forms a hydroxyl group (—OH) on the β-carbon.

$$CH_3-(CH_2)_n-\underset{\underset{H}{|}}{\overset{H}{\underset{\beta}{C}}}=\underset{\alpha}{C}-\overset{\displaystyle O}{\overset{\|}{C}}-S-CoA + H_2O \xrightarrow[\text{hydratase}]{\text{Enoyl-CoA}} CH_3-(CH_2)_n-\underset{\underset{H}{|}}{\overset{\overset{OH}{|}}{\underset{\beta}{C}}}-\underset{\underset{H}{|}}{\overset{\overset{H}{|}}{\underset{\alpha}{C}}}-\overset{\displaystyle O}{\overset{\|}{C}}-S-CoA$$

trans-Enoyl-CoA   β-Hydroxyacyl-CoA

Reaction 3   Oxidation

The secondary hydroxyl group on the β-carbon is oxidized to yield a ketone. The hydrogen atoms removed in the dehydrogenation reduce coenzyme NAD^+ to $NADH + H^+$. At this point, the β-carbon has been oxidized to a keto group.

$$CH_3-(CH_2)_n-\underset{\underset{H}{|}}{\overset{\overset{OH}{|}}{\underset{\beta}{C}}}-\underset{\underset{H}{|}}{\overset{\overset{H}{|}}{\underset{\alpha}{C}}}-\overset{\displaystyle O}{\overset{\|}{C}}-S-CoA + \boxed{NAD^+} \xrightarrow[\text{dehydrogenase}]{\text{β-Hydroxyacyl-CoA}} CH_3-(CH_2)_n-\underset{\beta}{\overset{\displaystyle O}{\overset{\|}{C}}}-\underset{\underset{H}{|}}{\overset{\overset{H}{|}}{\underset{\alpha}{C}}}-\overset{\displaystyle O}{\overset{\|}{C}}-S-CoA$$
$$+ \boxed{NADH} + H^+$$

β-Hydroxyacyl-CoA   β-Ketoacyl-CoA

Reaction 4   Cleavage

In the final step of β-oxidation, the fatty acid is cleaved at the β-carbon to yield a two-carbon acetyl-CoA and an acyl-CoA that is shorter by two carbon atoms. This new, shorter acyl-CoA continues to go through the β-oxidation cycle until it is entirely degraded to acetyl-CoA.

$$CH_3-(CH_2)_n-\underset{\beta}{\overset{\displaystyle O}{\overset{\|}{C}}}-\underset{\underset{H}{|}}{\overset{\overset{H}{|}}{\underset{\alpha}{C}}}-\overset{\displaystyle O}{\overset{\|}{C}}-S-CoA + HS-CoA \xrightarrow{\text{Thiolase}} CH_3-(CH_2)_n-\overset{\displaystyle O}{\overset{\|}{C}}-S-CoA + CH_3-\overset{\displaystyle O}{\overset{\|}{C}}-S-CoA$$

β-Ketoacyl-CoA   Acyl-CoA   Acetyl-CoA
(2 C atoms shorter)

Fatty Acid Length Determines Cycle Repeats

The number of carbon atoms in a fatty acid determines the number of times the cycle repeats and the number of acetyl-CoA units it produces. For example, the complete β-oxidation of capric acid (C_{10}) produces five acetyl-CoA groups, which is equal to one-half the number of carbon atoms in the chain. Because the final turn of the cycle produces two acetyl-CoA groups, the total number of times the cycle repeats is one less than the total number of acetyl groups it produces. Therefore, the C_{10} fatty acid goes through the cycle four times (see Figure 24.4).

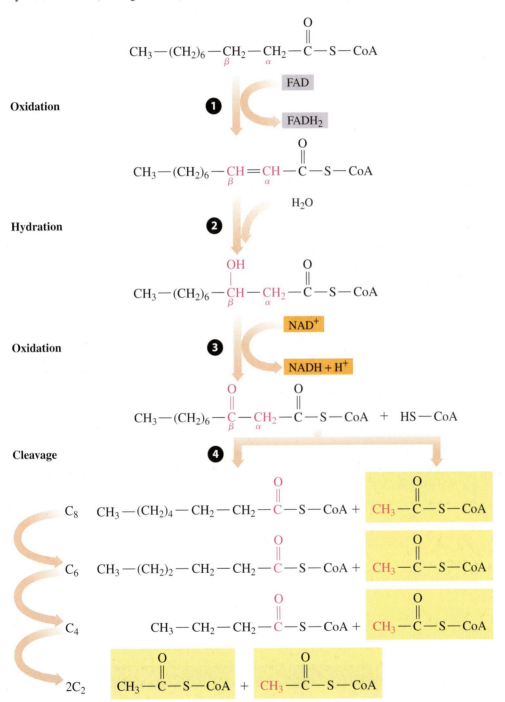

FIGURE 24.4 Capric acid (C_{10}) undergoes four oxidation cycles that repeat reactions 1–4 to yield 5 acetyl-CoA molecules, 4 NADHs, and 4 FADH$_2$s.

Q How many NADH and FADH$_2$ molecules are produced in one turn of the fatty acid cycle of β-oxidation?

Oxidation of Unsaturated Fatty Acids

The β-oxidation sequence we have described applies to saturated fatty acids with an even number of carbon atoms. However, the fats in our diets, particularly the oils, contain unsaturated fatty acids, which have one or more cis double bonds. The hydration reaction adds water to trans double bonds, not cis. When the double bond in an unsaturated fatty acid is ready for hydration, an isomerase forms a trans double bond between the α- and β-carbon atoms, which is the arrangement needed for the hydration reaction.

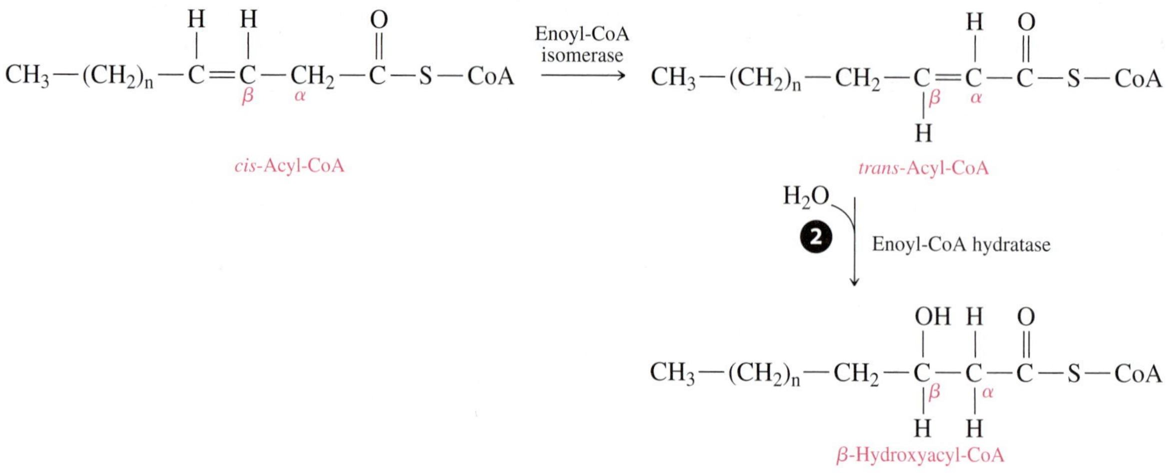

$$CH_3-(CH_2)_n-\underset{\beta}{C}=\underset{\alpha}{C}-CH_2-\overset{O}{\overset{\|}{C}}-S-CoA \xrightarrow[\text{isomerase}]{\text{Enoyl-CoA}} CH_3-(CH_2)_n-CH_2-\underset{\beta}{C}=\underset{\alpha}{C}-\overset{O}{\overset{\|}{C}}-S-CoA$$

cis-Acyl-CoA   *trans*-Acyl-CoA

$$H_2O \downarrow \quad \textbf{2} \quad \text{Enoyl-CoA hydratase}$$

$$CH_3-(CH_2)_n-CH_2-\underset{\underset{H}{\beta}}{\overset{OH}{\underset{|}{C}}}-\underset{\underset{H}{\alpha}}{\overset{H}{\underset{|}{C}}}-\overset{O}{\overset{\|}{C}}-S-CoA$$

β-Hydroxyacyl-CoA

Because the isomerization provides the trans double bond for the hydration in reaction 2, it bypasses the first reaction. Therefore, the energy released by the β-oxidation of an unsaturated fatty acid is slightly less because no $FADH_2$ is produced in that cycle.

SAMPLE PROBLEM 24.1 β-Oxidation

Match each of the following (**a–d**) with one of the reactions (**1–4**) in the β-oxidation cycle:

(1) first oxidation   (2) hydration   (3) second oxidation   (4) cleavage

a. Water is added to a trans double bond.
b. An acetyl-CoA is removed.
c. FAD is reduced to $FADH_2$.
d. Reaction that is bypassed during the oxidation of unsaturated fatty acids.

SOLUTION

a. (2) hydration   **b.** (4) cleavage   **c.** (1) first oxidation   **d.** (1) first oxidation

STUDY CHECK 24.1

Which coenzyme is needed in reaction 3 when a β-hydroxyl group is converted to a β-keto group?

CONCEPT CHECK 24.2   Number of β-Oxidation Cycles

Determine the number of β-oxidation cycles and number of acetyl-CoA molecules produced for cerotic acid (C_{26}).

ANSWER

Cerotic acid (C_{26}) requires 12 β-oxidation cycles, and produces 13 acetyl-CoA molecules.

QUESTIONS AND PROBLEMS

24.2 Oxidation of Fatty Acids

LEARNING GOAL: *Describe the metabolic pathway of β-oxidation.*

24.7 Where in the cell are fatty acids activated?

24.8 What is the function of carnitine in the degradation of fatty acids?

24.9 What coenzymes are required for β-oxidation?

24.10 When does an isomerization occur during the β-oxidation of a fatty acid?

24.11 In each of the following acyl-CoA molecules, identify the β-carbon:

a. $CH_3-CH_2-CH_2-CH_2-CH_2-CH_2-CH_2-\overset{\overset{\displaystyle O}{\|}}{C}-S-CoA$

b. $CH_3-(CH_2)_{14}-CH_2-CH_2-\overset{\overset{\displaystyle O}{\|}}{C}-S-CoA$

c. $CH_3-CH_2-CH=CH-CH_2-\overset{\overset{\displaystyle O}{\|}}{C}-S-CoA$

24.12 Draw the condensed structural formula for the product when each of the following undergoes the indicated reaction:

a. $CH_3-(CH_2)_{12}-CH=CH-\overset{\overset{\displaystyle O}{\|}}{C}-S-CoA + H_2O \xrightarrow{\text{Enoyl-CoA hydratase}}$

b. $CH_3-(CH_2)_6-CH_2-CH_2-\overset{\overset{\displaystyle O}{\|}}{C}-S-CoA \xrightarrow{\text{Acyl-CoA dehydrogenase}}$

c. $CH_3-(CH_2)_4-\overset{\overset{\displaystyle O}{\|}}{C}-CH_2-\overset{\overset{\displaystyle O}{\|}}{C}-S-CoA + HS-CoA \xrightarrow{\text{Thiolase}}$

24.13 Caprylic acid, $CH_3-(CH_2)_4-CH_2-CH_2-COOH$, is a C_8 fatty acid.
   a. Draw the condensed structural formula for the activated form of caprylic acid.
   b. Indicate the α- and β-carbon atoms in caprylic acid.
   c. State the number of β-oxidation cycles for the complete oxidation of caprylic acid.
   d. State the number of acetyl-CoAs from the complete oxidation of caprylic acid.

24.14 Lignoceric acid, $CH_3-(CH_2)_{20}-CH_2-CH_2-COOH$, is a C_{24} fatty acid found in peanut oil in small amounts.
   a. Draw the condensed structural formula for the activated form of lignoceric acid.
   b. Indicate the α- and β-carbon atoms in lignoceric acid.
   c. State the number of β-oxidation cycles for the complete oxidation of lignoceric acid.
   d. State the number of acetyl-CoAs from the complete oxidation of lignoceric acid.

24.3 ATP and Fatty Acid Oxidation

LEARNING GOAL

Calculate the total ATP produced by the complete oxidation of a fatty acid.

We can now determine the total energy yield from the oxidation of a particular fatty acid. In each β-oxidation cycle, one NADH, one FADH$_2$, and one acetyl-CoA are produced. From Section 23.3, we know that hydrogen ions and electrons transferred from NADH to coenzyme Q in electron transport generate sufficient energy to synthesize three ATPs, whereas FADH$_2$ leads to the synthesis of two ATPs. However, the greatest amount of energy produced from a fatty acid is generated by the production of the acetyl-CoA units that enter the citric acid cycle. We saw in Section 23.4 that one acetyl-CoA leads to the synthesis of 12 ATPs.

We have seen that capric acid, C_{10}, goes through four turns of the β-oxidation cycle, which produces five acetyl-CoA units. We also need to remember that activation of the capric acid requires two ATPs. We can calculate the ATP produced as follows:

ATP Production from β-Oxidation of Capric Acid (C_{10})	
Activation of Capric Acid to Capryl-CoA	−2 ATP
4 β-Oxidation Cycles	
$4 \text{ FADH}_2 \times \dfrac{2 \text{ ATP}}{\text{FADH}_2}$ (electron transport)	8 ATP
$4 \text{ NADH} \times \dfrac{3 \text{ ATP}}{\text{NADH}}$ (electron transport)	12 ATP
5 Acetyl-CoA	
$5 \text{ acetyl-CoA} \times \dfrac{12 \text{ ATP}}{\text{acetyl-CoA}}$ (citric acid cycle)	60 ATP
Total	78 ATP

Chemistry Link to Health

STORED FAT AND OBESITY

The storage of fat is an important survival feature in the lives of many animals. In hibernating animals, large amounts of stored fat provide the energy for the entire hibernation period, which can be several months. In camels, large amounts of calories are stored in the camel's hump, which is actually a huge fat deposit. When food resources are low, the camel can survive months without food or water by utilizing the fat reserves in the hump. Migratory birds preparing to fly long distances also store large amounts of fat. Whales are kept warm by a layer of body fat called "blubber" (which can be as thick as 2 feet) under their skin. Blubber also provides energy when whales must survive long periods of starvation. Penguins also have blubber, which protects them from the cold and provides energy when they are incubating their eggs.

Humans also have the capability to store large amounts of fat, although they do not hibernate or usually have to survive for long periods without food. When humans survived on sparse diets that were mostly vegetarian, about 20% of the dietary calories were from fat. Today, a typical diet includes more dairy products and foods with high fat levels, and as much as 60% of the calories are from fat. The U.S. Public Health Service now estimates that in the United States, more than one-third of adults are obese. Obesity is defined as a body weight that is more than 20% over an ideal weight. Obesity is a major factor in health problems such as diabetes, heart disease, high blood pressure, stroke, and gallstones, as well as some cancers and forms of arthritis.

At one time, we thought that obesity was simply a problem of eating too much. However, research now indicates that certain pathways in lipid and carbohydrate metabolism may cause excessive weight gain in some people. In 1995, scientists discovered that a hormone called *leptin* is produced in fat cells. When fat cells are full, high levels of leptin signal the brain to limit the intake of food. When fat stores are low, leptin production decreases, which signals the brain to increase food intake. Leptin acts on the liver and skeletal muscles, where it stimulates fatty acid oxidation in the mitochondria, which decreases fat stores.

Major research is currently being done to find the causes of obesity. Scientists are studying differences in the rate of leptin production, degrees of resistance to leptin, and possible combinations of these factors. After a person has dieted and lost weight, the leptin level drops. This decrease in leptin may cause an increase in hunger and food intake while slowing metabolism, which starts the weight-gain cycle all over again. Currently, studies are being made to assess the safety of leptin therapy following weight loss.

Marine mammals have thick layers of blubber that serve as insulation as well as energy storage.

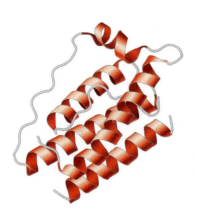

Leptin, shown here as a ribbon model, is an appetite-repressing hormone formed in the fat cells that consists of 146 amino acids.

A camel stores large amounts of fat in its hump.

SAMPLE PROBLEM 24.2   ATP Production from β-Oxidation

How much ATP will be produced from the complete β-oxidation of palmitic acid, a C_{16} saturated fatty acid?

SOLUTION

Analyze the Problem

Number of Carbon Atoms	Number of β-Oxidation Cycles	Number of FADH$_2$	Number of NADH	Number of Acetyl-CoAs
16	7	7	7	8

The complete oxidation of the 16-carbon palmitic acid requires seven β-oxidation cycles, which produce seven $FADH_2$ and seven NADH molecules. The total number of acetyl-CoA is eight. During electron transport, each $FADH_2$ produces two ATPs, and each NADH produces three ATPs. Each acetyl-CoA can produce 12 ATPs by way of the citric acid cycle. Two ATPs are utilized in the activation of palmitic acid to palmitoyl-CoA.

ATP Production from Palmitic Acid (C_{16})	
Activation of palmitic acid to palmitoyl-CoA	−2 ATP
$7 \, \cancel{FADH_2} \times \dfrac{2 \text{ ATP}}{\cancel{FADH_2}}$ (electron transport)	14 ATP
$7 \, \cancel{NADH} \times \dfrac{3 \text{ ATP}}{\cancel{NADH}}$ (electron transport)	21 ATP
$8 \, \cancel{acetyl\text{-}CoA} \times \dfrac{12 \text{ ATP}}{\cancel{acetyl\text{-}CoA}}$ (citric acid cycle)	96 ATP
Total	129 ATP

STUDY CHECK 24.2

Compare the total ATP from reduced coenzymes and from acetyl-CoA in the β-oxidation of palmitic acid.

Explore Your World

FAT STORAGE AND BLUBBER

Obtain four plastic freezer bags, masking tape, and some solid vegetable fat used for cooking. Fill a bucket or container with enough water to cover both of your hands. Add ice until the water feels very cold.

Place 3 or 4 tablespoons of the vegetable fat in one of the plastic bags. Place another plastic bag inside the first bag containing the fat. Tape the top edges of the two bags together, leaving the inside bag open. Using the remaining two plastic bags, place one inside the other, and tape the top edges together leaving the inside bag open. Now place one hand inside the bag with the vegetable fat and distribute the fat around until a layer of about 2/3 in. (2 cm) of the fat in the inner bag covers your hand. Place your other hand inside the other double bag and submerge both your hands in the ice water. Measure

the time it takes for one hand to feel uncomfortably cold. Remove your hands before they get too cold.

QUESTIONS

1. How effective is the double bag with "blubber" in protecting your hand from the cold?
2. How would increasing the amount of vegetable fat affect your results?
3. How does "blubber" help an animal survive starvation?
4. Why would animals in warm climates, such as camels and migratory birds, need to store fat?

QUESTIONS AND PROBLEMS

24.3 ATP and Fatty Acid Oxidation

LEARNING GOAL: *Calculate the total ATP produced by the complete oxidation of a fatty acid.*

24.15 Why is the energy of fatty acid activation from ATP to AMP considered the same as the hydrolysis of 2 ATP $\longrightarrow$ 2 ADP?

24.16 What is the number of ATP molecules obtained from one molecule of acetyl-CoA in the citric acid cycle?

24.17 Consider the complete oxidation of one molecule of behenic acid, $CH_3—(CH_2)_{18}—CH_2—CH_2—COOH$, ($C_{22}$), a fatty acid that is found in peanut and canola oils.
   a. How many cycles of β-oxidation are needed for the complete oxidation of behenic acid?
   b. How many molecules of acetyl-CoA are produced from the complete oxidation of behenic acid?
   c. How many ATP molecules are generated from the complete oxidation of one molecule of behenic acid?

24.18 Consider the complete oxidation of one molecule of stearic acid, $CH_3—(CH_2)_{14}—CH_2—CH_2—COOH$, a C_{18} fatty acid.
   a. How many cycles of β-oxidation are needed for the complete oxidation of stearic acid?
   b. How many molecules of acetyl-CoA are produced from the complete oxidation of stearic acid?
   c. How many ATP molecules are generated from the complete oxidation of one molecule of stearic acid?

TUTORIAL
Ketogenesis and Ketone Bodies

24.4 Ketogenesis and Ketone Bodies

When carbohydrates including glycogen are not available to meet energy needs, the body breaks down fatty acids, which undergo β-oxidation to acetyl-CoA. Normally, acetyl-CoA would enter the citric acid cycle for further oxidation and energy production. However, when large quantities of fatty acids are degraded, the citric acid cycle cannot utilize the full amount. As a result, acetyl-CoA accumulates in the liver, where acetyl-CoA combines to form compounds called **ketone bodies** in a pathway known as **ketogenesis** (see Figure 24.5).

Reaction 1   Condensation
In ketogenesis, two molecules of acetyl-CoA combine to form acetoacetyl-CoA, which reverses the last reaction in β-oxidation.

Reaction 2   Hydrolysis
The hydrolysis of acetoacetyl-CoA forms acetoacetate, a ketone body. Acetoacetate can enter the citric acid cycle for energy production, or break down into other ketone bodies.

Reaction 3   Reduction
Acetoacetate can be reduced to yield β-hydroxybutyrate, which is considered a ketone body even though it does not contain a keto group.

Reaction 4   Decarboxylation
Acetoacetate can also undergo decarboxylation to yield acetone.

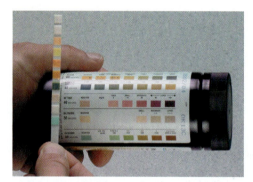

A test strip indicates the level of ketone bodies in a urine sample.

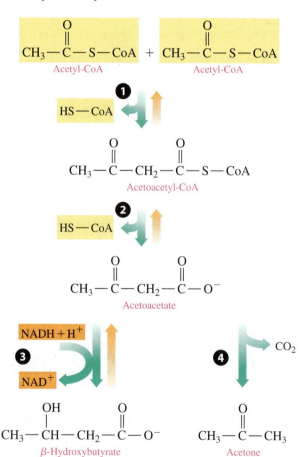

FIGURE 24.5 In ketogenesis, acetyl-CoA molecules combine to produce ketone bodies: acetoacetate, β-hydroxybutyrate, and acetone.

Q What condition in the body leads to the formation of ketone bodies?

Ketosis

The accumulation of ketone bodies may lead to a condition called **ketosis**, which occurs in severe diabetes, diets high in fat and low in carbohydrates, alcoholism, and starvation. Two of the ketone bodies are acids that produce H^+, which can lower the blood pH below 7.4. This condition, called **acidosis**, often accompanies ketosis. A drop in blood pH can interfere with the ability of the blood to carry oxygen and cause breathing difficulties.

CONCEPT CHECK 24.3 **Ketogenesis**

The process called ketogenesis takes place in the liver.

a. What are the conditions that promote ketogenesis?
b. What are the names of the three compounds that are called ketone bodies?
c. What ketone bodies are responsible for the acidosis that occurs in ketogenesis?

ANSWER

a. When excess acetyl-CoA cannot be processed by the citric acid cycle, acetyl-CoA enters the ketogenesis pathway, where it forms ketone bodies.
b. The ketone bodies in ketogenesis are acetoacetate, β-hydroxybutyrate, and acetone.
c. The formation of the ketone bodies acetoacetate and β-hydroxybutyrate decreases the pH of the blood (acidosis).

Chemistry Link to Health

KETONE BODIES AND DIABETES

Blood glucose is elevated within 30 minutes following a meal containing carbohydrates. The elevated level of glucose stimulates the secretion of the hormone *insulin* from the pancreas, which increases the flow of glucose into muscle and adipose tissue for the synthesis of glycogen. As blood glucose levels drop, the secretion of insulin decreases. When blood glucose is low, another hormone, *glucagon*, is secreted by the pancreas, which stimulates the breakdown of glycogen in the liver to yield glucose.

In *diabetes mellitus*, glucose cannot be utilized or stored as glycogen, because *insulin* is not secreted or does not function properly. In type 1, *insulin-dependent diabetes*, which often begins in childhood, the pancreas produces inadequate levels of insulin. This type of diabetes can result from damage to the pancreas by viral infections or from genetic mutations. In type 2, *insulin-resistant diabetes*, which usually occurs in adults, insulin is produced, but insulin receptors are not responsive. Thus, a person with type 2 diabetes does not respond to insulin therapy. *Gestational diabetes* can occur during pregnancy, but blood glucose levels usually return to normal after the baby is

born. Pregnant women with diabetes tend to gain weight and have large babies.

In all types of diabetes, insufficient amounts of glucose are available in the muscle, liver, and adipose tissue. As a result, liver cells synthesize glucose from noncarbohydrate sources (gluconeogenesis) and break down fat, which elevates the level of acetyl-CoA. Excess acetyl-CoA undergoes ketogenesis, and ketone bodies accumulate in the blood. The odor of acetone can be detected on the breath of a person with uncontrolled diabetes who is in ketosis.

In uncontrolled diabetes, the concentration of blood glucose exceeds the ability of the kidney to reabsorb glucose, and glucose appears in the urine. High levels of glucose increase the osmotic pressure in the blood, which leads to an increase in urine output. Symptoms of diabetes include frequent urination and excessive thirst. Treatment for diabetes includes diet changes to limit carbohydrate intake and may require medication such as a daily injection of insulin.

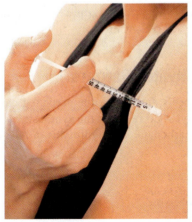
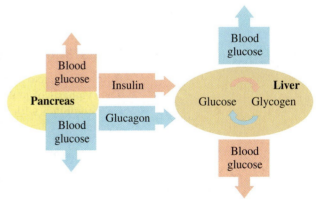

Diabetes can be treated with injections of insulin.

QUESTIONS AND PROBLEMS

24.4 Ketogenesis and Ketone Bodies

LEARNING GOAL: *Describe the pathway of ketogenesis.*

24.19 What is ketogenesis?

24.20 If a person were fasting, why would they have high levels of acetyl-CoA?

24.21 What type of reaction converts acetoacetate to β-hydroxybutyrate?

24.22 How is acetone formed from acetoacetate?

24.23 What is ketosis?

24.24 Why do diabetics produce high levels of ketone bodies?

24.5 Fatty Acid Synthesis

When the body has met all its energy needs and the glycogen stores are full, acetyl-CoA from the breakdown of carbohydrates and fatty acids is used to synthesize new fatty acids. In the pathway called **lipogenesis**, 2-carbon acetyl units are linked together to give a 16-carbon fatty acid, palmitic acid. Although the reactions appear much like the reverse of the reactions we discussed in fatty acid oxidation, the synthesis of fatty acids proceeds in a separate pathway with different enzymes. Fatty acid oxidation occurs in the mitochondria and uses FAD and NAD^+, whereas fatty acid synthesis occurs in the cytosol and uses the reduced coenzyme NADPH. NADPH is similar to NADH, except it has a phosphate group.

Synthesis of Acyl Carrier Protein (ACP)

In β-oxidation, acetyl and acyl groups are activated using coenzyme A (CoA—SH). In fatty acid synthesis, an acyl carrier protein (ACP—SH) activates the acyl compounds. In the ACP—SH molecule, the thiol and pantothenic acid (vitamin B_5) found in CoA are attached to a protein.

$$HS-CH_2-CH_2-\underset{\underset{\text{Aminoethanethiol}}{}}{N}-\overset{O}{\underset{}{C}}-CH_2-CH_2-\underset{\underset{\text{Pantothenic acid}}{}}{N}-\overset{O}{\underset{}{C}}-C-C-CH_2-O-\overset{O}{\underset{O^-}{P}}-O-CH_2-\text{Protein}$$

Aminoethanethiol   Pantothenic acid

Acyl carrier protein (ACP)
(HS–ACP)

Preparation of Activated Carriers

Before fatty acid synthesis can begin, the activated carriers must be synthesized. The synthesis of malonyl-ACP requires the synthesis of malonyl-CoA, when acetyl-CoA combines with bicarbonate. The hydrolysis of ATP provides the energy for the reaction.

$$CH_3-\overset{O}{\underset{}{C}}-S-CoA + HCO_3^- + ATP \xrightarrow{\text{Acetyl-CoA carboxylase}} {}^-O-\overset{O}{\underset{}{C}}-CH_2-\overset{O}{\underset{}{C}}-S-CoA + ADP + P_i + H^+$$

Acetyl-CoA   Malonyl-CoA

For fatty acid synthesis, the activated forms malonyl-ACP and acetyl-ACP are produced when the acyl group is combined with ACP—SH.

$$CH_3-\overset{\overset{\displaystyle O}{\|}}{C}-S-CoA + HS-ACP \xrightarrow[\text{transacylase}]{\text{Acetyl-CoA}} CH_3-\overset{\overset{\displaystyle O}{\|}}{C}-S-ACP + HS-CoA$$

Acetyl-CoA   Acetyl-ACP

$$\overset{\overset{\displaystyle O}{\|}}{C}-S-CoA + HS-ACP \xrightarrow[\text{transacylase}]{\text{Malonyl-CoA}} {}^-O-\overset{\overset{\displaystyle O}{\|}}{C}-CH_2-\overset{\overset{\displaystyle O}{\|}}{C}-S-ACP + HS-CoA$$

CoA   Malonyl-ACP

Synthesis of Fatty Acids (Palmitate)

The next four reactions occur in a cycle that adds two-carbon acetyl groups to a carbon chain.

Reaction 1   Condensation
Acetyl-ACP and malonyl-ACP condense to yield acetoacetyl-ACP and CO_2.

Reaction 2   Reduction
The keto group on the β-carbon is reduced to a hydroxyl group using hydrogen from the reduced coenzyme NADPH.

Reaction 3   Dehydration
The alcohol is dehydrated to form a trans double bond in *trans*-enoyl-ACP.

Reaction 4   Reduction
NADPH reduces the double bond to a single bond, which forms butyryl-ACP, a saturated four-carbon compound.

Cycle of Fatty Acid Synthesis Repeats

The cycle of fatty acid synthesis is repeated as the longer four-carbon butyryl-ACP reacts with another malonyl-ACP to produce hexanoyl-ACP. After seven cycles of fatty acid synthesis, the product, C_{16} palmitoyl-ACP, is hydrolyzed to yield palmitate and HS—ACP (see Figure 24.6).

Longer and Shorter Fatty Acids

Although we have looked at the synthesis of the fatty acid palmitate, shorter and longer fatty acids are also produced in cells. Shorter fatty acids are released before there are 16 carbon atoms in the chain. Longer fatty acids are produced with special enzymes that add two-carbon units to the carboxyl end of the fatty acid chain. An unsaturated cis bond can also be incorporated into a 10-carbon fatty acid followed by the same elongation reactions.

Regulation of Fatty Acid Synthesis

Fatty acid synthesis takes place primarily in the adipose tissue, where triacylglycerols are formed and stored. The hormone *insulin* stimulates the formation of fatty acids. When blood glucose is high, insulin moves glucose into the cells. In the cell, insulin stimulates glycolysis and the oxidation of pyruvate, thereby producing acetyl-CoA for fatty acid synthesis. During lipogenesis, the production of malonyl-CoA blocks the transport of acyl groups into the matrix of the mitochondria, which prevents their oxidation.

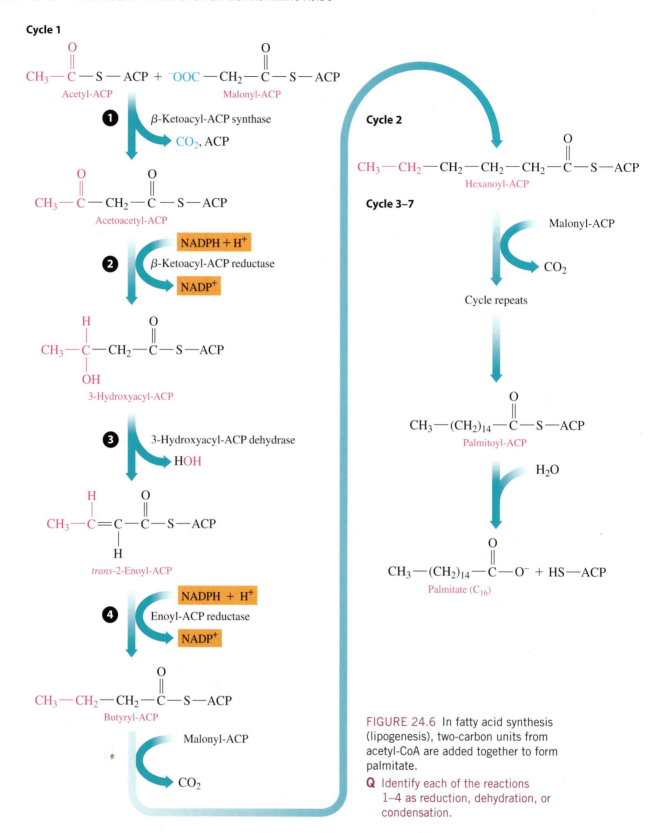

FIGURE 24.6 In fatty acid synthesis (lipogenesis), two-carbon units from acetyl-CoA are added together to form palmitate.

Q Identify each of the reactions 1–4 as reduction, dehydration, or condensation.

Comparison of β-Oxidation and Fatty Acid Synthesis

We have seen that many of the steps in the synthesis of palmitate are similar to those that occur in the β-oxidation of palmitate. Synthesis combines two-carbon units, whereas β-oxidation removes two-carbon units. Synthesis of fatty acids involves reduction and dehydration, whereas β-oxidation of fatty acids involves oxidation and hydration. We can distinguish between the two pathways by comparing some of their features in Table 24.1.

TABLE 24.1 A Comparison of β-Oxidation and Fatty Acid Synthesis

	β-Oxidation	Fatty Acid Synthesis (Lipogenesis)
Site	Mitochondrial matrix	Cytosol
Activated by	Glucagon	Insulin
	Low blood glucose	High blood glucose
Activator	Coenzyme A (HS—CoA)	Acyl carrier protein (ACP)
Initial Substrate	Fatty acid	Acetyl-CoA
Initial Coenzymes	FAD, NAD$^+$	NADPH
Types of Reactions	Oxidation	Reduction
	Hydration	Dehydration
	Cleavage	Condensation
Function	Cleaves two-carbon acyl group	Adds two-carbon acyl group
Final Product	Acetyl-CoA	Palmitate (C_{16}) or other fatty acids
Final Coenzymes	FADH$_2$, NADH	NADP$^+$

CONCEPT CHECK 24.4   **Fatty Acid Synthesis**

Malonyl-ACP is required for the elongation of fatty acid chains.

a. Complete the following equation for the formation of malonyl-ACP from the starting material acetyl-CoA:

   Acetyl-CoA + HCO$_3^-$ + ATP $\longrightarrow$

b. What enzyme catalyzes this reaction?
c. If malonyl-ACP is a three-carbon acyl group, why are only two carbon atoms added each time malonyl-ACP is combined with a fatty acid chain?

ANSWER

a. Acetyl-CoA combines with bicarbonate to form malonyl-CoA, which reacts with ACP to form malonyl-ACP.

   Acetyl-CoA + HCO$_3^-$ + ATP $\longrightarrow$ malonyl-CoA + ADP + P$_i$ + H$^+$

   Malonyl-CoA + HS—ACP $\longrightarrow$ malonyl-ACP + HS—CoA

b. The enzyme for this reaction is acetyl-CoA carboxylase.
c. In each cycle of fatty acid synthesis, a two-carbon acetyl group from the three-carbon group in malonyl-ACP adds to the growing fatty acid chain and one carbon forms CO$_2$.

QUESTIONS AND PROBLEMS

24.5 Fatty Acid Synthesis

LEARNING GOAL: *Describe the biosynthesis of fatty acids from acetyl-CoA.*

24.25 Where does fatty acid synthesis occur in the cell?

24.26 What compound is involved in the activation of acyl compounds in fatty acid synthesis?

24.27 What are the starting materials for fatty acid synthesis?

24.28 What is the function of malonyl-ACP in fatty acid synthesis?

24.29 Identify the reaction (**a–c**) catalyzed by each of the following enzymes (**1–3**):
   1. acetyl-CoA carboxylase   **2.** acetyl-CoA transacylase
   3. malonyl-CoA transacylase

   a. converts malonyl-CoA to malonyl-ACP
   b. combines acetyl-CoA with bicarbonate to give malonyl-CoA
   c. converts acetyl-CoA to acetyl-ACP

24.30 Identify the reaction (**a–d**) catalyzed by each of the following enzymes (**1–4**):
   1. β-ketoacyl-ACP synthase   **2.** β-ketoacyl-ACP reductase

   3. 3-hydroxyacyl-ACP dehydrase
   4. enoyl-ACP reductase

   a. catalyzes the dehydration of an alcohol
   b. converts a carbon–carbon double bond to a carbon–carbon single bond
   c. combines a two-carbon acetyl group with a three-carbon acyl group accompanied by the loss of CO$_2$
   d. reduces a keto group to a hydroxyl group

24.31 Determine the number of each of the following components involved in the synthesis of one molecule of capric acid, a C$_{10}$ fatty acid.
   a. HCO$_3^-$ **b.** ATP   **c.** acetyl-CoA
   d. malonyl-ACP   **e.** NADPH   **f.** CO$_2$ removed

24.32 Determine the number of each of the following components in the synthesis of one molecule of myristic acid, a C$_{14}$ fatty acid.
   a. HCO$_3^-$ **b.** ATP   **c.** acetyl-CoA
   d. malonyl-ACP   **e.** NADPH   **f.** CO$_2$ removed

no acids for the synthesis of new proteins
thesis of compounds such as nucleotides. We
major sources of energy, but when they are not
ostrates that enter energy-producing pathways.
s begins in the stomach, where hydrochloric acid
d activates enzymes such as *pepsin* that begin to
des move out of the stomach into the small intestine,
omplete the hydrolysis of the peptides to amino acids.
rough the intestinal walls into the bloodstream for trans-
).

24.3   **Digestion of Proteins**

nd products for the digestion of proteins?

SOLUTION

The digestion of proteins begins in the stomach and is completed in the small intestine to yield amino acids.

STUDY CHECK 24.3

What is the function of HCl in the stomach?

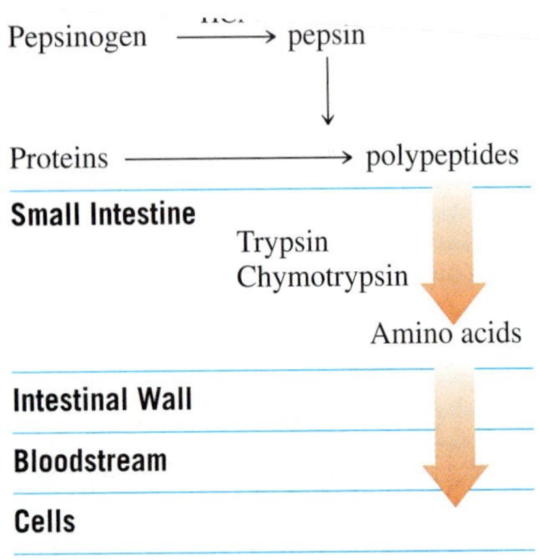

Pepsinogen ⟶ pepsin

Proteins ⟶ polypeptides

Small Intestine
     Trypsin
     Chymotrypsin

         Amino acids

Intestinal Wall

Bloodstream

Cells

FIGURE 24.7 Proteins are hydrolyzed to polypeptides in the stomach and to amino acids in the small intestine.

Q What enzyme, secreted into the small intestine, hydrolyzes peptides?

MC

TUTORIAL
Nitrogen in the Body

Protein Turnover

Our bodies are constantly replacing old proteins with new ones. The process of breaking down proteins and synthesizing new proteins is called **protein turnover**. Many types of proteins, including enzymes, hormones, and hemoglobin, are synthesized in the cells and then degraded. For example, the hormone insulin has a half-life of 10 minutes, whereas the half-life of lactate dehydrogenase is about 2 days, and hemoglobin is 120 days. Damaged and ineffective proteins are also degraded and replaced. While most amino acids are used to build proteins, other compounds also require nitrogen for their synthesis, as seen in Table 24.2 (see Figure 24.8).

TABLE 24.2   **Nitrogen-Containing Compounds**

Type of Compound	Example
Nonessential amino acids	Alanine, aspartate, cysteine, glycine
Proteins	Muscle protein, enzymes
Neurotransmitters	Acetylcholine, dopamine, serotonin
Amino alcohols	Choline, ethanolamine
Heme	Hemoglobin
Hormones	Thyroxine, epinephrine, insulin
Nucleotides (nucleic acids)	Purines, pyrimidines

Usually, we maintain a nitrogen balance in the cells so that the amount of protein we break down is equal to the amount that is reused. A diet that is high in protein, however, has a positive nitrogen balance because it supplies more nitrogen than we need. Because the body cannot store nitrogen, the excess is excreted as urea. A diet that does not provide sufficient nitrogen has a negative nitrogen balance, which is a condition that occurs during starvation and fasting.

Energy from Amino Acids

Normally, only a small amount (about 10%) of our energy needs is supplied by amino acids. However, more amino acids are used for energy in conditions such as fasting or starvation, when carbohydrate and fat stores are exhausted. If amino acids remain the

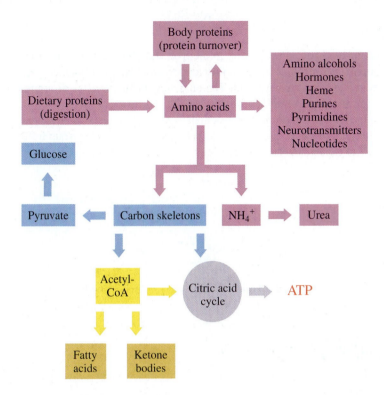

FIGURE 24.8 Proteins are used in the synthesis of nitrogen-containing compounds or degraded to urea and carbon skeletons that enter other metabolic pathways.

Q What are some compounds that require nitrogen for their synthesis?

only source of energy for a long period, the breakdown of body proteins eventually leads to a destruction of essential body tissues. In anorexia, the loss of protein decreases muscle mass and may severely weaken the heart muscle and impair heart function.

SAMPLE PROBLEM 24.4 Nitrogen Balance

With a positive nitrogen balance, why are excess amino acids excreted?

SOLUTION

Because the body cannot store nitrogen, amino acids that are not needed for the synthesis of proteins are excreted.

STUDY CHECK 24.4

Under what condition does the body have a negative nitrogen balance?

QUESTIONS AND PROBLEMS

24.6 Digestion of Proteins

LEARNING GOAL: *Describe the hydrolysis of dietary protein and absorption of amino acids.*

24.33 Where do dietary proteins undergo digestion in the body?

24.34 What is meant by protein turnover?

24.35 What are some nitrogen-containing compounds that need amino acids for their synthesis?

24.36 What is the fate of the amino acids obtained from a high protein diet?

24.7 Degradation of Amino Acids

When dietary protein exceeds the nitrogen needed for protein synthesis, the excess amino acids are degraded. The α-amino group is removed to yield an α-keto acid, which can be converted to an intermediate that will be used in another metabolic pathway. The carbon atoms from amino acids are used in the citric acid cycle as well as for the synthesis of fatty acids, ketone bodies, and glucose.

LEARNING GOAL

Describe the reactions of transamination and oxidative deamination in the degradation of amino acids.

TUTORIAL
Transamination and Deamination

Transamination

The degradation of amino acids occurs primarily in the liver. In a **transamination** reaction, an α-amino group is transferred from an amino acid to an α-keto acid, which produces a new amino acid and a new α-keto acid. The enzymes for the transfer of amino groups are known as *transaminases* or *aminotransferases*.

The α-keto acid often used in transamination reactions is α-ketoglutarate, which is converted to glutamate. We can write an equation to show the transfer of the amino group from alanine to α-ketoglutarate to yield glutamate, the new amino acid, and the α-keto acid pyruvate.

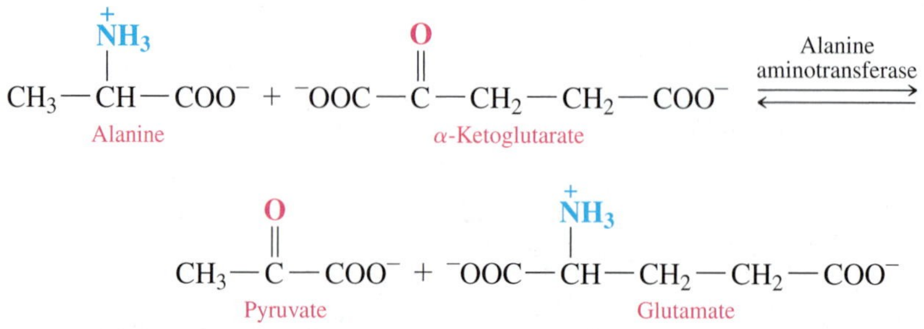

$$\underset{\text{Alanine}}{CH_3-\overset{\overset{+}{N}H_3}{\underset{|}{CH}}-COO^-} + \underset{\alpha\text{-Ketoglutarate}}{{}^-OOC-\overset{\overset{O}{\|}}{C}-CH_2-CH_2-COO^-} \xrightleftharpoons{\text{Alanine aminotransferase}}$$

$$\underset{\text{Pyruvate}}{CH_3-\overset{\overset{O}{\|}}{C}-COO^-} + \underset{\text{Glutamate}}{{}^-OOC-\overset{\overset{+}{N}H_3}{\underset{|}{CH}}-CH_2-CH_2-COO^-}$$

SAMPLE PROBLEM 24.5 Transamination

Write the equation for the transamination of glutamate and oxaloacetate by drawing the condensed structural formulas.

SOLUTION

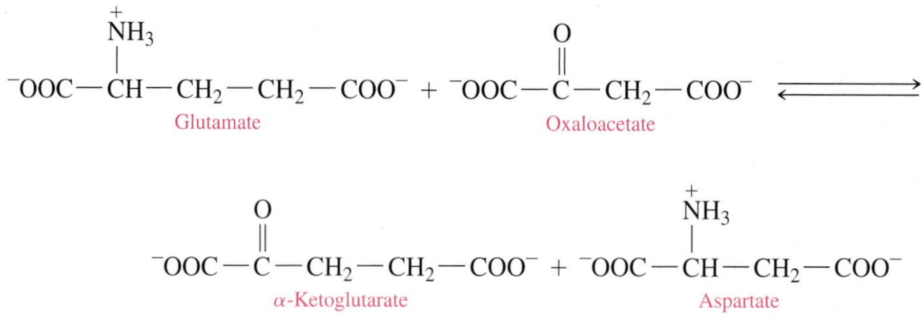

$$\underset{\text{Glutamate}}{{}^-OOC-\overset{\overset{+}{N}H_3}{\underset{|}{CH}}-CH_2-CH_2-COO^-} + \underset{\text{Oxaloacetate}}{{}^-OOC-\overset{\overset{O}{\|}}{C}-CH_2-COO^-} \xrightleftharpoons{}$$

$$\underset{\alpha\text{-Ketoglutarate}}{{}^-OOC-\overset{\overset{O}{\|}}{C}-CH_2-CH_2-COO^-} + \underset{\text{Aspartate}}{{}^-OOC-\overset{\overset{+}{N}H_3}{\underset{|}{CH}}-CH_2-COO^-}$$

STUDY CHECK 24.5

What is a possible name for the enzyme that catalyzes the reaction above?

Oxidative Deamination

In a process called **oxidative deamination**, the amino group in glutamate is removed as an ammonium ion, NH_4^+. The reaction is catalyzed by *glutamate dehydrogenase*, which uses NAD^+ as a coenzyme.

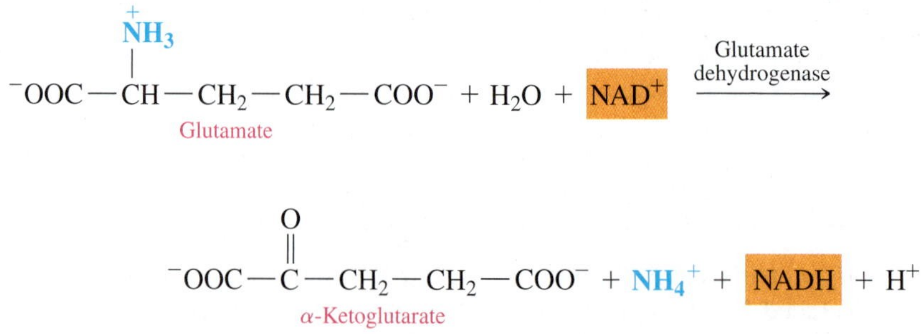

$$\underset{\text{Glutamate}}{{}^-OOC-\overset{\overset{+}{N}H_3}{\underset{|}{CH}}-CH_2-CH_2-COO^-} + H_2O + \boxed{NAD^+} \xrightarrow{\text{Glutamate dehydrogenase}}$$

$$\underset{\alpha\text{-Ketoglutarate}}{{}^-OOC-\overset{\overset{O}{\|}}{C}-CH_2-CH_2-COO^-} + NH_4^+ + \boxed{NADH} + H^+$$

Therefore, the amino group from any amino acid can be used to form glutamate, which undergoes oxidative deamination, converting the amino group to an ammonium ion.

Indicate whether each of the following represents a transamination or an oxidative deamination:

a. Glutamate is converted to α-ketoglutarate and NH_4^+.
b. Alanine and α-ketoglutarate react to form pyruvate and glutamate.
c. A reaction is catalyzed by glutamate dehydrogenase, which requires NAD^+.

ANSWER

a. Oxidative deamination occurs when the amino group in glutamate is removed as an ammonium ion.
b. Transamination occurs when an amino group is transferred from an amino acid to an α-ketoacid such as α-ketoglutarate.
c. Oxidative deamination is catalyzed by glutamate dehydrogenase, which requires NAD^+.

QUESTIONS AND PROBLEMS

24.7 Degradation of Amino Acids

LEARNING GOAL: *Describe the reactions of transamination and oxidative deamination in the degradation of amino acids.*

24.37 What are the reactants and products in transamination reactions?

24.38 What types of enzymes catalyze transamination reactions?

24.39 Draw the condensed structural formula for the α-keto acid produced from each of the following in transamination:

a. 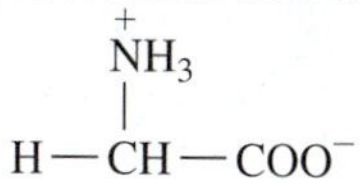
$$\overset{\overset{+}{N}H_3}{\underset{|}{H-CH-COO^-}} \quad \text{Glycine}$$

b. 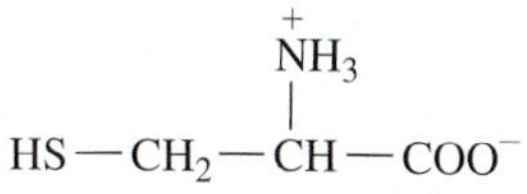
$$\overset{\overset{+}{N}H_3}{\underset{|}{HS-CH_2-CH-COO^-}} \quad \text{Cysteine}$$

c. 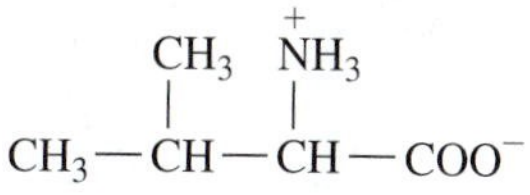
$$\overset{CH_3 \quad \overset{+}{N}H_3}{\underset{| \qquad |}{CH_3-CH-CH-COO^-}} \quad \text{Valine}$$

24.40 Draw the condensed structural formula for the α-keto acid produced from each of the following in transamination:

a. 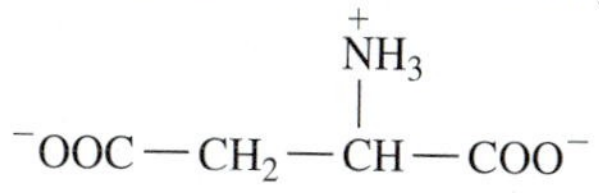
$$\overset{\overset{+}{N}H_3}{\underset{|}{^-OOC-CH_2-CH-COO^-}} \quad \text{Aspartate}$$

b. 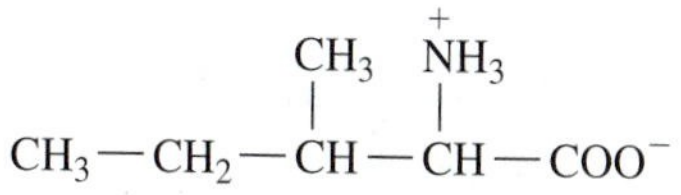
$$\overset{CH_3 \quad \overset{+}{N}H_3}{\underset{| \qquad |}{CH_3-CH_2-CH-CH-COO^-}} \quad \text{Isoleucine}$$

c. 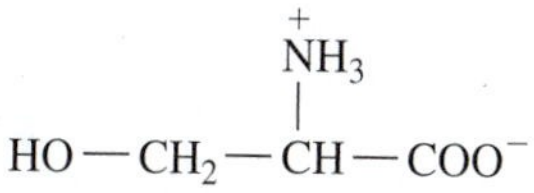
$$\overset{\overset{+}{N}H_3}{\underset{|}{HO-CH_2-CH-COO^-}} \quad \text{Serine}$$

24.41 Write the equation using condensed structural formulas for the oxidative deamination of glutamate.

24.42 How do all 20 amino acids produce ammonium ions in oxidative deamination?

24.8 Urea Cycle

In Section 24.7, we showed that the ammonium ion is the end product of amino acid degradation. However, the ammonium ion is toxic if it is allowed to accumulate. Thus, in the liver, ammonium ions are converted to urea using the **urea cycle**. The urea is transported to the kidneys to form urine.

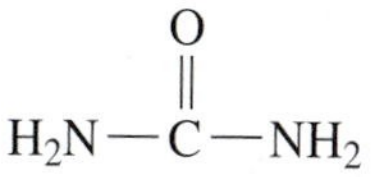

$$\underset{\text{Urea}}{H_2N-\overset{\overset{\displaystyle O}{\|}}{C}-NH_2}$$

In one day, a typical adult may excrete about 25–30 g of urea in the urine. This amount increases when a diet is high in protein. If urea is not properly excreted, it builds up quickly to a toxic level. To detect renal disease, the *blood urea nitrogen (BUN)* level is measured. If the BUN is high, protein intake must be reduced, and hemodialysis may be needed to remove toxic nitrogen waste from the blood.

Urea Cycle

The urea cycle in the liver cells consists of reactions that take place in both the mitochondria and cytosol (see Figure 24.9). In preparation for the urea cycle, ammonium

LEARNING GOAL

Describe the formation of urea from ammonium ion.

TUTORIAL
Detoxifying Ammonia in the Body

ions react with carbon dioxide from the citric acid cycle and two ATPs to yield carbamoyl phosphate.

$$NH_4^+ + CO_2 + 2\,ATP + H_2O \xrightarrow[\text{synthetase}]{\text{Carbamoyl phosphate}} H_2N-\overset{\displaystyle O}{\overset{\|}{C}}-O-\overset{\displaystyle O}{\underset{\displaystyle O^-}{\overset{\|}{P}}}-O^- + 2\,ADP + P_i$$

Carbamoyl phosphate

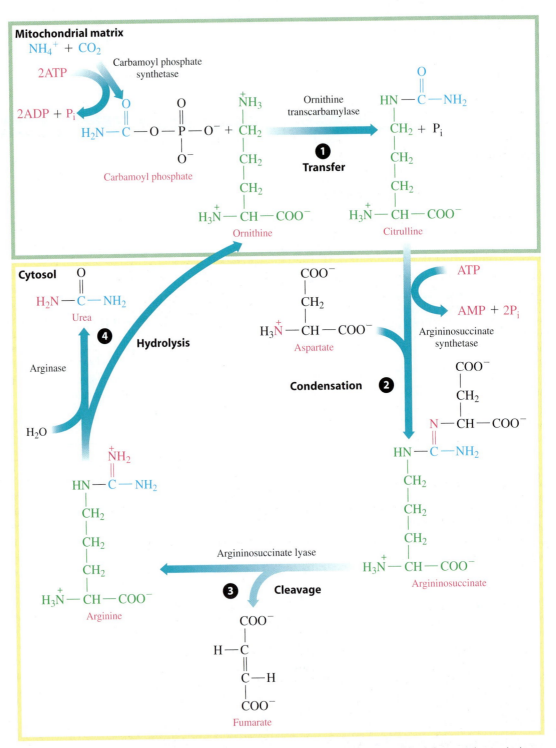

FIGURE 24.9 In the urea cycle, urea is formed from a carbon and nitrogen (blue) from carbamoyl phosphate (initially an ammonium ion from oxidative deamination) and a nitrogen atom from aspartate (pink).

Q Where in the cell is urea formed?

Reaction 1   Transfer of Carbamoyl Group

In the mitochondria, the carbamoyl group is transferred from carbamoyl phosphate to ornithine (an amino acid not found in proteins) to yield citrulline, which is transported across the mitochondrial membrane into the cytosol. The hydrolysis of the phosphate bond provides the energy to drive the reaction.

Reaction 2   Condensation with Aspartate

In the cytosol, citrulline condenses with the amino acid aspartate to form argininosucci-nate. The hydrolysis of ATP to AMP and two inorganic phosphates provides the energy for the reaction. The nitrogen atom in aspartate becomes the other nitrogen atom in the urea that is produced in the final reaction.

Reaction 3   Cleavage of Fumarate

The argininosuccinate undergoes a cleavage to yield fumarate, a citric acid cycle interme-diate, and arginine.

Reaction 4   Hydrolysis to Form Urea

The hydrolysis of arginine yields urea and ornithine, which returns to the mitochondria to repeat the cycle.

CONCEPT CHECK 24.6   Formation of Urea

Why would a person on a high-protein diet be instructed to drink large quantities of water?

ANSWER

A high-protein diet provides a large amount of protein that undergoes oxidative deami-nation in the liver. High levels of ammonium ion, NH_4^+, would result in the formation of large amounts of urea. The urea is transported to the kidneys where large amounts of water are needed to form urine for excretion. High levels of urea can be toxic.

SAMPLE PROBLEM 24.6   Urea Cycle

Indicate the reaction in the urea cycle where each of the following compounds is a reactant:

a. aspartate   **b.** ornithine   **c.** arginine

SOLUTION

a. Aspartate condenses with citrulline in reaction 2.
b. Ornithine accepts the carbamoyl group in reaction 1.
c. Arginine is cleaved in reaction 4.

STUDY CHECK 24.6

Name the products of each reaction in Sample Problem 24.6.

QUESTIONS AND PROBLEMS

24.8 Urea Cycle

LEARNING GOAL: *Describe the formation of urea from ammonium ion.*

24.43 Why does the body convert NH_4^+ to urea?

24.44 Where is the energy source for the formation of urea?

24.45 Draw the condensed structural formula for urea.

24.46 Draw the condensed structural formula for carbamoyl phosphate.

24.47 What is the source of carbon in urea?

24.48 How much ATP energy is required to drive one turn of the urea cycle?

24.9 Fates of the Carbon Atoms from Amino Acids

The carbon skeletons from the transamination of amino acids are used as intermediates of the citric acid cycle or other metabolic pathways. We can classify the amino acids according to the number of carbon atoms in those intermediates (see Figure 24.10). The amino acids that provide three-carbon compounds are converted to pyruvate. The amino acids with four carbon atoms are converted to oxaloacetate, and the five-carbon amino acids provide α-ketoglutarate. Some amino acids are listed twice because they can enter different pathways to form citric acid cycle intermediates.

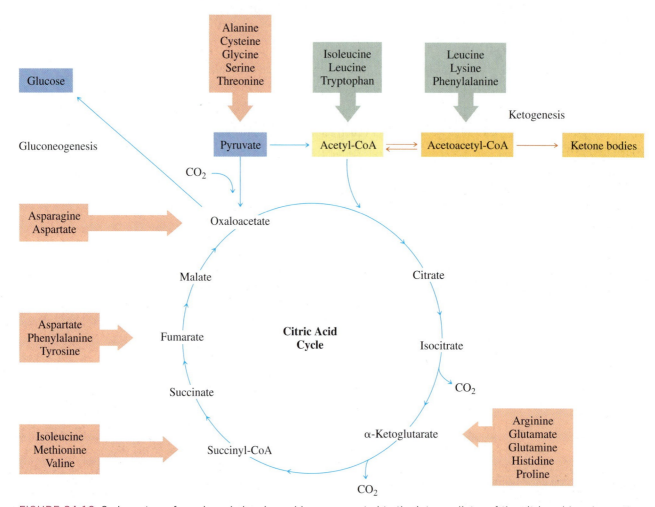

FIGURE 24.10 Carbon atoms from degraded amino acids are converted to the intermediates of the citric acid cycle or other pathways. Glucogenic amino acids (pink boxes) produce carbon skeletons that can form glucose, and ketogenic amino acids (green boxes) can produce ketone bodies.

Q Why is aspartate glucogenic, but leucine ketogenic?

A **glucogenic amino acid** generates pyruvate, α-ketoglutarate, succinyl-CoA, fumarate, or oxaloacetate, which can be converted to glucose by gluconeogenesis. A **ketogenic amino acid** produces acetoacetyl-CoA or acetyl-CoA, which can enter the ketogenesis pathway to form ketone bodies or the lipogenesis pathway to form fatty acids.

CONCEPT CHECK 24.7 **Degradation of Amino Acids**

What is the citric acid cycle intermediate formed by each of the following amino acids?

a. methionine　　　**b.** serine　　　**c.** glutamate

ANSWER

a. Carbon atoms from methionine form the citric acid cycle intermediate succinyl-CoA.

b. Carbon atoms from serine form the citric acid cycle intermediate oxaloacetate.

c. Carbon atoms from glutamate form the citric acid cycle intermediate α-ketoglutarate.

SAMPLE PROBLEM 24.7 **Degradation of Amino Acids**

Determine the citric acid cycle component and the number of ATP produced by each of the following amino acids:

a. proline   **b.** tyrosine   **c.** tryptophan

SOLUTION

Analyze the Problem

Amino Acid	Citric Acid Cycle Component	Coenzymes Produced	ATP Produced
Proline	α-Ketoglutarate	2 NADH, 1 GTP, FADH$_2$	$6 + 1 + 2 = 9$ ATP
Tyrosine	Fumarate	1 NADH	3 ATP
Tryptophan	Acetyl-CoA	3 NADH, 1 GTP, 1 FADH$_2$	$9 + 1 + 2 = 12$ ATP

a. Proline is converted to the citric acid cycle intermediate α-ketoglutarate. The reactions in the remaining part of the citric acid cycle from α-ketoglutarate to oxaloacetate produce two NADHs, one GTP, and one FADH$_2$. The two NADHs provide six ATPs, one GTP provides one ATP, and one FADH$_2$ provides two ATPs, for a total of nine ATPs from proline.

b. Tyrosine is converted to the citric acid cycle intermediate fumarate. The reactions in the remaining part of the citric acid cycle from fumarate to oxaloacetate produce one NADH, which provides three ATPs.

c. Tryptophan is converted to the citric acid cycle intermediate acetyl-CoA. The reactions in the citric acid cycle starting with acetyl-CoA produce three NADHs, one GTP, and one FADH$_2$. The three NADHs provide nine ATPs, one GTP provides one ATP, and one FADH$_2$ provides two ATPs, for a total of 12 ATPs from tryptophan.

STUDY CHECK 24.7

Why does the citric acid cycle component from leucine supply more ATP than the intermediate from phenylalanine?

QUESTIONS AND PROBLEMS

24.9 Fates of the Carbon Atoms from Amino Acids

LEARNING GOAL: *Describe where carbon atoms from amino acids enter the citric acid cycle on other pathways.*

24.49 What is the function of a glucogenic amino acid?

24.50 What is the function of a ketogenic amino acid?

24.51 What component of the citric acid cycle can be produced from the carbon atoms of each of the following amino acids?
a. alanine   **b.** asparagine
c. valine   **d.** glutamine

24.52 What component of the citric acid cycle can be produced from the carbon atoms of each of the following amino acids?
a. leucine   **b.** threonine
c. cysteine   **d.** arginine

24.10 Synthesis of Amino Acids

LEARNING GOAL

Illustrate how some nonessential amino acids are synthesized from intermediates in the citric acid cycle and other metabolic pathways.

Plants and bacteria such as *E. coli* produce all of their amino acids using NH_4^+ and NO_3^-. However, humans can synthesize only 9 of the 20 amino acids found in their proteins. The nonessential amino acids are synthesized in the body (discussed in Section 19.1), whereas the essential amino acids must be obtained from the diet (see Table 24.3). The amino acids arginine, cysteine, and tyrosine are essential in diets for infants and children due to their rapid growth requirements, but they are not essential amino acids for adults.

TABLE 24.3 Essential and Nonessential Amino Acids in Adults

Essential

Histidine	Phenylalanine
Isoleucine	Threonine
Leucine	Tryptophan
Lysine	Valine
Methionine	

Nonessential

Alanine	Glutamine
Arginine	Glycine
Asparagine	Proline
Aspartate	Serine
Cysteine	Tyrosine
Glutamate	

Some Pathways for Amino Acid Synthesis

A variety of pathways are involved in the synthesis of nonessential amino acids. When the body synthesizes nonessential amino acids, the α-keto acid carbon skeletons are obtained from the citric acid cycle or glycolysis and converted to amino acids by transamination (see Figure 24.11).

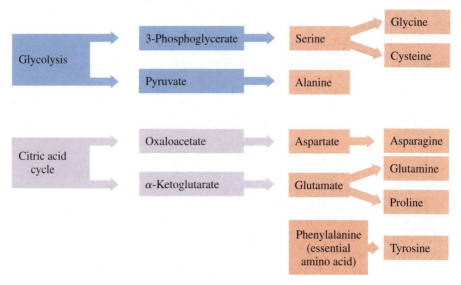

FIGURE 24.11 Nonessential amino acids are synthesized from intermediates of glycolysis and the citric acid cycle.

Q How is alanine formed from pyruvate?

Some of the amino acids are formed from a simple transamination by the reverse of the reactions we have seen in amino acid degradation. The transfer of an amino group from glutamate to pyruvate produces alanine.

$$\overset{\overset{+}{NH_3}}{^-OOC-\underset{|}{CH}-CH_2-CH_2-COO^-} + CH_3-\overset{\overset{O}{\|}}{C}-COO^- \xrightarrow{\text{Alanine aminotransferase}}$$

Glutamate   Pyruvate

$$CH_3-\overset{\overset{+}{NH_3}}{\underset{|}{CH}}-COO^- + {}^-OOC-\overset{\overset{O}{\|}}{C}-CH_2-CH_2-COO^-$$

Alanine α-Ketoglutarate

In another transamination using glutamate, oxaloacetate from the citric acid cycle is converted to aspartate.

$$\overset{\overset{+}{NH_3}}{^-OOC-\underset{|}{CH}-CH_2-CH_2-COO^-} + {}^-OOC-CH_2-\overset{\overset{O}{\|}}{C}-COO^- \xrightarrow{\text{Aspartate aminotransferase}}$$

Glutamate   Oxaloacetate

$$\overset{\overset{+}{NH_3}}{^-OOC-CH_2-\underset{|}{CH}-COO^-} + {}^-OOC-\overset{\overset{O}{\|}}{C}-CH_2-CH_2-COO^-$$

Aspartate α-Ketoglutarate

These two *aminotransferases* are abundant in the cells of the liver and heart, but they are present only in low levels in the bloodstream. When an injury or disease occurs, they are released from the damaged cells into the bloodstream. Elevated levels of *serum alanine aminotransferase* (ALT or SGPT) and *serum aspartate aminotransferase* (AST or SGOT) provide a means to diagnose the extent of damage to the liver or the heart.

The synthesis of the other nonessential amino acids requires several reactions in addition to transamination. For example, glutamine is synthesized when a second amino group is added to glutamate using the energy from the hydrolysis of ATP.

$$\overset{+}{N}H_3$$
$$^-OOC-\overset{|}{C}H-CH_2-CH_2-COO^- + NH_3 \xrightarrow[\text{ATP} \quad \text{ADP} + P_i]{\text{Glutamine synthetase}} {^-OOC}-\overset{\overset{+}{N}H_3}{\underset{}{\overset{|}{C}H}}-CH_2-CH_2-\overset{O}{\overset{||}{C}}-NH_2$$

Glutamate   Glutamine

Tyrosine, an aromatic amino acid with a hydroxyl group, is formed from phenylalanine, an essential amino acid.

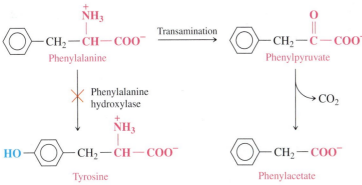

Phenylalanine $+ O_2 \xrightarrow{\text{Phenylalanine hydroxylase}}$ Tyrosine $+ H_2O$

Chemistry Link to Health

PHENYLKETONURIA (PKU)

In the genetic disease *phenylketonuria* (*PKU*), a person cannot convert phenylalanine to tyrosine because the gene for an enzyme, phenylalanine hydroxylase is defective. As a result, large amounts of phenylalanine accumulate. In a different pathway, phenylalanine undergoes transamination to form phenylpyruvate, which is decarboxylated to phenylacetate. Large amounts of these compounds are excreted in the urine.

In infants, high levels of phenylpyruvate and phenylacetate cause severe mental retardation. However, the defect can be identified at birth, and all newborns are now tested for PKU. By detecting PKU early, retardation is avoided by using an infant diet with proteins that are low in phenylalanine and high in tyrosine. It is also important to avoid the use of sweeteners and soft drinks containing aspartame, which contains phenylalanine as one of the two amino acids in its structure. In adulthood, some persons with PKU can eat a nearly normal diet as long as they are checked for phenylpyruvate periodically.

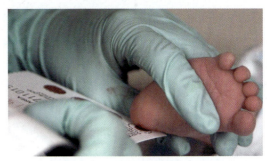

All newborns are tested for PKU.

Overview of Metabolism

In Chapters 22 through 24, we have seen that catabolic pathways degrade large molecules to small molecules that are used for energy production via the citric acid cycle and electron transport. We have also looked at the anabolic pathways that lead to the synthesis of larger molecules in the cell. In the overall view of metabolism, there are several branch points from which compounds may be degraded for energy or used to synthesize larger molecules. For example, glucose can be degraded to acetyl-CoA for the citric acid cycle to produce energy or converted to glycogen for storage. When glycogen stores are depleted, fatty acids are degraded for energy. Amino acids normally used to synthesize nitrogen-containing compounds in the cells can also be used for energy after they are degraded to intermediates of the citric acid cycle. In the synthesis of nonessential amino acids, α-keto acids of the citric acid cycle enter into a variety of reactions that convert them to amino acids through transamination by glutamate (see Figure 24.12).

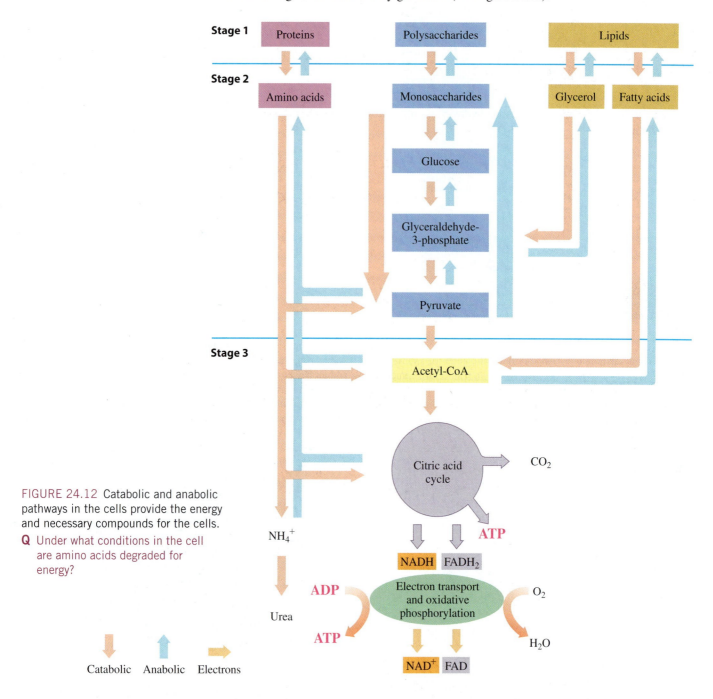

FIGURE 24.12 Catabolic and anabolic pathways in the cells provide the energy and necessary compounds for the cells.

Q Under what conditions in the cell are amino acids degraded for energy?

QUESTIONS AND PROBLEMS

24.10 Synthesis of Amino Acids

LEARNING GOAL: Illustrate how some nonessential amino acids are synthesized from intermediates in the citric acid cycle and other metabolic pathways.

24.53 What do we call the amino acids that humans can synthesize?

24.54 How do humans obtain the amino acids that cannot be synthesized in the body?

24.55 How is glutamate converted to glutamine?

24.56 What amino acid can be converted into the amino acid tyrosine?

24.57 What do the letters PKU mean?

24.58 How is PKU treated?

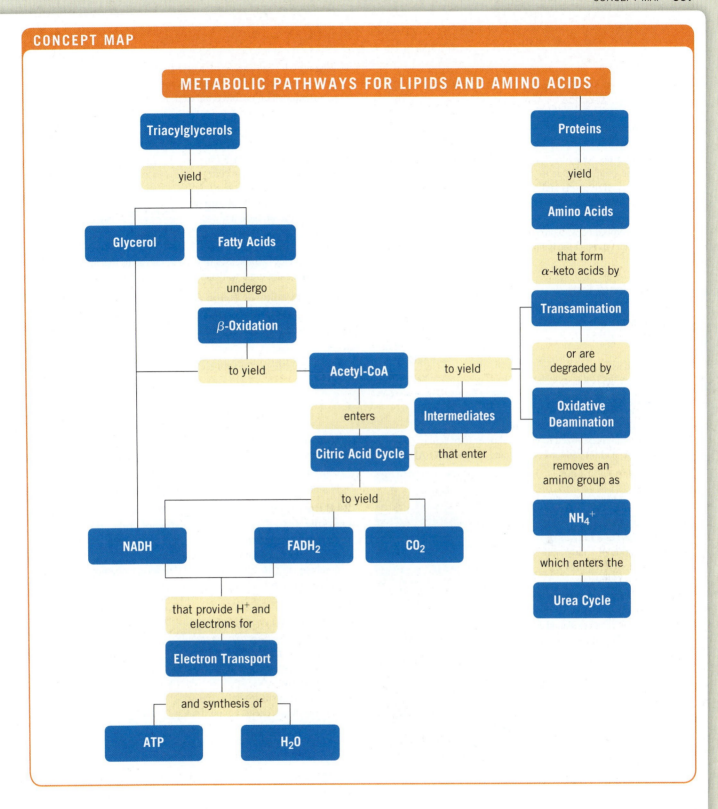

METABOLIC PATHWAYS FOR LIPIDS AND AMINO ACIDS

CHAPTER REVIEW

24.1 Digestion of Triacylglycerols

LEARNING GOAL: *Describe the sites and products obtained from the digestion of triacylglycerols.*

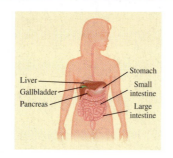

- Triacylglycerols are hydrolyzed in the small intestine to yield monoacylglycerols and fatty acids, which enter the intestinal wall and form new triacylglycerols.
- Triacylglycerols bind with proteins to form chylomicrons, which transport them through the lymphatic system and bloodstream to the tissues.

24.2 Oxidation of Fatty Acids

LEARNING GOAL: *Describe the metabolic pathway of β-oxidation.*

- When used as an energy source, fatty acids link to coenzyme A to be transported into the mitochondria, where they undergo β-oxidation.
- The acyl chain is oxidized to yield a shorter fatty acid, acetyl-CoA, and the reduced coenzymes NADH and FADH$_2$.

24.3 ATP and Fatty Acid Oxidation

LEARNING GOAL: *Calculate the total ATP produced by the complete oxidation of a fatty acid.*

- The activation of a fatty acid for β-oxidation requires an input of two ATPs.
- The energy obtained from a particular fatty acid depends on its length, with each oxidation cycle yielding five ATPs and an additional 12 ATPs from each acetyl-CoA that enters the citric acid cycle.

24.4 Ketogenesis and Ketone Bodies

LEARNING GOAL: *Describe the pathway of ketogenesis.*

- When high levels of acetyl-CoA are present in the cell, they enter the ketogenesis pathway, forming ketone bodies such as acetoacetate, which can cause ketosis and acidosis.

24.5 Fatty Acid Synthesis

LEARNING GOAL: *Describe the biosynthesis of fatty acids from acetyl-CoA.*

- When there is an excess of acetyl-CoA in the cell, the two-carbon acetyl-CoA units link together to synthesize palmitate, which is converted to triacylglycerols and stored in the adipose tissue.

24.6 Digestion of Proteins

LEARNING GOAL: *Describe the hydrolysis of dietary protein and absorption of amino acids.*

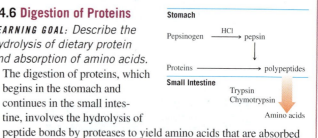

- The digestion of proteins, which begins in the stomach and continues in the small intestine, involves the hydrolysis of peptide bonds by proteases to yield amino acids that are absorbed through the intestinal wall and transported to the cells.

24.7 Degradation of Amino Acids

LEARNING GOAL: *Describe the reactions of transamination and oxidative deamination in the degradation of amino acids.*

- When the amount of amino acids in the cells exceeds that needed for the synthesis of nitrogen compounds, the process of transamination converts them to α-keto acids and glutamate. Oxidative deamination of glutamate produces ammonium ions and α-ketoglutarate.

24.8 Urea Cycle

LEARNING GOAL: *Describe the formation of urea from ammonium ion.*

- Ammonium ions from oxidative deamination combine with bicarbonate and ATP to form carbamoyl phosphate, which is converted to urea.

24.9 Fates of the Carbon Atoms from Amino Acids

LEARNING GOAL: *Describe where carbon atoms from amino acids enter the citric acid cycle or other pathways.*

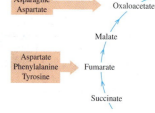

- The carbon atoms from the degradation of glucogenic amino acids enter into the citric acid cycle or gluconeogenesis as ketogenic amino acids that provide acetyl-CoA or acetoacetate for ketogenesis.

24.10 Synthesis of Amino Acids

LEARNING GOAL: *Illustrate how some nonessential amino acids are synthesized from intermediates in the citric acid cycle and other metabolic pathways.*

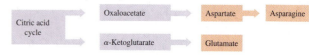

- Nonessential amino acids are synthesized when amino groups from glutamate are transferred to an α-keto acid obtained from glycolysis or the citric acid cycle.

SUMMARY OF KEY REACTIONS

Digestion of Triacylglycerols

$$\text{Triacylglycerols} + 2H_2O \xrightarrow{\text{Pancreatic lipase}} \text{monoacylglycerols} + 2 \text{ fatty acids}$$

Metabolism of Glycerol

$$\text{Glycerol} + \text{ATP} + \text{NAD}^+ \longrightarrow \text{dihydroxyacetone phosphate} + \text{ADP} + \text{NADH} + \text{H}^+$$

Transamination

$$
\underset{\text{Alanine}}{\overset{\overset{+}{N}H_3}{CH_3-CH-COO^-}} + \underset{\alpha\text{-Ketoglutarate}}{\overset{O}{{}^-OOC-C-CH_2-CH_2-COO^-}} \underset{\text{Alanine}\atop\text{aminotransferase}}{\rightleftharpoons}
$$

$$
\underset{\text{Pyruvate}}{\overset{O}{CH_3-C-COO^-}} + \underset{\text{Glutamate}}{\overset{\overset{+}{N}H_3}{{}^-OOC-CH-CH_2-CH_2-COO^-}}
$$

Oxidative Deamination

$$
\underset{\text{Glutamate}}{\overset{\overset{+}{N}H_3}{{}^-OOC-CH-CH_2-CH_2-COO^-}} + H_2O + NAD^+ \underset{\text{dehydrogenase}}{\overset{\text{Glutamate}}{\rightleftharpoons}}
$$

$$
\underset{\alpha\text{-Ketoglutarate}}{\overset{O}{{}^-OOC-C-CH_2-CH_2-COO^-}} + NH_4^+ + NADH + H^+
$$

KEY TERMS

acidosis Low blood pH resulting from the formation of acidic ketone bodies.

beta-(β-)oxidation The degradation of fatty acids that removes two-carbon segments from a fatty acid chain.

glucogenic amino acid An amino acid that provides carbon atoms for the synthesis of glucose.

ketogenesis The pathway that converts acetyl-CoA to four-carbon acetoacetate and other ketone bodies.

ketogenic amino acid An amino acid that provides carbon atoms for the synthesis of fatty acids or ketone bodies.

ketone bodies The products of ketogenesis: acetoacetate, β-hydroxybutyrate, and acetone.

ketosis A condition in which high levels of ketone bodies cannot be metabolized, leading to lower blood pH.

lipogenesis The synthesis of fatty acid in which two-carbon acetyl units link together to yield fatty acids, primarily palmitic acid.

oxidative deamination The loss of ammonium ion when glutamate is degraded to α-ketoglutarate.

protein turnover The amount of protein that we break down from our diet and utilize for synthesis of proteins and nitrogen-containing compounds.

transamination The transfer of an amino group from an amino acid to an α-keto acid.

urea cycle The process in which ammonium ions from the degradation of amino acids and CO_2 form carbamoyl phosphate, which is converted to urea.

UNDERSTANDING THE CONCEPTS

The chapter sections to review are given in parentheses at the end of each question.

24.59 Lauric acid, $CH_3-(CH_2)_8-CH_2-CH_2-COOH$, found in coconut oil, is a saturated C_{12} fatty acid. (24.2, 24.3)

Coconut oil contains lauric acid, a saturated C_{12} fatty acid.

a. Draw the condensed structural formula for the activated form of lauric acid.
b. Indicate the α- and β-carbon atoms in the acyl molecule.
c. How many cycles of β-oxidation are needed?
d. How many acetyl-CoA units are produced?
e. Calculate the total ATP yield from the complete β-oxidation of lauric acid by completing the following:

Activation	−2 ATP
___ FADH$_2$	___ ATP
___ NADH	___ ATP
___ Acetyl-CoA	___ ATP
Total	___ ATP

Peanuts contain arachidic acid, a saturated C_{20} fatty acid.

c. How many cycles of β-oxidation are needed?
d. How many acetyl-CoA units are produced?
e. Calculate the total ATP yield from the complete β-oxidation of arachidic acid by completing the following:

Activation	−2 ATP
___ FADH$_2$	___ ATP
___ NADH	___ ATP
___ Acetyl-CoA	___ ATP
Total	___ ATP

24.60 Arachidic acid CH_3—$(CH_2)_{16}$—CH_2—CH_2—COOH is a C_{20} fatty acid found in peanut and fish oils. (24.2, 24.3)
   a. Draw the condensed structural formula for the activated form of arachidic acid.
   b. Indicate the α- and β-carbon atoms in the acyl molecule.

ADDITIONAL QUESTIONS AND PROBLEMS

For instructor-assigned homework, go to www.masteringchemistry.com.

24.61 How are dietary triacylglycerols digested? (24.1)

24.62 What is a chylomicron? (24.1)

24.63 Why are the fats in the adipose tissues of the body considered the major form of stored energy? (24.1)

24.64 How are fatty acids obtained from stored fats? (24.1)

24.65 Why doesn't the brain utilize fatty acids for energy? (24.1)

24.66 Why don't red blood cells utilize fatty acids for energy? (24.1)

24.67 A triacylglycerol is hydrolyzed in the fat cells of adipose tissues and the fatty acid is transported to the liver. (24.1, 24.2)
   a. What happens to the glycerol?
   b. Where in the liver cells is the fatty acid activated for β-oxidation?
   c. What is the energy cost for activation of the fatty acid?
   d. What is the purpose of activating fatty acids?

24.68 Consider the β-oxidation of a saturated fatty acid. (24.2, 24.3)
   a. What is the activated form of the fatty acid?
   b. Why is the oxidation called β-oxidation?
   c. What reactions in the fatty acid cycle require coenzymes?
   d. What is the yield in ATP for one cycle of β-oxidation?

24.69 Identify each of the following as involved in β-oxidation or in fatty acid synthesis: (24.2, 24.3, 24.5)
   a. NAD$^+$
   b. occurs in the mitochondrial matrix
   c. malonyl-ACP
   d. cleavage of a two-carbon acetyl group
   e. acyl carrier protein
   f. acetyl-CoA carboxylase

24.70 Identify each of the following as involved in β-oxidation or in fatty acid synthesis: (24.2, 24.3, 24.5)
   a. NADPH
   b. takes place in the cytosol
   c. FAD
   d. oxidation of a hydroxyl group
   e. coenzyme A
   f. hydration of a double bond

24.71 The metabolism of triacylglycerols and carbohydrates is influenced by the hormones insulin and glucagon. Indicate the results of each of the following as stimulating fatty acid oxidation or fatty acid synthesis: (24.2, 24.3, 24.5)
   a. high blood glucose
   b. glucagon secreted

24.72 The metabolism of triacylglycerols and carbohydrates is influenced by the hormones insulin and glucagon. Indicate the results of each of the following as stimulating fatty acid oxidation or fatty acid synthesis: (24.2, 24.3, 24.5)
   a. low blood glucose
   b. insulin secreted

24.73 Why is ammonium ion that is produced in the liver converted immediately to urea? (24.8)

24.74 What compound is regenerated to repeat the urea cycle? (24.8)

24.75 Indicate the reactant in the urea cycle that reacts with each of the following compounds: (24.8)
   a. aspartate
   b. ornithine

24.76 Indicate the products in the urea cycle that are manufactured from the step that uses each of the following compounds: (24.8)
   a. arginine
   b. argininosuccinate

24.77 What component of the citric acid cycle can be produced from the carbon atoms of each of the following amino acids? (24.9)
   a. serine
   b. lysine
   c. methionine
   d. glutamate

24.78 What component of the citric acid cycle can be produced from the carbon atoms of each of the following amino acids? (24.9)
   a. glycine
   b. isoleucine
   c. histidine
   d. phenylalanine

24.79 How much ATP can be produced by the degradation of serine? (24.9)

24.80 Calculate the total ATP produced in the complete oxidation of caproic acid, $C_6H_{12}O_2$, and compare it with the total ATP produced from the oxidation of glucose, $C_6H_{12}O_6$. (24.3)

CHALLENGE QUESTIONS

24.81 A camel hump contains 14 kg of triacylglycerols. (24.2, 24.3)
   a. Using the value of 0.491 mole of ATP per gram of fat, how many moles of ATP could be produced by the fat in the camel's hump?

   b. If the hydrolysis of ATP releases 7.3 kcal/mole, how many kilocalories are produced by the utilization of the fat?

24.82 Identify each of the following reactions in the β-oxidation of palmitic acid, a C_{16} fatty acid, as **1.** activation, **2.** first dehydrogenation (oxidation), **3.** hydration, **4.** second dehydrogenation, or **5.** cleavage of acetyl-CoA. (24.2)

    a. Palmitoyl-CoA and FAD form α,β-unsaturated palmitoyl-CoA and $FADH_2$.

    b. β-Ketopalmitoyl-CoA forms myristyl-CoA and acetyl-CoA.

    c. Palmitic-acid, acetyl-CoA, and ATP form palmitoyl-CoA.

    d. α,β-Unsaturated palmitoyl-CoA and H_2O form β-hydroxypalmitoyl-CoA.

    e. β-Hydroxypalmitoyl-CoA and NAD^+ form β-ketopalmitoyl-CoA and $NADH + H^+$.

24.83 Draw the condensed structural formula for and give the name of the amino acid formed when the following α-keto acids undergo transamination with glutamate: (24.9, 24.10)

a. $CH_3-CH(CH_3)-C(=O)-C(=O)-O^-$

b. $CH_3-CH_2-CH(CH_3)-C(=O)-C(=O)-O^-$

c. $^-O-C(=O)-CH_2-C(=O)-C(=O)-O^-$

ANSWERS

Answers to Study Checks

24.1 NAD^+

24.2 Eight acetyl-CoAs give 96 ATPs; seven NADHs and seven $FADH_2$s give 35 ATPs.

24.3 HCl denatures proteins and activates enzymes such as pepsin.

24.4 In conditions such as fasting or starvation, a diet insufficient in protein leads to a negative nitrogen balance.

24.5 glutamate aminotransferase or glutamate transaminase

24.6 **a.** argininosuccinate
    b. citrulline
    c. urea and ornithine

24.7 Leucine forms the citric acid cycle intermediate acetyl-CoA that enters the beginning of the citric acid cycle to provide 12 ATPs. Phenylalanine forms the citric acid cycle intermediate fumarate that enters later in the citric acid cycle to provide three ATPs.

Answers to Selected Questions and Problems

24.1 The bile salts emulsify fat so that it forms small fat globules for lipase hydrolysis.

24.3 Fats are released from fat stores when blood glucose and glycogen stores are depleted.

24.5 Glycerol is converted to glycerol-3-phosphate, and then to dihydroxyacetone phosphate, an intermediate of glycolysis.

24.7 in the cytosol at the outer mitochondrial membrane

24.9 FAD, NAD^+, and $HS-CoA$

24.11 **a.** $CH_3-CH_2-CH_2-CH_2-CH_2-\underset{\beta}{CH_2}-CH_2-C(=O)-S-CoA$

    b. $CH_3-(CH_2)_{14}-\underset{\beta}{CH_2}-CH_2-C(=O)-S-CoA$

    c. $CH_3-CH_2-CH=CH-CH_2-CH_2-CH_2-\underset{\beta}{CH_2}-CH_2-C(=O)-S-CoA$

24.13 **a. and b.** $CH_3-(CH_2)_4-CH_2-\underset{\alpha}{\underset{\beta}{CH_2}}-C(=O)-S-CoA$

    c. three β-oxidation cycles   **d.** four acetyl-CoAs

24.15 The hydrolysis of ATP to AMP hydrolyzes ATP to ADP, and ADP to AMP, which provides the same amount of energy as the hydrolysis of two ATPs to two ADPs.

24.17 **a.** 10 β-oxidation cycles   **b.** 11 acetyl-CoAs
    c. 132 ATP from 11 acetyl-CoA (citric acid cycle) + 30 ATP from 10 NADH + 80 ATP from 10 $FADH_2$ − 2 ATP (activation) = 182 − 2 = 180 ATP (total)

24.19 Ketogenesis is the synthesis of ketone bodies from excess acetyl-CoA during fatty acid oxidation, which occurs when glucose is not available for energy, particularly in starvation, low-carbohydrate diets, fasting, alcoholism, and diabetes.

24.21 Acetoacetate undergoes reduction using $NADH + H^+$ to yield β-hydroxybutyrate.

24.23 High levels of ketone bodies lead to ketosis, a condition characterized by acidosis (a drop in blood pH values), excessive urination, and strong thirst.

24.25 in the cytosol of cells in liver and adipose tissue

24.27 acetyl-CoA, HCO_3^-, and ATP

24.29 **a.** (3) malonyl-CoA transacylase
    b. (1) acetyl-CoA carboxylase
    c. (2) acetyl-CoA transacylase

24.31 **a.** $4 HCO_3^-$ **b.** 4 ATP
    c. 5 acetyl-CoA   **d.** 4 malonyl-ACP
    e. 8 NADPH   **f.** $4 CO_2$ removed

24.33 The digestion of proteins begins in the stomach and is completed in the small intestine.

24.35 Hormones, heme, purines and pyrimidines for nucleotides, proteins, nonessential amino acids, amino alcohols, and neurotransmitters require nitrogen obtained from amino acids.

24.37 The reactants are an amino acid and an α-keto acid, and the products are a new amino acid and a new α-keto acid.

24.39 a. $H-\overset{\overset{\displaystyle O}{\|}}{C}-COO^-$ **b.** $HS-CH_2-\overset{\overset{\displaystyle O}{\|}}{C}-COO^-$

c. $CH_3-\overset{\overset{\displaystyle CH_3}{|}}{CH}-\overset{\overset{\displaystyle O}{\|}}{C}-COO^-$

24.41 $^-OOC-\overset{\overset{\displaystyle +}{\overset{\displaystyle NH_3}{|}}}{CH}-CH_2-CH_2-COO^- + H_2O + NAD^+ \xrightarrow{\overset{\text{Glutamate}}{\text{dehydrogenase}}}$
Glutamate

$^-OOC-\overset{\overset{\displaystyle O}{\|}}{C}-CH_2-CH_2-COO^- + NH_4^+ + NADH + H^+$
α-Ketoglutarate

24.43 NH_4^+ is toxic if allowed to accumulate in the liver.

24.45 $H_2N-\overset{\overset{\displaystyle O}{\|}}{C}-NH_2$

24.47 CO_2 from the citric acid cycle

24.49 Glucogenic amino acids are used to synthesize glucose.

24.51 a. oxaloacetate   **b.** oxaloacetate
c. succinyl-CoA   **d.** α-ketoglutarate

24.53 nonessential amino acids

24.55 Glutamine synthetase catalyzes the addition of an amino group to glutamate using energy from the hydrolysis of ATP.

24.57 phenylketonuria

24.59 a. and b. $CH_3-(CH_2)_8-\underset{\beta}{CH_2}-\underset{\alpha}{CH_2}-\overset{\overset{\displaystyle O}{\|}}{C}-S-CoA$

c. Five cycles of β-oxidation are needed.
d. Six acetyl-CoA units are produced.
e. Activation -2 ATP

$5 \text{ FADH}_2 \times \dfrac{2 \text{ ATP}}{\text{FADH}_2}$	10 ATP
$5 \text{ NADH} \times \dfrac{3 \text{ ATP}}{\text{NADH}}$	15 ATP
$6 \text{ acetyl-CoA} \times \dfrac{12 \text{ ATP}}{\text{acetyl-CoA}}$	72 ATP
Total	95 ATP

24.61 Triacylglycerols are hydrolyzed to monoacylglycerols and fatty acids in the small intestine, which reform as triacylglycerols in the intestinal lining for transport as lipoproteins to the tissues.

24.63 Fats can be stored in unlimited amounts in adipose tissue compared to the limited storage of carbohydrates as glycogen.

24.65 The fatty acids cannot diffuse across the blood–brain barrier.

24.67 a. Glycerol is converted to glycerol-3-phosphate and then to dihydroxyacetone phosphate, which can enter glycolysis or gluconeogenesis.
b. Activation of fatty acids occurs in the cytosol at the outer mitochondrial membrane.
c. The energy cost is equal to two ATPs.
d. Only acyl-CoA can move into the intermembrane space for transport by carnitine into the matrix.

24.69 a. β-oxidation   **b.** β-oxidation
c. fatty acid synthesis   **d.** β-oxidation
e. fatty acid synthesis   **f.** fatty acid synthesis

24.71 a. fatty acid synthesis   **b.** fatty acid oxidation

24.73 Ammonium ion is toxic if allowed to accumulate in the liver.

24.75 a. citrulline   **b.** carbamoyl phosphate

24.77 a. oxaloacetate   **b.** acetyl-CoA
c. succinyl-CoA   **d.** α-ketoglutarate

24.79 Serine is degraded to pyruvate, which is oxidized to acetyl-CoA. The oxidation produces $NADH + H^+$, which provides three ATPs. In one turn of the citric acid cycle, the acetyl-CoA provides 12 ATPs. Thus, serine can provide 15 ATPs.

24.81 a. 6900 moles of ATP
b. 5.0×10^4 kcal

24.83 a. $CH_3-\overset{\overset{\displaystyle CH_3}{|}}{CH}-\overset{\overset{\displaystyle +}{\overset{\displaystyle NH_3}{|}}}{CH}-\overset{\overset{\displaystyle O}{\|}}{C}-O^-$ Valine

b. $CH_3-CH_2-\overset{\overset{\displaystyle CH_3}{|}}{CH}-\overset{\overset{\displaystyle +}{\overset{\displaystyle NH_3}{|}}}{CH}-\overset{\overset{\displaystyle O}{\|}}{C}-O^-$ Isoleucine

c. $^-O-\overset{\overset{\displaystyle O}{\|}}{C}-CH_2-\overset{\overset{\displaystyle +}{\overset{\displaystyle NH_3}{|}}}{CH}-\overset{\overset{\displaystyle O}{\|}}{C}-O^-$ Aspartic acid

Combining Ideas from Chapters 21 to 24

CI.37 Identify each of the following as a substance that is part of the citric acid cycle, electron transport, or both: (23.1, 23.2, 23.3)
  a. GTP
  b. $CoQH_2$
  c. $FADH_2$
  d. cyt c
  e. succinate dehydrogenase
  f. complex I
  g. isocitrate
  h. NAD^+

CI.38 Use the value of 7.3 kcal per mole of ATP to determine the total kilocalories stored as ATP from each of the following: (23.4, 24.2, 24.3, 24.9)
  a. the reactions of 1 mole of glucose in glycolysis
  b. the oxidation of 2 moles of pyruvate to 2 moles of acetyl-CoA
  c. the complete oxidation of 1 mole of glucose to CO_2 and H_2O
  d. the β-oxidation of 1 mole of lauric acid, a C_{12} fatty acid
  e. the reaction of 1 mole of glutamate (from protein) in the citric acid cycle

CI.39 Acetyl-coenzyme A is the fuel for the citric acid cycle. It has the formula $C_{23}H_{38}N_7O_{17}P_3S$. (22.3, 23.1, 23.4)
  a. What are the components of acetyl-coenzyme A?
  b. What is the function of HS—CoA?
  c. Where does the acetyl group attach to HS—CoA?
  d. What is the molar mass (to three significant figures) of acetyl-CoA?
  e. How many moles of ATP are produced when 1.0 mg of acetyl-CoA completes one turn of the citric acid cycle?

CI.40 State if each of the following produces or consumes ATP: (22.5, 22.6, 23.1, 23.4, 24.2)
  a. citric acid cycle
  b. glucose forms two pyruvates
  c. pyruvate yields acetyl-CoA
  d. glucose forms glucose-6-phosphate
  e. oxidation of α-ketoglutarate
  f. transport of NADH across the mitochondrial membrane
  g. activation of a fatty acid

CI.41 Butter is a fat that contains 80% by mass triacylglycerols. Assume the triacylglycerol in butter is glyceryl tripalmitate. (17.4, 24.2, 24.3)

Butter is high in triacylglycerols.

  a. Write an equation for the hydrolysis of glyceryl tripalmitate.
  b. What is the molar mass of glyceryl tripalmitate, $C_{51}H_{98}O_6$?
  c. Calculate the ATP yield from the complete oxidation of 1 mole of palmitic acid.

  d. How many kilocalories are released from the palmitic acid in a 0.50-oz pat of butter?
  e. If running for exactly 1 h uses 750 kcal, how many pats of butter would provide the energy (kcal) for a 45-min run?

CI.42 Match these ATP yields with the given reactions: 2 ATP, 3 ATP, 6 ATP, 12 ATP, 18 ATP, 36 ATP, and 44 ATP. (22.5, 22.6, 23.4, 24.3)
  a. Glucose yields two pyruvates.
  b. Pyruvate yields acetyl-CoA.
  c. Glucose yields two acetyl-CoAs.
  d. Acetyl-CoA goes through one turn of the citric acid cycle.
  e. Caproic acid (C_6) is completely oxidized.
  f. $NADH + H^+$ is oxidized to NAD^+.
  g. $FADH_2$ is oxidized to FAD.

CI.43 Which of the following molecules will produce more ATP per mole when each is completely oxidized? (22.5, 22.6, 23.4, 24.3)
  a. glucose or maltose
  b. myristic acid, $CH_3—(CH_2)_{10}—CH_2—CH_2—COOH$, or stearic acid, $CH_3—(CH_2)_{14}—CH_2—CH_2—COOH$
  c. glucose or two acetyl-CoAs
  d. glucose or caprylic acid (C_8)
  e. citrate or succinate in one turn of the citric acid cycle

CI.44 Thalassemia is an inherited genetic mutation that limits the production of the beta chain needed for the formation of hemoglobin. If low levels of the beta chain are produced, there is a shortage of red blood cells (anemia). As a result, the body does not have sufficient amounts of oxygen. In one form of thalassemia, a single nucleotide is deleted in the DNA that codes for the beta chain. This mutation involves the deletion of thymine (T) from section 91 in the following coding strand of normal DNA: (21.4, 21.5, 21.6, 21.7, 21.8)

| 89 | 90 | 91 | 92 | 93 | 94 |

—AGT—GAG—CTG—CAC—TGT—GAC—A...

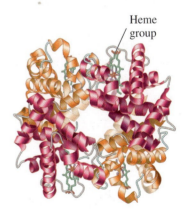

Heme group

The ribbon structure of hemoglobin shows the four polypeptide subunits; two (orange) are α-chains and two (red) are β-chains. The heme groups (green) in the four subunits bind oxygen.

a. Write the complementary (template) strand for this normal DNA segment.

b. Write the mRNA sequence from normal DNA using the template strand in part **a**.

c. What amino acids are placed in the beta chain by this portion of mRNA?

d. What is the order of nucleotides in the mutation?

e. Write the template strand for the mutated DNA segment.

f. Write the mRNA sequence from the mutated DNA segment using the template strand in part **e**.

g. What amino acids are placed in the beta chain by the mutated DNA segment?

h. What type of mutation occurs in this form of thalassemia?

i. How might the properties of this segment of the beta chain be different from the properties of the normal protein?

j. How might the level of structure in hemoglobin be affected if beta chains are not produced?

ANSWERS

CI.37 **a.** citric acid cycle **b.** electron transport
c. both **d.** electron transport
e. citric acid cycle **f.** electron transport
g. citric acid cycle **h.** both

CI.39 **a.** aminoethanethiol, pantothenic acid (vitamin B_5), and phosphorylated ADP

b. Coenzyme A carries an acetyl group to the citric acid cycle for oxidation.

c. The acetyl group links to the sulfur atom ($-S-$) in the aminoethanethiol part of CoA.

d. 809 g/mole

e. 1.5×10^{-8} mole of ATP

CI.41 **a.**

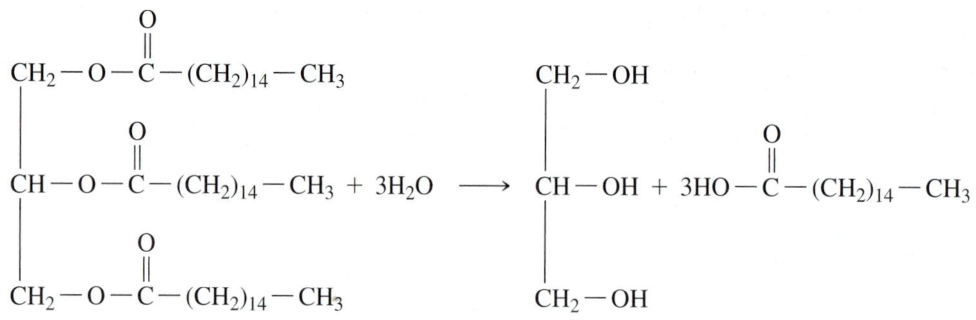

$$\begin{array}{l} CH_2-O-\overset{\overset{\displaystyle O}{\|}}{C}-(CH_2)_{14}-CH_3 \\[1em] CH-O-\overset{\overset{\displaystyle O}{\|}}{C}-(CH_2)_{14}-CH_3 \;+\; 3H_2O \;\longrightarrow \\[1em] CH_2-O-\overset{\overset{\displaystyle O}{\|}}{C}-(CH_2)_{14}-CH_3 \end{array}$$

$$\begin{array}{l} CH_2-OH \\[1em] CH-OH \;+\; 3HO-\overset{\overset{\displaystyle O}{\|}}{C}-(CH_2)_{14}-CH_3 \\[1em] CH_2-OH \end{array}$$

b. 806 g/mole
c. 129 moles of ATP
d. 36 kcal
e. 16 pats of butter

CI.43 **a.** maltose
b. stearic acid
c. glucose
d. caprylic acid
e. citrate

Credits

Glossary/Index